American Casebook Series
Hornbook Series and Basic Legal Texts
Nutshell Series

of

WEST PUBLISHING COMPANY

St. Paul, Minnesota 55102

ACCOUNTING
Fiflis and Kripke's Cases on Accounting for Business Lawyers, 687 pages, 1971.

ADMINISTRATIVE LAW
Davis' Basic Text on Administrative Law 3rd Ed., 617 pages, 1972.

Davis' Cases, Text and Problems on Administrative Law, 3rd Ed., about 625 pages, 1973.

Gellhorn's Administrative Law in a Nutshell, 336 pages, 1972.

ADMIRALTY
Healy and Currie's Cases on Admiralty, 872 pages, 1965.

AGENCY
Seavey and Hall's Cases on Agency, 431 pages, 1956.

Seavey's Text on Agency, 329 pages, 1964.

See Agency-Partnership.

AGENCY PARTNERSHIP
Henn's Cases on Agency, Partnership and Other Unincorporated Business Enterprises, 396 pages, 1972.

Seavey, Reuschlein & Hall's Cases on Agency and Partnership, 599 pages, 1962.

Steffen's Cases on Agency and Partnership, 3rd Ed., 733 pages, 1969.

ANTITRUST LAW
Oppenheim's Cases on Robinson-Patman Act, Pamphlet, 295 pages, 1967.

Oppenheim and Weston's Cases on Antitrust, 3rd Ed., 952 pages, 1968.

Oppenheim and Weston's Supplement, 1972.

BANKRUPTCY
MacLachlan's Text on Bankruptcy, 500 pages, 1956.

See Creditors' Rights.

Selected Commercial Statutes, about 1000 pages, 1973.

BILLS AND NOTES
Aigler and Steinheimer's Cases on Bills and Notes, 670 pages, 1962.

Britton's Text on Bills and Notes, 2nd Ed., 794 pages, 1961.

See Commercial Transactions.

See Negotiable Instruments.

BUSINESS ORGANIZATIONS
See Agency-Partnership.

See Corporations.

CIVIL PROCEDURE
See Pleading and Procedure.

CLINICAL TEACHING
Freeman and Weihofen's Cases on Clinical Law Training—Interviewing and Counseling, 506 pages, 1972.

COMMERCIAL PAPER
See Bills and Notes.

See Commercial Transactions.

See Negotiable Instruments.

COMMERCIAL TRANSACTIONS
Speidel, Summers and White's Teaching Materials on Commercial Transactions, 1144 pages, 1969.

Murray and White's Problem Teaching Materials on Commercial Transactions, about 300 pages, 1973.

White and Summers Text on the Uniform Commercial Code, 1054 pages, 1972.

Selected Commercial Statutes, about 1000 pages, 1973.

See Negotiable Instruments.

See Sales.

LAW SCHOOL PUBLICATIONS — Continued

...ADING

...ppy's Text on Common
...ng, 663 pages, 1969.
...Cases, Introduction to Civil
...re, 399 pages, 1950.
...n's Text on Common Law Plead-
...g, 3rd Ed., 644 pages, 1923.

OMMUNITY PROPERTY

Burby's Cases on Community Property,
4th Ed., 342 pages, 1955.
Huie's Texas Cases on Marital Property Rights, 681 pages, 1966.
Verrall and Sammis' Cases on California Community Property, 2nd Ed.,
398 pages, 1971.

CONFLICT OF LAWS

Cramton and Currie's Cases—Comments—Questions on Conflicts, 915
pages, 1968.
Ehrenzweig's Text on Conflicts, 824
pages, 1962.
Ehrenzweig's Conflicts in a Nutshell,
2nd Ed., 392 pages, 1970.
Ehrenzweig and Louisell's Jurisdiction
in a Nutshell, 3rd Ed., about 255
pages, 1973.
Goodrich's Text on Conflict of Laws, 4th
Ed., 483 pages, 1964.
Scoles and Weintraub's Cases on Conflict of Laws, 2nd Ed., 966 pages 1972.

CONSTITUTIONAL LAW

Lockhart, Kamisar and Choper's Cases
— Comments — Questions on Con-
stitutional Law, 3rd Ed., 1,487 pages,
1970.
Lockhart, Kamisar and Choper's Cases
on The American Constitution, 3rd
Ed., 1970.
Lockhart, Kamisar and Choper's Annual
Supplement.
See Constitutional Rights and Liberties.

CONSTITUTIONAL RIGHTS & LIBERTIES

Lockhart, Kamisar and Choper's Cases
on Constitutional Rights and Liberties, 3rd Ed., 1970.
Lockhart, Kamisar and Choper's Annual
Supplement.

CONSUMER CREDIT

Kripke's Cases on Consumer Credit, 454
pages, 1970.
Schrag's Cases on Consumer Credit,
2nd Ed., Pamphlet reprint from Cooper, et al. Law and Poverty, 2nd Ed.,
about 175 pages, 1973.

CONTRACTS

Calamari & Perillo's Text on Contracts,
621 pages, 1970.
Corbin's Cases on Contracts, 3rd Ed.,
1381 pages, 1947. 1953 Supplement,
36 pages.
Corbin's Text on Contracts, Student Edition, 1224 pages, 1952.
Freedman's Cases on Contracts, 658
pages, 1973.
Fuller and Eisenberg's Cases on Contracts, 1043 pages, 1972.
Jackson's Cases on Contract Law in a
Modern Society, about 1400 pages,
1973.
Simpson's Cases on Contracts, 592
pages, 1956.
Simpson's Text on Contracts, 2nd Ed.,
510 pages, 1965.
White and Summer's Text on the Uniform Commercial Code, 1054 pages,
1972.

COPYRIGHT

Nimmer's Cases on Copyright and Other Aspects of Law Pertaining to Literary, Musical and Artistic Works,
828 pages, 1971.
Nimmer's 1972 Supplement.

CORPORATIONS

Henn's Text on Corporations, 2nd Ed.,
956 pages, 1970.
Stevens and Henn's Statutes, Cases
on Corporations and Other Business
Enterprises, 1448 pages, 1965.
Stevens and Henn's Practice Projects
Supplement, 81 pages, 1965.

CORRECTIONS

Krantz' Cases on the Law of Corrections
and Prisoners' Rights, about 1085
pages, 1973.

CREDIT TRANSACTIONS

Maxwell & Riesenfeld's California Cases on Security Transactions, 371
pages, 1957.
Maxwell & Riesenfeld's Supplement, 68
pages, 1963.

CREDITORS' RIGHTS

Epstein's Teaching Materials on Debtor-
Creditor Relations, 525 pages, 1973.
Epstein's Debtor-Creditor Relations in a
Nutshell, 309 pages, 1973.
Riesenfeld's Cases on Creditors' Rem-
edies and Debtors' Protection, 669
pages, 1967.
Riesenfeld's Case and Statutory Sup-
plement, 1972.

CRIMINAL LAW

Dix and Sharlot's Cases on Criminal Law, about 1350 pages, 1973.

LaFave and Scott's Text on Criminal Law, 763 pages, 1972.

Miller's Text on Criminal Law, 649 pages, 1934.

Stumberg's Texas Cases on Criminal Law, 505 pages, 1954.

Stumberg and Maloney's Texas Cases Supplement, 117 pages, 1965.

CRIMINAL PROCEDURE

Hall, Kamisar, LaFave and Israel's Cases on Modern Criminal Procedure, 3rd Ed., 1456 pages, 1969.

Hall, Kamisar, LaFave and Israel's Cases on Basic Criminal Procedure, 3rd Ed., 617 pages, 1969.

Hall, Kamisar, LaFave and Israel's Annual Criminal Procedure Supplement.

Israel and LaFave's Constitutional Criminal Procedure in a Nutshell, 423 pages, 1971.

Federal Rules of Civil-Appellate-Criminal Procedure, Law School Edition, 296 pages, 1973.

DAMAGES

Crane's Cases on Damages, 3rd Ed., 337 pages, 1955.

McCormick's Text on Damages, 811 pages, 1935.

See Remedies.

DECEDENTS ESTATES

See Wills, Intestate Succession, Trusts, Gifts and Future Interests.

DICTIONARIES

Black's, one volume.
Bouvier's, two volumes.

DOMESTIC RELATIONS

Clark's Cases on Domestic Relations, 870 pages, 1965.

Clark's Text on Domestic Relations, 754 pages, 1968.

Paulsen's Cases on Family Law and Poverty, 2nd Ed., Pamphlet reprint from Cooper, et al. Law and Poverty, 2nd Ed., about 266 pages, 1973.

See Juvenile Courts.

EQUITY

Cook's Cases on Equity, 4th Ed., 1192 pp., 1948.

McClintock's Text on Equity, 2nd Ed., 643 pages, 1948.

Van Hecke, Leavell and Nelson's Cases on Equitable Remedies and Restitution, 2nd Ed., 717 pages, 1973.

See Remedies.

EVIDENCE

Broun and Meisenholder's Problems in Evidence, about 155 pages, 1973.

Cleary and Strong's Cases on Evidence, 967 pages, 1969.

McCormick, Elliott & Sutton's Cases on Evidence, 4th Ed., 1088 pages, 1971.

McCormick, Cleary, et al., Text on Evidence, 2nd Ed., 938 pages, 1972.

Rothstein's Evidence in a Nutshell, 406 pages, 1970.

FEDERAL ESTATE AND GIFT TAXATION

See Taxation.

FEDERAL INCOME TAXATION

See Taxation.

FEDERAL JURISDICTION AND PROCEDURE

Currie's Cases on Federal Courts, 823 pages, 1968.

Currie's Supplement, 1973.

Ehrenzweig and Louisell's Jurisdiction in a Nutshell, 3rd Ed., about 255 pages, 1973.

Forrester, Currier and Moye's Cases on Federal Jurisdiction and Procedure, 2nd Ed., 933 pages, 1970.

Forrester, Currier and Moye's Supplement, 1973.

Wright's Text on Federal Courts, 2nd Ed., 745 pages, 1970.

Wright's Supplement, 1972.

FUTURE INTERESTS

Gulliver's Cases on Future Interests, 624 pages, 1959.

Powell's Cases on Future Interests, 3rd Ed., 1961.

Simes Text on Future Interests, 2nd Ed., 355 pages, 1966.

See Wills, Intestate Succession, Trusts, Gifts and Future Interests.

GRATUITOUS TRANSFERS

See Wills, Intestate Succession, Trusts, Gifts and Future Interests.

AN DEVELOPMENT

on Housing, 2nd Ed.,
print from Cooper, et al.
overty, 2nd Ed., about 210
973.
iecki's Cases on Housing and
an Development, 697 pages, 1969.
nowiecki's Statutory Supplement
1969.
See Land Use.

INSURANCE

Keeton's Cases on Basic Insurance Law, 655 pages, 1960.
Keeton's Basic Text on Insurance Law, 712 pages, 1971.
Keeton's Case Supplement to Keeton's Basic Text, 398 pages, 1971.
Keeton's Programmed Problems in Insurance Law, 243 pages, 1972.
Keeton & Keeton's Compensation Systems, Pamphlet Reprint from Keeton & Keeton's Cases on Torts, 85 pages, 1971.
Vance's Text on Insurance, 3rd Ed., 1290 pages, 1951.

INTERNATIONAL LAW

Friedmann, Lissitzyn and Pugh's Cases on International Law, 1,205 pages, 1969.
Friedmann, Lissitzyn and Pugh's Supplement, 1972.

INTRODUCTION TO LAW

Fryer and Orentlicher's Cases on Legal Method and Legal System, 1,043 pages, 1967.
Kempin's Historical Introduction to Anglo-American Law in a Nutshell, 2nd Ed., 280 pages, 1973.
Kimball's Historical Introduction to Legal System, 610 pages, 1966.
Kinyon's Introduction to Law Study and Law Examinations in a Nutshell, 389 pages, 1971.
Smith's Cases on Development of Legal Institutions, 757 pages, 1965.
See Legal Method.

JURISPRUDENCE

Christie's Text and Readings on Jurisprudence—The Philosophy of Law, about 1050 pages, 1973.
Wu's Cases on Jurisprudence, 719 pages, 1958.

JUVENILE JUSTICE

Fox's Cases on Modern Juvenile Justice, 1012 pages, 1972.
Fox's The Law of Juvenile Courts in a Nutshell, 286 pages, 1971.

LABOR LAW

Oberer and Hanslowe's Cases on Labor Law, 1091 pages, 1972.
Oberer and Hanslowe's Statutory Supplement, 1972.
Sovern's Cases on Racial Discrimination in Employment, 2nd Ed., Pamphlet reprint from Cooper et al. Law and Poverty, 2nd Ed., about 160 pages, 1973.

LAND USE

Beuscher and Wright's Cases on Land Use, 788 pages, 1969.
Hagman's Cases on Public Planning and Control of Urban and Land Development, about 1025 pages, 1973.
Hagman's Text on Urban Planning and Land Development Control Law, 559 pages, 1971.

LEGAL BIBLIOGRAPHY

Cohen's Legal Research in a Nutshell, 2nd Ed., 259 pages, 1971.
How To Find The Law, with Special Chapters on Legal Writing, 6th Ed., 313 pages, 1965.
How To Find The Law Student Problem Book.
Rombauer's Legal Problem Solving, 2nd Ed., 212 pages, 1973.
Rombauer's Problem Supplement.

LEGAL ETHICS

Mellinkoff's Text on The Conscience of a Lawyer, 304 pages, 1973.
Pirsig's Cases on Professional Responsibility, 2nd Ed., 447 pages, 1970.

LEGAL HISTORY

Kempin's Historical Introduction to Anglo-American Law in a Nutshell, 2nd Ed., 280 pages, 1973.
Kimball's Historical Introduction to Legal System, 610 pages, 1966.
Radin's Text on Anglo-American Legal History, 612 pages, 1936.
Smith's Cases on Development of Legal Institutions, 757 pages, 1965.

LEGAL INTERVIEWING AND COUNSELING

See Clinical Teaching.

LEGAL METHOD—LEGAL SYSTEM

Fryer and Orentlicher's Cases on Legal Method and Legal System, 1043 pages, 1966.
See Introduction to Law.

LEGAL PROCESS

See Legal Method.

LAW SCHOOL PUBLICATIONS — Continued

LEGAL PROFESSION

See Legal Ethics.

LEGAL WRITING STYLE

Weihofen's Text on Legal Writing Style, 323 pages, 1961.
See Legal Bibliography.

LEGISLATION

Nutting, Elliott and Dickerson's Cases on Legislation, 4th Ed., 631 pages, 1969.

LOCAL GOVERNMENT LAW

Michelman and Sandalow's Cases on Government in Urban Areas, 1216 pages, 1970.
Michelman and Sandalow's 1972 Supplement.
Stason and Kauper's Cases on Municipal Corporations, 3rd Ed., 692 pages, 1959.
See Land Use.

MASS COMMUNICATION LAW

Gillmor and Barron's Cases on Mass Communication Law, 853 pages, 1969.
Gillmor and Barron's 1971 Supplement.

MORTGAGES

Osborne's Cases on Secured Transactions, 559 pages, 1967.
Osborne's Text on Mortgages, 2nd Ed., 805 pages, 1970.
See Sales.
See Secured Transactions.

MUNICIPAL CORPORATIONS

See Local Government Law.

NATURAL RESOURCES

Trelease, Bloomenthal and Geraud's Cases on Natural Resources, 1131 pages, 1965.

NEGOTIABLE INSTRUMENTS

Nordstrom and Clovis' Problems on Commercial Paper, 458 pages, 1972.
See Commercial Transactions.

OFFICE PRACTICE

A.B.A. Lawyer's Handbook, 557 pages, 1962.
See Clinical Teaching.

OIL AND GAS

Hemingway's Text on Oil and Gas, 486 pages, 1971.
Huie, Woodward and Smith's Cases on Oil and Gas, 2nd Ed., 955 pages, 1972.
See Natural Resources.

PARTNERSHIP

Crane and Bromberg's Text on Partnership, 695 pages, 1968.
See Agency-Partnership.

PATENTS

Choate's Cases on Patents, 1060 pages, 1973.

PERSONAL PROPERTY

Aigler, Smith and Tefft's Cases on Property, 2 Vols., 1339 pages, 1960.
Bigelow's Cases on Personal Property, 3rd Ed., 507 pages, 1942.
Fryer's Readings on Personal Property, 3rd Ed., 1184 pages, 1938.

PLEADING AND PROCEDURE

Brown, Karlen, Meisenholder, Stevens, and Vestal's Cases on Procedure Before Trial, 784 pages, 1968.
Cleary's Cases on Pleading, 2d Ed., 434 pages, 1958.
Cound, Friedenthal and Miller's Cases on Civil Procedure, 1075 pages, 1968.
Cound, Friedenthal and Miller's Cases on Pleading, Discovery and Joinder, 643 pages, 1968.
Cound, Friedenthal and Miller's Civil Procedure Supplement, 1972.
Ehrenzweig and Louisell's Jurisdiction in a Nutshell, 3rd Ed., about 255 pages, 1973.
Elliott & Karlen's Cases on Pleading, 441 pages, 1961.
Hodges, Jones and Elliott's Cases on Texas Trial and Appellate Procedure, 623 pages, 1965.
Hodges, Jones, Elliott and Thode's Cases on Texas Judicial Process Prior to Trial, 935 pages, 1966.
Karlen and Joiner's Cases on Trials and Appeals, 536 pages, 1971.
Karlen's Procedure Before Trial in a Nutshell, 258 pages, 1972.
McBaine's Cases on Introduction to Civil Procedure, 399 pages, 1950.
Federal Rules of Civil-Appellate-Criminal Procedure, Law School Edition, 296 pages, 1973.

POVERTY LAW

Cooper, Dodyk, Berger, Paulsen, Schrag and Sovern's Cases on Law and Poverty, 2nd Ed., about 1165 pages, 1973.

Cooper and Dodyk's Cases on Income Maintenance, 2nd Ed., Pamphlet reprint from Cooper, et al. Law and Poverty, 2nd Ed., about 400 pages, 1973.

LaFrance, Schroeder, Bennett and Boyd's Text on Law and the Poor, about 520 pages, 1973.

REAL PROPERTY

Aigler, Smith & Tefft's Cases on Property, 2 Vols., 1339 pages, 1960.

Berger's Cases on Housing, Pamphlet reprint from Dodyk, et al. Law and Poverty, 277 pages, 1969.

Browder, Cunningham & Julin's Cases on Basic Property Law, 2d Ed., 1397 pages, 1973.

Burby's Text on Real Property, 3rd Ed., 490 pages, 1965.

Jacobs' Cases on Landlord and Tenant, 2nd Ed., 815 pages, 1941.

Moynihan's Introduction to Real Property, 254 pages, 1962.

Phipps' Titles in a Nutshell—The Calculus of Interests, 277 pages, 1968.

Smith and Boyer's Survey of the Law of Property, 2nd Ed., 510 pages, 1971.

See Housing and Urban Development.

REMEDIES

Cribbet's Cases on Judicial Remedies, 762 pages, 1954.

Dobb's Text, on Remedies, 1067 pages, 1973.

Van Hecke, Leavell and Nelson's Cases on Equitable Remedies and Restitution, 2nd Ed., 717 pages, 1973.

Wright's Cases on Remedies, 498 pages, 1955.

York and Bauman's Cases on Remedies, 2nd Ed., about 1500 pages, 1973.

See Equity.

RESTITUTION

See Equity.
See Remedies.

REVIEW MATERIALS

Ballantine's Problems.
Burby's Law Refreshers.
Smith Reviews.

SALES

Nordstrom's Text on Sales, 600 pages, 1970.

Nordstrom and Lattin's Problems on Sales and Secured Transactions, 809 pages, 1968.

See Commercial Transactions.

SECURED TRANSACTIONS

Henson's Text on Secured Transactions, about 350 pages, 1973.
See Commercial Transactions.
See Sales.

SURETYSHIP AND GUARANTY

Osborne's Cases on Suretyship, 221 pages, 1966.

Simpson's Cases on Suretyship, 538 pages, 1942.

TAXATION

Chommie's Text on Federal Income Taxation, 2nd Ed., about 1000 pages, 1973.

Hellerstein's Cases on State and Local Taxation, 3rd Ed., 741 pages, 1969.

Kragen & McNulty's Cases on Federal Income Taxation, 1,182 pages, 1970.

Lowndes & Kramer's Text on Federal Estate and Gift Taxes, 2nd Ed., 951 pages, 1962.

McNulty's Federal Income Taxation in a Nutshell, 322 pages, 1972.

Rice's Problems in Federal Estate & Gift Taxation, 2nd Ed., 496 pages, 1972.

Rice's Problems in Federal Income Taxation, 2nd Ed., 589 pages, 1971.

TORTS

Green, Pedrick, Rahl, Thode, Hawkins and Smith's Cases on Torts, 1311 pages, 1968.

Green, Pedrick, Rahl, Thode, Hawkins and Smith's Cases on Injuries to Relations, 466 pages, 1968.

Keeton and Keeton's Cases on Torts, 1193 pages, 1971.

Prosser's Text on Torts, 4th Ed., 1208 pages, 1971.

TRADE REGULATION

See Anti-Trust Law.
See Unfair Trade Practices.

TRIAL AND APPELLATE PRACTICE

See Pleading and Procedure.

LAW SCHOOL PUBLICATIONS — Continued

TRUSTS

Bogert's Text on Trusts, 5th Ed., about 535 pages, 1973.

Powell's Cases on Trusts and Wills, 639 pages, 1960.

See Wills, Intestate Succession, Trusts, Gifts and Future Interests.

UNFAIR TRADE PRACTICES

Oppenheim's Cases on Unfair Trade Practices, 783 pages, 1965.

Oppenheim and Weston's Supplement.

Oppenheim's Robinson-Patman Act Pamphlet, 295 pages, 1967.

WATER LAW

Trelease's Cases on Water Law, 364 pages, 1967.

WILLS

Atkinson's Text on Wills, 2nd Ed., 975 pages, 1953.

Mennell's Cases on California Decedents' Estates, 566 pages, 1973.

Turrentine's Cases on Wills, 2nd Ed., 483 pages, 1962.

See Wills, Intestate Succession, Trusts, Gifts and Future Interests.

WILLS, INTESTATE SUCCESSION, TRUSTS, GIFTS AND FUTURE INTERESTS

Gulliver, Clark, Lusky and Murphy's Cases on Gratuitous Transfers: Wills, Intestate Succession, Trusts, Gifts and Future Interests, 1017 pages, 1967.

WORKMEN'S COMPENSATION

Malone and Plant's Cases on Workmen's Compensation, 622 pages, 1963.

CRIMINAL LAW
CASES AND MATERIALS

By

GEORGE E. DIX
Professor of Law, University of Texas

M. MICHAEL SHARLOT
Professor of Law, University of Texas

AMERICAN CASEBOOK SERIES

ST. PAUL, MINN.
WEST PUBLISHING CO.
1973

PREFACE

This book reflects a belief in the importance of the place of the substantive criminal law in the law school curriculum. All too often it appears that students lose interest in the subject upon learning that this is not the course in which *Miranda, Mapp,* and the other landmark criminal procedure decisions are to be analyzed. The student who measures his courses by the contribution he anticipates they will make to his law practice may be difficult to motivate in this area of study. Yet the substantive criminal law, more than any other subject in law school curriculums, poses the great questions of the relationship of the individual to the state. The goals of the criminal law and the unending debate over how they may best be achieved and at what cost to the values of our society should be part of the intellectual life of every thinking citizen and most especially every lawyer. Thus, something more than a vehicle by which the student may be familiarized with the law of crimes is essential to any meaningful criminal law course.

This book is designed to facilitate inquiry into the broadest issues involved in the decision to employ the state's ultimate sanction to coerce conduct. An attempt has been made to select cases and materials which are likely to evoke the interest of the students. Fact situations likely to spark emotional responses which must then be filtered through the requirements of the law may be found throughout the book. Insights from other fields of intellectual endeavor into the nature of human behavior are integrated with the case material, particularly in Parts II and VII. Preference has generally been given to more recent cases and efforts at codification in the belief that this will better reflect the collective experience of our society, and, in addition, will serve as an implicit illustration of the continuing importance of the subject matter.

Part I, the introductory portion, deals with the general framework of criminal law. Textual material dealing with the scope of criminal activity and the procedure for processing a criminal case is followed by material raising several procedural matters which we considered essential to an understanding of the context in which substantive criminal law issues are raised. A textual note in this section defines many traditional crimes in summary fashion, providing the student with a general background in the law of crimes. Detailed treatment of complex specific issues is left until later. Penalty provisions are also dealt with, and attention is devoted to the death penalty as well as to the Maryland Defective Delinquency Program, a major example of "indeterminant institutionalization."

Part II presents the criminalization issue in the context of the problems posed by alcohol-related activities. Emphasis is placed upon the complexity of both the basic legislative decision as to which, if any, alcohol-related activity is to be criminalized and of the judicial review of this decision in the form of the Powell v. Texas attack upon the constitutionality of criminal prohibition against public intoxication. Noncriminal compelled treatment is presented as a possible alternative to criminalization, and the functioning and effectiveness of criminal and noncriminal treatment systems are investigated. Empirical material dealing with the effectiveness of criminal "punishment" as well as other potential results of imposing criminal liability is presented in a manner enabling the teacher to discuss expectations that might be raised by application of the criminal sanction to alcohol-related activity as well as to other forms of antisocial behavior. Various legal issues raised by criminalization are presented, including the availability of a legally-enforceable "right to treatment." Efforts are made to acquaint the student with a theoretical framework for evaluating the criminalization decision in various contexts, to make clear the complexity of the decision and the factual issues upon which its resolution depends, and to provide some contact with the kinds of psychological and sociological materials available to help answer the factual questions posed.

Parts III through VI present the substantive criminal law. Only the homicide offenses are treated in a separate section. But in Part III issues concerning the meaning and appropriateness of various requirements of specific substantive crimes are dealt with in the context of the general requirements of act, state of mind, and results. Thus the material permits discussion of the differences between the traditional property acquisition offenses as well as the "act" requirements of offenses such as assault and kidnapping. Part IV covers the inchoate offenses, and Part V, as mentioned previously, deals with the homicide offenses. Those "defenses" that involve challenging the existence of an element of the offenses are covered in Part III along with the underlying requirements they "disprove"; Part VI deals with matters of justification and excuse.

In general, we concluded that the application of the criminal law to the psychologically abnormal offender presents special problems that should be dealt with as a whole. Much of the difficulty that is experienced in evaluating criminal law doctrine arises when the condition of a particular defendant forces the law to acknowledge that he is not one of the "normal" persons upon whom the assumptions of the criminal law are based. Consequently, we have endeavored to deal with most of the issues of substantive criminal law on the assumption that "normal" offenders are being processed and to treat separately the issue of what, if any, accommodations should be made for those situations in which the defendant is psychologically abnormal. The latter task is undertaken in Part VII of the casebook.

This section also, however, attempts to use the relationship between psychological abnormality and criminal liability as a vehicle for several purposes other than raising the doctrinal issues posed by the insanity defense and related matters. The introductory material explains "dynamic psychology" as a useful framework for attempting to answer many of the questions posed by the existing legal framework. In addition, an attempt is made to evaluate the use of expert testimony in litigation and to evaluate the effect of changes in doctrine upon practical results. Thus, quite extensive material from the Chicago jury study is presented, along with materials on the actual use of the insanity defense in practice. In an attempt to combine the issues raised by substantive definitions of crimes and the psychological abnormality of some (or many) offenders, the final portion of Part VII presents the California "diminished capacity" cases as an attempt to redefine the substantive law of homicide so as to provide a better vehicle for making defendants' psychological abnormality one of several factors considered in determining the "degree of guilt."

We anticipate that few if any teachers will seek to cover the entire material in a single course. But we hope that by providing a wide variety of material, much of which can be assigned as background reading, we are presenting a book that will enable teachers with different interests and areas of emphasis to tailor a course to fit their own specific needs. Parts II through VI, with portions of Part VII, could be used to teach a relatively traditional course stressing the doctrinal issues posed by substantive criminal law. Parts II and VII could be used in a shorter course dealing with the law's use of information regarding the causes of antisocial behavior and how such behavior can be modified.

We express our appreciation to the numerous authors and publishers who have given us permission to reproduce their materials in this volume. A special note of gratitude must go to the American Law Institute which kindly granted permission to reprint extensive portions of their copyrighted Model Penal Code (and the various tentative drafts) and the Model Code of Pre-Arraignment Procedure. In editing the materials reprinted in this book, we have left out citations and footnotes without any specific indication of such omissions. Footnotes retained from the original material are indicated by numbers. We have chosen not to renumber the footnotes that have been retained; consequently, the numbers appearing in the material are those assigned by the original authors. Footnotes indicated by letters are those we have inserted.

Students who wish guidance as to outside reading that may enrich or clarify sections of the book may be well advised to take advantage of the recent hornbook, Handbook on Criminal Law, published in 1972 by Professor Wayne R. LaFave and the late Professor Austin W. Scott, Jr. Also of significant aid are the two volumes of Working Papers of the National Commission on Reform of the Federal Criminal Laws, published in 1970. Somewhat older but more elaborate and by no means outdated is the commentary to the tentative drafts of the American Law Institute's Model Penal Code. Many excerpts from these volumes have been included but, of course, these are but the barest sampling of the thoughtful discussions contained therein. The best single source of information about the actual operation of the criminal justice system and recommendations for its improvement is The Challenge of Crime in a Free Society, A Report by the President's Commission on Law Enforcement and Administration of Justice, published in 1967, and the many Task Force Reports produced by the Commission. Finally, no finer overview of the problems of the criminal law can be recommended than the late Professor Herbert Packer's short volume, The Limits of the Criminal Sanction, published in 1968.

G.E.D.
M.M.S.

July 1, 1973

SUMMARY OF CONTENTS

SUMMARY OF CONTENTS

SUMMARY OF CONTENTS

SUMMARY OF CONTENTS

TABLE OF CONTENTS

TABLE OF CONTENTS

TABLE OF CONTENTS

TABLE OF CONTENTS

TABLE OF CONTENTS

TABLE OF CONTENTS

TABLE OF CONTENTS

TABLE OF CONTENTS

TABLE OF CONTENTS

TABLE OF CONTENTS

TABLE OF CONTENTS

TABLE OF CONTENTS

TABLE OF CONTENTS

TABLE OF CONTENTS

TABLE OF CONTENTS

TABLE OF CONTENTS

TABLE OF CONTENTS

TABLE OF CONTENTS

TABLE OF CONTENTS

REFERENCES TO THE PROPOSED FEDERAL CRIMINAL CODE

REFERENCES TO THE PROPOSED CRIMINAL CODE

REFERENCES TO THE MODEL PENAL CODE

TABLE OF CASES

The principal cases are in roman type. Cases cited or discussed are in ital. References are to Pages.

TABLE OF CASES

TABLE OF CASES

TABLE OF CASES

TABLE OF CASES

TABLE OF CASES

TABLE OF CASES

†

CASES AND MATERIALS
ON
CRIMINAL LAW

I. INTRODUCTION

A. THE CRIME PROBLEM

THE PRESIDENT'S COMMISSION ON LAW ENFORCEMENT AND ADMINISTRATION OF JUSTICE, THE CHALLENGE OF CRIME IN A FREE SOCIETY

18–24, 30–31, 43–45 (1967).

THE AMOUNT OF CRIME

*   *   *

The crimes that concern Americans the most are those that affect their personal safety—at home, at work, or in the streets. The most frequent and serious of these crimes of violence against the person are willful homicide, forcible rape, aggravated assault, and robbery. National statistics regarding the number of these offenses known to the police either from citizen complaints or through independent police discovery are collected from local police officials by the Federal Bureau of Investigation and published annually as a part of its report, "Crime in the United States, Uniform Crime Reports." The FBI also collects "offenses known" statistics for three property crimes: Burglary, larceny of $50 and over and motor vehicle theft. These seven crimes are grouped together in the UCR to form an Index of serious crimes. Figure 1 shows the totals for these offenses for 1965.

The Risk of Harm

Including robbery, the crimes of violence make up approximately 13 percent of the Index. The Index reports the number of incidents

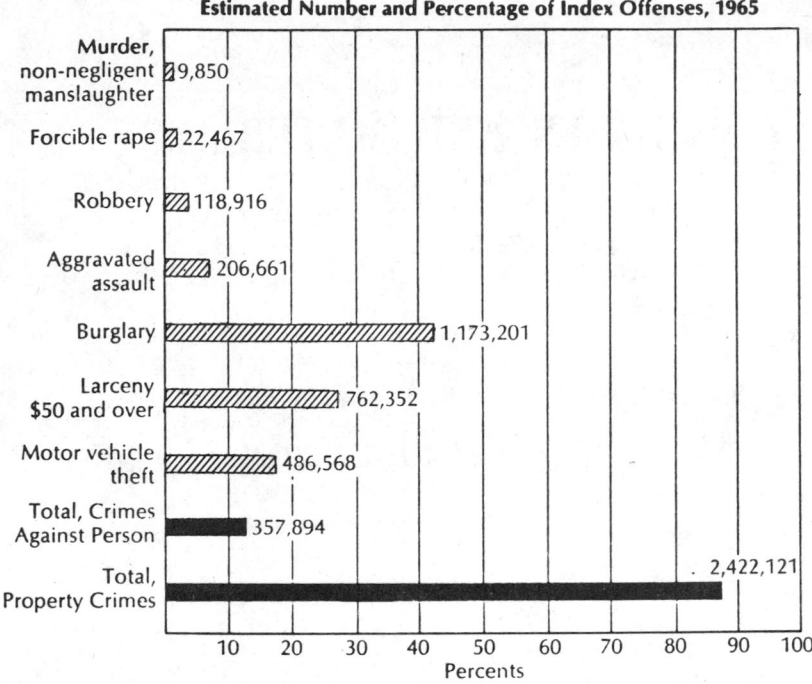

Estimated Number and Percentage of Index Offenses, 1965

SOURCE: Uniform Crime Reports, 1965, p. 51.

Figure 1

[A9004]

known to the police, not the number of criminals who committed them or the number of injuries they caused.

*   *   *

In summary, these figures suggest that, on the average, the likelihood of a serious personal attack on any American in a given year is about 1 in 550; together with the studies available they also suggest that the risk of serious attack from spouses, family members, friends, or acquaintances is almost twice as great as it is from strangers on the street. Commission and other studies, moreover, indicate that the risks of personal harm are spread very unevenly. The actual risk for slum dwellers is considerably more; for most Americans it is considerably less.

Except in the case of willful homicide, where the figures describe the extent of injury as well as the number of incidents, there is no national data on the likelihood of injury from attack. More limited studies indicate that while some injury may occur in two-thirds of all attacks, the risk in a given year of injury serious enough to require any degree of hospitalization of any individual is about 1 in 3,000 on the average, and much less for most Americans. These studies also suggest that the injury inflicted by family members or acquaintances is likely to be more severe than that from strangers. * * * [T]he risk of death from willful homicide is about 1 in 20,000.

Property Crimes

The three property crimes of burglary, automobile theft, and larceny of $50 and over make up 87 percent of Index crimes. The Index is a reasonably reliable indicator of the total number of property crimes reported to the police, but not a particularly good indicator of the seriousness of monetary loss from all property crimes. Commission studies tend to indicate that such non-Index crimes as fraud and embezzlement are more significant in terms of dollar volume. Fraud can be a particularly pernicious offense. It is not only expensive in total but all too often preys on the weak.

Many larcenies included in the Index total are misdemeanors rather than felonies under the laws of their own States. Auto thefts that involve only unauthorized use also are misdemeanors in many States. Many stolen automobiles are abandoned after a few hours, and more than 85 percent are ultimately recovered according to UCR studies. Studies in California indicate that about 20 percent of recovered cars are significantly damaged.

Other Criminal Offenses

The UCR Index does not and is not intended to assist in assessing all serious national crime problems. For example, offense statistics are not sufficient to assess the incidence of crime connected with corporate activity, commonly known as white-collar crime, or the total criminal acts committed by organized crime groups. Likewise, offense and arrest figures alone do not aid very much in analyzing the scope of professional crime—that is, the number and types of offenses committed by those whose principal employment and source of income are based upon the commission of criminal acts.

Except for larceny under $50 and negligent manslaughter, for which there are some national offenses-known-to-the-police data, knowledge of the volume and trends of non-Index crimes depends upon arrest statistics. Since the police are not able to make arrests in many cases, these are necessarily less complete than the "offenses known" statistics. Moreover, the ratio between arrests and the number of offenses differs significantly from offense to offense—as is shown, for example, by the high percentage of reported cases in which arrests are made for murder (91 percent) and the relatively low percentage for larceny (20 percent). Reporting to the FBI for arrests covers less than 70 percent of the population. However, because arrest statistics are collected for a broader range of offenses—28 categories including the Index crimes—they show more of the diversity and magnitude of the many different crime problems. Property crimes do not loom so large in this picture.

Nearly 45 percent of all arrests are for such crimes without victims or against the public order as drunkenness, gambling, liquor law violations, vagrancy, and prostitution. As table 2 shows, drunkenness alone accounts for almost one-third of all arrests. This is not neces-

TABLE 2. NUMBER AND RATE OF ARRESTS
FOR THE 10 MOST FREQUENT OFFENSES, 1965
(4,062 agencies reporting; total population 134,095,000)

Rank	Offense	Number	Rate (per 100,000 population)	Percent of total arrests
1	Drunkenness	1,535,040	1,144.7	31.0
2	Disorderly conduct	570,122	425.2	11.5
3	Larceny (over and under $50)	385,726	286.2	7.7
4	Driving under the influence	241,511	180.1	4.9
5	Simple assault	207,615	154.8	4.2
6	Burglary	197,627	147.4	4.0
7	Liquor laws	179,219	133.7	3.6
8	Vagrancy	120,416	89.8	2.4
9	Gambling	114,294	85.2	2.3
10	Motor vehicle theft	101,763	75.9	2.1
	Total, 10 most frequent offenses	3,651,333	2,722.9	73.7
	Arrests for all offenses	4,955,047	3,695.2	100.0

[A9005]

sarily a good indication of the number of persons arrested for drunkenness, however, as some individuals may be arrested many times during the year. Arrest statistics measure the number of arrests, not the number of criminals.

The Extent of Unreported Crime

Although the police statistics indicate a lot of crime today, they do not begin to indicate the full amount. Crimes reported directly to prosecutors usually do not show up in the police statistics. Citizens often do not report crimes to the police. Some crimes reported to the police never get into the statistical system. Since better crime prevention and control programs depend upon a full and accurate knowledge about the amount and kinds of crime, the Commission initiated the first national survey ever made of crime vicitimization. The National Opinion Research Center of the University of Chicago surveyed 10,000 households, asking whether the person questioned, or any member of his or her household, had been a victim of crime during the past year, whether the crime had been reported and, if not, the reasons for not reporting.

More detailed surveys were undertaken in a number of high and medium crime rate precincts of Washington, Chicago, and Boston by the Bureau of Social Science Research of Washington, D.C., and the Survey Research Center of the University of Michigan. All of the surveys dealt primarily with households or individuals, although some data were obtained for certain kinds of businesses and other organizations.

These surveys show that the actual amount of crime in the United States today is several times that reported in the UCR. As table 4 shows, the amount of personal injury crime reported to NORC is almost twice the UCR rate and the amount of property crime more than twice as much as the UCR rate for individuals. Forcible rapes were more than 3½ times the reported rate, burglaries three times, aggravated assaults and larcenies of $50 and over more than double, and robbery 50 percent greater than the reported rate. Only vehicle theft was lower and then by a small amount. (The single homicide reported is too small a number to be statistically useful.)

TABLE 4. COMPARISON OF SURVEY AND UCR RATES
(Per 100,000 population)

Index Crimes	NORC survey 1965–66	UCR rate for individuals 1965 [1]	UCR rate for individuals and organizations 1965 [1]
Willful homicide	3.0	5.1	5.1
Forcible rape	42.5	11.6	11.6
Robbery	94.0	61.4	61.4
Aggravated assault	218.3	106.6	106.6
Burglary	949.1	299.6	605.3
Larceny ($50 and over)	606.5	267.4	393.3
Motor vehicle theft	206.2	226.0	251.0
Total violence	357.8	184.7	184.7
Total property	1,761.8	793.0	1,249.6

[1] "Uniform Crime Reports," 1965, p. 51. The UCR national totals do not distinguish crimes committed against individuals or households from those committed against businesses or other organizations. The UCR rate for individuals is the published national rate adjusted to eliminate burglaries, larcenies, and vehicle thefts not committed against individuals or households. No adjustment was made for robbery.

[A9006]

Even these rates probably understate the actual amounts of crime. The national survey was a survey of the victim experience of every member of a household based on interviews of one member. If the results are tabulated only for the family member who was interviewed, the amount of unreported victimization for some offenses is considerably higher. Apparently, the person interviewed remembered more of his own victimization than that of other members of his family.

TRENDS IN CRIME

There has always been too much crime. Virtually every generation since the founding of the Nation and before has felt itself threatened by the spectre of rising crime and violence.

*   *   *

Unlike some European countries, which have maintained national statistics for more than a century and a quarter, the United States has maintained national crime statistics only since 1930. Because the rural areas were slow in coming into the system and reported poorly when they did, it was not until 1958, when other major changes were made in the UCR, that reporting of rural crimes was sufficient to allow a total national estimate without special adjustments. Changes in overall estimating procedures and two offense categories—rape and larceny—were also made in 1958. Because of these problems figures prior to 1958 and particularly those prior to 1940, must be viewed as neither fully comparable with nor nearly so reliable as later figures.

For crimes of violence the 1933–65 period, based on newly adjusted unpublished figures from the UCR, has been, as figure 3 shows, one of sharply divergent trends for the different offenses. Total numbers for all reported offenses have increased markedly; the Nation's population has increased also—by more than 47 percent since 1940. The number of offenses per 100,000 population has tripled for forcible rape and has doubled for aggravated assault during the period, both increasing at a fairly constant pace. The willful homicide rate has decreased somewhat to about 70 percent of its high in 1933, while robbery has fluctuated from a high in 1933 and a low during World War II to a point where it is now about 20 percent above the beginning of the postwar era. The overall rate for violent crimes, primarily due to the increased rate for aggravated assault, now stands at its highest point, well above what it has been throughout most of the period.

Property crime rates, as shown in figure 4, are up much more sharply than the crimes of violence. The rate for larceny of $50 and over has shown the greatest increase of all Index offenses. It is up more than 550 percent over 1933. The burglary rate has nearly doubled. The rate for auto theft has followed an uneven course to a point about the same as the rate of the early thirties.

The upward trend for 1960–65 as shown in table 6 has been faster than the long-term trend, up 25 percent for the violent crimes and 36 percent for the property crimes. The greatest increases in the period came in 1964, in forcible rape among crimes of violence and in vehicle theft among property crimes. Preliminary reports indicate that all Index offenses rose in 1966.

Arrest rates are in general much less complete and are available for many fewer years than are rates for offenses known to the police.

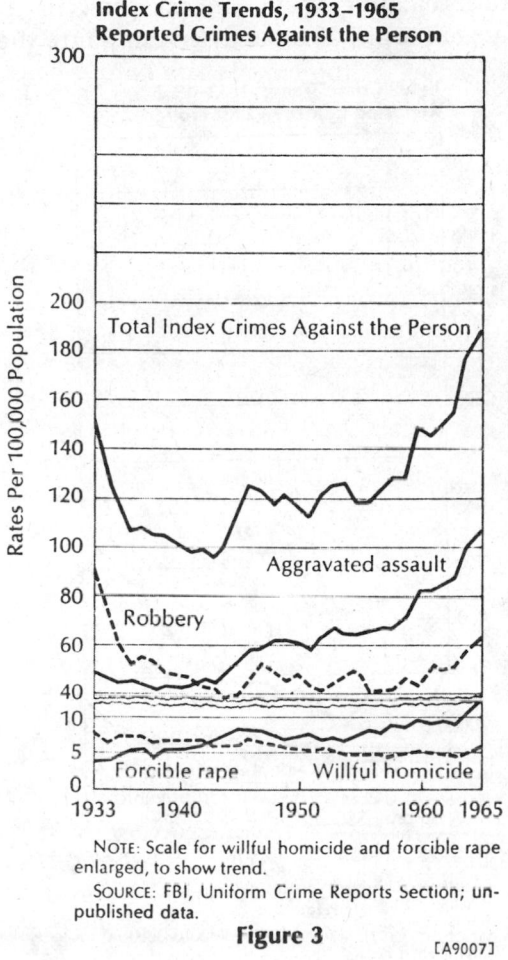

Index Crime Trends, 1933–1965
Reported Crimes Against the Person

NOTE: Scale for willful homicide and forcible rape
enlarged, to show trend.

SOURCE: FBI, Uniform Crime Reports Section; unpublished data.

Figure 3

[A9007]

However, they do provide another measure of the trend of crime.
For crimes of violence, arrest rates rose 16 percent during 1960–65,
considerably less than the 25 percent increase indicated by offenses
known to the police. For property crimes, arrest rates have increased
about 25 percent, as opposed to a 36 percent increase in offenses known
to the police during 1960–65. Figure 5 compares the 1960–65 trend for
arrests and offenses known for both crimes of violence and property
crimes.

Prior to the year 1933, shown in figures 3 and 4, there is no estimated national rate for any offenses. UCR figures for a sizable number of individual cities, however, indicate that the 1930–32 rates, at
least for those cities, were higher than the 1933 rates. Studies of such
individual cities as Boston, Chicago, New York, and others indicate
that in the twenties and the World War I years reported rates for many
offenses were even higher. A recent study of crime in Buffalo, N. Y.,
from 1854 to 1946 showed arrest rates in that city for willful homicide,

rape, and assault reaching their highest peak in the early 1870's, declining, rising again until 1918, and declining into the forties.

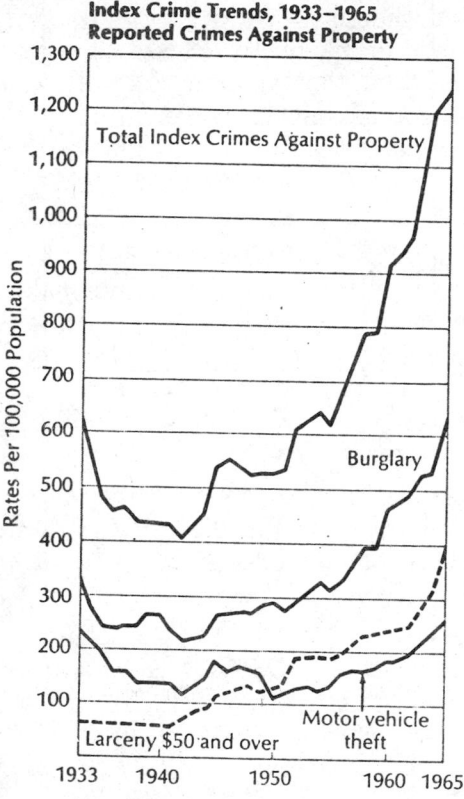

Index Crime Trends, 1933–1965
Reported Crimes Against Property

NOTE: The scale for this figure is not comparable with that used in Figure 3.

SOURCE: FBI, Uniform Crime Reports Section; unpublished data.

Figure 4

TABLE 6. OFFENSES KNOWN TO THE POLICE, 1960–65
(Rates per 100,000 population)

Offense	1960	1961	1962	1963	1964	1965
Willful homicide	5.0	4.7	4.5	4.5	4.8	5.1
Forcible rape	9.2	9.0	9.1	9.0	10.7	11.6
Robbery	51.6	50.0	51.1	53.0	58.4	61.4
Aggravated assault	82.5	82.2	84.9	88.6	101.8	106.6
Burglary	465.5	474.9	489.7	527.4	580.4	605.3
Larceny $50 and over	271.4	277.9	296.6	330.9	368.2	393.3
Motor vehicle theft	179.2	179.9	193.4	212.1	242.0	251.0
Total crimes against person	148.3	145.9	149.6	155.1	175.7	184.7
Total property crimes	916.1	932.7	979.7	1,070.4	1,190.6	1,249.6

SOURCE: FBI, Uniform Crime Reports Section, unpublished data.

[A9008]

Trends for crimes against trust, vice crimes, and crimes against public order, based on arrest rates for 1960–65, follow a much more checkered pattern than do trends for Index offenses. For some offenses this is in part due to the fact that arrest patterns change significantly from time to time, as when New York recently decided not to make further arrests for public drunkenness. Based on comparable places covering about half the total population, arrest rates during 1960–65 rose 13 percent for simple assault, 13 percent for embezzlement and fraud, and 36 percent for narcotics violations, while for the same period, the rates declined 24 percent for gambling and 11 percent for drunkenness.

The picture portrayed by the official statistics in recent years, both in the total number of crimes and in the number of crimes per 100,000 Americans, is one of increasing crime. Crime always seems to be increasing, never going down. Up 5 percent this year, 10 the next, and the Commission's surveys have shown there is a great deal more crime than the official statistics show. The public can fairly wonder whether there is ever to be an end.

This official picture is also alarming because it seems so pervasive. Crimes of violence are up in both the biggest and smallest cities, in the suburbs as well as in the rural areas. The same is true for property crimes. Young people are being arrested in ever increasing numbers. Offense rates for most crimes are rising every year and in every section of the country. That there are some bright spots does not change this dismal outlook. Rates for some offenses are still below those of the early thirties and perhaps of earlier periods. Willful homicide rates have been below the 1960 level through most of the last few years. Robbery rates continue to decline in the rural areas and small towns, and arrest rates for many non-Index offenses have remained relatively stable.

*   *   *

Assessing the Amount and Trend of Crime

Because of the grave public concern about the crime problem in America today, the Commission has made a special effort to understand the amount and trend of crime and has reached the following conclusions:

1. The number of offenses—crimes of violence, crimes against property and most others as well—has been increasing. Naturally, population growth is one of the significant contributing factors in the total amount of crime.

2. Most forms of crime—especially crimes against property—are increasing faster than population growth. This means that the risk of victimization to the individual citizen for these crimes is increasing, although it is not possible to ascertain precisely the extent of the

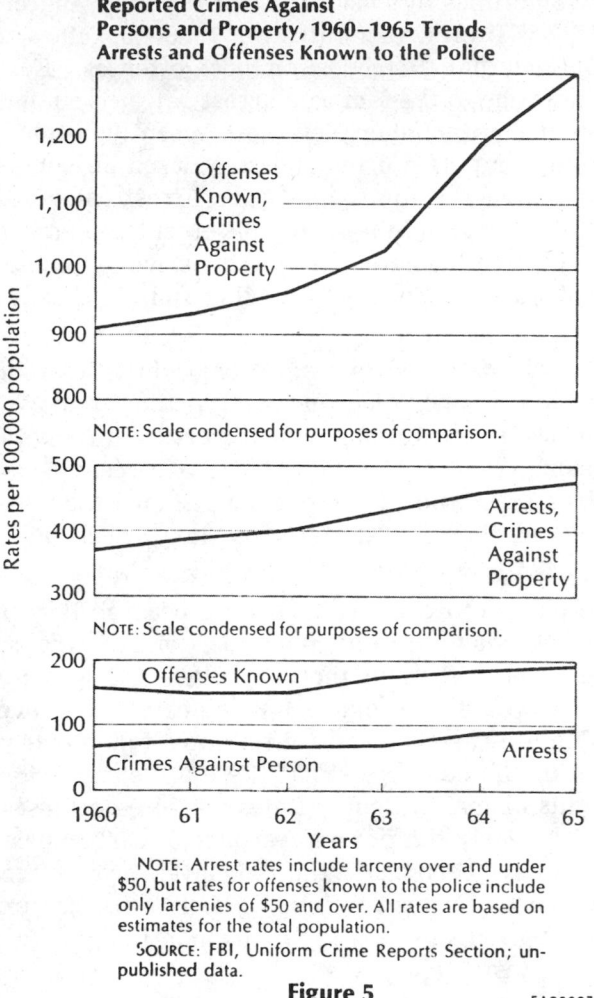

**Reported Crimes Against
Persons and Property, 1960–1965 Trends
Arrests and Offenses Known to the Police**

NOTE: Scale condensed for purposes of comparison.

NOTE: Scale condensed for purposes of comparison.

NOTE: Arrest rates include larceny over and under
$50, but rates for offenses known to the police include
only larcenies of $50 and over. All rates are based on
estimates for the total population.

SOURCE: FBI, Uniform Crime Reports Section; unpublished data.

Figure 5   [A9009]

increase.   All the economic and social factors discussed above support,
and indeed lead to, this conclusion.

The Commission found it very difficult to make accurate measure-
ments of crime trends by relying solely on official figures, since it is
likely that each year police agencies are to some degree dipping deeper
into the vast reservoir of unreported crime.   People are probably reporting more to the police as a reflection of higher expectations and
greater confidence, and the police in turn are reflecting this in their
statistics.   In this sense more efficient policing may be leading to higher rates of reported crime.   The diligence of the FBI in promoting more
complete and accurate reporting through the development of professional police reporting procedures has clearly had an important effect
on the completeness of reporting, but while this task of upgrading local
reporting is under way, the FBI is faced with the problem, in com-
puting national trends, of omitting for a time the places undergoing

changes in reporting methods and estimating the amount of crime that occurred in those places in prior years.

3.   Although the Commission concluded that there has been an increase in the volume and rate of crime in America, it has been unable to decide whether individual Americans today are more criminal than their counterparts 5, 10, or 25 years ago.   To answer this question it would be necessary to make comparisons between persons of the same age, sex, race, place of residence, economic status and other factors at the different times: in other words, to decide whether the 15-year-old slum dweller or the 50-year-old businessman is inherently more criminal now than the 15-year-old slum dweller or the 50-year-old business-man in the past.   Because of the many rapid and turbulent changes over these years in society as a whole and in the myriad conditions of life which affect crime, it was not possible for the Commission to make such a comparison.   Nor do the data exist to make even simple comparisons of the incidence of crime among persons of the same age, sex, race, and place of residence at these different years.

4.   There is a great deal of crime in America, some of it very serious, that is not reported to the police, or in some instances by the police.   The national survey revealed that people are generally more likely to report serious crimes to the police, but the percent who indicated they did report to the police ranged from 10 percent for consumer fraud to 89 percent for auto theft.   Estimates of the rate of victimization for Index offenses ranged from 2 per 100 persons in the national survey to 10 to 20 per 100 persons in the individual districts surveyed in 3 cities.   The surveys produced rates of victimization that were from 2 to 10 times greater than the official rates for certain crimes.

5.   What is needed to answer questions about the volume and trend of crime satisfactorily are a number of different crime indicators showing trends over a period of time to supplement the improved reporting by police agencies.   The Commission experimented with the development of public surveys of victims of crime and feels this can become a useful supplementary yardstick.   Further development of the procedure is needed to improve the reliability and accuracy of the findings.   However, the Commission found these initial experiments produced useful results that justify more intensive efforts to gather such information on a regular basis.   They should also be supplemented by new types of surveys and censuses which would provide better information about crime in areas where good information is lacking such as crimes by or against business and other organizations.   The Commission also believes that an improved and greatly expanded procedure for the collection of arrest statistics would be of immense benefit in the assessment of the problem of juvenile delinquency.

6.   Throughout its work the Commission has noted repeatedly the sharp differences in the amount and trends of reported crimes against

property as compared with crimes against persons. It has noted that while property crimes are far more numerous than crimes against the person, and so dominate any reported trends, there is much public concern about crimes against persons. The more recent reports of the UCR have moved far toward separating the reporting of these two classes of crime altogether.

*   *   *

7. The Commission believes that age, urbanization, and other shifts in the population already under way will likely operate over the next 5 to 10 years to increase the volume of offenses faster than population growth. Further dipping into the reservoirs of unreported crime will likely combine with this real increase in crime to produce even greater increases in reported crime rates. Many of the basic social forces that tend to increase the amount of real crime are already taking effect and are for the most part irreversible. If society is to be successful in its desire to reduce the amount of real crime, it must find new ways to create the kinds of conditions and inducements—social, environmental, and psychological—that will bring about a greater commitment to law-abiding conduct and respect for the law on the part of all Americans and a better understanding of the great stake that all men have in being able to trust in the honesty and integrity of their fellow citizens.

*   *   *

B. ASCERTAINMENT OF GUILT: THE INSTITUTIONAL FRAMEWORK

PRESIDENT'S COMMISSION ON LAW ENFORCEMENT AND ADMINISTRATION OF JUSTICE, THE CHALLENGE OF CRIME IN A FREE SOCIETY

7–12 (1967).

AMERICA'S SYSTEM OF CRIMINAL JUSTICE

*   *   *

The criminal justice system has three separately organized parts—the police, the courts, and corrections—and each has distinct tasks. However, these parts are by no means independent of each other. What each one does and how it does it has a direct effect on the work of the others. The courts must deal, and can only deal, with those whom the police arrest; the business of corrections is with those delivered to it by the courts. How successfully corrections reforms convicts determines whether they will once again become police business and influences the sentences the judges pass; police activities are subject to court scrutiny and are often determined by court decisions. And so reforming or reorganizing any part or procedure of the system changes other parts or procedures. Furthermore, the criminal process, the method by which the system deals with individual cases, is not a hodgepodge of random actions. It is rather a continuum—an orderly progression of events—some of which, like arrest and trial, are highly visible and some of which, though of great importance, occur out of public view. A study of the system must begin by examining it as a whole.

The chart on the following page sets forth in simplified form the process of criminal administration and shows the many decision points along its course. Since felonies, misdemeanors, petty offenses, and juvenile cases generally follow quite different paths, they are shown separately.

The popular, or even the lawbook, theory of everyday criminal process oversimplifies in some respects and overcomplicates in others what usually happens. That theory is that when an infraction of the law occurs, a policeman finds, if he can, the probable offender, arrests him and brings him promptly before a magistrate. If the offense is minor, the magistrate disposes of it forthwith; if it is serious, he holds the defendant for further action and admits him to bail. The case then is turned over to a prosecuting attorney, who charges the defendant with a specific statutory crime. This charge is subject to review by a judge at a preliminary hearing of the evidence and in many places if the offense charged is a felony, by a grand jury that can dismiss the charge, or affirm it by delivering it to a judge in the form of an indictment. If the defendant pleads "not guilty" to the charge he comes to trial; the facts of his case are marshaled by prosecuting and defense attorneys and presented, under the supervision of a judge, through witnesses, to a jury. If the jury finds the defendant guilty, he is sentenced by the judge to a term in prison, where a systematic attempt to convert him into a law-abiding citizen is made, or to a term of probation, under which he is permitted to live in the community as long as he behaves himself.

Some cases do proceed much like that, especially those involving offenses that are generally considered "major": serious acts of violence or thefts of large amounts of property. However, not all major cases follow this course, and, in any event, the bulk of the daily business of the criminal justice system consists of offenses that are not major—of breaches of the peace, crimes of vice, petty thefts, assaults arising from domestic or street-corner or barroom disputes. These and most other cases are disposed of in much less formal and much less deliberate ways.

* * *

What has evidently happened is that the transformation of America from a relatively relaxed rural society into a tumultuous urban one has presented the criminal justice system in the cities with a volume of cases too large to handle by traditional methods. One result of heavy caseloads is highly visible in city courts, which process many cases with excessive haste and many others with excessive slowness. In the interest both of effectiveness and of fairness to individuals, justice should be swift and certain; too often in city courts today it is, instead, hasty or faltering. Invisibly, the pressure of numbers has effected a series of adventitious changes in the criminal process. Informal short-

A general view of The Criminal Justice System

This chart seeks to present a simple yet comprehensive view of the movement of cases through the criminal justice system. Procedures in individual jurisdictions may vary from the pattern shown here. The differing weights of line indicate the relative volumes of cases disposed of at various points in the system, but this is only suggestive since no nationwide data of this sort exists.

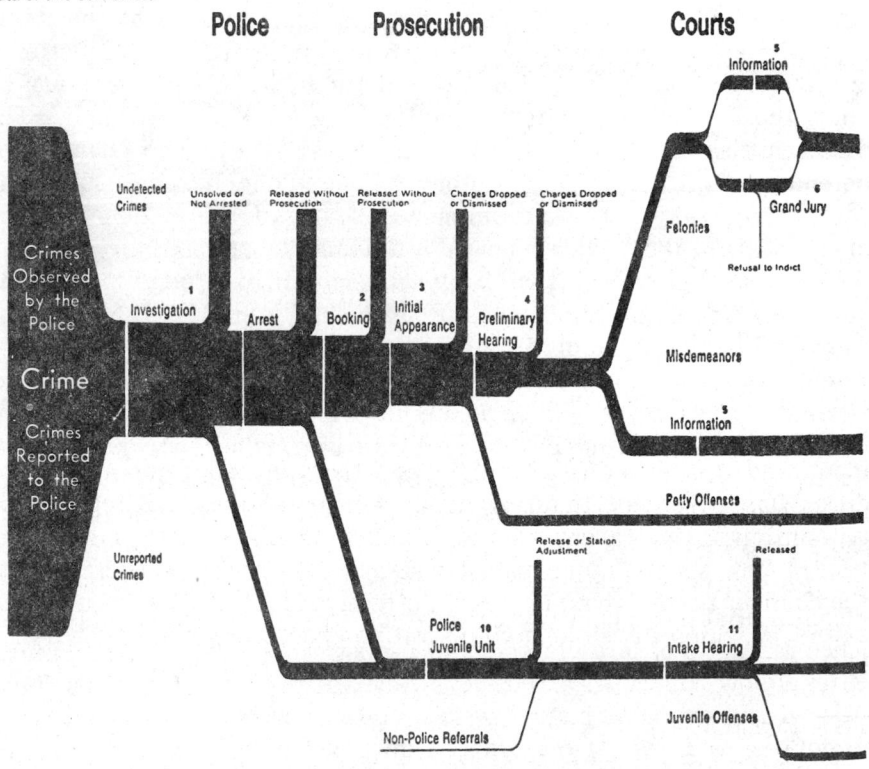

1   May continue until trial.

2   Administrative record of arrest. First step at which temporary release on bail may be available.

3   Before magistrate, commissioner, or justice of peace. Formal notice of charge, advice of rights. Bail set. Summary trials for petty offenses usually conducted here without further processing.

4   Preliminary testing of evidence against defendant. Charge may be reduced. No separate preliminary hearing for misdemeanors in some systems.

5   Charge filed by prosecutor on basis of information submitted by police or citizens. Alternative to grand jury indictment; often used in felonies, almost always in misdemeanors.

6   Reviews whether Government evidence sufficient to justify trial. Some States have no grand jury system; others seldom use it.

[A7374]

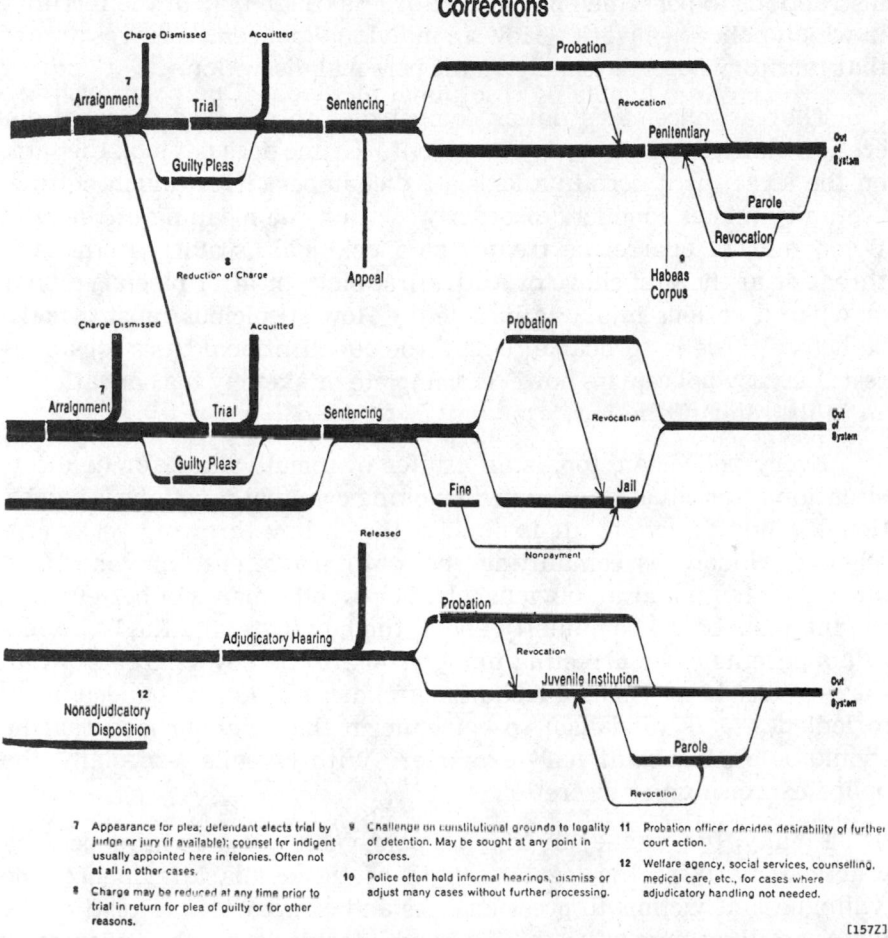

Corrections

7 Appearance for plea; defendant elects trial by judge or jury (if available); counsel for indigent usually appointed here in felonies. Often not at all in other cases.

8 Charge may be reduced at any time prior to trial in return for plea of guilty or for other reasons.

9 Challenge on constitutional grounds to legality of detention. May be sought at any point in process.

10 Police often hold informal hearings, dismiss or adjust many cases without further processing.

11 Probation officer decides desirability of further court action.

12 Welfare agency, social services, counselling, medical care, etc., for cases where adjudicatory handling not needed.

[157Z]

cuts have been used. The decision making process has often become routinized. Throughout the system the importance of individual judgment and discretion, as distinguished from stated rules and procedures, has increased. In effect, much decision making is being done on an administrative rather than on a judicial basis. Thus, an examination of how the criminal justice system works and a consideration of the changes needed to make it more effective and fair must focus on the extent to which invisible, administrative procedures depart from visible, traditional ones, and on the desirability of that departure.

THE POLICE

At the very beginning of the process—or, more properly, before the process begins at all—something happens that is scarcely discussed in lawbooks and is seldom recognized by the public: law enforcement policy is made by the policeman. For policemen cannot and do not arrest all the offenders they encounter. It is doubtful that they arrest most of them. A criminal code, in practice, is not a set of specific instructions to policemen but a more or less rough map of the territory in which policemen work.   How an individual policeman moves around that territory depends largely on his personal discretion.

That a policeman's duties compel him to exercise personal discretion many times every day is evident.   Crime does not look the same on the street as it does in a legislative chamber.   How much noise or profanity makes conduct "disorderly" within the meaning of the law? When must a quarrel be treated as a criminal assault: at the first threat or at the first shove or at the first blow, or after blood is drawn, or when a serious injury is inflicted?   How suspicious must conduct be before there is "probable cause," the constitutional basis for an arrest?   Every policeman, however complete or sketchy his education, is an interpreter of the law.

Every policeman, too, is an arbiter of social values, for he meets situation after situation in which invoking criminal sanctions is a questionable line of action.   It is obvious that a boy throwing rocks at a school's windows is committing the statutory offense of vandalism, but it is often not at all obvious whether a policeman will better serve the interests of the community and of the boy by taking the boy home to his parents or by arresting him.   Who are the boy's parents?   Can they control him?   Is he a frequent offender who has responded badly to leniency?   Is vandalism so epidemic in the neighborhood that he should be made a cautionary example?   With juveniles especially, the police exercise great discretion.

Finally, the manner in which a policeman works is influenced by practical matters: the legal strength of the available evidence, the willingness of victims to press charges and of witnesses to testify, the temper of the community, the time and information at the policeman's disposal.   Much is at stake in how the policeman exercises this discretion.   If he judges conduct not suspicious enough to justify intervention, the chance to prevent a robbery, rape, or murder may be lost. If he overestimates the seriousness of a situation or his actions are controlled by panic or prejudice, he may hurt or kill someone unnecessarily.   His actions may even touch off a riot.

THE MAGISTRATE

In direct contrast to the policeman, the magistrate before whom a suspect is first brought usually exercises less discretion than the law allows him.   He is entitled to inquire into the facts of the case, into whether there are grounds for holding the accused.   He seldom does. He seldom can.   The more promptly an arrested suspect is brought into magistrate's court, the less likelihood there is that much information about the arrest other than the arresting officer's statement will be available to the magistrate.   Moreover many magistrates, especially in big cities, have such congested calendars that it is almost impossible for them to subject any case but an extraordinary one to prolonged scrutiny.

In practice the most important things, by far, that a magistrate does are to set the amount of a defendant's bail and in some jurisdictions to appoint counsel. Too seldom does either action get the careful attention it deserves. In many cases the magistrate accepts a waiver of counsel without insuring that the suspect knows the significance of legal representation.

Bail is a device to free an untried defendant and at the same time make sure he appears for trial. That is the sole stated legal purpose in America. The Eighth Amendment to the Constitution declares that it must not be "excessive." Appellate courts have declared that not just the seriousness of the charge against the defendant, but the suspect's personal, family, and employment situation, as they bear on the likelihood of his appearance, must be weighed before the amount of his bail is fixed. Yet more magistrates than not set bail according to standard rates: so and so many dollars for such and such an offense.

The persistence of money bail can best be explained not by its stated purpose but by the belief of police, prosecutors, and courts that the best way to keep a defendant from committing more crimes before trial is to set bail so high that he cannot obtain his release.

THE PROSECUTOR

The key administrative officer in the processing of cases is the prosecutor. Theoretically the examination of the evidence against a defendant by a judge at a preliminary hearing, and its reexamination by a grand jury, are important parts of the process. Practically they seldom are because a prosecutor seldom has any difficulty in making a prima facie case against a defendant. In fact most defendants waive their rights to preliminary hearings and much more often than not grand juries indict precisely as prosecutors ask them to. The prosecutor wields almost undisputed sway over the pretrial progress of most cases. He decides whether to press a case or drop it. He determines the specific charge against a defendant. When the charge is reduced, as it is in as many as two-thirds of all cases in some cities, the prosecutor is usually the official who reduces it.

*　　　*　　　*

THE PLEA AND THE SENTENCE

When a prosecutor reduces a charge it is ordinarily because there has been "plea bargaining" between him and a defense attorney. The issue at stake is how much the prosecutor will reduce his original charge or how lenient a sentence he will recommend, in return for a plea of guilty. There is no way of judging how many bargains reflect the prosecutor's belief that a lesser charge or sentence is justified and how many result from the fact that there may be in the system at any one time ten times as many cases as there are prosecutors or judges or courtrooms to handle them, should every one come to trial. In form, a plea bargain can be anything from a series of careful conferences to a hurried consultation in a courthouse corridor. In content it can be anything from a conscientious exploration of the facts and dispositional alternatives available and appropriate to a defendant, to a perfunctory deal. If the interests of a defendant are to be properly protected while his fate is being thus invisibly determined, he obviously needs just as good legal representation as the kind he needs at a public trial. Whether or not plea bargaining is a fair and effective method of disposing of criminal cases depends heavily on whether or not defendants are provided early with competent and conscientious counsel.

Plea bargaining is not only an invisible procedure but, in some jurisdictions, a theoretically unsanctioned one. In order to satisfy the court record, a defendant, his attorney, and the prosecutor will at the time of sentencing often ritually state to a judge that no bargain has been made. Plea bargaining may be a useful procedure, especially in congested urban jurisdictions, but neither the dignity of the law, nor the quality of justice, nor the protection of society from dangerous criminals is enhanced by its being conducted covertly.

* * *

An enormously consequential kind of decision is the sentencing decision of a judge. The law recognizes the importance of fitting sentences to individual defendants by giving judges, in most instances, considerable latitude. For example the recently adopted New York Penal Code, which went into effect in autumn of 1967, empowers a judge to impose upon a man convicted of armed robbery any sentence between a 5-year term of probation and a 25-year term in prison. Even when a judge has presided over a trial during which the facts of a case have been carefully set forth and has been given a probation report that carefully discusses a defendant's character, background, and problems, he cannot find it easy to choose a sentence. In perhaps nine-tenths of all cases there is no trial; the defendants are self-confessedly guilty.

In the lower or misdemeanor courts, the courts that process most criminal cases, probation reports are a rarity. Under such circumstances judges have little to go on and many sentences are bound to be based on conjecture or intuition. When a sentence is part of a plea bargain, which an overworked judge ratifies perfunctorily, it may not even be his conjecture or intuition on which the sentence is based, but a prosecutor's or a defense counsel's. But perhaps the greatest lack judges suffer from when they pass sentence is not time or information, but correctional alternatives. Some lower courts do not have any probation officers, and in almost every court the caseloads of probation officers are so heavy that a sentence of probation means, in fact, releasing an offender into the community with almost no supervision. Few States have a sufficient variety of correctional institutions or treatment programs to inspire judges with the confidence that sentences will lead to rehabilitation.

CORRECTIONS

The correctional apparatus to which guilty defendants are delivered is in every respect the most isolated part of the criminal justice system. Much of it is physically isolated; its institutions usually have thick walls and locked doors, and often they are situated in rural areas, remote from the courts where the institutions' inmates were tried and from the communities where they lived. The correctional apparatus is isolated in the sense that its officials do not have everyday working relationships with officials from the system's other branches, like those that commonly exist between policemen and prosecutors, or prosecutors and judges. It is isolated in the sense that what it does with, to, or for the people under its supervision is seldom governed by any but the most broadly written statutes, and is almost never scrutinized by appellate courts. Finally, it is isolated from the public partly by its invisibility and physical remoteness; partly by the inherent lack of drama in most of its activities, but perhaps most importantly by the fact that the correctional apparatus is often used— or misused—by both the criminal justice system and the public as a rug under which disturbing problems and people can be swept.

The most striking fact about the correctional apparatus today is that, although the rehabilitation of criminals is presumably its major purpose, the custody of criminals is actually its major task. On any given day there are well over a million people being "corrected" in America, two-thirds of them on probation or parole and one-third of them in prisons or jails. However, prisons and jails are where four-fifths of correctional money is spent and where nine-tenths of correctional employees work. Furthermore, fewer than one-fifth of the people who work in State prisons and local jails have jobs that are not essentially either custodial or administrative in character. Many jails have nothing but custodial and administrative personnel. Of course many jails are crowded with defendants who have not been able to furnish bail and who are not considered by the law to be appropriate objects of rehabilitation because it has not yet been determined that they are criminals who need it.

What this emphasis on custody means in practice is that the enormous potential of the correctional apparatus for making creative decisions about its treatment of convicts is largely unfulfilled. This is true not only of offenders in custody but of offenders on probation and parole. Most authorities agree that while probationers and parolees need varying degrees and kinds of supervision, an average of no more than 35 cases per officer is necessary for effective attention; 97 percent of all officers handling adults have larger caseloads than that. In the juvenile correctional system the situation is somewhat better. Juvenile institutions, which typically are training schools, have a higher proportion of treatment personnel and juvenile probation and parole officers generally have lighter caseloads. However, these comparatively rich resources are very far from being sufficiently rich.

Except for sentencing, no decision in the criminal process has more impact on the convicted offender than the parole decision, which determines how much of his maximum sentence a prisoner must serve. This again is an invisible administrative decision that is seldom open to attack or subject to review. It is made by parole board members who are often political appointees. Many are skilled and conscientious, but they generally are able to spend no more than a few minutes on a case. Parole decisions that are made in haste and on the basis of insufficient information, in the absence of parole machinery that can provide good supervision, are necessarily imperfect decisions. And since there is virtually no appeal from them, they can be made arbitrarily or discriminatorily. Just as carefully formulated and clearly stated law enforcement policies would help policemen, charge policies would help prosecutors and sentencing policies would help judges, so parole policies would help parole boards perform their delicate and important duties.

C. ASCERTAINMENT OF GUILT: THE PROSECUTION'S BURDEN OF PROOF BEYOND A REASONABLE DOUBT

1. IN GENERAL

IN RE WINSHIP

Supreme Court of the United States, 1970.
397 U.S. 358, 90 S.Ct. 1068, 25 L.Ed.2d 368.

Mr. Justice BRENNAN delivered the opinion of the Court.

Constitutional questions decided by this Court concerning the juvenile process have centered on the adjudicatory stage at "which a determination is made as to whether a juvenile is a 'delinquent' as a result of alleged misconduct on his part, with the consequence that he may be committed to a state institution." In re Gault, 387 U.S. 1, 13, 87 S.Ct. 1428, 1436, 18 L.Ed.2d 527 (1967), *Gault* decided that, although the Fourteenth Amendment does not require that the hearing at this stage conform with all the requirements of a criminal trial or even of the usual administrative proceeding, the Due Process Clause does require application during the adjudicatory hearing of "the essentials of due process and fair treatment." Id., at 30, 87 S.Ct. at 1445. This case presents the single, narrow question whether proof beyond a reasonable doubt is among the "essentials of due process and fair treatment" required during the adjudicatory stage when a juvenile is charged with an act which would constitute a crime if committed by an adult.

* * *

I

The requirement that guilt of a criminal charge be established by proof beyond a reasonable doubt dates at least from our early years as a Nation. The "demand for a higher degree of persuasion in criminal cases was recurrently expressed from ancient times, [though] its crystallization into the formula 'beyond a reasonable doubt' seems to have occurred as late as 1798. It is now accepted in common law jurisdictions as the measure of persuasion by which the prosecution must convince the trier of all the essential elements of guilt." McCormick, Evidence, § 321, at 681–682 (1954); see also 9 Wigmore, Evidence, § 2497 (3d ed. 1940). Although virtually unanimous adherence to the reasonable-doubt standard in common-law jurisdictions may not conclusively establish it as a requirement of due process, such adherence does "reflect a profound judgment about the way in which law should be enforced and justice administered." Duncan v. Louisiana, 391 U.S. 145, 155, 88 S.Ct. 1444, 1451, 20 L.Ed.2d 491 (1968).

Expressions in many opinions of this Court indicate that it has long been assumed that proof of a criminal charge beyond a reasonable doubt is constitutionally required. * * * Mr. Justice Frankfurter stated that "[i]t is the duty of the Government to establish * * * guilt beyond a reasonable doubt. This notion—basic in our law and rightly one of the boasts of a free society—is a requirement and a safeguard of due process of law in the historic procedural content of 'due process.' " Leland v. Oregon, [343 U.S. 790, 802–803, 72 S.Ct. 1002, 1009 (1952)] (dissenting opinion). In a similar vein, the Court said in Brinegar v. United States, [338 U.S. 160, 174, 69 S.Ct. 1302, 1310 (1949)] that "[g]uilt in a criminal case must be proved beyond a reasonable doubt and by evidence confined to that which long experience in the common-law tradition, to some extent embodied in the Constitution, has crystallized into rules of evidence consistent with that standard. These rules are historically grounded rights of our system, developed to safeguard men from dubious and unjust convictions, with resulting forfeitures of life, liberty and property." Davis v. United States, [160 U.S. 469, 488, 16 S.Ct. 353, 358 (1895)] stated that the requirement is implicit in "constitutions * * * [which] recognize the fundamental principles that are deemed essential for the protection of life and liberty." In *Davis* a murder conviction was reversed because the trial judge instructed the jury that it was their duty to convict when the evidence was equally balanced regarding the sanity of the accused. This Court said: "On the contrary, he is entitled to an acquittal of the specific crime charged, if upon all the evidence, there is reasonable doubt whether he was capable in law of committing crime.   *   *   *   No man should be deprived of his life under the forms of law unless the jurors who try him are able, upon their consciences, to say that the evidence before them   *   *   *   is sufficient to show beyond a reasonable doubt the existence of every fact necessary to constitute the crime charged." Id., at 484, 493, 16 S.Ct., at 357, 360.

The reasonable-doubt standard plays a vital role in the American scheme of criminal procedure. It is a prime instrument for reducing the risk of convictions resting on factual error. The standard provides concrete substance for the presumption of innocence—that bedrock "axiomatic and elementary" principle whose "enforcement lies at the foundation of the administration of our criminal law." Coffin v. United States, [156 U.S. 432, 453, 15 S.Ct. 394, 403 (1895)]. As the dissenters in the New York Court of Appeals observed, and we agree, "a person accused of crime   *   *   *   would be at a severe disadvantage, a disadvantage amounting to a lack of fundamental fairness, if he could be adjudged guilty and imprisoned for years on the strength of the same evidence as would suffice in a civil case." 24 N.Y.2d, at 205, 299 N.Y.S.2d, at 422, 247 N.E.2d, at 259.

The requirement of proof beyond a reasonable doubt has this vital role in our criminal procedure for cogent reasons. The accused during a criminal prosecution has at stake interest of immense importance, both because of the possibility that he may lose his liberty upon conviction and because of the certainty that he would be stigmatized by the conviction. Accordingly, a society that values the good name and freedom of every individual should not condemn a man for commission of a crime when there is reasonable doubt about his guilt. As we said in Speiser v. Randall, [357 U.S. 513, 525–526, 78 S.Ct. 1332, 1342 (1958)]: "There is always in litigation a margin of error, representing error in factfinding, which both parties must take into account. Where one party has at stake an interest of transcending value —as a criminal defendant his liberty—this margin of error is reduced as to him by the process of placing on the other party the burden of *   *   *   persuading the factfinder at the conclusion of the trial of his guilt beyond a reasonable doubt. Due process commands that no man shall lose his liberty unless the Government has borne the burden of   *   *   *   convincing the factfinder of his guilt." To this end, the reasonable-doubt standard is indispensable, for it "impresses on the trier of fact the necessity of reaching a subjective state of certitude on the facts in issue." Dorsen & Rezneck, In re Gault and the Future of Juvenile Law, 1 Family Law Quarterly, No. 4, at 26 (1967).

Moreover, use of the reasonable-doubt standard is indispensable to command the respect and confidence of the community in applications of the criminal law. It is critical that the moral force of the criminal law not be diluted by a standard of proof which leaves people in doubt whether innocent men are being condemned. It is also important in our free society that every individual going about his ordinary affairs have confidence that his government cannot adjudge him guilty of a criminal offense without convincing a proper factfinder of his guilt with utmost certainty.

Lest there remain any doubt about the constitutional stature of the reasonable-doubt standard, we explicitly hold that the Due Process Clause protects the accused against conviction except upon proof beyond a reasonable doubt of every fact necessary to constitute the crime with which he is charged.

II

We turn to the question whether juveniles, like adults, are constitutionally entitled to proof beyond a reasonable doubt when they are charged with violation of a criminal law. The same considerations which demand extreme caution in factfinding to protect the innocent adult apply as well to the innocent child. * * *

We conclude, as we concluded regarding the essential due process safeguards applied in *Gault*, that the observance of the standard of proof beyond a reasonable doubt "will not compel the States to abandon or displace any of the substantive benefits of the juvenile process." *Gault*, supra, at 21, 87 S.Ct., at 1440.

Finally, we reject the Court of Appeals' suggestion that there is, in any event, only a "tenuous difference" between the reasonable-doubt and preponderance standards. The suggestion is singularly unpersuasive. In this very case, the trial judge's ability to distinguish between the two standards enabled him to make a finding of guilt which he conceded he might not have made under the standard of proof beyond a reasonable doubt. Indeed, the trial judge's action evidences the accuracy of the observation of commentators that "the preponderance test is susceptible to the misinterpretation that it calls on the trier of fact merely to perform an abstract weighing of the evidence in order to determine which side has produced the greater quantum, without regard to its effect in convincing his mind of the truth of the proposition asserted." Dorsen & Rezneck, supra, at 26–27.

III

In sum, the constitutional safeguard of proof beyond a reasonable doubt is as much required during the adjudicatory stage of a delinquency proceeding as are those constitutional safeguards applied in *Gault*—notice of charges, right to counsel, the rights of confrontation and examination, and the privilege against self-incrimination. We therefore hold, in agreement with Chief Judge Fuld in dissent in the Court of Appeals, "that, where a 12-year-old child is charged with an act of stealing which renders him liable to confinement for as long as six years, then, as a matter of due process * * * the case against him must be proved beyond a reasonable doubt." 24 N.Y.2d, at 207, 299 N.Y.S.2d at 423, 247 N.E.2d, at 260.

Reversed.

[The concurring opinion of Mr. Justice Harlan and the dissenting opinion of Mr. Chief Justice Burger, joined by Mr. Justice Stewart, are omitted.]

Mr. Justice BLACK, dissenting.

* * *

I admit a strong, persuasive argument can be made for a standard of proof beyond a reasonable doubt in criminal cases—and the majority has made that argument well—but it is not for me as a judge to say for that reason that Congress or the States are without constitutional power to establish another standard which the Constitution does not otherwise forbid. It is quite true that proof beyond a reasonable doubt has long been required in federal criminal trials. It is also true that this requirement is almost universally found in the governing laws of the States. And as long as a particular jurisdiction requires proof beyond a reasonable doubt, then the Due Process Clause commands that every trial in that jurisdiction must adhere to that standard. See Turner v. United States, 396 U.S. 398, 430, 90 S.Ct. 642, 24 L.Ed.2d 610 (1970) (Black, J., dissenting). But when, as here, a State through its duly constituted legislative branch decides to apply a different standard, then that standard, unless it is otherwise unconstitutional, must be applied to insure that persons are treated according to the "law of the land." The State of New York has made such a decision, and in my view nothing in the Due Process Clause invalidates it.

---

2. EXCEPTIONS AND THEIR VALIDITY

MORRISON v. CALIFORNIA

Supreme Court of the United States, 1934.
291 U.S. 82, 54 S.Ct. 281, 78 L.Ed. 664.

Mr. Justice CARDOZO delivered the opinion of the Court.

The appellants have been convicted of a conspiracy to violate the Alien Land Law of the state of California.

[Under the Alien Land Law, aliens ineligible for United States citizenship were not permitted to use or occupy real property, except to the extent provided in any treaty between the United States and the nation of which the alien was a citizen. A treaty between the United States and Japan provided for alien Japanese in the United States to own or lease houses, manufactories, warehouses, and shops, and to lease land for residential and commercial purposes. No provision was made in the treaty for use or ownership of agricultural land. Under the Alien Land Law, mere occupancy of land by an ineligible alien was not made criminal; conspiracy to violate the provisions of the act, however, was made criminal and punishable by up to two years incarceration, a fine of not more than five thousand dollars, or both.]

The indictment charges that the two appellants, Morrison and Doi, feloniously conspired to place Doi in the possession and enjoyment of agricultural land within the state; that possession was obtained, and the land used and cultivated, in execution of the conspiracy; and that Doi was an alien Japanese, ineligible to citizenship, and not protected in his possession by any treaty between the government of the United States and the government of Japan. These acts, if committed with the guilty knowledge of each defendant, make out a criminal conspiracy under the statutes of the state.

On the trial the state proved that Doi had gone upon the land and used it under an agreement with Morrison, but did not attempt to prove that he was not a citizen of the United States or that he was ineligible for citizenship. [Section 9a of the Alien Land Law provides] that as to these elements of the crime the burden of disproving guilt shall rest on a defendant. * * * There was an appeal to the District Court of Appeal for the Fourth District, where the judgment was affirmed. The court overruled the defendants' contention that, by the application of section 9a of the Alien Land Law * * * there had been a denial of due process of law under the Fourteenth Amendment of the Constitution of the United States. 13 P.2d 803.

* * *

A person of the Japanese race is a citizen of the United States if he was born within the United States. * * * He is a citizen, even though born abroad, if his father was a citizen, provided, however, that this privilege shall not exist unless the father was at some time a resident of the United States as well as a citizen, and provided also that such a child, who continues to reside abroad, shall, in order to receive the protection of this government, be required upon reaching the age of eighteen years to record at an American consulate his intention to become a resident and remain a citizen of the United States, and shall be further required to take the oath of allegiance to the United States upon attaining his majority. * * * But a person of the Japanese race, if not born a citizen, is ineligible to become a citizen, i.e., to be naturalized. The privilege of naturalization is confined to aliens who are "free white persons, and to aliens of African nativity and to persons of African descent." * * * "White persons," within the meaning of the statute, are members of the Caucasian race, as Caucasian is defined in the understanding of the mass of men. * * *

This court in Morrison v. California, 288 U.S. 591, 53 S.Ct. 401, 77 L.Ed. 970 passed upon a controversy as to the validity of section 9b of the California Alien Land Law, which, though akin to section 9a, has important elements of difference. This section (9b) provides in substance that, when it has been proved that the defendant has been in the use or occupation of real property, and when it has also been proved that he is a member of a race ineligible for citizenship under the naturalization laws of the United States, the defendant shall have the burden of proving citizenship as a defense. We sustained that enactment when challenged as invalid under the Fourteenth Amendment of the Federal Constitution. The state had given evidence with reference to the defendant, the occupant of the land, that by reason of his race he was ineligible to be made a citizen. With this evidence present, we held that the burden was his to show that by reason of his birth he was a citizen already, and thus to bring himself within a rule which has the effect of an exception. In the vast majority of cases, he could do this without trouble if his claim of citizenship was honest. The people, on the other hand, if forced to disprove his claim, would be relatively helpless. In all likelihood his life history would be known only to himself and at times to relatives or intimates unwilling to speak against him.

The ruling was not novel. The decisions are manifold that within limits of reason and fairness the burden of proof may be lifted from the state in criminal prosecutions and cast on a defendant. The limits are in substance these, that the state shall have proved enough to make it just for the defendant to be required to repel what has been proved with excuse or explanation, or at least that upon a balancing of convenience or of the opportunities for knowledge the shifting of the burden will be found to be an aid to the accuser without subjecting the accused to hardship or oppression. Special reasons are at hand to make the change permissible when citizenship vel non is the issue to be determined. Citizenship is a privilege not due of common right. One who lays claim to it as his, and does this in justification or excuse of an act otherwise illegal, may fairly be called upon to prove his title good. In accord with that view are decisions of this court in proceedings under the acts of Congress for the deportation of aliens. A Chinaman by race resisted deportation on the ground that, though a Chinaman, he had been born in the United States. The ruling was that as to the place of birth the burden was upon the alien, and not upon the government. The ruling also was that the imposition of that burden did not deprive the alien of his constitutional immunities. Chin Bak Kan v. United States, 186 U.S. 193, 200, 22 S.Ct. 891, 894, 46 L.Ed. 1121. "The inestimable heritage of citizenship is not to be conceded to those who seek to avail themselves of it under pressure of a particular exigency, without being able to show that it was ever possessed." Id.

We adhered to that principle in Morrison v. California, supra. Upon that basis, we approved the ruling of the Supreme Court of California (People v. Osaki, 209 Cal. 169, 286 P. 1025) that section 9b of the Alien Land Law casting upon a Japanese defendant the burden of proving citizenship after proof of his race had been given by the state was not an impairment of his immunities under the Federal Constitution. No point was made in the statement of jurisdiction or the supporting brief that the crime was conspiracy, and that one of the defendants belonged to the white race. The case was submitted as if both were Japanese.

The question is now as to section 9a. Obviously there is a wide difference between the scope of the two sections. Possession of agricultural land by one not shown to be ineligible for citizenship is an act that carries with it not even a hint of criminality. To prove such possession without more is to take hardly a step forward in support of an indictment. No such probability of wrongdoing grows out of the naked fact of use or occupation as to awaken a belief that the user or occupier is guilty if he fails to come forward with excuse or explanation. * * * "The legislature may go a good way in raising [a presumption] or in changing the burden of proof, but there are limits." McFarland v. American Sugar Co., 241 U.S. 79, 86, 36 S.Ct. 498, 501, 60 L.Ed. 899. What is proved must be so related to what is inferred in the case of a true presumption as to be at least a warning signal according to the teachings of experience. "It is not within the province of a legislature to declare an individual guilty or presumptively guilty of a crime." McFarland v. American Sugar Co., supra. There are, indeed, "presumptions that are not evidence in a proper sense but simply regulations of the burden of proof." Even so, the occasions that justify regulations of the one order have a kinship, if nothing more, to those that justify the others. For a transfer of the burden, experience must teach that the evidence held to be inculpatory has at least a sinister significance or, if this at times be lacking, there must be in any event a manifest disparity in convenience of proof and opportunity for knowledge, as, for instance, where a general prohibition is applicable to every one who is unable to bring himself within the range of an exception. The list is not exhaustive. Other instances may have arisen or may develop in the future where the balance of convenience can be redressed without oppression to the defendant through the same procedural expedient. The decisive considerations are too variable, too much distinctions of degree, too dependent in last analysis upon a common sense estimate of fairness or of facilities of proof, to be crowded into a formula. One can do no more than adumbrate them; sharper definition must await the specific case as it arises.

We turn to this statute and endeavor to assign it to its class. In the law of California there is no general prohibition of the use of agricultural lands by aliens, with special or limited provisos or exceptions. To the contrary, it is the privilege that is general, and only the prohibition that is limited and special. Without preliminary proof of race, occupation of the land is not even a suspicious circumstance. The inquiry must therefore be whether occupants so situated may be charged with the burden of proving themselves eligible and thus establishing their innocence.

First. The indictment is for conspiracy, and, indeed, the Alien Land Law creates no other crime. Morrison and Doi are charged to have conspired, but Doi alone is charged to be ineligible for citizenship. One might suppose from a reading of the statute that the burden of proof, even if shifted as to him, would be unaffected as to Morrison. The California courts, however, have cast the same burden upon both; and both have been convicted. * * *

Now, plainly as to Morrison, an imputation of knowledge is a wholly arbitrary presumption. He may never have seen Doi before the transfer of possession or afterwards. He may have made his agreement by an agent or over the telephone or by writings delivered through the mails. Even if lessor and lessee came together face to face, there is nothing to show whether Doi was a Japanese of the full blood, whose race would have been apparent to any one looking at him. Moreover, if his race was apparent, he may still have been a citizen, for anything that was known to Morrison or others. The statute does not make it a crime to put a lessee into possession without knowledge or inquiry as to race and place of birth. The statute makes it a crime to put an ineligible lessee into possession as the result of a willful conspiracy to violate the law. Nothing in the people's evidence gives support to the inference that Morrison had knowledge of the disqualifications of his tenant or could testify about them. What was known to him, so far as the evidence discloses, was known also to the people, and provable with equal ease. Only an arbitrary mandate could charge him with guilty knowledge as an inference of law if it were proved that Doi was not a citizen or eligible to become one. Still less can he be charged with such knowledge when Doi's disqualification is itself a mere presumption. In such circumstances the conviction of Morrison because he failed to assume the burden of disproving a conspiracy was a denial of due process that vitiates the judgment as to him. Nor is that the only consequence. Doi was not a conspirator, however guilty his own state of mind, unless Morrison had shared in the guilty knowledge and design. * * * The conviction failing as to the one defendant must fail as to the other. * * *

Second. The result will not be changed if we view the case on the assumption that possession by one ineligible, when it is the product of agreement, may be criminal as to the tenant who holds with guilty knowledge, though innocent as to the landlord who believes that all is lawful.

We have pointed out before that a lease of agricultural land, unaccompanied by evidence of the race of the lessee, conveys no hint of criminality. For the moment we assume, without intending to decide, that strong considerations of convenience, if they existed, might cast upon the tenant the burden of proving his qualifications and thus disproving guilt. The question will then be whether the normal burden of proof will so thwart or hamper justice as to create a practical necessity, without preponderating hardship to the defendant, for a departure from the usual rule.

In the vast majority of cases the race of a Japanese or a Chinaman will be known to any one who looks at him. There is no practical necessity in such circumstances for shifting the burden to the defendant. Not only is there no necessity; there is only a faint promotion of procedural convenience. The triers of the facts will look upon the defendant sitting in the courtroom and will draw their own conclusions. If more than this is necessary, the people may call witnesses familiar with the characteristics of the race, who will state his racial origin. The only situation in which the shifting of the burden can be of any substantial profit to the state is where the defendant is of mixed blood, the white or the African so preponderating that there will be no external evidence of another. But in such circumstances the promotion of convenience from the point of view of the prosecution will be outweighed by the probability of injustice to the accused. One whose racial origins are so blended as to be not discoverable at sight will often be unaware of them. If he can state nothing but his ignorance, he has not sustained the burden of proving eligibility, and must stand condemned of crime.

Reflection will satisfy that the chance of this injustice is not remote or shadowy. Let us assume a charge that agricultural land has been occupied by Filipinos not born in the United States, and not entitled to the privileges growing out of service in the army or the navy. 8 U.S.C. § 388 (8 USCA § 388). They are then ineligible for citizenship, and subject to indictment under the laws of California if they have gone into possession in aid of a conspiracy. But Filipinos have intermarried with many other peoples. They have intermarried with whites and with Negroes and mulattos. A laborer, born in Canada, his parents apparently mulattos, but one of his grandparents a Filipino, according to the charge in an indictment, would be ignorant in many cases whether he was a Filipino or an African. The admixture of oriental blood might be too slight for his race to be apparent to the eye, and family traditions are not always well preserved, especially when the descendants are men and women of humble origin, remote from kith and kin. The same possibility of injustice would be present where the occupant of the land is a descendant of Mexicans and Indians or an Eurasian, his ancestors partly Europeans and partly Asiatics.

The probability is thus apparent that the transfer of the burden may result in grave injustice in the only class of cases in which it will be of any practical importance. The statute does not say that the defendant shall be acquitted if he does not know his racial origin and is unable to make proof of it. What the effect of such a law would be, we are not required to consider. To the contrary, the statute says in substance that, unless he can and does prove it, he will have failed to discharge his burden, and will therefore be found guilty. Moreover, if he were to profess ignorance, and ignorance were an excuse, the trier of the facts might refuse to credit him. There can be no escape from hardship and injustice, outweighing many times any procedural convenience, unless the burden of persuasion in respect of racial origin is cast upon the people.

What has been written applies only to those provisions of the statute that prescribe the rule for criminal causes. Other considerations may or may not apply where the controversy is civil. We leave that question open.

The judgment is reversed, and the cause remanded for further proceedings not inconsistent with this opinion.

It is so ordered.

STUMP v. BENNETT

United States Court of Appeals for the Eighth Circuit, 1968.
398 F.2d 111, certiorari denied 393 U.S. 1001, 89 S.Ct. 483, 21 L.Ed.2d 466.

LAY, Circuit Judge. Ronald Maurice Stump, a state prisoner, appeals from the denial of his petition for a writ of habeas corpus in federal district court. Stump was convicted of murder in the second degree in the Polk County, Iowa, District Court in the slaying of one Michael Daly. On December 11, 1961, he was sentenced to a term of seventy-five years' imprisonment. Stump asserted as a sole defense at his trial that it was impossible for him to have been present at the place of the crime since he was driving on the highway between Des Moines and Knoxville when the shooting took place. He offered witnesses in an attempt to verify this fact. The state trial court placed upon the defendant the burden of proving his alibi by a preponderance of the evidence. * * *

After exhausting his state remedies, Stump petitioned for a writ of habeas corpus in the United States District Court for the Southern District of Iowa, alleging among other grounds that the state trial court's instructions placed upon the defendant the burden of proving his sole defense of alibi by the preponderance of the evidence * * *[.] We hold that the Iowa rule shifting the burden of proof to the defendant reached the level of constitutional error and was prohibited by the Fourteenth Amendment. We reverse and remand with directions.

*   *   *

I.

The Iowa trial court instructed the jury, in part, as follows:
"* * * *before you can acquit the defendant by reason of this defense* [alibi] you must find that he has established it by a preponderance or greater weight of the evidence bearing upon it." (Emphasis ours.)

There exist many bases for considering the instruction erroneous.

(a) The original premise behind placing the burden of proof upon the defendant is that "alibi" is an affirmative defense. * * *

This view has now been rejected by almost every state as well as by all federal courts which have had the proposition before them. * * * In asserting alibi the defendant simply denies the possibility of his having committed the crime by reason of being elsewhere when it was committed, whereas an affirmative defense generally applies to justification for his admitted participation in the act itself. * * *

(c) Upon a plea of alibi, the presumption of innocence is permanently shattered as to the evidence relating to (1) the presence of the defendant, (2) the time, and (3) the place of the crime itself. * * *

(d) By shifting the burden of proof to a person who claims to have been elsewhere at the time of the crime, there is created an irrational and arbitrary presumption of guilt. It arises not by reason of a proof of fact from which a fair inference might be drawn but from the mere happening that the defendant offers testimony in an attempt to establish innocence. When this occurs, unless the defendant can succeed in overbalancing the state's evidence, the jury is expressly told he cannot be acquitted by reason of his sole claim to innocence. There is thus a prejudgment of "a conclusion which the jury should reach of its own volition. * * * [T]his presumption would conflict with the overriding presumption of innocence with which the law endows the accused and which extends to every element of the crime. * * * [I]ncriminating presumptions are not to be improvised by the judiciary." See Morissette v. United States, 342 U.S. 246, 275, 72 S.Ct. 240, 256, 96 L.Ed. 288 (1952).

II.

However, as previously observed, mere error or confusion is not before us, unless we are convinced that it is so oppressive as to offend the due process clause. We resolve that question in the affirmative.

There are persuasive grounds to say that the denial of the presumption of innocence of an accused is a constitutional violation under the due process clause.

*   *   *

In Leland v. State of Oregon, 343 U.S. 790, 72 S.Ct. 1002, 96 L.Ed. 1302 (1952), the Supreme Court upheld the shifting of the burden of persuasion of a plea of insanity under Oregon law. And the majority opinion points out that although the federal courts do not condone shifting the burden of persuasion with regard to insanity, nevertheless such a procedural rule does not involve any constitutional right; thus Davis v. United States, 160 U.S. 469, 16 S.Ct. 353 (1895) was held not to be controlling. Whether or not one interprets the treatment of *Davis* in *Leland* as denying a constitutional status to the "presumption of innocence," this much is clear: when the burden of persuasion is shifted to the defendant to disprove essential elements of a crime, as it was in the instant case, then it is certain that the due process clause of the Fourteenth Amendment has been violated.   *   *   *

In the instant case, before the defendant assumed the burden of proof, the state produced an eye-witness who identified Stump as the assailant at the time and place of the murder. It is true, this is not a case where evidential gaps were filled by use of presumption. Cf. Tot v. United States, 319 U.S. 463, 63 S.Ct. 1241, 87 L.Ed. 1519 (1943). The vital prejudice here is that the instruction compels the jury to believe the state's evidence relating to the defendant's presence at the scene of the crime, unless the defendant is able to overcome its effect by preponderating proof. Thus, as Justice Adams early noted in dissent against the rule in State v. Hamilton, 57 Iowa 596, 11 N.W. 5, 6 (1881), the "true doctrine under such rule would seem to be that the evidence of guilt is aided by a presumption of guilt, if the evidence of innocence relied upon is the evidence of an alibi." The presumptive jump here is at least as dangerous as if it were made from an unrelated fact. In this case, it is created from no facts at all. Here the arbitrary, irrational presumption of guilt persists simply because a man may try to prove his only defense available, to-wit, non-presence.

It is clear that in Leland v. State of Oregon, supra, Mr. Justice Clark takes extreme care to point out (1) that the burden of persuasion as to the elements of the crime never shifts under Oregon law upon the plea of insanity, 343 U.S. at 795, 799, 800, 72 S.Ct. 1002, (2) that the state still has to prove all elements of the crime itself beyond a reasonable doubt, id. at 799, 72 S.Ct. 1002; (3) that the jury could acquit Leland if they found him mentally incapable of the requisite intent to sustain a first or second degree murder conviction, even though the proof fell short of legal insanity, id. at 794, 72 S.Ct. 1002; and (4) that the placing of the burden can be explained by the presumption of sanity recognized in all English courts, id. at 799, 72 S.Ct. 1002.

The defense of alibi is readily distinguishable from the plea of insanity. Basically, alibi relates to the presence of the defendant at the scene of the crime. Proof of the defendant's presence and participation is a wholly indispensable factor to the government's case; it is a *sine qua non* to sustain a verdict of guilty. In reality the Iowa instruction shifts the burden of persuasion on an essential element of the crime and thus requires the defendant to assume the onus of proving a negative averment, i. e., non-presence. In contrast to an insanity plea, Stump's defense did not admit the act in any way, or any element of the crime, but rather denied any knowledge of it. Nor is the shift here based upon any conflicting legal presumption involved, as in insanity.

It is also plain that the state cannot justify shifting the burden of persuasion on the basis of the standards set out in Morrison v. People of State of California, 291 U.S. at 88–93, 54 S.Ct. 281, for here the shift does subject the defendant to undue and arbitrary "hardship" and "oppression." There is no "excuse" or "explanation," nor any "balancing of convenience" nor "a greater opportunity for knowledge" on the defendant's part. In fact, under the Iowa statute, Iowa Code Ann. § 777.18, the defendant must give the names of all his witnesses as to the alibi issue to the state but the state has no reciprocal duty. Under such a rule, it is not easy to perceive how the defendant has the balance of knowledge.

* * *

NOTES

1. In Davis v. United States, 160 U.S. 469, 16 S.Ct. 353 (1895) the United States Supreme Court held that a federal district court committed reversible error when it instructed the jury that the defendant in a murder case was required to show to the jury's "reasonable satisfaction" that he was insane at the time of the crime and therefore not guilty.

2. The Iowa Supreme Court had defended its alibi instruction as follows:

> In the trial of a criminal case a defendant is not required to do anything. Even though he elects to do nothing the prosecution in order to convict must establish defendant's guilt beyond a reasonable doubt. This burden on the prosecution never shifts. It remains throughout the trial as a shield for defendant. Even in the absence of the alibi notice required by section 777.18, Code of Iowa, I.C.A., defendant may take the witness stand and testify to all material and relevant matters. He may testify that he was so far away and at such a specified place that he could not have been present at the scene of the crime. Such testimony thus presents the question of credibility for determination by the jury with the burden still resting on the prosecution. If the defendant voluntarily elects to go farther and call witnesses to testify in support of his alibi he must then give the notice required by statute. He assumes the offensive. He offers witnesses to testify that he could not possibly have committed the offense because he was too far away. This goes only to the testimony that he was at some specific place. If established it constitutes an absolute defense. To the extent that it may be an absolute defense it is affirmative in nature. Even though not affirmatively established it is still defensive against the prosecution's burden of establishing defendant's guilt beyond a reasonable doubt.
>
> * * * Our rules are, as they should be, designed for the protection of the innocent, without at the same time making the

conviction of the guilty impossible. We are not disposed to deviate from our well established and in our opinion sound rules.

State v. Stump, 254 Iowa 1181, 119 N.W.2d 210 (1963).

STATE v. SEGOVIA

Supreme Court of Idaho, 1969.
93 Idaho 208, 457 P.2d 905.

McFADDEN, Chief Justice. Appellants Florentino Segovia and Ramiro Hernandez Garcia were by a jury found guilty of illegal possession of a narcotic drug, following which they were sentenced to a term in the state penitentiary of not to exceed thirty months. They have appealed from their respective judgments of conviction.

During the course of trial, two police officers testified that on October 14, 1967 they were in their patrol car parked adjacent to a bar on Main Street in Boise, when they saw the defendants walk through the parking lot toward Main Street. The defendants were both smoking a cigarette, passing it back and forth between them. As they approached Main Street, one of the defendants dropped the cigarette, and both defendants turned the corner and went into the bar.

The officers testified they walked to where the cigarette was discarded, searched the area and found only one cigarette in the area, it being still lit and the other end still moist. The officers observed it was a home made cigarette, broke it open and identified the contents to be marihuana. The officers entered the bar and placed the defendants under arrest. A search of the defendants' persons produced another cigarette from Garcia's pocket which was also determined to contain marihuana. At the police station a more thorough search of their clothing produced loose marihuana and its residue.

At trial a pharmacist and medical technologist testified that he examined and tested by microscopic and eye examination and also performed chemical tests to the material in the cigarette obtained from the parking lot and from Garcia's person, and expressed his opinion that they contained marihuana.

On the basis of this testimony the jury found the defendants guilty as charged in the information, the charging part of which provides:

"That the said defendants * * * on or about the 14th day of October, 1967 in Boise, Ada County, Idaho, that is near the 807 Bar, then and there being, did then and there wilfully, intentionally, feloniously and unlawfully possess a narcotic drug, towit; marijuana (marihuana) without a written prescription therefor of a physician, dentist, podiatrist, osteopath or veterinarian licensed to practice in said state."

The statute under which the defendants were charged is I.C. § 37–3202 (enacted S.L.1967, Ch. 435, § 93, p. 1494), which provides:

"Except as otherwise provided in this act, every person who possesses any narcotic except upon the written prescription of a physician, dentist, podiatrist, osteopath or veterinarian licensed to practice in this state, may be punished by imprisonment in the state prison for a term of not to exceed ten (10) years."

No evidence was presented by the state to negate possession by the defendants of a prescription for the marihuana found in their possession, and the defendants contend that absent such proof by the state the facts as proven are insufficient to establish commission of the crime charged. In other words, the defendants assert that the burden is upon the state to negative the exception in I.C. § 37–3202. The state, on the other hand, contends that the burden is upon the defendants to prove that they are within the exception—that it was incumbent upon the defendants to produce a prescription authorizing their possession of the narcotic.

*   *   *

Prior to the enactment of the present narcotic law (S.L.1967, Ch. 435), Idaho's statutory provisions on narcotics (Title 37, Ch. 23) contained the following provision:

"In any complaint, information, or indictment, and in any action or proceedings brought for the enforcement of any provision of this act, it shall not be necessary to negative any exception, excuse, proviso, or exemption, contained in this act, and the burden of proof of any such exception, excuse, proviso, or exemption, shall be upon the defendant." I.C. § 37–2318.

In 1967, however, the legislature repealed this and all other sections of Chapter 23, Title 37. S.L.1967, Ch. 435, § 119, p. 1469.

In the absence of a statute, the general rule is that the burden is upon the state in a criminal case to negative any exception or proviso appearing in that part of the statute which defines the crime if the exception is "so incorporated with the language describing and defining the offense that the ingredients of the offense cannot be accurately and clearly described if the exception is omitted * * *." 41 Am. Jur.2d, Indictments and Informations, § 98, pp. 940–941. Under such circumstances, the state must aver in the information and prove at trial that the defendant is not within the exception to the statute.

*   *   *

It is our opinion that the exception contained in I.C. § 37–3202 is an integral part of the offense proscribed and is so incorporated with the description of the offense as to be a material element of it. The exception defines the scope of the general prohibition of I.C. § 37–3202 since it is not a crime to possess a narcotic drug pursuant to a valid prescription. The crime is defined as possession without a valid prescription, and thus the absence of such a prescription is of necessity a material element of the offense.

The state strenuously argues that the existence of a prescription is a matter peculiarly within the defendant's own knowledge and that to force the state to prove the non-existence of a prescription imposes an impossible burden upon the state. We do not agree. Whatever may be the situation in other jurisdictions, in Idaho the state has ready access to all prescriptions filled in the state. See I.C. § 37–3017, whereby copies of all *narcotic prescriptions* filled by pharmacists must be filed monthly with the Idaho State Board of Pharmacy. It is far from impossible for the state to establish a prima facie showing of the absence of a prescription. The fact that the legislature repealed the statute relieving the state of this burden and did not see fit to replace it with a comparable provision in the new statute regulating narcotic drugs (S.L.1967, Ch. 435) is a strong indication that the legislature intended for the state to assume this burden.

However, in regard to marihuana (defined by I.C. § 37–2704), the legislature classified this as a Class A narcotic drug, as follows:

> "IV MARIHUANA   (Cannabis sativa), its derivatives or compounds.   (Marihuana is not presently used for medicinal purposes in the United States.)"   I.C. § 37–2702 (S.L. 1967, Ch. 435, § 2, p. 1443).

By this classification, with the parenthetical statement that marihuana is not presently used for medicinal purposes, the legislature must have recognized that no prescription for such drug could be obtained, and intended that in a prosecution under the provisions of I.C. § 37–3202 for possession of the narcotic marihuana, it would be a useless act to require the state to prove absence of any prescription for the drug, when the law itself recognizes that no prescription is obtainable. Insofar as the instant case is concerned, the law itself by classification of marihuana as a drug not used for medicinal purposes, negates the burden on the state to prove absence of a prescription.

There being no burden on the state to prove absence of a prescription for marihuana and there being substantial evidence to sustain the judgments, the judgments of conviction are affirmed.

McQUADE and SPEAR, JJ., and NORRIS, D. J., concur.

BELLWOOD, D. J., concurs in the result.

MODEL PENAL CODE

(Proposed Official Draft, 1962).

Section 1.12. **Proof Beyond a Reasonable Doubt; Affirmative Defenses; Burden of Proving Fact When Not an Element of an Offense; Presumptions.**

(1) No person may be convicted of an offense unless each element of such offense is proved beyond a reasonable doubt. In the absence of such proof, the innocence of the defendant is assumed.

(2) Subsection (1) of this Section does not:

(a) require the disproof of an affirmative defense unless and until there is evidence supporting such defense; or

(b) apply to any defense which the Code or another statute plainly requires the defendant to prove by a preponderance of evidence.

(3) A ground of defense is affirmative, within the meaning of Subsection (2) (a) of this Section, when:

(a) it arises under a section of the Code which so provides; or

(b) it relates to an offense defined by a statute other than the Code and such statute so provides; or

(c) it involves a matter of excuse or justification peculiarly within the knowledge of the defendant on which he can fairly be required to adduce supporting evidence.

MODEL PENAL CODE, COMMENTS TO § 1.13, 110–11

(Tent. Draft No. 4, 1955).

No single principle can be conscripted to explain when these shifts of burden to defendants are defensible, even if the burden goes no further than to call for the production of some evidence. Neither the logical point that the prosecution would be called upon to prove a negative, nor the grammatical point that the defense rests on an exception or proviso divorced from the definition of the crime is potently persuasive, although both points have been invoked. * * * What is involved seems rather a more subtle balance which acknowledges that a defendant ought not be required to defend until some solid substance is presented to support the accusation but, beyond this, perceives a point where need for narrowing the issues, coupled with the relative accessibility of evidence to the defendant, warrants calling upon him to present his defensive claim. No doubt this point is reached more quickly if, given the facts the prosecution must establish,

the normal probabilities are against the defense, but this is hardly an
essential factor. Given the mere fact of an intentional homicide, no
one can estimate the probability that it was or was not committed in
self-defense. The point is rather that purposeful homicide is an event
of such gravity to society, and the basis for a claim of self-defense is
so specially within the cognizance of the defendant, that it is fair to
call on him to offer evidence if the defense is claimed. * * *

D. ASCERTAINMENT OF GUILT: THE DECISIONMAKERS
AND THEIR RESPECTIVE ROLES

At least three entities may be involved in the determination as
to whether, in a particular case, the prosecution has carried its burden
of proving guilt beyond a reasonable doubt. One is the trial judge.
The second is the trial jury. The last is the appellate court (or
courts) which review the conviction. This section deals with the role
of each of these in the guilt-determining process.

WYLEY v. WARDEN

United States Court of Appeals for the Fourth Circuit, 1967.
372 F.2d 742, certiorari denied 389 U.S. 863, 88 S.Ct. 121, 19 L.Ed.2d 131,
rehearing denied 389 U.S. 997, 88 S.Ct. 484, 19 L.Ed.2d 500.

SOBELOFF, Circuit Judge. This appeal by a state prisoner attacks on federal constitutional grounds Article XV, section 5 of the
Constitution of Maryland which leaves to the jury the final determination of the law as well as the facts in a criminal trial. The provision
reads as follows:

In the trial of all criminal cases, the Jury shall be the Judges
of Law, as well as of fact, except that the Court may pass
upon the sufficiency of the evidence to sustain a conviction.

On November 19, 1953 a jury in the Criminal Court of Baltimore
found Rodger Wyley guilty of first degree murder, without capital
punishment, and he was thereupon sentenced to prison for life. Wyley's petition for a writ of federal habeas corpus attacked his conviction on a number of grounds, but the only one which concerns us on
this appeal is whether the trial judge's instruction to the jury, given
in accordance with Article XV, section 5, denied defendant due pro-

cess and equal protection of the laws in violation of the Fourteenth Amendment.[1]

*   *   *

Appellant objects that charging that "in a criminal case the jury are the judges of the law as well as of the facts" permits them to apply any concept of law they see fit to his case, and that this amounts to a deprivation of due process of law. He further argues that the instruction permits the jury to reach a different legal conclusion in his case from that which they might reach in another case presenting identical facts, and so denies him the equal protection of the law.

*   *   *

The Maryland court has pointed out that juries in criminal cases are in reality not as unrestricted as the appellant suggests. The powers of the jury are hedged in a number of ways. Certain restraining powers lodged in the hands of the judges serve as a counterpoise. *   *   * And it is doubtful whether in actuality juries vary in their application of legal principles more widely than judges vary among themselves. Traditionally, this constitutional provision has been understood as permitting the trial judge to determine the admissibility of evidence and the competency of witnesses, and in 1950 an amendment to section 5 of Article XV explicitly empowered the court to pass on the legal sufficiency of the evidence. Yanch v. State, 201 Md. 296, 93 A.2d 749 (1953).[2] If the jury's view of the law has led them to a verdict of guilty and the court is of the opinion that the verdict is against the law, the trial judge may set the verdict aside and grant a new trial. An even more significant limitation is the acknowledged power of the court to take a case from the jury and direct a verdict of acquittal. In Chisley v. State, 202 Md. 87, 95 A.2d 577 (1953), decided the same year that our defendant was tried, the State argued that if there is *any* evidence of murder, there can be no determination by the trial court, as a matter of law, that the evidence was insufficient to prove first degree murder. The Court of Appeals, however, rejected this argument. It declared that the 1950 amendment to section 5, providing that "the Court may pass upon the sufficiency of

---

1. The trial judge, at the conclusion of all the evidence, gave the jury advisory instructions on the law, which he prefaced with the following remarks:

Members of the Jury, this is a criminal case and under the Constitution and the laws of the State of Maryland in a criminal case the jury are the judges of the law as well as of the facts in the case. So that whatever I tell you about the law while it is intended to be helpful to you in reaching a just and proper verdict in the case, it is not binding upon you as members of the jury and you may accept or reject it. And you may apply the law as you apprehend it to be in the case. *   *   *

2. Prior to the enactment of this amendment which added the words "except that the Court may pass upon the sufficiency of the evidence to sustain a conviction," the question of the legal sufficiency of the evidence was exclusively for the *jury* to determine. *   *   *

the evidence to sustain a conviction," not only gives the trial judge the power to direct an acquittal on the charge of murder, when there is *no* evidence of murder, but also empowers him to direct a verdict for the defendant even where there is some evidence of murder, but in the judge's understanding of the law the evidence is insufficient to go to the jury on the question of first degree murder.

Although a trial judge was always *permitted* to give advisory instructions, prior to 1950, he could not be *required* to give them, and a refusal to do so upon request of counsel was held not erroneous. But Rule 756, section b, of the Maryland Rules of Procedure, originally promulgated in 1950, now provides that the court *must* give advisory instructions if requested to do so by counsel.

Oddly, it has always been held that while juries are the judges of the law, a jury may not pass on the constitutionality of a statute.

Not only has the validity of Article XV, section 5 been repeatedly upheld by the state court, but the Supreme Court of the United States has had occasion to consider it, and failed to intimate any doubt of its constitutionality.   *   *   *

Potent and persuasive arguments have been leveled against the wisdom of the Maryland practice. * * * 5

The origin of the doctrine embodied in section 5 is not known with certainty. The principal theories propounded are the colonists' fear of tyrannical and arbitrary Crown judges, the large number of judges without legal training, and the capacity of a highly democratic tribunal, such as a jury, to decide matters, legal as well as factual, in small agricultural communities.[6] Whatever it was that generated the

5. See 9 Wigmore, Evidence § 2559 (3d ed. 1940) (terming the right of juries in criminal cases to repudiate the instructions of the judge and to determine the law for themselves an "ill-advised doctrine, defiant of the fundamentals of law"). Cf. Sparf and Hansen v. United States, 156 U.S. 51, 715, 15 S.Ct. 273, 39 L.Ed. 343 (1895) (holding that in *federal* criminal prosecutions, juries are the judges of the facts, under *binding* instructions by the judge on questions of law).

6. Howe, Juries as Judges of Criminal Law, 52 Harv.L.Rev. 582, 591 (1939). See Slansky v. State, 192 Md. 94, 101, 63 A.2d 599, 602 (1949).

The Maryland provision first appeared in the Constitution of 1851, after opposing views had been expressed in the Constitutional Convention as to the power of juries in criminal cases. It was thought to be merely a restatement of the common law, Franklin v. State, 12 Md. 236 (1858), but others have suggested that the delegates to the Convention may have been misled by Fox's Libel Act, never in force in Maryland, in which Parliament, dealing only with criminal libel cases, provided that jurors were not to be restricted to questions of fact, but "could give their verdict upon the whole matter in issue." Dennis, Maryland's Antique Constitutional Thorn, 92 U.Pa.L.Rev. 34, 37 (1943).

However, no less a political philosopher than John Adams was of the opinion that the jury was autonomous with respect to the law as well as the facts. According to him, the jury was not bound by the judge's opinion of the law. After expatiating upon the subject, he concluded:

The general Rules of Law and common Regulations of Society, under which ordinary Transactions ar-

rule, opponents maintain that the reasons for it no longer exist, and the rule has now been abandoned in all but two jurisdictions, although fifty years ago a similar system of adjudication still prevailed in at least ten states.[7] Among the fifty states, Maryland and Indiana today stand alone in their adherence to it. Even Indiana has substantially attenuated its provision by judicial modification, holding as early as 1889 that a trial court in a criminal case "is not required to neutralize the effect of its instructions by telling the jury that they are at liberty to disregard them, and to decide the law for themselves." * * *

[C]onstitutionality and wisdom are not interchangeable terms; a practice may be deemed unwise, yet not be unconstitutional, just as not every constitutionally permissible procedure is necessarily desirable. Moreover, our reluctance to intervene on the present record is heightened by the absence of any suggestion that this particular defendant was prejudiced by the court's advising the jury of its right to determine the law for itself. There is nothing to indicate that the jury did not faithfully follow the view of the law expressed in the trial judge's instructions, which are concededly unexceptionable; nor is there an intimation that a different verdict would have resulted if the judge could have given binding rather than advisory instructions. The jury extended the defendant the consideration of recommending against capital punishment. * * *

Neither on abstract principle nor in light of the operation of the provision in the instant case does this court find justification for disturbing the District Court's order of dismissal.

Affirmed.

range themselves, are well enough known to ordinary Jurors. The great Principles of the Constitution, are intimately known, they are sensibly felt by every Briton—it is scarcely extravagant to say, they are drawn in and imbibed with the Nurses Milk and first Air.

Now should the Melancholly Case arise, that the Judges should give their Opinions to the Jury, against one of these fundamental Principles, is a Juror obliged to give his Verdict generally according to this Direction, or even to find the fact specially and submit the Law to the Court. Every Man of any feeling or Conscience will answer, no. It is not only his right but his Duty in that Case to find the Verdict according to his own best Understanding, Judgment and Conscience, tho in Direct opposition to the Direction of the Court.

* * * * *

The English Law obliges no Man to decide a Cause upon Oath against his own Judgment, nor does it oblige any Man to take any Opinion upon Trust, or to pin his faith on the sleve of any mere Man.

Adams' Diary Notes on the Right of Juries, February 12, 1771, in 1 Legal Papers of John Adams 230 (Wroth & Zobel ed. 1965).

7. In addition to Maryland and Indiana, states providing such a system by constitution or statute were Arizona, Connecticut, Georgia, Illinois, Louisiana, Oregon, Pennsylvania, and Tennessee. Slansky v. State, 192 Md. 94, 104, 63 A.2d 599, 603 (1949).

UNITED STATES v. WILSON

United States District Court for the District of Columbia, 1959.
178 F.Supp. 881.

HOLTZOFF, District Judge.   The defendant Frank B. Wilson was convicted of murder in the first degree and moves for a new trial on the ground that the verdict was contrary to the weight of the evidence.

The indictment charged that on or about February 20, 1959, Frank B. Wilson purposely and with deliberate and premeditated malice murdered Florence E. Smith by means of shooting her with a pistol. * * * The specific charge against the defendant was that on the morning of February 20, 1959, at about seven o'clock, he entered the apartment of the deceased, with whom he had carried on a clandestine love affair, and fatally shot her.   In its instructions, the Court indicated to the jury that if the defendant was convicted, the jury might bring in a verdict of guilty of murder in the first degree, guilty of murder in the second degree, or guilty of manslaughter.   As stated, the jury returned a verdict of guilty of murder in the first degree.

At the close of the Government's case, as well as at the close of the entire case, the Court denied a motion made by the defendant to take the case away from the jury insofar as the charge of murder in the first degree was concerned.   It was the view of the Court, and it is still its view, that there was sufficient evidence to justify the submission of all of the issues to the jury.   There is, however, a very definite distinction between a motion for a judgment of acquittal and a motion to set aside the verdict on the ground that it is contrary to the weight of the evidence.   A motion for a judgment of acquittal raises the question of law whether there is any substantial evidence whatsoever justifying a conviction.   A motion to set aside the verdict on the ground that it is contrary to the weight of the evidence introduces an entirely different issue, namely, whether on weighing all of the evidence on both sides, it heavily preponderates against the verdict.

The effect of the two motions is also entirely different.   If a motion for a judgment of acquittal is granted, the result is a final disposition of the case and an acquittal of the defendant.   If a motion for a new trial is granted, the result is merely that the case will be tried before another jury and the parties will have a second opportunity to present the issues.

To set aside a verdict on the ground that it is contrary to the weight of the evidence is a very serious matter.   Verdicts of juries should not be treated lightly.   A great deal of respect must be accorded and much weight attached to the verdict of a jury.   I personally have a mounting sense of admiration for the type of justice that is generally meted out by the average jury. Nevertheless, all human beings are fallible. If a verdict is contrary to the weight of the evidence, it is the duty of the judge to set it aside. It is a duty that cannot be avoided, although the responsibility involved is great.

It must be borne in mind that there is no way of reviewing a verdict of a jury on the facts except by a motion for a new trial made before the trial judge. The Court of Appeals may not review the facts, that is, it may not reverse a conviction because it is contrary to the weight of the evidence. Its authority is limited to reviewing questions of law, in this instance whether there was sufficient evidence to submit the issue to the jury.

As just stated, the effect of granting a motion for a new trial is not to make a final disposition of the case, but merely to secure the decision of another jury. If a second jury reaches the same conclusion as the first it does not necessarily follow that the trial judge would set aside the second verdict. Only a short time ago, in the case of Frank v. Atlantic Greyhound Corp., D.C., 177 F.Supp. 922, I had set aside a verdict in a civil case on the ground that the damages awarded to the plaintiff were excessive. At the second trial approximately the same result was reached. I declined to set aside the second verdict as it seemed to me that two juries having practically agreed, substantial justice had been done.

The principles governing motions for a new trial are well established. I had occasion to review the authorities on the subject in United States v. Robinson, D.C., 71 F.Supp. 9, 10–11, and in the course of the discussion made the following remarks, after referring to motions for a directed verdict and motions for judgment notwithstanding the verdict:

> "On the other hand, on a motion for a new trial on the ground the verdict is against the weight of evidence, the power of the Court is much broader. On such an application, the Court may weigh the evidence and consider the credibility of witnesses. If the Court reaches the conclusion that the verdict is contrary to the weight of the evidence and that a miscarriage of justice may have resulted, the verdict may be set aside and a new trial granted. Naturally this authority should be exercised sparingly and with caution. It should be invoked only in exceptional cases in which the evidence preponderates heavily against the verdict.

*   *   *

The Court is convinced that in this case a verdict of guilty of murder in the second degree would have been in accord with the weight of evidence and would have been amply justified. The distinction between murder in the first degree and murder in the second degree is that the former, in addition to intent to kill, requires premeditation and deliberation, while murder in the second degree does not require any premeditation or deliberation and not even an intent to kill, if the killing is accompanied with malice. Under the law as it has been interpreted in the District of Columbia, in order that there may be sufficient premeditation and deliberation, some appreciable interval, no matter how brief, must elapse after the intent to kill is formed and before the killing is accomplished, and during that interval there must have been some reflection which would amount to premeditation and deliberation.

* * *

The verdict of guilty of murder in the first degree necessarily implies a finding of premeditation and deliberation in addition to the finding of intent to kill. The Court is of the opinion that the finding of intent to kill is sustained by the weight of the evidence, because such an intent may be implied from the very fact that a person fires a gun in the direction of another. The difficult question in this case is whether the finding that there was deliberation and premeditation, within the legal definition to which reference has just been made, is sustained by the weight of the evidence.

In order to reach a conclusion on this crucial question it is necessary to review the evidence briefly. As has been stated, the defendant and the deceased had been carrying on a love affair for a number of years. In fact, their relation was so close that the defendant had a key to her apartment, although they were not actually living in the same premises. The defendant was a taxicab driver and apparently was in the habit of calling to see the deceased at irregular hours, and at times when he happened to be cruising in the neighborhood of her home. Apparently during the few weeks preceding the homicide, the love affair between the deceased and the defendant did not have smooth sailing. On the occasion of the homicide at seven o'clock in the morning of February 20, 1959, it appears from the evidence that the defendant entered the apartment of the deceased by using his own key and surprised her. She was at that time getting ready to go to work and already had put on her coat. Her son was downstairs on the adjoining parking lot warming up his car and waiting for his mother. The defendant had a pistol in his overcoat pocket when he entered the apartment. There was an exchange of a few sentences between them and then he pulled out his pistol and shot the deceased several times.

The fact that the defendant was armed with a deadly weapon when he entered the apartment of the deceased is one item of evidence in support of an inference that there was premeditation and deliberation. It is because of this feature that the Court declined to take away from the jury the charge of murder in the first degree. Nevertheless, the weight to be accorded to the fact that the defendant was armed depends on circumstances. This fact would have great weight if the defendant had owned no weapon previously but acquired it for the occasion. It would have somewhat less weight if the defendant had been in possession of the weapon but was not in the habit of carrying it around. The significance is much weaker if the defendant was always in the habit of carrying the pistol. The evidence tends to show this was the case here. He claimed that as a taxicab driver he always carried the weapon in his cab as a protection against robberies, and on this occasion, since he was wearing an overcoat, he kept the pistol in his overcoat pocket. Obviously in carrying the pistol the defendant was violating the law, but this circumstance does not bear upon the issues of this case.

The theory of the Government was that the defendant arrived in the vicinity of the premises and lay in wait until the son left the apartment and then the defendant rushed in to kill the deceased. The Court is of the opinion that substantial evidence to support this hypothesis is lacking, and that there is no basis for such an inference. It is based entirely on speculation, suspicion and conjecture. It is, therefore, necessary to discard in its entirety the theory that the defendant lay in wait.

There appears to be no evidence supporting a finding of premeditation and deliberation other than the fact that the defendant entered the premises carrying a pistol in his overcoat pocket. This is not a case in which such a deduction is supported by evidence of prior threats or by some indication of a hostile attitude toward the deceased. On the contrary two days before the homicide the defendant wrote to the deceased what might be called popularly a love letter, in which he said in passing that he had no desire to hurt the deceased in any way.

What then is the evidence contradicting the inference of premeditation and deliberation? At the trial the defendant took the witness stand and testified that he entered the apartment of the deceased, unlocking the door with his key, and then he said on the stand: "And I actually cannot truthfully say that I remember shooting Florence. There wasn't any cause, and yet I can almost vividly recall my arm jumping like you would shoot a pistol, but I never heard no shots."

The Government introduced in evidence as part of its case a written statement made by the defendant to the police. That statement was quite different from his testimony on the stand and much more damaging to the defendant. The pertinent part of the statement reads as follows:

"This morning I got up early and went over there to talk to her. I had a key to the apartment and used to go in. She jumped up. 'I know you come over to hurt me. You got a gun or something.' She started screaming and then she started hollering. 'Go on and do it', or something. I saw red and I pulled the gun out of my right overcoat pocket and shot her, four times, I think. Then I tried to shoot myself, but the gun jammed."

Afterward the defendant left the premises, drove away in his cab, telephoned the police and surrendered. The Government naturally relies upon the defendant's confession to the police rather than his testimony on the witness stand, as the Government has a right to do.

The confession of the defendant to the police in effect admits the homicide but denies premeditation and deliberation as well as an intent to kill. It is an elementary principle that the jury is not bound to accept the entire confession. It may accept a part and reject the balance. It may believe the damaging admissions and discredit the exculpatory assertions. Assuming, however, that the jury rejects the exculpatory portions it may not draw an inference contrary to them unless there is affirmative evidence contradicting such assertions, be that evidence direct or circumstantial, from which the opposite deduction can be drawn. The jury had a right to discard the disclaimer of intention to kill and of premeditation and deliberation, but it might not draw an inference to the contrary, unless there is evidence to support it. In this case there is none except the fact that the defendant was armed. There were no eye witnesses to the murder. There is no circumstantial evidence other than the fact that the defendant was armed to support the theory that the murder was premeditated.

The Court has given a great deal of thought to this case since the time that the jury returned its verdict, because the responsibility resting on the Court is a heavy one. Manifestly, it cannot be avoided. After a great deal of reflection the Court has reached the conclusion that the verdict of guilty of murder in the first degree is contrary to the weight of the evidence as concerns the necessarily implied finding that there was premeditation and deliberation on the part of the defendant before he committed the homicide. As stated before, a verdict of murder in the second degree would have been fully warranted.

Under the circumstances, the Court has no alternative but to grant the motion for a new trial and this will be the order of the Court.

Motion for a new trial granted.

NOTES

1. Consider the following facts from Commonwealth v. Jenkins, 79 Montg.Co.L.R. 21 (Penn.Common Pleas, 1960):

A Jury found the defendant, Clifford Jenkins, guilty of rape. Defendant filed a motion for new trial and motion in arrest of judgment, assigning as reasons that the evidence was insufficient to sustain the verdict, that the verdict was against the weight of the evidence, contrary to law, and contrary to the charge of the trial judge. * * *

The Commonwealth's principal witness was Mary Cottone, who is 44 years of age, married 24 years to James Cottone, and who is the mother of two teen age children. Her husband is a road-paving contractor. In approximately 1958, the defendant, Clifford Jenkins, began working as an ordinary laborer for Mr. Cottone. According to Mrs. Cottone, on February 19, 1960, at about 2:00 p. m. while she was eating her lunch at her home, 633 Moore Street, Norristown, Pennsylvania, defendant knocked at her door, opened the door without invitation and approached the kitchen. He asked Mrs. Cottone where her husband was. She replied that he was out. Defendant then said he needed $25 because he did not have enough money to provide food for his wife and children, or to pay the electric company, which was threatening to shut off the electricity. Mrs. Cottone offered him $5. Defendant said, "Things are so black that I feel like doing something, so that the cops, city hall, can take care of my children and my wife, and I could be sent to jail." He grabbed her arm and throat. He seized a table knife and threatened to put it in her throat if she made an outcry. With one hand holding the knife at her back and with the other hand on her throat, he ordered her to proceed upstairs. She complied and at his command disrobed and submitted to intercourse against her will. Defendant arose, took the knife and ran out of the house. Mrs. Cottone went downstairs, locked the doors and telephoned Sam Bono telling him that she had been raped and asking him to have her husband, who was working nearby, call her. (Mr. Bono corroborated this.) Mrs. Cottone also promptly telephoned her son who was at a local high school, as a result of which the son came home to comfort her. Upon receiving the message from Mr. Bono, Mr. Cottone (who was a corroborating witness) telephoned his wife and discovered that she was screaming accusations against the defendant. Mr. Cottone rushed home as soon as he could. Mrs. Cottone's son and a policeman took her to the Sacred Heart Hospital.

Erwin Peikes, M. D., head of the Obstetrical Department at the hospital, examined Mrs. Cottone about 4:00 or 5:00 p. m. on the afternoon of her admission. His opinion was that Mrs. Cottone had had intercourse within six hours immediately previous to his examination. At the time of the examination, Mrs. Cottone was "upset, crying and hysterical."

Detective Paul Scharff interviewed Mrs. Cottone at the hospital. He also found her hysterical, and he observed bruise marks on the upper muscles of Mrs. Cottone's arms and throat.

*   *   *

Since his arrest, defendant in oral questioning and by written statement, admitted striking Mrs. Cottone in anger, but consistently denied the commission of rape. Defendant admittedly committed burglary in 1953 and pleaded guilty thereto. He testified that beginning in 1958 he visited the Cottone house and had sexual relations with Mrs. Cottone by mutual consent. In a sworn statement of the defendant taken by the police, but offered in evidence by the defendant, he deposed that about six months after he began working for Mr. Cottone, he visited the Cottone house and with the encouragement of Mrs. Cottone he had intercourse with her on the floor in the front room; that a couple of weeks later they had intercourse in the basement; that about a month after that they had intercourse in the front bedroom on a green blanket; that about two or three weeks after that, while in the basement, they repeated the performance on the green blanket; that they later had intercourse in the basement again, at which time she wore yellow underpants; that in November, 1959, this was repeated once in the living room on the floor (when she wore slacks), again in the same place (when she was wearing check slacks), again in the kitchen (when she wore slacks); and again in February, 1960, on the green blanket in the bed in the front bedroom, and later in the same day on the floor in the downstairs front room. (That was the day he fled from the house.)

* * *

According to his signed and sworn statement, which his counsel introduced in evidence, after having consentable intercourse with Mrs. Cottone on February 19, 1960, defendant heard a car drive into the driveway and a car door slammed shut outside of the Cottone house; defendant made a hasty exit via the back door and later telephoned Mrs. Cottone who told him "to get out of town . . . because the police is going to be looking for you. . . . Look, I had to tell my husband something."

Upon running out of the Cottone house, defendant admittedly went to the house of Raymond Lewis, 603 Arch Street, Norristown; asked to borrow a coat and cap and requested Mr. Lewis to telephone the defendant's wife telling her that the defendant would be late getting home because the police were searching for him.

* * *

Thereafter, the defendant moved about in Norristown, Philadelphia, and New York, knowing that the police were searching for him, until he was arrested in May, 1960. While he was fugitive and before he was arrested, defendant telephoned Assistant District Attorney Nelson, who had befriended him previously, to learn what, if any, charges had been preferred against defendant. He and Mr. Nelson agreed to meet one another in New York City, but Mr. Nelson, by reason of illness, was unable to keep the appointment.

On these facts, should a trial judge have let the issue of guilt or innocence go to the jury, i. e., should he have overruled a motion for a verdict of acquittal? Should the court now grant a motion for new trial? Should it make any difference in the way in which the court approaches either or both of these decisions whether the crucial issue is the defendant's state of mind at the time of the crime, as in Wilson, the victim's consent, as in the facts above, or the credibility of an eyewitness's identification, as in Pinkney v. State, 9 Md.App. 283, 263 A.2d 871 (1970)?

2. Some judicial opinions have suggested that a trial court should grant a new trial unless the evidence—especially if it is only circumstantial—excludes every other reasonable hypothesis other than the guilt of the defendant. Butler v. State, 104 Ga.App. 777, 123 S.E.2d 30 (1961); Scroggs v. State, 94 Ga.App. 28, 93 S.E.2d 583 (1956). Is this standard any different than the standard applied in the instant case, i. e., would it ever lead to different results? If so, would this be desirable?

3.   Despite the implications in Wilson to the contrary, it is generally held that the ruling of the trial court on a motion for new trial based on allegedly insufficient evidence to support the verdict is reviewable for abuse of discretion.   See Pinkney v. State, 9 Md.App. 283, 263 A.2d 871 (1970).   This appellate review may be available to both sides; the prosecution may be authorized to appeal from the granting of a motion for new trial. See State v. Saenz, 88 Ariz. 154, 353 P.2d 1026 (1960).   When the defendant appeals from denial of his motion for new trial, it has been held that the appellate court, in determining whether there has been an abuse of discretion, determines only whether there was substantial evidence to support the verdict.   State v. Morgan, 453 S.W.2d 932 (Mo.1970).   When the prosecution appeals, the role of the appellate court has been defined as follows:

> [T]he scope of review of an order granting a new trial is essentially the same in both civil and criminal prosecutions, taking into consideration the differences in the applicable burdens of proofs.   In a civil case, where the plaintiff has the burden to prove his case by a preponderance of the evidence, the trial court may properly grant a new trial provided that the "probative force of the evidence does not clearly preponderate in favor of the verdict" * * *.   In a criminal proceeding, on the other hand, where the prosecution has the burden to prove the guilt of the defendant beyond a reasonable doubt, the trial court does not abuse its discretion in granting a new trial unless the record shows that his guilt has been "proved beyond a reasonable doubt" * * *.

State v. A. Saenz, 88 Ariz. 154, 353 P.2d 1026, 1028 (1960).

4.   If a trial judge considers, in fixing sentence, what he views as deficiencies in the proof against the defendant, is this logically consistent with denying a motion for new trial based on allegedly insufficient evidence to support the verdict?   See Franklin v. State, 455 S.W.2d 479 (Mo. 1970), where the defendant has been found guilty by a jury which also assessed the penalty at death.   In exercising his right to reduce the sentence to life imprisonment, the trial judge explained, "Inasmuch as there is some doubt about the ability of the defendant to deliberate and premeditate this crime within the meaning of the law, the Court feels that sentence should be commuted to life imprisonment."   Does this necessarily mean that the same judge's prior action in overruling a motion for new trial was an abuse of discretion?   If not an abuse of discretion, was it nevertheless an unwise exercise of discretion?

5.   In several areas involving evidence thought to generally be particularly subject to suspicion, specific rules have developed in many jurisdictions for determining the adequacy of evidence to support a verdict.   Thus in many jurisdictions a conviction may not rest simply upon the uncorroborated testimony of an accomplice.   Evidence is sufficient to corroborate an accomplice's testimony only if it tends to connect the defendant with the offense.   State v. Thomas, 79 Ariz. 355, 290 P.2d 470 (1955).   Umsted v. State, 435 S.W.2d 156 (Tex.Crim.1968).   Perhaps a more widely applied requirement is that no conviction be permitted to rest upon a confession or admission of the defendant alone.   In order to be sufficient to support a conviction, however, the additional evidence need not tend to connect the

defendant with the offense. There are two alternative formulations of the criteria for determining the adequacy of such additional evidence. One approach requires that the additional evidence tend to prove the commission of a criminal act by someone; this is sometimes stated as a requirement of independent proof of the *corpus delicti*. See Barry v. State, 166 Tex. Cr.R. 372, 314 S.W.2d 90 (1958), reversing a conviction for murder by burning with fire because the evidence offered consisted of a confession other proof that a fire occurred and caused the victim's death; there was no proof, however, tending to show that the fire was of incendiary origin and therefore insufficient proof that a crime had been committed. The other formulation, applied in the federal courts, does not require that the independent proof tend to establish all elements of the corpus delicti but only that it tends to establish the trustworthiness of the confession. See Opper v. United States, 348 U.S. 84, 75 S.Ct. 158, 99 L.Ed. 101 (1954); Smith v. United States, 348 U.S. 147 (1954). See generally, McCormick on Evidence, § 158 (E. Cleary ed. 1972).

Some states, either by statute or case law, also have an absolute requirement of corroboration of the victim's testimony to support a conviction for rape. Some courts find a necessity for such evidence on the facts of particular cases. See generally the discussion in Smith v. State, 239 So. 2d 284 (Fla.App. 1970).

E. TRADITIONAL CRIMINAL OFFENSES

Although crimes are today almost entirely statutory, most have deep historical roots in the English common law. Specific issues concerning the elements of liability under some of these offenses will be dealt with later, but it is necessary at this point to take a preliminary look at the major criminal offenses. Understanding of the law's approach to defining criminal liability requires at least a basic knowledge of the major traditional offenses. Because of the wide variations among the manner in which various jurisdictions define different offenses, this summary must necessarily be quite general and may not correspond to the law of any particular jurisdiction.

Crimes are generally grouped according to the interest protected: security of the person, security of the habitation, security of rights in property, public health, safety, and morals, and public authority.

Offenses Against the Security of the Person

The major common law offense protecting the security of the person was, of course, homicide. At common law, unlawful homicides were either murder or manslaughter. A killing was murder if it was committed with "malice aforethought." As the subsequent material develops, the definition of the state of mind described by the term "malice aforethought" presents a variety of important issues. No degrees of murder were recognized at common law, although many subsequent codifications of the law of homicide have so divided murder. Manslaughter was of two types: voluntary and involuntary. Voluntary manslaughter was an intentional killing committed in a heat of passion induced by adequate provocation. Involuntary manslaughter consisted of an unintentional killing resulting from negligence or the commission of an unlawful act.

The crime of assault, a misdemeanor at common law, has been defined in a wide variety of ways. Some jurisdictions define the offense as an attempt to commit a battery. Under such a definition, the defendant must intend to commit a battery and engage in some activity designed to effectuate that intent. If, as is sometimes the case, the definition also requires the present ability to commit a battery, it is also necessary that there have been no inherent impediment to success. But under this definition, the reaction of the victim is of no legal significance. Probably a majority of jurisdictions include in the definition of assault threatening conduct engaged in with intent to injure or frighten the victim which does create in the victim a reasonable apprehension of immediate physical harm.

A battery is a successful assault, consisting of any application of force to the person of another. Modern American jurisdictions often distinguish between "simple" assaults and batteries and "aggravated" crimes of that nature. The latter consist of assaults and batteries performed under specified circumstances and carry a higher penalty.

Mayhem or maim at common law consisted of a violently inflicted injury rendering the victim less able to fight or annoy his enemy. Except where it took the form of castration, it was a misdemeanor. This offense is often retained in contemporary codes, although it is no longer restricted to injuries affecting the victim's ability to defend himself.

Rape consists, as it did at common law, of an act of intercourse with a woman not the wife of the perpetrator against her will and accomplished by actual or constructive force. At common law, a girl under the age of ten was legally incapable of consenting to intercourse, so any such act with her constituted rape. Modern statutes defining the crime of "statutory" rape generally set a significantly higher age at which a girl may give legally effective consent to intercourse. At common law rape was a felony, and it is also under contemporary statutes.

False imprisonment at common law consisted of any unlawful restraint upon a person's liberty and was a misdemeanor. It is retained in this form in most modern codes.

The common law misdemeanor of kidnapping consisted of the forcible abduction of another and the transportation of the victim to another country. Current statutes have greatly modified this offense in several ways. First, the seriousness of the crime has been increased. In many jurisdictions, at least some forms of kidnapping are categorized with the most serious felonies. Second, the extent to which the victim must be affected has been modified. Transportation to another country is not required; movement of any sort is often sufficient. In some jurisdictions, mere detention (if done with the requisite intent) is sufficient. Finally, some forms of kidnapping have been formulated so as to require detention or movement of the victim for certain specific purposes, such as the infliction of bodily harm, the obtaining of money or property, or the commission of some sexual offense.

Abortion, in its form as a common law misdemeanor, consisted of the destruction of a quickened fetus. The offense was not a homicide because the fetus was not regarded as a person for purposes of the law of homicide, although there was apparently some early authority to the contrary. There is some doubt as to the objective of the prohibition against abortion, especially as to whether the primary concern was with protecting the woman from a procedure that endangered her physical well-being, protecting the fetus' interest in "life," or protecting the community from a practice regarded as offensive or unethical. In any case, current statutes usually make abortion a felony and define it as the destruction of an unborn fetus (whether quickened or not) when this is not necessary to preserve the life or health of the woman.[a]

Offenses Against the Security of the Habitation

Two common law felonies were designed to protect the interest of the security of the habitation. Arson was committed by the malicious burning of a dwelling (or some building used in connection with it) belonging to or occupied by another. Modern criminal codes generally retain the offense in this form, although many have expanded it to cover the burning of structures other than residential dwellings.

Burglary consisted of a breaking and entry of the dwelling of another in the nighttime with the intent to commit a felony in the dwelling. Modern statutes often modify the crime of burglary by removing the requirement of a breaking, expanding the type of buildings protected, and eliminating the requirement that the offense be committed in the nighttime. The intent to commit even misdemeanor theft is often made a sufficient intent for the offense.

Offenses Against the Security of Interests in Property

The common law offenses related to the acquisition of property have an interesting historical development demonstrating an increas-

a. Most—if not all—existing abortion statutes are constitutionally defective in light of Roe v. Wade, — U.S. —, 93 S.Ct. 705, 35 L.Ed.2d 147 (1973) (reprinted at page 275) and Doe v. Bolton, — U.S. —, 93 S.Ct. 739, 35 L.Ed.2d 201 (1973).

ing willingness of the law to protect interests in personal property. In some jurisdictions the various offenses have to some extent been consolidated under the general title of "theft," but even such codifications often retain elements of the common law distinctions.

Robbery is an offense against both the security of the person and of interests in property. It consists of the taking and asportation of personal property from the person or the presence of another against his will by means of violence or placing the other in fear of personal safety with the intent to permanently deprive him of his interest in the property. It was apparently the initial common law property offense, although it was defined somewhat more narrowly.

Larceny, a felony at common law, consisted of a taking and asportation of personal property in the possession of another accomplished against the will of the other and by means of a trespass with the intent to permanently deprive the other of his interests in the property. Modern codes generally retain the offense as defined at common law, either as the separate offense of larceny or as one form of theft. Embezzlement was not a common law offense but was made a crime by early English statute. It is committed when one who has possession of another's property by virtue of a trust relationship fraudulently appropriates that property to a use inconsistent with the trust. The limited common law offense of cheating by use of false tokens was developed by early statutes into the crime of obtaining property by false pretenses. Under the early definitions, this offense required fraudulently causing another to part with ownership of property by means of false representations of fact known to be false. The statutory crime of "false pretenses" thus covered much of the gap left by the relatively restricted definitions of larceny and embezzlement.

Extortion was a misdemeanor at common law consisting of the unlawful collection by an official of an unlawful fee under color of his office. Thus it was an offense against the administration of justice. But in modern codes extortion has often been expanded (sometimes under the label of blackmail) to include obtaining property by means of a threat not sufficient to constitute robbery, including threats to do future (i.e., not immediate) bodily injury, to injure property, to accuse the victim of a crime, or to reveal certain types of information concerning the victim.

Several other offenses against property frequently found in modern criminal codes may have had their origin in common law. Forgery, clearly a misdemeanor at common law, consisted of a material false making or alteration of a writing or document of some legal significance with the intent to defraud. Current statutes often contain similar definitions. It is less clear whether receipt of stolen goods was a common law crime. It is, however, an offense in contemporary codes and requires a taking of possession of property which had been stolen knowing that it had been acquired in a manner constituting larceny (or theft). Similar doubt exists as to the origin of malicious mischief, which consists of malicious destruction of or injury to property of another.

Offenses Against the Public Health, Safety, Morals and Peace

There is a wide variety of offenses with roots in early English law that have in common only the fact that all are defined as crimes because the conduct prohibited has been viewed as infringing the broad interest of the state in maintaining the general public health, safety, and morality.

The misdemeanor of common nuisance consisted of creating a condition prejudicial to the health, safety, comfort, sense of decency, or property of the citizens at large by an act not warranted by law or by neglect of a duty imposed by law. It remains a criminal offense in some jurisdictions. Fornication—usually defined as intercourse between a man and woman not lawfully married—was not a common law offense, although the common law did prohibit any open and notorious lewdness and indecency, including open and notorious cohabitation. Incest—sexual relations between individuals related within the degrees of consanguinity or affinity within which marriage is prohibited—was not a common law offense, although there is dispute as to whether adultery—usually defined as illicit sexual relations in which at least one of the persons is married to someone other than the sexual partner—was such a crime. Bigamy, the marriage of another by one with a spouse living, was made criminal by statute in 1604. Contemporary criminal codes generally include fornication, adultery, incest, and bigamy.

Any willful and unjustifiable disturbance of the public peace was a common law misdemeanor, and is presently an offense in all American jurisdictions. The problem of mob action was dealt with by three offenses, consisting of progressive group activity. Unlawful assembly consisted of three or more persons assembled with intent to carry out any purpose by open force or in any manner such as would cause reasonable apprehension of a breach of the peace. Rout consisted of an unlawful assembly which had begun the accomplishment of the common objective. Riot was the execution of the unlawful purpose, that is, the accomplishment of the objective in a riotous manner. These offenses are retained to varying extents in modern codes.

Offenses Against Public Authority and the Administration of Justice

Treason was a common law offense but its definition was apparently quite uncertain. Later development of the offense by statute was significantly different in America than in England. Article 3, section 3 of the United States Constitution specifically provides that "treason against the United States shall consist only of levying war against them or in adhering to their enemies, giving them aid and comfort." State criminal codes often contain similar crimes, often expanded to prohibit treason against the state as well as the federal government.

Perjury, a misdemeanor at common law, is generally defined as the giving of testimony known to be false which is material to the proceeding and is given in a proceeding in which sworn testimony is permitted.   Subornation of perjury is simply the procuring by one person of another to commit perjury.

Bribery was clearly committed at common law when an officer connected with the administration of justice received a "reward" to influence his official behavior.   But it is unclear whether the crime extended to other governmental officials or to those who gave the "reward."   In any case, modern statutes generally define the offense broadly as the giving or receiving of a thing of value to influence any official act.

Two common law misdemeanors related to those who became involved with one who had committed an offense.   Misprision consisted of knowledge that a felony was to be committed or had been committed together with a failure to prevent its commission or to bring the offender to justice.   Compounding a felony consisted of agreeing for a consideration, with knowledge that a felony has been committed, not to prosecute the felony.   Both offenses are retained in some modern criminal codes, although the definition of misprision of felony has been modified—either by statute or judicial decision—to require significant affirmative assistance to the person who has committed the original offense.   At common law, one who received, relieved, comforted, or assisted another, knowing that he had committed a felony, was an accessory after the fact to the original felony and subject to the full punishment for it.   Contemporary statutes, however, define a separate offense of accessory after the fact to a felony and provide for an independent penalty, less than that provided for the original offense.

F.   PENALTY PROVISIONS AND GRADING OF CRIMINAL OFFENSES

PROBLEM

You, as a legislative draftsman, have been asked to assign proposed penalty provisions to the following offenses.

It is an offense to intentionally cause the death of a human being.

It is an offense for a male person to have sexual intercourse with a woman under the age of sixteen.

It is an offense to enter any dwelling with the intention of committing an offense therein.

It is an offense to inadvertently cause the death of a human being.

It is an offense to go upon the premises of another without the permission of the owner of those premises.

It is an offense for a male person to have sexual intercourse with a woman not his wife if such intercourse is accomplished against the expressed wishes of the woman and her resistance is overcome by means of force or the threats of force.

It is an offense to do any act knowing that such action endangers the life of another human being.

It is an offense for a person, knowing that the owner of premises does not desire his presence on those premises, to enter or remain upon the premises of another.

How would you go about the task? In making the necessary determinations, what factors would you consider?

---

1. THE TASK OF ASSIGNING PENALTIES

TASK FORCE ON ADMINISTRATION OF JUSTICE, THE PRESIDENT'S COMMISSION ON LAW ENFORCEMENT AND ADMINISTRATION OF JUSTICE, TASK FORCE REPORT: THE COURTS

15 (1967).

The penal codes of most jurisdictions are the products of piecemeal construction, as successive legislatures have fixed punishment for new crimes and adjusted penalties for existing offenses through separate sentencing provisions for each offense. As a result the sentencing distinctions among offenses are in excess of those which could rationally be drawn on the basis of relative harmfulness of conduct or the probable dangerousness of the offenders. In Wisconsin, for example, there are 16 variations in the statutory maximum terms of imprisonment for felonies upon a first conviction: 2, 3, 4, 5, 6, 7, 8, 10, 14, 20, 25, 35, and 40 years and life imprisonment. A study of the Oregon penal code revealed that the 1,413 criminal statutes contained a total of 466 different types and lengths of sentences.

The absence of legislative attention to the whole range of penalties may also be demonstrated by comparisons between certain offenses. A recent study of the Colorado statutes disclosed that a person convicted of first degree murder must serve 10 years before becoming eligible for parole, while a person convicted of a lesser degree of the same offense must serve at least 15 years; destruction of a house with fire is punishable by a maximum of 20 years' imprisonment, but destruction of a house with explosives carries a 10-year maximum. In California an offender who breaks into an automobile to steal the contents of the glove compartment is subject to a 15-year maximum sentence, but if he stole the car itself, he would face a maximum 10-year term.

Although each offense must be defined in a separate statutory provision, the number and variety of sentencing distinctions which result when legislatures prescribe a separate penalty for each offense are among "the main causes of the anarchy in sentencing that is so widely deplored."

WECHSLER AND MICHAEL, A RATIONALE FOR THE LAW OF HOMICIDE

37 Columbia Law Review 701, 1261, 1268–1270 (1937).

[S]ome one, legislator or administrator, must face the problem of ordering the severity of penalties within the limits of popular tolerance so that the welfare of individual offenders shall be sacrificed for the sake of deterrence only in those instances in which the sacrifice is most necessary and serves the most desirable ends. We must, therefore, address ourselves to an analysis of that problem. If we are right in believing that the core of the popular demand is for some gradation of the severity of punitive treatment in accordance with the actual or probable results of crimes of various sorts and the characters of criminals of various sorts, the major criteria for an ordered mitigation of punishment are, it will be observed, inherent in popular sentiment itself.

I. There are several reasons why the severity of penalties should be correlated with the relative undesirability of the behavior for which they are imposed. The more undesirable any kind of criminal behavior is, the less expedient it is to relax our efforts to prevent it, the more important it is that we make the incentive to avoid it, which the threat of punishment provides, as strong as it can be made. Moreover, such a correlation serves, as we have said, as an inducement to potential offenders to pursue their ends by the least undesirable criminal means; it also serves as an object lesson in relative evil which is not without some value as general moral education.

II. There are equally valid reasons why the severity of penalties should be correlated with the characters of individual offenders. The more numerous a potential offender's motives to refrain from criminal behavior apart from that of avoiding a threatened penalty, the more he is moved by them habitually, the greater his capacity to guide his conduct by such motives, the less need there is for a vigorous threat to counteract whatever desires to engage in criminal behavior he may have from time to time. Moreover, for the most part, the more severe a penalty, the greater is its incapacitative effect and the more likely it is to harm and the less likely to reform the actual offenders subjected to it. Obviously, the more dangerous men are, the more desirable it is that they be thoroughly incapacitated; the better the lives men can lead, the less desirable it is to debase them; the more likely it is that men are corrigible, the more tragic it is not to attempt to reform them.

Though these are, in our judgment, the major criteria for ordering the severity of punishment, they are not exhaustive. Two subordinate principles merit consideration. They are:

III. The severity of penalties should be correlated with the strength of the desires which motivate men to engage in criminal behavior of different sorts under different circumstances. The stronger the desire, the more need there is for severity in the threatened penalty in order to counteract it.

IV. The severity of penalties should also be correlated with the presence or absence of a discernible relation between the criminal act and some injustice done to the actor by another individual or even by society as a whole. Where such a relationship can be perceived, a mitigation of the penalty on that ground serves, as T. H. Green has pointed out,[25] to direct attention to and strengthen the popular awareness of the original injustice, a result that may be of value in preventing or remedying such injustices in the future. The greater the injustice, the less vigorous the efforts that are being made to deal with it, the more confidently the criminal act can be attributed to it as a cause, the stronger the case for mitigation for that reason becomes.

To the extent that these principles can be developed and employed, the severity of punishment should be susceptible of a rough ordering which is rationally adapted both to its primary deterrent purpose and to the other ends which even the punitive treatment of offenders should as far as possible serve.

AMERICAN BAR ASSOCIATION PROJECT ON MINIMUM STANDARDS FOR CRIMINAL JUSTICE, STANDARDS RELATING TO SENTENCING ALTERNATIVES AND PROCEDURES (COMMENTARY)

130, 143–54, 133–36, 157–58 (1967).[b]

There are two basic items of information which must be known about any prison sentence in order adequately to appraise its effect.

---

25. Lectures on the Principles of Political Obligation (1927) 193–4.

b. Copyright ©, 1967, by the American Bar Association. Reprinted with permission. The ABA Standards are printed in individual volumes. They may be ordered from the American Bar Association Circulation Dept., American Bar Center, 1155 East 60th

The first is the date beyond which, at all events, the offender must be released. This is * * * the "maximum" term to which he is subject. The second is the date at which he becomes eligible for discretionary release by parole authorities. This is * * * the "minimum" term.

*   *   *

Although there are wide differences in terminology, practically all forms of sentencing employed in this country involve at least to some extent the principle of indeterminacy. Parole authorities are almost always given some measure of discretion to release an offender prior to the expiration of the time when he must be released. As noted in comment *a* to section 3.1, the term "minimum sentence" is used here to designate the earliest time when discretion can be exercised in favor of parole. The spread between the minimum and the maximum is thus the degree of indeterminacy permitted by the sentence imposed.

The most obvious form of indeterminate sentencing occurs in states like California, Hawaii and Washington, where in most cases the sentencing judge commits for a legislatively fixed maximum term and the parole authorities are free to release the offender conditionally at any time. * * * A variation of this same principle exists in states like Alaska and Illinois, where the trial judges commit for both a minimum and a maximum term and the parole authorities are free to exercise their discretion within the range thus fixed. * * * A third approach is found in states like Florida and Minnesota, where either a very low minimum is fixed by statute independently of the maximum imposed, or where there is no minimum period at all. * * * Still a fourth variation of the same idea occurs in states like North Carolina and Virginia, which employ the so-called "definite" sentence. Under this approach, the commitment by the sentencing authority is for a fixed period of time. Indeterminacy is achieved by granting parole eligibility after a certain portion of that sentence has been served. Thus again, discretion over the actual period of detention is placed in the parole authorities. * * *

As can be seen by these random examples, there are numerous methods by which parole eligibility can be determined. Selection among them involves a judgment about the proper functions of three different agencies—the legislature, the court and the paroling authority. * * *

[Minimum Sentences]
The core of the debate between the Model Penal Code and the Model Sentencing Act involves the basic question of whether a minimum sentence should be authorized at all. The Model Sentencing Act

Street, Chicago, Illinois 60637, telephone (312) 493–0533. Cost is $2.00 per volume or $1 in lots of 10 or more, whether same or assorted titles.

flatly takes the position that there should be immediate parole eligibility—that there should be no minimum sentences even for the most serious of offenses. The Code is in full agreement with the proposition that the sentencing structure should be dominated by the principle of indeterminacy. But it is not in agreement that the timing of the parole decision should be entirely beyond legislative and judicial control. Judicial control is accomplished by authorizing the sentencing court to fix a minimum term within a range specified for each category of offenses; legislative control is manifested by the requirement that every commitment must be accompanied by a minimum term of at least one year.

It is helpful in assessing the dispute between these two highly respected model provisions to divide the issue into two parts: whether it is sound for the legislature to fix mandatory minimum terms which must be imposed irrespective of the circumstances; and whether the sentencing court should be authorized to impose a minimum term. Subsection (a) of this section deals with the first of these two questions.

It is quite common in this country for legislatures to provide mandatory minimum terms for certain offenses. The most consistent examples are those offenses which carry life imprisonment as the maximum term. Legislatively fixed minimum sentences in such cases range from an apparent low of seven years in Nevada, to thirty years in Maine. More common is the ten year minimum found in Alabama, Colorado, Idaho, Mississippi, North Carolina and Oregon and the fifteen year minimum found in the District of Columbia, Delaware, Iowa, Maryland, Utah and Virginia. * * *

In addition, legislatively fixed minimum terms are required in all prison sentences for other specific offenses named in the statutes of many jurisdictions. Perhaps the most criticized example of such mandatory minima is the federal narcotics statute which not only mandates a five, and in some cases a ten year prison term without parole, but which also denies eligibility for probation. * * *

Finally it should be noted that at least four states have adopted across-the-board minima for every prison sentence. In Massachusetts every sentence to the state prison must be for at least a two and one-half year minimum, while in Mississippi and New York all prison sentences must carry at least a one year minimum. In Florida, the term is six months. * * *

The argument most commonly advanced in favor of the imposition of a minimum term is based on community reassurance. The basic purpose of the criminal law is the protection of the public, and the public can only be assured that this purpose will be carried out if dangerous offenders are removed from society for at least a minimum period of time. A second argument is that it is destructive of the effective operation of parole boards to give them total freedom in every case. The parole decision should be a shared responsibility, and the minimum term is the way in which other agencies can participate in the process. A third point is that a minimum period of incarceration is an institutional necessity in order for any valid correctional program to have a meaningful chance to operate. Finally, a related argument is made that if a consensus can be reached on the minimum time needed in order to implement a valid correctional program, legislative specification of that term for every case will serve to emphasize to the sentencing court the nature of the decision being made, and to point up the difference between probation and institutionalization in more meaningful terms.

These four arguments, sometimes supplemented by general references to deterrence and the sureness of punishment, are the ones which are normally suggested in favor of the principle underlying a minimum term. * * *

Support for [the] position [that it is inappropriate for the legislature to prescribe minimum terms which must be imposed by the court without regard to the circumstances] must begin with a consideration of the arguments in favor of a minimum term. The most persuasive argument is the one that relies on the need for community reassurance that the law is performing its task of public protection. Not only is it important that the public in fact be protected, but it is important to develop the confidence in the legal system which is one of its necessary underpinnings.

Thus stated, the argument is ambiguous. Assuming that the minimum term can perform the function of developing this public confidence, the argument does not speak precisely to whether it should be the legislature, the court or some other agency which should determine the instances in which the protection of a minimum term is called for. There are some, however, who would use it for the proposition that the legislature can perform the task by adopting high, across-the-board minima for certain types of offenses. * * *

Public clamor for this position—and the political capitalization on it which feeds its growth—loses sight of the fact that it is at most only some offenders from whom the public needs this protection, and that the legislature is not in a position to identify the precise individuals who pose the feared risk. It is perfectly apparent that *every* robber and *every* mugger, and indeed *every* murderer, does not pose the same type of future danger to the community. The young adult who panics because he cannot find work and who robs to feed his starving family does not pose the same potential danger to the community as the sociopath who robs because his twisted values find that as convenient a way as any to make a living. * * *

The evil of the mandatory term is that it robs the system of the capacity to discriminate between offenders who do and offenders who do not deserve the harsh treatment which the minimum signifies. A far better way to attack the problem would be to arm the system with the funds and the facilities to enable it to identify the particular offenders from whom society legitimately needs protection.   *   *   *

There are several additional reasons why the mandatory minimum is a naive and destructive provision.   As noted, the definition of offenses is of necessity in general terms, and the varying circumstances in which an offense can occur will to a certainty lead to cases where all would agree that a long period of confinement is unwarranted.   Both judges and prosecuting officials recognize such cases when they arise, and are immediately put in a most awkward position.   They may either enforce the letter of the law and perpetrate a clear injustice, or they may ignore the law and defeat the apparent intent of the legislature.   Both results are destructive of the very public confidence in the system which is sought by the mandatory minimum term.

The process of nullification which comes about by judicial nonenforcement of mandatory provisions also illustrates another point which is often ignored in the heat of the moment which produces such legislation.   It is frequently stated by the proponents of mandatory minima that such devices are needed to prevent "soft" judges from being lenient toward dangerous offenders and to provide a sureness of punishment that will act as the great deterrent.   But the fact remains—whether the judge is right or whether he is wrong—that the judge has numerous discretionary means by which he can, and by by which judges do, defeat the intent of such legislation.   The intention to hamstring "soft" judges thus may boomerang to result in more lenient treatment—perhaps even acquittal—than even the judges themselves would desire.   The search for an alternative to the offense which carries the harsh minimum may not always produce an offense which provides an appropriate disposition.   The effect on the system, in any event, is that it becomes unmistakably truncated and artificial.

*   *   *

There is one last effect of the mandatory minimum sentence which should be noted.   The choice which is often presented between a plea to a lesser offense and the certainty of a brutal sentence upon conviction of the charged offense has clear coercive effects upon the supposedly consensual process of pleading guilty.   The mandatory minimum can stack the deck, as it were, in favor of inducing pleas to lesser offenses even though there may be a substantial chance of acquittal and even though the defendant may in fact not be guilty of the charged offense.   It can thus compromise the process by which guilt is determined.

It remains to consider the other arguments which have been advanced in favor of a minimum term.   The second argument noted above was that it is destructive of the effective operation of parole boards to give them total freedom, and that it tends to introduce conservatism by the board if it is to shoulder the entire burden in every case.

For reasons similar to those noted above, it would not seem that the objectives sought by this argument would be advanced by legislatively fixed minimum terms. The parole board is directed to make its judgments in terms of the case presented by each individual offender. The legislature, on the other hand, must make its judgments before the offender has identified himself by committing a crime. It would thus seem that to the extent that this argument is valid it is an argument for judicially imposed terms. The court is the only other agency in the process which is in a position to share in the parole decision by tailoring a minimum term to the particular offender.

There is another aspect of the mandatory minimum term which raises different questions. As noted above, in at least four states a reasonably short, across-the-board minimum is provided for every prison sentence, ranging from two and one-half years in Massachusetts to six months in Florida. * * *

This type of provision is supported, as the arguments stated above reflect, by the twin aims of assuring a sufficient time for the institution to undertake a meaningful corrections program and of emphasizing to the judge the practical fact that at least such a period of detention will be a necessary result from a sentence to prison. It is suggested, however, that neither objective justifies the requirement of such a minimum term in every prison sentence.

The danger, of course, is that classification and diagnosis of the individual will disclose that the offender is more likely to respond to probation than he is to a year's incarceration. The Model Penal Code guards against this possibility by authorizing the institution to return to the sentencing court and request resentencing. See Model Penal Code § 7.08(3), Appendix B, * * *. It would seem less cumbersome in such a case to authorize immediate parole eligibility than to require a return to the sentencing court. If the institution in fact needs a one year period or longer during which to implement a satisfactory program for a given offender, there is nothing about such immediate eligibility that would interfere. On the other hand, if the determination is that incarceration itself was a mistake, or that only a very short period of a few months together with parole supervision is a less damaging alternative, then the automatic minimum serves as a hindrance and the requirement of return to the court as an unnecessary clog on crowded dockets.

In addition, the idea that the trial judge needs to be put to a choice as drastic as one year versus probation in order to be forced to realize the nature of the decision he is making cannot support such a mandatory term. In the first place, this is a poor reason for refusing to rectify a mistake once it is discovered. More importantly, however, education of trial judges in the ways of the institutions to which they commit will apprise them of similar *de facto* minima which are bound to exist due to the classification procedures and the normal operation of the institution. It is thought better to require such judgments on the basis of the time institutions in fact need rather than by the erection of artificial mandatory periods during which perhaps unneeded and damaging detention must take place.

Finally, there is the point that it is somewhat inconsistent to authorize probation for an offense and at the same time to require a minimum period of incarceration if probation is rejected. Perhaps the most extreme example of this point is the federal offense which puts to the sentencing judge the choice of probation or twenty-five years, but nothing in between. See 18 U.S.C.A. § 2114 (1964); Smith v. United States, 284 F.2d 789, 791 n. 2 (5th Cir. 1960); United States v. Donovan, 242 F.2d 61, 64 (2d Cir. 1957). Only the degree of the vice differs. Whether the trial judge is to fluctuate minima or maxima within a given range, it is his function to grade offenders and he cannot do so effectively if he is faced with a gap in the alternatives which face him.

*   *   *

[T]he second aspect of the problem is whether the sentencing court should be authorized to impose a minimum if suited to the case before it. For while it may be undesirable to force the imposition of such a term, it by no means follows that a minimum term should not be permitted if the court deems it warranted in a particular case. * * *

The most compelling reason advanced in support of authority to impose a minimum sentence is the need to assure the community that a dangerous offender will be removed from society for a minimum period of time. The countervailing consideration is that in the heat of the moment—particularly if the judge is subject to the community pressures of an elected official—an unfair, irrevocable decision will be made. Equally possible, of course, is a decision which is informed at the time it is made, but which—though irrevocably made—is called into question by subsequent events. The vice of the minimum sentence is that it fails to allow for these possibilities.

[Maximum Sentence]

One of the questions which divided the American Law Institute in the formulation of its Model Penal Code was whether, assuming the court has determined to impose a prison sentence, the maximum term should be fixed in advance by the legislature for all offenses within a given class, or the sentencing judge should be authorized to fix the maximum term within a legislatively prescribed range. Present practice is divided between these two approaches, although the federal system and a clear majority of the states allow the sentencing judge a role in determining the maximum to be imposed. * * *

Argument in favor of a maximum term over which the sentencing judge is to have no control proceeds from the premise that the function of the maximum is to express the limit beyond which even the worst risks within a class of offenders should not be detained on the basis of past criminal behavior. Two judgments are therefore involved: the point at which this overall limit should be fixed and the nature of the risk provided by the particular offender. The first judgment is uniformly conceded to be for the legislature. The second arguably could be divided between judge and parole authority. The argument advanced by those who would place it exclusively with the parole authorities is that the decision which is required is one that can best be made on the basis of the hindsight provided by examination and diagnosis over time: the parole authorities are better able to determine the risk of release and the character of the offender at the time when parole is at issue than is the judge at the time of original sentencing.

In addition, proponents of no judicial control over the maximum argue that the best device by which to attack the pervasive problem of sentencing disparities is to reduce the variety of sentences available to the trial judge—and correspondingly to retain variations only when it is necessary to achieve a specific objective. The judgment which is thus expressed is that the gains of permitting judicial variation of the maximum are more than offset by the losses which result from uncontrollable sentencing disparities.

Finally, some critics have suggested that such a system will result in longer sentences. However, since the fixed maximum expresses a legislative judgment about how the worst offender within a given class should be treated, proponents have argued that less restraint is exerted on the parole authorities than is the case when the judge has purportedly tailored the maximum to the particular offender. The parole authorities would thus be encouraged to grade offenders on the basis of present condition, rather than intimidated by what can only be a judicial guess of future condition. In addition, parole authorities would not be limited by a judicially reduced sentence in cases where present condition did not warrant release. The conclusion is thus that while the *maximum* sentences imposed will necessarily be longer, time served may well be shorter, and at the least will be unaffected by a judicial judgment which because of its timing cannot be made upon optimum information.

On the other hand, those who are of the view that the judge should exercise control over the maximum sentence actually imposed answer that a legislatively-fixed maximum deprives the court of a necessary tool with which to grade the severity of a particular offense. The legislative grading of offenses is necessarily in broad categories, as are legislatively fixed ranges within which punishment is authorized. It ought to be the function of the sentencing judge to particularize the grading according to the severity of the offense and the character of the offender—to individualize the sentence, as this process is often described.

Dix & Sharlot Cs. Crim.Law ACB—5

Three further arguments are advanced in favor of judicial control. The first is an attack on the basic premise of the fixed-maximum proposal. The proposition that parole authorities are in a better position than judges to assess the readiness of the defendant to return to society needs more support than merely the advantage of more favorable timing. In particular, such a system would seem to call on more highly developed and more adequately funded correctional and parole facilities than many states have to date provided. In addition, the fact that judicial sentencing occurs in open court following an opportunity to present a case with the assistance of an attorney affords a visibility to the process which is normally absent before parole authorities, as well as greater procedural protection.

The second argument proceeds on the view that sentences in this country are already the longest in the world without any demonstration that such longevity is an aid rather than a hindrance to law enforcement. Permitting judicial control would be one way of reducing the sentences imposed, and also should effect the reduction of actual time served.

The third argument is based on wholly different considerations. The effect sought by the denial of discretion to determine the maximum sentence is a transfer of control to the parole authorities over the actual time to be served. Denying judicial control, the argument goes, will in fact frustrate rather than advance this objective. A great majority of convicted defendants—approaching ninety per cent in many jurisdictions—are convicted after a plea rather than a trial, and a majority of these tender their plea in the hope if not the expectation that sentencing leniency will be the reward. If the judge has no power to be lenient by reducing the otherwise legislatively fixed maximum, then the only concession left for the defendant to seek is charge reduction. Since the plea-bargaining process is so well entrenched, the practical result is a shift of discretion from the court to the prosecutor, rather than from the court to the parole authorities as is desired.

* * *

[Relationship Between Minimum and Maximum Sentences]

[There is also a] need for assurance that the principle of indeterminancy will not be undercut by the imposition of too high a minimum term. The laws of most states accomplish this by denying authority to impose a minimum term which approaches the maximum in severity. The "definite" sentence states, for example—those in which parole eligibility turns on a fixed percentage of the sentence imposed—have built into their system the requirement that there be an adequate spread between minimum and maximum terms. Thus, in the Virginia example given in comment *b*, supra, a twelve year sentence automatically means that the period between three and twelve years is indeterminate. This principle is likewise followed in most jurisdictions where the trial court is given discretion as to the minimum. In Alaska and the District of Columbia, for example, the sentencing court can select a minimum term at any point up to one-third of the maximum actually imposed. * * *

In some states, however, there is no limit on the minimum term which can be imposed. In one case, for example, an "indeterminate" sentence of 199 years (the minimum) to life (the maximum) was upheld, thus authorizing the parole authorities to release the offender at any time after the expiration of 199 years. See People v. King, 1 Ill. 2d 496, 16 N.E.2d 623 (1953), discussed in Note, Statutory Structures for Sentencing Felons to Prison, 60 Colum.L.Rev. 1134, 1145 n. 75 (1960). Such a sentencing structure has the effect of authorizing the trial judge to abandon the principle of indeterminacy, though in the name of the "indeterminate" sentence.

NOTES

1. To what extent is it reasonable to expect that the choice as to the severity of penalty will affect the incidence of the crime? Schwartz, The Effect in Philadelphia of Pennsylvania's Increased Penalties for Rape and Attempted Rape, 59 J.Crim.L., C. & P.S. 509 (1968) attempted to assess the effect of a change in penalties for rape and attempted rape. After a particularly offensive rape on April 3, 1966, the maximum penalty for rape with bodily injury was increased from fifteen years to life. A minimum of fifteen years was established; none had previously been imposed. For rape without bodily injury, the maximum was raised from fifteen to twenty years. The changes were widely publicized by news media and in Philadelphia were accompanied by an announcement that trials for such offenders would be speeded up. The statutory changes were signed by the governor on May 12, 1966. Schwartz compared the incidence of rapes and attempted rapes in Philadelphia during 1966 with 1965 and the period 1958 to 1965. This showed no significant decrease following the increased penalties. Nor was there any discernable reduction in the seriousness of the offenses following the enactment of heavier penalties for offenses involving bodily injury. What significance, if any, does this study have for the assignment of penalties for offenses? Explain. How might more helpful studies of the effect of penalties be structured? Cf. Ball, The Deterrent Concept in Criminology and Law, 46 J.Crim.L., C. & P.S. 347 (1955).

The classical criminologists argued that severity of penalty was irrelevant to the deterrent effect of criminal punishment and that greater certainty of punishment was more likely than greater severity to produce a deterrent effect. It has been argued that the results of experiments conducted by experimental psychologists confirm this. Jeffery, Criminal Behavior and Learning Theory, 56 J.C.L., C. & P.S. 294 (1965). Singer, Psychological Studies of Punishment, 58 Cal.L.Rev. 405 (1970) questions this. He reports finding no experimental evidence which directly contrasts the results of increased severity with those of increased certainty. The indirect evidence, Singer concludes, suggests that "a sufficiently severe punishment will suppress behavior effectively even if it is only occasional, whereas a mild punishment will permit complete recovery of the punished behavior even if it is administered every time [the behavior is performed]." Id. at 417.

The matter is complicated, he asserts, by the fact that delaying punishment has an effect equivalent to reducing its severity. As a result, "a five-year sentence beginning a year after the commission of a crime may not be as effective as a six-month sentence administered without delay." Id. at 421. When, however, society responds to continuing or increasing crime by increasing the severity of penalties, there is a corresponding desire to increase the procedural safeguards used to assure that the penalty is never imposed upon an innocent person. The delay caused by these procedural safeguards is likely to offset any effect the increased severity might have. Is this information helpful? If so, how?

2. Dix, Judicial Review of Sentences: Implications for Individual Disposition, 1969 Law & The Social Order 369, 413–15:

> The proposition that emphasis on individualization causes longer actual incarceration as well as longer potential incarceration finds some support in a comparison of definite and indeterminate sentencing practices. Table VII [omitted here] compares median sentences imposed upon offenders received during 1960 by institutions in several states. In those jurisdictions using both types of sentences, the indeterminate sentence meant longer potential incarceration—sometimes three times as long. In addition, maximum sentences in those jurisdictions imposing primarily indeterminate sentences were almost always longer than sentences imposed in juridictions imposing primarily definite sentences. Table VIII,

TABLE VIII

MEDIAN TIME SERVED BY OFFENDERS RELEASED IN 1960

	% of Offenders with Definite Sentences	Median Time Served (in months)		
		all	definite	indeterminate
United States	39.3	20.9	16.9	23.4
Jurisdictions Using Both Types of Sentences				
Georgia	36.1	22.0	22.8	21.5
Maryland	73.5	12.0	12.1	11.9
Nebraska	71.6	17.0	16.6	17.5
North Carolina	38.7	16.7	12.0	22.1
North Dakota	34.0	15.2	10.8	17.6
Texas	31.2	20.0	14.6	24.9
Jurisdictions Using Primarily Definite Sentences				
Delaware	100.0	14.5	14.5	–
Missouri	100.0	16.7	16.7	–
Montana	100.0	10.9	10.9	–
Rhode Island	100.0	21.9	21.9	–
South Carolina	100.0	17.0	17.0	–
Virginia	100.0	23.6	23.6	–
Wisconsin	92.6	15.2	14.8	28.3

	% of Offenders with Definite Sentences	Median Time Served (in months)		
		all	definite	indeterminate
Jurisdictions Using Primarily Indeterminate Sentences				
Arizona	0.5	20.8	–	20.8
Indiana	6.6	27.6	22.6	27.7
Michigan	2.1	20.3	56.3	20.0
New Hampshire	0.0	11.9	–	11.9
New York	0.0	28.6	–	28.6
Pennsylvania	0.3	31.2	–	31.2
West Virginia	6.4	27.3	64.0	22.3
Wyoming	0.0	13.0	–	13.0

Source: U. S. Dept. of Justice, Federal Bureau of Prisons, National Prisoner Statistics, Characteristics of State Prisoners 1960, at 70.

comparing median time actually served by offenders released during 1960, suggests that the exercise of parole discretion under the indeterminate sentences reduced this disparity but did not eliminate it. In some jurisdictions using both types of sentences, the parole authority was so exercised that those sentenced to indeterminate terms served less time than their counterparts serving definite terms; this was not always true, however. Most important, those states adopting a general policy of indeterminate sentencing generally required their offenders to serve significantly longer periods. Indeterminate sentencing, therefore, almost certainly means longer potential incarceration and—especially if the jurisdiction has adopted a general policy of near-exclusive use of indeterminate sentences—it also means longer actual incarceration.

Although definite sentences may involve the exercise of significant trial court individualization, it is probably true that indeterminate sentencing represents greater individualization. The opportunity for the exercise of discretionary individualization extends over a longer period of time (during the entire period of parole eligibility) and—although this is more questionable—correctional authorities are probably more likely than trial court judges to view their role as appropriately one of individualization at the expense of other factors such as uniformity and respect for upper limits on incarceration determined by the seriousness of the act for which liability was initially imposed. The general statistical inference is that the greater the opportunity for individualization, the longer the potential and actual incarceration is likely to be. This merely emphasizes that the acceptance of the propriety of individualization increases willingness to incarcerate longer, thus underlining the necessity of examining realistically the basis on which the ability to reliably individualize is accepted.

See, also Rubin, The Concept of Treatment in the Criminal Law, 21 S.C.L. Rev. 3, 5 (1968): "[T]his 'treatment' idea, indeterminate sentences, has had its principal effect increasing terms of imprisonment."

3. What impact is an increase in the severity of sentences imposed likely to have upon sentences actually served? Consider the following from U.

S. Department of Justice, Federal Bureau of Prisons Statistical Report, Fiscal Years 1969 and 1970 p. 16 (undated):

AVERAGE TIME SERVED AND AVERAGE SENTENCE LENGTH OF FIRST RELEASES FROM FEDERAL INSTITUTIONS

Fiscal Years 1960 - 1970 [Excludes Youth Corrections Act Releases]

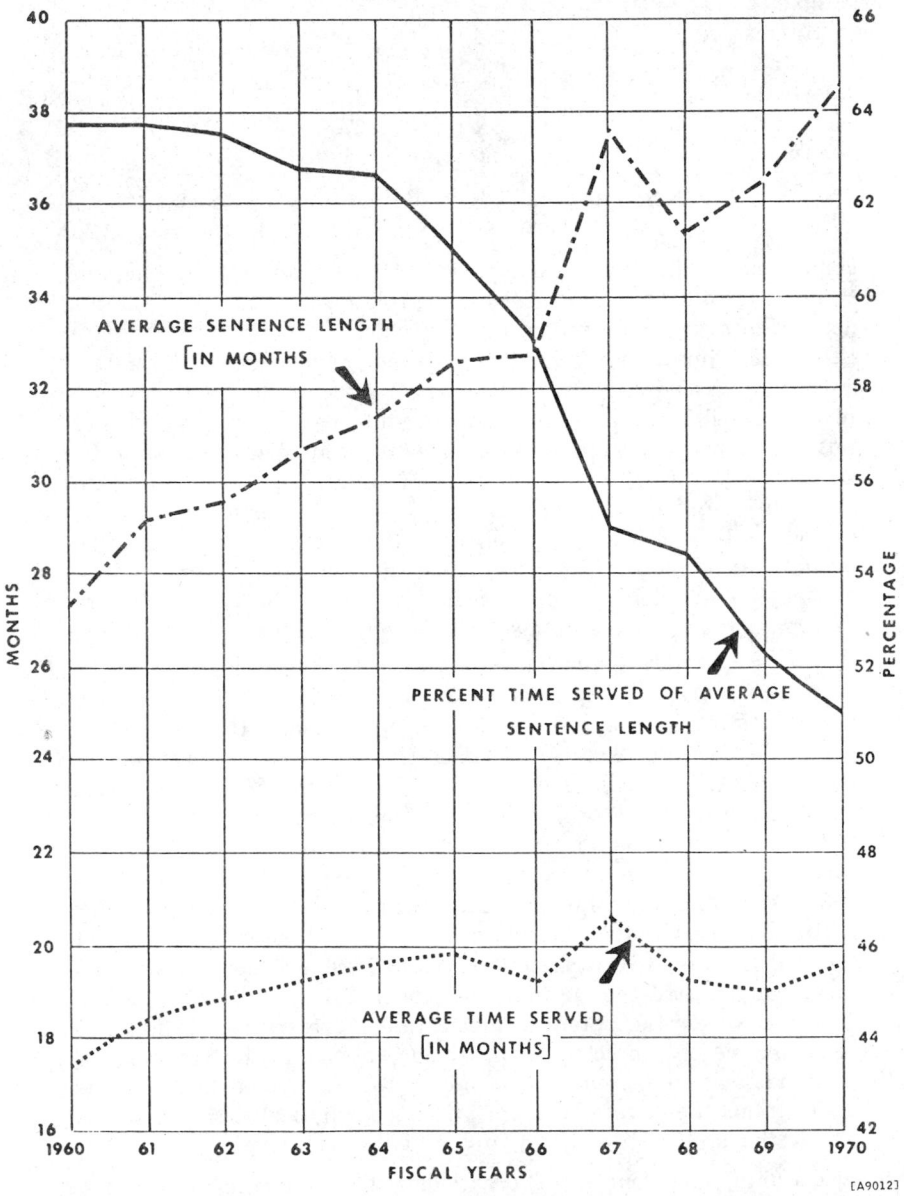

How might this be explained? If it is viewed as undesirable, how might it be changed?

4. Should the imposition of fines be treated differently than the imposition of other penalties? Consider the following provision of the New York Penal Law:

§ 80.00 Fine for felony

1. Criterion for fine. The court may impose a fine for a felony if the defendant has gained money or property through the commission of the crime.

2. Amount of fine. A sentence to pay a fine for a felony shall be a sentence to pay an amount, fixed by the court, not exceeding double the amount of the defendant's gain from the commission of the crime.

3. Determination of amount. As used in this section the term "gain" means the amount of money or the value of property derived from the commission of the crime, less the amount of money or the value of property returned to the victim of the crime or seized by or surrendered to lawful authority prior to the time sentence is imposed.

When the court imposes a fine for a felony the court shall make a finding as to the amount of the defendant's gain from the crime. If the record does not contain sufficient evidence to support such a finding the court may conduct a hearing upon the issue.

If this approach is proper when the offense is a felony, why should it not also be applied to the imposition of a fine for less serious offenses?

----

2. SPECIFIC PENALTIES

----

a. THE DEATH PENALTY

FURMAN v. GEORGIA

Supreme Court of the United States, 1972.
408 U.S. 238, 92 S.Ct. 2726, 33 L.Ed.2d 346.

PER CURIAM. Petitioner in No. 69–5003 was convicted of murder in Georgia and was sentenced to death pursuant to Ga.Code Ann. § 26–1005 (Supp.1971) (effective prior to July 1, 1969). 225 Ga. 253, 167 S.E.2d 628 (1969). Petitioner in No. 69–5030 was convicted of rape in Georgia and was sentenced to death pursuant to Ga. Code Ann. § 26–1302 (Supp.1971) (effective prior to July 1, 1969). 225 Ga. 790, 171 S.E.2d 501 (1969). Petitioner in No. 69–5031 was convicted of rape in Texas and was sentenced to death pursuant to Tex.Penal Code Ann., Art. 1189 (1961). 447 S.W.2d 932 (Tex.Ct. Crim.App.1969). Certiorari was granted limited to the following question: "Does the imposition and carrying out of the death penalty in [these cases] constitute cruel and unusual punishment in violation of the Eighth and Fourteenth Amendments?" 403 U.S. 952 (1971). The

Court holds that the imposition and carrying out of the death penalty in these cases constitutes cruel and unusual punishment in violation of the Eighth and Fourteenth Amendments. The judgment in each case is therefore reversed insofar as it leaves undisturbed the death sentence imposed, and the cases are remanded for further proceedings.

So ordered.

Mr. Justice DOUGLAS, Mr. Justice BRENNAN, Mr. Justice STEWART, Mr. Justice WHITE, and Mr. Justice MARSHALL have filed separate opinions in support of the judgments. The CHIEF JUSTICE, Mr. Justice BLACKMUN, Mr. Justice POWELL, and Mr. Justice REHNQUIST have filed separate dissenting opinions.

———

Mr. Justice BRENNAN, concurring.

* * * The Cruel and Unusual Punishments Clause, like the other great clauses of the Constitution, is not susceptible to precise definition. Yet we know that the values and ideals it embodies are basic to our scheme of government. And we know also that the Clause imposes upon this Court the duty, when the issue is properly presented, to determine the constitutional validity of a challenged punishment, whatever that punishment may be. In these cases, "[t]hat issue confronts us, and the task of resolving it is inescapably ours." Id., at 103.

I

We have very little evidence of the Framers' intent in including the Cruel and Unusual Punishments Clause among those restraints upon the new Government enumerated in the Bill of Rights. * * *

Several conclusions * * * emerge from the history of the adoption of the Clause. We know that the Framers' concern was directed specifically to the exercise of legislative power. They included in the Bill of Rights a prohibition upon "cruel and unusual punishments" precisely because the legislature would otherwise have had the unfettered power to prescribe punishments for crimes. Yet we cannot now know exactly what the Framers thought "cruel and unusual punishments" were. Certainly they intended to ban torturous punishments, but the available evidence does not support the further conclusion that *only* torturous punishments were to be outlawed. * * * [T]he Framers were well aware that the reach of the Clause was not limited to the proscription of unspeakable atrocities. Nor did they intend simply to forbid punishments considered "cruel and unusual" at the time. The "import" of the Clause is, indeed, "indefinite," and for good reason. A constitutional provision "is enacted, it is true, from an experience of evils, but its general language should not, therefore, be necessarily confined to the form that evil had theretofore taken. Time works changes, brings into existence new conditions and purposes. Therefore a principle to be vital must be capable of wider application than the mischief which gave it birth." Weems v. United States, 217 U.S., at 373.

It was almost 80 years before this Court had occasion to refer to the Clause. See Pervear v. The Commonwealth, 72 U.S. (5 Wall.) 475, 479–480 (1867). These early cases, as the Court pointed out in Weems v. United States, supra, at 369, did not undertake to provide "an exhaustive definition" of "cruel and unusual punishments." Most of them proceeded primarily by "looking backwards for examples by which to fix the meaning of the clause," id., at 377, concluding simply that a punishment would be "cruel and unusual" if it were similar to punishments considered "cruel and unusual" at the time the Bill of Rights was adopted. In Wilkerson v. Utah, 99 U. S., at 136, for instance, the Court found it "safe to affirm that punishments of torture * * * and all others in the same line of unnecessary cruelty, are forbidden." The "punishments of torture," which the Court labeled "atrocities," were cases where the criminal "was embowelled alive, beheaded, and quartered," and cases "of public dissection * * * and burning alive." Id., at 135. Similarly, in In re Kemmler, 136 U.S. 436, 446 (1890), the Court declared that "if the punishment prescribed for an offence against the laws of the State were manifestly cruel and unusual, as burning at the stake, crucifixion, breaking on the wheel, or the like, it would be the duty of the courts to adjudge such penalties to be within the constitutional prohibition." The Court then observed commenting upon the passage just quoted from Wilkerson v. Utah, supra, and applying the "manifestly cruel and unusual" test, that "[p]unishments are cruel when they involve torture or a lingering death; but the punishment of death is not cruel, within the meaning of that word as used in the Constitution. It implies there something inhuman and barbarous, something more than the mere extinguishment of life." 136 U.S., at 447.

Had this "historical" interpretation of the Cruel and Unusual Punishments Clause prevailed, the Clause would have been effectively read out of the Bill of Rights.

*   *   *

But this Court in *Weems* decisively repudiated the "historical" interpretation of the Clause. The Court, returning to the intentions of the Framers, "rel[ied] on the conditions which existed when the Constitution was adopted." * * *

In short, this Court finally adopted the Framers' view of the Clause as a "constitutional check" to ensure that "when we come to punishments, no latitude ought to be left, nor dependence put on the virtue of representatives." That, indeed, is the only view consonant with our constitutional form of government. If the judicial conclusion that a punishment is "cruel and unusual" "depend[ed] upon virtually unanimous condemnation of the penalty at issue," then, "[l]ike no other constitutional provision, [the Clause's] only function would be to legitimize advances already made by the other departments and opinions already the conventional wisdom." * * *

Judicial enforcement of the Clause, then, cannot be evaded by invoking the obvious truth that legislatures have the power to prescribe punishments for crimes. That is precisely the reason the Clause appears in the Bill of Rights. The difficulty arises, rather, in formulating the "legal principles to be applied by the courts" when a legislatively prescribed punishment is challenged as "cruel and unusual." In formulating those constitutional principles, we must avoid the insertion of "judicial conception[s] of * * * wisdom or propriety," Weems v. United States, 217 U.S., at 379, yet we must not, in the guise of "judicial restraint," abdicate our fundamental responsibility to enforce the Bill of Rights. * * *

II

Ours would indeed be a simple task were we required merely to measure a challenged punishment against those that history has long condemned. That narrow and unwarranted view of the Clause, however, was left behind with the 19th century. Our task today is more complex. We know "that the words of the [Clause] are not precise, and that their scope is not static." We know, therefore, that the Clause "must draw its meaning from the evolving standards of decency that mark the progress of a maturing society." Trop v. Dulles, * * * [356 U.S. 86, 100–01 (1958)]. That knowledge, of course, is but the beginning of the inquiry.

In Trop v. Dulles, supra, at 99, it was said that "[t]he question is whether [a] penalty subjects the individual to a fate forbidden by the principle of civilized treatment guaranteed by the [Clause]." It was also said that a challenged punishment must be examined "in light of the basic prohibition against inhuman treatment" embodied in the Clause. Id., at 100 n. 32. It was said, finally, that:

> "The basic concept underlying the [Clause] is nothing less than the dignity of man. While the State has power to punish, the [Clause] stands to assure that this power be exercised within the limits of civilized standards." Id., at 100.

At bottom, then, the Cruel and Unusual Punishments Clause prohibits the infliction of uncivilized and inhuman punishments. The State, even as it punishes, must treat its members with respect for their intrinsic worth as human beings. A punishment is "cruel and unusual," therefore, if it does not comport with human dignity.

This formulation, of course, does not of itself yield principles for assessing the constitutional validity of particular punishments. Nevertheless, even though "[t]his Court has had little occasion to give precise content to the [Clause]," ibid., there are principles recognized in our cases and inherent in the Clause sufficient to permit a judicial determination whether a challenged punishment comports with human dignity.

The primary principle is that a punishment must not be so severe as to be degrading to the dignity of human beings. Pain, certainly, may be a factor in the judgment. The infliction of an extremely severe punishment will often entail physical suffering. See Weems v. United States, 217 U.S., at 366. Yet the Framers also knew "that there could be exercises of cruelty by laws other than those which inflicted bodily pain or mutilation." Id., at 372. Even though "[t]here may be involved no physical mistreatment, no primitive torture," Trop v. Dulles, supra, at 101, severe mental pain may be inherent in the infliction of a particular punishment. See Weems v. United States, supra, at 366. That, indeed, was one of the conclusions underlying the holding of the plurality in Trop v. Dulles that the punishment of expatriation violates the Clause.[13] And the physical and mental suffering inherent in the punishment of *cadena temporal* was an obvious basis for the Court's decision in Weems v. United States that the punishment was "cruel and unusual."

More than the presence of pain, however, is comprehended in the judgment that the extreme severity of a punishment makes it degrading to the dignity of human beings. The barbaric punishments condemned by history, "punishments which inflict torture, such as the rack, the thumbscrew, the iron boot, the stretching of limbs and the like," are, of course, "attended with acute pain and suffering." O'Neil v. Vermont, 144 U.S. 323, 339 (1892) (Field, J., dissenting). When we consider why they have been condemned, however, we realize that the pain involved is not the only reason. The true significance of these punishments is that they treat members of the human race as nonhumans, as objects to be toyed with and discarded. They are thus inconsistent with the fundamental premise of the Clause that even the vilest criminal remains a human being possessed of common human dignity.

---

13. In a case from the Philippines Territory, the Court struck down a punishment that "ha[d] no fellow in American legislation." Weems v. United States, 217 U.S., at 377. After examining the punishments imposed, under both United States and Philippine law, for similar as well as more serious crimes, id., at 380–381, the Court declared that the "contrast" "exhibit[ed] a difference between unrestrained power and that which is exercised under the spirit of constitutional limitations formed to establish justice," id., at 381. And in Trop v. Dulles, supra, in which a law of Congress punishing wartime desertion by expatriation was held unconstitutional, it was emphasized that "[t]he civilized nations of the world are in virtual unanimity that statelessness is not to be imposed as punishment for crime." Id., at 102. When a severe punishment is not inflicted elsewhere, or when more serious crimes are punished less severely, there is a strong inference that the State is exercising arbitrary, "unrestrained power."

The infliction of an extremely severe punishment, then, like the one before the Court in Weems v. United States, from which "[n]o circumstance of degradation [was] omitted," 217 U.S., at 366, may reflect the attitude that the person punished is not entitled to recognition as a fellow human being. That attitude may be apparent apart from the severity of the punishment itself. In Louisiana ex rel. Francis v. Resweber, 329 U.S. 459, 464 (1947), for example, the unsuccessful electrocution, although it caused "mental anguish and physical pain," was the result of "an unforeseeable accident." Had the failure been intentional, however, the punishment would have been, like torture, so degrading and indecent as to amount to a refusal to accord the criminal human status. Indeed, a punishment may be degrading to human dignity solely because it is a punishment. A State may not punish a person for being "mentally ill, or a leper, or * * * afflicted with a venereal disease," or for being addicted to narcotics. Robinson v. California, 370 U.S. 660, 666 (1962). To inflict punishment for having a disease is to treat the individual as a diseased thing rather than as a sick human being. That the punishment is not severe, "in the abstract," is irrelevant; "[e]ven one day in prison would be a cruel and unusual punishment for the 'crime' of having a common cold." Id., at 667. Finally, of course, a punishment may be degrading simply by reason of its enormity. A prime example is expatriation, a "punishment more primitive than torture," Trop v. Dulles, 356 U.S., at 101, for it necessarily involves a denial by society of the individual's existence as a member of the human community.

In determining whether a punishment comports with human dignity, we are aided also by a second principle inherent in the Clause—that the State must not arbitrarily inflict a severe punishment. This principle derives from the notion that the State does not respect human dignity when, without reason, it inflicts upon some people a severe punishment that it does not inflict upon others. Indeed, the very words "cruel and unusual punishments" imply condemnation of the arbitrary infliction of severe punishments. And, as we now know, the English history of the Clause reveals a particular concern with the establishment of a safeguard against arbitrary punishments. See Granucci, "Nor Cruel and Unusual Punishments Inflicted:" The Original Meaning, 57 Calif.L.Rev. 839, 857–860 (1969).

This principle has been recognized in our cases. In Wilkerson v. Utah, 99 U.S., at 133–134, the Court reviewed various treatises on military law in order to demonstrate that under "the customs of war" shooting was a common method of inflicting the punishment of death. On that basis, the Court concluded:

"Cruel and unusual punishments are forbidden by the Constitution, but the authorities referred to [treatises on military law] are quite sufficient to show that the punishment of shooting as a mode of executing the death penalty for the crime of murder in the first degree is not included in that category, within the meaning of the [Clause]. Soldiers convicted of desertion or other capital military offenses are in the great majority of cases sentenced to be shot, and the ceremony for such occasions is given in great fulness by the writers upon the subject of courts-martial." Id., at 134–135.

The Court thus upheld death by shooting, so far as appears, solely on the ground that it was a common method of execution.

As Wilkerson v. Utah suggests, when a severe punishment is inflicted "in the great majority of cases" in which it is legally available, there is little likelihood that the State is inflicting it arbitrarily. If, however, the infliction of a severe punishment is "something different from that which is generally done" in such cases, Trop v. Dulles, 356 U.S., at 100 n. 32, there is a substantial likelihood that the State, contrary to the requirements of regularity and fairness embodied in the Clause, is inflicting the punishment arbitrarily. This principle is especially important today. There is scant danger, given the political processes "in an enlightened democracy such as ours," id., at 100, that extremely severe punishments will be widely applied. The more significant function of the Clause, therefore, is to protect against the danger of their arbitrary infliction.

A third principle inherent in the Clause is that a severe punishment must not be unacceptable to contemporary society. Rejection by society, of course, is a strong indication that a severe punishment does not comport with human dignity. In applying this principle, however, we must make certain that the judicial determination is as objective as possible. Thus, for example, Weems v. United States, 217 U.S., at 380, and Trop v. Dulles, 356 U.S., at 102–103, suggest that one factor that may be considered is the existence of the punishment in jurisdictions other than those before the Court. Wilkerson v. Utah, 99 U.S. 130 (1878), suggests that another factor to be considered is the historic usage of the punishment. Trop v. Dulles, supra, at 99, combined present acceptance with past usage by observing that "the death penalty has been employed throughout our history, and, in a day when it is still widely accepted, it cannot be said to violate the constitutional concept of cruelty." In Robinson v. California, 370 U.S., at 666, which involved the infliction of punishment for narcotics addiction, the Court went a step further, concluding simply that "in the light of contemporary human knowledge, a law which made a criminal offense of such a disease would doubtless be universally thought to be an infliction of cruel and unusual punishment."

The question under this principle, then, is whether there are objective indicators from which a court can conclude that contemporary society considers a severe punishment unacceptable. Accordingly, the judicial task is to review the history of a challenged punishment and to examine society's present practices with respect to its use. Legislative authorization, of course, does not establish acceptance. The acceptability of a severe punishment is measured not by its availability, for it might become so offensive to society as never to be inflicted, but by its use.

The final principle inherent in the Clause is that a severe punishment must not be excessive. A punishment is excessive under this principle if it is unnecessary: The infliction of a severe punishment by the State cannot comport with human dignity when it is nothing more than the pointless infliction of suffering. If there is a significantly less severe punishment adequate to achieve the purposes for which the punishment is inflicted, cf. Robinson v. California, supra, at 666; id., at 677 (DOUGLAS, J., concurring); Trop v. Dulles, supra, at 114 (BRENNAN, J., concurring), the punishment inflicted is unnecessary and therefore excessive.

*   *   *

Although the determination that a severe punishment is excessive may be grounded in a judgment that it is disproportionate to the crime, the more significant basis is that the punishment serves no penal purpose more effectively than a less severe punishment. This view of the principle was explicitly recognized by the Court in Weems v. United States, 217 U.S. 349 (1910). There the Court, reviewing a severe punishment inflicted for the falsification of an official record, found that "the highest punishment possible for a crime which may cause the loss of many thousands of dollars, and to prevent which the duty of the State should be as eager as to prevent the perversion of truth in a public document, is not greater than that which may be imposed for falsifying a single item of a public account." Id., at 381. Stating that "this contrast shows more than different exercises of legislative judgment," the Court concluded that the punishment was unnecessarily severe in view of the purposes for which it was imposed. Ibid. See also Trop v. Dulles, 356 U.S., at 111–112 (BRENNAN, J., concurring).

*   *   *

Since the Bill of Rights was adopted, this Court has adjudged only three punishments to be within the prohibition of the Clause. See Weems v. United States, 217 U.S. 349 (1910) (12 years in chains at hard and painful labor); Trop v. Dulles, 356 U.S. 86 (1958) (expatriation); Robinson v. California, 370 U.S. 660 (1962) (imprisonment for narcotics addiction). Each punishment, of course, was degrading to human dignity, but of none could it be said conclusively that it was fatally offensive under one or the other of the principles. Rather, these "cruel and unusual punishments" seriously implicated several of the principles, and it was the application of the principles in combination that supported the judgment. That, indeed, is not surprising. The function of these principles, after all, is simply to provide means by which a court can determine whether a challenged punishment comports with human dignity. They are, therefore, interrelated, and in most cases it will be their convergence that will justify the conclusion that a punishment is "cruel and unusual." The test, then, will ordinarily be a cumulative one: If a punishment is unusually severe, if there is a strong probability that it is inflicted arbitrarily, if it is substantially rejected by contemporary society, and if there is no reason to believe that it serves any penal purpose more effectively than some less severe punishment, then the continued infliction of that punishment violates the command of the Clause that the State may not inflict inhuman and uncivilized punishments upon those convicted of crimes.

III

The punishment challenged in these cases is death. Death, of course, is a "traditional" punishment, Trop v. Dulles, supra, at 100, one that "has been employed throughout our history," id., at 99, and its constitutional background is accordingly an appropriate subject of inquiry.

There is, first, a textual consideration raised by the Bill of Rights itself. The Fifth Amendment declares that if a particular crime is punishable by death, a person charged with that crime is entitled to certain procedural protections. We can thus infer that the Framers recognized the existence of what was then a common punishment. We cannot, however, make the further inference that they intended to exempt this particular punishment from the express prohibition of the Cruel and Unusual Punishments Clause. Nor is there any indication in the debates on the Clause that a special exception was to be made for death. If anything, the indication is to the contrary, for Livermore specifically mentioned death as a candidate for future proscription under the Clause. See * * * [1 Annals of Congress 754 (1789)]. Finally, it does not advance analysis to insist that the Framers did not believe that adoption of the Bill of Rights would immediately prevent the infliction of the punishment of death; neither did they believe that it would immediately prevent the infliction of other corporal punishments that, although common at the time, are now acknowledged to be impermissible.

There is also the consideration that this Court has decided three cases involving constitutional challenges to particular methods of inflicting this punishment. * * * These three decisions thus reveal that the Court, while ruling upon various methods of inflicting death, has assumed in the past that death was a constitutionally permissible punishment. Past assumptions, however, are not sufficient to limit the scope of our examination of this punishment today. The constitutionality of death itself under the Cruel and Unusual Punishments Clause is before this Court for the first time; we cannot avoid the question by recalling past cases that never directly considered it.

The question, then, is whether the deliberate infliction of death is today consistent with the command of the Clause that the State may not inflict punishments that do not comport with human dignity. I will analyze the punishment of death in terms of the principles set out above and the cumulative test to which they lead: It is a denial of human dignity for the State arbitrarily to subject a person to an unusually severe punishment that society has indicated it does not regard as acceptable and that cannot be shown to serve any penal purpose more effectively than a significantly less drastic punishment. Under these principles and this test, death is today a "cruel and unusual" punishment.

Death is a unique punishment in the United States. In a society that so strongly affirms the sanctity of life, not surprisingly the common view is that death is the ultimate sanction. This natural human feeling appears all about us. There has been no national debate about punishment, in general or by imprisonment, comparable to the debate about the punishment of death. No other punishment has been so continuously restricted, nor has any State yet abolished prisons, as some have abolished this punishment. And those States that still inflict death reserve it for the most heinous crimes. Juries, of course, have always treated death cases differently, as have governors exercising their commutation powers. Criminal defendants are of the same view. "As all practicing lawyers know, who have defended persons charged with capital offenses, often the only goal possible is to avoid the death penalty." Griffin v. Illinois, 351 U.S. 12, 28 (1956) (Burton and Minton, JJ., dissenting). Some legislatures have required particular procedures, such as two-stage trials and automatic appeals, applicable only in death cases. "It is the universal experience in the administration of criminal justice that those charged with capital offenses are granted special considerations." Ibid. See Williams v. Florida, 399 U.S. 78, 103 (1970) (all States require juries of 12 in death cases). This Court, too, almost always treats death cases as a class apart. And the unfortunate effect of this punishment upon the functioning of the judicial process is well known; no other punishment has a similar effect.

The only explanation for the uniqueness of death is its extreme severity. Death is today an unusually severe punishment, unusual in its pain, in its finality, and in its enormity. No other existing punishment is comparable to death in terms of physical and mental suffering. Although our information is not conclusive, it appears that there is no method available that guarantees an immediate and painless death. Since the discontinuance of flogging as a constitutionally permissible punishment, Jackson v. Bishop, 404 F.2d 571 (CA8

1968), death remains as the only punishment that may involve the conscious infliction of physical pain. In addition, we know that mental pain is an inseparable part of our practice of punishing criminals by death, for the prospect of pending execution exacts a frightful toll during the inevitable long wait between the imposition of sentence and the actual infliction of death. Cf. Ex parte Medley, 134 U.S. 160, 172 (1890). As the California Supreme Court pointed out, "the process of carrying out a verdict of death is often so degrading and brutalizing to the human spirit as to constitute psychological torture." People v. Anderson, 6 Cal.3d 628, 649, 493 P.2d 880, 894, 100 Cal.Rptr. 152, 166 (1972). Indeed, as Mr. Justice Frankfurter noted, "the onset of insanity while awaiting execution of a death sentence is not a rare phenomenon." Solesbee v. Balkcom, 339 U.S. 9, 14 (1950) (dissenting opinion). The "fate of ever-increasing fear and distress" to which the expatriate is subjected, Trop v. Dulles, 356 U.S., at 102, can only exist to a greater degree for a person confined in prison awaiting death.

The unusual severity of death is manifested most clearly in its finality and enormity. Death, in these respects, is in a class by itself. Expatriation, for example, is a punishment that "destroys for the individual the political existence that was centuries in the development," that "strips the citizen of his status in the national and international political community," and that puts "[h]is very existence" in jeopardy. Expatriation thus inherently entails "the total destruction of the individual's status in organized society." Id., at 101. "In short, the expatriate has lost the right to have rights." Id., at 102. Yet, demonstrably, expatriation is not "a fate worse than death." Id., at 125 (Frankfurter, J., dissenting). Although death, like expatriation, destroys the individual's "political existence" and his "status in organized society," it does more, for, unlike expatriation, death also destroys "[h]is very existence." There is, too, at least the possibility that the expatriate will in the future regain "the right to have rights." Death forecloses even that possibility.

Death is truly an awesome punishment. The calculated killing of a human being by the State involves, by its very nature, a denial of the executed person's humanity. The contrast with the plight of a person punished by imprisonment is evident. An individual in prison does not lose "the right to have rights." A prisoner retains, for example, the constitutional rights to the free exercise of religion, to be free of cruel and unusual punishments, and to treatment as a "person" for purposes of due process of law and the equal protection of the laws. A prisoner remains a member of the human family. Moreover, he retains the right of access to the courts. His punishment is not irrevocable. Apart from the common charge, grounded upon the recognition of human fallibility, that the punishment of death must inevitably be inflicted upon innocent men, we know that death has been the lot of men whose convictions were unconstitutionally secured in view of later, retroactively applied, holdings of this Court. The punishment itself may have been unconstitutionally inflicted, see With-erspoon v. Illinois, 391 U.S. 510 (1968), yet the finality of death precludes relief. An executed person has indeed "lost the right to have rights." * * *

In comparison to all other punishments today, then, the deliberate extinguishment of human life by the State is uniquely degrading to human dignity. I would not hesitate to hold, on that ground alone, that death is today a "cruel and unusual" punishment, were it not that death is a punishment of longstanding usage and acceptance in this country. I therefore turn to the second principle—that the State may not arbitrarily inflict an unusually severe punishment.

The outstanding characteristic of our present practice of punishing criminals by death is the infrequency with which we resort to it. The evidence is conclusive that death is not the ordinary punishment for any crime.

There has been a steady decline in the infliction of this punishment in every decade since the 1930's, the earliest period for which accurate statistics are available. In the 1930's, executions averaged 167 per year; in the 1940's, the average was 128; in the 1950's, it was 72; and in the years 1960–1962, it was 48. There have been a total of 46 executions since then, 36 of them in 1963–1964. Yet our population and the numbers of capital crimes committed have increased greatly over the past four decades. The contemporary rarity of the infliction of this punishment is thus the end result of a long-continued decline. That rarity is plainly revealed by an examination of the years 1961–1970, the last 10-year period for which statistics are available. During that time, an average of 106 death sentences were imposed each year. Not nearly that number, however, could be carried out, for many were precluded by commutations to life or a term of years, transfers to mental institutions because of insanity, resentences to life or a term of years, grants of new trials and orders for resentencing, dismissals of indictments and reversals of convictions, and deaths by suicide and natural causes. On January 1, 1961, the death row population was 219; on December 31, 1970, it was 608; during that span, there were 135 executions. Consequently, had the 389 additions to death row also been executed, the annual average would have been 52. In short, the country might, at most, have executed one criminal each week. In fact, of course, far fewer were executed. Even before the moratorium on executions began in 1967, executions totaled only 42 in 1961 and 47 in 1962, an average of less than one per week; the number dwindled to 21 in 1963, to 15 in 1964, and to seven in 1965; in 1966, there was one execution, and in 1967, there were two.

When a country of over 200 million people inflicts an unusually severe punishment no more than 50 times a year, the inference is strong that the punishment is not being regularly and fairly applied. To dispel it would indeed require a clear showing of nonarbitrary infliction.

Although there are no exact figures available, we know that thousands of murders and rapes are committed annually in States where death is an authorized punishment for those crimes. However the rate of infliction is characterized—as "freakishly" or "spectacularly" rare, or simply as rare—it would take the purest sophistry to deny that death is inflicted in only a minute fraction of these cases. How much rarer, after all, could the infliction of death be?

When the punishment of death is inflicted in a trivial number of the cases in which it is legally available, the conclusion is virtually inescapable that it is being inflicted arbitrarily. Indeed, it smacks of little more than a lottery system. The States claim, however, that this rarity is evidence not of arbitrariness, but of informed selectivity: Death is inflicted, they say, only in "extreme" cases.

Informed selectivity, of course, is a value not to be denigrated. Yet presumably the States could make precisely the same claim if there were 10 executions per year, or five, or even if there were but one. That there may be as many as 50 per year does not strengthen the claim. When the rate of infliction is at this low level, it is highly implausible that only the worst criminals or the criminals who commit the worst crimes are selected for this punishment. No one has yet suggested a rational basis that could differentiate in those terms the few who die from the many who go to prison. Crimes and criminals simply do not admit of a distinction that can be drawn so finely as to explain, on that ground, the execution of such a tiny sample of those eligible. Certainly the laws that provide for this punishment do not attempt to draw that distinction; all cases to which the laws apply are necessarily "extreme." Nor is the distinction credible in fact. If, for example, petitioner Furman or his crime illustrate the "extreme," then nearly all murderers and their murders are also "extreme." [48] Furthermore, our procedures in death cases, rather than

48. The victim surprised Furman in the act of burglarizing the victim's home in the middle of the night. While escaping, Furman killed the victim with one pistol shot fired through the closed kitchen door from the outside. At the trial, Furman gave his version of the killing:

"They got me charged with murder and I admit, I admit going to these folks' home and they did caught me 'in there and I was coming back out, backing up and there was a wire down there on the floor. I was coming out backwards and fell back and I didn't intend to kill nobody. I didn't know they was behind the door. The gun went off and I didn't know nothing about no murder until they arrested me, and when the gun went off I was down on the floor and I got up and ran. That's all to it." App. 54–55.

The Georgia Supreme Court accepted that version:

"The admission in open court by the 'accused * * * that during the period in which he was involved in the commission of a criminal act at the home of the deceased, he accidentally tripped over a wire in leaving the premises causing the gun to go off, together with other facts resulting in the selection of "extreme" cases for this punishment, actually sanction an arbitrary selection. For this Court has held that juries may, as they do, make the decision whether to impose a death sentence wholly unguided by standards governing that decision. Mc-Gautha v. California, 402 U.S. 183, 196–208 (1971). In other words, our procedures are not constructed to guard against the totally capricious selection of criminals for the punishment of death.

Although it is difficult to imagine what further facts would be necessary in order to prove that death is, as my Brother STEWART puts it, "wantonly and freakishly" inflicted, I need not conclude that arbitrary infliction is patently obvious. I am not considering this punishment by the isolated light of one principle. The probability of arbitrariness is sufficiently substantial that it can be relied upon, in combination with the other principles, in reaching a judgment on the constitutionality of this punishment.

When there is a strong probability that an unusually severe and degrading punishment is being inflicted arbitrarily, we may well expect that society will disapprove of its infliction. I turn, therefore, to the third principle. An examination of the history and present operation of the American practice of punishing criminals by death reveals that this punishment has been almost totally rejected by contemporary society.

* * *

Our practice of punishing criminals by death has changed greatly over the years. One significant change has been in our methods of inflicting death. Although this country never embraced the more violent and repulsive methods employed in England, we did for a long time rely almost exclusively upon the gallows and the firing squad. Since the development of the supposedly more humane methods of electrocution late in the 19th century and lethal gas in the 20th, however, hanging and shooting have virtually ceased. Our concern for decency and human dignity, moreover, has compelled changes in the circumstances surrounding the execution itself. No longer does our society countenance the spectacle of public executions, once thought desirable as a deterrent to criminal behavior by others. Today we reject public executions as debasing and brutalizing to us all.

Also significant is the drastic decrease in the crimes for which the punishment of death is actually inflicted. While esoteric capital crimes remain on the books, since 1930 murder and rape have ac-

and circumstances surrounding the death of the deceased by violent means, was sufficient to support the verdict of guilty of murder * *." Furman v. State, 225 Ga. 253, 254, 167 S.E.2d 628, 629 (1969).

About Furman himself, the jury knew only that he was black and that, ac-

cording to his statement at trial, he was 26 years old and worked at "Superior Upholstery." App. 54. It took the jury one hour and 35 minutes to return a verdict of guilt and a sentence of death. Id., at 64–65.

counted for nearly 99% of the total executions, and murder alone for about 87%. In addition, the crime of capital murder has itself been limited. As the Court noted in McGautha v. California, 402 U.S., at 198, there was in this country a "rebellion against the common-law rule imposing a mandatory death sentence on all convicted murderers." Initially that rebellion resulted in legislative definitions that distinguished between degrees of murder, retaining the mandatory death sentence only for murder in the first degree. Yet "[t]his new legislative criterion for isolating crimes appropriately punishable by death soon proved as unsuccessful as the concept of 'malice aforethought,'" ibid., the common-law means of separating murder from manslaughter. Not only was the distinction between degrees of murder confusing and uncertain in practice, but even in clear cases of first degree murder juries continued to take the law into their own hands: if they felt that death was an inappropriate punishment, "they simply refused to convict of the capital offense." Id., at 199. The phenomenon of jury nullification thus remained to counteract the rigors of mandatory death sentences. Bowing to reality, "legislatures did not try, as before, to refine further the definition of capital homicides. Instead they adopted the method of forthrightly granting juries the discretion which they had been exercising in fact." Ibid. In consequence, virtually all death sentences today are discretionarily imposed. Finally, it is significant that nine States no longer inflict the punishment of death under any circumstances, and five others have restricted it to extremely rare crimes.

*   *   *

The progressive decline in and the current rarity of the infliction of death demonstrate that our society seriously questions the appropriateness of this punishment today. The States point out that many legislatures authorize death as the punishment for certain crimes and that substantial segments of the public, as reflected in opinion polls and referendum votes, continue to support it. Yet the availability of this punishment through statutory authorization, as well as the polls and referenda, which amount simply to approval of that authorization, simply underscores the extent to which our society has in fact rejected this punishment. When an unusually severe punishment is authorized for wide-scale application but not, because of society's refusal, inflicted save in a few instances, the inference is compelling that there is a deep-seated reluctance to inflict it. Indeed, the likelihood is great that the punishment is tolerated only because of its disuse. The objective indicator of society's view of an unusually severe punishment is what society does with it. And today society will inflict death upon only a small sample of the eligible criminals. Rejection could hardly be more complete without becoming absolute. At the very least, I must conclude that contemporary society views this punishment with substantial doubt.

The final principle to be considered is that an unusually severe and degrading punishment may not be excessive in view of the purposes for which it is inflicted. This principle, too, is related to the others. When there is a strong probability that the State is arbitrarily inflicting an unusually severe punishment that is subject to grave societal doubts, it is likely also that the punishment cannot be shown to be serving any penal purpose that could not be served equally well by some less severe punishment.

The States' primary claim is that death is a necessary punishment because it prevents the commission of capital crimes more effectively than any less severe punishment. The first part of this claim is that the infliction of death is necessary to stop the individuals executed from committing further crimes. The sufficient answer to this is that if a criminal convicted of a capital crime poses a danger to society, effective administration of the State's pardon and parole laws can delay or deny his release from prison, and techniques of isolation can eliminate or minimize the danger while he remains confined.

The more significant argument is that the threat of death prevents the commission of capital crimes because it deters potential criminals who would not be deterred by the threat of imprisonment. The argument is not based upon evidence that the threat of death is a superior deterrent. Indeed, as my Brother MARSHALL establishes, the available evidence uniformly indicates, although it does not conclusively prove, that the threat of death has no greater deterrent effect than the threat of imprisonment. The States argue, however, that they are entitled to rely upon common human experience, and that experience, they say, supports the conclusion that death must be a more effective deterrent than any less severe punishment. Because people fear death the most, the argument runs, the threat of death must be the greatest deterrent.

It is important to focus upon the precise import of this argument. It is not denied that many, and probably most, capital crimes cannot be deterred by the threat of punishment. Thus the argument can apply only to those who think rationally about the commission of capital crimes. Particularly is that true when the potential criminal, under this argument, must not only consider the risk of punishment, but also distinguish between two possible punishments. The concern, then, is with a particular type of potential criminal, the rational person who will commit a capital crime knowing that the punishment is long-term imprisonment, which may well be for the rest of his life, but will not commit the crime knowing that the punishment is death. On the face of it, the assumption that such persons exist is implausible.

In any event, this argument cannot be appraised in the abstract. We are not presented with the theoretical question whether under any imaginable circumstances the threat of death might be a greater de-

terrent to the commission of capital crimes than the threat of imprisonment. We are concerned with the practice of punishing criminals by death as it exists in the United States today. Proponents of
this argument necessarily admit that its validity depends upon the
existence of a system in which the punishment of death is invariably
and swiftly imposed. Our system, of course, satisfies neither condition. A rational person contemplating a murder or rape is confronted not with the certainty of a speedy death, but with the slightest possibility that he will be executed in the distant future. The risk of
death is remote and improbable; in contrast, the risk of long-term
imprisonment is near and great. In short, whatever the speculative
validity of the assumption that the threat of death is a superior deterrent, there is no reason to believe that as currently administered the
punishment of death is necessary to deter the commission of capital
crimes. Whatever might be the case were all or substantially all
eligible criminals quickly put to death, unverifiable possibilities are an
insufficient basis upon which to conclude that the threat of death today has any greater deterrent efficacy than the threat of imprisonment.[54]

There is, however, another aspect to the argument that the punishment of death is necessary for the protection of society. The infliction of death, the States urge, serves to manifest the community's
outrage at the commission of the crime. It is, they say, a concrete
public expression of moral indignation that inculcates respect for the
law and helps assure a more peaceful community. Moreover, we are
told, not only does the punishment of death exert this widespread
moralizing influence upon community values, it also satisfies the
popular demand for grievous condemnation of abhorrent crimes and
thus prevents disorder, lynching, and attempts by private citizens to
take the law into their own hands.

The question, however, is not whether death serves these supposed purposes of punishment, but whether death serves them more
effectively than imprisonment. There is no evidence whatever that
utilization of imprisonment rather than death encourages private blood
feuds and other disorders. Surely if there were such a danger, the
execution of a handful of criminals each year would not prevent it.
The assertion that death alone is a sufficiently emphatic denunciation

54. There is also the more limited argument that death is a necessary
punishment when criminals are already serving or subject to a sentence
of life imprisonment. If the only punishment available is further imprisonment, it is said, those criminals will
have nothing to lose by committing
further crimes, and accordingly the
threat of death is the sole deterrent.
But "life" imprisonment is a misnomer
today. Rarely, if ever, do crimes
carry a mandatory life sentence without possibility of parole. That possibility ensures that criminals do not
reach the point where further crimes
are free of consequences. Moreover,
if this argument is simply an assertion
that the threat of death is a more
effective deterrent than the threat of
increased imprisonment by denial of
release on parole, then, as noted above,
there is simply no evidence to support
it.

for capital crimes suffers from the same defect. If capital crimes require the punishment of death in order to provide moral reinforcement for the basic values of the community, those values can only be undermined when death is so rarely inflicted upon the criminals who commit the crimes. Furthermore, it is certainly doubtful that the infliction of death by the State does in fact strengthen the community's moral code; if the deliberate extinguishment of human life has any effect at all, it more likely tends to lower our respect for life and brutalize our values. That, after all, is why we no longer carry out public executions. In any event, this claim simply means that one purpose of punishment is to indicate social disapproval of crime. To serve that purpose our laws distribute punishments according to the gravity of crimes and punish more severely the crimes society regards as more serious. That purpose cannot justify any particular punishment as the upper limit of severity.

There is, then, no substantial reason to believe that the punishment of death, as currently administered, is necessary for the protection of society. The only other purpose suggested, one that is independent of protection for society, is retribution. Shortly stated, retribution in this context means that criminals are put to death because they deserve it.

Although it is difficult to believe that any State today wishes to proclaim adherence to "naked vengeance," Trop v. Dulles, 356 U.S., at 112 (BRENNAN, J., concurring), the States claim, in reliance upon its statutory authorization, that death is the only fit punishment for capital crimes and that this retributive purpose justifies its infliction. In the past, judged by its statutory authorization, death was considered the only fit punishment for the crime of forgery, for the first federal criminal statute provided a mandatory death penalty for that crime. Act of April 30, 1790, c. 9, § 14, 1 Stat. 115. Obviously, concepts of justice change; no immutable moral order requires death for murderers and rapists. The claim that death is a just punishment necessarily refers to the existence of certain public beliefs. The claim must be that for capital crimes death alone comports with society's notion of proper punishment. As administered today, however, the punishment of death cannot be justified as a necessary means of exacting retribution from criminals. When the overwhelming number of criminals who commit capital crimes go to prison, it cannot be concluded that death serves the purpose of retribution more effectively than imprisonment. The asserted public belief that murderers and rapists deserve to die is flatly inconsistent with the execution of a random few. As the history of the punishment of death in this country shows, our society wishes to prevent crime; we have no desire to kill criminals simply to get even with them.

In sum, the punishment of death is inconsistent with all four principles: Death is an unusually severe and degrading punishment; there is a strong probability that it is inflicted arbitrarily; its rejection by contemporary society is virtually total; and there is no reason to believe that it serves any penal purpose more effectively than the less severe punishment of imprisonment. The function of these principles is to enable a court to determine whether a punishment comports with human dignity. Death, quite simply, does not.

IV

When this country was founded, memories of the Stuart horrors were fresh and severe corporal punishments were common. Death was not then a unique punishment. The practice of punishing criminals by death, moreover, was widespread and by and large acceptable to society. Indeed, without developed prison systems, there was frequently no workable alternative. Since that time, successive restrictions, imposed against the background of a continuing moral controversy, have drastically curtailed the use of this punishment. Today death is a uniquely and unusually severe punishment. When examined by the principles applicable under the Cruel and Unusual Punishments Clause, death stands condemned as fatally offensive to human dignity. The punishment of death is therefore "cruel and unusual," and the States may no longer inflict it as a punishment for crimes. Rather than kill an arbitrary handful of criminals each year, the States will confine them in prison. "The State thereby suffers nothing and loses no power. The purpose of punishment is fulfilled, crime is repressed by penalties of just, not tormenting, severity, its repetition is prevented, and hope is given for the reformation of the criminal." Weems v. United States, 217 U.S., at 381.

I concur in the judgments of the Court.

Mr. Justice STEWART, concurring.

*   *   *

I simply conclude that the Eighth and Fourteenth Amendments cannot tolerate the infliction of a sentence of death under legal systems that permit this unique penalty to be so wantonly and so freakishly imposed.

For these reasons I concur in the judgments of the Court.

Mr. Justice WHITE, concurring.

*   *   *

The imposition and execution of the death penalty are obviously cruel in the dictionary sense. But the penalty has not been considered cruel and unusual punishment in the constitutional sense because it was thought justified by the social ends it was deemed to serve. At the moment that it ceases realistically to further these purposes, however, the emerging question is whether its imposition in such circumstances would violate the Eighth Amendment. It is my view that it would, for its imposition would then be the pointless and needless extinction of life with only marginal contributions to any discernible social or public purposes. A penalty with such negligible returns to the State would be patently excessive and cruel and unusual punishment violative of the Eighth Amendment.

It is also my judgment that this point has been reached with respect to capital punishment as it is presently administered under the statutes involved in these cases. Concededly, it is difficult to prove as a general proposition that capital punishment, however administered, more effectively serves the ends of the criminal law than does imprisonment. But however that may be, I cannot avoid the conclusion that as the statutes before us are now administered, the penalty is so infrequently imposed that the threat of execution is too attenuated to be of substantial service to criminal justice.

Mr. Justice MARSHALL, concurring.

* * *

There is no more complex problem than determining the deterrent efficacy of the death penalty. "Capital punishment has obviously failed as a deterrent when a murder is committed. We can number its failures. But we cannot even know how many people have refrained from murder because of the fear of being hanged." This is the nub of the problem and it is exacerbated by the paucity of useful data. The United States is more fortunate than most countries, however, in that it has what are generally considered to be the world's most viable statistics.

* * *

Thorston Sellin, one of the leading authorities on capital punishment, has urged that if the death penalty deters prospective murderers, the following hypotheses should be true:

"(a) Murders should be less frequent in states that have the death penalty than in those that have abolished it, other factors being equal. Comparisons of this nature must be made among states that are as alike as possible in all other respects—character of population, social and economic condition, etc.—in order not to introduce factors known to influence murder rates in a serious manner but present in only one of these states.

"(b) Murders should increase when the death penalty is abolished and should decline when it is restored.

"(c) The deterrent effect should be greatest and should therefore affect murder rates most powerfully in those communities where the crime occurred and its consequences are most strongly brought home to the population.

"(d) Law enforcement officers would be safer from murderous attacks in states that have the death penalty than in those without it."   (Footnote omitted.)[99]

Sellin's evidence indicates that not one of these propositions is true.   This evidence has its problems, however.   One is that there are no accurate figures for capital murders; there are only figures on homicides and they, of course, include noncapital killings.   A second problem is that certain murders undoubtedly are misinterpreted as accidental deaths or suicides, and there is no way of estimating the number of such undetected crimes.   A third problem is that all homicides are not reported.   Despite these difficulties, most authorities have assumed that the proportion of capital murders in a State's or nation's homicide statistics remains reasonably constant, and that the homicide statistics are therefore useful.

Sellin's statistics demonstrate that there is no correlation between the murder rate and the presence or absence of the capital sanction.   He compares States that have similar characteristics and finds that irrespective of their position on capital punishment, they have similar murder rates.   In the New England States, for example, there is no correlation between executions and homicide rates.   The same is true for Mid-Western States, and for all others studied.   Both the United Nations and Great Britain have acknowledged the validity of Sellin's statistics.

Sellin's statistics also indicate that abolition and/or reintroduction of the death penalty had no effect on the homicide rates of the various States involved.   This conclusion is borne out by others who have made similar inquiries and by the experience of other countries.   Despite problems with the statistics, Sellin's evidence has been relied upon in international studies of capital punishment.

Statistics also show that the deterrent effect of capital punishment is no greater in those communities where executions take place than in other communities.   In fact, there is some evidence that imposition of capital punishment may actually encourage crime, rather than deter it.   And, while police and law enforcement officers are the strongest advocates of capital punishment, the evidence is overwhelming that police are no safer in communities which retain the sanction than in those which have abolished it.

There is also a substantial body of data showing that the existence of the death penalty has virtually no effect on the homicide rate in prisons.   Most of the persons sentenced to death are murderers, and murderers tend to be model prisoners.

*   *   *

There is but one conclusion that can be drawn from all of this—i. e., the death penalty is an excessive and unnecessary punishment

99. *   *   * [T. Sellin, The Death   Code Project of the American Law Institute 21 (1959).]
Penalty, A Report for the Model Penal

which violates the Eighth Amendment. The statistical evidence is not convincing beyond all doubt, but, it is persuasive.   *   *   *

In addition, even if capital punishment is not excessive, it nonetheless violates the Eighth Amendment because it is morally unacceptable to the people of the United States at this time in their history.

*   *   *

While a public opinion poll obviously is of some assistance in indicating public acceptance or rejection of a specific penalty, its utility cannot be very great. This is because whether or not a punishment is cruel and unusual depends, not on whether its mere mention "shocks the conscience and sense of justice of the people," but on whether people who were fully informed as to the purposes of the penalty and its liabilities would find the penalty shocking, unjust, and unacceptable.

In other words, the question with which we must deal is not whether a substantial proportion of American citizens would today, if polled, opine that capital punishment is barbarously cruel, but whether they would find it to be so in the light of all information presently available.

This is not to suggest that with respect to this test of unconstitutionality people are required to act rationally; they are not. With respect to this judgment, a violation of the Eighth Amendment is totally dependent on the predictable subjective, emotional reactions of informed citizens.

It has often been noted that American citizens know almost nothing about capital punishment. Some of the conclusions arrived at in the preceding section and the supporting evidence would be critical to an informed judgment on the morality of the death penalty: e. g., that the death penalty is no more effective a deterrent than life imprisonment, that convicted murderers are rarely executed, but are usually sentenced to a term in prison; that convicted murderers usually are model prisoners, and that they almost always become law-abiding citizens upon their release from prison; that the costs of executing a capital offender exceed the costs of imprisoning him for life; that while in prison, a convict under sentence of death performs none of the useful functions that life prisoners perform; that no attempt is made in the sentencing process to ferret out likely recidivists for execution; and that the death penalty may actually stimulate criminal activity.

This information would almost surely convince the average citizen that the death penalty was unwise, but a problem arises as to whether, it would convince him that the penalty was morally reprehensible. This problem arises from the fact that the public's desire for retribution, even though this is a goal which the legislature cannot constitutionally pursue as its sole justification for capital punishment, might influence the citizenry's view of the morality of capital punishment. The solution to the problem lies in the fact that no one has ever seriously advanced retribution as a legitimate goal of our society. Defenses of capital punishment are always mounted on deterrent or other similar theories. This should not be surprising. It is the people of this country who have urged in the past that prisons rehabilitate as well as isolate offenders, and it is the people who have injected a sense of purpose into our penology. I cannot believe that at this stage in our history, the American people would ever knowingly support purposeless vengeance. Thus, I believe that the great mass of citizens would conclude on the basis of the material already considered that the death penalty is immoral and therefore unconstitutional.

But, if this information needs supplementing, I believe that the following facts would serve to convince even the most hesitant of citizens to condemn death as a sanction: capital punishment is imposed discriminatorily against certain identifiable classes of people; there is evidence that innocent people have been executed before their innocence can be proved; and the death penalty wreaks havoc with our entire criminal justice system. * * *

Regarding discrimination, it has been said that "[i]t is usually the poor, the illiterate, the underprivileged, the member of the minority group—the man who, because he is without means, and is defended by a court appointed attorney—who becomes society's sacrificial lamb * * *." Indeed, a look at the bare statistics regarding executions is enough to betray much of the discrimination. A total of 3,859 persons have been executed since 1930, of which 1,751 were White and 2,066 were Negro. 3,334 of the executions were for murder; 1,664 of the executed murderers were White and 1,630 were Negro. 455 persons, including 48 Whites and 405 Negroes, were executed for rape. It is immediately apparent that Negroes were executed far more often than Whites in proportion to their percentage of the population. Studies indicate that while the higher rate of execution among Negroes is partially due to a higher rate of crime, there is evidence of racial discrimination.

* * *

There is also overwhelming evidence that the death penalty is employed against men and not women. Only 32 women have been executed since 1930, while 3,827 men have met a similar fate. It is difficult to understand why women have received such favored treatment since the purposes allegedly served by capital punishment seemingly are equally applicable to both sexes.

It also is evident that the burden of capital punishment falls upon the poor, the ignorant, and the underprivileged members of society. It is the poor, and the members of minority groups who are least able to voice their complaints against capital punishment. Their impotence leaves them victims of a sanction which the wealthier, better-represented, just-as-guilty person can escape. So long as the capital sanction is used only against the forlorn, easily forgotten members of society, legislators are content to maintain the status quo, because change would draw attention to the problem and concern might develop. Ignorance is perpetuated and apathy soon becomes its mate, and we have today's situation.

Just as Americans know little about who is executed and why, they are unaware of the potential dangers of executing an innocent man. Our "beyond-a-reasonable doubt" burden of proof in criminal cases is intended to protect the innocent, but we know it is not foolproof. Various studies have shown that people whose innocence is later convincingly established are convicted and sentenced to death.

* * *

Mr. Justice DOUGLAS, concurring.

* * *

In a Nation committed to Equal Protection of the laws there is no permissible "caste" aspect of law enforcement. Yet we know that the discretion of judges and juries in imposing the death penalty enables the penalty to be selectively applied, feeding prejudices against the accused if he is poor and despised, poor and lacking political clout, of if he is a member of a suspect or unpopular minority, and saving those who by social position may be in a more protected position.

* * *

The high service rendered by the "cruel and unusual" punishment clause of the Eighth Amendment is to require legislatures to write penal laws that are evenhanded, nonselective, and nonarbitrary, and to require judges to see to it that general laws are not applied sparsely, selectively, and spottily to unpopular groups.

A law that stated that anyone making more than $50,000 would be exempt from the death penalty would plainly fall, as would a law that in terms said that Blacks, those who never went beyond the fifth grade in school, or those who made less than $3,000 a year, or those who were unpopular or unstable should be the only people executed. A law which in the overall view reaches that result in practice has no more sanctity than a law which in terms provides the same.

Thus, these discretionary statutes are unconstitutional in their operation. They are pregnant with discrimination and discrimination is an ingredient not compatible with the idea of equal protection of the laws that is implicit in the ban on "cruel and unusual" punishments.

Any law which is nondiscriminatory on its face may be applied in such a way as to violate the Equal Protection Clause of the Fourteenth Amendment. Yick Wo v. Hopkins, 118 U.S. 356. Such conceivably might be the adding of a mandatory death penalty where equal or lesser sentences were imposed on the elite, a harsher one on the minorities or members of the lower castes. Whether a mandatory death penalty would otherwise be constitutional is a question I do not reach.

I concur in the judgments of the Court.

———————

Mr. Chief Justice BURGER, with whom Mr. Justice BLACKMUN, Mr. Justice POWELL, and Mr. Justice REHNQUIST join, dissenting.

*   *   *

I do not suggest that the presence of the word "unusual" in the Eighth Amendment is merely vestigial, having no relevance to the constitutionality of any punishment that might be devised. But where, as here, we consider a punishment well known to history, and clearly authorized by legislative enactment, it disregards the history of the Eighth Amendment and all the judicial comment that has followed to rely on the term "unusual" as affecting the outcome of these cases. Instead, I view these cases as turning on the single question whether capital punishment is "cruel" in the constitutional sense. The term "unusual" cannot be read as limiting the ban on "cruel" punishments or as somehow expanding the meaning of the term "cruel." For this reason I am unpersuaded by the facile argument that since capital punishment has always been cruel in the everyday sense of the word, and has become unusual due to decreased use, it is, therefore, now "cruel and unusual."

*   *   *

There are no obvious indications that capital punishment offends the conscience of society to such a degree that our traditional deference to the legislative judgment must be abandoned.

*   *   *

The rate of imposition of death sentences falls far short of providing the requisite unambiguous evidence that the legislatures of 40 States and the Congress have turned their backs on current or evolving standards of decency in continuing to make the death penalty available. For if selective imposition evidences a rejection of capital punishment in those cases where it is not imposed, it surely evidences a correlative affirmation of the penalty in those cases where it is imposed. Absent some clear indication that the continued imposition of the death penalty on a selective basis is violative of prevailing standards of civilized conduct, the Eighth Amendment cannot be said to interdict its use.

*   *   *

Capital punishment has also been attacked as violative of the Eighth Amendment on the ground that it is not needed to achieve legitimate penal aims and is thus "unnecessarily cruel." As a pure policy matter, this approach has much to recommend it, but it seeks to give a dimension to the Eighth Amendment that it was never intended to have and promotes a line of inquiry that this Court has never before pursued.

* * *

Apart from * * * isolated uses of the word "unnecessary," nothing in the cases suggests that it is for the courts to make a determination of the efficacy of punishments. The decision in Weems v. United States, 217 U.S. 349 (1910), is not to the contrary. In *Weems* the Court held that for the crime of falsifying public documents, the punishment imposed under the Philippine Code of 15 years' imprisonment at hard labor under shackles, followed by perpetual surveillance, loss of voting rights, loss of the right to hold public office and loss of right to change domicile freely, was violative of the Eighth Amendment. The case is generally regarded as holding that a punishment may be excessively cruel within the meaning of the Eighth Amendment because it is grossly out of proportion to the severity of the crime; some view the decision of the Court primarily as a reaction to the mode of the punishment itself. Under any characterization of the holding, it is readily apparent that the decision grew out of the Court's overwhelming abhorrence of the imposition of the particular penalty for the particular crime; it was making an essentially moral judgment, not a dispassionate assessment of the need for the penalty. The Court specifically disclaimed "the right to assert a judgment against that of the legislature of the expediency of the laws * * *." 217 U.S., at 378. Thus apart from the fact that the Court in *Weems* concerned itself with the crime committed as well as the punishment imposed, the case marks no departure from the largely unarticulable standard of extreme cruelty. However intractable that standard may be, that is what the Eighth Amendment is all about. The constitutional provision is not addressed to social utility and does not command that enlightened principles of penology always be followed.

By pursuing the necessity approach, it becomes even more apparent that it involves matters outside the purview of the Eighth Amendment. Two of the several aims of punishment are generally associated with capital punishment—retribution and deterrence. It is argued that retribution can be discounted because that, after all, is what the Eighth Amendment seeks to eliminate. There is no authority suggesting that the Eighth Amendment was intended to purge the law of its retributive elements, and the Court has consistently assumed that retribution is a legitimate dimension of the punishment of crimes. See Williams v. New York, 337 U.S. 241, 248 (1949); United States v. Lovett, 328 U.S. 303, 324 (1946) (Frankfurter, J., concurring). Furthermore, responsible legal thinkers of widely varying persuasions have debated the sociological and philosophical aspects of the retribution question for generations, neither side being able to convince the other. It would be reading a great deal into the Eighth

Amendment to hold that the punishments authorized by legislatures cannot constitutionally reflect a retributive purpose.

The less esoteric but no less controversial question is whether the death penalty acts as a superior deterrent. Those favoring abolition find no evidence that it does. Those favoring retention start from the intuitive notion that capital punishment should act as the most effective deterrent and note that there is no convincing evidence that it does not. Escape from this empirical stalemate is sought by placing the burden of proof on the States and concluding that they have failed to demonstrate that capital punishment is a more effective deterrent than life imprisonment. Numerous justifications have been advanced for shifting the burden, and they are not without their rhetorical appeal. However, these arguments are not descended from established constitutional principles, but are born of the urge to bypass an unresolved factual question. Comparative deterrence is not a matter that lends itself to precise measurement; to shift the burden to the States is to provide an illusory solution to an enormously complex problem. If it were proper to put the States to the test of demonstrating the deterrent value of capital punishment, we could just as well ask them to prove the need for life imprisonment or any other punishment. Yet I know of no convincing evidence that life imprisonment is a more effective deterrent than 20 years' imprisonment, or even that a $10 parking ticket is a more effective deterrent than a $5 parking ticket. In fact, there are some who go so far as to challenge the notion that any punishments deter crime. If the States are unable to adduce convincing proof rebutting such assertions, does it then follow that all punishments are suspect of being "cruel and unusual" within the meaning of the Constitution? On the contrary, I submit that the questions raised by the necessity approach are beyond the pale of judicial inquiry under the Eighth Amendment.

* * *

Mr. Justice BLACKMUN, dissenting.

* * *

7. I trust the Court fully appreciates what it is doing when it decides these cases the way it does today. Not only are the capital punishment laws of 39 States and the District of Columbia stricken down, but also all those provisions of the federal statutory structure that permit the death penalty apparently are voided. No longer is capital punishment possible, I suspect, for, among other crimes, treason, 18 U.S.C.A. § 2381; or assassination of the President, the Vice President, or those who stand elected to those positions, 18 U.S.C.A. § 1751; or assassination of a Member or member-elect of Congress, 18 U.S.C.A. § 351; or espionage, 18 U.S.C.A. § 794; or rape within the special maritime jurisdiction, 18 U.S.C.A. § 2031; or aircraft or motor vehicle destruction where death occurs, 18 U.S.C.A. § 34; or explosives offenses where death results, 18 U.S.C.A. § 844(d) and

(f); or train wrecking, 18 U.S.C.A. § 1992; or aircraft piracy, 49 U.S.C.A. § 1472(i). Also in jeopardy, perhaps, are the death penalty provisions in various Articles of the Uniform Code of Military Justice. 10 U.S.C.A. §§ 885, 890, 894, 899, 901, 904, 906, 913, 918, and 920. All these seem now to be discarded without a passing reference to the reasons, or the circumstances, that prompted their enactment, some very recent, and their retention in the face of efforts to repeal them.

8.   It is of passing interest to note a few voting facts with respect to recent federal death penalty legislation:

A.   The aircraft piracy statute, 49 U.S.C.A. § 1472(i), was enacted September 5, 1961. The Senate vote on August 10 was 92–0. It was announced that Senators Chavez, Fulbright, Neuberger, and Symington were absent but that, if present, all four would vote yea. It was also announced, on the other side of the aisle, that Senator Butler was ill and that Senators Beall, Carlson, and Morton were absent or detained, but that those four, if present, would vote in the affirmative. These announcements, therefore, indicate that the true vote was 100–0. 107 Cong. Rec. 15440. The House passed the bill without recorded vote. 107 Cong. Rec. 16849.

B.   The presidential assassination statute, 18 U.S.C.A. § 1751, was approved August 28, 1965, without recorded votes. 111 Cong. Rec. 14103, 18026, and 20239.

C.   The Omnibus Crime Control Act of 1970 was approved January 2, 1971. Title IV thereof added the congressional assassination statute that is now 18 U.S.C.A. § 351. The recorded House vote on October 7, 1970, was 341–26, with 63 not voting and 62 of those paired. 116 Cong. Rec. 35363–35364. The Senate vote on October 8 was 59–0, with 41 not voting, but with 21 of these announced as favoring the bill. 116 Cong. Rec. 35743. Final votes after conference were not recorded. 116 Cong. Rec. 42150, 42199.

It is impossible for me to believe that the many lawyer-members of the House and Senate—including, I might add, outstanding leaders and prominent candidates for higher office—were callously unaware and insensitive of constitutional overtones in legislation of this type. The answer, of course, is that in 1961, in 1965, and in 1970 these elected representatives of the people—far more conscious of the temper of the times, of the maturing of society, and of the contemporary demands for man's dignity, than are we who sit cloistered on this Court —took it as settled that the death penalty then, as it always had been, was not in itself unconstitutional. Some of those Members of Congress, I suspect, will be surprised at this Court's giant stride today.

*   *   *

Although personally I may rejoice at the Court's result, I find it difficult to accept or to justify as a matter of history, of law, or of constitutional pronouncement. I fear the Court has overstepped. It has sought and has achieved an end.

Mr. Justice POWELL, with whom THE CHIEF JUSTICE, Mr. Justice BLACKMUN, and Mr. Justice REHNQUIST join, dissenting.

* * *

One must conclude, contrary to petitioners' submission, that the indicators most likely to reflect the public's view—legislative bodies, state referenda and the juries which have the actual responsibility— do not support the contention that evolving standards of decency require total abolition of capital punishment. Indeed, the weight of the evidence indicates that the public generally has not accepted either the morality or the social merit of the views so passionately advocated by the articulate spokesmen for abolition. But however one may assess the amorphous ebb and flow of public opinion generally on this volatile issue, this type of inquiry lies at the periphery—not the core —of the judicial process in constitutional cases. The assessment of popular opinion is essentially a legislative, not a judicial, function.

* * *

Certainly the claim is justified that this criminal sanction falls more heavily on the relatively impoverished and underprivileged elements of society. The "have-nots" in every society always have been subject to greater pressure to commit crimes and to fewer constraints than their more affluent fellow citizens. This is, indeed, a tragic by-product of social and economic deprivation, but it is not an argument of constitutional proportions under the Eighth or Fourteenth Amendment. The same discriminatory impact argument could be made with equal force and logic with respect to those sentenced to prison terms. The Due Process Clause admits of no distinction between the deprivation of "life" and the deprivation of "liberty." If discriminatory impact renders capital punishment cruel and unusual, it likewise renders invalid most of the prescribed penalties for crimes of violence. The root causes of the higher incidence of criminal penalties on "minorities and the poor" will not be cured by abolishing the system of penalties. Nor, indeed, could any society have a viable system of criminal justice if sanctions were abolished or ameliorated because most of those who commit crimes happened to be underprivileged. The basic problem results not from the penalties imposed for criminal conduct but from social and economic factors that have plagued humanity since the beginning of recorded history, frustrating all efforts to create in any country at any time the perfect society in which there are no "poor," no "minorities" and no "underprivileged." The causes underlying this problem are unrelated to the constitutional issue before the Court.

* * *

[L]egislative judgments as to the efficacy of particular punishments are presumptively rational and may not be struck down under the Eighth Amendment because this Court may think that some alternate sanction would be more appropriate. Even if such judgments were within the judicial prerogative, petitioners have failed to show that there exist no justifications for the legislative enactments challenged in these cases. While the evidence and arguments advanced by petitioners might have proved profoundly persuasive if addressed to a legislative body, they do not approach the showing traditionally required before a court declares that the legislature has acted irrationally.

In two of the cases before us today juries imposed sentences of death after convictions for rape. In these cases we are urged to hold that even if capital punishment is permissible for some crimes, it is a cruel and unusual punishment for this crime. These petitioners rely on the Court's opinions holding that the Eighth Amendment, in addition to prohibiting punishments deemed barbarous and inhumane, also condemns punishments that are greatly disproportionate to the crime charged. * * * I find it quite impossible to declare the death sentence grossly excessive for all rapes. Rape is widely recognized as among the most serious of violent crimes, as witnessed by the very fact that it is punishable by death in 16 States and by life imprisonment in most other States. The several reasons why rape stands so high on the list of serious crimes are well known: It is widely viewed as the most atrocious of intrusions upon the privacy and dignity of the victim; never is the crime committed accidentally; rarely can it be said to be unpremeditated; often the victim suffers serious physical injury; the psychological impact can often be as great as the physical consequences; in a real sense, the threat of both types of injury is always present. For these reasons, and for the reasons arguing against abolition of the death penalty altogether, the excessiveness rationale provides no basis for rejection of the penalty for rape in all cases.

The argument that the death penalty for rape lacks rational justification because less severe punishments might be viewed as accomplishing the proper goals of penology is as inapposite here as it was in considering *per se* abolition. The state of knowledge with respect to the deterrent value of the sentence for this crime is inconclusive. Moreover, what has been said about the concept of retribution applies with equal force where the crime is rape. There are many cases in which the sordid, heinous nature of a particular crime, demeaning, humiliating and often physically or psychologically traumatic, will call for public condemnation. In a period in our country's history when the frequency of this crime is increasing alarmingly, it is indeed a grave event for the Court to take from the States whatever deterrent and retributive weight the death penalty retains.

Other less sweeping applications of the disproportionality concept have been suggested. Recently the Fourth Circuit struck down a death sentence in Ralph v. Warden, 438 F.2d 786 (C.A.4 1970), holding that the death penalty was an appropriate punishment for rape only where life is "endangered." Chief Judge Haynsworth, who joined in the panel's opinion, wrote separately in denying the State of Maryland's petition for rehearing in order to make clear the basis for his joinder. He stated that, for him, the appropriate test was not whether life was endangered, but whether the victim in fact suffered "grievous physical or psychological harm." Id., at 744. See Rudolph v. Alabama, 375 U.S. 889 (1963) (dissent from the denial of certiorari).

It seems to me that both of these tests depart from established principles and also raise serious practical problems. How are those cases in which the victim's life is endangered to be distinguished from those in which no danger is found? The threat of serious injury is implicit in the definition of rape; the victim is either forced into submission by physical violence or by the threat of violence. Certainly that test would provide little comfort for either of the rape defendants in the cases presently before us. Both criminal acts were accomplished only after a violent struggle. Petitioner Jackson held a scissors blade against his victim's neck. Petitioner Branch had less difficulty subduing his 65-year-old victim. Both assailants threatened to kill their victims. The alternate test, limiting the penalty to cases in which the victim suffers physical or emotional harm, might present even greater problems of application. While most physical effects may be seen and objectively measured, the emotional impact may be impossible to gauge at any particular point in time. The extent and duration of psychological trauma may not be known or ascertainable prior to the date of trial.

While I reject each of these attempts to establish specific categories of cases in which the death penalty may be deemed excessive, I view them as groping toward what is for me the appropriate application of the Eighth Amendment. While in my view the disproportionality test may not be used either to strike down the death penalty for rape altogether or to install the Court as a tribunal for sentencing review, that test may find its application in the peculiar circumstances of specific cases. Its utilization should be limited to the rare case in which the death penalty is rendered for a crime technically falling within the legislatively defined class but factually falling outside the likely legislative intent in creating the category. Specific rape cases (and specific homicides as well) can be imagined in which the conduct of the accused would render the ultimate penalty a grossly excessive punishment. Although this case-by-case approach may seem painfully slow and inadequate to those who wish the Court to assume an activist legislative role in reforming criminal punishments, it is the approach dictated both by our prior opinions and by a due recognition of the limitations of judicial power. This approach, rather than the majority's more pervasive and less refined judgment, marks for me the appropriate course under the Eighth Amendment.

*   *   *

Mr. Justice REHNQUIST, with whom THE CHIEF JUSTICE, Mr. Justice BLACKMUN, and Mr. Justice POWELL join, dissenting.

*   *   *

The task of judging constitutional cases imposed by Art. III cannot * * * be avoided, but it must surely be approached with the deepest humility and genuine deference to legislative judgment. Today's decision to invalidate capital punishment is, I respectfully submit, significantly lacking in those attributes. For the reasons well stated in the opinions of THE CHIEF JUSTICE, Mr. Justice POWELL, and Mr. Justice BLACKMUN, I conclude that this decision holding unconstitutional capital punishment is not an act of judgment, but rather an act of will. * * *

If there can be said to be one dominant theme in the Constitution, perhaps more fully articulated in The Federalist Papers than in the instrument itself, it is the notion of checks and balances. The Framers were well aware of the natural desire of office holders as well as others to seek to expand the scope and authority of their particular office at the expense of others. They sought to provide against success in such efforts by erecting adequate checks and balances in the form of grants of authority to each branch of the government in order to counteract and prevent usurpation on the part of the others.

This philosophy of the Framers is best described by one of the ablest and greatest of their number, James Madison, in Federalist No. 51:

> "In framing a government which is to be administered by men over men, the great difficulty lies in this: you must first enable the government to control the governed; and in the next place oblige it to control itself."

Madison's observation applies to the Judicial Branch with at least as much force as to the Legislative and Executive Branches. While overreaching by the Legislative and Executive Branches may result in the sacrifice of individual protections that the Constitution was designed to secure against action of the State, judicial overreaching may result in sacrifice of the equally important right of the people to govern themselves. The Due Process and Equal Protection Clauses of the Fourteenth Amendment were "never intended to destroy the States' power to govern themselves." Black, J., in Oregon v. Mitchell, 400 U.S. 112, 126 (1970).

The very nature of judicial review, as pointed out by Justice Stone in his dissent in the *Butler* case [297 U.S. 1, 78–79 (1936)] makes the courts the least subject to Madisonian check in the event that they shall, for the best of motives, expand judicial authority beyond the limits contemplated by the Framers. It is for this reason that judicial self-restraint is surely an implied, if not an expressed, condition of the grant of authority of judicial review. The Court's holding in these cases has been reached, I believe, in complete disregard of that implied condition.

---

b. EXPANDED TERMS FOR "ABNORMAL" OFFENDERS

DIRECTOR v. DANIELS

Circuit Court for Prince Georges County, Maryland, 1965.
Appendix to Director v. Daniels, 243 Md. 16, 221 A.2d 397 (1966).

It has been long recognized by many people, including criminologists, penologists, psychiatrists and judges, that there exists a group of offenders whose criminality results from and is related to a definite category of mental abnormality. These offenders have been of particular concern to society because usually they have long histories of persistent antisocial behavior which results from lack of emotional balance and control, and in some cases is accompanied by deficient intelligence.

It is clear that these individuals have a tendency to repeat their crimes, and they do not respond nor are they materially influenced by ordinary penological reformative measures as provided in the conventional penal institution.

Those studying the subject have recognized that these individuals, even though constituting an acute menace to society because of their criminal acts, are in fact mentally ill and should not be dealt with primarily as criminals and confined in a conventional prison, but should be placed in a special type institution. Such an institution they agree should be staffed with psychiatrists, psychologists, sociologists and social service workers, and should also include educational, vocational and recreational facilities and instructors, all of which enables the use of recognized psychiatric and psychological procedures and techniques on an intensive basis, for the purpose of changing and rehabilitating the character and personality make-up of the person, so that upon his release he will, hopefully, assume a useful role in society.

The advocates of this approach are cognizant of the fact that mental illness suffered by these offenders often is exceedingly difficult of cure, and will usually require confinement for considerable duration in order effectively to complete the treatment process. They recommend the use of an indeterminate sentence to an institution such as described above so that the offender's release will be related to a cure of the illness, and not merely to the passage of time. This concept recognizes, also, that some offenders may never be cured, and hence the indeterminate sentence would accomplish the protection of society but result in their confinement for life.

After extensive studies, Maryland adopted these concepts in 1951 when the Defective Delinquent Act was passed, and its operative facility, Patuxent Institution was completed and opened on January 1, 1955.

The initial cost of the Institution was $3,902,000 and the total cost of the physical plant to the present amounts to $7,579,560. The facility is located about midway between Baltimore and Washington, at Jessup, Maryland, is comprised of ten acres, fenced. Facilities include six guard houses, a multi-sectioned three-story defective delinquent building, a three-story diagnostic center, a kitchen-dining room, a gymnasium-theater, vocational shops and school area, a hospital (containing laboratory facilities, including electroencephalographic and electrocardiographic rooms, dental offices, examination and treatment rooms), administrative offices, a psychiatric isolation section, as well as other structures and units. The entire complex is interconnected by a ground-level tunnel.

Both the defective delinquent building and diagnostic center have tiers of cells containing standard items of furniture. The rated capacity of the Institution is 622 inmates, with the committed inmates being housed in the defective delinquent building, and those in a diagnostic status being confined in the diagnostic center.

Additional improvements are planned, which include a warehouse structure, home for maintenance supervisors, school building, chapel, additional shop space, and a "half-way" house.

The testimony discloses that from the Institution's opening in January, 1955, to July 1, 1965, a ten-year period, the Institution admitted 1,483 persons, of whom 1,222 were diagnosed by the staff. Of this number, 826 were recommended by the staff for commitment and original defective delinquent hearings were held. Either the court or jury found 581, or 82 percent, of those individuals to be defective delinquents. Up to July 1, 1965, there have been 347 rehearings under the provisions of the Act, and of that number, 185, or 53 percent, were found still to be defective delinquents.

SAS v. MARYLAND

United States Court of Appeals for the Fourth Circuit, 1964.
334 F.2d 506.

J. Spencer BELL, Circuit Judge. * * *

The first four sections of the [Defective Delinquency] Act provide for the establishment of the Patuxent Institution, the composition of its staff and its general administrative organization. It requires that the Director be a psychiatrist of at least five years experience in practice or teaching. Two of the Associate Directors must be psychiatrists with at least three years experience. An operating staff of psychiatrists, social workers, psychologists and sociologists is provided to operate the diagnostic clinic and to provide the treatment for the inmates of Patuxent.

Section five, the heart of the Act, defines the term defective delinquent as follows:

"Defective Delinquents

"§ 5. Defined.

"For the purposes of this article, a defective delinquent shall be defined as an individual who, by the demonstration of persistent aggravated antisocial or criminal behavior, evidences a propensity toward criminal activity, and who is found to have either such intellectual deficiency or emotional unbalance, or both, as to clearly demonstrate an actual danger to society so as to require such confinement and treatment, when appropriate, as may make it reasonably safe for society to terminate the confinement and treatment."

The remainder of the Act provides, in essence, that persons convicted of specified offenses may be thereafter tried as defective delinquents and if found to be such may be confined for an indeterminate period.

Section 6(a) lists the offenses conviction of which will subject one to trial for being a defective delinquent. It includes: (1) felonies; (2) serious misdemeanors; (3) crimes of violence; (4) certain sex crimes; and (5) two or more convictions for any offenses or crimes punishable by imprisonment in a Maryland criminal court. These classifications include both felons and rogues, vagabonds and other offenders against property. * * *

A convict may be examined for possible defective delinquency upon the request of the Department of Correction, the prosecuting State's Attorney in the criminal case, the convict or his attorney, or the convicting criminal court, "on any knowledge or suspicion of the presence of defective delinquency." Act, Section 6(b). This request may only be made if the convict has been sentenced to or is then serving a criminal sentence in a state penal institution. Act, Section 6(c). [A 1971 amendment to the statute prohibits an examination if the offender is within six months of expiration of his sentence.]

The request is filed with the convicting criminal court, which thereafter retains jurisdiction over the defendant. Act, Sections 6(d), (e).

[Each request must state the reasons for "suspecting or supposing the presence of defective delinquency" in the person sought to be examined. Act, Section 6(d). The statute does not state what, if any, factual finding must be made before an examination may be ordered. It simply provides that when a request has been filed, the court "may" order an examination and that the court "may" order an examination on its own initiative. Act, Section 6(b). Some courts, however, have made a factual finding that there exists "reasonable cause to believe that the defendant may be a defective delinquent" before ordering an examination. McNeil v. Director, 407 U.S. 245, 248, 92 S.Ct. 2083, 2086, 32 L.Ed.2d 719, 722 (1972).]

After the examination is ordered, the convict suspected of defective delinquency is transferred to Patuxent Institution and examined by a medical physician, a psychiatrist and a psychologist, who on the basis of their examination and study of the suspected defective delinquent and the circumstances of the originating crime, copies of any probation or other reports about him, and reports as to his social, physical, mental and psychiatric condition and history determine whether the suspected person is or is not a defective delinquent. Act, Section 7(a).

If the institutional report states that the suspected person is a defective delinquent, he is brought before the criminal court which sentenced him and is entitled to counsel of his choice and a jury trial. The right to speedy trial under the sixth amendment and Article 21 of the Maryland Declaration of Rights does not apply. McCloskey v. Director, 230 Md. 635, 187 A.2d 833 (1963). At the defective delinquency determination hearing, the state has the burden to establish, by a preponderance of the evidence, and not beyond a reasonable doubt, that the criminal is a defective delinquent. Purks v. Director, 226 Md. 43, 171 A.2d 726 (1961); Blizzard v. State, 218 Md. 384, 147 A.2d 227 (1958).

*   *   *

The state's evidence at the hearing is essentially that of expert witnesses, whose "expert findings and conclusions are to be accorded very serious consideration, particularly in a case such as this one, when the trial court almost necessarily must rely to a considerable degree on the opinions of expert witnesses." Palmer v. State, 215 Md. 142, 152, 137 A.2d 119, 125 (1957). See Purks v. State, 226 Md. 43, 171 A.2d 726 (1961). The institutional experts who testify for the state are not in a patient-physician relationship with the criminal and may testify as to matters learned from the criminal in interviews and tests, even if the same concerns prior criminal offenses and convictions and admissions of prior antisocial conduct. Simmons v. Director, 227 Md. 661, 177 A.2d 409 (1962); McDonough v. Director, 229 Md. 626, 183 A.2d 368 (1962); Purks v. State, supra. Extensive hearsay regarding the past social, physical, mental and psychiatric and criminal condition and history is admitted at the hearing over objection, since it is deemed that the Act requires the introduction of the same and that the purpose of the law would be defeated unless evidence of antecedent conduct is presented upon which to establish the propensity toward criminal activity. Simmons v. Director, supra; Fairbanks v. Director, 226 Md. 661, 173 A.2d 913 (1961).

The psychiatrist of the criminal's own choice, which must be furnished him by the state upon request, is not in the position of a medical expert in an adversary proceeding. He is considered to be "independent." He is required to submit a written report of his examination and findings to the court for consideration by the trier of fact. The defendant has no control over the admission of the report of this independent psychiatrist and the physician-patient relationship does not apply. Simmons v. Director, supra.

Defendant's counsel has access to the records and reports of Patuxent (and of the "independent" psychiatrist) which, presumably, he can put into evidence just as can the state. Act, Section 8. The defendant also has discovery procedures available to him pursuant to the Maryland Rules of Civil Procedure. Purks v. State, 226 Md. 43, 171 A.2d 726 (1961).

At a determination hearing the sole issue is "whether the person is a defective delinquent as defined in § 5." Act, Section 8(c). The trier of fact is precluded from considering whether treatment will aid defendant and whether any is available. Purks v. State, 226 Md. 43, 50, 171 A.2d 726 (1961); Queen v. Director, 226 Md. 664, 174 A.2d 351 (1961).

If the defendant is found not to be a defective delinquent, he is returned to the custody of the Department of Correction under his original criminal sentence, with credit for time spent in Patuxent and credit for behavior at Patuxent pursuant to the provisions of the state criminal code. Act, Section 9(a); Ann.Code of Md., Article 27, Section 688 (Supp.1962).

If the defendant is found to be a defective delinquent, the court is required to commit him to the Patuxent Institution, "for an indeterminate period without either maximum or minimum limits" and the sentence for the originating crime is suspended. Act, Section 9(b). The defective delinquent convict can be incarcerated at Patuxent Institution after his originating criminal sentence has expired, the purpose of his confinement being not to punish, but to receive "such confinement and treatment, when appropriate, as may make it reasonably safe for society to terminate the confinement and treatment." Act, Section 5. If he should escape this confinement, even if his originating criminal sentence has expired, he is guilty of the crime of escape under the provisions of the criminal code, Ann.Code of Md., Article 27, Section 139 (Supp.1963). See McCloskey v. Director, 230 Md. 635, 187 A.2d 833 (1963); Caparella v. State, 214 Md. 355, 135 A.2d 311 (1957).

During incarceration at Patuxent, the Institutional Board of Review may request the original criminal court to reinstate and reimpose the original criminal sentence upon the defective delinquent, who is then thereafter imprisoned in a penal institution, though he is still a defective delinquent. Act, Section 13(d).

Any person in the custody of the Patuxent Institution may be transferred by administrative decision, without a hearing, to the Department of Correction for imprisonment. Act, Section 16(d). This administrative transfer to a penal institution for imprisonment may take place regardless of whether the originating criminal sentence has expired. A convict sentenced to a determinate criminal sentence could, after defective delinquency determination, spend the rest of his life in the penitentiary.

During Patuxent confinement, the defective delinquent is subject to the term of his suspended original criminal sentence, and if released prior to its expiration, may be required to serve the remainder of that sentence. Act, Sections 10(a), 13(f).

While it is clear that a Patuxent inmate is subject to immediate and actual physical confinement without maximum or minimum limits, there is no requirement that he be given treatment unless the same is "appropriate." Act, Section 5. See Purks v. State, 226 Md. 43, 171 A.2d 726 (1961).

The Institutional Board of Review is required to review and re-examine each defective delinquent annually, utilizing examination procedures used in the first determination, and make a recommendation for the future status and treatment of each inmate so reviewed. Act, Section 13(b).

After a defective delinquent has been confined for two-thirds of his original criminal sentence or for a period of two years, whichever is longer, he may file a petition for redetermination of his defective delinquency. Act, Section 10(a). If the inmate is found not to be a defective delinquent, the court may discharge him from confinement or commit him under his original criminal sentence with credit for time spent at Patuxent and credit for behavior at Patuxent pursuant to the provisions of the criminal code. Act, Section 10(a); Ann.Code of Md., Article 27, Section 688 (Supp.1962). If the inmate is found to be a defective delinquent, excepting his application for leave to appeal, he is denied further petitions for review until intervals of not less than three years have elapsed. Act, Section 10(b).

The Act expressly saves the writ of habeas corpus to the defective delinquent, the Act, Section 10(c), who also has a post conviction remedy pursuant to the criminal code, Ann.Code of Md., Article 27, § 645A (Supp.1959). In neither proceeding can the defective delinquent raise the question of his defective delinquency on the merits.
* * *

DIRECTOR OF PATUXENT INSTITUTION v. DANIELS

Court of Appeals of Maryland, 1966.
243 Md. 16, 221 A.2d 397, certiorari denied 385 U.S. 940,
87 S.Ct. 307, 17 L.Ed.2d 219.

HAMMOND, Judge. * * *

This matter is * * * before this Court by direction of the Court of Appeals * * * whereby we are required to "determine whether his [Daniels'] continued detention at Patuxent [Institution], is a violation of his constitutional rights," after full hearing and making provision for adequate record of the proceedings with an explicit finding of fact and express conclusions of law.

We are directed to do this in light of the decision of the Federal Fourth Circuit Court of Appeals in Sas v. State of Maryland, 334 F.2d 506 (1964). The opinion in that case states that Maryland's Defective Delinquent Statute [Code, (1957) Article 31B], "is so serious a departure from traditional concepts of justice that it deserves a critical analysis on the broadest of terms after a careful factual development of its present operation."

* * *

All questions raised by all parties can be decided by answering the following:

I. Is the statutory definition of a Defective Delinquent as applied by the Maryland Courts sufficiently definitive to permit its practical application within Federal Constitutional limitations.

II. Are the objectives of the Act sufficiently implemented in its actual administration to support its categorization as a civil procedure, and to justify the elimination of conventional criminal procedural safeguards.

III. Are the procedures embodied in the statute and in Daniels' trial applied in such a manner as to offend the due process requirements of the Fifth Amendment and Fourteenth Amendment and the confrontation requirements of the Sixth Amendment.

IV. Does the Act, as interpreted and applied, permitting a defective delinquent to be found to be an actual danger to society, offend the Eighth Amendment's prohibition against cruel and unusual punishment when, as construed, it includes individuals whose conduct indicates a danger to property rights rather than violence to persons.

V. Does Patuxent in fact furnish treatment for treatable defective delinquents, as distinguished from other lawbreakers, which would support the Act under the "equal protection" clause of the Fourteenth Amendment.

A detailed finding of relevant facts is for convenience designated as Appendix "A", though nonetheless a part of this opinion, and will be referred to when appropriate in our conclusions.

I.

Legal Sufficiency of the Statutory Definition

*   *   *

This brings us to the question of whether or not the statutory definition of a defective delinquent as defined in Article 31B and as applied by the Maryland courts is sufficiently definitive to permit its practical application within constitutional limitations. The Act, Section 5, defines a defective delinquent as:

> " *   *   * an individual who, by the demonstration of persistent aggravated antisocial or criminal behavior, evidences a propensity toward criminal activity, and who is found to have either such intellectual deficiency or emotional unbalance, or both, as to clearly demonstrate an actual danger to society so as to require such confinement and treatment, when appropriate, as may make it reasonably safe for society to terminate the confinement and treatment."

It was noted by the *Sas* Court that this definition "was carefully drawn to conform to the definition approved by the [Supreme] Court [of the United States] in the Minnesota case," referring to State of Minnesota ex rel. Pearson v. Probate Court, 309 U.S. 270, 60 S.Ct. 523, 84 L.Ed. 744, (1940), wherein the Supreme Court upheld the constitutionality of Minnesota Sexual Psychopath Law.

From the voluminous testimony presented in this case we determine that the conclusion of the Fourth Circuit Court in *Sas* is justified when that court decided that the statutory definition was facially constitutional. We say this because the evidence before us clearly shows that there does in fact exist a class or group of persons falling within the definition, constituting a danger to the health and safety of people and who, with the aid of medical expert testimony, after appropriate examination, using recognized medical techniques, are discernible and recognizable by lay persons, including judge or jury. In fact, it is clear from the testimony of nearly all the eminent medical experts specializing in psychiatry testifying in this case that the defective delinquent definition as contained in the statute is no less vague and difficult of understanding or difficult of application to individual persons than are the M'Naghten or Durham rules used in testing criminal responsibility, or the civil insanity rule used in Maryland to determine the need for confinement in a mental hospital of persons suffering from mental disease sufficient to cause them to be "a danger to themselves or others". These same eminent medical experts, however, agree that there in fact does exist a medically recognizable group falling clearly within the definition in the Act's definition, and we so find.

*   *   *

II.

Civil Nature of the Act

The Maryland Court of Appeals in Eggleston v. State [209 Md. 504, 121 A.2d 644 (1963)] decided the Act was regulatory in character and therefore not penal but civil in nature. It becomes vital that there be a proper determination as to the correctness of this conclusion because only if the statute is regulatory can the precise criminal procedures required to uphold the constitutionality of a penal statute be dispensed with. If, on the other hand, the act is regulatory and therefore civil in nature, the Fourteenth Amendment of the Constitution's requirement is met if there is provided reasonable safeguards under the circumstances which include consideration of the fact that persons may be deprived of their liberty for the good of society and themselves. It seems clear that if there exists affirmative evidence that the act results from a legislative intent to regulate rather than punish, the law is deemed to be civil in nature. Kennedy v. Mendoza-Martinez, 372 U.S. 144, 83 S.Ct. 554, 9 L.Ed.2d 644 (1963). We conclude from the evidence before us that the legislative history of the Defective Delinquent Act clearly demonstrates that its sole objective and purpose was not penal but an effort to segregate a known group of mentally disordered people who are found guilty of criminal acts, by confining them in an institution housing only members of their group in a sole effort to protect society and provide treatment to effect, if possible, a cure of the illness. From the history it is clear that the legislative imposition of sanctions by restraining the individual results from studies that indicate that such restraint is necessary both for the protection of society and to provide medical treatment to further curative measures. In short, it is the State's effort to determine the cause of a criminal's acts and if associated with mental disorder to accomplish improvement under psychiatric supervision so that he may hopefully be released, no longer a danger to himself or society. This act now before the Court is so similar in design and has a legislative purpose so similar to the act that was before the Supreme Court in State of Minnesota, ex rel. Pearson v. Probate Court, supra, that we believe the decision of that court upholding the constitutionality of the Minnesota Sexual Psychopath Law is direct authority for our conclusion that this act is civil in nature. We further point out that the purpose of this act is so closely akin to the so-called "Sexual Psychopath" laws enforced in some twenty (20) states and the District of Columbia, that the decisions of the Courts in those jurisdictions that each of their laws is civil in nature is ample authority to conclude that the Maryland Act is regulatory. * * *

Assuming, however, that contrary to our finding here, there exists no conclusive evidence of legislative intent as to whether or not the act is penal or civil in nature, the answer to this question must be determined from the face of the Act after considering the following:

> " * * * [w]hether the sanction involves an affirmative disability or restraint, whether it has historically been regarded as a punishment, whether it comes into play only on a finding of scienter, whether its operation will promote the traditional aims of punishment—retribution and deterrence, whether the behavior to which it applies is already a crime, whether an alternative purpose to which it may rationally be connected is assignable for it, and whether it appears excessive in relation to the alternative purpose assigned." Kennedy v. Mendoza-Martinez, supra.

After considering these factors, we conclude that the statute on its face supports the conclusion that the act is civil in nature. We find this for the following reasons: Even though the sanction does involve an affirmative restraint it is provided only because it is deemed best for the protection of society and best for the protection and treatment of the individual that he be placed in a maximum security institution maintained solely for defective delinquents and not for other members of the criminal element. Historically, this type of sanction or restraint to accomplish the purposes of the Act has not been regarded as punishment but regulatory and is more akin to those laws consistently held to be civil in nature applicable to the "sexual psychopaths." Also this is true of laws involving loss of liberty by restraint of many mentally ill persons in mental hospitals in all of the states. The Maryland Act does not come into play on a finding of "scienter," because the person involved must before referral for diagnosis, already have been convicted of at least one criminal act and can be determined to be a "defective delinquent" only after there has been an intensive mental examination. The law on its face clearly shows that it was not enacted to promote the aims of punishment, retribution and deterrence, but its only purpose is for the protection of society, and the treatment of the individual to effectuate a cure if at all possible. The Act clearly demonstrates that "defective delinquency" is not a crime but is a mental condition that can only be diagnosed and determined to exist after a finding of guilt. There exist alternate purposes which are valid functions of the State as a part of its police power. They are the protection of society, coupled with a humanitarian attempt to treat, cure and rehabilitate those suffering from abnormal mental functioning. The sanctions or incarceration provided by the Act are not excessive in relation to these alternative purposes since most reputable psychiatrists agree that treatment cannot be related to a fixed period of confinement, as the length of time necessary for treatment and cure, if it can be obtained, is uncertain. In addition, experience has demonstrated that the indeterminate confinement is itself therapeutic, as it has a tendency to generate and motivate the individual to participate in the institutional program in order to help himself.

Based on the testimony, we fear that without the indeterminate provision in the Act, violence would be done to its basic concepts and purposes, and much of the good sought by this legislation would go for naught. The very qualities making up the nature of an individual at Patuxent, with his warped attitudes and distorted outlook, would dictate to him that he antisocially wait out his allotted time, resisting introspection and any kind of reappraisal of his makeup, and refusing to cooperate in receiving available therapy to any degree that would give promise of his ultimate rehabilitation.

We find that on the basis of present psychiatric and psychological knowledge, it can be accurately predicted that certain individuals will commit crimes. In cases where it is believed that a person at Patuxent still maintains his propensity for crime, it would be a tragic destruction of the purposes of this legislation, a disservice to society and not the least of the errors, a serious injustice to the individual to release him, uncured.

We therefore conclude that the Maryland Defective Delinquent Act is civil in nature under either test; that is, such a conclusion results from the legislative history and also the Act on its face supports this finding after taking into account the tests laid down by the Supreme Court in *Kennedy*.

The real question, however, Judge Bell asks in *Sas*, is " * * * whether the proposed objectives of the Act are sufficiently implemented in its actual administration to support its categorization as a civil procedure and justify the elimination of conventional criminal procedural safeguards * * * ". We are persuaded that there is much force in the respondent's argument that the answer to this question is a legislative rather than a judicial function. The *Kennedy* case seems to support the conclusion that the court's sole concern in this area is to determine whether or not the act is *reasonably calculated* to achieve its legislative purpose, leaving for the legislative and executive branches of the government a determination of whether in fact it is accomplishing its legislative purpose.

It would seem that the court's further concern after concluding that the Act was reasonably calculated to achieve its legislative purpose, only exists if the other branches of the government fail to act after a clear showing that it is ineffectual in accomplishing its purpose. We are aware of no responsible opinion of any professional group, and certainly there is no opinion of any of the witnesses testifying in this case, that the Act is clearly ineffectual in accomplishing its legislative purpose. On the contrary we conclude from the testimony by following the requirements of the Act, together with a utilization of medically accepted treatment techniques now being carried out at Patuxent, provides a procedure reasonably calculated to achieve the stated legislative purposes.

The testimony, we believe, justifies our determining that this legislation has proven to be a benefit to society as well as the individual and is becoming more so as results of knowledge gained from experiences at Patuxent and developments in psychiatry are evaluated and utilized.

Ten years is too short a time for anyone to know the extent of the ultimate accomplishments which may result from this vastly complex undertaking. Pioneering of necessity involves trial and error, but only in this way does civilization advance. What has been done up to now has not been ineffective and augurs well for the future.

All agree that the humane objectives, the protection of society and concern for the welfare of mentally ill persons are laudable. A benefit not to be overlooked is that the inmate while continuing to manifest pronounced symptoms of potentially dangerous antisocial behavior is protected, while confined, from the consequences to him, which would likely result from his being at large. We conclude that the Court has no power to interfere until its ineffectiveness is clearly demonstrated and the other branches of the government fail to act.

The petitioner argues that only a small number of individuals have been paroled or released during the ten (10) years of Patuxent's operation. Accepting this statement as true, we believe that such a result is understandable when it is considered that Patuxent was opened in 1955, that there necessarily ensued a period of nearly a year before there could be an adjudication after an examination that any individual was, in fact, a defective delinquent. The medical professional witnesses agreed that such a disorder is difficult of treatment and there exists no time table for cure. The illness does not await the discovery of a cure. The Act and its operation is admittedly an experimental one but we find nothing in the evidence to justify any conclusion that as administered it is unworkable or that it is not achieving its stated objectives. This we find is the conclusion of responsible psychiatrists, physicians, criminologists, and jurists who have studied in depth Patuxent Institution as it is being operated under the Defective Delinquent Act.

We further conclude from the evidence that the legislative and executive branches of the government are keeping abreast of and familiar with the operation of Patuxent Institution and the internal administration at Patuxent, in turn, is continually re-evaluating its treatment and release program in light of new developments in the psychiatric-medical field. * * *

We likewise conclude from all the evidence that the Act is not only intended to achieve its legislative purpose but the administrative procedures pursuant thereto are in accordance with the latest medically accepted practices and as administered are reasonably calculated to accomplish the Act's desired result—that is the protection of society, accompanied by an attempt to provide medical help for those unfortunate individuals who because of mental illness demonstrate a propensity to commit criminal acts. This is all the Federal Constitution requires. Kennedy v. Mendoza-Martinez, supra.

III.

Application of Procedures in Relation to
Due Process and Confrontation

*   *   *

While acknowledging the existence of [numerous] statutory and procedural safeguards, Daniels nevertheless contends that he has not been accorded due process in several respects, as hereafter enumerated and discussed.

Hearsay Evidence:

While hearsay evidence was received in Daniels' hearing when the Institution's report and finding were received in evidence, this was not violative of the Sixth Amendment [right to confront witnesses] because this was not a criminal prosecution, as heretofore discussed under heading II. The evidence under attack is part of a history and can be refuted under the procedure, both by a denial by the defendant and by the testimony of any other witnesses he sees fit to call.

Moreover, there appears to be nothing sacrosanct about the use of hearsay evidence; the weight is determined by the trier of the issue, and there are numerous exceptions under which hearsay evidence is properly received.

*   *   *

The discovery and other procedures which, under the statute and within Maryland's Rules, may be utilized by the defendant affords full protection against any possible damage resulting from the broadening of the hearsay rule in these hearings. *   *   *

After exposing the litmus to the atmosphere of reasonable necessity, we conclude that the mandatory procedures and the safeguards available, provide basic fairness and did not violate Daniels' right to due process.

Appellate Restrictions:

It is here contended that petitioner's rights were further violated because the procedure does not permit an absolute right of appeal, nor does the appellate court in applications for appeal under the Act consider the question of weight and sufficiency of the evidence or in the case of a pauper, review a transcript of the proceedings below.

*   *   *

We find * * * that special provisions concerning appeals in defective delinquent cases are within the proper prerogatives of the legislature.

* * *

Double Jeopardy:

Daniels believes that because he is confined at Patuxent after the expiration of his original sentence, his Constitutional rights have been violated in that he has been twice placed in jeopardy for the same offense.

* * *

The short answer to the petitioner's objection is that the commitment to Patuxent was a civil proceeding and does not involve his being placed in jeopardy for the commission of a crime.

* * *

IV.

Inclusion of Offenses Solely Against Property

We must summarily reject Daniels' contention that by his commitment to Patuxent, cruel and unusual punishment is being inflicted upon him, in violation of his rights under the Eighth Amendment. While it is true that the offense of which he was guilty and which became an indispensable ingredient to his confinement at Patuxent, was one against property not involving violence to the person, yet to confine such offenders appears to fall clearly within the area of valid legislative prerogatives (1) because Patuxent is not designed to punish but its purpose is to provide protective custody and treatment for members of a mentally ill group, until institutional confinement is no longer reasonably necessary. When this mental illness exists it is no less real because an outward manifestation has been an offense against property than an offense against a person. (2) One who is a menace to the property of others easily fits within the definition of a danger to society, and (3) the legislative power is not abused when it concludes that one only violating property rights is potentially a danger to the person of others. An arsonist may not know that there are occupants of the building he is setting fire to. A storehousebreaker may encounter the owner in the building. As Dr. Menninger said: "If you break one law, if you have nerved yourself up to defy social regulations and defy the order, and break one law, a sudden shift in the situation is very likely to precipitate the breaking of another law * * * Many prisoners start out with the idea of taking something, they are detected, they panic and then a subsequent act occurs which is very dangerous." We conclude that it is difficult if not impossible to limit consideration under the Act to persons whose only convictions involved violence to persons, since there always exists potential physical danger in crimes intended to concern only property.

V.

Quality of Treatment

We found from the evidence that treatment, in varying degrees, in a broad sense, is furnished to all defective delinquents at Patuxent. We have earlier concluded that the establishment by the legislature of a special category of criminal known as defective delinquents is within its constitutional powers.

* * *

Having concluded as a fact that Daniels has received or had had available to him (See Appendix "A") all of the treatment techniques available to other inmates at Patuxent, and also as generally recognized and utilized in the field of psychiatry it is obvious that he is not being denied equal protection of the law.

CONCLUSION

We conclude that the Act is constitutional and is being constitutionally applied, both generally and specifically as to Daniels.

APPENDIX A

COURT'S FINDINGS OF FACT

* * *

4. *Treatment of Inmates.*

Patuxent Institution furnishes treatment for inmates and presently experiences no deficiencies in staff, facilities, or finances substantially undermining the efficacy of the institution and the justification for the act, in that:

a. The aim of the treatment program at Patuxent is to develop internal controls within the individual in order that he may learn sufficient restraint to become a useful member of society. Otherwise stated, such aim is to enable defective delinquents, through treatment, to control their tensions, and, more specifically, to help the individual gain insight into his behavior, to accept responsibility for himself and others, to adjust with relationship to his peers and authority figures, to tolerate frustration and postpone gratification of instinctional demands.

b. The treatment program for defective delinquents has both formal and informal aspects and exists on all levels of communication between the inmates and their institutional environment. Underlying the treatment program is a philosophy which recognizes the desirability for total rehabilitation of the person, rather than mere improvement in his mental or emotional status. In addition to psychotherapeutics such as individual and group therapy, the treatment program, in furtherance of this aim, includes educational, vocational, religious, and recreational programs, together with provision for a highly structured social system, or "therapeutic milieu" within the institution. The graded tier system which, with its inclusion of tier counseling, is designed to build internal restraint, being based on the hypothesis that rewarding behavior which is socially desirable and personally beneficial to the inmate increases the frequency with which such behavior occurs and reduces the tendency toward antagonistic and undesirable behavior. In short, Patuxent utilizes a medically accepted treatment program adapted to the mental and emotional condition of the inmates.

c. Since defective delinquents usually require more than normal incentive to be motivated, cannot easily tolerate lack of discipline, and are deficient in ability to control their conflicts, their effectual treatment can best be carried out in a secure institutional environment, such as provided by Patuxent, with a definite reward and punishment system. Such treatment is not available and cannot feasibly be made available in State mental hospitals or State penal institutions.

d. The conventional mental hospital, whether State or private, deals with a distinctly different group of patients than Patuxent, in that within the former institutions are found individuals who, for the most part, have internalized their conflicts and do not "act out" against society, and thus such institutions can be operated as "open" hospitals. One of the chief characteristics of the defective delinquent is his inability to internalize these conflicts, resulting in "acting out" antisocial behavior. Moreover, all committed inmates at Patuxent have been found to be, in varying degrees, a danger to society, thus Patuxent must be operated as a maximum security institution. Experience has shown that when individuals possessing the characteristics of the defective delinquent are confined within mental hospitals, they are disruptive to the normal institutional program.

e. Confinement of defective delinquents at Patuxent, rather than in the State mental hospitals, has relieved what formerly was a most difficult situation and has made it possible and desirable for such mental hospitals to develop better "open" hospital programs for its general population, with greater freedom of movement.

f. The penal and correctional institutions under the jurisdiction of the Department of Correction have been ineffectual in developing or providing the specialized treatment and attention which defective delinquents require, and experience has indicated that when individuals possessing the characteristics of the defective delinquent are incarcerated in conventional penal institutions they are disruptive to the normal institutional program. Confinement of defective delinquents at Patuxent, rather than in the State's penal institutions, has enabled such institutions to develop more effective programs for the conventional prison population.

g. Both quantitatively and qualitatively, Patuxent's treatment program is more effective for the defective delinquent type person than that provided in the State's penal and correctional institutions.

h. The State's penal and correctional institutions are basically without functioning psychiatric treatment programs, and have no program even remotely approximating the graded tier concept in effect at Patuxent. Separation of inmates by tiers, in penal institutions of this State, is based purely on convenience to the operation and security.

i. Although treatment at Patuxent is not as intensive in the area of individual psychotherapeutic attention as that provided in private mental hospitals (though usually at prohibitive cost to the average citizen), treatment at Patuxent is superior in its milieu therapy, group therapy and post release programs to that provided by State or private mental hospitals, and is more comprehensive than either.

j. The operating budget requests, as well as the fiscal requirements, of Patuxent have been realistically met by the State as demonstrated by the figures heretofore given and the fact that the expenditures have increased year by year.

k. Patuxent presently provides effectual treatment for all treatable defective delinquents, including Daniels, denying treatment to none, in that:

(1) Patuxent's professional staff is adequate and competent as beginning August 15, 1965, the institution was authorized to employ twelve full-time psychiatrists (9.58 being then employed), nine psychologists (5.5 being then employed), and fourteen social workers (13 being then employed). With 485 patients on August 15, 1965, the professional staff to patient ratio was in full compliance with mental hospital staff standards promulgated by the American Psychiatric Association, and was materially higher than such ratios prevailing in the State penal and correctional institutions and in State mental hospitals in Maryland, as well as elsewhere in the country generally. Additionally, professional services of Patuxent's various advisory boards are available and are of value in the treatment program.

*   *   *

(5) All inmates are considered treatable and susceptible of help at Patuxent and the institution uses most of the recognized psychiatric treatment techniques. *   *   *
*   *   *

(6) Group therapy, which now enjoys almost universal acceptance, and in which use Patuxent pioneered, is now generally considered by experts to be the most effective form of treatment for defective delinquents. Presently 86% of the committed patients are regularly receiving this form of psychotherapy. All patients are afforded an opportunity to receive such therapy, and non-participation is due either to recent commitment, improper attitude or outright refusal.

(7) Individual therapy is also provided at Patuxent on a selective basis, but presently only four inmates are receiving this form of treatment, as experience there has demonstrated that defective delinquents generally do not respond well to this form of therapy.

(8) All committed inmates by virtue of the milieu therapy program are in a broad sense constantly receiving treatment.

(9) Treatment at Patuxent is effective and the environmental (milieu) therapy, which is different from the State penal institutions, is a substantial contributing factor. * * *

(10) The indeterminate sentence can be an incentive to treatment and rehabilitation of inmates, having therapeutic value in and of itself by motivating some patients to become amenable to treatment and making clear to all patients that they must participate in the treatment process in order to be helped and released.

(11) Though helpful, it is not indispensable to effective treatment at Patuxent that individuals be willing patients.

                         *   *   *

(14) Twenty percent of Patuxent's population are presently beyond the time of their original sentences.

(15) The incidence of successful adjustment in the community, of inmates released on parole demonstrates the effectiveness of the treatment program. The post release experience of patients committed to Patuxent, over a ten-year period, shows that of 581 patients committed to the institution, 155 or 27%, were released with results as follows:

Type of Release		Number	Risk Rate
I. Total released		155	
	Violated	64	41%
II. Court Releases without Institutional Board of Review (IBR) recommendation		129	
	Violated	62	48%
A. Above patients never on leave status		104	
	Violated	56	54%
B. Above patients who had been on parole but did not have IBR recommendation		25	
	Violated	7	28%
III. Total Released from Parole		51	
	Violated	9	18%
A. Same as item "B" in category II above		25	
	Violated	7	28%
B. IBR recommended		26	
	Violated	2	8%

"Risk rate" is based on the number who violated in a given category. It shows the risk to society when there is a release from Defective-Delinquency of a patient who falls into one of the above categories.

(16) Patuxent adopted the "live in-work out" program and 57 inmates on July 1, 1965, had participated in this program, with 16 violating its terms and committing new offenses.

(17) Patuxent's holiday and weekend leave program has resulted in a total of 148 inmates being given such leave up to July 1, 1965, 57 of whom started in 1965, being three times that of any previous year. Of these, 16 violated the terms of the leave program and 13 committed new offenses. All twenty-nine (29) were returned to the institution.

(18) A total of 24 inmates have been recommended by the Institutional Board of Review to the courts for outright release from their status as defective delinquents, nine such recommendations were made in 1965, twice the number as for all previous years of the institution's operation.

(19) The Patuxent treatment program includes a parole clinic, providing psychiatric aftercare to parolees. It meets regularly and provides both individual and group therapy for parolees, including family group therapy.

(20) Patuxent Institution, and the concept which it embodies, is accomplishing its purpose with increasing effectiveness, both because of the development of the science of psychiatry and from experience with the operation of the institution and dealing with the defective delinquent population there. It has been accorded positive recognition as a progressive institution, both nationally and internationally and among leading criminologists, penologists, psychiatrists and judges.

5. *Daniels' Treatment.*

As applied specifically to the petitioner we find as follows:

a. The aim of the treatment program for Daniels has not been necessarily to increase his intellectual performance, but to modify his social adaptabilities and his behavior to his environment, so that he can stay out in society as a functioning person, even though intellectually limited. Patuxent is attempting, through treatment, to have him modify his social behavior so as to handle his problems on a thinking rather than on an impulsive basis.

b. A specific educational program is available to and is participated in by Daniels.

c.   Although Daniels has proven not to respond particularly well to group therapy, he is susceptible of help, through application of a simple reality group therapy program. His institutional record with regard to such therapy is lacking in relation to the results reached. However, we do find that all therapy utilized at Patuxent which is appropriate to his condition is available to him.

6. *Irregularities at the Institution.*

There was considerable testimony of various incidents and conditions at Patuxent which if accepted by us as fact would indicate at least lapses in the treatment program and the efficient operation of the Institution. This testimony, while not wholly rejected, does not show such degree of flagrancy as to have a bearing on the constitutional questions here involved, either generally, or specifically as to Daniels. However, we hope that bringing them to light will be noted by the staff for future guidance and reference.

*   *   *

NOTES

1.   Prior to the litigation of the instant case, the validity of the Defective Delinquency program had been raised in federal litigation. A panel of the United States Court of Appeals for the Fourth Circuit upheld the statute creating the program on its face but remanded for further consideration by the District Court of the constitutionality of the program as applied. Sas v. Maryland, 334 F.2d 506 (4th Cir. 1964). On this remand, both sides agreed to postpone further federal litigation until the Maryland state courts had considered the issues. Following the decision by the Maryland Court of Appeals in the instant case, the federal litigation was again pursued. After considering the evidence taken in the state litigation and supplemental evidence, the District Court upheld the act on its face and its application. Sas v. Maryland, 295 F.Supp. 389 (D.Md.1969). The Fourth Circuit affirmed, Tippett v. Maryland, 436 F.2d 1153 (4th Cir. 1971), over the dissent of Judge Sobeloff who argued that the subjects of a Defective Delinquency proceeding were entitled to the presence of counsel at the final staff conference during the evaluation at Patuxent and to have the state establish defective delinquency by at least "clear and convincing evidence" at the judicial hearing. The United States Supreme Court granted certiorari. Murel v. Baltimore City Criminal Court, 404 U.S. 999, 92 S.Ct. 567, 30 L.Ed.2d 552 (1971). In Murel v. Baltimore City Criminal Court, 407 U.S. 355, 92 S.Ct. 2091, 32 L.Ed.2d 791 (1972) the writ of certiorari was dismissed as improvidently granted. Explaining its action, the Court noted that one of the four petitioners had been released from confinement and the other three were subject to criminal sentences which would bar their release should the case be decided in their favor. In addition, the court noted that the challenges to the Defective Delinquency statute had to be considered "in relation to the criteria, procedures, and treatment which the State of Maryland makes available to other persons, not defective delinquents, committed for compulsory

psychiatric treatment." Since the Maryland statutes governing civil commitment of the mentally ill were "presently undergoing substantial revision," the time was "particularly inappropriate" for consideration of the Defective Delinquency Program. Mr. Justice Douglas dissented on the ground that the Due Process Clause of the Fifth Amendment required the state to prove defective delinquency beyond a reasonable doubt:

> [In] In re Winship, [397 U.S. 385, 90 S.Ct. 1068, 25 L.Ed.2d 368 (1970)], dealing with the juvenile court we determined that "proof beyond a reasonable doubt" was constitutionally required "because of the possibility that [an individual might] lose his liberty" and because of the stigma of a criminal conviction. 397 U.S., at 363. * * *
>
> In the present case, petitioners were deprived of * * * their personal liberty * * * under a burden of proof which was constitutionally inadequate. * * *
>
> It is no answer to say that petitioners' commitments were in "civil" proceedings and that the requirement for proof beyond a reasonable doubt is required only in "criminal" cases. In re Gault, 387 U.S. 1, 87 S.Ct. 1428, 18 L.Ed.2d 527 (1967) [dealing with the juvenile court] and In re Winship, supra, specifically rejected this distinction and looked instead at the interests involved and the actual nature of the proceedings. * * * Nor would it be persuasive to argue that the difficulty in proving one's state of mind requires that the State be afforded the benefit of a lesser burden of proof. Proving a state of mind is no more difficult than many other issues with which courts and juries grapple each day.

2. Although the statute requires that the report from Patuxent be submitted within six months or before expiration of sentence, whichever occurs later (this was amended in 1971 to require submission within six months or three months before expiration of sentence, whichever occurs first), the Maryland Courts have construed the language to permit the retention of a subject committed for observation and examination beyond the expiration of his criminal sentence if the examination could not be completed because of the subject's refusal to cooperate with the examiners. State v. Musgrove, 241 Md. 521, 217 A.2d 247 (1966). In McNeil v. Director, 407 U.S. 245, 92 S.Ct. 2083, 32 L.Ed.2d 719 (1972) the Supreme Court considered the argument of Edward McNeil, who had been incarcerated at Patuxent for six years pursuant to a court order committing him for an examination and evaluation. His five-year sentence for assault had therefore expired, and he was being retained because the institution felt it could not complete the examination until and if he agreed to talk to the examining psychiatrists. Noting that the detention was pursuant to a court order based upon an ex parte determination that there was reasonable cause to believe that the subject was a defective delinquent, the Court found a denial of due process of law:

> [T]he State contends that petitioner has been committed merely for observation, and that a commitment for observation need not be

surrounded by the procedural safeguards (such as an adversary hearing) that are appropriate for a final determination of defective delinquency. Were the commitment for observation limited in duration to a brief period, the argument might have some force. But petitioner has been committed "for observation" for six years, and on the State's theory of his confinement there is no reason to believe it likely that he will ever be released. A confinement which is in fact indeterminate cannot rest on procedures designed to authorize a brief period of observation. * * * In these circumstances, it is a denial of due process to continue to hold [the petitioner] on the basis for an ex parte order committing him for observation. * * * The State contends that, by refusing to talk to psychiatrists, petitioner has prevented them from evaluating him, and made it impossible for the State to go forward with evidence at a hearing. Thus, it is argued, his continued confinement is analogous to civil contempt; he can terminate the confinement and bring about a hearing at any time by talking to the examining psychiatrists, and the State has the power to induce his cooperation by confining him.

Petitioner claims that he has a right under the Fifth Amendment to withhold cooperation, a claim we need not consider here. But putting that claim to one side, there is nevertheless a fatal flaw in the State's argument. For if confinement is to rest on a theory of civil contempt, then due process requires a hearing to determine whether petitioner has in fact behaved in a manner that amounts to contempt. At such a hearing it could be ascertained whether petitioner's conduct is willful, or whether it is a manifestation of mental illness, for which he cannot fairly be held responsible. Robinson v. California, 370 U.S. 660, 82 S.Ct. 1417, 8 L.Ed.2d 758 (1962). Civil contempt is coercive in nature, and consequently there is no justification for confining on a civil contempt theory a person who lacks the present ability to comply. Maggio v. Zeitz, 333 U.S. 56, 68 S.Ct. 401, 92 L.Ed. 476 (1947). Moreover, a hearing would provide the appropriate forum for resolution of petitioner's Fifth Amendment claim. Finally, if the petitioner's confinement were explicitly premised on a finding of contempt, then it would be appropriate to consider what limitations the Due Process Clause places on the contempt power. The precise contours of that power need not be traced here. It is enough to note that petitioner has been confined, potentially for life, although he has never been determined to be in contempt by a procedure that comports with due process. The contempt analogy cannot justify the State's failure to provide a hearing of any kind.

C. Finally, the State suggests that petitioner is probably a defective delinquent, because most noncooperators are. Hence, it is argued, his confinement rests not only on the purposes of observation, and of penalizing contempt, but also on the underlying purposes of the Defective Delinquency Law. But that argument proves too much. For if the Patuxent staff was prepared to conclude, on the basis of petitioner's silence and their observations of him over the years, that petitioner is a defective delinquent, then it is not true that he has prevented them from evaluating him. On that theory, they have long been ready to make their report to the Court, and the hearing on defective delinquency could have gone forward.

HODGES, CRIME PREVENTION BY THE INDETERMINATE SENTENCE LAW

128 Am.J. Psychiatry 291 (1971).c

From the opening in January 1955 through June 30, 1966, 1,340 diagnostic evaluations were made at Patuxent. The staff recommended that 896 persons be committed as defective delinquents. Court hearings resulted in 156 findings of "not found defective delinquent" and 740 commitments as defective delinquents.

The 156 men adjudicated "not defective delinquent" were returned to the Department of Corrections to serve out their original sentences. Since they were only evaluated at Patuxent and were not exposed to the treatment program, we shall refer to these men as the "untreated" group.

Of the 740 commitments to Patuxent, there were: 1) 26 men later released on legal technicalities; 2) 198 men released on subsequent court rehearings (inasmuch as these men entered the treatment program but were released by the court against Patuxent's advice, they constitute a "partially treated" group); and 3) 516 men who had court rehearings that did not result in release. Of this latter number, 156 improved enough to earn parole, while 360 others were still in confinement as of June 30, 1966. Since the Institutional Board of Review, on the recommendation of the staff, decides when a man should be granted parole, this group can be considered as "fully treated."

Using data on first admissions only, there were 129 men in the untreated group, 162 in the partially treated group, and 156 in the pa-

c. Reprinted from The American Journal of Psychiatry, volume 128, pages 291–295, 1971. Copyright 1971, the American Psychiatric Association.

INTRODUCTION

role group (see table 1). Omitting the uncertain cases in which persons were charged with an offense but the disposition was un-

TABLE 1
Postrelease Follow-Up

DISPOSITION	UNTREATED GROUP	PARTIALLY TREATED GROUP	FULLY TREATED GROUP (PAROLEES)
Convicted of new offense	95	111	57
No new offense	23	45	99
Charged, disposition unknown	11	6	—
Subtotal (men on first release)	129	162	156
Multiple releases	4	25	—
Died	4	6	—
Still confined by Department of Corrections on June 30, 1966	19	5	—
Subtotal (others)	27	36	—
Total	156	198	156

known, we find that recidivism occurred in 81 percent of the untreated group, 71 percent of the partially treated group, and in only 37 percent of the fully treated group. A comparison of the fully treated group with the untreated and partially treated groups gives a chi square of 54 and 40 respectively. Each of these values has a probability of .01, which is, of course, statistically significant.

Of the recidivists in the untreated group, 79 had committed one or more felonies, while 16 had been convicted of misdemeanors only. Of the partially treated group, 89 were convicted of felonies and 22 of misdemeanors only. Forty-two parolees had post-release felonies, while 15 had misdemeanors only (see table 2).

TABLE 2
Recidivism, by Type of Offense

OFFENSE	UNTREATED		PARTIALLY TREATED		FULLY TREATED (PAROLEES)	
	NUMBER	PERCENT	NUMBER	PERCENT	NUMBER	PERCENT
Felony	79	87	89	80	42	74
Misdemeanor only	16	13	22	20	15	26
Total	95		111		57	

An analysis of the types of felonies, based on the FBI crime index, appears in table 3. This index consists of personal crimes such

TABLE 3
Types of Felony Offenses

ITEM	UNTREATED GROUP	PARTIALLY TREATED GROUP	FULLY TREATED GROUP (PAROLEES)
Personal offenses			
Murder, manslaughter	3	1	2
Rape	2	3	1
Robbery	11	9	6
Aggravated assault	17	14	4
Other	6	3	2
Subtotal	39(49%)	30(34%)	15(36%)
Property offenses			
Burglary	16	29	14
Larceny	8	7	5
Car theft	10	15	2
Other	6	8	6
Subtotal	40(51%)	59(66%)	27(64%)
Total	79	89	42

as murder, forcible rape, robbery, and aggravated assault; and crimes against property such as burglary, larceny of goods valued at $50 or more, and auto theft. Maryland law defines larceny as a felony when the value of the stolen property is $100 or more; only such cases were scored as felonies in this study.

The felonies in the untreated group included 39 personal crimes and 40 property crimes. The partially treated group had 30 personal and 59 property offenses, while the fully treated group showed 15 personal and 27 property offenses. The higher proportion of personal offenses in the untreated group compared to the partially treated group is significant at the .05 level of probability; the same comparison with the fully treated group falls short of statistical significance.

Turning now to the group of 156 parolees, we note that 99 had no new offenses. Part of this rather favorable outcome is undoubtedly due to the policy of revoking the parole of those men who have violated their parole terms. Thus of the 99 men with no new offenses, 31 had to return to the institution for further treatment. Many of these later earned parole status again. It should be mentioned that parole is a carefully supervised experience and may include weekend furloughs, a work-out, live-in program, a study program, and a halfway house.   Also among the 99 parolees with no new offenses were 30 men who had gained complete release from parole.

*   *   *

It should be noted also that 80 percent of the 210 felony recidivists were released through court initiative, compared to 20 percent released on parole by the Patuxent staff.   It would seem that if the judges and juries had accepted the recommendations of the staff more often, the number of recidivists would have been smaller.

Discussion

The findings show that of a total of 807 men diagnosed as defective delinquents on first admission, 263 committed postrelease offenses; 95 of these recidivists came from the untreated group, 111 from the partially treated group, and 57 from the fully treated group.

Let us now ask how many recidivists there would have been in the same group of men if there had been no law on defective delinquents in Maryland.   The fact is that 81 percent of the group adjudicated as "not defective delinquents" did become recidivists. It seems reasonable to assume that the group committed by the courts as defective delinquents would have produced at least as high a percentage of recidivists as the group that was not committed.   Without the statute, the 807 men diagnosed as defective delinquents would have served fixed sentences in the Department of Corrections.   An 81 percent recidivist rate in this group would have produced 654 recidivists.

The difference between the 654 recidivists expected without this law and the 263 actual recidivists is 391;   this represents the approximate number of recidivists the law may be said to have prevented through June 1966.   Now, nearly five years later, I estimate the number of recidivists that the law has prevented to be well over 500.

Since the data show that the average recidivist has been convicted of several post-release offenses, the number of crimes that have been definitely prevented in this group was estimated at over 1,000 through June 1966.   By now this figure could easily have reached 1,500.   Recalling that there are on the average several unsolved offenses for every conviction, the volume of prevented crimes would seem to be even higher.   The effect of the law is of course cumulative, and each year adds a large increment to the volume of crime that this law is preventing.   FBI data on mobility of felony offenders strongly suggests that well over half of these prevented crimes would have occurred outside of Maryland.   Thus the benefits of this law have accrued to many states.

The data from this study tend to confirm the assumption that it is possible to identify a segment of the criminal population that probably will commit crimes if released after a fixed sentence.   The indeterminate sentence law appears to have been reasonably successful in achieving the dual purpose of protecting society from the defective delinquent while simultaneously handling him more effectively and humanely.

NOTES

1. Schreiber, Indeterminate Therapeutic Incarceration of Dangerous Criminals: Perspectives and Problems, 56 Va.L.Rev. 602, 615, 617, 619, 627–28 (1970) offers the following critical comments:

> A random sample conducted in 1965 of inmate records at Patuxent [82] demonstrates the uninformative nature of the "danger to society" standard. The sample discloses that nearly half of the inmates, who had been judged to pose an "actual danger to society" if released, had initially received criminal sentences of less than four years. The mean original sentence for inmates whose crimes could have resulted in ten-years' imprisonment was only 2.41 years.[83] Evidently, the judges who originally sentenced these inmates did not always regard them as especially dangerous to society. Such statistics cast grave doubts on the adequacy of the standards of Maryland's statutory scheme, under which men may remain in therapeutic confinement for as long as they live.

> * * *

> In past years, nearly one-half of Patuxent's inmates have been committed for acts other than assaultive crimes, and 96 of the 348 present inmates were convicted of property crimes, 40 of which did not endanger persons.[90] Such a result is inconsistent with the values of our society: human liberty deserves greater protection than property.

> * * *

> Experience at the Patuxent Institution confirms the difficulty of predicting dangerous behavior. Approximately 45 percent of those paroled by Patuxent have violated the terms of their parole, 26 percent by committing a new crime.[99] On the other hand, of the 432 inmates released by the courts contrary to the recommendations of Patuxent, all 432 of whom the staff believed were a danger to society at the time of their release, only 137, or 32 percent, committed new offenses.[100] These inaccurate predictions of dan-

---

82. Commission to Study Changes and Basis of Selection for Patuxent Institution, Report to Governor J. Millard Tawes (1965).

83. Id. at 47.

90. Letter from Dr. Arthur Kandel [Executive Secretary of Patuxent Institution, to the author, Jan. 6, 1970, copy on file at the Virginia Law Review].

99. Letter from Dr. Arthur Kandel, supra * * *. The statistics for the period 1959–69 show that 45% of the parolees violated their parole conditions, 26% by the commission of a new crime. 1969 Patuxent Institution Ann. Rep. 33–34.

100. Letter from Dr. Arthur Kandel, supra * * *. It should be noted that a number of those released by the courts had already been granted parole or leave by the institution. The Court decisions did, however, accelerate their complete release.

gerousness could have resulted in the needless incarceration of 295 individuals—68 percent of those released by court order over the staff's objections.

* * *

The rehabilitative effects of Patuxent's therapeutic approach are also open to question, even if any decrease in criminality is attributed to therapy rather than to other factors. Between 1955 and 1969, 333 inmates were paroled. Forty-five percent of these were returned to Patuxent, 26 percent for commission of a new offense and 19 percent for violating terms and conditions of parole or for other reasons.[139] This violation data should be compared with that for convicts who either did not undergo the therapeutic treatment at Patuxent or who were deemed insufficiently improved by it but were released by the courts against the staff recommendations. The rate of new offenses committed by these convicts was not substantially greater than for those considered to be "cured" by the institution.[140] The parole violation rate for other correction institutions in Maryland during the years 1965–1968 averaged about 10 percent.[141] Violation rates for other parts of the country range from 10 to 40 percent, and cluster around 25 percent.[142] Higher violation rates are to be expected at Patuxent, however, since its population primarily consists of hard-core, repeating offenders. Moreover, parole from Patuxent is more closely supervised for a longer period of time than is normal elsewhere, and the Board necessarily takes greater risks in granting parole. Prison systems should continue to offer inmates whatever benefits they can derive from psychotherapy, as imperfect as these may be. Nevertheless, the foregoing data falls short of supporting the effectiveness of an indeterminate sentence and therapeutic approach for rehabilitating prison inmates.

2. A number of jurisdictions have post-conviction procedures for indefinite detention of some offenders similar to the Maryland Defective Delinquency program but limited to sexual offenders. These are one version of the so-called "Sexual Psychopath Acts"; others provide for indefinite commitment before conviction of a criminal offense or before any charge has been filed. See generally The Mentally Disabled and the Law 341–75 (S. Brakel and R. Rock, eds., 2d ed. 1971). Although the precise language of the statutes varies, most apply to individuals who, because of mental disorder, have a propensity to the commission of sex offenses.

What procedures need be used in implementing such statutes? In Specht v. Patterson, 386 U.S. 605, 87 S.Ct. 1209, 18 L.Ed.2d 326 (1967) the Supreme Court held that for purposes of the constitutional requirement of

---

139. 1969 Patuxent Institution Ann. Rep. 33–34.

140. Between 1955 and 1969, 32% of those released from Patuxent by the courts contrary to the recommendation of the Board committed new offenses. Letter from Dr. Arthur Kandel, supra * * *.

141. Maryland Dep't of Parole and Probation, Five-Year Report 1965–1969, at 33–38 (1969).

142. See E. Sutherland, Principles of Criminology 652 (rev. ed. 1966). * * *

due process, such proceedings involved "the making of a new charge leading to criminal punishment" rather than merely the determination of the appropriate disposition of one convicted of an offense. Consequently, the Court declined to apply the flexible procedures it had approved for sentencing procedures in Williams v. New York, 337 U.S. 241, 69 S.Ct. 1079, 93 L.Ed. 1337 (1949). Williams held that during a normal sentencing procedure, the court was not required to hold hearings and to permit the defendant to participate in any hearings that may be held to determine the appropriate disposition. Due process, the Court held in Specht, means that in a Sex Offender proceeding the defendant is entitled to be present with counsel, to have an opportunity to be heard, to be confronted with the witnesses against him, to cross-examine these witnesses, and to offer evidence in his own behalf.

How "successful" are these programs? Kozol, Boucher, and Garofalo, The Diagnosis and Treatment of Dangerousness, 18 Crime and Delinquency 371 (1972) report on experience under the Massachusetts Sexually Dangerous Persons Act. This statute, similar to a number of others, permits the psychiatric examination of convicted offenders either before sentencing or during service of a sentence of imprisonment. If upon examination the offender is found by the examiners to be a sexually dangerous person, a court hearing may be held. If the court determines that the offender is a sexually dangerous person, he may then be committed to a treatment facility for an indefinite period. This study reports on 561 persons examined under this procedure. 304 were found by the examiners not to be sexually dangerous persons; these were then processed as "normal" offenders. In 257 cases, the examiners recommended a determination that the person was a sexually dangerous offender. In 226 cases, the court agreed; in 31 it did not. Of the 226 persons committed as sexually dangerous offenders, 82 were released by the medical authorities after an average of 43 months of treatment. 18 were released by courts against the advice of the medical authorities. The percentage of each category committing a serious assaultive crime after release was as follows:

304 offenders found by examiners not to be sexually dangerous offenders	8.6%
31 offenders found by examiners to be sexually dangerous persons but not committed by court	38.7%
82 offenders committed and released by medical authorities	6.1%
18 offenders committed but later released by court against recommendation of medical authorities	27.8%

Sexual offenders and specialized legal programs for dealing with them have stimulated a great deal of writing. For examinations of the Indiana program as it operates, see Cohen, Administration of the Criminal Sexual Psychopath Statute in Indiana, 32 Ind.L.J. 450 (1957) and Granucci and Granucci, Indiana's Sexual Psychopathic Act in Operation, 44 Ind.L.J. 555 (1969). For more general treatment of the issues, see, e. g., P. Gebhard, J. Gagnon, W. Pomeroy, and C. Christenson, Sex Offenders (1965); The Mentally Disabled and the Law 341–75 (S. Brakel and R. Rock, eds., 2d ed. 1971); Burick, An Analysis of the Illinois Sexually Dangerous Persons Act, 59 J.Crim.L., C. & P.S. 254 (1968); Sutherland, The Sexual Psychopath Laws, 40 J.Crim.L., C. & P.S. 543 (1950); Swanson, Sexual

Psychopath Statutes, 51 J.Crim.L., C. & P.S. 215 (1960); Tappan, Some Myths About the Sex Offender, 19 Fed.Prob. 7 (June 1955); Comment, Due Process for All—Constitutional Standards for Involuntary Civil Commitment and Release, 34 U.Chi.L.Rev. 633 (1967); Comment, The Validity of the Segregation of the Sexual Psychopath Under the Law, 26 Ohio St. L.J. 640 (1965).

A number of proposals would broaden "dangerous offender" provisions beyond "psychopaths" or "sexual psychopaths." Assuming that the major concern is the prevention of serious violent conduct on the part of offenders after release, what is the likelihood that workable criteria can be developed to isolate those offenders who pose a special high risk of such activity? Once isolated, this group could be subject to whatever therapeutic or incapacitating program was most appropriate. To be "workable," of course, the criteria must be one capable of application by correctional authorities to the large number of individuals convicted of criminal offenses. Wenk, Robison, and Smith, Can Violence Be Predicted? 18 Crime and Delinquency 393 (1972) reports an effort to develop practical criteria for such a task. The subjects used were 4,146 California Youth Authority wards admitted to a "reception center." The task was defined as formulating a criteria for defining a group that would include as many of the 104 wards that had committed a violent act within fifteen months of release and as few of the others as possible. The most optimistic expectation that the study offered—and one that it could not demonstrate success in reaching—would be the definition of a subgroup of about 450 of the 4,146 individuals which would contain half (52 of 104) of those who would subsequently commit violent offenses. If this expectation could be realized, what action should—or constitutionally could—be taken on the basis of it? Consider that anything done to all members of this group would involve "treating" or "incapacitating" eight harmless individuals for every truly dangerous individual, and would reach only half of the truly dangerous individuals.

3. To what extent, if any, should sentences of imprisonment which are within legislative limits be subject to constitutional attack on grounds of "excessiveness"? What standard should be used to resolve such attacks? Consider the following analysis by the California Supreme Court in In re Lynch, 8 Cal.3d 410, 105 Cal.Rptr. 217, 503 P.2d 921 (1972); Lynch attacked his life sentence for a second indecent exposure conviction on the ground that it violated the California state constitutional prohibition against cruel and unusual punishment:

> Petitioner urges, rather, that a life sentence *for indecent exposure* is cruel or unusual puunishment under the California Constitution because it is grossly disproportionate to the offense.

> No California court has yet held a statutory penalty unconstitutional on the ground it is disproportionate to the crime committed. The rule has been recognized, however, in several opinions considering the constitutionality of the death penalty. * * *

> A similar rule has evolved at the federal level in the interpretation of the cruel and unusual punishment clause of the Eighth Amendment. * * * [I]n the landmark case of Weems v. United States (1910) 217 U.S. 349, 30 S.Ct. 544, 54 L.Ed. 793 * * *,

a disbursing officer in a Philippine government bureau was convicted of making two false entries in his cash books. He was sentenced under a Philippine statute prescribing a minimum of 12 years' imprisonment for this crime, to be served in chains and at "hard and painful" labor, together with a fine, loss of numerous civil rights, and perpetual surveillance. The United States Supreme Court measured the statute against the cruel and unusual punishment clause of the Philippine Bill of Rights, which the court deemed to have the same meaning as the Eighth Amendment. Although undoubtedly influenced by the peculiar penalties imposed in addition to imprisonment, the court did not hold the law unconstitutional merely on the ground of the bizarre method of the punishment. Rather, the court quoted * * * an early Massachusetts case in which it was acknowledged that " '[imprisonment] in the State prison for a long term of years might be so disproportionate to the offense as to constitute a cruel and unusual punishment.' "

Reviewing in this light the minimum sentence permissible under the statute, the court observed that "Such penalties for such offenses amaze those who have formed their conception of the relation of a state to even its offending citizens from the practice of the American commonwealth, and believe that it is a precept of justice that punishment for crime should be graduated and proportioned to offense." The court concluded by invalidating the statute on the twofold ground that "It is cruel in its excess of imprisonment and that which accompanies and follows imprisonment. It is unusual in its character. Its punishments come under the condemnation of the bill of rights, both on account of their degree and kind."

* * *

Finally, the highest courts of our sister states have repeatedly invoked the rule of proportionality in applying their equivalents of our cruel or unusual punishment clause.[12] Thus in Workman v. Commonwealth (Ky.1968) 429 S.W.2d 374, a sentence of life imprisonment without possibility of parole for rape committed by juvenile defendants was held to be unconstitutionally disproportionate to the offense. In Cannon v. Gladden (1955) 203 Or. 629, 281 P.2d 233, a sentence of life imprisonment for assault with intent to commit rape was voided on this ground. In State v. Evans (1952) 73 Idaho 50, 245 P.2d 788, it was held in effect that life imprisonment for lewd and lascivious acts upon a child would be so excessive as to constitute cruel and unusual punishment. In Dembowski v. State (1968) 251 Ind. 250, 240 N.E.2d 815, a 25-year maximum indeterminate sentence for robbery was ruled unconstitutionally disproportionate to a lesser punishment for armed robbery. In State v. Kimbrough (1948) 212 S.C. 348, 46 S.E.2d 273, a sentence of 30 years at hard labor for burglary was held excessive. In People v. Lorentzen (1972) supra, 387 Mich. 167, 194

12. In certain states, it is true, the constitutional provision expressly directs that every penalty be proportioned to the offense. But the jurisdictions applying the rule are not limited to these few states.

N.W.2d 827, a mandatory minimum sentence of 20 years for selling marijuana was held so severe as to violate the cruel or unusual punishment clause.

Whether a particular punishment is disproportionate to the offense is, of course, a question of degree. The choice of fitting and proper penalties is not an exact science, but a legislative skill involving an appraisal of the evils to be corrected, the weighing of practical alternatives, consideration of relevant policy factors, and responsiveness to the public will; in appropriate cases, some leeway for experimentation may also be permissible. The judiciary, accordingly, should not interfere in this process unless a statute prescribes a penalty "out of all proportion to the offense" * * *, i. e., so severe in relation to the crime as to violate the prohibition against cruel or unusual punishment.

The courts have attempted to formulate a general description of that constitutional limit.

We conclude that in California a punishment may violate article I, section 6, of the Constitution if, although not cruel or unusual in its method, it is so disproportionate to the crime for which it is inflicted that it shocks the conscience and offends fundamental notions of human dignity.

To aid in administering this rule, we point to certain techniques used in the decisions discussed herein. First, a number of courts have examined the nature of the offense and/or the offender, with particular regard to the degree of danger both present to society. * * *

Also relevant to the question of proportionality is the nonviolent nature of the offense. * * *

Nor, finally, is nonviolence or absence of a victim a prerequisite to a finding of disproportionality. In appropriate cases the courts have nevertheless held the punishment excessive on the ground that no aggravating circumstances were shown. * * *

The second technique used by the courts is to compare the challenged penalty with the punishments prescribed in the *same jurisdiction* for *different offenses* which, by the same test, must be deemed more serious. The underlying but unstated assumption appears to be that although isolated excessive penalties may occasionally be enacted, e. g., through "honest zeal" generated in response to transitory public emotion, the Legislature may be depended upon to act with due and deliberate regard for constitutional restraints in prescribing the vast majority of punishments set forth in our statutes. The latter may therefore be deemed illustrative of constitutionally permissible degrees of severity; and if among them are found more serious crimes punished less severely than the offense in question, the challenged penalty is to that extent suspect.

*   *   *

Closely related to the foregoing is the third technique used in this inquiry, i. e., a comparison of the challenged penalty with the punishments prescribed for the *same offense* in *other jurisdictions* having an identical or similar constitutional provision. Here the assumption is that the vast majority of those jurisdictions will have prescribed punishments for this offense that are within the constitutional limit of severity; and if the challenged penalty is found to exceed the punishments decreed for the offense in a significant number of those jurisdictions, the disparity is a further measure of its excessiveness.

Does the analysis proposed by this court include anything it should not? Does it omit any relevant considerations? What result on the facts of Lynch?

---

c. PROBATION

TASK FORCE ON CORRECTIONS OF THE PRESIDENT'S COMMISSION ON LAW ENFORCEMENT AND ADMINISTRATION OF JUSTICE, TASK FORCE REPORT: CORRECTIONS

27, 7, 9, 30, 28 (1967).

Slightly more than half of the offenders sentenced to correctional treatment in 1965 were placed on probation—supervision in the community subject to the authority of the court. Table 1 sets forth data from the National Survey of Corrections and the Federal corrections system on the number of persons under probation on an average day in 1965 and the number in institutions or on parole. Also shown are estimates of what these populations are likely to be in 1975 on the basis of assumptions detailed in appendix B. As the table indicates, probation is the correctional treatment used for most offenders today and is likely to be used increasingly in the future.

Table 1.—Number of Offenders on Probation, and on Parole or in Institutions, 1965; Projections for 1975

Location of offender	1965		1975	
	Number	Percent	Number	Percent
Probation	684,088	53	1,071,000	58
Parole or institution	598,298	47	770,000	42
Total	1,282,386	100	1,841,000	100

SOURCES: 1965 data from National Survey of Corrections and special tabulations provded by the Federal Bureau of Prisons and the Administrative Office of the U.S. Courts; 1975 projections by R. Christensen, of the Commission's Task Force on Science and Technology, as described in Appendix B of this report.

[A9013]

* * *

The general underlying premise for the new directions in corrections [including the more frequent use of probation] is that crime and delinquency are symptoms of failures and disorganization of the community as well as of individual offenders. In particular, these failures are seen as depriving offenders of contact with the institutions that are basically responsible for assuring development of law-abiding conduct: sound family life, good schools, employment, recreational opportunities, and desirable companions, to name only some of the more direct influences. The substitution of deleterious habits, standards, and associates for these strengthening influences contributes to crime and delinquency.

The task of corrections therefore includes building or rebuilding solid ties between offender and community, integrating or reintegrating the offender into community life—restoring family ties, obtaining employment and education, securing in the larger sense a place for the offender in the routine functioning of society. This requires not only efforts directed toward changing the individual offender, which has been almost the exclusive focus of rehabilitation, but also mobilization and change of the community and its institutions. And these efforts must be undertaken without giving up the important control and deterrent role of corrections, particularly as applied to dangerous offenders.

*   *   *

The connection between social factors and crime was first systematically revealed in a series of studies carried on by Shaw and McKay at the University of Chicago during the 1920's.[1] These showed consistently high rates of delinquency in deteriorated areas within large cities, areas characterized by poverty and unemployment, residential mobility, broken homes, and evidence of disrupted social relationships such as mental illness, suicide, alcoholism, and narcotic addiction. Crime became in this perspective one of a wide array of symptoms of urban disorganization.

Other researchers undertook to explain the connection. One key to understanding delinquency in such deteriorated areas is the fact that people acquire the beliefs, values, attitudes, and habits of the groups with whom they are most closely associated. This idea is elaborated in Edwin Sutherland's theory of differential association, which hypothesized that people become delinquent to the extent that they participate in groups and neighborhoods where delinquent ideas and techniques are viewed favorably. The earlier, the longer, the more frequently, and the more intensely people participate in such social settings, the greater is the probability of their becoming delinquent.

An important corollary of this theory is that a person's attitude toward himself is determined by the evidence of support or opposition he sees in the responses of others toward him. If he receives praise,

1. [Footnotes renumbered.] See, for example, Clifford R. Shaw, Henry D. McKay, and others "Delinquency Areas, a Study of the Distribution of School Truants, Juvenile Delinquents, and Adult Offenders in Chicago" (Chicago: University of Chicago Press, 1929).

he comes to think of himself in the same light. When praise is associated with violations of society's codes and laws, the individual may accept nonconformity as a pathway to the favorable appraisals of others. The reverse, of course, is also true.

Other modern theories place emphasis on the concepts of "cultural disorganization" and "delinquent subcultures." Culture in this context refers to the system of goals and values that guide the conduct of a society's members. Cultural disorganization occurs when goals are contradictory and values conflicting. The term subculture describes a group that strongly endorses values and goals at odds with those of the dominant culture; a delinquent subculture is a system of values, beliefs, and practices that encourages participation in law violation and awards status on the basis of such participation.

Perhaps the development of these concepts most pertinent to reintegration as a mode of correctional treatment is that of Cloward and Ohlin [2] which built on work by Cohen [3] and others. It asserts that much delinquency is the result of inability to gain access to legitimate opportunities in our society, coupled with availability of illegitimate opportunities that are seized as alternatives by frustrated persons. Corrective action therefore should seek to increase the opportunities of the offender to succeed in law-abiding activities, while reducing his contacts with the criminal world.

Such theories have been formulated mainly in the context of crime by slum dwellers, particularly the young. The experiments and data on which they are based have most concerned this group, and their concentration on economic and social deprivation as the causative background of crime and delinquency reflects this perspective. But in fact these theories are not so exclusive in their implications. They can, for example, be applied to the many instances of middle-class and suburban delinquency in which school failure, family problems, and even the lack of exciting and challenging legitimate opportunities for use of leisure time are precipitating factors.

Nor do they deny that psychological causes operate in many criminal cases, particularly because the social and family disturbances on which they concentrate are also recognized today as important in psychological disturbance. Admittedly, however, further research and experimentation are necessary to develop these theories of social effect to the point where they can be of specific help in correctional treatment of particular offender types.

*   *   *

The main treatment implication of reintegration concepts is the value of community-based corrections. * * *

2. Richard A. Cloward and Lloyd E. Ohlin, "Delinquency and Opportunity" (Glencoe, Ill.: The Free Press, 1960).

3. See Albert K. Cohen, "Delinquent Boys: The Culture of the Gang" (Glencoe, Ill.: Free Press, 1955).

Probation was introduced initially as a humanitarian measure. The early pioneers simply wished to keep first offenders and minor recidivists from undergoing the corrupting effects of jail. They were volunteers—ministers and others—whose philosophy was that the offender was a deprived, perhaps uneducated person who needed help in adjusting to his environment.

During and after World War I, however, a marked change occurred in this orientation. As probation services continued to expand, there was increasing demand for professionally educated people, especially trained social workers, to serve as probation officers. The training of social workers, in turn, was profoundly influenced by the introduction of psychiatric, especially psychoanalytic, theory, and was primarily concerned with the individual and his emotional problems and deficiencies.

The emphasis was on seeing the offender as a disturbed person for whom some degree of psychotherapy was indicated. The professional probation caseworker, therefore, came to be valued for his ability to offer such individually oriented therapy.

More recent theories of reintegration * * * are now influencing the training of probation officers and place greater emphasis on developing the offender's effective participation in the major social institutions of the school, business, and the church, among others, which offer access to a successful, nondelinquent career. Experience with programs that have attempted rehabilitation in isolation from these institutions indicates that generally such efforts have only a marginal bearing on an offender's success or failure.

This point of view does not deny the importance of increasing individual capacity, but it does make clear that correctional techniques are nearsighted when they fail to take into account and make needed changes in an offender's social and cultural milieu. Successful adjustment on his part will often require some kind of personal reformation, but it will also usually require conditions within the community that will encourage his reintegration into nondelinquent activities and institutions.

                    *   *   *

There are many offenders for whom incarceration is the appropriate sanction—either because of their dangerousness or the seriousness of their offense, or both. But in the vast majority of cases where such a sanction is not obviously essential, there has been growing disenchantment with relying heavily on institutions to achieve correctional goals. The growing emphasis on community treatment is supported by several kinds of considerations.

* * * [T]he correctional strategy that presently seems to hold the greatest promise, based on social science theory and limited research, is that of reintegrating the offender into the community. A key element in this strategy is to deal with problems in their social

context, which means in the interaction of the offender and the community. It also means avoiding as much as possible the isolating and labeling effects of commitment to an institution. There is little doubt that the goals of reintegration are furthered much more readily by working with an offender in the community than by incarcerating him.

These justifications seem to be borne out by the record of probation services themselves. Probation services have been characteristically poorly staffed and often poorly administered. Despite that, the success of those placed on probation, as measured by not having probation revoked, has been surprisingly high. One summary analysis of outcomes observed in 11 probation studies indicates a success rate of from 60 to 90 percent.[4] A survey of probation effectiveness in such States as Massachusetts and New York and a variety of foreign countries provides similar results with a success rate at about 75 percent.[5] An exhaustive study was undertaken in California when 11,638 adult probationers granted probation during the period 1956-58 were followed up after 7 years. Of this group, almost 72 percent were successful in terms of not having their probation revoked.[6]

These findings were not obtained under controlled conditions, nor were they supported by data that distinguished among the types of offenders who succeeded or the types of services that were rendered. Nevertheless, all of the success rates are relatively high. They are the product of a variety of kinds of probation administered at different times and places. Even when interpreted skeptically, they are powerful evidence that a substantial number of persons can be placed on probation and have a relatively high rate of success.

 * * * [T]wo controlled experiments, one in Utah and one in California, [have attempted to measure] the relative effectiveness of institutionalization and community supervision under special conditions with small caseloads and specifically designed treatment programs were directly tested with randomly selected groups. In both instances the special community treatment was clearly superior in terms of reducing recidivism.

Perhaps the best known effort to determine the extent to which probation services could be used was a demonstration project conducted in Saginaw, Mich., over a 3-year period.[7] Here, trained probation officers with relatively low caseloads were assigned to an adult crim-

4. Ralph W. England, Jr., "What Is Responsible for Satisfactory Probation and Post-Probation Outcome?" Journal of Criminal Law, Criminology, and Police Science, 47:667–676 (March-April 1957).

5. Max Grunhut, "Penal Reform" (New York: The Clarendon Press, 1948), pp. 60–82.

6. George F. Davis, "A Study of Adult Probation Violation Rates by Means of the Cohort Approach," Journal of Criminal Law, Criminology, and Police Science, 55:70–85 (March 1964).

7. "The Saginaw Probation Demonstration Project," Michigan Crime and Delinquency Council of the National Council on Crime and Delinquency (New York: The Council, 1963).

inal court that had used probation a little more than the 50 percent average for the State. With full services available, including complete social histories for the use of the court at the time of sentencing, judges imposed prison sentences for only about 20 percent of all of the defendants who appeared before them. There is some evidence that the revocation rate for those granted probation was lower than in the prior 3-year period. Although these findings require more rigorous testing, they lend weight to the view that a high percentage of offenders can be supervised in the community and succeed.

Offenders can be kept under probation supervision at much less cost than in institutions. The National Survey found, for example, that the average State spends about $3,400 a year (excluding capital costs) to keep a youth in a State training school, while it costs only about one-tenth that amount to keep him on probation.

Objections might be raised as to the validity of such comparisons, since expenditures for probation services are now much too meager. However, with the 1-to-10 cost ratios prevailing, probation expenditures can clearly be increased several fold and still remain less expensive than institutional programs. This is especially true when construction costs, which now run up to and beyond $20,000 per bed in a correctional institution, are included. The differential becomes even greater if the cost of welfare assistance for the families of the incarcerated and the loss in taxable income are considered.

---

3. A PROPOSED CLASSIFICATION SCHEME

PROPOSED FEDERAL CRIMINAL CODE

(1971)

§ 3002. Classification of Offenses

(1) Felonies. Felonies are classified for the purpose of sentence into the following three categories:

(a) Class A felonies [including murder, kidnapping and forcible rape];

(b) Class B felonies [including manslaughter, arson, burglary of a dwelling at night, robbery with a deadly weapon, and theft of property exceeding $100,000 value]; and

(c) Class C felonies [including negligent homicide, aggravated assault, reckless endangerment of human life, burglaries not class B felonies, robberies not class B felonies, and theft of property exceeding $500 value but not exceeding $100,000 value].

* * *

Chapter 31.   Probation and Unconditional Discharge

§ 3101.   Criteria for Utilizing Chapter

(1) Eligibility.   A person who has been convicted of a federal offense may be sentenced to probation or unconditional discharge as provided in this Chapter.

(2) Criteria.   The court shall not impose a sentence of imprisonment upon a person unless, having regard to the nature and circumstances of the offense and to the history and character of the defendant, it is satisfied that imprisonment is the more appropriate sentence for the protection of the public because:

(a) there is undue risk that during a period of probation the defendant will commit another crime;

(b) the defendant is in need of correctional treatment that can most effectively be provided by a sentence to imprisonment * * *; or

(c) a sentence to probation or unconditional discharge will unduly depreciate the seriousness of the defendant's crime, or undermine respect for law.

(3) Factors to be Considered.   The following factors, or the converse thereof where appropriate, while not controlling the discretion of the court, shall be accorded weight in making determinations called for by subsection (2):

(a) the defendant's criminal conduct neither caused nor threatened serious harm to another person or his property;

(b) the defendant did not plan or expect that his criminal conduct would cause or threaten serious harm to another person or his property;

(c) the defendant acted under strong provocation;

(d) there were substantial grounds which, though insufficient to establish a legal defense, tend to excuse or justify the defendant's conduct;

(e) the victim of the defendant's conduct induced or facilitated its commission;

(f) the defendant has made or will make restitution or reparation to the victim of his conduct for the damage or injury which was sustained;

(g) the defendant has no history of prior delinquency or criminal activity, or has led a law-abiding life for a substantial period of time before the commission of the present offense;

(h) the defendant's conduct was the result of circumstances unlikely to recur;

(i) the character, history and attitudes of the defendant indicate that he is unlikely to commit another crime;

(j) the defendant is particularly likely to respond affirmatively to probationary treatment;

(k) the imprisonment of the defendant would entail undue hardship to himself or his dependents;

(*l*) the defendant is elderly or in poor health;

(m) the defendant did not abuse a public position of responsibility or trust; and

(n) the defendant cooperated with law enforcement authorities by bringing other offenders to justice, or otherwise.

Nothing herein shall be deemed to require explicit reference to these factors in a presentence report or by the court at sentencing.

§ 3102. Incidents of Probation

(1) Periods.   Unless terminated as provided in subsection (2), the periods during which a sentence to probation shall remain conditional and be subject to revocation are:

(a) for a felony, 5 years;

(b) for a misdemeanor, 2 years;

(c) for an infraction, 1 year.

(2) Early Termination.   The court may terminate a period of probation and discharge the defendant at any time earlier than that provided in subsection (1) if warranted by the conduct of the defendant and the ends of justice.

Chapter 32.   Imprisonment

§ 3201.   Sentence of Imprisonment: Incidents

(1) Authorized Terms.   The authorized terms of imprisonment are:

(a) for a Class A felony, no more than 30 years;

(b) for a Class B felony, no more than 15 years;

(c) for a Class C felony, no more than 7 years;

(d) for a Class A misdemeanor, no more than 1 year [6 months];

(e) for a class B misdemeanor, no more than 30 days.

Such terms shall be administered as provided in Part C of this Code.

(2) Components of Maximum Term for Indefinite Sentence.   A sentence of imprisonment of more than six months shall be an indefinite sentence.   The maximum term of every indefinite sentence imposed by the court shall include a prison component and a parole

component. The parole component of such maximum term shall be (i) one-third for terms of nine years or less; (ii) three years for terms between nine and fifteen years, and (iii) five years for terms more than fifteen years; and the prison component shall be the remainder of such maximum term. If, however, the parole component so computed is less than three years, the court may increase it up to three years.

(3) Minimum Term. An indefinite sentence for a Class A or B felony shall have no minimum term unless by the affirmative action of the court a term is set at no more than one-third of the prison component actually imposed. No other indefinite sentence shall have a minimum term. The court shall not impose a minimum term unless, having regard to the nature and circumstances of the offense and the history and character of the defendant, it is of the opinion that such a term is required because of the exceptional features of the case, such as warrant imposition of a term in the upper range under section 3202. The court shall set forth its reasons in detail. Except in the most extraordinary cases, the court shall obtain both a presentence report and a report from the Bureau of Corrections under section 3004 before imposing a minimum term.

(4) Minimum Term; Alternative; Further Powers. In lieu of imposing a minimum term, the court may make a recommendation to the Board of Parole as to when the defendant should first be considered for parole. The court shall not recommend a parole eligibility date which is beyond the time when the court could have fixed a minimum term under subsection (3). The court shall have the authority to reduce an imposed minimum term to time served upon motion of the Bureau of Corrections made at any time, upon notice to the United States Attorney.

§ 3202. Upper-Range Imprisonment for Dangerous Felons

(1) Authorization. The maximum term for a felony shall not be set at more than 20 years for a Class A felony, 10 years for a Class B felony or 5 years for a Class C felony unless, having regard to the nature and circumstances of the offense and the history and character of the defendant as it relates to that offense, the court is of the opinion that a term in excess of these limits is required for the protection of the public from further criminal conduct by the defendant because the defendant is a dangerous special offender.

(2) Definitions. A defendant is a dangerous special offender for purposes of this section if:

(a) he has previously been convicted of two or more felonies committed on occasions different from one another and from such felony and for one or more of such convictions he has been imprisoned prior to the commission of such felony, and less than five years have elapsed between the commission of such felony and either his release, on parole or otherwise, from imprisonment for one such conviction or his commission of the last such previous felony; or

(b) he committed such felony as part of a pattern of criminal conduct which constituted a substantial source of his income, and in which he manifested special skill or expertise; or

(c) his mental condition is abnormal, and makes him a serious danger to the safety of others, and he committed such felony as an instance of aggressive behavior with heedless indifference to the consequences of such behavior. An offender shall not be found to be a dangerous special offender under this paragraph unless the court has obtained a report from the Bureau of Corrections * * * which includes the results of a comprehensive psychiatric examination;

(d) such felony was, or he committed such felony in furtherance of, a conspiracy with three or more other persons to engage in a pattern of criminal conduct and he did, or agreed that he would, initiate, organize, plan, finance, direct, manage, or supervise all or part of such conspiracy or conduct, or give or receive a bribe or use force as all or part of such conduct; or

(e) he manifested his special dangerousness by using a firearm or destructive device in the commission of the offense or flight therefrom.

A conviction shown on direct or collateral review or at the hearing to be invalid or for which the defendant has been pardoned on the ground of innocence shall be disregarded for purposes of paragraph (a). In support of findings under paragraph (b), it may be shown that the defendant has had in his own name or under his control income or property not explained as derived from a source other than such conduct. For purposes of paragraph (b), a substantial source of income means a source of income which for any period of one year or more exceeds the minimum wage, determined on the basis of a forty-hour week and a fifty-week year, without reference to exceptions, under section 6(a)(1) of the Fair Labor Standards Act of 1938 (52 Stat. 1602, as amended 80 Stat. 838), and as hereafter amended, for an employee engaged in commerce or in the production of goods for commerce, and which for the same period exceeds fifty percent of the defendant's declared adjusted gross income under section 62 of the Internal Revenue Act of 1954 (68A Stat. 17, as amended 83 Stat. 655), and as hereafter amended. For purposes of paragraph (b), special skill or expertise in criminal conduct includes unusual knowledge, judgment or ability, including manual dexterity, facilitating the initiation, organizing, planning, financing, direction, management, supervision, execution or concealment of criminal conduct, the enlistment of accomplices in such conduct, the escape from detection or apprehension of such conduct, or the disposition of the fruits or proceeds of such conduct. For purposes of paragraphs (b) and (c), criminal conduct forms a pattern if it embraces criminal acts that have the same or similar purposes, results, participants, victims, or methods of commission, or otherwise are interrelated by distinguishing characteristics and are not isolated events.

(3) Notice. Whenever an attorney charged with the prosecution of a defendant in a court of the United States for an alleged felony committed when the defendant was over the age of twenty-one years has reason to believe that the defendant is a dangerous special offender such attorney, a reasonable time before trial or acceptance by the court of a plea of guilty or nolo contendere, may sign and file with the court, and may amend, a notice specifying that the defendant is a dangerous special offender who upon conviction for such felony is subject to the imposition of a sentence under subsection (1), and setting out with particularity the reasons why such attorney believes the defendant to be a dangerous special offender. In no case shall the fact that the defendant is alleged to be a dangerous special offender be an issue upon the trial of such felony, be disclosed to the jury, or be disclosed before any plea of guilty or nolo contendere or verdict or finding of guilty to the presiding judge without the consent of the parties. If the court finds that the filing of the notice as a public record may prejudice fair consideration of a pending criminal matter, it may order the notice sealed and the notice shall not be subject to subpoena or public inspection during the pendency of such criminal matter, except on order of the court, but shall be subject to inspection by the defendant alleged to be a dangerous special offender and his counsel.

(4) Hearing. Upon any plea of guilty or nolo contendere or verdict or finding of guilty of the defendant of such felony, a hearing shall be held, before sentence is imposed, by the court sitting without a jury. Except in the most extraordinary cases, the court shall obtain both a presentence report and a report from the Bureau of Corrections under section 3004 before holding a hearing under this subsection. The court shall fix a time for the hearing, and notice thereof shall be given to the defendant and the United States at least ten days prior thereto. The court shall permit the United States and counsel for the defendant, or the defendant if he is not represented by counsel, to inspect the presentence report sufficiently prior to the hearing as to afford a reasonable opportunity for verification. In extraordinary cases, the court may withhold material not relevant to a proper sentence, diagnostic opinion which might seriously disrupt a program of rehabilitation, any source of information obtained on a promise of confidentiality, and material previously disclosed in open court. A court withholding all or part of a presentence report shall inform the parties of its action and place in the record the rea-

sons therefor. The court may require parties inspecting all or part of a presentence report to give notice of any part thereof intended to be controverted. In connection with the hearing, the defendant and the United States shall be entitled to assistance of counsel, compulsory process, and cross-examination of such witnesses as appear at the hearing. A duly authenticated copy of a former judgment or commitment shall be prima facie evidence of such former judgment or commitment. If it appears by a preponderance of the information, including information submitted during the trial of such felony and the sentencing hearing and so much of the presentence report as the court relies upon, that the defendant is a dangerous special offender, the court shall sentence the defendant to imprisonment for an appropriate term as specified in subsection (1). The court shall place in the record its findings including an identification of the information relied upon in making such findings, and its reasons for the sentence imposed.

II. THE CRIMINALIZATION DECISION

The decision whether or to what extent to use the criminal law to deal with a social problem (whether to "criminalize" some or all aspects of the problem) is obviously an extremely complex one. Considerations as to the existence, definition, and seriousness of the social problem, the effectiveness of criminalization as a means of eliminating or minimizing the problem, alternative means of dealing with the social problem and their effectiveness, and potential adverse effects ("costs") of criminalization must all be considered. Professor Packer has defined the problem as follows:

> What are the criteria that ought to guide the exercise of * * * judgment regarding the appropriate occasions for invoking the criminal sanction? How are we to decide what kinds of conduct should be made criminal?
>
>   *   *   *
>
> In a sense, all limiting criteria reduce themselves to a simple prescription: first things first. The criminal sanction is the law's ultimate threat. Being punished for a crime is different from being regulated in the public interest, or being forced to compensate another who has been injured by one's conduct, or being treated for a disease. The sanction is at once uniquely coercive and, in the broadest sense, uniquely expensive. It should be reserved for what really matters.
>
> Considerations of several kinds enter into a determination of what "things" should be considered "first." On the credit side of the ledger are the social gains that will accrue from the successful prevention or reduction of the conduct in question, discounted by the prospects of achieving success (however defined). On the debit side are the moral and practical costs reckoned in terms of values other than the prevention of antisocial conduct. Finally, there is the question of alternatives: what other means of social control are available to achieve the same ends? The question of alternatives is particularly crucial. If there are readily available alternatives that avoid or minimize the formidable battery of objections and obstacles we have been considering, they must be carefully weighed. If there are not, we must face, rather than reject out of hand, the alternative of doing nothing.
> * * *

H. Packer, The Limits of the Criminal Sanction 250 (1968).
Initially, of course, the problem is one of legislative decision-making. But Robinson v. California and Powell v. Texas raise the question of

whether a similar analysis can—or should—be avoided when the legislative decision to criminalize is attacked in the courts on constitutional grounds.

It is generally difficult to discuss such matters in the abstract. Therefore, the following material presents, in addition to general considerations, selections discussing in some detail one of the many current social problems raising issues concerning the propriety of criminalization: alcohol intoxication or intoxication-related activity. For discussion, see H. Packer, The Limits of the Criminal Sanction 249–366 (1968); The President's Commission on Law Enforcement and Administration of Justice, Task Force Report: The Courts 97–107 (1967); The President's Commission on Law Enforcement and Administration of Justice, Task Force Report: Drunkenness (1967); Kadish, The Crisis of Overcriminalization, 374 Annals 157 (1967).

NOTE

For materials discussing the legal issues raised in this section, see Fingarette, Perils of Powell: In Search of A Factual Foundation for the "Disease Concept of Alcoholism," 83 Harv.L.Rev. 793 (1970); Greenawalt, "Uncontrollable" Actions and the Eighth Amendment: Implications of Powell v. Texas, 69 Colum.L.Rev. 927 (1969); Merrill, Drunkenness and Reform of the Criminal Law, 54 Va.L.Rev. 1135 (1968); Stern, Public Drunkenness: Crime or Health Problem, 374 Annals 147 (1967); Tao, Alcoholism as a Defense to Crime, 45 Notre Dame Law. 68 (1969); Tao, Criminal Drunkenness and the Law, 54 Iowa L.Rev. 1059 (1969).

A.   ALCOHOL USE AND ABUSE: A POTENTIAL SOCIAL PROBLEM

BLUM AND BRAUNSTEIN, MIND–ALTERING DRUGS AND DANGEROUS BEHAVIOR, IN THE PRESIDENT'S COMMISSION ON LAW ENFORCEMENT AND ADMINISTRATION OF JUSTICE, TASK FORCE REPORT: DRUNKENNESS

29, at 29–30 (1967).

In the case of alcohol use, unlike the situation with other drugs, we are fortunate to have recently completed national survey data on drinking practices which allow excellent estimates of who drinks how much in the United States. * * * 68 percent of all American adults have had at least one drink within the past year. Twenty-two percent of the population report they have never tried an alcoholic beverage. With reference to alcoholism, * * * the number of Americans who are alcoholics probably ranges between 4,500,000

* * * and 6,800,000 escapist heavy drinkers * * *. The "actual" number of alcoholics may be less or greater than the foregoing range, depending on the definition of alcoholism employed and the estimation method.

* * *

Among the 12 percent of the total population classified as heavy drinkers, 6 percent were found to be escape-oriented heavy drinkers or problem drinkers. * * * These escapist drinkers were older, of lower socioeconomic status and included more than an expected number of Negroes. They were people not well integrated in society. They were also people who worried about their drinking, who said they had more than their share of problems, who had unhappy childhoods, who claimed poor health, and who were dissatisfied with their achievements in life.

B. DEFINITION OF THE PROBLEM

BLUM AND BRAUNSTEIN, MIND–ALTERING DRUGS AND DANGEROUS BEHAVIOR, IN THE PRESIDENT'S COMMISSION ON LAW ENFORCEMENT AND ADMINISTRATION OF JUSTICE, TASK FORCE REPORT: DRUNKENNESS

29, at 34–35 (1967).

The effects of alcohol, as with other mind-altering drugs, depend upon the circumstances of use, past drug experience and personality of the individual, concurrent physiological status, dosage per body weight, rate of absorption (in turn dependent upon simultaneous food use, the other constituents of the alcoholic beverage employed, and the condition of the stomach and intestine) and the rate of excretion and detoxification. Route of administration matters as well, but since alcohol is usually taken by mouth this factor does not affect most calculations. In considering acute effects, blood alcohol levels are most clearly associated with its effects. For example at blood levels of 0.20 percent, depressed sensory and motor functions are marked, and loss of some social control occurs. At 0.50 percent drunkenness occurs, at 0.60 percent unconsciousness, and at 0.70 percent death. There are, of course, individual variations in this picture. A later effect, occurring several hours later and in conjunction with lowered blood sugar levels, is the well-known hangover, the causes of which are unknown * * *.

The prediction of chronic adverse effects is more difficult, for these are interrelated * * * with nutrition, exposure to stress, and a variety of other social and physiological circumstances. Alcoholism itself is associated with earlier than expected deaths and a

high frequency of cardiovascular disease, tuberculosis, and cirrhosis of the liver. Accidental deaths will also occur at a higher than average rate, these frequently involving persons other than the drinker.
* * *

Attention to the acute physical effects and chronic social and physical consequences should not allow us to overlook the adverse social effects arising from either occasional or frequent use when no alcoholism as such is present. One of the best illustrations of these hazards comes from a study of college drinking * * *. Alcoholism, because it takes some years to develop, is not found in college youth, but social complications and psychological distress do occur, most often among those drinking the most. On the basis of a questionnaire study, Straus and Bacon report that 17 percent of the men and 8 percent of the women have failed in a social obligation because of drinking, 11 percent of the men and 8 percent of the women have suffered damaged friendships because of alcohol, 4 percent of the men and 1 percent of the women have had an accident or injury attributable to drinking, and 2 percent of the men have experienced formal punishment or discipline (including arrest, expulsion, etc.) because of drinking. These foregoing are essentially progressive troubles; that is, the 2 percent disciplined are part of the 4 percent with accidents and part of the 11 percent with disrupted friendships. It is to be noted that 17 percent of the men and 10 percent of the women reported anxiety over their drinking, fearing dependency. Jellinek * * * gives as warning signs of progressive alcoholic disease the presence of blackouts, getting drunk when alone, early morning drinking, and being aggressive or destructive when drunk. Given the collegians' fears about their drinking future, it is interesting to learn that 18 percent of the men had had blackouts, 13 percent of the men had become drunk when alone, 16 percent of the men had drunk before or instead of breakfast, and 11 percent had behaved destructively at least once when drunk. Eight percent of the males reported two or more of these warning signs as did 1 percent of the females.

NOTES

1. To what extent, if any, should the law be concerned with the physical health of some drinkers? with their public appearances in an intoxicated condition? with their "disorderly conduct?" with their general life style? To what extent, if any, are other factors proper subjects of concern? Consider the following from Blum and Braunstein, Mind-Altering Drugs and Dangerous Behavior, in The President's Commission on Law Enforcement and Administration of Justice, Task Force Report: Drunkenness 29, at 35–37, 39, 40–43 (1967):

Alcohol and Suicide

* * *

Alcohol is clearly implicated in both suicide attempts and completed suicide. Alcoholics are more likely to commit suicide than nonalcoholics. However, nonalcoholics may also use alcohol in connection with their suicidal efforts. As a tentative finding one adds that when alcoholics commit suicide they are likely to have a history of prior suicide threats or attempts, to be depressed, not to be living in skid row or some other supporting-accepting environment but to lack any close or important relations with other people, and to be in older age brackets. There is not agreement among studies as to whether suicidal efforts occur most often among alcoholics when they are sober, slightly tipsy, intoxicated, or during the hangover phase. Except for cases of intentional acute alcohol poisoning, there are grounds for arguing—on insufficient evidence—that blood levels of alcohol will not be high since to succeed at suicide requires the capacity for muscle control and planful action. It is also reasonable to expect that the presence of alcoholism itself, along with its often disastrous social consequences, is of importance as a crucial element—in the mind of the alcoholic—in the suicide decision. On the other hand, viewed etiologically, the type of life events which lead to alcoholism per se are also likely to lead to suicide per se; or to be associated with a variety of other unhappy choices of conduct. Given this probability, it may be oversimplifying to say that alcoholism or alcohol use is *the* critical factor in suicides by drinking people. Nevertheless the presence of alcoholism and alcohol use is so great as to demand the conclusion that alcoholism or alcohol use are at least one critical factor in producing suicidal behavior.

SUICIDE AND ALCOHOL USE: SUMMARY

Alcoholics attempt and also complete suicide at a rate much higher than the nonalcoholic population. Drinking by nonalcoholics also appears to precede much suicidal behavior. Although alcoholism itself may not cause suicide—since the history and life circumstances of the drinker undoubtedly are necessary elements for a suicidal outcome—the presence of alcoholism is a strong warning of suicidal risk.   *   *   *

Alcohol and Traffic Accidents

*   *   *

Estimates on the percentage of accidents caused by drinking drivers compared to nondrinking drivers vary considerably, the range being from 1 to 50 percent. Unfortunately, sufficient care is not exercised in many studies in separating cause from involvement. In any case, alcohol is only a conditional variable among a number of other possible causative factors. Andréasson presents statistics as follows for various countries on the percentage of total traffic accidents where alcohol was involved: Spain, 1.5 percent; Belgium, 2.5 percent; France, 2 percent; Sweden, 2.9 percent; Israel, 0.2 percent; Finland, 7.6 percent; and Switzerland, 6.0 percent. In 25.4 percent of the fatal accidents in 1951 in California, a driver or pedestrian had been drinking.

The time at which the alcohol-related accidents are occurring is a relevant condition. Jeffcoate and Spriggs find that in accidents occurring after 10 p. m. alcohol is an associated factor in 50 percent of the cases. It is to be noted that many investigators hold that present police report statistics do not present an accurate measure of the extent of road accidents caused by drunken driving. Data derived from studies using chemical tests and controlled experimental methods reveal that the figures on alcohol involvement are much higher than conventional statistics suggest. The remainder of our alcohol and accidents discussion will confine itself to the controlled surveys and studies done under specified conditions.

*   *   *

Adequate studies * * * determine the blood alcohol levels of drivers involved in traffic accidents (personal injury and fatal motor and pedestrian accidents) and compare these figures with the blood alcohol levels of a control group of drivers or pedestrians who were not involved in the accident but were passing the accident site either at the time of the accident or at a later date. In addition, Smith and Popham contend it is ideal to sample only those drivers who are responsible for their accidents, differentiating out those who were innocent victims of someone else's error. We suspect that innocence is hard to establish, especially because defensive driving abilities may also be reduced by alcohol.

Results of investigations agree that there is an excess of drivers in accidents with levels of blood alcohol beginning at 0.04 to 0.05 percent as compared with now-accident controls. As alcohol level increases the percentage of such drivers included in accidents increases sharply. Smith and Popham state that drivers with 0.15 percent and over were present eight times more often in the accident than in the control group. On the basis of their findings, it was estimated that accident involvement with blood alcohol levels between 0.05 and 0.10 percent is 1½ times greater than below 0.05 percent and beyond 0.15 percent is approximately 10 times greater. * * *

What are the characteristics of the accident-involved "drinking and driving" population? Although popular belief has it that most alcoholic drivers are but social drinkers (normal, moderate, or heavy) the high levels of blood alcohol concentration present in the fatal car drivers and fatally injured pedestrians might lead one to wonder whether a sizable subgroup are not problem or pathological drinkers. From a statistical standpoint it is unlikely that most drinking drivers are alcoholics—only 1 out of every 14 to 20 citizens ($+/-$) is an alcoholic. Moreover some alcoholics rapidly become so drunk that they are unable to drive, or knowing themselves, take care not to drive. However, numerous studies analyzing the drinking patterns of accident-involved drivers reveal that a large proportion of them do have alcohol problems. Goldberg examined a group of arrested Swedish drunken drivers who were convicted for the second time on a drunken driving charge; 45.4 percent had alcohol problems compared to a problem rate of 8.8 percent for the general Swedish population. Selzer and Payne et al. (1963), investigated 67 persons arrested for driving while intoxicated in Ann Arbor, Mich. They found that 37 were alcoholics (55 percent), 10 were border-line cases (15 percent), and 4 were prealcoholic (6 percent)—a total of 76 percent with alcohol problems. Selzer and Weiss determined the incidence of chronic alcoholism in drivers responsible for fatal (nonpedestrian) traffic accidents in Washteran County, Mich. (1961–64). Of the 72 drivers, 40 percent were alcoholic, 10 percent were prealcoholic, and 50 percent were nonalcoholic. Of the 64 percent of the drivers who had been drinking prior to the accident, 75 percent were alcoholics or pre-alcoholics who usully had blood alcohol levels in excess of 0.14 percent. Forty-five of the alcoholic drivers had at least one prior arrest for drunk driving or drunk and disorderly conduct, and 16 had at one time driven with revoked licenses including 3 who had no license at the time of the accident. Also, alcoholic drivers were responsible for significantly more prior serious accidents and moving traffic violations than the nonalcoholic drivers. Two of the other alcoholic drivers had killed other persons in prior traffic accidents while driving in an intoxicated state!

* * * A study by the State of California Transportation Agency correlated the drunken drivers' alcohol level at the time of the fatal accident with their previous number of drunkenness arrests. The correlation was 0.92. That means that a drinking driver with high blood alcohol levels who kills someone nearly always (over 80 percent of the time) had prior drunk driving arrests. It is noteworthy that studies of the characteristics of problem drinkers involved in accidents show them as would be expected to be heavily drawn from the lower class. The chances are that this group is least likely to carry liability insurance and least able to pay indemnities to accident victims or their families. So it is that problem drinkers not only cause the most suffering and loss but are least likely to be able to make reparations. It would be useful to know what the actual insurance coverage of such drivers is. Such a study recommends itself.

49,000 deaths and 1,800,000 injuries [were caused] during 1965 in motor vehicle accidents. * * *

Alcohol and Crime

The basic question is, is alcohol related to crime? The basic answer is, "yes." When one gets away from the basic question and begins to seek an understanding of the many ways in which alcohol is implicated in criminality, the questions become more complex. * * *

Alcohol Implication by Type of Crime

In addition to the 55 percent of arrests that are for alcohol use offenses per se, a considerable number of other offenses are committed by persons—or suffered by victims—who have been drinking just prior to the commission of the offense. Some crimes show a high frequency of alcohol involvement; others a low one. Homicide for example is an alcohol-related crime; Cleveland in a Cincinnati study found that 44 percent of a sample of homicide victims had blood alcohol levels over 0.15 percent. Bullock in a Texas study found that 28.5 percent of a time sample of homicides took place in public places where liquor was served. Fisher in a Baltimore report states that 69 percent of homicide victims there had been drinking. Bowden and Wilson found 47 percent of homicide victims in Australia had been drinking. Shupe in an Ohio study found 43 percent of the homicide offenders had been drinking. Spain et al. found 87 percent of a small sample of homicide offenders had been drinking. The most comprehensive study of homicides is that by Wolfgang. Among 588 Philadelphia cases alcohol was *absent* from both victim and offender in only 36 percent of the cases. In 9 percent of the cases alcohol was present in the victim only; in 11 percent of the cases it was present in the offender only. In 44 percent of the cases it was present in *both* the victim and offender. Consequently in 64 percent of the homicide cases alcohol was a factor; and in the majority of these alcohol was present in both parties to the crime.

* * *

On the basis of the present data one can say that there is a strong link between alcohol and homicide and that the presumption is that alcohol plays a causal role as one of the necessary and precipitating elements for violence. Such a role is in keeping with the most probable effects of alcohol as a depressant of inhibition control centers in the brain—leading to release of impulses. One must keep in mind that even if alcohol is a necessary element for some murders, it is not necessary for all of them and further that alcohol use quite obviously does not necessarily lead to violence. An additional point is that alcohol use is likely to be but one element in a life pattern which increases the risk of being a homicide offender or victim (and it is sometimes chance which says which a person will turn out to be). For example, the Wolfgang study showed that 64 percent of the offenders and 47 percent of the victims had prior arrests. More important, the majority of these arrests were not for crimes against property (the predominant kind of nonalcohol use crime) but for crimes against person.

There is no study of other types of crime which compares with that of Wolfgang for careful and detailed analysis of persons and settings. Shupe examined blood and urine for alcohol in a group of 882 Columbus, Ohio, felons arrested either during or immediately after the offense. Presuming guilt, he found that alcohol was present more often in crimes of violence (e. g., 92 percent of the "cuttings" and concealed weapon arrests) and less often during more skilled offenses against property; e. g., 60 percent in forgery. The curious thing is that the 60 percent forgery figure is the lowest one. Two questions immediately arise. One is, given the criterion for inclusion in the study of immediate arrest during or after the offense, is it only inebriates who get caught right away? Perhaps "yes" since the majority of the alcohol blood levels of the arrested offenders were over 0.20. The second question is, what is the prevalence of alcohol in the blood for nonarrested persons in the same setting or with similar characteristics to the offenders? Quite possibly the arrests occurred among populations most of whom were accustomed to having some liquor inside them.

*   *   *

Criminal Histories of Alcoholics

Special attention is often given to chronic alcoholics, either sampled from skid row or clinics, or from prison, to learn about their criminality. For example, Clark, Hannigan, and Hart in a sample of 100 alcoholic felons report a preponderance of crimes of violence; only one planned skilled offense was committed by an alcoholic felon. Most men had extensive histories of past arrest on minor counts. As parolees alcoholics were said to have higher rates of recidivism. Blacker surveyed a Massachusetts alcoholic inmate sample and reported that the per man median number of past arrests was 58.5. One-third had only been arrested for alcohol use offenses, one-third for other minor crimes, and one-third for serious offenses, of these only one-third showing a recent felony arrest, a fact leading Blacker to conclude that one-sixth of these men were "potentially dangerous." Arai and Iijima examined Japanese offenders under the influence of alcohol at the time of their crime, the majority of whom proved to be alcoholics. Half of the sample had been involved in violent crimes, 30 percent in property offenses. The authors attribute at least one-quarter of the offenses to the specific presence of alcohol, that leading to emotional explosions and violence. Other offenses were said to be facilitated by the presence of alcohol.

Pittman and Gordon have done the most careful and detailed study of chronic offenders, in their case a sample of 187 chronic drunkenness offenders whose criminal careers were examined. All were imprisoned recidivists in New York State. The average frequency of arrest was 16.5 with the number of arrests increasingly progressing with age. Nearly one-quarter of all past arrests had been for other than drunkenness; these other crimes had not increased with age. The authors point out that inebriates who have as youths and young men been involved in theft, burglary, etc., change their conduct and show more intoxication offenses as they get older, age 35 to 40 being the critical period. The past histories of the inebriates showed gambling and homicide to be the least frequent but present other type of crimes; with increasing percentages of men involved in burglary (12 percent), larceny (23 percent), disorderly conduct (22 percent), and vagrancy (35 percent). One-third of the sample had been arrested only for alcohol use offenses. Thirty-seven percent had serious arrest records; many of their crimes being committed under the influence of alcohol. Pittman and Gordon remind us that many of their fellow inebriates had not committed such crimes. They suggest a "career" pattern, that many men who become drunkenness offenders started out with purer criminal interests but that they failed as criminals and drifted into alcoholism as an adjustment to criminal career failure. The authors find that the criminal career of the drunkenness offender is divided into two phases; under age 40 it is filled with many arrests unrelated to alcohol; afterwards their offenses are for alcohol use. (The authors are aware that arrest records are but a dim reflection of actual offenses.) Categorizing their men into three groups, approximately one-third with no crimes other than alcohol use, one-third with minor crimes, and one-third with serious crimes, they compared them on background characteristics and found no differences. Their proposal that criminal failures become alcoholics, gravitating to skid row, is limited to the special subgroup of one-third who started their offending career with property acquisition ambitions rather than alcohol interests per se.

Comment

It is difficult to do good work in any field and, when good work in social inquiry or science is done, it must lead to further questions and, necessarily, awareness of what we have not learned from what has been done before. The field of studies of alcohol involvement in crime is no different. * * * As a general statement most studies are simply descriptive and too easily conclude or imply that alcohol plays a critical role in the production of the crime reported. Blane has done a fine job of setting forth the limitations of much of the work done. He notes that research methods have been grossly inadequate all too often, that there has been no base of reason or theory to provide a framework for either inquiry or understanding, and that any criminal act is an outcome of many forces acting over time and in the situation. The presence of alcohol is only one such factor, and how alcohol affects conduct is conditional on what the user is like and what else is happening. At the very least a criminal outcome is the consequence of alcohol (dosage over time, concurrent physiological state, etc.) plus personality plus group or subcultural membership plus opportunity plus drinking circumstances plus other events. Even this additive scheme is insufficient, for the likelihood is one of interplay or interaction with differing outcomes each time one element in the drama of conduct is altered.

The weight of argument on alcohol leading to crime rarely considers alcohol as an inhibitor of crime, yet alcohol does suppress function as well as release inhibition. As a sedative or tranquilizer ("perhaps the best tranquilizer," said Leake and Silverman) it must account for the reduction of action too, some of that action criminal. * * *

On the basis of available information it is plausible to assume that alcohol does play an important and damaging role in the lives of offenders, particularly chronic inebriates and in the production of crime. Yet one cannot be sure on the basis of the work done to date that the alcohol use of offenders exceeds that of nonoffenders with similar social and personal characteristics (if any such match is possible). One cannot be sure that the alcohol use of offenders is any greater at the moments of their offense than during their ordinary noncriminal moments. One cannot be sure that the alcohol-using offenders would not have committed some offense had they not been drinking. One is not sure that the alcohol use of offenders differs from that of the other persons possibly present in the same or like situations which inspired or provoked the criminality of one and not the other. Finally, and this is an important point in view of the fact that all studies have been done on apprehended offenders, one does not know that the relationship now shown between alcohol use and crime is not in fact a relationship between being caught and being a drinker rather than in being a criminal and being a drinker. Given the foregoing questions and given the likelihood that people who do use alcohol to excess—and who explode into violence or sneak into thievery in the process—also have other characteristics which mark them as ones who disregard the welfare of their fellow men (and are equally unable to secure their own well-being), a prudent student of conduct will not hasten to label alcohol a cause and crime a result when it is equally likely that both alcohol excesses and crimes are "results."

2. H. Silving, Essays on Mental Incapacity and Criminal Conduct 251-53 (1967):

No doubt, since alcohol tends to reduce inhibitions, it "contributes" to this extent to crime. As reported by Henderson and Gillespie,[83] more than half of the 9028 persons proceeded against in Glasgow for Breach of the Peace (including Petty Assault) were found to be under the influence of intoxicating liquor at the time of the offense. The same writers point out that while few reliable figures are available to show how much alcohol contributes to other offenses or crimes, "authorities agree that it is an important factor in the genesis particularly of sexual and aggressive crimes (including suicide and murder.)" On the other hand, Banay concluded from results of his investigation of 3135 Sing Sing prisoners that, contrary to common belief, the contribution of alcoholism to crime is not very substantial and that it is greater in the minor than in the major crimes.[84] More significant than mere statistics of the apparent relationship between alcohol and criminal-

83. Henderson & Gillespie, A Textbook of Psychiatry 58–59 (8th ed., Oxford University Press, London 1956).

84. Banay, Alcohol and Aggression, in Alcohol, Science and Society, [Quarterly Journal of Studies on Alcohol [1945]] 143, at 147–149. In this study the incidence of inebriety was shown to be 25 per cent, whereas it was formerly estimated to be 60 per cent. The leading offense in this group of 3,135 prisoners, was among the inebriates, assault, while in the control group this crime took only fifth place. Of the acquisitive crimes, burglary was more common among the inebriate prisoners and grand larceny was more common among the noninebriate ones. The most aggressive of all crimes, homicide, constituted 9 per cent of the crimes committed by the inebriate group and 8 per cent by the noninebriate ones. Of the crimes most prominently associated in the public mind with habitual inebriety and acute intoxication, sex crimes, 7.5 per cent of the inebriates were committed to prison because of such crimes, while the ratio among the noninebriates was 5 per cent, so that the contribution of alcohol to this crime category was apparently substantiated. But, as the investigator remarked, criminal inebriates are generally known to be arrested more often for exhibitionism rather than for rape, while in noninebriate criminals the reverse is true.

ity is new insight into the meaning of "contribution." Banay contends that the mere quantitative relationship between alcohol and criminality, even assuming it to be substantial, would not by itself afford a proof that alcohol is the source of a person's dangerousness. Such proof would rather require establishment of a causal nexus between these two phenomena. As regards the causal problem, "[t]here is now an increasing tendency to consider that both alcohol and criminalism are caused by similar social and psychological factors" and that "[m]ore frequently is the relation of alcohol to crime one of a common cause rather than of cause and effect." [85] It follows that elimination of the practice of drinking would at best afford but a relative reduction of the scope of crime at present connected with alcohol consumption. In individuals disposed toward criminal conduct who are also alcohol consumers it is reasonable to assume that other methods of reducing inhibitions would probably lead to the same criminal results.[86]

Since criminal law must concern itself in the first place with serious crimes, it is of prime importance to notice that alcohol consumption does not determine the nature or gravity of the criminal conduct engaged in under the impact of intoxication. Banay's study has shown that there is "no greater homicidal tendency among inebriate criminals than among noninebriate criminals." [87] Since alcohol is known to reduce inhibitions, the question is posed as to why the release of aggression by drink does not operate in this instance, when it operates where lesser crimes are involved. Banay answers this question by suggesting that "[t]his extreme form of aggression [homicide] is so strongly inhibited that even intoxication does not release it more easily than the factors which account for it in noninebriates." In fact, the prevailing opinion is that alcohol "does not determine the type or form of behavior which follows, but only tends to make the form different from the usual." [88] Alcohol always has the same effect upon individuals, in the sense that it causes "a temporary loss of socialization as a process, rather than any specific types of accident, crime innovation or non-action." [89] But in what manner or form or on what levil this desocialization will express itself, in other words, "[t]he specific locus of the socialized behavior [which alcohol will affect]

85. Noyes & Kolb, [Modern Clinical Psychiatry] 167, (6th ed., 1963). For this reason one should not attribute too much importance to statistics, and there is no need to engage in an inquiry into the statistical methodology followed by Banay.

86. On this see Jellinek, [Effects of Small Amounts of Alcohol on Psychological Functions, in Alcohol, Science and Society (Quarterly Journal of Studies on Alcohol [1945])] at 84–86, 91.

87. Banay, supra, at 148.

88. Dr. Leon A. Greenberg, Director of the Laboratory of Applied Biodynamics and of the Yale Center of Alcoholic Studies, Address to the American Bar Association Section of Criminal Law, Third Session, August 30, 1960, 1960 Proceedings, p. 45, at 50–51.

89. Ibid.

is determined by factors other than the beverage of alcohol."[90] Traits which reveal themselves during intoxication represent the individual's basic personality. Always, the genesis of the crime antecedes the alcoholic indulgence or the alcohol addiction.[91]

C. THE PRESENT LEGAL APPROACH: CRIMINALIZATION OF DRUNKENNESS AND DRUNKEN BEHAVIOR

THE PRESIDENT'S COMMISSION ON LAW ENFORCEMENT AND ADMINISTRATION OF JUSTICE, TASK FORCE REPORT: DRUNKENNESS

1–3 (1967).

The Existing System

DRUNKENNESS LAWS

Drunkenness is punishable under a variety of laws, generally describing the offense as being "drunk in a public place," often without providing a precise definition of drunkenness itself. Some laws include as a condition that the offender is "unable to care for his own safety."

In some jurisdictions there are no laws prohibiting drunkenness, but any drunkenness that causes a breach of the peace is punishable. In Georgia and Alabama, for example, drunkenness that is manifested by boisterous or indecent conduct, or loud and profane discourse, is a crime. Other jurisdictions apply disorderly conduct statutes to those who are drunk in public. In Chicago, for example, the police, having no drunkenness law to enforce, use a disorderly conduct statute to arrest nondisorderly inebriates. Some jurisdictions permit police to make public drunkenness arrests under both State laws and local ordinances.

The laws provide maximum jail sentences ranging from 5 days to 6 months; the most common maximum sentence is 30 days. In some States an offender convicted of "habitual drunkenness" may be punished by a 2-year sentence of imprisonment.

THE OFFENDERS

The 2 million arrests for drunkenness each year involve both sporadic and regular drinkers. Among the number are a wide variety

90. Bowman and Jellinek, Alcoholic Mental Disorders, 2 Quarterly Journal of Studies on Alcohol 312, at 321 (1941).

91. Banay, supra, at 147.

of offenders—the rowdy college boy; the weekend inebriate; the homeless, often unemployed single man. How many offenders fall into these and other categories is not known. Neither is it known how many of the offenders are alcoholics in the medical sense of being dependent on alcohol. There is strong evidence, however, that a large number of those who are arrested have a lengthy history of prior drunkenness arrests, and that a disproportionate number involve poor persons who live in slums. In 1964 in the city of Los Angeles about one-fifth of all persons arrested for drunkenness accounted for two-thirds of the total number of arrests for that offense. Some of the repeaters were arrested as many as 18 times in that year.[8]

A review of chronic offender cases reveals that a large number of persons have, in short installments, spent many years of their lives in jail. In 1957 the Committee on Prisons, Probation and Parole in the District of Columbia studied six chronic offenders and found that they had been arrested for drunkenness a total of 1,409 times and had served a total of 125 years in penal institutions.[9] A recent article in a Syracuse, N. Y. newspaper illustrates the point even more succinctly:

> H_____ F_____, 69 appeared in police court for the 277th time on a public intoxication charge. F_____, who has served 16 years in the Jamesville Penitentiary in short terms on the charge, was returned there for a 6-month sentence.[10]

The great majority of repeaters live on "skid row"—a dilapidated area found in most large and medium-size cities in the United States. On skid row substandard hotels and roominghouses are intermingled with numerous taverns, pawn shops, cheap cafeterias, employment agencies that specialize in jobs for the unskilled, and religious missions that provide free meals after a service. Many of the residents—including the chronic drunkenness offenders—are homeless, penniless, and beset with acute personal problems.

*   *   *

OPERATION OF THE CRIMINAL SYSTEM AFTER ARREST

Following arrest, the drunk is usually placed in a barren cell called a "tank," where he is detained for at least a few hours. The tanks in some cities can hold as many as 200 people, while others

8. Statistics gathered by the Los Angeles Police Dep't. During 1964 there were 71,494 drunkenness arrests—47,401 of which involved 13,048 offenders. In 1955, 45,748 of the drunkenness arrests in Los Angeles involved 6,665 offenders. In 1961, 12,000 individuals accounted for approximately 30,000 of the 49,000 arrests in Atlanta, Ga. Dep't of Psychiatry, Emory Univ. School of Medicine, Alcohol Study Project 5 (unpublished 1963) [hereinafter cited as Emory Dep't of Psychiatry].

9. D.C.Comm. on Prisons, Probation, and Parole, Rep. 114–19 (1957).

10. Syracuse Herald American, Aug. 22, 1965, p. 30, col. 8.

hold only 1 or 2.   One report described the conditions found in a tank
in this way:

> Although he may have been picked up for his own pro-
> tection, the offender is placed in a cell, which may frequently
> hold as many as 40–50 men where there is no room to sit or
> lie down, where sanitary facilities and ventilation are inade-
> quate and a stench of vomit and urine is prevalent.

> The drunken behavior of some of the inmates is an added
> hazard.   It is questionable whether greater safety is achieved
> for the individual who is arrested for his safe keeping.[17]

The chronic alcoholic offender generally suffers from a variety
of ailments and is often in danger of serious medical complications,[18]
but medical care is rarely provided in the tank; and it is difficult to
detect or to diagnose serious illness since it often resembles intoxication.   Occasionally, chronic offenders become ill during pretrial detention and die without having received adequate medical attention.[20]

If the offender can afford bail, he usually obtains release after
he sobers up.[21]   In many jurisdictions an offender is permitted to for-

17.   Comm. on Alcoholism Community
Welfare Council of the Greater Sacra-
mento Area, Inc., The Alcoholic Law
Offender 4 (unpublished 1965).   Another tank was described in a 1966
newspaper article:

> There are at least two men in each
> 4 x 8 foot cell and three in some.
> * * *   The stench of cheap alcohol,
> dried blood, urine and excrement
> covers the cell blocks * * *.
> There are no lights in the cells
> * * *.   There are no mattresses.
> Mattresses wouldn't last the night a
> policeman explains.   And with pris-
> oners urinating all over them, they
> wouldn't be any good if they did
> last. * * *

Hoagland, Cell Blocks' Common De-
nominator: A Stench of Alcohol and
Dried Blood, Washington Post, March
29, 1966, p. A1, col. 3.

18.   Univ. of Minn. & Minneapolis Housing and Redevelopment Authority.   A
General Report on the Problem of
Relocating the Population of the Lower Loop Redevelopment Area 170 (unpublished 1958) ("health conditions in
this area are catastrophically bad").
The report provided a detailed description of illnesses which exist in
skid row areas and states that the
"tuberculosis rate in the lower loop
is 320 times as high as the rate for
the rest of the city."   Id. at 170.   See

also Dep't of Psychiatry, Temple
Univ., School of Medicine.   The Men
of Skid Row, A Study of Philadelphia's Homeless Man Population 88
(unpublished 1960) (57% of the men
reported one or more serious conditions).   Bogue's study [Bogue, Skid
Row in American Cities 222–23 (1963)]
depicted the great need for medical
care and observed that "among the
heavy drinkers, alcoholism is complicated by chronic sickness in a substantial portion of cases."

20.   Man, 52, Dies in Court Lockup,
Washington Post, Sept. 5, 1965, p. A3;
Man Detained as Drunk Dies From
Pneumonia, id., Dec. 15, 1965, p. D21,
cols. 1–2;   Man, 63, Found Dead in
Alexandria Jail Cell, id., Nov. 22,
1966, p. B4, cols. 1–2.   In the Pres.'s
Comm'n on Crime in the District of
Columbia, Rep. 476 (1966), it was re-
ported that "16 persons arrested for
intoxication died while in police cus-
tody in 1964–1965."

21.   Stationhouse bail permits the release of defendants pending a subsequent court appearance.   See generally Freed & Wald, Bail in the United
States (1964).   Outright release—with
no obligation to return to court—is
sometimes permitted by the police.
See LaFave, op. cit. supra note 16, at
440–42, for a variety of release systems ranging from outright police

feit bail routinely by not appearing in court.[22] Thus, if the arrested person has the few dollars required, he can avoid prosecution;[23] if he has no money, as is usually the case, he must appear in court.

Drunkenness offenders are generally brought before a judge the morning after their arrest, sometimes appearing in groups of 15 or 20. Rarely are the normal procedural or due process safeguards applied to these cases. Usually defendants are processed through the court system with haste and either released or sentenced to several days or weeks in jail.[25] In some cities only those offenders who request it are jailed. In others chronic offenders, who are likely to be alcoholics, are generally sent to jail.[27]

When a defendant serves a short sentence, he is fed, sheltered, and given access to available recreational facilities. In most institutions there is such a lack of facilities and financial resources that it is not possible to do more.

*   *   *

After serving a brief sentence, the chronic offender is released, more likely than not to return to his former haunts on skid row, with no money, no job, and no plans. Often he is rearrested within a matter of days or hours.

NOTE

A study of police handling of public drunkenness in Austin, Texas revealed that in 1968 43.3 percent of all arrests, excluding minor traffic

discretion to a payment to the city of $4.35. In Detroit the police have a "golden rule" procedure which resulted in 1965 in the release of 2,383 offenders out of a total of 8,715 drunkenness arrests. In Omaha, Neb., the majority of offenders are released after a few hours of detention. The Omaha system includes referral to community agencies following release, in appropriate cases. The police bring some offenders to the agencies where shelter and food are provided.

22. Bail or collateral forfeiture is common in some jurisdictions. The defendant pays $10 to $20, depending upon the stipulated amount in the jurisdiction, and he is not penalized for failing to return to court. See Pres.'s Comm'n on Crime in the District of Columbia, Rep. 477 (1966); Emory Dep't of Psychiatry 11.

23. In Washington, D.C., for example, approximately 20,000 of the 44,218 people arrested during 1965 obtained release by forfeiting $10 collateral. Pres.'s Comm'n on Crime in the District of Columbia, Rep. 475 (1966). In

Atlanta, Ga., approximately 20,000 of 49,805 arrests during 1961 resulted in ($15) collateral forfeitures. Emory Dep't of Psychiatry 11. Those who post and forfeit collateral avoid the risk of a jail sentence.

25. In Portland, Ore., for example, the first offense receives a suspended sentence, the second offense brings a 2-day jail sentence, and the fifth offense within a 12-month period brings a 6-month sentence. The Sunday Oregonian, April 17, 1966, p. F4, col. 4; Ore. Mental Health Div., Proceedings: The Alcoholic and the Court 39 (1963). In Atlanta, Ga., the fourth conviction within a 12-month period brings a fine, and the fifth conviction results in a 30-day jail sentence. Emory Dep't of Psychiatry 28. A 1957 study showed that 13,146 sentences out of 15,111 in Washington, D.C., were for 30 days or less. D.C. Comm. on Prisons, Probation, and Parole, Rep. 106 (1957).

27. See Pittman & Gordon, Revolving Door: A Study of the Chronic Police Case Inebriate 30, 125 (1958) * * *.

offenses, were for public drunkenness. If arrests for driving while intoxicated are included, the two offenses total 50.5 percent of all arrests. The author explains the discrepancy between these and national figures in two ways. First, Austin contains no "skid row" in which drunkenness offenders may lose themselves. Second, the police force of Austin is committed to vigorous enforcement of drunkenness laws as a means of retaining its reputation as a "clean town." Willis, Public Drunkenness in Austin, Texas 4–5 (prepared under the auspices of the Criminal Justice Project of the University of Texas Law School).

D. ISSUES FOR THE LAW

Once those matters with which the law is appropriately concerned are identified and the general current approach of the law is described, the next step must be an evaluation of this approach in light of available alternatives. This needs to be done on two levels. One involves the basic legislative decision as to what to criminalize. The other consists of the judicial decision as to the validity of various legislative resolutions of the first matter. Part 1 of this section focuses upon judicial evaluation of the constitutionality of one legislative response—the decision to criminalize practically all intoxication not in the person's own home or under other circumstances affording privacy. Part 2 addresses a related issue, the extent of precision necessary in defining those things that will be made criminal. Part 3 presents some alternative legislative responses that involve criminalization. Part 4, on the other hand, presents a legislative response involving use of noncriminal methods. Evaluation of all the issues arising in this section must be made in light of the material presented in Part E, but this material must in turn be considered with full understanding of the variety of ways in which the law may be used in this context.

1. CRIMINALIZATION OF PUBLIC DRUNKENNESS AS CRUEL AND UNUSUAL PUNISHMENT

ROBINSON v. CALIFORNIA

Supreme Court of the United States, 1962.
370 U.S. 660, 82 S.Ct. 1417, 8 L.Ed.2d 758, rehearing denied
371 U.S. 905, 83 S.Ct. 202, 9 L.Ed.2d 166.

Mr. Justice STEWART delivered the opinion of the Court.

A California statute makes it a criminal offense for a person to "be addicted to the use of narcotics." This appeal draws into question the constitutionality of that provision of the state law, as construed by the California courts in the present case.

The appellant was convicted after a jury trial in the Municipal Court of Los Angeles. The evidence against him was given by two Los Angeles police officers. Officer Brown testified that he had had occasion to examine the appellant's arms one evening on a street in Los Angeles some four months before the trial. The officer testified that at that time he had observed "scar tissue and discoloration on the inside" of the appellant's right arm, and "what appeared to be numerous needle marks and a scab which was approximately three inches below the crook of the elbow" on the appellant's left arm. The officer also testified that the appellant under questioning had admitted to the occasional use of narcotics.

Officer Lindquist testified that he had examined the appellant the follow morning in the Central Jail in Los Angeles. The officer stated that at that time he had observed discolorations and scabs on the appellant's arms, and he identified photographs which had been taken of the appellant's arms shortly after his arrest the night before. Based upon more than ten years of experience as a member of the Narcotic Division of the Los Angeles Police Department, the witness gave his opinion that "these marks and the discoloration were the result of the injection of hypodermic needles into the tissue into the vein that was not sterile." He stated that the scabs were several days old at the time of his examination, and that the appellant was neither under the influence of narcotics nor suffering withdrawal symptoms at the time he saw him. This witness also testified that the appellant had admitted using narcotics in the past.

The appellant testified in his own behalf, denying the alleged conversations with the police officers and denying that he had ever used narcotics or been addicted to their use. He explained the marks on his arms as resulting from an allergic condition contracted during his military service. His testimony was corroborated by two witnesses.

The trial judge instructed the jury that the statute made it a misdemeanor for a person "either to use narcotics, or to be addicted to the use of narcotics * * *. That portion of the statute referring to the 'use' of narcotics is based upon the 'act' of using. That portion of the statute referring to 'addicted to the use' of narcotics is based upon a condition or status. They are not identical. * * * To be addicted to the use of narcotics is said to be a status or condition and not an act. It is a continuing offense and differs from most other offenses in the fact that [it] is chronic rather than acute; that it continues after it is complete and subjects the offender to arrest at any time before he reforms. The existence of such a chronic condition may be ascertained from a single examination, if the characteristic reactions of that condition be found present."

The judge further instructed the jury that the appellant could be convicted under a general verdict if the jury agreed *either* that he was of the "status" *or* had committed the "act" denounced by the statute. "All that the People must show is either that the defendant did use a narcotic in Los Angeles County, or that while in the City of Los Angeles he was addicted to the use of narcotics * * *."

Under these instructions the jury returned a verdict finding the appellant "guilty of the offense charged."

* * *

Such regulation, it can be assumed, could take a variety of valid forms. A State might impose criminal sanctions, for example, against the unauthorized manufacture, prescription, sale, purchase, or possession of narcotics within its borders. In the interest of discouraging the violation of such laws, or in the interest of the general health or welfare of its inhabitants, a State might establish a program of compulsory treatment for those addicted to narcotics. Such a program of treatment might require periods of involuntary confinement. And penal sanctions might be imposed for failure to comply with established compulsory treatment procedures. Or a State might choose to attack the evils of narcotics traffic on broader fronts also—through public health education, for example, or by efforts to ameliorate the economic and social conditions under which those evils might be thought to flourish. In short, the range of valid choice which a State might make in this area is undoubtedly a wide one, and the wisdom of any particular choice within the allowable spectrum is not for us to decide. Upon that premise we turn to the California law in issue here.

It would be possible to construe the statute under which the appellant was convicted as one which is operative only upon proof of the actual use of narcotics within the State's jurisdiction. But the California courts have not so construed this law. Although there was evidence in the present case that the appellant had used narcotics in Los Angeles, the jury were instructed that they could convict him even if they disbelieved that evidence. The appellant could be convicted, they were told, if they found simply that the appellant's "status" or "chronic condition" was that of being "addicted to the use of narcotics." And it is impossible to know from the jury's verdict that the defendant was not convicted upon precisely such a finding.

* * *

This statute, therefore, is not one which punishes a person for the use of narcotics, for their purchase, sale or possession, or for antisocial or disorderly behavior resulting from their administration. It is not a law which even purports to provide or require medical treatment. Rather, we deal with a statute which makes the "status" of narcotic addiction a criminal offense, for which the offender may be prosecuted "at any time before he reforms." California has said that a person can be continuously guilty of this offense, whether or not he has ever used or possessed any narcotics within the State, and whether or not he has been guilty of any antisocial behavior there.

It is unlikely that any State at this moment in history would attempt to make it a criminal offense for a person to be mentally ill, or a leper, or to be afflicted with a venereal disease. A State might determine that the general health and welfare require that the victims of these and other human afflictions be dealt with by compulsory treatment, involving quarantine, confinement, or sequestration. But, in the light of contemporary human knowledge, a law which made a criminal offense of such a disease would doubtless be universally thought to be an infliction of cruel and unusual punishment in violation of the Eighth and Fourteenth Amendments. * * *

We cannot but consider the statute before us as of the same category. In this Court counsel for the State recognized that narcotic addiction is an illness.[8] Indeed, it is apparently an illness which may be contracted innocently or involuntarily.[9] We hold that a state law which imprisons a person thus afflicted as a criminal, even though he has never touched any narcotic drug within the State or been guilty of any irregular behavior there, inflicts a cruel and unusual punishment in violation of the Fourteenth Amendment. To be sure, imprisonment for ninety days is not, in the abstract, a punishment which is either cruel or unusual. But the question cannot be considered in the abstract. Even one day in prison would be a cruel and unusual punishment for the "crime" of having a common cold.

We are not unmindful that the vicious evils of the narcotics traffic have occasioned the grave concern of government. There are, as we have said, countless fronts on which those evils may be legitimately attacked. We deal in this case only with an individual provision of a particularized local law as it has so far been interpreted by the California courts.

Reversed.

Mr. Justice DOUGLAS, concurring.

While I join the Court's opinion, I wish to make more explicit the reasons why I think it is "cruel and unusual" punishment in the sense of the Eighth Amendment to treat as a criminal a person who is a drug addict. * * * [T]he principle that would deny power to exact capital punishment for a petty crime would also deny power to punish a person by fine or imprisonment for being sick. * * *

8. In its brief the appellee stated: "Of course it is generally conceded that a narcotic addict, particularly one addicted to the use of heroin, is in a state of mental and physical illness. So is an alcoholic." Thirty-seven years ago this Court recognized that persons addicted to narcotics "are diseased and proper subjects for [medical] treatment." Linder v. United States, 268 U.S. 5, 18, 45 S.Ct. 446, 449, 69 L.Ed. 819.

9. Not only may addiction innocently result from the use of medically prescribed narcotics, but a person may even be a narcotics addict from the moment of his birth. * * *

Mr. Justice HARLAN, concurring.

I am not prepared to hold that on the present state of medical knowledge it is completely irrational and hence unconstitutional for a State to conclude that narcotics addiction is something other than an illness nor that it amounts to cruel and unusual punishment for the State to subject narcotics addicts to its criminal law. * * * Since addiction alone cannot reasonably be thought to amount to more than a compelling propensity to use narcotics, the effect of ⌊the⌋ instruction was to authorize criminal punishment for a bare desire to commit a criminal act.

If the California statute reaches this type of conduct, * * * it is an arbitrary imposition which exceeds the power that a State may exercise in enacting its criminal law. Accordingly, I agree that the application of the California statute was unconstitutional in this case and join the judgment of reversal.

Mr. Justice CLARK, dissenting.

*   *   *

[T]he majority admits that "a State might establish a program of compulsory treatment for those addicted to narcotics" which "might require periods of involuntary confinement." I submit that California has done exactly that. The majority's error is in instructing the California Legislature that hospitalization is the *only treatment* for narcotics addiction—that anything less is a punishment denying due process. California has found otherwise after a study which I suggest was more extensive than that conducted by the Court. Even in California's program for hospital commitment of nonvolitional narcotic addicts—which the majority approves—it is recognized that some addicts will not respond to or do not need hospital treatment. As to these persons its provisions are identical to those of § 11721—confinement for a period of not less than 90 days. Section 11721 provides this confinement as treatment for the volitional addicts to whom its provisions apply, in addition to parole with frequent tests to detect and prevent further use of drugs. The fact that § 11721 might be labeled "criminal" seems irrelevant,* not only to the majority's own "treatment" test but to the "concept of ordered liberty" to which the States must attain under the Fourteenth Amendment. The test is the overall purpose and effect of a State's act, and I submit that California's program relative to narcotic addicts—including both the "criminal" and "civil" provisions—is inherently one of treatment and lies well within the power of a State.

*   *   *

* Any reliance upon the "stigma" of a misdemeanor conviction in this context is misplaced, as it would hardly be different from the stigma of a civil commitment for narcotics addiction.

Mr. Justice WHITE, dissenting.

If appellant's conviction rested upon sheer status, condition or illness or if he was convicted for being an addict who had lost his power of self-control, I would have other thoughts about this case. But this record presents neither situation. * * * [T]here was no evidence at all that appellant had lost the power to control his acts. * * * He was an incipient addict, a redeemable user, and the State chose to send him to jail for 90 days rather than to attempt to confine him by civil proceedings under another statute which requires a finding that the addict has lost the power of self-control. In my opinion, on this record, it was within the power of the State of California to confine him by criminal proceedings for the use of narcotics or for regular use amounting to habitual use.

* * *

POWELL v. TEXAS

Supreme Court of the United States, 1968.
392 U.S. 514, 88 S.Ct. 2145, 20 L.Ed.2d 1254.

Mr. Justice MARSHALL announced the judgment of the Court and delivered an opinion in which THE CHIEF JUSTICE, Mr. Justice BLACK, and Mr. Justice HARLAN join.

In late December 1966, appellant was arrested and charged with being found in a state of intoxication in a public place, in violation of Vernon's Ann.Texas Penal Code, Art. 477 (1952), which reads as follows:

"Whoever shall get drunk or be found in a state of intoxication in any public place, or at any private house except his own, shall be fined not exceeding one hundred dollars."

Appellant was tried in the Corporation Court of Austin, Texas, found guilty, and fined $20. He appealed to the County Court at Law No. 1 of Travis County, Texas, where a trial *de novo* was held. His counsel urged that appellant was "afflicted with the disease of chronic alcoholism," that "his appearance in public [while drunk was] * * * not of his own volition," and therefore that to punish him criminally for that conduct would be cruel and unusual, in violation of the Eighth and Fourteenth Amendments to the United States Constitution.

The trial judge in the county court, sitting without a jury, made certain findings of fact, * * * but ruled as a matter of law that chronic alcoholism was not a defense to the charge. He found appellant guilty, and fined him $50. There being no further right to appeal within the Texas judicial system, appellant appealed to this Court * * *.

I.

The principal testimony was that of Dr. David Wade, a Fellow of the American Medical Association, duly certificated in psychiatry. His testimony consumed a total of 17 pages in the trial transcript. Five of those pages were taken up with a recitation of Dr. Wade's qualifications. In the next 12 pages Dr. Wade was examined by appellant's counsel, cross-examined by the State, and re-examined by the defense, and those 12 pages contain virtually all the material developed at trial which is relevant to the constitutional issue we face here. Dr. Wade sketched the outlines of the "disease" concept of alcoholism; noted that there is no generally accepted definition of "alcoholism"; alluded to the ongoing debate within the medical profession over whether alcohol is actually physically "addicting" or merely psychologically "habituating"; and concluded that in either case a "chronic alcoholic" is an "involuntary drinker," who is "powerless not to drink," and who "loses his self-control over his drinking." He testified that he had examined appellant, and that appellant is a "chronic alcoholic," who "by the time he has reached [the state of intoxication] * * * is not able to control his behavior, and [who] * * * has reached this point because he has an uncontrollable compulsion to drink." Dr. Wade also responded in the negative to the question whether appellant has "the willpower to resist the constant excessive consumption of alcohol." He added that in his opinion jailing appellant without medical attention would operate neither to rehabilitate him nor to lessen his desire for alcohol.

On cross-examination, Dr. Wade admitted that when appellant was sober he knew the difference betwen right and wrong, and he responded affirmatively to the question whether appellant's act in taking the first drink in any given instance when he was sober was a "voluntary exercise of his will." Qualifying his answer, Dr. Wade stated that "these individuals have a compulsion, and this compulsion, while not completely overpowering, is a very strong influence, an exceedingly strong influence, and this compulsion coupled with the firm belief in their mind that they are going to be able to handle it from now on causes their judgment to be somewhat clouded."

Appellant testified concerning the history of his drinking problem. He reviewed his many arrests for drunkenness; testified that he was unable to stop drinking; stated that when he was intoxicated he had no control over his actions and could not remember them later, but that he did not become violent; and admitted that he did not remember his arrest on the occasion for which he was being tried. On cross-examination, appellant admitted that he had had one drink on the morning of the trial and had been able to discontinue drinking. In relevant part, the cross-examination went as follows:

"Q.   You took that one at eight o'clock because you wanted to drink?

"A.   Yes, sir.

"Q.   And you knew that if you drank it, you could keep on drinking and get drunk?

"A.   Well, I was supposed to be here on trial, and I didn't take but that one drink.

"Q.   You knew you had to be here this afternoon, but this morning you took one drink and then you knew that you couldn't afford to drink any more and come to court; is that right?

"A.   Yes, sir, that's right.

"Q.   So you exercised your will power and kept from drinking anything today except that one drink?

"A.   Yes, sir, that's right.

"Q.   Because you knew what you would do if you kept drinking that you would finally pass out or be picked up?

"A.   Yes, sir.

"Q.   And you didn't want that to happen to you today?

"A.   No, sir.

"Q.   Not today?

"A.   No, sir.

"Q.   So you only had one drink today?

"A.   Yes, sir."

On redirect examination, appellant's lawyer elicited the following:

"Q.   Leroy, isn't the real reason why you just had one drink today because you just had enough money to buy one drink?

"A.   Well, that was just give to me.

"Q.   In other words, you didn't have any money with which you could buy any drinks yourself?

"A.   No, sir, that was give to me.

"Q.   And that's really what controlled the amount you drank this morning, isn't it?

"A.   Yes, sir.

"Q.   Leroy, when you start drinking, do you have any control over how many drinks you can take?

"A.   No, sir."

Evidence in the case then closed. The State made no effort to obtain expert psychiatric testimony of its own, or even to explore with appellant's witness the question of appellant's power to control the frequency, timing, and location of his drinking bouts, or the substantial disagreement within the medical profession concerning the nature of the disease, the efficacy of treatment and the prerequisites for effective treatment. It did nothing to examine or illuminate what Dr. Wade might have meant by his reference to a "compulsion" which was "not completely overpowering," but which was "an exceedingly strong influence," or to inquire into the question of the proper role of such a "compulsion" in constitutional adjudication. Instead, the State contented itself with a brief argument that appellant had no defense to the charge because he "is legally sane and knows the difference between right and wrong."

Following this abbreviated exposition of the problem before it, the trial court indicated its intention to disallow appellant's claimed defense of "chronic alcoholism." Thereupon defense counsel submitted, and the trial court entered, the following "findings of fact":

"(1) That chronic alcoholism is a disease which destroys the afflicted person's will power to resist the constant, excessive consumption of alcohol.

"(2) That a chronic alcoholic does not appear in public by his own volition but under a compulsion symptomatic of the disease of chronic alcoholism.

"(3) That Leroy Powell, defendant herein, is a chronic alcoholic who is afflicted with the disease of chronic alcoholism."

Whatever else may be said of them, those are not "findings of fact" in any recognizable, traditional sense in which that term has been used in a court of law; they are the premises of a syllogism transparently designed to bring this case within the scope of this Court's opinion in Robinson v. State of California, 370 U.S. 660, 82 S.Ct. 1417, 8 L.Ed.2d 758 (1962). Nonetheless, the dissent would have us adopt these "findings" without critical examination; it would use them as the basis for a constitutional holding that "a person may not be punished if the condition essential to constitute the defined crime is part of the pattern of his disease and is occasioned by a compulsion symptomatic of the disease." * * *

The difficulty with that position, as we shall show, is that it goes much too far on the basis of too little knowledge. In the first place, the record in this case is utterly inadequate to permit the sort of informed and responsible adjudication which alone can support the announcement of an important and wide-ranging new constitutional principle. We know very little about the circumstances surrounding the drinking bout which resulted in this conviction, or about Leroy

Powell's drinking problem, or indeed about alcoholism itself. The trial hardly reflects the sharp legal and evidentiary clash between fully prepared adversary litigants which is traditionally expected in major constitutional cases. The State put on only one witness, the arresting officer. The defense put on three—a policeman who testified to appellant's long history of arrests for public drunkenness, the psychiatrist, and appellant himself.

Furthermore, the inescapable fact is that there is no agreement among members of the medical profession about what it means to say that "alcoholism" is a "disease." One of the principal works in this field states that the major difficulty in articulating a "disease concept of alcoholism" is that "alcoholism has too many definitions and disease has practically none." [2] This same author concludes that "*a disease is what the medical profession recognizes as such.*" In other words, there is widespread agreement today that "alcoholism" is a "disease," for the simple reason that the medical profession has concluded that it should attempt to treat those who have drinking problems. There the agreement stops. Debate rages within the medical profession as to whether "alcoholism" is a separate "disease" in any meaningful biochemical, physiological or psychological sense, or whether it represents one peculiar manifestation in some individuals of underlying psychiatric disorders.

Nor is there any substantial consensus as to the "manifestations of alcoholism." E. M. Jellinek, one of the outstanding authorities on the subject, identifies five different types of alcoholics which predominate in the United States, and these types display a broad range of different and occasionally inconsistent symptoms.[5] Moreover, wholly distinct types, relatively rare in this country, predominate in nations with different cultural attitudes regarding the consumption of alcohol. Even if we limit our consideration to the range of alcoholic symptoms more typically found in this country, there is substantial disagreement as to the manifestations of the "disease" called "alcoholism." Jellinek, for example, considers that only two of his five alcoholic types can truly be said to be suffering from "alcoholism" as a "disease," because only these two types attain what he believes to be the requisite degree of physiological dependence on alcohol. He applies the label "gamma alcoholism" to "that species of alcoholism in which (1) acquired increased tissue tolerance to alcohol, (2) adaptive cell metabolism * * *, (3) withdrawal symptoms and 'craving,' i. e., physical dependence, and (4) loss of control are involved." A "delta" alcoholic, on the other hand, "shows the first three characteristics of gamma alcoholism as well as a less marked form of the fourth characteristic—that is, instead of loss of control there is inability to abstain." Other authorities approach

2. E. Jellinek, The Disease Concept of Alcoholism 11 (1960).

5. Jellinek, supra, n. 2, at 35–41.

the problems of classification in an entirely different manner and, taking account of the large role which psychosocial factors seem to play in "problem drinking," define the "disease" in terms of the earliest identifiable manifestations of any sort of abnormality in drinking patterns.

Dr. Wade appears to have testified about appellant's "chronic alcoholism" in terms similar to Jellinek's "gamma" and "delta" types, for these types are largely defined, in their later stages, in terms of a strong compulsion to drink, physiological dependence and an inability to abstain from drinking. No attempt was made in the court below, of course, to determine whether Leroy Powell could in fact properly be diagnosed as a "gamma" or "delta" alcoholic in Jellinek's terms. The focus at the trial, and in the dissent here, has been exclusively upon the factors of loss of control and inability to abstain. Assuming that it makes sense to compartmentalize in this manner the diagnosis of such a formless "disease," tremendous gaps in our knowledge remain, which the record in this case does nothing to fill.

The trial court's "finding" that Powell "is afflicted with the disease of chronic alcoholism," which "destroys the afflicted person's will power to resist the constant, excessive consumption of alcohol" covers a multitude of sins. Dr. Wade's testimony that appellant suffered from a compulsion which was an "exceedingly strong influence," but which was "not completely overpowering" is at least more carefully stated, if no less mystifying. Jellinek insists that conceptual clarity can only be achieved by distinguishing carefully between "loss of control" once an individual has commenced to drink and "inability to abstain" from drinking in the first place. Presumably a person would have to display both characteristics in order to make out a constitutional defense, should one be recognized. Yet the "findings" of the trial court utterly fail to make this crucial distinction, and there is serious question whether the record can be read to support a finding of either loss of control or inability to abstain.

Dr. Wade did testify that once appellant began drinking he appeared to have no control over the amount of alcohol he finally ingested. Appellant's own testimony concerning his drinking on the day of the trial would certainly appear, however, to cast doubt upon the conclusion that he was without control over his consumption of alcohol when he had sufficiently important reasons to exercise such control. However that may be, there are more serious factual and conceptual difficulties with reading this record to show that appellant was unable to abstain from drinking. Dr. Wade testified that when appellant was sober, the act of taking the first drink was a "voluntary exercise of his will," but that this exercise of will was undertaken under the "exceedingly strong influence" of a "compulsion" which was "not completely overpowering." Such concepts, when juxtaposed in this fashion, have little meaning.

Moreover, Jellinek asserts that it cannot accurately be said that a person is truly unable to abstain from drinking unless he is suffering the physical symptoms of withdrawal. There is no testimony in this record that Leroy Powell underwent withdrawal symptoms either before he began the drinking spree which resulted in the conviction under review here, or at any other time. In attempting to deal with the alcoholic's desire for drink in the absence of withdrawal symptoms, Jellinek is reduced to unintelligible distinctions between a "compulsion" (a "psychopathological phenomenon" which can apparently serve in some instances as the functional equivalent of a "craving" or symptom of withdrawal) and an "impulse" (something which differs from a loss of control, a craving or a compulsion, and to which Jellinek attributes the start of a new drinking bout for a "gamma" alcoholic). Other scholars are equally unhelpful in articulating the nature of a "compulsion."

It is one thing to say that if a man is deprived of alcohol his hands will begin to shake, he will suffer agonizing pains and ultimately he will have hallucinations; it is quite another to say that a man has a "compulsion" to take a drink, but that he also retains a certain amount of "free will" with which to resist. It is simply impossible, in the present state of our knowledge, to ascribe a useful meaning to the latter statement. This definitional confusion reflects, of course, not merely the undeveloped state of the psychiatric art but also the conceptual difficulties inevitably attendant upon the importation of scientific and medical models into a legal system generally predicated upon a different set of assumptions.

II.

Despite the comparatively primitive state of our knowledge on the subject, it cannot be denied that the destructive use of alcoholic beverages is one of our principal social and public health problems. The lowest current informed estimate places the number of "alcoholics" in America (definitional problems aside) at 4,000,000, and most authorities are inclined to put the figure considerably higher. The problem is compounded by the fact that a very large percentage of the alcoholics in this country are "invisible"—they possess the means to keep their drinking problems secret, and the traditionally uncharitable attitude of our society toward alcoholics causes many of them to refrain from seeking treatment from any source. Nor can it be gainsaid that the legislative response to this enormous problem has in general been inadequate.

There is as yet no known generally effective method for treating the vast number of alcoholics in our society. Some individual alcoholics have responded to particular forms of therapy with remissions of their symptomatic dependence upon the drug. But just as there is no agreement among doctors and social workers with respect to the causes of alcoholism, there is no consensus as to why particular treatments have been effective in particular cases and there is no generally agreed-upon approach to the problem of treatment on a large scale. Most psychiatrists are apparently of the opinion that alcoholism is far more difficult to treat than other forms of behavioral disorders, and some believe it is impossible to cure by means of psychotherapy; indeed, the medical profession as a whole, and psychiatrists in particular, have been severely criticised for the prevailing reluctance to undertake the treatment of drinking problems. Thus it is entirely possible that, even were the manpower and facilities available for a full-scale attack upon chronic alcoholism, we would find ourselves unable to help the vast bulk of our "visible"—let alone our "invisible" —alcoholic population.

However, facilities for the attempted treatment of indigent alcoholics are woefully lacking throughout the country. It would be tragic to return large numbers of helpless, sometimes dangerous and frequently unsanitary inebriates to the streets of our cities without even the opportunity to sober up adequately which a brief jail term provides. Presumably no State or city will tolerate such a state of affairs. Yet the medical profession cannot, and does not, tell us with any assurance that, even if the buildings, equipment and trained personnel were made available, it could provide anything more than slightly higher-class jails for our indigent habitual inebriates. Thus we run the grave risk that nothing will be acomplished beyond the hanging of a new sign—reading "hospital"—over one wing of the jailhouse.

One virtue of the criminal process is, at least, that the duration of penal incarceration typically has some outside statutory limit; this is universally true in the case of petty offenses, such as public drunkenness, where jail terms are quite short on the whole. "Therapeutic civil commitment" lacks this feature; one is typically committed until one is "cured." Thus, to do otherwise than affirm might subject indigent alcoholics to the risk that they may be locked up for an indefinite period of time under the same conditions as before, with no more hope than before of receiving effective treatment and no prospect of periodic "freedom."

Faced with this unpleasant reality, we are unable to assert that the use of the criminal process as a means of dealing with the public aspects of problem drinking can never be defended as rational. The picture of the penniless drunk propelled aimlessly and endlessly through the law's "revolving door" of arrest, incarceration, release and re-arrest is not a pretty one. But before we condemn the present practice across-the-board, perhaps we ought to be able to point to some clear promise of a better world for these unfortunate people. Unfortunately, no such promise has yet been forthcoming. If, in addition to the absence of a coherent approach to the problem of treatment, we consider the almost complete absence of facilities and manpower for the implementation of a rehabilitation program, it is difficult to say in the present context that the criminal process is utterly lacking in social value. This Court has never held that anything in the Constitution requires that penal sanctions be designed solely to achieve therapeutic or rehabilitative effects, and it can hardly be said with assurance that incarceration serves such purposes any better for the general run of criminals than it does for public drunks.

Ignorance likewise impedes our assessment of the deterrent effect of criminal sanctions for public drunkenness. The fact that a high percentage of American alcoholics conceal their drinking problems, not merely by avoiding public displays of intoxication but also by shunning all forms of treatment, is indicative that some powerful deterrent operates to inhibit the public revelation of the existence of alcoholism. Quite probably this deterrent effect can be largely attributed to the harsh moral attitude which our society has traditionally taken toward intoxication and the shame which we have associated with alcoholism. Criminal conviction represents the degrading public revelation of what Anglo-American society has long condemned as a moral defect, and the existence of criminal sanctions may serve to reinforce this cultural taboo, just as we presume it serves to reinforce other, stronger feelings against murder, rape, theft, and other forms of antisocial conduct.

Obviously, chronic alcoholics have not been deterred from drinking to excess by the existence of criminal sanctions against public drunkenness. But all those who violate penal laws of any kind are by definition undeterred. The long-standing and still raging debate over the validity of the deterrence justification for penal sanctions has not reached any sufficiently clear conclusions to permit it to be said that such sanctions are ineffective in any particular context or for any particular group of people who are able to appreciate the consequences of their acts. Certainly no effort was made at the trial of this case, beyond a monosyllabic answer to a perfunctory one-line question, to determine the effectiveness of penal sanctions in deterring Leroy Powell in particular or chronic alcoholics in general from drinking at all or from getting drunk in particular places or at particular times.

III.

Appellant claims that his conviction on the facts of this case would violate the Cruel and Unusual Punishment Clause of the Eighth Amendment as applied to the States through the Fourteenth Amendment. The primary purpose of that clause has always been considered, and properly so, to be directed at the method or kind of punishment imposed for the violation of criminal statutes; the nature of the conduct made criminal is ordinarily relevant only to the fitness of the punishment imposed.

*   *   *

Appellant, however, seeks to come within the application of the Cruel and Unusual Punishment Clause announced in Robinson v. State of California, 370 U.S. 660, 82 S.Ct. 1417, 8 L.Ed.2d 758 (1962), which involved a state statute making it a crime to "be addicted to the use of narcotics." This Court held there that "a state law which imprisons a person thus afflicted [with narcotic addiction] as a criminal, even though he has never touched any narcotic drug within the State or been guilty of any irregular behavior there, inflicts a cruel and unusual punishment * * *." Id., at 667, 82 S.Ct., at 1420–1421.

On its face the present case does not fall within that holding, since appellant was convicted, not for being a chronic alcoholic, but for being in public while drunk on a particular occasion. The State of Texas thus has not sought to punish a mere status, as California did in *Robinson*; nor has it attempted to regulate appellant's behavior in the privacy of his own home. Rather, it has imposed upon appellant a criminal sanction for public behavior which may create substantial health and safety hazards, both for appellant and for members of the general public, and which offends the moral and esthetic sensibilities of a large segment of the community. This seems a far cry from convicting one for being an addict, being a chronic alcoholic, being "mentally ill, or a leper * * *." Id., at 666, 82 S.Ct., at 1420.

Robinson so viewed brings this Court but a very small way into the substantive criminal law. And unless *Robinson* is so viewed it is difficult to see any limiting principle that would serve to prevent this Court from becoming, under the aegis of the Cruel and Unusual Punishment Clause, the ultimate arbiter of the standards of criminal responsibility, in diverse areas of the criminal law, throughout the country.

It is suggested in dissent that *Robinson* stands for the "simple" but "subtle" principle that "[c]riminal penalties may not be inflicted upon a person for being in a condition he is powerless to change." Post, at 2171. In that view, appellant's "condition" of public intoxication was "occasioned by a compulsion symptomatic of the disease" of chronic alcoholism, and thus, apparently, his behavior lacked the critical element of *mens rea*. Whatever may be the merits of such a doctrine of criminal responsibility, it surely cannot be said to follow from *Robinson*. The entire thrust of *Robinson's* interpretation of the Cruel and Unusual Punishment Clause is that criminal penalties may be inflicted only if the accused has committed some act, has engaged in some behavior, which society has an interest in preventing, or perhaps in historical common law terms, has committed some *actus reus*. It thus does not deal with the question of whether certain conduct cannot constitutionally be punished because it is, in some sense, "involuntary" or "occasioned by a compulsion."

Likewise, as the dissent acknowledges, there is a substantial definitional distinction between a "status," as in *Robinson*, and a "condition," which is said to be involved in this case. Whatever may be the merits of an attempt to disinguish between behavior and a condition, it is perfectly clear that the crucial element in this case, so far as the dissent is concerned, is whether or not appellant can legally be held responsible for his appearance in public in a state of intoxication. The only relevance of *Robinson* to this issue is that because the Court interpreted the statute there involved as making a "status" criminal, it was able to suggest that the statute would cover even a situation in which addiction had been acquired involuntarily. 370 U.S., at 667, n. 9, 82 S.Ct., at 1420. That this factor was not determinative in the case is shown by the fact that there was no indication of how Robinson himself had become an addict.

Ultimately, then, the most troubling aspects of this case, were *Robinson* to be extended to meet it, would be the scope and content of what could only be a constitutional doctrine of criminal responsibility. In dissent it is urged that the decision could be limited to conduct which is "a characteristic and involuntary part of the pattern of the disease as it afflicts" the particular individual, and that "[i]t is not foreseeable" that it would be applied "in the case of offenses such as driving a car while intoxicated, assault, theft, or robbery." Post, at 2167, n. 2. That is limitation by fiat. In the first place, nothing in the logic of the dissent would limit its application to chronic alcoholics. If Leroy Powell cannot be convicted of public intoxication, it is difficult to see how a State can convict an individual for murder, if that individual, while exhibiting normal behavior in all other respects, suffers from a "compulsion" to kill, which is an "exceedingly strong influence," but "not completely overpowering." Even if we limit our consideration to chronic alcoholics, it would seem impossible to confine the principle within the arbitrary bounds which the dissent seems to envision.

It is not difficult to imagine a case involving psychiatric testimony to the effect that an individual suffers from some aggressive neurosis which he is able to control when sober; that very little alcohol suffices to remove the inhibitions which normally contain these aggressions, with the result that the individual engages in assaultive behavior without becoming actually intoxicated; and that the individual suffers from a very strong desire to drink, which is an "exceedingly strong influence" but "not completely overpowering." Without being untrue to the rationale of this case, should the principles advanced in dissent be accepted here, the Court could not avoid holding such an individual constitutionally unaccountable for his assaultive behavior.

Traditional common-law concepts of personal accountability and essential considerations of federalism lead us to disagree with appellant. We are unable to conclude, on the state of this record or on the current state of medical knowledge, that chronic alcoholics in general, and Leroy Powell in particular, suffer from such an irresistible compulsion to drink and to get drunk in public that they are utterly unable to control their performance of either or both of these acts and thus cannot be deterred at all from public intoxication. And in any event this Court has never articulated a general constitutional doctrine of *mens rea*.

We cannot cast aside the centuries-long evolution of the collection of interlocking and overlapping concepts which the common law has utilized to assess the moral accountability of an individual for his antisocial deeds. The doctrines of *actus reus*, *mens rea*, insanity, mistake, justification, and duress have historically provided the tools for a constantly shifting adjustment of the tension between the evolving aims of the criminal law and changing religious, moral, philosophical, and medical views of the nature of man. This process of adjustment has always been thought to be the province of the States.

Nothing could be less fruitful than for this Court to be impelled into defining some sort of insanity test in constitutional terms. Yet, that task would seem to follow inexorably from an extension of *Robinson* to this case. If a person in the "condition" of being a chronic alcoholic cannot be criminally punished as a constitutional matter for being drunk in public, it would seem to follow that a person who contends that, in terms of one test, "his unlawful act was the product of mental disease or mental defect," Durham v. United States, 94 U.S.App.D.C. 228, 241, 214 F.2d 862, 875, 45 A.L.R.2d 1430 (1954), would state an issue of constitutional dimension with regard to his criminal responsibility had he been tried under some different and perhaps lesser standard, e. g., the right-wrong test of *M'Naghten's Case*. The experimentation of one jurisdiction in that field alone indicates the magnitude of the problem. * * * But formulating a constitutional rule would reduce, if not eliminate, that fruitful experimentation, and freeze the developing productive dialogue between law and psychiatry into a rigid constitutional mold. It is simply not yet the time to write the Constitutional formulas cast in terms whose meaning, let alone relevance, is not yet clear either to doctors or to lawyers.

Affirmed.

Mr. Justice BLACK, whom Mr. Justice HARLAN joins, concurring.

While I agree that the grounds set forth in Mr. Justice MARSHALL's opinion are sufficient to require affirmance of the judgment here, I wish to amplify my reasons for concurring.

* * *

The rule of constitutional law urged by appellant is not required by Robinson v. State of California, 370 U.S. 660, 82 S.Ct. 1417, 8

L.Ed.2d 758 (1962). In that case we held that a person could not be punished for the mere status of being a narcotics addict. We explicitly limited our holding to the situation where no conduct of any kind is involved * * *[.] The argument is made that appellant comes within the terms of our holding in *Robinson* because being drunk in public is a mere status or "condition." Despite this many-faceted use of the concept of "condition," this argument would require converting *Robinson* into a case protecting actual behavior, a step we explicitly refused to take in that decision.

A different question, I admit, is whether our attempt in *Robinson* to limit our holding to pure status crimes, involving no conduct whatever, was a sound one. I believe it was. Although some of our objections to the statute in *Robinson* are equally applicable to statutes that punish conduct "symptomatic" of a disease, any attempt to explain *Robinson* as based solely on the lack of voluntariness encounters a number of logical difficulties. Other problems raised by status crimes are in no way involved when the State attempts to punish for conduct, and these other problems were, in my view, the controlling aspects of our decision.

Punishment for a status is particularly obnoxious, and in many instances can reasonably be called cruel and unusual, because it involves punishment for a mere propensity, a desire to commit an offense; the mental element is not simply one part of the crime but may constitute all of it. This is a situation universally sought to be avoided in our criminal law; the fundamental requirement that some action be proved is solidly established even for offenses most heavily based on propensity, such as attempt, conspiracy, and recidivist crimes. * * *

The reasons for this refusal to permit conviction without proof of an act are difficult to spell out, but they are nonetheless perceived and universally expressed in our criminal law. Evidence of propensity can be considered relatively unreliable and more difficult for a defendant to rebut; the requirement of a specific act thus provides some protection against false charges. See 4 Blackstone, Commentaries 21. Perhaps more fundamental is the difficulty of distinguishing, in the absence of any conduct, between desires of the day-dream variety and fixed intentions that may pose a real threat to society; extending the criminal law to cover both types of desire would be unthinkable, since "[t]here can hardly be anyone who has never thought evil. When a desire is inhibited it may find expression in fantasy; but it would be absurd to condemn this natural psychological mechanism as illegal."

In contrast, crimes that require the State to prove that the defendant actually committed some proscribed act involve none of these special problems. * * *

Mr. Justice WHITE, concurring in the result.

If it cannot be a crime to have an irresistible compulsion to use narcotics, Robinson v. State of California, 370 U.S. 660, 82 S.Ct. 1417, 8 L.Ed.2d 758, rehearing denied, 371 U.S. 905, 83 S.Ct. 202, 9 L.Ed.2d 166 (1962), I do not see how it can constitutionally be a crime to yield to such a compulsion. Punishing an addict for using drugs convicts for addiction under a different name. Distinguishing between the two crimes is like forbidding criminal conviction for being sick with flu or epilepsy but permitting punishment for running a fever or having a convulsion. Unless *Robinson* is to be abanboned, the use of narcotics by an addict must be beyond the reach of the criminal law. Similarly, the chronic alcoholic with an irresistible urge to consume alcohol should not be punishable for drinking or for being drunk.

Powell's conviction was for the different crime of being drunk in a public place. Thus even if Powell was compelled to drink, and so could not constitutionally be convicted for drinking, his conviction in this case can be invalidated only if there is a constitutional basis for saying that he may not be punished for being in public while drunk. The statute involved here, which aims at keeping drunks off the street for their own welfare and that of others, is not challenged on the ground that it interferes unconstitutionally with the right to frequent public places. No question is raised about applying this statute to the nonchronic drunk, who has no compulsion to drink, who need not drink to excess, and who could have arranged to do his drinking in private or, if he began drinking in public, could have removed himself at an appropriate point on the path toward complete inebriation.

The trial court said that Powell was a chronic alcoholic with a compulsion not only to drink to excess but also to frequent public places when intoxicated. Nothing in the record before the trial court supports the latter conclusion, which is contrary to common sense and to common knowledge.[1] The sober chronic alcoholic has no compulsion to be on the public streets; many chronic alcoholics drink at home and are never seen drunk in public. Before and after taking the first drink, and until he becomes so drunk that he loses the power to know where he is or to direct his movements, the chronic alcoholic with a home or financial resources is as capable as the nonchronic drinker of doing his drinking in private, of removing himself from public places and, since he knows or ought to know that he will

---

1. The trial court gave no reasons for its conclusion that Powell appeared in public due to "a compulsion symptomatic of the disease of chronic alcoholism." No facts in the record support that conclusion. The trial transcript strongly suggests that the trial judge merely adopted proposed findings put before him by Powell's counsel. The fact that those findings were of no legal relevance in the trial judge's view of the case is very significant for appraising the extent to which they represented a well-considered and well-supported judgment. For all these reasons I do not feel impelled to accept this finding, and certainly would not rest a constitutional adjudication upon it.

become intoxicated, of making plans to avoid his being found drunk in public. For these reasons, I cannot say that the chronic alcoholic who proves his disease and a compulsion to drink is shielded from conviction when he has knowingly failed to take feasible precautions against committing a criminal act, here the act of going to or remaining in a public place. On such facts the alcoholic is like a person with smallpox, who could be convicted for being on the street but not for being ill, or, like the epileptic, who would be punished for driving a car but not for his disease.[2]

The fact remains that some chronic alcoholics must drink and hence must drink *somewhere*. Although many chronics have homes, many others do not. For all practical purposes the public streets may be home for these unfortunates, not because their disease compels them to be there, but because, drunk or sober, they have no place else to go and no place else to be when they are drinking. This is more a function of economic station than of disease, although the disease may lead to destitution and perpetuate that condition. For some of these alcoholics I would think a showing could be made that resisting drunkenness is impossible and that avoiding public places when intoxicated is also impossible. As applied to them this statute is in effect a law which bans a single act for which they may not be convicted under the Eighth Amendment—the act of getting drunk.

It is also possible that the chronic alcoholic who begins drinking in private at some point becomes so drunk that he loses the power to control his movements and for that reason appears in public. The Eighth Amendment might also forbid conviction in such circumstances, but only on a record satisfactorily showing that it was not feasible for him to have made arrangements to prevent his being in pub-

---

2. Analysis of this difficult case is not advanced by preoccupation with the label "condition." In *Robinson* the Court dealt with "a statute which makes the 'status' of narcotic addiction a criminal offense * * *." 370 U.S., at 666, 82 S.Ct., at 1420. By precluding criminal conviction for such a "status" the Court was dealing with a condition brought about by acts remote in time from the application of the criminal sanctions contemplated, a condition which was relatively permanent in duration, and a condition of great magnitude and significance in terms of human behavior and values. Although the same may be said for the "condition" of being a chronic alcoholic, it cannot be said for the mere transitory state of "being drunk in public." "Being" drunk in public is not far removed in time from the acts of "getting" drunk and "going" into public, and it is not necessarily

a state of any great duration. And, an isolated instance of "being" drunk in public is of relatively slight importance in the life of an individual as compared with the condition of being a chronic alcoholic. If it were necessary to distinguish between "acts" and "conditions" for purposes of the Eighth Amendment, I would adhere to the concept of "condition" implicit in the opinion in *Robinson*; I would not trivialize that concept by drawing a nonexistent line between the man who appears in public drunk and that same man five minutes later who is then "being" drunk in public. The proper subject of inquiry is whether volitional acts brought about the "condition" and whether those acts are sufficiently proximate to the "condition" for it to be permissible to impose penal sanctions on the "condition."

lic when drunk and that his extreme drunkenness sufficiently deprived him of his faculties on the occasion in issue.

These prerequisites to the possible invocation of the Eighth Amendment are not satisfied on the record before us.[4] Whether or not Powell established that he could not have resisted becoming drunk on December 19, 1966, nothing in the record indicates that he could not have done his drinking in private or that he was so inebriated at the time that he had lost control of his movements and wandered into the public street. Indeed, the evidence in the record strongly suggests that Powell could have drunk at home and made plans while sober to prevent ending up in a public place. Powell had a home and wife, and if there were reasons why he had to drink in public or be drunk there, they do not appear in the record.

Also, the only evidence bearing on Powell's condition at the time of his arrest was the testimony of the arresting officer that appellant staggered, smelled of alcohol, and was "very drunk." Powell testified that he had no clear recollection of the situation at the time of his arrest. His testimony about his usual condition when drunk is no substitute for evidence about his condition at the time of his arrest. Neither in the medical testimony nor elsewhere is there any indication that Powell had reached such a state of intoxication that he had lost the ability to comprehend what he was doing or where he was. For all we know from this record, Powell at the time knew precisely where he was, retained the power to stay off or leave the streets, and simply preferred to be there rather than elsewhere.

4. A holding that a person establishing the requisite facts could not, because of the Eighth Amendment, be criminally punished for appearing in public while drunk would be a novel construction of that Amendment, but it would hardly have radical consequences. In the first place when as here the crime charged was being drunk in a public place, only the compulsive chronic alcoholic would have a defense to both elements of the crime —for his drunkenness because his disease compelled him to drink and for being in a public place because the force of circumstances or excessive intoxication sufficiently deprived him of his mental and physical powers. The drinker who was not compelled to drink, on the other hand, although he might be as poorly circumstanced, equally intoxicated, and equally without his physical powers and cognitive faculties, could have avoided drinking in the first place, could have avoided drinking to excess, and need not have lost the power to manage his movements. Perhaps the heavily intoxicated, compulsive alcoholic who could not have arranged to avoid being in public places may not, consistent with the Eighth Amendment, be convicted for being drunk in a public place. However, it does not necessarily follow that it would be unconstitutional to convict him for committing crimes involving much greater risk to society.

Outside the area of alcoholism such a holding would not have a wide impact. Concerning drugs, such a construction of the Eighth Amendment would bar conviction only where the drug is addictive and then only for acts which are a necessary part of addiction, such as simple use. Beyond that it would preclude punishment only when the addiction to or the use of drugs caused sufficient loss of physical and mental faculties. This doctrine would not bar conviction of a heroin addict for being under the influence of heroin in a public place (although other constitutional concepts might be relevant to such a conviction), or for committing other criminal acts.

It is unnecessary to pursue at this point the further definition of the circumstances or the state of intoxication which might bar conviction of a chronic alcoholic for being drunk in a public place. For the purposes of this case, it is necessary to say only that Powell showed nothing more than that he was to some degree compelled to drink and that he was drunk at the time of his arrest. He made no showing that he was unable to stay off the streets on the night in question.[5]

Because Powell did not show that his conviction offended the Constitution, I concur in the judgment affirming the Travis County court.

Mr. Justice FORTAS, with whom Mr. Justice DOUGLAS, Mr. Justice BRENNAN, and Mr. Justice STEWART join, dissenting.

*　　*　　*

I.

The issue posed in this case is a narrow one. There is no challenge here to the validity of public intoxication statutes in general or to the Texas public intoxication statute in particular. This case does not concern the infliction of punishment upon the "social" drinker—or upon anyone other than a "chronic alcoholic" who, as the trier of fact here found, cannot "resist the constant, excessive consumption of alcohol." Nor does it relate to any offense other than the crime of public intoxication.

The sole question presented is whether a criminal penalty may be imposed upon a person suffering the disease of "chronic alcoholism" for a condition—being "in a state of intoxication" in public—which is a characteristic part of the pattern of his disease and which, the trial court found, was not the consequence of appellant's volition but of "a compulsion symptomatic of the disease of chronic alcoholism." We must consider whether the Eighth Amendment, made applicable to the States through the Fourteenth Amendment, prohibits the imposition of this penalty in these rather special circumstances as "cruel and unusual punishment." This case does not raise any question as to the right of the police to stop and detain those who are intoxicated in public, whether as a result of the disease or otherwise; or as to

5. I do not question the power of the State to remove a helplessly intoxicated person from a public street, although against his will, and to hold him until he has regained his powers. The person's own safety and the public interest require this much. A statute such as the one challenged in this case is constitutional insofar as it authorizes a police officer to arrest any seriously intoxicated person when he is encountered in a public place. Whether such a person may be charged and convicted for violating the statute will depend upon whether he is entitled to the protection of the Eighth Amendment.

the State's power to commit chronic alcoholics for treatment. Nor does it concern the responsibility of an alcoholic for criminal *acts*. We deal here with the mere *condition* of being intoxicated in public.[2]

II.

As I shall discuss, consideration of the Eighth Amendment issue in this case requires an understanding of "the disease of chronic alcoholism" with which, as the trial court found, appellant is afflicted, which has destroyed his "will power to resist the constant, excessive consumption of alcohol," and which leads him to "appear in public [not] by his own volition but under a compulsion symptomatic of the disease of chronic alcoholism." It is true, of course, that there is a great deal that remains to be discovered about chronic alcoholism. Although many aspects of the disease remain obscure, there are some hard facts—medical and, especially, legal facts— that are accessible to us and that provide a context in which the instant case may be analyzed. We are similarly woefully deficient in our medical, diagnostic, and therapeutic knowledge of mental disease and the problem of insanity; but few would urge that, because of this, we should totally reject the legal significance of what we do know about these phenomena.

Alcoholism is a major problem in the United States. In 1956 the American Medical Association for the first time designated alcoholism as a major medical problem and urged that alcoholics be admitted to general hospitals for care. This significant development marked the acceptance among the medical profession of the "disease concept of alcoholism." Although there is some problem in defining the concept, its core meaning, as agreed by authorities, is that alcoholism is caused and maintained by something other than the moral fault of the alcoholic, something that, to a greater or lesser extent depending upon the physiological or psychological makeup and history of the individual, cannot be controlled by him. Today most alcohologists and qualified members of the medical profession recognize the validity of this concept. Recent years have seen an intensification of medical interest in the subject. Medical groups have become active in educating the public, medical schools, and physicians in the etiology, diagnosis, and treatment of alcoholism.

Authorities have recognized that a number of factors may contribute to alcoholism. Some studies have pointed to physiological

2. It is not foreseeable that findings such as those which are decisive here —namely that the appellant's being intoxicated in public was a part of the pattern of his disease and due to a compulsion symptomatic of that disease—could or would be made in the case of offenses such as driving a car while intoxicated, assault, theft, or robbery. Such offenses require independent acts or conduct and do not typically flow from and are not part of the syndrome of the disease of chronic alcoholism. If an alcoholic should be convicted for criminal conduct which is not a characteristic and involuntary part of the pattern of the disease as it afflicts him, nothing herein would prevent his punishment.

influences, such as vitamin deficiency, hormone imbalance, abnormal metabolism, and hereditary proclivity. Other researchers have found more convincing a psychological approach, emphasizing early environment and underlying conflicts and tensions. Numerous studies have indicated the influence of sociocultural factors. It has been shown, for example, that the incidence of alcoholism among certain ethnic groups is far higher than among others.

The manifestations of alcoholism are reasonably well identified. The late E. M. Jellinek, an eminent alcohologist, has described five discrete types commonly found among American alcoholics. It is well established that alcohol may be habituative and "can be physically addicting." It has been said that "the main point for the nonprofessional is that alcoholism is not within the control of the person involved. He is not willfully drinking."

Although the treatment of alcoholics has been successful in many cases, physicians have been unable to discover any single treatment method that will invariably produce satisfactory results. A recent study of available treatment facilities concludes as follows: [14]

"Although numerous kinds of therapy and intervention appear to have been effective with various kinds of problem drinkers, the process of matching patient and treatment method is not yet highly developed. There is an urgent need for continued experimentation, for modifying and improving existing treatment methods, for developing new ones, and for careful and well-designed evaluative studies. Most of the facilities that provide services for alcoholics have made little, if any, attempt to determine the effectiveness of the total program or of its components."

Present services for alcoholics include state and general hospitals, separate state alcoholism programs, outpatient clinics, community health centers, general practitioners, and private psychiatric facilities. Self-help organizations, such as Alcoholics Anonymous, also aid in treatment and rehabilitation.

The consequences of treating alcoholics, under the public intoxication laws, as criminals can be identified with more specificity. * * * Their arrest and processing place a tremendous burden upon the police, who are called upon to spend a large amount of time in arresting for public intoxication and in appearing at trials for public intoxication, and upon the entire criminal process.

It is not known how many drunkenness offenders are chronic alcoholics, but "[t]here is strong evidence * * * that a large number of those who are arrested have a lengthy history of prior drunkenness arrests." "There are instances of the same person being arrested as many as forty times in a single year on charges of

14. The Treatment of Alcoholism 13.

drunkenness, and every large urban center can point to cases of individuals appearing before the courts on such charges 125, 150, or even 200 times in the course of a somewhat longer period."

It is entirely clear that the jailing of chronic alcoholics is punishment. It is not defended as therapeutic, nor is there any basis for claiming that it is therapeutic (or indeed a deterrent). The alcoholic offender is caught in a "revolving door"—leading from arrest on the street through a brief, unprofitable sojourn in jail, back to the street and, eventually, another arrest. The jails, overcrowded and put to a use for which they are not suitable, have a destructive effect upon alcoholic inmates.

Finally, most commentators, as well as experienced judges, are in agreement that "there is probably no drearier example of the futility of using penal sanctions to solve a psychiatric problem than the enforcement of the laws against drunkenness."

> "If all of this effort, all of this investment of time and money, were producing constructive results, then we might find satisfaction in the situation despite its costs. But the fact is that this activity accomplishes little that is fundamental. No one can seriously suggest that the threat of fines and jail sentences actually deters habitual drunkenness or alcoholic addiction. * * * Nor, despite the heroic efforts being made in a few localities, is there much reason to suppose that any very effective measures of cure and therapy can or will be administered in the jails. But the weary process continues, to the detriment of the total performance of the law-enforcement function." [27]

III.

It bears emphasis that these data provide only a context for consideration of the instant case. They should not dictate our conclusion. The questions for this Court are not settled by reference to medicine or penology. Our task is to determine whether the principles embodied in the Constitution of the United States place any limitations upon the circumstances under which punishment may be inflicted, and, if so, whether, in the case now before us, those principles preclude the imposition of such punishment.

It is settled that the Federal Constitution places some substantive limitation upon the power of state legislatures to define crimes for which the imposition of punishment is ordered. In Robinson v. State of California, 370 U.S. 660, 82 S.Ct. 1417, 8 L.Ed.2d 758 (1962), the Court considered a conviction under a California statute making it a criminal offense for a person "[t]o be addicted to the use of narcotics." * * *

27. F. Allen, The Borderland of Criminal Justice 8–9 (1964).

This Court reversed Robinson's conviction on the ground that punishment under the law in question was cruel and unusual, in violation of the Eighth Amendment of the Constitution as applied to the States through the Fourteenth Amendment. * * *

Robinson stands upon a principle which, despite its subtlety, must be simply stated and respectfully applied because it is the foundation of individual liberty and the cornerstone of the relations between a civilized state and its citizens: Criminal penalties may not be inflicted upon a person for being in a condition he is powerless to change. In all probability, Robinson at some time before his conviction elected to take narcotics. But the crime as defined did not punish this conduct. The statute imposed a penalty for the offense of "addiction"—a condition which Robinson could not control. Once Robinson had become an addict, he was utterly powerless to avoid criminal guilt. He was powerless to choose not to violate the law.

In the present case, appellant is charged with a crime composed of two elements—being intoxicated and being found in a public place while in that condition. The crime, so defined, differs from that in *Robinson*. The statute covers more than a mere status. But the essential constitutional defect here is the same as in *Robinson*, for in both cases the particular defendant was accused of being in a condition which he had no capacity to change or avoid. The trial judge sitting as trier of fact found upon the medical and other relevant testimony, that Powell is a "chronic alcoholic." He defined appellant's "chronic alcoholism" as "a disease which destroys the afflicted person's will power to resist the constant, excessive consumption of alcohol." He also found that "a chronic alcoholic does not appear in public by his own volition but under a compulsion symptomatic of the disease of chronic alcoholism." I read these findings to mean that appellant was powerless to avoid drinking; that having taken his first drink, he had "an uncontrollable compulsion to drink" to the point of intoxication; and that, once intoxicated, he could not prevent himself from appearing in public places.

Article 477 of the Texas Penal Code is specifically directed to the accused's presence while in a state of intoxication, "in any public place, or at any private house except his own." This is the essence of the crime. Ordinarily when the State proves such presence in a state of intoxication, this will be sufficient for conviction, and the punishment prescribed by the State may, of course, be validly imposed. But here the findings of the trial judge call into play the principle that a person may not be punished if the condition essential to constitute the defined crime is part of the pattern of his disease and is occasioned by a compulsion symptomatic of the disease. This principle, narrow in scope and applicability, is implemented by the Eighth Amendment's prohibition of "cruel and unusual punishment," as we construed that command in *Robinson*. It is true that the command of the Eighth Amendment and its antecedent provision in the Bill of Rights of 1689 were initially directed to the type and degree of punishment inflicted. But in *Robinson* we recognized that "the principle that would deny power to exact capital punishment for a petty crime would also deny power to punish a person by fine or imprisonment for being sick." 370 U.S., at 676, 82 S.Ct., at 1425 (Mr. Justice DOUGLAS, concurring).

* * *

I would reverse the judgment below.

NOTES

1. Prior to the Supreme Court's decision in Powell, two United States Courts of Appeal had held that chronic alcoholics could not be convicted under public drunkenness statutes. Driver v. Hinnant, 356 F.2d 761 (4th Cir. 1966) was decided on Eighth Amendment cruel and unusual punishment grounds. Easter v. District of Columbia, 124 U.S.App.D.C. 33, 361 F.2d 50 (1966) rested upon the ground that legislative intent (evidenced by an extensive noncriminal program dealing with alcoholism) directed this result. Following Powell, a number of other courts rejected such arguments, often on reasoning that includes an evaluation of the evidence as inadequate to establish true involuntariness of the intoxication or appearance in public. See Budd v. Madigan, 418 F.2d 1032 (9th Cir. 1969), certiorari denied 397 U.S. 1053, 90 S.Ct. 1394, 25 L.Ed.2d 669 (1970); Vick v. State, 453 P.2d 342 (Alaska, 1969); People v. Hoy, 380 Mich. 597, 158 N.W.2d 436 (1968); Portland v. Juntunen, 488 P.2d 806 (Ore.App. 1971); Seattle v. Hill, 72 Wash.2d 786, 435 P.2d 692 (1967), certiorari denied 393 U.S. 872, 89 S.Ct. 163, 21 L.Ed.2d 142 (1968). The Minnesota Supreme Court, however, held in State v. Fearon, 283 Minn. 90, 166 N.W.2d 720 (1969) that legislative intent precluded the conviction of a chronic alcoholic under a statute declaring that "every person who becomes intoxicated by voluntarily drinking intoxicating liquor is guilty of the crime of drunkenness. . . ." In Upchurch v. State, 289 Minn. 520, 184 N.W.2d 607 (1971) the same court reviewed the revocation of probation of a defendant convicted of burglary. The defendant had asserted that he had been intoxicated at the time of the offense but that he thought he could "dry out." One condition of the probation was that the defendant not use intoxicating liquors. The defendant began drinking and was hospitalized. His probation was revoked when he refused to voluntarily remain hospitalized. Affirming the revocation and upholding the condition of probation prohibiting use of intoxicating liquors despite the allegedly involuntary nature of the defendant's drinking, the court stated, "The prospect of confinement is a compelling deterrent in a sufficient number of instances to justify the continuation of this probation practice." See generally, Stern, Handling Public Drunkenness: Reform Despite *Powell*, 55 A.B.A.J. 656 (1969).

2. Is the manner in which the issue is stated by any of the opinions satisfactory? If the function of legal doctrine is to provide a vehicle for organizing and evaluating all relevant considerations, does the doctrinal issue as posed by either the plurality or dissenting opinions do the job? Is the "data" set out by Mr. Justice Fortas in Part II of his opinion merely "a context for consideration of the instant case"? Should it be? Why

did Mr. Justice Fortas so describe the "data"? Consider the following alternative statement of the doctrinal issue: Given all of the benefits that might reasonably be expected to flow from such action weighed against the reasonably anticipatable "costs", was the legislative decision to authorize criminal conviction of a chronic alcoholic for being found in a state of intoxication in a public place so unreasonable as to constitute cruel and unusual punishment in violation of the Eighth Amendment? What arguments might be made for and against such a formulation of the issue?

3. To the extent that the underlying social problem is one of the "skid row derelict," would the rule advocated by the dissenters in Powell deal effectively with the problem? Consider the following from Murtagh, Arrests for Public Intoxication, 35 Fordham L.Rev. 1, 9–10 (1966). The subjects of the comments are the decisions in Easter v. District of Columbia and Driver v. Hinnant, but they may have some applicability to the Powell issue:

> Should the results in such cases depend on whether a derelict is a "chronic alcoholic?" Do not the opinions reveal a lack of perception of the nature of the skid row derelict? Do they not particularly fail to distinguish between chronic alcoholism and other forms of pathological drinking?

> It is not strange that the *Easter* and *Driver* opinions reflect an inability to identify with the derelict. The learned judges of those courts had probably been spared the experience of socializing with, or even meeting, a skid row derelict. Moreover, the derelict has been largely ignored by the behavioral sciences and is as yet almost a complete enigma. Most of the observations of the authors of the standard studies on skid row derelicts are impressionistic. * * *

> Nowhere is the lack of scientific data more evident than in the consideration of the derelict's involvement with alcohol. This is best expressed by McCarthy and Straus:

>> The impression still prevails * * * that the inhabitants of Skid Row or Bowery districts are nearly all addicted to alcohol. This belief is based on seemingly overwhelming evidence. * * *

>> Despite impressive external evidence of widespread excessive drinking among Bowery populations, data are not available for determining whether the drinking patterns of homeless men are consistent with clinical criteria of alcohol addiction. Few of these men seek or accept sustained professional treatment and nearly all resist personal questioning by an investigator. Psychological data on this population group are scant. Certain observations, necessarily impressionistic, suggest that some factors in the drinking behavior of many homeless men may be significantly different from those of persons who are classified clinically as addictive drinkers and that the commonly assumed synonymity of homelessness, vagrancy (and all equiv-

alent terms) with alcohol addiction may be technically erroneous. * * *[57]

Although pathological drinking is characteristic of a majority of the so-called homeless man population, *a substantial portion of these men should not be classified as addictive drinkers* * * *.[58]

This interesting hypothesis of McCarthy and Straus has been widely accepted. Bendiner states:

> [T]he Bowery Man's drinking style is less formidable than that of the respectable alcoholic. The Bowery Man rarely drinks alone with the singleminded objective of a quick knockout. He is a social drinker. And not only does he pass the bottle, but he must combine with his fellows to raise the price of one.
>
> He drinks to achieve a pleasant plateau from which he can survey the world and his fellows with some equanimity. He craves an illusion of friendship without the responsibilities that friends impose. His alcoholic haze fragments the harsh light of the world and diffuses it so that edges are blurred and the world is soft.[59]

After getting involved in the issue of alcoholism, the courts in the *Driver* and *Easter* cases appear to have assumed, contrary to the hypothesis of McCarthy and Straus, that all pathological drinkers are chronic alcoholics or addictive drinkers. If their reasoning were followed, the rulings would be limited to the percentage of derelicts who are addictive as distinquished from plateau and other problems drinkers.[a]

4. Biglow, Cohen, Liebson and Faillace, Abstinence or Moderation? Choice by Alcoholics, 10 Journal of Behavior Research and Therapy 209 (1972) reports on a study involving nineteen male "chronic alcoholics" referred from a hospital emergency room. During the period of the study, one ounce drinks of 95 proof liquor were available to the subjects upon their request. Upper limits upon consumption were enforced, but the subjects could consume up to six ounces of liquor in a two-hour period and up to ten or 24 ounces per day. On certain days each subject was given access to an "enriched environment" if he did not consume more than five ounces of liquor. The "enriched environment" included a recreational room, opportunity to socialize with staff members and other patients in the facility, the right to have visitors, a bedside chair and reading materials, a job that paid $1.00 per hour, and a regular diet. On those days when abstinence or moderation in drinking were rewarded by access to the en-

57. McCarthy & Straus, Nonaddictive Pathological Drinking Patterns of Homeless Men, 12 Q.J.Studies on Alcohol 602–03 (1951).

58. Id. at 609. (Emphasis added.)

59. Bendiner, ["Immovable Obstacle" in the Way of a New Bowery, N.Y.Times, January 21, 1962, § 6 (Magazine), p. 22].

a. Reprinted by permission of copyright holder from Fordham Law Review, Volume 35, pp. 1–14. Business Office: Fordham Law Review, Lincoln Center, 140 West 62nd Street, New York, N. Y. 10023. © 1966 by Fordham University Press.

riched environment, the subjects tended to drink but not to exceed the five ounce limit that determined their access to the "enriched environment." The nineteen subjects spent a total of 278 "subject days" under conditions offering such a choice.   Only 27 subject days (9.7 percent) involved consumption of over five ounces of liquor.   On the other hand, only 38 subject days (13.7 percent) involved total abstinence.   The remaining 213 subject days (76.6 percent) involved moderate drinking.   Those subjects that drank moderately tended to drink up to—but not beyond—the limit.   92.5 percent of the subject days involving moderate drinking were characterized by consumption of the five ounce limit.   How helpful is this study in resolving the issues posed by Powell?

2.   THE NEED TO BE PRECISE

Robinson v. California and Powell v. Texas deal with the basic policy decision of what to make criminal.   But the task of the law is not only to make such a decision but to embody it in a "rule." As with the decision to make given activity criminal, the decision as to how to express the result can best be initially approached by examining constitutional limitations upon possible solutions.   In the case of expressing the result, the basic constitutional limitation is the due process requirement of precision or, in negative terms, the defect of vagueness.   Consider, in light of the material in this chapter, the extent to which the statute involved in Powell v. Texas might be subject to attack on vagueness grounds.   Consider the same matter in regard to the various other statutes presented in this chapter as embodying various approaches—both criminal and noncriminal—towards alcohol-related activity.

PAPACHRISTOU v. JACKSONVILLE

Supreme Court of the United States, 1972.
405 U.S. 156, 92 S.Ct. 839, 31 L.Ed.2d 110.

Mr. Justice DOUGLAS delivered the opinion of the Court.

This case involves eight defendants who were convicted in a Florida municipal court of violating a Jacksonville, Florida, vagrancy ordinance.[1]   *   *   *   For reasons which will appear, we reverse.

1.   Jacksonville Ordinance Code § 26–57 provided at the time of these arrests and convictions as follows:

"Rogues and vagabonds, or dissolute persons who go about begging, common gamblers, persons who use juggling or unlawful games or plays, common drunkards, common night walkers, thieves, pilferers or pickpockets, traders in stolen property, lewd, wanton and lascivious persons, keepers of gambling places, common railers and brawlers, persons wandering or strolling around from place to place without any lawful purpose or object, habitual loafers, disorderly persons, persons neglecting all lawful business and habitually spending their time by frequenting houses of ill fame, gaming houses, or places where alcoholic beverages are sold or served, persons able to work but habitually living

At issue are five consolidated cases. Margaret Papachristou, Betty Calloway, Eugene Eddie Melton, and Leonard Johnson were all arrested early on a Sunday morning, and charged with vagrancy—"prowling by auto."

Jimmy Lee Smith and Milton Henry were charged with vagrancy—"vagabonds."

Henry Edward Heath and a co-defendant were arrested for vagrancy—"loitering" and "common thief."

Thoms Owen Campbell was charged with vagrancy—"common thief."

Hugh Brown was charged with vagrancy—"disorderly loitering on street" and "disorderly conduct—resisting arrest with violence."

The facts are stipulated. Papachristou and Calloway are white females. Melton and Johnson are black males. Papachristou was enrolled in a job-training program sponsored by the State Employment Service at Florida Junior College in Jacksonville. Calloway was a typing and shorthand teacher at a state mental institution located near Jacksonville. She was the owner of the automobile in which the four defendants were arrested. Melton was a Vietnam war veteran who had been released from the Navy after nine months in a veterans' hospital. On the date of his arrest he was a part-time computer helper while attending college as a full-time student in Jacksonville. Johnson was a tow-motor operator in a grocery chain warehouse and was a lifelong resident of Jacksonville.

At the time of their arrest the four of them were riding in Calloway's car on the main thoroughfare in Jacksonville. They had left a restaurant owned by Johnson's uncle where they had eaten and were on their way to a night club. The arresting officers denied that the racial mixture in the car played any part in the decision to make the arrest. The arrest, they said, was made because the defendants had stopped near a used-car lot which had been broken into several times. There was, however, no evidence of any breaking and entering on the night in question.

Of these four charged with "prowling by auto" none had been previously arrested except Papachristou who had once been convicted of a municipal offense.

upon the earnings of their wives or minor children shall be deemed vagrants and, upon conviction in the Municipal Court shall be punished as provided for Class D offenses."

Class D offenses at the time of these arrests and convictions were punishable by 90 days imprisonment, $500 fine, or both. Jacksonville Ordinance Code § 1–8 (1965). The maximum punishment has since been reduced to 75 days or $450. § 304.101 (1971). We are advised that that downward revision was made to avoid federal right-to-counsel decisions. The Fifth Circuit case extending right to counsel in misdemeanors where a fine of $500 or 90-days imprisonment could be imposed is Harvey v. Mississippi, 340 F.2d 263 (CA 5 1965).

[The details of the arrests in the other cases are omitted.]

Jacksonville's ordinance and Florida's statute were "derived from early English law," * * * and employ "archaic language" in their definitions of vagrants. The history is an often-told tale. The break-up of feudal estates in England led to labor shortages which in turn resulted in the Statutes of Laborers, designed to stabilize the labor force by prohibiting increases in wages and prohibiting the movement of workers from their home areas in search of improved conditions. Later vagrancy laws became criminal aspects of the poor laws. The series of laws passed in England on the subject became increasingly severe. But "the theory of the Elizabethan poor laws no longer fits the facts," Edwards v. California, 314 U.S. 160, 174, 62 S.Ct. 164, 167, 86 L.Ed. 119. The conditions which spawned these laws may be gone, but the archaic classifications remain.

This ordinance is void-for-vagueness, both in the sense that it "fails to give a person of ordinary intelligence fair notice that his contemplated conduct is forbidden by the statute," United States v. Harriss, 347 U.S. 612, 617, 74 S.Ct. 808, 812, 98 L.Ed. 989, and because it encourages arbitrary and erratic arrests and convictions. * * *

Living under a rule of law entails various suppositions, one of which is that "All [persons] are entitled to be informed as to what the State commands or forbids." Lanzetta v. New Jersey, 306 U.S. 451, 453, 59 S.Ct. 618, 619, 83 L.Ed. 888.

Lanzetta is one of a well-recognized group of cases insisting that the law give fair notice of the offending conduct. * * * In the field of regulatory statutes governing business activities, where the acts limited are in a narrow category, greater leeway is allowed. * * *

The poor among us, the minorities, the average householder are not in business and not alerted to the regulatory schemes of vagrancy laws; and we assume they would have no understanding of their meaning and impact if they read them. Nor are they protected from being caught in the vagrancy net by the necessity of having a specific intent to commit an unlawful act. * * *

The Jacksonville ordinance makes criminal activities which by modern standards are normally innocent. "Nightwalking" is one. Florida construes the ordinance not to make criminal one night's wandering, Johnson v. State, [Fla., 202 So.2d 852, 855,] only the "habitual" wanderer or as the ordinance describes it "common night walkers." We know, however, from experience that sleepless people often walk at night, perhaps hopeful that sleep-inducing relaxation will result.

"Persons able to work but habitually living on the earnings of their wives or minor children"—like habitually living "without visible means of support"—might implicate unemployed pillars of the community who have married rich wives.

"Persons able to work but habitually living on the earnings of their wives or minor children" may also embrace unemployed people out of the labor market, by reason of a recession or disemployed by reason of technological or so-called structural displacements.

Persons "wandering or strolling" from place to place have been extolled by Walt Whitman and Vachel Lindsay. The qualification "without any lawful purpose or object" may be a trap for innocent acts. Persons "neglecting all lawful business and habitually spending their time by frequenting * * * places where alcoholic beverages are sold or served" would literally embrace many members of golf clubs and city clubs.

Walkers and strollers and wanderers may be going to or coming from a burglary. Loafers or loiterers may be "casing" a place for a holdup. Letting one's wife support him is an intra-family matter, and normally of no concern to the police. Yet it may, of course, be the setting for numerous crimes.

The difficulty is that these activities are historically part of the amenities of life as we have known it. They are not mentioned in the Constitution or in the Bill of Rights. These unwritten amenities have been in part responsible for giving our people the feeling of independence and self-confidence, the feeling of creativity. These amenities have dignified the right of dissent and have honored the right to be nonconformists and the right to defy submissiveness. They have encouraged lives of high spirits rather than hushed, suffocating silence.

This aspect of the vagrancy ordinance before us is suggested by what this Court said in 1875 about a broad criminal statute enacted by Congress: "It would certainly be dangerous if the legislature could set a net large enough to catch all possible offenders, and leave it to the courts to step inside and say who could be rightfully detained, and who should be set at large." United States v. Reese, 92 U.S. 214, 221, 23 L.Ed. 563.

While that was a federal case, the due process implications are equally applicable to the States and to this vagrancy ordinance. Here the net cast is large, not to give the courts the power to pick and choose but to increase the arsenal of the police. * * *

Where the list of crimes is so all-inclusive and generalized as that one in this ordinance, those convicted may be punished for no more than vindicating affronts to police authority:

"The common ground which brings such a motley assortment of human troubles before the magistrates in vagrancy-type proceedings is the procedural laxity which permits 'conviction' for almost any kind of conduct and the existence of

the House of Correction as an easy and convenient dump-
ing-ground for problems that appear to have no other immediate solution." Foote, Vagrancy Type Law and Its Administration, 104 U.Pa.L.Rev. 603, 631.

Another aspect of the ordinance's vagueness appears when we
focus, not on the lack of notice given a potential offender, but on the
effect of the unfettered discretion it places in the hands of the Jacksonville police. Caleb Foote, an early student of this subject, has
called the vagrancy-type law as offering "punishment by analogy."
Id., at 609. Such crimes, though long common in Russia, are not
compatible with our constitutional system. We allow our police
to make arrests only on "probable cause," a Fourth and Fourteenth
Amendment standard applicable to the States as well as to the Federal Government. Arresting a person on suspicion, like arresting a
person for investigation, is foreign to our system, even when the
arrest is for past criminality. Future criminality, however, is the
common justification for the presence of vagrancy statutes. See
Foote, op. cit. supra, at 625. Florida has indeed construed her vagrancy statute "as necessary regulations," *inter alia*, "to deter vaga-
bondage and prevent crimes." Johnson v. State, Fla., 202 So.2d
852; Smith v. State, Fla., 239 So.2d 250, 251.

A direction by a legislature to the police to arrest all "suspicious"
persons would not pass constitutional muster. A vagrancy prosecution may be merely the cloak for a conviction which could not be obtained on the real but undisclosed grounds for the arrest. People v.
Moss, 309 N.Y. 429, 131 N.E.2d 717. But as Chief Justice Hewart
said in Frederick Dean, 18 Cr.App.Rep. 133, 134 (1924):

> "It would be in the highest degree unfortunate if in any
> part of the country those who are responsible for setting in
> motion the criminal law should entertain, connive at or co-
> quette with the idea that in a case where there is not enough
> evidence to charge the prisoner with an attempt to commit
> a crime, the prosecution may, nevertheless, on such insuf-
> ficient evidence, succeed in obtaining and upholding a con-
> viction under the Vagrancy Act, 1824."

Those generally implicated by the imprecise terms of the ordinance—poor people, nonconformists, dissenters, idlers—may be required to comport themselves according to the life-style deemed appropriate by the Jacksonville police and the courts. Where, as here,
there are no standards governing the exercise of the discretion granted by the ordinance, the scheme permits and encourages an arbitrary
and discriminatory enforcement of the law. It furnishes a convenient tool for "harsh and discriminatory enforcement by prosecuting officials, against particular groups deemed to merit their dis-
pleasure." Thornhill v. Alabama, 310 U.S. 88, 97–98, 60 S.Ct. 736,
742, 84 L.Ed. 1093. It results in a regime in which the poor and

the unpopular are permitted to "stand on a public sidewalk * * * only at the whim of any police officer." * * *

The implicit presumption in these generalized vagrancy standards—that crime is being nipped in the bud—is too extravagant to deserve extended treatment. Of course, vagrancy statutes are useful to the police. Of course they are nets making easy the roundup of so-called undesirables. But the rule of law implies equality and justice in its application. Vagrancy laws of the Jacksonville type teach that the scales of justice are so tipped that that evenhanded administration of the law is not possible. The rule of law, evenly applied to minorities as well as majorities, to the poor as well as the rich, is the great mucilage that holds society together.

The Jacksonville ordinance cannot be squared with our constitutional standards and is plainly unconstitutional.

Reversed.

Mr. Justice POWELL and Mr. Justice REHNQUIST took no part in the consideration or decision of this case.

NOTES

1. Consider the following comment by Mr. Justice Frankfurter, dissenting in Winters v. New York, 333 U.S. 507, 68 S.Ct. 665, 92 L.Ed. 840 (1948):

[The] requirement of fair notice that there is a boundary of prohibited conduct not to be overstepped is included in the conception of "due process of law." The legal jargon for such failure to give forewarning is to say that the statute is void for "indefiniteness."

But "indefiniteness" is not a quantitative concept. It is not even a technical concept of definite components. It is itself an indefinite concept. There is no such thing as "indefiniteness" in the abstract, by which the sufficiency of the requirement expressed by the term may be ascertained. The requirement is fair notice that conduct may entail punishment. But whether notice is or is not "fair" depends upon the subject matter to which it relates. Unlike the abstract stuff of mathematics, or the quantitatively ascertainable elements of much of natural science, legislation is greatly concerned with the multiform psychological complexities of individual and social conduct. Accordingly, the demands upon legislation, and its responses, are variable and multiform. That which may appear to be too vague and even meaningless as to one subject matter may be as definite as another subject matter of legislation permits, if the legislative power to deal with such a subject is not to be altogether denied. The statute books of every State are full of instances of what may look like unspecific definitions of crime, of the drawing of wide circles of prohibited conduct.

In these matters legislatures are confronted with a dilemma. If a law is framed with narrow particularity, too easy opportunities are afforded to nullify the purposes of the legislation. If the legislation is drafted in terms so vague that no ascertainable line is drawn in advance between innocent and condemned conduct, the purpose of the legislation cannot be enforced because no purpose is defined. It is not merely in the enactment of tax measures that the task of reconciling these extremes—of avoiding throttling particularity or unfair generality—is one of the most delicate and difficult confronting legislators. The reconciliation of these two contradictories is necessarily an empiric enterprise largely depending on the nature of the particular legislative problem.

What risks do the innocent run of being caught in a net not designed for them? How important is the policy of the legislation, so that those who really like to pursue innocent conduct are not likely to be caught unaware? How easy is it to be explicitly particular? How necessary is it to leave a somewhat penumbral margin but sufficiently revealed by what is condemned to those who do not want to sail close to the shore of questionable conduct? These and like questions confront legislative draftsmen. Answers to these questions are not to be found in any legislative manual nor in the work of great legislative draftsmen. They are not to be found in the opinions of this Court. These are questions of judgment, peculiarly within the responsibility and the competence of legislatures. The discharge of that responsibility should not be set at naught by abstract notions about "indefiniteness."

If "indefiniteness" or "vagueness" is not definable as an abstract matter, how should the judicial decision as to whether, in a specific context, the legislature has been "too indefinite" or "too vague" be made? Is the question whether, given the possible justifications for imprecision and the potential costs of such imprecision, the legislative judgment that the imprecision was worth the risks was "unreasonable?" If so, what factors—in addition to those enumerated by Mr. Justice Frankfurter—might be considered? See Note, The Void-For-Vagueness Doctrine in the Supreme Court, 109 U.Penn.L.Rev. 67 (1961).

2. In Giaccio v. Pennsylvania, 382 U.S. 399, 86 S.Ct. 518, 15 L.Ed. 2d 447 (1966) the Court struck down a statute authorizing the imposition of court costs upon an acquitted defendant in a nonfelony case "whenever the jury shall [so] determine." Explaining, the Court stated:

[A] law fails to meet the requirements of Due Process if it is so vague and standardless that it * * * leaves judges and jurors free to decide, without any legally fixed standards, what is prohibited and what is not in each particular case. * * * [The statute at issue] contains no standards at all, nor does it place any conditions of any kind upon the jury's power to impose costs upon a defendant who has been found by the jury to be not guilty of a crime charged against him. * * * Certainly one of the basic purposes of the Due Process Clause has always been to protect a person against having the Government impose burdens upon him except in accordance with the valid laws of the land. Implicit in this constitutional safeguard is the premise that the law must be one that carries an understandable meaning with legal standards that courts must enforce. This state Act as written does not even begin to meet this constitutional requirement.

382 U.S. at 402–03. Is this an indication of another interest that the constitutional requirement of precision is intended to protect? Does not efficient administration of a court system—on both the trial and appellate levels—require that the participants have laws to work with that are reasonably precise? If so, does the constitutional requirement of precision serve the purpose of furthering the administrative efficiency of the judicial system, either expressly or implicitly? Is it important whether or not it does so?

Compare with Giaccio the more recent decision in McGautha v. California, 402 U.S. 183, 91 S.Ct. 1454, 28 L.Ed.2d 711 (1971), that Fourteenth Amendment standards were not violated by authorization of juries to impose the death penalty or life imprisonment, even though no attempt was made to provide any guidance for the making of this decision. The Court explained its result as follows:

> To identify before the fact those characteristics of criminal homicides and their perpetrators which call for the death penalty, and to express these characteristics in language which can be fairly understood and applied by the sentencing authority, appear to be tasks which are presently beyond present human ability.

*   *   *

> In light of history, experience, and the present limitations of human knowledge, we find it quite impossible to say that committing to the untrammelled discretion of the jury the power to pronounce life or death in capital cases is offensive to anything in the Constitution. The States are entitled to assume that jurors confronted with the truly awesome responsibility of decreeing death for a fellow human will act with due regard for the consequences of their decision and will consider a variety of factors, many of which will have been suggested by the evidence or by the arguments of defense counsel. For a court [or legislature?—ed.] to attempt to catalog the appropriate factors in this elusive area could inhibit rather than expand the scope of consideration, for no list of circumstances would ever be really complete. The infinite variety of cases and facets to each case would make general standards either meaningless "boiler-plate" or a statement of the obvious that no jury would need.

402 U.S. at 204, 207–08. Does this mean that there cannot be situations in which the difficulty of drafting standards for doing something is so great that due process requires that the task not be undertaken until more precision can be achieved? If so, is this appropriate?

3. Is the due process requirement of precision in language applicable only to statutes imposing "criminal" liability? In Giaccio v. Pennsylvania, 382 U.S. 399, 86 S.Ct. 518, 15 L.Ed.2d 447 (1966) the Supreme Court considered the validity of a state statute which authorized the jury in a nonfelony case to impose costs of the prosecution upon an acquitted defend-

ant. Responding to the argument that the statute did not impose criminal liability, the Court stated:

> Whatever label be given the * * * Act, there is no doubt that it provides the State with a procedure for depriving an acquitted defendant of his liberty and his property. Both liberty and property are specifically protected by the Fourteenth Amendment against any state deprivation which does not meet the standards of due process, and this protection is not to be avoided by the simple label a State chooses to fasten upon its conduct or its statute. So here this state Act whether labeled "penal" or not must meet the challenge that it is unconstitutionally vague.

382 U.S. at 402. But isn't the nature of the liability imposed—whether "criminal" or "civil"—relevant to the degree of precision that will be required of a legislature? In other words, might not certain language that would be unconstitutionally vague in a criminal statute survive attack if it was used in imposing noncriminal liability?

The District of Columbia Code authorizes the hospitalization of a mentally ill person determined to be "likely to injure himself or other persons if allowed to remain at liberty." D.C.Code 1967, § 21–545(b). This has been upheld against attack on due process vagueness grounds. See In re Alexander, 336 F.Supp. 1305 (D.D.C.1972).

---

3. OTHER APPROACHES TO CRIMINALIZATION OF ALCOHOL-RELATED ACTIVITY

The statute at issue in Powell v. Texas is obviously only one of a number of different ways in which the criminal law might be used to deal with alcohol-related activity. Consider the following as a far from exhaustive selection of alternatives. Evaluate them not only in light of the legal issues raised in the preceding sections but also in view of the material in the remainder of this chapter.

UNITED STATES CONSTITUTION AMENDMENT XVIII. LIQUOR PROHIBITION

(Repealed by section 1 of Amendment XXI).

Section 1. After one year from the ratification of this article the manufacture, sale, or transportation of intoxicating liquors within, the importation thereof into, or exportation thereof from the United States and all territories subject to the jurisdiction thereof for beverage purposes is hereby prohibited.

NORTH DAKOTA CENTURY CODE

(1971 Supp.)

§ 5–01–09. Delivery to certain persons unlawful.

Any person delivering alcoholic beverages to a person under twenty-one years of age, an habitual drunkard, an incompetent, or an intoxicated person is guilty of a misdemeanor * * *.

WISCONSIN STATUTES ANNOTATED

176.26 Liquor; beer and ale; sale forbidden; to whom [b]

(1) When any person shall by excessive drinking of intoxicating liquors, or fermented malt beverages misspend, waste or lessen his estate so as to expose himself or family to want, or the town, city, village or county to which he belongs to liability for the support of himself or family, or so as thereby to injure his health, endanger the loss thereof, or to endanger the personal safety and comfort of his family or any member thereof, or the safety of any other person, or the security of the property of any other person, or when any person shall, on account of the use of intoxicating liquors or fermented malt beverages, become dangerous to the peace of any community, the wife of such person, the supervisors of such town, the mayor, chief of police or aldermen of such city, the trustees of such village, the county superintendent of the poor of such county, the chairman of the county board of supervisors of such county, the district attorney of such county or any of them, may, in writing signed by her, him or them, forbid all persons knowingly to sell or give away to such person any intoxicating liquors or fermented malt beverages, for the space of one year and in like manner may forbid the selling, furnishing, or giving away of any such liquors or fermented malt beverages, knowingly to such person by any person in any town, city or village to which such person may resort for the same. A copy of said writing so signed shall be personally served upon the person so intended to be prohibited from obtaining any such liquor or beverage.

(2) And the wife of such person, the supervisors of any town, the aldermen of any city, the trustees of any village, the county superintendent of the poor of such county, the mayor of any city, the chairman of the county board of supervisors of such county, the district attorney or sheriff of such county, may, by a notice made and signed as aforesaid, in like manner forbid all persons in such town, city or village, to sell or give away intoxicating liquors or drinks or fermented malt beverages to any person given to the excessive use of such liquors, drinks or beverages, specifying such person, and

b. As to the constitutional validity of this statute, see Wisconsin v. Constantineau, 400 U.S. 433, 91 S.Ct. 507, 27 L.Ed.2d 515 (1971).

such notice shall have the same force and effect when such specified person is a nonresident as is herein provided when such specified person is a resident of said town, city or village.

[Section 176.28 makes the sale or gift of liquor to such a person a misdemeanor.]

NEW YORK PENAL LAW

(1967)

§ 240.40   Public intoxication

A person is guilty of public intoxication when he appears in a public place under the influence of alcohol, narcotics, or other drug to the degree that he may endanger himself or other persons or property, or annoy persons in his vicinity.

Public intoxication is a violation [and punishable by not more than fifteen days imprisonment, a fine of not more than $250, or both].

JACKSONVILLE, FLORIDA ORDINANCE CODE

(1971)

§ 26.57   Vagrants

[C]ommon drunkards   *   *   *   shall be deemed vagrants and, upon conviction in the Municipal Court shall be punished [by up to 75 days imprisonment, a fine of $450, or both].

ALASKA STATUTES

(1970)

Sec. 11.45.032.

Public drunkenness.   (a) A person who (1) is drunk in a private place, not his own property or his usual place of abode, or in a public place, to the annoyance of another, or (2) drinks intoxicating liquor on a public street or sidewalk, or on the premises of a public carrier or business establishment offering goods or services to the public, which is not licensed to dispense intoxicating liquor, upon conviction, is guilty of a misdemeanor, and is punishable by a fine of not more than $300, or by imprisonment for not more than 30 days, or by both.

(b) Any part of a sentence requiring a person convicted under this section to serve more than five days in jail shall be suspended subject to reasonable conditions relating to the rehabilitation of the offender, which may include commitment to a program or facility approved or provided by the Department of Health and Welfare for medical or rehabilitative services, if the court finds

> (1) that at the time of the offense the defendant was not under a suspended sentence; and

> (2) that the defendant was not convicted of another crime arising from the same incident.

(c) Notwithstanding the provisions of (b) of this section a court may continue the confinement imposed under this section for more than five days if it finds that

> (1) there is reason to believe that the release of the defendant would be detrimental to his health or safety or to the safety of the community; and

> (2) there is no suitable alternative to jail custody for the defendant available in the community.

(d) Nothing in this section precludes the court from exercising its discretion to suspend an entire sentence in an appropriate case.

MARYLAND ANNOTATED CODE

(1971)

§ 123. Drunkenness and disorderly conduct generally; habitual offenders.

(a) No person * * * shall be intoxicated and endanger the safety of another person or property and no person * * * shall be intoxicated or drink any alcoholic beverage in a public place or in or upon any public conveyance and cause a public disturbance.

> * * *

(d) Any person violating the prohibitions of this section shall be deemed guilty of a misdemeanor; and upon conviction thereof, shall be subject to a fine of not more than fifty dollars, or be confined in jail for a period of not more than sixty days or be both fined and imprisoned in the discretion of the court.

(e) A person who shall have been convicted or have forfeited collateral under * * * this section three (3) times in the preceding twelve (12) months shall be deemed an habitual offender and may be committed by the court to an appropriate alcoholism treatment facility for a period of not more than sixty (60) days. * * *

4. NONCRIMINAL COMPELLED "TREATMENT": A POTENTIAL ALTERNATIVE TO CRIMINALIZATION

TEXAS CIVIL STATUTES

(1970 Supp.)

Art. 5561c. Alcoholism

Purpose

Section 1. The purpose of this Act is to prevent broken homes and the loss of lives by creating the Texas Commission on Alcoholism, which shall co-ordinate the efforts of all interested and affected State and local agencies; develop educational and preventive programs; and promote the establishment of constructive programs for treatment aimed at the reclamation, rehabilitation and successful re-establishment in society of alcoholics. Alcoholism is hereby recognized as an illness and a public health problem affecting the general welfare and the economy of the State. Alcoholism is further recognized as an illness subject to treatment and abatement and the sufferer of alcoholism is recognized as one worthy of treatment and rehabilitation. The need for proper and sufficient facilities, programs and procedures within the State for the control and treatment of alcoholism is hereby recognized. It is hereby declared that the procedure for commitment of alcoholics as hereinafter provided for is not punitive but is a committal for treatment of an illness affecting not only the individual involved but the public welfare as well.

Construction of the Act

Sec. 2. This Act shall be liberally construed to accomplish the purpose herein sought.

Definitions

Sec. 3. As used in this Act, (a) "Commission" means the Texas Commission on Alcoholism.

*   *   *

(c) An "alcoholic" means any person who chronically and habitually uses alcoholic beverages to the extent that he has lost the power of self control with respect to the use of such beverages, or while chronically and habitually under the influence of alcoholic beverages endangers public morals, health, safety or welfare.

(d) "Alcoholism," as used herein, has reference to any condition of abnormal behavior or illness leading directly or indirectly to the chronic and habitual use of alcoholic beverages.

Texas Commission on Alcoholism

Sec. 4. Commission established. (a) There is hereby created a Commission to be known as the Texas Commission on Alcoholism, hereinafter called the Commission. The Commission shall consist of six (6) members to be appointed by the Governor * * *[.]

Admission and Certification of Alcoholics

Sec. 9. (a) The county judge of the county where an alleged alcoholic resides may certify or remand him or her to the custody of the Commission or its authorized representative for the treatment and rehabilitation of such alcoholic, upon proper proof as hereinafter provided, and with the consent in writing of the Commission or its authorized representative.

(b) The Court may remand an alcoholic to the Commission or its authorized representative for treatment when it is properly shown to the court upon petition or application filed by the alleged alcoholic's husband, wife, child, mother, father, next of kin, next friend, or the county health officer, that such a person is an alcoholic, is a resident of the county, is over eighteen years of age, and is not capable of, or is unfit properly to conduct himself or herself, or to conduct and look after his or her affairs or is dangerous to himself, or others, or has lost the power of self-control because of use of alcohol. Such a petition or application must show that the alleged alcoholic is in actual need of care and treatment and that his or her detention, care and treatment would improve his health.

(c) Upon filing of a petition or application, the court shall set a day for the hearing, which hearing must be held not less than five (5) days and no more than fourteen (14) days from the filing of the petition. The alleged alcoholic shall be personally served with a copy of the petition or application and the order fixing the time of hearing of the same by the sheriff of the county in which he is found and the court may proceed to hear the cause at the stated time, with or without the presence of the alleged alcoholic and with or without an answer by him, provided such service is perfected at least three (3) days prior to the hearing. The court shall inform relatives of the alleged alcoholic and other persons to appear at the hearing to give evidence in the cause. The judge may, in his discretion or upon request, require an alleged alcoholic to be examined by the county health officer, or by other physicians, as the court may direct, the results of which examination to be considered by the court at the hearing of the application for commitment. If in the county court in which a petition or application is filed, a Certificate of Medical Examination for Alcoholism is filed showing that the proposed patient has been examined within five (5) days of the filing of the Certificate and stating the opinion of the examining physician that the proposed patient is an alcoholic and because of his alcoholism is likely to cause injury to himself or others if not immediately restrained, the Judge may order any health or peace officer to take the proposed patient into protective custody and immediately transport him to a designated mental hospital or other suitable place and detain him pending order of the court; provided, however, that in no event shall the proposed patient be denied the hearing prescribed above to be held not less than five (5) days and no more than fourteen (14) days from the filing of the petition.

(d) If the alleged alcoholic admits the allegations of the application, or if the court finds that the material allegations of the application have been proven, it shall issue the proper certificate for his or her commitment or remand to the Commission or its authorized representative for such confinement and treatment as the Commission shall direct. Upon such a finding, the court shall order that he or she be remanded to the Commission or its authorized representative for a period of not less than fifteen (15) days nor more than three (3) months as the necessity of the case may require, subject, however, to earlier discharge at the discretion of the Commission.

*   *   *

Habeas Corpus by Persons Committed to the Commission

Sec. 11.   If a writ of habeas corpus to be obtained in behalf of a person committed to and confined by an order of a court and it appears at the hearing on the return of such writ that such person may properly be discharged, or if the person's condition is such that it will be safe for him or her or others for him or her to be released, the judge before whom the hearing is held shall so direct; but if it appears from the condition of such person that he or she requires treatment, he or she shall be remanded to the care and custody of the Commission or its authorized representative for such treatment.

*   *   *

Rights as Citizens

Sec. 16.   No person who is committed for treatment under the provisions of this Act, either through voluntary application or involuntary procedure, shall forfeit or be abridged thereby of any of his or her rights as a citizen of the United States or of the State of Texas. The record of any individual committed for treatment, guidance and rehabilitation shall be confidential and the contents thereof shall not be divulged except on order of a court of competent jurisdiction.

NOTE

See Kuhn, Civil Commitment of Alcoholics in Texas, 1 Am.J.Crim.L. 335 (1972); Comment, Civil Commitment of Alcoholics in Texas, 48 Texas L.Rev. 159 (1969).

NORTH DAKOTA CENTURY CODE

(1971 Supp.)

5-01-05.1   Public intoxication—Assistance—Medical care.

A peace officer shall have authority to take any apparently intoxicated person to his home, to a local hospital, or, whenever such person constitutes a danger to himself or others, to a jail for purposes of detoxification. A duly licensed physician of such local hospital shall have authority to hold such person for treatment up to seventy-two hours. Such intoxicated person shall not be held in jail because of intoxication more than twenty-four hours. An intoxicated person shall not be placed in a jail unless a jailer is constantly present within hearing distance and medical services are provided when the need is indicated. Upon placing such person in a hospital or jail, said peace officer shall notify the intoxicated person's family as soon as possible. Any additional costs incurred by the city or county on account of an intoxicated person shall be recoverable from such person.

5-01-05.2   No prosecution for intoxication.

No person shall be prosecuted in any court solely for public intoxication. Law enforcement officers may utilize standard identification procedures on all persons given assistance because of apparent intoxication.

5-01-05.3   Disturbing the peace—Disorderly conduct—Penalty.

Any person who commits an act which disturbs the public peace or constitutes disorderly conduct is guilty of a misdemeanor.

NOTES

1. Would the existence of a statutory provision such as that from the Texas or North Dakota Code above be desirable as a matter of general policy? Would its existence have any effect upon the resolution of policy question as to what intoxication-related conditions or activities should be criminalized? Upon the *Powell* issue? If so, what effect would it have? Would the answers to these questions depend upon any additional factors? If so, which ones? Would the answers be affected if the statute had a different criteria for determining who is subject to compelled treatment? Would they be affected if the procedure for compelling treatment was different than that provided in the statute? What alternative criterion or procedures might be provided for, and what might the effect upon the criminalization issue and the *Powell* question be if they were provided for? In answering these questions, consider the material in this section as well as in II(E).

For an argument in favor of a broad criterion, see Selzer, Alcoholism and the Law, The Need for Detection and Treatment, 56 Mich.L.Rev. 237 (1957) urging compelled treatment for the alcoholic "whether or not he creates a nuisance or breaks laws" on the ground that the alternative "is tantamount to permitting an insidious form of suicide." Id. at 244. Compare the following from Hutt, Modern Trends in Handling the Chronic Offender: The Challenge of the Courts, 19 S.Carolina L.Rev. 305, 320 (1967):

I am wholly opposed to any form of involuntary treatment except in two limited areas. I do believe that, in a situation where a person is not mentally competent to make a rational choice as to whether he wishes to undergo treatment, a court has a right and a duty to make that choice for him. Thus, if a person is mentally incompetent and also is an alcoholic, involuntary treatment may be appropriate. But this is the very rare case. The vast majority of chronic alcoholics do not suffer from severe mental illness. For these people, involuntary treatment is not appropriate.

Some would argue that any person who fails voluntarily to accept treatment for his alcoholism must ipso facto be considered mentally incompetent to make a rational choice. This is obviously fallacious. A person who chooses not to undergo surgery for heart disease is not considered mentally incompetent to make that choice. Nor is a person who chooses not to undergo a simple vaccination against disease or any other form of medical treatment that might be considered by the majority of our population to be an obviously intelligent step. In our democratic society, we respect the free choice of the individual to accept treatment or to reject it.

When a derelict alcoholic becomes so debilitated that he is virtually dying in the street, however, he is obviously not in a position to make a rational choice about treatment.

A court should have the power, under those limited circumstances, to commit him for treatment until he once again is capable of making a rational choice. But this does not mean an indeterminate sentence, or indeed any commitment longer than about thirty days. The unfortunate plight of the derelict inebriate cannot lead us to deprive him of his liberty on humanitarian grounds any more than it should lead us to deprive him of his liberty on criminal grounds.

2. To what extent is coercion necessary? Consider the experience of the Vera Institute's Bowery program in New York City as described in R. Nimmer, Two Million Unnecessary Arrests 128–141 (1971). The Project maintains a detoxification center where individuals may be detoxified under medical supervision and a social service staff that refers detoxified individauls to other programs. In addition to accepting "walk in" cases, the Project sends two-man rescue teams into the Bowery streets. These teams *offer* assistance only to persons so obviously intoxicated or debilitated that they are unable to take care of themselves on the street. No coercion is used, in fact as well as in theory. Despite frequent refusals of admission to walk in cases, about 25 percent of the total patient load consists of such walk ins. Approximately sixty percent of the persons approached by the rescue teams accept the offer to take them to the detoxification center. Approximately sixty to seventy percent of patients accept post-detoxification referrals to other programs. After it became clear that the Project was removing too few persons from the street to satisfy community pressure, an out-patient medical clinic was established

to provide medical care to Bowery inhabitants whether or not intoxicated. During the clinic's first year of operation, the rescue teams approached 4,717 men on the street who appeared to be in need of medical attention; only 689 (14 percent) refused the offer of help from the clinic.

To what extent does such a program adequately meet the demands responsible for public intoxication laws and their enforcement? To what extent does it meet the problems with which the law ought to be concerned? What effect does this experience with a noncoercive program have upon the arguments for replacing criminal liability with a program of compulsory "treatment"?

SZASZ, ALCOHOLISM: A SOCIO-ETHICAL PERSPECTIVE

6 Washburn L.J. 255, 258-63, 266-67 (1967).

The demand that alcoholism be considered an illness constitutes a late stage in a moral revolution that has swept the Western world during the past century. [I]t has manifested itself in the redefining of diverse types of behavior—from homosexuality to political "extremism"—as expressions of mental illness. No doubt those who strive to medicalize human problems are usually well-intentioned. The consequences of their actions are none the less morally and socially disastrous. Their posture is essentially one of medical prohibitionism: they combat drinking (or smoking, or certain types of sexual practices) not as a sin or a crime, but as a disease. The upshot is deprivation of personal liberties in the name of medical help.

I believe that before we accept or reject the disease concept of alcoholism, we ought to understand exactly what is meant by it.

First, the view that alcoholism is a disease may be held on the ground that the excessive use of alcohol causes specific illnesses, such as chronic gastritis and cirrhosis of the liver. Properly understood, this view is unobjectionable. It is misleading, however, because it confuses the *cause of an illness* with the *illness itself*. Excessive drinking may cause cirrhosis, but does this suffice to define the act of chronic imbibing as a disease? If we say yes, we shall have to label every other activity that predisposes to or causes illness as an illness. This would render not only excessive drinking as an illness, but also excessive eating and smoking. Furthermore, since many occupations are hazardous to health and life, these too would have to be classified as diseases.

Second, the view that alcoholism is a disease may be held on the ground that the alcoholic undergoes periodic episodes of acute intoxication, during which he is physically ill and may even die. Properly understood, this view also is unobjectionable. Acute alcoholism is a state of poisoning. As such, it is a disease. The difficulty with this view (as with the previous one) is that the poisoning is self-induced. To be sure, from a patho-physiological point of view, it is immaterial how a person becomes poisoned. But from a socio-ethical point of view, this "how" is very significant. In other words, the alcoholic both resembles and differs from the diabetic—just as the soldier who shoots himself in the foot (to be evacuated from the front lines) both resembles and differs from his buddy wounded by the enemy. From a surgical point of view, both soldiers are injured. But from the point of view of law, military discipline, and morals, their conditions could not differ more sharply. * * *

Third, the view that alcoholism is a disease may be held on the ground that the alcoholic suffers from a genetic or biochemical dysfunction which interferes with the proper metabolism of alcohol; he thus becomes the victim of the peculiar interaction between alcohol and his particular body chemistry. I am not competent to pass on the validity of this hypothesis. However, even if it proves to be correct, the same socio-ethical considerations apply to it as to the first two views. Even though the alcoholic's physiological makeup might differ from that of other men, his alcoholism still depends on whether and how much he drinks. Assuming the existence of a medical disability such as postulated by this hypothesis, the individual suffering from it may be compared to a person who is allergic to ragweed pollen. The first few times such a person succumbs to the effects of alcohol (or ragweed pollen), his illness resembles ordinary diseases (such as pneumonia or cancer of the stomach). But once he grasps the nature of his "sensitivity," he must be held responsible —not, to be sure, for his sensitivity itself, but for protecting himself (and others) from its forseeable consequences. In this view, the individual predisposed to alcoholism who imbibes is like the man with ragweed allergy who plants ragweed on his lawn and spends his leisure time in late August working in his yard.

Fourth and last, the view that alcoholism is a disease may be held on the ground that the alcoholic suffers from a defect of his personality as a result of which he uses alcohol in an excessive and intemperate fashion. This view differs from those previously listed in that it identifies the excessive drinking itself as a manifestation of illness. According to the first three propositions alcoholism is a bodily (organic) illness; according to this last one, it is a mental (emotional) illness. This view of alcoholism aptly illustrates my contention that mental illness is a myth and a metaphor. What we call "mental illness" is a type of action or conduct: we call a person "mentally ill" when he behaves in certain "abnormal" ways. Thus the term "mental illness" is but a new name for certain types of social performances or roles.

Students of alcoholism usually emphasize that the alcoholic drinks "compulsively." Marty Mann, for example, defines alcoholism as "a disease which manifests itself chiefly by the uncontrollable drinking of the victim * * * " [10]

I, on the other hand, stress the issue of choice and freedom in the use (and abuse) of alcohol. Physicians, someone might object, do not speak of the freedom to suffer from cancer or hypertension. Why, then, do I speak of the freedom to suffer from alcoholism? This question strikes at the heart of the differences between cancer and alcoholism, and more generally, between bodily and mental diseases.

The disease concept of alcoholism, in contrast to, say, the disease concept of cancer, is confused and confusing because it fails to distinguish between the individual's helplessness and hence lack of responsibility for falling ill—and his power and hence responsibility for trying to recover from an illness. The medical profession has been woefully remiss—especially in addressing the lay public—in failing to clarify this difference.

*   *   *

When we say that a person is ill, we mean either that he suffers from an anatomical or physiological disorder of his body, or that he assumes the role of patient, or both. The point to remember is that sickness as a physical condition and as a social role are two quite different things and that they may vary independently from one another.

From a socio-ethical point of view, the single most important fact about being a medical patient is that the sick role must be assumed voluntarily. In general, the state does not have the right to cast the adult citizen in the role of patient; nor does it have the right to cast the citizen who defines himself as sick into the role of non-patient. Accordingly, a person may be ill (in the sense of having a disease), but may prefer not to assume the sick role. Most of us have made such a decision when, for example, we have a severe cold but go about our ordinary business and accept our usual responsibilities, rather than go to bed and seek medical help. Conversely, a person may be healthy (in the sense of not having a disease), but may prefer to assume the sick role. We may offer illness as an excuse for avoiding an obligation to go to the office or a party. Let us look at the implications of these concepts for the problem of alcoholism.

The alcoholic, it is claimed, does not choose to be an alcoholic. According to Mann, "He has lost the power of choice in the matter of drinking, and that is precisely the nature of his disease, alcoholism." Although I disagree with this statement, let us for the present discussion assume that it is true. The assertion that the alcoholic has no choice in the matter of drinking can only mean that he does not choose to crave alcohol any more than the cancer patient craves a

10. M. Mann, Primer on Alcoholism 3 (1950).

malignancy; it cannot mean that, given his craving, he cannot choose to take certain steps to alter it (such as joining Alcoholics Anonymous). Whether or not alcoholism is a disease, a crucial and frequent psychological and social characteristic of the person who drinks to excess happens to be that he does not wish to be "treated" for it. In this respect, the alcoholic resembles the Jehovah's Witness suffering from a bleeding peptic ulcer who refuses a blood transfusion for it. The ordinary medical patient, let us remember, has the right to be sick and refuse treatment. When we proclaim the alcoholic as sick, are we prepared to accord him this same right? Or do we intend to view his illness as similar to mental disease—that is, as a condition for which the patient lacks understanding and one, moreover, that threatens the safety of others—and hence prescribe involuntary treatment for it?

Since we have chosen this second course, it is quite clear that the fundamental purpose of defining alcoholism as a disease is to bring it under the umbrella of mental illness and so justify the involuntary hospitalization and treatment of the so-called patient. * * *

The proposition that alcoholism is a disease disguises and obscures several fundamental moral problems. Do we, as American citizens, have a right to ingest drugs and other substances (e.g., alcohol, amphetamines, barbiturates, nicotine, fatty foods, etc.), if we so choose? Further, if we take certain drugs but act as responsible and law-abiding citizens, do we have the right to be unmolested by the government? Lastly, if we take drugs and break social customs or laws, do we have the right to be treated as undesirable individuals or as persons accused of crime, rather than as involuntary (mental) patients?

* * *

[L]et us assume that [a] hypothetical alcoholic disturbs the peace while under the influence of alcohol. How should the law regard his conduct? Two important decisions have already been handed down by * * * courts finding that alcoholics are ill and that, although they may be forcibly retained for treatment, they are not criminals and should be hospitalized rather than imprisoned. These decisions may be due to fuzzy thinking, or a desire to use doctors instead of jailers to control undesirable social behavior, or both. For the alcoholic who comes before the courts must, by definition, be a person who has disturbed *someone*. The man who drinks himself into oblivion in his own bedroom whence he does not emerge until he is sober is not a candidate for imprisonment. The alternative between jailing and hospitalizing "the alcoholic" is thus a spurious one. It applies only to the individual who is *publicly* intoxicated (or who commits some other crime). But in such a case, it is not the drinking itself that is, or ought to be, of interest to the courts, but rather the socially deviant conduct that provoked and justified the man's arrest. Intoxication with alcohol is of course no more a cause of crime than is any other bodily state or illness. The alcoholic *knows* he is an alcoholic and owes society the same responsibility for controlling his behavior, drunk or sober, as any other man. If we were really serious about regarding chronic alcoholism as a disease—and used this assertion not merely as a rhetorical device but as a morally binding proposition—we would arrive at an attitude toward alcoholic misbehavior diametrically opposite to the currently prevalent view.

Blindness, everyone will admit, is an organic disability of considerable proportions. Does it excuse the blind person from socially deviant or inept behavior? No, it does not, and should not. "In the law's appraisal,"—according to the late Professor Edmond Cahn—"a blind man is not of a different species from one who has the sight of his eyes. A blind man is simply another member of the total society; he must take suitable and reasonable precautions for his and others' safety. So must a man who is too short, or too heavy, or whose reflexes are slowing with the years; so also must every one of us. . . . Persons who are afflicted and disabled must not be categorized even by themselves as an inferior or pitiable species. They are, on the contrary men in all essentials like their neighbors—with the needs, duties, dignities, and singular potentialities of the genus." [16]

Among the needs, duties, dignities, and singular potentialities of the alcoholic I would emphasize his obligation to assume responsibility for his drinking and its consequences. From this point of view, there cannot be such a category as the "alcoholic criminal." Like all classes, this one is created by man and may be abolished by him. In the United States, we do not recognize, as separate categories, the "obese criminal" or the "Jewish criminal" or the "syphilitic criminal." So far as the law is concerned, all these men are individuals "accused of crime," or, if convicted, "criminals." In my opinion, the demonstrable disadvantage of creating a category of "alcoholic offenders" far outweighs its alleged advantages.

KITTRIE, THE DIVESTMENT OF CRIMINAL LAW AND THE COMING OF THE THERAPEUTIC STATE

1 Suffolk U.L.Rev. 43, 43–44, 65–67, 69–76 (1967).

Criminal law in the United States has been undergoing a process of divestment resulting in the relinquishment of its jurisdiction over many of its prior subjects and subject areas. Many classes of criminal offenders are no longer subject to its sanctions. * * *

This divestment, carried out in the name of the new social aims of therapy and rehabilitation * * * as contrasted with crim-

----

16. E. Cahn, The Moral Decision, Right and Wrong in the Light of American Law 220–21 (1956).

inal law's emphasis upon retribution, incapacitation and deterrence, has produced new types of borderland proceedings, lodged between the civil and criminal law. * * * This process began * * * with the recognition in the early 19th century that the institutionalization of the insane should be separated from the incarceration of criminals. * * *

The process of divestment has continued through a similar recognition, at the end of the 19th century, that juveniles, likewise, should not be subject to traditional criminal sanctions and proceedings. * * * Through subsequent legislative and judicial actions [in some jurisdictions], psychopaths * * * drug addicts * * * and alcoholics were similarly outside the boundaries of criminal law.

What are the specific reasons for the divestment of criminal law and what social needs does it fulfill? What are the major reasons for dissatisfaction with criminal law resulting in the divestment procedure?

The first factor to be considered is the influence of canon law which bases punishment upon moral guilt. * * * The growing recognition that certain classes of offenders are incapable of guilt because affected mentally, has resulted in the exemptions of lunatics and idiots from criminal sanctions as early as the beginning of the 14th century. * * * Over the years, [the] standards have been liberalized in various jurisdictions and could now well encompass a broader segment of mentally affected offenders. * * *

The second factor is the humanistic awakening which distinguished the ill and the immature from the evil and considered the punishment of those who require treatment as inhumane and morally objectionable. * * *

Having commenced with religious and humanitarian considerations against the applicability of criminal sanctions, the process of divestment continued under the steam generated by other factors. One of these was the growing disillusionment with the determinate sentence utilized under the criminal law. * * *

The traditional standard of criminal law has been to fit the punishment to the crime, not to the criminal. Society, acting through the modern legislature, continues in setting criminal penalties that respond to the severity of the crime. Yet the severity of the crime provides no meaningful measure for the time or tools required by society to deal with a particular offender. The conduct of an alcoholic charged with disturbing the peace is not extremely offensive and, consequently, the penalties prescribed for him are not severe. Yet, the reformation of an alcoholic may require more time and facilities than the rehabilitation of the passion murderer whose conduct is extremely condemnable and thus traditionally results in more severe criminal sanctions. As long as society's emphasis was upon the punishment of the offender and the deterrence of others, a punishment which fits the crime was perfectly in order. Once the emphasis began shifting to the rehabilitation of the offender and his return to society as an unlikely future delinquent, the traditional system of penalties appeared totally inappropriate. The answer was therefore sought outside criminal law, under a non-criminal "parens patriae" system in which the period of detention and the applicable sanctions are responsive to the therapeutic needs of the delinquent rather than the nature of his offense.

Additionally, the movement for the divestment of criminal justice allows for the replacement of penal facilities with therapeutically oriented institutions. Increasingly, it has been recognized that traditional punitive sanctions are not effective as means of social control. Society has increasingly undertaken, therefore, in the case of selected offenders or others posing a threat to social tranquility, to deemphasize punishment and to emphasize therapy. Divestment thus allows for new experimental programs, in hospitals rather than prisons.

The shift from a penal or punitive orientation to a therapeutic one is also looked upon by behavioral scientists as allowing for a better rehabilitation atmosphere and potential. Relevant in this connection is the concept of "double-expectancy" as described by Psychiatrist George Sturup.[92] According to Sturup, offenders respond according to what they perceive society expects of them. The offender who is tagged as a criminal responds to the negative social expectation that he perceives and recovery is therefore inadequate; the offender who is tagged ill responds to the perception of a much more positive social expectation and recovery is better.

Resort to non-criminal proceedings has the further effect of dispensing with some of the cumbersome formalism and procedural requirements of criminal law: counsel, adversary hearing, jury, non-hearsay evidence, etc. Accordingly, the courts have repeatedly emphasized the civil or non-criminal nature of these new proceedings and the inapplicability of the criminal law standards. * * * The non-criminal process also professes the laudatory desire and policy of removing the criminal stigma from those who are either too young or too lacking medically and mentally to be forever branded.

Finally, the divestment of criminal law and the substitution of civil proceedings permits another drastic departure from the criminal law standards, by allowing the treatment of a general condition or status, considered hazardous to society, instead of waiting until the commission of a prohibited overt act. Traditionally, criminal law is primarily a system designed to deal with criminals after the fact. Thus, while the general public's awareness of criminal sanctions is expected to exert a deterring influence and to curb prohibited con-

92. George Sturup, Superintendent of Herstedvester Institution, Denmark, A Situational Approach to Behavior Disorders, reprinted from the Leeds Symposium on Behavior Disorders, 25–27 March (1965).

duct, the actual sanctions of criminal law do not, generally, come into use until after a criminal act has indeed been carried out or attempted.   The non-criminal procedures, on the other hand, have been utilized as a means of preventive control for prospective offenders: the mentally ill person likely to become dangerous to himself or others, the mental defective likely to produce defective offspring, the child exposed to dangerous influences.   In being directed towards crime prevention, not merely crime management, the non-criminal proceedings have appealed and will undoubtedly demonstrate an ever increasing appeal to those seeking new tools for society's struggle against crime and delinquency.

*   *   *

Upon initial observation the increasing function of the state in the "parens patriae" and therapeutic role appears to go hand in hand with scientific progress and with the newer concepts of public welfare.   It is not surprising therefore that the advent of the "parens patriae" state has been warmly welcomed.   *   *   *

More recent and more searching scrutiny raises serious questions regarding both the conceptual and substantive framework and the procedural safeguards which apply to the exercise of therapeutic functions by the state.   Clearly, the sovereign's assumption of a broad "parens patriae" role also necessitates the exercise of comprehensive responsibility and extensive powers   *   *   *.

By emphasizing the therapeutic function of the state and by giving sympathetic consideration to mental and other aberrations, the therapeutic state acts to hasten the divestment of criminal justice. Yet this divestment, which increasingly frees persons from criminal responsibility, is not the final step in the process.   The need for social defense does not permit the complete release of the recognized or prospective delinquent.   What is resorted to, therefore, as a means of both therapy and social defense is the non-criminal incarceration and treatment—still involuntary or even coercive and quite often resulting in even more objectionable deprivations of liberty than are possible under the criminal process.

*   *   *   These still comparatively new areas of non-criminal treatment raise a host of legal and non-legal questions.   Foremost is the question of the basic balance between society's right to protect and improve itself and its members through preventive measures and the individual's right to liberty or, otherwise phrased, to be left alone. How much of a social hazard must one be demonstrated to be before society may step in?   And may society involuntarily seek to remedy one's status, absent a dangerous act on his part?   This is in essence the question of substantive due process.   The traditional approach of our Anglo-American society has been for the state to step in only once an anti-social act has been committed or once "clear and present danger" has been demonstrated.   Our society seeks generally not to control a status but an act.   *   *   *   Yet in the therapeutic "parens

patriae" realm we often ignore the question of whether a particular offense had been committed. Instead we are often triggered to exercise therapeutic sanctions by a finding of the general social undesirability of one's condition or status.

Beyond the substantive questions regarding the exercise of state sanctions, even in the name of the "parens patriae", absent an overt "clear and present" danger, there also looms the question of procedural due process. Assuming that a non-criminal program is being utilized to accomplish a therapeutic social aim, what procedural safeguards must be required in order to protect the rights of the person allegedly requiring treatment? How carefully should the disabling medical or mental status be defined by law? Should there be a requirement of proof of previous anti-social behavior? Should there be a right to a hearing and counsel? Does an administrative confinement or one based on a medical certificate, without prior hearing, suffice if followed by an opportunity for judicial review? Should the state be required to disclose the record upon which it proceeds against a certain person? What should be the term of the therapeutic treatment —determinate or indeterminate? Should the social sanctions depend on the availability of treatment and should the person against whom sanctions are exercised have the right to treatment?

E.   FACTORS RELEVANT TO THE RESOLUTION OF THE LEGAL ISSUES

---

1.   THE NATURE OF CRIMINAL LIABILITY

HENRY M. HART, JR., THE AIMS OF THE CRIMINAL LAW

23 Law and Contemporary Problems 401, 402–06 (1958).

What do we mean by "crime" and "criminal"?   *   *   *

A great deal of intellectual energy has been misspent in an effort to develop a concept of crime as "a natural and social phenomenon" abstracted from the functioning system of institutions which make use of the concept and give it impact and meaning. But the criminal law, like all law, is concerned with the pursuit of human purposes through the forms and modes of social organization, and it needs always to be thought about in that context as a method or process of doing something.

What then are the characteristics of this method?

1.   The method operates by means of a series of directions, or commands, formulated in general terms, telling people what they must

or must not do. Mostly, the commands of the criminal law are "must-nots," or prohibitions, which can be satisfied by inaction. "Do not murder, rape, or rob." But some of them are "musts," or affirmative requirements, which can be satisfied only by taking a specifically, or relatively specifically, described kind of action. "Support your wife and children," and "File your income tax return."

2. The commands are taken as valid and binding upon all those who fall within their terms when the time comes for complying with them, whether or not they have been formulated in advance in a single authoritative set of words. They speak to members of the community, in other words, in the community's behalf, with all the power and prestige of the community behind them.

3. The commands are subject to one or more sanctions for disobedience which the community is prepared to enforce.

Thus far, it will be noticed, nothing has been said about the criminal law which is not true also of a large part of the noncriminal, or civil, law. The law of torts, the law of contracts, and almost every other branch of private law that can be mentioned operate, too, with general directions prohibiting or requiring described types of conduct, and the community's tribunals enforce these commands. What, then, is distinctive about the method of the criminal law?

Can crimes be distinguished from civil wrongs on the ground that they constitute injuries to society generally which society is interested in preventing? The difficulty is that society is interested also in the due fulfillment of contracts and the avoidance of traffic accidents and most of the other stuff of civil litigation. The civil law is framed and interpreted and enforced with a constant eye to these social interests. Does the distinction lie in the fact that proceedings to enforce the criminal law are instituted by public officials rather than private complainants? The difficulty is that public officers may also bring many kinds of "civil" enforcement actions—for an injunction, for the recovery of a "civil" penalty, or even for the detention of the defendant by public authority. Is the distinction, then, in the peculiar character of what is done to people who are adjudged to be criminals? The difficulty is that, with the possible exception of death, exactly the same kinds of unpleasant consequences, objectively considered, can be and are visited upon unsuccessful defendants in civil proceedings.

If one were to judge from the notions apparently underlying many judicial opinions, and the overt language even of some of them, the solution of the puzzle is simply that a crime is anything which is *called* a crime, and a criminal penalty is simply the penalty provided for doing anything which has been given that name. So vacant a concept is a betrayal of intellectual bankruptcy. Certainly, it poses no intelligible issue for a constitution-maker concerned to decide whether to make use of "the method of the criminal law." Moreover, it is false to popular understanding, and false also to the understanding embodied in existing constitutions. By implicit assumptions that are more impressive than any explicit assertions, these constitutions proclaim that a conviction for crime is a distinctive and serious matter—a something, and not a nothing. What is that something?

4. What distinguishes a criminal from a civil sanction and all that distinguishes it, it is ventured, is the judgment of community condemnation which accompanies and justifies its imposition. As Professor Gardner wrote not long ago, in a distinct but cognate connection:

> The essence of punishment for moral delinquency lies in the criminal conviction itself. One may lose more money on the stock market than in a court-room; a prisoner of war camp may well provide a harsher environment than a state prison; death on the field of battle has the same physical characteristics as death by sentence of law. It is the expression of the community's hatred, fear, or contempt for the convict which alone characterizes physical hardship as punishment.

If this is what a "criminal" penalty is, then we can say readily enough what a "crime" is. It is not simply anything which a legislature chooses to call a "crime." It is not simply antisocial conduct which public officers are given a responsibility to suppress. It is not simply any conduct to which a legislature chooses to attach a "criminal" penalty. It is conduct which, if duly shown to have taken place, will incur a formal and solemn pronouncement of the moral condemnation of the community.

5. The method of the criminal law, of course, involves something more than the threat (and, on due occasion, the expression) of community condemnation of antisocial conduct. It involves, in addition, the threat (and, on due occasion, the imposition) of unpleasant physical consequences, commonly called punishment. But if Professor Gardner is right, these added consequences take their character as punishment from the condemnation which precedes them and serves as the warrant for their infliction. Indeed, the condemnation plus the added consequences may well be considered, compendiously, as constituting the punishment. Otherwise, it would be necessary to think of a convicted criminal as going unpunished if the imposition or execution of his sentence is suspended.

In traditional thought and speech, the ideas of crime and punishment have been inseparable; the consequences of conviction for crime have been described as a matter of course as "punishment." The Constitution of the United States and its amendments, for example, use this word or its verb form in relation to criminal offenses no less than six times. Today, "treatment" has become a fashionable euphemism for the older, ugly word. This bowdlerizing of the Constitution and of conventional speech may serve a useful purpose in discouraging unduly harsh sentences and emphasizing that punishment is not an end in itself. But to the extent that it dissociates the treatment of criminals from the social condemnation of their conduct which is implicit in their conviction, there is danger that it will confuse thought and do a disservice.

At least under existing law, there is a vital difference between the situation of a patient who has been committed to a mental hospital and the situation of an inmate of a state penitentiary. The core of the difference is precisely that the patient has not incurred the moral condemnation of his community, whereas the convict has.

NOTE

Does it really make any significant difference whether a criminal or civil approach is taken to alcohol-related activity? Is there likely to be any difference between a system in which at least some of those who engage in antisocial alcohol-related activity are compelled on a noncriminal basis to receive treatment and one in which all are convicted of crimes but the disposition is to a program of treatment? Can these questions be answered by examining the language of the statutory frameworks? If not, what else must be considered?

_____

2. JUSTIFICATION AND FUNCTIONS OF CRIMINALIZATION

_____

H. L. A. HART, MURDER AND THE PRINCIPLES OF PUNISHMENT: ENGLAND AND THE UNITED STATES

52 Nw.U.L.Rev. 433, 448–49 (1957).c

[W]e must distinguish two questions commonly confused. They are, first "Why do men in fact punish?" * * * The second question * * * is "What justifies men in punishing? Why is it morally good or morally permissible for them to punish?" It is clear that no demonstration that in fact men have punished or do punish for certain reasons can amount *per se* to a justification for this practice unless we subscribe to what is itself a most implausible moral position, namely, that whatever is generally done is justified or morally right * * *.

When this simple point is made clear and the two questions * * * are forced apart, very often the objector to the utilitarian position will turn out to be a utilitarian of a wider and perhaps more

c. Reprinted by special permission of the Northwestern University Law Review (Northwestern University School of Law), Copyright © 1958, Vol. 52, No. 4.

imaginative sort. He will perhaps say that what justifies punishment is that it satisfies a popular demand (perhaps even for revenge) and explain that it is good that it satisfies this demand because if it did not there would be disorder in society, disrespect for the law, or even lynching. Such a point of view, of course, raises disputable questions of fact * * *. Nevertheless, this objection itself turns out to be a utilitarian position, emphasizing that the good to be secured by punishment must not be narrowly conceived as simply protecting society from the harm represented by the particular type of crime punished but also as a protection from a wider set of injuries to society.

----

a. CRIMINALIZATION AND PUNISHMENT AS RETRIBUTION

P. BRETT, AN INQUIRY INTO CRIMINAL GUILT

51 (1963).

The retributive theory of punishment can be formulated in a number of ways. Its distinguishing feature is that it asks for no further justification of the right to punish than that the offender has committed a wrong. "Judicial punishment * * * can never serve merely as a means to further *another* good, whether for the offender himself or of society, but must always be inflicted on him for the sole reason that he *has committed a crime.* * * * The law of punishment is a categorical imperative, and woe to him who crawls through the serpentine windings of the happiness theory seeking to discover something which in virtue of the benefit it promises will release him from the duty of punishment or even from a fraction of its full severity." Thus Kant expounded the theory, and he based it upon his view that man must always be treated as an end in himself and never as a means of achieving some other end. Kant's position here is an intuitive one, with which one can only either agree or disagree in the light of one's own intuitions. Other formulations of the retributive theory are likewise intuitive, and occasionally they take on a somewhat mystical tinge, as with Hegel's view that crime is a negation and punishment a negation of that negation.

NOTES

1. Can a reasonable argument be made that criminalization of some or all intoxication-related conditions or activities can be justified on a retribution theory of punishment? How might such an argument be formulated? Should the retributive theory be a factor in making the legislative criminalization decision? In deciding the *Powell* issue?

2. Insofar as retributive notions provide the justification for criminal punishment, do they also suggest a limitation upon those who may be punished? Consider the following:

> The aim of criminal legislation is to prevent the perpetration of acts classified as criminal (because they are regarded as being socially damaging). * * * I can subscribe fully to this premise, and would only add the rider that, if by putting it forward it is sought to suggest, as does Barbara Wooton, that the purpose of penal legislation is *not* retribution for guilt, then the point rests on a misunderstanding. For this is something no one has even claimed. The so-called retributivist theories are not concerned with the *purpose* of penal law (its intended effects) but with the moral basis for sentencing a particular person and for the kind and extent of the punishment imposed. The substance of the retributivist's case is that the guilt requirement sets a moral limitation upon the state's right to pursue its preventive aims.

Ross, The Campaign Against Punishment, 14 Scandinavian Studies in Law 109, 124–25 (1970).

---

b. CRIMINALIZATION AND PUNISHMENT AS A REFLECTION OF MORALITY

P. DEVLIN, THE ENFORCEMENT OF MORALS

9 (1965).

I think it is clear that the criminal law as we know it is based upon moral principle. In a number of crimes its function is simply to enforce a moral principle and nothing else.

J. MILL, UTILITARIANISM: LIBERTY AND REPRESENTATIVE GOVERNMENT 73 [d]

The sole end for which mankind is warranted, individually or collectively, in interfering with the liberty of action of any of their number is self-protection. That the only purpose for which power can be rightfully exercised over any member of a civilized community, against his will, is to prevent harm to others. His own good, whether physical or moral, is not a sufficient warrant. He cannot rightfully be compelled to do or forbear because it will be better for him to do so, because it will make him happier, because, in the opinion of others, to do so would be wise, or even right. These are good reasons for remonstrating with him, or reasoning with him or persuading him, or entreating him but not for compelling him, or visiting him with any evil in case he do otherwise. To justify that, the conduct from

[d]. From the book Utilitarianism: Liberty and Representative Government by John Stuart Mill. Everyman's Library Edition. Published by E. P. Dutton & Co., Inc. and used with their permission.

which it is desired to deter him must be calculated to produce evil to some one else. The only part of the conduct of any one, for which he is amenable to society, is that which concerns others. In the part which merely concerns himself, his independence is, of right, absolute.

NOTES

1. Is Mill's analysis helpful in determining what conduct or conditions should be criminalized? Consider the following from Nagel, The Enforcement of Morals, The Humanist, May/June 1968, 21, at 21–22:[e]

Mill offers two formulations—a broader and a narrower one —for his principle to distinguish between conduct that does and conduct that does not fall within the scope of permissible social control. i) According to the broad formulation, a person's actions are matters for legitimate social scrutiny only if they are of "concern" to others, but not if they "merely concern himself." On this criterion for deciding on the justifiability of social control, the relevant question to ask is not whether an action is performed in private (e. g., within the walls of a man's home) or in public, but whether it has *consequences* that in some way may affect other men. However, as has often been noted, there are few if any actions, even when done in private, which can be guaranteed to have no effects whatsoever on others than the actors themselves, so that on this formulation of the principle the domain of conduct that is reserved for the exercise of individual liberty is at best extremely narrow.

ii) In point of fact, it is not upon this broad formulation of his principle that Mill relies, but on the narrowed one according to which no adult member of a civilized community can be rightfully compelled to perform or to desist from performing an act, unless the action or the failure to perform it is likely to produce *harm* or *evil* to others. But it takes little to see that even on this narrower injunction relatively few human actions are in principle excluded from social regulation. For example, a successful courtship may bring joy to a lover but acute anguish to his rival; the acclaim won by a musician or a scientist may produce self-destructive feelings of inferiority in those who do not achieve such distinction; and the vigorous expression of heterodox opinions may cause severe distress in those hearing them. Mill himself was fully aware of this and qualified his principle by excluding from the class of actions he regarded as "harmful to others" (in the sense that they are subject to social control) many actions which, though they may affect others adversely by causing them physical or mental pain, he designated as merely "inconveniences"; and he maintained that society should tolerate such inconveniences, without attempting to control the actions that are their source, on

e. This article first appeared in The Humanist May/June 1968 and is reprinted by permission.

the ground that this is the price men must be prepared to pay for the enjoyment of individual liberty.

However, the actions mentioned by Mill as productive of inconveniences only, rather than of serious evils that warrant social intervention, are in some instances highly idiosyncratic; but they frequently also reflect attitudes and standards of conduct that were held by many other men of Mill's time and station in life. Thus, he saw in the prohibition of the sale of alcoholic beverages an infringment of personal liberty, despite the social evils that excessive consumption of alcohol may produce; and he maintained that though a person attempting to cross an unsafe bridge should be warned of the risk he is incurring, no public official would be warranted in forcibly preventing the person from exposing himself to danger.   But Mill also believed that society is justified in compelling parents to educate their young; that society is warranted in forbidding marriages between individuals who cannot prove that they have the means to support a family; and that contracts between persons should be prohibited, even if no one else is affected by the agreements, when the parties bind themselves to abide by some arrangement for an indefinite number of years, if not in perpetuity, without the power to revoke the agreement.   On the other hand, though Mill had no doubt that society must tolerate fornication and gambling, he evaded answering the question whether a person should be free to be a pimp or a gambling-house keeper.

I do not believe it is possible to state a firm rule underlying Mill's selection of conduct for inclusion in the category of actions whose consequences for others are merely annoying inconveniences, rather than serious evils that justify the adoption of some form of social regulation.   Indeed, it is obvious that his principle for demarcating a realm of behavior which is exempt from social control excludes virtually *nothing* from the scope of justifiable legal enactment—*unless* some agreement is first reached on what to count as "harm or evil to others." But two points are no less clear; i) an explication of what is to be understood as harmful to others (in the sense of warranting some type of social control), cannot escape reference to some more or less explicit and comprehensive system of moral and social assumptions—more fully articulated than Mill's, whether or not the moral theory involved in the explication is one about which reasonable men may differ; and ii), even when agreement on general moral principles can be taken for granted, it may be difficult to decide whether a given type of conduct is indeed harmful to others, especially if the circumstances under which the actions take place may vary considerably, or if the number of individuals who engage in them should increase.   Each point merits brief comment.

i) There are various categories of behavior whose harmful character (as distinct from its mere inconvenience to others) is in general not disputed in our society—for example, actions resulting in physical injury to others, or in depriving them of their **possessions** (as in theft) ; and no elaborate moral theory is usually invoked in justifying legal measures designed to prevent such actions. Nevertheless, the point needs stressing that though in a given society certain kinds of conduct seem unquestionably harmful, the classification of such conduct as harmful may, and frequently does, involve far-reaching assumptions about the public weal—assumptions which may be modified for a variety of reasons, and which may not be operative in other societies. This is evident when we reflect that even in our own society not all actions resulting in physical injury to others, or in depriving others of their possessions, are held to be harmful in the sense here relevant. Thus the infliction of physical injury on others in duels or feuds currently counts as action that is harmful, but the infliction of such injury is not so regarded when it occurs in boxing contests, in acts of self-defense, or in many though not in all surgical operations. Moral assumptions and considerations of social policy surely control this classification of such conduct; and there have been societies in which those actions have been classified differently.

* * *

In short, attempts such as Mill's to delimit a priori a realm of conduct that is exempt from social regulation, presupposes a fairly detailed moral philosophy that articulates what actions are to count as harmful to others. But the discussion thus far has also suggested that unless individual freedom (as the maximum non-interference with individual conduct) is taken as an inalienable and absolute right, which must never be compromised or curtailed for the sake of satisfying other human needs (such as security from physical want or the development of human excellence), there appear to be no determinate and fixed limits to the scope of justifiable legal regulation of conduct.

ii) I * * * will now comment on the second point mentioned earlier. Given some explication of the notion of "harm (or evil) to others," the question whether a certain form of conduct is indeed harmful can be settled only by an empirical study of its consequences—it cannot be resolved by appeal to uncriticized custom or by considering that conduct in isolation from the enormously complex field of human relations in which it may actually be embedded. Now it may in principle be always possible to find reliable answers to such questions, and frequently such answers are undoubtedly available; but it is also the case that in a large number of instances adequate answers are difficult to obtain. Thus to mention a trivial example, it appears quite certain in the light of current physical and biological knowledge that the kind of clothing a man wears, especially in the privacy of his home, has no "harmful" consequences for others—although in this connection some geneticists have raised (but as far as I know not resolved) the question whether the kind of clothing men wear affects the mutation rate of genes, and therefore the character of the gene stock in in-breeding human populations. On the other hand, while there are reasons to believe that were artificial insemination practiced with the full consent of both parties to a marriage, no undesirable consequences would ensue either for those directly involved or for anyone else, no one can say today with any surety what effects the practice might have on the institution of the family or on current systems of property relations, if the practice were to become widespread. More generally, one should not ignore the truism that men's actions have unintended consequences; and Hegel was at least partly correct in his claim that the owl of Minerva spreads its wings only when the dusk begins to fall.

These comments must not be construed to mean that no deliberate changes in policies of social control in respect to some type of conduct should ever be made, until thoroughly competent knowledge becomes available concerning the likely consequences for others of the proposed policy change. For the desired knowledge can often be acquired only if the change is instituted; and refusal to make a change in the absence of fully adequate knowledge of its consequences is itself a policy decision, whose own likely effects may also be unknown to us. The conclusion that does emerge from these observations is that the distinction between conduct which is merely of concern to the actors (and hence, according to Mill, should be excluded from the scope of the law), and conduct that affects others adversely (and hence may be a proper subject for social regulation) cannot be drawn precisely or once for all, and may require repeated revision as conditions change and our funded knowledge grows.

P. DEVLIN, THE ENFORCEMENT OF MORALS

9–10 (1965).f

What makes a society of any sort is community of ideas, not only political ideas but also ideas about the way its members should behave and govern their lives; these latter ideas are its morals. Every society has a moral structure as well as a political one: or rather, since that might suggest two independent systems, I should say that the structure of every society is made up both of politics and morals. Take, for example, the institution of marriage. Whether a man should be allowed to take more than one wife is something about which every society has to make up its mind one way or the other. In England we believe in the Christian idea of marriage and therefore adopt monogamy as a moral principle. Consequently the Christian institution of marriage has become the basis of family life and so part of the structure of our society. It is there not because it is Christian. It has got there because it is Christian, but it remains there because it is built into the house in which we live and could not be removed without bringing it down. The great majority of those who live in this country accept it because it is the Christian idea of marriage and for them the only true one. But a non-Christian is

f. From Morals and the Criminal Law included in The Enforcement of Morals   by Lord Devlin, published by Oxford University Press.

bound by it, not because it is part of Christianity but because, rightly or wrongly, it has been adopted by the society in which he lives. It would be useless for him to stage a debate designed to prove that polygamy was theologically more correct and socially preferable; if he wants to live in the house, he must accept it as built in the way in which it is.

We see this more clearly if we think of ideas or institutions that are purely political. Society cannot tolerate rebellion; it will not allow argument about the rightness of the cause. Historians a century later may say that the rebels were right and the Government was wrong and a percipient and conscientious subject of the State may think so at the time. But it is not a matter which can be left to individual judgement.

The institution of marriage is a good example for my purpose because it bridges the division, if there is one, between politics and morals. Marriage is part of the structure of our society and it is also the basis of a moral code which condemns fornication and adultery. The institution of marriage would be gravely threatened if individual judgements were permitted about the morality of adultery; on these points there must be a public morality. But public morality is not to be confined to those moral principles which support institutions such as marriage. People do not think of monogamy as something which has to be supported because our society has chosen to organize itself upon it; they think of it as something that is good in itself and offering a good way of life and that it is for that reason that our society has adopted it. I return to the statement that I have already made, that society means a community of ideas; without shared ideas on politics, morals, and ethics no society can exist. Each one of us has ideas about what is good and what is evil; they cannot be kept private from the society in which we live. If men and women try to create a society in which there is no fundamental agreement about good and evil they will fail; if, having based it on common agreement, the agreement goes, the society will disintegrate. For society is not something that is kept together physically; it is held by the invisible bonds of common thought. If the bonds were too far relaxed the members would drift apart. A common morality is part of the bondage. The bondage is part of the price of society; and mankind, which needs society, must pay its price.

Common lawyers used to say that Christianity was part of the law of the land. That was never more than a piece of rhetoric * * * [.] What lay behind it was the notion which I have been seeking to expound, namely that morals—and up till a century or so ago no one thought it worth distinguishing between religion and morals—were necessary to the temporal order.

H. L. A. HART, SOCIAL SOLIDARITY AND THE
ENFORCEMENT OF MORALITY

35 U.Chi.L.Rev. 1, 8–13 (1967).

If we ask in relation to theories such as Lord Devlin's * * * precisely what empirical claim they make concerning the connection between the maintenance of a common morality and the existence of society, some further disentangling of knots has to be done.

It seems a very natural objection to such theories that if they are to be taken seriously * * * the justification which they attempt to give for the enforcement of social morality is far too general. It is surely both possible and good sense to discriminate between those parts of a society's moral code (assuming it has a single moral code) which are essential for the existence of a society and those which are not. Prima facie, at least, the need for such a discrimination seems obvious even if we assume that the moral code is only to be enforced where it is supported by "sentiments which are strong and precise" * * * or by "intolerance, indignation and disgust" * * *. For the decay of all moral restraint or the free use of violence or deception would not only cause individual harm but would jeopardise the existence of a society since it would remove the main conditions which make it possible and worthwhile for men to live together in close proximity to each other. On the other hand the decay of moral restraint on, say, extramarital intercourse, or a general change of sexual morality in a permissive direction seems to be quite another matter and not obviously to entail any such consequences as "disintegration" or "men drifting apart."

It seems, therefore, worthwhile pausing to consider two possible ways of discriminating within a social morality the parts which are to be considered essential.

(i) The first possibility is that the common morality which is essential to society, and which is to be preserved by legal enforcement, is that part of its social morality which contains only those restraints and prohibitions that are essential to the existence of any society of human beings whatever. Hobbes and Hume have supplied us with general characterisations of this moral minimum essential for social life: they include rules restraining the free use of violence and minimal forms of rules regarding honesty, promise keeping, fair dealing, and property. It is, however, quite clear that * * * Devlin * * * [does not mean] that only those elements, which are to be found in common morality, are to be enforced by law * * *. Quite clearly the argument * * * concerns moral rules which may differ from society to society * * *

(ii) The second possibility is this: the morality to be enforced, while not coextensive with every jot and tittle of an existent moral code, includes not only the restraints and prohibitions such as those relating to the use of violence or deception which are necessary to any society whatever, but also what is essential for a particular society. The guiding thought here is that for any society there is to be found, among the provisions of its code of morality, a central core of rules or principles which constitutes its pervasive and distinctive style of life. Lord Devlin frequently speaks in this way of what he calls monogamy adopted "as a moral principle," and of course this does deeply pervade our society in two principal ways. First, marriage is a *legal* institution and the recognition of monogamy as the sole legal form of marriage carries implications for the law related to wide areas of conduct: the custody and education of children, the rules relating to inheritance and distribution of property, etc. Second, the principle of monogamy is also morally pervasive: monogamous marriage is at the heart of our conception of family life, and with the aid of the law has become part of the structure of society. Its disappearance would carry with it vast changes throughout society so that without exaggeration we might say that it had changed its character.

On this view the morality which is necessary to the existence of society is neither the moral minimum required in all societies (Lord Devlin himself says that the polygamous marriage in a polygamous society may be an equally cohesive force as monogamy is in ours), nor is it every jot and tittle of a society's moral code. What is essential and is to be preserved is the central core. On this footing it would be an open and empirical question whether any particular moral rule or veto, *e. g.,* on homosexuality, adultery, or fornication, is so organically connected with the central core that its maintenance and preservation is required as a vital outwork or bastion. There are perhaps traces of some of these ideas in Lord Devlin * * *. But even if we take this to be the position, we are still not really confronted with an empirical claim concerning the connection of the maintenance of a common morality and the prevention of disintegration or "drifting apart." Apart from the point about whether a particular rule is a vital outwork or bastion of the central core, we may still be confronted only with the unexciting tautology depending now on the identification of society, not with the whole of its morality but only with its central core or "character" and this is not the disintegration thesis.

*   *   *

What is required to convert the last mentioned position into the disintegration thesis? It must be the theory that the maintenance of the core elements in a particular society's moral life is in fact necessary to prevent disintegration, because the withering or malignant decay of the central morality is a disintegrating factor. But even if we have got thus far in identifying an empirical claim, there would of course be very many questions to be settled before anything empirically testable could be formulated. What are the criteria in a complex society for determining the existence of a single recognised morality or its central core? What is "disintegration" and "drifting apart" under modern conditions? I shall not investigate these difficulties but I shall attempt to describe in outline the types of evidence that might conceivably be relevant to the issue if and when these difficulties are settled. They seem to be the following:

(a) Crude historical evidence in which societies—not individuals —are the units. The suggestion is that we should examine societies which have disintegrated and enquire whether their disintegration was preceded by a malignant change in their common morality. This done, we should then have to address ourselves to the possibility of a causal connection between decay of a common morality and disintegration. But of course all the familiar difficulties involved in macroscopic generalisations about society would meet us at this point, and anyone who has attempted to extract generalisations from what is called the decline and fall of the Roman Empire would know that they are formidable. To take only one such difficulty: suppose that all our evidence was drawn from simple tribal societies or closely knit agrarian societies * * * We should not, I take it, have much confidence in applying any conclusions drawn from these to modern industrial societies. Or, if we had, it would be because we had some well developed and well evidenced theory to show us that the differences between simple societies and our own were irrelevant to these issues as the differences in the size of a laboratory can safely be ignored as irrelevant to the scope of the generalisations tested by laboratory experiments. * * *

(b) The alternative type of evidence must be drawn presumably from social psychology and must break down into at least two subforms according to the way in which we conceive the alternatives to the maintenance of a common morality. One alternative is general uniform *permissiveness* in the area of conduct previously covered by the common morality. The lapse, for example, of the conception that the choices between two wives or one, heterosexuality or homosexuality, are more than matters of personal taste. This (the alternative of permissiveness) is what Lord Devlin seems to envisage or to fear when he says: "The enemy of society is not error but indifference," and "Whether the new belief is better or worse than the old, it is the interregnum of disbelief that is perilous." On the other hand the alternative may not be permissivenes but *moral pluralism* involving divergent submoralities in relation to the same area of conduct.

To get off the ground with the investigation of the questions that either of these two alternatives opens up, it would be reasonable to abandon any general criteria for the disintegration of society in favour of something sufficiently close to satisfy the general spirit of the disintegration thesis. It would be no doubt sufficient if our evidence were to show that malignant change in a common morality led to a general increase in such forms of antisocial behavior as would infringe what seem the minimum essentials: the prohibitions and restraints of violence, disrespect for property, and dishonesty. We should then require some account of the conceivable psychological mechanisms supposed to connect the malignant decay of a social morality with the increase in such forms of behavior. Here there would no doubt be signal differences between the alternatives of permissiveness and moral pluralism. On the permissiveness alternative, the theory to be tested would presumably be that in the "interregnum conditions," without the discipline involved in the submission of one area of life, *e. g.,* the sexual, to the requirements of a common morality, there would necessarily be a weakening of the general capacity of individuals for self control. So, with permissiveness in the area formally covered by restrictive sexual morality, there would come increases in violence and dishonesty and a general lapse of those restraints which are essential for any form of social life. This is the view that the morality of the individual constitutes a seamless web. There is a hint that this, in the last resort, is Lord Devlin's view of the way in which the "interregnum" constitutes a danger to the existence of society: for he replied to my charge that he had assumed without evidence that morality was a seamless web by saying that though "[s]eamlessness presses the simile rather hard," "most men take their morality as a whole." But surely this assumption cannot be regarded as obviously true. The contrary view seems at least equally plausible: permissiveness in certain areas of life (even if it has come about through the disregard of a previously firmly established social morality) might make it easier for men to submit to restraints on violence which are essential for social life.

If we conceive the successor to the "common morality" to be not permissiveness but moral pluralism in some area of conduct once covered by a sexual morality which has decayed through the flouting of its restrictions, the thesis to be tested would presumably be that where moral pluralism develops in this way quarrels over the differences generated by divergent moralities must eventually destroy the minimal forms of restraints necessary for social cohesion. The counter-thesis would be that plural moralities in the conditions of modern large scale societies might perfectly well be mutually tolerant. To many indeed it might seem that the counter-thesis is the more cogent of the two, and that over wide areas of modern life, sometimes hiding behind lip service to an older common morality, there actually are divergent moralities living in peace.

NOTE

Does Lord Devlin's argument provide significant support for any particular position on the criminalization of intoxication-related conditions or activities issue? On the *Powell* issue? How would Mr. Justice Marshall answer the second question? Would it be necessary to know additional facts before either of the initial two questions could be answered? If so, what facts? How might these matters be investigated?

c. CRIMINALIZATION AND PUNISHMENT AS SATISFYING A PSYCHOLOGICAL URGE TO PUNISH

F. ALEXANDER AND H. STAUB, THE CRIMINAL, THE JUDGE, AND THE PUBLIC

5–9, 13, 9, 213–15 (1931).

In general, any restriction of an impulse is undertaken or accepted as a result of two factors: fear of pain and expectation of pleasure. Such restrictions are expressions of the adjustment which our subjective instinctive drives make to the objective demands of reality. One renounces the satisfaction of certain impulses either because such gratification is impossible, or because such gratification would cause more pain than the renunciation. In order to avoid the pain of immediate gratification of an impulse, it is not infrequently sufficient to defer such a gratification to the future and in the meantime bear a certain amount of tension; such a postponement may also serve as an insurance of gratification with which external circumstances might otherwise interfere for the present. Freud called this process the evolution of the individual from the pleasure principle to the reality principle. The reality principle thus represents nothing else but the pleasure principle which adjusted itself to the demands of reality.

Human instinctual drives demand expression, gratification. Reality puts obstacles in the way of expression; the reality principle consists of a purposive adjustment of the instinctual demands to the available possibilities of gratification. It is quite natural that renunciation goes just as far as it is possible, not further. Thus an equilibrium is established between renunciation and gratification of the demands of one's impulses. If an added renunciation is demanded, the equilibrium becomes disturbed.

The whole process of education is based on this principle. Education presents a systematic guidance in the direction of adjustment of the instinctual originally asocial, impulses of the child to the demands of the educator. The adjustment to society, like the adjustment to reality, is based on the evolutionary transition from the pleasure principle to the reality principle. The unpleasant or painful sensations, which we experience when our actions do not honor the demands of nature, correspond in the field of education and in the domain of social life in general to *punishment*.

* * * Fear of punishment and hope of being loved thus represent the two social regulators of human instinctive life. Freud came to these simple formulations in his last two works on instinctual life. ("The Ego and the Id," and "Inhibition, Symptom and Anxiety.")

* * *

Thus, fear of punishment and of not being loved (this, too, is a special form of punishment) are the two factors of education; later, throughout the life of the adult, these two factors remain the chief regulators of the instinctual life of man. Our analytical experience shows us that the conscious self-restraint of one's instinctual life plays but a very modest role as compared with the above-mentioned emotional factors. The fundamental principle of all adjustment is that of obtaining pleasure and of avoiding pain.

These considerations contain a silent recognition of the following fact: in the case of each restriction of our instinctual life, we deal with an outer world whose power to restrict this instinctual life happens to be stronger than our instinctual demands; it does not matter particularly who or what happens to be the representative of this restricting outer world; it may be Nature, educator, public leader, or the stronger social class. This process of restriction of our instinctual expressions, i. e., the adjustment to a stronger, restricting force brings about a state of equilibrium; in this state our psychic apparatus renounces just the minimal necessary amount of its wishes in order to obtain the greatest possible security in the matter of gratifying the remaining instinctual demands. What is called social order means just the equilibrium between the renunciation of instinctual demands and the assured gratification; it is a sort of a contract between the powers which restrict our instinctual expression and the instinctual demands of the individual. The very sensitive, emotional regulator of this equilibrium is the *sense of justice*. This is not developed as a result of the knowledge of the demands of the law. As Ihering in his *The Battle for Justice* well recognized, it is an indicator that functions purely instinctively, it is something comparable to anxiety (fear) or, according to Ihering, pain. Fear is the signal of a coming danger. The sense of justice acts in a similar way; whenever the accepted instinctual gratifications, which were acquired through such bitter restrictions of one's instinctual life, are threatened the sense of justice feels injured. Man senses with astounding precision when his acquired right (and each right was once acquired) is in some way threatened or diminished; to each violation of his right, he reacts with strong notice that the contract has been violated; this he does by means of freeing himself from some of the restrictions of his instinctual life which he heretofore accepted. Thus a regression takes place; man regresses from instinctual inhibition to instinctual expression.

*   *   *

The sense of justice must be recognized as one of the foundations of social life. It may be considered as a sort of an inner psychic regulator, which automatically guarantees certain self-imposed restrictions in the interest of the community. * * * [A]ny injury to this sense of justice brings about an embitterment and rebellion, and the individual finds himself, as a result, unwilling to continue the renunciation which he observed heretofore. Under the latter circumstances, the continuation of law and order becomes possible only

through the increase of the external power of the law. We must remember that within every law-abiding citizen there must live a police
officer, for it is practically impossible to keep law and order only
by means of external compulsion; the psycho-economic significance
of the citizens' voluntary readiness to support the law becomes self-
evident; this readiness, as we have seen is based upon the common
sense of justice remaining uninjured. When the public shows undisturbed confidence in the legal institutions and their official representatives, then we may say that the common sense of justice is in
harmony with the demands of the powers that be.

*   *   *

The great sensitivity of the sense of justice, the violation of
which is capable of setting afire the emotions of masses of people,
is explained particularly by the fact that the contract on which the
above-mentioned equilibrium is based is concluded between two parties, one of which is much weaker than the other.

The Ego accomplishes the self-restriction of its instinctual demands with great difficulty; it makes this sacrifice in favor of the
stronger party (society) only because it expects a compensation, the
nature of which we described as being loved. The social manifestations of this being loved is public recognition, respect, the whole
scale of social recognition, from individual liberty granted to every
citizen to the highest public distinctions. These compensations make
it easier to bear the limitations of individual sovereignty. If, however, these compensations are not forthcoming, if an individual is
treated unjustly, his fellow members of the same community, to whom
the same might happen, perceive it as a betrayal, for it appears then
that one gained nothing by renunciation. Thus, one rebels; there appears a spiteful determination to live out fully and unrestrainedly all
those instinctual drives which one held heretofore in check.

This is the reason why one feels so stirred and provoked when
a miscarriage of justice occurs and either an innocent man is convicted by mistake and thus treated like a criminal, or when it comes
to light that too harsh a sentence has been imposed as a result of
arbitrary judgment of those in power.

*   *   *   [I]n the case of escape from justice, however, every
member of the community feels that he was wronged, for a man who
violated the law escaped punishment; he was forgiven, as it were,
for a transgression which is forbidden the righteous member of the
community. We deal in both cases with the struggle for the individual freedom of one's instinctual drives; it is a protest against the
restriction of these drives. It is as if the individual member of the
community said to himself: "If other people are punished unjustly,
then *my* personal freedom is also in danger, or if *another* escapes
the punishment he deserves, why should *I* continue to conform?"

These simple psychological considerations lead to the understanding of one of the fundamental motives which prompts the public demand for the expiation of offenses. To put it in psychoanalytical language, the failure to punish an offender means to us a threat to our own repressive trends. * * *

We can state now that the power of the Superego over our instinctive life is undermined, not only when some one is punished unjustly and too severely, but also when the offender escapes punishment and thus fails to pay for his offense. Unwarranted acquittal means simply that the court permits the defendant to do things which we prohibit to ourselves. Under such circumstances, the righteous member of the community finds himself facing the following dilemma: he must either give up his own inhibitions and give in to his own anti-social tendencies, or he must demand that the offender be punished without fail. "What I do not allow myself must not be allowed others; if others are not called upon to pay for their violations of the law, then I shall not abide by my self-imposed restrictions."

We may say, then, that what creates the public demand for atonement is one's anxiety lest his own Superego be overturned and that one's own impulses, which have been curbed with so much difficulty, might break through to expression. This anxiety is quite justified, because before our Superego was set up, our unbridled impulses kept us always in a state of painful conflict with the outside world. Was not the Superego set up for the purpose of ridding ourselves of or escaping from such painful situations? Moreover, the original pressure of our instinctual drives remains so strong that man's Superego, if it is to preserve its power of repression, always needs the support of outside authorities. Hence, in the case of every violation of the law, our Ego makes an appeal for the atonement of the transgression; it does this in order to enforce the opposition of the Superego against the pressure of its instincts. The example of a criminal has a stimulating effect on our own repressed impulses, and increases the pressure coming from them. That is why our Ego needs the constant reinforcement of our Superego; it can obtain this reinforcement only from those in authority, who are the prototype of our Superego. If the Ego can show that the secular authorities agree with the Superego, then it is able to keep the instinctual impulses in check; if, however, these secular authorities happen to disavow the Superego by setting a guilty man free, then the individual feels that no support is given him to counteract a pending breaking through of his own antisocial tendencies. The demand that every crime should be expiated represents, then, a defense reaction on the part of the Ego against one's own instinctual drives; the Ego puts itself at the service of the inner repressing forces, in order to retain the state of equilibrium, which must always exist between the repressed and the repressing forces of the personality. The demand that the lawbreaker be punished is thus a demonstration against one's own inner drives, a demonstration which tends to keep these drives amenable to control: "I forbid the lawbreaker what I forbid myself."

NOTE

Is the Alexander and Staub argument based upon a retributive theory of criminal liability and punishment? Should it be entitled to any weight in the decision whether—or to what extent—to criminalize intoxication-related conditions or activities? In the *Powell* decision? Can these questions be answered without first having more information? If not, what additional information is necessary?

---

d. CRIMINALIZATION AND PUNISHMENT AS A SYMBOLIC DESIGNATION OF PUBLIC MORES

GUSSFIELD, ON LEGISLATING MORALS: THE SYMBOLIC PROCESS OF DESIGNATING DEVIANCE

56 Cal.L.Rev. 54, 57–59 (1968).g

Analysis of the designation of public norms begins with a distinction between instrumental and symbolic functions of governmental acts. Acts of officials, legislative enactments, and court decisions clearly affect behavior in an instrumental manner; they directly influence the actions of people. The National Labor Relations Act and the Taft-Hartley Act, for example, have deeply affected the conditions of collective bargaining in the United States. Tariff legislation directly affects the prices of import commodities. The instrumental function of such law lies in its enforcement; unenforced it has little instrumental effect.

Symbolic aspects of law and government, however, do not depend for their effect on enforcement. They are symbolic in a sense close to that used in literary analysis. The symbolic act "invites consideration rather than overt action." Symbolic behavior has meaning beyond its immediate significance in its connotation for the audience that views it. The symbol "has acquired a meaning which is added to its immediate intrinsic significance." The use of the wine and wafer in the Mass or the importance of the national flag cannot be appreciated without knowing their symbolic meaning for the users. In analyzing law as symbolic we are oriented less to its behavioral consequences than to its meaning as an act or gesture important in itself, as a symbol.

A governmental agent's act may have symbolic import because it affects the designation of public norms. The courtroom decision or the legislative act often glorifies the values of one group and demeans those of another. Government actions can be seen as ceremonial and ritual performances, designating the content of public morality. Law is not only a means of social control but also symbolizes the public affirmation of social ideals and norms. The statement, promulgation, or announcement of law has a symbolic dimension unrelated to its function of influencing behavior through enforcement.

Students of government and law recognize that these two functions, instrumental and symbolic, may often be separated in more than the analytical sense. Many laws are honored as much in the breach as in the performance. Proscribed behavior which nevertheless regularly occurs in a socially organized manner and is unpunished has been described as a "patterned evasion of norms." The kinds of crimes discussed here quite clearly fall into this category. Gambling, prostitution, abortion and public drunkenness are all common modes of behavior although prohibited by law. Such systematic evasion may mediate conflict between cultures; the law can proclaim one set of norms as public morality and use another set of norms in actually controlling behavior.

Even where patterned evasion of norms exists, however, the passage of legislation, the acts of officials, and decisions of judges do have significance as gestures of public affirmation. First, the affirmation of a norm as the public norm prevents recognition of the norm violator's existence by the public. The existence of law quiets and comforts those whose interests and sentiments it embodies. Second, public affirmation of a moral norm directs the major institutions of the society to its support. Despite the fact of a patterned practice of abortion in the United States, obtaining abortions does require access to subterranean social structure and is not as easy as obtaining an appendectomy. Law has instrumental functions even where there is patterned evasion.

The third impact of public affirmation is the one that most interests us here. Affirmation through law and governmental acts expresses the public worth of one subculture's norms relative to those of others, demonstrating which cultures have legitimacy and public domination. Accordingly it enhances the social status of groups carrying the affirmed culture and degrades groups carrying that which is condemned as deviant. We have argued elsewhere, for example, that the significance of Prohibition in the United States lay less in its enforcement than in the fact that it occurred. Enforcement of Prohibition law apparently was often limited by the unwillingness of "Dry" forces to utilize all their political strength for fear of creating intensive opposition. The "Dry" forces gained great satisfaction from the passage and maintenance of the legislation itself.

Whatever its instrumental effects, public designation of morality itself generates deep conflict. The designating gesture is a dramatic event, "since it invites one to consider the matter of motives in a perspective that, being developed in the analysis of drama, treats language and thought primarily as modes of action." Therefore, designation of behavior as violating public norms confers status and honor on those groups with conventional cultures and derogates those whose cultures are considered deviant. My analysis of the American temperance movement has shown how the issue of drinking and abstinence became a politically significant focus for the conflicts between Protestant and Catholic, rural and urban, native and immigrant, middle class and lower class in American society, as an abstinent Protestant middle class attempted to control the public affirmation of morality in drinking. Victory or defeat thus symbolized the status and power of the opposing cultures, indicating that legal affirmation or rejection can have symbolic as well as instrumental importance.

NOTES

1. Assuming that Gussfield is correct, is his statement merely an interesting observation or does it have some relevance for legal issues? Specifically, if he is correct, what results might flow from a decision to criminalize all intoxication-related activity? Would these results be significantly different if the law did not formally brand them as "criminal" but made clear that they were disapproved and if committed rendered the person committing them subject to "treatment" until it was likely that he would not repeat them? Would they be different if the formal law was silent as to intoxication but prohibited any unreasonably disturbing behavior, whether related to intoxication or not?

2. Would the results Gussfield predicts flow from a formal passage of a statute, without regard to the manner or extent of its enforcement? Once a statute was passed, would its enforcement have any affect upon the results that he discusses? Suppose, for example, that despite Furman v. Georgia, 408 U.S. 238, 92 S.Ct. 2726, 33 L.Ed.2d 346 (1972) (reprinted at page 71) a state legislature enacts a broad death penalty provision. Because of *Furman*, however, the death penalty is never imposed upon a defendant or executed if imposed.

---

e. CRIMINALIZATION AND CONVICTION AS PREVENTIVE MEASURES

(1) PUNISHMENT AS A MEANS OF DETERRING, MORALIZING AND THE LIKE

ANDENAES, THE GENERAL PREVENTIVE EFFECTS OF PUNISHMENT

114 U.Pa.L.Rev. 949–51 (1966).[h]

In continental theories of criminal law, a basic distinction is made between the effects of punishment on the man being punished—individual prevention or special prevention—and the effects of punishment upon the members of society in general—general prevention. The characteristics of special prevention are termed "deterrence," "reformation" and "incapacitation," and these terms have meanings similar to their meanings in the English speaking world. General prevention, on the other hand, may be described as the *restraining influences emanating from the criminal law and the legal machinery.*

By means of the criminal law, and by means of specific applications of this law, "messages" are sent to members of a society. The criminal law lists those actions which are liable to prosecution, and it specifies the penalties involved. The decisions of the courts and actions by the police and prison officials transmit knowledge about the law, underlining the fact that criminal laws are not mere empty threats, and providing detailed information as to what kind of penalty might be expected for violations of specific laws. To the extent that these stimuli restrain citizens from socially undesired actions which they might otherwise have committed, a general preventive effect is secured. While the effects of special prevention depend upon how the law is implemented in each individual case, general prevention occurs as a result of an interplay between the provisions of the law and its enforcement in specific cases. In former times, emphasis was often placed on the physical exhibition of punishment as a deterrent influence, for example, by performing executions in public. Today it is customary to emphasize the *threat* of punishment as such. From this point of view the significance of the individual sentence and the execution of it lies in the support that these actions give to the law. It may be that some people are not particularly sensitive to an abstract threat of penalty, and that these persons can be motivated toward conformity only if the penalties can be demonstrated in concrete sentences which they feel relevant to their own life situations.

The effect of the criminal law and its enforcement may be *mere deterrence.* Because of the hazards involved, a person who contemplates a punishable offense might not act. But it is not correct to regard general prevention and deterrence as one and the same thing. The concept of general prevention also includes the *moral* or *sociopedagogical* influence of punishment. The "messages" sent by law and the legal processes contain factual information about what would be risked by disobedience, but they also contain proclamations specifying that it is *wrong* to disobey. * * *

The moral influence of the criminal law may take various forms. It seems to be quite generally accepted among the members of society that the law should be obeyed even though one is dissatisfied with it and wants it changed. If this is true, we may conclude that the law as an institution itself to some extent creates conformity. But more important than this formal respect for the law is respect for the values which the law seeks to protect. It may be said that from law and the legal machinery there emanates a flow of propaganda which favors such respect. Punishment is a means of expressing social disapproval. In this way the criminal law and its enforcement supplement and enhance the moral influence acquired through education and other non-legal processes. Stated negatively, the penalty neutralizes the demoralizing consequences that arise when people witness crimes being perpetrated.

Deterrence and moral influence may both operate on the conscious level. The potential criminal may deliberate about the hazards involved, or he may be influenced by a conscious desire to behave lawfully. However, with fear or moral influence as an intermediate link, it is possible to create unconscious inhibitions against crime, and perhaps to establish a condition of habitual lawfulness. In this case, illegal actions will not present themselves consciously as real alternatives to conformity, even in situations where the potential criminal would run no risk whatsoever of being caught.

General preventive effects do not occur only among those who have been informed about penal provisions and their applications. Through a process of learning and social imitation, norms and taboos may be transmitted to persons who have no idea about their origins—in much the way that innovations in Parisian fashions appear in the clothing of country girls who have never heard of Dior or Lanvin.

Making a distinction between special prevention and general prevention is a useful way of calling attention to the importance of legal punishment in the lives of members of the general public, but the distinction is also to some extent an artificial one. The distinction is simple when one discusses the reformative and incapacitative effects of punishment on the individual criminal. But when one discusses the deterrent effects of punishment the distinction becomes less clear. Suppose a driver is fined ten dollars for disregarding the speed limit. He may be neither reformed or incapacitated but he might, perhaps, drive more slowly in the future. His motivation in subsequent situations in which he is tempted to drive too rapidly will not differ fundamentally from that of a driver who has not been fined; in other words a general preventive effect will operate. But for the driver who has been fined, this motive has, perhaps, been strengthened by the recollection of his former unpleasant experience. We may say that a general preventive feature and special preventive feature here act together.

NOTES

1. Which of the potential preventive effects of punishment should be relied upon in evaluating the propriety of criminalizing intoxication-related offenses? How should this choice be made?

2. Which, if any, persons who commit intoxication-related acts does the material suggest are most likely to be specially prevented (in Andenaes' terminology) from reoffending? Why? Which persons who might commit such acts are most likely to be "generally deterred"? Why? Do we

know enough about the actual or potential effects of punishing any category of offenders to rely upon such considerations in making the criminalization decisions? In making the *Powell* decision?

3. Schwartz and Orleans, On Legal Sanctions, 34 U.Chi.L.Rev. 274 (1967) report on a limited but interesting attempt to investigate the motivation of law-compliance. Compliance with federal income tax requirements was the subject. Four groups of taxpayers were selected at random. Members of three were interviewed prior to filing their 1962 tax returns; the fourth served as a control. Members of one group (the "sanction" group) were asked questions intended to accentuate the possibility of punishment for failure to comply with the legal requirements. Members of another group (the "conscience" group) were asked questions designed to emphasize moral reasons for compliance with tax statutes. Members of the third group (the "placebo" group) were asked neutral questions. The tax returns of all four groups for 1961 and 1962 were then compared as to adjusted gross income reported. The change between the two years for all four groups was as follows:

Group	Mean Increase or Decrease in Adjusted Gross Income
"Conscience" group	804 dollar increase
"Sanction" group	181 dollar increase
"Control" group	13 dollar decrease
"Placebo" group	87 dollar decrease

Although acknowledging that the results of the study were not always statistically significant, the authors offer the following conclusion:

The results * * * give some evidence to support the following propositions:

1. Compliance can be increased by threat of punishment.
2. Appeals to conscience can be a more effective instrument than sanction threat for securing compliance.

Id. at 299.

BALL, WHY PUNISHMENT FAILS, AMERICAN JOURNAL OF CORRECTIONS

19–21 (Jan.-Feb., 1969).[i]

One of the principal barriers to better understanding of the relationship between punishment and behavior has been our essentially rationalistic view of "human nature." The fact is that both the opponents and the advocates of a punitive approach to crime have be-

---

i. Reprinted with the permission of the American Correctional Association.

come ensnared in a set of mistaken assumptions; each faction seems to believe that man learns like a machine, responding automatically toward reward and away from punishment. In its extreme form this idea was elaborated more than a century ago by the pioneer of penology, Jeremy Bentham. According to his principle of the *felicific calculus,* man is fundamentally oriented in terms of avoiding pain (punishment) and attaining pleasure (reward); he calculates his conduct continuously so as to minimize the former and maximize the latter. Although few today would go as far as Bentham, most modern learning theory remains consistent with his outline.

Such pictures of man do little justice to the realities of his conduct. One has only to look about to realize that human behavior is not so mechanical, not so simple, and not easy to understand and predict. The actions of men are often foolish, inexpedient, and puzzling; this is what makes human behavior so singularly *human.* Man's reactions to punishment are occasionally paradoxical and are not to be explained by some contemporary version of the *felicific calculus.* * * *

One especially promising approach [to understanding the failure of punishment] lies in the careful distinction between frustration-instigated and motivation-instigated behavior.

The distinction between frustration-instigated and motivation-instigated behavior came about nearly two decades ago as a result of the psychologist Maier's experiments with rats. Maier argued that modern learning theory (which is largely within the "felicific calculus" tradition) could not account for the behavior of animals under conditions of frustration. After a short while in the frustration situation many of Maier's subjects developed responses which had no "adaptive" value. That is, the responses were neither adequate to the situation nor superior to any number of any other possible responses. Thus, the behavior pattern adopted by any given animal was maintained rigidly, without the animal's once attempting an alternative, despite the fact that the response was punished frequently. Even more striking was the fact that many animals would not abandon their responses even when punishment was instituted on every occasion.

After review of these experiments and examination of the effects of frustration on human subjects, Maier concludes that such behavior cannot be adequately accounted for by the ordinary viewpoint. He argues that motivation and frustration are qualitatively different instigators of behavior, which he believes must be described by different principles. The type of behavior which takes place with a goal in view tends to fit the "felicific calculus" or "pleasure-pain principle" closely. Since this motivation-instigated action has purpose it is properly approached on the basis of typical learning theory. It is flexible and adaptive, and the learner profits from experience of advances (reward) and setbacks (punishment). Frustration-instigated behavior, in contrast, is not goal-oriented behavior in the usual sense. The consequence of the action is not always a determining factor. A variety of modern research indicates that men under stress just do not behave with computer-like reason in the selection of behavior options.

Since there is no apparent reason for frustration-instigated behavior, such behavior appears senseless when regarded from the "felicific calculus" point of view. We simply cannot understand why a person who is punished will not reform under the pressure. We tend to overlook the possibility that behavior resulting from extreme frustration may represent a terminal response to the frustration itself rather than a rational means to any end. The possibility that satisfaction simply comes in temporary relief and tension-reduction explains the observation that frustration often produces behavior logically unrelated to alleviation of the frustrating conditions. * * *

Thus, punishment tends to aggravate [some] human reactions, which are frequently connected with a long history of prior frustration. One who has settled upon criminal behaviors may become even more set in his ways after experience with punitive conditions. One who has resigned himself ("Born to Lose") may become even more negativistic. One who has turned to aggressive outbursts may leave the punitive situation much more prone to violent aggression than when he entered. And one whose frustrations have made him progressively more dependent may find a home in the institution, returning to its protection time and again.

* * *

This interpretation would by no means result in elimination of every punishment and all frustrations of institutional life. Such a thing is currently impossible. The argument does imply that frustration should be handled more judiciously, with full knowledge of the reasons that it may make a bad problem worse. Having a more balanced view of man's nonrational behavior patterns, and perceiving that these are among the most human of reactions, we will stand in a much better position to design effective treatment programs.

NOTE

How—and to what extent, if any—is Ball's point affected by the fact that Maier's experiments were conducted with rats? Does it cast doubt upon his conclusion that some human activity is connected with frustration and is not subject to the deterrent impact of punishment? Does it call into serious question whether that human criminal activity which is connected with frustration can be identified? What are the conditions in which humans may find themselves that are analogous to the conditions Maier imposed upon his rats? Cf. Singer, Psychological Studies of Punishment, 58 Cal.L.Rev. 405, 407–09 (1970).

CHAMBLISS, TYPES OF DEVIANCE AND THE EFFECTIVENESS OF LEGAL SANCTIONS

1967 Wis.L.Rev. 703, 712–17 (1967).

[The author first reviews a number of sociological studies of the effect of the death penalty, responses of parking violators to increased sanctions, white collar crimes, and shoplifting.]

The preceding summary of research findings on the deterrent influence of punishment on various types of crimes suggests some interesting contrasts.   First is the contrast between acts that are "expressive" and acts that are "instrumental."   Murder as an expressive act is quite resistant to punishment as a deterrent, as is drug addiction; instrumental acts, such as violating parking regulations and shoplifting by middle-class housewives, are more likely to be influenced by the threat or imposition of punishment.

The other major distinction suggested by the research is between persons who are highly committed to crime as a way of life and persons whose commitment is low. * * * More generally, one could say that persons with a high commitment perceive group support, conceive of themselves as criminal, and pattern their way of life around their involvement in criminality.   Persons with low commitment would, of course, exhibit the reverse of these characteristics.

By combining these two dimensions of criminality and offender, it is possible to construct a typology of criminal acts with clear implications for the likelihood that a combination of offender and offense will respond to punishment by reducing their involvement in crime. The hypothesis is that where a high commitment to crime as a way of life is combined with involvement in an act that is expressive, one finds the greatest resistance to deterrence through threat of punishment.   At the other extreme are acts where commitment to crime is low and where the act is instrumental (such as the Snitch, the white-collar criminal, or the parking law violator).   Here we would expect both general and specific deterrence to be maximally effective * * *[.]

While we can assert with some confidence that the remaining two types—high commitment-instrumental and low commitment-expressive—will fall between the two polar types, it is somewhat more difficult to know which of these types will be more responsive to punishment.   It seems likely, however, that the impulsive nature of expressive acts, even when commitment to crime is low, will make such acts less amenable to punishment than instrumental acts, even though commitment is high.

We have, then, the following hierarchy of types that can be ranked according to whether or not they are likely to be deterred by punishment or the threat of it:

Most likely to be deterred: low commitment-instrumental
high commitment-instrumental

Least likely to be deterred: low commitment-expressive
high commitment-expressive

In considering this typology, it must be stressed that the sociological types represented by it do not correspond perfectly with legal types. * * * For example, the legal category "murder" contributes cases to at least three of the four sociological types. Probably in over 90 percent of the cases, murder is an expressive act where the commitment to crime as a way of life is low. Typically, murder occurs in an argument between two people. But there are other types of murder that would fit into the instrumental category of offenses; gangland murders, which constitute only a very small portion of the total number of murders, would, of course, be such a type. Murdering someone to collect insurance and sundry other profit-making schemes would represent instrumental types of offenses where commitment is probably low.

Ironically, most of the criminal-legal effort is devoted to processing and sanctioning those persons *least* likely to be deterred by legal sanctions. Most arrests and most convictions are for relatively minor offenses, most of which are unlikely to be deterred by imposing sanctions. * * * [W]ell over 80 percent of the arrests made by the police are for relatively minor offenses. Although some of these offenses might be responsive to sanctions, most will not. Drunkenness accounts for a larger share of arrests made than any other single offense—in 1965, 1,535,040 arrests were for drunkenness, and this represents almost one-third of the total arrests made. Furthermore, when drunkenness-related offenses are added together, they constitute *almost 50 percent* of all criminal arrests.

NOTES

1. Consider the following comment on Chambliss' distinctions:

The analytical value of Chambliss' distinction is doubtful. It does not seem self-evident that expressive acts are less influenced by social sanctions than are instrumental acts. Experience from social intercourse shows that the fear of even mild social sanctions often leads to the suppression of expressive acts (for example, yawning, picking one's nose, or crying out angrily).

Moreover, the distinction does not seem very clear. For instance, Chambliss considers the use of narcotics a typically expressive act. It may seem pedantic to object that taking the drug is instrumental in bringing about the ultimate effects of the drug. But certainly the purchase or possession of the drug is instrumental in relation to the later use. Criminal acts to obtain the drug or to obtain money to buy it are even more clearly instrumental. Yet experience seems to show that the desperate addict is deterred no more from committing these instrumental acts than he is from committing the expressive act—use of the drug. Thus, what leads to a lack of deterrent effect is not the expressive character of drug use, but rather the overwhelming motivating power of the addiction. That carefully planned acts are more easily deterred than those that result from a sudden, emotional impulse is an old proposition. The latter acts are probably more commonly labeled expressive. Apart from this distinction, however, referring to the act as expressive or instrumental does not seem to give a significant clue to the problem. A much more detailed analysis is needed.

Andenaes, Deterrence and Specific Offenses, 38 U.Chi.L.Rev. 537, 538–39 (1971).

2. Can the law justifiably rely upon an expectation that criminal punishment will have a general preventive effect? Consider the following from Lukas, A Criminologist Looks at Criminal Guilt in Social Meaning of Legal Concepts: Criminal Guilt 121–22 (1950):

[T]he Roman Empire devised a criminal code under which, though crime was a hurt to the community which must be revenged, it was provided that the revenge would be proportionate to the injury inflicted on the victim. However, penal codes and the manner in which they are popularly interpreted are often poles apart—then, as now. The record plainly shows that despite the avowed purpose of the Roman code, punishments were totally disproportionate, and their infliction at times brought a touch of carnival to the occasions. During the Emperor Constantine's reign (early fourth century), Christianity having become the Empire's official religion, the Church arrogated to itself some of the power to prosecute those who offended against moral sanctions as well as ecclesiastic edicts. Criminal courts were distinct from civil courts, and were separated from the administration of government. Their status was unchallenged as the final arbiter of guilt. Evil wills were sinful; hence the Church exhorted the evildoer to seek penitence. From that to atonement was but a short step, and from atonement to harsh punishment was shorter still.

This was held to be expiation of sin, reminiscent of the primitive posture toward crime. But it also gave impetus to the new doctrine of "deterrence." Because the presumably enlightened Church could not appear to descend to the level of primitive revenge, it engaged in the derived rationalization that severe punishment would serve to deter unknown others from committing similar offenses. That pseudo-scientific apology for punishment, artlessly distinguished from punishment for its own sake, has survived and flowered—like a hardy perennial—into the present. It is probably superfluous to remark that there was no convincing proof then—just as there is none now—that punishment in any form acts as an effective deterrent.

The deterrence doctrine now, just as it was in Constantine's day, is one of the many disingenuous excuses for criminal justice, and is woven inextricably into the more ancient tragic pattern of man's unremitting effort to shift to a substitute his own unexpressed criminal impulses.

Andenaes, General Prevention—Illusion or Reality?, 43 J.Crim.L., C. & P.S. 176, 180–81 (1952) [j]:

The disagreement over the importance of general prevention is of course largely due to the fact that its effectiveness cannot be measured. We do not know the true extent of crime. In certain areas of crime there is reason to believe that the figures available for offenses which are prosecuted and punished corresponds roughly to the true incidence of crime. In other areas recorded crimes represent only a small fraction of the true incidence. We know still less about how many people *would* have committed crimes if there had been no threat of punishment. There is a certain lesson to be drawn from the events following upon changes in the law or in other circumstances important to general prevention—such as police efficiency. We can also get somewhere by the use of common sense and psychology. But even so, it can hardly be denied that any conclusion as to the real nature of general prevention involves a great deal of guesswork. Claims based on the "demands of general prevention," therefore, can often be used to cloak strictly retributive demands for punishment or mere conservative resistance to change. On the other hand, it is just as possible that the importance of general prevention is seriously overlooked by those who are mainly interested in a more efficacious treatment of the individual offender.

On the other hand we might also ask, what do we really know about the individual-preventive effect of punishment? We have figures on recidivism to tell how large a proportion of ex-convicts commit new crimes. Yet, even aside from the significant error that comes from the fact that figures on recidivism only cover cases where the ex-convict is *caught* committing a new crime, the figures can tell us nothing of how great the recidivism would have been if there had been no punishment, or a different punishment. We might compare recidivism according to the different methods of treatment—e. g. recidivism after the use of probation or recidivism after use of special non-penal measures, as opposed to recidivism after ordinary punishment. But the results can hardly be sure, because the different methods of treatment will always be applied against different sorts of law-breakers. If the most promising of these are selected for probation and their recidivism figures are better than others', this is no proof that probation is superior in terms of individual prevention. (If the result were the opposite, however, there would be grounds for more concrete con-

j. Reprinted by special permission of the Journal of Criminal Law, Criminology & Police Science (Northwestern University School of Law), Copyright © 1952, Vol. 43, No. 2.

clusions). On the whole we can say that recidivism statistics are no more useful in measuring the individual-preventive effect of punishment than the ordinary crime statistics are useful in measuring its general-preventive effect. Both in an evaluation of individual prevention and of general prevention we can resort only to judgment based on psychology, practical experience and common sense.

Andenaes, The Morality of Deterrence, 37 U.Chi.L.Rev. 649, 663–64 (1970):

[I]t is often asserted that there is no scientific proof for the general preventive effects of punishment, and it may be argued that it is morally unjustifiable to inflict punishment on the basis of a belief which is not corroborated by scientific evidence. The burden of proof, it is sometimes said, is on those who would invoke punishment. Others may answer that the burden of proof is on those who would experiment at the risk of society by removing or weakening the protection which the criminal law now provides.

Two points should be made. First, our lack of knowledge of general prevention may be exaggerated. In some areas of criminal law we have experiences which come as close to scientific proof as could be expected in human affairs. In many other areas it seems reasonably safe to evaluate the general preventive effects of punishment on a common sense basis. Modern psychology has shown that the pleasure-pain principle is not as universally valid as is assumed, for instance, in Bentham's penal philosophy. Nevertheless, it is still a fundamental fact of social life that the risk of unpleasant consequences is a very strong motivational factor for most people in most situations.

Second, even in questions of social and economic policy we rarely are able to base our decisions on anything which comes close to strict scientific proof. Generally we must act on the basis of our best judgment. In this respect, the problems of penal policy are the same as problems of education, housing, foreign trade policy, and so on. The development of social science gradually provides a better factual foundation for decisions of social policy, but there is a long way to go. Besides, research always lags behind the rapid change of social conditions.

However, it is undeniable that punishment—the intentional infliction of suffering—is a special category among social policies. It contrasts sharply with the social welfare measures which characterize our modern state. This calls for caution and moderation in its application. I do not think the legal concept of "burden of proof" is very useful in this context. The balance that should be struck between defense of society and humaneness towards the offender can hardly be expressed in a simple formula. The solution of the conflict will depend on individual attitudes. Some people identify more with the values threatened by criminal behavior; others identify more with the lawbreaker. But certainly punishment should not be imposed precipitously. History provides a multitude of examples of shocking cruelty based on ideas of deterrence, often in combination with ideas of just retribution.

Morris and Zimring, Deterrence and Corrections, 381 Annals 137, 138–39 (1969):

> Our dedication to corrections must not lead us to repudiate deterrence. Our criminal-law system has deterrence as its primary and essential postulate. And there are many examples of the threat of punishment under the criminal law clearly influencing human behavior. Honest reader, consider your income tax return, and what it would be like were you assured that it could not be checked. If we have misjudged you, consider the impact on your neighbor's tax return! On the other hand, there are many areas where variations in the severity of the penal sanction seem to be irrelevant to the incidence of the behavior threatened—capital punishment as distinguished from protracted imprisonment for homicide; the gross increase in sanctions for narcotics offenses; and, generally, variations in minima and maxima of terms of imprisonment for a wise diversity of criminal offenses. Here, as elsewhere, the compelling lesson is that it is foolish in the extreme to offer general propositions about crime and criminals. We must address ourselves [to] the diversity of our purposes and the varieties of human behavior we seek to influence.

3. Sociological researchers have provided some material bearing on this issue, but it is difficult to evaluate because of complex methodological differences and difficulties. Gibbs, Crime, Punishment, and Deterrence, 48 Southwestern Social Science Quarterly 515 (1968) compared certainty of punishment for homicide (the number of prison admissions related to homicides known to police), severity of punishment for homicide (median number of months served by those imprisoned), and homicide rates. He found a distinct inverse association between both certainty and severity of punishment and the homicide rate in various jurisdictions. The degree of association was much greater for certainty than severity, although Gibbs believed that the statistics "caution[ed] against entirely rejecting the possibility that severity in some way operates as a deterrent." Id. at 525. He concluded that the overall results of the study "question[ed] the common assertion that no evidence exists of a relationship between legal reactions to crime and the crime rate". Id. at 529–30. Similar results were reached by Gray and Martin, Punishment and Deterrence: Another Analysis of Gibbs' Data, 50 Social Science Quarterly 389 (1969), using other methods of statistical analysis. Their methodology, however, did not substantiate Gibbs' conclusion that certainty was more important than severity.

Tittle, Crime Rate and Legal Sanctions, 16 Social Problems 409 (1969) compared certainty and severity of punishment with the rates of the F.B.I.'s "index crimes"—homicide, rape, assault, larceny, robbery, burglary, and auto theft. In each category, he found a negative association between certainty and crime rate. This was much stronger in more highly urbanized areas. Variations among the offenses is clear from the following list of associations:

All Felonies	−.45
Sex Offenses	−.57
Assault	−.46
Larceny	−.37
Robbery	−.36
Burglary	−.31
Homicide	−.17
Auto Theft	−.08

Tittle notes that there is an almost perfect negative rank order correlation between this list and one ranking offenses by offense rate. What might account for the variations? Tittle suggests that the likelihood of being punished at all for auto theft is so small that changes in this factor are unlikely to affect offenders. He also suggests that the likelihood of being punished for homicide is so high that variations in certainty are similarly unlikely to have any effect.

Tittle also found—for all offenses except homicide—a positive correlation between severity and crime rate. Controlling for urbanization in regard to nonhomicide crimes, however, eliminated any association whatsoever. This led him to the conclusion that "severity alone is simply irrelevant to the control of deviance." Id. at 416.

Chiricos and Waldo, Punishment and Crime: An Examination of Some Empirical Evidence, 18 Social Problems 200 (1970) reached similar results, although they concluded that the evidence was not strong enough to justify reliance upon deterrence as a matter of policy. Their attempts to find a relationship between changes in certainty or severity of punishment and crime rate led to data with no discernible pattern.

4. It seems likely that some alcohol-related activity can be deterred by the threat of punishment. Andenaes, Deterrence and Specific Offenses, 38 U.Chi.L.Rev. 537, 546–53 (1971) discusses the impact in Great Britain of legislation criminalizing driving with a much lower proportion of alcohol in the blood than had previously been the case and authorizing tests of a suspect's breath and blood. He notes a decrease in traffic accidents, especially those likely to involve intoxicated drivers. "My personal view," he concludes, "is that the major factor in the success of the British legislation is mere deterrence." See also, Little, A Theory and Empirical Study of What Deters Drinking Drivers, If, When and Why! 23 Ad.L.Rev. 23 (1970), 23 Ad.L.Rev. 169 (1971).

5. Note the following caution from Hawkins, Punishment and Moral Responsibility, 7 Mod.L.Rev. 205, 206 (1944):

> The vice in regarding punishment entirely from the points of view of reformation and deterrence lies * * * in forgetting that a just punishment is deserved. The punishment of men then ceases to be essentially different from the training of animals, and the way is open for the totalitarian state to undertake the forcible improvement of its citizens * * *.

(2) Criminal Conviction as a Means of Providing "Treatment"

K. MENNINGER, THE CRIME OF PUNISHMENT

253, 257-61 (1968).k

The medical use of the word *treatment* implies a program of presumably beneficial action prescribed for and administered to one who seeks it. The purpose of treatment is to relieve pain, correct disability, or combat an illness. Treatment may be painful or disagreeable but, if so, these qualities are incidental, not purposive.

*   *   *

When the community begins to look upon the expression of aggressive violence as the symptom of an illness or as indicative of illness, it will be because it believes doctors can do something to correct such a condition. At present, some better-informed individuals do believe and expect this. However angry at or sorry for the offender, they want him "treated" in an effective way so that he will cease to be a danger to them. And they know that the traditional punishment, "treatment-punishment," will not effect this.

What *will*? What effective treatment is there for such violence? It will surely have to begin with motivating or stimulating or arousing in a cornered individual the wish and hope and intention to change his methods of dealing with the realities of life. Can this be done by education, medication, counseling, training? I would answer *yes*. It can be done successfully in a majority of cases, if undertaken in time.

The present penal system and the existing legal philosophy do not stimulate or even expect such a change to take place in the criminal. Yet change is what medical science always aims for. The prisoner, like the doctor's other patients, should emerge from his treatment experience a different person, differently equipped, differently functioning, and headed in a different direction from when he began the treatment.

It is natural for the public to doubt that this can be accomplished with criminals. But remember that the public used to doubt that change could be effected in the mentally ill. *   *   * The average length of time required for restoring a mentally ill patient to health in [one particular] hospital has been reduced from years, to months, to weeks. Four-fifths of the patients living there today will be back in their homes by the end of the year. There are many empty beds, and the daily census is continually dropping.

What Is This Effective Treatment?

If these "incurable" patients are now being returned to their homes and their work in such numbers and with such celerity, why not something similar for offenders? Just what are the treatments used to effect these rapid changes? Are they available for use with offenders?

The forms and techniques of psychiatric treatment used today number in the hundreds. Psychoanalysis; electroshock therapy; psychotherapy; occupational and industrial therapy; family group therapy; milieu therapy; the use of music, art, and horticultural activities; and various drug therapies—these are some of the techniques and modalities of treatment used to stimulate or assist the restoration of a vital balance of impulse control and life satisfaction. No one patient requires or receives all forms, but each patient is studied with respect to his particular needs, his basic assets, his interests, and his special difficulties. In addition to the treatment modalities mentioned, there are many facilitations and events which contribute to total treatment effect: a new job opportunity (perhaps located by a social worker) or a vacation trip, a course of reducing exercises, a cosmetic surgical operation or a herniotomy, some night school courses, a wedding in the family (even one for the patient!), an inspiring sermon. Some of these require merely prescription or suggestion; others require guidance, tutelage, or assistance by trained therapists or by willing volunteers. A therapeutic team may embrace a dozen workers—as in a hospital setting—or it may narrow down to the doctor and the spouse. Clergymen, teachers, relatives, friends, and even fellow patients often participate informally but helpfully in the process of readaptation.

All of the participants in this effort to bring about a favorable change in the patient, i. e., in his vital balance and life program, are imbued with what we may call a *therapeutic attitude*. This is one in direct antithesis to attitudes of avoidance, ridicule, scorn, or punitiveness. Hostile feelings toward the subject, however justified by his unpleasant and even destructive behavior, are not in the curriculum of therapy or in the therapist. This does not mean that therapists approve of the offensive and obnoxious behavior of the patient; they distinctly disapprove of it. But they recognize it as symptomatic of continued imbalance and disorganization, which is what they are seeking to change. * * * A patient may cough in the doctor's face or may vomit on the office rug; a patient may curse or scream or even struggle in the extremity of his pain. But these acts are not "punished." Doctors and nurses have no time or thought for inflicting unnecessary pain even upon patients who may be difficult, disagreeable, provocative, and even dangerous. It is their duty to care for them, to try to make them well, and to prevent them from doing themselves or others harm. This requires love, not hate.

This is the deepest meaning of the therapeutic attitude. Every doctor knows this; every worker in a hospital or clinic knows it (or should). * * *

"But you were talking about the mentally ill," readers may interject, "those poor, confused, bereft, frightened individuals who yearn for help from you doctors and nurses. Do you mean to imply that willfully perverse individuals, our criminals, can be similarly reached and rehabilitated? Do you really believe that effective treatment of the sort you visualize can be applied to people *who do not want any help,* who are so willfully vicious, so well aware of the wrongs they are doing, so lacking in penitence or even common decency that punishment seems to be the only thing left?"

Do I believe there is effective treatment for offenders, and that they *can* be changed? *Most certainly and definitely I do.* Not all cases, to be sure; there are also some physical afflictions which we cannot cure at the moment. Some provision has to be made for incurables—pending new knowledge—and these will include some offenders. But I believe the majority of them would prove to be curable. The willfulness and the viciousness of offenders are part of the thing for which they have to be treated. These must not thwart the therapeutic attitude.

NOTES

1. Is it reasonable or realistic to expect correctional programs to seek to change behavior by use of methods patterned upon techniques used in treating the "mentally ill?" Compare P. Tappan, Crime, Justice and Correction 523–24 (1960):

The Role of Clinical Methods in Prevention and Treatment

In the light of the extremely exiguous facilities available for clinical treatment and the wide prevalence of relatively serious disorders in the general population, it appears desirable to employ measures of individual or intensive psychiatric therapy with prisoners only when there is reasonable ground to believe that their criminality was directly related to a psychiatric deviation and that treatment may significantly reduce the danger of criminal conduct. It is not a specific objective of the criminal law or the correctional system to alleviate the mental or emotional distress of offenders. The effort to accomplish this can be justified only in so far as it may result in increased public protection through diminishing criminality. At the present level of knowledge and technique, we cannot be exact in making the decisions called for here, but there is no sound reason to believe that psychiatric ministration to offenders displaying ordinary emotional difficulties will curtail their crimes more effectively than present measures of correctional treatment do. A large proportion of offenders who have drawn their attitudes and behavior from the criminal norms of antisocial minorities display no more and possibly less psychological distress than does the ordinary man in the street.

The primary legal and correctional objective is to protect the public against criminal recidivism with reasonable economy and humanity. This means using effective measures of control and correctional treatment of many sorts, derived from the various behavioral and social disciplines. The increasingly prevalent emphasis today upon psychotherapy and the removal of emotional problems as *the* means of prevention and reformation is an illusory diversion. The ends of deterrence, incapacitation, and rehabilitation must be sought through widely varied methods and in some instances, at least, the result should be to increase the frustrations and guilt feelings of those who are criminally inclined. Psychiatry, psychology, and casework, all important phases of correctional treatment, will fulfill their potential roles in that field best by adapting their specialized techniques to the essential objectives of correction rather than by attempting to alleviate neurosis or other discomforts on a wholesale basis. As psychiatrists and clinical psychologists incorporate a criminological orientation, they should contribute more fully to the prevention and treatment of crime. This will involve not only a refinement of their diagnostic skills but also instructing nonclinical workers in the treatment approaches that are most effective in reorienting the antisocial toward authority and reality. It is quite apparent that clinical specialists will not be able themselves to carry on individual psychotherapy with offenders to any considerable extent, either in institutions or in the community.

2. Robison and Smith, Effectiveness of Correctional Programs, 17 Crime and Delinquency 67 (1971) examined the results of research done in the California correctional system in an effort to determine the extent to which research results supported theoretical assertions that recidivism could be reduced by use of institutional programs rather than probation, longer periods of institutionalization, group counseling during incarceration, smaller caseloads during postsentence parole supervision, or parole supervision upon completion of sentence rather than immediate and complete discharge. The findings, Robison and Smith report, "strongly suggest" that "there is no evidence to support any program's claim of superior rehabilitative efficacy." Id. at 80. In evaluating the effectiveness of "treatment" during imprisonment, Robison and Smith reported an unpublished study comparing the recidivism rate or the rate of return to prison, either for violation of parole or upon a new conviction, of prison inmates who voluntarily choose to participate in group counseling, inmates compelled to participate in such counseling, inmates who voluntarily choose not to participate in group counseling, and a control group not offered the opportunity to participate in group counseling. The rates of recidivism after three years were as follows:

compelled treatment	51% recidivated
voluntary treatment	49
voluntary nonparticipants	55
control group	48

The differences among the groups were not statistically significant.

3. To the extent that "treatment" is the objective of the law, how is attainment of that objective impeded by use of the criminal process? Consider the following comment by MacCormick, Correctional Views on Alcohol, Alcoholism, and Crime, 9 Crime and Delinquency 15, 22–23 (1963): [1]

A.A. Groups in Jail

In many a county institution which in other respects does not rise above the level of [other] jails * * * the visits of members of Alcoholics Anonymous, the meetings of A.A. groups, the opportunity to join local groups after release, and the A.A. members who will be waiting on discharge day for any man or woman who wants their help cast rays of light for the alcoholic.

Last spring (1962) the General Service Office of Alcoholics Anonymous announced that there were 502 A.A. groups in prisons and jails with a total reported membership of 20,451. Of these groups, 405 were in the United States and the remainder in Canada and nine other countries.

Except in the larger jails, which can provide appropriate meeting space and usually have a more enlightened attitude toward alcoholism and Alcoholics Anonymous, A.A. groups in jails operate under great handicaps. They must frequently hold meetings in cramped, poorly lighted, and grimy quarters. Many prisoners are not in good enough physical and mental condition to participate, and others are discouraged by the officials or by fellow inmates from attending group meetings. Anyone who is thinking of establishing an A.A. group in a jail should bear in mind that many sheriffs and jailers understand A.A.'s aims and have respect for what it has accomplished, but others still view it with distrust—especially when A.A. members who were formerly inmates of the jail come in to conduct meetings. Then, too, some jail personnel who understand its aims do not have the same understanding of its methods: the necessity for closed meetings, for having A.A. members conduct the meetings, and for non-A.A. institution officials to resist their natural desire to take charge.

* * * The A.A. groups have had, and are having today, substantial success with jail inmates during their confinement and after they come out. Those who have achieved sobriety include not only the Skid Row or Bowery type of alcoholic, but also men and women who have found their way back from the shadows to the respected positions which they had once held in the business and professional world.

Other Correctional Programs

Although, in my opinion, A.A. has the most significant program, in terms of success in salvaging alcoholics, to be found in any of our county jails, it is not the only bright spot in the jail picture. A number of large county institutions, dealing with the typical jail population, have reasonably adequate physical facilities and person-

---

I. Reprinted, with permission of the National Council on Crime and Delinquency, from Crime and Delinquency, January 1963, pp. 22–23.

nel and have developed well-rounded programs of rehabilitation, some of which are aimed particularly at the alcoholic. One of the most highly rated, for example, is the Santa Rita Rehabilitation Center, operated by the sheriff of Alameda County (California), about twenty-five miles from Oakland. The U.S. Bureau of Prisons has consistently listed it among the top county penal facilities of the country.

Santa Rita is a medium-security institution which utilizes the temporary buildings and other facilities of a World War II naval installation. It has a population of about 1,000 prisoners, about 10 per cent of whom are women. Approximately 70 per cent present problems of alcoholism or narcotic addiction. About 5 per cent of the population are alcoholics under voluntary or civil court commitments; the other alcoholics are sentenced misdemeanants.

Most of the prisoners live in barracks and are employed on the large farm or in other maintenance and productive activities providing helpful work and some vocational training. The institution is surrounded by a low wire fence and, in spite of the small degree of security maintained, the escape rate is low—less than three per 1,000 inmates. The medical program includes a physical examination, X-rays, and blood tests for each inmate, followed by treatment at the institution's infirmary or at outside hospitals if needed. A doctor and a male nurse are on duty eight hours a day, and the doctor is on call for the remaining sixteen hours. Through the public school systems of nearby communities, a program of academic education that leads to the issuance of elementary certificates and high school diplomas is carried on. Religious programs, casework, counseling, and other resources and services are utilized in the attempt to rehabilitate all types of inmates.

The Center's Alcoholic Clinic carries on the special program for alcoholics. It is directed by a full-time resident psychiatrist and has a staff of four mental health therapists and two probation officers assigned by the county probation department to serve as counselors in close association with the Clinic.

In the first year of its existence (1950), 1,400 alcoholics were seen at the Clinic; since that date, at least a thousand a year have received its services. Among the treatment techniques used at the Clinic are (1) the use of tranquilizers, sedatives, and Vitamin B for treatment of acute cases, particularly those with delirium tremens, (2) use of Antabuse in the Clinic and issuance of a 30-day supply to the alcoholic when he leaves the institution (Antabuse treatment is used, however, only when the alcoholic has also received psychotherapy), (3) an initial psychiatric interview not only for fact-finding and diagnosis but also for orientation and treatment, (4) both individual and group psychotherapy, necessarily on a short-term basis, (5) individual counseling by the four mental health therapists and the two probation officers, and (6) full use of the Alcoholics Anonymous program.

To what extent does—or might—the criminal process result in "treatment" of the drunkenness offender? Compare the following comments:

> The criminal justice system appears ineffective to deter drunkenness or to meet the problems of the chronic alcoholic offender. What the system usually does accomplish is to remove the drunk from public view, detoxify him, and provide him with food, shelter, emergency medical services, and a brief period of forced sobriety. As presently constituted, the system is not in a position to meet his underlying medical and social problems.

President's Commission on Law Enforcement and Administration of Justice, The Challenge of Crime in a Free Society 235 (1967).

> Dr. John H. Lindberg, a specialist in internal medicine, testified that he gave Mr. Hill a physical examination and found no physical evidence of alcoholism, but readily diagnosed him as a chronic addictive alcoholic from his medical history. He said that Mr. Hill, considering his frequent drunkenness over so long a time, showed very little deterioration of the brain cells—a surprising lack of an expected consequence. Dr. Lindberg testified that alcoholism, unrelieved and untreated, produces cirrhosis of the liver, i. e., destruction of liver cells and their replacement by scar tissue, and that this inevitably causes death.

> If uninterrupted drunkenness is a direct cause of death, then undeniably frequent periods of confinement in a clean city jail with nourishing food during 20 years of chronic addictive alcoholism, were of beneficial therapeutic effect. Defendant's medical history contributes to the idea that laws against public drunkenness are designed to protect not only society but the offender too. Although we would not recommend jail confinement as a suitable substitute for medical, psychiatric and social therapy in the treatment of alcoholism, we observe that, in the absence of any other available alternatives, the afflicted person derives considerable benefit and protection from it. So did Mr. Hill.

> Undoubtedly a beneficial therapy must have intervened to keep the defendant in so good a physical condition that, after 20 years of chronic addictive alcoholism, his doctor could find no physical symptoms of the sickness and had to rely exclusively on a case history to confirm the diagnosis of chronic addictive alcoholism. It thus seems reasonable to conclude that Mr. Hill's frequent periods of confinement in jail, following his bouts of drunkenness, were to a large degree responsible for his continuing physical health.

Seattle v. Hill, 72 Wash.2d 786, 435 P.2d 692, 696 (1967).

4. As an alternative to the "treatment" approach suggested by Dr. Menninger, reconsider the use of probation as described in The President's Commission on Law Enforcement and Administration of Justice, Task Force Report: Corrections 28 (1967) reprinted at page 135, supra.

Dix & Sharlot Cs. Crim.Law ACB—17

PRESIDENT'S COMMISSION ON LAW ENFORCEMENT AND ADMINISTRATION OF JUSTICE, THE CHALLENGE OF CRIME IN A FREE SOCIETY

133–34 (1967).

The limited statistics available indicate that approximately one-half of those arrested are dismissed by the police, a prosecutor, or a magistrate at an early stage of the case. Some of these persons are released because they did not commit the acts they were originally suspected of committing, or cannot be proved to have committed them, or committed them on legally defensible grounds.   *   *   *

However, others who are released probably did commit the offense for which they were arrested.   *   *   *   In [some of these] the police, or more often prosecutors, have exercised the discretion that is traditionally theirs to decline to prosecute offenders whose conduct appears to deviate from patterns of law-abiding conduct, or who present clear medical, mental, or social problems that can be better dealt with outside the criminal process than within it.   *   *   *   [P]ersons whose offenses arise from drinking or mental problems [are often dealt with in this manner,] if the offenses are minor.   *   *   *

Procedures are needed to identify and divert from the criminal process mentally disordered or deficient persons. Not all members of this group are legally insane   *   *   *   under traditional legal definitions.   *   *   *   While recognizing the importance of the long-standing controversies over the definitions of criminal responsibility   *   *   *   the Commission does not believe it has a substantial contribution to make to their resolution. It is more fruitful to discuss, not who can be tried and convicted as a matter of law, but how the officers of the administration of criminal justice should deal with people who present special needs and problems. In common prosecutorial practice this question is, and the Commission believes should be, decided on the basis of the kind of correctional program that appears to be most appropriate for a particular offender. The Commission believes that, if an individual is to be given special therapeutic treatment, he should be diverted as soon as possible from the criminal process. It believes further that screening procedures capable of identifying mentally disordered or deficient offenders as early in the process as possible can be improved by training law enforcement and court officers to be more sensitive to signs of mental abnormality and by making specialized diagnostic services more readily available to the police and the courts.

*   *   *

In some communities a beginning has been made in providing alternatives other than charge or outright dismissal. In several cities the police or prosecutors conduct hearings at which the attempt is made to settle disputes, to arrange restitution or damages, to calm family quarrels, and to obtain promises to keep the peace in the future. In some places the judge participates in this process, and there are procedures to place defendants under informal probation supervision without conviction. The laws of at least five states * * * specifically provide for such dispositions, and they appear to be used in other places without specific statutory authority.

Alternative ways of disposing of criminal cases that involve close supervision or institutional commitment without conviction, call for protections from their abuse, protections that should be roughly comparable to those of the criminal law. Experience with civil procedures for the commitment of the mentally ill, for so-called sexual psychopaths, and for similar groups demonstrates that there are dangers of such programs developing in ways potentially more oppressive than those foreclosed by the careful traditional protections of the criminal law. When the alternative noncriminal disposition involves institutionalization or prolonged or intrusive supervision of the offender in the community, the disposition should be reviewed by the court.

The effect of these recommendations might well be to alter the responsibilities of the prosecutor and defense counsel and require more effort on their part early in the case. But these procedures would result in the early elimination of many cases from the process and thus relieve the system from some of its caseload burden without sacrificing the proper administration of justice. The additional investment of manpower and talent would not appear as great as that required to make existing practice work with equal effectiveness.

Of course, implementation of this recommendation is heavily dependent on the availability to the prosecutor, defense counsel, and the courts of adequate factual information on offenders and of appropriate facilities and programs in the community for the diagnosis and management of offenders who are diverted.

SPRINGER, NEW HOPE OFFERED TO REFORM DRUNKS

Austin Statesman, February 8, 1973, p. A25, col. 1–2.

Austin's Municipal Court judges and officials from the local Alcohol Reform Center are now wielding a pair of judicial scissors with which they hope to snip the jail-to-street-to-jail yoyo of many of the city's drunks.

The alcoholic reform program for persons arrested by city police for public drunkenness began Jan. 30, according to Gil Ortiz, director of the Alcohol Reform Center * * *.

Ortiz said the rehabilitation program offered the city drunks is the same set of lecture, films, therapy and counseling sessions the center holds for persons required to take an alcoholic rehabilitation course as a condition of their probation for a drinking-related offense.

Two ARC officials visit the city jail twice a day—once at 7 a. m. and again at 7 p. m.—to screen those persons arrested in the previous 12 hours for public drunkenness.

"We look for the younger drinkers, those in their 20s or 30s, who are starting to show signs of a drinking problem," Ortiz said.

The ARC * * * is not a detoxification center and cannot handle longtime alcoholics or "regulars" Ortiz said. "We try to get the ones who are starting to become repeaters and make them aware."

After ARC officials pinpoint a likely candidate for their alcohol reform school, they visit the individual in city jail before he enters a plea before a judge at the twice-daily "jail call."

"We fully explain the program to him—it's wholly voluntary," Ortiz said.

If the alcoholic program candidate agrees to attend the thrice-weekly sessions, he then must enter a plea of "guilty" or "no contest" to the public drunkenness charge.

According to presiding municipal Court Judge Allen Hill, the ARC-screened drunk is brought before the city judge, who accepts the individual's plea and assesses the maximum fine—$102.50.

"The payment of the fine is suspended pending completion of the program worked out by ARC," Judge Hill said. "Dismissal of the case will be considered upon completion of that program."

*   *   *

"The $100 fine is certainly an incentive for many persons to stay in the program," the judge said.

NOTES

1. To what extent would it be appropriate to abandon efforts to change existing criminal prohibitions covering alcohol related activity in reliance upon the development of diversion programs such as those discussed by the President's Commission? Should—and would—the actual or potential existence of such diversionary programs have any impact upon the resolution of the constitutional issue posed in *Powell*? Explain.

2. Would the ability of society to "treat" some individuals now criminally liable under laws relating to alcohol offenses be impeded by reliance upon diversion rather than decriminalization (or reduced criminalization)?

3. Could a diversionary program reasonably be expected to work in the context of the skid row alcoholic? To what extent would the success of such programs depend upon activity of the prosecutor and defense counsel? Are skid row alcoholics likely to be involved in criminal litigation to which lawyers on either side will devote much effort?

4. To what extent, if any, does the diversion program described here endanger or violate the rights of the individuals involved? Consider that

in Argersinger v. Hamlin, 407 U.S. 25, 92 S.Ct. 2006, 32 L.Ed.2d 530 (1972) the Supreme Court held that the right to representation by publicly-provided counsel applied to any defendant incarcerated as the result of his criminal conviction. In a portion of the article not reproduced above, it is noted that less than half of the fines assessed for public drunkenness in Austin were paid, "with the non-paying drunks electing to 'lay out' their fines in jail." Does the program endanger or violate this right to counsel? Consider also that in Williams v. Illinois, 399 U.S. 235, 90 S.Ct. 2018, 26 L. Ed.2d 586 (1970) the Supreme Court held that an indigent could not be incarcerated for nonpayment of a fine where no alternative methods of payment (other than lump sum immediate payment of the entire amount assessed) were made available and the total amount of time the indigent would spend in incarceration exceeded the period to which the court could have sentenced the defendant. In Tate v. Short, 401 U.S. 395, 91 S.Ct. 668, 28 L.Ed.2d 130 (1971) the Court held that an indigent defendant in a Texas Municipal Court, which lacked any authority to directly order a defendant jailed, could not be jailed for nonpayment of a fine where no alternatives to lump sum immediate payment of the entire amount was made available. Does the program described above endanger the equal protection right enforced in these decisions?

5. As a means of structuring diversion programs more adequately, consider the following provisions of the Tentative Draft of the American Law Institute's Model Code of Prearraignment Procedure:

Section 320.5   Agreement To Dismiss Or Suspend The Charge

(1) *Agreements Permitted.* The parties may agree to any one or more of the following dispositions of the case:

*   *   *

(c) that the prosecution will be suspended for a period up to one year on the condition that the defendant not engage in specific activities and conduct related to the conduct on which the charge against him was based;

(d) that the prosecution will be suspended for a period up to one year on the condition that the defendant participate in a supervised rehabilitation program which may include treatment, counseling, training and education;

(e) that the prosecutor will file an information charging the defendant with a specified crime to which the defendant will plead guilty; and

(f) that the defendant will plead guilty to a specified crime on the condition that the sentence to be imposed upon him will be consistent with terms agreed to by the parties.

(2) *Further Limitations.* The agreed disposition permitted by Subsections (1)(c) and (d) of this Section shall be subject to the further limitations specified in Section 320.6 * * *.

(3) *Stipulations.* The agreement of the parties pursuant to this Section may include stipulations concerning the admissibility into evidence of specified testimony, evidence or depositions in the

event that the dismissal or suspension of the prosecution is terminated and there is a trial on the charge.

(4) *Record of the Agreement.* An agreement pursuant to this Section shall be in writing, and a copy signed by the defendant and the respective counsel shall be filed with the court.

Section 320.6   Limitations On Agreements Involving Conditional Suspension of Prosecution

Agreements pursuant to Subsections 320.5(c) and (d) shall be subject to the limitation set forth in this section 320.6.

(1) *Agreement to Be No More Onerous than if Defendant on Probation.* The terms of the agreement shall not be more onerous than those which could be imposed on a defendant placed on probation after conviction of the crime charged in the complaint.

(2) *Limitation on Commitment to Custodial Institution.* The agreement shall not provide for the defendant's commitment for more than thirty days to an institution imposing custodial controls other than reasonable curfew restrictions during the nighttime, unless, the court, at the hearing provided in Section 320.7, determines that there exist grounds, independent of the pending prosecution, to commit the defendant to such institution involuntarily.

(3) *Limitation on Obligation to Reside away from Home.* The agreement shall not require the defendant to reside in any designated place other than his own home or that of a member of his immediate family, except that the defendant may be required to reside in a residential facility for persons participating in a particular program of training or rehabilitation if (a) it is necessary to reside there in order to participate fully in the program, and (b) the rules of the residence facility, other than those relating to reasonable curfew restrictions during the nighttime, permit the defendant free ingress and egress.

Section 320.7   Judicial Approval of Agreements Involving Conditional Suspension of Prosecution

(1) *When Required.* An agreement pursuant to Subsection 320.5(1)(c) or (d) of this Code shall not take effect until it has been reviewed and approved by the court having jurisdiction to try the offense charged in the complaint.

(2) *Additional Required Judicial Determinations.* The court's approval shall be subject to its making the following additional determinations:

(a) by inquiry of the defendant personally and by such other inquiry as it deems appropriate, that the defendant's consent to the agreement is a product of an informed choice, that he is aware of and understands the alternative courses available to him including his right to a preliminary hearing if applicable and his right to trial, and that he understands the terms and consequences of the agreement;

(b) that the agreement does not exceed the limitations set forth in Sections 320.5 and 320.6; and

(c) that the parties have considered the facts relevant to an appropriate disposition with respect to the defendant and that the terms of the agreement and any psychiatric or other special rehabilitation program agreed upon appear generally suited to the defendant's needs, furnish the public adequate protection, and do not unreasonably restrict the defendant's freedom, taking into account the fact that he has not been convicted of the crime charged. The court may order its probation service to conduct an investigation to assist it in ruling on the agreement.

(3) *Statement of Reasons for Disapproval of the Agreement.* If the court determines to disapprove the agreement it shall give the parties the reasons for its determination and afford them the opportunity to modify the agreement accordingly. The court shall not, however, participate in discussions concerning the terms of a plea agreement. A decision by the court disapproving an agreement shall not be subject to appeal.

(4) *Approval of the Agreement; Release from Custody.* If the court determines to approve the agreement it shall enter an order to that effect, and the defendant shall be released on his own recognizance if he is in custody, unless the agreement provides for commitment pursuant to Subsection 320.6(2).

Section 320.8   Termination, Modification And Extension Of The Agreement

(1) *Modification by Mutual Consent.* At any time within the period agreed upon for a conditional dismissal or suspension of the prosecution pursuant to Subsections 320.5(1)(c) and (d), the parties may by mutual consent modify the terms of the agreement. The agreement as modified shall be subject to the provisions of Sections 320.5 and 320.6 and shall be reviewed by the court pursuant to Section 320.7.

(2) *Termination by Prosecutor for Violation or Misrepresentation.* If the defendant violates a material condition of the agreement or if at any time within six months after the date of the agreement it appears that the defense misrepresented facts in a way materially affecting the agreement, the prosecutor may, after affording the defendant an opportunity to be heard in accordance with Section 320.9, request permission from the court to terminate the agreement and reinstate the prosecution. As an alternative to such termination, the defendant and the prosecutor may agree, pursuant to Subsection (1), to a modification of the agreement reasonably related to the defendant's violation or to the newly ascertained facts. In the event of such modification, the period of the agreement may be extended up to one additional year from the date of modification.

(3) *Termination by the Defendant.* The defendant may terminate the agreement at any time by furnishing written notice of such revocation to the prosecutor or the court. Prior to accepting

such consent and permitting reinstatement of the prosecution, the court shall give the defendant an opportunity to consult with counsel. Upon the court's acceptance of such consent, the prosecutor may reinstate the prosecution.

(4) *Resumption of Prosecution.* If the prosecution is reinstated, the court shall enter such order as is appropriate, taking into account the passage of time and any change of circumstances, in order to effectuate the resumption of the prosecution. The court shall determine the stage of the proceedings at which the prosecution shall be resumed. Such order shall designate a period, no longer than permitted in Subsection 340.2(1), during which an indictment or information may be filed, and filing within such period shall constitute compliance with that Subsection.

(5) *Termination and Dismissal by Court for Misrepresentation by Prosecution.* If the court finds that the defendant's consent to the agreement was obtained as a result of a material misrepresentation made by the prosecutor or anyone under his control and that the interests of justice so require, the court may direct that the defendant be released from his obligations under the agreement and that the prosecution be dismissed with prejudice.

(6) *Termination by Lapse of Time.* Upon the expiration of the agreement in accordance with its terms, the court shall dismiss the complaint and prosecution of the defendant for the conduct on which the complaint was based shall thereafter be barred.

Section 320.9   Procedure On Allegation Of Violation Or Misrepresentation

(1) *Notice and Hearing.* A defendant alleged to have violated a material term of the agreement or to have made a misrepresentation materially affecting the agreement shall be given written notice of the facts alleged against him and shall be entitled to a hearing before the prosecutor to determine whether such violation or misrepresentation in fact occurred and, if so, whether the prosecution should be reinstated or the agreement modified. The defendant shall be entitled to be represented by counsel at the hearing. The rules of evidence shall not govern the procedure at the hearing, but the defendant shall have the right to confront and cross-examine any witnesses against him. A record shall be made of the hearing.

(2) *Judicial Review.* If the prosecutor determines to reinstate the prosecution, the defendant may make a motion before the court to continue the dismissal or suspension of the prosecution on the ground that the record does not support the prosecutor's determination or that the prosecutor has not complied with the provisions of Subsection (1) of this Section. The court may hear witnesses in addition to those heard at the hearing before the prosecutor.

A Model Code of Pre-Arraignment Procedure (Tent. Draft No. 5, 1972).

6. To what extent would the answers to the questions above differ if instead of the program described above being at issue, the matter concerned a defendant charged with forcible rape who was offered as an al-

ternative to "regular processing" as a criminal defendant the opportunity to admit himself to a psychiatric facility until the staff felt that he no longer posed a danger to the community? For a study of diversion programs for narcotics addicts and a discussion of the dangers posed by such programs, see Note, Addict Diversion: An Alternative Approach for the Criminal Justice System, 60 Geo.L.J. 667 (1972). See also Brakel, Diversion from the Criminal Process: Informal Discretion, Motivation, and Formalization, 48 Denver L.J. 211 (1971); Warder and Zalk, Non-Trial Disposition of Criminal Offenders: A Case Study, 5 J.L.Reform 453 (1972).

---

3. "COSTS" OF CRIMINALIZATION

---

a. INFRINGEMENTS UPON PERSONAL PRIVACY

GRISWOLD v. CONNECTICUT

Supreme Court of the United States, 1965.
381 U.S. 479, 85 S.Ct. 1678, 14 L.Ed.2d 510.

Mr. Justice DOUGLAS delivered the opinion of the Court.

Appellant Griswold is Executive Director of the Planned Parenthood League of Connecticut. Appellant Buxton is a licensed physician and a professor at the Yale Medical School who served as Medical Director for the League at its Center in New Haven—a center open and operating from November 1 to November 10, 1961, when appellants were arrested.

They gave information, instruction, and medical advice to *married persons* as to the means of preventing conception. They examined the wife and prescribed the best contraceptive device or material for her use. Fees were usually charged, although some couples were serviced free.

The statutes whose constitutionality is involved in this appeal are §§ 53–32 and 54–196 of the General Statutes of Connecticut (1958 rev.). The former provides:

"Any person who uses any drug, medicinal article or instrument for the purpose of preventing conception shall be fined not less than fifty dollars or imprisoned not less than sixty days nor more than one year or be both fined and imprisoned."

Section 54–196 provides:

"Any person who assists, abets, counsels, causes, hires or commands another to commit any offense may be prosecuted and punished as if he were the principal offender."

The appellants were found guilty as accessories and fined $100 each, against the claim that the accessory statute as so applied violated the Fourteenth Amendment. * * *

Coming to the merits, we are met with a wide range of questions that implicate the Due Process Clause of the Fourteenth Amendment. Overtones of some arguments suggest that Lochner v. New York, 198 U.S. 45, 25 S.Ct. 539, 49 L.Ed. 937, should be our guide. But we decline that invitation * * *. We do not sit as a super-legislature to determine the wisdom, need, and propriety of laws that touch economic problems, business affairs, or social conditions. This law, however, operates directly on an intimate relation of husband and wife and their physician's role in one aspect of that relation.

The association of people is not mentioned in the Constitution nor in the Bill of Rights. The right to educate a child in a school of the parents' choice—whether public or private or parochial—is also not mentioned. Nor is the right to study any particular subject or any foreign language. Yet the First Amendment has been construed to include certain of those rights.

By Pierce v. Society of Sisters, [268 U.S. 510 (1925)], the right to educate one's children as one chooses is made applicable to the States by the force of the First and Fourteenth Amendments. By Meyer v. Nebraska, [262 U.S. 390 (1923)], the same dignity is given the right to study the German language in a private school. In other words, the State may not, consistently with the spirit of the First Amendment, contract the spectrum of available knowledge. The right of freedom of speech and press includes not only the right to utter or to print, but the right to distribute, the right to receive, the right to read and freedom of inquiry, freedom of thought, and freedom to teach—indeed the freedom of the entire university community. * * * Without those peripheral rights the specific rights would be less secure. And so we reaffirm the principle of the Pierce and the Meyer cases.

In NAACP v. Alabama, 357 U.S. 449, 462, 78 S.Ct. 1163, 2 L. Ed.2d 1488, 1499, we protected the "freedom to associate and privacy in one's associations," noting that freedom of association was a peripheral First Amendment right. Disclosure of membership lists of a constitutionally valid association, we held, was invalid "as entailing the likelihood of a substantial restraint upon the exercise by petitioner's members of their right to freedom of association." Ibid. In other words, the First Amendment has a penumbra where privacy is protected from governmental intrusion. In like context, we have protected forms of "association" that are not political in the customary sense but pertain to the social, legal, and economic benefit of the members. In Schware v. Board of Bar Examiners, 353 U.S. 232, 77 S.Ct. 752, 1 L.Ed.2d 796, 64 A.L.R.2d 288, we held it not permissible to bar a lawyer from practice, because he had once been a member of the Communist Party. The man's "association with that Party" was not shown to be "anything more than a political faith in a political party" (id., at 244, 1 L.Ed.2d at 804, 64 A.L.R.2d 288) and was not action of a kind proving bad moral character. Id., at 245–246, 1 L.Ed.2d at 805, 64 A.L.R.2d 288.

Those cases involved more than the "right of assembly"—a right that extends to all irrespective of their race or ideology. The right of "association," like the right of belief is more than the right to attend a meeting; it includes the right to express one's attitudes or philosophies by membership in a group or by affiliation with it or by other lawful means. Association in that context is a form of expression of opinion; and while it is not expressly included in the First Amendment its existence is necessary in making the express guarantees fully meaningful.

The foregoing cases suggest that specific guarantees in the Bill of Rights have penumbras, formed by emanations from those guarantees that help give them life and substance. * * *

Various guarantees create zones of privacy. The right of association contained in the penumbra of the First Amendment is one, as we have seen. The Third Amendment in its prohibition against the quartering of soldiers "in any house" in time of peace without the consent of the owner is another facet of that privacy. The Fourth Amendment explicitly affirms the "right of the people to be secure in their persons, houses, papers, and effects, against unreasonable searches and seizures." The Fifth Amendment in its Self-Incrimination Clause enables the citizen to create a zone of privacy which government may not force him to surrender to his detriment. The Ninth Amendment provides: "The enumeration in the Constitution, of certain rights, shall not be construed to deny or disparage others retained by the people."

The Fourth and Fifth Amendments were described in Boyd v. United States, 116 U.S. 616, 630, 6 S.Ct. 524, 29 L.Ed. 746, 751, as protection against all governmental invasions "of the sanctity of a man's home and the privacies of life." We recently referred in Mapp v. Ohio, 367 U.S. 643, 656, 81 S.Ct. 1684, 6 L.Ed.2d 1081, 1090, 84 A.L.R.2d 933, to the Fourth Amendment as creating a "right to privacy, no less important than any other right carefully and particularly reserved to the people." * * *

We have had many controversies over these penumbral rights of "privacy and repose." * * * These cases bear witness that the right of privacy which presses for recognition here is a legitimate one.

The present case, then, concerns a relationship lying within the zone of privacy created by several fundamental constitutional guarantees. And it concerns a law which, in forbidding the *use* of contraceptives rather than regulating their manufacture or sale, seeks to achieve its goals by means having a maximum destructive impact upon that relationship. Such a law cannot stand in light of the familiar principle, so often applied by this Court, that a "governmental purpose to control or prevent activities constitutionally subject to state regulation may not be achieved by means which sweep unnecessarily broadly and thereby invade the area of protected freedoms." NAACP v. Alabama, 377 U.S. 288, 307, 84 S.Ct. 1302, 12 L.Ed.2d 325, 338. Would we allow the police to search the sacred precincts of marital bedrooms for telltale signs of the use of contraceptives? The very idea is repulsive to the notions of privacy surrounding the marriage relationship.

We deal with a right of privacy older than the Bill of Rights— older than our political parties, older than our school system. Marriage is a coming together for better or for worse, hopefully enduring, and intimate to the degree of being sacred. It is an association that promotes a way of life, not causes; a harmony in living, not political faiths; a bilateral loyalty, not commercial or social projects. Yet it is an association for as noble a purpose as any involved in our prior decisions.

Reversed.

Mr. Justice GOLDBERG, whom the Chief Justice and Mr. Justice BRENNAN join, concurring.

I agree with the Court that Connecticut's birth-control law unconstitutionally intrudes upon the right of marital privacy, and I join in its opinion and judgment.

I do agree that the concept of liberty protects those personal rights that are fundamental, and is not confined to the specific terms of the Bill of Rights. My conclusion that the concept of liberty is not so restricted and that it embraces the right of marital privacy though that right is not mentioned explicitly in the Constitution is supported both by numerous decisions of this Court, referred to in the Court's opinion, and by the language and history of the Ninth Amendment. In reaching the conclusion that the right of marital privacy is protected, as being within the protected penumbra of specific guarantees of the Bill of Rights, the Court refers to the Ninth Amendment. I add these words to emphasize the relevance of that Amendment to the Court's holding.

Mr. Justice WHITE, concurring in the judgment.

*   *   *

[The] decisions affirm that there is a "realm of family life which the state cannot enter" without substantial justification. * * *

The Connecticut anti-contraceptive statute deals rather substantially with this relationship. * * * [T]he clear effect of these statutes, as enforced, is to deny disadvantaged citizens of Connecticut, those without either adequate knowledge or resources to obtain private counseling, access to medical assistance and up-to-date information in respect to proper methods of birth control. In my view, a statute with these effects bears a substantial burden of justification when attacked under the Fourteenth Amendment. * * *

An examination of the justification offered, however, cannot be avoided by saying that the Connecticut anti-use statute invades a protected area of privacy and association or that it demeans the marriage relationship. The nature of the right invaded is pertinent, to be sure, for statutes regulating sensitive areas of liberty do, under the cases of this Court, require "strict scrutiny," Skinner v. Oklahoma, 316 U.S. 535, 541, 62 S.Ct. 1110, 86 L.Ed. 1655, 1660, and "must be viewed in the light of less drastic means for achieving the same basic purpose." Shelton v. Tucker, 364 U.S. 479, 488, 81 S.Ct. 247, 5 L.Ed.2d 231, 237. "Where there is a significant encroachment upon personal liberty, the State may prevail only upon showing a subordinating interest which is compelling." Bates v. Little Rock, 361 U.S. 516, 524, 80 S.Ct. 412, 4 L.Ed.2d 480, 486. See also McLaughlin v. Florida, 379 U.S. 184, 85 S.Ct. 283, 13 L.Ed.2d 222. But such statutes, if reasonably necessary for the effectuation of a legitimate and substantial state interest, and not arbitrary or capricious in application, are not invalid under the Due Process Clause.

As I read the opinions of the Connecticut courts and the argument of Connecticut in this Court, the State claims but one justification for its anti-use statute. There is no serious contention that Connecticut thinks the use of artificial or external methods of contraception immoral or unwise in itself, or that the anti-use statute is founded upon any policy of promoting population expansion. Rather, the statute is said to serve the State's policy against all forms of promiscuous or illicit sexual relationships, be they premarital or extramarital, concededly a permissible and legitimate legislative goal.

Without taking issue with the premise that the fear of conception operates as a deterrent to such relationships in addition to the criminal proscriptions Connecticut has against such conduct, I wholly fail to see how the ban on the use of contraceptives by married couples in any way reinforces the State's ban on illicit sexual relationships. Connecticut does not bar the importation or possession of contraceptive devices; they are not considered contraband material under state law, and their availability in that State is not seriously disputed. The only way Connecticut seeks to limit or control the availability of such devices is through its general aiding and abetting statute whose operation in this context has been quite obviously ineffective and whose most serious use has been against birth-control clinics rendering advice to married, rather than unmarried, persons. Indeed, after over 80 years of the State's proscription of use, the legality of the sale of such devices to prevent disease has never been expressly passed upon, although it appears that sales have long occurred and have only infrequently been challenged. This "undeviating policy

* * * throughout all the long years * * * bespeaks more than prosecutorial paralysis." Poe v. Ullman, 367 U.S. 497, 502, 81 S.Ct. 1752, 6 L.Ed.2d 989, 995. Moreover, it would appear that the sale of contraceptives to prevent disease is plainly legal under Connecticut law.

In these circumstances one is rather hard pressed to explain how the ban on use by married persons in any way prevents use of such devices by persons engaging in illicit sexual relations and thereby contributes to the State's policy against such relationships. Neither the state courts nor the State before the bar of this Court has tendered such an explanation. It is purely fanciful to believe that the broad proscription on use facilitates discovery of use by persons engaging in a prohibited relationship or for some other reason makes such use more unlikely and thus can be supported by any sort of administrative consideration. Perhaps the theory is that the flat ban on use prevents married people from possessing contraceptives and without the ready availability of such devices for use in the marital relationship, there will be no or less temptation to use them in extramarital ones. This reasoning rests on the premise that married people will comply with the ban in regard to their marital relationship, notwithstanding total nonenforcement in this context and apparent nonenforcibility, but will not comply with criminal statutes prohibiting extramarital affairs and the anti-use statute in respect to illicit sexual relationships, a premise whose validity has not been demonstrated and whose intrinsic validity is not very evident. At most the broad ban is of marginal utility to the declared objective. A statute limiting its prohibition on use to persons engaging in the prohibited relationship would serve the end posited by Connecticut in the same way, and with the same effectiveness, or ineffectiveness, as the broad anti-use statute under attack in this case. I find nothing in this record justifying the sweeping scope of this statute, with its telling effect on the freedoms of married persons, and therefore conclude that it deprives such persons of liberty without due process of law.

[The concurring opinion of Mr. Justice HARLAN and the dissenting opinions of Mr. Justice BLACK and Mr. Justice STEWART have been omitted.]

STANLEY v. GEORGIA

Supreme Court of the United States, 1969.
394 U.S. 557, 89 S.Ct. 1243, 22 L.Ed.2d 542.

Mr. Justice MARSHALL delivered the opinion of the Court.

An investigation of appellant's alleged bookmaking activities led to the issuance of a search warrant for appellant's home. Under authority of this warrant, federal and state agents secured entrance. They found very little evidence of bookmaking activity, but while looking through a desk drawer in an upstairs bedroom, one of the federal agents, accompanied by a state officer, found three reels of eight-millimeter film. Using a projector and screen found in an upstairs living room, they viewed the films. The state officer concluded that they were obscene and seized them. Since a further examination of the bedroom indicated that appellant occupied it, he was charged with possession of obscene matter and placed under arrest. He was later indicted for "knowingly hav[ing] possession of * * * obscene matter" in violation of Georgia law. Appellant was tried before a jury and convicted. * * *

Appellant raises several challenges to the validity of his conviction. We find it necessary to consider only one. Appellant argues here, and argued below, that the Georgia obscenity statute, insofar as it punishes mere private possession of obscene matter, violates the First Amendment, as made applicable to the States by the Fourteenth Amendment. For reasons set forth below, we agree that the mere private possession of obscene matter cannot constitutionally be made a crime.

The court below saw no valid constitutional objection to the Georgia statute, even though it extends further than the typical statute forbidding commercial sales of obscene material. It held that "[i]t is not essential to an indictment charging one with possession of obscene matter that it be alleged that such possession was 'with intent to sell, expose or circulate the same.'" Stanley v. State, supra, 224 Ga., at 261, 161 S.E.2d, at 311. The State and appellant both agree that the question here before us is whether "a statute imposing criminal sanctions upon the mere [knowing] possession of obscene matter" is constitutional. In this context, Georgia concedes that the present case appears to be one of "first impression * * * on this exact point," but contends that since "obscenity is not within the area of constitutionally protected speech or press," Roth v. United States, 354 U.S. 476, 485, 77 S.Ct. 1304, 1309, 1 L.Ed.2d 1498 (1957), the States are free, subject to the limits of other provisions of the Constitution to deal with it any way deemed necessary, just as they may deal with possession of other things thought to be detrimental to the welfare of their citizens. If the State can protect the body of a citizen, may it not, argues Georgia, protect his mind?

It is true that Roth does declare, seemingly without qualification, that obscenity is not protected by the First Amendment. * * * However, neither Roth nor any subsequent decision of this Court dealt with the precise problem involved in the present case. Roth was convicted of mailing obscene circulars and advertising, and an obscene book, in violation of a federal obscenity statute. * * * Moreover, none of this Court's decisions subsequent to Roth involved prosecution for private possession of obscene materials. Those cases dealt with the power of the State and Federal Governments to prohibit or regulate certain public actions taken or intended to be taken with respect to obscene matter. * * *

In this context, we do not believe that this case can be decided simply by citing *Roth*. *Roth* and its progeny certainly do mean that the First and Fourteenth Amendments recognize a valid governmental interest in dealing with the problem of obscenity. But the assertion of that interest cannot, in every context, be insulated from all constitutional protections. Neither *Roth* nor any other decision of this Court reaches that far. As the Court said in *Roth* itself, "[c]easeless vigilance is the watchword to prevent * * * erosion [of First Amendment rights] by Congress or by the States. The door barring federal and state intrusion into this area cannot be left ajar; it must be kept tightly closed and opened only the slightest crack necessary to prevent encroachment upon more important interests." 354 U.S., at 488, 77 S.Ct., at 1311. *Roth* and the cases following it discerned such an "important interest" in the regulation of commercial distribution of obscene material. That holding cannot foreclose an examination of the constitutional implications of a statute forbidding mere private possession of such material.

It is now well established that the Constitution protects the right to receive information and ideas. "This freedom [of speech and press] * * * necessarily protects the right to receive * * *." Martin v. City of Struthers, 319 U.S. 141, 143, 63 S.Ct. 862, 863, 87 L.Ed. 1313 (1943) * * *. This right to receive information and ideas, regardless of their social worth is fundamental to our free society. Moreover, in the context of this case—a prosecution for mere possession of printed or filmed matter in the privacy of a person's own home—that right takes on an added dimension. For also fundamental is the right to be free, except in very limited circumstances, from unwanted governmental intrusions into one's privacy.

These are the rights that appellant is asserting in the case before us. He is asserting the right to read or observe what he pleases —the right to satisfy his intellectual and emotional needs in the privacy of his own home. He is asserting the right to be free from state inquiry into the contents of his library. Georgia contends that appellant does not have these rights, that there are certain types of materials that the individual may not read or even possess. Georgia justifies this assertion by arguing that the films in the present case are obscene. But we think that mere categorization of these films as "obscene" is insufficient justification for such a drastic invasion of personal liberties guaranteed by the First and Fourteenth Amendments. Whatever may be the justifications for other statutes regulating obscenity, we do not think they reach into the privacy of one's own home. If the First Amendment means anything, it means that a State has no business telling a man, sitting alone in his own house, what books he may read or what films he may watch. Our whole constitutional heritage rebels at the thought of giving government the power to control men's minds.

And yet, in the face of these traditional notions of individual liberty, Georgia asserts the right to protect the individual's mind from the effects of obscenity. We are not certain that this argument amounts to anything more than the assertion that the State has the right to control the moral content of a person's thoughts. To some, this may be a noble purpose, but it is wholly inconsistent with the philosophy of the First Amendment. As the Court said in Kingsley International Pictures Corp. v. Regents, 360 U.S. 684, 688–689, 79 S.Ct. 1362, 1365, 3 L.Ed.2d 1512 (1959), "[t]his argument misconceives what it is that the Constitution protects. Its guarantee is not confined to the expression of ideas that are conventional or shared by a majority. * * * And in the realm of ideas it protects expression which is eloquent no less than that which is unconvincing." Nor is it relevant that obscene materials in general, or the particular films before the Court, are arguably devoid of any ideological content. The line between the transmission of ideas and mere entertainment is much too elusive for this Court to draw, if indeed such a line can be drawn at all. Whatever the power of the state to control public dissemination of ideas inimical to the public morality, it cannot constitutionally premise legislation on the desirability of controlling a person's private thoughts.

Perhaps recognizing this, Georgia asserts that exposure to obscene materials may lead to deviant sexual behavior or crimes of sexual violence. There appears to be little empirical basis for that assertion.[9] But more important, if the State is only concerned about printed or filmed materials inducing antisocial conduct, we believe that in the context of private consumption of ideas and information we should adhere to the view that "[a]mong free men, the deterrents ordinarily to be applied to prevent crime are education and punishment for violations of the law * * *." Whitney v. California, 274 U.S. 357, 378, 47 S.Ct. 641, 649, 71 L.Ed. 1095 (1927) (Brandeis, J., concurring). See Emerson, Toward a General Theory of the First Amendment, 72 Yale L.J. 877, 938 (1963). Given the present state of knowledge, the State may no more prohibit mere possession of obscene matter on the ground that it may lead to antisocial conduct than it may prohibit possession of chemistry books on the ground that they may lead to the manufacture of homemade spirits.

It is true that in *Roth* this Court rejected the necessity of proving that exposure to obscene material would create a clear and pres-

9. See, e. g., Cairns, Paul, & Wishner, Sex Censorship: The Assumptions of Anti-Obscenity Laws and the Empirical Evidence, 46 Minn.L.Rev. 1009 (1962); see also M. Jahoda, The Impact of Literature: A Psychological Discussion of Some Assumptions in the Censorship Debate (1954), summarized in the concurring opinion of Judge Frank in United States v. Roth, 237 F.2d 796, 814–816 (C.A.2d Cir. 1956).

ent danger of antisocial conduct or would probably induce its recipients to such conduct. 354 U.S., at 486–487, 77 S.Ct., at 1309–1310. But that case dealt with public distribution of obscene materials and such distribution is subject to different objections. For example, there is always the danger that obscene material might fall into the hands of children, see Ginsberg v. New York, *supra*, or that it might intrude upon the sensibilities or privacy of the general public. No such dangers are present in this case.

Finally, we are faced with the argument that prohibition of possession of obscene materials is a necessary incident to statutory schemes prohibiting distribution. That argument is based on alleged difficulties of proving an intent to distribute or in producing evidence of actual distribution. We are not convinced that such difficulties exist, but even if they did we do not think that they would justify infringement of the individual's right to read or observe what he pleases. Because that right is so fundamental to our scheme of individual liberty, its restriction may not be justified by the need to ease the administration of otherwise valid criminal laws. See Smith v. California, 361 U.S. 147, 80 S.Ct. 215, 4 L.Ed.2d 205 (1959).

We hold that the First and Fourteenth Amendments prohibit making mere private possession of obscene material a crime.[11] *Roth* and the cases following that decision are not impaired by today's holding. As we have said, the States retain broad power to regulate obscenity; that power simply does not extend to mere possession by the individual in the privacy of his own home. Accordingly, the judgment of the court below is reversed and the case is remanded for proceedings not inconsistent with this opinion.

It is so ordered.

Judgment reversed and case remanded.

[Mr. Justice BLACK concurred in a separate opinion. Mr. Justice STEWART, joined by Mr. Justice BRENNAN and Mr. Justice WHITE, concurred in the result only on the ground that the film had been seized in violation of the Fourth Amendment.]

---

11. What we have said in no way infringes upon the power of the State or Federal Government to make possession of other items, such as narcotics, firearms, or stolen goods, a crime. Our holding in the present case turns upon the Georgia statute's infringement of fundamental liberties protected by the First and Fourteenth Amendments. No First Amendment rights are involved in most statutes making mere possession criminal.

Nor do we mean to express any opinion on statutes making criminal possession of other types of printed, filmed, or recorded materials. See, e. g., 18 U.S.C.A. § 793(d), which makes criminal the otherwise lawful possession of materials which "the possessor has reason to believe could be used to the injury of the United States or to the advantage of any foreign nation * * *." In such cases, compelling reasons may exist for overriding the right of the individual to possess those materials.

NOTE

In Eisenstadt v. Baird, 405 U.S. 438, 92 S.Ct. 1029, 31 L.Ed.2d 349 (1972), aff'g 429 F.2d 1398 (1st Cir. 1970), the Supreme Court invalidated Baird's conviction for giving a young woman a package of contraceptive vaginal foam. The conviction was based upon a Massachusetts statute prohibiting the distribution of contraceptives except to married persons upon a physician's prescription. Mr. Justice Brennan, speaking for the Court, declined to address himself to whether under *Griswold* a state could bar the distribution of contraceptives to married persons. Rather, the decision was based upon Equal Protection grounds:

> If under *Griswold* the distribution of contraceptives to married persons cannot be prohibited, a ban on distribution to unmarried persons would be equally impermissible. It is true that in *Griswold* the right of privacy in question inhered in the marital relationship. Yet the marital couple is not an independent entity with a mind and heart of its own, but an association of two individuals each with a separate intellectual and emotional make-up. If the right of privacy means anything, it is the right of the *individual*, married or single, to be free from unwarranted governmental intrusion into matters so fundamentally affecting a person as the decision whether to bear or beget a child. * * *

> On the other hand, if *Griswold* is no bar to a prohibition on the distribution of contraceptives, the State could not, consistently with the Equal Protection Clause, outlaw distribution to unmarried but not to married persons. In each case the evil, as perceived by the State, would be identical, and the underinclusion would be invidious. * * *

405 U.S. at 454, 92 S.Ct. at 1038.

ROE v. WADE

Supreme Court of the United States, 1973.
— U.S. —, 93 S.Ct. 705, 35 L.Ed.2d 147.

Mr. Justice BLACKMUN delivered the opinion of the Court.

This Texas federal appeal and its Georgia companion, Doe v. Bolton, present constitutional challenges to state criminal abortion legislation. * * *

We forthwith acknowledge our awareness of the sensitive and emotional nature of the abortion controversy, of the vigorous opposing views, even among physicians, and of the deep and seemingly absolute convictions that the subject inspires. One's philosophy, one's experiences, one's exposure to the raw edges of human existence, one's religious training, one's attitudes toward life and family and their values, and the moral standards one establishes and seeks to observe, are all likely to influence and to color one's thinking and conclusions about abortion.

In addition, population growth, pollution, poverty, and racial overtones tend to complicate and not to simplify the problem.

Our task, of course, is to resolve the issue by constitutional measurement free of emotion and of predilection.

*   *   *

The Texas statutes that concern us here are Arts. 1191–1194 and 1196 of the State's Penal Code. These make it a crime to "procure an abortion," as therein defined, or to attempt one, except with respect to "an abortion procured or attempted by medical advice for the purpose of saving the life of the mother." Similar statutes are in existence in a majority of the States.

*   *   *

The principal thrust of appellant's attack on the Texas statutes is that they improperly invade a right, said to be possessed by the pregnant woman, to choose to terminate her pregnancy. Appellant would discover this right in the concept of personal "liberty" embodied in the Fourteenth Amendment's Due Process Clause; or in personal, marital, familial, and sexual privacy said to be protected by the Bill of Rights or its penumbras, see Griswold v. Connecticut, 381 U.S. 479 (1965); Eisenstadt v. Baird, 405 U.S. 438 (1972); id., at 460 (WHITE, J., concurring); or among those rights reserved to the people by the Ninth Amendment, Griswold v. Connecticut, 381 U.S., at 486 (Goldberg, J., concurring). *   *   *

The Constitution does not explicitly mention any right of privacy. In a line of decisions, however, going back perhaps as far as Union Pacific R. Co. v. Botsford, 141 U.S. 250, 251 (1891), the Court has recognized that a right of personal privacy, or a guarantee of certain areas or zones of privacy, does exist under the Constitution. In varying contexts the Court or individual Justices have indeed found at least the roots of that right in the First Amendment, Stanley v. Georgia, 394 U.S. 557, 564 (1969); in the Fourth and Fifth Amendments, Terry v. Ohio, 392 U.S. 1, 8–9 (1968), Katz v. United States, 389 U.S. 347, 350 (1967), Boyd v. United States, 116 U.S. 616 (1886), see Olmstead v. United States, 277 U.S. 438, 478 (1928) (Brandeis, J. dissenting); in the penumbras of the Bill of Rights, Griswold v. Connecticut, 381 U.S. 479, 484–485 (1965); in the Ninth Amendment, id., at 486 (Goldberg, J., concurring); or in the concept of liberty guaranteed by the first section of the Fourteenth Amendment, see Meyer v. Nebraska, 262 U.S. 390, 399 (1923). These decisions make it clear that only personal rights that can be deemed "fundamental" or "implicit in the concept of ordered liberty," Palko v. Connecticut, 302 U.S. 319, 325 (1937), are included in this guarantee of personal privacy. They also make it clear that the right has some extension to activities relating to marriage, Loving v. Virginia, 388 U.S. 1, 12 (1967), procreation,

Skinner v. Oklahoma, 316 U.S. 535, 541–542 (1942), contraception, Eisenstadt v. Baird, 405 U.S. 438, 453–454 (1972); id., at 460, 463–465 (WHITE, J., concurring), family relationships, Prince v. Massachusetts, 321 U.S. 158, 166 (1944), and child, rearing and education, Pierce v. Society of Sisters, 268 U.S. 510, 535 (1925), Meyer v. Nebraska, supra.

This right of privacy, whether it be founded in the Fourteenth Amendment's concept of personal liberty and restrictions upon state action, as we feel it is, or, as the District Court determined, in the Ninth Amendment's reservation of rights to the people, is broad enough to encompass a woman's decision whether or not to terminate her pregnancy. The detriment that the State would impose upon the pregnant woman by denying this choice altogether is apparent. Specific and direct harm medically diagnosable even in early pregnancy may be involved. Maternity, or additional offspring, may force upon the woman a distressful life and future. Psychological harm may be imminent. Mental and physical health may be taxed by child care. There is also the distress, for all concerned, associated with the unwanted child, and there is the problem of bringing a child into a family already unable, psychologically and otherwise, to care for it. In other cases, as in this one, the additional difficulties and continuing stigma of unwed motherhood may be involved. All these are factors the woman and her responsible physician necessarily will consider in consultation.

On the basis of elements such as these, appellants and some *amici* argue that the woman's right is absolute and that she is entitled to terminate her pregnancy at whatever time, in whatever way, and for whatever reason she alone chooses. With this we do not agree. Appellants' arguments that Texas either has no valid interest at all in regulating the abortion decision, or no interest strong enough to support any limitation upon the woman's sole determination, is unpersuasive. The Court's decisions recognizing a right of privacy also acknowledge that some state regulation in areas protected by that right is appropriate. As noted above, a state may properly assert important interests in safeguarding health, in maintaining medical standards, and in protecting potential life. At some point in pregnancy, these respective interests become sufficiently compelling to sustain regulation of the factors that govern the abortion decision. The privacy right involved, therefore, cannot be said to be absolute. In fact, it is not clear to us that the claim asserted by some *amici* that one has an unlimited right to do with one's body as one pleases bears a close relationship to the right of privacy previously articulated in the Court's decisions. The Court has refused to recognize an unlimited right of this kind in the past. Jacobson v. Massachusetts, 197 U.S. 11 (1905) (vaccination); Buck v. Bell, 274 U.S. 200 (1927) (sterilization).

We therefore conclude that the right of personal privacy includes the abortion decision, but that this right is not unqualified and must be considered against important state interests in regulation.

*   *   *

Where certain "fundamental rights" are involved, the Court has held that regulation limiting these rights may be justified only by a "compelling state interest," * * * and that legislative enactments must be narrowly drawn to express only the legitimate state interests at stake.

*   *   *

The District Court held that the appellee failed to meet his burden of demonstrating that the Texas statute's infringement upon Roe's rights was necessary to support a compelling state interest, and that, although the defendant presented "several compelling justifications for state presence in the area of abortions," the statutes outstripped these justifications and swept "far beyond any areas of compelling state interest." 314 F.Supp., at 1222–1223. Appellant and appellee both contest that holding. Appellant, as has been indicated, claims an absolute right that bars any state imposition of criminal penalties in the area. Appellee argues that the State's determination to recognize and protect prenatal life from and after conception constitutes a compelling state interest. As noted above, we do not agree fully with either formulation.

A. The appellee and certain *amici* argue that the fetus is a "person" within the language and meaning of the Fourteenth Amendment. In support of this they outline at length and in detail the well-known facts of fetal development. If this suggestion of personhood is established, the appellant's case, of course, collapses, for the fetus' right to life is then guaranteed specifically by the Amendment. The appellant conceded as much on reargument. On the other hand, the appellee conceded on reargument that no case could be cited that holds that a fetus is a person within the meaning of the Fourteenth Amendment.

The Constitution does not define "person" in so many words. Section 1 of the Fourteenth Amendment contains three references to "person." The first, in defining "citizens," speaks of "persons born or naturalized in the United States." The word also appears both in the Due Process Clause and in the Equal Protection Clause. "Person" is used in other places in the Constitution: in the listing of qualifications for representatives and senators. Art. I, § 2, cl. 2, and § 3, cl. 3; in the Apportionment Clause, Art. I, § 2, cl. 3; in the Migration and Importation provision, Art. I, § 9, cl. 1; in the Emolument Clause, Art. I, § 9, cl. 8; in the Electors provisions, Art. II, § 1, cl. 2, and the superseded cl. 3; in the provision outlining qualifications for the office of President, Art. II, § 1, cl. 5; in the Extradition provisions, Art. IV, § 2, cl. 2, and the superseded Fugitive Slave cl. 3; and in the Fifth, Twelfth, and Twenty-second Amendments as well as in §§ 2 and 3 of the Fourteenth Amendment. But in nearly all these instances, the use of the word is such that it has application only postnatally. None indicates, with any assurance, that it has any possible pre-natal application.

All this, together with our observation * * * that throughout the major portion of the 19th century prevailing legal abortion practices were far freer than they are today, persuades us that the word "person," as used in the Fourteenth Amendment, does not include the unborn. * * *

This conclusion, however, does not of itself fully answer the contentions raised by Texas, and we pass on to other considerations.

B. The pregnant woman cannot be isolated in her privacy. She carries an embryo and, later, a fetus, if one accepts the medical definitions of the developing young in the human uterus. See Dorland's Illustrated Medical Dictionary, 478–479, 547 (24th ed. 1965). The situation therefore is inherently different from marital intimacy, or bedroom possession of obscene material, or marriage, or procreation, or education, with which *Eisenstadt, Griswold, Stanley, Loving, Skinner, Pierce,* and *Meyer* were respectively concerned. As we have intimated above, it is reasonable and appropriate for a State to decide that at some point in time another interest, that of health of the mother or that of potential human life, becomes significantly involved. The woman's privacy is no longer sole and any right of privacy she possesses must be measured accordingly.

Texas urges that, apart from the Fourteenth Amendment, life begins at conception and is present throughout pregnancy, and that, therefore, the State has a compelling interest in protecting that life from and after conception. We need not resolve the difficult question of when life begins. When those trained in the respective disciplines of medicine, philosophy, and theology are unable to arrive at any consensus, the judiciary, at this point in the development of man's knowledge, is not in a position to speculate as to the answer.

It should be sufficient to note briefly the wide divergence of thinking on this most sensitive and difficult question. * * *

In areas other than criminal abortion the law has been reluctant to endorse any theory that life, as we recognize it, begins before live birth or to accord legal rights to the unborn except in narrowly defined situations and except when the rights are contingent upon live birth. * * *

In view of all this, we do not agree that, by adopting one theory of life, Texas may override the rights of the pregnant woman that are at stake. We repeat, however, that the State does have an important and legitimate interest in preserving and protecting the health of the pregnant woman, whether she be a resident of the State or a nonresident who seeks medical consultation and treatment there, and that it has still *another* important and legitimate interest in protecting the potentiality of human life. These interests are separate and distinct. Each grows in substantiality as the woman approaches term and, at a point during pregnancy, each becomes "compelling."

With respect to the State's important and legitimate interest in the health of the mother, the "compelling" point, in the light of present medical knowledge, is at approximately the end of the first trimester. This is so because of the now established medical fact * * * that until the end of the first trimester mortality in abortion is less than mortality in normal childbirth. It follows that from and after this point, a State may regulate the abortion procedure to the extent that the regulation reasonably relates to the preservation and protection of maternal health. Examples of permissible state regulation in this area are requirements as to the qualifications of the person who is to perform the abortion; as to the licensure of that person; as to the facility in which the procedure is to be performed, that is, whether it must be a hospital or may be a clinic or some other place of less-than-hospital status; as to the licensing of the facility; and the like.

This means, on the other hand, that, for the period of pregnancy prior to this "compelling" point, the attending physician, in consultation with his patient, is free to determine, without regulation by the State, that in his medical judgment the patient's pregnancy should be terminated. If that decision is reached, the judgment may be effectuated by an abortion free of interference by the State.

With respect to the State's important and legitimate interest in potential life, the "compelling" point is at viability. This is so because the fetus then presumably has the capability of meaningful life outside the mother's womb. State regulation protective of fetal life after viability thus has both logical and biological justifications. If the State is interested in protecting fetal life after viability, it may go so far as to proscribe abortion during that period except when it is necessary to preserve the life or health of the mother.

Measured against these standards, Art. 1196 of the Texas Penal Code, in restricting legal abortions to those "procured or attempted by medical advice for the purpose of saving the life of the mother," sweeps too broadly. The statute makes no distinction between abortions performed early in pregnancy and those performed later, and it limits to a single reason, "saving" the mother's life, the legal justification for the procedure. The statute, therefore, cannot survive the constitutional attack made upon it here.

*   *   *

This holding, we feel, is consistent with the relative weights of the respective interests involved, with the lessons and example of medical and legal history, with the lenity of the common law, and with the demands of the profound problems of the present day. The decision leaves the State free to place increasing restrictions on abortion as the period of pregnancy lengthens, so long as those restrictions are tailored to the recognized state interests. The decision vindicates the right of the physician to administer medical treatment according to his professional judgment up to the points where important state interests provide compelling justifications for intervention. Up to those points the abortion decision in all its aspects is inherently, and primarily, a medical decision, and basic responsibility for it must rest with the physician. If an individual practitioner abuses the privilege of exercising proper medical judgment, the usual remedies, judicial and intra-professional, are available.

The opinions of Mr. Justice STEWART, concurring, Chief Justice BURGER, concurring Mr. Justice DOUGLAS, concurring, Mr. Justice REHNQUIST, dissenting, and Mr. Justice WHITE (joined in by Mr. Justice REHNQUIST)', dissenting, are omitted.

NOTES

1. In Doe v. Bolton, —— U.S. ——, 93 S.Ct. 739, 35 L.Ed.2d 201 (1973) the Court held invalid state statutory requirements that all abortions be performed in a hospital, that the hospital be accredited by the Joint Commission on Accreditation of Hospitals, that each abortion be approved by the hospital staff abortion committee, that the performing physician's decision to perform an abortion be confirmed by two other physicians, and that the woman upon whom the abortion is performed be a resident of the state.

2. In United States v. Moses, 12 Crim.L.Rptr. 2198 (D.C.Super.Ct., 1972) the court struck down a statute prohibiting solicitation for purposes of prostitution. In the course of its opinion, the court concludes that there is insufficient governmental interest to support a blanket prohibition against prostitution (as well as fornication, sodomy and adultery) and solicitation for prostitution. Emphasis is placed on the fact that the crime consists of words (and thus invokes First Amendment free speech factors) as well as "the Constitutional right of the individual to control the use and function of his or her own body."

3. What, if any, limits do the "right of privacy" cases place upon the extent to which the criminal law can be used to deal with alcohol-related problems? Could, for example, consumption of alcoholic beverages be prohibited, except pursuant to a physician's prescription? Could possession for personal use be prohibited? Could simply being intoxicated be made an offense? Even if the law is read so as not to impose an absolute prohibition upon defining a given act as a crime, does any similarity between the case at issue and those in *Griswold, Stanley* and *Eisenstadt* suggest a factor to be weighed in the policy decision as to criminalization?

What, if any, limits do the "right of privacy" cases place upon the extent to which noncriminal measures may be taken to deal with alcohol-related problems? Can mere intoxication be made the basis for noncriminal but compulsory detention for sobering-up? Can frequent intoxication be made the basis for compulsory treatment? Can physical addiction to alcohol be made a basis for compulsory treatment? What, if any, is the relevance of the noncriminal nature of the measures taken to a determination of whether a right of privacy is being violated?

b. "OPERATIONAL" COSTS

Although use of the law is almost certain to infringe upon personal privacy to some extent, there are also a variety of other "costs" of the use of the law in various ways that may arise in the actual administration of enforcement programs. This section presents material concerning the operation of both heavily-criminalized and noncriminal "civil" treatment programs. In considering the material, consider especially what "costs" the administration of various programs is likely to involve, the extent to which such costs are an inherent aspect of such programs, and whether—or to what extent—the costs could, as a practical matter, be eliminated or reduced.

(1) HEAVILY-CRIMINALIZED SYSTEMS

TRIVETTE v. STATE

District Court of Appeals of Florida, 1971.
244 So.2d 173.

DOWNEY, JAMES C., Associate Judge. This is an appeal from a judgment and sentence of the Court of Record of Broward County sentencing appellant to two and one-half years probation as the result of his plea of nolo contendere to an information charging him with possession of marijuana.

It appears that defendant-appellant, age 21, and another young man were walking south on the west side of U. S. Highway #1 in the City of Hollywood, Florida at approximately 1:30 a. m. The area was otherwise deserted. A police officer on routine patrol proceeding north on said highway passed the two boys and as he did so he observed that " * * * they took special notice of me. They both turned and looked at me, and the defendant * * * appeared to be putting something in his right pocket, turning away * * * ". The officer turned his police car around, stopped defendant and his companion and asked for their identification. Defendant furnished his but the companion had none. The officer interrogated them as to their destination and other general matters, though he could not remember the questions verbatim. He testified that defendant "appeared to be drowsy, sleepy. He didn't answer the questions as if he were in a clear mind. I was shining the flashlight in his eyes and his eyes were dilated. When I asked him questions his mind appeared to wander to other things". The officer concluded that the defendant was intoxicated and arrested him for public intoxication. On cross-examination the officer testified that defendant was cooperative, showed him his identification, didn't cause any trouble, and nothing was smelled on his breath. Further, on cross-examination it was called to the officer's attention that he didn't mention the fact that defendant and his companion had long hair and wore bell bottoms, and he was asked if that added something to his reason for stopping them. He answered: "Yes sir. I will tell you something sir: Anyone out at that time of the day, I would stop". After placing the defendant under arrest for public intoxication, the officer searched him and found what appeared to be marijuana, whereupon he arrested him for possession thereof.

Defendant pled not guilty at his arraignment and filed a motion to suppress the evidence found on his person on the ground that the search was made pursuant to an unlawful arrest. The trial court heard testimony in support of the motion and denied it. Thereafter, defendant changed his plea from not guilty to nolo contendere, specifically noting it was being done in view of the court's previous ruling denying his motion to suppress. * * *

Since the crime for which the defendant was initially arrested, and as a result of which the search was made, was a misdemeanor and the arrest having been made without a warrant, the decision here must of course turn upon a finding vel non that the officer had probable cause to arrest the defendant for public intoxication. Thus, the elements of the crime of public intoxication become vital. Is the required degree of intoxication so extreme as to meet the standard related in People v. Williams, City Ct.1961, 215 N.Y.S.2d 841, that a man is intoxicated "when he falls flat on his face and hangs on to the grass to keep from falling off the earth", or "not drunk is he who from the floor can rise again and drink once more, but drunk is he who prostrate lies and can neither drink nor rise"? Or is the more enlightened rule that arrived at in the Williams case, supra, that a person is intoxicated when there is an impairment of his capacity to think and/or act correctly and/or when he has lost, even in part, the control of his physical and mental faculties? We think that fairly states the rule. In Clowney v. State, Fla.1958, 102 So.2d 619, the Supreme Court of Florida held that a person is intoxicated when he is under the influence of intoxicants to such extent as to deprive him of full possession of his normal faculties. * * * [I]t is not necessary to constitute public intoxication that the defendant attract attention thereby, or that he annoy, molest, disgust, or be offensive to others, for that would constitute disorderly conduct. * * *

We know that probable cause means a reasonable ground of suspicion, supported by circumstances sufficiently strong in themselves to warrant a cautious man in the belief that the person accused is guilty of the offense with which he is charged * * *.

Turning now to the facts and circumstances confronting the police officer and analyzing them as a whole rather than the effect of each item in isolation * * * it must be conceded that their impact is not overwhelming. However, as stated in State v. Profera, Fla. App.1970, 239 So.2d 867, citing Jackson v. United States, 1962, 112 U.S.App.D.C. 260, 302 F.2d 194:

" ' * * * (P)robable cause is not to be evaluated from a remote vantage point of a library, but rather from the viewpoint of a prudent and cautious police officer on the scene at the time of arrest. The question to be answered is whether such an officer in the particular circumstances, conditioned by his observations and information, and guided by the whole of his police experience, reasonably could have believed that a crime had been committed by the person to be arrested.' "

The trial court having considered the effect of the circumstances in their totality: the time of night, the deserted street, the taking of unusual note of the passing police car, the turning away to put something in his pocket, the dilated eyes, his unclear mind, his mind wandering to other things when asked a question, found they were sufficient to give a reasonable man cause to believe the defendant was intoxicated. He heard the testimony pro and con, observed the witnesses and resolved the conflicts against the appellant.   *   *   *

Having failed to demonstrate error, the decision appealed from is affirmed.

NOTES

1. The Fourth Amendment requirement that seizures of the person and searches be "reasonable" has been interpreted to mean that an arrest may be made only upon "probable cause," i. e., if the officer is aware of facts and circumstances sufficient to warrant a prudent man in believing that the person had committed or was committing a crime. E.g., Beck v. Ohio, 379 U.S. 89, 85 S.Ct. 223, 13 L.Ed.2d 142 (1964). When an arrest is made, a search of the individual and the area within his immediate control may be made without obtaining a search warrant. Chimel v. California, 395 U.S. 752, 89 S.Ct. 2034, 23 L.Ed.2d 685 (1969). A police officer may also make brief investigatory stops even if he lacks probable cause in the traditional sense. Cf. Terry v. Ohio, 392 U.S. 1, 88 S.Ct. 1868, 20 L.Ed.2d 889 (1968). But more than mere suspicion is necessary; probably some objective basis for believing that the investigatory stop will give rise to information of value in discharging the officer's duties to prevent and detect crime is sufficient. Pursuant to such an investigatory stop, a limited "frisk" of the subject's outer clothing is permissible if there is reason to believe such a frisk is necessary to preserve the safety of the officer or that of others. Terry v. Ohio, 392 U.S. 1, 88 S.Ct. 1868, 20 L.Ed.2d 889 (1968). But this frisk may extend only so far as is necessary to find any weapons the suspect may have; if it is used to search for evidence of a crime, it is "unreasonable." Sibron v. New York, 392 U.S. 40, 88 S.Ct. 1889, 20 L.Ed.2d 917 (1968). Under the exclusionary rule of Mapp v. Ohio, 367 U.S. 643, 81 S.Ct. 1684, 6 L.Ed.2d 1081 (1961), evidence obtained by means of an unreasonable search or seizure (or any "fruits" thereof) are inadmissible as evidence in a criminal prosecution.

To what extent might the existence of some alcohol-related offenses permit or encourage police officers to evade the restrictions upon investigations imposed by the case law under the Fourth Amendment? See Foote, Vagrancy-Type Law and Its Administration, 104 U.Pa.L.Rev. 603 (1956), suggesting that vagrancy-type crimes (which often include "habitual drunkenness") do provide a method of circumventing restrictions. "To the extent that the police actually are hampered by the restrictions of the ordinary law of arrest, by the illegality of arrests on mere suspicion alone, and by defects and loopholes of substantive criminal law, vagrancy-type statutes facilitate the apprehension, investigation or harrassment of suspected criminals. When suspects can be arrested for nothing else, it is often possible to 'go and vag them.' " Id. at 614. What impact should—or would —the response to this query have upon the validity of the statute defining the offense? See Fenster v. Leary, 20 N.Y.2d 309, 229 N.E.2d 426 (1967).

2. President's Commission on Law Enforcement and Administration of Justice, Task Force Report; Drunkenness 1–2 (1967):

> Two million arrests in 1965—one of every three arrests in America—were for the offense of public drunkenness.[1] The great volume of these arrests places an extremely heavy load on the operations of the criminal justice system. It burdens police, clogs lower criminal courts, and crowds penal institutions throughout the United States.

*   *   *

> The police do not arrest everyone who is under the influence of alcohol.[12] Sometimes they will help an inebriate home. It is when he appears to have no home or family ties that he is most likely to be arrested and taken to the local jail.[13]

> One policeman assigned to a skid row precinct in a large eastern city recently described how he decided whom to arrest:

> > I see a guy who's been hanging around; a guy who's been picked up before or been making trouble. I stop him. Sometimes he can convince me he's got a job today or got

1. 1965 FBI Uniform Crime Reports 117 (table 25). In 1965, 1,516,548 drunkenness arrests were reported by 4,043 agencies, embracing a total population of 125,139,000. Projections based upon these figures indicate that there were over 2 million arrests in the entire country during 1965. An undetermined number of additional arrests for drunkenness are made under disorderly conduct, vagrancy, loitering, and related statutes. See, e. g., Foote, Vagrancy-Type Law and Its Administration, 104 U.Pa.L.Rev. 603 (1956) (discussion of interchanging of statutes for like purposes); Murtagh, Arrests for Public Intoxication, 35 Fordham L. Rev. 1–7 (1966) (description of the prior New York City practice of using a disorderly conduct statute to arrest nondisorderly inebriates).

12. It is often the express policy of a police department to refrain from arresting a person for drunkenness in cases in which he may be placed in a taxicab or he is with friends who are able to escort him home. See, e. g., 1 Columbus, Ohio, Police Dep't Training Bull., rev. Aug. 1958, unit 6, p. 2; Pres.'s Comm'n on Crime in the District of Columbia, Rep. 475 (1966), citing letter from District of Columbia Police Chief John B. Layton to Pres.'s Comm'n on Crime in the District of Columbia, Apr. 1, 1966.

13. The police make this determination by observing, *inter alia*, the apparent affluence of the inebriate. Moreover, the lack of funds for transportation will influence the determination to arrest. The result is that the poor are more likely to be arrested than the well-to-do. See Pres.'s Comm'n on Crime in the District of Columbia, Rep. 475 (1966). See also Washington Daily News, Dec. 21, 1965, p. 5, at p. 35 (interview with precinct commanding officer: "We do tend to enforce the laws more rigidly on 14th Street than in, say, Crestwood, a better part of the precinct.").

something to do. He'll show me a slip showing he's supposed
to go to the blood bank, or to work. I let him go. But if it
seems to me that he's got nothing to do but drink, then I bring
him in.[14]

Drunkenness arrest practices vary from place to place. Some
police departments strictly enforce drunkenness statutes, while
other departments are known to be more tolerant. In fact, the
number of arrests in a city may be related less to the amount of
public drunkenness than to police policy. Some of the wide variations in police practices can be seen in the table below that compares drunkenness arrests by two police departments known to be
guided by policies of strict enforcement (Atlanta, Ga., and Washington, D. C.) to arrests by a department that is considered more
tolerant (St. Louis, Mo.).

In some large and medium-size cities, police departments have
"bum squads" that cruise skid rows and border areas to apprehend inebriates who appear unable to care for their own safety, or
who are likely to annoy others.[15] Such wholesale arrests sometimes
include homeless people who are not intoxicated.[16]

* * *

Comparison of Drunkenness Arrests in Three Cities

	Popu-lations 1965 estimates	Number of arrests (1965)			(Percentage of all arrests) accounted for by:	
		Drunken-ness arrests	Disorderly conduct and vagrancy arrests	All arrests	Drunk arrests	Drunk, disorderly, and vagrancy arrests
Washington, D.C._____	802,000	44,792	21,338	86,464	51.8	76.5
St. Louis, Mo._____	699,000	2,445	5,994	44,701	5.5	18.9
Atlanta, Ga._____	522,000	48,835	22,379	92,965	52.5	76.6

[A9014]

14. Interview with a police officer assigned to a large-city skid row by a
staff member of the Vera Institute of
Justice.

15. LaFave, Arrest: The Decision to
Take a Suspect Into Custody 441 n. 13
(1965).

16. The Atlanta Alcohol Study Project
found that there are a "significant
number of individuals who are arrested for public intoxication and who are

not drunk at the time of arrest."
Emory Dep't of Psychiatry 18. Similar findings were reported in other
cities; see, for example, reports by
Klein, The Criminal Law Process vs.
the Public Drunkenness Offender in
San Francisco, 1964 (unpublished, on
file at Stanford Univ. Institute for the
Study of Human Problems), and by
Nash, Habitats of Homeless Men in
Manhattan, Nov. 1964 (unpublished, on
file at Columbia Univ. Bureau of Applied Social Research).

ROSS, HAYES, FRIEL AND KERPER, A DESCRIPTIVE STUDY OF THE SKID ROW ALCOHOLIC IN HOUSTON, TEXAS

42–44 (1970) (Criminal Justice Monograph, Vol. II, No. 2, Institute of Contemporary Corrections and the Behavioral Sciences, Sam Houston State University).

Houston Police Department statistics show that of the 61,985 arrests made by the Houston Police Department in 1966, 26,453 were for public intoxication. Police officials estimate that of the 26,543 arrests, approximately two thirds (65%) to three fourths (75%) were made among the bottom ten per cent of the alcoholic community. This "bottom ten per cent" includes the "skid row bum," the "wino," and the "sociopathic-hobohemian" who inhabit the "Avenue" or skid row section in Houston. From interviews with Houston police patrolmen who work the skid row area the problems that arise most often invoke the police practice called "keeping the peace" rather than "law enforcement" which demands more stringent control. The procedures employed in keeping the peace are not determined by legal mandates so much as they are responses to certain demand conditions. Major among these conditions is the concentration of certain types mentioned above, such as the "skid row bum," the "wino," et cetera. As Bittner points out, the lives of the inhabitants of skid row are in most instances lacking in prospective coherence.[1] The consequent reduction of predictability constitutes the main problem of keeping the peace on skid row. One of the major complaints made by the subjects in the research sample was: "I was just standing there, minding my own business, and they picked me up and charged me with being drunk." This type of arrest is most often the result of a police practice known as "sweeping the street." Answering a disturbance call to a point within the "Avenue" section the Police will arrest, not only those involved in the "disturbance," but all others in sight who have the appearance of being a "skid row bum," a "wino," et cetera. This tendency to proceed against persons mainly on the basis of perceived risk rather than on the basis of culpability, springs from the desire of the patrolmen to reduce the aggregate total of troubles in the area. It is easier to eliminate all sources of "trouble" by mass arrest than painstakingly evaluate individual cases of "trouble," on merit.

NOTES

1. To what extent may the situations described here be regarded as a "cost" of some alcohol-related offenses? Consider the possibility that insofar as the existence of an offense of public intoxication constitutes a

1. Egon Bittner, "The Police on Skid-Row, American Sociological Review, Vol. 32, No. 5 (October 1967), 712–715.

demand upon law enforcement agencies for its enforcement, enforcement may be too difficult or impossible unless "short cuts" are taken which infringe or endanger other rights. This argument is often made in the context of marijuana regulation: the existence of a prohibition against possession of marijuana for personal use creates too costly an incentive for improper police enforcement activities. See Note, Possession of Marijuana in San Mateo County: Some Social Costs of Criminalization, 22 Stan.L.Rev. 101, 115 (1969), stating that of 80 marijuana prosecutions studied, one-fifth raised "serious questions for the critical observer as to whether the officer had probable cause either to search or to arrest." Need such a situation—if it exists—be a "cost" of criminalization? Why not simply restrict enforcement to those situations in which enforcement can be had without infringement of other rights? Is this practical? How might it be done? By excluding evidence obtained by improper methods from a subsequent prosecution, thereby removing the incentive for such enforcement techniques? For an exhaustive examination of the effectiveness of such an exclusionary rule, see Oaks, Studying the Exclusionary Rule in Search and Seizure, 37 U.Chi.L.Rev. 665 (1970). What practical problems would you anticipate in the enforcement of a right to exclusion by the subjects of the procedures of the Houston, Texas police described above?

2. To what extent would "decriminalization" prevent the costs described above? Arrests and detentions without any intent to bring formal charges have been documented in the drunkenness area. See W. LaFave, Arrest 439–49 (1965). If community pressure to "keep the streets clean" remained after repeal or invalidation of public intoxication crimes, to what extent would the lot of present subjects of improper enforcement techniques be improved? If criminal penalties were replaced by authorizations for involuntary treatment, would it be likely that the means used to "collect" individuals for such treatment would be less offensive than those presently used? Why?

---

(2) NONCRIMINAL COMPELLED TREATMENT SYSTEMS

COMMENT, CIVIL COMMITMENT OF ALCOHOLICS IN TEXAS

48 Texas L.Rev. 159, 164–70 (1969).

III. CIVIL COMMITMENT IN TRAVIS COUNTY

A. The Commitment Process

In Travis County, the authority for civil commitment of alcoholics is vested, by Statute, in County Judge J. H. Watson. Judge Watson minimizes the importance of article 5561c as a guideline to involuntary civil commitment. For example, while section 9(c) requires that the hearing be at least five days subsequent to the filing of the petition and that notice be perfected at least three days prior to the hearing, Judge Watson states that he does not pay any attention to those periods because delay may cause increased danger to or even the death of the alleged alcoholic or other persons. He feels that it is impossible to define chronic alcoholism and that a strict definition is not necessary because he "has a feel for those who should be committed" for treatment as alcoholics. If it is proper for anyone to make such a "common-sense-based-on-experience" judgment, Judge Watson is well qualified to do so. He has had many years of experience in dealing with alcoholics and is a member of the Austin Council on Alcoholism.

*   *   *

The county judge is also required by statute to find that the material allegations of the petition are true before he may order a commitment. Judge Watson asserts, however, that he "does not commit, the doctor does." The doctor can be any medical doctor, but invariably it is either the Director of Mental Health of Texas, Doctor Richard J. Alexander, or one of the two doctors working under him. In practice, Dr. Alexander is solely responsible for almost all of the involuntary commitments of alcoholics in Travis County. He believes that if a person is found to be a chronic alcoholic, he should be committed. He states that he has read the alcoholic commitment statute, but does not regard it in his commitment decisions. A person is a "chronic alcoholic" to Dr. Alexander if "his habitual drinking interferes with his social or economic standing." Overt physical disabilities commonly thought to be alcohol-caused, such as delirium tremens and chronic brain syndrome, will almost always lead to a recommendation for commitment without any inquiry into the social or economic disruption caused by the condition. Dr. Alexander does not make a physical examination, which he finds to be an ineffective method of determining whether or not a person is an habitual drinker. Instead, he looks for "signposts of the habit," like a present state of intoxication, an emaciated condition, a lack of appetite, advanced age, and the occurrence of blackout spells.

Dr. Alexander feels that he is better qualified than the average person to make the commitment determination, not because he is a medical doctor, but because he has had experience with alcoholism and knows the methods and shortcomings of alcoholic treatment. He does not recognize the distinctions made by E. M. Jellinek between different types of alcoholics. This statement does not reflect on the medical competence of Dr. Alexander, but it does emphasize that he uses a broad, functional definition of alcoholism rather than making a technically refined determination of the person's condition.

As for involuntarily committing an alcoholic who is not harming any person and is not causing trouble for anyone other than himself, Dr. Alexander feels that this person should be committed. He gives two reasons for this feeling. First, he is convinced that talking to an alcoholic does no good at all and that, to achieve any results, medical treatment is essential. Secondly, he feels strongly that he is justified in committing the person because an alcoholic lacks the capacity to make a rational decision concerning his own welfare.

After determining that a person is a chronic alcoholic and that commitment is necessary, Dr. Alexander calls Judge Watson on the telephone and discusses the case with him. The commitment follows. The Doctor feels that this procedure may be "unfair, in a sense," but his conscience is soothed by his benevolent purpose. He admits quite frankly that he acts as "judge and jury" for the commitment decision. He describes himself as a "committing doctor," that is, one who is not timid in prescribing its use. * * *

The commitment, indeed, is made with very little provision for safeguarding the rights of the alleged alcoholic. The possibility of a "railroading" does exist and this possibility does worry Dr. Alexander. In contrast, Judge Watson feels that the concern about railroading is the result of a fetish of law professors for protection of the individual when no real danger of prejudice exists, and that though some people may be railroaded, the possibility is too remote for worry.

B.   *The Post Commitment Remedies and the Indefinite Commitment*

After the alleged alcoholic is committed, he becomes one of the 140 patients who enter the Alcoholic Rehabilitation Center (A.R.C.) of the Austin State Hospital each month. Dr. Larry M. Wharton, Director of the Alcoholic Rehabilitation Center, assumes upon each patient's arrival that the person is a chronic alcoholic, and he makes no further inquiry into the propriety of the commitment. The patient, if necessary, is detoxified in a medical hospital separate from the A.R.C. and then is started on a structured life plan that subjects him to the stresses of societal living in a controlled environment.

(1) Appeal

The alleged alcoholic has the right to appeal the commitment decision to the district court, if he does so within five days. * * * Dr. Wharton states that his patients are not advised of their right to appeal. * * *

(2) Writ of Habeas Corpus

It is Dr. Wharton's policy to retain a patient for two to four weeks, even though the patient continually objects to his confinement and totally rejects treatment. * * * Dr. Wharton * * * feels that the delay is justified because the patient lacks the mental capacity to make a rational decision concerning his own welfare. He states that the toxic effects of the alcohol in the patient's system may last as long as thirty days. After this period, a rapid transition often takes place that, according to the Doctor, is "as if someone turned on a light and suddenly he's with the program [of treatment]."

If the patient still refuses treatment, after the initial time period, Dr. Wharton, as a matter of course, will consider his release. This voluntary release is granted only if Dr. Wharton is convinced that the patient, on his own, would not be dangerous to himself or to others. * * *

In practice, the broad discretion given the treating doctor seldom threatens the patient's rights: because of the crowded conditions of the A.R.C., the doctor generally resolves all doubts concerning the patient's condition in favor of the patient's liberty. * * *

McKEIVER v. PENNSYLVANIA

Supreme Court of the United States, 1971.
403 U.S. 528, 91 S.Ct. 1976, 29 L.Ed.2d 647.

Mr. Justice BLACKMUN announced the judgment of the Court and an opinion in which the Chief Justice, Mr. Justice STEWART, and Mr. Justice WHITE join.

These cases present the narrow but precise issue whether the Due Process Clause of the Fourteenth Amendment assures the right to trial by jury in the adjudicative phase of a state juvenile court delinquency proceeding.

*   *   *

The issue arises understandably, for the Court in a series of cases already has emphasized due process factors protective of the juvenile:

*   *   *

From [the] * * * cases * * * it is apparent that:

1.   Some of the constitutional requirements attendant upon the state criminal trial have equal application to that part of the state juvenile proceeding that is adjudicative in nature. Among these are the rights to appropriate notice, to counsel, to confrontation and to cross-examination, and the privilege against self-incrimination. Included, also, is the standard of proof beyond a reasonable doubt.

2.   The Court, however, has not yet said that *all* rights constitutionally assured to an adult accused of crime also are to be enforced or made available to the juvenile in his delinquency proceeding. * * *

The right to an impartial jury "[i]n all criminal prosecutions" under federal law is guaranteed by the Sixth Amendment. Through the Fourteenth Amendment that requirement has now been imposed upon the States "in all criminal cases which—were they to be tried in a federal court—would come within the Sixth Amendment's guarantee." This is because the Court has said it believes "that trial by jury in criminal cases is fundamental to the American scheme of justice." Duncan v. Louisiana, 391 U.S. 145, 149, 88 S.Ct. 1444, 20 L.Ed.2d 491, 496 (1968); Bloom v. Illinois, 391 U.S. 194, 210–211, 88 S.Ct. 1477, 20 L.Ed.2d 522, 533, 534 (1968).

This, of course, does not automatically provide the answer to the present jury trial issue, if for no other reason than that the juvenile court proceeding has not yet been held to be a "criminal prosecution," within the meaning and reach of the Sixth Amendment, and also has not yet been regarded as devoid of criminal aspects merely because it usually has been given the civil label.

*   *   *

[W]e conclude that trial by jury in the juvenile court's adjudicative stage is not a constitutional requirement. We so conclude for a number of reasons:

1. The Court has refrained, in the cases heretofore decided, from taking the easy way with a flat holding that all rights constitutionally assured for the adult accused are to be imposed upon the state juvenile proceeding. * * *

2. There is a possibility, at least, that the jury trial, if required as a matter of constitutional precept, will remake the juvenile proceeding into a fully adversary process and will put an effective end to what has been the idealistic prospect of an intimate, informal protective proceeding.

*   *   *

4. The Court specifically has recognized by dictum that a jury is not a necessary part even of every criminal process that is fair and equitable. Duncan v. Louisiana, 391 U.S., at 149–150 n. 14, and at 158, 20 L.Ed.2d at 496, and, at 501.

5. The imposition of the jury trial on the juvenile court system would not strengthen greatly, if at all, the factfinding function, and would, contrarily, provide an attrition of the juvenile court's assumed ability to function in a unique manner. It would not remedy the defects of the system. Meager as has been the hoped-for advance in the juvenile field, the alternative would be regressive, would lose what has been gained, and would tend once again to place the juvenile squarely in the routine of the criminal process.

6. The juvenile concept held high promise. We are reluctant to say that, despite disappointments of grave dimensions, it still does not hold promise, and we are particularly reluctant to say, as do the Pennsylvania petitioners here, that the system cannot accomplish its rehabilitative goals. So much depends on the availability of resources, on the interest and commitment of the public, on willingness to learn, and on understanding as to cause and effect and cure. In this field, as in so many others, one perhaps learns best by doing. We are reluctant to disallow the States further to experiment and to seek in new and different ways the elusive answers to the problems of the young, and we feel that we would be impeding that experimentation by imposing the jury trial. The States, indeed, must go forward. If, in its wisdom, any State feels the jury trial is desirable in all cases, or in

certain kinds, there appears to be no impediment to its installing a system embracing that feature. That, however, is the State's privilege and not its obligation.

* * *

12. If the jury trial were to be injected into the juvenile court system as a matter of right, it would bring with it into that system the traditional delay, the formality and the clamor of the adversary system and, possibly, the public trial. * * *

13. Finally, the arguments advanced by the juveniles here are, of course, the identical arguments that underlie the demand for the jury trial for criminal proceedings. The arguments necessarily equate the juvenile proceeding—or at least the adjudicative phase of it—with the criminal trial. Whether they should be so equated is our issue. Concern about the inapplicability of exclusionary and other rules of evidence, about the juvenile court judge's possible awareness of the juvenile's prior record and of the contents of the social file; about repeated appearances of the same familiar witnesses in the persons of juvenile and probation officers and social workers—all to the effect that this will create the likelihood of prejudgment—chooses to ignore, it seems to us, every aspect of fairness, of concern, of sympathy, and of paternal attention that the juvenile court system contemplates.

If the formalities of the criminal adjudicative process are to be superimposed upon the juvenile court system, there is little need for its separate existence. Perhaps that ultimate disillusionment will come one day, but for the moment we are disinclined to give impetus to it.

Affirmed.

[The opinions of Mr. Justice WHITE (concurring), Mr. Justice HARLAN (concurring), Mr. Justice BRENNAN (concurring and dissenting), and Mr. Justice DOUGLAS (dissenting) are omitted.]

NOTES

1. In In re Gault, 387 U.S. 1, 87 S.Ct. 1428, 18 L.Ed.2d 527 (1967), the Court held that due process applied to juvenile court delinquency proceedings and required that a child who was the subject of such proceedings be accorded the rights to appropriate notice, to representation by counsel, to confrontation of witnesses and to cross examination of them, and to the privilege against compelled self incrimination. Explaining its decision, the Court said:

> From the inception of the juvenile court system, wide differences have been tolerated—indeed insisted upon—between the procedural rights accorded to adults and those of juveniles. In practically all jurisdictions, there are rights granted to adults which are withheld from juveniles. In addition to the specific problems involved in the present case, for example, it has been held that the juvenile is not entitled to bail, to indictment by grand jury, to a

public trial or to trial by jury. It is frequent practice that rules governing the arrest and interrogation of adults by the police are not observed in the case of juveniles.

*   *   *

The early reformers were appalled by adult procedures and penalties, and by the fact that children could be given long prison sentences and mixed in jails with hardened criminals. They were profoundly convinced that society's duty to the child could not be confined by the concept of justice alone. They believed that society's role was not to ascertain whether the child was "guilty" or "innocent," but "What is he, how has he become what he is, and what had best be done in his interest and in the interest of the state to have him from a downward career." The child—essentially good, as they saw it—was to be made "to feel that he is the object of [the state's] care and solicitude," not that he was under arrest or on trial. The rules of criminal procedure were therefore altogether inapplicable. The apparent rigidities, technicalities, and harshness which they observed in both substantive and procedural criminal law were therefore to be discarded. The idea of crime and punishment was to be abandoned. The child was to be "treated" and "rehabilitated" and the procedures, from apprehension through institutionalization, were to be "clinical" rather than punitive.

These results were to be achieved, without coming to conceptual and constitutional grief, by insisting that the proceedings were not adversary, but that the state was proceeding as *parens patriae.*
*   *   *

Accordingly, the highest motives and most enlightened impulses led to a peculiar system for juveniles, unknown to our law in any comparable context. The constitutional and theoretical basis for this peculiar system is—to say the least—debatable. And in practice, * * * the results have not been entirely satisfactory. Juvenile Court history has again demonstrated that unbridled discretion, however benevolently motivated, is frequently a poor substitute for principle and procedure. * * * The absence of substantive standards has not necessarily meant that children receive careful, compassionate, individualized treatment. The absence of procedural rules based upon constitutional principle has not always produced fair, efficient, and effective procedures. Departures from established principles of due process have frequently resulted not in enlightened procedure, but in arbitrariness. * * *

Failure to observe the fundamental requirements of due process has resulted in instances, which might have been avoided, of unfairness to individuals and inadequate or inaccurate findings of fact and unfortunate prescriptions of remedy. * * *

It is claimed that juveniles obtain benefits from the special procedures applicable to them which more than offset the disadvantages of denial of the substance of normal due process. As we shall discuss, the observance of due process standards, intelligently and not ruthlessly administered, will not compel the States to abandon or displace any of the substantive benefits of the juvenile process. But it is important, we think, that the claimed benefits of the juvenile process should be candidly appraised. Neither sentiment nor folklore should cause us to shut our eyes, for example, to such startling findings as that reported in an exceptionally reliable study of repeaters or recidivism conducted by the Stanford Research Institute for the President's Commission on Crime in the District of Columbia. This Commission's Report states:

> "In fiscal 1966 approximately 66 percent of the 16- and 17-year-old juveniles referred to the court by the Youth Aid Division had been before the court previously. In 1965, 56 percent of those in the Receiving Home were repeaters. The SRI study revealed that 61 percent of the sample Juvenile Court referrals in 1965 had been previously referred at least once and that 42 percent had been referred at least twice before." Id., at 773.

Certainly, these figures and the high crime rates among juveniles * * * could not lead us to conclude that the absence of constitutional protections reduces crime, or that the juvenile system, functioning free of constitutional inhibitions as it has largely done, is effective to reduce crime or rehabilitate offenders. We do not mean by this to denigrate the juvenile court process or to suggest that there are not aspects of the juvenile system relating to offenders which are valuable. But the features of the juvenile system which its proponents have asserted are of unique benefit will not be impaired by constitutional domestication. For example, the commendable principles relating to the processing and treatment of juveniles separately from adults are in no way involved or affected by the procedural issues under discussion. Further, we are told that one of the important benefits of the special juvenile court procedures is that they avoid classifying the juvenile as a "criminal." The juvenile offender is now classed as a "delinquent." There is, of course, no reason why this should not continue. It is disconcerting, however, that this term has come to involve only slightly less stigma than the term "criminal" applied to adults. It is also emphasized that in practically all jurisdictions, statutes provide that an adjudication of the child as a delinquent shall not operate as a civil disability or disqualify him for civil service appointment. There is no reason why the application of due process requirements should interfere with such provisions.

Beyond this, it is frequently said that juveniles are protected by the process from disclosure of their deviational behavior. * * * This claim of secrecy, however, is more rhetoric than reality. Disclosure of court records is discretionary with the judge in most jurisdictions. Statutory restrictions almost invariably apply only to the court records, and even as to those the evidence is that many courts routinely furnish information to the FBI and the military, and on request to government agencies and even to private employers. Of more importance are police records. In most States the police keep a complete file of juvenile "police contacts" and have complete discretion as to disclosure of juvenile records. Police departments receive requests for information from the FBI and other law-enforcement agencies, the Armed Forces, and social service agencies, and most of them generally comply. Private employers word their application forms to produce information concerning juvenile arrests and court proceedings, and in some jurisdictions information concerning juvenile police contacts is furnished private employers as well as government agencies.

In any event, there is no reason why, consistently with due process, a State cannot continue if it deems it appropriate, to provide and to improve provision for the confidentiality of records of police contacts and court action relating to juveniles. * * *

Further, it is urged that the juvenile benefits from informal proceedings in the court. The early conception of the Juvenile Court proceeding was one in which a fatherly judge touched the heart and conscience of the erring youth by talking over his problems, by paternal advice and admonition, and in which, in extreme situations, benevolent and wise institutions of the State provided guidance and help "to save him from a downward career." Then, as now, goodwill and compassion were admirably prevalent. But recent studies have, with surprising unanimity, entered sharp dissent as to the validity of this gentle conception. They suggest that the appearance as well as the actuality of fairness, impartiality and orderliness—in short, the essentials of due process—may be a more impressive and more therapeutic attitude so far as the juvenile is concerned. * * *

Ultimately, however, we confront the reality of that portion of the Juvenile Court process with which we deal in this case. A boy is charged with misconduct. The boy is committed to an institution where he may be restrained of liberty for years. It is of no constitutional consequence—and of limited practical meaning—that the institution to which he is committed is called an Industrial School. The fact of the matter is that, however euphemistic the title, a "receiving home" or an "industrial school" for juveniles is an institution of confinement in which the child is incarcerated for a greater or lesser time. His world becomes "a building with whitewashed walls, regimented routine and institutional hours * * *." Instead of mother and father and sisters and brothers and friends and classmates, his world is peopled by guards, custodians, state employees, and "delinquents" confined with him for anything from waywardness to rape and homicide.

In view of this, it would be extraordinary if our Constitution did not require the procedural regularity and the exercise of care implied in the phrase "due process."

2. Given the above cases dealing with the juvenile justice system, to what extent may a person be noncriminally compelled to receive treatment without being accorded all of the procedural rights made available to one who is criminally prosecuted? What effect does the answer to this question have upon the desirability of noncriminal compelled treatment

as an alternative means of dealing with the problem of intoxication-related conditions and activities?

3. Given the results of the study of Texas commitment standards and procedures under the statute appearing at page 204, supra, is it reasonable to expect that a formal requirement that standard criminal procedural rights be accorded will have any significant effect in practice? Why?

---

c. INDIRECT EFFECTS OF DECRIMINALIZATION

WYATT v. STICKNEY

United States District Court for the Middle District of Alabama, 1971.
325 F.Supp. 781.

JOHNSON, Chief Judge.   This is a class action that was initiated by guardians of patients confined at Bryce Hospital, Tuscaloosa, Alabama * * *.

Bryce Hospital is located in Tuscaloosa, Alabama, and is a part of the mental health service delivery system for the State of Alabama. Bryce Hospital has approximately 5,000 patients, the majority of whom are involuntarily committed through civil proceedings by the various probate judges in Alabama.

Included in the Bryce Hospital patient population are between 1,500 and 1,600 geriatric patients who are provided custodial care but no treatment. The evidence is without dispute that these patients are not properly confined at Bryce Hospital since these geriatric patients cannot benefit from any psychiatric treatment or are not mentally ill. Also included in the Bryce patient population are approximately 1,000 mental retardates, most of whom receive only custodial care without any psychiatric treatment. Thus, the evidence reflects that there is considerable confusion regarding the primary mission and function of Bryce Hospital since certain nonpsychotic geriatric patients and the mental retardates, and perhaps other non-mentally ill persons, have been and remain committed there for a variety of reasons.

The evidence further reflects that Alabama ranks fiftieth among all the states in the Union in per-patient expenditures per day. This Court must, and does, find from the evidence that the programs of treatment in use at Bryce Hospital prior to the [recent] reorganization that has resulted in the unit-team approach were scientifically and medically inadequate. These programs of treatment failed to conform to any known minimums established for providing treatment for the mentally ill.

The patients at Bryce Hospital, for the most part, were involuntarily committed through noncriminal procedures and without the constitutional protections that are afforded defendants in criminal proceedings. When patients are so committed for treatment purposes they unquestionably have a constitutional right to receive such individual treatment as will give each of them a realistic opportunity to be cured or to improve his or her mental condition. Rouse v. Cameron, 125 U.S.App.D.C. 366, 373 F.2d 451; Covington v. Harris, 136 U.S.App.D.C. 35, 419 F.2d 617. Adequate and effective treatment is constitutionally required because, absent treatment, the hospital is transformed "into a penitentiary where one could be held indefinitely for no convicted offense." Ragsdale v. Overholser, 108 U.S.App.D.C. 308, 281 F.2d 943, 950 (1960). The purpose of involuntary hospitalization for treatment purposes is *treatment* and not mere custodial care or punishment. This is the only justification, from a constitutional standpoint, that allows civil commitments to mental institutions such as Bryce. According to the evidence in this case, the failure of Bryce Hospital to supply adequate treatment is due to a lack of operating funds. The failure to provide suitable and adequate treatment to the mentally ill cannot be justified by lack of staff or facilities. Rouse v. Cameron, supra. * * *

There can be no legal (or moral) justification for the State of Alabama's failing to afford treatment—and adequate treatment from a medical standpoint—to the several thousand patients who have been civilly committed to Bryce's for treatment purposes. To deprive any citizen of his or her liberty upon the altruistic theory that the confinement is for humane therapeutic reasons and then fail to provide adequate treatment violates the very fundamentals of due process.

* * *

A failure on the part of the defendants to implement fully, within six months from the date of this order, a treatment program so as to give each of the treatable patients committed to Bryce facility a realistic opportunity to be cured or to improve his or her mental condition, will necessitate this Court's appointing a panel of experts in the area of mental health to determine what objective and subjective hospital standards will be required to furnish adequate treatment to the treatable mentally ill in the Bryce facility. This will include an order requiring a full inspection of the existing facilities, a study of the operational and treatment practices and programs, and recommendations that will enable this Court to determine what will be necessary in order to render the Bryce facilities a mental health unit providing adequate and effective treatment, in a constitutional sense, for the patients who have been involuntarily committed and are confined there.

NOTES

1. Under Alabama law, a person can be involuntarily committed to the state's mental hospitals if he is found by a court to be "sufficiently deficient or defective mentally to require that, for his own or others' wel-

fare, he be moved to the insane hospital for restraint, care and treatment."
Ala.Code Ann., Tit. 45, § 205 (1959).

2. Compare with the instant case the following statement by the United States Court of Appeals for the District of Columbia concerning the evidence necessary to establish that a "right to treatment" is not being violated:

> The hospital need not show that the treatment will cure or improve the patient but only that there is a bona fide effort to do so. This requires the hospital to show that initial and periodic inquiries are made into the needs and conditions of the patient with a view to providing suitable treatment for him, and that the program provided is suited to his particular needs. * * *

> The effort should be to provide treatment which is adequate in light of present knowledge. Some measures which have therapeutic value for the particular patient may be too insubstantial in comparison with what is available. On the other hand, the possibility of better treatment does not necessarily prove that the one provided is unsuitable or inadequate.

Rouse v. Cameron, 125 U.S.App.D.C. 366, 373 F.2d 451 (1966).

3. Would a person compelled to undergo involuntary treatment for chronic alcoholism have a legally-enforceable "right to treatment"? Would a person detained for a limited period while he "sobered up"? If so, does the information in this section suggest that it could be established that such a right to treatment was not being violated? What would be necessary for such a showing? Would it make any difference whether the noncriminal "commitment" was for a limited period as opposed to one to last until the person was "cured" (or until he no longer met whatever criterion the law established for compelling such treatment)? What effect, if any, would answers to these questions have upon the decision to criminalize? Upon the decision as to the constitutional validity of a decision to criminalize? If noncriminal compelled confinement would be improper because of denial of the right to treatment, could the matter be avoided by "criminalizing"?

4. The "right to treatment" of the mentally ill has given rise to much discussion. See, e. g., Bazelon, Implementing the Right to Treatment, 36 U.Chi.L.Rev. 742 (1969); Birnbaum, A Rationale for the Right, 57 Geo.L.J. 752 (1969); Halpern, A Practicing Lawyer Views the Right to Treatment, 57 Geo.L.J. 782 (1969); Katz, The Right to Treatment—An Enchanting Legal Fiction? 36 U.Chi.L.Rev. 755 (1969).

NIMMER, THE PUBLIC DRUNK: FORMALIZING THE POLICE ROLE AS A SOCIAL HELP AGENCY

58 Geo.L.J. 1089, 1090–91, 1105–1113 (1970).

[T]he current trend is to officially redefine public drunkenness as a public health concern. In most jurisdictions where such a view predominates and a treatment-oriented program has been introduced, the police still are retained as the primary intake mechanism for the detoxification center, a medical "sobering-up station." The police reaction to this formal redefinition of their role has not always met the expectations or the desires of the planners of the new programs. * * *

This * * * is a study of police response to the formal redefinition of their role in the handling of drunks in Washington, D. C. and, more particularly, their response to the District of Columbia Rehabilitation Act (the Hagan Act). In addition to providing a basis for discussion of the difficulties involved in restructuring the official definition of the police role, this analysis will aid an evaluation of the effects of the Act's detoxification program. Inasmuch as the detoxification approach contemplates providing medical help to intoxicated men who are found in public, and offers referral to more extensive rehabilitation programs, the response of the police determines, to a large extent, how well the program reaches the target class of public inebriates.

* * *

[T]he District of Columbia Alcoholic Rehabilitation Act of 1967 (the Hagan Act) [53] * * * [established] a broad program of alcoholic rehabilitation services in the District. Of particular concern here, since it most directly involves the police, are the provisions of the Act establishing a public health system to replace the criminal laws relating to public intoxication. The Hagan Act directs all public officials in the District to "take cognizance of the fact that public intoxication shall be handled as a public health problem rather than as a criminal offense * * *." In line with this redefinition, the new law directs the District Government to establish one or more detoxification centers with a total capacity of no more than 150 beds. These centers are to provide "appropriate medical services for intoxicated persons, including initial examination, diagnosis, and classification." The medical director of each center is empowered to determine whether an individual should be admitted to this facility as a patient, or be transported to some other public health facility. Those who are admitted as "voluntary" patients may be required to remain until sober or no longer incapacitated, but in no event may they be held longer than 72 hours. The Center is required to accept persons brought in by the police and walk-in admissions on an equal basis.

Since the Public Health Department did not, and has not, established additional detoxification facilities, the Hagan Act had the effect of making the existing Center responsible for the entire city. In order to deal with the expected increase in admissions, the treatment program at the Center was modified. Whereas the original demonstration program called for holding each patient from three to five days

---

53. Pub.L. No. 90–452, 82 Stat. 618
(codified in scattered sections of 14, 24,
25 D.C.Code Ann.).

at the Center, the modification called for release after one day and, in situations in which there continued to exist extreme physical problems, referral to a subsection of the District's long-term treatment facility. Thus, the Center was able to accommodate up to 60 men each day.

Although police use of the Center increased after the new legislation, it continued to remain remarkably low when compared to the arrest rates that the District had previously experienced. During the summer of 1969, police admissions exceeded the self-admission rate for the first time. Recent admissions records indicate that the police use of the Center has leveled off to approximately a one-to-one ratio with walk-ins, or an average of less than 500 per month. This reflects an annual rate of 6,000, or one-seventh of the arrest rate in the years prior to *Easter*. If not for the fact that the Center also admits walk-in patients, it would be substantially underemployed most of the time.

Thus, an issue confronting the new system is the fact that at no time prior to or following the Hagan Act has the rate of police admissions to the Detoxification Center approximated the arrest level traditional in Washington.[60] Although the Center has been filled to capacity because of the heavy intake of self-admitted patients, the fact of this non-use by the police is significant. The self-admitted inebriates are those whose physical condition is such as to enable them to walk into the Center, or whose family or friends have taken them there. Police admissions are designed to reach those whose immediate physical condition or location prevents them from reaching the Center without assistance, and who have no family or friends to bring them in. To the extent that the police are now leaving these persons on the street, the Center fails to reach perhaps the most important portion of those intended to benefit by it.

Since there is nothing to indicate that the lower arrest rate reflects any decrease in the number of public inebriates on the streets of Washington, the explanation for the decrease must be sought within the police department and the new system. Research indicates that the cause of the lower level of official police contacts with public inebriates can best be discussed in terms of two broad categories: (1)

60.

	1966 to 1967 Drunkenness Arrests		1968 to 1969 Police-Referred Admissions	
Nov.	1966	3566	1968	188
Dec.		2411		207
Jan.	1967	2844	1969	247
Feb.		2368		356
March		3039		474
April		3055		619
May		2698		609

Arrest statistics were supplied by the Metropolitan Police Department. Detoxification admission statistics were supplied by the Public Health Dep't.

confusion concerning police authority and (2) exercise of police discretion not to become involved with intoxicated men.

[Discussion of the general confusion regarding police authority to take inebriates to a facility is omitted.]

The relatively low level of use of the Hagan Act is not caused solely by confusion concerning police authority. Even if this confusion were cleared up, the level of use would probably increase only slightly. This underemployment is best explained as an exercise of police discretion.

An officer who observes a public inebriate has three alternatives: (1) take him to the Detoxification Center; (2) handle him informally (send him home, take him to a church mission, etc.); or (3) ignore the situation. Present attitudes within the department indicate that, of these three, the detoxification alternative would be the least frequently taken. These attitudes are not a product of the statutory preference for sending the inebriate home or to a hospital; the statutory language merely restates a pre-existing departmental policy statement. The Hagan Act would seldom be invoked for even the homeless and indigent. Influencing the exercise of discretion at every police level, rather, are the notions that handling the intoxicated is no longer a task deserving substantial police effort and that the Hagan treatment approach is an inappropriate way of dealing with these persons.

Inappropriate task.

The [previous] strict enforcement of the drunkenness law * * * did not result from a determination that, in the abstract, the task should occupy a large portion of the time of patrolmen. Rather, it developed in response to police perception of strong community pressure to remove the intoxicated men from the street and, to a lesser extent, because the patrolmen felt that arrest and confinement benefitted the destitute inebriate and provided him with an otherwise unavailable service. * * * [T]he police perception of community attitudes was affected by * * * subsequent events. Reform and court pressure combined with a decreased level of public complaint to cause the police, individually and as a department, to make an informal reassessment of their enforcement priorities. Even before the public health law was enacted, the drunkenness arrest rate had dropped, and the police were leaving many destitute inebriates untouched on the streets.

Significantly enough, the reassessment was made at a time of increased public concern over violent behavior. In Washington, this increased awareness was stimulated by the severe rioting in early 1968. The public inebriate was no longer considered an important police concern or as a desirable focus for substantial resource commitment. Moreover, even before the riots, departmental resources were insufficient to deal with violent crime while at the same time being heavily allocated to the handling of the public drunk. The five percent of all police manhours devoted to drunkenness arrests represented a substantial drain on police time, while the vehicles needed to transport the men represented a substantial burden on the already limited vehicular resources of the department. In light of these factors, the reordering of priorities which occurred appears to have been inevitable.

The enactment of the Hagan Act itself cooperated in bringing about the reordering of priorities. The tenor of the hearings on the bill and the bill itself is that public drunkenness is not properly a criminal problem but rather a public health problem. This influenced the police in different ways. Insofar as the police view themselves as primarily a criminal agency and tend to consider "non-criminal" tasks as incidental low-priority operations, many now assert that they can no longer be troubled with handling the inebriate. A small minority of the patrolmen, moreover, go so far as to assume that what is not a "criminal problem" is not a "police problem." As one patrolman noted, "It's no longer our problem, the bill takes it out of our hands."

Official policies of the police department itself recognize the distinction between public health activity and crime control. An order of the department states that "it is the policy of this department to cooperate to the fullest extent practicable (short of diverting substantial police manpower from law enforcement tasks to the Detoxification Center Program) with the Department of Public Health program * * *." Moreover, since it did not adjust its internal evaluation criteria after the Hagan Act, the department now effectively discourages drunkenness pick-ups. Under the Hagan Act, a police pick-up of an intoxicated man is not considered to be an arrest. Under an evaluation system premised upon the number of arrests made by an officer, these pick-ups are not counted, but are evaluated on a par with assisting a pregnant woman to reach a hospital. This removes what had been a strong incentive for individual patrolmen to make drunkenness arrests, their one time status as a low risk, readily available method of enhancing one's evaluation within the department.

Inappropriate Treatment.

The detoxification program introduces a series of assumptions and a treatment orientation which conflicts with the previously existing approach of the police and the criminal system. The conflict is not stated simply by referring to the difference in formal labels— "criminal" and "public health"—for police activities often were designed to benefit the indigent inebriates.

The emphasis of the detoxification process in Washington is upon short-term compulsory confinement with longer confinement available if the patient desires it. This must be compared to the 30-day confinement given to the average indigent defendant under the previous system. The longer-term model was functional in removing the men from the streets for long periods. It also was interpreted as being beneficial to the men by giving them time to dry out, recuperate from extended drinking, and rebuild their physical condition. Now, the police derisively observe, the men are back on the streets the next day. The new system, moreover, provides an expensive and relatively plush environment for the men. Although the medical supervision is recognized as desirable, the police seem to prefer a spartan though not punishment-oriented facility. The new program "molly-coddles" the men, they contend, and permits them to abuse the beneficence of the state.

These differences of view create a gulf between the new system as the patrolmen see it and the system as the public health and reform elements see it. Nevertheless, no attempt has been made to bridge the gulf with lines of communication. Planners of the new law paid too little attention to the police role in implementing the new system. They either mistakenly assumed that the police would recognize the benefits of the new approach or failed to appreciate the amount of discretion police possess in enforcing the law. Since the law's enactment, there has been no attempt by the Public Health Department to instruct patrolmen on their role in the new system. No course on the subject of detoxification is offered at the police academy, and Public Health personnel are uninterested in establishing one. The command structure of the Police Department, moreover, sees no need to take the initiative in establishing such instruction. This lack of communication, in addition to doing nothing to moderate the friction within the police department caused by a program imposed from without, permits the long held views of the police to go unchallenged. Measured according to their previously held interpretation of the needs of the men and how best to treat them, their conclusion that the new system is inappropriate is not surprising.

NOTES

1. What "costs" does the Nimmer study suggest might be involved in decriminalization? How reliable are the study's conclusions? What, if any, relevance does this information have for the criminalization and *Powell* issues?

2. Consider as an alternative to the Washington D. C. program described in the Nimmer study the following proposal from Proposal for the Manhattan Bowery Project, in Task Force on Drunkenness of the President's Commission on Law Enforcement and Administration of Justice, Task Force Report: Drunkenness 58, at 60–61 (1967):

> Seven days a week, the Bowery and its immediate vicinity would be patrolled by a three-men team composed of a lodging house clerk, a rehabilitated alcoholic, and a plainclothes policeman. The New York Police Department has tentatively agreed to make available the necessary police coverage. Rehabilitated alcoholics

would be recruited from graduates of programs operated by the Salvation Army, Bowery Mission, Volunteers of America, and Fellowship Center. The lodging house clerks would be paid out of the project's budget.

The street team would seek out and offer assitance to homeless alcoholics who are either prone, intoxicated, or in a state of physical deterioration. If the offer of help is accepted, the man would ordinarily be transported to the infirmary facility described below. Should the man refuse transportation to the infirmary, alternative forms of assistance would be offered; for example, the man could be driven to a lodging house or to a facility maintained by the Salvation Army or the Bowery Mission.

The street patrol would send men who seemed dangerously ill to a hospital immediately rather than transporting them to the infirmary first. The patrol would summon an ambulance for any man who was unconscious, unable to walk, incoherent, or in some acute medical emergency. The ambulance would transport such a man to a nearby hospital.

The function of the policeman would be to protect both the civilian team members and the derelicts from assault or infringement of their rights. The policeman would also act as driver of one of two unmarked station wagons which would be supplied to the project by the Police Department. In appropriate cases, the police officer would summon an ambulance on the car's radio.

---

4. EFFECTIVENESS OF CRIMINALIZATION AND THE ALTERNATIVES

The material above has, to some extent, raised questions and provided some basis for predicting the extent to which behavior related to alcohol use is likely to respond to various measures that may follow either criminal conviction or noncriminal detention for "treatment." This section presents some of the scanty evidence available bearing upon how individuals do in fact respond to some of the measures involved. When considered in light of the previous material, it also raises the question of whether the results that can reasonably be expected of the various means of using the law to deal with alcohol-related problems justifies their employment.

a. RESPONSE TO TRADITIONAL CRIMINAL SANCTIONS
OF IMPRISONMENT AND FINES

LOVALD AND STUB, THE REVOLVING DOOR: REACTIONS OF CHRONIC DRUNKENNESS OFFENDERS TO COURT SANCTIONS

59 J.Crim.L., C. & P.S. 525, 525–27, 529 (1968).m

In 1957 there were 11,031 arrests for public intoxication in Minneapolis, Minnesota. As a result of police surveillance and action, a total of 5,763 persons appeared in Municipal Court to answer charges of drunkenness or such related charges as drunk and disorderly conduct. In a manner typical of most lower courts in the United States, the cases were disposed of either by committing the individual to the workhouse, imposing a fine, or suspending the charge. Although a majority of these individuals were not arrested and punished again for their drinking behavior (even a suspended sentence may entail a tongue-lashing from the presiding judge), a total of 1,649 did reappear in Municipal Court on a drunkenness charge at least once more during that year. These individuals contributed to what has been called the "revolving door" phenomenon of our lower courts.

* * *

Although we may hypothesize that in general punishment does not deter acts of drunkenness, individuals caught in the process of the revolving door may, in fact, react differently to the type of sanction imposed by the court. It is generally thought that the lower courts tend to incarcerate recidivists; therefore, the possibility that a fine or even a suspended sentence may account for variability in the reactions of recidivists to court actions may be overlooked. The purpose of the present paper is to investigate the reactions to various "degrees" of punishment meted out to the 1649 Minneapolis recidivists.

Procedures

* * *

The data were obtained as part of a study of the Minneapolis Skid Row district. The files of the Minneapolis Police Department and of the Minneapolis Municipal Court were made available to the investigators working on this project. All "prisoner showup sheets" and court records for the entire year of 1957 were extracted from these files, and the information from each source was collated. The following information was obtained for each person arrested in Minneapolis who

m. Reprinted by special permission of the Journal of Criminal Law, Criminology & Police Science (Northwestern University School of Law), Copyright ©, 1968, Vol. 59, No. 4.

subsequently appeared in Municipal Court (N = 5763): (1) charge; (2) day and month of arrest; (3) sex of offender; (4) home address of offender; (5) court sentences; and (6) court disposition (i. e., final court action).

Since there were so few females in the sample, only males were included in the analyses. Persons arrested on a drunkenness or related charge two or more times during 1957 were classified as chronic offenders.

The three most common court dispositions used in American lower courts for offenders found guilty of public intoxication are jail sentences, fines, and suspended sentences. In the present study, the nature of the disposition is treated as the *independent* variable. The *dependent* variable is operationalized as the period of time between court appearances for drunkenness or a related charge.

*   *   *

Findings

Tables 1 and 2 suggest that the revolving door actually describes social phenomena somewhat more complex than simply the repetitious punishment of persons whose drinking behavior is judged illegal. The most striking fact revealed by these findings is that, regardless of the number of arrests, court fines apparently have a greater deterrent effect than workhouse sentences. Five of the six comparisons show longer periods of time between arrests when offenders are given fines compared to workhouse sentences. Three of the six F ratios are significant.

Thus with one exception fines apparently inhibit future offenses more effectively than is the case for a jail or suspended sentence. This is especially surprising since a drunkenness offense cannot occur while the individual is serving a jail sentence. With respect to Skid Row offenders, Table 1 shows that upon the second arrest a mean of 73 days had transpired after the first arrest of offenders who had been fined, compared to 60 days for those given jail sentences and 62 days for those given suspended sentences. Although the analysis yields a nonsignificant F ratio, the comparison does show the trend we have been discussing—a greater inhibitive effect for fines than for jail sentences. The same pattern is obtained for the non-Skid Row sample upon the second arrest, and the trend is significant (see Table 2). It should be noted that the mean number of days since the first arrest is consistently higher than for the Skid Row group.

A similar pattern characterizes Skid Row offenders who reappear in court after a third arrest—

TABLE 1

Comparison of Reactions by Skid Row Chronic Drunkenness Offenders to Types of Court Dispositions by Chronology of Court Appearance, Minneapolis Municipal Court, 1957

Court Appearance	Court Disposition Previous Appearance	N	Mean Number of Days Since Last Appearance	F	P
After Second Arrest	Workhouse Fine Suspended	425 104 320	60. 73. 62.	1.691	P > .05
After Third Arrest	Workhouse Fine Suspended	366 46 118	49. 74. 42.	6.310	P < .01
After Fourth Arrest	Workhouse Fine Suspended	233 32 87	49. 35. 43.	1.564	P > .05

[A7100]

TABLE 2

Comparison of Reactions by Non-Skid Row Chronic Drunkenness Offenders to Types of Court Dispositions by Chronology of Court Appearance, Minneapolis Municipal Court, 1957

Court Appearance	Court Disposition Previous Appearance	N	Mean Number of Days Since Last Appearance	F	P
After Second Arrest	Workhouse Fine Suspended	274 254 272	69. 85. 70.	4.267	P < .05
After Third Arrest	Workhouse Fine Suspended	201 94 71	52. 55. 52.	0.109	P > .05
After Fourth Arrest	Workhouse Fine Suspended	135 39 40	55. 63. 33.	4.207	P < .05

[A7101]

74 days for those who had been fined, compared to 49 days for jail sentences and 42 days for suspended sentences (see Table 1). These differences are significant. The same pattern emerges for the non-Skid Row sample after the third arrest, but it does not reach significance (see Table 2). Only after the *fourth arrest* does a jail sentence seem to result in the greatest period of time between offenses for Skid Row individuals (49 days, compared to 35 days for fines and 43 days for suspended sentences), but the differences are not significant. The Skid Row sample continues to show the same pattern as for second and third arrests; the F ratio is significant for the fourth arrest.

The reactions of Skid Row offenders to court sanctions shows a remarkably similar pattern to those offenders living in other parts of Minneapolis. Tables 1 and 2 show some variation in response pattern when type of court disposition is included. When this factor is omitted from the analysis, however, a comparison of weighted means for each of the three court appearances, regardless of previous disposition, reveals an identical pattern—that is, for both Skid Row offenders and offenders living in other parts of Minneapolis, the periods of time between arrests decrease following each court appearance.

*   *   *

Discussion

*   *   *

We may hypothesize that variations in frequency of drunkenness arrests are partly a function of the ability to absorb financial sacrifice resulting from indulgence in drinking. Our findings show that financial loss apparently deters future drunkenness episodes more effectively than does incarceration. In addition to difficulty in raising money for fines, the use of "the drinking money" for this purpose may act as a further deterrent. Thus, the economic status of the Skid Row resident may provide one reason why the workhouse sentence is less of a deterrent than a fine to future drunkenness behavior. Many of the men living on Skid Row rely solely on monthly OASI or public assistance checks. During a period of imprisonment, an offender is unable to spend any money, and he may find an extra check waiting for him at his place of residence upon his release. The individual who is fined for his drinking offense must spend money that might otherwise be used to buy liquor. A court fine is a luxury few can afford. Our data indicate no difference in length of time between arrests for the workhouse sentence and the suspended sentence. Neither of these two types of court sanctions involve a financial loss.

Another aspect of Skid Row life may be linked to the revolving door. Skid Row residents attach no particular stigma to serving time in jail. This does not mean that Skid Row lacks a normative structure, but rather that middle class norms do not operate there. Knowledge that a man has served a jail sentence has little if any effect upon his status in the community, since Skid Row residents regard a month in jail (especially during the winter) as a good way to recuperate from the effects of cheap liquor, poor food, and haphazard sleeping arrangements.

---

b. RESPONSE TO "TREATMENT"

DITMAN, CRAWFORD, FORGY, MOSKOWITZ AND MacANDREW, A CONTROLLED EXPERIMENT ON THE USE OF COURT PROBATION FOR DRUNK ARRESTS

124 Am.J. Psychiatry 160 (1967).[n]

The courts are increasingly coming to view chronic drunk offenders as sick people who deserve treatment rather than punishment,

n. Reprinted from The American Journal of Psychiatry, volume 124, pages 160–63, 1967. Copyright 1967, the American Psychiatric Association.

although there is no available body of evidence which clearly indicates the relative effectiveness of these two approaches.

We have been studying this matter for the past four and a half years in the San Diego Municipal Court. During this time, there have been various reports of municipal court programs throughout the country, programs using such approaches as probation, referral to clinic treatment, Alcoholics Anonymous, court-sponsored honor classes, halfway houses, and camps instead of jail sentences. However, for two reasons little if anything can be safely concluded from the reports. First, they do not record and compare the results from different approaches in a systematic fashion, and second, other factors, such as various changes over a period of time, are confounded with the variations in approach so that therapeutic differences cannot properly be attributed to the programs per se. Until such deficiencies as these are corrected in controlled studies, claims for the particular value of any one program over another are of dubious worth.

Our previous work has led us to expect that the use of probation with suspended sentence would be an effective way both of getting the chronic drunk offender into treatment and of decreasing the likelihood of his being rearrested. The first study was a pilot program in which chronic drunk offenders were probated to Alcoholics Anonymous. If this failed, they were probated to clinic treatment, and if clinic treatment also failed, they were sent to an honor camp for six months. A marked decrease in the over-all number of drunk arrests in the city resulted.

We next instituted a controlled study to compare the effectiveness of three different "treatments." In this study a chronic drunk offender was defined as one who has had either two drunk arrests in the previous three months or three drunk arrests in the previous year. When such individuals came before the court and were found guilty, they were fined $25 and given a 30-day sentence suspended as a condition of a one-year probation. Other conditions of probation were that they complete an 80-item biographical questionnaire and that they abstain from alcoholic beverages for one year.

Each offender was then assigned to one of three treatment conditions: no treatment; alcoholic clinic; or Alcoholics Anonymous. To avoid bias, the judge followed a random assignment schedule. It was also required that each offender report back to the court at the end of six months. Evidence of cooperation in clinic treatment was given to the court by the clinic. In Alcoholics Anonymous such evidence was brought to the court by the offender in the form of signed statements from AA secretaries proving attendance at five meetings within 30 days. If the offender failed to comply, a bench warrant was issued for his arrest. Those unable to pay the $25 fine served one day in jail for each $5 and were then released to probation and one of the three treatments.

Our sample consisted of 301 chronic drunk arrestees who came before the San Diego Municipal Court between July 1964 and January 1965. Ninety percent were men with a median age in the early 40s. They had an average of 12 prior drunk arrests, with one exemplary case having a total of 153. (Not too surprisingly, he became one of our treatment failures.)

*   *   *

Results

*   *   *

Two independent sources of information were used to ascertain whether or not an individual was subsequently rearrested: a local police "rap" sheet and the State of California Criminal Identification and Investigation Report, which purports to list all arrests made in California for any offense and at least some arrests made elsewhere in the U.S.A. All offenders were followed for at least one year after their conviction. On all but seven of the 301 cases at least one of these reports was available, and on 241 cases both reports were obtained.

It was observed that relationships were usually clearer for the 241 complete data cases; thus figures based upon only these offenders will be presented here. *   *   *

TABLE 1
Number of Rearrests Among 241 Offenders in Three Treatment Groups

TREATMENT GROUP	REARRESTS			
	NONE	ONE	TWO OR MORE	TOTAL
No treatment	32 (44%)	14 (19%)	27 (37%)	73
Alcoholism clinic	26 (32%)	23 (28%)	33 (40%)	82
Alcoholics Anonymous	27 (31%)	19 (22%)	40 (47%)	86
Total	85	56	100	241

[A9010]

TABLE 2
Time Before Rearrest in Three Treatment Groups

TREATMENT GROUP	NO REARRESTS	AFTER FIRST MONTH OF TREATMENT	WITHIN FIRST MONTH OF TREATMENT	TOTAL
No treatment	32 (44%)	25 (34%)	16 (22%)	73
Alcoholism clinic	26 (32%)	39 (47%)	17 (21%)	82
Alcoholics Anonymous	27 (31%)	40 (47%)	19 (22%)	86
Total	85	104	52	241

[A9011]

While Table 1 seems to suggest that the no-treatment condition was more effective than either Alcoholics Anonymous or clinic treatment, the chi-square tests of these frequencies failed to reach statistical significance at the .05 level of confidence. Even when Table 1 was collapsed so that the two treatments were lumped together and one or more arrests were lumped together, chi-square still did not quite achieve the .05 level of significance.

Another way of looking at the effectiveness of these three treatment conditions is to determine the length of time that elapsed before the recidivists became treatment failures. As can be seen in Table 2, the no-treatment condition again comes out on top; and again there is little difference between Alcoholics Anonymous and clinic treatment. Once more, however, the chi-square test failed to indicate that this trend was statistically significant at the .05 level of confidence.

*　　*　　*

Discussion

The failure of both Alcoholics Anonymous and the alcoholism clinic to produce fewer recidivists than did no treatment at all ought to be of great concern. Some of the present writers were quite optimistic about the possibilities of enforced referral to treatment, but the early encouraging anecdotal reports are not borne out by present data.

Possible reasons for this are: 1) the 30 days in jail suspended for one year was so powerful that any additional efforts such as treatment had little meaning to the offender; 2) even if the treatment had been initiated by the offender, the number of treatment sessions required as a condition of probation may have been too few to achieve positive results; or 3) the conditions of court-imposed referral confronted the offender with an anxiety-producing situation which may have *increased* the likelihood that he would resume his previous drinking pattern.

Be this as it may, the present data offer no support for a general policy of forced referrals to brief treatment. It is too early to tell whether a policy of *selective referral* would be of benefit. If such differential trends as we have described stand up under cross-validation, they would seem to offer some hope for the future. The data from which to construct such an empirically based referral strategy are still being collected.

NOTES

1. Selzer and Holloway, A Follow-Up of Alcoholics Committed to a State Hospital, 18 Q.J. Studies of Alcohol 98 (1957) report on a follow-up study of 83 patients committed to a Michigan mental hospital in 1948–49. At the time of the study (1955), 35 percent of the sample were "frequently intoxicated" despite the compelled treatment. 22 percent were completely abstinent, however, and 19 percent were only moderate drinkers with good adjustment to their life situations, causing the authors to conclude that "41 percent of the patients who could be evaluated were essentially rehabilitated." Id. at 118. They further commented:

These results must be viewed in the light of knowledge that almost every patient was an unwilling participant in the effort to rehabilitate him. Since these patients displayed little or no realistic

motivation towards obtaining help for their problem, they are probably representative of alcoholics in the community least likely to
recover from their illness if left to their own devices.

Id. at 119.

But consider the significance of these results in light of other studies.
LeMere, What Happens to Alcoholics, 109 Am.J.Psychiatry 674 (1953)
reported that 21 percent of untreated alcoholics either became abstinent
or moderated their drinking. Cowen, A Six Year Follow-up of a Series of
Committed Alcoholics, 15 Q.J. Studies Alcohol 413 (1954) reported that
of 68 alcoholics given "hardly more than custodial care" in a state mental
hospital for 60 days, 37 percent were "substantially improved" six years
later.

What significance do these two studies have for the resolution of
the criminalization and Powell issues? Does the Lovald and Stub study
suggest that in resolving these issues it should be assumed that even skid-
row chronic alcoholics are somewhat receptive to criminal punishment?
Does the Ditman, et al. study suggest that treatment is no more advantageous than simply ignoring the offender? than holding him criminally
liable? How much information should there be—and of what quality
should it be—before the criminalization and *Powell* issues should be resolved? Can inaction be justified before enough information of the desired quality is available? Does it depend upon the state of the existing
law, i. c., what is presently criminalized and what provisions are made
for "treatment"?

2. On the issue of whether nonvoluntary treatment can ever be successful, consider the following from Plaut, Some Major Issues in De
veloping Community Services for Persons with Drinking Problems, in
Task Force on Drunkenness of the President's Commission on Law Enforcement and Administration of Justice, Task Force Report: Drunkenness 120, at 127 (1967):

The Issue of Motivation

    In virtually all facilities providing treatment for problem
drinkers, much importance is attached to the issue of motivation.
Often the key screening criterion is the patient's motivation (or
sincerity) in relation to stopping drinking. Few facilities are
interested in working with patients whom they define as inadequately motivated. It is assumed that motivation is an all-or-none
phenomenon. If present, then the patient can be worked with; if
absent, nothing can be done until the patient really wants to stop
his drinking. It is almost as though the motivated patient is seen
as worthy of assistance and the nonmotivated one as not. The
earlier attitude of rejecting all problem drinkers has been shifted
to an acceptance of those who fit a certain image and a rejection
of the remainder. Many workers believe there are clear-cut stages
through which problem drinkers pass before becoming true alcoholics. In some clinics considerable staff time is spent in determining whether patients are true alcoholics—even though the treatment implications of such labeling are unclear.

The tendency to place the onus on the patient when treatment fails needs to be replaced by the view that each such occurrence is a challenge for the therapist and the agency to develop better and more effective techniques. If current approaches and techniques are effective with only a certain proportion of the target group, then further study and the development of new methods and approaches are required. Evidence is accumulating that changes in the organization, operation, and treatment philosophy of an agency can have a substantial effect on its ability to work with the supposedly unmotivated patient. For example, recent work at the Massachusetts General Hospital has demonstrated that such changes can radically increase the proportion of the referred patients who come into an alcoholism clinic for treatment and who remain in treatment. A similar experiment has been reported in improving the utilization of alcoholism clinic services by women released from a correctional institution. Too frequently the use of motivation as a criterion for the screening of patients functions as a way of excluding those from variant cultural backgrounds, particularly persons from lower socioeconomic strata who are not comfortable with the whole style of operation of most clinics which are geared to middle-class clients. These clinics usually emphasize talking about one's problems, involving other family members in the treatment, and coming in a fixed time every week—all of which may be alien concepts for many lower class persons.

3. For an evaluation of the literature regarding the use of drugs to treat alcoholism, see Viamontes, Review of Drug Effectivenss in the Treatment of Alcoholism, 128 Am.J. Psychiatry 1570 (1972). Eighty percent of the 107 studies reviewed involved no control group but rather "involved the clinical impression of an investigator rather than objectively valid, reasearch-based evaluation." After noting that "only in the uncontrolled studies was any degree of success claimed," Viamontes concludes that "no drug has been proved to be better than a placebo [a substance physically resembling medication but without the medication's chemical characteristics] in the treatment of chronic alcoholism."

III. PRINCIPLES OF CRIMINAL LIABILITY

INTRODUCTORY NOTE

Crimes are generally—and perhaps constitutionally must be—statutory. Nevertheless, it is often difficult or impossible to evaluate the liability of defendants from the face of the offenses with which they are charged. With the possible exception of some of the recently revised statutory criminal codes, most statutory schemes were initially written as codifications of the common law of crimes and have received only piecemeal revision. Thus many statutory definitions of crimes must be read in light of the common law of crimes to determine the elements of the offense, and recourse must often be had to general defenses which may or may not be codified in the statutory scheme.

The material in Parts III–VII makes almost no attempt to deal directly with the definition of particular common law offenses. Rather, it proposes a scheme of analysis which is designed to provide the facility and background necessary to deal with a body of law that is essentially statutory. Basically the task is to define the elements of liability, given the statute and general principles of substantive and constitutional law, and to ascertain the defenses to liability in light of the same factors.

The analysis proposed here is a three-step one. The first step is the ascertainment of the elements of the offense, those matters as to which the prosecution must introduce sufficient evidence to avoid a directed verdict of not guilty. For the sake of convenience and clarity, it is valuable to consider elements of offenses in terms of four categories. A particular crime may not contain an element in each category, although to some extent constitutional considerations may require that a crime require proof of some element in each of the first two categories:

1. The "Act". Although the latin phrase "actus reus" has a much broader meaning, it is valuable to think of the act required for liability in terms of what physical activity must be shown on the part of the accused. The statutory definition may rather specifically describe the type of physical activity, as, for example, requiring that the defendant have been "driving". Or, it may make no attempt to describe the required physical activity, in which case any action or failure to act that meets general requirements will suffice.

2. The State of Mind. For policy reasons, the criminal law is concerned with the accused's conscious state of mind

315

at the time of the offense. Probably all offenses require that the trier of fact be convinced beyond a reasonable doubt that the accused was, at the time he performed the physical act required for liability, aware of something, but the state of mind required differs drastically among offenses.

3. Circumstances. Some offenses require a showing of the existence of particular circumstances. These differ from results (see the fourth category) in that there is no necessity of a causal relationship between the accused's actions and circumstances, while such a relationship must be shown between his actions and results. Circumstances may serve an important policy purpose, or they may be of relatively minor importance. Federal crimes, for example, often require the showing of circumstances for the purpose of establishing federal jurisdiction over the offense.

4. Results. A number of offenses require that a particular result be shown to have occurred. It is important to differentiate between circumstances and results because the complex problems of causation arise only in regard to the latter.

The second step of the analysis involves the ascertainment of any so-called "defenses" which are really means of disproving one of the elements of the offense. Most often this amounts to disproving the state of mind required for the crime. Proof of a defendant's mistake as to the facts at the time of his acts, for example, may well serve simply to raise in the jury's mind a reasonable doubt as to whether he entertained the requisite state of mind.

The final step involves consideration of defenses in the true sense. These are matters which, if established to the satisfaction of the trier of fact, prevent (or reduce) liability despite proof of all elements of the offense. One who kills to preserve his own life, for example, may have entertained an awareness that his action would cause the death of the victim that suffices (under most statutes) for second degree murder; yet if the elements of self defense are established he is relieved of liability.

While one should not pretend that the substantive criminal law may be analyzed "scientifically" it may be helpful to visualize the basic framework of analysis through the following formula: $\text{Act} + \text{State of Mind} \xrightarrow{\text{Causation}} \text{Results} = \text{Liability}$. In considering the material which follows periodically pause to place it within the framework of the above formula. See whether a reduction in the importance of any particular element in the definition of an offense is accompanied by a compensatory increase in the emphasis given another element on the left of the equation or a reduction to the right of it, and, if so, reflect on why this is the case.

During the course of the examination of substantive criminal law in the following material, it might occasionally be worthwhile to refer to the following statutes, using the material as a guide to interpreting more precisely the elements of the crimes created by the statutes. In some cases, reference to analogous common law crimes might be helpful. In others, the only assistance will be provided by general principles of criminal liability.

Ariz. Rev. Stat. (1956)

§ 13–822. Contributing to delinquency and dependency; punishment; procedure

A. A person who by any act, causes, encourages or contributes to the * * * delinquency of a child * * *, or who for any cause is responsible therefore is guilty of a misdemeanor punishable by a fine not exceeding three hundred fifty dollars, by imprisonment in the county jail for not to exceed one year, or both.

18 U.S.C.A.

§ 488. Making or possessing counterfeit dies for foreign coins

Whoever, within the United States, without lawful authority, makes any die, hub, or mold, or any part thereof * * * in the likeness or similitude, as to the design or the inscription thereon, of any die, hub, or mold designated for the coining of the genuine coin of any foreign government; or

Whoever, without lawful authority, possesses any such die, hub, or mold, or any part thereof, or conceals, or knowingly suffers the same to be used for the counterfeiting of any foreign coin—

Shall be fined not more than $5,000 or imprisoned not more than five years, or both.

Maryland Code Ann. (1971)

Art. 27 § 111A. Opening gate of another's pasture, etc.

Any person who shall willfully and maliciously open the gate of another's field, pasture, or enclosure, enclosing livestock, shall be guilty of a misdemeanor, and upon conviction thereof shall be subject to imprisonment for a period of not more than one year or to a fine of not more than five hundred dollars ($500.00), or to both imprisonment and fine.

A. THE "ACT"

1. GENERAL REQUIREMENT OF AN ACT

Conceptually, it is possible to include within the "act" required for criminal liability not only the physical activity which the accused must be shown to have performed but also the circumstances under which it was performed and the consequences of it. It is more satisfactory, however, to differentiate "circumstances" and "results" from the act required, as this forces a more thorough examination of the proof necessary for liability. As to the constitutional necessity that a crime require proof of some act on the part of the accused, review Robinson v. California, supra, as interpreted by Mr. Justice Marshall in Powell v. Texas, supra. Aside from any possible constitutional imperative, the act requirement places an obvious restriction on the authority of the state to employ the criminal sanction. Given that it marks an extreme outer limit on the exercise of governmental power, the student should consider whether the requirement is desirable, and why. Consider also whether it is of any practical importance: For purposes of determining whether the state may employ the criminal sanction; for purposes of determining the severity of the sanction which may be employed?

Several of the most basic questions regarding the requirement of an "act" are raised in this section. What is the significance, if any, of the requirement that the "act" be "willed" or "voluntary"? In particular, after becoming familiar with the "state of mind" requirement, Section III. B, infra, the student should reconsider the *Mercer* case, infra, to decide whether the issues involved there could not have been as effectively analyzed and resolved without any reference whatever to the "act" requirement.

In this regard consider the view of Profesor Perkins:

It is sometimes said that no crime has been committed unless the harmful result was brought about by a "voluntary act." Analysis of such a statement will disclose, however, that as so used the phrase "voluntary act" means no more than the mere word "act." An act must be a willed movement or the omission of a possible and legally-required performance. This is essential to the *actus reus* rather than to the *mens rea*. "A spasm is not an act."

* * * A positive act (willed movement) always has a voluntary element and hence the phrase "voluntary act" is merely tautological as so applied. A negative act may be either a forbearance or an unintentional omission of a legally-required performance. The former is voluntary, the latter is not. If a watchman charged with the duty of

lowering the gates at a crossing whenever a train is approaching fails to do so on a particular occasion, with fatal consequences to a motorist, the death is due to his (negative) act. But it would be absurd to speak of this act as "voluntary" if he was inattentive and did not know the train was approaching. As his legal duty required him to be attentive in this regard his want of knowledge of the need for immediate action will not excuse him, but it leaves his failure wholly unintentional. Hence the assertion that there is no crime without a "voluntary act" is redundant as to positive action and incorrect as to negative action.

Furthermore, such an assertion invites confusion in two directions—first because the modifier may be improperly extended to the legally-recognized consequences of the act, and second because it may raise a false issue as to the meaning of the word "voluntary." As to the first, assume the unintentional, but fatal, discharge of a weapon which had been pointed unlawfully at the deceased with no thought other than to intimidate him. The intentional pointing of the weapon was an act and the resulting death is imputable to the pointer. It is not improper to hold the slayer guilty of criminal homicide in certain cases of this nature, but to speak of the "shooting" or the "killing" as voluntary or intentional is merely confusion of words. * * * the notion of a "voluntary act" as requisite to criminal guilt may result in the jury's being confused by argument of counsel to the effect that defendant's act was committed under the stress and strain of difficult circumstances and hence was not "voluntary." If the harm was caused by a willed movement of the defendant it was caused by his "act" no matter how much "pressure" he may have been under at the moment. Perkins, Criminal Law 749–50 (1969).

18 U.S.C.A. § 1792 provides, in pertinent part: "Whoever conveys * * * from place to place [within a Federal penal institution] any * * * weapon * * * designed to kill, injure or disable any officer, agent, employee or inmate thereof * * *. Shall be imprisoned not more than ten years." Does a prisoner violate this provision if, while carrying a knife under his clothing, he walks from his cell pursuant to a guard's order? What if he is running a knife across a sander in the prison workshop and, on the approach of his foreman, he drops it to the floor? Which of the following factors would control your interpretation: the meaning of the verb "convey"; the "voluntariness" of the conduct; or the purpose of the statute given the fact that mere possession of a knife by an inmate is not criminal? Compare United States v. Meador, 456 F.2d 197 (10th Cir. 1972) with United States v. Bedwell, 456 F.2d 448 (10th Cir. 1972).

To what extent is a failure to act sufficient for liability? To what extent may a defendant be held liable if the acts relied upon are performed by someone other than himself, i. e., to what extent may "vicarious liability" be imposed?

PROPOSED FEDERAL CRIMINAL CODE (1971)

✳ § 301.   Basis of Liability for Offenses

(1) Conduct. A person commits an offense only if he engages in conduct, including an act, an omission, or possession, in violation of a statute which provides that the conduct is an offense.

(2) Omissions. A person who omits to perform an act does not commit an offense unless he has a legal duty to perform the act.

(3) Publication Required. A person does not commit an offense if he engages in conduct in violation only of a statute or regulation thereunder that has not been published.

Comment

Federal criminal law does not, at present, contain statutes stating basic conditions of liability. Chapter 3 would make the treatment and understanding of these issues clear and uniform.

Subsection (1) states the minimum condition of criminal liability: a person must engage in conduct; that he has a certain status or that certain circumstances exist will not render him criminally liable. Conduct includes omissions and possessions. The issue of the voluntariness of the conduct, i. e., whether or not it is conscious and the result of determination or effort, is not dealt with explicitly in this subsection because, while doing so would have limited utility, it would raise the possibility of evasion of limitations placed on defenses such as intoxication and mental illness through inquiries as to voluntariness.

Subsection (2) restates present federal law: a person is not liable for an omission unless he has a duty to act.

Subsection (3) constitutes the basic prohibition against secret criminal laws.

STATE v. MERCER

Supreme Court of North Carolina, 1969.
275 N.C. 108, 165 S.E.2d 328.

Separate indictments charged defendant with the first degree murder on September 14, 1967, of (1) Myrtle R. Mercer, defendant's wife, (2) Ida Mae Dunn, and (3) Jeffrey Lane Dunn, Ida's five-year-old son. * * *

There was evidence tending to show the facts narrated below.

Defendant, a member of the United States Army for 19½ years, was stationed at Fort Benning, Georgia, at the time of the trial.

Defendant and Myrtle Mercer were married in Fayetteville, N. C., in April, 1965. Thereafter, he was stationed at duty posts in and out of the United States. Myrtle Mercer, Ida Mae Dunn, and Jeffrey Lane

Dunn, Ida's five-year-old boy, lived together in Wilson, N. C. Defendant visited Myrtle in Wilson from time to time when on leaves. He was thirty-nine; Myrtle was twenty-three.

Marital difficulties developed. Defendant had heard that Myrtle was having affairs with other men. He thought Myrtle's relationship with Ida involved more than normal affection. As time passed, defendant's strong affection for Myrtle was not reciprocated.

On July 6, 1967, defendant received a letter from Myrtle, referred to in the evidence as a "Dear John" letter, in which she told him she was tired of being tied down and wanted to come and go as she pleased. In a letter mailed August 10th from Kentucky (where he was then stationed), defendant wrote Myrtle: "Please don't make me do something that will send both of us to our graves." Also: "I could never see you with another man, and I would die and go to hell before I would see you with some other man, and take myself with you."

In September, 1967, defendant obtained a ten-day leave "to come home and see if he could get straightened out with his wife. * * *" Defendant told his first sergeant that "if he did not get straightened out he would not be back."

On September 13, 1967, defendant visited the house in Wilson where Myrtle, Ida, and Jeffrey lived. He talked with Myrtle. However, she would not discuss their marital problems and did not want him to stay at that house.

Defendant stayed at the home of his cousin, Mrs. Mable Owens, in Tarboro. He left there on the morning of September 14, 1967, and arrived at Myrtle's around noon. She would not talk with him. (Note: Defendant testified Myrtle at that time gave him some clothes, a camera and a paper bag containing a pistol he had given to her for her protection.) At the conclusion of this visit, he returned to the home of Mrs. Owens. Sometime during the day defendant bought a pint of vodka and had two drinks from it.

About 8:30 p. m., Mrs. Owens, at the request of defendant, drove defendant to Myrtle's house in Wilson. The two children of Mrs. Owens accompanied them. Defendant knocked. There was no response. The house was unlighted and apparently no one was there. They left and visited defendant's brother (in Wilson) for some twenty-five or thirty-five minutes. While there, defendant telephoned Myrtle's house. The line was busy. They went back to Myrtle's house. Defendant asked Mrs. Owens if she and her children would go into the house with him. She replied that they would wait in the car.

Defendant went to the front door and knocked several times. There was no answer. Defendant shot at the door twice, pushed it open with his foot and went inside. At that time, a light came on in the front bedroom. Someone said, "Ervin, don't do that." Defendant fired three or four shots killing Myrtle instantly and fatally wounding Ida and Jeffrey. He then left the house. A neighbor called the police.

*   *   *

Defendant was arrested at the home of his brother in Wilson, a few hours after the fatal shots were fired. He accompanied the officers to a lot behind Myrtle's house where the gun which inflicted the fatal injuries was hidden.

Testimony of defendant, in addition to that referred to above, is set out in the opinion. It tended to show he was completely unconscious of what transpired when Myrtle, Ida and Jeffrey were shot.

In each case, the jury returned a verdict of guilty of murder in the second degree. *   *   *

BOBBITT, Judge.

*   *   *

The court's final instructions were as follows: "(T)he Court instructs you that the evidence in regard and surrounding the alleged loss of memory by the defendant will be considered by you *on the question of premeditation and deliberation in the charge of murder in the first degree.* * * * if you find from the evidence, not by the greater weight, nor by the preponderance, but if the defendant has satisfied you—merely satisfied you—that he lost consciousness, sufficient consciousness, to the extent that he did not have sufficient time to *premeditate or deliberate,* that is, if he did not have sufficient time to form in his mind the intent to kill, under the definition of *premeditation* and *deliberation,* then it would be your duty to return a verdict of not guilty of murder in the first degree, because the Court has instructed you if the State has failed to satisfy you of the element of *premeditation* or *deliberation,* or if there arises in your minds a reasonable doubt in regard to those two elements or either one of those two elements, it would be your duty to return a verdict of not guilty. And further in regard, when you come to consider those elements of *premeditation* and *deliberation,* if the defendant has satisfied you, not beyond a reasonable doubt, not by the greater weight of the evidence, but has merely satisfied you that he lost consciousness to such an extent that he was unable to *premeditate,* and was unable to *deliberate,* according to the definition of those terms that the law has given you, then he could not be guilty of murder in the first degree, and it would be your duty to return a verdict of not guilty as to murder in the first degree, under those circumstances. Now, *the Court feels that those are the only two elements in the case in which this evidence in regard to his loss of consciousness applies,* and the Court has ruled that there is no element of legal insanity in the evidence." (Our italics.)

Defendant's assignment of error, based on his exception to the foregoing portion of the charge, must be sustained. Defendant testified he was completely unconscious of what transpired when Myrtle, Ida and Jeffrey were shot. The court instructed the jury that this evidence was for consideration *only* in respect of the elements of premeditation and deliberation in first degree murder. This restriction of the legal significance of the evidence as to defendant's unconsciousness was erroneous.

* * *

"If a person is in fact unconscious at the time he commits an act which would otherwise be criminal, he is not responsible therefor. The absence of consciousness not only precludes the existence of any specific mental state, but also excludes the possibility of a voluntary act without which there can be no criminal liability." 1 Wharton's Criminal Law and Procedure (Anderson), § 50, p. 116.

"Unconsciousness is a complete, not a partial, defense to a criminal charge." 21 Am.Jur.2d, Criminal Law § 29, p. 115.

"*Unconsciousness.* A person cannot be held criminally responsible for acts committed while he is unconscious. Some statutes broadly exempt from responsibility persons who commit offenses without being conscious thereof. Such statutes, when construed in connection with other statutes relating to criminal capacity of the insane and voluntarily intoxicated, do not include within their protection either insane or voluntarily intoxicated persons, and are restricted in their contemplation to persons of sound mind suffering from some other agency rendering them unconscious of their acts * * *." 22 C.J.S. Criminal Law § 55, p. 194.

Defendant contends he had no knowledge of and did not consciously commit the act charged in the indictments. He does not contend he was insane. Unconsciousness and insanity are separate grounds of exemption from criminal responsibility.

* * *

There was no evidence defendant was a somnambulist or an epileptic. Nor was there evidence he was under the influence of intoxicants or narcotics. Under cross-examination, defendant testified his only previous "blackout" experience, which was of brief duration, occurred when he received and read the "Dear John" letter.

Upon the present record, defendant was entitled to an instruction to the effect the jury should return verdicts of not guilty if in fact defendant was *completely* unconscious of what transpired when Myrtle, Ida and Jeffrey were shot.

* * *

It should be understood that unconsciousness, although always a factor of legal significance, is not a complete defense under all circumstances. Without undertaking to mark the limits of the legal principles applicable to varied factual situations that will arise from time to time, but solely by way of illustration, attention is called to the following: In California, "unconsciousness produced by voluntary intoxication does not render a defendant incapable of committing a crime." People v. Cox, 67 Cal.App.2d 166, 153 P.2d 362, and cases cited. In Colorado, a person who precipitates a fracas and as a result is hit on the head and rendered semi-conscious or unconscious cannot maintain that he is not criminally responsible for any degree of homicide above involuntary manslaughter, or that he is not criminally responsible at all. Watkins v. People, 158 Colo. 485, 408 P.2d 425. In Oklahoma, a motorist is guilty of manslaughter if he drives an automobile with knowledge that he is subject to frequent blackouts, when his continued operation of the automobile is in reckless disregard to the safety of others and constitutes culpable or criminal negligence. Carter v. State, [376 P.2d 351 (Okl.Cr.1962)]; Smith v. Commonwealth, [268 S.W.2d 937 (Ky.1954)]. As to somnambulism, see Fain v. Commonwealth, [78 Ky. 183 (1879)], and Lewis v. State, 196 Ga. 755, 27 S.E.2d 659.

POWELL v. TEXAS

United States Supreme Court, 1968.
392 U.S. 514, 88 S.Ct. 2145, 20 L.Ed.2d 1254.

[The opinion of Mr. Justice MARSHALL for the Court, from which this excerpt is taken, is more fully reprinted at page 168].

Appellant * * * seeks to come within the application of the Cruel and Unusual Punishment Clause announced in Robinson v. California, 370 U.S. 660 (1962), which involved a state statute making it a crime to "be addicted to the use of narcotics." This Court held there that "a state law which imprisons a person thus afflicted [with narcotic addiction] as a criminal, even though he has never touched any narcotic drug within the State or been guilty of any irregular behavior there, inflicts a cruel and unusual punishment * * *." Id., at 667.

On its face the present case does not fall within that holding, since appellant was convicted, not for being a chronic alcoholic, but for being in public while drunk on a particular occasion. The State of Texas thus has not sought to punish a mere status, as California did in *Robinson*; nor has it attempted to regulate appellant's behavior in the privacy of his own home. Rather, it has imposed upon appellant a criminal sanction for public behavior which may create substantial health and safety hazards, both for appellant and for members of the general public and which offends the moral and esthetic sensibilities of a large segment of the community. This seems a far cry from convicting one for being an addict, being a chronic alcoholic, being "mentally ill, or a leper * * *." Id., at 666.

Robinson so viewed brings this Court but a very small way into the substantive criminal law. And unless *Robinson* is so viewed it is difficult to see any limiting principle that would serve to prevent this Court from becoming, under the aegis of the Cruel and Unusual Punishment Clause, the ultimate arbiter of the standards of criminal responsibility, in diverse areas of the criminal law, throughout the country.

It is suggested in dissent that *Robinson* stands for the "simple" but "subtle" principle that "[c]riminal penalties may not be inflicted upon a person for being in a condition he is powerless to change." *Post*, at 567. In that view, appellant's "condition" of public intoxication was "occasioned by a compulsion symptomatic of the disease" of chronic alcoholism, and thus, apparently, his behavior lacked the critical element of *mens rea*. Whatever may be the merits of such a doctrine of criminal responsibility, it surely cannot be said to follow from *Robinson*. The entire thrust of *Robinson*'s interpretation of the Cruel and Unusual Punishment Clause is that criminal penalties may be inflicted only if the accused has committed some act, has engaged in some behavior, which society has an interest in preventing or perhaps in historical common law terms, has committed some *actus reus*. It thus does not deal with the question of whether certain conduct cannot constitutionally be punished because it is, in some sense, "involuntary" or "occasioned by a compulsion."

Mr. Justice BLACK, whom Mr. Justice HARLAN joins, concurring.

Punishment for a status is particularly obnoxious, and in many instances can reasonably be called cruel and unusual, because it involves punishment for a mere propensity, a desire to commit an offense; the mental element is not simply one part of the crime but may constitute all of it. This is a situation universally sought to be avoided in our criminal law; the fundamental requirement that some action be proved is solidly established even for offenses most heavily based on propensity, such as attempt, conspiracy, and recidivist crimes.[4] In fact, one eminent authority has found only one isolated instance, in all of Anglo-American jurisprudence, in which criminal responsibility was imposed in the absence of any act at all.[5]

The reasons for this refusal to permit conviction without proof of an act are difficult to spell out, but they are nonetheless perceived and universally expressed in our criminal law. Evidence of propensity can be considered relatively unreliable and more difficult for a de-

---

4. As Glanville Williams puts it, "[t]hat crime requires an act is *invariably* true if the proposition be read as meaning that a private thought is not sufficient to found responsibility." Williams, Criminal Law—the General Part 1 (1961). (Emphasis added.) For the requirement of some act as an element of conspiracy and attempt, see id., at 631, 663, 668; R. Perkins, Criminal Law 482, 531–532 (1957).

5. Williams, supra, n. 4, at 11.

fendant to rebut; the requirement of a specific act thus provides some protection against false charges. See 4 Blackstone, Commentaries 21. Perhaps more fundamental is the difficulty of distinguishing, in the absence of any conduct, between desires of the day-dream variety and fixed intentions that may pose a real threat to society; extending the criminal law to cover both types of desire would be unthinkable, since "[t]here can hardly be anyone who has never thought evil. When a desire is inhibited it may find expression in fantasy; but it would be absurd to condemn this natural psychological mechanism as illegal."

In contrast, crimes that require the State to prove that the defendant actually committed some proscribed act involve none of these special problems. In addition, the question whether an act is "involuntary" is, as I have already indicated, an inherently elusive question, and one which the State may, for good reasons, wish to regard as irrelevant. In light of all these considerations, our limitation of our *Robinson* holding to pure status crimes seems to me entirely proper.

NOTES

1. As Mr. Justice Marshall makes clear there must be "some act * * * some behavior" before criminal penalties may be imposed. The Court in *Robinson* explictly included "possession of narcotics" in its recitation of acts which might properly be criminalized. Is possession an "act" or "behavior"? The Proposed Texas Penal Code would provide in § 6.02:

"Possession is a voluntary act if the possessor knowingly obtains or receives the thing possessed or is aware of his control of the thing for a sufficient time to permit him to terminate his control."

The Committee on Revision comments:

"Although possession is often treated in the criminal law as the equivalent of an act, it is not strictly speaking a bodily movement so this section is necessary to treat it as such.

"The section does not determine whether an actor must know the nature of the thing possessed or just know that he possesses a thing; this issue is determined by the definition of the specific (possessory) offense involved * * *."

The question of whether it is necessary that the possession be "knowing" is examined later.

2. If the mere possession of drugs is criminalized should there be any requirement that the amount possessed be sufficient, as to either quantity or quality, for use? Does possession of a lesser amount involve behavior which, in Mr. Justice Marshall's words, "society has an interest in preventing."? Compare Pelham v. State, 164 Tex.Cr.R. 226, 298 S.W.2d 171 (1957) (to constitute marijuana within meaning of possession statute amount must be capable of being applied to the use commonly made thereof) and Greer v. State, 163 Tex.Cr.R. 377, 292 S.W.2d 122 (1956) (chemically identifiable trace of heroin on moist piece of cotton insufficient to war-

rant conviction for possession) with Jordan v. United States, 416 F.2d 338 (9th Cir. 1969), certiorari denied 397 U.S. 920, 90 S.Ct. 930, 25 L.Ed.2d 101 (1970) (Federal law only requires that some measurable amount of narcotic drug be contained in the substance which is the subject of the indictment), Massiate v. State, 365 S.W.2d 802 (Tex.Ct.Crim.App.1963) (caring for 29 marijuana plants so immature at seizure that they would contain only microscopic bits of narcotic, if any, sufficient to sustain conviction of possession; punishment, life (two prior felony convictions), Getters v. State, 170 Tex.Cr.R. 331, 340 S.W.2d 806 (1960) (2/100 of a gram of marijuana leaf plus 5 grams of seeds which police chemist testified "contained no narcotics" were together sufficient to make a cigarette and therefore to sustain conviction; punishment, 10 years (second conviction) and Tomlin v. State, 170 Tex.Cr.R. 108, 338 S.W.2d 735 (1960) (1700 micrograms of heroin equivalent to one capsule of 3% heroin all of which was destroyed in the course of analysis by the prosecution held sufficient to sustain conviction of possession; punishment, life (three prior convictions)). In State v. Siirila, —— Minn. ——, 193 N.W.2d 467, 10 Cr.L. 2287 (1971) the eighteen year old defendant appealed his conviction and 20 year sentence for possession of marijuana on the grounds that 1/2800 of an ounce—too small to permit chemical analysis but identified by microscopic examination— discovered by police vacuuming of the lining and pockets of his jacket was not a usable amount. An earlier, but quite similar, opinion in this case may be found summarized at 8 Cr.L. 2429 (March 10, 1971).

3. As is suggested by the definition of possession quoted in note 1 supra, the contraband need not be actually possessed in the sense of being on the person of the possessor. The ambit of possession statutes is significantly broadened by the doctrine of "constructive possession" which extends culpability to situations where the defendant may be found to have been "in a position to exercise dominion or control" over the contraband. United States v. Holland, 445 F.2d 701, 703 (D.C.Cir.1971). See Annotation, 91 A.L.R.2d 810. An especially common problem in this area arises where the alleged possession is not only constructive but joint; as where the contraband is found in a car or room occupied by more than one person. See Folk v. State, 11 Md.App. 508, 275 A.2d 184 (1971).

4. As is indicated by the following case, joint, constructive possession of the prohibited drug has not been the minimum "behavior" on which the use of the criminal sanction has been predicated.

CRAWFORD v. UNITED STATES

District of Columbia Court of Appeals, 1971.
278 A.2d 125.

Before GALLAGHER, REILLY and YEAGLEY, Associate Judges.

GALLAGHER, Associate Judge. Appellant was charged with carrying a pistol without a license and possession of implements of a crime—narcotics paraphernalia. A jury found him not guilty of carrying a pistol without a license and rendered a special verdict finding him guilty of possession of one hypodermic needle and one hypodermic syringe found under the front seat of the car he was driving. He was found not guilty of possession of implements of a crime as to other narcotics paraphernalia found in the rear seat. Appellant was sentenced to serve 180 days in jail.

At the close of the Government's case in chief and again upon final submission of the case, appellant moved for judgment of acquittal contending the Government's evidence was insufficient to support a finding that he was in possession of the narcotics paraphernalia. The trial judge denied the motions and appellant now contends this was reversible error.

The Government's evidence consisted of the following: Officer Richardson testified that he stopped appellant's car for speeding and while waiting for appellant (who had alighted from the car) to produce his license he noticed a syringe at the foot of one of the occupants in the rear seat.[3] Upon the arrival of other officers he had called by radio, the occupants were removed from the car. He then recovered two pieces of tinfoil, a spoon, two syringes and one needle from the rear seat and one syringe and needle protruding from beneath the front seat on the driver's side where appellant had been sitting. A pistol was also recovered from the rear seat. A Detective Dotson testified that he examined appellant at the precinct on the day of the arrest and found ten to twenty "individual needle marks—small punctures on the arm." The Government chemist testified that neither the spoon nor the aluminum foil recovered contained any narcotics. He could not testify each syringe positively contained heroin because the sample he tested was a composite from all three syringes; and consequently, he could not testify specifically that there was heroin in the syringe found under appellant's seat.[a]

"A motion for acquittal must be granted when the evidence, viewed in the light most favorable to the Government, is such that a reasonable juror must have a reasonable doubt as to the existence of any of the essential elements of the crime." * * * If, on the other hand, the evidence is such that a reasonable man might or might not have a reasonable doubt as to the defendant's guilt, the case should go to the jury. We think the motions were properly denied under this standard.

Possession in this instance could have been either actual or constructive, i. e., the exercise of, or right to exercise, dominion and control over the narcotics paraphernalia under appellant's seat. See Hill v. District of Columbia, D.C.App., 264 A.2d 145, 146 (1970); cf.

---

3. There were three youths in the rear seat and one in the front passenger seat in addition to appellant.

a. Is there any point to requiring that the drug paraphernalia contain at least a trace of the prohibited drugs? In a jurisdiction which permits conviction of possession of less than a usable amount?

Garza v. United States, 395 F.2d 899, 901 (5th Cir. 1967). There is no question but that appellant did not have actual possession of the needle and syringe at the time of his arrest. But appellant had been present in the automobile immediately before the officer noticed the paraphernalia protruding from under the seat where appellant had just been seated. He had been driving the car immediately prior to the time the articles were recovered in plain view from beneath that seat. He was the owner of the vehicle. The single needle and syringe were certainly within his reach. Additionally, puncture marks were found on his arm which indicated he was a user of drugs. Garza v. United States, supra, 385 F.2d at 900. From these facts it was reasonable to infer that appellant had dominion and control over the needle and syringe under his seat. Viewing the evidence in the light most favorable to the Government, as we must, we conclude it was adequate to support the jury's finding that appellant had possession of that needle and syringe.

Appellant also contends that possession of a single hypodermic needle and syringe alone will not support a conviction under the statute [5] without proof of specific intent to use the instruments to commit a crime since they do not in themselves raise "sinister" implications. See McKoy v. United States, D.C.App., 263 A.2d 649, 651 (1970). He raises this point for the first time on appeal. "[O]ur power to notice errors raised for the first time on appeal is discretionary, and will be exercised only where the error alleged is 'plain error' and clearly prejudicial to the appellant." Bunter v. United States, D.C.App., 245 A.2d 839, 842 (1968). Our review of the record in this case reveals no such plain error. We conclude upon the record before us that there existed sufficient independent circumstantial evidence of appellant's intent above and beyond his mere possession of a single needle and syringe to support his conviction of possession of implements of a crime. Therefore, we are not met with the issue posed by appellant that possession of the needle and syringe, standing alone, would not violate the statute.

This court has recognized the use of surrounding circumstances to evidence the requisite criminal intent under the statute. McKoy v. United States, supra. In the present case appellant possessed a hypodermic needle and syringe but, in addition, two other syringes and one other needle, with two pieces of foil and a spoon, were found in the rear seat of the automobile driven by appellant. While it is true that the jury found that appellant did not possess these items in the rear seat, this is not to say that he did not know of their presence.

---

5. D.C.Code 1967, § 22–3601 provides in part:

No person shall have in his possession in the District any instrument, tool, or other implement for picking locks or pockets, or that is usually employed, or reasonably may be employed in the commission of any crime, if he is unable satisfactorily to account for the possession of the implement. * * *

And their presence would indicate an apparent intention to administer narcotics illegally, if this had not already been done. These materials constituted a narcotics "kit" and thus appellant was in the immediate company of others who had this "kit." There was evidence that at least one of the syringes contained heroin, though which one could not be determined due to the nature of the chemist's test. Further, ten to twenty puncture marks were observed on appellant's left forearm by Detective Dotson indicating appellant was a drug user.

We believe that these circumstances taken together, and when viewed in a light most favorable to the Government, were sufficient for the jury to conclude that appellant possessed the hypodermic needle and syringe with the intent to use them for a criminal purpose.

For these reasons, the judgment of the trial court is

Affirmed.

PEOPLE v. PAGNOTTA

Court of Appeals of New York, 1969.
25 N.Y.2d 333, 253 N.E.2d 202, 305 N.Y.S.2d 484.

JASEN, Judge. On this appeal, the defendant questions the constitutionality of subdivision 5 of section 1533 of the former Penal Law, Consol.Laws, c. 40, which made it a misdemeanor to loiter in the common areas of a building for the purpose of unlawfully using or possessing any narcotic drug.[b]

On November 29, 1965, while on patrol in Kings County, Patrolman John Connelly of the New York City Police Department saw the defendant and two others enter a building. Since the defendant was known by Officer Connelly to be a narcotics addict, the officer's suspicions were aroused and he entered an adjoining building and went to the roof. He crossed over to the roof of the building which he had seen the defendant enter, and when he opened the door from the roof to the stairs, he came upon defendant and his two companions on the stair landing. Defendant had a bottle cap containing a liquid in his hand and one of the other men had a hypodermic needle and an eyedropper. (A subsequent search of the third man found glassine

[b]. Section 1533 (subd. 5) of the former Penal Law provided:
"Permitting use of building for nuisance.
"A person who: * * *
*   *   *   *   *   *
"5. Uses, resorts to or loiters about any stairway, staircase, hall, roof, elevator, cellar, courtyard or any passageway of a building for the purpose of unlawfully using or possessing any narcotic drug,
"Is guilty of a misdemeanor." Compare D.C.Code 1967, § 22–1515(a): "Who-

ever is found in the District in [an] * * * establishment * * * where * * * any narcotic drug is sold, administered, or dispensed without a license shall, if he knew that it was such an establishment and if he is unable to give a good account of his presence in the establishment, be imprisoned for not more than one year or fined not more than $500, or both." See Cook v. United States, 272 A.2d 444 (D.C.Ct.App.1971).

envelopes in his possession which laboratory tests indicated were completely empty.) When defendant saw the officer he dropped the bottle cap, spilling the liquid, none of which was recovered.

Defendant and his cohorts were placed under arrest and charged with possession of narcotics instruments and violations of subdivision 5 of section 1533 of the former Penal Law.

The charges against one of the defendant's companions were dismissed with the consent of the District Attorney when it was found that the glassine envelopes which the man had in his possession were completely empty. The other companion, who had held the eyedropper and needle, was accepted for treatment under article IX of the Mental Hygiene Law, Consol.Laws, c. 27.

At the defendant's trial, Officer Connelly testified on the basis of his experience in making narcotics arrests and his training at the police narcotics school, that bottle caps are commonly used by narcotics addicts as "cookers". Heroin is put into the cap along with a quantity of water to dissolve the drug and the mixture is then drawn up into an eyedropper and injected into the vein by means of a hypodermic needle.

The Trial Judge dismissed the charge of possession of narcotics instruments which had been placed against defendant, because a bottle cap or "cooker" is not one of the instruments enumerated in the statute. (See former Penal Law, § 1747-e.) However, defendant was found guilty of violating subdivision 5 of section 1533 of the former Penal Law and was sentenced to 60 days in the New York City Workhouse.

On this appeal, defendant contends that the People failed to prove beyond a reasonable doubt that he was loitering *for the purpose of* possessing or using a narcotic drug. He argues that the People failed to establish the presence of any narcotic drug in his possession or in the possession of his companions, and he claims that at best the facts of this case raise a mere suspicion as to possession. In addition, defendant asserts that dismissal of the charges against the companion who only had the glassine envelopes supports his position that possession of narcotics is needed to sustain a charge under subdivision 5 of section 1533.

Inasmuch as the statute makes loitering for the purpose of using or possessing a narcotic drug a crime, it was unnecessary for the People to prove that the unrecovered liquid was in fact heroin, so long as it was shown that the defendant and his friends had congregated with the purpose of using or possessing drugs. Furthermore, even though the District Attorney may have consented to a dismissal as to the companion who had the envelopes, this does not mandate that possession be proven, nor may it be raised as some sort of collateral estoppel in regard to this defendant. * * *

While it is true that the People were unable to actually prove that the liquid in the cooker was in fact a narcotic drug, the circumstances of the gathering, the possession of narcotics implements by one of defendant's companions and the expert testimony of the police officer in regard to the common practice of narcotics addicts support the inference that the defendant and his companions had gathered to take narcotic drugs. To be sure, the evidence upon which guilt is found in this case is merely circumstantial; however, the facts support no other inference. The hypothesis of guilt flows naturally from and is consistent with all the facts proven. Moreover, all these facts are clearly inconsistent with innocence and exclude to a moral certainty every hypothesis but guilt. * * *

Defendant also challenges subdivision 5 of section 1533 of the former Penal Law as being unconstitutional due to vagueness and lack of proper purpose.

There is a strong presumption that a statute duly enacted by the Legislature is constitutional. * * *

Of course, a statute must be sufficiently definite to give a reasonable man subject to it notice of the nature of what is prohibited and what is required of him. Moreover, in order to be upheld as constitutional, a law which places some restriction upon an individual's freedom of action in the name of the police power must bear some reasonable relation to the public good. A statute which fails to distinguish between innocent conduct and action which is calculated to cause harm may not be sustained. In People v. Diaz, 4 N.Y.2d 469, 176 N.Y.S.2d 313, 151 N.E.2d 871, we held that a statute which made it illegal to lounge or loiter about any street in the City of Dunkirk failed to draw this distinction. Likewise, in Fenster v. Leary, 20 N.Y. 2d 309, 282 N.Y.S.2d 739, 229 N.E.2d 426, we overturned a statute which made it a crime for an individual to have no visible means of support and to live without employment. In that case we ruled that such conduct in no way impinged on the rights of others and had only the most tenuous connection with commission of a crime and disruption of public order.

We hold the statute in the present case is not too vague, and is a completely reasonable restriction upon the individual for the public good. The statute makes it illegal to loiter about any "stairway, staircase, hall, roof, elevator, cellar, courtyard or any passageway of a building for the purpose of unlawfully using or possessing any narcotic drug". The statute does not penalize mere loitering as did the statute in *Diaz*, but rather prohibits loitering for the purpose of committing the crime of unlawfully using or possessing narcotic drugs. (Cf. People v. Johnson, 6 N.Y.2d 549, 190 N.Y.S.2d 694, 161 N.E.2d 9, where we upheld a statute making it a crime to loiter in a school building; the majority holding it to be common knowledge that school authorities often are harassed by loiterers who are usually present for some illegitimate purpose.)

However, the defendant argues that subdivision 5 of section 1533 has no reasonable purpose and was merely intended as a catchall to prevent a suspect from being set free in a case where evidence was illegally seized or where there is insufficient evidence to sustain a conviction for any of the substantive narcotics offenses. With this appraisal we do not agree.

[It appears that the Legislature in enacting the statute before us sought to prevent generally idle and dissolute persons engaged in the unlawful traffic of narcotics, from drawing together for that purpose in places frequented by other citizens, thereby endangering public health, morals and tranquility] This protection of innocent citizens from drug users is a very crucial problem. As has recently been pointed out by several newspaper articles, in some of our poorer urban areas where drug use is high, innocent citizens are often beaten, robbed, and even murdered by drug addicts. (See, e. g., New York Times, Sept. 24, 1969, p. 1, col. 2.) It is completely reasonable and proper for the Legislature to protect these citizens from accidentally stumbling into the midst of such miscreants in the common areas of buildings.

Finally, defendant argues that the statute punishes an individual for a bare desire to commit a criminal act, and he cites People v. Rizzo, 246 N.Y. 334, 158 N.E. 888, 55 A.L.R. 711, as authority for the proposition that it is impermissible to make criminal the mere intent to commit a crime.

Defendant's reliance upon *Rizzo* is misplaced. In *Rizzo* the defendant and his cohorts planned to rob a bank messenger carrying a payroll. They armed themselves and proceeded to cruise the neighborhood looking for the messenger, who never appeared. During this period the police arrested the defendant and his companions and charged them with attempted robbery. This court reversed their conviction, holding the acts of the defendants too remote from the consummation of the crime of robbery to be considered an attempt.

In the case at bar, the defendant and his companions were gathered for the obvious purpose of taking heroin. They had the needle and eyedropper, the cooker, and, apparently, the heroin ready for use. But for the entrance of Officer Connelly, they probably would have succeeded in injecting the fluid which was in the cooker within the next few moments. It is hard to conceive of any other set of circumstances which would have found them closer to consummation of the act of using drugs. Furthermore, it is of no significance that the liquid in the cooker was not proven to be heroin for even if the defendant and his companions were about to use some innocent substance which they mistakenly believed to be heroin, they would still be guilty of a violation of subdivision 5 of section 1533 because they were loitering *for the purpose* of using a narcotic drug.

A more difficult case might have been presented if the defendant and his companions merely congregated without any narcotics instruments to await the possible delivery of drugs which they would later possess and use.

However, these are not the facts of this case. That there may be marginal cases in which it is difficult to determine whether certain conduct is criminal is not sufficient reason to declare the language of a statute unconstitutionally vague. (Roth v. United States, 354 U.S. 476, 491, 77 S.Ct. 1304, 1 L.Ed.2d 1498; United States v. Harriss, 347 U.S. 612, 618, 74 S.Ct. 808, 98 L.Ed. 989.)

The statute in this case is clear and unambiguous. It prohibits loitering or congregating for the purpose of committing a criminal act. It certainly is a reasonable legislative response to a critical problem.

Accordingly, the judgment of the Appellate Term should be affirmed.

FULD, C. J., and BURKE, SCILEPPI, BERGAN, BREITEL and GIBSON, JJ., concur.

Judgment affirmed.

PEOPLE v. SHAUGHNESSY

District Court, Nassau County, New York, 1971.
66 Misc.2d 19, 319 N.Y.S.2d 626.

JOHN S. LOCKMAN, Judge. On October 9th, 1970, shortly before 10:05 p. m., the Defendant in the company of her boy friend and two other youngsters proceeded by automobile to the vicinity of the St. Ignatius Retreat Home, Searingtown Road, Incorporated Village of North Hills, Nassau County, New York. The Defendant was a passenger and understood that she was headed for the Christopher Morley Park which is located across the street from the St. Ignatius Retreat Home and has a large illuminated sign, with letters approximately 8 inches high, which identifies the park. As indicated, on the other side of the street the St. Ignatius Retreat Home has two pillars at its entrance with a bronze sign on each pillar with 4 to 5 inch letters. The sign is not illuminated. The vehicle in which the Defendant was riding proceeded into the grounds of the Retreat House and was stopped by a watchman and the occupants including the Defendant waited approximately 20 minutes for a Policeman to arrive. The Defendant never left the automobile.

The Defendant is charged with violating Section 1 of the Ordinance prohibiting entry upon private property of the Incorporated Village of North Hills, which provides: "No person shall enter upon any privately owned piece, parcel or lot of real property in the Village of North Hills without the permission of the owner, lessee or occupant thereof. The failure of the person, so entering upon, or found to be on, such private property, to produce upon demand, the written permission of the owner, lessee or occupant to enter upon, or to be on, such real property, shall be and shall constitute presumptive evidence of the violation of this Ordinance."

The Defendant at the conclusion of the trial moves to dismiss on the grounds that the statute is unconstitutional. Since the Ordinance is Malum Prohibitum, in all likelihood the Ordinance is constitutional. * * *

However, it is unnecessary to pass upon the constitutionality of the Ordinance since there is another basis for dismissal.

The problem presented by the facts in this case brings up for review the primary elements that are required for criminal accountability and responsibility. It is only from an accused's voluntary overt acts that criminal responsibility can attach. An overt act or a specific omission to act must occur in order for the establishment of a criminal offense. * * *

The physical element required has been designated as the *Actus Reus*. The mental element is of course better known as the *Mens Rea*. While the mental element may under certain circumstances not be required as in crimes that are designated as *Malum Prohibitum,* the *Actus Reus* is always necessary. It certainly can not be held to be the intent of the legislature to punish involuntary acts. * * *

The principle which requires a voluntary act or omission to act had been codified in the Revised Penal Law, Section 15.10 and reads as follows in part: "The minimal requirement for criminal liability is the performance by a person of conduct which includes a *voluntary act or the omission to perform an act* which he is physically capable of performing * * *"

The legislature may prescribe that an act is criminal without regard to the doer's intent or knowledge, but an involuntary act is not criminal (with certain exceptions such as involuntary acts resulting from voluntary intoxication).

In the case at bar, the People have failed to establish any act on the part of the Defendant. She merely was a passenger in a vehicle. Any action taken by the vehicle was caused and guided by the driver thereof and not by the Defendant. If the Defendant were to be held guilty under these circumstances, it would dictate that she would be guilty if she had been unconscious or asleep at the time or even if she had been a prisoner in the automobile. There are many situations which can be envisioned and in which the trespass statute in question would be improperly applied to an involuntary act. One might conceive of a driver losing control of a vehicle through mechanical failure and the vehicle proceeding onto private property which is the subject of a trespass.

Although the Court need not pass on the question, it might very well be proper to hold the driver responsible for his act even though he was under the mistaken belief that he was on his way to Christopher Morley Park. The legislature has provided statutes which make mistakes of fact or lack of knowledge no excuse in a criminal action. However, if the driver had been a Defendant, the People could have established an act on the part of the Defendant driver, to wit, turning his vehicle into the private property.

In the case of the Defendant now before the Court, however, the very first and essential element in criminal responsibility is missing, an overt voluntary act or omission to act and, accordingly, the Defendant is found not guilty.

STATE v. BUGGER

Supreme Court of Utah, 1971.
25 Utah 2d 404, 483 P.2d 442.

TUCKETT, Justice. The defendant was found guilty of a violation of Section 41–6–44, U.C.A.1953, and from that conviction he has appealed to this court.

During the night of July 28, 1969, the defendant was asleep in his automobile which was parked upon the shoulder of a road known as Tippet's Lane in Davis County. The automobile was completely off the traveled portion of the highway and the motor was not running. An officer of the Highway Patrol stopped at the scene and discovered the defendant was asleep. With some effort the officer succeeded in awakening the defendant, at which time the officer detected the smell of alcohol and arrested the defendant for being in actual physical control of the vehicle while under the influence of intoxicating liquor.

The complaint charges the defendant with the violation of the statute above referred to which provides as follows:

> It is unlawful and punishable as provided in subsection (d) of this section for any person who is under the influence of intoxicating liquor to drive or be in actual physical control of any vehicle within this state.

The defendant is here challenging the validity of the statute on the grounds of vagueness. However, we need not decide the case upon that ground. That part of the statute which states: "be in actual physical control of any vehicle" has been before the courts of other jurisdictions which have statutes with similar wordings. The word "actual" has been defined as meaning "existing in act or reality; * * * in action or existence at the time being; present; * * *."

The word "physical" is defined as "bodily," and "control" is defined as "to exercise restraining or directing influence over; to dominate; regulate; hence, to hold from actions; to curb." The term in "actual physical control" in its ordinary sense means "existing" or "present bodily restraint, directing influence, domination or regulation." It is clear that in the record before us the facts do not bring the case within the wording of the statute. The defendant at the time of his arrest was *not* controlling the vehicle, nor was he exercising any dominion over it. It is noted that the cases cited by the plaintiff in support of its position in this matter deal with entirely different fact situations, such as the case where the driver was seated in his vehicle on the traveled portion of the highway; or where the motor of the vehicle was operating; or where the driver was attempting to steer the automobile while it was in motion; or where he was attempting to brake the vehicle to arrest its motion.

We are of the opinion that the facts in this case do not make out a violation of the statute and the defendant's conviction is reversed. We do not consider it necessary to discuss the other claimed errors raised by the defendant.

CALLISTER, C. J., and HENRIOD and CROCKETT, JJ., concur.

ELLETT, Justice (dissenting).

I dissent.

The statute formerly made it unlawful for a person under the influence of intoxicating liquor to drive any vehicle upon any highway within this state. The amendment added a provision making it unlawful to be in actual physical control of a vehicle while under the influence of intoxicating liquor. It removed the need to be upon a highway before the crime was made out and did away with the necessity of driving before a crime was committed.

The reason for the change is obvious. It is better to prevent an intoxicated person in charge of an automobile from getting on the highway than it is to punish him after he gets on it. The amended statute gives officers a right to arrest a drunk person in the control of an automobile and thus prevent him from wreaking havoc a minute later by getting in traffic, or from injuring himself by his erratic driving.

It does not matter whether the motor is running or is idle nor whether the drunk is in the front seat or in the back seat. His potentiality for harm is lessened but not obviated by a silent motor or a backseat position—provided, of course, that he is the one in control of the car. It only takes a flick of the wrist to start the motor or to engage the gears, and it requires only a moment of time to get under the wheel from the back seat. A drunk in control of a motor vehicle has such a propensity to cause harm that the statute intended to make it criminal for him to be in a position to do so.

Restraining the movement of a vehicle is controlling it as much as moving it is. A person finding a drunk in the back seat of a car parked in one's driveway is likely to learn who is in control of that car if he should attempt to move it. A drunk may maliciously block one's exit, and in doing so he is in control of his own vehicle.

I think the defendant in this case was in control of his truck within the meaning of the statute even though he may have been asleep. He had the key and was the only one who could drive it. The fact that he chose to park it is no reason to say he was not in control thereof.

I, therefore, think that we should consider the question which he raises in his brief as to the validity of the statute.

Cases wherein an attack was made on statutes like ours have been decided in a number of jurisdictions. They hold the statute good.

In the case of State v. Webb, 78 Ariz. 8, 274 P.2d 338 (1954), the defendant was intoxicated and asleep in a truck parked next to some barricades in a lane of traffic. An officer passed by and observed no one in the car. Later he returned and found the defendant "passed out." The statute made it a crime to be in actual physical control of a car while under the influence of intoxicating liquor. The defendant contended that the wording of the statute was not meant to apply to a situation where the car was parked and that it was only concerned with the driving of an automobile and other acts and conduct of a positive nature. In holding that the statute was applicable to the conduct of the defendant, the court said:

> An intoxicated person seated behind the steering wheel of a motor vehicle is a threat to the safety and welfare of the public. The danger is less than that involved when the vehicle is actually moving, but it does exist.

In the case of Parker v. State, 424 P.2d 997 (Okl.Cr.App.1967), the appellant challenged the constitutionality of a statute making it unlawful for "any person who is under the influence of intoxicating liquor to drive, operate, or be in actual physical control of any motor vehicle within this state." There the defendant (appellant) claimed that the statute was unconstitutional in that it was so vague and indefinite that a person charged thereunder would be deprived of due process of law. The court held that the statute did not violate any of appellant's constitutional rights.

Under a similar statute the Montana Supreme Court in State v. Ruona, 133 Mont. 243, 321 P.2d 615 (1958), held that the statute was not void for vagueness, and in doing so said:

> * * * Thus one could have "actual physical control" while merely parking or standing still so long as one was keeping the car in restraint or in position to regulate its move-

ments. Preventing a car from moving is as much control and dominion as actually putting the car in motion on the highway. Could one exercise any more regulation over a thing, while bodily present, than prevention of movement or curbing movement. As long as one were physically or bodily able to assert dominion, in the sense of movement, then he has as much control over an object as he would if he were actually driving the vehicle.

* * * * * * * *

* * * [I]t is quite evident that the statute in the instant case is neither vague nor uncertain. * * *

The appellant here claims some federally protected rights in that he says he was improperly arrested. It is difficult for me to see where that has anything to do with guilt or innocence. If he were improperly arrested, he would have an action against the officer for false arrest, but surely our courts have not lost contact with reality to the extent that we turn a guilty man free simply "because the constable may have blundered".

From what has been said above, there is absolutely no merit to this claim. By being in control of an automobile while under the influence of intoxicating liquor, the defendant was guilty of a misdemeanor which was in the presence of the officer, and the officer had a right and a duty to arrest him.

The defendant was found guilty in the court below of being in actual physical control of his truck while he was under the influence of intoxicating liquor. He does not dispute that he was drunk. If the statute is good, we should not attempt to overrule the trier of the facts and find that the defendant was not the one actually controlling his truck.

I would affirm the judgment of the trial court.

WHEELER v. GOODMAN

United States District Court, W.D. North Carolina, 1969 (three judge).
306 F.Supp. 58.

CRAVEN, Circuit Judge. This is a suit under the Civil Rights Act, 42 U.S.C.A. § 1983 (1964), to obtain injunctive and other relief and to have the North Carolina vagrancy statute, N.C.Gen.Stat. § 14–336 (1953),[1] declared unconstitutional. After a hearing be-

1. The North Carolina statute was first enacted in 1905, but it has antecedents as early as the English statute of 1349. Today, the vagrancy statute reads, as follows:
§ 14–336. *Persons classed as vagrants.*
—If any person shall come within

any of the following classes, he shall be deemed a vagrant, and shall be fined not exceeding fifty dollars or imprisoned not exceeding thirty days: Provided, however, that this limitation of punishment shall not be binding except in cases of a first

fore a single district judge, defendants, the Charlotte, North Carolina, police, were enjoined preliminarily from unconstitutional interrogations, searches, seizures, and arrests, as well as from interference with plaintiffs' freedoms of expression and association. Wheeler v. Goodman, 298 F.Supp. 935 (W.D.N.C.1969). * * * A three-judge court has been convened to consider the constitutionality of the vagrancy statute. We hold N.C.Gen.Stat. § 14–336 unconstitutional because it is vague and overbroad; because it punishes mere status; and because it invidiously discriminates against those without property, all in violation of the Fourteenth Amendment.

I.

The twelve plaintiffs are minors, represented here by next friend. They are commonly called "hippies," a term applied to certain persons, usually young, whose standards, attitudes, and dress differ in certain special ways from the norm. The Charlotte police, on their own initiative, decided that the plaintiffs were undesirable and harassed them systematically. The harassment was designed to discourage the plaintiffs' associations with one another and to dissuade them from visiting and occupying a certain residence leased by several of the plaintiffs for a home. The police action succeeded, and the house was abandoned by the plaintiffs for fear of further harassment.

The police misbehavior was described in almost incredible detail by the district judge. See Wheeler v. Goodman, 298 F.Supp. 935 (W.D. N.C.1967). We need not repeat that description, but we note that there were fifteen instances of police harassment between December 13, 1968, and January 18, 1969, inclusive. The harassment included unlawful threats, interrogations, searches, and seizures, as well as the service of two unlawful eviction notices. During one of these instances, on January 9, 1969, several officers entered the premises leased by plaintiffs and arrested eighteen persons inside the house for vagran-

offense, and in all other cases such person may be fined or imprisoned, or both, in the discretion of the court:

1. Persons wandering or strolling about in idleness who are able to work and have no property to support them.

2. Persons leading an idle, immoral or profligate life, who have no property to support them and who are able to work and do not work.

3. All persons able to work having no property to support them and who have not some visible and known means of a fair, honest and reputable livelihood.

4. Persons having a fixed abode who have no visible property to support them and who live by stealing or by trading in, bartering for or buying stolen property.

5. Professional gamblers living in idleness.

6. All able-bodied men having no other visible means of support who shall live in idleness upon the wages or earnings of their mother, wife or minor children, except of male children over eighteen years old.

7. Keepers and inmates of bawdyhouses, assignation houses, lewd and disorderly houses, and other places where illegal sexual intercourse is habitually carried on: Provided, that nothing here is intended or shall be construed as abolishing the crime of keeping a bawdyhouse, or lessening the punishment by law for such crime.

cy.   The police said they had gone to the residence on a "routine patrol," but the only reason offered for the entry and arrests was some "profane talk," which the police said they overheard while standing in the street outside the house.   The police took plaintiffs to the station and thumbprinted them.   Several of the plaintiffs were photographed.   The cases were heard the next day and all the plaintiffs were released under a *"nolle prosequi* with leave," which means the prosecution is "suspended," but can be reopened at the state's whim.

During the period of harassment the police discovered no evidence of illegality.   Seemingly, the plaintiffs never committed any crime; nor was there probable cause to suppose that they did.

*   *   *

Here plaintiffs' real offense (to the police) consisted of their being hippies.   They were at home—not wandering about idly or otherwise.   It was enough to initiate oppressive police action that plaintiffs seemed "vaguely undesirable," * * *.

Freedom to conform to community behavior patterns is not liberty, but state regimentation.   There can never be total freedom of action for the individual, since behavior that is harmful to others cannot be permitted.   But toleration of nonconformity is the test of a mature, established government.   In the United States belief and noninjurious behavior are not punishable.   A man is free to be a hippie, a Methodist, a Jew, a Black Panther, a Kiwanian, or even a Communist, so long as his conduct does not imperil others, or infringe upon their rights.   In short, it is no crime to be a hippie.   Hughes v. Rizzo, 282 F.Supp. 881, 884 (E.D.Penn.1968).

The equal protection clause of the Fourteenth Amendment requires that a statutory classification be reasonable, as well as necessary to accomplish a permissible state policy.   McLaughlin v. Florida, 379 U.S. 184, 85 S.Ct. 283, 13 L.Ed.2d 222 (1964).   Sections 1 through 4 and 6 of the vagrancy statute are written in terms of "classes." Those with property are exempt and may live idly, blessed by the criminal law.   Those without property must be gainfully employed, and it is no excuse that there may be no jobs available.   If Washington decides to cool the economy by permitting unemployment to rise from three to five percent, the number of vagrants will increase considerably, for criminal intent is not an element of the offense.   Under Section 3 of the statute, for example, it is enough for guilt that a man (1) be able to work, (2) lack property, and (3) have no fair, honest job. To make poverty and misfortune criminal is contrary to our fundamental beliefs, and to arrest and prosecute a person under this statute violates the Fourteenth Amendment.   The equal protection clause of that Amendment does not permit the unreasonable classifications made by this statute: idleness and poverty, without fault, cannot be made the elements of a crime, and one cannot be punished as a vagrant on the premise that he may commit a crime in the future because he is presently poor and unemployed.

The due process clause of the Fourteenth Amendment prohibits as cruel and unusual the punishment of status. Robinson v. California, 370 U.S. 660, 82 S.Ct. 1417, 8 L.Ed.2d 758 (1962). Sections 1 through 4 and 6 of the statute attempt to punish economic status without mens rea. No overt act is required to convict for vagrancy—only indigency and idleness coupled with the ability to work.   *   *   *

Sections 5 and 7 require separate analysis. These sections depart completely from the traditional and historical meaning of vagrancy. In these sections the North Carolina General Assembly attributes the status of vagrant to gamblers, madams, and prostitutes. Professional gamblers and keepers and inmates of bawdy houses may well be evil persons who ought to be controlled by the sanctions of the criminal law. But to suppose, indeed, conclusively presume, that they are vagrants is irrational nonsense. One might as sensibly deem them to be Franciscan monks or murderers. One need only watch television or visit Las Vegas to observe that not all professional gamblers lack property and that many are not idle. As for inmates of bawdy houses, the legislative premise that they are visited only by the poor is manifestly absurd. Libido afflicts both the rich and poor with fine impartiality.

Where there is no rational connection between premise and conclusion, even legislative presumptions must fail. See Leary v. United States, 395 U.S. 6, 89 S.Ct. 1532, 23 L.Ed.2d 57 (1969); United States v. Romano, 382 U.S. 136, 86 S.Ct. 279, 15 L.Ed.2d 210 (1965).

Nor can Sections 5 and 7 be saved on the theory that the legislature used "vagrant" in a special sense, as a coined word without reference to its meaning at common law. Such a purpose appears very unlikely in the context of a statute using "vagrant" in its traditional sense in five other sections. But the result would be, nevertheless, unconstitutional. Status—even that of a gambler or prostitute—may not be made criminal. Powell v. Texas, 392 U.S. 514, 88 S.Ct. 2145, 20 L.Ed.2d 1254 (1968); Robinson v. California, 370 U.S. 660, 82 S.Ct. 1417, 8 L.Ed.2d 758 (1962). The *acts* of gambling, prostitution, and operating bawdy houses are criminally punishable, of course, but the state cannot create the special status of vagrant for persons who commit those illegal acts and then punish the status instead of the act. The due process clause of the Fourteenth Amendment is violated by the statute's attempt to do so.

*   *   *

Although we must invalidate the vagrancy statute, we are not indifferent to the problems of the police. A statute that will allow the police to stop crime before it starts is both necessary and desirable. The extent to which idleness breeds crime is not established on this record, or otherwise, as far as we know. Assuming the relationship, however, the North Carolina statute goes too far. Crime prevention is not an absolute value. Methods of prevention are constantly weighed against the personal liberties enshrined in the Constitution. Here the outrageous police action under color of the vagrancy statute is far too high a price to pay for crime prevention. This conclusion is especially valid where, as here, crime prevention can be accomplished by legitimate means.[9] We reiterate, however, that the record does not suggest that the plaintiffs ever contemplated any criminal activity.

* * *

NOTE

An interesting discussion of the history and use of vagrancy statutes is found in Mr. Justice Douglas' opinion in Papachristou v. Jacksonville, reprinted in part at page 192. There, for a unanimous court, the vagrancy ordinance of the City of Jacksonville was held void for vagueness.

---

2. LIABILITY BASED ON FAILURE TO ACT

JONES v. UNITED STATES

United States Court of Appeals for the District of Columbia, 1962.
113 U.S.App.D.C. 352, 308 F.2d 307.

WRIGHT, Circuit Judge. Appellant, together with one Shirley Green, was tried on a three-count indictment charging them jointly with (1) abusing and maltreating Robert Lee Green, (2) abusing and maltreating Anthony Lee Green, and (3) involuntary manslaughter through failure to perform their legal duty of care for Anthony Lee Green, which failure resulted in his death. At the close of evidence, after trial to a jury, the first two counts were dismissed as to both defendants. On the third count, appellant was convicted of involuntary manslaughter. Shirley Green was found not guilty.

Appellant urges several grounds for reversal. We need consider but two. First, appellant argues that there was insufficient evidence as a matter of law to warrant a jury finding of breach of duty in the

---

9. Despite innovative court decisions of the last decade that have made law enforcement more difficult, the police are not yet, and we hope will never be, helpless to prevent crime. Arrests may still be made upon probable cause to believe a crime has been committed, Wong Sun v. United States, 371 U.S. 471, 83 S.Ct. 407, 9 L.Ed.2d 441 (1963); Henry v. United States, 361 U.S. 98, 80 S.Ct. 168, 4 L.Ed.2d 134 (1959), search warrants may yet be procured, Spinelli v. United States, 393 U.S. 410, 89 S.Ct. 584, 21 L.Ed.2d 637 (1969); Aguilar v. Texas, 378 U.S. 108, 114 n. 4, 84 S.Ct. 1509, 12 L.Ed.2d 723 (1964); Jones v. United States, 362 U.S. 257, 268, 80 S.Ct. 725, 4 L.Ed.2d 697 (1960), and "stop and frisk" laws, properly drawn, enable investigation of suspicious conduct, as well as interrogations of those suspected of criminal intent, Peters v. New York, 392 U.S. 40, 88 S.Ct. 1889, 20 L.Ed.2d 917 (1968); Terry v. Ohio, 392 U.S. 1, 88 S.Ct. 1868, 20 L.Ed.2d 889 (1968). Moreover, legislation has been proposed that would give the police extensive power to stop and interrogate persons for investigative purposes. Model Code of Prearraignment Procedure, Art. 2 (1969) (Tent.Draft No. 2).

care she rendered Anthony Lee. Alternatively, appellant argues that the trial court committed plain error in failing to instruct the jury that it must first find that appellant was under a legal obligation to provide food and necessities to Anthony Lee before finding her guilty of manslaughter in failing to provide them. The first argument is without merit. Upon the latter we reverse.

A summary of the evidence, which is in conflict upon almost every significant issue, is necessary for the disposition of both arguments. In late 1957, Shirley Green became pregnant, out of wedlock, with a child, Robert Lee, subsequently born August 17, 1958. Apparently to avoid the embarrassment of the presence of the child in the Green home, it was arranged that appellant, a family friend, would take the child to her home after birth. Appellant did so, and the child remained there continuously until removed by the police on August 5, 1960. Initially appellant made some motions toward the adoption of Robert Lee, but these came to naught, and shortly thereafter it was agreed that Shirley Green was to pay appellant $72 a month for his care. According to appellant, these payments were made for only five months. According to Shirley Green, they were made up to July 1960.

Early in 1959 Shirley Green again became pregnant, this time with the child Anthony Lee, whose death is the basis of appellant's conviction. This child was born October 21, 1959. Soon after birth, Anthony Lee developed a mild jaundice condition, attributed to a blood incompatability with his mother. The jaundice resulted in his retention in the hospital for three days beyond the usual time, or until October 26, 1959, when, on authorization signed by Shirley Green, Anthony Lee was released by the hospital to appellant's custody. Shirley Green, after a two or three day stay in the hospital, also lived with appellant for three weeks, after which she returned to her parents' home, leaving the children with appellant. She testified she did not see them again, except for one visit in March, until August 5, 1960. Consequently, though there does not seem to have been any specific monetary agreement with Shirley Green covering Anthony Lee's support,[5] appellant had complete custody of both children until they were rescued by the police.

With regard to medical care, the evidence is undisputed. In March, 1960, appellant called a Dr. Turner to her home to treat Anthony Lee for a bronchial condition. Appellant also telephoned the doctor at various times to consult with him concerning Anthony Lee's diet and health. In early July, 1960, appellant took Anthony Lee to Dr. Turner's office where he was treated for "simple diarrhea." At this time the doctor noted the "wizened" appearance of the child and told appellant to tell the mother of the child that he should be taken to a hospital. This was not done.

5. It was uncontested that during the entire period the children were in appellant's home, appellant had ample means to provide food and medical care.

On August 2, 1960, two collectors for the local gas company had occasion to go to the basement of appellant's home, and there saw the two children. Robert Lee and Anthony Lee at this time were age two years and ten months respectively. Robert Lee was in a "crib" consisting of a framework of wood, covered with a fine wire screening, including the top which was hinged. The "crib" was lined with newspaper, which was stained, apparently with feces, and crawling with roaches. Anthony Lee was lying in a bassinet and was described as having the appearance of a "small baby monkey." One collector testified to seeing roaches on Anthony Lee.

On August 5, 1960, the collectors returned to appellant's home in the company of several police officers and personnel of the Women's Bureau. At this time, Anthony Lee was upstairs in the dining room in the bassinet, but Robert Lee was still downstairs in his "crib." The officers removed the children to the D. C. General Hospital where Anthony Lee was diagnosed as suffering from severe malnutrition and lesions over large portions of his body, apparently caused by severe diaper rash. Following admission, he was fed repeatedly, apparently with no difficulty, and was described as being very hungry. His death, 34 hours after admission, was attributed without dispute to malnutrition. At birth, Anthony Lee weighed six pounds, fifteen ounces—at death at age ten months, he weighed seven pounds, thirteen ounces. Normal weight at this age would have been approximately 14 pounds.

Appellant argues that nothing in the evidence establishes that she failed to provide food to Anthony Lee. She cites her own testimony and the testimony of a lodger, Mr. Wills, that she did in fact feed the baby regularly. At trial, the defense made repeated attempts to extract from the medical witnesses opinions that the jaundice, or the condition which caused it, might have prevented the baby from assimilating food. The doctors conceded this was possible but not probable since the autopsy revealed no condition which would support the defense theory. It was also shown by the disinterested medical witnesses that the child had no difficulty in ingesting food immediately after birth, and that Anthony Lee, in the last hours before his death, was able to take several bottles, apparently without difficulty, and seemed very hungry. This evidence, combined with the absence of any physical cause for nonassimilation, taken in the context of the condition in which these children were kept, presents a jury question on the feeding issue.

Moreover, there is substantial evidence from which the jury could have found that appellant failed to obtain proper medical care for the child. Appellant relies upon the evidence showing that on one occasion she summoned a doctor for the child, on another took the child to the doctor's office, and that she telephoned the doctor on several occasions about the baby's formula. However, the last time a doctor saw the child was a month before his death, and appellant admitted that on that occasion the doctor recommended hospitalization.

Appellant did not hospitalize the child, nor did she take any other steps to obtain medical care in the last crucial month. Thus there was sufficient evidence to go to the jury on the issue of medical care, as well as failure to feed.

Appellant also takes exception to the failure of the trial court to charge that the jury must find beyond a reasonable doubt, as an element of the crime, that appellant was under a legal duty to supply food and necessities to Anthony Lee. Appellant's attorney did not object to the failure to give this instruction, but urges here the application of Rule 52(b).

The problem of establishing the duty to take action which would preserve the life of another has not often arisen in the case law of this country.[7] The most commonly cited statement of the rule is found in People v. Beardsley, 150 Mich. 206, 113 N.W. 1128, 1129, 13 L.R.A.,N.S., 1020:

> "The law recognizes that under some circumstances the omission of a duty owed by one individual to another, where such omission results in the death of the one to whom the duty is owing, will make the other chargeable with manslaughter. * * * This rule of law is always based upon the proposition that the duty neglected must be a legal duty, and not a mere moral obligation. It must be a duty imposed by law or by contract, and the omission to perform the duty must be the immediate and direct cause of death. * * *"

There are at least four situations in which the failure to act may constitute breach of a legal duty. One can be held criminally liable: first, where a statute imposes a duty to care for another;[8] second, where one stands in a certain status relationship to another;[9] third, where one has assumed a contractual duty to care for another; and fourth, where one has voluntarily assumed the care of another and so secluded the helpless person as to prevent others from rendering aid.

It is the contention of the Government that either the third or the fourth ground is applicable here. However, it is obvious that in any of the four situations, there are critical issues of fact which must be passed on by the jury—specifically in this case, whether appellant had entered into a contract with the mother for the care of Anthony Lee or, alternatively, whether she assumed the care of the child and

7. The problem has evoked considerable study. See, e. g., Holmes, The Common Law, p. 278 (1881); Moreland, A Rationale of Criminal Negligence, ch. 10 (1944); Hughes, Criminal Omissions, 67 Yale L.J. 590, 620–626 (1958); Annot., 10 A.L.R. 1137 (1921).

8. See, e. g., D.C.Code, § 22–902; Craig v. State, 220 Md. 590, 155 A.2d 684.

9. A.L.R. Annot., supra, Note 7 (parent to child); Territory v. Manton, 8 Mont. 95, 19 P. 387 (husband to wife); Regina v. Smith, 8 Carr. & P. 153 (Eng. 1837) (master to apprentice); United States v. Knowles, 26 Fed.Cas. 800 (No. 15,540) (ship's master to crew and passengers); cf. State v. Reitze, 86 N. J.L. 407, 92 A. 576 (innkeeper to inebriated customers).

secluded him from the care of his mother, his natural protector. On both of these issues, the evidence is in direct conflict, appellant insisting that the mother was actually living with appellant and Anthony Lee, and hence should have been taking care of the child herself, while Shirley Green testified she was living with her parents and was paying appellant to care for both children.

In spite of this conflict, the instructions given in the case failed even to suggest the necessity for finding a legal duty of care. The only reference to duty in the instructions was the reading of the indictment which charged, inter alia, that the defendants "failed to perform their legal duty." A finding of legal duty is the critical element of the crime charged and failure to instruct the jury concerning it was plain error.

* * *

Reversed and remanded.

NOTES

1. One of Mrs. Clark's twin girls dies at four months of age due to a combination of medical factors of a continuing nature, malnutrition, dehydration, fecal impaction. Mrs. Clark never sought medical aid though she had access to a telephone. Is she criminally responsible? For what offense? State v. Clark, 5 Conn.Cir. 699, 261 A.2d 294 (1969).

2. The following statute is proposed for your jurisdiction. Would you support it or not? What if any changes would you recommend?

Liability for Omission. A person shall be criminally responsible for a result if he fails to take action to prevent that result, but for his failure to take action the result would not have occurred, and the failure to take action constitutes a substantial deviation from common decency. In determining whether a failure to act constitutes a substantial deviation from common decency the following factors shall be taken into account:

1. the seriousness of the result,

2. the likelihood that the result would occur without action,

3. any burden or risk which taking action would have required the person to assume, and

4. any responsibility of the person for creating the need for action.

Compare this proposal with that of the Proposed Texas Penal Code.

Sec. 6.03 Criminal Responsibility for Omission

A person does not commit an offense if his criminal responsibility is based solely on an omission to perform a voluntary act unless:

(1) the law defining the offense imposes criminal responsibility for the omission; or

(2) a duty to perform the omitted voluntary act is imposed by statute.

Statutes quite similar to the first proposal are found in European Codes. Feldbrugge, "Good and Bad Samaritans," 14 Am.J.Comp.L. 630 (1966). The Texas proposal is typical of the Anglo-American approach to this issue. Why do you think there is this difference? Which is preferable in dealing with the following problems?

a. A, from the safety of his home, sees a young woman being assaulted by a man on a deserted street in the early hours of the morning. She cries for aid, screaming: "Oh my God, he stabbed me! Please help me!" A shouts at the assailant who stops momentarily but then pursues the victim. A takes no further action and the victim is again struck. The police, responding to a call from B who passes by after the assault has ended, arrive within two minutes after being notified. The victim dies on the way to the hospital.

b. A, a physician who has stopped at a rural restaurant while on vacation, hears a distraught young man announce that his wife is in very painful labor in a car outside. He asks if there is a doctor there or nearby. A does not respond but gets in his car and drives away. For want of proper assistance the woman and child perish.

c. Assume that the young man in #2 is rushing his wife to the hospital when he is involved in a minor accident with A who is at least partly to blame. The young man's car is disabled but A, fearing loss of his license because of prior violations and possible criminal penalties if his involvement is discovered by the police, flees the scene. Because the woman can't be taken to the hospital in time she and the child perish.

d. A, a school-crossing guard, leaves her post to obtain a cup of coffee on a bitterly cold winter day. A first-grader, slightly late for school, dashes across the street and is struck and killed by a car.

e. A group of air traffic controllers call in sick in a wage dispute knowing that there are insufficient replacements. In the course of diverting planes from that area, a mistake is made by an inexperienced substitute and a crash ensues killing all aboard.

3. Can one be convicted of a criminal omission in the absence of knowledge of the duty to act? See Lambert v. California, 355 U.S. 225, 78 S.Ct. 240, 2 L.Ed.2d 228 (1957) reprinted at page 456. If it had been established that the defendant in *Jones* had contracted to care for the child would a defense of ignorance as to the scope of her duties been permitted?

4. What relevance, if any, does the law regarding liability for failure to act have to the criminalization of possession?

5. Defendant, as secretary-treasurer of a local union, was under a statutory duty to file an annual financial report of the union with the Secretary of Labor. He is charged with willfully violating the statute on the grounds that although aware of this duty the report was not filed. May he defend his failure on the grounds that it was impossible for him to comply? United States v. Spingola, 464 F.2d 909 (7th Cir. 1972).

3. SPECIFIC REQUIREMENTS IMPOSED BY SUBSTANTIVE LAW

In the substantive definition of a number of crimes, no attempt is made to define the "act" which the defendant must have committed. In such cases—the homicide offenses are perhaps the best example—any voluntary physical movement or failure to move that meets general requirements is sufficient. The substantive definition of other crimes, however, contains a more limited definition of the "act" which must have been performed. The following material presents cases dealing with such limited definitions in a number of offenses. In regard to each, consider the policy reasons for limiting those acts which will give rise to liability, and the extent to which the specific definition of the required act well serves those policies.

a. IMPORTANCE OF STATUTORY DEFINITIONS

STATE v. DECINA

Court of Appeals of New York, 1956.
2 N.Y.2d 133, 138 N.E.2d 799.

FROESSEL, Judge. At about 3:30 p. m. on March 14, 1955, a bright, sunny day, defendant was driving, alone in his car, in a northerly direction on Delaware Avenue in the city of Buffalo. The portion of Delaware Avenue here involved is 60 feet wide. At a point south of an overhead viaduct of the Erie Railroad, defendant's car swerved to the left, across the center line in the street, so that it was completely in the south lane, traveling 35 to 40 miles per hour.

It then veered sharply to the right, crossing Delaware Avenue and mounting the easterly curb at a point beneath the viaduct and continued thereafter at a speed estimated to have been about 50 or 60 miles per hour or more. During this latter swerve, a pedestrian testified that he saw defendant's hand above his head; another witness said he saw defendant's left arm bent over the wheel, and his right hand extended towards the right door.

A group of six schoolgirls were walking north on the easterly sidewalk of Delaware Avenue, two in front and four slightly in the rear, when defendant's car struck them from behind. One of the girls escaped injury by jumping against the wall of the viaduct. The bodies of the children struck were propelled northward onto the street and the lawn in front of a coal company, located to the north of the Erie viaduct on Delaware Avenue. Three of the children, 6 to 12 years old, were found dead on arrival by the medical examiner, and a fourth child, 7 years old, died in a hospital two days later as a result of injuries sustained in the accident.

[Testimony was received from Dr. Wechter, a resident physician at the facility to which appellant was taken after the accident.]

The direct examination was then continued, the doctor being permitted to state the conversation with defendant over objection and exception. He asked defendant how he felt and what had happened. Defendant, who still felt a little dizzy or blurry, said that as he was driving he noticed a jerking of his right hand, which warned him that he might develop a convulsion, and that as he tried to steer the car over to the curb he felt himself becoming unconscious, and he thought he had a convulsion. He was aware that children were in front of his car, but did not know whether he had struck them.

Defendant then proceeded to relate to Dr. Wechter his past medical history.

On the basis of this medical history, Dr. Wechter made a diagnosis of Jacksonian epilepsy, and was of the opinion that defendant had a seizure at the time of the accident. Other members of the hospital staff performed blood tests and took an electroencephalogram during defendant's three-day stay there. The testimony of Dr. Wechter is the only testimony before the trial court showing that defendant had epilepsy, suffered an attack at the time of the accident, and had knowledge of his susceptibility to such attacks.

Defendant was indicted and charged with violating section 1053–a of the Penal Law, Consol.Laws, c. 40.

We turn first to the subject of defendant's cross appeal, namely, that his demurrer should have been sustained, since the *indictment* here does not charge a crime. The indictment states essentially that defendant, *knowing* "that he was subject to epileptic attacks or other disorder rendering him likely to lose consciousness for a considerable period of time", was culpably negligent "in that he *consciously* undertook to and *did operate* his Buick sedan on a public highway" (emphasis supplied) and "while so doing" suffered such an attack which caused said automobile "to travel at a fast and reckless rate of speed, jumping the curb and driving over the sidewalk" causing the death of 4 persons. In our opinion, this clearly states a violation of section 1053–a of the Penal Law. The statute does not require that a defendant must deliberately intend to kill a human being, for that would be murder. Nor does the statute require that he knowingly and consciously follow the precise path that leads to death and destruction. It is sufficient, we have said, when his conduct manifests a "disregard of the consequences which may ensue from the act, and indifference to the rights of others. No clearer definition, applicable to the hundreds of varying circumstances that may arise, can be given. Under a given state of facts, whether negligence is culpable is a question of judgment." People v. Angelo, 246 N.Y. 451, 457, 159 N.E. 394, 396.

Assuming the truth of the indictment, as we must on a demurrer, this defendant knew he was subject to epileptic attacks and seizures that might strike *at any time*. He also knew that a moving motor vehicle uncontrolled on a public highway is a highly dangerous instrumentality capable of unrestrained destruction. With this *knowledge*, and without anyone accompanying him, he deliberately took a chance by making a conscious choice of a course of action, in disregard of the consequences which he knew might follow from his conscious act, and which in this case did ensue. How can we say as a matter of law that this did not amount to culpable negligence within the meaning of section 1053–a?

To hold otherwise would be to say that a man may freely indulge himself in liquor in the same hope that it will not affect his driving, and if it later develops that ensuing intoxication causes dangerous and reckless driving resulting in death, his unconsciousness or involuntariness at that time would relieve him from prosecution under the statute. His awareness of a condition which he knows may produce such consequences as here, and his disregard of the consequences, renders him liable for culpable negligence, as the courts below have properly held. To have a sudden sleeping spell, an unexpected heart or other disabling attack, without any prior knowledge or warning thereof, is an altogether different situation, and there is simply no basis for comparing such cases with the flagrant disregard manifested here.

It is suggested in the dissenting opinion that a new approach to licensing would prevent such disastrous consequences upon our public highways. But would it—and how and when? The mere possession of a driver's license is no defense to a prosecution under section 1053–a; nor does it assure continued ability to drive during the period of the license. It may be noted in passing, and not without some significance, that defendant strenuously and successfully objected to the district attorney's offer of his applications for such license in evidence, upon the ground that whether or not he was licensed has nothing to do with the case. Under the view taken by the dissenters, this defendant would be immune from prosecution under this statute even if he were unlicensed. Section 1053–a places a personal responsibility on each driver of a vehicle—whether licensed or not—and not upon a licensing agency.

Accordingly, the Appellate Division properly sustained the lower court's order overruling the demurrer, as well as its denial of the motion in arrest of judgment on the same ground.

DESMOND, Judge (concurring in part and dissenting in part).

Section 1053–a of the Penal Law describes the crime of "criminal negligence in the operation of a vehicle resulting in death". Declared to be guilty of that crime is "A person who operates or drives any vehicle of any kind in a reckless or culpably negligent manner, whereby a human being is killed". The essentials of the crime are, therefore, first, vehicle *operation* in a culpably negligent *manner*, and, second, the resulting death of a person. This indictment asserts that defendant violated section 1053–a, but it then proceeds in the language quoted in the next-above paragraph of this opinion to describe the way in which defendant is supposed to have offended against that statute.   That descriptive matter (an inseparable and controlling ingredient of the indictment, Code Crim.Proc. §§ 275, 276; People v. Dumar, 106 N.Y. 502, 13 N.E. 325) shows that defendant did *not* violate section 1053–a.   No *operation* of an automobile in a reckless manner is charged against defendant.   The excessive speed of the car and its jumping the curb were "caused", says the indictment itself, by defendant's prior "attack and loss of consciousness".   Therefore, what defendant is accused of is *not* reckless or culpably negligent driving, which necessarily connotes and involves consciousness and volition.   The fatal assault by this car was after and because of defendant's failure of consciousness.   To say that one drove a car in a reckless manner in that his unconscious condition caused the car to travel recklessly is to make two mutually contradictory assertions.   One cannot be "reckless" while unconscious.   One cannot while unconscious "operate" a car in a culpably negligent manner or in any other "manner".   The statute makes criminal a particular kind of knowing, voluntary, immediate operation.   It does not touch at all the involuntary presence of an unconscious person at the wheel of an uncontrolled vehicle.   To negative the possibility of applying section 1053–a to these alleged facts we do not even have to resort to the rule that all criminal statutes are closely and strictly construed in favor of the citizen and that no act or omission is criminal unless specifically and in terms so labeled by a clearly worded statute, People v. Benc, 288 N.Y. 318, 323, 43 N.E.2d 61, 63, and cases cited.

Tested by its history section 1053–a has the same meaning: penalization of conscious operation of a vehicle in a culpably negligent manner.   It is significant that until this case (and the Eckert case, 2 N.Y. 2d 126, 157 N.Y.S.2d 551, 138 N.E.2d 794, handed down herewith) no attempt was ever made to penalize, either under section 1053–a or as manslaughter, the wrong done by one whose foreseeable blackout while driving had consequences fatal to another person.

NOTES

1.   Did the majority in *Decina* evade the act requirement?   Is there any function of the doctrine that was not satisfied by the majority's analysis and did that analysis focus on conduct or state of mind?

2.   The relevant statute in *Decina*, 1053–a, carried a maximum penalty of five years and/or $1,000.   It was the source, in part, of two provisions in the new New York Penal Code:

§ 125.10   Criminally negligent homicide

A person is guilty of criminally negligent homicide when, with criminal negligence, he causes the death of another person.

Criminally negligent homicide is a class E felony.   (one to four years).

§ 125.15   Manslaughter in the second degree

A person is guilty of manslaughter in the second degree when:

1.   He recklessly causes the death of another person   .   .   .

Manslaughter in the second degree is a class C felony. (one to fifteen years).

How would Mr. Decina have fared under these provisions? Would the analysis have been the same?

---

b.   PROPERTY ACQUISITION OFFENSES

The following cases all involve the misappropriation or attempted misappropriation of property without any threat to the person of another. They illustrate only a handful of the many statutory formulations which, largely as a function of history, attempt to distinguish among various crimes of acquisition: e. g., theft, theft by false pretext, conversion by a bailee, theft from the person, shoplifting, acquisition of property by theft, swindling, embezzlement, extortion, receiving or concealing embezzled or stolen property. The various statutes turn in their application on such niceties as whether or not the accused obtained possession of the property by trespass (larceny as contrasted with embezzlement) or whether the owner in reliance on the accused's misrepresentations of fact delivered mere possession or title (larceny by trick as contrasted with false pretenses). The fine distinctions required in the application of these laws have produced considerable appellate litigation.

(1) LARCENY

ROGERS v. STATE

Supreme Court of Arkansas, 1970.
458 S.W.2d 369.

FOGLEMAN, Justice.   Appellant was convicted of the larceny of a boat and trailer belonging to Maxwell's Esso Station. His appeal questions the sufficiency of the evidence to support the jury verdict. Viewing it in the light most favorable to the state, we find it sufficient.

Morris Maxwell, proprietor of the station, kept boats and motors as stock-in-trade. On the night preceding February 5, 1970, he left one boat resting on a trailer chained to a light pole on the north side of the station. About 2:30 a. m. on February 5, Officers Paul Wood and Harold Flowers were patrolling the street in front of the station and saw a Thunderbird automobile backed up to the boat and a man standing behind the auto. They drove their patrol car to the next driveway on the street and watched the car at the station. When they saw this car pull out from the station, they pursued it to a driveway of a fire station on another street and blocked the Thunderbird there as the driver attempted to turn it around. The driver was identified by Paul Wood as the defendant and the person seen behind the vehicle at Maxwell's station. The officers looked into this automobile and saw a pair of bolt cutters lying on the right front floorboard. There was a trailer hitch on the rear of this vehicle. The defendant was arrested and searched. He had a small, cheap .22 caliber gun in a coat pocket. The officers then returned to the Maxwell station with the defendant in custody. There they found that the boat had been moved from its previous position and the chain by which it was secured to the lamp post cut.

The bolt cutters and chain were taken to the police station and on February 6 delivered by the Chief of Police to Paul McDonald, who was in charge of the State Police Firearms Identification Laboratory. McDonald testified that when a tool is manufactured, machine marks are left which are identifiable in the marks made by that tool. It was his opinion that the severed link of the chain had been cut by that particular set of cutters. It was stipulated that the boat and trailer were never removed from Maxwell's premises.

The principal argument advanced by appellant is that the evidence fails to show that the defendant ever had such possession and control of the boat and trailer adverse to the owner to constitute the crime of larceny. This argument is based upon the fact that the tongue of the trailer supporting the boat was only lifted off a block upon which it rested, and that no evidence showed that the trailer was ever hitched to defendant's automobile. We find this argument invalid.

We have said that the requisite element of asportation in larceny cases may be found from the slightest removal of goods from the place where they were left by the owner. The fact that the property was not actually removed from the owner's premises does not make the thief's dominion over it incomplete nor preclude a finding that there was an asportation. Banks v. State, 133 Ark. 169, 202 S.W. 43. In cases from other jurisdictions, it has been held that: moving a safe in a building five feet before the owner arrived is an asportation, Caruso v. State, 205 Tenn. 211, 326 S.W.2d 434 (1958); removal only a hair's breadth is sufficient, Gettinger v. State, 13 Neb. 308, 14 N.W. 403 (1882); the slightest change of location is sufficient, Lundy v. State, 60 Ga. 143 (1878); the least removal of a thing from the place it was located is sufficient, Wombles v. Commonwealth, 317 S.W.2d 169 (Ky.Ct.App.1958); the act of asportation is complete when the property taken is moved from its original position regardless of however slight may be the change of position, Blakeney v. State, 31 Ala. App. 154, 13 So.2d 424 (1942), reversed for error in instructions, Blakeney v. State, 244 Ala. 262, 13 So.2d 430 (1943).

It was reasonable for the jury to infer that appellant, with larcenous intent, cut the chain by which the boat and trailer had been fastened to the light pole, and removed them from their original position where they were supported by a concrete block in order to fasten the tongue of the trailer to the hitch on his vehicle. The evidence was sufficient to show asportation and felonious intent.

The judgment is affirmed.

RAY v. UNITED STATES

Court of Appeals of the District of Columbia, 1967.
229 A.2d 161.

MYERS, Associate Judge. After trial by the court, appellant was found guilty of petit larceny of United States property in violation of 18 U.S.C.A. § 641.[1]

Appellant was employed by a professional mover who was an independent contractor of the United States government. On the day of the alleged larceny, appellant's duties were to transport and deliver several chairs and a typewriter from a storage area in the city to the warehouse area of the Department of Commerce. After part of his load had been transferred from the truck to the warehouse, appellant was seen carrying an adding machine covered with wrapping paper out of the storage room of the warehouse. His explanation was that he was temporarily moving the adding machine to free space on a skid, thus permitting him to keep his entire load together. Although testimony differed as to how far he carried the machine, it is clear he never went beyond the warehouse area or carried the machine outside the building. On these facts, we feel the trial judge erred as a matter of law in his finding of guilt beyond a reasonable doubt.

Larceny from the United States is merely a codification of common law larceny, with the owner specified in the statute. As such it retains the common law elements of asportation and intent. While we are mindful that the slightest moving or taking may constitute an asportation when viewed with other circumstances, appellant had the government's permission, as a normal incident of his employment duties, to move and carry certain articles in and around the warehouse area. This he had done on previous occasions. Under principles of agency, he had the implied permission to touch, move and carry other articles in the same area to facilitate the proper performance of his duties. He would be guilty of larceny only if his possession of the adding machine was clearly adverse and contrary to the interest of its rightful owner, the United States. Since it was without doubt within appellant's scope of employment to pick up and carry articles for the purpose of rearranging items stored, some other act on the part

---

1. The information charged that he did "unlawfully embezzle, steal, purloin and knowingly convert to his own use and use of another, and without authority sell, convey and dispose of an adding machine, a thing of value of the United States and of a department or agency thereof."

of appellant would be necessary to allow a reasonable inference of criminal intent. Although intent is generally a question for the trier of fact, we find no substantial evidence from which criminal intent could be inferred here, and, without intent, the element of asportation in this case fails for want of adequate showing.

Reversed with directions to enter a judgment of acquittal.

---

(2) EMBEZZLEMENT

STATE v. WILLIAMS

Supreme Court of Iowa, 1970.
179 N.W.2d 756.

BECKER, Justice. Defendant was indicted and tried for the crime of embezzlement by bailee, section 710.4, Code of Iowa, 1966.[1] Jury verdict of guilty was returned, defendant's post trial motions were overruled and he was sentenced to the State Penitentiary for a term not exceeding five years. He appeals. We reverse.

The embezzlement charge is an outgrowth of a business arrangement between defendant, his father and Liberty Livestock Farms, a partnership owned by Dwaine Clark and Dr. Joe Graham. Both Earl Williams, defendant's father and Dwaine Clark, one of the partners, were deceased at time of trial.

The parties mentioned entered into an agreement under which the partnership was to deliver 35 head of Hampshire open gilt hogs and 2 boars to defendant and his father for breeding purposes. Defendant and his father were to keep the hogs long enough to farrow and raise two litters of pigs. Thereafter the partnership was to receive one hog from each litter plus the return of the hogs originally delivered.

The 35 gilts and two boars were delivered as agreed to the farm owned by defendant's father and operated by defendant. Defendant took delivery of the animals.

The contract provided the gilts were to be large enough to breed and the boars large enough for service. One of the State's witnesses notes that he talked to defendant after the hogs were delivered and received complaints that the hogs were too small. Defendant claims the hogs were too small and were returned.

The contract contemplated defendant and his father would have the hogs on their farm for over a year. Delivery was made February 24, 1967. Frank Madera told of visiting defendant's farm and seeing

---

1. "Embezzlement by bailee. Whoever embezzles or fraudulently converts to his own use, or secretes with intent to embezzle or fraudulently convert to his own use, money, goods, or property delivered to him, or any part thereof, which may be the subject of larceny, shall be guilty of larceny and punished accordingly."

the hogs in early April 1967. Dwaine Clark died May 27, 1967. His son-in-law, Leo Seuferer, took over the management of the partnership, discovered the contract for 35 gilts and two boars in the active file but took no further action until February 3, 1968, when he went to defendant's farm to check on the animals. Neither defendant nor his father was at home. Seuferer looked around the premises but saw no hogs. Two days later he reached defendant on the telephone and asked how the hogs were getting along. Defendant said they were doing fine. Seuferer then said he had been at the farm the previous Saturday and did not see any hogs on the farm. The telephone then went dead and Seuferer could not immediately reestablish connections.

Later the same evening Seuferer again called defendant and said he wanted to pick up the animals belonging to Liberty Livestock Farms. Defendant said he and his father did not have the animals, they had only been on the farm about a week when they were picked up. Defendant said he had been thinking about another deal when Seuferer had called earlier in the evening.

Defendant acknowledges the above telephone calls but denies the substance of the conversation. He denied he hung up on the first conversation and said that during the second conversation he told Seuferer Dwaine Clark had picked up the hogs.

Defendant did not produce the hogs and Seuferer then took the matter to the county attorney. The result was the instant indictment.

The first line of defense was that the State did not generate a jury question on all essential elements of the crime charged. The affirmative portion of the defense was that the hogs were returned to their rightful owners. Defendant contends the hogs were too small for proper breeding when delivered. His father was dissatisfied and called Dwaine Clark. Defendant's wife testified Dwaine Clark and a trucker came and took the hogs away while defendant was working in the fields. She was in the house. Earl Williams, defendant's father, went out and helped load the animals.

Since Dwaine Clark, the manager of the partnership that owned the hogs, died May 1967, shortly after the hogs were delivered and Earl Williams, defendant's father, died July 20, 1968, three weeks before defendant was indicted, the only person active in the contract, and still alive, was defendant. No evidence was produced as to how the partnership kept track of its hogs, what books were kept on financial transactions or what, if any, evidence the partnership papers contained as to whether the hogs in question had or had not been returned. In this regard the sole evidence was by James Clark and Leo Seuferer. Both said to the best of their knowledge no hogs had been returned but they did not know what, if anything, Dwaine Clark might have done about the hogs in April 1967. Seuferer said he found the contract under which the hogs were delivered in the active files maintained by Dwaine Clark at the time of his death in May 1967. Dr. Graham was an inactive partner and knew nothing about the matter.

*   *   *

Embezzlement was not a crime at common law, 2 Burdick, Law of Crime, § 574, p. 351; 29A C.J.S. Embezzlement § 2, p. 4. In Iowa embezzlement and all other crimes are wholly statutory. State v. Wallace, 259 Iowa 765, 772, 145 N.W.2d 615.

Chapter 710, Code, 1966, deals with embezzlement in several sections which define distinct and separate crimes; i. e., embezzlement by public officers, § 710.1; by bailee, § 710.4; by agents, § 710.9; et cetera. These crimes are similar but not subject to identical rules, State v. Cavanaugh, 214 Iowa 457, 460, 236 N.W. 96.

The different crimes of embezzlement covering different situations are noted here because of a rule laid down in State v. Bryan, 40 Iowa 379, 381, 382:

"The crime with which the defendant is charged, is that of converting the money which came into his hands as treasurer to his own use. The rule is too well established to require citation of authorities to verify it, that conversion may be shown either by direct proof of the fact of conversion, or by proof of a demand and refusal. Where the fact of conversion is sought to be proved by evidence of a demand and refusal, it may always be met and neutralized by evidence showing an excuse for this refusal; and when the excuse shown is sufficient, then the evidence of a demand and refusal does not establish the fact of conversion. * * *

"But this doctrine does not apply to the crime of embezzlement as defined by the next section of our statute, (Code, 3909). (Now § 710.5, at that time § 710.3, embezzlement by bailee had not been enacted.) There the doctrine relied upon by appellant's counsel and vindicated by the authorities they cite applies."

The State's brief relies on the above rule: " * * * The State showed that appellant signed an agreement to lease certain hogs, the hogs were delivered to appellant and when the lease expired a demand was made on appellant to return the hogs and the hogs were never returned. Obviously the State sustained its burden in proving the elements of the crime in question and the case was properly submitted to the jury." If the rule applies to embezzlement by bailee there is sufficient evidence for a jury case. This rule, under which the State need only show receipt of the property, demand and refusal to redeliver, is peculiar to embezzlement by public officials. State v. Bryan, supra, so states. Reference to section 710.1 relating to public officials will show the wealth of prohibited acts provided in the section and a rational basis for the rule.

In cases charging embezzlement by persons other than public officials a different rule applies. Ordinarily, fraudulent conversion to defendant's use must be shown. Cf. Footnote 1. See also, 2 Burdick, Law of Crime, § 575, p. 353: " * * * the accused must have fraudulently converted the property; and under most statutes, there must be an intent to defraud."

We have had little occasion in the past to consider the quantum of proof of conversion required necessary in cases of this kind. In similar cases there has always been proof of some overt act of defendant which is inconsistent with the rights of the true owner of the property; State v. Dykes (Iowa, 1968), 158 N.W.2d 154 (sale of corn at other than designated elevator); State v. Christiansen, 231 Iowa 525, 1 N.W.2d 623 (admitted collection of monies retained by agent and kept by him); State v. Schumacher, 162 Iowa 231, 143 N. W. 1110 (use of company funds to purchase grain options); State v. Boggs, 166 Iowa 452, 147 N.W. 934 (pledge of nonowned contract as security for personal loan); State v. Rowell, 172 Iowa 208, 154 N.W. 488 (commingling and use of funds by agent. The funds belonged to the principal). Other cases to the same effect could be cited. In each case, where conviction has been sustained there has been some evidence, direct or circumstantial, of wrongful conversion. We can find no such evidence here.

The subject, as it relates to demand and refusal, is best covered by Perkins on Criminal Law, Second Ed., chapter 4 (D), p. 293, where he quotes People v. Ward (1901), 134 Cal. 301, 304, 66 P. 372, 373:

" 'A demand, followed by a refusal *if the other essential facts exist,* is evidence of embezzlement, and sometimes indispensable evidence of it; *but it is the fraudulent and felonious conversion of the money or other property that constitutes the offense,* and that may often be proved without a demand' " (Emphasis supplied.)

Except in the case of public officials our statutes ordinarily require a showing of conversion of the property to the use of the embezzler. This may be done by circumstantial evidence and the State is entitled to all reasonable inferences to be taken from the factual circumstances shown. Here the State relied entirely on circumstantial evidence to prove defendant converted the property to his own use.

* * *

We know of no other case with a similar factual situation; i. e., where the accused defendant was one of two joint bailees either of whom could have disposed of the bailed property. There is no direct evidence that either bailee actually did so act. The possible activity of the deceased father is simply not met as an issue in the State's case. This alone is a fatal weakness under the foregoing rule long recognized in this court.

Nor is there any substantial evidence to eliminate the very real possibility that the bailor Dwaine Clark did not come and take the hogs away. The jury's obvious rejection of defendant's contention

in this regard is not enough "to exclude a reasonable doubt that defendant was innocent of the charge". The negative factor of rejection of defendant's story does not relieve the State of its affirmative
burden to prove its case. Defendant's evidence is to be considered but
here it did not add to the weight of the State's case. There was no
effort, beyond the finding of the papers with the "active files", to show
the partnership still charged defendant and his father with possession
of the hogs at the time of Clark's death.

The books of the partnership may or may not have been sufficiently detailed to show the location and number of hogs to which
the partnership claimed ownership. If such evidence was available
it was not produced. In the absence of such evidence and because
of the death of Mr. Clark, the jury was left to speculate as to what
the active partner did or did not do between the date of delivery of
the hogs and the date of his death. As in the case of the possible
activity of defendant's father, this dearth of evidence constitutes a
fatal weakness in the State's case.

The rule applicable to public officials as to demand and nonde-
livery is inapplicable here. The record is completely silent as to what
happened to the hogs. The evidence permits rational hypothesis inconsistent with defendant's guilt. As was asked in State v. Daves,
259 Iowa 584, 591, 144 N.W.2d 879, 884:

"The evidence is circumstantial. Can we say it is sufficient to
allow the jury to find every rational hypothesis of innocence has
been negatived as required by the cases? State v. Whisler, 231 Iowa
1216, 3 N.W.2d 525, 527; State v. Sigman, 220 Iowa 146, 149, 261
N.W. 538; State v. Bricker, 178 Iowa 297, 306–307, 159 N.W. 873;
State v. Vandewater, not reported in Iowa, 176 N.W. 883, 884." As
in State v. Daves, supra, the answer must be negative under the record made.

What has been said here makes moot the other points relied upon by defendant. The motion for directed verdict made at the close
of all the evidence should have been sustained.

Reversed.

MOORE, C. J., and MASON, RAWLINGS, LeGRAND and
UHLENHOPP, JJ., concur.

LARSON, STUART and REES, JJ., dissent.

(3) FALSE PRETENSES

POLLARD v. STATE

Supreme Court of Mississippi, 1971.
244 So.2d 729.

ROBERTSON, Justice. The appellant, Norman Pollard, was indicted, tried and convicted in the Circuit Court of Lee County, of the crime of false pretense (giving a bad check), and was sentenced to serve a term of three years in the State Penitentiary and to pay a fine of $250.00.

The appellant assigned as error: the granting of State's Instruction No. 1; the refusal to direct a verdict for the defendant * * *

Appellant had a sideline of buying used cars, repairing and improving them, and then selling them at a profit. He was a young married man with no capital and operated on a shoestring. He had been doing business for some months with Ronald Michael and Charles Baxter, of B & M Motors, Inc., Baldwyn, Mississippi.

On September 5, 1968, Pollard gave B & M Motors a $2,550.00 check for three used cars. September 5th was on Thursday, and Pollard testified that he asked Ronald Michael to hold the check until the following week. The proof showed that the check was held until the following Tuesday, September 10th, when it was deposited to the account of B & M Motors. Michael explained that B & M Motors was charged a flat exchange fee of $5.00 whether he deposited $1,000.00 or $50,000.00, so he usually waited until after the auction sale on Monday to make his deposit. The $2,550.00 check of Pollard was returned because of insufficient funds.

At the November, 1968, term of Circuit Court, Pollard was indicted for the crime of false pretense, (the giving of a bad check for $2,550.00 and receiving value for the check in the form of three used cars). The one indispensable element of this offense is the receiving of value for the check at the very time it is delivered. In other words, the seller parts with something of value on the belief that the check is good at that particular time. * * *

The gravamen of the offense was succinctly stated in Jackson v. State, 251 Miss. 529, 170 So.2d 438 (1965):

"So an essential element of the offense under section 2153 is the making and delivering of the check to another person for value, *and thereby obtaining from such other person money, goods, or other property of value.*" (Emphasis added). 251 Miss. at 531, 170 So.2d at 439.

It would appear that the transaction between Pollard and B & M Motors was a credit sale, and not an exchange for value based on the belief that Pollard's check was good at that particular moment.

If Pollard is to be believed, he was doing business on a hold-check basis, received the cars on Thursday and his check was deposited the following Tuesday. This would indicate a credit sale.

If Michael is to be believed, he frequently allowed dealers to take cars one day and mail in a check several days later. He testified that he had followed this practice with Pollard on two or three occasions. This also would indicate a credit sale based on Michael's confidence in the purchaser generally. Michael had followed this procedure with Pollard just a week before. Pollard had taken delivery of two used cars on August 24, 1968, and his check to B & M Motors was dated August 27, 1968. Michael's uncertain testimony about this transaction was:

> "A   I'm saying it is a possibility that—it's been a long time, Mr. Parker, that he could have bought the cars, come by my place and bought the cars, verbally bought them, and said that when I send after the cars or when somebody brings them to me I'll send the check back or I'll put the check in the mail. There is that possibility, which I do that on numerous occasions.
>
> "Q   You have done that for him on numerous occasions, is that right?
>
> "A   No, probably a couple of times, but I do that with all of my dealers. *I had no reason to doubt the man wouldn't send me the check.*
>
> "Q   In fact you had no reason to doubt that he wouldn't send you the $2550 check?
>
> "A   I didn't—
>
> "Q   Isn't that a fact?
>
> "A   I thought the check was good when he gave it to me, I'll tell that.
>
> "Q   You had delivered his cars before that hadn't you?
>
> "A   I'm not sure when they delivered the cars on the $2550 check.
>
> "Q   That's all my questions.
>
> *   *   *   *   *   *   *   *   *   *
>
> "A   I believe he took those cars that day, Mr. McCreary I believe took those cars down there, I'm not sure." (Emphasis added).

This Court said in Grenada Coca Cola Co. et al. v. Davis, 168 Miss. 826, 151 So. 743 (1934):

> "The so-called bad check law does not cover the obtaining of goods where the goods had already been delivered, had passed completely out of the possession of the seller and

away from his hands and premises in a previously completed transaction or transactions, *although those transactions may have been at previous hours on the same day. There must be an exchange for the check at the time of delivery.* The bad check law is severe enough without extending it by construction so as to include past deliveries, to say nothing of the question of the constitutional validity of such a statute if it were so construed." (Emphasis added.) 168 Miss. at 832, 151 So. at 744.

In the later case of Broadus v. State, 205 Miss. 147, 38 So.2d 692 (1949), this Court again interpreted the bad check law:

"In the case at bar, the pressing machinery had been delivered to the agent of Broadus and the agent had completely removed them from the possession and premises of Fowler and had departed from Roses Hill for Escatawpa, and had been gone for some thirty minutes before Broadus came up and delivered the check to Fowler in payment for same. When Fowler let the machinery leave his possession and control without demanding and receiving the purchase price, he extended credit for same, Broadus did not obtain the machinery with the check, for he had already, before that time, obtained the machinery. He obtained nothing with the check. The check was given in discharge of a pre-existing debt. The bad check law has no application here." 205 Miss. at 150–151, 38 So.2d at 693.

The court should have directed a verdict for the Defendant Pollard.

* * *

Judgment reversed and defendant discharged.

GILLESPIE, P. J., and RODGERS, JONES and INZER, JJ., concur.

NOTES

1. The essential elements of larceny, the oldest and most important of the acquisitive offenses, are that the offender, by trespass, takes and carries away another's personal property with intent to steal it.

In *Rogers* the only dispute was whether the defendant had taken and carried away the property—that is, whether the asportation requirement had been satisfied. The element of trespass was present not because the station was not open for business at 2:30 a. m. but because all that is needed is a taking from the possession of the owner without his consent. The result would have been the same if these actions had been performed during business hours. One of the more difficult theoretical problems with respect to the trespass requirement is where the owner has voluntarily surrendered actual possession as where an employer has given some property to an employee for his use in the employer's business. In such situations the courts have solved the problem by creating the fiction of constructive possession so that the employee is said to have mere custody and his taking is deemed to be trespassory, i. e., from the employer's possession.

Taking (caption) and carrying away (asportation) have traditionally been viewed as separate elements. The former refers to the thief's exercise of control over the property, either directly or through an innocent third party, the latter to some movement, however slight, of the property. In practice the distinction is unimportant and in some states it has been abandoned. Thus, Vernon's Tex.Code Ann. Art. 1412 (Penal) provides:

> To constitute 'taking' it is not necessary that the property be moved any distance from the place of taking; it is sufficient that it has been in the possession of the thief, though it may not be moved out of the presence of the person deprived of it * * *.

It should be noted that the requisite larcenous intent, which was inferred in *Rogers,* is an intent to steal which has been defined in the Model Penal Code Section 223(1) as:

> (a) to withhold property of another permanently or for so extended a period as to appropriate a major portion of its economic value, or with intent to restore only upon payment of reward or other compensation; or (b) to dispose of the property so as to make it unlikely that the owner will recover it.

The intent and the larcenous conduct must coincide. Normally, there will be little difficulty with this requirement since intent may be readily inferred from conduct. However, where, as in *Ray,* the conduct is consistent with the continued possession by the owner such an inference would not be reasonable. As may be seen from the MPC definition, if the taker is unaware that the property is that of another or believes that he has a claim of right to it the intent requirement is not satisfied. The existence of such states of mind is made an affirmative defense by MPC section 223.1(3). Thus, the unexplained possession of recently stolen property is commonly said to permit the inference that the possessor committed the crime by which the property was taken from its owner. Does casting the burden on the defendant to explain his possession raise serious problems with respect to the defendant's enjoyment of his constitutional right not to testify? See, e. g., State v. Young, 217 So.2d 567 (Fla.1968). A rather special problem is where the property is taken with intent merely to use it temporarily, as in joyriding. This has frequently been treated as a separate and less serious offense.

2. Why did the prosecutor in *Williams* proceed on embezzlement rather than larceny? What element of larceny was missing? What additional element is required for embezzlement? Is there any justification for differentiating between embezzlement by a public officer and by a bailee?

3. Was either larceny or embezzlement a viable alternative for the prosecution in *Pollard*? Why?

4. It should be noted in connection with *Pollard* that "bad check" laws were enacted because of difficulties encountered in fitting this activity within the traditional requirement that in obtaining property by false pretenses there must be reliance by the victim on a false representation with respect to a past or present fact. Cf. Chaplin v. United States, 157 F.2d 697

(D.C.Cir. 1946). Unlike the statute in *Pollard* most such laws do not require that property be obtained as a result of the check. It is sufficient that the check be given with the requisite state of mind; usually knowledge of insufficient funds and an intent to defraud.

5. If one by false representations—perhaps even as to future facts—obtains possession of property, as where one borrows property by lying, the crime of false pretenses does not lie since there title must pass. Instead, assuming the offender has converted the property, the charge would be larceny by trick.

6. Dissatisfaction with such hairsplitting has led to efforts at consolidating the various theft offenses. An example is the following sections of the Proposed Federal Criminal Code (1971):

§ 1731. Consolidation of Theft Offenses

(1) Construction. Conduct denominated theft in sections 1732 to 1734 constitutes a single offense designed to include the separate offenses heretofore known as larceny, stealing, purloining, embezzlement, obtaining money or property by false pretenses, extortion, blackmail, fraudulent conversion, receiving stolen property, and the like.

(2) Charging Theft. An indictment or information charging theft under sections 1732 to 1734 which fairly apprises the defendant of the nature of the charges against him shall not be deemed insufficient because it fails to specify a particular category of theft. The defendant may be found guilty of theft under such an indictment or information if his conduct falls under any of sections 1732 to 1734, so long as the conduct proved is sufficiently related to the conduct charged that the accused is not unfairly surprised by the case he must meet.

§ 1732. Theft of Property

A person is guilty of theft if he:

(a) knowingly takes or exercises unauthorized control over, or makes an unauthorized transfer of an interest in, the property of another with intent to deprive the owner thereof;

(b) knowingly obtains the property of another by deception or by threat with intent to deprive the owner thereof, or intentionally deprives another of his property by deception or by threat; or

(c) knowingly receives, retains or disposes of property of another which has been stolen, with intent to deprive the owner thereof.

§ 1733. Theft of Services

A person is guilty of theft if:

(a) he intentionally obtains services known by him to be available only for compensation, by deception, threat, false token or other means to avoid payment for the services; or

(b) having control over the disposition of services of another to which he is not entitled, he knowingly diverts those services to his own benefit or to the benefit of another not entitled thereto.

Where compensation for services is ordinarily paid immediately upon their rendition, as in the case of hotels, restaurants, and comparable establishments, absconding without payment or making provision to pay is prima facie evidence that the services were obtained by deception.

§ 1735.   Grading of Theft Offenses Under Sections 1732 to 1734

(1) Class B Felony.   Theft under sections 1732 to 1734 is a Class B felony if the property or services stolen exceed $100,000 in value or are acquired or retained by a threat to commit a Class A or Class B felony or to inflict serious bodily injury on the person threatened or on any other person.

(2) Class C Felony.   Theft under sections 1732 to 1734 is a Class C felony if:

(a) the property or services stolen exceed $500 in value;

(b) the property or services stolen are acquired or retained by threat and (i) are acquired or retained by a public servant by a threat to take or withhold official action, or (ii) exceed $50 in value;

(c) the property or services stolen exceed $50 in value and are acquired or retained by a public servant in the course of his official duties;

(d) the property stolen is a firearm, ammunition, explosive or destructive device or an automobile, aircraft or other motor-propelled vehicle;

(e) the property consists of any government file, record, document or other government paper stolen from any government office or from any public servant;

(f) the defendant is in the business of buying or selling stolen property and he receives, retains or disposes of the property in the course of that business;

(g) the property stolen consists of any implement, paper, or other thing uniquely associated with the preparation of any money, stamp, bond, or other document, instrument or obligation of the United States;

(h) the property stolen consists of a key or other implement uniquely suited to provide access to property the theft of which would be a felony and it was stolen to gain such access; or

(i) the property is stolen from the United States mail and is first class mail or air mail.

(3) Class A Misdemeanor.   All other theft under sections 1732 to 1734 is a Class A misdemeanor, unless the requirements of subsection (4) or (5) are met.

(4) Class B Misdemeanor. Theft under sections 1732 to 1734 of property or services of a value not exceeding $50 shall be a Class B misdemeanor if:

(a) the theft was not committed by threat;

(b) the theft was not committed by deception by one who stood in a confidential or fiduciary relationship to the victim of the theft; and

(c) the defendant was not a public servant or an officer or employee of a financial institution who committed the theft in the course of his official duties.

The special classification provided in this subsection shall apply if the offense is classified under this subsection in the charge or if, at sentencing, the required factors are established by a preponderance of the evidence.

(5) Infraction. Theft under section 1733 of services of a value not exceeding $10 shall be an infraction if the defendant was not a public servant who committed the theft in the course of his official duties. The special classification provided in this subsection shall apply if the offense is classified under this subsection in the charge or if, at sentencing, the required factors are established by a preponderance of the evidence.

§ 1741. Definitions for Theft and Related Offenses

In sections 1731 to 1741:

(a) "deception" means: (i) creating or reinforcing a false impression, including false impressions as to fact, law, status, value, intention or other state of mind; but deception as to a person's intention to perform a promise shall not be inferred from the fact alone that he did not substantially perform the promise unless it is part of a continuing scheme to defraud; or (ii) preventing another from acquiring information which would affect his judgment of a transaction; or (iii) failing to correct a false impression which the actor previously created or reinforced, or which he knows to be influencing another to whom he stands in a fiduciary or confidential relationship; or (iv) failing to correct an impression which the actor previously created or reinforced and which the actor knows to have become false due to subsequent events; or (v) failing to disclose a lien, adverse claim or other impediment to the enjoyment of property which he transfers or encumbers in consideration for the property obtained or in order to continue to deprive another of his property, whether such impediment is or is not valid, or is or is not a matter of official record; or (vi) using a credit card, charge plate, or any other instrument which purports to evidence an undertaking to pay for property or services delivered or rendered to or upon the order of a designated person or bearer (A) where such instrument has been stolen, forged, revoked or cancelled, or where for any other reason its use by the actor is unauthorized, and (B) where the actor does not have the intention and ability to meet all obligations to the issuer arising out of his use of the instrument; or (vii) any other scheme to defraud. The term "deception" does not, however, include falsifications as to matters having no pecuniary significance, or puffing by statements unlikely to deceive ordinary persons in the group addressed. "Puffing" means an exaggerated commendation of wares in communications addressed to the public or to a class or group;

(b) "deprive" means: (i) to withhold property or to cause it to be withheld either permanently or under such circumstances that a major portion of its economic value, or its use and benefit, has, in fact, been appropriated; or (ii) to withhold property or to cause it to be withheld with the intent to restore it only upon the payment of a reward or other compensation; or (iii) to dispose of property or use it or transfer any interest in it under circumstances that make its restoration, in fact, unlikely.

* * *

(e) "obtain" means: (i) in relation to property, to bring about a transfer or purported transfer of an interest in the property, whether to the actor or another; or (ii) in relation to services, to secure performance thereof;

(f) "property" means any money, tangible or intangible personal property, property (whether real or personal) the location of which can be changed (including things growing on, affixed to, or found in land and documents although the rights represented thereby have no physical location), contract right, chose-in-action, interest in or claim to wealth, credit, or any other article or thing of value of any kind. "Property" also means real property the location of which cannot be moved if the offense involves transfer or attempted transfer of an interest in the property;

(g) "property of another" means property in which a person other than the actor or in which a government has an interest which the actor is not privileged to infringe without consent, regardless of the fact that the actor also has an interest in the property and regardless of the fact that the other person or government might be precluded from civil recovery because the property was used in an unlawful transaction or was subject to forfeiture as contraband. Property in possession of the actor shall not be deemed property of another who has a security interest therein, even if legal title is in the creditor pursuant to a conditional sales contract or other security agreement. "Owner" means any person or a government with an interest in property such that it is "property of another" as far as the actor is concerned;

(k) "threat" means an expressed purpose, however communicated, to (i) cause bodily injury in the future to the person threatened or to any other person; or (ii) cause damage to property; or (iii) subject the person threatened or any other person to physical confinement or restraint; or (iv) engage in other conduct constituting a crime; or (v) accuse anyone of a crime; or (vi) expose a secret or publicize an asserted fact, whether true or false, tending to subject a person living or deceased, to hatred, contempt, or ridicule or to impair another's credit or business repute; or (vii) reveal any information sought to be concealed by the person threatened; or (viii) testify or provide information or withhold testimony or information with respect to another's legal claim or defense; or (ix) take or withhold official action as a public servant, or cause a public servant to take or withhold official action; or (x) bring about or continue a strike, boycott, or other similar collective action to obtain property or deprive another of his property which is not demanded or received for the benefit of the group which the actor purports to represent; or (xi) cause anyone to be dismissed from his employment, unless the property is demanded or obtained for lawful union purposes; or (xii) do any other act which would not in itself substantially benefit the actor or a group he represents but which is calculated to harm another person in a substantial manner with respect to his health, safety, business, employment, calling, career, financial condition, reputation, or personal relationship. Upon a charge of theft, the receipt of property in consideration for taking or withholding official action shall be deemed to be theft by threat regardless of whether the owner voluntarily parted with his property or himself initiated the scheme.

There are, of course, many other offenses against property which are not covered by these provisions, but all of the significant ones involve invasions or threatened invasions of socially valued interests in addition to our interest in protecting the enjoyment of property. Thus arson is generally punished more severely than would be the theft of the same property or its destruction by other means because of the special dangers posed by fire to persons and other property. Robbery is distinguished from other thefts because it involves the use or threatened use of force against the person. Similarly, burglary, although commonly engaged in for purposes of theft has traditionally been viewed more seriously than mere theft because it is thought to threaten the sense of security justifiably reposed in a place.

---

(4) ROBBERY

PEOPLE v. HELLER

Appellate Court of Illinois, 1971.
131 Ill.App.2d 799, 267 N.E.2d 685.

SCOTT, Justice. Defendant was indicted and tried by a jury in Tazewell County for armed robbery and robbery. He was found guilty of robbery and sentenced to the penitentiary for a term of four to twelve years. The charge arises out of an incident that occurred on October 21, 1969, in a tavern in Creve Coeur, Illinois, known as the Harbor Lights. The complaining witness, Peter Horvath, was tending bar on the night in question in the Harbor Lights, the same being a tavern, pool hall and restaurant establishment owned by Horvath's mother. He testified that early in the morning at approximately 2:30 or 3:00 A.M., two men came into the establishment, played three games of pool, ordered and ate "three chili dogs" taking them approximately twenty to twenty-five minutes. No one else was in the establishment. He identified defendant as one of the two men. He stated that defendant's accomplice gave him a $10.00 bill to change and while he was looking for change the accomplice struck him on the right temple knocking him down. He testified that defendant and his accomplice then took money from the cash register in the amount of approximately $100.00 and the defendant removed a gun from a small drawer near the register, the gun apparently being the property of Horvath or his mother. The defendant then pointed the gun at him and said twice that he would kill him. The two men then left the store.

*　　*　　*

Defendant next contends the court erred in failing to direct a verdict to the charge of armed robbery. The contention here is that the failure to so direct a verdict, acting together with an erroneous instruction given by the court and inflammatory remarks made by the State's Attorney, prejudiced the defendant and caused the jury to reach a compromise verdict. The instructions given by the court will be commented on later in this opinion.

The testimony establishes that the gun did not come into play until and at the same time the money was taken from the cash register. Defendant contends the gun was no more than a part of the property taken. This is not accurate for the testimony shows the gun was pointed at Horvath and that the defendant threatened to kill him. Defendant nonetheless claims, not without merit, that the weapon was not used in the commission of the crime nor in perfecting an escape. The substance of the argument is that despite the obvious intimidation of Horvath with the gun and despite the use of the gun while the robbery was in effect, this should not change the crime from robbery to armed robbery.

The question immediately arises as to whether the act of using the gun cannot be considered along with the robbery as a continuous series of events constituting a single occurrence. People v. Watson, 110 Ill.App.2d 343, 249 N.E.2d 293.

To sustain a conviction for robbery the force or threat of force must proceed or be contemporaneous with the taking of the property, People v. Jones, 290 Ill. 603, 125 N.E. 256, yet it is acknowledged by the authorities that the taking of property may be peaceful but the departure with the same may be forceful. In People v. Jones, supra, defendant apparently lifted the wallet of the complaining witness, who was intoxicated. The latter then accused the defendant of taking his wallet and defendant responded by striking him and knocking him out. The court there said:

> "There was no evidence of a struggle to retain possession of the pocketbook, but only an accusation of the theft after it occurred, which the plaintiff in error resented by assaulting the accuser."

In 58 A.L.R. 656, that authority says:

> "Though the decisions are not without conflict, the general rule requires that, in the offense of robbery, force or putting in fear be employed before, or at the time of, the taking of property, and does not permit a charge of robbery to be sustained by showing a retention of property, or an attempt to escape, by force or putting in fear." Citing People v. Jones, supra.

No case directly in point has been suggested by either party and People v. Jones cannot, we believe, be quoted as placing Illinois within that general rule.

In People v. Brown, 76 Ill.App.2d 362, 222 N.E.2d 227, a case involving a simple robbery, the court held that force exerted after the taking was sufficient to sustain the robbery charge. The complaining witness was asleep in an elevated train in the city of Chicago. He awoke and saw a man with his wallet taking money from it. He reached for his wallet and was struck by a second man and knocked back into his seat. The three men, all accomplices, left the train with his money. The court in denying defendant's contention that robbery had not been proven stated:

> "The series of events—the taking of the wallet, the attempt to recover it by Dickerson, and the striking of Dickerson * * *—constituted a single incident or occurrence or the 'res gestae' of the crime."

In People v. Chambliss, 69 Ill.App.2d 459, 217 N.E.2d 422, the force took place after the taking of a wallet and after the complaining witness chased the thief after he had felt someone take his wallet from his pocket. The court quotes with approval from 46 Am.Jur., Robbery, Sec. 21, where it is stated:

> "Thus, if a struggle *immediately ensues* to keep possession of the property and the thief overcomes the resistance * * * the violence is sufficient to constitute the act a robbery."

The court there referred to the force applied after the taking as the "res gestae of the crime."

We feel that the use of a dangerous weapon at any point of a robbery, so long as it can reasonably be said to be a part of a single occurrence or incident—or put another way, a part of the "res gestae of the crime", will constitute armed robbery.

In the case at bar we believe there was sufficient evidence to go to the jury on the question of armed robbery. So long as the assailant wielded a gun it is impossible to say what further resistance the victim may have put forth. No error was committed by the lower court in permitting the jury to consider the armed robbery count and certainly under these circumstances the defendant was not prejudiced.

NOTES

1. Defendant asks a stranger for money in order to get his pregnant wife to the hospital for the delivery. The stranger takes out his wallet and the defendant snatches it from his hand. Is this robbery? Jones v. State, 467 S.W.2d 453 (Tex.Crim.App. 1971). What if he seized a woman's bag from her shoulder?

2. Defendant is retained by an 84 year old woman for some repair work to cost $25. He and two other men come to her house, do the work, and present a bill for $600. She pays $300 because, according to her testimony, she was frightened by the demand even though none of the men were impolite. Is this robbery? Is it any crime? Should it be? Parnell v. State, 389 P.2d 370 (Okla.Crim.App. 1964).

3. Robbery is not consolidated into theft in the Proposed Federal Criminal Code, but rather is retained as a separate offense in the following provision:

§ 1721. Robbery

(1) Offense. A person is guilty of robbery if, in the course of committing a theft, he inflicts or attempts to inflict bodily injury upon another, or threatens or menaces another with imminent bodily injury.

(2) Grading. Robbery is a Class A felony if the actor fires a firearm or explodes or hurls a destructive device or directs the force of any other dangerous weapon against another. Robbery is a Class B felony if the robber possesses or pretends to possess a firearm, destructive device or other dangerous weapon, or menaces another with serious bodily injury, or inflicts bodily injury upon another, or is aided by an accomplice actually present. Otherwise robbery is a Class C felony.

(3) Definitions. In this section:

(a) an act shall be deemed "in the course of committing a theft" if it occurs in an attempt to commit theft, whether or not the theft is successfully completed, or in immediate flight from the commission of, or an unsuccessful effort to commit, the theft;

(b) "dangerous weapon" means a weapon the possession of which under the circumstances indicates an intent or readiness to inflict serious bodily injury.

(5) EXTORTION

STATE v. HARRINGTON

Supreme Court of Vermont, 1969.
260 A.2d 692.

HOLDEN, Chief Justice. The respondent John B. Harrington has been tried and found guilty of the offense of threatening to accuse Armand Morin of Littleton, New Hampshire, of the crime of adultery. The indictment charges that the threat was maliciously made with the intent to extort $175,000 and to compel Morin to do an act against his will in violation of 13 V.S.A. § 1701.^c

At the outset the respondent acknowledges that there is no serious conflict in the material evidence presented to the jury. The main effort of his appeal challenges the jurisdiction and the sufficiency of the evidence to sustain the conviction.

At the time of the alleged offense the respondent was engaged in the general practice of law in a firm with offices in Burlington, Vermont. Early in March, 1968, he was consulted by Mrs. Norma Morin, the wife of the alleged victim, Armand E. Morin. Mrs. Morin had separated from her husband because of his recent and severe physical abuse. Prior to their separation they owned and operated the Continental 93 Motel in Littleton, New Hampshire, where the Morins maintained a residential apartment. The respondent learned the marital estate of the parties had a net value of approximately $500,000. Mrs. Morin reported to the respondent that her husband had also been guilty of numerous marital infidelities with different women at the motel. Mrs. Morin also disclosed that she had been guilty of marital misconduct which apparently had been condoned.

During the first conference the respondent advised Mrs. Morin that, because of her residence in New Hampshire, she could not undertake divorce proceedings in Vermont for at least six months and for her to obtain a divorce in New Hampshire it would be necessary that she obtain counsel from that state. Mrs. Morin indicated she wished to retain Mr. Harrington to represent her.

On one of the subsequent conferences a friend of Mrs. Morin's, who accompanied her to the respondent's office, suggested that an effort should be made to procure corroborative evidence of Mr. Morin's marital misconduct. To this end, the floor plan of the motel was discussed and a diagram prepared. At this time a scheme was designed to procure the services of a girl who would visit the motel in an effort to obtain corroborative evidence of Morin's infidelity.

c. A person who maliciously threatens to accuse another of a crime or offense, or with an injury to his person or property, with intent to extort money or other pecuniary advantage, or with intent to compel the person so threatened to do an act against his will, shall be imprisoned in the state prison not more than two years or fined not more than $500.00.

After some screening, a Mrs. Mazza, who had been suggested by the respondent, was selected to carry out the assignment. The respondent explained to Mrs. Mazza the purpose of her employment and the results she was expected to accomplish and provided her with a "cover story" to explain her registration and presence as a guest at the Continental 93 Motel. Warning Mrs. Mazza against enticement and entrapment, the respondent instructed the employee to be "receptive and available," but not aggressive. The agreement with Mrs. Mazza was that she would be paid one hundred dollars at the time she undertook the assignment and one hundred dollars when her mission was completed.

Mrs. Morin was without funds at the time. A contingent fee agreement was signed by Mrs. Morin and the firm of Harrington and Jackson, by the respondent. The agreement was dated March 5, 1968 and provided that in the event a satisfactory property settlement was obtained, the respondent's firm was to receive twelve and a half percent of the settlement, in addition to reimbursement for expenses advanced by counsel. Electronic listening and recording equipment was ordered and delivered by air.

On the afternoon of March 6 the respondent and two office associates traveled to St. Johnsbury in two vehicles. Mrs. Mazza continued on to Littleton unaccompanied. She registered on arrival at the Continental 93 Motel under the name of Jeanne Raeder. She called the respondent at St. Johnsbury from a public telephone and informed him of her room number and location. Mrs. Mazza later delivered the key to her room to the respondent to enable him to procure a duplicate. The respondent, representing that he was a book salesman, registered at the motel and procured a room directly above that occupied by Mrs. Mazza. He was accompanied by a junior associate and an investigator,—both employed by the respondent's law firm.

During the next day Mrs. Mazza attracted Mr. Morin's attention. The sequence of events which followed led to an invitation by Morin for her to join him at his apartment for a cocktail. Mrs. Mazza accepted. Later she suggested that they go to her room because Mr. Morin's young son was asleep in his quarters. Morin went to Mrs. Mazza's room about midnight. Soon after the appointed hour the respondent and his associates entered the room. With one or more cameras, several photographs were taken of Morin and Mrs. Mazza in bed and unclothed. Morin grabbed for one camera and broke it.

During the time of her stay at the motel Mrs. Mazza carried an electronic transmitter in her handbag. By means of this device, her conversations with Morin were monitored by the respondent and his associates.

The respondent and his companions checked out of the motel at about one in the morning. Before doing so, there was a brief confrontation with Morin. According to Morin's testimony, the respondent demanded $125,000. Morin testified—"at that time I made him an offer of $25,000 to return everything he had, and in a second breath I retracted the offer."

The following day the respondent conferred with Mrs. Morin and reported the events of the trip to New Hampshire. He asked Mrs. Morin to consider reconciliation over the weekend. On March 11, 1968, Mrs. Morin informed the respondent she decided it was too late for reconciliation. With this decision, the respondent dictated, in the presence of Mrs. Morin, a letter which was received in evidence as State's Exhibit 1. The letter was addressed to Armand Morin at Littleton, New Hampshire, and was placed in the United States mail at Burlington the same day.

The communication is designated personal and confidential. The following excerpts are taken from the full text:

"—Basically, your wife desires a divorce, and if it can be equitably arranged, she would prefer that the divorce be as quiet and as undamaging as possible.

This letter is being written in your wife's presence and has been completely authorized by your wife. The offer of settlement contained herein is made in the process of negotiation and is, of course, made without prejudice to your wife's rights.

It is the writer's thinking that for the children's sake, for your sake, and for Mrs. Morin's sake, that neither the courts in New Hampshire nor in Vermont should become involved in this potentially explosive divorce. If a suitable 'stipulation or separation agreement' can be worked out, the writer would recommend a Mexican, Stipulation-Divorce. This divorce would be based upon the catch-all grounds 'Incompatability'. A Mexican divorce of this type can be obtained when both parties have agreed as to terms of separation and have executed certain powers of attorney, etc., which this office can provide. With incompatability as the grounds, it is actually immaterial who goes down for the 48 hour period necessary to obtain the divorce in the State of Chihuahua. Mrs. Morin is willing to go; however, if a settlement can be reached, she has no objection to your going.

Mrs. Morin is willing to give up the following:

1. All of her marital rights, including her rights to share in your estate.

2. All of her right, title, and interest, jointly or by reason of marital status, that she has in and to, any or all property

of the marriage, including the Continental 93 Motel, the three (3) farms in Vermont, the capital stock that you own, the house in Lindenville, the joint venture in land in East Burke, all personal property except as is specifically hereinafter mentioned and in short, all rights that she may now have or might acquire in the future, as your wife. Furthermore, any such settlement would include the return to you of all tape recordings, all negatives, all photographs and copies of photographs that might in any way, bring discredit upon yourself. Finally, there would be an absolute undertaking on the part of your wife not to divulge any information of any kind or nature which might be embarrassing to you in your business life, your personal life, your financial life, of your life as it might be affected by the Internal Revenue Service, the United States Customs Service, or any other governmental agency.—"

The letter goes on to specify the terms of settlement required by Mrs. Morin, concerning custody of the minor child, her retention of an automobile and the disposition of certain designated personal effects. It further provides:

"5. Mrs. Morin would waive all alimony upon receipt of One Hundred Seventy Five Thousand Dollars ($175,000)—."

The sum of $25,000 is specified to be paid at the signing of the separation agreement, with the balance due according to a schedule of payments over the period of eighteen months.

The letter continues:

"—At the present time Mrs. Morin is almost without funds. She did have the $200 that you gave her when she left and she does have the $1500 in Canadian bills from the 'found' money. Because of her shortage of money, and, because she is badly missing David, and finally, because she cannot continue for any substantial period of time to live in the present vacuum, the writer must require prompt communication from you with respect to the proposed settlement contained herein. This letter is being dictated on March 11 and you should have it in your possession by March 13, at the latest. Unless the writer has heard from you on or before March 22, we will have no alternative but to withdraw the offer and bring immediate divorce proceedings in Grafton County. This will, of course, require the participation by the writer's correspondent attorneys in New Hampshire. If we were to proceed under New Hampshire laws, without any stipulation, it would be necessary to allege, in detail, all of the grounds that Mrs. Morin has in seeking the divorce. The writer is, at present, undecided as to advising Mrs. Morin whether or not to file for 'informer fees' with respect to the Internal Revenue Service and the United States Customs Service. In any event, we would file, alleging adultery, including affidavits, alleging extreme cruelty and beatings, and asking for a court order enjoining you from disposing of any property, including your stock interests, during the pendency of the proceeding.

The thought has been expressed that you might, under certain circumstances, decide to liquidate what you could and abscond to Canada or elsewhere. The writer would advise you that this would in no way impede Mrs. Morin's action. You would be served by publication and under those circumstances, I am very certain that all property in New Hampshire and in Vermont, would be awarded, beyond any question, to Mrs. Morin.

With absolutely no other purpose than to prove to you that we have all of the proof necessary to prove adultery beyond a reasonable doubt, we are enclosing a photograph taken by one of my investigators on the early morning of March 8. The purpose of enclosing the photograph as previously stated, is simply to show you that cameras and equipment were in full operating order.—"

It was stipulated that the letter was received by Morin in Littleton, New Hampshire "in the due course of the mail."

Such is the evidence upon which the respondent was found guilty. * * *

Turning to the other grounds advanced in the motion for acquittal, the respondent maintains his letter (State's Exhibit 1) does not constitute a threat to accuse Morin of the crime of adultery. He argues the implicit threats contained in the communication were "not to accuse of the CRIME of adultery but to bring an embarrassing, reputation-ruining divorce proceeding, in Mr. Morin's county of residence unless a stipulation could be negotiated." (Brief of Respondent-Appellant, p. 13.)

In dealing with a parallel contention in State v. Louanis, 79 Vt. 463, 467, 65 A. 532, 533, the Court answered the argument in an opinion by Chief Judge Rowell. "The statute is aimed at blackmailing, and a threat of any public accusation is as much within the reason of the statute as a threat of a formal complaint, and is much easier made, and may be quite as likely to accomplish its purpose. There is nothing in the statute that requires such a restricted meaning of the word 'accuse'; and to restrict it thus, would well nigh destroy the efficacy of the act."

The letter, marked "personal and confidential," makes a private accusation of adultery in support of a demand for a cash settlement.

An incriminating photograph was enclosed for the avowed purpose of demonstrating "we have all of the proof necessary to prove adultery beyond a reasonable doubt." According to the writing itself, cost of refusal will be public exposure of incriminating conduct in the courts of New Hampshire where the event took place.

In further support of motion for acquittal, the respondent urges that the totality of the evidence does not exclude the inference that he acted merely as an attorney, attempting to secure a divorce for his client on the most favorable terms possible. This, of course, was the theory of the defense.

*   *   *

At the time of the writing, the respondent was undecided whether to advise his client to seek "informer fees." One of the advantages tendered to Morin for a "quiet" and "undamaging" divorce is an "absolute undertaking" on the part of the respondent's client not to inform against him in any way. The Internal Revenue Service, the United States Customs Service and other governmental agencies are suggested as being interested in such information. Quite clearly, these veiled threats exceeded the limits of the respondent's representation of his client in the divorce action. Although these matters were not specified in the indictment, they have a competent bearing on the question of intent. State v. Louanis, supra, 79 Vt. at 467, 65 A. 532.

Apart from this, the advancement of his client's claim to the marital property, however well founded, does not afford legal cause for the trial court to direct a verdict of acquittal in the background and context of his letter to Morin. A demand for settlement of a civil action, accompanied by a malicious threat to expose the wrongdoer's criminal conduct, if made with intent to extort payment, against his will, constitutes the crime alleged in the indictment. Commonwealth v. Coolidge, 128 Mass. 55, 58; O'Neil v. State, 237 Wis. 391, 296 N.W. 96, 135 A.L.R. 719, 724, and cases annotated at 729.

The evidence at hand establishes beyond dispute the respondent's participation was done with preconceived design. The incriminating evidence which his letter threatens to expose was wilfully contrived and procured by a temptress hired for that purpose. These factors in the proof are sufficient to sustain a finding that the respondent acted maliciously and without just cause, within the meaning of our criminal statutes. State v. Muzzy, 87 Vt. 267, 269, 88 A. 895; Compare, State v. Sylvester, 112 Vt. 202, 206, 22 A.2d 505. The sum of the evidence supports the further inference that the act was done with intent to extort a substantial contingent fee to the respondent's personal advantage.

*   *   * The evidence of guilt is ample to support the verdict and the trial was free from errors in law.

Judgment affirmed.

NOTES

1. Robbery and extortion are both aggravated forms of larceny. In the former the taking is from or in the presence of the person by means of violence or intimidation. But where the intimidation is not a threat of immediate harm to the possessor or some one in his company, or is not of physical harm the surrender of the property in response would not constitute robbery. Extortion and blackmail statutes have been created to cover these situations. These very similar offenses have sometimes been distinguished by a statutory requirement that for extortion the accused be a public official whereas blackmail involves private citizens. United States v. Nardello, 393 U.S. 286, 89 S.Ct. 534, 21 L.Ed.2d 487 (1969), provides an interesting examination of this distinction and its possible affect on the application of the Federal Travel Act (18 U.S.C.A. § 1952, prohibiting interstate travel in furtherance of "extortion") to defendants who allegedly operated a scheme to "shake down" persons lured into homosexual situations.

Although extortion and blackmail are distinguishable from the crime of false pretenses inasmuch as there may be neither misrepresentations nor an intent to defraud involved, it has been suggested, see, e. g., Proposed Federal Criminal Code (1971) (reprinted at page 365), they be included in the consolidation of theft offenses. Does the employment of threats, particularly those of future violence, invade a distinct social interest to the extent that it is more appropriate to treat this crime as equivalent to robbery?

2. If the defendant has obtained the property without the use of force or intimidation but employs these to effect his escape or to retain the property, may he be charged with robbery? Compare Mason v. Commonwealth, 200 Va. 253, 105 S.E.2d 149 (1958) (defendant had already passed television set to his accomplice through broken window of victim's store when victim struck him and defendant responded with pistol shots) with People v. Phillips, 201 Cal.App.2d 383, 19 Cal.Rptr. 839 (1962) ($3.00 worth of gasoline had been placed in car at request of defendant before he displayed gun to effect his escape). What public policy is served by drawing such distinctions?

3. Can a defendant be guilty of robbery if the state's evidence shows that although he threatened to blow off the head of teller X, thereby putting her "in fear of immediate injury to ˣ ˣ ˣ her person", he took the money from the cash drawer of teller Y who was not present. State v. Hawkins, 418 S.W.2d 921 (Mo.1967).

4. What interest deserving protection is threatened by attempts to obtain money in exchange for a promise not to reveal the truth? Do Harrington and/or Nardello answer this question? Should the result be the same if the accused had not participated in the creation of the compromising situation? Is it extortion if law enforcement officials require a drug offender to "make" a certain number of cases for them in order to avoid prosecution?

c. OFFENSES AGAINST THE HABITATION

HOUCHIN v. STATE

Court of Criminal Appeals of Oklahoma, 1970.
473 P.2d 925.

BUSSEY, Judge. Clifford Rhea Houchin was charged, tried and convicted in the District Court of Oklahoma County with the crime of Burglary in the Second Degree After Former Convictions of Felonies, and from the judgment and sentence fixing his punishment at ten years imprisonment in the state penitentiary, he appeals.

Briefly stated, the evidence discloses that Houchin, hereinafter referred to as defendant, removed a box containing a television set from the trunk of a car belonging to Dorothy Davis. He was observed placing this television set in the trunk of his car and arrested by Officer Kerlick. The evidence further discloses that the trunk of the Davis' car was not closed because of the height of the box containing the television set, and that it had been secured by a nylon cord which was broken when the defendant opened the trunk.

It is first contended by the defendant that the evidence was not sufficient to support the verdict of the jury for the reason that there was no "breaking and entering" as contemplated by the provisions of 21 O.S. § 1435, the same providing:

> "Every person who breaks and enters any building or any part of any building, room, booth, tent, railroad car, automobile, truck, trailer, vessel or other structure or erection in which any property is kept, with intent to steal therein or to commit any felony, is guilty of burglary in the second degree."

We are of the opinion that this assignment of error is without merit. In Lumpkin v. State, 25 Okl.Cr. 108, 219 P. 157 (1923), this Court stated, and has continued to follow, the following rule:

> "It is a familiar principle that a breaking, necessary to constitute the crime of burglary, may be by any act of physical force, however slight, by which obstruction to entering is forcibly removed and the opening and closing of a door to enter a building may constitute a breaking * * *"

In the instant case it is apparent that the nylon cord which was broken when the defendant opened the trunk, served the purpose of a lock or latch, the breaking of which to gain entry falls squarely within the purview of 21 O.S. § 1435, supra.[1]

---

1. In Landry v. State, 96 Tex.Cr.R. 417, 258 S.W. 172, which involved a prosecution for burglary, the court found that the requisite "breaking" was present where the defendant, in order to obtain entrance to a garage, unfastened a wire in order that the door might be opened.

It is next contended that there was no evidence of entry as required by 21 O.S. § 1435 and for that reason his Demurrers and Motions to Dismiss were improperly overruled. We are of the opinion that this assignment of error is also without merit, for it is readily apparent that the box containing the television set was in the trunk of Mrs. Davis' automobile and that in order to remove the box from said trunk and place it in his own vehicle, the defendant, of necessity, had to place his hands inside the trunk.

* * *

The judgment and sentence appealed from is accordingly affirmed.

NOTES

1. Assume the state's burglary statute prohibits entry with intent to commit a felony and defines entry, in part, as follows:

> The entry is not confined to the entrance of the whole body; it may consist of the entry of any part for the purpose of committing a felony or theft * * * or by the introduction of any instrument for the purpose of taking from the house any personal property, although no part of the body of the offender should be introduced.

Does this statute cover one who: raises a window in such a manner that his fingers are within the house; uses an iron bar to break a window and pry apart bars on the window; bores a hole in a corn storehouse so that the corn runs out; throws a brick through a window? On what basis are the distinctions, if any, to be made? See Russell v. State, 158 Tex. Crim. 350, 255 S.W.2d 881 (1953).

2. The Proposed Federal Criminal Code (1971) would provide:

§ 1711. Burglary

(1) Offense. A person is guilty of burglary if he willfully enters or surreptitiously remains in a building or occupied structure, or a separately secured or occupied portion thereof, when at the time the premises are not open to the public and the actor is not licensed, invited or otherwise privileged to enter or remain, as the case may be, with intent to commit a crime therein.

(2) Grading. Burglary is a Class B felony if:

(a) the offense is committed at night and is knowingly perpetrated in the dwelling of another; or

(b) in effecting entry or while in the premises or in immediate flight therefrom, the actor inflicts or attempts to inflict bodily injury or physical restraint on another, or menaces another with imminent serious bodily injury, or is armed with a firearm, destructive device or other weapon the possession of which under the circumstances indicates an intent or readiness to inflict serious bodily injury.

Otherwise burglary is a Class C felony.

§ 1719.   Definitions for Sections 1711 to 1719

In sections 1711 to 1719:

(a) "occupied structure" means a structure or vehicle:

(i) where any person lives or carries on business or other calling; or

(ii) which is used for overnight accommodation of persons.

Any such structure or vehicle is deemed to be "occupied" regardless of whether a person is actually present;

* * *

(e) "night" means the period between 30 minutes past sunset and 30 minutes before sunrise.

Notice that the above proposal abandons common law requirements that there be a "breaking", that it be at night and that it be into a dwelling. How would you explain these changes in the definition of the prohibited conduct? Is the resulting expansion of criminalization desirable? Can there be any justification for retaining burglary as a separate offense? Is there any conduct which we wish to deter which could not be punished in the absence of a burglary provision?

------

d.   CRIMES AGAINST THE PERSON [d]

(1) ASSAULT

PEOPLE v. ABRAMS

Supreme Court of Illinois, 1971.
48 Ill.2d 446, 271 N.E.2d 37.

PER CURIAM.   A jury in the circuit court of Cook County found each of the 11 defendants guilty of violating one or more of the statutes or ordinances under which complaints had been filed. The defendant Arnold Abrams was convicted of selling liquor without a license in violation of the Municipal Code of the City of Chicago and was fined $200. The defendant Florence Levinsohn, convicted on two complaints of aggravated assault and on two complaints of battery, received a sentence of two months on each charge. The sentences were ordered to run concurrently. She was also convicted of disorderly conduct and of interfering with a police officer in the performance of his duties, both violations of the Municipal Code, and fined $200 and $100 respectively on these charges. Convictions of disorderly conduct were entered against the other defendants, Helen Ketterer, Michael Kemper, Maury Lubet, William E. Simpson, Leslie Friedman, Robert Lane, Maxwell Primack, Preston Browning and Russell DuPree. Fines of $200 were imposed against these defend-

------

d. Homicide, the most important of all crimes against the person and, indeed, of all crimes, is treated separately in Part V.

ants. Excepting the defendant Helen Ketterer, each of these defendants was also found guilty of interfering with a police officer in the performance of his duties and was fined $100. Constitutional questions raised give this court jurisdiction on direct appeal.

On the evening of April 8, 1967, the Chicago Peace Council and the Student Mobilization Committee to End the War in Vietnam sponsored a "send-off" party which was held at the home of Mr. and Mrs. Arnold Abrams in Chicago. The party's object was to raise funds for the transportation of the groups' representatives to New York City, where a march protesting the war in Vietnam was to be held on April 15. Leaflets announcing the date, place, time, charge for admission, and purpose of the proposed party had been placed at several public locations in the neighborhood. The leaflets bore the request "R.S.V.P." and two telephone numbers were given.

Sergeant Lewis Smith of the Chicago Police Department obtained one of the announcements on April 8 and brought it to the attention of Lieutenant Cassidy at the 21st District Police Station. Early that evening the lieutenant informed Officers Andrew Alinovich and Donald Duffy of the party, gave them the announcement and instructions to go to the Abramses' house in order, according to testimony given by the police at trial, to make an "investigation and surveillance" and to "discover what was going on there." The two officers, who were not in uniform, arrived at the Abramses' house at about 9:15 P.M. They entered the house and purchased two tickets of admission at a table set up just inside the entranceway to the house. The officers did not identify themselves at this time nor were they asked to do so. Upon entering the officers observed two signs taped to a door in the entry hall which read: "Ice 75¢—drinks free," "Cups 30¢—beer free," and "No drinks served to minors under 21 years of age." They remained in the house for about 10 minutes. They said they observed odors of alcohol on the breaths and from drinking cups of a number of young persons who appeared to be underage.

Upon returning to their car Officers Alinovich and Duffy resumed normal patrol activity for about an hour and then returned to the district station at 10:30 P.M. There they met with Lieutenant Cassidy and Sergeant Smith. After a discussion of "probable violations" of law, the lieutenant instructed Alinovich and Duffy to return to the house. The record is not clear concerning the purpose of this second visit to the Abramses' house. It cannot be determined whether the officers were instructed to make arrests or whether they were only to continue their investigation. The two officers left the station, and about one-half hour later by pre-arrangement met three other officers near the Abramses' house. After a brief discussion, the five officers proceeded directly to the house, arriving at approximately 11:50 P.M. No attempt was made at any time to procure a search or an arrest warrant.

As the officers reached the admission table inside the door, they were stopped by either the defendant Florence Levinsohn or by Mrs. Alice Peurala, and were asked if they were police officers. They identified themselves as officers and were then informed that their presence was not desired. Several persons were congregated at the table, including the defendants Mrs. Abrams and Mrs. Levinsohn. The officers were asked if they had a search warrant and were told they could not enter without a warrant. Officer Alinovich testified that he informed Mrs. Levinsohn that a crime had been committed in his presence and that, therefore, no warrant was necessary. According to Alinovich's testimony, the offense he referred to involved a youth seated at the admission table. At his request the youth handed Alinovich a styrofoam cup, which the officer said contained an alcoholic beverage. The evidence is conflicting as to whether the cup was on the table or in the boy's hand when first noticed by Alinovich: When the cup was handed to the officer a minor scuffle developed. Alinovich testified that Mrs. Levinsohn, claiming the cup belonged to her, reached for the cup and in her efforts to take it struck him several times. According to the testimony of the officers, Alinovich handed the cup to officer Hines and then Mrs. Levinsohn struck Hines. Mrs. Abrams and Mrs. Levinsohn testified, however, that when Mrs. Levinsohn reached for the cup, Officer Hines took hold of her. Mrs. Abrams then, they said, pulled Mrs. Levinsohn behind her. Throughout this incident, Mrs. Abrams and others standing near the door were insisting that the officers leave the house until they had obtained a search warrant.

* * *

[The court's very extensive discussion of the fourth amendment issue and of the constitutionality of the ordinances relating to disorderly conduct and interfering with a police officer in the performance of his duties, is omitted.]

A contention of the defendant Florence Levinsohn is that the complaints which charged her with aggravated assault and with battery were fatally defective in that they failed to charge the respective offenses. Section 111–3 of the Code of Criminal Procedure, consistently with the requirement of our constitution that an accused be apprised of the nature and cause of the accusation (Ill.Const. art. II, sec. 9, S.H.A.; see also People v. Heard, Ill., 266 N.E.2d 340), provides in part: "(a) A charge shall be in writing and allege the commission of an offense by: * * * (3) Setting forth the nature and elements of the offense charged." (Ill.Rev.Stat.1969, ch. 38, par. 111–3(a) (3).) Where the nature and elements of the offense with which the accused is intended to be charged are not set forth in the complaint, it fails to state an offense and is subject to dismissal under section 114–1(a) (8) of the Code of Criminal Procedure. (Ill. Rev.Stat.1969, ch. 38, par. 114–1(a) (8).) It is sufficient to allege an offense in the language of a statute if the words so far particularize the offense that by their use alone an accused is informed with reasonable certainty of the precise offense with which he is charged (People v. Mills, 40 Ill.2d 4, 237 N.E.2d 697), or by specifically alleging all the facts which constitute the crime. See People v. Vraniak, 5 Ill.2d 384, 389, 125 N.E.2d 513; People v. Barnes, 314 Ill. 140, 145, 145 N.E. 391.

Two of the complaints charged that Mrs. Levinsohn committed the offense of "aggravated assault" against Officers Andrew Alinovich and Kenneth Hines. They alleged that she, knowing Alinovich and Hines to be police officers engaged in official duties, "did without lawful authority strike the officer(s) about the arms and body," thereby placing them in reasonable apprehension of receiving a battery. The statute defining this offense provides in part: "(a) A person commits an aggravated assault, when, in committing an assault, he: * * * (6) Knows the individual assaulted to be a peace officer * * * while such officer is engaged in the execution of any of his official duties." (Ill.Rev.Stat.1969, ch. 38, par. 12–2(a) (6).) To commit an assault, including an aggravated assault, one without lawful authority must engage "in conduct which places another in reasonable apprehension of receiving a battery." (Ill.Rev.Stat.1969, ch. 38, par. 12–1.) Assault is an offense distinct from battery. If there has been any touching or other form of physical contact with the victim, a battery has been committed and not an assault, assuming the presence of the other requirements for a battery. The Comments to section 12–1 of the Criminal Code (assault) observe: "It should be emphasized that an assault does not involve a touching. If a touching occurs, by any means, it is a battery." (See Committee Comments, S. H.A. ch. 38, § 12–1.) Too, the Comments to the section which defines aggravated assault note: "If there is a touching the offense would not come within this section but should be prosecuted under the attempt, battery, or aggravated battery section." (Committee Comments, S.H.A. ch. 38, § 12–2.) Considering this, it must be concluded that the assault complaints failed to charge the offense of aggravated assault. The conduct alleged that the officers had been struck and therefore assault was not charged. The complaints were fatally defective and the judgments of conviction thereunder must be reversed. See People v. Heard, Ill., 266 N.E.2d 340; People v. Billingsley, 67 Ill.App.2d 292, 297–301, 213 N.E.2d 765.

Considering the complaints which assertedly charge the defendant Levinsohn with battery we note that the statute defining the offense states: "(a) A person commits battery if he intentionally or knowingly without legal justification and by any means, (1) causes bodily harm to an individual or (2) makes physical contact of an insulting or provoking nature with an individual." (Ill.Rev.Stat.

Dix & Sharlot Cs. Crim.Law ACB—25

1969, ch. 38, par. 12–3.)   The complaints here alleged that the defendant Levinsohn committed the offense of battery against Officers Alinovich and Hines in that she "knowingly and intentionally and without legal justification made physical contact with complainant herein without the consent of said complainant."   It is, of course, essential that a complaint allege all the material facts constituting the offense charged.   (See People v. Vraniak, 5 Ill.2d 384, 389, 125 N.E.2d 513; People v. Strong, 363 Ill. 602, 605, 2 N.E.2d 942.)   The complaints here did not charge either that the physical contact was of an insulting or provoking nature or caused bodily harm, the alternative elements of the offense.   Thus, the complaints for battery were also fatally defective and the judgments of conviction thereunder must be reversed.

*   *   *

For the reasons given, the judgments of conviction against the defendant Florence Levinsohn for aggravated assault and for battery are reversed.   The remaining judgments of the circuit court of Cook County are reversed and the causes remanded for a new trial.

Reversed in part, and reversed and remanded in part.

UNDERWOOD, Chief Justice (dissenting in part):

I disagree with the majority's finding that the complaints charging defendant Levinsohn with aggravated assault are fatally defective and do not charge an offense.   These complaints alleged that, knowing Alinovich and Hines to be police officers engaged in official duties, defendant "did without lawful authority strike the officer(s) about the arms and body" thereby placing them in reasonable apprehension of receiving a battery.   Examination of the relevant statutes as stated in the majority opinion reveals that the statutory language varies from that used in the complaint only in that defendant's conduct, which created the reasonable apprehension, is described.   Since this conduct involved touching, however, the majority finds that it no longer constituted assault.   Sole reliance for this curious result is placed on the Committee Comments to § 12—1 and § 12—2 of the Criminal Code.   (S.H.A., ch. 38, §§ 12—1, 12—2, pp. 697 and 700.) These comments are clearly intended only to emphasize the fact that no touching is required for assault or aggravated assault, while physical contact is required for battery.   They cannot reasonably be read, in my opinion, to preclude prosecution for assault where touching is involved.   This point becomes even more apparent when one considers the majority's treatment of the complaint charging Levinsohn with battery against the same two police officers.   The rejection of this complaint because it did not allege that the physical contact complained of was of an insulting or provoking nature, or that it caused bodily harm, clearly indicates that all intentional physical contact without legal justification does not constitute a battery.   No element of the offense of aggravated assault is absent from the complaint in question. The additional allegation of physical contact is, at most, unnecessary surplusage which does not constitute a fatal defect, and ought to be so treated. People v. Adams, 46 Ill.2d 200, 204, 263 N.E.2d 490; People v. Figgers, 23 Ill.2d 516, 179 N.E.2d 626; People v. Crawford, 23 Ill.2d 605, 179 N.E.2d 667.

DAVIS and RYAN, JJ., join in this dissent.

OTT v. STATE

Court of Special Appeals of Maryland, 1971.
11 Md.App. 259, 273 A.2d 630.

ANDERSON, Judge. Appellant, Harry Clifford Ott, was convicted in the Criminal Court of Baltimore by a jury of the crime of common law assault, and was sentenced to a term of one year under the jurisdiction of the Department of Correctional Services.

It is contended in this appeal that:

* * *

2) that the evidence was insufficient to sustain the conviction, and that the State failed to prove the necessary *mens rea* to establish the guilt of the appellant.

From the evidence adduced by the State, on February 18, 1969, Leo Zimmerman, a constable with the Peoples' Court of Baltimore City, accompanied by Edward Connor, a collection agent, went to the home of Harry C. Ott and Maxine Ott, his wife, located at 2057 Druid Park Drive. He had in his possession a writ of *fieri facias* (commonly called a fi-fa) issued by Chief Judge Tippett of the Peoples' Court of Baltimore City for the purpose of collecting a judgment. Zimmerman and Connor arrived at the Ott home at approximately 2:20 p. m. and were admitted by Mrs. Ott. Zimmerman showed her his badge and explained to her that he was there to execute a writ, or it could be settled by payment of the debt to Mr. Connor. Present in the home at the time was David Perry, a son of Mrs. Ott by a former marriage. About ten minutes after their arrival, Mr. Ott arrived on the premises. He became loud and disorderly and, although Zimmerman showed him his badge and the writ, he refused to listen and informed them that no matter who they were they had better get out or he was going to kill them. Zimmerman told Connor to call the police and after Connor left he tried to calm Ott down, but Ott refused to listen and said he would throw them out. Connor returned and told Zimmerman that he had called the police. When Ott heard the police had been summoned, he said: "You better all get out of here or I'm going to make you get out. I'm going to kill you all." He then ran upstairs and returned with a gun in his pocket with the butt protruding out and his hand on the butt. At that time, he said: "I'm going to kill all of you if you don't get out of here." As he said this, his stepson grabbed his hand and after a struggle disarmed him. Zimmerman testified he was frightened as was everyone else in the room. At this time the police arrived and upon being informed what had happened, the officer asked the stepson where the gun was, and Perry gave it to the police officer and appellant was placed under arrest.

The witness, Edward Connor, supported in detail the testimony of the witness Zimmerman. He testified that appellant refused to listen to any explanation about the writ but became very loud and abusive and threatened to kill them. He observed appellant with the gun in his pocket and his hand on the pistol grip and at that time appellant's stepson grabbed his hand and wrestled the gun away from him. When the police wagon arrived, he ran out and called them in real quick.

Baltimore City Police Officer Richard Bernhartz testified that when he arrived appellant was very emotional, nervous and excited and was hollering. After receiving certain information, he requested the gun and Perry, Ott's stepson, got the gun and turned it over to him. When the chamber was opened, the gun contained one bullet.

This concluded the State's case. At this time the State confessed a plea of not guilty to the first count of the indictment (assault with intent to murder) and the court denied the defendant's motion for judgment of acquittal to the second count (common law assault).

Appellant's first witness was his wife, Maxine Ott. She testified that at the time of the alleged assault she was under the care of her doctor for a heart condition. She denied that she was the one who admitted Zimmerman and Connor and was under the impression that they had pushed their way in after her son had opened the door. She stated that Connor had threatened to take all her possessions and had yelled at her causing her to feel faint. She further stated that her husband arrived home at this time and ordered the two men out of the house. She said at this time it looked like Constable Zimmerman was reaching for his gun and at this point her husband ran upstairs and got a gun. She denied hearing her husband make any threats.

Appellant, testifying in his own behalf, stated that when he returned home he found Zimmerman and Connor inside the house and that Connor was standing over his wife yelling at her. He told both men to get out, and when he thought Zimmerman was reaching for his gun he ran upstairs to get his gun, claiming he thought the two men might be hold-up men. On cross-examination he admitted to numerous other convictions of assault and disorderly conduct.

Appellant's final witness was his stepson, David Perry. He testified it was he who admitted Zimmerman and Connor to the house; that Zimmerman said something about being a constable and having a writ in his hand and asked if Mr. Ott was home. When told he was not, he said he had a matter of importance to discuss with him about furniture, and as the door was partly opened, Zimmerman completed opening the door and, together with Connor, walked in. As they entered the house, his mother, Mrs. Ott, came though the doorway from the dining room and the two men began talking with her. During the discussion the talking was louder than usual but he did not understand much about it as they were all talking at once. However, his mother did say that she was sick and had a heart condition. About 5 or 10 minutes after they arrived, his stepfather, Mr. Ott, arrived. Upon his arrival, the first thing he did was to rush up to where the discussion was taking place and tell them "to get the hell out of the house." He saw the smaller man reach inside his jacket and at that time Mr. Ott turned and ran up the steps. He ran up after him but Ott got back first. He had a gun in his hand when he got to the bottom of the steps and stuck it in his pocket. He managed to take the gun away from him. It had one bullet in it.

On cross-examination he admitted that he knew Zimmerman was a constable and that the conversation between Zimmerman, Connor and his mother was normal conversation up to the time of appellant's arrival, and while it was a little louder than usual, it was not sufficient to upset anyone. He stated that it was only after Mr. Ott arrived that the discussion became very loud. He admitted that Zimmerman and Connor tried to explain to appellant why they were there but Ott refused to listen.

On redirect examination he stated that "the loud talk and all" was Harry Ott's fault.

Appellant then renewed his motion for judgment of acquittal, which was denied.

I

*   *   *

Assault has been defined as any attempt to apply the least force to the person of another. The attempt is made when there is any action or conduct reasonably tending to create apprehension in another and that the person engaged therein is about to apply such force to him. An apparent intention to inflict a battery and an apparent ability to carry out such intention is sufficient. A specific purpose to inflict a particular injury is not necessary. General malevolence or recklessness is sufficient; but mere negligence does not suffice. Williams v. State, 4 Md.App. 643, 244 A.2d 619; Hochheimer, Crimes and Criminal Procedure, Sec.Ed. §§ 253, 254, 256.

The exhibition of a gun to a victim in such a manner as to cause apprehension that it would be used to inflict harm upon him is an assault. Tender v. State, 2 Md.App. 692, 237 A.2d 65.

From the evidence in this case the jury could find appellant guilty of assault. After threatening to kill Connor and Zimmerman appellant ran upstairs and returned with a revolver which was clearly visible and renewed his threat. His actions and conduct tended to create apprehension in Zimmerman and with a weapon in his possession appellant had an apparent ability to carry out his threats. Zimmerman testified he was frightened and the jury could well so find.

We further point out that it is not necessary that there be a specific purpose to do a particular injury in order to prove the necessary *mens rea*. General malevolence or recklessness is sufficient. Williams v. State, supra. The jury could infer general malevolence from appellant's threats to kill coupled with his obtaining the gun.

We find the evidence sufficient to sustain the conviction.

NOTE

As is indicated by the *Abrams* opinion, assault and battery are separate and distinct offenses. It is generally agreed that the unlawful application of force to the person of another is a battery but assault is more difficult to define. An attempted battery which fails will, in most jurisdictions, be deemed an assault. But what if the accused has pointed the gun at his victim and pulled the trigger but unknown to either the gun is unloaded? In a minority of jurisdictions this is not an assault because the accused did not have "present ability" to commit a battery. Yet it would seem that the accused is a proper subject for the criminal sanction. Is he distinguishable from the accused who has pointed the gun and pulled the trigger knowing it to be unloaded but intending to frighten his victim? Under statutes such as that involved in *Abrams,* and in a majority of American jurisdictions, such conduct is an assault since it "places another in reasonable apprehension of receiving a battery". What should be the result if the victim was not conscious of the accused's attempt to frighten him?

---

(2) KIDNAPPING

PEOPLE v. ADAMS

Court of Appeals of Michigan, 1971.
34 Mich.App. 546, 192 N.W.2d 19.

LEVIN, Judge. The defendant, Otis L. Adams, appeals his conviction of kidnapping.

Kidnapping is now a statutory, not a common-law crime. The relevant portion of our statute makes it unlawful to "wilfully, maliciously and without lawful authority * * * forcibly or secretly confine or imprison any other person within this state against his will." But every forcible confinement is not the capital offense of kidnapping.

Our kidnapping statute, like most, is so all-encompassing in its literal breadth that unless its operative effect is confined by objective standards it would be void for overbreadth.

Where a kidnapping statute does not in terms require a "carrying away" of the victim, an asportation requirement or, as a substitute, the element of secrecy, has been judicially read into and made a part of the definition of the crime.

There are two basic kidnapping patterns. In one, the victim is seized and removed to another place; in the other, the victim is confined in the place where he is found. In the first, an asportation or movement of the victim is an essential element; in the second, movement is not an element, but secrecy of the confinement is required.

In this case the people do not charge that the victim was secretly confined. The information charged the defendant Otis Adams with "forcibly confining and imprisoning" his victim—the word "secretly" in the statutory phrase "forcibly or secretly confine" was omitted when the charge was drawn.

To save the Michigan kidnapping statute, insofar as it applies to nonsecret confinements, from a declaration of unconstitutionality because of overbreadth we read it as requiring an asportation. A confinement (other than a secret confinement) without a movement of the victim is not kidnapping. And, for reasons which we will spell out, every movement of the victim of an assaultive crime incidental to the commission of that crime is not kidnapping; the asportation must have a significance independent of the assault in order to manifest the capital and separate offense of kidnapping.

In this case the victim, a prison official, was seized in Jackson State Prison by Adams and other inmates and moved from one part of the prison to another. The seizure and movement occurred in the presence of prison guards; the exact location of both the victim and of the defendant Adams was at all times known to prison guards who had the place cordoned off and surrounded by overwhelming armed force. It is not claimed that Adams ever intended to remove his victim from the prison or that he intended to attempt to effect an escape. This is not the usual hostage pattern, nor is it the usual kidnapping pattern.

I.

Facts

On the morning of October 18, 1965, Adams consumed substantial quantities of alcohol and barbiturates in the company of several other inmates of Jackson Prison. Their conversation turned to the grievances—real or imagined—which they felt against the prison administration.

Shortly after 11:00 a. m., Adams and inmate Edward Whitehead went to the main dining hall of the prison where lunch was being served. Adams cut into the serving line ahead of other inmates and was told by a guard to go to the end of the line. Adams directed some verbal abuse at the guard, then proceeded with Whitehead to the prison's 4-block, a cell block in the northwest portion of the prison. Adams' conduct aroused the attention of two unarmed prison guards who followed him to 4-block.

Because this was the lunch hour, several hundred prisoners were milling about 4-block. The presence of Adams and Whitehead, plus a third inmate, Alvin Shaw, all of whom were highly agitated, as well as the two guards and the hundreds of milling prisoners, led to a disturbance of uncertain proportions.

At this time Inspector Joseph Dembosky, the highest ranking uniformed prison officer, was notified of the disturbance in 4-block. He immediately proceeded to the area and thrust himself into the center of the milling crowd.

Before Inspector Dembosky could take any action, he was seized from behind by inmate Whitehead, who held a knife to his throat. Adams also produced a knife which he used to wave back the prisoners pressing in on Inspector Dembosky and Whitehead. At the trial Inspector Dembosky testified that at this point he said, "Can't we talk about this?" Another witness testified that Dembosky said, "Can't we go somewhere and talk about this?" Adams, Whitehead and Shaw, all of whom had knives, then accompanied Dembosky at knifepoint out of 4-block into the prison yard.

There were approximately one thousand inmates in the yard as Dembosky, Whitehead, Shaw and Adams left 4-block. Inspector Dembosky testified that he felt that there was danger of a riot if the party remained in the yard. He suggested that they go to the prison gymnasium to talk things over. Instead, he was forced to accompany Whitehead, Shaw, and Adams to the prison hospital, which was roughly 1500 feet from the entrance to 4-block. During their journey to the hospital, the armed inmates repeatedly shouted warnings to the heavily-armed tower guards that Inspector Dembosky would be killed if they were fired upon.

Shortly before reaching the hospital building, the group was joined by another inmate, Milton Thomas, who was also armed. Together, immediately after entering the hospital, they seized two guards, a prison doctor, and an inmate elevator operator named Hubbard. Shaw, Whitehead, Thomas, and Adams, together with Inspector Dembosky and the other victims, then proceeded to the doctor's lounge on the fifth floor of the hospital.

Adams and his cohorts erected barricades around the lounge. Over an intercom, they repeatedly demanded to see various prison officials, as well as the warden, to air their grievances. They also demanded to see a newspaper reporter. There were repeated warnings that Inspector Dembosky would be killed if they were fired upon.

During the hours that followed, the armed inmates displayed contradictory behavior toward their captives. The physician was released when Adams ascertained that he had a heart condition. Thomas told the warden to notify the pregnant wife of one of the captive guards that he would not be harmed. Contrastingly, inmate Hubbard was severely beaten by Adams, then released as an example of Adams' serious intentions.

A number of prison officials visited the fifth floor landing to discuss grievances. A newspaper reporter summoned to the scene was occupied for almost three hours in recording these grievances. Adams repeatedly expressed his fear of being shot by guards when he left the fifth floor.

After about 5½ hours, Shaw, Whitehead, Thomas, and Adams were persuaded to abandon their barricaded position. Upon being given assurances that they would not be shot, they released their captives unharmed. They then proceeded to the deputy warden's office, where they surrendered their weapons.

The reprehensible nature of Adams' action does not alter our duty to determine whether the evidence against him is sufficient to support his conviction for kidnapping Inspector Dembosky.

II.

The statute and its overbreadth

* * *

What is immediately obvious about the language of our kidnapping statute is the extraordinary range of conduct it might proscribe.

In the phrase "forcible confinement or imprisonment," the word "imprisonment" is clearly a narrower term than "confinement"; every "imprisonment" would be a "confinement." The word "forcible" adds little, if anything, to the word "confine." "Confine," in the sense in which it is used in this statute, clearly speaks of an involuntary restraint of the liberty of the individual, which, of necessity, is brought about by the use of some force. Similarly, as to the words "against his will." If the confinement was voluntary, it would mean that the victim was confined although he was free to leave—an obvious contradiction of terms.

Since "confine" in this context strongly implies force of some kind, the offense is complete when the actor "wilfully, maliciously and without lawful authority" confines the victim. And, since in the ordinary case there is likely to be no question of lawful authority (and besides, lawful authority negatives "malice"), and since the wilfulness required by law does not enlarge the requirement of malice, *violation of the terms of the statute occurs whenever the actor "maliciously confines" any other person.*

"Malice, in its common acceptation, means ill will toward some person. In its legal sense, it applies to a wrongful act committed intentionally against that person, without legal justification or excuse." Bonkowski v. Arlan's Department Store (1970), 383 Mich. 90, 99, 174 N.W.2d 765, 768.

*   *   *

Accordingly, freed of its tautology, the kidnapping statute, simply put, makes it kidnapping to *intentionally confine another person without legal justification or excuse.*

It will be observed that the statute makes no reference to the duration or circumstances of the confinement. Literally construed, the statute leads to absurd results. The trespasser who momentarily locks a caretaker in his cottage is placed on the same footing as the professional criminal who invades a home, seizes the occupants at gunpoint, transports them to a secret hideout, and holds them for ransom. The robber who orders his victim to stand motionless while his wallet is removed is guilty of the same crime as the robber who forces his victim to drive for miles to a deserted location, where he is terrorized and abandoned. A group of college students who invade a dean's office, wrongfully confining its occupants, commit the same offense as a gang of rapists who seize a woman and remove her from her family to a place of isolation.

Shopkeepers who wrongfully detain suspected shoplifters, cabdrivers who purposely deliver passengers to the wrong destinations, tavernkeepers who bar exits until bar bills have been paid, all may be subject to civil damage actions, but a sensible penology rebels at the classification of such acts as capital offenses.

As emphatically as these examples offend a rational penal code, they scarcely embrace all the varieties if technically culpable, but scarcely menacing, conduct which violates a statutory ban on "intentional confinement" of any other person.

*   *   *

[The Court's discussion of the problems posed by statute under the void-for-vagueness doctrine (see section II.D.2. supra) is omitted. The Court concluded that a literal reading of the statute would expose perpetrators of virtually every crime against the person to capital sanctions in the discretion of prosecutors, judges and juries. To avoid such results and thereby preserve the statute the court turned to an analysis of its substance.]

III.

Substantive law of kidnapping

At common law, kidnapping required an asportation of the victim out of the country. Kidnapping was a misdemeanor, and was viewed merely as an aggravated form of false imprisonment; the aggravating factor was the removal of the victim from the sovereign's protection.[20]

Kidnapping statutes in the United States have abolished the requirement that a national or a regional boundary be breached.

Modification of the asportation element of the common-law crime was not the only American statutory departure from the common law. Public revulsion against the wave of carefully-planned and often brutal kidnappings for ransom of the 1920's and 1930's resulted in the imposition of heavy penalties,[23] including the death penalty, for kidnappers, and passage of the Federal Kidnapping Act, the so-called Lindbergh Law. It was in 1931 that Michigan imposed a maximum sentence of life imprisonment for kidnapping.

Another characteristic of kidnapping legislation has been its failure to distinguish between the crimes of kidnapping and false imprisonment. Michigan, along with most States, does not have a separate false imprisonment statute.

These matters aside, the principal question that has perplexed American courts in construing kidnapping legislation has been the degree of asportation required to transform an assault, robbery, or other crime into kidnapping. Torn between the common-law rule that a most significant asportation was required, and the obvious legislative intention to broaden the scope of the offense, the courts, virtually without exception, endorsed the idea that any asportation, however slight, was sufficient to constitute kidnapping.

Representative of this formulation were the opinions of the California Supreme Court in People v. Chessman (1951), 38 Cal.2d 166, 192, 238 P.2d 1001, 1017, and People v. Wein (1958), 50 Cal.2d 383, 399, 400, 326 P.2d 457, 466. In *Chessman,* the defendant forced his victim to move 22 feet to his automobile, where he sexually assaulted her. The Court held that, "It is the fact, not the distance, of forcible removal which constitutes kidnapping in this state." In *Wein,* the Court applied the *Chessman* standard to uphold the kidnapping conviction of a defendant who forced his victims to move from room in their own homes during a series of robberies and rapes. These holdings

---

20. For discussions of the common law crime of kidnapping, see Perkins on Criminal Law (2d ed.), p. 176; Note, A Rationale of the Law of Kidnapping, 53 Colum.L.Rev. 540 (1953).

23. See Model Penal Code, Tentative Draft No. 11, comment p. 11, fn. 1: "Kidnapping (or some category of it) is punishable by life imprisonment or death in all States except Alaska (10 years), Connecticut (50 years), Minnesota (40 years), New Hampshire (25 years), and North Dakota (20 years). Where kidnapping is divided into degrees, even simple kidnapping is punishable by life imprisonment, in some States, and the maximum in other States is commonly 10–25 years."

* * *

Modern legislation, as an inducement to the felon to release his victim unharmed, reserves the capital offense of kidnapping for cases where the victim is not voluntarily released free of serious physical injury. See, e. g., New York Penal Law, McKinney's Consol.Laws, c. 40, § 135.00 et seq.; Model Penal Code, § 212, et seq.; Study Draft of a New Federal Criminal Code, § 1631.

came under sharp criticism,[27] but were accurate reflections of the state of the law until quite recently.

The first significant departure from the "any asportation" requirement came in another California case, Cotton v. Superior Court (1961), 56 Cal.2d 459, 464, 15 Cal.Rptr. 65, 68, 364 P.2d 241, 244. A labor dispute led to the invasion of a farm worker's camp by union members. Several braceros were assaulted and dragged about the camp during the ensuing riot. The California Supreme Court ruled that the assailants could not be convicted of kidnapping, saying that "all 'asportation' in the instant case would appear to be only incidental to the assault and rioting." The Court declared that it should avoid "absurd consequences" in application of the kidnapping laws; it warned that a literal reading of the California statute "could result in a rule that every assault could also be prosecuted for kidnapping." The Court ignored, it did not overrule, *Chessman* and *Wein,* but the significance of *Cotton* was not lost on the commentators.

A few years after *Cotton* was decided, the New York Court of Appeals articulated a new approach to the asportation requirement. In People v. Levy (1965), 15 N.Y.2d 159, 164, 256 N.Y.S.2d 793, 796, 204 N.E.2d 842, 844, the defendants accosted the victims, who had just arrived at their home in an automobile. One of the defendants took the wheel, and the victims, husband and wife, were driven about city streets for twenty minutes, covering twenty-seven blocks. During this journey the victims were robbed of money and jewelry.

The defendants were convicted by a jury of kidnapping under the New York statute, which provided that a person who "confines" another with intent to "cause him * * * to be confined" against his will is guilty of kidnapping. The Court of Appeals reversed. Central to the Court's holding was its concern that the broad statutory definition, "could literally overrun several other crimes, notably robbery and rape, and in some circumstances assault, since detention and sometimes confinement, against the will of the victim, frequently accompany these crimes * * * It is a common occurrence in robbery, for example, that the victim be confined briefly at gunpoint or bound and detained, or moved into and left in another room or place.

"It is unlikely that these restraints, sometimes accompanied by asportation, which are incidents to other crimes and have long been treated as integral parts of other crimes, were intended by the Legislature in framing its broad definition of kidnapping to constitute a separate crime of kidnapping, even though kidnapping might sometimes be spelled out literally from the statutory words." The Court

27. See Model Penal Code, Tentative Draft No. 11, p. 14, fn. 9 as to *Chessman. Wein* was termed the *reductio ad absurdum* case in Packer, The Case for Revision of the Penal Code, 13 Stan.L.Rev. 252, 259, fn. 41 (1961).

overruled a contrary prior decision [31] and held that the kidnapping statute was to be limited in its application "to 'kidnapping' in the conventional sense in which that term has now come to have acquired meaning."

Left unresolved in *Levy* was the precise degree of asportation necessary to constitute "kidnapping in the conventional sense." The opinion did, however, revive the requirement that some meaningful asportation must accompany the crime. In a subsequent case the Court of Appeals declared that "the direction of the criminal law has been to limit the scope of the kidnapping statute, with its very substantially more severe penal consequences, to true kidnapping situations and not to apply it to crimes which are essentially robbery, rape or assault and in which some confinement or asportation occurs as a subsidiary incident." People v. Lombardi (1967), 20 N.Y.2d 266, 270, 282 N.Y.S. 2d 519, 521, 229 N.E.2d 206, 208. But, in a still more recent case, the Court held that "the more complicated nature of the asportation" pursued in the defendant's efforts to kill the victim, removed the case from the *Levy-Lombardi* rule.

The reasoning of the New York Court of Appeals was not accepted by other courts. Several jurisdictions expressly rejected the idea that a substantial asportation was necessary under broadly-worded kidnapping statutes.

In 1969, by a 6-to-1 decision the California Supreme Court overruled its prior constructions in the *Chessman-Wein* line of cases. People v. Daniels (1969), 71 Cal.2d 1119, 1139, 80 Cal.Rptr. 897, 910, 459 P.2d 225, 238, clearly repudiates the doctrine that any asportation of the victim is sufficient to constitute kidnapping. There the victims had been forced to move about in their apartments during the commission of crimes of robbery and rape. The Court declared:

> "We hold that the intent of the Legislature * * * was to exclude from [the statute's] reach not only 'standstill' robberies * * * but also those in which the movements of the victim are merely incidental to the commission of the robbery and do not substantially increase the risk of harm over and above that necessarily present in the crime of robbery itself."

A few months ago the California Supreme Court elaborated on its decision in *Daniels*. See People v. Timmons (1971), 4 Cal.3d 411, 93 Cal.Rptr. 736, 482 P.2d 648, where the Court held that the defendant's acts in entering the robbery victims' automobile and directing them to drive it some five city blocks, in order to facilitate the robbery, did not constitute kidnapping since the acts did not "substan-

31. People v. Florio, * * * In *Florio* a girl was enticed into an automobile and driven from Manhattan to an isolated spot in Queens where she was raped.

tially" increase "the risk that the victim may suffer significant physical injuries over and above those to which a victim of the underlying
crime [robbery] is normally exposed."   Similarly, see People v. Smith
(1971), 4 Cal.3d 426, 93 Cal.Rptr. 743, 482 P.2d 655, where the Court
held that the crime of kidnapping had not been committed where, in
the course of robbing a hotel, the defendant caused the night clerk to
move about the office and up to a second floor room.

Having reviewed the authorities in some detail, we approach decision.

IV.

The asportation requirement and the standard by which it is applied

We hold that, except in those relatively rare cases where the victim is intentionally locked in the place where he is found and
there secretly isolated and confined, a reasonable construction of our
kidnapping statute requires an asportation of the victim before the
crime of kidnapping is complete.   Still to be answered is the extent of
the asportation required.

We believe that the history of kidnapping jurisprudence in this
country demonstrates the futility of attempting to calculate the requisite asportation in terms of linear measurement.   The harm sought to
be prevented is not movement of the victim, but his removal from one
place to another and attendant increased risks to the victim.   The actual distance the victim is transported does not necessarily correspond
with the invasion of his physical interest.   An asportation of 50 feet
may in some cases expose the victim to precisely those abuses which
kidnapping statutes are designed to prevent; in other cases, an asportation of 500 feet may alter the victim's situation not at all.

We have concluded that under the kidnapping statute a movement
of the victim does not constitute an asportation unless it has significance independent of the assault.   And, unless the victim is removed from the environment where he is found, the consequences of
the movement itself to the victim are not independently significant
from the assault—the movement does not manifest the commission
of a separate crime—and punishment for injury to the victim must be
founded upon crimes other than kidnapping.

A comprehensive scheme for dealing with this offense rests within the province of the legislature, not the courts.   The standard we apply today does, however, discriminate with some certainty between conduct which ought clearly to be punished under the kidnapping statute and conduct which falls within the scope of other crimes.[36]

36.   While, as Judge Gillis points out, this case does not involve movement of a victim incident to a robbery or rape, it does involve movement inci- dent to a felonious assault which, too, is a separate crime.

Indeed, under Michigan law there is little reason to charge kidnapping where the movement is incidental to an armed robbery or a rape because both of those offenses are punishable by life sentences and in Michigan all

V.

The standard applied to the facts of this case

To define "environment" restrictively, *e. g.,* the mere geographic location of the victim, would be to return to the "any movement" concept. The relevant environment is the totality of the surroundings, animate and inanimate.

Applying these criteria to the assault on Inspector Dembosky, we conclude that Adams did not commit the crime of kidnapping. The movement of Inspector Dembosky did not remove him from the prison environment. As his duties customarily took him throughout the entire prison, it cannot be said that moving him from the confused, threatening situation in 4-block to the fifth floor hospital was independently significant from the assault.

The purpose of the movement was neither to avoid detection nor to expose Inspector Dembosky to an increased risk of harm. He was moved to reduce the risk of escalation by providing a cooling-off period. When he was first assaulted the inspector asked, "Can't we talk about this?" And, when the group moved off, he suggested that they go to the prison gymnasium. Instead he was required to accompany the assailants to the fifth floor of the prison hospital. This case is not like a case of street assault where the victim is seized on a thoroughfare and pulled into a dark alley or into an automobile to prevent detection so that the assault can be completed in greater privacy; such a movement might have significance independent of the assault.

The evidence does not support a contention that the movement to the fifth floor of the hospital exposed the inspector to an increased risk of harm because it made his rescue more difficult. Adams and the other men were armed with knives. There is no evidence, no reason to suppose or infer that they were less likely to use their knives if a confrontation with rescuers had occurred at 4-block than at the fifth floor landing of the hospital. Might not the presence at 4-block of hundreds of milling men have made rescue there more difficult? Might not one of the three agitated, perhaps still intoxicated and narcotized, assailants reacted mortally on the spur of the moment to a taunting challenge from an unseen voice in the milling throng? Un-

sentences, with few exceptions, run concurrently. It is only where the other offense is punishable by a sentence less than life that there is likely to be an issue whether movement incidental to the commission of that offense constituted the separate crime of kidnapping.

Accordingly, the likelihood is that in Michigan kidnapping will be charged for a street assault most frequently where the assailant failed to consummate his objective, the prosecutorial purpose in charging kidnapping being to aggravate the penalty for the unsuccessful attempt. The degree of asportation that should be required to justify a kidnapping prosecution in such a case is beyond the scope of this opinion.

der the circumstances we are satisfied that the evidence does not support a finding that the movement had significance adverse to Inspector Dembosky independent of the continuing assault.[39]

The inspector was seized in Jackson Prison. It is an atypical place, an armed enclosure that no one can enter or leave without passing through guarded entranceways. Movement from one building to another in Jackson Prison, for purposes of the kidnapping statute, is not significantly different than movement from one room to another in a building, especially where, as here, the movement was under surveillance of armed guards who had the enclosure protected and there was no intention on the part of Adams or the other felons themselves to leave or to remove Inspector Dembosky from the prison.

The movement of Inspector Dembosky did not make the apprehension of the felons less likely, nor did the movement make it less likely that the inspector would be released unharmed. It provided a cooling-off period—which Inspector Dembosky himself wisely sought. It provided time for these impetuous, desperate men to reflect and to draw back from worse folly.

Adams' conduct was highly dangerous and indefensible. The prison and prosecutorial authorities are understandably anxious to see that he is severely punished. Prison guards and officials like Inspector Dembosky mingle with frustrated, assaultive desperate men. An assault upon any of them is a serious breach of discipline; punishment should be clear, certain and severe.

Michigan, unlike other jurisdictions, does not have a specific statute making assault by a prisoner on a prison guard or official a crime carrying special penalties. In Michigan, assault upon a prison guard is treated no differently than assault outside of prison walls. The maximum penalties are relatively mild for the kind of aggravated conduct indulged in by Adams and his confederates. That is a good reason for the legislature to amend the penal code to provide adequate sanctions for an assault by a prisoner. It is not a reason for transforming, without legislative authorization, what under present law may

---

39. It is important in this case to make clear what we do not decide as well as what we hold so that our opinion is not misread.

The taking of a hostage may be the offense of kidnapping. In the hostage situation, if the victim is removed from the environment where he is found, the removal will generally have significance adverse to the victim independent of the assault and the offense of kidnapping will be completed upon his removal from the environment. Even if the victim is not so removed, if the actor intends to remove him from the environment where he is found and commits an overt act going beyond mere preparation, that would be attempted kidnapping. If the victim is seized with intent "to extort money or other valuable thing" or to hold the victim "to service against his will" that too *may* be kidnapping even though there has been no asportation * * *

Nor do we express any opinion as to when a seizure of a person on the street incidental to the commission or attempted commission of another offense (*e. g.*, rape, robbery) becomes the separate offense of kidnapping. * * *

be nothing more than a felonious assault, into an offense which carries with it a possible life sentence.

Criminal statutes, in contrast with the common law, may not be expanded to meet new problems beyond the contemplation of the legislature when the statute was enacted.[42]

Reversed.

42. At common law there was a clear distinction between false imprisonment, kidnapping and extortion.

False imprisonment was a common-law misdemeanor and consisted of compelling a person to remain where he is or go somewhere else against his will by an unlawful exercise or show of force. Perkins on Criminal Law (2d ed.), p. 171.

Kidnapping was aggravated false imprisonment. However, it was also a misdemeanor at common law and consisted of forcible abduction or stealing of a person from his own country and sending him into another. Perkins on Criminal Law (2d ed.), p. 176.

Common-law extortion, also a misdemeanor, was the collection of an unlawful fee by an officer under color of office. Perkins on Criminal Law (2d ed.), p. 367.

* * *

Robbery is the taking from the person of another or in his presence of money or other property which may be the subject of larceny by force and violence or by assault or putting in fear (M.C.L.A. § 750.530 [Stat.Ann.1954 Rev. § 28.798]); and, if committed with a dangerous weapon or any article used or fashioned in a manner to lead the person so assaulted to reasonably believe it to be a dangerous weapon, it is armed robbery. M.C.L.A. § 750.529 (Stat.Ann.1971 Cum.Supp. § 28.797).

* * *

It is apparent from the history of the development of these statutes that kidnapping historically and definitionally is a different crime from false imprisonment or extortion or robbery.

The kidnapping statute is not a catch-all, a means of aggravating the penalties—to fill in a gap in the law—so that penalties as severe as those that can be meted out for extortion, armed robbery and kidnapping can be imposed for "extortion" not involving threatened assault on a relative. We

may not properly engraft an additional pattern and provide by judicial interpretation that any detention of a person for the purpose of extracting any advantage whatsoever is kidnapping even though there is no meaningful asportation and no secrecy, or that where "extortion" is involved the quality of the asportation required to establish kidnapping need not be of the kind required where extortion is not present * * *.

All the foregoing shows the difficulty of trying to make a statute * * * designed for one purpose, based upon certain definitional assumptions long established, do another job.

* * *

In the construction of criminal statutes a court is not at liberty to evolve the law much the same as if the court were developing the common law. It is the prerogative of the legislature, not the courts, to define a new crime. "There is no crime whatever punishable by our laws except by virtue of a statutory provision." In the Matter of Lamphere (1886), 61 Mich. 105, 108, 27 N.W. 882, 883.

"The spirit of the doctrine which denies to the federal judiciary power to create crimes forthrightly admonishes that we should not enlarge the reach of enacted crimes by constituting them from anything less than the incriminating components contemplated by the words used in the statute. And where Congress borrows terms of art in which are accumulated the legal tradition and meaning of centuries of practice, it presumably knows and adopts the cluster of ideas that were attached to each borrowed word in the body of learning from which it was taken and the meaning its use will convey to the judicial mind unless otherwise instructed. In such case, absence of contrary direction may be taken as satisfaction with widely accepted definitions, not as a departure from them." Morissette v. United States

J. H. GILLIS, Presiding Judge (dissenting).

Unlike my Colleagues, I am satisfied that there was sufficient evidence from which the jury could lawfully find defendant Adams guilty of kidnaping. Accordingly, I would affirm defendant's conviction.

In my view, the majority misapply the teachings of such cases as People v. Levy, People v. Lombardi and People v. Daniels. And, as a result, the majority reach what I consider to be an absurd result. This case is not one in which the restraint and forcible movement of Inspector Dembosky can be characterized solely as "incident[s] to other crimes and * * * integral parts of other crimes." People v. Levy, 15 N.Y.2d at 164–165, 256 N.Y.S.2d at 796, 204 N.E.2d at 844. This case does not involve movement of the victim incident to robbery (People v. Levy, *supra*; People v. Daniels, *supra*); nor does it involve asportation incident to rape (People v. Lombardi, *supra*; People v. Daniels, *supra*).

In People v. Miles (1969), 23 N.Y.2d 527, 539, 540, 297 N.Y.S.2d 913, 922, 245 N.E.2d 688, 694, 695, the New York Court of Appeals explained the *Levy-Lombardi* rationale as follows:

> "In the *Levy* and *Lombardi* cases, and especially in the *Levy* case, the restraint and asportation were parts of the crimes ultimately committed. The robbery and the rapes could not be committed in the forms planned without the limited asportations there involved. Indeed, in any robbery, there is a restraint of 'false imprisonment' and in every rape there is a similar restraint and often removal in some limited sense. It is this kind of factual merger with the ultimate crime of the preliminary, preparatory, or concurrent action that the rule is designed to recognize, and thus prevent unnatural elevation of the 'true' crime to be charged.

> *   *   *   *   *   *   *   *   *   *

> "Moreover, *the rule has no purpose of ignoring as independent crimes alternative or optional means used in commit-*

(1951), 342 U.S. 246, 263, 72 S.Ct. 240, 249, 96 L.Ed. 288, 300.

*   *   *

An asportation is the gist of the offense of kidnapping. If we sustain a conviction for kidnapping on evidence that the victim of the confinement has been held a "substantial" period of time and exposed to "serious" risk of harm even though there was not an asportation having significance independent of the assault, then most every assaultive crime can be the capital offense of kidnapping if the prosecutor so charges and a jury so finds.

We acknowledge that we have, indeed, by our construction of Michigan's kidnapping statute defined the crime. But we have done so in the context that the Michigan Supreme Court has not defined the crime and, unless defined, the statute would be void for overbreadth. It is the traditional role of the judiciary to pass on the constitutionality of a statute and to construe it, if possible, to preserve its constitutionality.

ting another crime which, by the gravity and even horrendousness of the means used, constitute and should constitute a separately cognizable offense.

* * * * * * * * * *

"In short, the *Levy-Lombardi* rule was designed to prevent gross distortion of lesser crimes into a much more serious crime by excess of prosecutorial zeal. *It was not designed to merge 'true' kidnappings into other crimes merely because the kidnappings were used to accomplish ultimate crimes of lesser or equal or greater gravity.*" (Emphasis supplied.)

Nothing in this record suggests to me an excess of prosecutorial zeal. Accordingly, the *Levy-Lombardi* rule is inapposite. In my view, Adams' conduct could lawfully be considered "true" kidnaping.

In People v. Congdon (1889), 77 Mich. 351, 354, 43 N.W. 986, the Michigan Supreme Court noted that the gist of the offense under the kidnaping statute is the involuntariness of the seizure. Similarly, the United States Supreme Court has stated that "the involuntariness of seizure and detention * * * is the very essence of the crime of kidnaping." Chatwin v. United States (1946), 326 U.S. 455, 464, 66 S.Ct. 233, 237, 90 L.Ed. 198, 203. On the facts as recited in the majority opinion, it clearly appears that the jury could find that Inspector Dembosky had been involuntarily seized.

Moreover, "the gravity and even horrendousness", People v. Miles, 23 N.Y.2d at 539, 297 N.Y.S.2d at 922, 245 N.E.2d at 694, of Adams' conduct serves to distinguish this case from mere false imprisonment. Inspector Dembosky was confined against his will for a substantial period of time. He was exposed to serious risk of harm. Thus, Inspector Dembosky was subjected to the very abuses the kidnaping statute is intended to prevent. It follows that we should not, as a matter of law, refuse to characterize defendant Adams' conduct as kidnaping. At least, on this record, the jury should be permitted to so find.

I have discovered but two cases which factually resemble this case of *Adams*. In each, a prison guard was forcibly seized and held against his will within the prison by inmates. Jury convictions of kidnaping were affirmed in both cases on the law and the facts. The evidence was held sufficient to justify the verdicts. See State v. Randall (1960), 137 Mont. 534, 353 P.2d 1054, and State v. Frodsham (1961), 139 Mont. 222, 362 P.2d 413. See, also, People v. Shaw (1968), 11 Mich.App. 255, 160 N.W.2d 761. Such should be the result in this case.

Defendant's other contentions are without merit. His conviction should be affirmed.

NOTE

Marcellus enticed Steve, a thirteen year old boy, into accompanying him into the woods to see some squirrels. Once there Marcellus committed a vicious and apparently unprovoked assault. He is tried and convicted for both felonious assault and common law kidnapping; he receives sentences of ten years for the former and twenty-eight for the latter. On his appeal from the kidnapping conviction Marcellus argues that there was no kidnapping since Steve was never deprived of his liberty. Is there merit to this position? Should he face a possible life sentence for conduct that is arguably indistinguishable from a similar assault following an accidental meeting in the woods? Are these distinguishable? Should he be faced with a kidnapping charge if he had simply slapped Steve after inveigling him into the woods? See State v. Murphy, 280 N.C. 1, 184 S.E.2d 845 (1971).

---

4. LIMITATION UPON TREATING ONE ACT OR RELATED ACTIVITY AS MORE THAN ONE CRIME AND IMPOSING CUMULATIVE PENALTIES

In 1305, William Wallace, a notorious traitor, was "drawn for treason, hanged for robbery and homicide and disembowelled for sacrilege, beheaded as an outlaw and quartered for divers depredations." 2 Pollack and Maitland, History of English Law 501 (2nd ed. 1905). More recently, the Supreme Court of Ohio upheld two charges of first degree murder (in attempting to perpetrate a robbery, and with premeditation), guilty verdicts on both, and two sentences (death and life imprisonment) for the slaying of a single person. State v. Ferguson, 175 Ohio St. 390, 195 N.E.2d 794 (1964). Although the practical effect of such multiple punishment on Wallace and Ferguson was probably minimal, the problem of multiple punishment for arguably related or identical activity has today become of greater significance. First, as the severity of punishment for single offenses as decreased there is a greater sense of disproportion in cumulative punishment for what seems essentially the same conduct. Second, the frequency with which such issues arise has increased as the number of separate offenses, with considerable overlapping application, has been multiplied. The following material raises a number of questions in this area. Commentators have provided extensive discussion of the matter. E. g., Horack, The Multiple Consequences of a Single Criminal Act, 21 Minn.L.Rev. 805 (1937); 43 Notre Dame Law 1017 (1968); Note, Twice in Jeopardy, 75 Yale L.J. 262 (1965); Comment, Statutory Implementation of Double Jeopardy Clauses: New Life for a Moribund Constitutional Guarantee, 65 Yale L.J. 339 (1956).

SMITH-HURD ILL. ANN. STAT. CH. 38.

§ 1–7. Judgment, Sentence and Related Provisions

* * *

(m) Consecutive and Concurrent Sentences.

When a person shall have been convicted of 2 or more offenses which did not result from the same conduct, either before or after sentence has been pronounced upon him for either the court in its discretion may order that the term of imprisonment upon any one of the convictions may commence at the expiration of the term of imprisonment upon any other of the offenses.

McKINNEY CONSOL. LAWS OF N. Y. (PENAL LAW)

§ 70.25 Concurrent and Consecutive Terms of Imprisonment

* * *

2. When more than one sentence of imprisonment is imposed on a person for two or more offenses committed through a single act or omission, or through an act or omission which in itself constituted one of the offenses and also was a material element of the other, the sentences must run concurrently.

3. Where consecutive definite sentences of imprisonment are not prohibited by subdivision two of this section and are imposed on a person for offenses which were committed as parts of a single incident or transaction, the aggregate of the terms of such sentences shall not exceed one year.

BLOCKBURGER v. UNITED STATES

Supreme Court of the United States, 1932.
284 U.S. 299, 52 S.Ct. 180, 76 L.Ed. 306.

Mr. Justice SUTHERLAND delivered the opinion of the Court.

The petitioner was charged with violating provisions of the Harrison Narcotic Act * * * [.] The indictment contained five counts. The jury returned a verdict against petitioner upon the second, third, and fifth counts only. Each of these counts charged a sale of morphine hydrochloride to the same purchaser. The second count charged a sale on a specified day of ten grains of the drug not in or from the original stamped package; the third count charged a sale on the following day of eight grains of the drug not in or from the original stamped package; the fifth count charged the latter sale also as having been made not in pursuance of a written order of the purchaser as required by the statute. The court sentenced petitioner to five years' imprisonment and a fine of $2,000 upon each count, the terms of imprisonment to run consecutively; and this judgment was affirmed on appeal. (C.C.A.) 50 F.(2d) 795.

The principal contentions here made by petitioner are as follows: (1) That, upon the facts, the two sales charged in the second and third counts as having been made to the same person constitute a single offense; and (2) that the sale charged in the third count as having been made not from the original stamped package, and the same sale charged in the fifth count as having been made not in pursuance of a written order of the purchaser, constitute but one offense, for which only a single penalty lawfully may be imposed.

One. The sales charged in the second and third counts, although made to the same person, were distinct and separate sales made at different times. It appears from the evidence that, shortly after delivery of the drug which was the subject of the first sale, the purchaser paid for an additional quantity, which was delivered the next day. But the first sale had been consummated, and the payment for the additional drug, however closely following, was the initiation of a separate and distinct sale completed by its delivery.

The contention on behalf of petitioner is that these two sales, having been made to the same purchaser and following each other, with no substantial interval of time between the delivery of the drug in the first transaction and the payment for the second quantity sold, constitute a single continuing offense. The contention is unsound. The distinction between the transactions here involved and an offense continuous in its character is well settled, as was pointed out by this court in the case of In re Snow, 120 U.S. 274, 7 S.Ct. 556, 30 L.Ed. 658. There it was held that the offense of cohabiting with more than one woman, created by the Act of March 22, 1882, c. 47, 22 Stat. 31 (now 18 U.S.C.A. § 514) was a continuous offense, and was committed, in the sense of the statute, where there was a living or dwelling together as husband and wife. The court said (pages 281, 286 of 120 U.S., 7 S.Ct. 556, 559):

> "It is, inherently, a continuous offense, having duration; and not an offense consisting of an isolated act. * * *
>
> "A distinction is laid down in adjudged cases and in text-writers between an offense continuous in its character, like the one at bar, and a case where the statute is aimed at an offense that can be committed uno ictu."

The Narcotic Act does not create the offense of engaging in the business of selling the forbidden drugs, but penalizes any sale made in the absence of either of the qualifying requirements set forth. Each of several successive sales constitutes a distinct offense, however closely they may follow each other. The distinction stated by Mr. Wharton is that, "when the impulse is single, but one indictment lies, no matter how long the action may continue. If successive impulses are separately given, even though all unite in swelling a common stream of action, separate indictments lie." Wharton's Criminal Law (11th Ed.) § 34. Or, as stated in note 3 to that section, "The test is whether the individual acts are prohibited, or the course of action which they constitute. If the former, then each act is punishable separately. * * * If the latter, there can be but one penalty."

In the present case, the first transaction, resulting in a sale, had come to an end. The next sale was not the result of the original impulse, but of a fresh one—that is to say, of a new bargain. The question is controlled, not by the Snow Case, but by such cases as that of Ebeling v. Morgan, 237 U.S. 625, 35 S.Ct. 710, 59 L.Ed. 1151. There the accused was convicted under several counts of a willful tearing, etc., of mail bags with intent to rob. The court (page 628 of 237 U.S., 35 S.Ct. 710, 711) stated the question to be "whether one who, in the same transaction, tears or cuts successively mail bags of the United States used in conveyance of the mails, with intent to rob or steal any such mail, is guilty of a single offense, or of additional offenses because of each successive cutting with the criminal intent charged." Answering this question, the court, after quoting the statute, section 189, Criminal Code, (U.S.C. title 18, § 312 [18 USCA § 312]) said (page 629 of 237 U.S., 35 S.Ct. 710, 711):

> "These words plainly indicate that it was the intention of the lawmakers to protect each and every mail bag from felonious injury and mutilation. Whenever any one mail bag is thus torn, cut, or injured, the offense is complete. Although the transaction of cutting the mail bags was in a sense continuous, the complete statutory offense was committed every time a mail bag was cut in the manner described, with the intent charged. The offense as to each separate bag was complete when that bag was cut, irrespective of any attack upon, or mutilation of, any other bag."

Two. Section 1 of the Narcotic Act creates the offense of selling any of the forbidden drugs except in or from the original stamped package; and section 2 creates the offense of selling any of such drugs not in pursuance of a written order of the person to whom the drug is sold. Thus, upon the face of the statute, two distinct offenses are created. Here there was but one sale, and the question is whether, both sections being violated by the same act, the accused committed two offenses or only one.

The statute is not aimed at sales of the forbidden drugs qua sales, a matter entirely beyond the authority of Congress, but at sales of such drugs in violation of the requirements set forth in sections 1 and 2, enacted as aids to the enforcement of the stamp tax imposed by the act.

Each of the offenses created requires proof of a different element. The applicable rule is that, where the same act or transaction constitutes a violation of two distinct statutory provisions, the test to be applied to determine whether there are two offenses or only one is whether each provision requires proof of an additional fact which the other does not. Gavieres v. United States, 220 U.S. 338, 342, 31 S.Ct. 421, 55 L.Ed. 489, and authorities cited. In that case this court quoted from and adopted the language of the Supreme Court of Massachusetts in Morey v. Commonwealth, 108 Mass. 433: "A single act may be an offense against two statutes; and if each statute requires proof of an additional fact which the other does not, an acquittal or conviction under either statute does not exempt the defendant from prosecution and punishment under the other." * * * Applying the test, we must conclude that here, although both sections were violated by the one sale, two offenses were committed.

* * *

Judgment affirmed.

NOTE

In Gavieres v. United States, 220 U.S. 338, 31 S.Ct. 421, 55 L.Ed. 489 (1911) the defendant had been convicted of two offenses by the Philippine courts based upon "the same words and conduct." One conviction was under an ordinance of the city of Manila which prohibited disorderly conduct, including boisterous or rude conduct. The second conviction was under an article of the Philippine Penal Code which prohibited insulting a public official by word of mouth in his presence. The "single question" presented by the case, the Court stated, was whether the defendant had been twice placed in jeopardy for the same offense in violation of a federal statute applicable to Philippine criminal prosecutions. The Court had previously held that the statute applied to the Philippines the prohibition against double jeopardy as that prohibition had developed under the Federal Constitution. Affirming the conviction, the Court stated:

> It is to be observed that the protection intended and specifically given is against second jeopardy for the *same offense*. The question, therefore, is, Are the offenses charged, and of which a conviction has been had * * *, identical? An examination of the ordinance show that the gist of the offense under it was misbehaving in an indecent manner in a public place open to public view. It was not necessary to charge or prove * * * any outrage, insult, or threat to a public official or agent of the authorities. * * *

> In the second case it was charged, as was essential to conviction, that the misbehavior in deed and word was addressed to a public official. In this view we are of opinion that while the transaction charged is the same in each case, the offenses are different. * * * While it is true that the conduct of the accused was one and the same, two offenses resulted, each of which had an element not embraced in the other.

Id. at 341–42, 343.

The same result was reached, without citation of *Gavieres*, by a split court in Bell v. Kansas, 452 F.2d 783 (10th Cir. 1972). There the petitioner had first been convicted in the municipal court of Topeka, Kansas for the misdemeanor of carrying a concealed weapon. He was fined $100 and sentenced to 90 days in jail. He was then tried and convicted in a Kansas district court for violating a state statute prohibiting convicted felons from possessing a pistol. Because of his prior record he was sentenced, as a habitual criminal, to not less than 15 years.

Is there any reason why the test announced in *Gavieres* for determining the applicability of the double jeopardy clause to a subsequent prosecution should not be applied when the two charges are brought in the same proceeding, as in *Blockburger*?

GORE v. UNITED STATES

Supreme Court of the United States, 1958.
357 U.S. 386, 78 S.Ct. 1280, 2 L.Ed.2d 1405, rehearing denied
358 U.S. 858, 79 S.Ct. 13, 3 L.Ed.2d 92.

Mr. Justice FRANKFURTER delivered the opinion of the Court.

This is a prosecution under an indictment containing six counts for narcotics offenses. Four counts were based on provisions of the Internal Revenue Code of 1954 and two counts on the Narcotic Drugs Import and Export Act, as amended. The first three counts derive from a sale on February 26, 1955, of twenty capsules of heroin and three capsules of cocaine; the last three counts derive from a sale of thirty-five capsules of heroin on February 28, 1955. Counts One and Four charged the sale of the drugs, on the respective dates, not "in pursuance of a written order" of the person to whom the drugs were sold on the requisite Treasury form, in violation of § 4705(a) of the Internal Revenue Code of 1954, 26 U.S.C.A. § 4705(a). Counts Two and Five charged the sale and distribution of the drugs on the respective dates not "in the original stamped package or from the original stamped package," in violation of § 4704(a) of the Internal Revenue Code of 1954, 26 U.S.C.A. § 4704(a). Counts Three and Six charged facilitating concealment and sale of the drugs on the respective dates, with knowledge that the drugs had been unlawfully imported, in violation of § 2(c) of the Narcotic Drugs Import and Export Act, as amended by the Act of November 2, 1951, 65 Stat. 767. In short, Congress had made three distinct offenses in connection with the vending of illicit drugs, and the petitioner, having violated these three independent provisions, was prosecuted for all three as separate wrongdoings, despite the fact that these violations of what Congress had proscribed were compendiously committed in single transactions of vending. Duly tried before a jury, petitioner was convicted, and no question touching the conviction is before us. In controversy is the legality of the sentences imposed by the trial court. These were imprisonment for a term of one to five years, imposed on each count, the sentences on the first three counts to run consecutively, the sentences on the remaining three counts to run concurrently with those on the first three counts. Thus the total sentence was three to fifteen years. Petitioner moved, under 28 U.S.C. § 2255, 28 U.S.C.A. § 2255, to vacate the sentence, claiming that for all three counts a sentence as for only one count could be imposed. The motion was denied and the Court of Appeals affirmed, 100 U.S.App.D.C. 315, 244 F.2d 763, with expressions of doubt by two of the judges, who felt themselves bound by Blockburger v. United States, 284 U.S. 299, 52 S.Ct. 180, 76 L.Ed. 306. We brought the case here, 355 U.S. 903, 78 S.Ct. 335, 2 L.Ed.2d 259, in order to consider whether some of our more recent decisions, while not questioning Blockburger but moving in related areas may not have impaired its authority.

We adhere to the decision in Blockburger v. United States, supra. The considerations advanced in support of the vigorous attack against it have left its justification undisturbed, nor have our later decisions generated counter currents.

*   *   *

We are strongly urged to reconsider Blockburger by reading the various specific enactments of Congress as reflecting a unitary congressional purpose to outlaw nonmedicinal sales of narcotics. From this the conclusion is sought to be drawn that since Congress had only a single purpose, no matter how numerous the violations by an offender, of the specific means for dealing with this unitary purpose, the desire should be attributed to Congress to punish only as for a single offense when these multiple infractions are committed through a single sale. We agree with the starting point, but it leads us to the opposite conclusion. Of course the various enactments by Congress extending over nearly half a century constitute a network of provisions, steadily tightened and enlarged, for grappling with a powerful, subtle and elusive enemy. If the legislation reveals anything, it reveals the determination of Congress to turn the screw of the criminal machinery—detection, prosecution and punishment—tighter and tighter. The three penal laws for which petitioner was convicted have different origins both in time and in design. The present § 2(c) of the Narcotic Drugs Import and Export Act derives from an enactment of February 9, 1909, § 2, 35 Stat. 614. The present § 4705 (a) of the Internal Revenue Code of 1954 derives from the Act of December 17, 1914, § 2, 38 Stat. 785, 786. The present § 4704(a) of the Internal Revenue Code of 1954 derives from the Revenue Act of 1918, § 1006, 40 Stat. 1057, 1130 (1919). It seems more daring than convincing to suggest that three different enactments, each relating to a separate way of closing in on illicit distribution of narcotics, passed at three different periods, for each of which a separate punishment was declared by Congress, somehow or other ought to have carried with them an implied indication by Congress that if all these three different restrictions were disregarded but, forsooth, in the course of one transaction, the defendant should be treated as though he committed only one of these offenses.

This situation is *toto coelo* different from the one that led to our decision in Bell v. United States, 349 U.S. 81, 75 S.Ct. 620, 99 L.Ed. 905. That case involved application of the Mann Act, 18 U.S.C.A. § 2421,—a single provision making it a crime to transport a woman in interstate commerce for purposes of prostitution. We held that the transportation of more than one woman as a single transaction is to be dealt with as a single offense, for the reason that when Congress has not explicitly stated what the unit of offense is, the doubt will be judicially resolved in favor of lenity. It is one thing for a single transaction to include several units relating to proscribed conduct under a single provision of a statute. It is a wholly different thing to evolve a rule of lenity for three violations of three separate offenses created by Congress at three different times, all to the end of dealing more and more strictly with, and seeking to throttle more and more by different legal devices, the traffic in narcotics. Both in the unfolding of the substantive provisions of law and in the scale of punishments, Congress has manifested an attitude not of lenity but of severity toward violation of the narcotics laws. Nor need we be detained by two other cases relied on, United States v. Universal C. I. T. Credit Corp., 344 U.S. 218, 73 S.Ct. 227, 231, 97 L.Ed. 260, and Prince v. United States, 352 U.S. 322, 77 S.Ct. 403, 1 L.Ed.2d 370. In the former we construed the record-keeping provisions of the Fair Labor Standards Act, 29 U.S.C.A. § 201 et seq., as punishing "a course of conduct." Of the Prince case, it suffices to say that the Court was dealing there "with a unique statute of limited purpose." 352 U.S. at page 325, 77 S.Ct. at page 405.

Finally, we have had pressed upon us that the Blockburger doctrine offends the constitutional prohibition against double jeopardy. If there is anything to this claim it surely has long been disregarded in decisions of this Court, participated in by judges especially sensitive to the application of the historic safeguard of double jeopardy. In applying a provision like that of double jeopardy, which is rooted in history and is not an evolving concept like that of due process, a long course of adjudication in this Court carries impressive authority. Certainly if punishment for each of separate offenses as those for which the petitioner here has been sentenced, and not merely different descriptions of the same offense, is constitutionally beyond the power of Congress to impose, not only Blockburger but at least the following cases would also have to be overruled: [citations omitted]
* * *

Suppose Congress, instead of enacting the three provisions before us, had passed an enactment substantially in this form: "Anyone who sells drugs except from the original stamped package and who sells such drugs not in pursuance of a written order of the person to whom the drug is sold, and who does so by way of facilitating the concealment and sale of drugs knowing the same to have been unlawfully imported, shall be sentenced to not less than fifteen years' imprisonment: *Provided, however,* That if he makes such sale in pursuance of a written order of the person to whom the drug is sold he shall be sentenced to only ten years' imprisonment: *Provided further,* That if he sells such drugs in the original stamped package he shall also be sentenced to only ten years' imprisonment: *And provided further,* That if he sells such drugs in pursuance of a written order and from a stamped package, he shall be sentenced to only five years' imprisonment." Is it conceivable that such a statute would not be within the power of Congress? And is it rational to find such a statute constitutional but to strike down the Blockburger doctrine as violative of the double jeopardy clause?

In effect, we are asked to enter the domain of penology, and more particularly that tantalizing aspect of it, the proper apportionment of punishment. Whatever views may be entertained regarding severity of punishment, whether one believes in its efficacy or its futility, see Radzinowicz, The History of English Criminal Law: The Movement for Reform, 1750–1833, *passim,* these are peculiarly questions of legislative policy. Equally so are the much mooted problems relating to the power of the judiciary to review sentences. First the English and then the Scottish Courts of Criminal Appeal were given power to revise sentences, the power to increase as well as the power to reduce them. See 7 Edw. VII, c. 23, § 4(3); 16 & 17 Geo. V, c. 15, § 2(4). This Court has no such power.

Affirmed.

Mr. Chief Justice WARREN dissenting.

The problem of multiple punishment is a vexing and recurring one. It arises in one of two broad contexts: (a) a statute or a portion thereof proscribes designated conduct, and the question is whether the defendant's conduct constitutes more than one violation of this proscription. Thus, murdering two people simultaneously might well warrant two punishments but stealing two one-dollar bills might not. (b) Two statutes or two portions of a single statute proscribe certain conduct, and the question is whether the defendant can be punished twice because his conduct violates both proscriptions. Thus, selling liquor on a Sunday might warrant two punishments for violating a prohibition law and a blue law, but feloniously entering a bank and robbing a bank, though violative of two statutes, might warrant but a single punishment.

In every instance the problem is to ascertain what the legislature intended. Often the inquiry produces few if any enlightening results. Normally these are not problems that receive explicit legislative consideration. But this fact should not lead the judiciary, charged with the obligation of construing these statutes, to settle such questions by the easy application of stereotyped formulae. It is at the same time too easy and too arbitrary to apply a presumption for or against multiple punishment in all cases or even to do so one way in one class of cases and the other way in another. Placing a case in the category of unit-of-offense problems or the category of overlapping-statute problems may point up the issue, but it does not resolve it.

Where the legislature has failed to make its intention manifest, courts should proceed cautiously, remaining sensitive to the interests of defendant and society alike. All relevant criteria must be considered and the most useful aid will often be common sense. In this case I am persuaded, on the basis of the origins of the three statutes involved, the text and background of recent amendments to these statutes, the scale of punishments prescribed for second and third offenders, and the evident legislative purpose to achieve uniformity in sentences, that the present purpose of these statutes is to make sure that a prosecutor has three avenues by which to prosecute one who traffics in narcotics, and not to authorize three cumulative punishments for the defendant who consummates a single sale.

[The dissenting opinion of Mr. Justice DOUGLAS for himself and Mr. Justice BLACK, and the dissenting opinion of Mr. Justice BRENNAN are omitted].

IRBY v. UNITED STATES

United States Court of Appeals for the District of Columbia, 1967.
129 U.S.App.D.C. 17, 390 F.2d 432.

ON REHEARING EN BANC

Before BAZELON, Chief Judge, and DANAHER, BURGER, WRIGHT, McGOWAN, TAMM and LEVENTHAL, Circuit Judges, sitting *en banc*.

McGOWAN, Circuit Judge, with whom Circuit Judges DANAHER, BURGER, and TAMM join:

In 1958 appellant, represented by counsel, pleaded guilty to the housebreaking and robbery counts of a 9-count indictment, and received consecutive sentences of two to eight years on the one, and four to twelve years on the other. The other counts were then dismissed. In 1965 he moved under 28 U.S.C.A. § 2255 to regain his liberty on the ground that the two sentences could not validly have been made to run consecutively. The District Court denied the motion in a long opinion which explored with care the single legal issue raised by the motion. 250 F.Supp. 983 (1965). Upon appeal, a panel of this court reversed, one judge dissenting (No. 19,988, decided March 15, 1967). The Government's petition for rehearing *en banc* was granted; and, after rehearing, the District Court's judgment is herewith affirmed.

I

Because of the existence of District Judge (now Circuit Judge) Robinson's opinion referred to above, there is no occasion for us to cover the same ground in reaching the same result. He recognized, as this court has recently had occasion to do, that there are circumstances where it cannot safely be assumed that simply because the legislature has defined two separate crimes with differing elements and prescribed separate punishments for them, it contemplated that such punishments can be consecutively inflicted.[1] The nature of the two criminal specifications, and of the course of conduct in which both crimes may be thought to have been committed, may be such as to raise a doubt as to a legislative purpose to encompass both punishments. In such a case, an aid to the divination of such purpose in the form of a so-called "rule of lenity" has been devised to the end of barring double punishment where there is substantial doubt as to whether Congress would have intended it to be imposed.

A majority of the panel which first heard this appeal thought that there was a sufficiently "substantial doubt about what Congress intended" as to cause the rule of lenity to operate. This point of view was conscientiously and competently urged upon us by appellant's appointed counsel, who has served his client faithfully and well here as in the District Court. However, we agree with the District Court that the degree of doubt discernible on this record does not warrant invocation of the rule of lenity. We note in this regard the District Court's analysis of the historic differences in concept between housebreaking as a crime against property, on the one hand, and robbery as a crime against the person, on the other.

It is not novel that Congress has differentiated between housebreaking and robbery in terms of the one as an invasion of the security of the dwelling, and the other as an intrusion upon the security of the person. This was a distinction familiar to the common law, and it was perpetuated in the statutes found to have been violated here. Stealing something worth $1000 may be only an aggravation of the misdeed involved in stealing something worth $10. But taking something, whatever its worth, from another's person by force and putting in fear brings in a new and different interest which it

---

1. Ingram v. United States, 122 U.S. App.D.C. 334, 353 F.2d 872 (1965); Davenport v. United States, 122 U.S. App.D.C. 344, 353 F.2d 882 (1965). These cases involved a single act directed against a single interest, i. e., violent assault upon the person of another. We held consecutive sentences to be improper because of the doubt created under these circumstances as to whether Congress would have intended double punishments to be imposed. The doubt is much less pronounced in a case like the one before us where two discrete protected interests are involved, and where the course of conduct, although perhaps continuous in its flow, nevertheless affords an opportunity for discrimination by the actor between such interests before both are infringed.

has been thought important to protect, namely, the person threatened as distinct from the property taken.

One who wrongfully goes into a house to pilfer what he can find may or may not start out with a purpose to rob, if necessary. If he consciously entertains both purposes from the beginning, it can be said that he sets out with an intent to commit both larceny and robbery, or crimes against both property and person, if the opportunity presents itself. In such circumstances, he will be guilty of housebreaking in either event once he crosses the threshold, but, if he retires upon finding the house occupied and without robbing the occupant, he has made the decision which saves him from punishment for robbery. The point is, of course, that his invasion of the premises to steal does not irrevocably commit him to rob from the person of anyone he finds there. The choice is still his up to the moment of confrontation.[2] If he decided to rob, consecutive punishments are not made available solely as a means of exacting greater retribution. Congress could well have conceived of them as a deterrent to compromising the safety of the person as well as the security of the premises. They illuminate the differing dangers to society inherent in stealing what one finds in a vacant house, and robbing the occupant as well when he proves to be at home. We cannot, at any rate, say with confidence that Congress did not contemplate some additional disincentive for the latter.[3]

2. We do not think that the indictment can be characterized as asserting that appellant's course of conduct was motivated by a single criminal intent. In the housebreaking count, he was charged with entering a dwelling "with intent to steal property of another." In the robbery count, he was charged with taking two rings from the person and from the immediate possession of a named complainant "by force and violence and against resistance and by sudden and stealthy seizure and snatching and by putting in fear." The two are not the same, and they are fully consistent with either concurrent or consecutive ciminal purposes of a different order. The Supreme Court has, of course, been alert to prohibit double punishment for the commission of a federally-created crime and for the attempt to do so. See Prince v. United States, 352 U.S. 322, 77 S.Ct. 403, 1 L.Ed.2d 370 (1957).

3. The drafters of the American Law Institute's Model Penal Code were ex-

plicitly conscious of the unfairness involved in the imposition of "cumulative penalties * * * for entering with intent to steal and for stealing, although ordinarily attempt merges in the completed offense." Although proposing a burglary offense not essentially unlike our housebreaking statute, they added a ban on duplicate penalties in these terms:

Multiple Convictions. A person may not be convicted both for burglary and for the offense which it was his purpose to commit after the burglarious entry or for an attempt to commit that offense, unless the additional offense constitutes a felony of the first or second degree.

They went on, however, to define robbery in a manner similar to our robbery statute, and made it a felony of the second degree. See Model Penal Code (Proposed Official Draft) § 221.1 incorporating Commentary of Tentative Draft No. 11, at 56, 61.

II

The problems in this area are not easy. It was for this reason that the court *en banc* decided to seek the views of a disinterested *amicus curiœ*. There has been forthcoming, as a result of this appointment, a very helpful brief which has supplied us with useful research information,[4] as well as with imaginative reflections upon the judicial approach most cognizant of both the public and private interests involved.

Amicus has concluded that the rule of lenity has a very limited utility indeed as a touchstone of the propriety of consecutive sentences. He suggests that it be abandoned in favor of a supervisory rule to the effect that consecutive sentences may not be imposed for offenses arising out of a single course of conduct unless the sentencing judge (1) finds from the facts that the defendant was not motivated by a single intent and objective, and (2) recites his reasons for believing that consecutive sentences are necessary to achieve at least one of the recognized sentencing goals.

Were this proposal to be deemed wholly meritorious, it could have no application to this case, for the reason that it would require a remand hearing to try to assemble and reconstruct facts which happened nearly a decade ago. The sentencing judge is dead; and it is a commonplace that the passage of even a few years makes it difficult to pursue factual inquiries. An attack on consecutive sentences is one which should be made at the time the sentences are imposed, when

---

4. *Amicus* has discussed at length the law as to consecutive sentencing in certain states, notably California and Illinois. The former has had, for nearly a century, a statutory ban on double punishments for "an act or omission which is made punishable in different ways by different provisions" of the Code. Directly indicative in itself of a legislative purpose in the matter of consecutive sentences, the statute has nevertheless had a checkered career of judicial interpretation, culminating in a rule to the effect that whether an act is single or not is to be derived from the intent and objective of the actor Neal v. State, 55 Cal.2d 11, 9 Cal.Rptr. 607, 357 P.2d 839 (1960). It was held in that case that one who threw gasoline into the bedroom of a sleeping couple for the purpose of killing them could not be punished for both attempted murder and arson. We suggest that, on the facts, this ruling is not unlike our holdings in *Davenport* and *Ingram*, Note 1, supra; and we recognize that, as *Neal* suggests, there is no utter conclusiveness to a technical distinc-

tion between crimes against property and person, respectively. Illinois also has a statutory limitation of consecutive sentences, although it appears to have followed, rather than preceded, judicial development. The case which that statute is reputed to have codified invalidated consecutive sentences for assault wtih intent to rape and assault with intent to murder, People v. Stingley, 414 Ill. 398, 111 N.E.2d 548, cert. denied, 345 U.S. 959, 73 S.Ct. 945, 97 L.Ed. 1379 (1959); and again we suggest that this holding is arguably within the range of our decisions in *Davenport* and *Ingram*. The distinction between all those cases and this, at least on the facts as we have to assume them to be in this case, is that here the course of conduct admitted of interruption and alteration in response to the deterrent influence of additional punishment. That possibility is what disables us from seriously doubting that Congress, absent any explicit declaration of its intent, can be taken to have disclaimed any such purpose to deter.

there is the opportunity to make a meaningful inquiry into the facts. It is not suited to the vehicle of belated collateral attack.

It is true that where, as here, consecutive sentencing was founded upon a guilty plea, the record is singularly uninformative in respect of those facts which would be most helpful in any appraisal of the Congressional will. Any judge contemplating consecutive sentences in such a situation hereafter would be well advised to cause the record to show the factual circumstances surrounding the commission of the crimes. Such a practice would enable the judicial process to function better at all levels because it would facilitate the search for the legislative intent which primarily defines the limits of the sentencing power.

The judgment of the District Court is

Affirmed.

LEVENTHAL, Circuit Judge (concurring):

I concur in the judgment, since I agree that it is possible that a combination at one scene of a housebreaking, with intent to commit larceny, and a robbery, may reflect sufficiently separate criminal purposes to permit consecutive punishment. While they may also, I think, be so integrated as to preclude consecutive punishment, that objection is one that should ordinarily be put forward when sentence is imposed, or timely in a motion to reduce the sentence. In any event, as will be indicated, I do not believe that appellant's pleading asserted the factual predicate necessary to sustain the conclusion that the "sentence was in excess of the maximum authorized by law."

A new approach, such as that suggested by amicus curiae,[1] is left by the court to future consideration, and that seems right to me. In exploring approaches and pondering consequences, we may be aided by the analyses generated by the tensions of the adversary system, and, if they are available, by reflections of a sentencing judge whose attention has been directed to the elements of the approach advanced for consideration.

* * *

BAZELON, Chief Judge, with whom J. SKELLY WRIGHT, Circuit Judge, concurs (dissenting):

There are two questions before us. The first is whether, in some cases, the D. C. housebreaking and robbery statutes prohibit cumulative punishment. The second is whether Irby's is one of those cases.

The answer to the first question depends entirely upon statutory construction. The issue is whether Congress authorized cumulative

1. Amicus curiae recommended that this court remand for resentencing in accordance with new criteria which would, inter alia, condition consecutive punishments on a prerequisite finding that a sentence in excess of the maximum available for the most serious offense is necessary to achieve recognized sentencing goals.

punishment not whether the trial judge properly exercised judicial sentencing discretion. No doubt, the process of statutory construction, which entails examining the history of these common law crimes, the legislative history of the statutes, the words of each statute, and the relationship between them is very difficult. But the process is not necessarily more difficult here than in many other contexts in which we must construe statutes. In any event, the difficulty of the process does not excuse us from our duty.

We depend upon statutory construction because the authority to punish resides in the legislature, not in the courts, and we cannot arrogate to ourselves authority which has not been granted. Neither can we assume that Congress wanted separate punishment simply because it created separate crimes. To do so would be to allow the prosecutor and the trial judge almost unfettered discretion to multiply punishment since often it takes nothing more than a fertile imagination to spin several crimes out of a single transaction. The cases are perfectly clear that the legality of cumulative punishment depends on more than a finding that separate crimes have been committed. Indeed, the Supreme Court has established a "rule of lenity" which requires courts to forego cumulative punishment when there is a doubt about what Congress intended.

*   *   *

The Government does not challenge the validity of the rule of lenity. Nonetheless, the Government argues that these two crimes should be punishable cumulatively simply because they are separate offenses—historically separate as well as codified in separate statutes. It may be that housebreaking and robbery were distinct offenses at common law. It should be noted, though, that both burglary (the common law predecessor to housebreaking) and robbery were thought to be aggravated forms of the same crime—larceny. Further, certain activity punishable at common law only as a larceny now violates both the housebreaking and robbery statutes. In any event, even if the housebreaking and robbery statutes had more distinct ancestors, that fact would not determine whether the two crimes could be punishable separately.

On the issue of separate punishment, the common law and legislative history are even more ambiguous. Around the time of codification there was a lively debate about the legality of cumulative punishment for crimes similar to housebreaking and robbery. Congress does not seem to have taken any position when it codified the D.C. laws, for there is no provision in the original D.C. Code (or the present one) about cumulative punishment. And there is no mention of this problem in the Congressional reports and debates which preceded passage of the Code.

We must turn, then, to the statutes themselves. The housebreaking statute reads as follows: "Whosoever shall, either in the night or in the daytime, break and enter, or enter without breaking, any dwelling * * * whether at the time occupied or not * * * with intent * * * to commit any criminal offense, shall be imprisoned for not more than fifteen years." 22 D.C.Code § 1801 (1961). Housebreaking, by the terms of the statute, is committed in preparation for some other criminal offense which is intended at the time of entry. It seems most likely that Congress, instead of desiring to punish for both the preparation and the completion, created two separate crimes in order to punish those housebreakers who are thwarted and who do not complete the intended crime.

The Supreme Court faced a similar situation in Prince v. United States. There the defendant was convicted of robbing a federally insured bank and entering the bank with intent to commit a felony. The Supreme Court reasoned that:

> It is a fair inference from the wording in the Act, uncontradicted by anything in the meager legislative history, that the unlawful entry provision was inserted to cover the situation where a person enters a bank for the purpose of committing a crime, but is frustrated for some reason before completing the crime. The gravamen of the offense is not in the act of entering, which satisfies the terms of the statute even if it is simply walking through an open, public door during normal business hours. Rather the heart of the crime is the intent to steal. This mental element merges into the completed crime if the robbery is consummated.

Therefore, the Supreme Court held that Congress did not intend to punish cumulatively for the preparation and the completed crime.

A similar inference is warranted here, since, as in *Prince*, our statute defines housebreaking as entry with intent to commit another crime. And, as in *Prince*, the gravamen of the offense is not simply the act of entering, which need not be forcible to satisfy the terms of the statute. Indeed, it is possible that a person may be guilty of housebreaking although he has not committed a criminal trespass as long as he enters the premises with the required criminal intent.

Even if a criminal trespass is a necessary prerequisite to a finding of housebreaking, it is evident that the illegal act of entry is not the gravamen of housebreaking. If nothing more than entering without permission were involved, a penalty in the order of six months would probably be thought enough by Congress. However, Congress provided a much stiffer penalty for housebreaking. And the likely reason is that Congress believed that entry with an intent to commit another crime would often, in fact, lead to that other crime. As in *Prince*, the intent to commit another crime is at the heart of the offense. By deterring housebreaking Congress meant also to deter the intended crime which might follow. If so, then the housebreaking statute punishes for the possibility or probability of the intended crime. We do not think Congress would have wanted to impose punishment of fifteen years for the probability of the intended crime and an additional fifteen years for the crime itself.

Under this analysis, however, cumulative punishment is prohibited only if the crime defendant in fact committed was the same as the crime he intended to commit when he entered the dwelling. This seems to be the question which divides the court. The majority does not think "the indictment can be characterized as asserting that appellant's course of conduct was motivated by a single criminal intent." Judge Leventhal thinks the record is unclear and would require more specific allegations of a single intent. We think the record is clear enough to show that Irby had only one criminal purpose when he committed the two crimes.

According to the indictment, Irby entered the complainant's dwelling with an "intent to steal [his] property." While in the house, Irby carried out his intention and stole two rings worth $2,200.

The fact that in order to steal he did things which made his crime robbery, as opposed, for example, to grand larceny or petit larceny, does not negate the fact that what he did within the house was motivated by the same criminal purpose ("to steal property of another") as his illegal entry.

Furthermore, it is significant that Irby was originally charged with carrying a dangerous weapon and assault with a dangerous weapon. If these charges are correct, they suggest that when Irby entered the dwelling he was already prepared to use "force and violence" (i. e., to commit robbery) if necessary.

A California state court was faced with a similar situation in Downs v. State.[21] There two men broke into an office building and were engaged in looting the safe when the janitors entered the room. The two men then tied the janitors up at gunpoint. The state argued that consecutive sentences for burglary and robbery should be upheld since the trier of fact could have found that the intent to commit robbery originated only after the janitors arrived on the scene. The California court disagreed:

> Regardless of the wording of the information, petitioner entered the telephone building with the single purpose to rifle its safe, hoping no doubt that this could be accomplished without interference, but prepared for that event by carrying a gun which he intended to and did threateningly use to consummate the crime. * * * The information, had it been worded with strict accuracy, would have accused peti-

21. 202 Cal.App.2d 609, 20 Cal.Rptr. 922 (1962).

tioner of entering to commit *either theft or robbery* as might become necessary.[22]

Unless courts are willing to reason in this fashion, no limits can be placed on cumulative punishment in housebreaking cases. A defendant can rarely demonstrate what his mental state was when he entered the dwelling. His original intent must be inferred from his later conduct. If there are facts suggesting a departure from the original intent, the Government should have the burden of asserting them.[24]

We think the record sufficiently shows that defendant entered the dwelling with the objective of stealing property, by force if necessary, and that he carried out this objective. Since there is substantial doubt that Congress intended cumulative punishment in this situation, the rule of lenity must be applied. Irby should have been punished for either housebreaking or robbery but not both consecutively.

NOTES

1. If Irby had only committed theft within the house could he properly be sentenced consecutively for both burglary (housebreaking) and larceny? See Maynes v. People, 169 Colo. 186, 454 P.2d 797 (1969). What if he commits rape after entry; can he be sentenced for both burglary and rape? Should the answer be affected by the intent with which the burglary was committed; the intent of the legislature in enacting the two prohibitions; both? See Walton v. State, 448 S.W.2d 690 (Tenn.Cr.App. 1969).

2. Is the reliance of the dissent in *Irby* on Prince v. United States, 352 U.S. 322, 77 S.Ct. 403, 1 L.Ed.2d 370 (1957), well placed? Does a law criminalizing entering a federally insured bank with intent to commit a felony have any purpose other than to facilitate prosecution of would-be bank robbers who reveal their intention by conduct short of an attempt? Is the purpose of a housebreaking or burglary statute similarly limited?

WHITTON v. STATE

Supreme Court of Alaska, 1970.
479 P.2d 302.

DIMOND, Justice. A jury found appellant guilty of the crime of robbery and of the crime of using a firearm during commission of the same robbery. Appellant raises several points on this appeal in support of his contention that a new trial should be ordered.

---

22. Id. at 614, 20 Cal.Rptr. at 925 (emphasis in original).

24. If, for example, defendant entered a dwelling equipped with burglar's tools, burlap bag, etc., but then raped an occupant, the Government could use the possession of the tools as evidence that his intended and actual crimes were different.

Double Jeopardy.

In Count I of the indictment appellant was charged with robbery. This was in accordance with a statute making one guilty of the crime of robbery if he steals or takes anything of value from a person by force or violence or by putting such person in fear. In Count II of the indictment, appellant was charged with the crime of using or carrying a firearm during the commission of a robbery. This was in accordance with another statute which makes it a felony to use or carry a firearm during the commission of robbery or other designated offenses. Appellant argues that the two separate statutory offenses are essentially one crime, and that when he was sentenced for both he was placed in jeopardy twice for the same offense in violation of his constitutional rights.

It is within the traditional scope of legislative power to deter anti-social behavior by enacting laws proscribing, under the pain of punishment certain courses of human conduct considered to be detrimental to an ordered society. In the course of regulating authoritatively the essential relations between the members of society, the legislature has allocated certain property rights to individuals, groups or collective units. It is in recognition and for the protection of those rights that laws have been enacted which provide for the infliction of punishment upon one who takes the property of another.

In criminal laws of this nature, society is asserting its basic interest in the protection of the person and his property. This interest may vary according to the circumstances in which the person is unlawfully deprived of his property. Such varying degrees of interest are expressed in criminal statutes which prescribe different punishments for what may be considered as one basic offense against a person's property rights, but which, because of the circumstances in which the property is taken from the person, are considered by society to be more or less grave.

This is exemplified by the statutes pertinent to this case. The legislature has made it a crime to steal or take from another anything of value. When this crime is committed without force or violence, and without putting the victim in fear, it is called larceny from the person, punishable by imprisonment for not less than one year nor more than five years. When the crime is committed by force or violence, or by putting the victim in fear, it is called robbery and the punishment is increased to a maximum of 15 years imprisonment. And when the robbery is committed while using or carrying a firearm, the punishment is even more severe—imprisonment for not less than 10 years for the first offense, and for not less than 25 years for a second or subsequent offense.

*   *   *

We cannot question the wisdom of the legislature in imposing a more stringent penalty for robbery where a firearm is involved.

The inherent nature and purpose of a firearm is such as to create a danger of loss of life or serious injury to the person so as to merit the inhibiting force of a law imposing a minimum prison term of 10 years for one who commits a robbery in this manner. The question that we must decide is whether, where there is a single criminal event, one may be punished for two crimes—robbery, and robbery while using or carrying a firearm.

* * *

At best the legislative intent in this regard is obscure. Since it is conceivable that separate, distinct offenses may have been intended, we feel we must pass upon the question of whether separate punishments may be imposed for the commission of separate statutory offenses arising from a single criminal event.

It is a fundamental concept, expressed in criminal statutes providing a single sentence of imprisonment for each distinct crime, that a defendant may not be punished more than once for the same offense. But frequently the legislature will isolate and make criminal a number of steps arising out of one transaction, so that a defendant may be convicted and punished for multiple offenses arising out of a single activity. This type of legislation promotes the law-making body's legitimate objective of attacking a basic, unitary social evil by different legal devices, to the end that such evil will be entirely obliterated and all avenues of escape for offenders will be closed.

The need to protect the individual from being punished more than once for the same offense, and the necessity of allowing the legislature freedom to effectively deal with a social evil in a variety of ways reflect the competing interests of the individual and society. How to fairly balance such interests has been a perplexing problem. One attempt to solve the problem has been through a rule of law which is applied for the purpose of determining whether a single criminal activity or transaction constitutes more than one offense. If there are, for example, two distinct statutory offenses arising out of one transaction, and one offense requires proof of an additional fact which the other does not, then according to that rule there are two separate offenses and not just one, and the defendant may be punished for both.

This rule was enunciated and applied by the Supreme Court of the United States in Blockburger v. United States in 1932.

* * *

The rule in *Blockburger* is commonly referred to as the "same-evidence" test because, put another way, it means that different violations constitute one offense only when proof of all of them is established by the same evidence. Although this test has been widely used by the courts, it has been increasingly criticized as not coping satisfactorily with the problem it was designed to solve. Legislative refinement of an essentially unitary criminal episode into numerous separate violations of the law has resulted in a proliferation of offenses capable of commission by a person at one time and in one criminal transaction. Since each violation by definition will usually require proof of a fact which the others do not, application of the same-evidence test will mean that each offense is punishable separately. But as the separate violations multiply by legislative action, the likelihood increases that a defendant will actually be punished several times for what is really and basically one criminal act.

Recognizing the limitations of the same-evidence rule, attempts have been made to meet the problem in other ways. Some courts have adopted the same-transaction test. This means that there may be only one punishment if a number of separate statutory violations arise out of a single criminal act or transaction. We believe that there are as many difficulties inherent in this method as with the same-evidence rule. Where a court is faced with the problem of whether to impose multiple sentences, it tries to determine whether the separate statutory violations for which the defendant was convicted amounted to the same offense. Under the same-transaction test, the different violations would amount collectively to the same offense if they all arose in the course of the same criminal act or transaction. But a single course of criminal conduct may involve violations of different statutes, with differences in acts performed, in means of perpetration, and intent. The question then arises as to just what is a single criminal transaction. It may be just as difficult in some cases to determine whether the wrongful course of conduct involved constitutes a single criminal transaction as it is to determine whether such conduct, involving separate statutory violations, amounts to the same offense.

A person may break into a house with the intent to steal some money. He has committed the crime of burglary. As he enters he is confronted by the owner, and within seconds he shoots the owner with intent to kill him, leaves him for dead, takes the money he came after, and departs. Some of the crimes with which he could be charged are burglary, assault with a dangerous weapon, assault with intent to kill and robbery. In one sense there was a single criminal transaction, because the separate criminal acts, in the brief time in which they were committed, were unitary events since they merge one into the other. On the other hand, this general criminal act or transaction may not really be characterized as single or one, because four distinct and separate acts were committed, with distinguishing characteristics, which the legislature had the right to denominate as entirely different crimes. The same-transaction test, therefore, will not always provide a solution to the problem of when separate violations of the law constitute the same offense.

In more recent years the United States Supreme Court has adopted what is called a rule of lenity. This rule, briefly stated, is that where Congress has enacted a number of statutory criminal prohibitions which a defendant may have violated in a single transaction, and the question is whether the multiple sentences should be imposed, doubt as to what Congress intended will be resolved against turning a single transaction into multiple offenses. Thus, unless it is clear that Congress has intended there be multiple punishments, the legislative silence will be construed in favor of lenity, i. e., of imposing only one sentence for different statutory violations that amount to a single or unitary criminal event. * * *

The rule of lenity focuses on legislative intent, or the lack of it. But there are difficulties here also, as there may well be with any test that may be devised. It is seldom an easy thing to know what the legislature intended in this area of criminal law. As Judge Leventhal has stated in his concurring opinion in Irby v. United States, "for the most part there is no ascertainable legislative intent on cumulation of punishment in relation to any particular offense or group of offenses * * *." Furthermore, it is conceivable that the legislature may well have intended that multiple punishments be imposed for separate statutory offenses arising out of one criminal episode, and if legislative intent must govern in such a case it would follow that a person may well be punished more than once for the same offense.

This brings us to the point of our major concern—the constitutional prohibition against double jeopardy. The fifth amendment to the federal constitution provides that a person shall not "be subject for the same offense to be twice put in jeopardy of life and limb." This constitutional guarantee is applicable to the states through the fourteenth amendment.[20] Its purpose, as stated by the United States Supreme Court in Green v. United States was to prevent the government from making "repeated attempts to convict an individual for an alleged offense, thereby subjecting him to embarrassment, expense and ordeal and compelling him to live in a continuing state of anxiety and insecurity, * * *"[21] As stated more recently in Ashe v. Swenson, the double jeopardy clause "stands as a constitutional barrier against possible tyranny by an overzealous prosecutor."[22]

The question before us is whether the double jeopardy provision protects against multiple punishments for the same offense. The United States Supreme Court in 1941 in Holiday v. Johnston[23]

20. Benton v. Maryland, 395 U.S. 784, 89 S.Ct. 2056, 23 L.Ed.2d 707 (1969).

21. Green v. United States, 355 U.S. 184, 187, 78 S.Ct. 221, 223, 2 L.Ed.2d 199, 204 (1957).

22. 397 U.S. 436, 456, 90 S.Ct. 1189, 1200, 25 L.Ed.2d 469, 482 (1970) [concurring opinion of Justices Brennan, Douglas and Marshall].

23. 313 U.S. 342, 349, 61 S.Ct. 1015, 1017, 85 L.Ed. 1392, 1396 (1941).

held that it did not. This view had support in decisions of other courts.[24] On the other hand, there have been decisions going the other way in holding that the constitutional prohibition against double jeopardy does protect an accused against double punishment for the same offense.[25]

* * *

The *Gore* case appears to be the latest decision by the United States Supreme Court on the question of double jeopardy as it bears on multiple punishments for what might amount to a single or "the same" criminal offense. Assuming that *Gore* stands for the proposition that the constitutional prohibition against double jeopardy does not pertain to multiple punishments, we would be obliged to follow that interpretation under the supremacy clause of the federal constitution. But this would be the case only as to the United States Constitution. Alaska has its own constitutional provision relating to double jeopardy, and as to that we are free to make our own interpretations as long as they do not detract from minimum national standards for the protection of human rights as established by the United States Supreme Court in decisions interpreting the federal constitution.

Alaska's constitution provides that "no person shall be put in jeopardy twice for the same offense." The present dictionary meaning of "jeopardy", as it pertains to a person, is the loss or injury or hazard or peril or danger to which one may become exposed. When a person is convicted of a crime, he has been exposed to the danger of loss of his freedom by way of imprisonment. The conviction of the offense places him in jeopardy. If this one conviction makes him liable for two sentences, instead of one, then the loss or peril to which he has been exposed—double punishment—has placed him in jeopardy twice for the same offense. We believe that multiple punishments for one or "the same" offense violate our constitutional inhibition against double jeopardy.

When we speak of the "present dictionary meaning" of double jeopardy we are not unaware of Justice Frankfurter's view in *Gore* that the meaning of that term cannot be decided from the dictionary, that since the principle of double jeopardy is derived from history, its historical origin must be examined to ascertain its significance and scope, and that the principle of double jeopardy is not an evolving concept like that of due process. We do not depreciate history as a valuable means of ascertaining the scope of a constitutional safe-

24. Calvaresi v. United States, 216 F.2d 891, 902 (10th Cir. 1954); White v. Pescor, 155 F.2d 902, 904 (8th Cir. 1946). *See* Consecutive Sentences in Single Prosecutions: Judicial Multiplication of Statutory Penalties, 67 Yale L.J. 916, 918–19 (1958); Statutory Implementation of Double Jeopardy Clauses: New Life for a Moribund Constitutional Guarantee, 65 Yale L.J. 339, 350 (1956).

25. Tritico v. United States, 4 F.2d 664, 665 (5th Cir. 1925); Murphy v. United States, 285 F. 801, 817 (7th Cir. 1923).

guard. * * * Our point is that history must not be used in a constrictive or limiting way in the area of human rights.

We respectfully disagree with Justice Frankfurter's view that double jeopardy is not an evolving concept as due process is. What in fact today is "jeopardy" as it relates to a criminal offense according to the existing common understanding of the term, may not have been even contemplated at the time the federal constitutional provision was adopted, or for that matter, the Alaska constitutional provision. Our constitution, at least in its Declaration of Rights in Article I where the prohibition against double jeopardy is found, is not static. It is a viable, active thing, designed to serve the needs of humanity and society with the ability to accommodate to changes which inevitably occur with the progress of our civilization.

We hold that Alaska's constitutional prohibition against double jeopardy prevents one from receiving multiple prison sentences for the same offense. We know it is not an easy thing to determine in every case when two or more statutory violations constitute the same offense. This problem has been the subject of a considerable amount of thoughtful discussion and debate among courts and legal commentators. We have discussed briefly the "same-evidence" and "same-transaction" tests. Variations of these tests are the "material element" test, the "single intent" test and the "gravamen of the offense" test.

We have also spoken of the rule of lenity and the attempt to focus on legislative intent. It has been suggested that the problem be met by ascertaining legislative purpose from a consideration of the social norms or interests or values sought to be vindicated by criminal statutes, and the various objectives of the criminal law such as reformation, rehabilitation, retribution, isolation and deterrence.

*   *   *

Also related to legislative purpose are the rules devised by Kirchheimer.[47] It is his belief that there is a lack of legislative intent to impose multiple punishments (1) where two statutes are alternative, i. e., where conviction under one is inconsistent with conviction under the other for the same criminal conduct, (2) where one offense is included in another, as where violation of the second offense always involves violation of the first, (3) where one offense is preparatory, in that it is ordinarily committed in preparation for another, and (4) where several statutes are not usually violated together, where they seem to be designed to protect the same social interest and, therefore, where the inference is created that the function of the multiple statutes is only to allow alternative punishment.[48]

47. Kirchheimer, The Act, the Offense and Double Jeopardy, 58 Yale L.J. 513 (1949).

48. Kirchheimer's suggested rules are discussed in the commentary. Twice in Jeopardy, 75 Yale L.J. 262, 318–20 (1965).

More recently proposed solutions relate to the intent of the criminal. In 1967 Judge Leventhal, in his concurring opinion in Irby v. United States, expressed the belief that the rule focusing on changes in extent and direction of the defendant's criminal intention provided a basis for permitting cumulative punishment that is related to mens rea. In that same case the majority opinion referred to an amicus curiae suggestion that in determining whether to impose multiple punishments, attention should be directed to whether the defendant was motivated by a single intent or objective, and to the necessity of achieving recognized sentencing goals. In 1969 the Supreme Court of California stated that multiple punishments would not be permitted where there is a course of conduct composing an indivisible transaction. The divisibility of the course of conduct would depend upon the objective of the defendant, and if all the offenses were incident to one objective, the defendant could be punished for any one of them but not for more than one.[52]

We realize that the problem involved cannot be solved by the easy application of a pat mechanical formula. This is evident from the critical and discerning discussion of the subject by the courts and legal writers. But the problem has to be met so that society's very basic interest in deterring criminal behavior can be vindicated, and at the same time so that the individual's constitutional right not to be placed in jeopardy more than once for the same offense can be protected. As Judge Leventhal stated in *Irby*: "[W]hen there is need our law has traditions and mechanisms for coping with even difficult factual questions."

The problem we are faced with has arisen by reason of legislative division or refinement of what may be a unitary criminal episode into a number of statutory offenses, with differences based upon intent or means or method of perpetration. In determining whether several statutory violations constitute the same offense for double jeopardy purposes, we will no longer follow the same-evidence test as enunciated in Blockburger v. United States, * * *.

We now meet the problem in another way, with confidence that it can be solved, by focusing upon the quality of the differences, if any exist, between the separate statutory offenses, as such differences relate to the basic interests sought to be vindicated or protected by the statutes.

The trial judge first would compare the different statutes in question, as they apply to the facts of the case, to determine whether there were involved differences in intent or conduct. He would then judge any such differences he found in light of the basic interests of society to be vindicated or protected, and decide whether

52. People v. Bauer, 1 Cal.3d 368, 82 Cal.Rptr. 357, 362, 461 P.2d 637, 642 (1969).

those differences were substantial or significant enough to warrant multiple punishments. The social interests to be considered would include the nature of personal, property or other rights sought to be protected, and the broad objectives of criminal law such as punishment of the criminal for his crime, rehabilitation of the criminal, and the prevention of future crimes.

If such differences in intent or conduct are significant or substantial in relation to the social interests involved, multiple sentences may be imposed, and the constitutional prohibition against double jeopardy will not be violated. But if there are no such differences, or if they are insignificant or insubstantial, then only one sentence may be imposed under double jeopardy. Ordinarily the one sentence to be imposed will be based upon or geared to the most grave of the offenses involved, with degrees of gravity being indicated by the different punishments prescribed by the legislature.

In the event the trial judge decides, under the test we have established, that multiple sentences may be imposed without contravening the double jeopardy provision, the reasons for his determination must affirmatively appear in the record. There should be a statement by the judge of the relevant factual and other considerations which led him to such a decision, in order that the constitutional legitimacy of the multiple sentences may be fully reviewed on appeal.

The test we adopt to determine whether different statutory violations amount to the same offense is quite close to the view advocated by Justice Rutledge in 1942,[59] and which has been recommended as a proper view in a recent law review article written by Michael McElroy.[60] Our test undoubtedly will be subject to criticism, as Justice Rutledge's has been, for failure to provide a method or rule for determining when differences between statutory offenses are substantial or insubstantial. It is true that the test of whether differences in acts are substantial is not as precise as one would wish. But the test is by no means obscure or lacking in meaning. The law constantly uses similarly indefinite concepts, such as "justice", "fairness", "reasonableness", and many others.

We have stated the factors to be considered by the sentencing judge. We can go no further. At this point, reason and judgment must be exercised. There is no practicable way of formulating in advance any precise standards for the proper or "reasonable" exercise of such reason and judgment.

If the rule we have adopted is lacking in definiteness, the danger of prejudice, either to society or to the individual, is not grave. If

59. District of Columbia v. Buckley, 75 U.S.App.D.C. 301, 128 F.2d 17, 21–22 (1942) [concurring opinion of Justice Wiley Rutledge].

60. McElroy, Double Jeopardy: The Ephemeral Guarantee, 5 Crim.L.Bull. 375, 399 (1969).

mistakes are made in the imposition of sentences, there are remedies both for the individual and society. Where the imposition of multiple sentences violates a defendant's constitutional protection against double jeopardy, he may appeal to this court and have his constitutional right vindicated. Where the sentencing judge makes a mistake in favor of the individual and against society's interest, in erroneously determining that two or more criminal violations constitute the same offense when they should properly be treated as separate offenses, the state may seek review by this court on the ground that the sentences are too lenient. It is true that under our statutory authority to review sentences at the instance of the state, the legislature has provided that we are not authorized to increase a sentence if we find it too lenient. But we are authorized to express our views as to the state's claim of excessive leniency. If we determine that a sentencing judge has mistakenly applied the test we have prescribed for determining identity of offenses, and has imposed too lenient a sentence, we shall state the reasons for our determination in a written, published opinion. This will have the salutary effect of further clarifying this area of criminal law and of obviating the making of the same or similar mistakes in future sentencings.

We apply the test we have adopted to this case. Money was taken from persons in a restaurant by appellant and his two accomplices who were armed with a rifle and a pistol. Since the presence of the firearms means that the money was taken by force or violence, or by putting the victims in fear, the crime committed was robbery. And since the force or violence or fear was created specifically by the use of the firearms, the more serious crime of robbery with a firearm was also committed.

The more serious crime differs from the less serious in that there can be the crime of robbery with or without a firearm. But the intent and conduct involved in the former encompasses the intent and conduct involved in the latter. Since the more serious offense already proscribes and punishes the activity of the less serious offense, the differences between the two offenses must be deemed insubstantial or insignificant in relation to the social interests involved.

The result is that the two separate statutory crimes constitute the "same offense" for purposes of double jeopardy. A single sentence was all that could properly be imposed under the double jeopardy provision of our constitution.

It could be urged that double jeopardy is not involved because the two sentences, each of which was for 10 years, were to run concurrently. The practical effect of this, it could be argued, is that appellant has really received only one 10-year sentence instead of two. We could not agree with this contention. We pointed out in Gray v. State that there are collateral disadvantages that follow from receiving two concurrent sentences, such as the prejudicial effect on the prisoner's chances of parole. Since the likelihood or lack of it of being released on parole is a critical factor in relation to imprisonment and the consequent deprivation of liberty, this collateral consequence of concurrent sentences does affect jeopardy in a very substantial way. Where two sentences are imposed for the same offense, even though they are for the same period of time and are to run concurrently, the constitutional prohibition against double jeopardy has been violated.[e]

* * *

NOTES

1. California Penal Code section 654 represents a legislative effort to deal with these problems. It provides: "an act or omission which is made punishable in different ways by different provisions of this code may be punishable under either of such provisions but in no case can it be punished under more than one." In Neal v. State, 55 Cal.2d 11, 9 Cal. Rptr. 607, 357 P.2d 839 (1960), the California Supreme Court was required to interpret this provision. There the petitioner had thrown gasoline into a couple's bedroom and ignited it. The couple were severely burned. Neal was convicted on two counts of attempted murder and one count of arson, and the judge directed that the sentences for the attempted murders run consecutively. The applicability of section 654 was said to turn on "whether a separate and distinct act can be established as the basis of each conviction". 357 P.2d at 843. The court recognized, that few crimes are the result of a single physical act and noted that section 654 was also applicable where the multiple offenses resulted from an indivisible course of criminal conduct. The divisibility of the conduct was to be determined by the intent and objective of the actor: "If all of the offenses were incident to one objective, the defendant may be punished for any one of such offenses but not for more than one." Ibid. Here, the court concluded, the arson was merely the means of perpetrating the crime of attempted murder and therefore conviction for both arson and attempted murder violated section 654; Neal could be punished only for the more serious offense. The court then turned to, and upheld the two consecutive attempted murder sentences.

> The two attempted murder convictions, however, present a different problem. The purpose of the protection against multiple punishment is to insure that the defendant's punishment will be commensurate with his criminal liability. A defendant who commits an act of violence with the intent to harm more than one

---

e. *Compare* State v. Ranne, 80 N.M. 188, 453 P.2d 209 (1969) (state double jeopardy clause not offended by convictions for both robbery and aggravated burglary with consecutive sentences since theft, a necessary element of robbery, is not necessarily involved in aggravated burglary) *with* Lawson v. State, 33 So.2d 405 (Ala.App.1948) (separate punishments for grand larceny and burglary violates double jeopardy). Cf. Householder v. Ramey, 485 P.2d 247 (Okl.Cr.1971) (trial of defendant for rape after his conviction of kidnapping (for the purpose of that rape) would violate both a statutory prohibition of multiple punishment and a constitutional bar on double jeopardy).

person or by a means likely to cause harm to several persons is more culpable than a defendant who harms only one person. For example, a defendant who chooses a means of murder that places a planeload of passengers in danger, or results in injury to many persons, is properly subject to greater punishment than a defendant who chooses a means that harms only a single person.
357 P.2d at 844.

Is the argument against multiple punishment where one offense was a means towards another satisfying? If three defendants hijack a truck and two briefly kidnap the driver in order to facilitate the successful escape of the third with the truck, should they be subject to conviction and sentence for both robbery and kidnapping? Does your answer differ if the jurisdiction is California or the District of Columbia? See United States v. Wolford, 444 F.2d 876 (D.C.Cir. 1971). Are the means selected for the achievement of a criminal objective without significance in the sentencing process? If so, how do you explain the *Neal* court's illustration of the bomb on a plane?

In Ladner v. United States, 358 U.S. 169, 79 S.Ct. 209, 3 L.Ed.2d 199 (1958), petitioner claimed that it had been error to punish him twice —two ten year sentences to run consecutively—for a single discharge of a shotgun injuring two federal officers in violation of 18 U.S.C.A. § 254. The Court, after concluding that the legislative history shed no light on the Congressional intention as to the appropriate unit of prosecution, found that the statute might as reasonably be read either way. Therefore, pursuant to the rule of lenity it adopted the less harsh construction and remanded for a hearing on the question of whether, in fact, only a single shot had been fired. Is the interest of the Federal Government in protecting its officers distinguishable from the interest of the state which was involved in *Neal*? Presumably, under the *Ladner* analysis firing two shots at one officer would have justified two sentences. What purpose of the criminal law is served by such distinctions?

The California Supreme Court was again forced to explain the meaning of section 654 in a case where the petitioner had driven a car while his license was suspended and while under the influence of alcohol. He was sentenced for both offenses and contended that such multiple punishment violated section 654. Can this single physical act which simultaneously violates two statutes representing distinct state interests be divided into two criminal offenses because the act involved two subjective elements—knowledge of the license suspension and being under the influence of alcohol? See In re Hayes, 69 Cal.Rptr. 310, 442 P.2d 366 (Cal.1968), vacated on rehearing, 70 Cal.2d 604, 75 Cal.Rptr. 790, 451 P.2d 430 (1969).

An excellent analysis of the efforts of the California Supreme Court to implement its multiple punishment statute is Phillip E. Johnson's "Multiple Punishment and Consecutive Sentences: Reflections on the *Neal* Doctrine", 58 Calif.L.Rev. 357 (1970). The author is highly critical of the doctrine as "difficult to apply" and as bearing "no apparent relationship to any sentencing policy or philosophy." Id. at 377. The alleged irrelevance of the doctrine to the problem of excessive punishment is, in large measure, a function of California's indeterminate sentencing system under which judges do not fix the term of imprisonment but only sentence to the term prescribed by law. The decision as to date of release within applicable statutory maxima and minima, is entirely within the discretion of the California Adult Authority. The author would attack the problem by prohibiting consecutive sentences and limiting the discretion of the Adult Authority. However, much of the article's discussion is of value to an understanding of the difficulties in implementing such statutes. In particular, the questions raised by the author on pages 363–69 are recommended.

2. The preceding cases can be categorized in various ways. You will notice that the problems of multiple charges, convictions and punishments arise in three basic fact patterns. First, there are those like *Gore* and *Hayes* where a single, distinct physical action violates more than one statutory provision. Then there are the more common cases where during a single episode or arguably integrated course of conduct more than one crime is committed; usually pursuant to the attempt or accomplishment of a single criminal objective. *Irby* and *Walton* are examples. Finally, there is the situation such as that in *Neal* where by a single act two or more persons are injured in violation of the same statutory prohibition. Are such distinctions useful in resolving the multiple punishment and allied issues? If so, how and can the cases be readily fitted within these categories? To what extent is the particularity with which the pertinent actus reus is defined helpful? Can any of these questions be answered apart from basic decisions as to the purposes of the criminal law and their relative importance at the time of sentencing?

Another way in which these cases may be distinguished is in the techniques by which the problems raised are analyzed and resolved. Thus, legislative intent is employed as a guideline in *Gore, Irby* and *Maynes*, while the doctrine of merger is discussed in *Wolford* and *Walton*. In *Whitton* and *Gore* the possibility of using double jeopardy as a rationale for resolution is examined while in the remaining cases a statutory effort at resolution is applied. Overlapping with these vehicles are efforts to employ the offender's intent or notions of separable societal interests as talismans. Do you find any of these approaches promising? Are they easily employed? Can case of application be achieved without the sacrifice of legitimate and important social interests?

3. The Fifth Amendment's prohibition against placing a defendant "twice in jeopardy" represents a constitutional policy of finality for the defendant's benefit in federal criminal proceedings. A power in government to subject the individual to repeated prosecutions for the same offense would cut deeply into the framework of procedural protections which the Constitution establishes for the conduct of a criminal trial. And society's awareness of the heavy personal strain which a criminal trial represents for the individual defendant is manifested in the willingness to limit the Government to a single criminal proceeding to vindicate its very vital interest in enforcement of criminal laws. Both of these considerations are expressed in Green v. United States, 355 U.S. 184, 187–188 (1957), where the Court noted that the policy underlying this provision "is that the State with all its resources and power should not be allowed to make repeated attempts to convict an individual for an alleged offense, thereby subjecting him to em-

barrassment, expense and ordeal and compelling him to live in a continuing state of anxiety and insecurity, as well as enhancing the possibility that even though innocent he may be found guilty."

Are the concerns underlying the double jeopardy clause thus expressed by Mr. Justice Harlan for the Court in United States v. Jorn, 400 U.S. 470, 479, 91 S.Ct. 547, 554, 27 L.Ed.2d 543, 553 (1971) the same as those with which the cases of this section have grappled? Was it necessary or reasonable to transfer the test enunciated in *Gavieres* to the *Blockburger* and *Gore* situation? Can a test designed to protect a narrower and more readily cognizable value be satisfactorily applied to give expression to the broader and more diffuse concern which underlies the multiple punishment cases?

4. It must be recognized that multiplication of charges with their inherent dangers of multiple convictions and punishment is not merely a function of the increase in the number of separate yet overlapping criminal prohibitions. Nor is it merely the result of prosecutorial vindictiveness.

Cumulative pressures lead prosecutors to multiply the individual counts in an indictment or information. There is a high degree of uncertainty at the time of charge as to just what the proof at trial will be. The speed which is essential to a humane and efficient system of criminal administration compounds this uncertainty, for a prosecutor often must draw the charge very shortly after the crime or arrest and is not free to engage in extensive discovery and investigation while the defendant is in custody awaiting trial.

The sixth amendment right to a grand jury indictment has been understood severely to restrict the prosecutor's right to amend indictments, and this combines with the rules concerning variance to place a heavy penalty on the prosecutor who does not plead to cover every contingency of proof at trial. Returning to the hypothetical concerning the forgery of the social security check, reliance solely upon a forgery charge is likely to lead to disaster if, as is too often sadly the case, the expert handwriting witness lacks credibility or the person who accepted the check proves a weak identification witness at trial. In such a situation, however, it is likely that the theft of the instrument from the mail or its possession by the defendant can be independently proved without these weak witnesses.

Rules of criminal pleading also lead a prosecutor to break down his charge into as many counts of individual offenses as possible. The prosecutor is justifiably apprehensive of violating the hypertechnical rules of multiplicity and duplicity which are said to be related to the defendant's sixth amendment right to be specifically informed of the precise charges against him. A parallel pressure is exerted by the prosecutor's desire to present the judge and jury with narrow, clear issues of fact.

The dynamics of criminal justice administration also contribute to the multiplication of charges. Most criminal charges are disposed of by a plea of guilty, which often is the product of explicit or tacit negotiations between prosecutor and defense counsel.

The multiplication of charges provides both lawyers with leverage for negotiation, even when as a practical matter there can be only one conviction or sentence and the likelihood of consecutive sentences is remote. Often a defendant can be persuaded to plead guilty to one charge on the assurance that the remaining 27 counts will be dismissed. Some judges express resentment when a prosecutor presents a 1 count indictment or information, complaining that this unduly restricts their sentencing flexibility.

Finally, the impact of the multiplicity of charges on proof at trial must be recognized. Some judges will not allow proof of similar acts not charged in the indictment and sometimes a prosecutor will be limited in showing the entire transaction if it includes other criminal offenses not charged. All of these pressures to charge as large a number of offenses as possible tend to be aggravated by the prosecutor's perception of himself as the avenging agent of society. Certainly there is often more emotion than sense in the 100 count indictment, but the existing rules provide few countervailing pressures, or even escapes, through which the prosecutor can avoid the multiplication of charges.

Rosett, Arthur I. and Green, Richard A., Working Papers of the National Commission on Reform of Federal Criminal Laws, Vol. I, at 335–36 (1970).

5. Multiple convictions in a single prosecution pose a less substantial problem than does multiple punishment. This is reflected in the concurrent sentence doctrine announced in Hirabayashi v. United States, 320 U.S. 81, 63 S.Ct. 1375, 87 L.Ed. 1774 (1943), under which if the defendant has been convicted on more than one count and received concurrent sentences the courts have discretion, if they affirm one conviction carrying an equal or greater sentence, to decline to review any other conviction. This doctrine was reconsidered in Benton v. Maryland, 395 U.S. 784, 89 S.Ct. 2056, 23 L.Ed.2d 707 (1969), where the Court held that the concurrence of sentences did not preclude, as a matter of jurisdiction, consideration of an attack on only one of the petitioner's convictions. The Court was satisfied that the possible adverse consequences collateral to multiple convictions, such as use for enhancement under habitual offender statutes, were sufficient to give the case an adversary cast and make it justiciable. The Court suggested, without deciding, that the *Hirabayashi* rule might remain as one of judicial convenience. See United States v. Tyler, 466 F.2d 920, 924 (9th Cir. 1972).

6. The proposed federal statutes which follow represent a new effort to deal with all of these problems. They recognize that the heart of the issue is that of multiple punishment and that that problem cannot be satisfactorily resolved through the logical gymnastics performed in the preceding opinions. Under these proposals when will multiple punishment be possible? Should it be where defendant has, in a single episode, killed his wife and two children, State ex rel. Stangvik v. Tahash, 281 Minn. 353, 161 N.W.2d 667 (1968); where defendant in the course of an armed robbery, almost chokes one person to death and gouges out the eye of another, State v. Boag, 104 Ariz. 362, 453 P.2d 508 (1969).

PROPOSED FEDERAL CRIMINAL CODE (1971)

§ 703.   Prosecution for Multiple Related Offenses

(1) Multiple Related Charges. When the same conduct of a defendant may establish the commission of more than one offense, the defendant may be prosecuted for each such offense.

(2) Limitation on Separate Trials. Unless otherwise ordered by the court to promote justice, a defendant shall not be subject to separate trials for multiple offenses (a) based on the same conduct, (b) arising from the same criminal episode, or (c) based on a series of acts or omissions motivated by a common purpose or plan and which result in the repeated commission of the same offense or affect the same person or persons or their property, if such offenses are within the jurisdiction of the court and known to the United States Attorney at the time the defendant is arraigned on the first indictment or information.

Comment

*   *   *

This section sets forth rules for prosecution of a defendant for related offenses. Subsection (1) recognizes that multiple charges must be permitted, despite the possibility of abuse from overcharging, because of the uncertainty at the time of charging as to what the proof at trial will be, the constitutional restriction on amending indictments, and the requirement that the defendant be informed of the precise charges against him. Subsection (2) codifies present federal practice, but makes joinder compulsory unless otherwise ordered by the court. Note that, while the offenses to be joined are those known to the prosecutor at the time of the first indictment or information, only multiple *trials* of such offenses are prohibited. Thus the prosecution is not barred from filing additional charges before trial on the first takes place.

Separate trials "to promote justice" will include severance of counts against one defendant so that he can be tried jointly with other defendants on one or more counts.

Since § 705 bars subsequent prosecution for offenses required to be joined by this section, double jeopardy protection is extended well beyond the existing protection which applies only when offenses are "identical."

No limit on multiple convictions is established. Limitations on multiple convictions could be provided; but to require the court or prosecutor to choose one of several offenses to submit to the jury or upon which to enter judgment could result in an unjustified windfall to the defendant, where the charge for the offense chosen is dismissed on appeal. Accordingly, limitations have been placed instead on sentencing (§ 3204).

§ 3204. Concurrent and Consecutive Terms of Imprisonment

(1) Authority of Court. When multiple sentences of imprisonment are imposed on a person at the same time or when a term of imprisonment is imposed on a person who is already subject to an undischarged term of imprisonment, the sentences shall run concurrently or consecutively as determined by the court. Sentences shall run concurrently unless otherwise specified by the court.

(2) Multiple Sentences. A defendant may not be sentenced consecutively for more than one offense to the extent:

(a) one offense is an included offense of the other;

(b) one offense consists only of a conspiracy, attempt, solicitation or other form of preparation to commit, or facilitation of, the other; or

(c) the offenses differ only in that one is defined to prohibit a designated kind of conduct generally and the other to prohibit a specific instance of such conduct.

(3) Maximum Limits Where Felony Involved. The aggregate maximum of consecutive sentences to which a defendant may be subject shall not exceed the maximum term authorized by section 3201(1) for the most serious felony involved, except that a defendant being sentenced for two or more Class C felonies may be subject to an aggregate maximum not exceeding that authorized by section 3201(1) for a Class B felony if each Class C felony was committed as part of a different course of conduct or each involved a substantially different criminal objective [and a defendant being sentenced for two or more Class B felonies may be subject to an aggregate maximum not exceeding that authorized by section 3201(1) for a Class A felony if each Class B felony was committed as part of a different course of conduct or each involved a substantially different criminal objective].

(4) Maximum Limits for Misdemeanors. When sentenced only for misdemeanors, a defendant may not be consecutively sentenced to more than one year, except that a defendant being sentenced for two or more Class A misdemeanors may be subject to an aggregate maximum not exceeding that authorized by section 3201(1) for a Class C felony if each Class A misdemeanor was committed as part of a different course of conduct or each involved a substantially different criminal objective.

(5) Criteria and Reasons. The court shall not impose a consecutive sentence unless, having regard to the nature and circumstances of the offense and the history and character of the defendant, it is of the opinion that such a term is required because of the exceptional features of the case, for reasons which the court shall set forth in detail.

(6) Application to Multiple Proceedings. The limitations provided in this section shall apply not only when a defendant is sentenced at one time for multiple offenses but also when a defendant is sentenced at different times for multiple offenses all of which were committed prior to the imposition of any sentence for any of them. Sentences imposed both by other federal courts and by any state or local courts shall be counted in applying these limitations.

(7) Effect of Consecutive Terms. In determining the effect of consecutive sentences and the manner in which they will be served, the Board of Parole shall treat the defendant as though he has been committed for a single term which is the aggregate of the maximum terms validly imposed. Any such term longer than six months shall have the following incidents:

(a) the parole component of such single term shall be:
(i) one-third for terms of nine years or less, except that, if one-third of such single term is less than three years, the parole component shall be the aggregate of the parole components of the terms imposed, but no more than three years;
(ii) three years for terms between nine and fifteen years, and
(iii) five years for terms more than fifteen years;

(b) the minimum term, if any, shall constitute the aggregate of all validly imposed minimum terms.

(8) Effect of State Sentences. Subject to any permissible cumulation of sentences explicitly authorized by this section, the Bureau of Corrections shall automatically award credit against the maximum term and any minimum term of any federal sentence for all time served in a state or local institution since the commission of the federal offense or offenses.

Comment

Subsection (1) continues the authority of a federal court to impose either concurrent or consecutive terms in the case of conviction for more than one offense. Subsection (2) prohibits consecutive sentences in three situations where the multiple crimes result from one criminal objective. An alternative and more general statement might be: "The court shall not impose consecutive sentences for offenses which were committed as part of a single course of conduct during which there was no substantial change in the nature of the criminal objective." In the event that subsections (3) and (4) are not adopted, some such limitation on the open-ended imposition of consecutive terms would be appropriate.

Subsections (3) and (4) would substantially change federal law by setting, for consecutive sentences, a maximum other than the total authorized for the combined offenses. The principle underlying subsection (3) is that multiple offenders may, like persistent offenders, evidence dangerousness which justifies a long sentence. It applies whenever a defendant is sentenced for a felony and for any other crime. Sentences for all crimes may be aggregated up to the upper range maximum for the most serious felony involved.

Class C felonies may be aggregated into the Class B felony range. The felonies must, however, be parts of different courses of conduct or involve substantially different criminal objectives. Thus, stealing a check from the mails, forging and then uttering it would not permit consecutive sentences into the Class B felony range, but stealing the check, assaulting the postal inspector who was investigating the case and bribing a witness would permit such cumulation.

The bracketed addition reflects a substantial body of opinion in the Commission that an additional deterrent is necessary to prevent repetition of Class B offenses, which embrace egregious misconduct, e.g., rape, armed robbery, and that such repeated misconduct may warrant incapacitation for as long a period as commission of a single Class A felony. The counter consideration is that the authorized limits for a Class B sentence are high enough for these purposes and that the Class A felony range should be available only for a few specifically defined and especially heinous offenses.

Subsection (4) sets forth the general rule when a defendant is sentenced only for misdemeanors. Sentences may be cumulated to a maximum of one year. When, however, a defendant is convicted of unrelated Class A misdemeanors he may be consecutively sentenced into the Class C felony sentence range.

Subsection (5) is designed to assure a reasoned use of consecutive sentences. Subsection (6) complements the last sentence of subsection (1); the sentence imposed will run concurrently with other sentences, state or federal, in the absence of affirmative action by the court. Subsection (7) provides that, for such purposes as determining the proper facility for confinement, a defendant must be treated as subject to one sentence, even though consecutive sentences have been imposed, and indicates how the various components are to be determined.

B. THE STATE OF MIND

COWAN, TOWARDS AN EXPERIMENTAL DEFINITION OF CRIMINAL MIND, IN PHILOSOPHICAL ESSAYS IN HONOR OF EDGAR ARTHUR SINGER, JR.

163 (F. Clarke and M. Nahm eds. 1942).

In the 17th year of the reign of Edward IV, Brian pronounced his celebrated dictum that a man is responsible only for his words and deeds and not for his thoughts, because "the devil himself knoweth not the mind of man." What the learned judge apparently took to be an axiomatic rule of evidence has become a part of the substantive law of contracts in the form of the doctrine of objective intent. Contract law is now taken to be concerned only with intent as outwardly manifested by the conduct of the parties.

Similarly, the law of torts is almost exclusively occupied with the external behavior of the parties. Only in the case of intentional wrongs does it purport to refer to states of mind as qualifying responsibility. The great body of non-intentional torts applies what are called "objective standards." In determining negligence, for instance, the law does not inquire whether the harmful act was accompanied by a culpable state of mind. On the contrary, it merely decides whether the defendant failed to conform to external standards of reasonably expectable conduct. His state of mind is immaterial. Anglo-American *civil* law, therefore, has from the earliest times indicated that, with certain few exceptions, objective intent is the only kind of intent with which it is prepared to deal.

The theory of the *criminal* law is different. Here it is still felt necessary to investigate a man's secret thought, or absence of thought, whenever intention, or malice, or even negligence is an element of the crime in question.

NOTES

1. The so-called subjective theory of criminal liability assumes that state of mind and therefore "mind" itself is ascertainable. This underlying assumption has been called into question on both practical and theoretical grounds.

The practical ground is based upon difficulty of proof. If there is such a "thing" as state of mind, it is nevertheless so subjective and difficult of proof that it is unrealistic to believe that an individual's state of mind at a past time can generally be reliably determined. Thus, it is argued, the criminal law should not attempt to make criminal liability turn on state of mind.

The theoretical ground is more basic. This view holds that "mind" is a mere abstraction and therefore it is artificial to treat states of mind as if they actually existed. Rather than waste time attempting to infer an offender's state of mind from his behavior, this view holds that the law would better serve its purposes if it regarded the so-called mind as the criminal behavior itself rather than using the behavior as evidence from which to infer "mind". See T. Cowan, Towards an Experimental Definition of Criminal Mind, in Philosophical Essays in Honor of Edgar Arthur Singer, Jr. (F. Clarke and M. Nahm eds. 1942); Cowan, A Critique of the Moralistic Conception of Criminal Law, 97 U.Pa.L.Rev. 502, 510 (1949). In fact, Cowan represents, the law in fact does this by procedural devices such as the presumption that a person "intends" the natural consequences of his act. Inserting the concept of "state of mind", he concludes, merely serves to confuse analysis.

2. The historical development of the criminal law's emphasis upon an alleged offender's state of mind (the mens rea requirement) is traced in the following portions of Sayre, Mens Rea, 45 Harv.L.Rev. 974, 981–83, 988–89, 993–94 (1932):[f]

[S]tudy of the early law seems to show that up to the twelfth century the conception of *mens rea* in anything like its present sense was nonexistent. In certain cases at least criminal liability might attach irrespective of the actor's state of mind. But because the old records fail to set forth a *mens rea* as a general requisite of criminality one must not reach the conclusion that even in very early times the mental element was entirely disregarded. The very nature of the majority of the early offenses rendered them impossible of commission without a criminal intent. Waylaying and robbery are impossible without it; so is rape; and the same is roughly true of housebreaking. * * *

Furthermore, the intent of the defendant seems to have been a material factor, even from the very earliest times, in determining the extent of punishment.

By the end of the twelfth century two influences were making themselves strongly felt. One was the Roman law[;] * * * the Roman law conceptions of *dolus* and *culpa* required careful consideration of the mental element in crime.

A second influence, even more powerful, was the canon law, whose insistence upon moral guilt emphasized still further the mental element in crime. * * * Henceforth, the criminal law of England, developing in the general direction of moral blameworthiness, begins to insist upon a *mens rea* as an essential element of criminality. * * *

We can trace the changed attitude in the new generalizations concerning the necessity of an evil intent which are found scattered through the Year Books in the remarks of judges and counsel * * *. We sense it in the growing insistence upon more and more sharply defined mental requisites as essentials of the common-law felonies. We find it fermenting in the form of new defenses which show the absence of an evil mind and therefore of criminal liability-defenses such as infancy or insanity or compulsion.

* * *

By the second half of the seventeenth century, it was universally accepted law that an evil intent was as necessary for felony as the act itself. * * *

At the outset when the *mens rea* necessary for criminality was based on general moral blameworthiness, the conception was an exceedingly vague one. As a result of the slow judicial process of discriminating one case from another and "talking of diversities," much sharper and more precise lines gradually came to be drawn as to the exact mental requisites for various crimes. Since each felony involved different social and public interests, the mental requisites for one almost inevitably came to differ from those of another.

f. Reprinted from 45 Harvard Law Review 974 (1932).

REMINGTON AND HELSTAD, THE MENTAL ELEMENT IN CRIME—A LEGISLATIVE PROBLEM

1952 Wis.L.Rev. 644, 678.

If the problem of the mental element in crime is difficult and confused, that is due in large part to the fact that it is comparatively a neglected area in the law. While the scope of the criminal law is continually being expanded through legislative enactment, little attention has been given to broad aspects such as the mental state required. * * * The problem is not easy. In fact it is perhaps as difficult as any in the law, but the need for improvement is imperative and with some effort much improvement can be made. The solution requires * * * awareness of the problem, a willingness to face squarely the policy determinations that must be made, and once those determinations are made, careful attention to the drafting [and interpretation] of criminal statutes so as to assure that the basis of liability is clearly expressed.

---

1. TYPES OF STATES OF MIND

PROPOSED FEDERAL CRIMINAL CODE

(1971).

§ 302 **Requirements of Culpability**

(1) Kinds of Culpability. A person engages in conduct:

(a) "intentionally" if, when he engages in the conduct, it is his purpose to do so;

(b) "knowingly" if, when he engages in the conduct, he knows or has a firm belief unaccompanied by substantial doubt that he is doing so, whether or not it is his purpose to do so;

(c) "recklessly" if he engages in the conduct in conscious and clearly unjustifiable disregard of a substantial likelihood of the existence of the relevant facts or risks, such disregard involving a gross deviation from acceptable standards of conduct * * *;

(d) "negligently" if he engages in the conduct in unreasonable disregard of a substantial likelihood of the existence of the relevant facts or risks, such disregard involving a gross deviation from acceptable standards of conduct; and

(e) "willfully" if he engages in the conduct intentionally, knowingly, or recklessly.

WEINREB, COMMENT ON BASIS OF CRIMINAL LIABILITY; CULPABILITY; CAUSATION, IN WORKING PAPERS OF THE NATIONAL COMMISSION ON REFORM OF FEDERAL CRIMINAL LAWS

106–28 (1970).

2. *Subsection (1). Kinds of Culpability.* * * *

The degrees of culpability, or categories of mental state, are reduced to four; culpable conduct is conduct in which a person engages *intentionally, knowingly, recklessly,* or *negligently.* All other statutory formulations are eliminated. The four degrees of culpability that are retained express the significant distinctions found by the courts, and are adequate for all the distinctions which can and should be made to accomplish the purposes of a Federal Criminal Code.

"Intentionally." The highest degree of culpability is present when a person engages in conduct *intentionally,* that is "when he engages in the conduct, it is his purpose to do so, whether or not there is a further objective toward which the conduct is directed."

The law can properly single out conceptually and functionally the person who engages in prohibited conduct with the very purpose of engaging in it, who adopts as a guide to his conduct the doing of a prohibited act (or failing to do a required act), the possessing of a prohibited article, or the accomplishing of a prohibited objective. A common way to describe conduct intentional in this sense is to say that it is done "on purpose." [51]

*　　*　　*

"Knowingly." A high, but not the highest, degree of culpability is present when a person engages in conduct *knowingly,* that is "when he engages in the conduct, he knows or has a firm belief unaccompanied by substantial doubt that he is doing so, whether or not it is his purpose to do so."

In many situations, there may be little reason for the criminal law to distinguish between a man who engages in prohibited conduct purposefully and a man who engages in the same conduct not on purpose but knowing that he is doing so. Both are consciously conducting themselves in a way that the law prohibits. In some situations, however, it seems reasonable that the law should distinguish between a man who wills that a particular act or result take place and another who is merely willing that it should take place. The distinction is drawn between the main direction of a man's conduct and the (antici-

---

51. The choice of the word "intentionally" rather than "purposely" for this category of conduct was made because the former is more familiar to the law. Also, the latter word may too easily suggest a requirement of a particular purpose rather than simply that conduct be purposive. The Model Penal Code makes the latter word primary and provides that the two have the same meaning. The California, Illinois, Michigan, and New York Codes use the word "intentionally."

pated) side effects of his conduct. For example, a man might intentionally blow up the grocery store next to the post office, with knowledge that the post office will be blown up as well. A category of conduct in which a person engages knowingly is warranted not only to allow a distinction between purposeful and knowing conduct but also because in most cases it will be sufficient for liability that a person engaged in prohibited conduct knowingly, whether or not it was his purpose to do so.

* * *

"Recklessly." A different order of culpability is present when a person engages in conduct *recklessly*, that is "he engages in the conduct in conscious [,] and [plain and] clearly unjustifiable disregard of a substantial likelihood of the existence of the relevant facts [, such disregard involving a gross deviation from acceptable standards of conduct]."

* * *

Addition of the concluding clause, "such disregard involving a gross deviation from acceptable standards of conduct," would import into the definition of recklessness the distinction between negligence for civil cases and criminal negligence recognized (at least) in the crime of manslaughter. * * *

[A]lthough the courts have regularly used phrases like "simple" and "gross" negligence, it is doubtful whether such shades of meaning have substantive significance. If it is established that a person has consciously disregarded a likelihood that he is engaging in prohibited conduct, and that his disregard is (plain and) clearly unjustifiable, that may be all that can meaningfully be said. To ask a jury to determine also whether his conduct violates standards of conduct "grossly" or only "simply" is very likely to entrust to it the power to judge the conduct at large without standards.

"Negligently." The lowest degree of culpability is involved when a person acts *negligently*, that is, "he engages in the conduct in unreasonable disregard of a substantial likelihood of the existence of the relevant facts [, such disregard involving a gross deviation from acceptable standards of conduct]."

* * *

The formulation used distinguishes negligent conduct from reckless conduct by requiring only an "unreasonable" disregard for the former, in comparison with the requirement of "conscious and [plain and] clearly unjustifiable" disregard for the latter. The major difference is that the negligent person need not be aware of the likelihood that he is engaging in the prohibited conduct. Because he may not be aware, it seems more appropriate to talk of "unreasonable" rather than "unjustifiable" disregard; the former word more easily encompasses a negligent failure to be aware of, as well as a negligent failure to give sufficient weight to, the danger involved. In addition, the omission of the word "clearly," which appears in the definition of reckless conduct, emphasizes the difference in degree between the two levels of culpability. Aside from the distinction drawn between recklessness and negligence on the basis of awareness, the formulations allow a jury to conclude that although the defendant was conscious of a risk, the nature and extent of the risk or the manner or degree of the defendant's disregard of it or the reasons for his disregard of it indicate that he was not reckless, but only negligent. Since all of these elements are relevant to the question whether a person was reckless or entirely without fault, it should be possible to reach the middle ground of negligence on the same basis.

Again, the clause "such disregard involving a gross deviation from acceptable standards of conduct" is added in brackets at the end. For the reasons discussed above, its inclusion is not recommended.

* * *

"Willfully." There may be no word in the Federal criminal lexicon which has caused as much confusion as the word "willfully" (or "willful"). In ordinary speech, the word probably connotes something between purpose and malice, and also something of obstinacy. Despite the confusion that the word has engendered, it has an accepted place in Federal criminal law and can be eliminated only with difficulty. The next best thing to eliminating it entirely is to attempt to give it a clear, fixed meaning. This has been done by providing that a person engages in conduct "willfully" if he engages in it "intentionally," "knowingly," or "recklessly." So confined, the word offers a useful means of referring to the more serious degrees of culpability. None of its connotations have significance for the criminal law.

2. THE STANDARD STATE OF MIND REQUIREMENT FOR CRIMINAL LIABILITY: "GENERAL INTENT"

REGINA v. PEMBLITON

Court of Criminal Appeal, 1874.
12 Cox Crim. Cases 607.

LORD COLERIDGE, C. J.—I am of opinion that this conviction must be quashed. The facts of the case are these. The prisoner and some other persons who had been drinking in a public house were turned out of it at about 11 p.m. for being disorderly, and they then began to fight in the street near the prosecutor's window. The prisoner separated himself from the others, and went to the other side of the street, and picked up a stone, and threw it at the persons he had been fighting with. The stone passed over their heads, and broke a large plate glass window in the prosecutor's house, doing damage to an amount exceeding 5*l*. The jury found that the prisoner threw the stone at the people he had been fighting with, intending to strike one or more of them with it, but not intending to break the window. The question is whether under an indictment for unlawfully and maliciously committing an injury to the window in the house of the prosecutor the proof of these facts alone, coupled with the finding of the jury, will do? Now I think that is not enough. The indictment is framed under the 24 & 25 Vict. c. 97, s. 51. The Act is an Act relating to malicious injuries to property, and sect. 51 enacts that whosoever shall unlawfully and maliciously commit any damage, &c., to or upon any real or personal property whatsoever of a public or a private nature, for which the punishment is hereinbefore provided, to an amount exceeding 5l shall be guilty of a misdemeanor. There is also the 58th section which deserves attention. "Every punishment and forfeiture by this Act imposed on any person maliciously committing any offence, whether the same be punishable upon indictment or upon summary conviction, shall equally apply and be enforced whether the offence shall be committed from malice conceived against the owner of the property in respect of which it shall be committed, or otherwise." It seems to me on both these sections that what was intended to be provided against by the Act is the wilfully doing an unlawful Act, and that the Act must be wilfully and intentionally done on the part of the person doing it, to render him liable to be convicted. Without saying that, upon these facts, if the jury had found that the prisoner had been guilty of throwing the stone recklessly, knowing that there was a window near which it might probably hit, I should have been disposed to interfere with the conviction, yet as they have found that he threw the stone at the people he had been fighting with intending to strike them and not intending to break the window, I think the conviction must be quashed. I do not intend to throw any doubt on the cases which have been cited and which show what is sufficient to constitute malice in the case of murder. They rest upon the principles of the common law, and have no application to a statutory offence created by an Act in which the words are carefully studied.

UNITED STATES v. BYRD

United States Court of Appeals for the Second Circuit, 1965.
352 F.2d 570.

ANDERSON, Circuit Judge. [Defendant, an office auditor for the Internal Revenue Service, was convicted of receiving an unauthorized fee in connection with his official tasks.]

On this appeal Byrd claims that the trial court committed plain error in its charge to the jury in failing to include criminal intent as one of the essential elements of the offense alleged in the three counts. There was no exception taken to the court's instructions but the appellant asserts that there were several other mistakes in the charge of sufficient gravity to constitute plain error. We conclude that, in the circumstances of this case, the omission of criminal intent as one of the enumerated essential elements of the offense charged, constituted plain error and that, therefore, the judgment must be reversed and the case remanded for a new trial.

By failing specifically to instruct the jury that criminal intent was an essential element of the offense, the court left what it did say about intent and the act being knowingly committed, unrelated to the other elements of the crime and omitted any instruction that criminal intent was an element which the Government, to convict, was required to prove beyond a reasonable doubt. While it did not define criminal intent as such, it did give one of the generally used definitions of "knowingly"[1] which in the circumstances of the case would have sufficed, because a finding that one acts knowingly presupposes that he was apprised of all of the facts which constitute the offense.

> "Ordinarily one is not guilty of a crime unless he is aware of the existence of all those facts which make his conduct criminal. That awareness is all that is meant by the mens rea, the 'criminal intent', necessary to guilt, * * *."

United States v. Crimmins, 123 F.2d 271, 272 (2d Cir.1941).

Examining the charge as a whole, however, this definition stands entirely unrelated to the other essential elements of the crime. What its significance is in the case and how it should be treated by the jury is left to conjecture. * * *

* * * [T]he court's treatment of the issue might have survived the test of plain error, Rule 52(b) F.R.Crim.P., except for its specific delineation of the essential elements of the offense.

The instructions which bore on intent came in the early part of the charge. Thereafter the court gave fairly full explanations of types of evidence, rulings on evidence, evaluation of testimony, an analysis of Government and defense evidence, the definition of accomplice and the cautionary remarks on dealing with accomplices' testimony, a reading of the applicable statute and comments on the three counts of the indictment. Then toward the end of the charge the court specified the essential elements of each of the offenses charged as follows:

> "1. That the defendant was an employee of the United States.
>
> 2. That he was acting in connection with the revenue laws of the United States.

---

1. "Now, the word 'knowingly,' as used in the indictment, means that the act or acts which were committed by the defendant were done voluntarily and purposely, not because of a mistake or inadvertence or in good faith.

Now, the knowledge may be proven by the defendant's conduct and by all the facts and circumstances surrounding the case.

No person can intentionally avoid knowledge by closing his eyes to facts which prompt him to investigate.

* * *"

3.   That he received a fee not prescribed by law.

4.   That he received a fee for the performance of a duty."

It briefly mentioned how the jury should handle the separate counts and then said,

"Now, if you find, after such examination, that the government has proven all the four elements which I have just described to you beyond a reasonable doubt as to any of these counts, then he should be convicted on that count."

Thus in the very climax of the charge the court in short explicit terms gave the jury what they would naturally regard as the nub of the law of the case and which, coming at the end of the exposition of the law, gave them what they were most likely to hold in their minds and apply to the facts in their deliberations, and which, not only completely omitted criminal intent as an essential element but, specifically told the jury that, if they found the other four elements which were mentioned, they had a duty to convict.

Byrd made no special attack on the element of intent, for he denied accepting any bribes. The jury disbelieved him. But to sustain a conviction the Government had to prove and the jury had to find criminal intent. It was an unavoidable issue in the case.

We conclude that the court's failure to explain the relevance of criminal intent to the other factors in the case and to describe it as one of the essential elements of the offense, requiring, as such, proof beyond a reasonable doubt, was tantamount to no instruction at all on the subject. There was, therefore, plain error which requires reversal even though no exception was taken below to the charge as given.

PROPOSED FEDERAL CRIMINAL CODE

(1971).

§ 302.   Requirements of Culpability

*   *   *

(2) Where Culpability Not Specified. If a statute or regulation thereunder defining a crime does not specify any culpability and does not provide explicitly that a person may be guilty without culpability, the culpability that is required is willfully. Except as otherwise expressly provided or unless the context otherwise requires, if a statute provides that conduct is an infraction without including a requirement of culpability, no culpability is required.

(3) Factors to Which Requirement of Culpability Applies.

(a) Except as otherwise expressly provided, where culpability is required, that kind of culpability is required with respect to every element of the conduct and to those attendant circumstances specified in the definition of the offense, except that where the required culpability is "intentionally", the culpability required as to an attendant circumstance is "knowingly."

(b) Except as otherwise expressly provided, if conduct is an offense if it causes a particular result, the required kind of culpability is required with respect to the result.

(c) Except as otherwise expressly provided, culpability is not required with respect to any fact which is solely a basis for federal jurisdiction or for grading.

(d) Except as otherwise expressly provided, culpability is not required with respect to facts which establish that a defense does not exist, if the defense is defined in Part A of this Code [covering all generally applicable defenses] or Chapter 10 [covering attempt, facilitation, solicitation, conspiracy, and regulatory offenses and defenses related to those offenses]; otherwise the least kind of culpability required for the offense is required with respect to such facts.

(e) A factor as to which it is expressly stated that it must "in fact" exist is a factor for which culpability is not required.

(4) Specified Culpability Requirement Satisfied by Higher Culpability. If conduct is an offense if a person engages in it negligently, the conduct is an offense also if a person engages in it intentionally, knowingly, or recklessly. If conduct is an offense if a person engages in it recklessly, the conduct is an offense also if a person engages in it intentionally or knowingly. If conduct is an offense if a person engages in it knowingly, the conduct is an offense also if a person engages in it intentionally.

(5) No Requirement of Awareness that Conduct is Criminal. Culpability is not required as to the fact that conduct is an offense, except as otherwise expressly provided in a provision outside this Code.

WEINREB, COMMENT ON BASIS OF CRIMINAL LIABILITY; CULPABILITY; CAUSATION, IN 1 WORKING PAPERS OF THE NATIONAL COMMISSION ON REFORM OF FEDERAL CRIMINAL LAWS

118–21, 129 (1970).

This section follows the example of the Model Penal Code and other recent codifications in their efforts to restate the general requirement of culpability ("mens rea") in a limited number of relatively specific principles. It defines a group of specific mental states and provides that, unless a law explicitly provides otherwise, one of them must accompany conduct for it to be criminal. In addition, it provides general rules of statutory construction with respect to the requirement of culpability.

There is no comparable Federal statute now. The "mental element" of Federal crimes is specified in the definitions of the crimes, which definitions are frequently modified, if not indeed distorted, in judicial decisions. If one looks to the statutes alone, the specifications of mental states form a staggering array[.]   *   *   *

Unsurprisingly, the courts have been unable to find substantive correlates for all these varied descriptions of mental states, and, in fact, the opinions display far fewer mental states than the statutory language. Not only does the statutory language not reflect accurately or consistently what are the mental elements of the various crimes; there is no discernible pattern or consistent rationale which explains why one crime is defined or understood to require one mental state and another crime another mental state or indeed no mental state at all.

Perhaps the best illustration of the confusion engendered by existing statutory formulations of the mental element in Federal crimes is that surrounding the word "willfully."   *   *   *

[T]he courts, including the Supreme Court, have endowed the requirement of willfulness with the capacity to take on whatever meaning seems appropriate in the statutory context. Similarly, the mental state that accompanies an act done corruptly has been variously described.

The courts have been equally unclear about the meaning of the requirement that conduct be intentional, or even when there is such a requirement.   *   *   *

An issue basic to the proposed Federal Code is resolved in this subsection. Insofar as it provides that, in the absence of an explicit provision to the contrary, willfulness is a requirement of all crimes, the subsection states a presumption that conduct is a crime only if a person engages in it intentionally, knowingly, or recklessly. The subsection also, however, does acknowledge that some conduct may be declared criminal even though a person engages in it not culpably.

*   *   *

NOTES

1. Given the fact that Byrd made "no special attack on the element of intent," was the trial court's instruction so importantly defective as to justify finding it "plain error?" Is there any real likelihood that the result would have been different had the proper instruction been given? If the answer to either of these questions is negative, how can the apparent importance which the court seems to attach to instructions on intent be justified?

2.   In State v. Hatley, 72 N.M. 377, 384 P.2d 252 (1963), the defendant was charged with mayhem, based upon striking a blow that put out the eye of the victim.   Challenging the adequacy of the proof against him, the defendant argued that there was no proof of "intent to maim" and that if the victim had not turned his head at the moment of the blow the injury to the eye would not have resulted.   Affirming the conviction, the appellate court stated:

> We think the conduct of appellant falls well within the rule so as to make him liable for the consequences of an unlawful act, even though such consequences may not have been intended.   One who, in the commission of a wrongful act, commits another wrong not meant by him, is nevertheless liable for the latter wrong.   * * *   Here, the appellant deliberately committed the crime of assault and battery, and, in so doing, committed mayhem.

Id. at 382, 384 P.2d at 252.

Is it significant that in *Pembliton* the injury intended was to a person and that resulting was to property, while in *Hatley* both the injury intended and that caused were to a person?   Was the injury intended more severe than that actually caused in either *Pembliton* or in *Hatley*?   If so, is this relevant?

3.   The Texas Penal Code contains the following provisions:

Art. 42.   Act done by mistake a felony.

One intending to commit a felony and who in the act of preparing for or executing the same shall through mistake or accident do another act which, if voluntarily done, would be a felony, shall receive the punishment affixed to the felony actually committed.

Art. 44.   Felony done by mistake.

One intending to commit a misdemeanor and who in the act of preparing for or executing the same shall through mistake commit a felony shall receive the lowest punishment affixed to the felony.

What results on the facts of *Pembliton* if these statutes are applicable?   Is this desirable?   What arguments can be made for and against the positions embodied in the Texas statutes?

4.   See generally, P. Brett, An Inquiry into Criminal Guilt (1963);   H. Packer, The Limits of the Criminal Sanction 103–35 (1968);   Acimovic, Conceptions of Culpability in Contemporary American Criminal Law, 26 La.L.Rev. 28 (1965);   Binavince, The Ethical Foundation of Criminal Liability, 33 Fordham L.Rev. 1, 1965);   Dubin *Mens Rea* Reconsidered: A Plea for a Due Process Concept of Criminal Responsibility, 18 Stan.L.Rev. 323 (1966);   Hughes, Book Review, 16 Stan.L.Rev. 470 (1964);   Levitt, Extent and Function of the Doctrine of Mens Rea, 17 Ill.L.Rev. 578 (1923);   Mueller, On Common Law Mens Rea, 42 Minn.L.Rev. 1043 (1958);   Packer, Mens Rea and the Supreme Court, 1962 Sup.Ct.Rev. 107;   Perkins, A Rationale of Mens Rea, 52 Harv.L.Rev. 905 (1939);   Turner, The Mental Element in Crimes at Common Law, 6 Camb.L.J. 31 (1936);   Wechsler, On Culpability and Crime: The Treatment of "Mens Rea" in the Model Penal Code, 339 Annals 26 (1962).   See also Weiler, The Supreme Court of Canada and the Doctrines of Mens Rea, 49 Can.B.Rev. 280 (1971).

5. The position of the Proposed Federal Criminal Code and of the Model Penal Code—that in the absence of a specific indication to the contrary "willfullness" would be required—was defended by the draftsmen of the Model Penal Code as representing "what is usually regarded as the common law position." Model Penal Code, Comments to § 2.02, 127 (Tent.Draft No. 4, 1955). It also, according to the comments, "represents the most convenient norm for drafting purposes, since when purpose or knowledge is to be required, it is normal to so state; and negligence ought to be viewed as an exceptional basis of liability." Id. In view of this, can the analysis of the Proposed Federal Criminal Code be satisfactorily applied to criminal statutes in existing codes as a framework for analysis, an aid in construction, or both?

Why should negligence be regarded as "an exceptional basis of liability," to be used only where the legislative intent to impose it is extremely clear? Consider the following:

> Since negligence involves no *mens rea*, the question is raised as to the advisability of punishing negligent conduct with criminal sanctions. Professor Edwin Keedy responded to this question as follows: "If the defendant, being mistaken as to the material facts, is to be punished because his mistake is one an average man would not make, punishment will sometimes be inflicted *when the criminal mind does not exist*. Such a result is contrary to fundamental principles, and is plainly unjust, for a man should not be held criminal because of lack of intelligence." [10] This argument is persuasive, especially when considered in conjunction with the traditional concepts and goals of criminal punishment.
>
> The concept of criminal punishment is based on one, or a combination, of four theories: deterrence, retribution, rehabilitation and incapacitation.
>
> The deterrence theory of criminal law is based on the hypotheses that the prospective offender knows that he will be punished for any criminal activity, and, therefore, will adjust his behavior to avoid committing a criminal act. This theory rests on the idea of "rational utility," i. e., prospective offenders will weigh the evil of the sanction against the gain of the contemplated crime. However, punishment of a negligent offender in no way implements this theory, since the negligent harm-doer is, by definition, unaware of the risk he imposes on society. It is questionable whether holding an individual criminally liable for acts the risks of which he has failed to perceive will deter him from failing to perceive in the future.
>
> The often-criticized retributive theory of criminal law presupposes a "moral guilt," which justifies society in seeking its revenge against the offender. This "moral guilt" is ascribed to those forms of conduct which society deems threatening to its very existence, such as murder and larceny. However, the negligent harm-doer has not actually committed this type of morally reprehensible act,

10. Keedy, Ignorance and Mistake in the Criminal Law, 22 Harv.L.Rev. 75, 84 (1908) (Emphasis added.)

but has merely made an error in judgment. This type of error is an everyday occurrence, although it may deviate from a normal standard of care. Nevertheless, such conduct does not approach the moral turpitude against which the criminal law should seek revenge. It is difficult to comprehend how retribution requires such mistakes to be criminally punished.

It is also doubtful whether the negligent offender can be rehabilitated in any way by criminal punishment. Rehabilitation presupposes a "warped sense of values" which can be corrected. Since inadvertence, and not a deficient sense of values, has caused the "crime," there appears to be nothing to rehabilitate.

The underlying goal of the incapacitation theory is to protect society by isolating an individual so as to prevent him from perpetrating a similar crime in the future. However, this approach is only justifiable if less stringent methods will not further the same goal of protecting society. For example, an insane individual would not be criminally incarcerated, if the less stringent means of medical treatment would afford the same societal protection. Likewise, with a criminally negligent individual, the appropriate remedy is not incarceration, but "to exclude him from the activity in which he is a danger."

The conclusion drawn from this analysis is that there appears to be no reasonable justification for punishing negligence as a criminal act under any of these four theories. It does not further the purposes of deterrence, retribution, rehabilitation or incapacitation; hence, there is no rational basis for the imposition of criminal liability on negligent conduct.

This view, favoring exclusion of negligence from the criminal law, is not without support. The chief exponent of this position is Professor Jerome Hall, who maintains that there are persuasive historical, ethical and scientific reasons to support the exclusionary argument.[16]

Hall's historical ground rests upon a continuing trend toward restricting criminal negligence in many Anglo-American legal systems. In addition, the same trend can be noted in civil law systems, where negligence is not criminally punishable absent a specific provision to that effect. Such provisions are very few. While Hall recognizes that history is often a dubious ground upon which to support a thesis, he argues that a long and sustained movement, such as that limiting the applicability of criminal negligence, places the burden of retention upon the proponents of penalization. This burden, Hall maintains, has not been carried.

Professor Hall's ethical argument is based on the premise that, throughout the long history of ethics, the essence of fault has been voluntary harm-doing. He maintains that this requirement of voluntary action becomes even more persuasive in the penal law, because no one should be criminally punished unless he has clearly

16. Hall, Negligent Behavior Should be Excluded from Penal Liability, 63 Colum.L.Rev. 632 (1963).

acted immorally, by voluntarily harming someone. Negligence, of course, cannot be classified as voluntary harm-doing. Therefore, no fault is involved and accordingly no punishment is justified.

In addition, Hall suggests scientific arguments for the exclusion of negligence from penal liability. One contention is that the incorporation of negligence into the penal law imposes an impossible function on judges, namely, to determine whether a person, about whom very little is known, had the competence and sensitivity to appreciate certain dangers in a particular situation when the facts plainly indicate that he did not exhibit that competence. Also, Hall maintains that "the inclusion of negligence bars the discovery of a scientific theory of penal law, i. e., a system of propositions inter-relating variables that have a realistic foundation in fact and values."

Comment, Is Criminal Negligence A Defensible Basis for Penal Liability?, 16 Buffalo L.Rev. 749, 750–52 (1967).[g] See also Fletcher, The Theory of Criminal Negligence: A Comparative Analysis, 119 U.Pa.L.Rev. 401 (1971); Note, Negligence and the General Problem of Criminal Liability, 81 Yale L.J. 949 (1972).

----

3. STATES OF MIND BEYOND "GENERAL INTENT"

NOTE: THE DISTINCTION BETWEEN "SPECIFIC" AND "GENERAL" INTENT

The case law often speaks of "specific" or "general" intents, but there is wide disagreement concerning the meaning of these terms. Compare the following uses of the terminology:

State v. Daniels, 109 So.2d 896, 899 (La.1958):

> "[S]pecific intent is present when from the circumstances the offender must have subjectively desired the prohibited result; whereas general intent exists when from the circumstances the prohibited result may reasonably be expected to follow from the offender's voluntary act, irrespective of any subjective desire to have accomplished such result."

State v. Binders, 24 Conn.Sup. 214, 216, 189 A.2d 408, 409 (1962):

> "Crimes are either mala in se or mala prohibita, and intent is a necessary element. In crimes which are mala in se, a specific intent, a wrongful intent, to commit the crime must be established, but in crimes that are mala prohibita the only intent requisite to a conviction is the intent or purpose to do the prohibited act."

R. Perkins, Criminal Law 762 (2nd ed. 1969):

> "Some crimes require a specified intention in addition to
> the intentional doing of the *actus reus* itself * * *. The
> physical part of the crime of larceny, for example, is the
> trespassory taking and carrying away of the personal goods
> of another, but this may be done intentionally, deliberately,
> and with full knowledge of all the facts and complete under-
> standing of the wrongfulness of the act, without constituting
> larceny. If this willful misuse of another's property is done
> with the intention of returning it * * * the special
> mens-rea requirement of larceny is lacking * * *. This
> additional requirement is a 'specific intent,' an additional
> intent specifically required for guilt of the particular of-
> fense."

What difference does it make whether a particular state of mind be
proven is labeled "specific" or "general" intent? Consider the following cases and raise the issue again when the defenses of mistake
of fact and intoxication are considered.

NOTE

Consider the following proposed offenses in the Proposed Federal Criminal Code. What reasons might be urged in support of the decisions as to
the state of mind requirements of the offenses?

§ 1344. Hindering Proceedings by Disorderly Conduct

(1) Intentional Hindering. A person is guilty of a Class A
misdemeanor if he intentionally hinders an official proceeding by
noise or violent or tumultuous behavior or disturbance.

(2) Reckless Hindering. A person is guilty of an offense if he
recklessly hinders an official proceeding by noise or violent or
tumultuous behavior or disturbance. The offense is a class B misdemeanor if it continues after explicit official request to desist.
Otherwise it is an infraction.

§ 1361. Bribery

(1) Offense. A person is guilty of bribery, a Class C felony, if
he knowingly offers, gives or agrees to give to another, or solicits,
accepts or agrees to accept from another, a thing of value as consideration for:

(a) the recipient's official action as a public servant; or

(b) the recipient's violation of a known legal duty as a
public servant.

(2) Defense Precluded. It is no defense to a prosecution under
this section that a recipient was not qualified to act in the desired
way whether because he had not yet assumed office, or lacked
jurisdiction, or for any other reason.

(3) Prima Facie Case. A prima facie case is established under this section upon proof that the actor knew that a thing of pecuniary value was offered, given or agreed to be given by, or solicited, accepted or agreed to be accepted from, a person having an interest in an imminent or pending (a) examination, investigation, arrest, or judicial or administrative proceeding, or (b) bid, contract, claim, or application, and that interest could be affected by the recipient's performance or nonperformance of his official action or violation of his known legal duty as a public servant.

§ 1705. Criminal Mischief

(1) Offense. A person is guilty of an offense if he:

(a) willfully tampers with tangible property of another so as to endanger person or property;

(b) willfully damages tangible property of another; or

(c) negligently damages tangible property of another by fire, explosives, or other dangerous means listed in section 1704(1).

(2) Grading. The offense is:

(a) a Class C felony if the actor intentionally causes pecuniary loss in excess of $5,000 or damages tangible property of another by means of an explosive or a destructive device; and

(b) a Class A misdemeanor if the actor recklessly causes pecuniary loss in excess of $5,000 or if the actor intentionally causes pecuniary loss in excess of $500.

Otherwise the offense is a Class B misdemeanor.

------

a. AWARENESS OF THE LAW CREATING AND DEFINING THE OFFENSE

LAMBERT v. CALIFORNIA

Supreme Court of the United States, 1957.
355 U.S. 225, 78 S.Ct. 240, 2 L.Ed.2d 228.

Mr. Justice DOUGLAS delivered the opinion of the Court.

Section 52.38(a) of the Los Angeles Municipal Code defines "convicted person" as follows:

"Any person who, subsequent to January 1, 1921, has been or hereafter is convicted of an offense punishable as a felony in the State of California, or who has been or who is hereafter convicted of any offense in any place other than the State of California, which offense, if committed in the State of California, would have been punishable as a felony."

Section 52.39 provides that it shall be unlawful for "any convicted person" to be or remain in Los Angeles for a period of more than five days without registering; it requires any person having a place of abode outside the city to register if he comes into the city on five occasions or more during a 30-day period; and it prescribes the information to be furnished the Chief of Police on registering.

Section 52.43(b) makes the failure to register a continuing offense, each day's failure constituting a separate offense.

Appellant, arrested on suspicion of another offense, was charged with a violation of this registration law. The evidence showed that she had been at the time of her arrest a resident of Los Angeles for over seven years. Within that period she had been convicted in Los Angeles of the crime of forgery, an offense which California punishes as a felony. Though convicted of a crime punishable as a felony, she had not at the time of her arrest registered under the Municipal Code. At the trial, appellant asserted that § 52.39 of the Code denies her due process of law and other rights under the Federal Constitution, unnecessary to enumerate. The trial court denied this objection. The case was tried to a jury which found appellant guilty. The court fined her $250 and placed her on probation for three years. Appellant, renewing her constitutional objection, moved for arrest of judgment and a new trial. This motion was denied. On appeal the constitutionality of the Code was again challenged. The Appellate Department of the Superior Court affirmed the judgment, holding there was no merit to the claim that the ordinance was unconstitutional. The case is here on appeal. * * * The case having been argued and reargued, we now hold that the registration provisions of the Code as sought to be applied here violate the Due Process requirement of the Fourteenth Amendment.

The registration provision, carrying criminal penalties, applies if a person has been convicted "of an offense punishable as a felony in the State of California" or, in case he has been convicted in another State, if the offense "would have been punishable as a felony" had it been committed in California. No element of willfulness is by terms included in the ordinance nor read into it by the California court as a condition necessary for a conviction.

We must assume that appellant had no actual knowledge of the requirement that she register under this ordinance, as she offered proof of this defense which was refused. The question is whether a registration act of this character violates due process where it is applied to a person who has no actual knowledge of his duty to register, and where no showing is made of the probability of such knowledge.

We do not go with Blackstone in saying that "a vicious will" is necessary to constitute a crime, 4 Bl.Comm. 21, for conduct alone without regard to the intent of the doer is often sufficient. There is wide latitude in the lawmakers to declare an offense and to exclude elements of knowledge and diligence from its definition. * * * But we deal here with conduct that is wholly passive—mere failure to register. It is unlike the commission of acts, or the failure to act under circumstances that should alert the doer to the consequences of his deed. * * * The rule that "ignorance of the law will not excuse" is deep in our law, as is the principle that of all the powers of local government, the police power is "one of the least limitable." District of Columbia v. Brooke, 214 U.S. 138, 149, 29 S.Ct. 560, 563, 53 L.Ed. 941. On the other hand, due process places some limits on its exercise. Engrained in our concept of due process is the requirement of notice. Notice is sometimes essential so that the citizen has the chance to defend charges. Notice is required before property interests are disturbed, before assessments are made, before penalties are assessed. Notice is required in a myriad of situations where a penalty or forfeiture might be suffered for mere failure to act. [citations omitted] These cases involved only property interests in civil litigation. But the principle is equally appropriate where a person, wholly passive and unaware of any wrongdoing, is brought to the bar of justice for condemnation in a criminal case.

Registration laws are common and their range is wide. * * * Many such laws are akin to licensing statutes in that they pertain to the regulation of business activities. But the present ordinance is entirely different. Violation of its provisions is unaccompanied by any activity whatever, mere presence in the city being the test. Moreover, circumstances which might move one to inquire as to the necessity of registration are completely lacking. At most the ordinance is but a law enforcement technique designed for the convenience of law enforcement agencies through which a list of the names and addresses of felons then residing in a given community is compiled. The disclosure is merely a compilation of former convictions already publicly recorded in the jurisdiction where obtained. Nevertheless, this appellant on first becoming aware of her duty to register was given no opportunity to comply with the law and avoid its penalty, even though her default was entirely innocent. She could but suffer the consequences of the ordinance, namely, conviction with the imposition of heavy criminal penalties thereunder. We believe that actual knowledge of the duty to register or proof of the probability of such knowledge and subsequent failure to comply are necessary before a conviction under the ordinance can stand. As Holmes wrote in The Common Law, "A law which punished conduct which would not be blameworthy in the average member of the community would be too severe for that community to bear." Id., at 50. Its severity lies in the absence of an opportunity either to avoid the consequences of the law or to defend any prosecution brought under it. Where a person did not know of the duty to register and where there was no proof of the probability of such knowledge, he may not be convicted consistently with due process. Were it otherwise, the evil would be as great as it is when the law is written in print too fine to read or in a language foreign to the community.

Reversed.

Mr. Justice BURTON, dissents because he believes that, as applied to this appellant, the ordinance does not violate her constitutional rights.

Mr. Justice FRANKFURTER, whom Mr. Justice HARLAN and Mr. Justice WHITTAKER join, dissenting.

The present laws of the United States and of the forty-eight States are thick with provisions that command that some things not be done and others be done, although persons convicted under such provisions may have had no awareness of what the law required or that what they did was wrongdoing. The body of decisions sustaining such legislation, including innumerable registration laws, is almost as voluminous as the legislation itself. The matter is summarized in United States v. Balint, 258 U.S. 250, 252, 42 S.Ct. 301, 302, 66 L.Ed. 604: "Many instances of this are to be found in regulatory measures in the exercise of what is called the police power where the emphasis of the statute is evidently upon achievement of some social betterment rather than the punishment of the crimes as in cases of *mala in se.*"

Surely there can hardly be a difference as a matter of fairness, of hardship, or of justice, if one may invoke it, between the case of a person wholly innocent of wrongdoing, in the sense that he was not remotely conscious of violating any law, who is imprisoned for five years for conduct relating to narcotics, and the case of another person who is placed on probation for three years on condition that she pay $250, for failure, as a local resident, convicted under local law of a felony, to register under a law passed as an exercise of the State's "police power." Considerations of hardship often lead courts, naturally enough, to attribute to a statute the requirement of a certain mental element—some consciousness of wrongdoing and knowledge of the law's command—as a matter of statutory construction. Then, too, a cruelly disproportionate relation between what the law requires and the sanction for its disobedience may constitute a violation of the Eighth Amendment as a cruel and unusual punishment, and, in respect to the States, even offend the Due Process Clause of the Fourteenth Amendment.

But what the Court here does is to draw a constitutional line between a State's requirement of doing and not doing. What is this but a return to Year Book distinctions between feasance and nonfeasance—a distinction that may have significance in the evolution of common-law notions of liability, but is inadmissible as a line between constitutionality and unconstitutionality. * * *

If the generalization that underlies, and alone can justify, this decision were to be given its relevant scope, a whole volume of the United States Reports would be required to document in detail the legislation in this country that would fall or be impaired. I abstain from entering upon a consideration of such legislation, and adjudications upon it, because I feel confident that the present decision will turn out to be an isolated deviation from the strong current of precedents—a derelict on the waters of the law. Accordingly, I content myself with dissenting.

NOTE

The response of the California courts to the United States Supreme Court's decision was to grant a new trial. Mrs. Lambert sought a writ of prohibition enjoining such retrial, primarily on the ground that the Supreme Court decision held that the ordinance was invalid. The trial court refused to issue the writ and this was first reversed by the District Court of Appeal. Lambert v. Municipal Court, 334 P.2d 605 (Cal.App.1959). Upon rehearing, however, the District Court of Appeal vacated its initial opinion and order and affirmed. Lambert v. Municipal Court, 343 P.2d 81 (Cal. App.1959). In the second opinion the court noted that the prosecution's brief asserted that the records established that Mrs. Lambert was advised by a deputy probation officer to register with the Los Angeles Police Department in accordance with the city's regulation. On appeal to the California Supreme Court, the judgment of the District Court of Appeals was reversed and the trial court was ordered to issue the writ on the authority of another case holding such municipal ordinances void as encroaching upon an area preempted by state legislation. Lambert v. Municipal Court, 53 Cal. 2d 690, 349 P.2d 984, 3 Cal.Rptr. 168 (1960).

UNITED STATES v. INTERNATIONAL MINERALS & CHEMICAL CORP.

Supreme Court of the United States, 1971.
402 U.S. 558, 91 S.Ct. 1697, 29 L.Ed.2d 178.

Mr. Justice DOUGLAS delivered the opinion of the Court.

The information charged that appellee shipped sulfuric acid and hydrofluosilicic acid in interstate commerce and "did knowingly fail to show on the shipping papers the required classification of said property, to wit, Corrosive Liquid, in violation of 49 CFR 173.427."

18 U.S.C.A. § 834(a) gives the Interstate Commerce Commission power to "formulate regulations for the safe transportation" of "corrosive liquids" and 18 U.S.C.A. § 834(f) states that whoever "knowingly violates any such regulation" shall be fined or imprisoned.

Pursuant to the power granted by § 834(a) the regulatory agency promulgated the regulation already cited which reads in part:

"Each shipper offering for transportation any hazardous material subject to the regulations in this chapter, shall describe that article on the shipping paper by the shipping name prescribed in § 172.5 of this chapter and by the classification prescribed in § 172.4 of this chapter, and may add a further description not inconsistent therewith. Abbreviations must not be used." 49 CFR § 173.427.

The District Court * * * ruled that the information did not charge a "knowing violation" of the regulation and accordingly dismissed the information, 318 F.Supp. 1335.

Here as in United States v. Freed, 401 U.S. 601, 91 S.Ct. 1112, 28 L.Ed.2d 356, which dealt with the possession of hand grenades, strict or absolute liability is not imposed; knowledge of the shipment of the dangerous materials is required. The sole and narrow question is whether "knowledge" of the regulation is also required. It is in that narrow zone that the issue of *"mens rea"* is raised; and appellee bears down hard on the provision in 18 U.S.C.A. § 834(f) that whoever "knowingly violates any such regulation" shall be fined, etc.

Boyce Motor Lines, Inc. v. United States, 342 U.S. 337, 72 S.Ct. 329, on which the District Court relied is not dispositive of the issue. It involved a regulation governing transporting explosive, inflammable liquid, and the like and required drivers to "avoid, so far as practicable, and, where feasible, by prearrangement of routes, driving into or through congested thoroughfares, places where crowds are assembled, streetcar tracks, tunnels, viaducts, and dangerous crossings." The statute punished whoever "knowingly" violated the regulation. Id., at 339, 72 S.Ct. at 330. The issue of *"mens rea"* was not raised below, the sole question turning on whether the standard of guilt was unconstitutionally vague. Id., at 340, 72 S.Ct. 330–331. In holding the statute was not void for vagueness we said:

> "The statute punishes only those who knowingly violate the Regulation. This requirement of the presence of culpable intent as a necessary element of the offense does much to destroy any force in the argument that application of the Regulation would be so unfair that it must be held invalid. That is evident from a consideration of the effect of the requirement in this case. To sustain a conviction, the Government not only must prove that petitioner could have taken another route which was both commercially practicable and appreciably safer (in its avoidance of crowded thoroughfares, etc.) than the one it did follow. It must also be shown that petitioner knew that there was such a practicable, safer route and yet deliberately took the more dangerous route through the tunnel, or that petitioner willfully neglected to exercise its duty under the Regulation to inquire into the availability of such an alternative route.

> * * *

> "In an effort to give point to its argument, petitioner asserts that there was no practicable route its trucks might have followed which did not pass through places they were required to avoid. If it is true that in the congestion surrounding the lower Hudson there was no practicable way of

crossing the River which would have avoided such points of danger to a substantially greater extent than the route taken, then petitioner has not violated the Regulation. But that is plainly a matter for proof at the trial. We are not so conversant with all the routes in that area that we may, with no facts in the record before us, assume the allegations of the indictment to be false. We will not thus distort the judicial notice concept to strike down a regulation adopted only after much consultation with those affected and penalizing only those who knowingly violate its prohibition." Id., at 342–343, 72 S.Ct. at 331–332.

The *"mens rea"* that emerged in the foregoing discussion was not knowledge of the regulation but knowledge of the more safe and the less safe routes within the meaning of the regulation. * * *

We * * * see no reason why the word "regulations" should not be construed as a shorthand designation for specific acts or omissions which violate the Act. The Act, so viewed, does not signal an exception to the rule that ignorance of the law is no excuse and is wholly consistent with the legislative history.

The principle that ignorance of the law is no defense applies whether the law be a statute or a duly promulgated and published regulation. In the context of these 1960 amendments we decline to attribute to Congress the inaccurate view that that Act requires proof of knowledge of the law, as well as the facts, and intended to endorse that interpretation by retaining the word "knowingly." We conclude that the meager legislative history of the 1960 amendments makes unwarranted the conclusion that Congress abandoned the general rule and required knowledge of both the facts and the pertinent law before a criminal conviction could be sustained under this Act.

So far as possession, say, of sulfuric acid is concerned the requirement of *"mens rea"* has been made a requirement of the Act as evidenced by the use of the word "knowingly." A person thinking in good faith that he was shipping distilled water when in fact he was shipping some dangerous acid would not be covered. * * *

There is leeway for the exercise of congressional discretion in applying the reach of *"mens rea."* United States v. Balint, 258 U.S. 250, 42 S.Ct. 301, 66 L.Ed. 604. United States v. Murdock, 290 U.S. 389, 54 S.Ct. 223, 78 L.Ed. 381, closely confined the word "wilfully" in the income tax law to include a purpose to bring about the forbidden result * * *.

In *Balint* the Court was dealing with drugs, in *Freed* with hand grenades, in this case with sulfuric and other dangerous acids. Pencils, dental floss, paper clips may also be regulated. But they may be the type of products which might raise substantial due process questions if Congress did not require, as in *Murdock,* *"mens rea"* as to each ingredient of the offense. But where, as here and as in *Balint* and *Freed,* dangerous or deleterious devices or products or obnoxious waste materials are involved, the probability of regulation is so great that anyone who is aware that he is in possession of them or dealing with them must be presumed to be aware of the regulation.

Reversed.

Mr. Justice STEWART, with whom Mr. Justice HARLAN and Mr. Justice BRENNAN join, dissenting.

This case stirs large questions—questions that go to the moral foundations of the criminal law. Whether postulated as a problem of *"mens rea,"* of "willfulness," of "criminal responsibility," or of *"scienter,"* the infliction of criminal punishment upon the unaware has long troubled the fair administration of justice. * * * But there is no occasion here for involvement with this root problem of criminal jurisprudence, for it is evident to me that Congress made punishable only knowing violations of the regulation in question. That is what the law quite clearly says, what the federal courts have held, and what the legislative history confirms.

The statutory language is hardly complex. Section 834(a) of Title 18, U.S.C.A., gives the regulatory agency power to "formulate regulations for the safe transportation" of, among other things, "corrosive liquids." Section 834(f) provides that "[w]hoever knowingly violates any such regulation shall be fined not more than $1,000 or imprisoned not more than one year, or both." In dismissing the information in this case because it did not charge the appellee shipper with knowing violation of the applicable labeling regulation, District Judge Porter did no more than give effect to the ordinary meaning of the English language.

* * *

The Court today * * * grants to the Executive Branch what Congress explicitly refused to grant * * *. It effectively deletes the word "knowingly" from the law. I cannot join the Court in this exercise, requiring as it does such a total disregard of plain statutory language, established judicial precedent, and explicit legislative history.

A final word is in order. Today's decision will have little practical impact upon the prosecution of interstate motor carriers or institutional shippers. For interstate motor carriers are members of a regulated industry, and their officers, agents, and employees are required by law to be conversant with the regulations in question. As a practical matter, therefore, they are under a species of absolute liability for violation of the regulations despite the "knowingly" requirement. This, no doubt, is as Congress intended it to be. Cf. United States v. Dotterweich, 320 U.S. 277, 64 S.Ct. 134, 88 L.Ed. 48; United States v. Balint, 258 U.S. 250, 42 S.Ct. 301, 66 L.Ed. 604.

Likewise, prosecution of regular shippers for violations of the regulations could hardly be impeded by the "knowingly" requirement, for triers of fact would have no difficulty whatever in inferring knowledge on the part of those whose business it is to know, despite their protestations to the contrary. The only real impact of this decision will be upon the casual shipper, who might be any man, woman, or child in the Nation. A person who had never heard of the regulation might make a single shipment of an article covered by it in the course of a lifetime. It would be wholly natural for him to assume that he could deliver the article to the common carrier and depend upon the carrier to see that it was properly labeled and that the shipping papers were in order. Yet today's decision holds that a person who does just that is guilty of a criminal offense punishable by a year in prison. This seems to me a perversion of the purpose of criminal law.

I respectfully dissent from the opinion and judgment of the Court.

---

b. STATES OF MIND REQUIRED BY THE PROPERTY ACQUISITION OFFENSES

VIRGIN ISLANDS v. WILLIAMS

United States Court of Appeals for the Third Circuit, 1970.
424 F.2d 526.

HASTIE, Chief Judge. This case presents the question whether larceny as defined by the Virgin Islands Code can be committed without an intent to deprive the owner permanently of his property.

The five juvenile appellants have been convicted of petit larceny under 14 V.I.C. §§ 1081, 1084. It was stipulated at the beginning of the hearing that the defendants had taken five horses from a pasture in St. Croix, ridden them to another part of the island several miles away, returned them to the general area from which they had been taken and released them. One horse subsequently died of injuries sustained during this unauthorized excursion.

At the close of the prosecution's case and again after all the evidence had been presented, the defendants moved to dismiss the complaint on the basis that there was no proof of an intent to deprive the owners of the horses permanently. The court denied the motion ruling that the Virgin Islands Code does not require proof of such an intent to establish larceny.

Section 1081 of title 14, Virgin Islands Code, defines larceny as " * * * the unlawful taking, stealing, carrying, leading, or driving away the personal property of another." This definition contains no mention of any requisite intent. In these circumstances, the process of interpretation begins with the consideration that the specific intent to deprive the owner permanently of his property is an essential element of the crime of larceny at common law. Absent a clear indication of legislative purpose, we are reluctant to assume that the omission of any mention of intent in the statute which makes "larceny" a crime was intended to eliminate that important and long-accepted element from the crime. * * *

In the tradition of Anglo-American law the crime of larceny is a major felony and as such is not intended to cover the less serious wrong of temporary appropriation of another's property. In the Virgin Islands larceny is deemed such a serious crime that, if the value of the stolen property exceeds $100, the wrongdoer is subject to imprisonment for up to ten years. 14 V.I.C. § 1083. In these circumstances, as had been said at common law, a "momentary loss of possession is not what has been guarded against with such severe penalties. What the law means to prevent is the loss of it wholly and forever * * *." Holmes, The Common Law 71 (1881).

At least one situation of temporary appropriation of property is treated separately by the Virgin Islands Code, and less severe penalties are provided. The unauthorized use of a motor vehicle, however valuable, or bicycle with no intent permanently to deprive the owner of possession is a lesser crime, distinct from larceny. 14 V.I.C. § 1381. One convicted under that section " * * * shall be fined not more than $500 or imprisoned not more than 1 year, or both." We are unable to believe that the Territorial Legislature intended that the "joy-rider" who wrongfully takes even a valuable horse from its pasture for an unauthorized ride should be punishable ten times more severely than one who similarly appropriates an automobile.

If the legislature of the Virgin Islands determines, as it has for motor vehicles and bicycles, that the unauthorized temporary taking of horses is a sufficiently serious wrong, it may properly make such misappropriation criminal. But it has not yet done so.

The judgment will be reversed.

NOTES

1. Does the state of mind required for larceny require that the defendant affirmatively desire the permanent deprivation of the owner's interest? That he know or have a firm belief unaccompanied by a substantial doubt that such deprivation will occur? Or is it sufficient that he was aware of a certain risk that the deprivation would occur? In Commonwealth v. Salerno, 356 Mass. 642, 255 N.E.2d 318 (1970) the defendant had apparently taken a parked car from Worcester, Massachusetts. He drove it to Leominster, Massachusetts where it was used the next morning as the "get-away" car in an armed robbery. That afternoon the car was found, apparently abandoned, in a parking lot behind a Leominster theater. In affirming the defendant's conviction for theft of the car, the court commented, "One who takes property without the authority of the owner and so uses or disposes of it as to show indifference whether the owner recovers possession may be found to intend to deprive the owner of it permanently." Compare W. LaFave and A. Scott, Handbook on Criminal

Law 637 (1972), who suggest that the state of mind required is the "intent to deprive the owner of his possession of the property either permanently or for an unreasonable length of time, or [the intent] to use it in such a way that the owner will probably be thus deprived of his property." Would the court in Salerno have come out as it did if it had applied this requirement? Which is preferable?

2. Samuels, Permanently to Deprive, New Law Journal, March 21, 1968, at 281:

Why should not dishonest borrowing amount to stealing? The reasons given by the Criminal Law Revision Committee are in para. 56 of their report. Borrowing is essentially different from stealing. It would constitute a considerable extension of the criminal law, when there is no existing serious evil. It might have undesirable social consequences. Quarrelling neighbours and families would be able to threaten one another with prosecution. Students and young people sharing accommodation who might be tempted to borrow one another's property in disregard of a prohibition by the owner would be in danger of acquiring a criminal record. It would be difficult for the police to avoid being involved in wasteful and undesirable investigations into alleged offences which had no social importance. It is difficult to see how the provision could be framed in a way which would satisfactorily exclude trivial cases and meet these objections. * * *

The counter-arguments in favour of making dishonest borrowing a criminal offence are, it is submitted, overwhelming. The reform of the law of theft should be moving towards the concept of dishonest economic deprivation and away from the traditional concept of a physical taking with intent permanently to deprive. The new code should be expressed in terms of simple and comprehensive general principle, and it should not be necessary to have to make special provision for taking and driving away aeroplanes and for removing Goyas, a provision anyway rightly recognising that dishonest borrowing should be criminal. The complete usurpation clause is difficult to construe, complicated, and anyway an admission that the permanently to deprive concept is by itself inadequate. The jury are unlikely to be enlightened by such a clause being put to them in the summing up in every theft case, as presumably it would have to be. My lecture notes in my car are "taken" when my car is criminally taken and driven away. The car and the notes are recovered, after the lecture. Is this complete usurpation? Naturally in order to be criminal the borrowing would have to be dishonest, and the defence of claim of right or subjectively reasonable belief that the owner would have consented if he has been asked would apply. The man in the street readily recognises "pinching" when he sees it, he does not require or accept the permanently to deprive concept. At the time of taking the thief is not always too sure whether he is going to retain or return the stuff. As for the dishonest student borrowing without authority to the grave inconvenience of a colleague, why should he be protected and privileged? Perhaps an exception should be made for "borrowing" the mascot of a rival college in a student rag, though the student rag is not dishonest. The suggestion that neighbours and families would threaten one another with prosecution is naive. Is knowledge of the subtleties of the criminal law so widespread? And are the police no longer to be trusted to be capable of exercising their discretion not to prosecute in their traditionally responsible manner? It is a crime for a boy of 11 to take an apple from an orchard, but there are few prosecutions. The existence of a civil remedy for the owner against the unauthorised borrower is more of a theoretical than a practical argument. The concept of permanently to deprive is not found in Canada and many other common law jurisdictions.

R. v. COCKBURN

Court of Appeal, Criminal Division, 1967.
[1968] 1 All E.R. 466.

WINN, L.J., delivered the following judgment of the court: The appellant was employed as manager of a shop of Peter Dominic, Ltd., wine merchants in Halifax. He was dismissed on Apr. 17, not for any matter connected with this charge. The next day the area manager carried out a check of the cash at the shop, and found that about £107 was missing. The appellant then and subsequently maintained that he certainly knew nothing about any shortage to the extent of £107; he had not taken any such amount at all, but he somewhat belatedly admitted that he did take £50 from the till on the previous Saturday. He said that he had intended to cover that £50 withdrawal by a cheque, but it was discovered on the Monday before he had time to put the cheque in. It appears that the appellant was helped by his own daughter in a most remarkably loose and rash fashion in as much as she gave him from time to time bunches of blank cheques which she had signed on her own bank account with authority from her to fill them in with any amount that he might require, and to put those cheques into his employers' till against money that he took from the till. He said that his practice was to put a note into the till when he did not immediately put a cheque, but as and when he found himself with a cheque and at the till he would put one of his daughter's cheques in the till. It is right to say that all his daughter's cheques had been met up to the relevant date, a total of nine of them, some given in payment of her account and some with the daughter's authority in the manner that I have indicated. He apparently was receiving an allowance of about £10 a week from a trust fund left by his late wife, but he was not operating any bank account of his own at the material time.

The point raised by counsel for the appellant is that it is a good defence in law to a charge of larceny of a sum of money if the defendant is able to satisfy the jury, or if it remains open in the minds of the jury as a reasonable possibility, that he intended to replace the money taken with its currency equivalent and had resources available to him which would enable him to make that replacement. The court is quite satisfied that that submission of counsel is founded on, and very ill-founded on, a passage in a report of R. v. Williams [1] which was before the Court of Criminal Appeal in 1953, when the court was presided over by LORD GODDARD, C. J., and PARKER and BYRNE, JJ., were the other two members of the court. There is in the Weekly Law Reports a passage [2] which this court sincerely hopes will for the future be disregarded entirely by the Bar and all others who have occasion from time to time to refer to R. v. Williams [1]. There is no corresponding passage in the Law Reports [3], or in the Criminal Appeal Reports [4], and I venture to think that beyond peradventure LORD GODDARD himself must have checked those reports, the Law Reports and the Criminal Appeal Reports, and taken good care to see that the passage which I am about to read did not appear in those official reports. The passage reads as follows [2]:

> "It is one thing if a person with good credit and plenty of money uses somebody else's money which may be in his possession and which may have been entrusted to him or which he may have had the opportunity of taking, merely intending to use those coins instead of some of his own which he has only to go to his room or to his bank to obtain. No jury would then say that there was any intent to defraud or any fraudulent taking, it is quite another matter if the person who takes the money is not in a position to replace it at the time but only has a hope or expectation that he will be able to do so in the future * * * "

I venture to think that quite probably, LORD GODDARD, C. J., felt about that passage what I myself not only feel but now say: that it is an extremely dangerous and misleading statement. It does not appear in the other reports that I have mentioned.

The fact of the matter, however, is this: that whereas larceny may vary very greatly indeed to the extent, one might say, of the whole heavens between grave theft and a taking which, whilst technically larcenous, reveals no moral obloquy and does no harm at all, it is nevertheless quite essential always to remember what are the elements of larceny and what are the complete and total elements of larceny, that is to say, taking the property of another person against the will of that other person without any claim of right so to do, and with the intent at the time of taking it permanently to deprive the owner of it. If coins, half a crown, a 10s. note, a £5 note, whatever it may be, are taken in all the circumstances which I have already indicated with the intention of spending or putting away somewhere

---

1. [1953] 1 All E.R. 1068; [1953] 1 Q.B. 660.

2. [1953] 2 W.L.R. 937 at p. 942.

3. [1953] 1 Q.B. 660.

4. (1953), 37 Cr.App.Rep. 71.

those particular coins or notes, albeit not only hoping but intending and expecting reasonably to be able to replace them with their equivalent, nevertheless larceny has been committed because with full appreciation of what is being done, the larcenous person, the person who commits the offence, has taken something which he was not entitled to take, had no claim of right to take, without the consent of the owner, and is in effect trying to force on the owner a substitution to which the owner has not consented.

*   *   *

Appeal against conviction dismissed.   Sentence varied.

STATE v. MILLS

Supreme Court of Arizona, 1964.
96 Ariz. 377, 396 P.2d 5.

LOCKWOOD, Vice Chief Justice. Defendants appeal from a conviction on two counts of obtaining money by false pretenses in violation of A.R.S. §§ 13–661.A.3. and 13–663.A.1.[1]

The material facts, viewed " *   *   *   in the light most favorable to sustaining the conviction,"   *   *   *   are as follows: Defendant William Mills was a builder and owned approximately 150 homes in Tucson in December, 1960. Mills conducted his business in his home. In 1960 defendant Winifred Mills, his wife, participated in the business generally by answering the telephone, typing, and receiving clients who came to the office.

In December 1960, Mills showed the complainant, Nathan Pivowar, a house at 1155 Knox Drive and another at 1210 Easy Street, and asked Pivowar if he would loan money on the Knox Drive house. Pivowar did not indicate at that time whether he would agree to such a transaction. Later in the same month Nathan Pivowar told the defendants that he and his brother, Joe Pivowar, would loan $5,000 and $4,000 on the two houses. Three or four days later Mrs. Mills, at Pivowar's request, showed him these homes again.

Mills had prepared two typed mortgages for Pivowar. Pivowar objected to the wording, so in Mills' office Mrs. Mills, retyped the mortgages under Pivowar's dictation. After the mortgages had been recorded on December 31, 1960, Pivowar gave Mills a bank check for $5,791.87, some cash, and a second mortgage formerly obtained from Mills in the approximate sum of $3,000. In exchange Mills gave Pivowar two personal notes in the sums of $5,250.00 and $4,200.00 and the two mortgages as security for the loan.

---

1. A.R.S. § 13–661.A. (1956) defines "theft" to include:
"3. Knowingly and designingly, by any false or fraudulent representa-
tion or pretense, defrauding any other person of money, labor or property, whether real or personal."

Although the due date for Mills' personal notes passed without payment being made, the complainant did not present the notes for payment, did not demand that they be paid, and did not sue upon them. In 1962 the complainant learned that the mortgages which he had taken as security in the transaction were not first mortgages on the Knox Drive and Easy Street properties. These mortgages actually covered two vacant lots on which there were outstanding senior mortgages. On learning this, Pivowar signed a complaint charging the defendants with the crime of theft by false pretenses.

On appeal defendants contend that the trial court erred in denying their motion to dismiss the information. They urge that a permanent taking of property must be proved in order to establish the crime of theft by false pretenses. Since the complainant had the right to sue on the defendants' notes, the defendants assert that complainant cannot be said to have been deprived of his property permanently.

Defendants misconceive the elements of the crime of theft by false pretenses. Stated in a different form, their argument is that although the complainant has parted with his cash, a bank check, and a second mortgage, the defendants intend to repay the loan.

Defendants admit that the proposition of law which they assert is a novel one in this jurisdiction. Respectable authority in other states persuades us that their contention is without merit. A creditor has a right to determine for himself whether he wishes to be a secured or an unsecured creditor. In the former case, he has a right to know about the security. If he extends credit in reliance upon security which is falsely represented to be adequate, he has been defrauded even if the debtor intends to repay the debt. His position is now that of an unsecured creditor; at the very least, an unreasonable risk of loss has been forced upon him by reason of the deceit. This risk which he did not intend to assume has been imposed upon him by the intentional act of the debtor, and such action constitutes an intent to defraud.

* * *

The cases cited by defendants in support of their contention are distinguishable from the instant case in that they involved theft by larceny. Since the crime of larceny is designed to protect a person's possessory interest in property whereas the crime of false pretenses protects one's title interest, the requirement of a permanent deprivation is appropriate to the former. Accordingly, we hold that an intent to repay a loan obtained on the basis of a false representation of the security for the loan is no defense.

UNITED STATES v. POWELL

United States District Court for the Eastern District of Virginia, 1968.
294 F.Supp. 1353, affirmed 413 F.2d 1037 (4th Cir. 1969).

KELLAM, District Judge.   Charged under Title 18 § 641 of
U.S.C.A. with embezzlement of funds of the United States Post Office Department aggregating $1,393.56, entrusted to his care as a
postal clerk, Langston B. Powell entered a plea of not guilty, waived
jury trial and was found guilty by the Court.   Defendant moved for
judgment of acquittal at the conclusion of the government's case, and
renewed his motion at the close of all of the evidence.   The motion
was denied, and defendant was found guilty.   Following the finding
of guilty, defendant again moved for judgment of acquittal.   Ruling
on this motion was continued to enable counsel to file a written memo-
randum of authorities.

Defendant contends the evidence fails to show (a) a criminal intent, and (b) a fraudulent appropriation of the money by him.   In
substance, defendant admits the funds in question came into his hands
in his capacity as a postal employee, and that when an audit of the
funds was made the funds were missing.   But, he says he thereafter
made good on the shortage, and there has been no showing "there was
a fraudulent appropriation of the money by the defendant."   That is,
the government has not shown what he did with the funds.   Defendant says the prosecution must establish how he spent the money,
whether in high living, gambling, etc.

The offense charged in the indictment is that defendant did "embezzle certain funds of the United States Post Office Department
*   *   *   in the care and custody" of defendant.   Embezzlement is
the fraudulent or felonious conversion or appropriation of property
which has rightfully or lawfully come into the hands of the converter.
It is defined in Moore v. United States, 160 U.S. 268, 269, 16 S.Ct. 294,
295, 40 L.Ed. 422, in these words:

> Embezzlement is the fraudulent appropriation of prop-
> erty by a person to whom such property has been entrusted,
> or into whose hands it has lawfully come.   It differs from
> larceny in the fact that the original taking of the property
> was lawful, or with the consent of the owner, while in lar-
> ceny the felonious intent must have existed at the time of the
> taking.

*   *   *   Embezzlement presupposes that the money or property came
to the possession of the accused lawfully and/or with the consent of
the owner, and that a fiduciary relationship exists between the owner
and accused.   The elements are (1) a trust or fiduciary relationship,
(2) that the property claimed embezzled is embraced within the meaning of the statute, (3) that it came into the possession or care of accused by virtue of his employment, (4) it is property of another, (5)

that his dealing therewith constituted a fraudulent conversion or appropriation of same to his own use, and (6) such was with the intent to deprive the owner thereof.

When one wrongfully and intentionally embezzles or misappropriates the property of another which is lawfully in his possession to his own use, the offense is complete. The mere fact he intends subsequently to return the property or to make restitution to the rightful owner does not relieve his wrongful act; nor does it destroy the criminal nature of the act or excuse him. Hence, the mere fact that defendant at a subsequent date made restitution of the amount of the shortage does not wipe out the offense.

Accused offered no explanation of the shortage except to say he did not use the funds for his personal use.   *   *   *

The motion for judgment of acquittal is denied. Upon the evidence heard by the court, the defendant is adjudged guilty as charged.

NOTE

Is any policy served by differences in the states of mind required for larceny, embezzlement, and obtaining property by false pretenses? Should any such difference be retained? Consider the consolidated offense of theft as defined in the Proposed Federal Criminal Code (1971), reprinted at page 365, supra.

---

4. PROOF OF STATE OF MIND

STATE v. CARLSON

Supreme Court of Wisconsin, 1958.
5 Wis.2d 595, 93 N.W.2d 354.

In the early morning of September 1, 1957, a serious fire occurred at the home of Frank Haecker at 3053 North Booth Street in the city of Milwaukee. Bernice Bonner, who lived with her husband in a second floor apartment in the building, died as a result of the fire.

The fire was at the rear of the building and the officers of the fire department particularly examined an enclosed area at the rear where steps go down to the basement and there are wooden stairs leading to the first and second floors. The cause of the fire could not be determined.

Carlson had been seen at the fire by a neighbor and after several of the neighbors were interviewed, the police picked Carlson up on Tuesday morning, September 3rd.   *   *   *

[H]e started to cry and said he could remember squeezing the matches and the candles when he ran away; that he didn't get the idea of starting the fire until he was at the rear of the Haecker home.

Carlson explained that he had struck a match, lit a bag and the light from the flame revealed two candles; that he lit one candle and held it under an innertube until the innertube began to hiss and bubble. He said he then became frightened, tried to squeeze out the fire and ran away. He said the innertube was underneath the steps in the enclosure at the rear of the Haecker home. He described the route he followed and the places where he discarded the matches and candles.

Carlson and the officers next went to the Haecker home and he pointed out the place where he had started the fire. He then showed them where he had discarded the matches next to an ashbox and the officers picked up book matches imprinted with the name, address, and business of Carlson's uncle. The two candles were also retrieved from a sewer which he pointed out. * * *

Still later, at the safety building, Carlson was questioned and the questions and answers taken down and typewritten. In this statement Carlson told of going to the restaurant after he left his uncle's, then going to Haeckers; going down toward the basement, finding the innertube underneath the stairs and lighting the matches and candle. He also said that after running away he returned to the same restaurant. * * *

[Carlson was tried and convicted of arson of a building and third degree murder.]

At the trial, Carlson testified that he went to the restaurant, had a hamburger and lemonade, walked to Haecker's, noticed there was no light, remembered an innertube he had seen underneath the steps when he was there earlier in the week and had thought of asking for. He wanted it to take to the lake so that his little cousin could use it for swimming. He went down toward the basement, lit a match to see where the tube was, held the match too long and burned his fingers. He threw the match away and it ignited a paper bag but the burning bag did no damage. He intended to use his matches to examine the tube for leakage of air. He saw the candles, lit one and held it to the left of the tube so that he could tell if there was any escaping of air. The flame flickered; he wasn't sure whether air was escaping so he held the candle closer; then the tube started to smolder and opened up and started to burn away. He put out the candle and squeezed the innertube with his hand, pushing the sides around the fire to smother it. He then left, taking the candles. He returned to the restaurant, made a remark about the clock not being on the wall, and the waiter looked at his watch and said that it was 25 minutes to one. Carlson washed his hands, played some selections on the juke box and had a hamburger and lemonade, the same as on the first occasion when he was in the restaurant. He heard the fire trucks just as he was finishing. He testified that he had told the police officers at first that he couldn't have started the fire. The reason he said that was that he "was pretty positive that I had extinguished that little bit that I had there."

* * *

FAIRCHILD, Justice. * * * Was there sufficient Proof of intent? * * * Sec. 943.02(1)(a), Stats., provides for the punishment of anyone who "by means of fire, intentionally damages any building of another without his consent." Sec. 939.23(3), Stats., provides in part: " 'Intentionally' means that the actor either has a purpose to do the thing or cause the result specified or believes that his act, if successful, will cause that result * * *."

It is virtually conceded that Carlson's activity under the stairway caused the fire and the damage to the Haecker house. It is clear that the fire was a natural and probable consequence of acts which he admitted to the officers, i. e. lighting a paper bag and holding a lighted candle to an innertube until it began to burn. It is true that in all his statements and testimony, Carlson said he tried to extinguish the fire in the tube before leaving the scene and that upon the trial he testified that both the bag and the tube were ignited accidently as a result of innocent (even if negligent) acts. The jury was not bound to believe either of these statements. There were also several facts which might tend to discredit his statements. Among others: Carlson's running away, his disposal of the matches and candles, his return to the restaurant, and remaining there until the fire was discovered, and his failure to give the officers the explanation which he gave on the trial.

The law presumes that a person intends the natural and probable consequences of his own acts but the presumption may be rebutted. Carlson, by his statements to the officers, furnished proofs of acts by him which caused the fire as a natural and probable consequence. At the trial he endeavored to rebut the presumption by ascribing an innocent purpose to his acts and by describing the acts somewhat differently from the way he described them to the officers. He failed to raise a reasonable doubt in the minds of the jurors.

SULLATESKEE v. STATE

Court of Criminal Appeals of Oklahoma, 1967.
428 P.2d 736.

BRETT, Judge. Gladys Juanita Sullateskee was charged in the Municipal Criminal Court of the City of Tulsa, Tulsa County, Oklahoma, with having in her possession 556 bottles of tax paid alcoholic beverage with intent to sell same, without having first procured a license therefor from the Oklahoma Alcoholic Beverage Control Board.

A jury was waived and the case tried to the Judge of said Court, the Hon. Luther P. Lane, who found the defendant guilty and assessed punishment at a fine of $25. Appeal has been perfected to this Court.

Defendant's only contention for reversal is that the State introduced no evidence to show that the whiskey found was in the possession of the defendant, with an intent on the part of the defendant to sell same.

The State introduced but one witness, a police officer of the City of Tulsa, who testified that he had a search warrant for the Rainbow Bar, located in the city of Tulsa. On direct examination he testified:

"A The Rainbow Bar is located on the southwest corner of Second and Detroit. We entered the Bar and served the warrant on Mrs. Sullateskee, and then searched the premises, and there is a room located on the southwest portion of the Bar, and in there we found approximately 50 cases, or 556 bottles of tax paid whiskey.

* * * * * * * * * *

"Q Who was in charge of the premises when you arrived that evening, Officer Glanz? A *Mr.* Sullateskee.

Q Had you ever been in that place, any time prior? A Yes sir.

Q Who was in charge of the premises on those times prior? A Different barmaids.

Q Is Mrs. Sullateskee a barmaid, or the owner, if you know? A She is a barmaid.

By the Court: Do you know who the owner is? A Yes, sir, the owner was R. E. Herrington."

The court also asked the witness: "Was there anything on the wall that would indicate they had a license? " To which witness replied: "No, sir, they were not holders of Federal or State alcohol Beverage license."

The court further asked: "Whatever happened to Herrington?" and the witness replied, "His beer license was revoked, and the Bar was closed." By the court: "By the County Judge? A Yes, sir."

The officer further testified that 13 persons were arrested for being drunk. On cross-examination he testified that he asked the defendant about a key to the room where the liquor was found, and she said she did not have one, and the officers were forced to break the lock. He stated also that he did not see any liquor bottles in the place of business, but the 13 persons arrested were drunk.

In the within case, specific intent was an element of the crime charged, and in order to make out a case, it was necessary for the

State to prove as an independent fact the intent charged—to sell alcoholic beverages. There was no proof that the defendant had possession or control of the liquor seized, or that she had "on the same date, or within fifteen days prior thereto [as provided in Tit. 37 O.S.A. § 568] sold any such beverage." We think the rule stated in 22 C.J.S. Criminal Law § 32, pg. 117, is appropriate, when the statute requires specific intent, as does this Oklahoma statute:

> "A specific criminal intent is not presumed, and conviction cannot be had on the basis of an imputed intent. The general rule, stated infra § 34, that a criminal intention will be presumed from the commission of the unlawful act does not apply. No intent in law or mere presumption, differing from the intent in fact, can be allowed to supply the place of proof of the requisite specific intent."

And, 21 Am.Jur.2d, § 82, at page 164 states:

> "If a specific intent is required by statute to constitute a crime, such intent enters into the nature of the act itself and must be alleged and proved."

Admittedly, specific intent may be, and most generally is, proved by circumstantial evidence. However, in the instant case even though one admits that the circumstantial evidence is sufficient to show the intent, *on the part of someone,* to sell the alcoholic beverages, such is not applicable to this defendant.

In the instant case the crime charged was: "possession with intent to sell". However, there was no positive showing that this defendant was the owner, or operator, of the Rainbow Bar; nor was there any actual proof that the defendant had sold, or offered to sell, any of the liquor. Instead, the prosecution proved by its own witness that one R. E. Herrington owned the establishment.

The case at bar can readily be distinguished from Lambert v. State, Okl.Cr., 374 P.2d 783, cited by both the defendant and the State, in that in the Lambert case the officers found a federal liquor license hanging on the wall, which this Court held showed the intent to sell the liquor found. In the instant case, no such license was found.

> The trial judge stated, at the conclusion of the trial:

> "I will hold that the presence of drunks indicate, and with a large quantity of liquor like that, there is some selling going on."

There is little doubt in our minds that, from a practical point of view, the judge was quite right in his ultimate conclusion; but nonetheless, such is not sufficient to support the proof required for the element of "specific intent", which was included in the charge against this defendant.

From a careful consideration of the evidence introduced, we are of the opinion that the prosecution failed to prove that this defendant was in possession of the alcoholic beverage found, with intent to sell the same.

It follows, therefore, that the judgment and sentence of the Municipal Criminal Court of the City of Tulsa must be, and the same is hereby reversed.

NIX, P. J., and BUSSEY, J., concur.

---

5. STATES OF MIND LESS THAN "GENERAL INTENT": THE "STRICT LIABILITY" OFFENSES

UNITED STATES v. BALINT

Supreme Court of the United States, 1922.
258 U.S. 250, 42 S.Ct. 301, 66 L.Ed. 604.

Mr. Chief Justice TAFT delivered the opinion of the Court.

* * * The indictment charged [the defendants] with unlawfully selling to another a certain amount of a derivative of opium and a certain amount of a derivative of coca leaves, not in pursuance of any written order on a form issued in blank for that purpose by the Commissioner of Internal Revenue, contrary to the provisions of section 2 of the [Narcotic Act of December 17, 1914] * * * The defendants demurred to the indictment on the ground that it failed to charge that they had sold the inhibited drugs knowing them to be such. The statute does not make such knowledge an element of the offense. The District Court sustained the demurrer and quashed the indictment. The correctness of this ruling is the question before us.

While the general rule at common law was that the scienter was a necessary element in the indictment and proof of every crime, and this was followed in regard to statutory crimes even where the statutory definition did not in terms include it (Rex v. Sleep, 8 Cox, 472), there has been a modification of this view in respect to prosecutions under statutes the purpose of which would be obstructed by such a requirement. It is a question of legislative intent to be construed by the court. It has been objected that punishment of a person for an act in violation of law when ignorant of the facts making it so, is an absence of due process of law. But that objection is considered and overruled in Shevlin-Carpenter Co. v. Minnesota, 218 U.S. 57, 69, 70, 30 S.Ct. 663, 666, 54 L.Ed. 930, in which it was held that, in the prohibition or punishment of particular acts, the state may in the maintenance of a public policy provide "that he who shall do them shall do them at his peril and will not be heard to plead in defense good faith or ignorance." Many instances of this are to be found in regulatory measures in the exercise of what is called the police power where the emphasis of the statute is evidently upon achievement of some social betterment rather than the punishment of the crimes as in cases of mala in se. * * *

So, too, in the collection of taxes, the importance to the public of their collection leads the Legislature to impose on the taxpayer the burden of finding out the facts upon which his liability to pay depends and meeting it at the peril of punishment. Again where one deals with others and his mere negligence may be dangerous to them, as in selling diseased food or poison, the policy of the law may, in order to stimulate proper care, require the punishment of the negligent person though he be ignorant of the noxious character of what he sells.

The question before us, therefore, is one of the construction of the statute and of inference of the intent of Congress. The Narcotic Act has been held by this court to be a taxing act with the incidental purpose of minimizing the spread of addiction to the use of poisonous and demoralizing drugs. * * * It is very evident from a reading of [section 2 of the Narcotics Act] that the emphasis of the section is in securing a close supervision of the business of dealing in these dangerous drugs by the taxing officers of the Government and that it merely uses a criminal penalty to secure recorded evidence of the disposition of such drugs as a means of taxing and restraining the traffic. Its manifest purpose is to require every person dealing in drugs to ascertain at his peril whether that which he sells comes within the inhibition of the statute, and if he sells the inhibited drug in ignorance of its character, to penalize him. Congress weighed the possible injustice of subjecting an innocent seller to a penalty against the evil of exposing innocent purchasers to danger from the drug, and concluded that the latter was the result preferably to be avoided. Doubtless considerations as to the opportunity of the seller to find out the fact and the difficulty of proof of knowledge contributed to this conclusion. We think the demurrer to the indictment should have been overruled.

Judgment reversed.

MORISSETTE v. UNITED STATES

Supreme Court of the United States, 1952.
342 U.S. 246, 72 S.Ct. 240, 96 L.Ed. 288.

Mr. Justice JACKSON delivered the opinion of the Court.

This would have remained a profoundly insignificant case to all except its immediate parties had it not been so tried and submitted to the jury as to raise questions both fundamental and far-reaching in federal criminal law, for which reason we granted certiorari.

On a large tract of uninhabited and untilled land in a wooded and sparsely populated area of Michigan, the Government established a practice bombing range over which the Air Force dropped simulated bombs at ground targets. These bombs consisted of a metal cylinder about forty inches long and eight inches across, filled with sand and enough black powder to cause a smoke puff by which the strike could be located. At various places about the range sings read "Danger—Keep Out—Bombing Range." Nevertheless, the range was known as good deer country and was extensively hunted.

Spent bomb casings were cleared from the targets and thrown into piles "so that they will be out of the way." They were not stacked or piled in any order but were dumped in heaps, some of which had been accumulating for four years or upwards, were exposed to the weather and rusting away.

Morissette, in December of 1948, went hunting in this area but did not get a deer. He thought to meet expenses of the trip by salvaging some of these casings. He loaded three tons of them on his truck and took them to a nearby farm, where they were flattened by driving a tractor over them. After expending this labor and trucking them to market in Flint, he realized $84.

Morissette, by occupation, is a fruit stand operator in summer and a trucker and scrap iron collector in winter. An honorably discharged veteran of World War II, he enjoys a good name among his neighbors and has had no blemish on his record more disreputable than a conviction for reckless driving.

The loading, crushing and transporting of these casings were all in broad daylight, in full view of passers-by, without the slightest effort at concealment. When an investigation was started, Morissette voluntarily, promptly and candidly told the whole story to the authorities, saying that he had no intention of stealing but thought the property was abandoned, unwanted and considered of no value to the Government. He was indicted, however, on the charge that he "did unlawfully, wilfully and knowingly steal and convert" property of the United States of the value of $84, in violation of 18 U.S.C. § 641, 18 U.S.C.A. § 641, which provides that "whoever embezzles, steals, purloins, or knowingly converts" government property is punishable by fine and imprisonment. Morissette was convicted and sentenced to imprisonment for two months or to pay a fine of $200. The Court of Appeals affirmed, one judge dissenting.

On his trial, Morissette, as he had at all times told investigating officers, testified that from appearances he believed the casings were cast-off and abandoned, that he did not intend to steal the property, and took it with no wrongful or criminal intent. The trial court, however, was unimpressed, and ruled: "[H]e took it because he thought it was abandoned and he knew he was on government property. * * * That is no defense. * * * I don't think anybody can have the defense they thought the property was abandoned on another man's piece of property." The court stated: "I will not permit you to show this man thought it was abandoned. * * * I hold in this case that there is no question of abandoned property." The court refused to submit or to allow counsel to argue to the jury whether Morissette acted with innocent intention. It charged: "And I instruct you that if you believe the testimony of the government in this case, he intended to take it. * * * He had no right to take this property. * * * [A]nd it is no defense to claim that it was abandoned, because it was on private property. * * * And I instruct you to this effect: That if this young man took this property (and he says he did), without any permission (he says he did), that was on the property of the United States Government (he says it was), that it was of the value of one cent or more (and evidently it was), that he is guilty of the offense charged here. If you believe the government, he is guilty. * * * The question on intent is whether or not he intended to take the property. He says he did. Therefore, if you believe either side, he is guilty." Petitioner's counsel contended, "But the taking must have been with a felonious intent." The court ruled, however: "That is presumed by his own act."

The Court of Appeals suggested that "greater restraint in expression should have been exercised", but affirmed the conviction because, "As we have interpreted the statute, appellant was guilty of its violation beyond a shadow of doubt, as evidenced even by his own admissions." Its construction of the statute is that it creates several separate and distinct offenses, one being knowing conversion of government property. The court ruled that this particular offense requires no element of criminal intent. This conclusion was thought to be required by the failure of Congress to express such a requisite and this Court's decisions in United States v. Behrman, 258 U.S. 280, 42 S.Ct. 303, 66 L.Ed. 619, and United States v. Balint, 258 U.S. 250, 42 S.Ct. 301, 66 L.Ed. 604.

I.

In those cases this Court did construe mere omission from a criminal enactment of any mention of criminal intent as dispensing with it. If they be deemed precedents for principles of construction generally applicable to federal penal statutes, they authorize this conviction. Indeed, such adoption of the literal reasoning announced in those cases would do this and more—it would sweep out of all federal crimes, except when expressly preserved, the ancient requirement of a culpable state of mind. We think a résumé of their historical background is convincing that an effect has been ascribed to them more comprehensive than was contemplated and one inconsistent with our philosophy of criminal law.

The contention that an injury can amount to a crime only when inflicted by intention is no provincial or transient notion. It is as universal and persistent in mature systems of law as belief in freedom of the human will and a consequent ability and duty of the normal individual to choose between good and evil. A relation between some mental element and punishment for a harmful act is almost as instinctive as the child's familiar exculpatory "But I didn't mean to," and has afforded the rational basis for a tardy and unfinished substitution of deterrence and reformation in place of retaliation and vengeance as the motivation for public prosecution. Unqualified acceptance of this doctrine by English common law in the Eighteenth Century was indicated by Blackstone's sweeping statement that to constitute any crime there must first be a "vicious will." Common-law commentators of the Nineteenth Century early pronounced the same principle, although a few exceptions not relevant to our present problem came to be recognized.

Crime, as a compound concept, generally constituted only from concurrence of an evil-meaning mind with an evil-doing hand, was congenial to an intense individualism and took deep and early root in American soil. As the states codified the common law of crimes, even if their enactments were silent on the subject, their courts assumed that the omission did not signify disapproval of the principle but merely recognized that intent was so inherent in the idea of the offense that it required no statutory affirmation. Courts, with little hesitation or division, found an implication of the requirement as to offenses that were taken over from the common law. The unanimity with which they have adhered to the central thought that wrongdoing must be conscious to be criminal is emphasized by the variety, disparity and confusion of their definitions of the requisite but elusive mental element. However, courts of various jurisdictions, and for the purposes of different offenses, have devised working formulae, if not scientific ones, for the instruction of juries around such terms as "felonious intent," "criminal intent," "malice aforethought," "guilty knowledge," "fraudulent intent," "wilfulness," "scienter," to denote guilty knowledge, or "mens rea," to signify an evil purpose or mental culpability. By use or combination of these various tokens, they have sought to protect those who were not blameworthy in mind from conviction of infamous common-law crimes.

However, the Balint and Behrman offenses belong to a category of another character, with very different antecedents and origins. The crimes there involved depend on no mental element but consist only of forbidden acts or omissions. This, while not expressed by the Court, is made clear from examination of a century-old but accelerating tendency, discernible both here and in England, to call into existence new duties and crimes which disregard any ingredient of intent. The industrial revolution multiplied the number of workmen exposed to injury from increasingly powerful and complex mechanisms, driven by freshly discovered sources of energy, requiring higher precautions by employers. Traffic of velocities, volumes and varieties unheard of came to subject the wayfarer to intolerable casualty risks if owners and drivers were not to observe new cares and uniformities of conduct. Congestion of cities and crowding of quarters called for health and welfare regulations undreamed of in simpler times. Wide distribution of goods became an instrument of wide distribution of harm when those who dispersed food, drink, drugs, and even securities, did not comply with reasonable standards of quality, integrity, disclosure and care. Such dangers have engendered increasingly numerous and detailed regulations which heighten the duties of those in control of particular industries, trades, properties or activities that affect public health, safety or welfare.

While many of these duties are sanctioned by a more strict civil liability,[13] lawmakers, whether wisely or not,[14] have sought to make such regulations more effective by invoking criminal sanctions to be applied by the familiar technique of criminal prosecutions and convictions. This has confronted the courts with a multitude of prosecutions, based on statutes or administrative regulations, for what have been aptly called "public welfare offenses." These cases do not fit neatly into any of such accepted classifications of common-law offenses, such as those against the state, the person, property, or public morals. Many of these offenses are not in the nature of positive aggressions or invasions, with which the common law so often dealt, but are in the nature of neglect where the law requires care, or inaction where it imposes a duty. Many violations of such regulations result in no direct or immediate injury to person or property but merely create the danger or probability of it which the law seeks to

---

13. The development of strict criminal liability regardless of intent has been roughly paralleled by an evolution of a strict civil liability for consequences regardless of fault in certain relationships, as shown by Workmen's Compensation Acts, and by vicarious liability for fault of others as evidenced by various Motor Vehicle Acts.

14. Consequences of a general abolition of intent as an ingredient of serious crimes have aroused the concern of responsible and disinterested students of penology. Of course, they would not justify judicial disregard of a clear command to that effect from Congress, but they do admonish us to caution in assuming that Congress, without clear expression, intends in any instance to do so.

Radin, Intent, Criminal, 8 Encyc.Soc.Sci. 126, 130, says, " * * * as long as in popular belief intention and the freedom of the will are taken as axiomatic, no penal system that negates the mental element can find general acceptance. It is vital to retain public support of methods of dealing with crime." * * *

Sayre, Public Welfare Offenses, 33 Col. L.Rev. 55, 56, says: "To inflict substantial punishment upon one who is morally entirely innocent, who caused injury through reasonable mistake or pure accident, would so outrage the feelings of the community as to nullify its own enforcement."

Hall, Prolegomena to a Science of Criminal Law, 89 U. of Pa.L.Rev. 549, 569, appears somewhat less disturbed by the trend, if properly limited, but, as to so-called public welfare crimes, suggests that "There is no reason to continue to believe that the present mode of dealing with these offenses is the best solution obtainable, or that we must be content with this sacrifice of established principles. *The raising of a presumption of knowledge might be an improvement.*" (Italics added.)

* * *

minimize. While such offenses do not threaten the security of the state in the manner of treason, they may be regarded as offenses against its authority, for their occurrence impairs the efficiency of controls deemed essential to the social order as presently constituted. In this respect, whatever the intent of the violator, the injury is the same, and the consequences are injurious or not according to fortuity. Hence, legislation applicable to such offenses, as a matter of policy, does not specify intent as a necessary element. The accused, if he does not will the violation, usually is in a position to prevent it with no more care than society might reasonably expect and no more exertion than it might reasonably exact from one who assumed his responsibilities. Also, penalties commonly are relatively small, and conviction does no grave damage to an offender's reputation. Under such considerations, courts have turned to construing statutes and regulations which make no mention of intent as dispensing with it and holding that the guilty act alone makes out the crime. This has not, however, been without expressions of misgiving.

The pilot of the movement in this country appears to be a holding that a tavernkeeper could be convicted for selling liquor to an habitual drunkard even if he did not know the buyer to be such. Later came Massachusetts holdings that convictions for selling adulterated milk in violation of statutes forbidding such sales require no allegation or proof that defendant knew of the adulteration. * * *

After the turn of the Century, a new use for crimes without intent appeared when New York enacted numerous and novel regulations of tenement houses, sanctioned by money penalties. Landlords contended that a guilty intent was essential to establish a violation. Judge Cardozo wrote the answer: "The defendant asks us to test the meaning of this statute by standards applicable to statutes that govern infamous crimes. The analogy, however, is deceptive. The element of conscious wrongdoing, the guilty mind accompanying the guilty act, is associated with the concept of crimes that are punished as infamous. * * * Even there it is not an invariable element. * * * But in the prosecution of minor offenses there is a wider range of practice and of power. Prosecutions for petty penalties have always constituted in our law a class by themselves. * * * That is true, though the prosecution is criminal in form." Tenement House Department of City of New York v. McDevitt, 1915, 215 N.Y. 160, 168, 109 N.E. 88, 90.

Soon, employers advanced the same contention as to violations of regulations prescribed by a new labor law. Judge Cardozo, again for the court, pointed out, as a basis for penalizing violations whether intentional or not, that they were punishable only by fine "moderate in amount", but cautiously added that in sustaining the power so to fine unintended violations "we are not to be understood as sustaining to a like length the power to imprison. We leave that question open."

People ex rel. Price v. Sheffield Farms-Slawson-Decker Co., 1918, 225 N.Y. 25, 32–33, 121 N.E. 474, 476, 477.

Thus, for diverse but reconcilable reasons, state courts converged on the same result, discontinuing inquiry into intent in a limited class of offenses against such statutory regulations.

Before long, similar questions growing out of federal legislation reached this Court. Its judgments were in harmony with this consensus of state judicial opinion, the existence of which may have led the Court to overlook the need for full exposition of their rationale in the context of federal law. In overruling a contention that there can be no conviction on an indictment which makes no charge of criminal intent but alleges only making of a sale of a narcotic forbidden by law, Chief Justice Taft, wrote: "While the general rule at common law was that the *scienter* was a necessary element in the indictment and proof of every crime, and this was followed in regard to statutory crimes even where the statutory definition did not in terms include it * * *, there has been a modification of this view in respect to prosecutions under statutes the purpose of which would be obstructed by such a requirement. It is a question of legislative intent to be construed by the court. * * *" United States v. Balint, supra, 258 U.S. 251–252, 42 S.Ct. 302.

*   *   *

On the same day, the Court determined that an offense under the Narcotic Drug Act does not require intent, saying, "If the offense be a statutory one, and intent or knowledge is not made an element of it, the indictment need not charge such knowledge or intent." United States v. Behrman, supra, 258 U.S. at page 288, 42 S.Ct. at page 304.

Of course, the purpose of every statute would be "obstructed" by requiring a finding of intent, if we assume that it had a purpose to convict without it. Therefore, the obstruction rationale does not help us to learn the purpose of the omission by Congress. And since no federal crime can exist except by force of statute, the reasoning of the Behrman opinion, if read literally, would work far-reaching changes in the composition of all federal crimes.

*   *   *

It was not until recently that the Court took occasion more explicitly to relate abandonment of the ingredient of intent, not merely with considerations of expediency in obtaining convictions, nor with the *malum prohibitum* classification of the crime, but with the peculiar nature and quality of the offense. We referred to "* * * a now familiar type of legislation whereby penalties serve as effective means of regulation", and continued, "such legislation dispenses with the conventional requirement for criminal conduct—awareness of some wrongdoing. In the interest of the larger good it puts the burden of acting at hazard upon a person otherwise innocent but standing in responsible relation to a public danger." But we warned: "Hardship there doubtless may be under a statute which thus penalizes the transaction though consciousness of wrongdoing be totally wanting." United States v. Dotterweich, 320 U.S. 277, 280–281, 284, 64 S.Ct. 134, 136, 88 L.Ed. 48.

Neither this Court nor, so far as we are aware, any other has undertaken to delineate a precise line or set forth comprehensive criteria for distinguishing between crimes that require a mental element and crimes that do not. We attempt no closed definition, for the law on the subject is neither settled nor static. The conclusion reached in the Balint and Behrman cases has our approval and adherence for the circumstances to which it was there applied. A quite different question here is whether we will expand the doctrine of crimes without intent to include those charged here.

Stealing, larceny, and its variants and equivalents, were among the earliest offenses known to the law that existed before legislation; they are invasions of rights of property which stir a sense of insecurity in the whole community and arouse public demand for retribution, the penalty is high and, when a sufficient amount is involved, the infamy is that of a felony, which, says Maitland, is " * * * as bad a word as you can give to man or thing." State courts of last resort, on whom fall the heaviest burden of interpreting criminal law in this country, have consistently retained the requirement of intent in larceny-type offenses. If any state has deviated, the exception has neither been called to our attention nor disclosed by our research.

Congress, therefore, omitted any express prescription of criminal intent from the enactment before us in the light of an unbroken course of judicial decision in all constituent states of the Union holding intent inherent in this class of offense, even when not expressed in a statute. Congressional silence as to mental elements in an Act merely adopting into federal statutory law a concept of crime already so well defined in common law and statutory interpretation by the states may warrant quite contrary inferences than the same silence in creating an offense new to general law, for whose definition the courts have no guidance except the Act. Because the offenses before this Court in the Balint and Behrman cases were of this latter class, we cannot accept them as authority for eliminating intent from offenses incorporated from the common law. Nor do exhaustive studies of state court cases disclose any well-considered decisions applying the doctrine of crime without intent to such enacted common-law offenses, although a few deviations are notable as illustrative of the danger inherent in the Government's contentions here.

The Government asks us by a feat of construction radically to change the weights and balances in the scales of justice. The purpose and obvious effect of doing away with the requirement of a guilty intent is to ease the prosecution's path to conviction, to strip the

defendant of such benefit as he derived at common law from innocence of evil purpose, and to circumscribe the freedom heretofore allowed juries. Such a manifest impairment of the immunities of the
individual should not be extended to common-law crimes on judicial
initiative.

The spirit of the doctrine which denies to the federal judiciary
power to create crimes forthrightly admonishes that we should not
enlarge the reach of enacted crimes by constituting them from anything less than the incriminating components contemplated by the
words used in the statute. And where Congress borrows terms of
art in which are accumulated the legal tradition and meaning of centuries of practice, it presumably knows and adopts the cluster of ideas
that were attached to each borrowed word in the body of learning
from which it was taken and the meaning its use will convey to the
judicial mind unless otherwise instructed. In such case, absence of
contrary direction may be taken as satisfaction with widely accepted
definitions, not as a departure from them.

We hold that mere omission from § 641 of any mention of intent
will not be construed as eliminating that element from the crimes
denounced.

II.

It is suggested, however, that the history and purposes of § 641
imply something more affirmative as to elimination of intent from
at least one of the offenses charged under it in this case. The argument does not contest that criminal intent is retained in the offenses
of embezzlement, stealing and purloining, as incorporated into this
section. But it is urged that Congress joined with those, as a new,
separate and distinct offense, knowingly to convert government property, under circumstances which imply that it is an offense in which
the mental element of intent is not necessary.

Congress has been alert to what often is a decisive function of
some mental element in crime. It has seen fit to prescribe that an
evil state of mind, described variously in one or more such terms as
"intentional," "wilful," "knowing," "fraudulent" or "malicious," will
make criminal an otherwise indifferent act, or increase the degree
of the offense or its punishment. Also, it has at times required a
specific intent or purpose which will require some specialized knowledge or design for some evil beyond the common-law intent to do injury. The law under some circumstances recognizes good faith or
blameless intent as a defense, partial defense, or as an element to be
considered in mitigation of punishment. And treason—the one crime
deemed grave enough for definition in our Constitution itself—requires not only the duly witnessed overt act of aid and comfort to the
enemy but also the mental element of disloyalty or adherence to the
enemy. In view of the care that has been bestowed upon the sub-

ject, it is significant that we have not found, nor has our attention been directed to, any instance in which Congress has expressly eliminated the mental element from a crime taken over from the common law.

*　　　*　　　*

We find no grounds for inferring any affirmative instruction from Congress to eliminate intent from any offense with which this defendant was charged.

III.

As we read the record, this case was tried on the theory that even if criminal intent were essential its presence (a) should be decided by the court (b) as a presumption of law, apparently conclusive, (c) predicated upon the isolated act of taking rather than upon all of the circumstances. In each of these respects we believe the trial court was in error.

NOTES

1. Is "strict liability" appropriate or defensible in regard to those "regulatory offenses" as to which it has traditionally been imposed? Consider the following comments from Mueller, Mens Rea and the Law Without It, 58 W.Va.L.Rev. 34, 37–38, 50, 59–60 (1955):

The reasons for * * * [imposing strict liability in regard to such offenses] have been variously stated: If "mens rea" were required, (1) the enforcement of the statute would be impeded; or (2) the courts would be overburdened; or (3) justice would be hampered; or (4) fraudulent defenses could be fabricated, etc. Prima facie such claims can be just as easily made as refuted. The often stated reason here listed under (1), for instance, seems to be nothing more than a woman's "because", and proves no more.

(2) supra, is a little more specific. It is certainly true that there is hardly any aspect of human activity which has escaped control by the law. When we eat, the (pure food and drug) law eats with us; when we walk, the (traffic) law walks with us; and even the health and soundness of our sleep is regulated by law. To litigate every one of the regulated problems of daily life would surely hamper the administration of justice. But what good will it do to punish indiscriminately, regardless of guilt or innocence, merely to save the time it would take to determine the validity of a defense? And what of the deterrent effect of such a frustrating law? Would it not ease the burden on the court and reduce the length of the court calendar much more if, for instance, in January we would prosecute only blond culprits, in February only bald ones, in March brunettes, etc.? That would at least deter some of the culprits some of the time, whereas absolute criminal liability is totally without deterrent effect. * * *

Ad (3) it might be answered that absolute criminal liability surely is not the vehicle to unhamper criminal justice. If any-

thing, it does away with justice altogether by distributing penalties indiscriminately. *Ad* (4) it will suffice to ask: what crime
is there which is not subject to the interposition of fraudulent
defenses? Surely the temptation for tricking one's way out of
a jam is much greater in crimes threatening serious consequences
than it is in petty offenses.

*   *   *

[It has been feared that the enforcement of the regulatory
schemes would bog down if strict liability were not imposed.]

Now then, how can a law deter anybody which inflicts punishment for the mere doing of the outward act? Is it not manifest that a law which punishes without caring about the factual and
moral blamelessness of a defendant thereby frustrates him and the
community at large? Why should the citizen bother to use care
if the courts do not bother whether or not he used care, inflicting
punishment in any event? Punishment which befalls the innocent
and the guilty alike, like hay fever, hail or hurricane, can have
no good effect at all, except perhaps for insurance companies, for
whom it creates a new insurable interest.

*   *   *

[It has also been argued that unless strict liability were imposed, "many unscrupulous persons would not hesitate to fabricate
such facts as would be needful to accomplish" the assertion of a
defense of mistake of fact.]

The ease of manufacturing surreptitious or fraudulent defenses is, as any lawyer knows, not confined to such cases. * *
Since the temptation to fabricate defenses is even greater in prosecutions in which the stakes are higher, for instance in murder
prosecutions, why then not dispense with "mens rea" altogether
and make every act, e. g., the killing of a human being, conclusive
evidence of a criminal intent to do the act, e. g., killing a human
being conclusive evidence of a criminal intent, thus murder?

* * * All other arguments in favor of absolute criminal
liability failing, it has sometimes been reasoned that the raising
of issues in defense of regulatory violations would require dealing
with collateral and irrelevant issues. Hence, too much time, in
proportion to the slightness of the offense, would have to be devoted to the matter if the defendant were permitted to present an
elaborate defense, or, indeed, any defense. It has been said that
courts would never be able to clear their calendars if in this vast
mass of petty offenses a judge, or a jury, were to try all defensive
facts. Speediness of "justice" is said to be the compelling reason for absolute criminal liability.

If this were truly the only, or major, reason for resort to
absolute criminal liability, then it would be sheer folly to dispense
with the "mens rea" and nevertheless to consider all defensive
arguments for the purpose of possibly mitigating the punishment
* * *. Of course, this only goes to show that the "speediness
of justice" argument is absurd. The choice does not lie between

speedy justice and slow justice, but between speedy injustice and justice of whatever celerity we can achieve by whatever court reform may be necessary. Justice ought to be speedy, but absolute criminal liability is not apt to achieve it.

* * *

[It has also been argued in support of strict liability that "as the penalty is slight, no great injustice is perpetrated by enforcing this type of statute regardless of knowledge".]

Are we compelled to prefer small injustice over justice? I do not think that the writer regarded this point as a major reason for the imposition of absolute criminal liability. But even as collateral support it fails miserably. Such reasoning may be appropriate in a country where absolutism and dictatorial utility sacrifice life, liberty and property to the Moloch state, but not here.

2. What, if any, significance upon "strict liability" issues does the following observation concerning the administration of such offenses have?

* * * [B]oth legislature and court have in substantial measure sanctioned the imposition of liability under the food and drug sections containing no express fault requirement upon persons who violate the provisions completely through inadvertence or mistake and without any measure of subjective fault. These sections are not self-executing, however; the enforcement policies of the Wisconsin department of agriculture play an important role in determining the practical working significance of these provisions.

The general policy of the department has been to refrain from prosecuting inadvertent violations of the food and drug sections until a specific warning has been given and the violator has had ample opportunity to cease the offending action or correct the offensive condition. The considerations underlying this policy are many. Some of the more clearly defined factors include: (1) The department believes that the most effective control and the best public relations can be achieved by co-operation with the regulated group and correction of the average offender, coupled with selective prosecution of only the uncooperative recalcitrant minority. (2) The state would incur substantial cost from large numbers of food and drug prosecutions. (3) Administrative officers and field inspectors alike share a natural reluctance to be responsible for the imposition of punishment for a wholly unintended violation by a defendant free from any subjective fault. (4) The department faces the necessity of convincing the appropriate district attorney to institute prosecution, even after the inspector has decided that prosecution is desirable and has prepared a case. Evidence that a warning has been issued to the prospective defendant and has been ignored will often encourage a district attorney, who might otherwise be hesitant to do so, to prosecute. (5) Courts and juries may be reluctant to find an offender guilty even in the face of conclusive evidence of an actual violation, unless this evidence is accompanied by some showing of moral culpability, or subjective fault, such as might be provided by proof of failure to heed an express warning issued by the department.

Standard operating procedure calls for the issuance of a warning notice by the field inspector immediately upon discovery of an inadvertently offensive condition or action. If the offender does not make the required corrections immediately, he may be given several more warnings and opportunities to evince a willingness to co-operate with the department before prosecution is instituted. The final decision to prosecute is usually made by the administrative head of the division concerned, who is kept constantly informed of the progress of each case. There are several offenses under the cognizance of the department, however, which manifestly demonstrate guilty intent and knowledge on the part of the offender. When an inspector uncovers a violation of this type he is authorized to institute prosecution through the district attorney immediately without either the issuance of a warning to the offender or notification to the division head. An example of this type of offense is "watering of milk" * * *.

A case history selected from the correspondence files of the dairy and food division of the department presents a vivid illustration of the department's technique of issuing warning notices before resorting to prosecution. A field inspector discovered unsanitary conditions in a small town cheese factory, particularly in relation to milk cans and milk trucks. Warning notices were issued on March 18, 1953, May 13, 1953, July 28, 1953, August 5, 1953, February 3, 1954, and June 21, 1954. Finally, on July 9, 1954, prosecution was instituted under section 97.32, which provides a penalty for any cheese factory operator who does "maintain his premises and utensils in an insanitary condition." Defendant was found guilty and fined $100.

Another case from the same file illustrates the department's policy of prosecuting only upon a showing of subjective fault and unwillingness to co-operate on the part of the violator. Prosecution had been instituted under section 97.32 against a dairy farmer for maintaining his milking machine and equipment in an unsanitary condition. In court, the defendant argued that this was his first offense, that he had co-operated fully with the department in the past, and that he had hired a contractor who would begin immediate construction of a milkhouse on defendant's farm. Convinced of defendant's sincerity, the department dropped the charge upon payment of costs by the defendant.

To a certain extent the practical effect of these enforcement policies is to nullify the significance of the liability without fault character of the food and drug sections, since prosecution under them takes place only when the defendant has demonstrated subjective fault by showing a conscious intent to violate or, at least, a wilful heedlessness in failing to respond to repeated warnings. However, the liability without fault character of these provisions is still of prime importance to successful regulation of foods and drugs because the necessity of proving guilty knowledge or intent to the satisfaction of the court or jury would in many instances present an insurmountable burden to the department and greatly hinder efforts at control and regulation. This would be true even in many cases of conscious and advertent violation.

Consider the example of a cheesemaker who insists in spite of repeated warnings upon using only the bare minimum of milk fat permissible under statutory standards, thus producing on the narrowest possible margin of safety. It is inevitable that such methods will result in continued occasional production of below-standard cheese. If the cheesemaker refuses to raise his standards so as to insure the production of only above-minimum cheese, he will, under existing department policy, be prosecuted each time he turns out a substandard batch. His actual subjective intent, however, is to produce only cheese which will meet the statutory standards. It would therefore be impossible for the department to regulate his conduct if proof of subjective fault on his part were essential to conviction under the sections involved.

It is apparent that both (1) the liability without fault food and drug sections, which eliminate the necessity of proving intent or knowledge on the part of the violator, and (2) the self-imposed area of administrative tolerance within which warnings are issued by the department and opportunities for correction are held out to offenders before prosecution under these sections, are essential components of the existing policy of food and drug regulation in Wisconsin.

In actual effect then the principal functional significance of the liability without fault character of the food and drug sections is not to make possible wholesale conviction of inadvertent offenders untinted by subjective fault; it is rather to provide widened areas of administrative discretion within which the department of agriculture can administer and enforce the regulations with greater flexibility and effectiveness than would be possible if proof of subjective fault were necessary.

Comment, Liability Without Fault in the Food and Drug Statutes, 1956 Wis.L.Rev. 641, 653–55.

3. For discussions of "strict" liability offenses, see Starrs, The Regulatory Offense in Historical Perspective, in Essays in Criminal Science (G. Mueller ed. 1961); Packer, Mens Rea and the Supreme Court, 1962 Sup.Ct.Rev. 107; Borre, Public Welfare Offenses: A New Approach, 52 J.Crim.L.C. & P.S. 418 (1961); Sayre, Public Welfare Offenses, 33 Colum.L.Rev. 55 (1933); Wasserstrom, Strict Liability in the Criminal Law, 12 Stan.L.Rev. 731 (1960); Comment, Liability Without Fault: Logic and Potential of a Developing Concept, 1970 Wis.L.Rev. 1201.

UNITED STATES v. FREED

Supreme Court of the United States, 1971.
401 U.S. 601, 91 S.Ct. 1112, 28 L.Ed.2d 356, rehearing denied
403 U.S. 912, 91 S.Ct. 2201.

Mr. Justice DOUGLAS delivered the opinion of the Court.

[Defendants were indicted for possessing and conspiring to possess hand grenades not registered under the National Firearms Act.] * * *

The District Court * * * granted the motion to dismiss on two grounds * * * (2) the conspiracy "to possess destructive devices" and the possession charged do not allege the element of scienter. The case is here on direct appeal. * * *

We * * * conclude that the District Court erred in dismissing the indictment for absence of an allegation of scienter.

The Act requires no specific intent or knowledge that the hand grenades were unregistered. It makes it unlawful for any person "to receive or possess a firearm which is not registered to him." [12] By the lower court decisions at the time that requirement was written into the Act the only knowledge required to be proved was knowledge that the instrument possessed was a firearm. See Sipes v. United States, 8 Cir., 321 F.2d 174, 179, and cases cited.

The presence of a "vicious will" or *mens rea* (Morissette v. United States, 342 U.S. 246, 251, 72 S.Ct. 240, 243, 96 L.Ed. 288) was long a requirement of criminal responsibility. But the list of exceptions

---

12. Section 26 U.S.C.A. § 5812(a) provides:
"A firearm shall not be transferred unless (1) the transferor of the firearm has filed with the Secretary or his delegate a written application, in duplicate, for the transfer and registration of the firearm to the transferee on the application form prescribed by the Secretary or his delegate; (2) any tax payable on the transfer is paid as evidenced by the proper stamp affixed to the original application form; (3) the transferee is identified in the application form in such manner as the Secretary or his delegate may by regulations prescribe, except that, if such person is an individual, the identification must include his fingerprints and his photograph; (4) the transferor of the firearm is identified in the application form in such manner as the Secretary or his delegate may by regulations prescribe; (5) the firearm is identified in the application form in such manner as the

Secretary or his delegate may by regulations prescribe; and (6) the application form shows that the Secretary or his delegate has approved the transfer and the registration of the firearm to the transferee. Applications shall be denied if the transfer, receipt, or possession of the firearm would place the transferee in violation of law."

Section 26 U.S.C.A. § 5812(b) provides:
"The transferee of a firearm shall not take possession of the firearm unless the Secretary or his delegate has approved the transfer and registration of the firearm to the transferee as required by subsection (a) of this section."

Section 26 U.S.C.A. § 5841(b) provides:
"Each manufacturer, importer, and maker shall register each firearm he manufactures, imports, or makes. Each firearm transferred shall be registered to the transferee by the transferor."

grew, especially in the expanding regulatory area involving activities affecting public health, safety, and welfare. Id., at 254, 72 S.Ct. at 245. The statutory offense of embezzlement, borrowed from the common-law where scienter was historically required, was in a different category.[13] Id., at 260–261, 72 S.Ct., at 248–249.

> " * * * where Congress borrows terms of art in which are accumulated the legal tradition and meaning of centuries of practice, it presumably knows and adopts the cluster of ideas that were attached to each borrowed word in the body of learning from which it was taken and the meaning its use will convey to the judicial mind unless otherwise instructed." Id., at 263, 72 S.Ct., at 250.

At the other extreme is Lambert v. California, 355 U.S. 225, 78 S.Ct. 240, 2 L.Ed.2d 228, in which a municipal code made it a crime to remain in Los Angeles for more than five days without registering if a person had been convicted of a felony. Being in Los Angeles is not *per se* blameworthy. The mere failure to register, we held, was quite "unlike the commission of acts, or the failure to act under circumstances that should alert the doer to the consequences of his deed." Id., at 228, 78 S.Ct., at 243. The fact that the ordinance was a convenient law enforcement technique did not save it.

> "Where a person did not know of the duty to register and where there was no proof of the probability of such knowledge, he may not be convicted consistently with due process. Were it otherwise, the evil would be as great as it is when the law is written in print too fine to read or in a language foreign to the community." Id., 229–230, 78 S.Ct., 243–244.

In United States v. Dotterweich, 320 U.S. 277, 284, 64 S.Ct. 134, 138, 88 L.Ed. 48, a case dealing with the imposition of a penalty on a corporate officer whose firm shipped adulterated and misbranded

---

13. As respects the *Morissette* case, Marshall, Intention—In Law and Society (1968), p. 138, says:

"The defendant wished to take government property from a government bombing range, he had the capacity to take it, he had the opportunity, he tried and succeeded in taking it (his wish was fulfilled, his act accomplished). For recovery in a tort action no more would have to be shown to establish liability, but the court held that to make his action criminal 'a felonious intent,' *mens rea*, had to be established. This could not be presumed from his actions, which were open, without concealment, and in the belief—according to his statement—that the property had been abandoned. In other words, for the happening to be criminal, the wish had to be to accomplish something criminal. So in discussing intent we may have wishes of two different characters: one giving a basis for civil liability (the wish to take property not one's own), and another which would support criminal liability as well as civil (taking property with criminal intent)."

drugs in violation of the Food and Drug Act, we approved the penalty "though consciousness of wrong-doing be totally wanting."

The present case is in the category neither of *Lambert* nor *Morissette*, but is closer to *Dotterweich*. This is a regulatory measure in the interest of the public safety, which may well be premised on the theory that one would hardly be surprised to learn that possession of hand grenades is not an innocent act. They are highly dangerous offensive weapons, no less dangerous than the narcotics involved in United States v. Balint, 258 U.S. 250, 254, 42 S.Ct. 301, 303, 66 L.Ed. 604, where a defendant was convicted of sale of narcotics against his claim that he did not know the drugs were covered by a federal act. * * *

Reversed.

[Mr. Justice BRENNAN's concurring opinion appears at page 533, infra.]

NOTE

The penalty provision of the National Firearms Act, 26 U.S.C.A. § 5871, provides for a fine of no more than $10,000 or imprisonment for not more than ten years or both. Is this relevant? Should it have been controlling?

PEOPLE v. HERNANDEZ

Supreme Court of California, 1964.
61 Cal.2d 529, 39 Cal.Rptr. 361, 393 P.2d 673.

PEEK, Justice. By information defendant was charged with statutory rape. (Pen.Code, § 261, subd. 1.) Following his plea of not guilty he was convicted as charged by the court sitting without a jury and the offense determined to be a misdemeanor.

Section 261 of the Penal Code provides in part as follows: "Rape is an act of sexual intercourse, accomplished with a female not the wife of the perpetrator, under either of the following circumstances: 1. Where the female is under the age of 18 years; * * * ."

The sole contention raised on appeal is that the trial court erred in refusing to permit defendant to present evidence going to his guilt for the purpose of showing that he had in good faith a reasonable belief that the prosecutrix was 18 years or more of age.

The undisputed facts show that the defendant and the prosecuting witness were not married and had been companions for several months prior to January 3, 1961—the date of the commission of the alleged offense. Upon that date the prosecutrix was 17 years and 9 months of age and voluntarily engaged in an act of sexual intercourse with defendant.

In support of his contention defendant relies upon Penal Code, § 20, which provides that "there must exist a union, or joint operation of act and intent, or criminal negligence" to constitute the commission of a crime. He further relies upon section 26 of that code which provides that one is not capable of committing a crime who commits an act under an ignorance or mistake of fact which disapproves any criminal intent.

Thus the sole issue relates to the question of intent and knowledge entertained by the defendant at the time of the commission of the crime charged.

Consent of the female is often an unrealistic and unfortunate standard for branding sexual intercourse a crime as serious as forcible rape. Yet the consent standard has been deemed to be required by important policy goals. We are dealing here, of course, with statutory rape where, in one sense, the lack of consent of the female is not an element of the offense. In a broader sense, however, the lack of consent is deemed to remain an element but the law makes a conclusive presumption of the lack thereof because she is presumed too innocent and naive to understand the implications and nature of her act. The law's concern with her capacity or lack thereof to so understand is explained in part by a popular conception of the social, moral and personal values which are preserved by the abstinence from sexual indulgence on the part of a young woman. An unwise disposition of her sexual favor is deemed to do harm both to herself and the social mores by which the community's conduct patterns are established. Hence the law of statutory rape intervenes in an effort to avoid such a disposition. This goal, moreover, is not accomplished by penalizing the naive female but by imposing criminal sanctions against the male, who is conclusively presumed to be responsible for the occurrence.

The assumption that age alone will bring an understanding of the sexual act to a young woman is of doubtful validity. Both learning from the cultural group to which she is a member and her actual sexual experiences will determine her level of comprehension. The sexually experienced 15-year old may be far more acutely aware of the implications of sexual intercourse than her sheltered cousin who is beyond the age of consent. A girl who belongs to a group whose members indulge in sexual intercourse at an early age is likely to rapidly acquire an insight into the rewards and penalties of sexual indulgence. Nevertheless, even in circumstances where a girl's actual comprehension contradicts the law's presumption, the male is deemed criminally responsible for the act, although himself young and naive and responding to advances which may have been made to him.[1]

1. The inequitable consequences to which we may be led are graphically illustrated by the following excerpt from State v. Snow (Mo.1923) 252 S.W. 629 at page 632:

"We have in this case a condition and not a theory. This wretched girl was young in years but old in sin and shame. A number of callow youths, of otherwise blameless lives

The law as presently constituted does not concern itself with the relative culpability of the male and female participants in the prohibited sexual act. Even where the young woman is knowledgeable it does not impose sanctions upon her. The knowledgeable young man, on the other hand, is penalized and there are none who would claim that under any construction of the law this should be otherwise. However, the issue raised by the rejected offer of proof in the instant case goes to the culpability of the young man who acts *without* knowledge that an essential factual element exists and has, on the other hand, a positive, reasonable belief that it does not exist.

The primordial concept of *mens rea*, the guilty mind, expresses the principle that it is not conduct alone but conduct accompanied by certain specific mental states which concerns, or should concern the law. In a broad sense the concept may be said to relate to such important doctrines as justification, excuse, mistake, necessity and mental capacity, but in the final analysis it means simply that there must be a "joint operation of act and intent," as expressed in section 20 of the Penal Code, to constitute the commission of a criminal offense. The statutory law, however, furnishes no assistance to the courts beyond that, and the casebooks are filled to overflowing with the courts' struggles to determine just what state of mind should be considered relevant in particular contexts. In numerous instances culpability has been completely eliminated as a necessary element of criminal conduct in spite of the admonition of section 20 to the contrary. * * * More recently, however, this court has moved away from the imposition of criminal sanctions in the absence of culpability where the governing statute, by implication or otherwise, expresses no legislative intent or policy to be served by imposing strict liability. * * *

Statutory rape has long furnished a fertile battleground upon which to argue that the lack of knowledgeable conduct is a proper defense. The law in this state now rests, as it did in 1896, with this court's decision in People v. Ratz, 115 Cal. 132, at pages 134 and 135, 46 P. 915, at page 916, where it is stated: "The claim here made is not a new one. It has frequently been pressed upon the attention of courts, but in no case, so far as our examination goes, has it met with favor. The object and purpose of the law are too plain to need comment, the crime too infamous to bear discussion. The protection of society, of the family, and of the infant, demand that one who has carnal intercourse under such circumstances shall do so in peril of the fact, and he will not be heard against the evidence to urge his belief

* * * fell under her seductive influence. They flocked about her, * * * like moths about the flame of a lighted candle and probably with the same result. The girl was a common prostitute * * *. The boys were immature and doubtless more sinned against than sinning.

They did not defile the girl. She was a mere 'cistern for foul toads to knot and gender in.' Why should the boys, misled by her, be sacrificed? What sound public policy can be subserved by branding them as felons? Might it not be wise to ingraft an exception in the statute?"

that the victim of his outrage had passed the period which would make his act a crime." The age of consent at the time of the Ratz decision was 14 years, and it is noteworthy that the purpose of the rule, as there announced, was to afford protection to young females therein described as "infants." * * *

The rationale of the Ratz decision, rather than purporting to eliminate intent as an element of the crime, holds that the wrongdoer must assume the risk; that, subjectively, when the act is committed, he consciously intends to proceed regardless of the age of the female and the consequences of his act, and that the circumstances involving the female, whether she be a day or a decade less than the statutory age, are irrelevant. There can be no dispute that a criminal intent exists when the perpetrator proceeds with utter disregard of, or in the lack of grounds for, a belief that the female has reached the age of consent. But if he participates in a mutual act of sexual intercourse, believing his partner to be beyond the age of consent, with reasonable grounds for such belief, where is his criminal intent? In such circumstances he has not consciously taken any risk. Instead he has subjectively eliminated the risk by satisfying himself on reasonable evidence that the crime cannot be committed. If it occurs that he has been misled, we cannot realistically conclude that for such reason alone the intent with which he undertook the act suddenly becomes more heinous.

While the specific contentions herein made have been dealt with and rejected both within and without this state, the courts have uniformly failed to satisfactorily explain the nature of the criminal intent present in the mind of one who in good faith believes he has obtained a lawful consent before engaging in the prohibited act. As in the Ratz case the courts often justify convictions on policy reasons which, in effect, eliminate the element of intent. The Legislature, of course, by making intent an element of the crime, has established the prevailing policy from which it alone can properly advise us to depart.

We have recently given recognition to the legislative declarations in sections 20 and 26 of the Penal Code, and departed from prior decisional law which had failed to accord full effect to those sections as applied to charges of bigamy. (People v. Vogel, supra, 46 Cal.2d 798, 299 P.2d 850.) We held there that a good faith belief that a former wife had obtained a divorce was a valid defense to a charge of bigamy arising out of a second marriage when the first marriage had not in fact been terminated. Pertinent to the instant contention that defendant's intent did not suddenly become more criminal because it later developed that he had been misled by the prosecutrix, are the following comments appearing in Vogel at page 804 of 46 Cal.2d, at page 854 of 299 P.2d: "Nor would it be reasonable to hold that a person is guilty of bigamy who remarries in good faith in reliance on a judgment of divorce or annulment that is subsequently found not to be the 'judgment of a competent Court' * * *. Since it is often difficult for laymen to know when a judgment is not that of a competent court, we cannot reasonably expect them always to have such knowledge and make them criminals if their bona fide belief proves to be erroneous." Certainly it cannot be a greater wrong to entertain a bona fide but erroneous belief that a valid consent to an act of sexual intercourse has been obtained.

Equally applicable to the instant case are the following remarks, also appearing at page 804 of 46 Cal.2d, at page 855 of 299 P.2d of the Vogel decision: "The severe penalty imposed for bigamy, the serious loss of reputation conviction entails, * * * and the fact that it has been regarded for centuries as a crime involving moral turpitude, make it extremely unlikely that the Legislature meant to include the morally innocent to make sure the guilty did not escape."

We are persuaded that the reluctance to accord to a charge of statutory rape the defense of a lack of criminal intent has no greater justification than in the case of other statutory crimes, where the Legislature has made identical provision with respect to intent. " 'At common law an honest and reasonable belief in the existence of circumstances, which, if true, would make the act for which the person is indicted an innocent act, has always been held to be a good defense. * * * So far as I am aware it has never been suggested that these exceptions do not equally apply to the case of statutory offenses unless they are excluded expressly or by necessary implication.' " (Matter of Application of Ahart, 172 Cal. 762, 764–765, 159 P. 160, 161–162, quoting from Regina v. Tolson, [1889] 23 Q.B.D. 168, s. c., 40 Alb.L.J. 250.) Our departure from the views expressed in Ratz is in no manner indicative of a withdrawal from the sound policy that it is in the public interest to protect the sexually naive female from exploitation. No responsible person would hesitate to condemn as untenable a claimed good faith belief in the age of consent of an "infant" female whose obviously tender years preclude the existence of reasonable grounds for that belief. However, the prosecutrix in the instant case was but three months short of 18 years of age and there is nothing in the record to indicate that the purposes of the law as stated in Ratz can be better served by foreclosing the defense of a lack of intent. This is not to say that the granting of consent by even a sexually sophisticated girl known to be less than the statutory age is a defense. We hold only that in the absence of a legislative direction otherwise, a charge of statutory rape is defensible wherein a criminal intent is lacking.

For the foregoing reasons People v. Ratz, supra, 115 Cal. 132, 46 P. 915, and People v. Griffin, supra, 117 Cal. 583, 49 P. 711 are overruled, and People v. Sheffield, 9 Cal.App. 130, 98 P. 67 is disapproved to the extent that such decisions are inconsistent with the views expressed herein.

Some question has been raised that the offer of proof of defendant's reasonable belief in the age of the prosecutrix was insufficient to justify the pleading of such belief as a defense to the act. It is not our purpose here to make a determination that the defendant entertained a reasonable belief. Suffice to state that the offer demonstrated a sufficient basis upon which, when fully developed, the trier of fact might have found in defendant's favor. We conclude that it was reversible error to reject the offer.

The judgment is reversed.

NOTES

1. Other courts considering the same issue as is raised in the instant case have rejected the California Supreme Court's conclusion. E. g., State v. Superior Court, 104 Ariz. 440, 454 P.2d 982 (1969); Eggleston v. State, 4 Md.App. 124, 241 A.2d 433 (1968); People v. Doyle, 16 Mich. App. 242, 167 N.W.2d 907 (1969) ("Current social and moral values make more realistic the California view that a reasonable and honest mistake of age is a valid defense to a charge of statutory rape * * * but this court is bound to follow the law presently in effect."); State v. Moore, 105 N.J. Super. 567, 253 A.2d 579 (1969); State v. Fulks, 83 S.D. 433, 160 N.W. 2d 418 (1968). See generally, Annot., 8 A.L.R.3rd 1100 (1966). The cases seldom discuss any constitutional issues which might be raised by interpreting statutory rape statutes as to provide for no defense based upon mistake of age. Why might this be? But see Commonwealth v. Moore, 269 N.E.2d 636 (Mass.1971), in which the defendant was charged with "carnally knowing and abusing" a minor. The victim testified she had an identification card showing her age as eighteen and that she told the defendant she was that age. In addition, the victim had been convicted of prostitution and placed on probation; apparently the police officers, the lawyer representing her, the trial court judge, and the probation officer assumed she was eighteen. Nevertheless, the court held that no affirmative defense of mistake of age was available and that this "strict" liability did not deny the defendant due process of law.

2. If a statutory rape statute permits an accused to raise consent as a defense if the girl was over fifteen years of age at the time of the intercourse and was "previously unchaste," may a defendant assert a reasonable (although mistaken) belief in the girl's lack of chastity and (if consent is shown) thereby secure acquittal? See State v. Vicars, 186 Neb. 311, 183 N.W.2d 241 (1971).

3. To what extent do—and should—other sexual crimes involving minor victims impose strict liability? See State v. Morse, 281 Minn. 378, 161 N.W.2d 699 (1968) holding that a reasonable mistake as to the age of the victim was no defense to a charge of taking indecent liberties with a minor. "In fact situations where the underage female is the aggressor and her male partner the real victim, it is likely that the good judgment of prosecutors and jurors will prevent a miscarriage of justice." 161 N.W. 2d at 703.

4. Despite the California Supreme Court's decision in People v. Vogel, 46 Cal.2d 798, 299 P.2d 850 (1956) bigamy has often been re-

garded as imposing strict liability in regard to that element requiring proof
of the existence of a prior spouse. See Moore, Bigamy, A Crime Though
Unwittingly Committed, 30 U.Cin.L.Rev. 35 (1961); Annot., 56 A.L.R.2d
905 (1957). The Supreme Court seems to have approved, or at least not
disapproved. See Williams v. North Carolina, 325 U.S. 226, 238, 65 S.Ct.
1092, 1099, 89 L.Ed. 1577 (1945). Is this appropriate? Explain. Would
it be significant if the statute specifically provided, as many do, for a defense consisting of proof that the prior spouse had been absent for a specified number of years during which time the defendant had no knowledge
that the spouse was alive?

5. Consider the treatment of the issues raised in the instant case
by the following sections of the Proposed Federal Criminal Code (1970):

§ 1641. Rape

(1) Offense. A male who has sexual intercourse with a
female not his wife is guilty of rape if:

(a) he compels her to submit by force, or by threat of
imminent death, serious bodily injury, or kidnapping, to be
inflicted on any human being;

(b) he has substantially impaired her power to appraise
or control her conduct by administering or employing without
her knowledge intoxicants or other means with intent to prevent resistance; or

(c) the victim is less than ten years old.

(2) Grading. Rape is a Class A felony if in the course of the
offense the actor inflicts serious bodily injury upon the victim,
or if his conduct violates subsection (1) (c), or if the victim is not
a voluntary companion of the actor and has not previously permitted him sexual liberties. Otherwise rape is a Class B felony.

§ 1645. Corruption of Minors

(1) Offense. A male who has sexual intercourse with a female
not his wife or any person who engages in deviate sexual intercourse with another or causes another to engage in deviate sexual
intercourse is guilty of an offense if the other person is less than
sixteen years old and the actor is at least five years older than
the other person.

(2) Grading. The offense is a Class C felony, except when
the actor is less than twenty-one years old, in which case it is a
Class A misdemeanor.

§ 1648. General Provisions for Sections 1641 to 1647

(1) Mistake as to Age. In sections 1641 to 1647: (a) when
the criminality of conduct depends on a child's being below the age
of ten, it is no defense that the actor did not know the child's age,
or reasonably believed the child to be older than ten; (b) when
criminality depends on the child's being below a critical age older

than ten, it is an affirmative defense that the actor reasonably be-lieved the child to be of the critical age or above.

* * *

(3) Prompt Complaint. No prosecution may be instituted or maintained under sections 1641 to 1647 unless the alleged offense was brought to the notice of public authority within three months of its occurrence or, where the alleged victim was less than sixteen years old or otherwise incompetent to make complaint, within three months after a parent, guardian or other competent person specifi-cally interested in the victim, other than the alleged offender, learned of the offense.

* * *

[(5) Testimony of Complainants. No person shall be con-victed of any felony under sections 1641 to 1645 upon the uncor-roborated testimony of the alleged victim. Corroboration may be circumstantial. In a prosecution before a jury for an offense under sections 1641 to 1647, the jury shall be instructed to evalu-ate the testimony of a victim or complaining witness with special care in view of the emotional involvement of the witness and the difficulty of determining the truth with respect to alleged sexual activities carried out in private.]

The earlier Study Draft had contained the following additional provision:

(3) Sexually Promiscuous Complainants. It is an affirmative defense to prosecution under sections 1645 * * * that the alleged victim had, prior to the time of the offense charged, en-gaged promiscuously in sexual relations with others.

This was deleted from the final draft, according to the comment, because it attempted "to reduce an issue of credibility to a fixed rule."

SPEIDEL v. STATE

Supreme Court of Alaska, 1969.
460 P.2d 77.

DIMOND, Justice. Appellant was convicted by a jury of failure to return a rented motor vehicle. From this conviction an appeal has been taken.

The indictment alleged a violation of AS 28.35.026. Appellant moved to dismiss the indictment because the statute failed to provide for proof of criminal intent before conviction. The motion was denied.

At trial it was shown that appellant had rented an automobile from Avis Rent-A-Car Company pursuant to a signed agreement, and had failed to return the automobile at the time stated in the agree-ment. In regard to the allegation that AS 28.35.026 failed to require proof of criminal intent, the trial judge said:

I find that the statute does require an element of intent as such as to constitute * * * wilfull conduct on the part of the person charged that his indifference must be a conscious indifference * * * whether the wrong is done to the owner. * * *

AS 28.35.026 provides:

(a) A person in possession of a motor vehicle under an agreement in writing which requires him to return the vehicle to a particular place or at a particular time who refuses or wilfully neglects to return it to the place and at the time specified in the agreement in writing, or who secretes, converts, sells or attempts to sell the vehicle or any part of it is, upon conviction, punishable by imprisonment for not more than five years, or by a fine of not more than $1,000, or by both.

(b) As used in this section, "wilfully neglects" means omits, fails, or forbears, with a conscious purpose to injure, or without regard for the rights of the owner, or with indifference whether a wrong is done the owner or not.

Appellant asserts that the trial court's interpretation of AS 28.-35.026 is incorrect. He states that failure to return a rented automobile under the statute is a felony and requires proof of criminal intent for conviction. He argues that AS 28.35.026 has no criminal intent requirement and is, therefore, invalid.

It is said to be a universal rule that an injury can amount to a crime only when inflicted by intention—that conduct cannot be criminal unless it is shown that one charged with criminal conduct had an awareness or consciousness of some wrongdoing.

But this rule is not without exception. During the past century there has been an ever increasing tendency to impose new duties with criminal sanctions which disregard any ingredient of intent. This has been caused primarily by the industrial revolution, out of which grew the necessity of imposing more stringent duties on those connected with particular industries, trades, properties, or activities that affect public health, safety or welfare. * * * The statute under consideration here, however, does not represent what could be classified as a "public welfare offense." The health, safety and welfare of the public is not involved. All that the statute is concerned with is the protection of one select group of persons in the business community—those who rent automobiles.

Moreover, as was indicated in *Morissette* [v. United States, 342 U.S. 246 (1952)], penalties for public welfare offenses "commonly are relatively small, and conviction does no grave damage to an offender's reputation." That is not true here. The penalty is not small—the offender under AS 28.35.026 is subject to conviction of a felony and imprisonment for a term of five years. This would do considerable damage to one's reputation. The basis for dispensing with the requirement of criminal intent with respect to "public welfare" types of offenses has no application in this case.

It is true that one will sometimes find felony statutes that are silent on the subject of criminal intent. But these are instances where the states have codified the common law of crimes, and their courts have assumed that the omission of the requirement of criminal intent did not signify disapproval of the principle but merely recognized that intent was so inherent in the idea of the offense that it needed no statutory affirmation. Thus, as to felony-type offenses codified from the common law, the courts have found an implication of intent. Representative of these instances are larceny-type offenses where the state courts have consistently retained a requirement of criminal intent.

But the statute under consideration is not of that type. It is not silent as to the mental elements of the acts made criminal, so as to give rise to the inference that criminal intent is inherent in the idea of the offense denounced. A person is guilty of a crime under AS 28.35.026 if he "willfully neglects" to return a motor vehicle to the owner. The term "willfully neglects" is defined as meaning—

> omits, fails, or forbears, with a conscious purpose to injure, or without regard for the rights of the owner, or with indifference whether a wrong is done the owner or not.

By defining "willfully neglects" so specifically, the legislature has indicated that the ordinary criminal or felonious intent, as in the case of larceny (the intent to deprive the owner permanently of the property taken), is not inherent in the offense of failing to return a rented automobile. In place of inherent criminal intent the legislature has substituted something else. The question is whether this substitution meets the conventional requirement for criminal conduct in this kind of case, i. e., the infliction of injury on the owner of a vehicle by intention, with awareness of some wrongdoing.

By one of the definitions of "willfully neglects" the statute makes it a criminal offense to fail to return a motor vehicle "with conscious purpose to injure." Here the statute incorporates an element of conscious wrongdoing or criminal intent. To that extent the statutory offense meets the conventional requirement of criminal conduct.

But that is not so as to the other definitions which make it a crime to fail to return a motor vehicle "without regard for the rights of the owner" or "with indifference whether a wrong is done the owner or not." Under this terminology it is possible for one to be found guilty of the offense when there was an entire lack of any conscious deprivation of property or intentional injury. If one fails to return an automobile out of neglect, without any intention to deprive the owner of his property or to convert the property to his own use, or of doing wrong to the owner, he is made guilty of a felony although he may have acted unwittingly or inadvertently or negligently. This is contrary to the general conditions of penal liability requiring not only the doing of some act by the person to be held liable, but also the existence of a guilty mind during the commission of the act.

Although an act may have been objectively wrongful, the mind and will of the doer of the act may have been innocent. In such a case the person cannot be punished for a crime, unless it is one such as the "public welfare" type of offense, which we have discussed, where the penalties are relatively small and conviction does no great damage to an offender's reputation. Under the terms of AS 28.35.026 there is no escape from a felony conviction and a possible five-year prison term for simple neglectful or negligent failure to return a rented automobile at the time specified in the rental agreement. To make such an act, without consciousness of wrongdoing or intention to inflict injury, a serious crime, and criminals of those who fall within its interdiction, is inconsistent with the general law. To convict a person of a felony for such an act, without proving criminal intent, is to deprive such person of due process of law. To the extent that AS 28.35.-026 permits that to happen, it is invalid and of no effect.

------

6. "DEFENSES" CONSISTING OF "DISPROOF" OF STATE OF MIND

------

a. IGNORANCE OR MISTAKE OF FACT

REGINA v. PRINCE

Court for Crown Cases Reserved, 1875.
L.R. 2 Cr.Cas.Res. 154.

BRETT, J. In this case the prisoner was indicted under 24 & 25 Vict. c. 100, s. 55, for that he did unlawfully take an unmarried girl, being under the age of sixteen years, out of the possession and against the will of her father. And, according to the statement of the case, we are to assume that it was proved on a trial that he did take an unmarried girl out of the possession and against the will of her father, and that when he did so the girl was under the age of sixteen years. But the jury found that the girl went with the prisoner willingly, that she told the prisoner that she was eighteen years of age, that he believed that she was eighteen years of age, and that he had reasonable grounds for so believing. The question is, whether upon such proof and such findings of the jury, the prisoner ought or ought not, in point of law, to be pronounced guilty of the offence with which he was charged. He, in fact, did each and everything which is enumerated in the statute as constituting the offence to be punished, if what he did was done unlawfully within the meaning of the statute. If what he did was unlawful within the meaning of the statute, it seems impossible to say that he ought not to be convicted. If what he did was not unlawful within the meaning of the statute, it seems impossible to say that he ought to be convicted. The question, therefore, is, whether the findings of the jury, which are in favour of the prisoner, prevent what he is proved to have done from being unlawful within the meaning of the statute. It cannot, as it seems to me, properly be assumed that what he did was unlawful within the meaning of the statute, for that is the very question to be determined.

Now, on the one side, it is said that the prisoner is proved to have done every particular thing which is enumerated in the Act as constituting the offence to be punished, and that there is no legal justification for what he did, and, therefore, that it must be held, as a matter of law, that what he did was unlawful within the meaning of the statute, and that the statute was therefore satisfied, and the crime completed. On the other side, it is urged that if the facts had been as the prisoner believed them to be, and as by the findings of the jury he might reasonably believe them to be, and was deceived into believing them to be, he would have been guilty of no criminal offence at all, and therefore he had no criminal intent at all, and therefore that what he did was not criminally unlawful within the meaning of the criminal statute under which he was indicted.

* * *

[I]f the facts had been as the prisoner, according to the findings of the jury, believed them to be, and had reasonable ground for believing them to be, he would have done no act which has ever been a criminal offence in England; he would have done no act in respect of which any civil action could have ever been maintained against him; he would have done no act for which, if done in the absence of the father, and done with the continuing consent of the girl, the father could have had any legal remedy.

* * *

Upon all the cases I think it is proved that there can be no conviction for crime in England in the absence of a criminal mind or mens rea.

Then comes the question, what is the true meaning of the phrase. I do not doubt that it exists where the prisoner knowingly does acts which would constitute a crime if the result were as he anticipated, but in which the result may not improbably end by bringing the offence within a more serious class of crime. As if a man strikes with a dangerous weapon, with intent to do grievous bodily harm, and kills, the result makes the crime murder. The prisoner has run the risk. So, if a prisoner do the prohibited acts, without caring to consider what the truth is as to facts—as if a prisoner were to abduct a girl under sixteen without caring to consider whether she was in truth under sixteen—he runs the risk. So if he without abduction defiles a girl who is in fact under ten years old, with a belief that she is between ten and twelve. If the facts were as he believed he would be committing the lesser crime. Then he runs the risk of his crime resulting in the greater crime. It is clear that ignorance of the law does not excuse. It seems to me to follow that the maxim as to mens rea applies whenever the facts which are present to the prisoner's mind, and which he has reasonable ground to believe, and does believe to be the facts, would, if true, make his acts no criminal offence at all.

It may be true to say that the meaning of the word "unlawfully" is, that the prohibited acts be done without justification or excuse; I, of course, agree that if there be a legal justification there can be no crime; but I come to the conclusion that a mistake of facts, on reasonable grounds, to the extent that if the facts were as believed the acts of the prisoner would make him guilty of no criminal offence at all, is an excuse, and that such excuse is implied in every criminal charge and every criminal enactment in England. I agree with Lord Kenyon that "such is our law," and with Cockburn, C. J., that "such is the foundation of all criminal procedure."

The following judgment (in which Cockburn, C. J., Mellor, Lush, Quain, Denman, Archibald, Field, and Lindley, JJ., and Pollock, B., concurred) was delivered by

BLACKBURN, J.   *   *   *

The question   *   *   *   is reduced to this, whether the words in 24 & 25 Vict. c. 100, s. 55, that whosoever shall take "any unmarried girl, being under the age of sixteen, out of the possession of her father," are to be read as if they were "being under the age of sixteen, and he knowing she was under that age." No such words are contained in the statute, nor is there the word "maliciously," "knowingly," or any other word used that can be said to involve a similar meaning.

*   *   *

[W]e are of opinion that the intention of the legislature sufficiently appears to have been to punish the abduction, unless the girl, in fact, was of such an age as to make her consent an excuse, irrespective of whether he knew her to be too young to give an effectual consent, and to fix that age at sixteen.   *   *   *

We think   *   *   *   that the conviction in the present case should stand.

The following judgment (in which Kelly, C. B., Cleasby, Pollock, and Amphlett, BB., and Grove, Quain, and Denman, JJ., concurred) was delivered by

BRAMWELL, B. The question in this case depends on the construction of the statute under which the prisoner is indicted. That enacts that "whosoever shall unlawfully take any unmarried girl under the age of sixteen out of the possession and against the will of her father or mother, or any other person having the lawful care or charge or her, shall be guilty of a misdemeanor." * * * [T]he question is, has the prisoner taken an unmarried girl under the age of sixteen out of the possession of and against the will of her father? In fact, he has; but it is said not within the meaning of the statute, and that that must be read as though the word "knowingly," or some equivalent word, was in; and the reason given is, that as a rule the mens rea is necessary to make any act a crime or offence, and that if the facts necessary to constitute an offence are not known to the alleged offender, there can be no mens rea. I have used the word "knowingly;" but it will, perhaps, be said that here the prisoner not only did not do the act knowingly, but knew, as he would have said, or believed, that the fact was otherwise than such as would have made his act a crime; that here the prisoner did not say to himself, "I do not know how the fact is, whether she is under sixteen or not, and will take the chance," but acted on the reasonable belief that she was over sixteen; and that though if he had done what he did, knowing or believing neither way, but hazarding it, there would be a mens rea, there is not one when, as he believes, he knows that she is over sixteen.

It is impossible to suppose that, to bring the case within the statute, a person taking a girl out of her father's possession against his will is guilty of no offence unless he, the taker, knows she is under sixteen; that he would not be guilty if the jury were of opinion he knew neither one way nor the other. Let it be, then, that the question is whether he is guilty where he knows, as he thinks, that she is over sixteen. This introduces the necessity for reading the statute with some strange words introduced; as thus: "Whosoever shall take any unmarried girl, being under the age of sixteen, and not believing her to be over the age of sixteen, out of the possession," &c. Those words are not there, and the question is, whether we are bound to construe the statute as though they were, on account of the rule that the mens rea is necessary to make an act a crime. I am of opinion that we are not, nor as though the word "knowingly" was there, and for the following reasons: The act forbidden is wrong in itself, if without lawful cause; I do not say illegal, but wrong. I have not lost sight of this, that though the statute probably principally aims at seduction for carnal purposes, the taking may be by a female with a good motive. Nevertheless, though there may be such cases, which are not immoral in one sense, I say that the act forbidden is wrong.

Let us remember what is the case supposed by the statute. It supposes that there is a *girl*—it does not say a woman, but a girl—something between a child and a woman; it supposes she is in the *possession* of her father or mother, or other person having lawful *care or charge* of her; and it supposes there is a *taking*, and that that taking is *against the will* of the person in whose possession she is. It is, then, a *taking* of a *girl,* in the *possession* of some one, *against his will.* I say that done without lawful cause is wrong, and that the legislature meant it should be at the risk of the taker whether or no she was under sixteen. I do not say that taking a woman of fifty from her brother's or even father's house is wrong. She is at an age when she has a right to choose for herself; she is not a *girl,* nor of such tender age that she can be said to be in the *possession* of or under the *care or charge* of anyone. I am asked where I draw the line; I answer at when the female is no longer a girl in anyone's possession.

But what the statute contemplates, and what I say is wrong is the taking of a female of such tender years that she is properly called a *girl,* can be said to be in another's *possession,* and in that other's *care or charge.* No argument is necessary to prove this; it is enough to state the case. The legislature has enacted that if anyone does this wrong act, he does it at the risk of her turning out to be under sixteen. This opinion gives full scope to the doctrine of the mens rea. If the taker believed he had the father's consent, though wrongly, he would have no mens rea; so if he did not know she was in anyone's possession, nor in the care or charge of anyone. In those cases he would not know he was doing the *act* forbidden by the statute—an act which, if he knew she was in possession and in care or charge of anyone, he would know was a crime or not, according as she was under sixteen or not. He would not know he was doing an act wrong in itself, whatever was his intention, if done without lawful cause.

*   *   *

DENMAN, J. I agree in the judgment of my Brothers Bramwell and Blackburn, and I wish what I add to be understood as supplementary to them. *   *   *

In the present case the jury found that the defendant had done everything required to bring himself within the clause as a misdemeanant, unless the fact that he bonâ fide and reasonably believed the girl taken by him to be eighteen years old constituted a defence. That is in other words, unless such bonâ fide and reasonable belief prevented them from saying that the defendant in what he did acted "unlawfully" within the meaning of the clause. The question, therefore, is whether, upon this finding of the jury, the defendant did unlawfully do the things which they found him to have done.

The solution of this question depends upon the meaning of the word "unlawfully" in s. 55. If it means "with a knowledge or belief that every single thing mentioned in the section existed at the moment of the taking," undoubtedly the defendant would be entitled to an acquittal, because he did not believe that a girl of under sixteen was being taken by him at all. If it only means "without lawful excuse" or justification, then a further question arises, viz. whether the defendant had any lawful excuse or justification for doing all the acts mentioned in the clause as constituting the offence, by reason, merely, that he bonâ fide and reasonably believed the girl to be older than the age limited by the clause. Bearing in mind the previous enactments relating to the abduction of girls under sixteen, 4 & 5 Phil. & Mary, c. 8, s. 2, and the general course of the decisions upon those enactments, and upon the present statute, and looking at the mischief intended to be guarded against, it appears to me reasonably clear that the word "unlawfully," in the true sense in which it was used, is fully satisfied by holding that it is equivalent to the words "without lawful excuse," using those words as equivalent to "without such an excuse as being proved would be a complete legal justification for the act, even where all the facts constituting the offence exist."

Cases may easily be suggested where such a defence might be made out, as for instance, if it were proved that he had the authority of a Court of competent jurisdiction, or of some legal warrant, or that he acted to prevent some illegal violence not justified by the relation of parent and child, or school-mistress, or other custodian, and requiring forcible interference by way of protection.

In the present case the jury find that the defendant believed the girl to be eighteen years of age; even if she had been of that age, she would have been in the lawful care and charge of her father, as her guardian by nature * * *[.] Her father had a right to her personal custody up to the age of twenty-one, and to appoint a guardian by deed or will, whose right to her personal custody would have extended up to the same age. The belief that she was eighteen would be no justification to the defendant for taking her out of his possession, and against his will. By taking her, even with her own consent, he must at least have been guilty of aiding and abetting her in doing an unlawful act, viz. in escaping against the will of her natural guardian from his lawful care and charge. This, in my opinion, leaves him wholly without lawful excuse or justification for the act he did, even though he believed that the girl was eighteen, and therefore unable to allege that what he has done was not unlawfully done, within the meaning of the clause. In other words, having knowingly done a wrongful act, viz. in taking the girl away from the lawful possession of her father against his will, and in violation of his rights as guardian by nature, he cannot be heard to say that he thought the girl was of an age beyond that limited by the statute for the offence charged against him. He had wrongfully done the very thing contemplated by the legislature: He had wrongfully and knowingly violated the father's rights against the father's will. And he cannot set up a legal defence by merely proving that he thought he was committing a different kind of wrong from that which in fact he was committing.

Conviction affirmed.

NOTE

What are the differences in the ways which the various opinion writers in *Prince* see ignorance or mistake as to a matter of fact as affecting criminal liability? Which is appropriate? Should mistake or ignorance of fact serve to "disprove" state of mind? (How can a negative response to such a question be defended?) Should any distinction be made between ignorance and mistake of fact? If ignorance or mistake of fact is relevant to the existence of the state of mind required for the crime, should it be limited to that (or should an "affirmative defense" of ignorance or mistake of fact be recognized)? Would it be more desirable to have such an "affirmative defense" instead of permitting use of ignorance or mistake of fact to "disprove" state of mind? In either case, how might such an affirmative defense be formulated?

UNITED STATES v. SHORT

United States Court of Military Appeals, 1954.
4 USCMA 437, 16 CMR 11.

ROBERT E. QUINN, Chief Judge. A general court-martial in Japan convicted the accused of assault with intent to commit rape, and sentenced him to dishonorable discharge, total forfeitures, and confinement at hard labor for ten years. The convening authority modified the sentence by reducing the period of confinement to five years. A board of review affirmed the conviction and the modified sentence. We granted review to consider the correctness of the law officer's general instructions and his denial of certain defense requests for specific instructions.

The events of this case took place on November 28, 1952, in Tokyo. At about 11:30 p. m., two Japanese girls, Yayoi Tomobe and Tokiko Okano, left the shop in which they worked to dispose of some waste paper in a public latrine located across the street. Apparently as the girls were crossing the street, they were approached from behind by the accused and his companion, Private O'Rourke. From their speech, Okano deduced that the "foreigners" were intoxicated. She was frightened. Calling out to Tomobe to run, Okano ran back to the shop. Tomobe, however, tripped over a stone. As she regained her balance, she was caught under her right arm by the accused. The accused spoke to her in English. Although she had learned some English in school, she was "so scared and * * * surprised" that she did not know what was said, except that there was mention of yen. She was then pulled to the front of the latrine and pushed in. The accused entered and closed the door.

Tomobe tried to get away from the accused, but he was "very big." She was "scared" and "had no strength to go out." While the accused did not punch, kick, or otherwise inflict bodily harm upon her, he fondled her person against her protests. She kept saying "No" in Japanese as loudly as she could. She pushed the accused away, but he was "so strong that [she] was unable to hold him away."

In the meantime, Okano, having seen Tomobe pulled into the latrine, reported to the manager of the shop. He immediately went to the latrine and opened the door. He heard Tomobe saying "No," and he saw the accused holding her. However, just then O'Rourke tapped him on the shoulder and he made no further effort to interfere. Instead, he went to a police box, located approximately forty feet from the latrine, and reported the matter to the Japanese policemen. They hastened to the latrine. One of the policemen opened the door, and in Japanese called out to the accused to stop. In the same language, the accused replied that it was all right. Then he was forcibly removed from the latrine, and taken to the police box.

At the trial, the accused admitted fondling Tomobe, as set out in the specification. However, he denied that he acted unlawfully. He testified that when he saw Tomobe, he thought she was a prostitute since the area was known to be frequented by them. He "propositioned" her, and after some negotiation they agreed on a price of 500 yen. Tomobe showed him the latrine; he previously did not know of its existence. Inside Tomobe helped him in his efforts to "make love to her." Although he was "under the influence," he was generally aware of what he was doing. When the police entered the latrine, he thought that they wanted to arrest the girl as a prostitute. He told them that it was all right because he was anxious to protect her.

*   *   *

Before giving his instructions, the law officer discussed them with both counsel in a recorded out-of-court hearing. Each counsel submitted requests for specific instructions. With some modification, one of the three offered by the prosecution was accepted; the two submitted by the defense were rejected. The defense requests are as follows:

*   *   *

"In order to constitute an offense, the accused must think victim is not consenting because he must intend not only to have carnal knowledge of the woman but to do so by force.

"The guilt or innocence of the accused depends on the circumstances as they appear to him."

*   *   *

Turning to the second request, the accused argues that this instruction sought, in essence, to present a defense of mistake of fact. It is axiomatic that, before a failure to instruct on a defense may be alleged as ground for error, the evidence must show that the defense was reasonably raised. United States v. Sandoval, 4 USCMA 61, 15 CMR 61. We assume for the purposes of this case that sufficient evidence appears in the record from which it may reasonably be inferred the accused believed that Tomobe consented to his "proposition." However, the question still to be answered is whether the instruction requested is legally correct. The accused stresses the similarity of the requested instruction to that in McQuirk v. State, 84 Ala. 435, 4 So. 775. In that case the accused was charged with rape. The evidence showed that the prosecutrix was weakminded. The defendant maintained that he believed she had consented to the act. He requested the following instruction which was denied by the trial judge:

> "If the jury believe, from the evidence, that the conduct of the prosecutrix was such towards the defendant, at the time of the alleged rape, as to create in the mind of the defendant the honest and reasonable belief that she had consented, or was willing for defendant to have connection with her, they must acquit the defendant."

On appeal the conviction was reversed because of the failure of the trial judge to give the requested instruction.

It is immediately apparent that the requested instruction in this case is markedly different from that in McQuirk. It fails to qualify the accused's belief by requiring that it be reasonable and honest. * * * This omission is substantial. The requested instruction also assumes too much. When consent is in issue, whether or not it was given is a question of fact for the court. It, not the accused, must determine whether the woman's conduct was such as to lead the accused to believe she had consented to his acts. The accused's personal evaluation of the circumstances is but one factor to be considered by the court; it is not conclusive. There are other objectionable elements in the request * * * but we need not further elaborate upon them. There may be occasions when a request to instruct is technically defective but still sufficiently challenging in content to require the law officer to instruct on the subject matter in spite of the defect. * * * However, nothing in the instant request suggested a material issue that was not adequately covered in the general instructions.

The decision of the board of review is affirmed.

BROSMAN, Judge (concurring in part and dissenting in part):

* * * Here the evidence seems to me to have raised reasonably the possibility that the accused believed the prosecutrix was acceding to his overtures. The principal opinion suggests that such a belief, to be effective, must be both reasonable and honest. For this its author cites United States v. Perruccio, 4 USCMA 28, 15 CMR 28, where an unreasonable—and thus negligent—mistake of fact was deemed no defense to a prosecution for negligent homicide. On the other hand, a mistake of fact may be negligent and yet negate the intent or knowledge required for conviction of certain offenses. United States v. Lampkins, 4 USCMA 31, 15 CMR 31. Within which category do rape and assault with intent to commit rape fall?

Rape—like unpremeditated murder—has ordinarily been treated as requiring only a general criminal intent. Thus, drunkenness, even in excessive degree, would probably not constitute a defense to this crime—that is, as serving to belie the accused's necessary intent. However, assault with intent to commit rape would seem to occupy a quite different position—since the very designation of the offense indicates the requirement of a specific intent. Clearly, then, drunkenness could operate to negate the intent required for conviction of such an assault. An *unreasonable* mistake of fact could perhaps not serve to deny criminal liability for a consummated rape. But could it negative the prerequisites for a finding of guilt of assault with intent to commit rape—just as an unreasonable mistake of fact is said to destroy liability for larceny by false pretenses?

* * *

Assault with intent to commit rape demands proof of an assault on the prosecutrix accompanied by an intent to have unlawful sexual intercourse by force and without her consent—a purpose to overcome any resistance by force. Manual for Courts-Martial United States, 1951, paragraph 213*d*(1) (*c*). If the woman consents to the application of force to her body, there would presumably be no assault in the first instance. Of course, if she had consented to sexual intercourse—that is, if her "will" favored such a result—she would also ordinarily have consented to that fondling which frequently precedes the act of coition. Thus, acts like those before us here would not partake of their usual character of a battery. See Manual, supra, paragraph 207*a*, page 371.

Ignorance or mistake of fact—if reasonable—normally provides a defense to an accused. Manual, paragraph 154*a*(3). Ignorance of law usually constitutes no excuse—although it may negate the existence of the specific intent required in certain offenses. Idem, paragraph 154*a*(4). While consent in some areas may be a matter of law * * * I would suppose that the type of consent with which we are now dealing is "factual" in nature, and that a mistake as to the woman's attitude would constitute one of fact. Thus, if the accused believed reasonably that the Japanese girl here was consenting to his proposals, he would be exonerated, I should think, even from the crime of assault. On the other hand, an unreasonable mistake on his part would not affect his liability for assault, in violation of the Uniform Code, Article 128, 50 U.S.C.A. § 722.

But if an assault is to be found here—on the theory there was neither consent nor a reasonable mistake with regard thereto—does not the accused's mistake reenter the picture? One possibility is that the trier of fact may conclude that the girl did not consent, and that no reasonable man would have thought she did, but that the accused—because of drunkenness or some variety of mild sexual complex which destroyed his realism—genuinely believed that she was acquiescent. His purpose simply was to enjoy sexual relations with her under the circumstances presented to him. Those circumstances he unreasonably construed to amount to an invitation on her part. However, he did not intend coitus under any other circumstances. This might be because (a) he did not desire intercourse without full consent; or (b) because he was just not the sort of person who worries about hypothetical problems. When an accused fondles a woman against a background of the frame of mind just mentioned, I would suppose him to be wanting in that variety of criminal purpose required for assault with intent to rape. One may well lack an intention to overcome resistance when nothing is present which seems to suggest the possibility of its presence.

It may be regarded as anomalous to conclude that an accused may be exonerated from guilt of assault with intent to commit rape because of an unreasonable mistake, whereas he could have been convicted lawfully of rape had penetration been effected under the same misapprehension. It is to be observed, however, that the anomaly is no greater than that involved in holding that an assault with intent to murder requires a specific intent to kill, whereas the crime of murder may be made out with a lesser intent. See United States v. Woodson, 3 USCMA 372, 12 CMR 128. The fact of the matter is that a specific intent is, by definition, required for the present finding. The evidence, in my view, raised the possibility that a mistake of fact on the accused's part precluded that intent.

* * *

Regardless of whether the offered—and denied—instruction was entirely accurate in phrasing, it is manifest that the law officer was put on notice to see to it that the court-martial was instructed correctly on mistake of fact.

* * *

It follows from what has been said that, as to mere assault, the accused is not entitled to an instruction on mistake of fact, unless the possibility of a *reasonable* mistake was raised by the evidence. On the other hand, as to assault with intent to rape, he is so entitled *regardless* of reasonableness. * * *

I would reverse the decision of the board of review and order a rehearing.

NOTES

1. How can a requirement that a mistake of fact be "reasonable" be reconciled with the state of mind requirement? Is there any way the distinction of the dissenting judge between "general" and "specific" intent crimes can be defended?

2. Howard, The Reasonableness of Mistake in the Criminal Law, 4 U.Queens L.J. 45 (1961) suggests that the confusion concerning whether a mistake need be reasonable results from a failure to distinguish mistake as a defense to a crime requiring "general intent" and mistake offered as a defense to a crime for which negligence is sufficient. In the former case, he suggests, no reasonableness is necessary; in the latter, only a reasonable mistake prevents liability.

3. For general discussions of mistake of fact, see Haddad, The Mental Attitude Requirement in Criminal Law—and Some Exceptions, 59 J. Crim.L., C. & P.S. 4, 11–21 (1968); Hall, Ignorance and Mistake in Criminal Law, 33 Ind.L.J. 1, 2–14 (1957); Keedy, Ignorance and Mistake in the Criminal Law, 22 Harv.L.Rev. 81–88 (1908); Perkins, Ignorance and Mistake in Criminal Law, 88 U.Pa.L.Rev. 35, 54–65 (1939).

PROPOSED FEDERAL CRIMINAL CODE (1971)

§ 304. Ignorance or Mistake Negating Culpability

A person does not commit an offense if when he engages in conduct he is ignorant or mistaken about a matter of fact or law and the ignorance or mistake negates the kind of culpability required for commission of the offense.

---

b. IGNORANCE OR MISTAKE OF LAW

PROPOSED FEDERAL CRIMINAL CODE (1971)

§ 304. Ignorance or Mistake Negating Culpability
[For text of this section, see above.]

§ 609. Mistake of Law

Except as otherwise expressly provided, a person's good faith belief that conduct does not constitute a crime is an affirmative defense if he acted in reasonable reliance upon a statement of the law contained in:

    (a) a statute or other enactment;

    (b) a judicial decision, opinion, order or judgment;

    (c) an administrative order or grant of permission; or

    (d) an official interpretation of the public servant or body charged by law with responsibility for the interpretation, administration or enforcement of the law defining the crime.

Comment

This section sets forth those circumstances under which a person is excused from criminal liability for his conduct because he mistakenly believed his conduct did not constitute a crime. The defense is not available for infractions where proof of culpability is generally not required. Mistake of law is an affirmative defense; it must be established by a preponderance of the evidence. See § 103(3). Note that the reliance must be "reasonable," and that good faith is explicitly required. In most instances, it would be unreasonable for a layman to fail to consult a lawyer, and would not be in good faith if he failed to make full disclosure to him of all relevant facts. * * *

An alternative preferred by a substantial body of opinion in the Commission would limit the defense to situations where knowledge of the law might be regarded as especially relevant to culpability, e. g., tax and draft evasion, conflict of interest. This approach is premised on the view that " * * * to admit the excuse at all would be to encourage ignorance * * *." Holmes, The Common Law 41 (Howe ed. 1963). Consequently, it is argued, mistake of law ought only be a defense where knowledge of the law is an element of the offense. It is argued for the view embodied in the text, however, that it does not "encourage ignorance" since it explicitly requires a good faith effort by the accused to inform himself from usually reliable sources, and puts the burden of proof on the defendant.

NOTES

1. The study draft of the proposed federal code did not contain the words "good faith" that now appear before "belief." What, if anything, did the insertion of these words add to the section?

2. For general discussions, see Hall, Ignorance and Mistake in Criminal Law, 33 Ind.L.J. 1, 14–44 (1957); Hall and Seligman, Mistake of Law and Mens Rea, 8 U.Chi.L.Rev. 641 (1941); Keedy, Ignorance and Mistake in the Criminal Law, 22 Harv.L.Rev. 81, 88–96 (1908); Mueller-Rappard, The Mistake of Law as a Defense, 36 Temple L.Q. 261 (1963); Perkins, Ignorance and Mistake in Criminal Law, 88 U.Pa.L.Rev. 35, 36–53 (1939); Ryu and Silving, Error Juris: A Comparative Study, 24 U.Chi.L.Rev. 421 (1957).

---

(1) IGNORANCE OR MISTAKE AS TO THE LAW PROHIBITING THE CRIMINAL ACT

LAMBERT v. CALIFORNIA

Supreme Court of the United States, 1957.
355 U.S. 225, 78 S.Ct. 240, 2 L.Ed.2d 228.

[The opinion in this case is reprinted at page 456.]

ZAKRASEK v. STATE

Supreme Court of Indiana, 1926.
197 Ind. 249, 150 N.E. 615.

TRAVIS, J. Appellant was tried and found guilty by a jury, as charged in count 1 of an affidavit of two counts. Count 1 charged that he did unlawfully purchase, receive, manufacture, transport, ship, possess, sell, barter, exchange, give away, furnish, and otherwise handle and dispose of intoxicating liquor. He appeals from the judgment upon the verdict and assigns as error the overruling of his motion for a new trial by the trial court.

The only legal cause alleged for a new trial, is that the verdict of the jury is contrary to law. * * * Appellant admits by his brief that, on May 12, 1925, the date alleged in the affidavit as the time of the offense charged, he was in possession of 30 gallons of wine. The contention of appellant is that by section 4, p. 145, c. 48, Acts 1925 (section 2717, Burns' 1926), the Legislature did not intend to make mere possession of intoxicating liquor a crime, and, if that was the intention of the Legislature when it passed the act of 1925, some time should have been set within which persons then in possession of intoxicating liquor could have destroyed the same before they would be guilty of violation of the law.

In support of this contention, appellant says that, under the prohibition laws passed in 1917 (Acts 1917, p. 15, c. 4) and in 1923 (Acts 1923, p. 70, c. 23), as interpreted by the courts, it was not a crime to possess intoxicating liquor. Knowing such judicial interpretation, and not actually knowing the existence of the act passed in March, 1925, which became a law by proclamation of the Governor April 28, 1925, when he was thus charged with this alleged crime May 12, 1925, the verdict of guilty is contrary to law. Appellant's proposition and the reason for it are without merit. All persons are charged with knowledge of the criminal laws which define crimes, and the fact, if it be a fact, that until the day he was charged with this crime he was ignorant that the act which created the crime had been passed by the Legislature and had become a law is of no avail to excuse him for the crime charged. * * *

The verdict is not contrary to law.

Judgment affirmed.

WRIGHT v. GEORGIA

Supreme Court of the United States, 1963.
373 U.S. 284, 83 S.Ct. 1240, 10 L.Ed.2d 349.

Mr. Chief Justice WARREN delivered the opinion of the Court.

Petitioners, six young Negroes, were convicted of breach of the peace for peacefully playing basketball in a public park in Savannah, Georgia, on the early afternoon of Monday, January 23, 1961.

* * *

Petitioners' principal contention in this Court is that the breach of the peace statute did not give adequate warning that their conduct violated that enactment in derogation of their rights under the Due Process Clause of the Fourteenth Amendment of the Constitution of the United States. * * *

* * * [I]t is said that the petitioners were guilty of a breach of the peace because a park rule reserved the playground for the use of younger people at the time. However, neither the existence nor the posting of any such rule has been proved. Cf. Lambert v. California, 355 U.S. 225, 228, 78 S.Ct. 240, 242, 2 L.Ed.2d 228. The police officers did not inform them of it because they had no knowledge of any such rule themselves. Furthermore, it is conceded that there was no sign or printed regulation which would give notice of any such rule.

* * *

Under any view of the facts alleged to constitute the violation it cannot be maintained that petitioners had adequate notice that their conduct was prohibited by the breach of the peace statute. It is well established that a conviction under a criminal enactment which does not give adequate notice that the conduct charged is prohibited is violative of due process. * * *

Reversed.

STATE v. STRIGGLES

Supreme Court of Iowa, 1926.
202 Iowa 1318, 210 N.W. 137.

ALBERT, J. We gather from the record and arguments of counsel the following history of the case at bar:

It appears that in the early part of 1923 there was installed in several places of business in the city of Des Moines a gum or mint vending machine. The machine and its workings are fully set out in the opinion in the case of State v. Ellis, 200 Iowa 1228, 206 N.W. 105, filed at the November, 1925, sitting of this court. In that opinion it was judicially determined that such machine was a gambling device within the inhibition of the statute.

On August 1, 1923, in several proceedings then pending in the municipal court of the city of Des Moines, a decision was rendered holding that such machine was not a gambling device. The distributors of the machine in question thereupon secured a certified copy of said decree, and equipped themselves with a letter from the county attorney, and also one from the mayor of the city, stating that such machine was not a gambling device. Thus equipped they presented themselves to appellant, Striggles, who conducted a restaurant in the city of Des Moines, and induced him to allow them to install a machine in his place of business.

Subsequent thereto, in the early part of 1925, the Polk county grand jury returned an indictment against appellant in which it charged that he did "willfully and unlawfully keep a house, shop, and place * * * resorted to for the purpose of gambling, and he * * * did then and there willfully and unlawfully permit and suffer divers persons, * * * in said house, shop, and place * * * to play a certain machine * * * being then and there a gambling device." On entering a plea of not guilty, the appellant was put on trial. He offered in evidence the aforesaid certified copy of the judgment decree of the court, and the letters from the county attorney and the mayor, which were properly objected to and the objection sustained. The appellant while testifying was permitted by the court to say that the exhibits had been presented to him before he permitted the machine to be installed. He was then asked by his counsel whether he relied on the contents of the papers when he gave his permission for installation of the machine. Objection to this line of testimony was sustained. He was also asked whether he would have permitted the machine to be installed had he believed it to be a gambling device. He was not permitted to answer this question.

* * * There is no case cited, nor can we find one on diligent search, holding that the decision of an inferior court can be relied upon to justify the defendant in a criminal case in the commission of the act which is alleged to be a crime. We are disposed to hold * * * that, when the highest court of jurisdiction passes on any given proposition, all citizens are entitled to rely upon such decision; but we refuse to hold that the decisions of any court below, inferior to the Supreme Court, are available as a defense under similar circumstances.

The testimony offered, if available to the appellant, must be on the theory that it goes to prove his intention. It is settled law that in prohibitive statutes covering misdemeanors, where no provision is made as to intention, and the word "knowingly" or other apt words are not employed to indicate that knowledge is the essential element of the crime, intention is not an element of the crime. Especially is this so where the act is forbidden by statute in the aid of the police power of the state. * * * We are therefore of the opinion that the ruling of the district court in excluding this testimony was right.

NOTE

Suppose the government had previously, in widely-circulated documents, taken the position that new legislation was needed because existing legislation did not cover the device in issue in the instant case. Would this have had any impact upon the outcome of the instant case? What if the government had asserted a need for legislation to clarify an ambiguous point of existing law? Cf. United States v. Laub, 385 U.S. 475, 87 S.Ct. 574, 17 L.Ed.2d 526 (1967).

HUNTER v. STATE

Supreme Court of Tennessee, 1928.
158 Tenn. 63, 12 S.W.2d 361.

CHAMBLISS, J. This appeal is from a conviction of embezzlement by a public officer, under section 6574, Shan. Code. Hunter was trustee of Hamilton county, and he failed to account for $31,239.48 of public funds. His defense is and was that he acted, in appropriating to his own use these funds, under the belief, supported by the advice of counsel, that chapter 101 of the Acts of 1921, passed prior to his election, and in effect during his term, known as the Salary Law, was unconstitutional, leaving in force the former law which vested all fees of the office in the trustee. * * *

In effect, the sole question for consideration is whether or not belief in the unconstitutionality of an act of the Legislature, supported by the advice of counsel, is competent to rebut such proof of criminal intent, if any, as is essential under the embezzlement statute to a conviction of a public officer who has converted and appropriated public funds to his personal use.

* * *

The authorities uniformly recognize and give effect to this distinction between mistakes of fact and ignorance of the law, sometimes excusing the accused in the first case, but refusing always to do so in the latter. The claim of belief in the unconstitutionality of a law comes, of course, within the latter class. It is a plea of ignorance of the law which is never admissible to excuse crime.

* * *

In the noted case of U. S. v. Anthony, 24 Fed.Cas. p. 829, No. 14459, in which Susan B. Anthony was convicted of voting illegally, the United States Circuit Court for the Northern District of New York, affirming the judgment, rejected the insistence of the defendant that the state Constitution, which denied to her the right to vote, contravened the Federal Constitution and was therefore void, and held that she could not, when prosecuted, defend on the ground of her belief in the unconstitutionality of the state law. Said the court, "Miss Anthony knew that she was a woman, and that the Constitution of this State prohibits her from voting. She intended to violate that provision—intended to test it, perhaps, but certainly, intended to violate it. * * * There was no ignorance of any fact. * * * She takes the risk, and she cannot escape the consequences. It is said, and authorities are cited to sustain the position, that there can be no crime unless there is a culpable intent, and that, to render one criminally responsible a vicious will must be present. * * * To constitute a crime, it is true that there must be a criminal intent, but it is equally true that knowledge of the facts of the case is always held

to supply this intent.   *   *   *   No system of criminal jurisprudence
can be sustained upon any other principle." This language might
readily be paraphrased and made to fit the case before us. It enun-
ciates the rule and draws the distinction here applicable. Moreover,
we have here a case not so much of ignorance of the law, either as
to existence or interpretation, as of conscious and purposeful repudiation of its authority. The plaintiff in error, committed by his obligation of office to its observance, has challenged the power of the
General Assembly to enact it, and has usurped the exclusive prerogative of the courts to adjudge its invalidity. This no man may
do with impunity.

It results that we find no error, and the judgment is affirmed.

UNITED STATES v. BERRIGAN

United States District Court for Maryland, 1968.
283 F.Supp. 336, convictions affirmed 417 F.2d 1002, 1009 (4th Cir. 1969),
certiorari denied 397 U.S. 909, 90 S.Ct. 907, 25 L.Ed.2d 90.

NORTHROP, District Judge. The defendants before this court
are charged in three counts that they did willfully

1. injure property of the United States;

2. mutilate records filed in a public office of the United
States; and

3. hinder the administration of the Military Selective Service Act.

Defendants wish to proffer an opening statement to the jury
as to what they would present for their defense. Specifically, they
contend that, by virtue of what they have read, heard, and seen, the
war in Vietnam is immoral and illegal; and that the United States,
in carrying on the war in Vietnam, is violating certain precepts of
international law, constitutional law, and judgments which were
handed down at Nurnberg.

To serve as a foundation and a basis for their beliefs, defendants wish to produce in court, among other evidence, "the outstanding experts" on international law who would testify that the acts of
the United States government in Vietnam are illegal. Their conduct,
they say, was prompted by their belief that the United States is acting illegally and was intended to prevent criminal acts from being
committed. Because this belief prompted their acts, they argue
that the necessary *mens rea* is lacking.

Initially, it must be pointed out that in law once the commission of a crime is established—the doing of a prohibited act with the
necessary intent—proof of a good motive will not save the accused
from conviction.   *   *   *   This point is best illustrated and highlighted by those cases where a defendant has been found guilty of

murder even though the motive advanced for justification was of the highest and most selfless level. For example, a man drowns his children because he loves them and wants to prevent their suffering in poverty; and a man poisons his wife, at her request, to end her agony from an incurable disease.

Counsel for defendants candidly admits that there is no precedent for the proposition advanced here, namely that any citizen is justified in mutilating and damaging government property and interfering with vital governmental functions—all acts specifically prohibited by penal statutes—if he reasonably believes that the government is acting illegally under international and possibly constitutional law.

*   *   *

That there is no legal precedent for defendants' proposition is not surprising. No civilized nation can endure where a citizen can select what law he would obey because of his moral or religious belief. It matters not how worthy his motives may be. It is axiomatic that chaos would exist if an individual were permitted to impose his beliefs upon others and invoke justification in a court to excuse his transgression of a duly-enacted law. *   *   *

[N]o matter how reasonably, sincerely, or deeply these defendants believed that the government was acting illegally does not go to the question whether they sincerely and honestly believed that *their* acts were lawful and thus negate the specific intent necessary for conviction, namely willfulness. Thus, the proposition presented here is to be distinguished from a case where a defendant believed that he was acting within the law, although subsequently it turns out that he was mistaken as to the applicable law.

In essence, the defendants are arguing not that they were legally justified in acting the way they chose to, or that they had a *bona fide* belief that they were legally justified, but that their lofty motives and sincerely-held convictions negate criminal intent.

*   *   *

Finally, counsel contends that these defendants should be allowed to present to the jury what is popularly known as the "Nurnberg Defense." The trial of the Nazi war criminals at Nurnberg was premised on the generally accepted view that there are, as a part of international law, certain crimes against peace and humanity which are punishable. The Nurnberg Trial, 6 F.R.D. 69 (1946). It is urged here that the belief of these defendants that the United States was waging a war of aggression, and thus committing a crime against peace, justified the acts charged.

It is not clear what standing these defendants have to raise the legality of this country's involvement in Vietnam when they have not been called to serve in the armed forces, are not directly affected by our government's actions in that country, and are not even directly affected by the Selective Service apparatus. As pointed out by Judge Charles E. Wyzanski in an article in the February 1968 issue of the Atlantic Monthly:

"As the Nuremberg verdicts show, merely to fight in an aggressive war is no crime. What is a crime is *personally* to fight by foul means." [Emphasis supplied.]

The important element in this defense, assuming its applicability in an American court, is the individual responsibility which is necessary before it can be raised. These defendants do not have standing to raise the validity of governmental actions, either under international law or constitutional law, on the grounds that the rights of parties not before this court are violated. * * *

But irrespective of the lack of standing of these defendants to raise the issue of the legality of the government's actions as they relate to the Vietnam situation, the proffered defense suffers from a more fundamental bar. It is clear that there are certain questions of substantive law, that is, "political questions", which are not cognizable in our courts because of the nature of our governmental system which is based upon a separation of functions among different branches of the government. * * *

The activities of these defendants were directed towards the Selective Service System, which system counsel has admitted is not criminal or illegal in and of itself. What is called into question here is the utilization of the armed forces by the executive and legislative branches. It cannot be disputed that the recognition of belligerency abroad, and the measures necessary to meet a crisis to preserve the peace and safety of this country, is uniquely an executive and a legislative responsibility. Whether the actions by the executive and the legislative branches in utilizing our armed forces are in accord with international law is a question which necessarily must be left to the elected representatives of the people and not to the judiciary. This is so even if the government's actions are contrary to valid treaties to which the government is a signatory. * * *

Counsel will govern themselves accordingly, and the court's instructions to the jury will reflect this decision if any transgression makes it necessary.

UNITED STATES v. MOYLAN

United States Court of Appeals, Fourth Circuit, 1969.
417 F.2d 1002, certiorari denied 397 U.S. 910, 90 S.Ct. 908, 25 L.Ed.2d 91.

SOBELOFF, Circuit Judge. The defendants [in United States v. Berrigan, supra] appeal their conviction in the United States District Court for the District of Maryland for violation of three federal statutes proscribing the mutilation of Government records, destruction of Government property and interference with the administration of the Selective Service System. The facts are uncontroverted. At 12:50 P.M. on May 17, 1968, the appellants entered the office of Local Board No. 33 in Catonsville, Maryland and removed approximately 378 I–A, I–Y and II–A files to an adjacent parking lot where they burned the files with homemade napalm. The appellants, men and women with sincere and strong commitments, readily admit the commission of these acts as a protest against the war in Vietnam.

The appeal is based on asserted error in the trial court's instructions to the jury. The appellants claim that: (1) The trial court erred in charging the jury on the definition of criminal intent and the meaning of "willfully," and (2) That the trial judge should have informed the jury that it had the power to acquit the defendants even if they were clearly guilty of the offenses, or at least that the court should have permitted their counsel so to argue to the jury.

I

For the appellants to be convicted of the crimes for which they were indicted, they must have acted knowingly (50 App.U.S.C. § 462 (a)) or willfully (18 U.S.C. §§ 1361, 2071(a)). The trial court instructed the jury to the effect that the willful intent requisite to constitute a violation of the statutes involved is the intent on the part of the accused to commit the proscribed acts with knowledge that they were violating the statute. Defense counsel urged upon the court a more expansive interpretation of the word "willful" as used in the statutes, namely that no violation occurred unless defendants performed the admitted acts with a bad purpose or motive. Their position was and is that since they acted from good motives, i. e., to protest a war which they sincerely believed was not only illegal but immoral, they could not have "willfully" violated the statutes and must be acquitted. We agree with the interpretation of the trial judge.

To read the term "willfully" to require a bad purpose would be to confuse the concept of intent with that of motive. The statutory requirement of willfulness is satisfied if the accused acted intentionally, with knowledge that he was breaching the statute. While the trial judge allowed evidence to be freely admitted concerning the defendants' motives, whatever motive may have led them to do the act is not relevant to the question of the violation of the statute, but is rather an element proper for the judge's consideration in sentencing.

*   *   *

II

Appellants' second contention is that the trial judge should have informed the jury, as requested, that it had the power to acquit even if appellants were clearly guilty of the charged offenses. They maintain that the judge should have told the jury this or permitted their counsel to argue it to the jury in the face of the judge's instruction on the law. Appellants reason that since the jury has "the power to bring in a verdict in the teeth of both law and facts," then the jury should be told that it has this power. Furthermore, the argument runs, the jury's power to acquit where the law may dictate otherwise is a fundamental necessity of a democratic system. Only in this way, it is said, can a man's actions be judged fairly by society speaking through the jury, or a law which is considered too harsh be mitigated.

In the early history of the American Colonies and for a time after the Revolution juries were nearly always recognized as having the power to judge both law and fact. * * *

In criminal cases juries remained the judges of both law and fact for approximately fifty years after the Revolution. However, the judges in America, just as in England after the Revolution of 1688, gradually asserted themselves increasingly through their instructions on the law.

We recognize, as appellants urge, the undisputed power of the jury to acquit, even if its verdict is contrary to the law as given by the judge and contrary to the evidence. This is a power that must exist as long as we adhere to the general verdict in criminal cases, for the courts cannot search the minds of the jurors to find the basis upon which they judge. If the jury feels that the law under which the defendant is accused is unjust, or that exigent circumstances justified the actions of the accused, or for any reason which appeals to their logic or passion, the jury has the power to acquit, and the courts must abide by that decision.

Concededly, this power of the jury is not always contrary to the interests of justice. For example, freedom of the press was immeasurably strengthened by the jury's acquittal of John Peter Zenger of seditious libel, a violation of which, under the law as it then existed and the facts, he was clearly guilty. In that case Andrew Hamilton was allowed to urge the jury, in the face of the judge's charge, "to see with their own eyes, to hear with their own ears, and to make use of their consciences and understanding in judging of the lives, liberties, or estates of their fellow subjects."

No less an authority than Dean Pound has expressed the opinion that "Jury lawlessness is the great corrective of law in its actual administration." However, this is not to say that the jury should be encouraged in their "lawlessness," and by clearly stating to the jury that they may disregard the law, telling them that they may decide according to their prejudices or consciences (for there is no check to insure that the judgment is based upon conscience rather than prejudice), we would indeed be negating the rule of law in favor of the rule of lawlessness. This should not be allowed.

* * *

III

As an undercurrent throughout the trial and interwoven with appellants' assertions of error is an appeal to morality as justification for their conduct. The argument consists of two closely related strands. They argue that the motivation for their action was moral in the sense that they intended to protest a war which is outrageous to their individual standards of humanity. Therefore, their actions are said to be not punishable regardless of the literal violation of a statute. Moreover, appellants argue that apart from their motivation, which is subjective, the war in Vietnam is in fact illegal and immoral and hence their acts in protest of this war were themselves moral acts for which they must be similarly immunized from punishment. In effect, the appellants focus upon the means by which an organized society treats those citizens who choose to commit an act of civil disobedience in the name of justice.

From the earliest times when man chose to guide his relations with fellow men by allegiance to the rule of law rather than force, he has been faced with the problem how best to deal with the individual in society who through moral conviction concluded that a law with which he was confronted was unjust and therefore must not be followed. Faced with the stark reality of injustice, men of sensitive conscience and great intellect have sometimes found only one morally justified path, and that path led them inevitably into conflict with established authority and its laws. Among philosophers and religionists throughout the ages there has been an incessant stream of discussion as to when, if at all civil disobedience, whether by passive refusal to obey a law or by its active breach, is morally justified. However, they have been in general agreement that while in restricted circumstances a morally motivated act contrary to law may be ethically justified, the action must be non-violent and the actor must accept the penalty for his action. In other words, it is commonly conceded that the exercise of a moral judgment based upon individual standards does not carry with it legal justification or immunity from punishment for breach of the law.

The defendants' motivation in the instant case—the fact that they engaged in a protest in the sincere belief that they were breaking the law in a good cause—cannot be acceptable legal defense or justification. Their sincerity is beyond question. It implies no disparagement of their idealism to say that society will not tolerate the means they choose to register their opposition to the war. If these defendants were to be absolved from guilt because of their moral certainty that the war in Vietnam is wrong, would not others who might commit breaches of the law to demonstrate their sincere belief that the country is not prosecuting the war vigorously enough be entitled to acquittal? Both must answer for their acts.

We are not called upon in this case to establish guidelines for determining in what extreme circumstances, if any, governmental acts may be resisted. We confine ourselves to this case and hold only that the law does not allow the seizure of public records and their mutilation or destruction, even when this is done as an act of conscience to dramatize the protest of a presumed evil. The acts of these appellants are not as extreme as some committed by other dissenters. Nevertheless, this publicly exploited action cannot be dismissed as *de minimis*. To encourage individuals to make their own determinations as to which laws they will obey and which they will permit themselves as a matter of conscience to disobey is to invite chaos. No legal system could long survive if it gave every individual the option of disregarding with impunity any law which by his personal standard was judged morally untenable. Toleration of such conduct would not be democratic as appellants claim, but inevitably anarchic.

The judgment below is

Affirmed.

NOTES

1. Should the substantive criminal law in the context of these (or similar) cases make any attempt to exempt some or any who commit the act because of a commitment to a moral value they hold above the obligation to obey the criminal law? If so, how should this be done? Should the state of mind requirement be modified so as to require something absent in such cases? How might such a requirement be formulated? Or would it be more appropriate to provide an affirmative defense?

2. If some provision is made for such exemptions, should it apply to the facts of the instant case? Consider also the following: The defendant was a physician and member of the armed forces. As chief of dermatology services at a military hospital, he was ordered to provide training for "special service aidmen," who would serve in the Vietnam war. He refused and is charged with disobeying the order. May he assert as a defense the argument that the aidmen would, while in Vietnam, commit acts in violation of international law? Cf. United States v. Levy, 39 Court Martial Reports 672 (1967). The "Nuremberg Defense" aspect of the case is discussed in 9 Harv.Inter.L.J. 169 (1968). For general discussions, see D'Amato, Gould, and Woods, War Crimes and Vietnam: The 'Nuremberg Defense' and the Military Service Register, 57 Cal.L.Rev. 1055 (1969); Ferencz, War Crimes Law and the Vietnam War, 17 Am.U.L.Rev. 403 (1968); Woetzel, Comment on the Nuremberg Principles and Conscientious Objection with Special Reference to War Crimes, 16 Cath.Law. 257 (1970).

3. If no such attempt to exempt such individuals should be made, should evidence of motive be admissible? Should counsel be permitted to argue to the jury that it should use its inherent power to acquit despite proof of guilt beyond a reasonable doubt? If such evidence is received or such argument permitted, why not instruct the jury concerning the matter? Could the jurors be told anything that would be helpful? What would this be?

---

(2) IGNORANCE OR MISTAKE REGARDING LAW OTHER THAN THAT PROHIBITING THE CRIMINAL ACT

MODEL PENAL CODE (TENT. DRAFT NO. 4, 1955)

Comment to § 2.02, p. 131.

[T]he general principle that ignorance or mistake of law is no excuse is usually greatly overstated; it has no application when the circumstances made material by the definition of the offense include a legal element. * * * The law involved is not the law defining the offense; it is some other legal rule that characterizes the attendant circumstances that are material to the offense.

RICHARDSON v. UNITED STATES

United States Court of Appeals for the District of Columbia, 1968.
131 U.S.App.D.C. 168, 403 F.2d 574.

EDGERTON, Senior Circuit Judge. Appellant was charged with robbery (count one), assault with a dangerous weapon (count two), and carrying a dangerous weapon (count three). A jury found him guilty as charged on count one, guilty of simple assault on count two and not guilty on count three.

The complaining witness Snowden testified that appellant and another held him up at gunpoint and took $98 from his wallet. Appellant testified that Snowden, who had recently been convicted of a gambling offense, owed him a $270 gambling debt which he had several times unsuccessfully tried to collect. He admitted reaching into Snowden's wallet and removing $138 without his consent, but denied having a gun. His mother corroborated his story of the gambling debt and testified that Snowden was a known gambler.

The chief ground of this appeal is the trial court's denial of appellant's request for the following standard instruction:

Evidence has been introduced that the defendant believed that he had a right to take the property he is alleged to have stolen.

If a person takes the property of another, but does so in the good faith belief that he has a right to take the property, the specific intent essential to the crime of robbery is lacking.

The Government must prove beyond a reasonable doubt that the defendant acted with the specific intent to steal. If you have a reasonable doubt whether or not the defendant acted with a specific intent to steal, you must find him not guilty.

I.

A defendant is not guilty of robbery unless he has a specific intent to take the property of another. Jackson v. United States, 121 U.S. App.D.C. 160, 348 F.2d 772 (1965). Viewing the evidence most favorably to the defendant, as we must where he appeals from the denial of a favorable instruction, he believed in good faith that he was entitled to the money. If so, he did not have that specific intent. We therefore find that the requested instruction should have been given.[2]

The government's position seems to be that no instruction on a claim of right is necessary unless the defendant had a legally enforceable right to the property he took. But specific intent depends upon a state of mind, not upon a legal fact. If the jury finds that the defendant believed himself entitled to the money, it cannot properly find that he had the requisite specific intent for robbery. * * *

The government urges affirmance for policy reasons, claiming that a reversal of this robbery conviction would encourage violent takings and would frustrate the policy of the law that a successful gambler may not recover his winnings from the loser. But "The taking and carrying away of the property of another in the District of Columbia without right to do so" is a misdemeanor. D.C.Code (1967 ed.) § 22–1211. Since this section can be violated without specific intent, it provides a deterrent to self-help by a winning gambler without rejecting the principle that specific intent turns on the actor's state of mind and not upon an objective fact.

*   *   *

Reversed.

NOTES

1. What was the subject matter of the mistake which would entitle Richardson to acquittal if believed by the jury? Was it the law defining robbery in the District of Columbia? Was it the property law of the District of Columbia defining rights in the property of debtors and the procedures for enforcing those rights? Is the answer crucial? If so, why should it be?

2. Accord: State v. Steele, 150 Wash. 466, 273 P. 742 (1929). The majority rule in cases involving a forceful taking of money under color of a liquidated debt is that the requisite specific intent for robbery is lacking.

2.   The court in the instant case rejected the following argument made by the appellee:

> There is no law in this jurisdiction on whether claim of right can be a defense to robbery.[4] We submit on policy grounds that such a defense should not apply to these facts while recognizing that the rejection thereof must be consistent with the requirement that the "commission of the crime of robbery requires the specific intent to deprive the victim of * * * [his] property." Jackson v. United States, 121 U.S.App.D.C. 160, 161, 348 F.2d 772, 773 (1965).

> Cases on claim of right as a defense to robbery involve three general types of situations: (1) where a defendant has a liquidated, legally enforceable claim against a complainant; (2) where he has a legal claim but for an unliquidated amount; and (3) where as a loser at gambling he retakes his losses from a winner or as a winner he takes his winnings from a loser. In the first type, where the forceful taking is under color of a liquidated, legally enforceable claim, most courts hold that there is no robbery on the theory that the requisite intent to steal is lacking. E. g., People v. Gallegos, 130 Colo. 232, 274 P.2d 608 (1954); Butts v. Commonwealth, 145 Va. 800, 133 S.E. 764 (1926);[5] People v. Butler, 55 Cal.Rptr. 511, 421 P.2d 703 (S.Ct.1967). There is, however, law to the contrary. Moyers v. State, 186 Ga. 446, 197 S.E. 846 (1938). Frazier v. State, 342 S.W.2d 115 (Tex.Cr.App.1961). See Gettinger v. State, 13 Neb. 308, 14 N.W. 403 (1882) (claim of right no defense in larceny prosecution). In *Moyers*, where there was a forceful taking without consent to satisfy a liquidated claim for services rendered, the court equated with the specific intent to steal the intent to convert to the use of the taker property to which the taker in fact had no title or right of possession. 197 S.E. at 848–49.

> In contrast to the majority rule for liquidated claims, the cases do not allow a claim of right defense for an unliquidated claim. State v. Austin, 60 Wash.2d 227, 373 P.2d 137 (1962). Thomas v. State, 165 Miss. 897, 148 So. 225 (1933). Henderson v. State, 149 Tex.Cr. 167, 192 S.W.2d 446 (1946).[7] Tipton v. State, 23 Okla.Cr. 86, 212 Pac. 612 (1912). The rationale in these cases is that it violates public policy to allow a defendant to bypass the courts and determine for himself the value of a claim which may not even be valid.

4.   In Mills v. United States, 97 U.S.App. D.C. 131, 228 F.2d 645 (1955), a prosecution for housebreaking and larceny, this Court held that the jury should have been instructed that if defendant took the property with the consent of the person he believed to be its owner, there was no intent to steal it. Here, however, the taking was by force and against the will of the owner, not with a consent real or imagined, and the claim upon which the taking was predicated was legally unenforceable.

5.   In both *Gallegos* and *Butts*, the defendant held up his employer for wages claimed in good faith to be due. In neither case was there a prosecution claim that the amount taken was not in fact due.

7.   In *Henderson*, for example, A and B, each driving a car, had a collision. After a short interval B returned to the scene of the accident, demanded $15 damages from A and then took $5 from him by force.

Our research has located only one case corresponding to the fact situation at bar, that is, where the winner at gambling forcefully extracts his winnings from the loser. State v. Steele, 150 Wash. 466, 273 Pac. 742 (1929). The lower court had denied a defense request for an instruction that if the property involved was taken under an honest belief of entitlement, however ill-founded that belief was, the requisite intent for robbery was absent. The Supreme Court ruled the instruction should have been given. That the wager may have been won by dishonest means did not matter, the court said, because if the defendants nonetheless entertained a good faith belief of entitlement, there was no intent to steal.

Where the loser retakes his losses, the cases are divided. In Texas if losses incurred in a fair gambling transaction are voluntarily surrendered, the loser retaking by force is guilty of robbery even though he believes he is entitled to retake. Murphy v. State, 133 Tex.Cr. 504, 109 S.W.2d 488 (1937). Blair v. State, 34 Tex. Cr. 488, 31 S.W. 368 (1895). This criminal doctrine is in the context of a civil rule which leaves the parties in *status quo*—the winner cannot recover his winnings nor can the loser recover his losses voluntarily surrendered.[8] See Coker v. State, 71 Tex.Cr. 504, 160 S.W. 366 (1913). Other states permit the claim of right defense. People v. Rosen, 11 Cal.2d 147, 78 P.2d 727 (1938). People v. Hughes, 11 Utah 100, 39 Pac. 492 (1895). State v. Hardin, 96 Ariz. 56, 406 P.2d 406 (1965) (dictum). In *Rosen*, the leading authority for this position, defendant lost more than $1,000 at "Tango", an illegal gambling game, over several months. On the night of the offense he took $198 back at gunpoint. In California, as in Texas, the civil law left the parties to such a game in *status quo*. The court held that defendant's evidence that he was acting under a good faith belief of entitlement should have been admitted and the defense request for a claim of right instruction should have been granted. If illegal gambling losses were sought to be recaptured the court felt there could be no intent to steal because "the law recognizes no title or right to possession in the winner." 78 P.2d at 728. Of course in the case at bar there was no defect, at least as to appellant, Snowden's ownership or right to possession in the money taken. The dissenting opinion in *Rosen* discerned an adverse social effect in the majority ruling—"The recognition by law of the policy contended for would have the direct effect of menacing life by encouraging violence and breaches of the peace." 78 P.2d at 730.

In our view, a rule that the forceful taking of what is clearly another person's property because the assailant had a belief mistaken as a matter of law that he had a right to it not only would serve to offer encouragement to violence and thus endanger life but would also frustrate the clear policy of the civil law of this jurisdiction that a gambler cannot recover his winnings from the loser. Where the claim is barred by law, more is involved than the

8. In this jurisdiction the rule is all in favor of the loser—he can recover his losses voluntarily surrendered, by suit. 16 D.C.Code § 1702.

policy also applicable here that disputes should be settled in court, not by force.[9] A good faith, although mistaken, belief of a right to property as a defense to robbery could not easily be limited to a case with some sympathetic defense appeal where a gambler has "welched" on a bet. Suppose A agreed to pay B $10,000 if B turned over to A evidence of a sordid incident in A's past life. After B did so A refused to pay. Believing he is entitled to the $10,000, B extracts it from A at gunpoint. In our view, it is absurd to say that because of this belief in the validity of an illegal contract (as is the gambling contract at bar), B is not guilty of robbery. Or suppose A, a poor man, really believes he is entitled to take money by force from B, a rich man, because of his need and the disparity in their economic positions. As a practical matter, we submit, the law cannot tolerate such a defense, and neither should it permit the same defense in the case at bar.

Finally, the rejection of a claim of right defense on these facts does not result in appellant being convicted of robbery where he does not have the requisite specific intent to deprive the victim permanently of his property. Obviously there is evidence from which the jury could have concluded that appellant intended to deprive Snowden permanently of the sum of money taken. And in fact that money was property in Snowden's possession [10] in which he had good title and the right to possession, at least as against appellant, and against which appellant had no enforceable claim. See Moyers v. State, supra.

Brief for Appellee at 7–10, Richardson v. United States, 131 U.S.App.D.C. 168, 403 F.2d 574 (1968).

9. In a discussion rejecting claim of right to collect on a debt as a defense to robbery, the following appears in 135 Am.St.Reps. at 487:
"But assuming * * * [the creditor took only the amount to which he was entitled], an accord with the principle that such was his right would land us just a couple of thousand years back. There would be no longer need for courts of justice. Every creditor would carry his court of appeal in his hip pocket! And if the demand of one's debt is not robbery, what is it? * * * A man has a sum of money on his person, and is stopped by two or more of his creditors, each of whom levels a revolver at him and demands payment of his claim. If he hasn't enough for all, it would be as perfectly consistent to charge him with giving a fraudulent preference to the one who first took his money vi et armis as to say that such taking is not robbery."

10. Levin v. United States, 119 U.S. App.D.C. 156, 338 F.2d 265 (1965), defines larceny as an offense against possession.

UNITED STATES v. FREED

Supreme Court of the United States, 1971.
401 U.S. 601, 91 S.Ct. 1112, 28 L.Ed.2d 356.

[Mr. Justice DOUGLAS' opinion for the Court appears on page 492, supra.]

Mr. Justice BRENNAN, concurring in the judgment of reversal.

* * *

[A]lthough I reach the same result as the Court on the intent the Government must prove to convict, I do so by another route.

* * *

In regard to the first two elements of the offense, (1) possession of items that (2) are hand grenades, the general rule in favor of some intent requirement finds confirmation in the case law under the provisions replaced by the present amendments. Those cases held that a conviction of an individual for illegal possession of unregistered firearms had to be supported by proof that his possession was "willing and conscious" and that he knew the items possessed were firearms. E. g., Sipes v. United States, 321 F.2d 174, 179 (C.A.8 1963); United States v. Decker, 292 F.2d 89 (C.A.6 1961). Congress did not disapprove these cases, and we may therefore properly infer that Congress meant that the Government must prove knowledge with regard to the first two elements of the offense under the amended statute.

The third element—the unregistered status of the grenades—presents more difficulty. Proof of intent with regard to this element would require the Government to show that the appellees knew that the grenades were unregistered or negligently or recklessly failed to ascertain whether the weapons were registered. It is true that such a requirement would involve knowledge of law, but it does *not* involve "consciousness of wrongdoing" in the sense of knowledge that one's actions were prohibited or illegal. Rather, the definition of the crime, as written by Congress, requires proof of circumstances which involve a legal element, namely whether the grenades were registered in accordance with federal law. The knowledge involved is solely knowledge of the circumstances which the law has defined as material to the offense. * * *

Therefore, as with the first two elements, the question is solely one of congressional intent. And while the question is not an easy one, two factors persuade me that proof of *mens rea* as to the unregistered status of the grenades is not required. First, as the Court notes, the case law under the provisions replaced by the current law dispensed with proof of intent in connection with this element. Sipes v. United States, supra. Second, the firearms covered by the Act are major weapons such as machineguns and sawed-off shotguns; deceptive weapons such as flashlight guns and fountain pen guns; and major destructive devices such as bombs, grenades, mines, rockets, and large calibre weapons including mortars, anti-tank guns, and bazookas. Without exception, the likelihood of governmental regulation of the distribution of such weapons is so great that anyone must be presumed to be aware of it. In the context of a taxing and registration scheme, I therefore think it reasonable to conclude that Congress dispensed with the requirement of intent in regard to the unregistered status of the weapon, as necessary to effective administration of the statute.

NOTES

1. Does *Freed* present an issue of "mistake of fact," "mistake of law," or "strict liability"? Are these categories mutually exclusive? Should they be? Are Justices Douglas and Brennan agreed on the formulation of the issue? If not, which is correct? Does it make any difference?

2. Mr. Justice Brennan states that "Proof of intent with regard to the third element—the unregistered status of the grenades would require the government to show that the appellees knew that the grenades were unregistered or negligently or recklessly failed to ascertain whether the weapons were registered. It is true that such a requirement would involve knowledge of law * * *" Is this necessarily true? Why? Could there ever be a case in which the defendant was aware of a sufficient risk that the firearms were not registered to make conviction appropriate, but was unaware of a registration requirement in the federal statutory law?

3. Mr. Justice Brennan further suggests that if "knowledge of the law" were required, this would not involve "'consciousness of wrongdoing' in the sense of knowledge that one's actions were prohibited or illegal." Is this accurate? If so, is it of any significance? Could one have this "knowledge of the law" without awareness of the substance of the National Firearms Act? How likely is it that one could have this knowledge of the law yet still be unaware that the actions were prohibited by the National Firearms Act? Of what, if any, significance is the answer to this question?

STATE v. McDERMOTT

Circuit Court of Connecticut, Appellate Division, 1965.
3 Conn.Cir. 524, 220 A.2d 38.

DEARINGTON, Judge. The defendant was convicted on a charge of trespassing in violation of § 53–103 of the General Statutes [1] and has appealed. * * *

The following facts were found: On March 22, 1965, the defendant was a union representative of International Union of District 50, Unit-

---

1. "Sec. 53–103. Trespass. Any person who, without right, enters or remains upon the premises of another after having been forbidden to do so by the owner of such premises or his authorized agent, either directly or by clear and legible signs posted thereon, shall be fined not more than fifty dollars."

ed Mine Workers of America, Local 14977. This local had entered into a contract with the Robertson Paper Box Company of Montville on behalf of certain employees of the company. The contract covered labor-management relations and was in effect on the day in question. It was the defendant's duty to see to it that the employees obtained their rights under the contract. On the day in question, the defendant arranged with O'Neill, personnel manager of Robertson, to confer with Burdick, a shop steward, in the personnel office. At this meeting the defendant learned that company representatives were in the process of conducting a discussion with certain employees concerning union activities. A preliminary discussion was to be held in an office located in the production area. Without permission, the defendant left the personnel office and proceeded to the production area. Arriving there, he was told that the employees would be represented by Dolzenchuk, the union president. The defendant was then told to leave by Lockwood, a company foreman, and later by O'Neill. The defendant refused to leave, asserting he had a right to be present in the absence of Dolzenchuk. Dolzenchuk was late for work and arrived some twenty minutes later, at which time the defendant left the production area.

The court reached the following conclusions: (1) The contract did not give the defendant the right to remain in the production area. (2) The defendant did not obtain such a right by virtue of § 31–105(7) of the General Statutes. (3) The defendant did remain in the production area "without right" in violation of § 53–103 of the General Statutes.

*   *   *

*   *   *   [T]he defendant contends that the words "without right" appearing in § 53–103 of the General Statutes must be equated with knowledge that the defendant intentionally committed the act the commission of which resulted in a violation of the law. In this respect he argues that if he believed he had a lawful right to be where he was such belief negates guilt, that is, an honest mistake of law excuses him from the consequences of his act. It is not claimed that the defendant did not intentionally commit the act. He was requested to leave, and he chose to remain on the ground that he had the lawful right to do so. We first consider the question of the defendant's belief that his act was not of an unlawful nature. "It is a rule which is deep in our law, that ignorance of the law or mistake as to its meaning is no excuse and is not ordinarily a defense to a criminal prosecution." 22 C.J.S. Criminal Law § 48, p. 183. This rule applies whether the offense is malum prohibitum or malum in se. Blumenthal v. United States, 8 Cir., 88 F.2d 522. "If a man intentionally adopts certain conduct in certain circumstances known to him, and that conduct is forbidden by the law under those circumstances, he intentionally breaks the law in the only sense in which the law ever considers intent." Ellis v. United States, 206 U.S. 246, 257, 27 S.Ct. 600, 602,

51 L.Ed. 1047. The defendant also contends that the state failed to prove a specific intent to commit the crime. Whether proof of scienter is essential, as claimed by the defendant, is a matter of legislative intent. State v. Sul, 146 Conn. 78, 86, 147 A.2d 686. In State v. Turner, 60 Conn. 222, 22 A. 542, the defendant was charged with violating § 1454 of the Revision of 1888 in that he entered upon land of another without permission for the purpose of fishing. On appeal, he contended that he had no criminal intent to violate the law and that without such an intent he could not be found guilty. The court construed the statute (p. 229) as imposing a penalty when the thing forbidden was done, no matter how innocently. While the defendant in the instant case is charged under a different statute, we think the analogy as it relates to intent is the same. The difference between the two statutes arises from the words "without right" which appear in the statute under review (§ 53–103). While under the provisions of § 1454 (as amended, § 53–108) permission to go upon the property of another could only be derived through the owner, the legislature in § 53–103 extended such permission to include any right of entry, whether derived from the owner or otherwise. But if such a right is not shown, the prohibition has been transgressed, and this is so irrespective of intent. The defendant's assignment of error in respect to the foregoing contentions is without foundation.

We have examined the entire record and are satisfied that the trial court's conclusions were conclusions which could be reached legally and logically and that there was adequate evidence to prove the defendant guilty as charged.

There is no error.

---

(3) Ignorance or Mistake of Law Based Upon Advice of Counsel

UNITED STATES v. PAINTER

United States Court of Appeals for the Fourth Circuit, 1963.
314 F.2d 939, certiorari denied 374 U.S. 831, 83 S.Ct. 1873, 10 L.Ed.2d 1054.

SOBELOFF, Chief Judge. After a trial extending over six days a jury in the United States District Court for the Southern District of West Virginia found Finley McAdoo Painter guilty on a five-count indictment charging use of the mails, and of radio and television in interstate commerce, with intent to defraud. 18 U.S.C.A. §§ 1341, 1343. The main contention made on this appeal is that the evidence was not sufficient to warrant the jury's finding that he had devised a scheme to defraud, and that therefore the District Court should have directed a judgment of acquittal in accordance with the defendant's motion. Our reading of the record compels us to hold that the conviction must stand.

A recital of the proof adduced by the Government necessarily begins with October 9, 1959, when Painter launched an extensive advertising campaign to encourage the general public to invest in a real estate project. Nine days later he organized and became sole owner of a company chartered as the Credit Discount Corporation. Prospective investors were told that Credit Discount owned a valuable 140-acre parcel of land known as the Peck Farm, situated adjacent to Huntington, West Virginia, and that this property was to be subdivided, developed, and improved by housing construction. It was represented that the company would pay eight to twelve per cent interest on all loans of $1000 or more "plus the return of entire principal in 12 months" and that such investments would be "fully secured by 12-month corporate notes." The advertisements further proclaimed that Credit Discount held "numerous properties over the city" and that it "had more than double the amount of assets to take care of these notes."

For more than a year Painter persisted in relaying to the public by mail, radio, television, and personal interview his promises of quick profits. That success of the promotional campaign depended upon interstate communications is undisputed. The messages apparently bore fruit, for it is conceded that about a dozen persons relied thereon and invested a total of $24,000. And yet it is a striking fact that Credit Discount never took title to the Peck Farm or refunded, with but one exception, any portion of the principal sum to the investors.

The record discloses that the Peck Farm was not acquired until December 14, 1959, when it was conveyed for the first time not to Credit Discount, but to State Motor Sales, Inc., another company also controlled by Painter as sole shareholder. On February 17, 1960, he and his wife incorporated a third entity and named it the Credit Realty Corporation. Shortly thereafter State Motor Sales transferred the Peck Farm to the new company. After holding this property for less than four months, Credit Realty reconveyed it to State Motor Sales on July 18. Later still, the Peck Farm was transferred back to Credit Realty, but not once did it pass to Credit Discount, which purportedly held the real estate as security for the "fully secured" corporate notes issued to investors. The debtor, Credit Discount, remained wholly without assets during the entire period, except for a brief interlude when it was in possession of two other properties of relatively inconsequential value.

As the Peck Farm, the very keystone of the financial structure, shuttled back and forth between interlocking corporations at his personal whim, Painter continued to assure his investors that it was Credit Discount's primary asset. The confusion created by the deceptive similarity of the two corporate names, Credit Discount and Credit Realty, was compounded by joining both corporations in the same advertising.   According to Philip R. Reeder, office manager for Credit Discount, this strategy was intended to cause the public to associate the corporations as one, rather than to distinguish between them as separate entities.

Meanwhile, barren of assets and thus insulated from potential claims of its creditors, Credit Discount was being steadily drained by Painter of its investment funds as they were received.   This callous abuse of his position of trust was nowhere better portrayed than in Reeder's testimony.   He swore that Painter instructed him to divert the Credit Discount money into the bank account of State Motor Sales, then in serious financial difficulty.   He testified explicitly that Painter avowed to him that the purpose of these transfers was to make certain that these funds would be beyond the reach of the investors when their notes matured.   Checks were drawn on Credit Discount's account to cover overdrafts of State Motor Sales to purchase a pair of airplanes, to make political contributions, and for other uses known only to Painter and unrelated to the purpose for which persons had been led to advance their money.   Whether they were technically "investors" or, as they were sometimes called, "lenders," is immaterial. Additional witnesses substantially corroborated Reeder and certified copies of cancelled checks were introduced as government exhibits. While the Government was unable at trial to trace each and every defalcation,[5] there is significance in Painter's inability to offer to his investors any explanation of the ultimate disposition of their money when his financial empire finally collapsed in December, 1960.   Judgment was entered against the now insolvent State Motor Sales in the sum of $71,000 on a lis pendens earlier filed by a creditor bank, thereby choking off what remained of the investment funds and freezing all assets, including the Peck Farm.   Needless to say, Credit Discount was without funds to satisfy its investors' claims.   The Peck Farm remained undeveloped.

In the circumstances here disclosed, we cannot escape the conclusion that there was "substantial evidence which, taken in the light most favorable to the United States, tends to show that the defendant is guilty beyond a reasonable doubt."   Bell v. United States, 185 F.2d 302, 310 (4th Cir., 1950).   From a series of transactions the court preliminarily, and later the jury, could properly infer that Painter had devised a scheme for a major campaign of deceit through the mails, radio, and television to obtain funds on the strength of false assurances as to Credit Discount's financial strength, and then to divert the proceeds to his personal use.   The deliberately false statements and sub-

5.   Conversion of money to the defendant's private use was not an essential element to be proved by the Government, United States v. Bagdasian, 291 F.2d 163, 164 (4th Cir., 1961), although evidence of such misappropriation is clearly relevant and admissible.   United States v. Crosby, 294 F.2d 928, 947 (2d Cir., 1961).

sequent conversion of funds by one who had assumed a fiduciary position constituted a patent fraud on the investors whom he had solicited.

Painter argues that he did exactly as promised, making interest payments on the loans until the filing of lis pendens interrupted his plan to go through with the real estate project. The suggestion apparently is that the defendant actually believed that the enterprise would ultimately show a profit and that if he had been permitted to go on he would have performed his promises to repay the principal in full within twelve months. The clear answer is that no amount of honest belief that his corporate enterprise would eventually succeed can excuse the willful misrepresentations by which the investors' funds were obtained. An investor may be defrauded if his reliance is induced by deliberately false statements of fact, and the defendant's optimism as to the future is no defense. Moreover, the scheme to defraud may consist of suggestions and promises as to the future, not made in good faith but with deceptive intent. The testimony here was such that either or both forms of fraud could be found.

*   *   *

The final point raised by the appellant requires only brief exploration. He claims that he was guided in part by legal counsel. On this record we cannot accord finality to his answer that in pursuing the actions under inquiry he had obtained a legal opinion. In judging whether the defendant's behavior was honest or corrupt, this is a circumstance the jury was entitled to weigh and consider as part of the entire context of the case. If in good faith reliance upon legal advice given him by a lawyer to whom he has made full disclosure of the facts, one engages in a course of conduct later found to be illegal, the trier of fact may in appropriate circumstances conclude that the conduct was innocent because "the guilty mind" was absent. * * * But consultation with lawyer confers no automatic immunity from the legal consequences of conscious fraud. * * *

The crucial question here is the defendant's state of mind in issuing the interstate communications. The question being one for the jury and having been appropriately submitted, the conviction stands upon solid ground.

Affirmed.

NOTES

1. Given the facts of the case and the statute under which the defendant was prosecuted, could a jury have concluded that because of consultation with counsel the defendant lacked a "guilty mind"? If so, what would the consultation have to have involved?

2. Consider the following portion of a charge to the jury by Chief Judge Wyzanski in the trial of a prosecution for using the mails to defraud:

> I must now deal with a particular problem in connection with intent, and that has to do with a defendant or other person who

acts upon the advice of counsel. Now if an individual having at his command all the relevant facts before taking any action places all the relevant facts before a competent attorney whom he believes to act in good faith and asks that attorney his opinion, and that attorney having considered all the relevant facts, and speaking in advance of any action taken, indicates that the conduct is lawful, under such circumstances you cannot find that the client has knowingly, intentionally violated the law, if he acts in accordance with expert counsel, chosen in a disinterested and honest way, and acting, so far as the client knows, in a disinterested and honest way.

Now it may happen that the client consults his lawyer mid-way in the course of his action. If he consults him mid-way, anything which is done pursuant to the advice of counsel after the consultation also is conduct as to which one cannot say that the client has acted in a fraudulent or dishonest or knowingly and intentionally unlawful way. But, of course, everything depends on whether there has been placed before the lawyer everything which is relevant and whether the lawyer has been selected in an honest and disinterested way, and whether, so far as the client knows, the lawyer has acted in an honest and disinterested way.

You do not as a client get an immunity bath by going around and talking to a lawyer. You have to tell the lawyer everything you know that is relevant. You have to have selected your lawyer honestly and, so far as you know, the lawyer has to be acting honestly, and the opinion he gives you will protect you with respect to what you do afterwards. He isn't a Court giving a judgment with respect to what you did before. He can't give you a retroactive bath of immunity.

And in this situation you the jury are entitled to take into account in connection with the defendants the degree to which they did or did not lay their knowledge before a lawyer in advance of some or all of their conduct, and the degree to which they made a selection with integrity, and the degree to which they had a right to assume that the lawyer was acting with integrity.

I am sure that you will have in mind, without my specifically calling it to your attention, that the New Hampshire defendants had as their counsel, at least at some stages of this matter, Mr. Connor, and you will bear in mind what the testimony was with respect to what was laid before Mr. Connor and what opinions he gave.

I think it only fair for me to point out to you that Mr. Connor for a considerable period of time had been representing the New Hampshire defendants with respect to litigation, and that he had represented them in the New Hampshire State Courts, and he undoubtedly had been giving advice of some kind to the defendants for a very long period of time.

We also know that in October of 1965, if not earlier, and it is up to you, he, as he said, took into account the Federal Trade Commission Order, Exhibit 32-A, and he took into account the State Court proceedings, and he took into account certain State Lottery and other Statutes. It does not appear from what he said, if I remember correctly, but you can correct my memory, you are not bound by what I remember of the evidence, if I remember correctly he did not take into account the statute, 18 United States Code, Section 1341, the Mail Fraud Statute under which this Indictment in this case has been laid.

United States v. Interstate Engineering Corp., 288 F.Supp. 402 (D.N.H. 1967).

3. Does permitting use of advice of counsel only as a means of "disproving" the existence of the state of mind required for guilt adequately do the job? Should there be an "affirmative defense" of advice of counsel? If so, what should be its scope?

LONG v. STATE

Supreme Court of Delaware, 1949.
65 A.2d 489.

PEARSON, Judge, delivering the opinion of the court:

The defendant Long was married to his first wife in Wilmington, and resided there with her for thirty years prior to their separation in October 1945. On September 21, 1946, he went to Arkansas. He had been pensioned from the police force, and had been in bad health for a number of years. He testified that he went to Arkansas on account of his health because he "thought it would be a better climate"; also that he went there to obtain a divorce; and that he intended "to leave Delaware permanently and take up a permanent domicile in Arkansas". His health improved there. He returned to Wilmington for a few days in November "for business reasons" and spent the Christmas holidays in Wilmington. On December 3, he renewed his Delaware automobile registration for six months ending June 30, 1947. He remained in Arkansas for the statutory period of residence required for divorce in that state, and instituted divorce proceedings against his wife in the Chancery Court of Garland County. On January 7, 1947, that court entered a decree of absolute divorce. The decree recites publication of a notice and the mailing of a registered letter with a copy of the complaint to defendant's wife, a nonresident of Arkansas. She did not appear in the proceeding. She testified before the lower court here that she was not "served with any divorce papers" and did not receive any mail or a registered letter from Arkansas. On the same day the divorce decree was granted, defendant left Arkansas and returned to Wilmington where he has since resided. While in Wilmington during the Christmas holidays of 1946, he had been offered a job in a hospital there. He accepted this job after the divorce decree was granted and began work on January 13, 1947. On January 25, he was married to a second wife in Wilmington. This marriage was the subject of the bigamy prosecution under Rev.Code of Del. Sec. 5254.

*　　*　　*

* * * [E]rror is assigned for the refusal of the lower court to receive evidence relating to adultery of defendant's first wife, and relating to defendant's mistake in applying law to the facts with respect to the validity of the Arkansas divorce. In his brief, defendant makes the following statement of facts in this connection:

"Prior to the defendant's decision to go to Arkansas he discussed the question of securing a divorce with a Delaware attorney (not his present attorney). Shortly prior to that time he had been advised by certain men, * * * that they had lived in adultery with defendant's wife. The evidence would have borne out these facts and shown with specificity by the men themselves that they had registered at certain Wilmington hotels and the names under which they had registered and that sexual relations were had. These facts were known to the Delaware attorney. In his discussion with the Delaware attorney he stated he was 'fed up with Wilmington' and that his health had been bad and that he wanted to get away. He also stated, upon being advised that he could get a divorce in Delaware, that he did not want to further embarrass his children by getting a divorce on the ground of adultery, especially since a number of them had just come out of the service and were attempting to make their way in Wilmington.

"He was advised by the Delaware attorney to go to Arkansas for the divorce and that it would be 'just as good as if obtained in Delaware.' He was advised and knew that he could secure a divorce in Delaware for approximately one-tenth of the total cost in Arkansas. * * *

"* * * After he had returned from Arkansas he decided to remarry, which marriage is the basis for the present prosecution. Before deciding on marriage, he went to the same Delaware attorney and inquired whether he was free to remarry and whether the divorce was good in view of the fact that he had returned to Delaware and changed his intention of living in Arkansas for an indefinite period of time. He was advised that the divorce was good and that he was free to remarry. He then made arrangements with the Reverend Harris for the marriage. Reverend Harris, due to hearsay statements he had read in the newspapers, was suspicious of the validity of the divorce in Arkansas. The Reverend Harris decided, after conferring with the defendant, to visit the Delaware attorney himself and, upon doing so, was advised that the divorce was good and the defendant was free to remarry.

"The defendant conferred a final time with his attorney before applying for a marriage application and defendant's Delaware counsel appeared with him and signed his second marriage application as guarantor in the Office of the Clerk of the Peace for New Castle County. He also offered evidence to the Clerk of the Peace that he was legally divorced and free to remarry."

*   *   *

The evidence of defendant's consulting an attorney and following his advice was refused on * * * [the ground] that defendant's mistake was one of law, and is a case "to which the maxim 'ignorantia juris non excusat' applies." * * *

We turn now to the ground that this is a case to which the ignorance of law maxim applies. In many crimes involving a *specific* criminal intent, an honest mistake of law constitutes a defense if it negatives the specific intent. State v. Pullen, 3 Pennewill, 184, 50 A. 538 (larceny); State v. Collins, 1 Marv. 536, 41 A. 144 (embezzlement); see also Perkins: Ignorance and Mistake in Criminal Law, 88 Univ. of Pa.Law Rev. 35, 45, 46. As to crimes not involving a specific intent, an honest mistake of law is usually, though not invariably, held not to excuse conduct otherwise criminal. (Perkins article, pp. 41–45 and cases cited.) A mistake of law, where not a defense, may nevertheless negative a general criminal intent as effectively as would an exculpatory mistake of fact. Thus, mistake of law is disallowed as a defense in spite of the fact that it may show an absence of the criminal mind. The reasons for disallowing it are practical considerations dictated by deterrent effects upon the administration and enforcement of the criminal law, which are deemed likely to result if it were allowed as a general defense. As stated in the Perkins article, supra, p. 41: " * * * But if such ignorance were available as a defense in every criminal case, this would be a constant source of confusion to juries, and it would tend to encourage ignorance at a point where it is peculiarly important to the state that knowledge should be as widespread as is reasonably possible. In the language of one of the giants of the profession, this is a point at which 'justice to the individual is rightly outweighed by the larger interests on the other side of the scales.' " Quoting from Holmes: The Common Law, p. 48.

Similar considerations are involved when we disallow ignorance or mistake of law as a defense to a defendant who engages in criminal conduct (even though not obviously immoral or anti-social) where his ignorance or mistake consists merely in (1) unawareness that such conduct is or might be within the ambit of any crime; or (2) although aware of the existence of criminal law relating to the subject of such conduct, or to some of its aspects, the defendant erroneously concludes (in good faith) that his particular conduct is for some reason not subject to the operation of any criminal law. But it seems to us significantly different to disallow mistake of law where (3) together with the circumstances of the second classification, it appears that before engaging in the conduct, the defendant made a bona fide, diligent effort, adopting a course and resorting to sources and means at least as appropriate as any afforded under our legal system, to ascertain and abide by the law, and where he acted in good faith reliance upon the results of such effort. It is inherent in the way our legal system functions that the criminal law consequences of any particular contemplated conduct cannot be determined in advance with certainty. Not until after the event, by final court decision, may the consequences be definitely ascertained. Prior to the event, the ultimate that can be ascertained about the legal consequences consists of predictions of varying degrees of probability of eventuation. Hence, in the sense in which we are concerned with the expression, a "mistake of law" of the second or third classification refers to the failure of predictions of legal consequences to come to pass. No matter how logical, plausible and persuasive may be the bases for a prediction (assumptions, abstract legal rules, reasoning, etc.,) a mistake of law arises if the prediction does not eventuate; and there is no mistake of law if the prediction eventuates.

With these thoughts in mind, let us examine how the considerations which justify the rejection of a mistake of the first and second classifications operate with respect to a mistake of the third classification. The objection of tending to "encourage ignorance" of the law would hardly seem applicable. The very conditions of the third classification include a diligent effort, in good faith, by means as appropriate as any available under our legal system, to acquire knowledge of the relevant law. The objection of difficulties of proof, including facilitation of subterfuge, is applicable, if at all, in a far less degree than in the case of mistakes of the first and second classifications. For them, the facts are essentially confined to the defendant's subjective state of mind. The conditions of the third classification are not so limited. They include an affirmative showing of effort to abide by the law, tested by objective standards rather than the defendant's subjective state of mind.

Any deterrent effects upon the administration of the criminal law which might result from allowing a mistake of the third classification as a defense seem greatly outweighed by considerations which favor allowing it. To hold a person punishable as a criminal transgressor where the conditions of the third classification are present would be palpably unjust and arbitrary. Most of the important reasons which support the prohibition of ex post facto legislation are opposed to such a holding. It is difficult to conceive what more could be reasonably expected of a "model citizen" than that he guide his conduct by "the law" ascertained in good faith, not merely by efforts which might seem adequate to a person in his situation, but by efforts as well designed to accomplish ascertainment as any available under our system. We are not impressed with the suggestion that a mistake under such circumstances should aid the defendant only in inducing more lenient punishment by a court, or executive clemency after conviction. The circumstances seem so directly related to the defendant's behavior upon which the criminal charge is based as to constitute an integral part of that behavior, for purposes of evaluating it. No excuse appears for dealing with it piecemeal. We think such circumstances should entitle a defendant to full exoneration as a matter of right, rather than to something less, as a matter of grace. Unless there be

aspects of the particular crime involved which give rise to considerations impelling a contrary holding,—some special, cogent reasons
why "justice to the individual is rightly outweighed by the larger interests on the other side of the scales"—a mistake of the third classification should be recognized as a defense.

We find nothing about the crime of bigamy under our statute
which calls for a contrary holding. As previously decided, an absence of general criminal intent is a defense to this crime. As to the
acts involved in the crime, remarriage is obviously neither immoral
nor anti-social in our culture. These aspects lie in the circumstance
that the defendant has a spouse living from whom a divorce has not
been obtained which our courts will recognize as valid. The matters
to which a mistake of law might relate are legal questions concerning
marriage and divorce. It is a gross understatement to say that such
questions are more frequently perplexing than obvious to a layman.
For these reasons, the defense seems appropriate and we hold it available in prosecutions for bigamy.   *   *   *

Here, from the evidence rejected by the lower court, the jury
might have found substantially as follows: (1) that prior to his second marriage, defendant consulted a reputable Delaware attorney
for the purpose of ascertaining whether such marriage would be lawful or unlawful in Delaware, and so that he might abide by the law;
(2) that the attorney advised him that the proposed remarriage would
not be unlawful; (3) that he relied on this advice, honestly believing
his remarriage lawful; (4) that his efforts to ascertain the law were
at all times diligent and in good faith, not by way of subterfuge, and
such that there was no better course for ascertaining the law than
that which he followed; and hence, that he made a full disclosure to
the attorney of the relevant circumstances as well as of what he proposed to do, and that he had no substantial reason to believe that the
advice received was ill-founded, such as circumstances reasonably
indicating that the attorney was incompetent to give advice about
this matter, or had not given the question sufficient consideration,
or that the advice was lacking in candor. Assuming that the Arkansas decree be held invalid here, such findings would constitute a
defense to the present charge as a mistake of law of the third classification. They would meet the test of bona fide, diligent efforts,
as well designed to accomplish ascertainment of the law as any available under our system. The conditions indicated furnish safeguards
against pretext and fraud. The defendant would have the burden of
demonstrating that his efforts were well nigh exemplary. It would
not be enough merely for him to say that he had relied on advice of
an attorney, unless the circumstances indicated that his conduct
throughout in seeking to ascertain the law and in relying on advice
received manifested good faith and diligence beyond reproach. We
see no occasion to assume that recognizing such a defense would
foster dishonest practices among attorneys. These might well be ex-

pected to be deterred by the availability of disciplinary measures for non-professional conduct. Moreover, although erroneous advice might save a defendant from criminal responsibility for acts in reliance on it, the same acts would in many instances incur substantial civil responsibility and financial loss. The risk of possible disingenuous resort to the defense does not seem to us sufficient to warrant withholding it from those acting in good faith. Accordingly, the evidence should have been submitted to the jury under proper instructions.

A new trial should be awarded for the reasons set forth in this opinion.

An order accordingly will be entered.

------

c. INTOXICATION

UNITED STATES v. WILLIAMS

United States District Court for the District of Maryland, 1971.
332 F.Supp. 1.

HERBERT F. MURRAY, District Judge. In this case the defendant was charged in a two-count indictment under Title 18, U.S.C.A. Sections 2113(a) and (b) with robbery of a branch of the Maryland National Bank in Cambridge, Maryland on December 4, 1970. [The relevant portions of the statute were as follows:

§ 2113.　Bank robbery and incidental crimes

(a) Whoever, by force and violence, or by intimidation, takes, or attempts to take, from the person or presence of another any property or money or any other thing of value belonging to, or in the care, custody, control, management, or possession of, any bank, credit union, or any savings and loan association　*　*　*

Shall be fined not more than $5,000 or imprisoned not more than twenty years, or both.

(b) Whoever takes and carries away, with intent to steal or purloin, any property or money or any other thing of value exceeding $100 belonging to, or in the care, custody, control, management, or possession of any bank, credit union, or any savings and loan association, shall be fined not more than $5,000 or imprisoned not more than ten years, or both　*　*　*]

The case was tried non-jury on September 13 and 14, 1971.

The basic facts are not in dispute. In a stipulation signed by government counsel, the defendant and his counsel, it was agreed that on the date set out in the indictment, the defendant went into the bank in Cambridge, Maryland and requested a loan from a branch officer of the bank. The officer declined to grant the defendant a loan. Thereafter the defendant walked up to Mrs. Martina Bennett, a teller, and handed to her a note stating "This is a stickup". Mrs. Bennett gave him all her cash, and defendant then left the bank with the money. It was also stipulated that Mrs. Bennett was intimidated by defendant giving her the note and for that reason turned over to defendant the funds in her drawer. An audit made immediately after the robbery showed the defendant had taken $4,727 of the bank's money.

While defendant thus does not contest the fact that a robbery occurred and he committed it, his counsel urges upon the Court that an essential element of the crime is lacking. It is contended that the two sections of the bank robbery statute on which the counts in the indictment are based both require a specific intent to steal, and that at the time of the robbery defendant was so intoxicated from alcohol and drugs that he was incapable of forming such specific intent.

The threshold legal questions thus are whether voluntary intoxication can negative specific intent as an element of crime and, if so, whether the offenses charged in either or both counts of the indictment require proof of specific intent. If specific intent is an element of the offense in either count of the indictment, the factual question then arises as to whether on all the evidence the degree of defendant's intoxication was such as to create a reasonable doubt that defendant had a specific intent to steal when the robbery took place.

It is clear from the cases that while voluntary intoxication is ordinarily no defense to crime, it may have that effect if specific intent is an element of the crime. * * *

The rule has also been adopted by the American Law Institute. Model Penal Code, Tentative Draft No. 9, Section 2-08.

Thus in the area of criminal responsibility as affected by voluntary intoxication, a distinction must be drawn between so-called "general intent" to commit a crime and a "specific intent" to do a particular criminal act.

These terms are often used in the cases but seldom defined. * *

Did Congress in the several subsections of the bank robbery statute create "general intent" crimes or "specific intent" crimes? Some cases uncritically lump all subsections of the statute under the "specific intent" label. Other cases ascribe more careful draftsmanship to the Congress, and find a specific intent an element of the crime only in those subsections of the statute where the language "with intent" is used.

Thus, in United States v. DeLeo, 422 F.2d 487 (1st Cir. 1970), cert. den. 397 U.S. 1037, 90 S.Ct. 1355, 25 L.Ed.2d 648 (1970), the indictment was under 18 U.S.C.A. Sections 2113(a) and (d). On appeal the defendant contended that the crime was of the common law larceny genus requiring allegation and proof of specific intent. The Court rejected this argument, stating at pages 490–491:

> "Six specific crimes are set out in Section 2113. Felonious intent is specifically incorporated in the definition of two of them: entering a federally insured institution with intent to commit a felony (a—second paragraph), and taking property with intent to steal or purloin (b). However, it is not made part of the crimes of taking by force and violence or by intimidation (a—first paragraph); knowingly receiving stolen property (c); assaulting or putting in jeopardy the life of a person by a dangerous weapon (d); or killing a person, or forcing a person to accompany him, while in the course of committing one of the other offenses or avoiding apprehension or confinement for any of them (e).

> "This differentiation shows careful draftsmanship. Entering and taking can be innocent acts, and therefore require felonious intent to constitute crime; receiving stolen property can be innocent, unless done knowingly. However, the other offenses described acts which, when performed, are so unambiguously dangerous to others that the requisite mental element is necessarily implicit in the description. * * *

The Court in the present case concludes as a matter of law * * that the act of the defendant, which he admits of taking by intimidation from the presence of another money belonging to the bank, constitutes a violation of subsection (a) of the statute as charged in Count I of the indictment. The Court rejects as a defense to the crime charged in Count I of the indictment any voluntary intoxication of the defendant.

As to Count II of the indictment, the Court feels that historically and legally the contention of the defendant is correct, and that a specific intent to steal is an element of the crime. The Court on a review of all the evidence in the case is satisfied beyond a reasonable doubt that defendant when he took and carried away money belonging to the bank exceeding $100 in value did so with the intent to steal or purloin.

The Court in finding as a fact that defendant had the intent to steal is not unmindful of the fact that there was substantial evidence to show that defendant had imbibed significant quantities of alcohol and drugs, but the Court from all the evidence finds beyond a reasonable doubt that he both had the capacity to and did intend to steal when he took the bank's money. The basis for the Court's finding in this regard requires some reference to the evidence of defendant's taking of alcohol and drugs and his condition at the time of the robbery.

In testifying on his own behalf, defendant claimed that as a result of an argument with his wife he started drinking with a companion around 9:00 A.M. on December 3, 1970, the day before the robbery and over the next fourteen hours the two consumed three fifths of whiskey, of which defendant had about half. During this period defendant also took 6 or 7 "yellow jackets" or barbiturate pills. Between midnight on December 3 and the occurrence of the robbery around 1:00 P.M. on December 4, defendant claims that he and a companion drank an additional one or one and a half fifths of whiskey, of which defendant had all but half a pint. In addition, sometime in this latter period defendant took some LSD pills, with the result that he had only "spotty" recollection of events the morning of the robbery. Defendant does recall going into the bank and talking with the branch officer, and leaving the bank stuffing money under his jacket, but disclaims any recollection of confronting the teller, presenting her with a "stickup" note and actually receiving from her over $4,000 in cash.

The witnesses who actually observed the defendant on the day of the robbery indicate he had been drinking but not that he was drunk. A cab driver named Hopkins who drove the defendant at 6:00 A.M. to redeem his watch and then to a drive-in said his eyes were red and he had been drinking. His speech was "heavy" and he did not seem to walk normally.

Mrs. Florence Brannock, a teller in the bank, spoke briefly with defendant when he asked for the loan department and directed him to the branch officer. She felt he smelled strongly of cheap wine or alcohol and that his speech while understandable was not normal— it was a little "slurred" or "thick".

Branch Officer John Bramble testified that the defendant came into his office seeking a $400 loan for Christmas. In their conversation defendant gave his place of employment, said he owned a 1969 Chevrolet and had an account in the Farmer's and Merchant's bank across the street. The witness said he could smell a strong odor of alcohol on the defendant's breath and felt he was under the influence of liquor and that he also appeared somewhat nervous. After declining to grant the defendant a loan, the witness watched the defendant walk towards the lobby of the bank and could not remember anything unusual about the defendant's walk.

Mrs. Martina Bennett, a cash teller, recalled that a little after 1:00 P.M. a man approached from the side aisle of the bank. She recalled having seen him previously at Mrs. Brannock's desk. He put a note on her counter and said nothing. At first she thought he might be deaf and read the note. It was printed in pencil on a torn piece of paper and read "This is a stickup". She noticed that he had his right hand in his jacket pocket which was thrust forward pointing at her as though he had a gun. She was terrified and afraid he was going to shoot her. She put all her money on the counter, but she did not see what he did with it, although she believes he dropped some and then picked it up. She noticed nothing unusual about the defendant's appearance and did not smell any alcohol. When he was standing before her he did not appear to waver, but his eyes did appear sleepy. She watched him walk away from her counter and down a flight of four steps leading to the lobby entrance.

A cab driver witness named Wilson Wright testified defendant and two other men approached him around 5:00 P.M. on December 4, 1970 in Salisbury, Maryland. He took the men to two different destinations in Salisbury and then the defendant and one of the men hired him to take them to Hartsville, South Carolina where the other man, "Charles", lived. The witness noticed the defendant had a large sum of money in a bag, which the defendant said was earned in five years of work in Vietnam. The witness said the defendant looked and acted normal while they were in Salisbury, but en route to Virginia the defendant and his companions were drinking from two fifths of whiskey and the defendant fell into a deep sleep about 8:30 P.M. About 4:00 A.M. the witness left the two men off at a house in Hartsville, South Carolina, and that was the last he saw of the defendant.

The testimony as to acts of the defendant closest in time to the robbery was given by the owner of a small store in Cambridge, George Heist. His store is located about two blocks from the bank. He recalled that the defendant came into his store about noon and asked for a piece of paper to figure a bill. The defendant reached for a sales pad but the witness did not want the defendant to use the pad and gave him a piece of paper instead. The defendant turned around with his back to the witness and put the piece of paper on top of some stocking boxes and started to write. Apparently dissatisfied, he balled up the piece of paper and threw it on the floor. Defendant reached again for the witness' sales pad, which the witness again refused to give him, tearing off a piece of old calendar paper instead. Defendant again turned around and wrote some more, and then left the store.

The witness said that the defendant while in his store seemed coherent, didn't stagger, and acted normally except for trying to take his sales pad twice. However, because the defendant "seemed a little high on something" he decided, after the defendant left the store, to read what was on the balled up piece of paper. It read "This is a stick". Although defendant on leaving the store walked away from and not towards the bank, the witness appropriately concluded a robbery might be in prospect and got a policeman to whom he gave a description of the defendant. Later he heard the fire whistle blow about 1:00 P.M., which was a signal that the bank had been robbed.

Dr. Leonard Rothstein, a private psychiatrist called by defendant, had an interview examination with defendant on May 24, 1971 and also talked to defendant's wife. The defendant gave the doctor a history of abusing alcohol since age 19, and told the doctor he was drinking beer all day before the robbery and took some "yellow jackets" in the evening, and some LSD in the morning before the robbery. Dr. Rothstein found no significant evasiveness in the defendant and no discrepancies between defendant's account and his wife's.

On the basis of defendant's account to him and his examination the doctor expressed the opinion that at the time of the offense the defendant had no psychosis or structural alteration in the brain. However, the doctor concluded from what the defendant told him of his ingestion of alcohol and drugs that the higher centers governing the making of judgments, control of behavior and retention of experience in memory had been affected. While the defendant knew what he was doing, his judgment about the appropriateness of his actions and his ability to control them were severely impaired. From the history the doctor concluded the defendant had taken the alcohol and drugs voluntarily and with knowledge from previous experience of their probable effect. In response to a hypothetical question asked on cross examination by counsel for the government, the doctor admitted that if the defendant had not taken alcohol and drugs before the offense, he would at the time have had no psychiatric illness and would have had the capacity to conform his conduct to the requirements of the law.

Dr. William Fitzpatrick, who had examined the defendant on July 15, 1971 at the request of the government, was called as an expert psychiatric witness by the defense. He related a personal history and account of the offense given him by the defendant very similar to that related by defendant's own expert, Dr. Rothstein. He found the defendant of normal intelligence with no evidence of psychosis or structural brain disorder. From the history he judged defendant to be a passive dependent personality of the type more likely to abuse alcohol than the average person. Although from defendant's own account he was an episodic heavy user of alcohol and drugs, he did not find evidence that he was an alcoholic or a drug addict. He felt that because defendant was a passive dependent type he had a condition something short of total mental health. However, had the defendant not taken alcohol and drugs at time of the offense, he would not consider that defendant lacked criminal responsibility or capacity to conform his conduct to the requirements of the law. Although the doctor did not know the quantity of alcohol or drugs defendant consumed before the offense, he assumed the defendant was intoxicated at the time and that his intoxication was self-induced with knowledge on the part of the defendant that he would get drunk if he drank. He admitted that if he assumed a lesser degree of intoxication he would have to alter his opinion, but his opinion that defendant at the time of the offense could not conform his conduct to the requirements of the law was based on assumed intake of large quantities of alcohol. However, the doctor honestly disclaimed any opinion on whether defendant could specifically intend to rob a bank.

In expressing their conclusions, both psychiatrists obviously had in mind the ALI formulation [of the insanity defense] contained in Model Penal Code, Section 4.01, approved in this circuit in United States v. Chandler, 393 F.2d 920 (1968). [Under this formulation, "a person is not responsible for criminal conduct if at the time of such conduct as a result of mental disease or defect he lacks substantial capacity either to appreciate the criminality of his conduct or to conform his conduct to the requirements of law."] However, defense counsel disclaimed any contention that this standard was applicable in determining the issue of the criminal responsibility of this defendant. In this connection it is noted that Section 2.08(3) of the Model Penal Code provides "Intoxication does not, in itself, constitute mental disease within the meaning of Section 4.01."

As then Circuit Judge Burger stated in Heideman v. United States, 104 U.S.App.D.C. 128, 259 F.2d 943, at p. 946 (1958): "Drunkenness, while efficient to reduce or remove *inhibitions*,* does not readily negate *intent*.* " (* Footnotes omitted)

The Court believes that the defendant had taken alcohol and drugs to the point of being "under the influence" but that he was not so intoxicated as not to understand what he was doing or to not have the intention to steal from the bank. There is a marked difference between the accounts of the persons who observed defendant and defendant's own account as to his condition. It appears from a witness called by the defense that he was able to write a "stickup" note shortly before the robbery, to go into the bank, hold a coherent conversation about a loan, present the note, obtain over $4,000 in cash, none of which has been returned, and make good his escape. The Court concludes beyond a reasonable doubt that defendant had the intent to steal from the bank as required for conviction under Count II, and that he is in any event guilty under Count I of the indictment. If an intent to steal is an element of the offense charged in Count I, the Court finds that intent proved as to Count I also. The Court therefore finds the defendant guilty as charged in both counts of the indictment.

NOTES

1. When a case such as the instant case is submitted to a jury, how are they likely to consider the evidence of the defendant's intoxication? Is it likely that they actually do consider it only as evidence tending to disprove the existence of a specific intent required by the definition of the crime? If not, what (if anything) should the law do?

2. Hutchison, Tuchie, Gray and Steinberg, A Study of the Effects of Alcohol on Mental Functions, 7 Crim.L.Q. 343 (1965) describe the ability to identify oneself, relate certain items of personal history, and to orient oneself as to time and place as "the usual basis of the average person's ap-

praisal of whether a person is mentally impaired." Id. at 348. In the authors' experiment, these abilities remained unimpaired by intoxication although other mental processes were impaired. Does the court in Williams seem to be simply applying this layman's appraisal to the case? Is this appropriate? If so, could the so-called intoxication defense be reformulated to better provide for this? How?

3.   Hutchison, Tuchie, Gray and Steinberg, A Study of the Effects of Alcohol on Mental Functions, 7 Crim.L.Q. 343 (1965) note that although it is "common practice" when drunkenness is raised as a defense to a criminal charge to call a psychiatrist to testify, there have been "surprisingly few" experimental studies of any value in ascertaining the mental impairment caused by a given degree of intoxication. Most of the experimental work, the authors observe, deals with the impairment of physical actions by intoxication. Given this deficiency, the authors describe an experiment "undertaken to provide data relevant to the task of the expert witness" called to testify as to the state of mind of an accused who was intoxicated at the time of the offense. Eight individuals drank whiskey until their blood alcohol was approximately 1.0 parts per 1,000 (ascertained by a Breathalyzer). The subjects were then given a battery of tests, and their performance while intoxicated was compared with their performance while sober. The results, concluded the authors, showed that the effects of drinking upon mental functions are not uniform. No effect was noted upon the subjects' ability to relate their personal histories or to orient themselves as to time and place. Nor was their ability to repeat a sequence of digits spoken by the examiner impaired. But other functions were adversely affected, including attention (as measured by the subjects' ability to repeat in reverse order a sequence of digits spoken by the examiner) and learning efficiency (as measured by the subjects' ability, after the examiner has read off a short list of word pairs, to accurately give the second word of each pair as the examiner gives the first). Also affected was the subjects' abstract thinking capacity, as measured by their ability to abstract essential likenesses or common properties from apparently dissimilar objects or events, i. e., "In what way are good and evil alike?" This ability, the authors note, "is not only a reliable measure of general intelligence but is recognized as 'a measure of the logical character of the subject's thinking processes.'" Id. at 349. The subjects' ability to recognize certain pictures that had been shown to them during the period of intoxication was not significantly impaired, but they did demonstrate a significantly reduced ability to recall the title they had given the picture (in response to the examiner's request) earlier.

To what extent does this information assist in evaluating the criminal liability of someone like Williams? If it can be assumed that Williams' intoxication was at least no less than that of the subjects of the Hutchison, et al. study, does the study suggest that Williams did not have the specific intent required by the robbery statute? Hutchison, et al. describe their findings as supporting the clinical observation that impairment of mental functioning can occur at relatively low concentrations of blood alcohol. But is this impairment of the kind or degree that might reasonably be expected to affect criminal liability by showing the nonexistence of a specific intent? How might researchers provide data more helpful in resolving the factual questions raised by the traditional formulation of the "intoxication defense?"

4. To what extent would the relevance of intoxication to liability for serious criminal acts be simplified by enactment of the following statute:

Dangerous Intoxication.

A person is guilty of an offense if he takes or permits to be administered to him intoxicating substances while aware of a substantial and unjustifiable risk that he will become intoxicated and, while intoxicated, commit acts that except for his intoxication would be crimes.

What penalty should be assigned to the offense of "dangerous intoxication?" Should the penalty be related to the penalty assigned to the crime which the offender was aware he might commit? Should it be related to the number of crimes the offender was aware he might commit? The number actually committed?

5. It is generally held that intoxication from substances other than alcohol have the same effect upon criminal liability as alcohol intoxication. Is this appropriate? Consider the following from Commonwealth v. Campbell, 445 Pa. 388, 284 A.2d 798, 801 (1971):

Defendant contends that the law with respect to voluntary intoxication is [as it is] because human experience has shown the effects of taking alcohol are predictable, but not predictable with LSD [and therefore LSD intoxication should be permitted to result in complete acquittal]. The expert testimony in this case (if believed * * *) showed * * * that LSD produces widely varying results among different persons and even different results with the same person on different occasions. This distinction of nonpredictability of effect on the human body is devoid of any adequate legal justification based upon legal precedent, or reason, or policy considerations for a radical change and departure from our law of criminal responsibility. The very fact that the effects of a voluntary, nonmedical use of a hallucinogenic drug are predictably unforeseeable should require Courts to decide in the public interest that this is not legally sufficient to completely exculpate a person from murder or any criminal act.

6. What arguments could be made for or against the enactment of the following statute:

Effect of Intoxication Upon Criminal Liability.

(a) Except under the circumstances described in subsection (b), no person shall be convicted of an offense committed while intoxicated if it is found that [Alternative A: except for such intoxication he would not have committed the offense.] [Alternative B: his intoxication so reduces his culpability that given general community standards of accountability and blameworthiness he should not be held liable.]

(b) If a person, contemplating the commission of an offense, becomes intoxicated as a means of causing or enabling himself to commit the offense, he shall be liable for that offense without regard to subsection (a).

7. From a purely tactical point of view, should evidence of intoxication be introduced by a defendant? What factors should be taken into account in making this decision? In which of the cases in this section was the attempt to put before the jury evidence that the defendant was intoxicated a wise tactical decision by defense counsel?

8. See generally Baumgartner, The Effect of Drugs on Criminal Responsibility, Specific Intent, and Mental Competency, 8 Am.Crim.L.Q. 118 (1970); Paulson, Intoxication as a Defense to Crime, 1961 U.Ill.L.Forum 1; Note, Volitional Fault and the Intoxicated Criminal Offender, 36 U.Cin. L.Rev. 258 (1967); Annot., Modern Status of the Rules as to Voluntary Intoxication as Defense to Criminal Charge, 8 A.L.R.3d 1236 (1966). For a historical analysis, see Singh, History of the Defense of Drunkenness in English Criminal Law, 49 L.Q.Rev. 528 (1933). For comparative purposes, see Bryden, Mens Rea and the Intoxicated Offender, 1968 Juridical Review 48 (Scottish) and Parker and Beck, The Intoxicated Offender—A Problem of Responsibility, 44 Can.B.Rev. 563 (1966) (Canadian). The relationship between the "insanity" defense and the voluntary intoxication "defense," especially in one who exhibits symptoms of mental illness when intoxicated, is discussed in Comment, The Mentally Impaired and Voluntarily Intoxicated Offender, 1972 Wash.U.L.Q. 160.

PEOPLE v. HOOD

Supreme Court of California, 1969.
1 Cal.3d 444, 82 Cal.Rptr. 618, 462 P.2d 370.

TRAYNOR, Chief Justice. An indictment charged defendant in Count I with assault with a deadly weapon upon a peace officer, Alfred Elia (Pen.Code, § 245, subd. (b)), in Count II with battery upon a peace officer, Donald Kemper (Pen.Code, §§ 242, 243), and in Count III with assault with intent to murder Officer Elia (Pen.Code § 217). A jury found him guilty on Counts I and III and not guilty on Count II, and the trial court entered judgment on the verdicts. The trial court also ordered that "Defendant shall serve the sentence in Count Three only * * * as the sentence in Count One * * * is withheld and will only be imposed if the sentence for Count Three is not carried out for any reason. * * *" Defendant appeals.

On September 11, 1967, at about 2:00 a. m., defendant, his brother Donald, and a friend, Leo Chilton, all of whom had been drinking for several hours, knocked on the door of the house of Susan Bueno, defendant's former girlfriend, and asked if they could use the bathroom. Susan said no, but defendant forced his way in and started to hit her. He knocked her to the floor and kicked her. Donald Hood then took Susan aside, and defendant, Chilton, and Gene Saunders, a friend of Susan's who was staying at the house, went to the kitchen and sat down.

Gilbert A. Nielsen, Susan's next-door neighbor, was awakened by the sound of Susan's screams and called the police. Officers Elia and Kemper responded to his call.   After talking to Nielsen, they went to Susan's house, knocked on the door, which was opened by Stella Gonzales, Susan's cousin, and asked if "Susie" was there.   Miss Gonzales said, "Yes, just a minute," and in a few seconds Susan came running to the door crying.   Officer Elia asked Susan if she had been beaten and who did it.   She pointed to the kitchen and said, "They're in there right now."   The two officers walked through the living room, where Susan, Susan's seven-year-old son Ronnie, and Stella remained, and went into the kitchen.   There they observed defendant on the right-hand side of the room leaning against a door.   On the left side of the kitchen, the three other men were seated at a table. Officer Elia walked to the middle of the room and questioned the men at the table.   Defendant interrupted the questioning and asked Officer Elia if he had a search warrant.   Officer Elia replied that he did not need one since the person who rented the house had given him permission to enter.   Defendant then directed a stream of obscenities at Officer Elia, who turned and, according to his testimony, started to place defendant under arrest for a violation of Penal Code section 415 (using vulgar, profane, or indecent language within the presence or hearing of women or children).   He got no further than to say, "Okay fella, you are * * *," when defendant swung at him with his fist.   When Officer Kemper attempted to go to Officer Elia's assistance, Donald Hood jumped on him from behind.   During the ensuing struggle, Officer Elia fell with defendant on top of him in a corner of a pantry adjoining the kitchen at the rear.   While struggling on the floor, Officer Elia felt a tug at his gun belt and then heard two shots fired.

A third officer, Laurence Crocker, who had arrived at the house shortly after the other two officers, came into the kitchen as the scuffle between Officer Elia and defendant was beginning.   After he had control of Donald Hood, he looked across the kitchen and saw defendant with a gun in his right hand.   He testified that defendant pointed the gun towards Officer Elia's midsection and pulled the trigger twice.

Both Officers Crocker and Kemper testified that after the shots, defendant's arm came up over his head with the revolver in his hand. The struggle continued into the bathroom.   Defendant was finally subdued when Officer Elia regained possession of the gun and held it against the side of defendant's neck.   Officer Elia then noticed that defendant had shot him once in each leg.

The foregoing evidence is clearly sufficient to support the verdicts.

Defendant contends that the court * * * erred in instructing on the effect of intoxication with respect to the offenses charged in both Counts I and III.

*   *   *

The judgment must also be reversed as to Count III, for the court gave hopelessly conflicting instructions on the effect of intoxication. * * *

To guide the trial court on retrial, we consider the question of the effect of intoxication on the crime of assault with a deadly weapon.

Many cases have held that neither assault with a deadly weapon nor simple assault is a specific intent crime. A number of these cases held that an assault with a deadly weapon could be predicated on reckless, as well as intentional, conduct. " 'Where the act is both unlawful and wrongful, and well calculated to inflict serious personal injury, the law will imply malice and an unlawful intention and override any actual intention existing in the mind of the aggressor. Thus, while it is not an assault to fire a gun in the air for the purpose of frightening another, it is an assault, without regard to the aggressor's intention, to fire a gun at another or in the direction in which he is standing. The law will not tolerate such a reckless disregard for human life.' " (People v. Peak, supra, 66 Cal.App.2d 894, 901, 153 P.2d 464, 467, quoting from 4 Am.Jur., § 6, p. 130.) "[Pen.Code § 245] provides that 'Every person who commits an assault * * * with a deadly weapon or instrument or by any means or force *likely to produce great bodily injury*,' is guilty of that offense. The *intention* to actually injure another is not mentioned in that section. * * * If a rifle is deliberately and unlawfully fired toward another person in a manner 'likely to produce great bodily injury,' an assault with a deadly weapon may be accomplished even if the defendant does not really intend to *hit* the victim." (People v. Corlett, supra, 67 Cal.App.2d 33, 54–55, 153 P.2d 595, 605.) (See also People v. Vasquez (1927) 85 Cal.App. 575, 259 P. 1005.)

The first clear signs of doubt that an assault with a deadly weapon was not a specific intent crime are found in People v. Carmen (1951) 36 Cal.2d 768, 228 P.2d 281. * * *

The opinion then expressly disapproved the cases that had held reckless conduct to be a sufficient basis for assault. * * *

The distinction between specific and general intent crimes evolved as a judicial response to the problem of the intoxicated offender. That problem is to reconcile two competing theories of what is just in the treatment of those who commit crimes while intoxicated. On the one hand, the moral culpability of a drunken criminal is frequently less than that of a sober person effecting a like injury. On the other hand, it is commonly felt that a person who voluntarily gets drunk and while in that state commits a crime should not escape the consequences. (See Hall, General Principles of Criminal Law (2d ed. 1960), p. 537.)

Before the nineteenth century, the common law refused to give any effect to the fact that an accused committed a crime while intoxicated. The judges were apparently troubled by this rigid traditional rule, however, for there were a number of attempts during the early part of the nineteenth century to arrive at a more humane, yet workable, doctrine. The theory that these judges explored was that evidence of intoxication could be considered to negate intent, whenever intent was an element of the crime charged. As Professor Hall notes, however, such an exculpatory doctrine could eventually have undermined the traditional rule entirely, since some form of *mens rea* is a requisite of all but strict liability offenses. (Hall, Intoxication and Criminal Responsibility, 57 Harv.L.Rev. 1045, 1049.) To limit the operation of the doctrine and achieve a compromise between the conflicting feelings of sympathy and reprobation for the intoxicated offender, later courts both in England and this country drew a distinction between so-called specific intent and general intent crimes.

Specific and general intent have been notoriously difficult terms to define and apply, and a number of textwriters recommend that they be abandoned altogether. (Hall, General Principles of Criminal Law, supra, p. 142; Williams, Criminal Law—The General Part (2d ed. 1961) § 21, p. 49.) Too often the characterization of a particular crime as one of specific or general intent is determined solely by the presence or absence of words describing psychological phenomena—"intent" or "malice," for example—in the statutory language of defining the crime. When the definition of a crime consists of only the description of a particular act, without reference to intent to do a further act or achieve a future consequence, we ask whether the defendant intended to do the proscribed act. This intention is deemed to be a general criminal intent. When the definition refers to defendant's intent to do some further act or achieve some additional consequence, the crime is deemed to be one of specific intent. There is no real difference, however, only a linguistic one, between an intent to do an act already performed and an intent to do that same act in the future.

The language of Penal Code section 22, drafted in 1872 when "specific" and "general" intent were not yet terms of art, is somewhat broader than those terms: "No act committed by a person while in a state of voluntary intoxication is less criminal by reason of his having been in such condition. But whenever the actual existence of any particular purpose, motive, or intent is a necessary element to constitute any particular species or degree of crime, the jury may take into consideration the fact that the accused was intoxicated at the time, in determining the purpose, motive, or intent with which he committed the act." Even this statement of the relevant policy is no easier to apply to particular crimes. We are still confronted with the difficulty of characterizing the mental element of a given crime as a particular purpose, motive, or intent necessary to constitute the offense, or as something less than that to which evidence of intoxication is not pertinent.

Even if we assume that the presence or absence of words clearly denoting mental activity is a valid criterion for determining the significance of intoxication, our present problem is not resolved. The difficulty with applying such a test to the crime of assault or assault with a deadly weapon is that no word in the relevant code provisions unambiguously denotes a particular mental element, yet the word "attempt" in Penal Code section 240 strongly suggests goal-directed, intentional behavior. This uncertainty accounts for the conflict over whether assault is a crime only of intention or also of recklessness.

We need not reconsider our position in *Carmen* that an assault cannot be predicated merely on reckless conduct. Even if assault requires an intent to commit a battery on the victim, it does not follow that the crime is one in which evidence of intoxication ought to be considered in determining whether the defendant had that intent. It is true that in most cases specific intent has come to mean an intention to do a future act or achieve a particular result, and that assault is appropriately characterized as a specific intent crime under this definition. An assault, however, is equally well characterized as a general intent crime under the definition of general intent as an intent merely to do a violent act. Therefore, whatever reality the distinction between specific and general intent may have in other contexts, the difference is chimerical in the case of assault with a deadly weapon or simple assault. Since the definitions of both specific intent and general intent cover the requisite intent to commit a battery, the decision whether or not to give effect to evidence of intoxication must rest on other considerations.

A compelling consideration is the effect of alcohol on human behavior. A significant effect of alcohol is to distort judgment and relax the controls on aggressive and anti-social impulses. (Beck and Parker, The Intoxicated Offender—A Problem of Responsibility (1966), 44 Can.B.Rev. 563, 570–573; Muelberger, Medico-Legal Aspects of Alcohol Intoxication (1956), 35 Mich.St.B.J. 36, 40–41.) Alcohol apparently has less effect on the ability to engage in simple goal-directed behavior, although it may impair the efficiency of that behavior. In other words, a drunk man is capable of forming an intent to do something simple, such as strike another, unless he is so drunk that he has reached the stage of unconsciousness. What he is not as capable as a sober man of doing is exercising judgment about the social consequences of his acts or controlling his impulses toward anti-social acts. He is more likely to act rashly and impulsively and to be susceptible to passion and anger. It would therefore be anomalous to allow evidence of intoxication to relieve a man of responsibility for the crimes of assault with a deadly weapon or simple assault, which are so frequently committed in just such a manner. As the court said in Parker v. United States (1966) 123 U.S.App.D.C. 343, 359 F.2d 1009, 1012–1013, "Whatever ambiguities there may be in distinguishing between specific and general intent to determine whether drunkenness constitutes a defense, an offense of this nature is not one which requires an intent that is susceptible to negation through a showing of voluntary intoxication."

Those crimes that have traditionally been characterized as crimes of specific intent are not affected by our holding here. The difference in mental activity between formulating an intent to commit a battery and formulating an intent to commit a battery for the purpose of raping or killing may be slight, but it is sufficient to justify drawing a line between them and considering evidence of intoxication in the one case and disregarding it in the other.[7] Accordingly, on retrial the court should not instruct the jury to consider evidence of defendant's intoxication in determining whether he committed assault with a deadly weapon on a peace officer or any of the lesser assaults included therein. People v. Fanning, supra, 265 Cal.App.2d 729, 71 Cal.Rptr. 641, and any case implying the contrary are disapproved.

NOTE

Not all American jurisdictions permit evidence of voluntary intoxication to be used to negate even "specific" intents. See, e. g., Chittum v. Commonwealth, 211 Va. 12, 174 S.E.2d 779 (1970), holding that evidence of voluntary intoxication need not be considered in determining whether defendant charged with kidnapping and attempted rape was capable of forming the requisite state of mind.

7. It should be pointed out that the fact that intent may be inferred from the defendant's conduct does not affect the nature of the requisite intent. Whether the intent be merely to do that which was done or to do a further act or achieve a particular consequence, the jury may infer from defendant's acts that defendant acted with the requisite intent, if such an inference is warranted by the evidence. As the Court of Appeal said in People v. Fanning, supra, 265 Cal.App.2d 729, 734 n. 4, 71 Cal.Rptr. 641, 644, in discussing whether assault was a specific or a general intent crime, "The confusion seems to be, in part at least, traceable to the rule that the intent may be inferred from the act. (People v. McCoy, 25 Cal.2d 177, 194–195, 153 P.2d 315.) The fact that one element of a crime may be inferred from proof of another does not decrease the number of elements." In the crimes of simple assault and assault with a deadly weapon, the jury may infer from defendant's conduct that he entertained the necessary intent to commit an injury. Such an inference does not affect the nature of that intent or determine what significance should be accorded to evidence of intoxication.

ROBINSON v. CALIFORNIA

Supreme Court of the United States, 1962.
370 U.S. 660, 82 S.Ct. 1417, 8 L.Ed.2d 758, rehearing denied
371 U.S. 905, 83 S.Ct. 202, 9 L.Ed.2d 166.

[The opinion in this case is reprinted at page 163, supra].

POWELL v. TEXAS

Supreme Court of the United States, 1968.
392 U.S. 514, 88 S.Ct. 2145, 20 L.Ed.2d 1254.

[The opinion in this case is reprinted at page 168, supra].

STATE v. GUIDEN

Supreme Court of Wisconsin, 1970.
46 Wis.2d 328, 174 N.W.2d 488.

FACTS.

On July 15, 1968, a criminal complaint was issued, charging Charles Jackson, Robert Norwood and defendant Joshua Guiden with burglary * * * and with operating an automobile without the owner's consent * * *[.] On January 22, 1969, the charge against the defendant of operating without consent was dropped on motion of the state. On February 3, 1969, the court accepted the guilty plea of defendant to the burglary charge and found the defendant guilty. Defendant appeals.

ROBERT W. HANSEN, Justice. The defendant seeks to withdraw his guilty plea and have a new trial ordered as "* * * necessary to correct a manifest injustice." * * *

The principal argument of the defendant on this appeal is that he was intoxicated at the time of the burglary and hence incapable of forming the required criminal intent to burglarize.[3] The record here is more complete than would ordinarily be the case in a hearing on a plea of guilty. This is because, by stipulation of prosecution and defense, the testimony in the trial of the co-defendant Norwood (who was found not to have participated in the burglary and was acquitted) was incorporated by reference in the hearing on defendant's plea.

At the Norwood trial the defendant himself took the stand to testify that at the time of the burglary he was "I suppose kind of tipsy," "I was feeling kind of high," "I was sort of half intoxicated."

---

3. Sec. 939.42, Stats., provides: " * * * An intoxicated or drugged condition of the actor is a defense only if such condition: * * * (2) Negatives the existence of a state of mind essential to the crime." * * *

The "intoxicated or drugged condition" to which the statute refers is not the condition of alcohol-induced incandescence or being well-lit that lowers the threshold of inhibitions or stirs the impulse to criminal adventures. It is that degree of complete drunkenness which makes a person incapable of forming intent to perform an act or commit a crime. To be relieved from responsibility for criminal acts it is not enough for a defendant to establish that he was under the influence of intoxicating beverages. He must establish that degree of intoxication that means he was utterly incapable of forming the intent requisite to the commission of the crime charged.

The physical facts, as well as the defendant's testimony, do not provide a basis for finding here such inability to form intent to burglarize. While Norwood was sleeping in the back of the car, the defendant and Jackson parked the auto in the lot at the television store. After some talk about getting a television set, Jackson got out of the car and the defendant followed. As the defendant got to the corner, he heard a window break. Jackson came around the corner, holding two television sets, one of which he handed to the defendant. Jackson then got into the car and started driving away, to prove again that there is indeed no honor among thieves. Carrying the television set he had been given by Jackson, the defendant ran after the car. The car stopped, and co-defendants Jackson and Norwood got out and started running, with the police officers in hot pursuit. Norwood fell almost immediately, but Jackson and the defendant kept running and were captured a short time later and some distance away. The contention of the defendant has to be that he was sober enough to know enough to run after the car and away from the officers with the stolen TV set, but too drunk to form an intent to burglarize. The contention is not very persuasive. The capacity to form intent is to be inferred from the acts and conduct of a defendant, as well as from his self-description of his state of sobriety. Here his actions speak at least as loud as his words, and both establish that he was not unable to intend to do what he did do.[4]

*   *   *

Judgment affirmed.

NOTES

1. Does the instant case fall far short of holding that if an individual during a state of voluntary intoxication demonstrates his capability to do an act which, if performed by a sober person in the circumstances would permit the inference that he had the "specific" intent required for the

---

4. "Intent is a state of mind existing at the time a person commits an offense. If intent required definite and substantive proof, it would be almost impossible to convict, absent facts disclosing a culmination of the intent. The mind of an alleged offender, however, may be read from his acts, conduct and inferences fairly deducible from all the circumstances." 13 Am.Jur.2d, Burglary, sec. 52, p. 352, cited with approval in Strait v. State (1969), 41 Wis. 2d 552, 559, 164 N.W.2d 505.

crime, he may then be found guilty despite the extent of his intoxication? If this is the essence of the opinion, is the intoxication "defense" of any value?

2. Should voluntary intoxication continue to be relevant to criminal liability only insofar as it "disproves" state of mind? Consider the following materials in regard to how an "affirmative defense" based upon intoxication or use of intoxicants might be formulated.

COMMONWEALTH v. INGRAM

Supreme Court of Pennsylvania, 1970.
440 Pa. 239, 270 A.2d 190.

BELL, Chief Justice. On the evening of April 24, 1967, at approximately 8:30 P.M., Huriel Hildreth, the deceased, and Eugene Butler entered Margie's Bar at Second Street and Allegheny Avenue, in the City of Philadelphia. According to the testimony of Butler, an *eyewitness* to the homicide, they entered the bar so Hildreth could make a long-distance telephone call. The telephone was located in the rear of the bar, adjacent to a pool table where defendant-appellant Ingram and others were playing pool. Hildreth was making his telephone call when appellant requested him to move because Hildreth was blocking appellant from taking his next shot. Hildreth refused. Appellant walked over to the bar, grabbed a beer bottle, broke it, came back, and with its jagged edges struck Hildreth on the side of his face, causing him to fall off the chair in which he was seated. Appellant went back to the bar and broke another beer bottle and returned and struck and slashed the other side of Hildreth's face while he was still on the floor. Appellant returned to the bar a third time and broke a third bottle, and was about to resume his attack on Hildreth, but was stopped by the bartender and other patrons.

Butler was finally able to get Hildreth to his feet and immediately took him to the hospital. Hildreth died in the hospital that morning at 5:00 A.M. At the autopsy, the Commonwealth proved that death was caused by the severing of Hildreth's jugular vein by a jagged instrument.

The jury returned a verdict of guilty of murder in the second degree. Appellant then filed post-trial motions for a new trial and in arrest of judgment. The lower Court denied these motions and sentenced appellant to a term of not less than five years nor more than fifteen years. From the judgment of sentence, defendant took this appeal.

* * *

Appellant raises * * * as grounds for a new trial * * * whether it was error for the lower Court not to charge the jury that it could consider the degree of appellant's *voluntary intoxication* on the question of whether he had the requisite state of mind to have the legal *malice* which is necessary for first- or second-degree murder, and, if not, whether he could be guilty of voluntary or involuntary manslaughter * * *.

Appellant and other witnesses testified that he (the appellant) was intoxicated and had been drinking for almost four hours prior to his attacks on Hildreth. Appellant's testimony disclosed a clear recollection of all his actions and activities both before and after he slashed Hildreth with the broken bottles, but he said he had no recollection of breaking any bottle or of attacking the deceased.[1]

Appellant bases his requested charge (1) on the testimony of himself and several other witnesses that he was intoxicated, (2) also the testimony of Bernard Cowitz, M.D., a psychoanalyst, and (3) on a drastic change in the long-established law of Pennsylvania with respect to voluntary intoxication.

Dr. Cowitz testified that "as a result of alcohol ingest, very probably and very likely he [appellant] had no recollection of this incident," and that "there was a very definite possibility that at the time of this alleged offense that Mr. Ingram was not aware of his actions, as the result of the ingestion of alcohol." On the basis of the above-mentioned evidence, appellant requested a charge that would allow the jury (1) to consider whether his voluntary intoxication rendered him incapable of having the *requisite malice for either* first- or second-degree murder, and (2) to consider that the degree of his intoxication could reduce the killing to voluntary manslaughter. He argues that if the degree of intoxication can reduce a killing from murder in the first degree to murder in the second degree, it can and should be legally adequate to reduce the killing to voluntary manslaughter.[2] For the reasons hereinafter stated, we disagree.

*   *   *

In Commonwealth v. Commander, 436 Pa. 532, pages 536–537, 260 A.2d 773, page 776, this Court said: " 'Murder' * * * is * * * an unlawful killing of another [human being] with malice aforethought express or implied * * *.

" ' "Malice express or implied is the criterion and absolutely essential ingredient of murder. Malice in its legal sense exists not only where there is a particular ill will, but also whenever there is a wickedness of disposition, hardness of heart, wanton conduct, cruelty, recklessness of consequences and a mind regardless of social duty. Legal malice may be inferred and found from the attending circumstances. * * *

---

1. It is interesting to note that appellant had just won three games of pool and was aware of the fact that Hildreth occupied the spot from which he could make his best shot.

2. If appellant's contentions are sound, it would follow arguably and possibly logically that voluntary intoxication, like insanity, would absolve him of murder and of voluntary, as well as involuntary, manslaughter.

In Commonwealth v. Walters, 431 Pa. 74, pages 82, 83, 244 A.2d 757, page 762, a *unanimous* Court said: "The law on both voluntary manslaughter and intoxication as a defense to murder is clear. In Commonwealth v. Paese, 220 Pa. 371, 373, 69 A. 891, 892 (1908), we defined voluntary manslaughter quite explicitly. 'To reduce an intentional blow, stroke or wounding, resulting in death, to voluntary manslaughter, there must be sufficient cause of provocation and a state of rage or passion, without time to cool, placing the prisoner beyond the control of his reason, and suddenly impelling him to the deed. If any of these be wanting—if there be provocation without passion, or passion without a sufficient cause of provocation, or there be time to cool, and reason has resumed its sway, the killing will be murder: Commonwealth v. Drum, 58 Pa. 9 (17.)' This explanation retains vitality today. * * * The evidence in the present case furnishes no real proof whatsoever that [appellant] acted in the heat of passion. * * *

"On the other hand, there was considerable evidence that appellant was seriously intoxicated at the time of the stabbing. In fact, the trial judge at sentencing stated specifically that this was the reason he agreed to accept the Commonwealth's certification that the crime was murder in the second degree. The law is quite clear that *intoxication can lower the degree of guilt,* but it remains *murder.* 'Intoxication sufficient to deprive the mind of power to form a design with deliberation and premeditation, and to properly judge the legitimate consequences of an act, will reduce a killing from murder in the first degree to murder in the second degree.' * * *

Appellant makes a frontal assault on one of the most basic bulwarks of our law. In Commonwealth v. Reid, 432 Pa. 319, page 322, 247 A.2d 783, page 785, this Court said: "Generally speaking, voluntary drunkenness neither exonerates nor excuses a person for his criminal acts. However, where the charge is felonious homicide, intoxication which is so great as to make the accused incapable of forming a wilful, deliberate, and premeditated design to kill, or incapable of judging his acts and their consequences, may serve to reduce the crime of murder from the first to the second degree. Commonwealth v. Simmons, supra. See also Commonwealth v. Walters, 431 Pa. 74, 244 A.2d 757 (1968)." This has been the well-established and frequently reaffirmed law of Pennsylvania, and we believe there is no reason or justification for any change. * * *

Our well-reasoned policy and well-established law have been adopted or followed by the overwhelming majority of States which continuue to maintain the same policy. 8 A.L.R.3rd 1,236, Voluntary Intoxication—Defense (1966); Hall, Intoxication and Criminal Responsibility, 57 Harv.L.Rev. 1,045 (1944).[6]

6. We note that there are some States—for instance, California and Arizona—which allow intoxication to negate malice. In these States, there are *statutes, legislatively enacted,* which direct the jury to consider intoxication affecting "any particular purpose, motive or intent" necessary for crime.

Moreover, the facts in the instant case create an important factual presumption of malice. Appellant attacked a vital part of Hildreth's body (face and throat) with a deadly weapon (jagged edges of broken beer bottles), thereby raising a factual presumption that the homicide was both intentional and malicious. As this Court recently said in Commonwealth v. Winebrenner, 439 Pa. 73, pages 78–80, 265 A.2d 108, page 112: "It is true that malice is an absolutely essential ingredient of murder (cases supra). *Legal malice* may be inferred and found from the attending circumstances, and, like the specific intent to kill, may be inferred from the intentional use, without legal excuse or legal justification, of a deadly weapon on a vital part of another human body * * *.

Appellant seeks to have the evidence of his voluntary intoxication (which the jury does not have to believe * * *) to be of such a nature and degree, that the jury could consider it to *completely rebut* this presumption of malice. The practical effect of this would be to allow an intoxicated man to feloniously take the life of another man with a gun, knife or any other dangerous weapon, including a broken beer bottle, and be convicted only of voluntary manslaughter (or indeed found not guilty of any crime), while the same man with one drink or a few drinks, or completely sober, would be convicted of murder. As was so well and wisely said in State v. Arsenault, 152 Me. 121, 124 A.2d 741, 746: "The Court is unanimous in its opinion that the rule regarding the defense of insanity should never be extended to apply to voluntary intoxication in a murder case. It would not only open wide the door to defenses built on frauds and perjuries, but would build a broad, easy turnpike for escape. All that the crafty criminal would require for a well-planned murder * * * would be a revolver in one hand to commit the deed, and a quart of intoxicating liquor in the other with which to build his excusable defense." [8]

We see no reason or logic, or realistic principles of law, to subject a man who *voluntarily* becomes intoxicated to any different standards of criminal responsibility for second degree murder or voluntary manslaughter than a sober man.

*   *   *

Judgment of sentence affirmed.

Section 22 of California Penal Code, and Ariz.Rev.Stat. 13–132. These jurisdictions have concepts and classifications of homicide wholly inapposite to that which we have in Pennsylvania.

8. The Model Penal Code, [as well as the proposed Federal Criminal Code, reprinted at page 567, infra] generally considered as a *liberal* statement of criminal law and theory, also clearly rejected intoxication as a defense for consideration by the jury if the defendant had committed a homicide with "recklessness under circumstances manifesting extreme indifference to the value of human life." Sections 2.08(2), 210.2(1) (b). We note in passing that the Model Penal Code—unlike the well-established law of Pennsylvania—does not use the generic term "malice" in its definition of murder, but substitutes "recklessness under circumstances manifesting an extreme indifference to the value of human life."

NOTE

On what basis did the Pennsylvania Supreme Court reject the defendant's contention that jury should have been charged to consider his intoxication in determining whether he was guilty of murder or voluntary manslaughter? Was the definition of voluntary manslaughter significant or controlling? Was the absence of a statute making intoxication relevant to the existence of "any particular purpose, motive or intent" significant or controlling? (If by case law intoxication can be used to "disprove" premeditation, is any such statute needed?) Was the "presumption" of malice arising from the use of a deadly weapon significant or controlling? Was the possibility that awareness of an extremely high risk of death (a type of recklessness) was a sufficient state of mind for murder significant or controlling? If the defendant had been permitted to use intoxication to "disprove" malice aforethought, does it necessarily follow that it might also be used to absolve him of any homicide offense?

PROPOSED FEDERAL CRIMINAL CODE (1971)

§ 502. Intoxication

(1) *Defense Precluded.* Except as provided in subsection (3), intoxication is not a defense to a criminal charge. Intoxication does not, in itself, constitute mental disease within the meaning of section 503. Evidence of intoxication is admissible whenever it is relevant to negate or to establish an element of the offense charged.

(2) *Recklessness.* A person is reckless with respect to an element of an offense even though his disregard thereof is not conscious, if his not being conscious thereof is due to self-induced intoxication.

(3) *When a Defense.* Intoxication which (a) is not self-induced, or (b) if self-induced, is grossly excessive in degree, given the amount of the intoxicant, to which the actor does not know he is susceptible, is an affirmative defense if by reason of such intoxication the actor at the time of his conduct lacked substantial capacity either to appreciate its criminality or to conform his conduct to the requirements of law.

(4) *Definitions.* In this section:

(a) "intoxication" means a disturbance of mental or physical capacities resulting from the introduction of alcohol, drugs or other substances into the body;

(b) "self-induced intoxication" means intoxication caused by substances which the actor knowingly introduces into his body, the tendency of which to cause intoxication he knows or ought to know, unless he introduces them pursuant to medical advice or under such circumstances as would otherwise afford a defense to a charge of crime.

Comment

This section largely codifies existing law as to when or whether intoxication is a defense to a criminal charge.   *   *   *

The Congress and the Advisory Committee on the Federal Rules of Criminal Procedure should give consideration to requiring pretrial notice of these defenses.

NOTE

Probably the most difficult issue posed by the Proposed Federal Code as well as by other model statutory formulations relates to the question of whether intoxication should be permitted to "disprove" recklessness when that is sufficient for guilt. Present law is generally stated as in accord with the position of the Proposed Federal Code. See W. LaFave and A. Scott, Criminal Law 346–47 (1972). The commentary to the Model Penal Code defends this position as follows:

> Those who oppose a special rule [making intoxication unavailable to "disprove" recklessness] draw strength initially from the presumptive disfavor of any special rules of liability.   *   *   * [They] draw further strength from the proposition that it is precisely the awareness of the risk in recklessness that is the essence of its moral culpability—a culpability dependent on the magnitude of the specific risk advertently created. When that risk is greater in degree than that which the actor perceives at the time of getting drunk, as is frequently the case, the result of a special rule is bound to be a liability disproportionate to culpability.   *   *   *

> The case thus made is worthy of respect, but there are strong considerations on the other side. We mention first the weight of the prevailing law   *   *   *. Beyond this, there is the fundamental point that awareness of the potential consequences of excessive drinking on the capacity of human beings to gauge the risks incident to their conduct is by now so dispersed in our culture that we believe it fair to postulate a general equivalence between the risks created by the conduct of the drunken actor and the risks created by his conduct in becoming drunk. Becoming so drunk as to destroy temporarily the actor's power of perception and of judgment is conduct which plainly has no affirmative social value to counterbalance the potential danger. The actor's moral culpability lies in engaging in such conduct. Added to this are the impressive difficulties posed in litigating the foresight of any particular actor at the time when he imbibes and the relative rarity of cases where intoxication really does engender unawareness as distinguished from imprudence. These considerations lead us to propose, on balance, that the Code declare that unawareness of a risk of which the actor would have been aware had he been sober be declared immaterial.

Model Penal Code § 2.08, comment (Tent.Draft No. 9, 1959).

ROBERTS v. STATE

Supreme Court of Wisconsin, 1969.
41 Wis.2d 537, 164 N.W.2d 525.

HALLOWS, Chief Justice.   It is not and cannot be seriously contended that Roberts did not shoot and kill Mrs. Elfriede Howe with a .12 gauge shotgun about 3:00 o'clock a. m. on March 11, 1967, in her home in Columbus, Wisconsin.   Roberts was an acquaintance of Mrs. Howe, the mother of two children whose husband was in Vietnam. Early in the evening of March 10th Mrs. Howe and her friend Mrs. Kath visited several taverns in and around Columbus.   In these taverns they saw and talked to Roberts.   On the previous day Roberts had borrowed Mrs. Howe's automobile and at one tavern an argument arose between them concerning the car.   Mrs. Howe objected to the attentions of Roberts and asked the bartender to remove him from the bar but nothing was done.

After Mrs. Howe and Mrs. Kath left the tavern, the argument with Roberts continued and Mrs. Howe told Roberts to leave her alone. Roberts is reported to have told Mrs. Howe she would be sorry she made a fool out of him in the tavern.   This apparently referred to a remark Mrs. Howe made that Roberts should leave her alone and he was no good.   Upon returning home accompanied by Mrs. Kath, Mrs. Howe locked the door.   About 2:30 in the morning Mrs. Howe received a phone call and she told her caller to leave her alone and hung up the receiver.

The prosecution claims Roberts came to Mrs. Howe's home about 3:00 o'clock in the morning, broke the glass in the door and entered the kitchen holding a .12 gauge shotgun.   Mrs. Kath testified Roberts told Mrs. Howe several times he was going to kill her before the night was over but he was going to let her suffer a while first.   Roberts again accused Mrs. Howe of making a fool out of him.   While Mrs. Kath was out of the kitchen, she heard a shot and returning saw Mrs. Howe lying on the floor between the kitchen and the dining room and Roberts standing in front of her with the shotgun in his hand.

Roberts claims he was intoxicated at the time of the shooting and the record is replete with testimony of his heavy drinking for many years and during the evening prior to the killing.   According to his testimony, on the day before the shooting he consumed a pint of brandy at work and five large glasses of beer after work before dinner.   He then returned Mrs. Howe's car and he and Mrs. Howe consumed several drinks of water and brandy.   At one tavern that evening he drank two to four 12-ounce bottles of beer and between three and six brandy drinks.   At another tavern Roberts claimed he drank between 10 and 20 drinks of 84-proof brandy and another drink in the third tavern about 12:30 a. m.   From that time on Roberts claims he was unable to recall any events until he was awakened in jail about six hours later.

It is claimed that in the last tavern Mrs. Howe exclaimed so others could hear that Roberts was an ex-convict, had beaten his mother and former wife, and was no good. At the trial, several bartenders testified, Roberts took the stand, and medical testimony was introduced by both sides. The trial court found Roberts was not drunk when he shot Mrs. Howe.

Roberts argues he was drunk at the time of the shooting and was a chronic alcoholic which condition he claims is a separate affirmative defense to criminal responsibility. This is the first case in this state which raises chronic alcoholism *per se* as a separate and independent defense to the charge of first degree murder. The argument is based on the premise that chronic alcoholism is a disease which incapacitates a sufferer from responsibility for his acts because the disease determines his action.

We think there is a distinction between chronic alcoholism and an addiction to alcohol even if such addiction could be considered such a disabling disease. Not every person commonly called a "chronic alcoholic" is addicted to the point where he has a physiological or psychological dependency upon alcohol and his drinking is so involuntary and compulsive that one might argue he is irresponsible for his acts. No doubt the testimony classified Roberts as a chronic alcoholic at least to a moderate or mild degree, but the evidence is clear he could control his drinking up to the point of intoxication and was not addicted to alcohol.

*　　*　　*

Roberts was found not intoxicated and this is sustained by evidence which the trial court had a right to believe. We cannot on this record find, which would be necessary for a reversal, that Roberts as a matter of law was not only drunk but drunk involuntarily and but for that he would not have shot Mrs. Howe. Roberts could control his drinking and therefore any intoxication was not involuntary. Besides, his shooting another person and his entering another's house without consent and with intent to commit a felony are not characteristics or an involuntary part of the pattern of chronic alcoholism or symptomatic of the disease.

Roberts argues he has a defense under sec. 939.42(1), Stats.[2] If Roberts had been intoxicated to the point that he could not distinguish between right and wrong in respect to the shooting of Mrs. Howe when he shot her (old *M'Naghten* test) and such intoxication was involuntary because he suffered from a type of chronic alcoholism which compels involuntary drinking to satisfy a psychological or physiological

2. 939.42 Intoxication. An intoxicated or a drugged condition of the actor is a defense only if such condition:

   (1) Is involuntarily produced and renders the actor incapable of distinguishing between right and wrong in regard to the alleged criminal act at the time the act is committed; or * * *

   (2) Negatives the existence of a state of mind essential to the crime.

dependency thereon, Roberts would have a defense. But the evidence does not prove such involuntariness or drunkenness.

It is also quite plain that under subsec. (2) of sec. 939.42, Stats., Roberts has no defense because although he was drinking he did intend to kill Mrs. Howe. On several occasions he stated to Mrs. Howe he was going to kill her. The shooting was no accident. The trigger pressure of the gun was an unusually high pressure of 14 pounds and the gun was not likely to go off by accident. The trial court was not required to believe Roberts' testimony that he had blacked out around 12:30 in the morning and had no recollection of shooting Mrs. Howe.

*   *   *

In the instant case, the trial court found Roberts' drinking did not impair his capacity for entertaining a felonious intent and we cannot say that it was in error. We think sec. 939.42, Stats., has no application to the facts.

NOTE

Parker v. State, 7 Mo.App. 167, 254 A.2d 381 (1969): Lord Hale, in 1 Pleas of the Crown, Ch. IV, pp. 29–33 (1847) recognized three types of "idiocy, madness and lunacy" under the general name of "dementia". The third type was "dementia affectata, namely drunkenness".

"This vice doth deprive men of the use of reason, and puts many men into a perfect, but temporary phrenzy; and therefore, according to some Civilians, such a person committing homicide, shall not be punished simply for the crime of homicide, but shall suffer for his drunkenness answerable to the nature of the crime occasioned thereby; so that yet the formal cause of his punishment is rather the drunkenness, than the crime committed in it: but by the laws of England such a person shall have no privilege by this voluntary contracted madness, but shall have the same judgment as if he were in his right senses. But yet there seems to be two allays to be allowed in this case. 1. That if a person by the unskillfulness of his physician, or by the contrivance of his enemies, eat or drink such a thing as causeth such a temporary or permanent phrenzy, as aconitum or nux vomica, this puts him into the same condition, in reference to crimes, as any other phrenzy, and equally excuseth him. 2. That although the simplex phrenzy occasioned immediately by drunkenness excuse not in criminals, yet if by one or more such practices, an habitual or fixed phrenzy be caused, though this madness was contracted by the vice and will of the party, yet this habitual and fixed phrenzy thereby caused puts the man into the same condition in relation to crimes, as if the same were contracted involuntarily at first." pp. 31–33.

Thus Hale, as the law does today, distinguished between temporary insanity caused by voluntary drunkenness and that caused by involuntary drunkenness and he recognized that permanent insanity, even though caused by voluntary drinking, excused the commission of a crime.

The rule of law with respect to responsibility for criminal conduct as affected by voluntary intoxication which has been consistently followed by the majority of courts in the United States is substantially that stated by Lord Hale. Regardless of what test is applicable to determining insanity, the majority distinguish between (1) the mental effect of voluntary intoxication which is the immediate result of a particular alcoholic bout; and (2) an alcoholic psychosis[3] resulting from long continued habits of excessive drinking. The first does not excuse responsibility for a criminal act; the second may. In other words, if a person drinks intoxicating liquor and is sane both prior to drinking and after the influences of the intoxicant has worn off, but is insane by the applicable test while under the influence of the intoxicant, he comes under the first category. If he is insane whether or not he is directly under the influence of an intoxicant, even though that insanity was caused by voluntary drinking, he comes under the second category. The cases usually refer to the first category as a "temporary" insanity and the second category as a "permanent", "fixed" or "settled" insanity. These terms may be an oversimplification. What "permanent", "fixed" or "settled" means within the frame of reference is that the insanity not only existed while a person was under the influence of intoxicating spirits as an immediate result of imbibing, but existed independent of such influence, even though the insanity was caused by past imbibing. So if a person while in the throes of delirium tremens which may meet the test for insanity, commits a crime, he is not responsible for his criminal conduct, although such defect, resulting remotely from excessive drinking is only a temporary toxic state. It would seem that the distinction, notwithstanding the language of the cases, is not so much between temporary and permanent insanity as it is one between the direct results of of drinking, which are voluntarily sought after, and its remote and undesired consequences. We adopt the majority view.

---

3. The term "alcoholic psychosis" has been defined as "Insanity due to alcohol", Davidson, Forensic Psychiatry, p. 316 (1952), and as "grave mental disorder found in connection with excessive use of alcohol which was imbibed because of defective personality integration and resulting unsolved conflicts", Cavanaugh & McGoldrick, Fundamental Psychiatry, p. 426 (1958).

C. RESULTS AND THE REQUIREMENT OF CAUSATION

A number of crimes, including but by no means restricted to the homicide offenses, require proof of the occurrence of a result and of a causal relationship between the defendant's acts and that result. Problems of causation—especially of so-called "proximate" causation—present some of the most perplexing matters with which the substantive criminal law must deal.

WEINREB, COMMENT ON BASIS OF CRIMINAL LIABILITY; CULPABILITY; CAUSATION, IN 1 WORKING PAPERS OF THE NATIONAL COMMISSION ON REFORM OF FEDERAL CRIMINAL LAWS

142–43 (1970).

The principles governing attribution of consequences to a person's conduct for purposes of criminal liability are not ordinarily stated collectively as a coherent body of doctrine. Still less often have such principles been codified. * * *

If anything but for which an event would not have occurred is a cause of the event, there are any number of "causes" of every event. The presence of oxygen in the air and the physical properties of paper are as much causes, in that sense, of the burning of a piece of paper as is touching a lit match to the paper. When we select a cause as *the cause,* the selection is based on some principle that reflects our interests. By making the selection, we focus our attention on some aspect of the situation, usually one which we think is under our control, so that we can assure or prevent a repetition of the occurrence. If someone drops a cup and it breaks, we are more likely to say "You should be more careful," than to say "I wish the floor were not so hard"; but if an infant drops the cup, we are likely to say "We'll have to get him a plastic cup," instead of "He really must not drop things." As a crude and preliminary approximation of ordinary speech and understanding it is fair to say that we distinguish the cause of an event from the (necessary) conditions of an event according to our interests, which usually but not always means that we single out as the "cause" some element of the situation which we can control and describe as "conditions" other necessary elements. Some necessary conditions are taken so much for granted—for example, the presence of oxygen in the air, the physical properties of paper—that unless some curious feature of the situation focuses our attention on them, we do not mention them even as conditions. Without some frame of reference, the question, "What is (are) the cause(s) of X?" is as meaningless as the question, "What are all the conditions but for which X would not have occurred?" Ordinarily the frame of reference is clear and is supplied by commonsense out of common experience.

The inadequacy of principles of causation in the criminal law reflects uncertainty about the basis of criminal liability in situations where results are important to liability. We are not certain whether the assailant who gives the hemophiliac a light blow that causes a bruise from which the hemophiliac dies should be punished for assault or homicide; or whether all the senators should be punished as Caesar's murderers even though any dozen could have stayed away from the Forum on the fateful day without changing the result.

PEOPLE v. HEBERT

California District Court of Appeal, 1964.
228 Cal.App.2d 514, 39 Cal.Rptr. 539.

SHINN, Presiding Justice. Henry Hebert was charged with the murder of Charles Swallow, pleaded not guilty, and after a trial by jury was convicted of involuntary manslaughter, a lesser included offense. Probation was denied and he was sentenced to the state prison. Defendant was represented by the Public Defender. Appeal is brought from the judgment in propria persona.

Defendant was a patron in a Venice bar, drinking beer but not intoxicated, when the victim entered at about 11 p. m. According to all the witnesses who testified on the subject, Swallow appeared to be either drunk or ill; the barmaid refused him service. He sat on a stool near defendant and an argument arose between them. It was established that defendant, while standing, hit Swallow in the face with his fist while Swallow was sitting on a bar stool, and that the assault was without sufficient provocation. When hit, the victim was knocked to the floor. Defendant testified that Swallow asked him for a quarter, which was refused, and Swallow said "All I done for you niggers, I can't get anything out of you" and defendant said "That is where you are wrong, man." Swallow shoved him, put his hand into his coat pocket and said "I ought to cut your throat"; Swallow did not fall off the bar stool but that after he was hit another patron said "watch that knife," grabbed Swallow around the waist and pulled him off the stool. This other patron did not testify, nor was any knife found. No one actually saw Swallow fall, but several witnesses heard him fall. There was sufficient evidence to prove that the victim was knocked off the bar stool by the force of defendant's blows and that his head hit the wooden barroom floor with what one witness described as a loud "thud."

Officers arrived about ten minutes later. Swallow was lying on the floor on his back, but apparently conscious. Officers assisted him to a sitting position and thought he was not seriously injured, but was intoxicated. They partly carried, partly dragged him to a patrol car and took him to the police station for booking for being intoxicated in a public place. Thelma McCord, the barmaid, testified that the two officers dragged Swallow from the place where he lay on the floor to the sidewalk; one officer lifted Swallow by holding onto his belt in the rear; the other lifted at his head; Swallow's feet were dragging; at the sidewalk the officers dropped him on his face; the drop was 12 to 14 inches; he was perfectly limp. The two officers testified that they partly carried, partly dragged Swallow to the sidewalk, sat him down in a sitting position and then laid him gently on his back; they did not drop him.

The officers arrived at the station with the victim about 35 minutes after the altercation. According to the officers, during the booking procedure and just after Swallow was searched and he was standing with his hands high against a wall, he was observed to fall over backwards with his arms at his sides and "completely rigid as though a plank were falling"; his buttocks hit the floor first and then the back of his head; his head bounced about six inches off the floor and fell back, striking the floor a second time. The floor was concrete with an asphalt tile covering. Immediately after hitting the floor he started bleeding from one ear and within a few seconds from both ears. He was removed to a hospital where he died that morning.

The determinative question on the trial was whether defendant's act of striking decedent and knocking him to the floor was a proximate cause of death.

Dr. Kade, autopsy surgeon for the Los Angeles County Coroner's office, testified that there were three areas of injury to the head, each caused by a separate impact; one to the nasal area, causing a fracture of the nasal bones; one to the left rear of the skull, causing severe hemorrhaging; and a third to the right rear portion of the skull, causing additional fracturing and hemorrhaging. The nasal fracture was apparently due to the direct blows of defendant; the injury to the left rear of the skull was the most serious and the injury was more consistent with the decedent's having struck his head on the wooden barroom floor than with his falling and striking his head on the concrete floor at the police station. In the opinion of the witness, the injury to the left rear of the skull was received as the result of decedent's being knocked off the bar stool. Both these injuries to the brain caused hemorrhaging, and either one, in Dr. Kade's opinion, would have resulted in a loss of consciousness. It was the opinion of Dr. Kade that the injury to the right side of decedent's head was caused at the police station when decedent suddenly lost consciousness and fell backward. The opinion of Dr. Kade was stated on cross-examination as follows: "In my opinion, death was caused by the two blows to the rear of the head. Whether the injury causing the fracture of the nasal bone would have been enough to cause death in and of itself, is difficult for me to establish, since there were these two additional injuries to the back of the head."

The witness was questioned further on cross-examination: "Q You feel at this time, Doctor, that it is difficult for you to say that the damage to the nasal area and the front of the skull there, that that would have been sufficient in and of itself to have brought about death; is that right? A Well, it is difficult to say because it is a conjectural question. It is like saying, if a boat is on fire and there is an explosion on board and the boat sinks would the fire have been enough to destroy the boat by itself had there not been an explosion. It is trying to infer what would have happened or could have happened if something else didn't happen. But the something else did happen and so I would be hesitant to conjecture about what could or might have happened under other circumstances." And when questioned further on cross-examination, he answered as follows: "Q Well, when you stated earlier, Doctor, that you felt it would be speculative or conjectural for you to say that the damage to the front part of the skull was sufficient in itself to be fatal, did you mean that you felt it was conjectural, too conjectural or speculative for you to testify under oath that such damage could cause death in and of itself? A No, I did not. It is my opinion that it easily could have, but I did not wish to state it as an absolute certainty that it would have definitely and unequivocally have caused death as an inevitable result in and of it-self. It is my opinion that the greatest likelihood, the greatest medical probability is that it would have been sufficient to cause death. But I hesitate to state it as an absolute certainty."

The statement of the doctor that death resulted from the blows on the rear portions of the skull is clear enough. His opinion with respect to the probable consequences of the blow which fractured the nasal bones was an expression of his belief that the blow "easily could have" and that according "to the greatest medical probability" would have been sufficient to cause death. The force of this opinion was not destroyed by the stated qualification that he was not saying that death would have been the inevitable result of the blow or would have followed as an absolute certainty. The opinions expressed with respect to the probable consequences of the blow to the face, considered with the opinion that the major brain hemorrhage resulted from the fall on the barroom floor left no doubt that the opinion of the doctor was that the injuries in the barroom were probably fatal.

The evidence of the several injuries, the blow to the face, the fall in the barroom, the incident on the sidewalk and the fall in the police station presented the critical question as to the proximate cause of the death.

Upon this issue the primary factual question was whether the injuries received in the barroom would have resulted in death. Defendant was responsible for all the injuries inflicted in the barroom and if the jury had found those injuries to have been so severe as to have resulted in death the fact that other injuries were suffered later would have been immaterial. The only support for a finding of the jury that the injuries in the barroom were fatal would have been the opinion expressed by Dr. Kade. The jury was not required to give full effect to his opinion, and could have doubted that the fatal injuries were suffered in the barroom incident. It is of common knowledge that a blow which causes a broken nose does not ordinarily cause death. The picture of deceased taken at the police station merely showed him lying on his back with his head on the floor. There was evidence that his head bounced after hitting the floor. It was a matter of pure speculation which side of the skull hit the floor first. Moreover, the opinion of the doctor that the most serious fall was the one in the barroom was inconsistent with the fact that it was the fall in the police station that caused immediate bleeding from both ears. If it was doubted that the first injuries would have produced a fatal result and that death would have resulted despite the injuries received in the police station, the question necessarily arose whether defendant was responsible for the consequences of the later fall. It was, therefore, vitally important that the jury be adequately and correctly instructed on the doctrine of proximate cause.

The court instructed that in order to find the defendant guilty of either murder or involuntary manslaughter the jury must find that the injury inflicted by defendant was a proximate cause of the death and that "The proximate cause of an injury is that cause which, in natural and continuous sequence, unbroken by any efficient intervening cause, produces the injury, and without which the result would not have occurred. It is the efficient cause—the one that necessarily sets in operation the factors that accomplish the injury."

The court also instructed as follows: "You are instructed that to be a legal cause of death, a defendant's act must be its proximate cause, not merely its possible cause. A defendant's act may be considered the proximate cause of the death of another though it is not the immediate cause, if it is the ultimate cause. But where there is a supervening cause the defendant's act cannot be considered a proximate cause. The fact, if it be a fact, that the deceased or some other person or persons were guilty of negligence, which was a contributory cause of the death involved in the case, is not deemed to be a supervening cause and is no defense to a criminal charge if the defendant's own conduct was a proximate cause of the death." We are of the opinion that these instructions were wholly inadequate.

It has been the practice for many years to instruct in the language of the first quoted instruction, but we do not believe it was a satisfactory or sufficient instruction to give in the present case where the question of proximate cause was an intricate and difficult one to be resolved by the jury. We do not say the instruction misstates the law, but only that in the present case it was unclear and confusing as a statement of the doctrine of proximate cause. * * *

There have been many attempts to phrase an all-purpose definition of proximate cause, but we think that in ordinary circumstances all the definitions have had their roots in the doctrine of foreseeability. We think the jury should have been instructed in clear and simple language as to the measure of the responsibility of defendant for the acts which caused Swallow's death. He was responsible not only for the injuries inflicted in the barroom, but for any later injuries to Swallow that were reasonably foreseeable, and which he would not have sustained if in a normal condition. The issue here was clearcut and vital and should have been submitted to the jury upon the test of foreseeability. Instead of being submitted in this simple form, the issue was confused by the use in the first instruction of the terms "natural and continuous sequence," "efficient intervening cause" and "necessarily sets in operation the factors that accomplish the result." And in the second quoted instruction, we find "superseding cause" added. The jury was given no definition of "efficient intervening cause" or "supervening cause." These are vague and confusing terms, at best, and the jury should not have been left to guess at their meaning and their application to the facts. What test was the jury to apply in determining their meaning? Do the terms "intervening" and "supervening" mean the same thing, or have they different meanings? What would be an "efficient intervening cause" or "supervening cause" that would break the chain of causation? Would the chain remain unbroken even though the later event was one that was extraordinary and unpredictable? The instructions did not answer these questions.

We cannot doubt that in an effort to understand the full purport of the instructions the minds of the jurors would have been distracted from the question of foreseeability of future injury. They were told to look for an "efficient intervening cause" or a "supervening cause" as if it made no difference whether after-occurring causes were reasonably foreseeable. The fall in the police station, judged from appearances, was extremely serious, as evidenced by the bleeding from both ears. The jury could well have believed that except for that fall death would not have occurred. Of course, the question was not whether that particular event might occur, but whether any serious injury was likely to occur because of Swallow's condition. Defendant had a duty to anticipate the common and ordinary consequences of his act, and these he was responsible for. They could be said to be the direct consequences. But the fall in the police station could have been found to be an extraordinary and abnormal occurrence, not reasonably foreseeable as a result of the first injuries. The failure of the court to instruct that defendant would have been responsible for the consequences of the injuries received after Swallow was taken from the barroom only if further injury was reasonably to be anticipated, and the giving of instructions that enabled the jury to hold him responsible for later injuries even if the same were not reasonably foreseeable was prejudicial and reversible error.

The judgment is reveresd.

NOTES

1.   Does the court in the instant case hold or suggest that the concept of "intervening superceding cause" is not a helpful or appropriate one? If it does, is it correct? In answering, consider the following:

> An intervening force is a force which is neither operating in the defendant's presence, nor at the place where the defendant's act takes effect at the time of the defendant's act, but comes into effective operation at or before the time of the damage. Thus where a a fire is started in a then existing wind, the wind is not an intervening force, but a condition existing at the time of the defendant's act.

McLaughlin, Proximate Cause, 39 Harv.L.Rev. 149, 159–60 (1925).   Can the phrase "superceding cause" reasonably be defined in any way other than as a factor causally related to the result which, for reasons of policy, will be given the legal effect of rendering the cause which it supercedes not a legally-recognized cause of the result? See R. Perkins, Criminal Law 698 (2nd ed. 1969). As so defined, what analytical value might these concepts have?

2.   What difference, if any, would it—or should it—make whether Swallow's falls from the stool, on the sidewalk, and in the police station were causally related to his intoxication, the defendant's blows, negligence, conscious indifference, or intentional conduct on the part of police officers, or any combination of these?

3.   What difference, if any, would it—or should it—make whether (or to what extent) at the time of Swallow's death he was hemorrhaging from the fracture of the nasal bone, the injury to the left rear of the skull, and the injury to the right rear of the skull? Whether (or to what extent) he had hemorrhaged from these injuries between each injury and the time of death?

MODEL PENAL CODE

(Tent. Draft No. 4, 1955).

Section 2.03.   Causal Relationship Between Conduct and Result; Divergence Between Result Designed or Contemplated and Actual Result or Between Probable and Actual Result

(1) Conduct is the cause of a result when:

(a) it is an antecedent but for which the result in question would not have occurred; and

(b) the relationship between the conduct and result satisfies any additional causal requirements plainly imposed by law.

(2) When purposely or knowingly causing a particular result is a material element of an offense, the element is not established if the

actual result is not within the purpose or the contemplation of the actor unless:

> (a) the actual result differs from that designed or contemplated, as the case may be, only in the respect that a different person or different property is injured or affected or that the injury or harm designed or contemplated would have been more serious or more extensive than that caused; or

> (b) the actual result involves the same kind of injury or harm as that designed or contemplated and is not too accidental in its occurrence to have a just bearing on the actor's liability or on the gravity of his offense. [Alternative: and it occurs in a manner which the actor knows or should know is rendered substantially more probable by his conduct.]

(3) When recklessly or negligently causing a particular result is a material element of an offense, the element is not established if the actual result is not within the risk of which the actor is aware, or in the case of negligence, of which he should be aware unless:

> (a) the actual result differs from the probable result only in the respect that a different person or different property is injured or affected or that the probable injury or harm would have been more serious or more extensive than that caused; or

> (b) the actual result involves the same kind of injury or harm as the probable result and is not too accidental in in its occurrence to have a just bearing on the actor's liability or on the gravity of his offense. [Alternative: and it occurs in a manner which the actor knows or should know is rendered substantially more probable by his conduct.]

Commentary

Section 2.03. Causal relationship between conduct and result; Divergence between result designed or contemplated and actual result or between probable and actual result

1. This section is concerned with offenses that are so defined that causing a particular result is a material element of the offense, as in the case of homicide, theft, etc. It undertakes to define the causality relationship that should generally be required to establish liability for such offenses and to deal with inevitable problems incident to variations between the actual result of conduct and the result sought or contemplated by the actor or probable under the circumstances of the action. These problems are now faced as issues of "proximate causation" and they present enormous difficulty, especially in homicide, because of the vague meaning of that term. Rather than

seek to systematize variant and sometimes inconsistent rules in different areas in which the problem has arisen, the section undertakes a fresh approach to what appear to be the central issues.

2. Paragraph 1(a) treats but-for cause as the causality relationship that normally should be regarded as sufficient, in the view that this is the simple, pervasive meaning of causation that is relevant for purposes of penal law. When concepts of "proximate causation" disassociate the actor's conduct and a result of which it was a but-for cause, the reason always inheres in the judgment that the actor's culpability with reference to the result, i. e., his purpose, knowledge, recklessness or negligence, was such that it would be unjust to permit the result to influence his liability or the gravity of the offense of which he is convicted. Since this is so, the draft proceeds upon the view that problems of this kind ought to be faced as problems of the culpability required for conviction and not as problems of "causation."

Paragraph 1(b) contemplates, however, that this general position may prove unacceptable in dealing with particular offenses. In that event, additional causal requirements may be imposed explicitly, such, for example, as a temporal limitation with respect to causing death.

3. Paragraphs (2) and (3) are drafted on the theory stated. They assume that liability requires purpose, knowledge, recklessness or negligence with respect to the result which is an element of the offense and deal explicitly with variations between the actual result and that designed, contemplated or threatened, as the case may be, stating when the variation is considered immaterial.

4. Paragraph (2) is addressed to the case where the culpability requirement with respect to the result is purpose or knowledge, i. e. where purposely or knowingly causing a specified result is a material element of the offense. Here if the actual result is not within the purpose or the contemplation of the actor, the culpability requirement is not established, except in the circumstances set forth in sub-paragraphs (a) and (b).

Sub-paragraph (a) deals with the situation where the actual result differed from the result designed or contemplated only in the respect that a different person or different property was injured or affected or that the injury or harm designed or contemplated was more serious or more extensive than that caused. Such variations between purpose or contemplation and result are made immaterial, as almost certainly would be the view under existing law.

Sub-paragraph (b) deals with the situation where the actual result involved the same kind of injury or harm as that designed or contemplated but the precise injury inflicted was different or occurred in a different way. Here the draft makes no attempt to catalogue the possibilities, e. g., to deal with the intervening or concurrent causes, natural or human; unexpected physical conditions; distinctions between the infliction of mortal or non-mortal wounds. It deals only with the ultimate criterion by which the significance of such possibilities ought to be judged, presenting two alternative formulations. The first proposes that the question to be faced is whether the actual result is "too accidental in its occurrence to have a just bearing on the actor's liability or on the gravity of his offense." The alternative proposes that the issue turn on whether the actual result "occurs in a manner which the actor knows or ought to know is rendered substantially more probable by his conduct."

It may be useful in appraising either treatment of the problem to note that what will usually turn on the determination will not be the criminality of a defendant's conduct but rather the gravity of his offense. Since the actor, by hypothesis, has sought to cause a criminal result or has been reckless or negligent with respect to such a result, he will be guilty of some crime under a well-considered penal code even if he is not held for the actual result, i. e. he will be guilty of attempt, assault or some offense involving risk creation, such as reckless driving. Thus the issue in penal law is very different than in torts. Only in form is it, in penal law, a question of the actor's liability. In substance, it is a question of the severity of sentence which the Court is authorized or obliged to impose. Its practical importance thus depends on the disparity in sentence for the various offenses that may be involved, e. g. the sentences for an attempted and completed crime.

How far a Model Code ought to attribute importance in the grading of offenses to the actual result of conduct, as distinguished from results attempted or threatened, presents an issue of some difficulty which is of general importance in the Code. It may be said, however, that distinctions of this order are to some extent essential, at least when the severest sanctions are involved. For juries will not lightly find convictions that will lead to the severest types of sentences unless the resentments caused by the infliction of important injuries have been aroused. Whatever abstract logic may suggest, a prudent legislator cannot disregard these facts of life in the enactment of a penal code.

It may be added that attributing importance to the actual result does not substantially detract from the deterrent efficacy of the law, at least in dealing with cases of purposeful misconduct. One who attempts to kill and thus expects to bring about the result punishable by the gravest penalty, is unlikely to be influenced in his behavior by the treatment that the law provides for those who fail in such attempts; his expectation is that he is going to succeed. See Michael and Wechsler, A Rationale of the Law of Homicide, 37 Columbia L. Rev. 1261, 1294–1298.

Viewed in these terms, it may be said that either the proposed or the alternative formulation should suffice for the exclusion of those situations where the actual result is so remote from the actor's purpose or contemplation that juries can be expected to believe that it should have no bearing on the actor's liability for the graver offense or, stated differently, on the gravity of the offense of which he is convicted. If, for example, the defendant attempted to shoot his wife and missed, with the result that she retired to her parents' country home and then was killed in falling off a horse, no one would think that the defendant should be held guilty of murder, though he did intend her death and his attempt to kill her was a but-for cause of her encounter with the horse. Both court and jury would regard the actual result as "too accidental in its occurrence to have a just bearing on the actor's liability or on the gravity of his offense." Alternatively, they would regard the actual result as one which did not occur in a manner that the actor knew or should have known was rendered substantially more probable by his conduct when he attempted to shoot his wife to death.

It is in closer cases that a difference in result might be expected. Thus, if the defendant in the case supposed had shot his wife and in the hospital she had contracted a disease which was medically unrelated to the wound (though related to her presence in the hospital), her death from the disease may well be thought to have been rendered substantially more probable by the defendant's conduct, as presumably he should have known. Yet juries might regard it as a too unusual result to justify convicting him of murder. The advantage of putting the issue squarely to the jury's sense of justice is that it does not attempt to force a result which the jury may resist. It also leaves the principle flexible for application to the infinite variety of cases likely to arise. The argument for the alternative is, on the other hand, that flexibility will involve inequality of application; that if the actual result was foreseen or foreseeable as a substantial probability, there can be no injustice in holding the actor responsible for its occurrence, nor is there any reason to expect that jury action will nullify such a rule.

In the Reporter's view, either formulation is acceptable. What is important is to free the law from the encrusted precedents on "proximate causation", offering a principle that will permit both courts and juries to begin afresh in facing problems of this kind.

5. Paragraph (3) deals with the case where recklessness or negligence is the required kind of culpability and where the actual result is not within the risk of which the actor was aware, or, in the case of negligence, of which he should have been aware. The principles proposed to govern are the same as in the case where purposely or knowingly causing the specified result is the material element of the crime. If the actual result differed from the probable result only in the respect that a different person or different property was injured or affected, the variation is declared to be inconsequential. In

other situations, if the actual result involved the same kind of injury or harm as the probable result, the question asked is whether it was too accidental in its occurrence to have just bearing on the actor's liability or on the gravity of his offense or, if the alternative is preferred, whether the result occurred in a manner which the actor knew or should have known was rendered substantially more probable by his conduct. The governing considerations are the same as in the situation dealt with by paragraph (2).

WEINREB, COMMENT ON BASIS OF CRIMINAL LIABILITY; CULPABILITY; CAUSATION, IN 1 WORKING PAPERS OF THE NATIONAL COMMISSION ON REFORM OF FEDERAL CRIMINAL LAWS

144–46 (1970).

The only statutory attempt in this country to develop a general explanatory formula of causal relation in criminal cases is that of the Model Penal Code (§ 2.03). As the commentary to the Model Penal Code observes, its formula does not systematize the "variant and sometimes inconsistent rules" that have developed, but "undertakes a fresh approach." The inadequacy of the Code's formulation illustrates the difficulties involved.

The basic provision of the Model Penal Code adopts "but for" causation as the general test; it is both necessary and, unless "additional causal requirements" are specifically imposed, sufficient. This provision does not clearly state the accepted rule or easily lead to the correct result in cases of "concurrent causation."

Even though all of the senators may have intended to kill Caesar and all of them stabbed him, under the Model Penal Code's formulation none would be criminally liable for his death since (so I shall assume) he would have died even though any one of them had held back his knife. Even a senator who stabbed Caesar through the heart would not be liable, since, so Anthony tells us (act 3, scene 2) "sweet Caesar's blood" was streaming from all the wounds.

The Model Penal Code's reliance on "but for" causation as ordinarily enough for liability ignores the cases in which it is not essential to liability. There are situations in which, for purposes of the criminal law, we are properly "interested" in more than one cause of an occurrence, even though none of them alone is necessary or more than one of them are alone sufficient. The paradigm is a situation in which each of two or more persons engages in conduct that fully satisfies the definition of a crime but in which there is only "one" harmful consequence.

A and *B* simultaneously shoot at *X*, both intending to kill him. The bullets enter *X's* body at the same time. Each wound is sufficient to cause death and would alone cause

death in the same amount of time.   X dies from the joint
effect of both wounds.

We are just as properly interested if neither of the wounds alone
would cause death but the facts are otherwise the same.   (Such a set
of facts is, of course, hardly likely to occur.   It is not so unlikely
that, for lack of evidence, a situation should be treated as if it occurred
as described.)

This point was discussed during the American Law Institute's discussion of the Model Penal Code.   It was concluded that the matter
would be clarified in the commentary to the section.   In the discussion, Professor Wechsler indicated that he believed the Model Penal
Code's statement was acceptable, evidently on the basis that the specific result caused by concurrent causes would not have occurred but
for the operation of each.   While this is a permissible construction
of the language, it is a strain on ordinary usage, which does not attend so carefully to details of this kind in the face of the major fact
of a death.

Additional sections of the Model Penal Code's formulation deal
with cases in which the actual result is not intended or is not within
the risk created by the actor's conduct, by providing that there is no
causal relation in such cases unless either the actual and the intended
or probable results differ only in respects generally irrelevant to the
criminal law (the specific person or property injured; the greater seriousness of the intended or probable harm) or the actual result is
similar to ("involves the same kind of injury or harm as") the intended or probable result, and "is not too remote or accidental in its
occurrence to have a [just] bearing on the actor's liability or on the
gravity of his offense."   This formulation breaks down in precisely
those cases in which difficulties arise, those covered by the last clause.
Of the alternative formulations, that which omits the word "just"
states the problem without resolving it (by use of the question-begging
word "too"); that which includes the word "just" (in addition to
using the word "too") refers to an inapt standard for resolving it—
that the connection between a result and conduct but for which the
result would not have occurred is remote or accidental does not, unless the words "remote" and "accidental" are given special (question-
begging) meaning, affect the justice of holding the actor liable for
his conduct.

Illustrative of an alternative to the Model Penal Code's reliance
on "but for" causation as the basic test, is the following, drafted for
consideration in the Federal Code:

> A causal connection between a person's conduct and an
> occurrence does not exist if:
>
> > (a) the person's conduct was not sufficient to cause
> > the occurrence without the cooperation of one or more
> > events or the conduct of one or more persons; and

(b) without the cooperation of the person's conduct, another event or the conduct of another person was
sufficient to cause the occurrence.

Such a provision, which does not attempt to state what causation
is but only what, in some circumstances, it is not, leads to the correct result in many cases of concurrent causation by providing that a
person's conduct is not the cause of a result if someone else's conduct
or some other event is both necessary and sufficient to produce the result. Where conduct is not sufficient to cause an occurrence and
there is present and identifiable other conduct or some event which is
sufficient to cause the occurrence, common understanding would probably regard the latter as the cause. However, the provision, at best,
offers no guidance in the case of sequential, as opposed to concurrent causes. (If A shoots X, as a result of which X goes to the
hospital, and while he is there (i) the hospital burns down, or (ii) the
wound becomes infected, or (iii) a doctor stabs X inadvertently, or
(iv) a doctor stabs X deliberately, and X dies, in which of the four
cases should A be liable for X's death?) Even though the provision
attempts to say only when causation is not present, it is readily perceived as indicating when causation is present. If we understand the
provision to refer only to concurrent and not sequential causes, it is
only because, without relying on the provision, we have a sense of
when an act or event causes an occurrence. (If the provision is not
so understood, A would, or at least might, be liable for X's death in
all of the cases described, which would surely be the wrong result at
least in case (iv) and possibly in others as well.)

The provision gives limited guidance, and even that only because
of our independent understanding of the very concept of causation
which the provision attempts partially to illuminate.

A final possibility is not to provide what shall or shall not count
as a causal relation, but to list factors which shall be relevant to a
determination that conduct did or did not cause a result. One might,
for example, specify as such factors the extent to which the conduct
manifests the danger which is realized in the result or the extent to
which the actor's conduct singles him out as the person responsible
for the result. All such "factors," however, are either make-weights
which collapse on analysis or depend finally on the concept of causation which they are intended to clarify.

PROPOSED FEDERAL CRIMINAL CODE

(1971).

§ 305. Causal Relationship Between Conduct and Result

Causation may be found where the result would not have occurred but for the conduct of the accused operating either alone or concurrently with another cause, unless the concurrent cause was clearly sufficient to produce the result and the conduct of the accused clearly insufficient.

Comment

Rules governing causation have never been specified in federal criminal statutes. The major problem in enunciating such rules is presented by situations in which two or more factors "cause" the result. This section is a modified "but for" test with a proviso that excludes those situations in which the concurrent cause was clearly sufficient to produce the result and the accused's conduct clearly insufficient. An alternative approach would be to have no specific provision on causation, leaving the matter to judge-made law. While the proposed section may not be useful in all cases where causation must be explained, it is intended to be an aid to uniformity and clarification whenever it does apply.

NOTE

Weinreb, Comment on Basis of Criminal Liability; Culpability; Causation, in 1 Working Papers of the National Commission on Reform of Federal Criminal Laws 147 (1970) explained the Proposed Federal Code's position as follows:

> The drafters of the basic provisions on liability have been unable to develop an explanatory formula of causation which is both accurate and meaningful. All such formulae, whether cast in terms of what is necessary or sufficient to establish a causal relationship or, more tentatively, in terms of what is relevant to the existence of a causal relationship, flounder in precisely those cases where the existence of the relationship is in doubt. To omit a section defining causation generally will simply acknowledge the absence of any such general provision in Federal criminal law.

STATE EX REL. SCHULTER v. RORAFF

Supreme Court of Wisconsin, 1968.
39 Wis.2d 342, 159 N.W.2d 25, certiorari denied 393 U.S. 1066,
89 S.Ct. 716, 21 L.Ed.2d 709.

The order appealed from quashed an alternative writ of prohibition which the plaintiff Roger Schulter had obtained to prevent the defendant County Judge Leonard Roraff of La Crosse County from proceeding in a case entitled State of Wisconsin v. Roger Schulter.

That case arose out of an automobile accident which occurred on May 15, 1967, on a county trunk highway in La Crosse county. Schulter, aged 23 years, was the owner of an automobile which he allowed Peter Cavadini, a 17-year-old boy, to drive. Besides Schulter and Cavadini, the other passengers included a man of 28 years and three other 17-year-old boys. The Schulter car collided with an automobile owned and operated by Peter Fink, which contained three passengers. In the collision the four 17-year-old boys in the Schulter car and a passenger in the Fink car were killed.

A coroner's inquest was held pursuant to sec. 966.01, Stats., and the evidence disclosed the passengers in the Schulter car had been drinking beer purchased by Schulter and the other adult passenger. Blood tests showed Peter Cavadini had alcohol in his blood amounting to .142 percent, which under sec. 885.235, Stats., is relevant evidence on the issue of intoxication. The coroner's jury returned a verdict finding the negligent driving of Cavadini caused the accident; that his blood alcohol level affected his ability to drive the Schulter car and the furnishing of the beer to the minor Cavadini by Schulter and allowing him to drive the car under these conditions was the proximate cause of the deaths.

Schulter as a result of the inquest was charged with two counts of contributing to the delinquency of a child in violation of sec. 947.15, Stats.; the first count charged a felony because the deaths were involved; the second count charged only the misdemeanor of contributing to the delinquency of the children by furnishing them fermented malt beverage.

HALLOWS, Chief Justice. * * *

It is claimed sec. 947.15, Stats., is unconstitutional because it is arbitrary [and] unreasonable * * *. It is specifically argued that the statute increased the penalty for contributing to the delinquency of a child from that of a misdemeanor to the punishment of a felony if death is a consequence of the delinquency. It is argued this increased penalty has no substantial relationship to the purpose sought to be accomplished by the section and there is no requirement of a criminally relevant connection between the delinquent acts and the death such as foreseeability, a dangerous activity, or a felonious act. What punishment is to be related to a particular crime is within the province of the legislature and the relating process is governed by the constitution to the extent no cruel and inhuman punishment is permitted and due process and equal protection are afforded.

We think the consequences of the act and their seriousness may be a proper consideration in fixing the severity of the punishment. Foreseeability or intent that the specific consequences occur are not necessary to due process or to a crime. Acts which result in death frequently carry increased penalties over the same act which does not result in death, i. e., sec. 940.03, felony murder. We think there is sufficient connection even if it is only causation between the proscribed act of contributing to the delinquency of a child and death resulting from such delinquency to make an increased penalty reasonable and not arbitrary even though death is unintended or unforeseen.

* * *

Order affirmed.

NOTE

Wis.Stat.Ann. § 947.15 (1970 Supp.) provides as follows:

(1) The following persons may be fined not more than $500 or imprisoned not more than one year in county jail or both, and if death is a consequence may be fined $1,000 or imprisoned not more than 5 years:

(a) Any person 18 or older who intentionally encourages or contributes to the delinquency or neglect of any child; * * *

(2) An act or failure to act contributes to the delinquency or neglect of a child, although the child does not actually become neglected or delinquent, if the natural and probable consequence of that act or failure to act would be to cause the child to become delinquent or neglected.

Can concepts of causation be meaningfully applied in the absence of the forbidden harm? On what basis is it to be decided whether "the natural and probable consequence" of an act would be to cause delinquency if that result has not occurred? If "intentionally" in subsection (1) (a) supra means that the state must establish an intent to cause "delinquency or neglect" the statute would be consistent with the doctrine of attempt, but what if it refers only to the state of mind with which the defendant performed the act—that is he did not act inadvertently—later claimed to have probable effect of causing delinquency? In State v. Hodges, 254 Ore. 21, 457 P.2d 491 (1969), the portion of the Oregon "contributing-to-delinquency" statute which criminalized "any act which manifestly tends to cause any child to become a delinquent child" was held unconstitutional on its face. This language had, in an earlier case, been interpreted as limited to acts "of such a character that the court could hold as a matter of law that such conduct would, if unchecked, produce delinquency in a victim." Id. at 492. In holding that the challenged language provided inadequate notice to the public and uncontrolled discretion to judge and jury the court faced the state's argument that "the jury should be permitted to exercise its own common sense and good judgment on the causes of delinquency." Id. at 494. The court responded:

"* * * but this argument begs the question. Without a legislative declaration of standards, the trial court would have no basis for submitting one case to a jury and refusing to submit another case to a jury. Further, the trial jury would have no basis for deciding that a given course of conduct tended to endanger the welfare of a child, or that it had no such tendency. Some degree of ad hoc legislation by juries in finding defendants not guilty may be unavoidable and socially desirable to ease the edges of the criminal law, but the free-wheeling power to legislate so as to find a defendant guilty should not be institutionalized in a criminal statute. Such a statute not only creates a serious danger of inequality in the administration of the criminal law, but it runs squarely contrary to the purpose of Oregon Constitution, Art. I, § 21, which prohibits the delegation of legislative power." Ibid.

RAMIREZ v. STATE

Supreme Court of Arizona, 1916.
18 Ariz. 272, 158 P. 640.

ROSS, C. J. Appellant appeals from a judgment of conviction of murder in the second degree. * * *

At the trial the facts developed that appellant and one Leandro Maldonado, at about 12:30 o'clock of the night of June 27, 1915, were proceeding along the main highway from Lowell to Bisbee. They were carrying a number of bottles of mescal and three canteens of mescal that they had brought from Naco. Walter Brooks, who was head watchman for the Copper Queen Mining Company, in some way not explained by the evidence, the appellant, and Maldonado came together and became involved in a fight, resulting in Brooks' death. Five shots were fired, one of which took effect in the body of Maldonado, and at least two struck the deceased. Maldonado's testimony was that deceased attacked him without any warning; that deceased shot at him once or twice, when they grappled with each other; that in the struggle they fell and rolled off the grade into an arroyo. He then wrested the pistol from Brooks and shot him. Appellant, who was then standing near by and over them, told Maldonado to "shoot him another shot, finish killing him," which he did; that then, "believing he was dead, I says to my partner, 'Let him alone; he is dead now; let's go.'" Appellant then said: "Wait for me, partner; let me throw some rocks on him."

About 200 feet from where this took place Luz Romero and her son, Gregorio Romero, lived. Their attention was attracted by the gunshots, and also the talk of the combatants. They testified to seeing one of the parties lift rocks and drop or throw them toward the ground, and to hearing groans proceeding from that point as the rocks were thrown. They saw two parties leave the scene of trouble, one going toward Bisbee and the other in the direction of Lowell. A few minutes thereafter the body of deceased was found with his head and face so crushed and beaten as that his friends were not able to recognize him. A number of rocks were lying around near and on his head, bespattered with blood and covered with hair. Appellant's hat was found lying near the corpse, and a few days later, when he was arrested, he was wearing the deceased's hat.

* * *

The contention that the verdict is contrary to the evidence is based upon the allegation in the information as to the means used in killing the deceased. The charge is, "did * * * kill and murder one Walter Brooks * * * by * * * beating him with rocks and shooting him." It is urged by appellant that, granting the evidence shows that he did beat the deceased with rocks, it was after the deceased had been fatally and mortally wounded, and after the extinction of life. If it were possible to disconnect appellant from the trouble prior to the throwing of the rocks, still the evidence shows that the very instant the rocks were being thrown at Brooks many and repeated groans were heard, thus indicating that life was not extinct.

We think the evidence amply sustains the verdict. The judgment is affirmed.

NOTES

1. Should a distinction be drawn between one who kills a victim about to expire from other causes and one who kills a victim who would otherwise have lived for a significant period of time? If so, is causation doctrine an appropriate vehicle for drawing such a distinction?

2. Suppose, on the facts of the instant case, Maldonado instead of Ramirez had been prosecuted for murder. Would—and should—Ramirez's actions relieve Maldonado from liability?

PEOPLE v. ELDER

Supreme Court of Michigan, 1894.
100 Mich. 515, 59 N.W. 237.

HOOKER, J. Defendant appeals from a conviction of manslaughter. He was a bartender, and, in an altercation with the deceased, struck him, and knocked him down, whereupon one Nixon, a bystander, kicked him, from which kick death resulted. The theory of the prosecution was that there was preconcert of action on the part of Nixon and the defendant. The defendant denies this; claiming that defendant had no reason to expect any assistance from Nixon, or to anticipate his interference, and that he did not induce it. In his charge to the jury, the trial judge said, "On the part of the defendant, I give you the instructions which I now read." This was followed by the reading of several requests, in which the law was stated correctly upon this subject. The fifth was as follows: "If it shall appear to you, from the evidence, that Elder did not himself inflict the blow or do the injury which resulted in the death of Lowden, and that Nixon, by his own motion, while the encounter between Elder and Lowden was going on, rushed in, uninvited by Elder, and inflicted the injuries which produced Lowden's death, then you must acquit the prisoner." To this the court added as follows: "Unless, I have added, you find that his assault upon Lowden contributed and produced the conditions that deprived the deceased of the power of resistance, and enabled Nixon the better to inflict great bodily injury on the deceased, if you find that the cause of death was the wounds or injury he received on that occasion." The requests upon the part of the defendant were followed by those of the prosecution, 22 in number, most of which were given, and which seem to have concluded the charge. The first was as follows: "If you find that the respondent assaulted Lowden, and felled him to the floor, putting the body of the deceased in such a position that he was helpless to protect himself from Nixon, and rendered it possible for Nixon to kick him, such act upon the respondent's part was unlawful; and if decedent's death was caused by the defendant's act, the kicking given by Nixon, or both combined, then they are equally guilty of the death caused." This request, and the addition to defendant's fifth, were in direct contradiction of the earlier requests given upon defendant's part, where the jury were instructed that the defendant could not be convicted if the death was caused by acts of Nixon, for which he was not responsible, and which he did not induce or anticipate. The discussion of this subject, which appears to have been the important point in the case, was left with the requests, and the addition which has been mentioned. We fear that the jurors were misled by the first request of the prosecution, which, in plain terms, told them they might convict the defendant if he had "assaulted Lowden, and felled him to the floor, putting his body in such a position that he was helpless to protect himself from Nixon, and rendered it possible for Nixon to kick him, if such kicks caused death." Equally faulty was the implication contained in the addition to defendant's fifth request,—that if defendant's assault "deprived the deceased of the power of resistance, and enabled Nixon the better to inflict great bodily injury on the deceased." The case of People v. Carter, 96 Mich. 583, 56 N.W. 79, which seems to have been relied upon by the prosecution, was quite a different case from this. In that case the defendant felled the deceased by a blow while he was engaged in a fight with another, whereupon that other immediately kicked him. It was held that if the jury could find that the defendant volunteered to aid another in his fight, for the purpose of aiding him to whip the deceased, they were joint wrongdoers, responsible for each other's acts. In this case the defendant's contention was that he was not a volunteer in another's cause, but that the other volunteered in his, without his request or expectation. He was entitled to have his theory properly submitted to the jury. The judgment must be reversed, and a new trial ordered. The other justices concurred.

STATE v. CLARK

Superior Court of New Jersey, 1968.
104 N.J.Super. 67, 248 A.2d 559, affirmed 110 N.J.Super. 562, 266 A.2d 315,
certiorari denied 401 U.S. 958, 91 S.Ct. 988, 28 L.Ed.2d 243.

GALANTI, B. P., J. C. C. (temporarily assigned).

Defendant pleaded non vult on December 2, 1963 to indictment No. S–94–63 on the charge of homicide. He was sentenced to the New Jersey State Prison for not less than 15 nor more than 25 years. Defendant has filed an application for post-conviction relief on the following grounds:

1. There is newly discovered medical evidence which indicates that his acts were not the natural and probable cause of the death of the victim.

* * *

The first contention presents a question of novel impression in the State of New Jersey * * *

Dr. Robert M. Livingston testified that he examined the records concerning the victim's hospital stay and also examined the autopsy reports; that she died as a result of the lack of blood before the operation and insufficient blood transfusions during her stay in the recovery room; that she was not a prime risk for surgery; that had he been the operating surgeon he would have operated a second time (he further criticized the hysterectomy and removal of the cervix), and that if more blood had been transfused into her after the operation she would have lived.

Dr. Frank Drews, Jr., testified that he examined and operated on the deceased and saw her in the emergency room; he described the course of the projectile; he testified that there were eight perforations in the small bowel; he described the operation and that the deceased never responded thereto and that she was never without blood from the moment she entered surgery until her expiration. He described the county physician's autopsy report. He also described the course of the bullet, the amount of blood and time of the transfusions, and that she died from shock and damage caused by the gunshot wound.

The question of responsibility for homicide where the victim's death resulted from the intervening treatment or mistreatment of the wound or injury inflicted by the accused, not from the wound or injury itself, is a novel question before a New Jersey court. Consequently an exhaustive search of the authorities in other jurisdictions for guidance in dealing with this novel problem has been made.

* * *

In Odenal v. State, 128 Tenn. 60, 157 S.W. 419 (Sup.Ct.1913), the court dealt with this problem in the following manner:

> "The rule on this subject, supported by the weight of authority, is that, to exonerate the accused from the charge of causing death by a dangerous wound unlawfully inflicted, it must appear, *not only that the operation was performed in a grossly negligent and unskillful manner, but also that it was the sole cause of the death* and not one of a series of intermediate causes, following in the train of injury, the original cause. One who unlawfully inflicts a dangerous wound upon another is held for the consequences flowing from such injury, whether the sequence be direct or through the operation of intermediate agencies dependent upon arising out of the original cause. One of these dependent occurrences is the necessity of surgical aid, which may eventuate as the immediate cause of death. Surgical aid must be employed, with the attendant risks. Surgeons are not infallible. They are required to have and exercise only reasonable skill, measured by the rules of their art or profession. When the accused inflicts the injury that necessitates the operation, he is held to assume the risk attendant on it. Much is required before the surgeon can be substituted for the defendant."

New Jersey has no case law on this particular point; the closest it seems New Jersey comes to dealing with this general type of a problem is in State v. Loray, 41 N.J. 131, 195 A.2d 289 (1963), where in dealing with a blow to a person with a preexisting heart condition, we find the Supreme Court looking to the Iowa court and other authorities for guidance and deciding the fact that a victim of an assault is in a weakened condition or suffers from disease and as a result succumbs to a blow which might not be fatal to a person in perfect health does not lessen the criminal responsibility for causing death. We know of no duty imposed upon a victim to supply a guarantee of good health to a robber.

* * * In the present case defendant Clark shot his wife; she received medical treatment which this court finds was in the usual course of practice that good practitioners adopt and, consequently, defendant is chargeable with her death.

* * * I find as a fact that the wife's death was not caused by a supervening act disconnected with any act of defendant.

For all of these reasons the application for post-conviction relief is denied.

NOTES

1. Why should Clark be held "responsible" for the failure on the part of medical personnel to give his victim adequate blood transfusions if Elder is not responsible for the injuries inflicted by Nixon? Is one more or

less an "intervening act" than the other? Is one more or less the "natural result" of the initial injury than the other? Is one more or less foreseeable than the other?

2. Should Clark's conviction be reversed if adequate proof were presented that the medical treatment of his victim was negligent and that but for that negligence death would not have occurred?

3. In *Jordan*, 40 Crim.App. 158 (Eng.1956), the defendant's conviction of murder (sentence, death) was quashed on the basis of new evidence indicating that the victim died not from the defendant's perforation of his intestine but from pneumonia which resulted from medical treatment which was "palpably wrong" and "not normal." Id. at 157, 158. The court's judgment was based upon the testimony of two medical witnesses who apparently had not been involved in the treatment of the deceased. Following the court's action a medical board of inquiry found that the treatment had been "devoted and exemplary". Williams, Causation in Homicide, [1957] Crim.L.Rev. (Eng.) 429, 430, 510. An interesting critical piece on *Jordan* is Camps & Havard, Causation in Homicide—A Medical View, [1957] Crim.L.Rev. (Eng.) 576 which concludes:

> In future when victims of homicidal assaults survive long enough to receive hospital treatment it may well become a routine of the defence to impeach the medical treatment in order to show that the treatment was 'not normal.' There must be a strong body of opinion to agree with the old authorities that the point is legally irrelevant providing a wound has been given which is dangerous to life and the treatment has been adopted bona fide by competent medical attendants. The consequence of this change in the substantive law of homicide may be greater than has been appreciated. In particular, the courts may find themselves involved in protracted, undesirable, and, it is respectfully submitted, unnecessary investigations into the medical treatment of victims of homicidal assaults. Id. at 585.

If Jordan is absolved of murder as a result of the acts of the medical personnel should they be charged with some form of negligent homicide? If not, why?

4. It was, of course, possible to reindict and convict Jordan of some lesser offense. What value or values are served by thus reducing his liability? Are these the same values which would limit his liability if his victim had recovered and then died in an auto mishap?

5. In many American jurisdictions, the common law rule that one may not be convicted of murder unless the victim died within a year and one day from the time the fatal blow was given or the cause of death administered is applied. See, e. g., Louisville E. & St. L. R. Co. v. Clarke, 152 U.S. 230, 239 (1894). In Commonwealth v. Ladd, 402 Pa. 164, 166 A.2d 501 (1966) the Pennsylvania Supreme Court interpreted the requirement as only a common law rule of evidence which the court was empowered to change, and abandoned it. Seeing the purpose of the requirement as preventing prosecutions in which the passage of time would make it too difficult to accurately ascertain the cause of death, the court concluded that advances in crime detection and medicine were such that the interest in accuracy would be served by putting no restriction upon the time within which

prosecutions might be brought and requiring "proof of causation of conventional quality" at the trial.   Musmanno, J. dissented, arguing that despite advances in crime detection and medicine there remains a real danger of unjustified prosecutions if the year and a day requirement was removed. He pointed to specifically the facts of the case—the victim had died of pneumonia thirteen months after being assaulted by the defendant—as demonstrating the difficult issues the rule was designed to withdraw from courts' consideration.

Should other courts and legislatures follow this lead?

PEOPLE v. GEIGER

Michigan Court of Appeals, 1968.
10 Mich.App. 339, 159 N.W.2d 383.

BURNS, Judge.   Defendant appeals from a circuit court jury conviction of manslaughter.   C.L.1948, § 750.321 (Stat.Ann.1954 Rev. § 28.553).

Sometime after 11 p. m., May 6, 1965, defendant confronted his estranged wife, Sharon Geiger, in the parking lot of a bar in Prudenville, Michigan, as she was about to enter the bar with Joan Greening. Joan Greening testified that she and Mrs. Geiger had had only one drink at another bar prior to meeting the defendant, that Mrs. Geiger's health appeared normal and that she observed no black and blue marks or abrasions upon Mrs. Geiger that evening.   Joan Greening further testified that she was told by the defendant to wait for Mrs. Geiger in the bar, but that she waited in the parking lot and observed the defendant talking to his wife and trying to force her into the car; he then "threw" her into the car and drove away.

State police officers who had interrogated the defendant after the alleged offense testified that defendant told them the couple drove to the Prudenville elementary school playing field.   They argued and got out of the car.   Defendant struck his wife "two or three times" with his open hand and pushed her to the ground in such a manner that she bumped her head against the car.   When Mrs. Geiger failed to get up and appeared unconscious, defendant picked her up and placed her in his car.   He then allegedly attempted to clean her after driving a short distance to a house trailer which the Geigers had rented until May 1, 1965.

Early in the morning on May 7, defendant left his wife in the trailer and drove to James Meigs' house where defendant had been residing while he and his wife were separated.   Meigs was awakened around 3:15 a. m., at which time defendant persuaded Meigs to help move the automobile which Mrs. Geiger had driven to the bar.   After taking the vehicle to Mrs. Geiger's parents' home, defendant finally replied to Meigs' inquiries as to what was going on; defendant stated that he might be "facing a murder rap."

Between 3:30 a. m. and 4:30 a. m., May 7, defendant aroused his employer, asked for $100 and was given $50 in order to get away for a few days.

Defendant apparently returned to the house trailer, placed his wife in the front seat of his car and put a blanket over her. He drove south for approximately 186 miles and at 7:30 a. m. or 8 a. m., stopped at the Addison Community Hospital, Addison, Michigan, where his wife was pronounced dead.

Doctor Gordon J. Hammersley performed an autopsy and testified that Sharon Geiger had been struck about the face and body by a blunt object such as a hand or a fist. The deceased's external marks of violence included swelling around both eyes, the chin, both lips, the right forearm, the left hand, both shoulders and the neck. There were facial abrasions and dried blood covering the right side of her face. Also present were small hemorrhages in the covering of the brain. The medical cause of death was "aspiration of the gastric contents into the air passages with resultant shock, asphyxia, collapse and pulmonary edema." In other words, sometime after the beating Sharon Geiger had attempted to vomit and had choked to death on her own vomitus.

Defendant was charged with first-degree murder, but the jury was instructed only as to second-degree murder and manslaughter. Defendant contends that the instructions regarding second-degree murder should not have been submitted to the jury because there were no proofs showing malice.

Defendant further argues, however, that the immediate cause of death, asphyxiation, renders a finding of malice impossible. It is true that the likelihood of death resulting from the head wounds *per se* was medically improbable. Nevertheless, the likelihood of death resulting as a natural and probable consequence of the beating was within the range of medical testimony from which a jury could find a causal connection between the assault and Mrs. Geiger's act of vomiting. The pathologist who performed the autopsy testified as follows:

"Q. [prosecuting attorney] Now my question to you is this: These blows on the head, these blows to the side of the face, or whatever the blows were, did they have anything to do with the asphyxiation?

"A. Yes, I think they did in that they indicated a trauma which resulted in minor brain and subarachnoid damage that probably caused some degree of cerebral concussion, probably a temporary thing. That would contribute to the diminution of laryngeal reflexes which would allow the asphyxiation.

"Q. In other words, if she hadn't had the blows to the head, blows to the side of the face, or the blows on the other parts of her body, would she have been able to—excuse my words—vomit and bring this content of the stomach up?

"A.   I would think that she would have been able to vomit and remove it from her body in normal fashion."

26 Am.Jur., Homicide, § 52, p. 195, states:

"It is not indispensable to a conviction that the wounds be necessarily fatal and the direct cause of death. It is sufficient that they cause death indirectly through a chain of natural effects and causes unchanged by human action."

The evidence in this case would permit a jury to find that the injuries were " 'reasonably calculated to cause death' " and that the wounds " 'contributed mediately or immediately to the death.' "

———

COMMONWEALTH v. FEINBERG

Supreme Court of Pennsylvania, 1969.
433 Pa. 558, 253 A.2d 636.

JONES, Justice.   Appellant Max Feinberg owned and operated a cigar store in the skid-row section of Philadelphia.   One of the products he sold was Sterno, a jelly-like substance composed primarily of methanol and ethanol and designed for cooking and heating purposes.   Sterno was manufactured and sold in two types of containers, one for home use and one for industrial use.   Before September, 1963, both types of Sterno contained approximately 3.75% methanol, or wood alcohol, and 71% ethanol, or grain alcohol; of the two types of alcohols, methanol is far more toxic if consumed internally.   Beginning in September of 1963, the Sterno company began manufacturing a new type of industrial Sterno which was 54% methanol.   The cans containing the new industrial Sterno were identical to the cans containing the old industrial Sterno except in one crucial aspect: on the lids of the new 54% methanol Sterno were imprinted the words "Institutional Sterno.   Danger.   Poison.   For use only as a Fuel.   Not for consumer use.   For industrial and commercial use.   Not for home use."   A skull and crossbones were also lithographed on the lid.   The carton in which the new Sterno cans were packaged and shipped did not indicate that the contents differed in any respect from the old industrial Sterno.

According to its records, Sterno Corporation sent only one shipment of the new Sterno to the Philadelphia area; that shipment went to the Richter Paper Company and was received on December 17, 1963.   Charles Richter, president of the firm, testified that his company in turn, made only one sale of the new industrial Sterno, and that was to appellant.   Richter testified that his records indicated that appellant received the Sterno on December 21 and, since Richter had not opened any of the cartons, he was unaware that he was selling appellant a new type of industrial Sterno. On December 27, Richter received a call from appellant informing him that the cartons contained a new type of Sterno and that appellant wished to return the portion of his order that he had not sold. The unused cartons were picked up by Richter's deliveryman the next day.

Meanwhile, between December 21 and December 28, appellant had sold approximately 400 cans of the new industrial Sterno. Between December 23 and December 30, thirty-one persons died in the skid-row area as a result of methanol poisoning. In many of the cases the source of the methanol was traced to the new industrial Sterno. Since appellant was the only retail outlet of this type of Sterno in Philadelphia, he was arrested and indicted on thirty-one counts charging involuntary manslaughter and on companion bills charging violations of the Pharmacy Act (Act of September 27, 1961, P.L. 1700, § 1 et seq., 63 P.S. § 390–1 et seq.)

Appellant was convicted on seventeen counts of involuntary manslaughter and on twenty-five counts of violating the Pharmacy Act by Judge Charles L. Guerin, sitting without a jury. Judge Guerin held that appellant had violated the Pharmacy Act and that, therefore, he was guilty of a misdemeanor-manslaughter in each of the seventeen cases. Five of the manslaughter convictions were appealed to the Superior Court which affirmed four of them, although on a different theory. Commonwealth v. Feinberg, 211 Pa.Super. 100, 234 A.2d 913 (1967). In writing for a six-judge majority, Judge Montgomery held that appellant had not violated the Pharmacy Act and, therefore, was not guilty of a misdemeanor-manslaughter, but that the evidence justified the conclusion that appellant was guilty of involuntary manslaughter. * * *

The second issue in this case is whether appellant is guilty of involuntary manslaughter in each or any of the four appeals presently before us. The Penal Code defines involuntary manslaughter as a death "happening in consequence of an unlawful act, or the doing of a lawful act in an unlawful way * * *." (Act of June 24, 1939, P.L. 872, § 703, 18 P.S. § 4703) Since we have determined that appellant did not violate the Pharmacy Act in selling the new industrial Sterno, the second portion of this statutory definition must be controlling. When a death results from the doing of an act lawful in itself but done in an unlawful manner, in order to sustain a conviction for manslaughter the Commonwealth must present evidence to prove that the defendant acted in a rash or reckless manner. The conduct of the defendant resulting in the death must be such a departure from the behavior of an ordinary and prudent man as to evidence a disregard of human life or an indifference to the consequences. Furthermore, there must be a direct causal relationship between the defendant's act and the deceased's death. Commonwealth v. Root, 403 Pa. 571, 170 A.2d 310, 82 A.L.R.2d 452 (1961).

We have searched in vain for cases from this Commonwealth involving factual situations similar to the one now before us. We have, however, found four cases from other jurisdictions which are on point. In the leading case, Thiede v. State, 106 Neb. 48, 182 N. W. 570 (1921), the defendant gave the deceased moonshine containing methanol, the drinking of which resulted in his death. While noting that the defendant had violated the state prohibition laws, the court refused to rest the manslaughter conviction on this statutory violation, holding that the manufacturing and distribution of moonshine was merely malum prohibitum and not malum per se. The court continued, "We cannot go so far as to say that [dispensing moonshine], prompted perhaps by the spirit of good-fellowship, though prohibited by law, could ever, by any resulting consequence, be converted into the crime of manslaughter; *but, where the liquor by reason of its extreme potency or poisonous ingredients,* is dangerous to use as an intoxicating beverage, where the drinking of it is capable of producing direct physical injury, other than as an ordinary intoxicant, and of perhaps endangering life itself, *the case is different, and the question of negligence enters; for, if the party furnishing the liquor knows, or was apprised of such facts that he should have known, of the danger, there then appears from his act a recklessness which is indifferent to results.* Such recklessness in the furnishing of intoxicating liquors, in violation of law, may constitute such an unlawful act as, if it results in causing death, will constitute manslaughter." (106 Neb. at 57, 58, 182 N.W. at 573.) (Emphasis added.)

We conclude, after studying the record, that appellant fits within the black-letter rule laid down in *Thiede* and that the Commonwealth has made out all the elements necessary to warrant a conviction for involuntary manslaughter. First, the record establishes that appellant sold the Sterno with the knowledge that at least some of his customers would extract the alcohol for drinking purposes. * * * Second, appellant was aware, or should have been aware, that the Sterno he was selling was toxic if consumed. The new industrial Sterno was clearly marked as being poisonous. Even the regular Sterno is marked "Caution. Flammable. For Use only as a Fuel" and if consumed internally may have serious consequences. * * *

Appellant presses several contentions for our consideration. First, he claims that the Commonwealth has not established the necessary causal link between the sale of the Sterno and the deaths, citing Commonwealth v. Root, supra. We cannot agree. First, appellant sold the Sterno knowing, or having reason to know, that some of his customers would consume it. Second, some of his customers did consume the new industrial Sterno and died as a result. The Commonwealth's expert toxicologist testified that in several of the cases death could only have resulted from consumption of the new as opposed to the regular Sterno. Since appellant was the only retail outlet for the new Sterno in Philadelphia, these persons must have died from drinking Sterno purchased in appellant's store. Third, *Root* does not help the appellant. *Root* involved a drag racing situation. The decedent died when he negligently passed the defendant on a two-lane road and collided with a truck. This Court held that the defendant could not be held criminally responsible for the deceased's death because there was no direct causal connection between the defendant's act in engaging in a drag race and the deceased's death. The court in *Thiede,* in answering an argument similar to the one now made by appellant, stated: "Defendant contends that the drinking of liquor, by deceased was his voluntary act and served as an intervening cause, breaking the causal connection between the giving of the liquor by defendant and the resulting death. The drinking of the liquor, in consequence of defendant's act, was, however, what the defendant contemplated. Deceased, it is true, may have been negligent in drinking, but, where the defendant was negligent, then the contributory negligence of the deceased will be no defense in a criminal action." (106 Neb. at 58, 59, 182 N.W. at 574)

*   *   *

PEOPLE v. SCOTT

Court of Appeals of Michigan, 1971.
29 Mich.App. 549, 185 N.W.2d 576.

J. H. GILLIS, Presiding Judge. Defendant appeals as of right from a conviction by jury of involuntary manslaughter, M.C.L.A. § 750.321 (Stat.Ann.1954 Rev. § 28.553).

The defendant, after engaging in an exchange of verbal hostilities with the occupants of a police patrol car, attempted to force the vehicle off the road. A chase ensued and a radio alert was relayed to other cars in the vicinity. An unmarked patrol car, in pursuit of defendant, collided at an intersection with a DSR bus, killing one of the officers in the patrol car.

The single issue raised on appeal is whether trial court committed reversible error when it instructed the jury that to find the defendant guilty of involuntary manslaughter it must be established that the defendant's negligence was "a" proximate cause of the police officer's death and whether the court further erred in rejecting the defendant's contention that his negligence must constitute "the" proximate cause.

*   *   *

Michigan courts have traditionally held that a conviction for involuntary manslaughter, especially when committed with an automobile, may be sustained if the trier of fact is

"[Able to] determine [that] the defendant was guilty of gross and culpable negligence in the operation of his motor

vehicle and that said gross negligence in the operation of
such motor vehicle was the proximate cause of the death of
the deceased." People v. Layman (1941), 299 Mich. 141, 145,
146, 299 N.W. 840, 841.

*   *   *

Defendant stipulates, on appeal, that the speed and manner in
which he was operating his car was such as could be deemed wilful
and wanton disregard for the safety of others. It is the contention
of the people that because the defendant readily admits that his driving was grossly negligent, that that erratic driving then becomes the
proximate cause of the death of the police officer. They contend that
if the defendant's driving had not been in violation of state law, the
police would never have given chase and the death would not have
occurred. Further, it is their contention that even if there were another independent cause for the officer's death, the jury could still
find the defendant guilty of the offense charged if they found that his
gross negligence was "a proximate cause" of the death. We find this
logic unacceptable.

The trial judge's charge to the jury defined "proximate cause"
to be

"A direct and producing cause of the damage or injury.
It doesn't have to be 'the' direct. The reason I say 'a' direct
is that there can be more than one proximate cause of the
damage or injury complained of * * *. As far as you
[the jury] are concerned in this case, it is up to you to determine whether there was a causal connection between the
driving of the defendant, if you find there was improper
driving, and the end result * * *. There can be more
than one proximate cause, as I told you."

*   *   *

The court, in its definition of "proximate cause," has adopted
the civil law definition and applied it to a criminal prosecution.

*   *   *

If the tort liability concept of proximate cause were applied in
criminal homicide prosecutions, the conduct of the decedent would
have to be considered. That conduct would be examined not to prove
that it was merely an additional proximate cause, but rather to determine whether it amounted to a subsequent wrongful act and thus
superseded the original conduct chargeable to defendant. The trial
court properly instructed the jury that they could find defendant
not guilty if they determined that deceased's conduct was the sole
cause of the collision. However, the court did give the instruction
that the defendant could be found guilty if it was determined that
both defendant and deceased had acted negligently. Such a charge
is in opposition to the fundamental principles of criminal responsi-

bility. It is axiomatic that "criminal guilt under our law is personal fault." People v. Sobczak (1955), 344 Mich. 465, 470, 73 N.W.2d 921, 923. "It is the very essence of our deep-rooted notions of criminal liability that guilt be personal and individual." [3] Commentary on Commonwealth v. Redline, 391 Pa. 486, 137 A.2d 472 (1958), reiterates why the tort standard of proximate cause is unacceptable in criminal prosecutions:

> "A closer causal connection between the felony and the killing than the proximate-cause theory normally applicable to tort cases should be required because of the extreme penalty attaching to a conviction for felony murder and the difference between the underlying rationales of criminal and tort law. The former is intended to impose punishment in appropriate cases while the latter is primarily concerned with who shall bear the burden of a loss." [4]

Other states have agreed with the reasoning adopted by Pennsylvania and have compelled their triers of fact, when implementing "proximate causation" in criminal prosecutions, to find that the defendant's act be the proximate cause of the homicide charged. * * *

The people, here, as in People v. Marshall (1961), 362 Mich. 170, 174, 106 N.W.2d 842, actually seek from us an "interpretation of the manslaughter statute which would impose open-ended criminal liability". This we cannot do. It is true as a general rule of law:

> "That a person engaged in the commission of an unlawful act is legally responsible for all of the consequences which may naturally or necessarily flow or result from such unlawful act." People v. Barnes, 182 Mich. 179, 197, 148 N.W. 400, 406 (1914).

But before this principle of law can have any application in this case before us, it must first appear that the defendant's act was grossly negligent and that the resulting homicide was *the* natural or necessary result of *the act* of [the defendant]." *Barnes, supra,* p. 198, 148 N.W. p. 406. (Emphasis supplied.) * * *

While there are no Michigan cases which are factually similar, there are many Michigan cases dealing with involuntary manslaughter,

> "[W]hich make it clear that to sustain a conviction of manslaughter the conduct of the accused must have been the immediate and direct cause of the death." People v. Ogg (1970), 26 Mich.App. 372, 400, 182 N.W.2d 570, 584, dis-

---

3. Sayre, "Criminal Responsibility for the Acts of Another," 43 Harvard Law Review 689, 716 (1930).

4. Note, 71 Harvard Law Review 1565, 1566 (1958).

sent by Danhof, J. and cases cited. See also: People v. Beardsley (1907), 150 Mich. 206, 113 N.W. 1128.

Although neither party is able to cite authority which requires that the defendant's criminally negligent act be the only direct and proximate cause of the ensuing homicide, this Court feels that the reasoning proffered by the Pennsylvania court in Commonwealth v. Root, 403 Pa. 571, 170 A.2d 310 (1961), constitutes the better standard. In criminal prosecutions there must be a more direct causal connection between the criminal conduct of the defendant and the homicide charged than is required by the tort liability concept of proximate cause.

Reversed and remanded for new trial not inconsistent herewith.

COMMONWEALTH v. ATENCIO

Supreme Judicial Court of Massachusetts, 1963.
345 Mass. 627, 189 N.E.2d 223.

WILKINS, Chief Justice. Each defendant has been convicted upon an indictment for manslaughter in the death of Stewart E. Britch and upon an indictment for illegally carrying a firearm, namely a revolver, on his person in violation of G.L. c. 269, § 10 (as amended through St.1957, c. 688, § 23). * * *

Facts which the jury could have found are these. On Sunday, October 22, 1961, the deceased, his brother Ronald, and the defendants spent the day drinking wine in the deceased's room in a rooming house in Boston. At some time in the afternoon, with reference to nothing specific so far as the record discloses, Marshall said, "I will settle this," went out, and in a few minutes returned clicking a gun, from which he removed [all but?—eds.] one bullet. Early in the evening Ronald left, and the conversation turned to "Russian roulette."

The evidence as to what happened consisted of testimony of police officers, who took statements of the defendants, and testimony of one defendant, Atencio. The evidence did not supply all the facts. For example, the source and ownership of the revolver were not made clear. The jury could have found that it was produced by the deceased and that he suggested the "game," or they might have found neither to be the fact. There was evidence that Marshall earlier had seen the revolver in the possession of the deceased, and that the latter handed it to Marshall, who put it in the bathroom under the sink. Later when the deceased accused him of stealing it, he brought it back from the bathroom, and gave it to the deceased. Any uncertainty is not of prime importance. The "game" was played. The deceased and Atencio were seated on a bed, and Marshall was seated on a couch. First, Marshall examined the gun, saw that it contained one cartridge, and, after spinning it on his arm, pointed it at his head, and pulled the trigger. Nothing happened. He handed the gun to Atencio, who repeated the process, again without result. Atencio passed the gun to the deceased, who spun it, put to his head and pulled the trigger. The cartridge exploded, and he fell over dead.

1. There is no controversy as to definition. Involuntary manslaughter may be predicated upon wanton or reckless conduct.   *   *

We are of opinion that the defendants could properly have been found guilty of manslaughter. This is not a civil action against the defendants by the personal representative of Stewart Britch. In such a case his voluntary act, we assume, would be a bar. Here the Commonwealth had an interest that the deceased should not be killed by the wanton or reckless conduct of himself and others. State v. Plaspohl, 239 Ind. 324, 327, 157 N.E.2d 579. Such conduct could be found in the concerted action and coöperation of the defendants in helping to bring about the deceased's foolish act. The jury did not have to believe testimony that the defendants at the last moment tried to dissuade the deceased from doing that which they had just done themselves.

The defendants argue as if it should have been ruled, as matter of law, that there were three "games" of solitaire and not one "game" of "Russian roulette." That the defendants participated could be found to be a cause and not a mere condition of Stewart Britch's death. It is not correct to say that his act could not be found to have been caused by anything which Marshall and Atencio did, nor that he would have died when the gun went off in his hand no matter whether they had done the same. The testimony does not require a ruling that when the deceased took the gun from Atencio it was an independent or intervening act not standing in any relation to the defendants' acts which would render what he did imputable to them. It is an oversimplification to contend that each participated in something that only one could do at a time. There could be found to be a mutual encouragement in a joint enterprise. In the abstract, there may have been no duty on the defendants to prevent the deceased from playing. But there was a duty on their part not to coöperate or join with him in the "game." Nor, if the facts presented such a case, would we have to agree that if the deceased, and not the defendants, had played first that they could not have been found guilty of manslaughter. The defendants were much more than merely present at a crime. It would not be necessary that the defendants force the deceased to play or suggest that he play.

We are referred in both briefs to cases of manslaughter arising out of automobiles racing upon the public highway. When the victim is a third person, there is no difficulty in holding the drivers, including the one whose car did not strike the victim (Brown v.

Thayer, 212 Mass. 392, 99 N.E. 237), or in whose car a victim was not a passenger. Nelson v. Nason, 343 Mass. 220, 221, 177 N.E.2d 887.

In two cases the driver of a noncolliding car has been prosecuted for the death of his competitor, and in both cases an appellate court has ruled that he was not guilty of manslaughter. In Commonwealth v. Root, 403 Pa. 571, 170 A.2d 310, 82 A.L.R.2d 452, the competitor drove on the wrong side of the road head-on into an oncoming truck and was killed. The court held (p. 580, 170 A.2d p. 314) that "the tort liability concept of proximate cause has no proper place in prosecutions for criminal homicide and more direct causal connection is required for conviction. * * * In the instant case, the defendant's reckless conduct was not a sufficiently direct cause of the competing driver's death to make him criminally liable therefor." In Thacker v. State, 103 Ga.App. 36, 117 S.E.2d 913, the defendant was indicted for the involuntary manslaughter of his competitor in a drag race who was killed when he lost control of his car and left the highway. The court said (p. 39, 117 S.E.2d p. 915) that the indictment "fails to allege any act or acts on the part of the defendant which caused or contributed to the loss of control of the vehicle driven by the deceased, other than the fact that they were engaged in a race at the time."

Whatever may be thought of those two decisions, there is a very real distinction between drag racing and "Russian roulette." In the former much is left to the skill, or lack of it, of the competitor. In "Russian roulette" it is a matter of luck as to the location of the one bullet, and except for a misfire (of which there was evidence in the case at bar) the outcome is a certainty if the chamber under the hammer happens to be the one containing the bullet.

2. Each defendant excepted to the denial of a request to the effect that if he urged the deceased not to pull the trigger, the jury would be warranted in finding that the defendant did not show a reckless disregard of the deceased's safety, and would be warranted in finding him not guilty. We do not agree with the defendants' contention that the request was not given in substance. Very near the close of the charge the judge instructed the jury, "If any one of these defendants abandoned or quit the roulette before it was completed, before the shot was fired, then, of course, he would not be responsible or guilty of the shooting."

NOTES

1. If it had been Scott's car, rather than that of the pursuing officer, which had crashed and caused a death would there be any doubt as to his culpability? See Tegethoff v. State, 220 So.2d 399 (Fla.Dist.Ct.App.1969). Is this because no other actor intervened or because the crash may be viewed as a natural result of such conduct? Wasn't police pursuit, with its attendant dangers, a natural result of Scott's conduct? Would holding Scott

responsible for the results of the officer's mishap serve to deter such flight? Would it violate our sense of fairness? Would holding the officer liable for the results of his apparently reckless pursuit deter such pursuit? Would it violate our sense of fairness?

2. In Pereira v. United States, 347 U.S. 1, 74 S.Ct. 358, 98 L.Ed. 435 (1954), the Supreme Court was faced with the question of whether the appellant had "caused" a check to be mailed pursuant to a scheme to defraud. Writing for a unanimous Court (as to this point) Chief Justice Warren announced: "That question is easily answered. Where one does an act with knowledge that use of the mails will follow in the ordinary course of business, or where such use can reasonably be foreseen, even though not actually intended, then he 'causes' the mails to be used." Id. at 8–9. If this standard were applied to Scott would the result change? Is there any reason it should not be applied?

3. Is *Atencio* to be distinguished from *Scott* because the chances of a fatal result in Russian roulette are greater than in high speed auto chases? Because of the comparative lack of social utility of the two activities? Because the driving skills of the pursuing officer in *Scott*, or the lack thereof, are a variable for which the defendant should not be held responsible? Is the *Scott* court's reliance on *Root* (described in *Feinberg* and *Atencio*) well-placed given the voluntary participation of the decedent there?

TEXAS STATE BAR COMMITTEE ON REVISION OF THE PENAL CODE, TEXAS PENAL CODE, A PROPOSED REVISION (1970)

§ 6.07. Causation: Criminal Responsibility for Causing a Result

(a) Subject to the additional requirements in Subsections (b) and (c), an element of an offense requiring that an actor cause a result is established if the result would not have occurred as it did but for the actor's conduct.

(b) If the offense requires that the actor intentionally or knowingly cause a result, he is criminally responsible for the result if the result that actually occurred:

(1) was desired or contemplated, whether the desire or contemplation extended to natural events or the conduct of another; or

(2) was desired or contemplated and occurred in a manner not too accidental, or by a means not too dependent on another's volitional act, to have a just bearing on the actor's criminal responsibility or the gravity of his offense.

(c) If the offense requires that the actor recklessly or with criminal negligence cause a result, he is criminally responsible for the result if the result that actually occurred:

(1) was within the risk perceived or that which should have been perceived, whether the risk extended to natural events or the conduct of another; or

(2) was within the risk perceived or that which should have been perceived and occurred in a manner not too accidental, or by a means not too dependent on another's volitional act, to have a just bearing on the actor's criminal responsibility or the gravity of his offense.

(d) An actor is nevertheless criminally responsible for causing a result if the only difference between what actually occurred and what he desired, contemplated, or risked is that a different person or property was injured, harmed, or otherwise affected.

Committee Comment

* * *

Variance Between Manner or Means Desired, Contemplated, or Risked and Result as it Actually Occurred

A particular result (e. g., death, destruction of property, a false statement) is a material element of most offenses in this code. To convict of such an offense, therefore, requires the state to prove beyond a reasonable doubt that (1) the result actually occurred and that (2) the defendant intentionally, knowingly, recklessly, or with criminal negligence—depending on the culpable mental state required for the offense—caused the result. * * *

If an actor has the requisite culpable mental state with regard to a proscribed result, but because of an additional cause the result occurs in a manner or by a means different from what he desired, contemplated, or risked, Subsections (b) (2) and (c) (2) set out the factors the trier of facts must consider in determining whether to hold the actor criminally responsible for the result as it actually occurred. * * * [T]he section asks the trier of facts whether it is just to hold the actor criminally responsible for the proscribed result even though, because of an additional cause, it occurred in a manner or by a means he did not desire, contemplate, or risk. The standards for determining justness are whether the manner of occurrence was too accidental or the means of occurrence too dependent on another's conduct. * * *

It should be noted that if an actor intentionally engages in conduct, but the proscribed result comes about in a manner or by a means he did not desire or contemplate, he will nevertheless be guilty of a lesser included offense, usually a criminal attempt under Section 15.01. The phrase "gravity of his offense" in Subsections (b) (2) and (c) (2) emphasizes this point and makes clear, for example, that an actor who shoots another with intent to kill, but inflicts a nonmortal wound, whereupon the other dies a week later in the hospital when it is burned to the ground by a maniac—that although the actor is not guilty of murder, he is guilty of attempted murder.

D. COMPLICITY

The law of "parties" is the doctrinal device by which the criminal law defines the outer limits of liability for activity indirectly related to a crime. At common law, participants in—or "parties to—felonies [a] were categorized as follows:

Principal in the First Degree	One who, with the requisite state of mind, performed the criminal act or directly caused the criminal result, either with his own hand, with an instrument or a non-human agent, or by means of an innocent human agent.
Principal in the Second Degree	One who was actually or constructively present at the scene of the crime and who, with the required state of mind, aided, counseled, commanded, or encouraged the principal in the first degree.
Accessory Before the Fact	One neither actually nor constructively present at the scene of the crime who, with the requisite state of mind, ordered, counseled, encouraged or otherwise aided and abetted the principal in the first degree.
Accessory After the Fact	One who, with knowledge of the commission of an offense by an offender, concealed the offender or gave him some other assistance to prevent his detection, arrest, trial, or punishment.

All participants in misdemeanors were simply principals. Concealment or assistance of a misdemeanant did not give rise to criminal liability at all.

Initially, all participants in a felony were subject to the same penalty without regard to which category they fell into. But it was soon recognized that the involvement of an accessory after the fact rendered him significantly less culpable than other participants. This category was set aside as a separate offense, independent of the felony of the individual aided or concealed, and penalty was assigned to it that was less severe than that assigned to the offense committed by the assisted felon. Although no jurisdiction still retains unmodified the common law of parties, statutory changes have been widely varied.

---

a. Treason was the sole exception. All participants in treason were regarded as principals.

Most, however, retain the basic notion of the common law of parties, that all who aid or abet the commission of a serious offense are subject to the same punishment as the person who actually commits it.

Clearly the law of parties (or its modern statutory progeny) is significant insofar as it defines the liability of those whose activity is only indirectly related to the offense. At common law, however, the law of parties had other implications. Jurisdictional complexities arose because of the common law rule that an accessory was punishable only where his act of accessoryship was committed, not where the final offense was committed. Strict attitudes towards pleading resulting in holdings that a defendant must be charged with the specific form of liability that the proof showed at trial; one charged as a principal in the first degree could not be convicted if the proof at trial showed that he was an accessory before the fact. (This was not expanded, however, to distinguish between the two degrees of principals.) Finally, the liability of an accessory was tied to that of the principal. Thus an accessory could not be tried before the principal and anything which prevented the conviction of the principal also prevented conviction of the accessory. This was even expanded to the point of holding that reversal of the principal's conviction required reversal of the conviction of the accessory.

Many of the procedural implications of the law of parties have been modified by statutes, and other offenses have been created in many jurisdictions to supplement that defining the accessory after the fact as guilty of an offense as a means of dealing with those whose actions impede official investigation of crime. The emphasis on the following material, then, is upon the law of parties as it defines the outer limits of liability for conduct other than that consisting of the criminal act itself or conduct directly causing the criminal result.

---

1. LIABILITY AS AN AIDER AND ABETTOR OR INCITOR

PROBLEM

Consider the liability of Macchia for making the likeness of a ten dollar bill on the theory that he aided and abetted Villari. The facts are from United States v. Garguilo, 310 F.2d 249 (2d Cir. 1962).

The Government's principal witnesses were Mario Villari, owner of Graphic Printing Company, a co-defendant who pleaded guilty, and Albert Della Monica, a photographer and long-time friend of the Garguilo family, whose innocence was not questioned. Villari first met Garguilo in Magistrate's Court on August 17, 1960, while both were waiting to pay traffic fines; Villari told Garguilo he was in the printing business and gave Garguilo his card. About a month later Garguilo came to Villari's shop on West 53rd Street in Manhattan. Joseph Macchia was with him. According to Villari, Garguilo introduced Macchia as "Tony", saying "that he is buddy-buddy, that they do everything together as a group." Garguilo took Villari "on the side", approximately 25 feet away from Macchia, and, placing his arm around Villari's shoulder, asked Villari to join him in a counterfeiting endeavor; Villari said he was not interested and the two visitors left about ten minutes after they had arrived. There is no evidence that Macchia talked about counterfeiting or anything else.

Sometime during the summer of 1961, Garguilo came to Della Monica's photography studio in Brooklyn and asked to be taught how to develop a picture and make a copy. He came "several times," "about a week or so". He had Macchia with him "only once or two" of these times. Garguilo introduced Macchia to Della Monica as "my friend, Joe". After Garguilo had learned how to develop pictures, he "started to practice himself" and apparently did so regularly at Della Monica's studio; Macchia was there "two or three times" in all, never alone but always with Garguilo. Garguilo borrowed a camera and other photographic equipment from Della Monica, explaining that he was going into the advertising business and needed the camera to make copies. Inquiries by Della Monica as to Garguilo's progress produced no satisfactory response. There was no evidence that Macchia witnessed the loan of the equipment or participated in its use.

In July, 1961, Garguilo returned to Villari's printing shop. The record is not altogether plain whether there were two or three visits during July, but it is clear that Garguilo was alone on each of them. Assuming that there were three, the first was devoted to a general request for help, which Villari declined, as he had a year before; on the second, Garguilo asked Villari to check his negatives of $10 bills, which Villari again refused to do; on the third, Villari "succumbed", looked at the negatives, which Garguilo carried in a newspaper, through a "view box" and pronounced them too dark, whereupon Garguilo destroyed them.

Garguilo again came to Villari's shop in early August, 1961. This time Macchia accompanied him. Garguilo had brought some more negatives which Villari viewed and found "pretty good"— good enough so that he "burnt in" a plate. This was done with Macchia two or three feet away, "very close". The plate being blurred and inadequate, Garguilo erased it, whereupon he and Macchia "went away. They took the negatives with them and went away." Who carried the negatives is not clear. Villari testified this was the last he saw of Macchia.

Garguilo came to Villari's shop a few days later with some more negatives. Again a plate was "burnt in", found inadequate, and destroyed.

One of Garguilo's visits to the printing shop was witnessed by Secret Service Agent Motto. He testified that on August 11, 1961, he saw Garguilo and another man drive up in an automobile. Garguilo got out, carying a newspaper wrapped tightly under his arm, and went into the building where Villari's shop was located. He remained for approximately one hour. Then he and Villari came out, got in the car in which the other man was seated, and drove off. Motto could not identify the man who stayed in the car; he did estimate the man's age, height and weight, but there is nothing to tell whether these estimates bear any correspondence with Macchia or whether the unidentified man was the driver. Toward the end of August, Secret Service Agents searched Villari's shop and found the erased plate of early August, which bore Garguilo's fingerprints.

The * * * other evidence against Macchia was that, when brought before an Assistant United States Attorney for questioning, he admitted that he knew Garguilo, that on several occasions he accompanied Garguilo to the photographer in Brooklyn, and that several times he went to a printing place with him. He claimed, however, "that he never went up to the printer's establishment but merely sat on the stoop." Macchia also admitted that he knew what was in the newspaper taken out of the car by Garguilo, but refused to say what this was.

---

18 UNITED STATES CODE

§ 2. Principals

(a) Whoever commits an offense against the United States or aids, abets, counsels, commands, induces or procures its commission, is punishable as a principal.

(b) Whoever willfully causes an act to be done which if directly performed by him or another would be an offense against the United States, is punishable as a principal.

CALIFORNIA PENAL CODE

§ 30. Classification

CLASSIFICATION OF PARTIES TO CRIME. The parties to crimes are classified as:

1. Principals; and,
2. Accessories.

§ 31. Principals defined

WHO ARE PRINCIPALS. All persons concerned in the commission of a crime, whether it be felony or misdemeanor, and whether they directly commit the act constituting the offense, or aid and abet in its commission, or, not being present, have advised and encouraged its commission, and all persons counseling, advising, or encouraging children under the age of fourteen years, lunatics or idiots, to commit any crime, or who, by fraud, contrivance, or force, occasion the drunkenness of another for the purpose of causing him to commit any crime, or who, by threats, menaces, command, or coercion, compel another to commit any crime, are principals in any crime so committed.

ILLINOIS STAT., CH. 38

§ 5–2. When Accountability Exists

A person is legally accountable for the conduct of another when:

(a) Having a mental state described by the statute defining the offense, he causes another to perform the conduct, and the other person in fact or by reason of legal incapacity lacks such a mental state; or

(b) The statute defining the offense makes him so accountable; or

(c) Either before or during the commission of an offense, and with the intent to promote or facilitate such commission, he solicits, aids, abets, agrees or attempts to aid, such other person in the planning or commission of the offense. However, a person is not so accountable, unless the statute defining the offense provides otherwise, if:

(1) He is a victim of the offense committed; or

(2) The offense is so defined that his conduct was inevitably incident to its commission; or

(3) Before the commission of the offense, he terminates his effort to promote or facilitate such commission, and does one of the following: wholly deprives his prior efforts of effectiveness in such commission, or gives timely warning to the proper law enforcement authorities, or otherwise makes proper effort to prevent the commission of the offense.

PROPOSED FEDERAL CRIMINAL CODE

(1971).

§ 401. Accomplices

(1) Liability Defined. A person may be convicted of an offense based upon the conduct of another person when:

(a) acting with the kind of culpability required for the offense, he causes the other to engage in such conduct; or

(b) with intent that an offense be committed, he commands, induces, procures, or aids the other to commit it or, having a legal duty to prevent its commission, he fails to make proper effort to do so; or

(c) he is a co-conspirator and his association with the offense meets the requirements of either of the other paragraphs of this subsection.

A person is not liable under this subsection for the conduct of another person when he is either expressly or by implication made not accountable for such conduct by the statute defining the offense or related provisions, because he is a victim of the offense or otherwise.

(2) Defenses Precluded. Except as otherwise provided, in any prosecution in which the liability of the defendant is based upon the conduct of another person, it is no defense that:

(a) the defendant does not belong to the class of persons who, because of their official status or other capacity or characteristic, are by definition of the offense the only persons capable of directly committing it; or

(b) the person for whose conduct the defendant is being held liable has been acquitted, has not been prosecuted or convicted or has been convicted of a different offense, or is immune from prosecution, or is otherwise not subject to justice.

§ 1002. Criminal Facilitation

(1) Offense. A person is guilty of criminal facilitation if he knowingly provides substantial assistance to a person intending to commit a crime which is, in fact, a felony, and that person, in fact, commits the crime contemplated, or a like or related felony, employing the assistance so provided. The ready lawful availability from others of the goods or services provided by a defendant is a factor to be considered in determining whether or not his assistance was substantial. This section does not apply to a person who is either expressly or by implication made not accountable by the statute defining the felony facilitated or related statutes.

(2) *Defense Precluded.* Except as otherwise provided, it is no defense to a prosecution under this section that the person whose conduct the defendant facilitated has been acquitted, has not been prosecuted or convicted, has been convicted of a different offense, is immune from prosecution, or is otherwise not subject to justice.

(3) *Grading.* Facilitation of a Class A felony is a Class C felony. Facilitation of a Class B or Class C felony is a Class A misdemeanor.

NOTE

The Study Draft's section dealing with criminal facilitation is discussed in Comment, *A New Crime: Criminal Facilitation,* 18 Loyola L.Rev. 103 (1972).

———

a. THE EXTENT OF PARTICIPATION NECESSARY

THE QUEEN v. CONEY

Queens Bench, 1882.
[1881] 8 Q.B. 534.

CAVE, J. In this case I am of opinion that the direction to the jury was wrong, and consequently that the conviction ought not to stand.

The prisoners were charged in one count with a common assault on one Burke, and in another count with a like assault on one Mitchell.

The evidence was that on the 16th of June last, at the close of Ascot races, Burke and Mitchell had engaged in a fight near the road from Ascot to Maidenhead; that a ring was formed with posts and ropes; that a large number of persons were present looking on, some of whom were undoubtedly encouraging the fight; that the men fought for some time; and that the three prisoners were seen in the crowd, but were not seen to do anything, and there was no evidence how they got there or how long they stayed there.

The chairman of quarter sessions directed the jury in the words of Russell on Crimes, vol. i. p. 818: "There is no doubt that prize-fights are illegal, indeed just as much so as that persons should go out to fight with deadly weapons, and it is not at all material which party strikes the first blow, and all persons who go to a prize-fight to see the combatants strike each other, and who are present when they do so are, in point of law, guilty of an assault." And the chairman added, in the words of Littledale, J., in Rex v. Murphy [6 C. & P. 103]: "If they were not casually passing by, but stayed at the place, they encouraged it by their presence, although they did not say or do anything." [As to Coney, Gilliam, and Tully, who had been shown only to have been spectators, the jury returned a verdict of guilty, but indicated that it was in consequence of the direction as they found the three not to have been aiding and abetting.]

By [his] direction I gather that the chairman laid down as matter of law, first, that the actual fighters in a prize-fight are guilty of an assault; and, secondly, that if any person is shewn to have been present in the crowd looking on at the fight, that is not merely evidence, but, if unexplained, conclusive proof that he was aiding and abetting the assault. That seems to be the natural meaning of the language used, and that, from the finding of the jury, appears to me to be the sense in which they understood it. They found a verdict of guilty against five of the prisoners who I presume, were proved to have taken some active part, or to have been there for the purpose of encouraging the fight, and as to the three prisoners in question they found that they were guilty of an assault, and yet that they were not aiding and abetting, which is to my mind an inconsistent finding. Indeed on no other supposition can I understand the verdict, for the evidence against the three prisoners, and especially against Gilliam, is quite consistent with their being labourers working near or persons going quietly home from the races, who observing a crowd, went up to see what the matter was, and finding it was a fight stayed some short time looking on.

* * *

It was next contended that the chairman was wrong in directing the jury in the words of Littledale, J., in Rex v. Murphy [supra,] that if the prisoners were not merely casually passing by, but stayed at the place, they encouraged it by their presence, although they did not say or do anything.

Now it is a general rule in the case of principals in the second degree that there must be participation in the act, and that although a man is present whilst a felony is being committed, if he takes no part in it, and does not act in concert with those who commit it, he will not be a principal in the second degree merely because he does not endeavour to prevent the felony, or apprehend the felon.

* * * Where presence may be entirely accidental, it is not even evidence of aiding and abetting. Where presence is primâ facie not accidental it is evidence, but no more than evidence, for the jury.

* * *

This summing-up unfortunately appears to me capable of being understood in two different ways. It may mean either that mere presence unexplained is evidence of encouragement, and so of guilt, or that mere presence unexplained is conclusive proof of encouragement, and so of guilt. If the former is the correct meaning, I concur in the law so laid down, if the latter, I am unable to do so. It appears to me that the passage tending to convey the latter view is that which was read by the chairman in this case to the jury, and I cannot help thinking that the chairman believed himself, and meant to direct the jury, and at any rate I feel satisfied that the jury understood him to mean, that mere presence unexplained was conclusive of proof of encouragement, and so of guilt; and it is on this ground I hold that this conviction ought not to stand.

MATHEW, J.

* * *

It was contended that the presence of persons shewn to have assembled for the purpose of witnessing prize-fights did not prove that they were aiding and abetting, and only afforded evidence from which a jury might draw that inference, and it was urged that the decisions upon which the Chairman of Quarter Sessions had acted were wrong, and ought to be overruled. It was argued that even though the combatants might be criminally responsible, it did not follow that spectators were chargeable with any offence. As to the latter class it was contended that the direction to the jury should have been, that it was for them to say whether the defendants were encouraging, or assisting the combatants, and that if it were not shewn that anything had been said or done by a particular spectator, the jury would be justified in acquitting him.

If this contention were correct some subtle distinctions would have to be made in dealing with the question of the criminality of persons present at prize-fights. For instance, it would be clear that those persons who helped to keep the ring, and so to provide sufficient space for the combatants, were aiding and abetting; but those who, in conformity with the arrangements made by the ring-keepers, remained outside the ring with the same object, would not be aiding and abetting unless the jury thought fit to say so. I cannot see the grounds for this distinction.

Many illustrations given to us of the mistake into which it was suggested that Littledale and Patteson, JJ., had fallen, were due, as it seems to me, to a misapprehension of the meaning of their decisions. Those judges never intended to say that the mere fact of presence at the place where a prize-fight was going on was proof of an intention to aid and abet. What I understand their lordships to have laid down is, that where a person was shewn to have been present as a spectator for the purpose of watching the fight, and with no other object, he was encouraging the combatants in their criminal purpose, and was therefore aiding and abetting. To submit to a jury in such a case the question of the guilt of spectators, is to treat, what seems to me a clear matter of law, as a doubtful question of fact. It is to intimate to the jury that they will not be wrong in determining that question in favour of the accused, and the practical result would be, that spectators would, as a general rule, escape conviction and punishment. As, without spectators, I believe there would be no prize-fights, the Courts would thus have surrendered the principal means of discouraging the disgraceful exhibitions in question, which there was some reason to hope, under the pressure of the law, were gradually being discontinued.

I have no doubt in this case that the defendants were spectators, and that the jury meant to find and properly found that they were so; and I am of opinion that they are rightly convicted.

STEPHEN, J. I entirely agree with the judgment delivered by my Brother Cave. * * *

Upon the question whether bare voluntary presence at a prize-fight is, in itself, either an aiding or abetting of the combatants, or conclusive evidence of it, I have only one remark to add to my Brother Cave's judgment. I think that the chairman rightly apprehended the ruling of Littledale, J., in Rex v. Murphy, [supra], and that that ruling was wrong. In that case it was alleged by the prosecution that Murphy acted as second in the fight. The witnesses for the defence denied this, and said that Murphy neither did nor said anything. Littledale, J., told the jury upon this, that persons who are at a fight, in consequence of which death ensues, "are all guilty of manslaughter if they encourage it by their presence; I mean if they remained present during the fight. I say that if they were not casually passing by, but stayed at the place, they encouraged it by their presence, although they did not do or say anything." I do not think that such cases as were suggested during the argument, cases of persons voluntarily witnessing a prize-fight for some innocent, or even laudable purpose, were present to the mind of Littledale, J., when he said this. It would be unfair to construe language, chosen on the spur of the moment, and in reference to the facts of a particular case, as it is necessary to construe an Act of Parliament; but I think the learned judge cannot have meant to say less, than that a person who looks on at a prize-fight out of mere curiosity does thereby aid and abet the fight. It would have served no purpose to say anything short of this. No one could doubt Murphy's guilt if he acted as second, or did any other positive act to encourage the fight. He was either in that position, or he was a mere spectator, and the whole point of the judge's charge is, that in either case he was guilty. In this, I think, that Littledale, J., went too far, being no doubt desirous of providing an easy and summary mode of suppressing prize-fights. It may, or may not, be desirable to make it a criminal offence to look on at a prize-fight in the absence of a lawful excuse to be proved by the spectator, but I think we should be making, instead of interpreting the law, if we were to say that such conduct is now a crime. * * *

POLLOCK, B. In my judgment this conviction should stand. * * *

Before I deal with the direction of the chairman, which relates to the legal effect to be given to the presence of the prisoners in this particular case, I must notice what appears to me to be the true ground upon which the decisions of judges have been based, when they have ruled that those who remain and look on whilst a fight is going on encourage it by their presence, and are guilty of an illegal act; and also the wide distinction which exists between the case of persons standing by to witness a prize-fight, and that of persons standing by and witnessing an attack by a mob, the setting fire to a building or any other illegal act of violence such as was referred to in the course of the argument.

With reference to this part of the case we ought not, when considering what is the true character of an act, to lay aside all knowledge of human nature and all experience of the habits of mankind. These appear to me to be the basis of, and necessarily to be interwoven with and form a part of all law, whether criminal or otherwise; and, when I look at the case in this light, I see no true analogy between a crowd of persons voluntarily collected round a fight, and those who in a public street or elsewhere are present whilst an illegal act (the sight of which in itself cannot reasonably be supposed to give pleasure to any one) is going on. In the one case it is usually the bystanders collected around who create and who are responsible for the fight as a matter of interest and amusement to themselves. In the other, unless there be some overt act by gesture or word which denotes assistance or encouragement, it would be contrary to all reason to infer that the bystanders were taking any part in the illegal act. Again, when a prize-fight takes place but two can fight, and but some half dozen can assist the combatants, it is however almost of the very essence of the thing that a large number should be present as mere spectators, who could not consistently with the object of the whole proceeding actively interfere. On the contrary, where acts of violence take place, it is to say the least more probable that those who intend to encourage them will not remain mere passive spectators, but will in some measure take an active part.

In my view of the law, [the summing-up] correctly laid it down as applicable to the particular case in hand. No doubt it did not exhaust the subject, or deal with all the possible cases, or all the supposititious cases which were put during the argument before us. It was said that instances might occur of persons being present at a fight such as this, or even at this fight, who yet would not be doing an illegal act; thus a weak man might be hemmed in by the crowd and so be present against his will; the father or mother of one of the combatants might be there to dissuade him, if possible, from entering upon or continuing the contest; a very short man might be at the outer edge of the crowd and so unable either to see or to apprehend what was going on, and that these persons would not be guilty of an illegal act. This is quite true, but surely it has no bearing upon the facts proved here, nor could the chairman have alluded to such cases without travelling very wide from the facts proved, and distracting the minds of the jury from the question to be considered in the particular case. The chairman's own direction is confined to "all persons who go to a prize-fight to see the combatants." The quotation from Littledale, J., is not so accurate, because it may appear to affirm the proposition that all persons who stay at the place encourage the fight, but even as to this it states what I think is sound law, unless it be taken to include persons staying for some cause which makes it legal, or to include those curious and exceptional instances mentioned during the argument. Few propositions of law can be applied during a summing-up, even in criminal cases, so as to be sufficient and complete in omnibus; nor need they be, since the office of a summing-up is not to propound the law exhaustively, but to explain so much of its as relates to and is called for by the particular case which the jury have to try.

COMMONWEALTH v. PERRY

Supreme Judicial Court of Massachusetts, 1970.
357 Mass. 149, 256 N.E.2d 745.

QUIRICO, Justice. The defendant was found guilty by a jury on two indictments * * *. Indictment No. 41,760 charges that the defendant being armed with a revolver assaulted George Salibe with intent to rob him. Indictment No. 41,761 charges that the defendant being armed with a revolver assaulted William Kempner with intent to rob him and did rob and steal a wallet and some money from his person. The case is before us on the defendant's exceptions to the trial judge's denial of his motions for directed verdicts of not guilty and his motion to suppress certain evidence.

At 9:30 P.M. on November 6, 1968, Kempner and Salibe were working as clerks at the Murray Kempner Company liquor store in the Dorchester district of Boston. Three men entered the store. One of the men had a gun, and they robbed Kempner of his wallet and some money and assaulted Salibe with the intent to rob him. Both clerks testified that the defendant was not one of the three robbers who entered the store, and that they had never seen him before.

The defendant did not testify. The only evidence relating to him was testimony from a police sergeant who said that he arrested him on March 26, 1969, that he "gave the defendant the warnings required by the Miranda Case," that "he advised him of no other rights," and that the defendant then made a statement to him as follows: On November 6, 1968, he was at the apartment of one Carlson on Beacon Street in Boston, and that one Wiggins and Gary Murphy were also there. Wiggins and Murphy talked about holding up a liquor store later that night. Murphy had formerly been a truck driver in the area of the Kempner liquor store and he suggested that they hold up that store. They all agreed and they went to that area by public transit. The defendant had formerly lived with a sister in that area and on occasions he had made purchases at the Kempner store. In view of this he feared that he would be recognized. He therefore arranged with the other three that after the holdup they would pick him up at the Y.M.C.A. which was a block away from the store. He waited at the Y.M.C.A. for them, but they did not come. He then went to his home in Boston by the public transit system. Wiggins came to his home about 11 P.M. that evening. They discussed the holdup and Wiggins said they got no money from the store. Wiggins told him that Murphy stayed near the door with a gun and Carlson went to the register looking for money. Two or three days later the defendant met Carlson who also told him they got no money.

The police sergeant testified that the Y.M.C.A. was about 400 feet from the entrance to the Kempner store. This was not a statement made by the defendant. There was no evidence whether the Y.M.C.A. was on the same street as the liquor store, or whether it was possible to see from one place to the other.

The motions for directed verdicts of not guilty raise the question whether there was sufficient evidence of the defendant's guilt to warrant submission of the cases to the jury. Although each indictment charges the defendant as a principal, he could be convicted on proof that he was an accessory before the fact to the crimes charged.

There was evidence that the defendant knew the three persons who entered the liquor store and committed the robbery and assault, that he associated with them, and that he was in their company both before and after the robbery. But that, without more, is not enough to convict the defendant on either charge. There can be no finding of guilt by association. *   *   *

There was also evidence that the defendant knew before the robbery and assault that Carlson, Wiggins and Murphy were going to the liquor store to commit those crimes, and that he knew later that they had committed them. But mere knowledge that a crime is to be committed, even when coupled wih subsequent concealment of the completed crime, does not make one guilty as an accessory before the fact or as a principal to the crime about which he has knowledge. *   *   *

The Commonwealth's evidence is also deficient in that it does not show that the defendant counseled, hired or otherwise procured the three other persons to commit the robbery or the assault with intent to rob, or that he did any other act which would make him an accessory before the fact to such crimes. It appears that it was Murphy who counseled and procured the others to rob the liquor store. Moreover, the Commonwealth made no showing that there was an agreement for the defendant to stand by, at or near the scene of the crimes to render aid, assistance or encouragement to the perpetrators if it became necessary, or to assist them in making their escape from the scene.

Finally, there was no showing that he was in any location or position where he could aid in any way in the commission of the crimes. Commonwealth v. Knapp, 9 Pick. 495, 517. He did not act as a lookout or decoy for the perpetrators of the crimes. He had no car or other means by which he could assist them to escape.   * * *

There may possibly be enough evidence to warrant the jury in finding that the defendant conspired with Carlson, Wiggins and Murphy to commit the robbery and the assault charged in the indictments. But even that, without more, would not be sufficient to convict the defendant on the basis that he was either an accessory before the fact or a principal to the substantive crimes charged.   * * *

In view of this state of the evidence we are convinced that it was not sufficient to be submitted to the jury on the theory either that the defendant was an accessory before the fact or that he was a principal. The denial of his motions for directed verdicts of not guilty was error.

* * *

Exceptions sustained.

Judgments for the defendant.

NOTE

Reconsider the court's conclusion that even if the defendant conspired to commit the robbery and the assault he is not for that reason alone guilty of the substantive crimes in light of the material on conspiracy.

STATE v. COBB

Supreme Court of Missouri, 1969.
444 S.W.2d 408.

STORCKMAN, Judge. A jury convicted the defendant Harold Cobb of burglary in the second degree and stealing in connection therewith * * *. He attacks the sufficiency of the evidence to support the verdict * * *.

On February 27, 1967, at approximately 4:25 a. m., in response to a burglar alarm, a police patrol car was dispatched to a drug store owned and operated by Bingaman's No. 1 United Super Market, Inc., which was located at the State Fair Shopping Center in Sedalia. It had been raining and the pavement was wet. The evidence most favorable to the verdict shows that when the patrol car arrived at the parking lot the police officers, James Tuttle and Charles Shepherd, saw a GTO Pontiac automobile occupied by the defendant and three other persons about 20 feet from the north door of the drug store, sometimes referred to as Bing's or Bing's No. 1. The lights on the Pontiac were completely off and it was moving slowly. As the patrol car entered the parking lot, the Pontiac accelerated and was driven rapidly from the parking lot. As it turned left on Limit Avenue, the rear end "fishtailed" and the car skidded into a ditch; it then came back across the highway and stalled in the middle of the road and crossways of it.

The police officers stopped their patrol car near the stalled Pontiac and ordered the occupants to get out on the driver's side. Ernest Greer was driving and left the car first. The defendant Cobb was riding on the right side of the front seat and got out next. A boy by the name of Herbert Horton and a girl whose name was once given as Courtney Bell were in the back seat and got out last. As the occupants of the Pontiac were getting out, a second patrol car occupied by officers Robert Lewis and James Curry arrived and assisted in searching the occupants, handcuffing them, and taking them to the police station.

An investigation at the drug store disclosed that a window beside the front door had been broken. The dimensions of the window were estimated by some witnesses as 6 feet by 4 feet and by others as 3 feet wide by 8 or 10 feet high. Approximately half or ¾ths of the glass had been broken out of the window. The opening was large enough to admit a man's body. There were fragments of glass both inside and outside the building. A heavy metal container or basket for carrying four gallons of milk was found on the walk immediately in front of the broken window. There were fragments of glass in the container.

A number of bottles containing prescription drugs which were on a shelf when the store was closed the night before were missing. The missing articles were found in a carton on the floor of the Pontiac automobile behind the right front seat occupied by the defendant Cobb. The drug items were identified at the trial as being the property of the owner of the store and as having been stolen from the store.

The GTO Pontiac was a two-door sports model with bucket seats in front. To permit a person to leave or enter the back seat, one of the side doors had to be opened and then the back of the front seat pushed forward. If the door was not opened first, the back of the front seat when pushed forward would strike and get caught on the door handle.

The defendants Cobb and Greer were the only witnesses for the defense. Their testimony tended to show that they and two other men left Kansas City for Jefferson City in two automobiles at about 8:30 p. m. on the day before the burglary was committed. The men were accompanied by four girls, two of whom were students at Lincoln University. After they arrived in Jefferson City, they spent some time at a cafe drinking 3.2 beer since the students were not required to check into the University until midnight. On the return trip to Kansas City, the occupants of the GTO Pontiac were the defendants Greer and Cobb, Herbert Horton, and Courtney Bell who was referred to as a sixteen-year old girl.

According to the testimony of Cobb and Greer, Horton was driving the GTO, Greer was on the right side of the front seat, and Cobb and the girl were in the rear seat. Cobb testified that he did not know what time they left Jefferson City, that he went to sleep shortly thereafter and was aware of nothing that happened until he was awakened by lights of the patrol car flashing on the stalled GTO in Sedalia and Horton saying that everybody must get out.

Greer testified that he, too fell asleep on the return trip but that Horton awakened him in Sedalia and told him he was going to look for a girl he knew there. Greer went back to sleep and after an hour or two Horton again awakened him and asked for money to get sandwiches and coffee. They were at a filling station and Greer went in and relieved himself, returned to the car, again fell asleep, and the next time he woke up was when the officers told him to get out of the car. Greer denied that he was the driver of the Pontiac and testified that the car belonged to a friend of Horton's but the testimony as to ownership was quite vague and uncertain.

The defendant Cobb testified that he was twenty-seven years old at the time of the trial. It is not a vital factor in the case, but there is some indication in the record that Horton and the girl as well as Greer, were under seventeen when the crime was committed.

The appellant contends that the state failed to prove that he burglarized the store or that he aided or abetted or associated himself with the venture in any way and, therefore, the verdict and judgment are contrary to the evidence and against the greater weight of the credible evidence. He relies mainly on State v. Irby, Mo., 423 S.W.2d 800, for the proposition that something more than mere presence at the scene of the crime must be shown in order to convict; on State v. Castaldi, Mo., 386 S.W.2d 392, for the proposition that evidence that the accused had an opportunity to commit a crime or which merely raises a suspicion or gives rise to conjecture is insufficient to support a judgment of conviction; and on State v. Butler, Mo., 310 S.W.2d 952, for the proposition that some form of affirmative participation must be shown. These rules are well recognized but more than mere presence and an opportunity to commit the crime are involved in this case.

The presence of the accused at the place of the commission of a criminal offense may be considered along with other incriminating evidence to determine if the total circumstances raise a reasonable inference that the accused was a participant or an aider or abettor in the crime. * * * Evidence fairly showing any form of affirmative participation in a crime is sufficient to support a conviction. * * * Even in cases where the evidence is wholly circumstantial, the evidence tending to support the verdict must be considered as true, contrary evidence must be disregarded, and every reasonable inference in support of the verdict must be indulged. * * * For present purposes we must disregard entirely the testimony of Cobb and Greer that Cobb was asleep at the time the burglary and stealing occurred.

*   *   *

An inference of guilt is permissible from the unexplained possession of property recently stolen in a burglary and the inference exists both as to the offense of burglary and of stealing. * * * However, the jury determines the credibility of the defendant's explanation of his possession of the stolen property, and even though such explanation was not impeached, the jury was entitled to disbelieve it and draw an inference unfavorable to him based on his possession. * * * Quite understandably, the jury did not believe the defendant's story that he slept through the din that must have attended the breaking of the large window of the drug store with a 10-pound metal milk carrier approximately 20 feet from the automobile, the disturbance of depositing the stolen drugs in the rear portion of the two-door GTO Pontiac, and the unusual movements of rapid acceleration, fishtailing and skidding of the car. We hold that the evidence was sufficient to make a case for the jury and it supports the verdict returned.

* * *

DONNELLY, Judge (dissenting).

I would apply the following rules to the facts in this case:

(1) A recent, unexplained, and exclusive possession of stolen property will support an inference of the guilt of the possessor.

(2) To "create an inference of guilt, the term 'exclusive' does not mean that the possession must be separate from all others * * *." State v. Oliver, 355 Mo. 173, 176, 195 S.W.2d 484, 486.

(3) However, in situations where joint possession is claimed, there must be *other* evidence to connect defendant with the offense. State v. Oliver, supra; State v. Crawford, 59 Utah 39, 201 P. 1030.

In my opinion, the "other evidence" adduced in this case is not sufficient to show defendant *participated in the burglary*.

I respectfully dissent.

SEILER, J., concurs.

NOTES

1. Was it ever made clear to the jury what extent of participation they must infer from the unexplained possession of the stolen goods in order to find the defendant guilty? Suppose Cobb had not been asleep; would he be liable for the crimes? If neither the appellate court nor the trial court ever address themselves to the extent of participation necessary for a finding of guilt, can this failure be justified by the existence of the permissible inference of guilt from possession of the stolen items?

2. To what extent—or under what circumstances—may a passenger in an automobile involved in a fatal accident be liable for the death of the victim on the theory that he aided and abetted the driver? See, e. g., Flippen v. State, 211 Tenn. 507, 365 S.W.2d 895 (1963).

STATE v. SPILLMAN

Supreme Court of Arizona, 1970.
105 Ariz. 523, 468 P.2d 376.

HAYS, Justice. Defendant Erich Spillman was charged by information with two counts of forcible rape of Marguerite Basko. Count II of the complaint alleged that defendant raped Margie Basko * * * and Count I charged that defendant aided and abetted another rape of Miss Basko by one Gilbert Felix * * *. Trial on both charges was held in the Maricopa County Superior Court, at which the jury returned a verdict of guilty to Count I. The jury was unable to reach a verdict on Count II. The trial court sentenced defendant to a term of not less than five nor more than seven years at the Arizona State Prison. Defendant appeals from this conviction and sentence.

The alleged crimes purportedly took place in a downtown Phoenix flower shop around 11:00 p. m. on the night of April 4, 1967. Margie Basko, eighteen and a half years of age and a student at Arizona State University, was living at home with her parents near 40th Street and Thomas Road in East Phoenix. About 9 p. m. that evening, she received a telephone call from her former boyfriend, Bill Dickerson, who related that he had shown her picture to a couple of male acquaintances who wanted to drive over to her house to meet her. Margie agreed to their coming over, and about a half hour later, defendant and Gilbert Felix arrived at the Basko home and identified themselves as Dickerson's friends. Margie had never met either of the young men before, but invited them into the house, conversed with them for a few minutes, and introduced them to her parents. Afterward, the two men asked her to go out with them for a coke. Margie received permission from her mother to go out for a few minutes, and left the Basko home with defendant and Felix in defendant's Jaguar automobile. They drove from her home to a flower shop where defendant worked in downtown Phoenix.

After looking around the flower shop for about five minutes, the three went upstairs to the office of the shop, which was furnished with a couch and desk. While Margie sat on the couch, defendant Spillman showed her a copy of Playboy magazine and a book called "Sexes." Felix went downstairs to fix a drink, and Spillman moved next to Margie on the couch and tried to kiss her. Margie thwarted the gesture by pushing him away, and defendant did not persist. Felix returned with a drink, and defendant immediately proceeded downstairs.

While defendant was downstairs, Felix attempted several times to kiss Margie. Each time she told him to stop and pushed him away. She got up from the couch and started to walk away, but Felix pursued her over to a corner and held her against the wall. At this time the lights went out. Felix somehow got Margie back over to the couch, where he allegedly forcibly raped her. Margie testified at defendant's trial that while Felix was having intercourse with her, defendant Spillman returned upstairs, knelt beside her on the couch, and said "What's the matter." Felix then got off of her and Margie stood up from the couch and pulled up her pants. Defendant forced her back down on the couch and allegedly proceeded to rape her.

Defendant and Felix drove Margie back to her home, and let her off around midnight. Margie went inside and reported the incident to her mother. The police were called shortly thereafter, and defendant was arrested the next day, April 5. Gilbert Felix was not apprehended until several months later.

The information filed against Gilbert Felix was identical to that filed against defendant, that is, Count II of rape and Count I of aiding and abetting a rape. Felix was tried separately from and subsequent to defendant. At the time of Felix' trial, Count I, the aiding and abetting charge was dropped, and the jury subsequently found Felix not guilty of rape. In this appeal, defendant Spillman contends that his conviction of aiding and abetting Felix' rape cannot stand for the reason that Felix, the actual perpetrator of the alleged rape, was acquitted. The argument is made that where, as here, there is no question as to the identity of the party allegedly committing the forcible rape, the acquittal of the principal establishes that no forcible rape took place at all, thus invalidating the conviction for aiding and abetting. We do not agree.

* * *

Aiding and abetting is an independent and distinct substantive offense, and it is not necessary to try and convict the perpetrator of a criminal act before an aider and abettor can be tried. * * * But where a principal has been acquitted of a criminal act, can his accomplice, in a separate trial, be convicted of aiding and abetting that criminal act? We hold that he can.

The State is never required to prove more than the allegations contained in an information in order to sustain the conviction of an aider and abettor. Where, as here, a principal and an aider and abettor are jointly charged in the same information, and the aider and abettor is tried first, there can be no truthful allegation that the principal has been convicted of the crime. What is required at the trial of the aider and abettor is proof, complete and convincing, of the guilt of the principal. Justice demands that the principal crime be fully proved, since the guilt of the aider and abettor depends upon the commission of the principal crime. Thus, whether or not the principal is convicted or acquitted in a separate trial can have no bearing on the trial of the aider and abettor, if the evidence shows the latter guilty. Society is no less injured by the illegal acts of the aider and abettor even though the principal himself escapes conviction. In order to convict an aider and abettor, justice demands no more than the information properly charge and the evidence convincingly show that a crime was committed by the principal. * * * We hold that defendant's conviction * * * was not made invalid by the fact that Gilbert Felix was later acquitted of rape.

Defendant also contends that the evidence introduced at his trial was insufficient to support a conviction of aiding and abetting rape. Specifically, defendant contends that the evidence failed to show that he "assist(ed) in the commission of an act (the rape), either by active participation in it or in some manner advising or encouraging it," State v. Roberts, 85 Ariz. 252, 254, 336 P.2d 151, 152 (1959), or that he "(stood) in the same relation to the crime as the criminal, approach(ed) it from the same angle, touch(ed) it at the same point and possess(ed) criminal intent," State v. Bearden, supra, 99 Ariz. at 3, 405 P.2d at 886. A thorough review of the record, in a light most favorable to the allegations of the State, compels us to agree with defendant's position.

The evidence is clear and undisputed that Margie Basko voluntarily accompanied defendant and Felix to the flower shop where the alleged rapes occurred. She clearly testified that she was not in any fear and in no way felt coerced in either going to the flower shop or in going upstairs to the office of the shop. Margie unequivocally explained to the trial court that the first time she began to feel frightened was after defendant had gone downstairs leaving her alone upstairs with Felix. When Felix grabbed her and assaulted her, defendant was out of the room. Defendant did not return to the upstairs office until after the rape had commenced.

Nowhere does the evidence indicate that defendant assisted in any way, either physically or by advice and encouragement, Felix' alleged rape of Margie Basko. The State makes much of the fact that the lights to the upstairs office went out at the time Felix had Margie pinned against the wall. Margie testified that she did not douse the lights and that she did not see Felix turn off a light switch. Such testimony, however, is insufficient to link defendant with the act of turning out the lights in aid of Felix. The State failed to introduce evidence as to the location of the light switch in the room or building. In addition, testimony was never offered concerning any discussion between Felix and Spillman which would indicate a plot, scheme or agreement to rape Margie Basko.

In Carroll v. State, 90 Ariz. 411, 368 P.2d 649 (1962), we held that the mere presence of a defendant at the scene of a crime is insufficient to establish guilt. The evidence in this case, concerning Gilbert Felix' alleged rape of Margie Basko, indicates nothing more than defendant Erich Spillman being present, somewhere in the building, at the time Felix assaulted Margie. Without evidence indicating defendant Spillman's complicity in the crime, defendant's conviction for aiding and abetting a rape cannot stand.

The judgment of conviction is reversed.

NOTES

1. Compare United States v. Prince, 430 F.2d 1324 (4th Cir. 1970), reversing a conviction for aiding and abetting a hunting companion in taking a rail bird from a boat powered by a motor in violation of federal law on the ground that while the appeal was pending the companion was tried as a principal and acquitted. What arguments can be made for the result in *Prince*? Is the acquittal of the principal logically inconsistent with the guilt of the aider and abettor? Does not the verdict in the principal's trial simply establish that on this occasion the prosecution failed to meet its especially high burden of proof of the principal's guilt, a determination in no way conclusive as to the actual guilt of the principal? What policy would be served by granting an alleged aider and abettor the "windfall" of acquittal?

2. If Spillman had the requisite state of mind, is there any real doubt that he performed sufficient acts to give rise to liability? In view of the victim's potential reluctance to accompany a single man, might not Spillman's actions in accompanying Felix be sufficient? If not, would his furnishing the transportation to the scene of the crime? Even if he did not turn off the lights, is it not arguable that his conduct at the flower shop facilitated the rape?

Is there adequate evidence of the requisite state of mind? Does not the testimony of the apparently coordinated activity of Spillman and Felix together with Spillman's lack of surprise at the time he came upon Felix and the victim permit the inference that he knew Felix intended to accomplish intercourse with the victim, by force if necessary? Would this be enough, or would it be necessary to establish that Spillman believed that such force would in fact be necessary?

3. Is there any helpful way to describe in general terms what nature of activity related to an offense committed by another will give rise to liability for aiding and abetting? Is the matter one of describing the acts of the potential aider and abettor, or is it one of describing the requisite impact (or likely impact) upon the principal? Consider Perkins, Parties to Crime, 89 U.Pa.L.Rev. 581, 598 (1941), who makes the following comment concerning the encouragement necessary for liability as a principal in the second degree: "Guilt or innocence of the abettor * * * is not determined by the quantum of his advice or encouragement. If it is rendered to induce another to commit the crime and actually has this effect, no more is required." Cf. Commonwealth v. Pierce, 437 Pa. 266, 263 A.2d 350 (1970). Is it accurate to say that there is guilt as an aider and abettor if one, with the requisite state of mind, does any act within the meaning of the general principle that an act is required for criminal liability, or fails to act under circumstances making that failure sufficient for liability under general principles, and there is a resulting significant impact upon the principal in the commission of the crime? Must some impact, (i. e., a "result" factually and proximately caused by the alleged aider and abettor) be proved, or is it sufficient that the accused's act would generally tend to cause such an impact?

b. THE STATE OF MIND NECESSARY

WYATT v. UNITED STATES

United States Court of Appeals, Tenth Circuit, 1968.
388 F.2d 395.

HILL, Circuit Judge. * * * [A]ppellant Chandler attacks the sufficiency of the evidence to sustain his conviction * * * [of] aiding and abetting in the sale of non-tax-paid liquor to Agent Carpenter * * *.

Carpenter, an undercover agent and the Government's witness, testified that on August 14 he went to "Sonny Boy's" place in Guthrie, Oklahoma, and there he contacted Sonny Boy and asked him if he could buy some whiskey. Sonny Boy, not having any whiskey, directed him to go see Quinnon Chandler. Carpenter testified that he did go to the residence of Quinnon Chandler. Further: "When I arrived, I walked up to the front door and knocked and was invited into the house. Inside the house I observed Chester Chandler and Quinnon Chandler, they said they were glad to see me and told me to come out in the garage and see what they had. I walked out into the garage with Quinnon Chandler and Chester Chandler and observed seventeen and one-half gallons of moonshine whiskey inside the garage. After a brief conversation, I agreed to purchase six gallons of whiskey that night. After the agreement was made, Quinnon Chandler took two gallons, Chester Chandler took the four gallons in the case and placed them in the front of my vehicle, which was a Corvair with a trunk in the front. After the six gallons of whiskey was placed in the, in my vehicle, I asked Quinnon Chandler how much I owed him for the six gallons of whiskey, and he replied $36.00. I then paid Quinnon Chandler $36.00 for the six gallons of non-tax-paid whiskey, non-tax paid spirits." To be guilty of the crime of "aiding and abetting" one does not have to have an active stake in the outcome of the crime but merely participate therein. * * * Clearly and without any doubt, appellant Chandler participated here to the extent of helping his brother carry the illegally sold alcohol to the purchaser's car.

* * *

Affirmed.

STATE v. GLADSTONE

Supreme Court of Washington, 1970.
78 Wash.2d 306, 474 P.2d 274.

HALE, Justice. A jury found defendant Bruce Gladstone guilty of aiding and abetting one Robert Kent in the unlawful sale of marijuana. Deferring imposition of sentence, the court placed defendant on probation. He appeals * * * contending that the evidence as a matter of law was insufficient to sustain a verdict of guilty. His point, we think, is well taken.

* * *

Gladstone's guilt as an aider and abettor in this case rests solely on evidence of a conversation between him and one Douglas Mac-Arthur Thompson concerning the possible purchase of marijuana from one Robert Kent. There is no other evidence to connect the accused with Kent who ultimately sold some marijuana to Thompson.

* * *

The conversation between defendant and Thompson occurred at defendant's residence. Douglas MacArthur Thompson, a 25-year-old student at the University of Puget Sound in Tacoma and an employee of the Internal Revenue Service of the United States, had done some investigative work for the government. From time to time, the Tacoma Police Department engaged him to investigate the use, possession and sale of narcotics, principally marijuana, among college students. When working for the Tacoma Police Department, he operated under the control and direction of the department's narcotics detail.

Thompson testified that Lieutenant Seymour and Detective Gallwas of the narcotics detail asked him to attempt a purchase of marijuana from Gladstone. During the evening of April 10, 1967—between 10 and 11 o'clock—the two officers and Thompson drove in a police car to the vicinity of defendant's apartment. Thompson went to Gladstone's door alone, beyond the hearing and out of the sight of the two officers. He knocked at the door and Gladstone responded. Thompson asked Gladstone if he would sell him some marijuana. Describing this incident, Thompson testified as follows:

Well, I asked—at the time Gladstone told me that he was—he did not have enough marijuana on hand to sell me any, but he did know an individual who had quite a sufficient quantity and that was very willing to sell and he named the individual as Robert Kent, or Bob Kent as he put it, and he gave me directions to the residence and he—due to the directions I asked him if, you know, if he could draw me a map and he did.

When Thompson said he asked Gladstone to draw the map for him, he added, "I'm not sure whether he did give me the exact address or not, he told me where the residence was." He said that Gladstone then with pencil and paper sketched the location of Kent's place of residence. Thompson had no prior knowledge of where Kent lived, and did not know if he might have marijuana or that he had ever possessed it.

The two officers then took Thompson to Kent's residence where marijuana was purchased. The actual purchase was made by Thompson directly from Kent while Officer Gallwas and Lieutenant Seymour stayed in the police car. Kent was subsequently arrested and convicted of selling Thompson approximately 8 ounces of marijuana—the very sale which defendant here was convicted of aiding and abetting.

That ended the prosecution's case. Even if it were accorded all favorable inferences, there appears at this point a gap in the evidence which we feel as a matter of law is fatal to the prosecution's cause. Neither on direct examination nor under cross-examination did Thompson testify that he knew of any prior conduct, arrangements or communications between Gladstone and Kent from which it could be even remotely inferred that the defendant had any understanding, agreement, purpose, intention or design to participate or engage in or aid or abet any sale of marijuana by Kent. Other than to obtain a simple map from Gladstone and to say that Gladstone told him Kent might have some marijuana available, Thompson did not even establish that Kent and the defendant were acquainted with each other. Testimony of the brief conversation and Gladstone's very crude drawing consisting of 8 penciled lines indicating where Kent lived constitute the whole proof of the aiding and abetting presented.

* * *

If all reasonable inferences favorable to the state are accorded the evidence, it does not, in our opinion, establish the commission of the crime charged. That vital element—a nexus between the accused and the party whom he is charged with aiding and abetting in the commission of a crime—is missing. The record contains no evidence whatever that Gladstone had any communication by word, gesture or sign, before or after he drew the map, from which it could be inferred that he counseled, encouraged, hired, commanded, induced or procured Kent to sell marijuana to Douglas Thompson as charged, or took any steps to further the commission of the crime charged. He was not charged with aiding and abetting Thompson in the purchase of marijuana, but with Kent's sale of it.

* * *

[E]ven without prior agreement, arrangement or understanding, a bystander to a robbery could be guilty of aiding and abetting its commission if he came to the aid of a robber and knowingly assisted him in perpetrating the crime. But regardless of the modus operandi and with or without a conspiracy or agreement to commit the crime and whether present or away from the scene of it, there is no aiding and abetting unless one " 'in some sort associate himself with the venture, that he participate in it as in something that he wishes to bring about, that he seek by his action to make it succeed.' " Nye & Nissen v. United States, 336 U.S. 613, 619, 69 S.Ct. 766, 769, 93 L.Ed. 919 (1949).

Although an aider and abettor need not be physically present at the commission of the crime to be held guilty as a principal, his conviction depends on proof that he did something in association or connection with the principal to accomplish the crime. Learned Hand, J., we think, hit the nail squarely when, in United States v. Peoni, 100 F.2d 401, 402 (2d Cir. 1938), he wrote that, in order to aid and abet another to commit a crime, it is necessary that a defendant

> in some sort associate himself with the venture, that he participate in it as in something that he wishes to bring about, that he seek by his action to make it succeed. All the words used—even the most colorless, "abet"—carry an implication of purposive attitude towards it.

* * *

Another case—and one nearly identical with the instant case—affirms the foregoing principles. In Morei v. United States, 127 F.2d 827 (6th Cir. 1942), undercover narcotic agents approached the defendant, a physician, and asked him to sell them narcotics. The doctor told the agents he had none, but gave the agents the name of another party and advised the agent to tell the latter that the doctor had sent him. The doctor added that "he will take care of you." The agents did arrange a purchase of illegal narcotics from the person to whom the doctor had referred them, and the doctor was thereupon charged with aiding and abetting in the sale.

After tracing the common-law distinction between a principal in the second degree and an accessory before the fact and pointing out that an aider and abettor must at least procure, counsel or command another to commit the felony actually committed, the court said, at 830:

> It is not necessary that there should be any direct communication between an accessory before the fact and the principal felon; it is enough if the accessory direct an intermediate agent to procure another to commit the felony, without naming or knowing of the person to be procured. *A person is not an accessory before the fact, unless there is some sort of active proceeding on his part; he must incite, or procure, or encourage the criminal act, or assist or enable it to be done, or engage or counsel, or command the principal to do it.* Halsbury, supra, § 531. [9 Halsbury, Laws of England § 531 (1909)]. * * *
>
> * * * It is not to be assumed that Congress, in defining as a principal, one who "procures the commission of an offense," and using almost the identical language by which the common law defined aiders, abettors, and accessories, was providing for a new crime theretofore unknown. If the criterion for holding that one is guilty of procuring the commission of an offense, is that the offense would not have been committed except for such a person's conduct or revela-

tion of information, it would open a vast field of offenses that have never been comprehended within the common law by aiding, abetting, inducing or procuring.   *   *   *

*   *   *   [T]he only thing Dr. Platt did was to give Beach the name of Morei as a man from whom he might secure heroin to dose horses in order to stimulate them in racing.   This is not the purposive association with the venture that, under the evidence in this case, brings Dr. Platt within the compass of the crime of selling or purchasing narcotics, either as principal, aider and abettor, or accessory before the fact.   (Italics ours.)

*   *   *

It would be a dangerous precedent indeed to hold that mere communications to the effect that another might or probably would commit a criminal offense amount to an aiding and abetting of the offense should it ultimately be committed.

There being no evidence whatever that the defendant ever communicated to Kent the idea that he would in any way aid him in the sale of any marijuana, or said anything to Kent to encourage or induce him or direct him to do so, or counseled Kent in the sale of marijuana, or did anything more than describe Kent to another person as an individual who might sell some marijuana, or would derive any benefit, consideration or reward from such a sale, there was no proof of an aiding and abetting, and the conviction should, therefore, be reversed as a matter of law.   Remanded with directions to dismiss.

HAMILTON, Justice (dissenting).

*   *   *

The statutory language and the overt action it contemplates does *   *   *   give rise to the requirement that the aider or abettor entertain a conscious intent, *i. e.*, knowledge and intent that his action will instigate, induce, procure or encourage perpetration of the primary crime.   *   *   *

The question to be resolved, then, in the instant case is whether the evidence sustains the jury's conclusion that the appellant entertained the requisite intent to render him culpable as an aider or abettor.

*   *   *

Although the evidence in the case is conflicting, the jury was entitled to believe   *   *   *   that prior to the evening of April 10, 1967, when Thompson talked to appellant, *Thompson and the Tacoma Police Department were unaware of Kent or his association with marijuana;* *   *   *   *that Thompson approached Kent and told him "Gladstone had sent me" whereupon Kent invited him to a room and sold him some marijuana for $30* *   *   *.

Based upon the * * * inferences reasonably derivable there-from, I am satisfied that the jury was fully warranted in concluding that appellant, when he affirmatively recommended Kent as a source and purveyor of marijuana, entertained the requisite conscious design and intent that his action would instigate, induce, procure or encourage perpetration of Kent's subsequent crime of selling marijuana to Thompson. Furthermore, insofar as an element of preconcert be concerned, certainly the readiness with which the passwords, "Gladstone had sent me," gained a stranger's late evening entree to Kent's domain and produced two illegal sales strongly suggests, if not conclusively establishes, the missing communal nexus which the majority belabors.

NOTE

Perkins, Parties to Crime, 89 U.Pa.L.Rev. 581, 603–04 (1941), in discussing the liability as an accessory before the fact of one conducting a lawful business who becomes aware that one purchasing his wares or services intends to use them in the commission of a crime, concludes as follows: "[T]he gravity of the social harm resulting from the unlawful conduct is used to determine whether mere knowledge of the intended use will be sufficient * * *. A seller who completes the sale of goods after correctly divining that the purchaser is buying them as an agent of an armed combination attempting to overthrow the government, thereby 'voluntarily aids the treason'. * * * But the mere knowledge of one party to transaction that the other intends later to make an unlawful use of the property will not of itself be sufficient * * * if [the offense] is of a relatively minor nature. * * * It is otherwise, even as to such an offense, if the one charged as an inciter has not only had knowledge of the intended offense but has gone out of his way to promote it, as by packing the goods sold in an unusual manner to conceal their identity." How can such a position be defended on policy grounds?

PEOPLE v. POPLAR

Court of Appeals of Michigan, 1969.
20 Mich.App. 132, 173 N.W. 732.

J. H. GILLIS, Presiding Judge. Defendant was charged, as an aider and abettor, of breaking and entering, and of assault with intent to commit murder. * * * Defendant was found guilty on both counts by a jury and on appeal alleges that the denial of his motions * * * for a directed verdict was error.

The breaking and entering was of the Oak Park recreation building in Flint and was carried out in the early morning of December 3, 1964, by Alfred Williams and Clifford Lorrick. When the manager of the building discovered the two men, Williams shot him in the face with a shotgun. Defendant allegedly acted as a lookout.

* * *

Lorrick * * * testified for the prosecution at defendant's trial. He stated that he met defendant and Williams in a bar the night before the breaking and entering and left with them and two others. The five men allegedly drove around for a while before stopping to pick up some tools. They then took the tools and placed them in back of the bowling alley. An unsuccessful attempt to enter was made at that time. The group continued to drive around and during that time a shotgun that was in the car accidentally discharged, blowing a hole in the windshield. Just before the actual breaking and entering, the defendant, after getting out of the car with Lorrick and Williams, proceeded to a house directly across from the bowling alley. Lorrick testified that defendant went to see if anybody was watching.

Defendant took the stand and testified that he was in no way involved in the plans of Lorrick and Williams. He stated that the purpose of his going to the house across the street was to seek a friend who he thought would help him find employment.

[It was not] * * * error for the trial court to deny defendant's motion for directed verdict on the issue of whether defendant aided and abetted in the breaking and entering by acting as a lookout. The circumstances leading up to the offense, coupled with Lorrick's testimony, present sufficient evidence which, if believed by the jury, would support a conviction under the statute.

Since the jury found that defendant acted as a lookout, a more difficult question is whether defendant may be found guilty, as an aider and abettor, of assault with intent to commit murder.

Where a crime requires the existence of a specific intent, an alleged aider and abettor cannot be held as a principal unless he himself possessed the required intent or unless he aided and abetted in the perpetration of the crime knowing that the actual perpetrator had the required intent. * * *

There was no evidence that defendant harbored any intent to commit murder. Therefore, "knowledge of the intent of Hill [Williams] to kill the deceased is a necessary element to constitute him [defendant] a principal. This, however, may be established either by direct or circumstantial evidence from which knowledge of the intent may be inferred." Lee v. State (1948), 152 Tex.Cr.R. 401, 214 S.W. 2d 619.

A typical case of this kind is one where, as here, a crime not specifically within the common intent and purpose is committed during an escape. Convictions for aiding and abetting such crimes have been carefully scrutinized. In People v. Knapp (1872), 26 Mich. 112, the defendant had gathered with several other men in an upper story of his building for the purpose of having forcible sexual intercourse with the deceased against her will. In order to avoid arrest, all the parties jumped out of a window. After the defendant had jumped, the deceased was either pushed or thrown out of the window by one of the other men present. As a result, she suffered injuries from which she died. Knapp was tried separately on an information charging him and the others with murder and was convicted of manslaughter. In reversing the conviction, the Court stated,

"The conviction of manslaughter could only have been under certain portions of the charge, permitting the jury to find it in case the injury was caused in an attempt of the various persons assembled in the paint shop to avoid an arrest. The language of the court, repeated nearly in the same terms twice, was as follows:

" 'In this case, if the jury should be satisfied (beyond the doubt that I have spoken of) that these defendants combined for the purpose of inducing this girl to go to that shop for the purpose of prostitution, and that they did induce her to go, and while at the shop all had connection with her, and, in order to avoid arrest or exposure, threw her out of the window, without the intention of killing her, but by it she received injuries which caused her death, it would be manslaughter, because they were engaged in an act against public morals, and unlawful.'

"And the court refused to charge that, if the act was done under these circumstances without the concurrence of Knapp, he should not be convicted. Also refused to charge, that if the parties attempted to escape, and one of them, without the knowledge or consent of the other, helped or threw the deceased out of the window, then, none but those actually engaged in the act are liable for the consequences.

"The effect of these rulings was practically to hold that parties who have combined in a wrong purpose must be presumed, not only to combine in some way in escaping arrest, but also to be so far bound to each other as to be responsible severally for every act done by any of them during the escape.

"It is impossible to maintain such a doctrine. *It is undoubtedly possible for parties to combine in order to make an escape effectual, but no such agreement can lawfully be inferred from a combination to do the original wrong. There can be no criminal responsibility for any thing not fairly within the common enterprise, and which might be expected to happen if occasion should arise for any one to do it.* In other words, the principle is quite analogous to that of agency, where the liability is measured by the express or implied authority. And the authorities are quite clear, and reasonable, which deny any liability for acts done in escaping, which were not within any joint purpose or combination (citing authority).

"This ruling must have been of controlling weight with
the jury. There is evidence tending to show that some person other than Knapp pushed, or threw, the deceased out of
the window; but, if the testimony is all before us, it has very
little, if any, bearing upon Knapp's complicity in the act
which caused her death. He jumped out first, according to
the clear current of evidence, and it is not easy to discover
in the record, proof of his part in any conspiracy or agreement, in pursuance or execution of which it can be inferred
she was put out of the window." (pp. 114, 115) (Emphasis
supplied.)

* * *

Whether the crime committed was fairly within the scope of the
common unlawful enterprise is a question of fact for the jury. In
the present case, the evidence tends to show that the gun with which
the victim was shot was removed from the trunk of the car to the
front seat. It is not clear whether the defendant was present when
the gun was moved but he was aware of its presence inside the car.
Since the record also fails to reveal whether or not defendant knew
that the gun was taken into the bowling alley, the question is whether
it was proper for the jury to infer from the circumstantial evidence
that the defendant entertained the requisite intent to render him liable as a principal for assault with intent to commit murder.

In our opinion the jury could reasonably infer from the defendant's knowledge of the fact that a shotgun was in the car that he was
aware of the fact that his companions might use the gun if they were
discovered committing the burglary or in making their escape. * *
If the jury drew that inference, then it could properly conclude that
the use of the gun was fairly within the scope of the common unlawful enterprise and that the defendant was criminally responsible
for the use by his confederates of the gun in effectuating their escape.

Affirmed.

---

c. RENUNCIATION OR WITHDRAWAL

COMMONWEALTH v. HUBER

Court of Quarter Sessions, Montgomery County, Pennsylvania, 1958.
15 D. & C.2d 726.

GROSHENS, J. Defendant was indicted * * * on the charge
of accessory before the fact to robbery, and on * * * the charge
of accessory after the fact to robbery.

At the trial before the Hon. Harold G. Knight, sitting without a
jury, defendant was found guilty of accessory before the fact.

Defendant's motions for a new trial and in arrest of judgment
are now before the court for disposition. In support of his motions,

defendant contends in his brief: (a) That the Commonwealth failed to prove his guilt beyond a reasonable doubt, and (b) that defendant withdrew from any plan or scheme of robbery so as to make him not guilty as an accessory before the fact.

* * *

The happening of the robbery was not in dispute at the trial, as counsel for defendant admitted in open court that a robbery had taken place. The issue was narrowed down to defendant's connection with the robbery.

To prove defendant's implications the Commonwealth called the two police officers who investigated the case and one of the principals to the robbery. Both police officers testified defendant freely admitted to them three days after the robbery that he had furnished the rifle used in the robbery and the naptha type fluid used on the victim, that he knew a "hold-up" was planned, that he had been asked to accompany the principals which he refused to do, that defendant had gone to the police station on the night of the robbery where he learned that the robbery had taken place and that he went forthwith to the home of one of the principals to get his rifle back.

One of the three principals, Ernest Farr, testified that defendant knew of the plan and that defendant furnished the rifle and naptha (ether).

Defendant took the stand in his own defense and corroborated much of the Commonwealth's evidence. For example defendant testified concerning his rifle and his knowledge of its proposed use in a conversation with John Goodwin, one of the principals:

" 'Sure, you can borrow it,', and I asked him what he was going to do with it, and he said:

" 'I am going to rob somebody.' "

By the Court:

"Q. Going to what?

"A. He said he was going to rob somebody.

"Q. Rob somebody?

"A. That's it."

By Mr. Pearlstine:

"Q. And then what did you say to him about that?

"A. I just laughed right then, and then Landis, Dave Landis came in and I hadn't had a chance to talk to him again till we got down to my place.

"Q. Did Goodwin at that time say anything about you going with him or where they were going or anything like that or what they planned to?

"A. Yes, at that time he asked me to go along.

"Q. What did you say?

"A. I said no I had a date at first; and then he was persistent and it seemed like he wanted me to go and I says: *'No I ain't going to get involved in anything like that'* (Italics supplied)

"Q. Did you or not think he was serious at the time?

"A. No, I did not."

* * *

Certainly, the Commonwealth's evidence of aid given by this defendant, supported as it is by defendant's own testimony, amply supports the finding of guilt. The defense of withdrawal remains but to be considered.

The aid given by defendant to the principals in the perpetration of the robbery was supplying the rifle and the naptha type fluid which were indubitably used by the principals. To "aid" literally means to "help". A rifle, for instance, may be of great help to a robber. A pointed rifle is one of the oldest and most effective methods to cow a person into the quick and docile relinquishment of his wallet. Hence, a person who supplies an avowed robber with a rifle which is shortly thereafter used by the robber in a robbery may be said to have aided the robber.

The fact that this defendant was asked to participate in the robbery as a principal, and that he refused, does not constitute such a withdrawal as would relieve him of criminal liability as an accessory before the fact. Had this defendant demanded and received back his rifle, or had he reported the principals to the police in time to thwart the robbery, then he could be said to have withdrawn successfully. Having placed the rifle in the hands of John Goodwin who, according to defendant's own testimony, told defendant "he was going to rob somebody", defendant committed himself to a sequence of events from which he could only extricate himself by getting his rifle out of the hands of John Goodwin before the robbery, or by thwarting the robbery in some other way. The "aid" in this case was the rifle. Therefore, to effectively withdraw made it incumbent upon defendant to get the rifle out of the hands of John Goodwin, or the equivalent thereof. He did neither of these things. He did, however, go to the police station where he learned of the perpetration of the robbery. He then rushed posthaste to get his rifle, not to withdraw from the crime, but to get incriminating evidence out of the possession of a principal who was then the object of a police investigation.

* * *

[D]efendant's motions for a new trial and in arrest of judgment are dismissed, and defendant is ordered to appear for sentence at miscellaneous court on Friday, March 28, 1958.

NOTES

1. Suppose Huber had sought Goodwin to get the rifle back, but was unable to find him despite thorough search? Suppose he had retrieved the rifle because he learned of increased police surveillance of prime robbery targets, but the others nevertheless committed the robbery using a knife one of them already had?

2. The Study Draft of the Proposed Federal Criminal Code (1970) contained this portion of § 401 which was left out of the final version

> (3) Affirmative Defense of Renunciation and Withdrawal. It is an affirmative defense in a prosecution under subsection (1) that, under circumstances manifesting a voluntary and complete renunciation of his culpable intent, the defendant attempted to prevent the commission of the offense by taking affirmative steps which substantially reduced the likelihood of the commission thereof. A renunciation is not "voluntary and complete" if it is motivated in whole or in part by (a) a belief that circumstances exist which increase the probability of detection or apprehension of the defendant or an accomplice or which make more difficult the consummation of the offense, or (b) a decision to postpone the offense until another time or to substitute another victim or another but similar objective.

Was this desirable? How might it be justified?

There was no equivalent provision in § 1002, Criminal Facilitation. How could this be justified, if the above provision in § 401 was appropriate?

---

2. LIABILITY FOR CONDUCT AFTER THE COMMISSION OF AN OFFENSE

---

18 UNITED STATES CODE

§ 3. Accessory after the fact

Whoever, knowing that an offense against the United States has been committed, receives, relieves, comforts or assists the offender in order to hinder or prevent his apprehension, trial or punishment, is an accessory after the fact.

Except as otherwise expressly provided by any Act of Congress, an accessory after the fact shall be imprisoned not more than one-half the maximum term of imprisonment or fined not more than one-half the maximum fine prescribed for the punishment of the principal, or both; or if the principal is punishable by death, the accessory shall be imprisoned not more than ten years.

§ 4. Misprision of felony

Whoever, having knowledge of the actual commission of a felony cognizable by a court of the United States, conceals and does not as soon as possible make known the same to some judge or other person in civil or military authority under the United States, shall be fined not more than $500 or imprisoned not more than three years, or both.

UNITED STATES v. FOY

United States Court of Appeals for the Seventh Circuit, 1969.
416 F.2d 940.

KERNER, Circuit Judge. Defendant was indicted for violation of 18 U.S.C.A. § 1071, harboring and concealing a person from arrest. A jury found defendant guilty and from this conviction he appeals.

On October 19, 1967 an appeal bond of Bernard Francis Ryan was revoked and a bench warrant was issued for his arrest. The next morning, F.B.I. agents drove to an apartment building in Chicago, Illinois in which a friend of Ryan's, Leona Phebus, lived. Ryan was known to frequent her residence. When the agents arrived, they saw Ryan's car outside. Two agents entered the front of the building while two other agents entered through the rear. Four minutes elapsed from the time the agents knocked on the door until Leona Phebus let them in. In the apartment the agents met the defendant Foy. Phebus and Foy were told that the agents had an arrest warrant for Ryan based on the revocation of his bond. The agents also told them that if they failed to tell the whereabouts of Ryan they would be guilty of harboring and concealing a fugitive. Both Foy and Phebus told the agents that they had not seen Ryan since the previous afternoon. The agents were allowed to search the entire apartment but they could not find Ryan. Two agents left to try another place but later called back to say that Ryan was not at the other place. Then, one of the agents at the Phebus apartment found Ryan on a ledge outside the bedroom window. He was ordered to come in and was arrested. Phebus and Foy were both indicted for harboring and concealing Ryan. Phebus pled guilty but refused to testify at the trial of Foy. The court was asked to issue a writ of habeas corpus ad testificandum for production of Ryan but the court refused.

Since there was no evidence that Foy told Ryan to hide on the ledge, the essential question before the court is whether Foy's statement that he had not seen Ryan since the previous afternoon and did not know where he was, violated 18 U.S.C.A. § 1071.

18 U.S.C.A. § 1071 provides:

> Whoever harbors or conceals any person for whose arrest a warrant * * * has been issued under the provisions of any law of the United States, so as to prevent his discovery and arrest, after notice or knowledge of the fact that a warrant * * * has been issued * * * shall be fined.
> * * *

In United States v. Shapiro, 113 F.2d 891, 130 A.L.R. 147 (2nd Cir. 1940), the court having before it 18 U.S.C.A. § 246, the predecessor of § 1071, held that the words "harbor" and "conceal" must be construed narrowly, not to include all forms of assistance. "These are active verbs, which have the fugitive as their object." 113 F.2d at 892. The court concluded that weekly payments of $250 to the fugitive, the purpose of the payments being to allow him to evade arrest, did not come within the proscribed behavior. The court in United States v. Biami, 243 F.Supp. 917 (E.D.Wis.1965), held that the refusal to admit the police officers into the apartment where the fugitive was, constituted harboring and concealing under § 1071. Here, the agents were admitted into the apartment and were allowed to completely search it. There was no evidence that defendant took any action "to hide, secrete or keep out of sight" or "to lodge, to care for after secreting the offender" as the terms conceal and harbor are defined in United States v. Thornton, 178 F.Supp. 42, 43 (E.D.N.Y.1959). In *Thornton* the defendant left Denver, Colorado with the fugitive because FBI notices that the fugitive was wanted were posted in a Denver hotel, traveled with the fugitive to Brooklyn, New York and rented a room in his name for himself and the fugitive in Brooklyn. The court in United States v. Giampa, 290 F.2d 83 (2nd Cir. 1961), held that defendant's conduct in leasing an apartment in his name for the fugitive, shopping for food for the fugitive and refusing to let Federal narcotics agents into the apartment constituted a violation of § 1071. Here, the false statement of defendant that he did not know where Ryan was, without any further acts of concealment, did not impose a real barrier to the discovery of Ryan. While there are many negative or passive acts which would fall within the statutory prohibition, we do not think that a failure to disclose the location of a fugitive is the type of assistance contemplated by "harbor and conceal" as used in § 1071. The statute proscribes acts calculated to obstruct the efforts of the authorities to effect arrest of the fugitive, but it does not impose a duty on one who may be aware of the whereabouts of the fugitive, although having played no part in his flight, to reveal this information on pain of criminal prosecution.

The government relies heavily on Stamps v. United States, 387 F. 2d 993 (8th Cir. 1967), claiming that the facts are identical with those in the case before us. While in *Stamps* the court was not confronted with the issue of sufficiency of the evidence, the defendant, there, committed various acts calculated and determined to prevent the arrest of the fugitive: one, defendant refused to let officers in the apartment; two, after police had left, defendant removed the fugitive from the apartment and placed him in the apartment of a neighbor; and three, after the fugitive had left the building, defendant picked him up in a car and tried to drive away. We do not think the facts in *Stamps* lend any support to the government's argument in the case before us.

For the foregoing reasons we reverse.

Reversed.

KNOCH, Senior Circuit Judge (dissenting).

I am very reluctant to disagree with my colleagues; yet I believe that we should draw some distinction between mere mute refusal to assist the officers and deliberate misstatements of fact designed to mislead the police so as to prevent the fugitive's discovery and arrest. On the specific circumstances of this case, I would affirm.

NOTES

1. How, on policy grounds, might the interpretation of the words "harbor" and "conceal" used by the court in the instant case be defended? Would the result have been the same if there had been proof that Foy was aware of Ryan's guilt and Foy was charged as an accessory after the fact under 18 U.S.C.A. § 3? Cf. State v. Young, 7 Ohio App.2d 194, 220 N.E.2d 146 (1966). But contrast People v. Duty, 269 Cal.App.2d 97, 74 Cal.Rptr. 606 (1969); McClain v. State, 10 Md.App. 106, 268 A.2d 572 (1970). If he was charged with misprision of felony under 18 U.S.C.A. § 4? Should the words "receives" and assists" (in 18 U.S.C.A. § 3) and "conceals" (in 18 U.S.C.A. § 4) be interpreted in the same manner as "harbours" and "conceals" in 18 U.S.C.A. § 1071?

2. Goldberg, Misprision of Felony: An Old Concept in a New Context, 52 A.B.A.J. 148, 149–50 (1966):

> Unfortunately, the courts have interpreted "conceals" [in statutes making misprision of felony an offense, such as 18 U.S.C.A. § 4] as requiring a positive act, thus effectively emasculating the statute by merging it into the general accessory provisions of the law. The history of misprision of felony strongly suggests that this interpretation is erroneous. The Supreme Court of Vermont in 1907 defined the offense in its traditional sense:
>
>> Misprision of felony is * * * a criminal neglect either to prevent a felony from being committed or to bring the offender to justice after its commission, but without such previous concert with or subsequent assistance of him as will make the concealer an accessory before or after the fact.[17]
>
> Thus defined, misprision of felony would be a very salutary influence in our distressed society. If limited by its terms to serious crimes, perhaps only serious crimes against the person, few injustices are likely to result. Then Chief Justice Marshall's concern that "It may be the duty of a citizen to accuse every offender, and to proclaim every offence which comes to his knowledge; but the law which would punish him in every case for not performing this duty is too harsh for man"[19] need not deter legislators from passing a much-needed law. In the case which elicited Marshall's compassion, the defendant had advanced money to his son-in-law in an attempt to save him from the consequences of forgery. The law which would punish such behavior and even require a man to report his family's peculations to the police *is* too harsh. Restricting the opera-

17. Vermont v. Wilson [67 Atl. 533,] 533 [(1907)].

19. Marbury v. Brooks, 7 Wheat. 556, 575–76 (1822).

tion of the law to serious crimes (and perhaps exempting certain degrees of consanguinity) ought to remove this objection.

Exceptions must also be made for conflicting legal duties. A lawyer is legally obliged not to divulge information confidentially revealed to him by his client regarding a committed felony. Nor may a doctor broadcast his patient's confidential communications, nor a clergyman his parishioner's. Misprision of felony statutes must allow for these obligations to be respected without fear of lawbreaking.

It may finally be objected that a legal duty to report criminal acts to the authorities would be so novel in most American jurisdictions that even responsible citizens would unavoidably break the law. But all Americans are familiar with their legal duty to report serious traffic accidents to the police. It is about time we consider violent assault on persons as important as automobile crashes.

3. The tendency in recent legislative revision has been to replace accessory-after-the-fact statutes and misprision crimes with offenses defined in terms of interfering with law enforcement activity. Consider the extent to which the following sections of the Proposed Federal Criminal Code adequately serve the purposes which ought to be served:

§ 1303. Hindering Law Enforcement

(1) Offense. A person is guilty of hindering law enforcement if he intentionally interferes with, hinders, delays or prevents the discovery, apprehension, prosecution, conviction or punishment of another for an offense by:

(a) harboring or concealing the other;

(b) providing the other with a weapon, money, transportation, disguise or other means of avoiding discovery or apprehension;

(c) concealing, altering, mutilating or destroying a document or thing, regardless of its admissibility in evidence; or

(d) warning the other of impending discovery or apprehension other than in connection with an effort to bring another into compliance with the law.

(2) Grading. Hindering law enforcement is a Class C felony if the actor:

(a) knows of the conduct of the other and such conduct constitutes a Class A or Class B felony; or

(b) knows that the other has been charged with or convicted of a crime and such crime is a Class A or Class B felony.

Otherwise hindering law enforcement is a Class A misdemeanor.

§ 1304. Aiding Consummation of Crime

(1) Offense. A person is guilty of aiding consummation of crime if he intentionally aids another to secrete, disguise, or convert the proceeds of a crime or otherwise profit from a crime.

(2) Grading. Aiding consummation of a crime:

(a) is a Class C felony if the actor knows of the conduct of the other and such conduct constitutes a Class A or Class B felony; and

(b) is a Class A misdemeanor if the actor knows of the conduct of the other and such conduct constitutes a Class C felony or a Class A misdemeanor.

Otherwise aiding consummation of a crime is a Class B misdemeanor.

§ 1353. False Reports to Security Officials

(1) Offense. A person is guilty of a Class B misdemeanor if he:

(a) gives false information to a law enforcement officer with intent to falsely implicate another; or

(b) falsely reports to a law enforcement officer or other security official the occurrence of a crime of violence or other incident calling for an emergency response when he knows that the incident did not occur. "Security official" means fireman or other public servant responsible for averting or dealing with emergencies involving public safety.

The comment to the Proposed Draft of Section 1353 contained the following:

A significant issue * * * is whether there should be criminal sanctions at all for false reports to officials other than the type dealt with in subsection (1)(b), in view of the dangers presented in making criminal the conduct of persons who thoughtlessly make reports and in view of the potential of official abuse. These dangers might be lessened if the prohibition were limited to written (or even signed) statements, if it is required that notice of the statute be given to a reporting individual, and if distinctions were made among kinds of investigators in order to avoid application of the section to a casual street encounter. The potential for official abuse could also be lessened by requiring corroboration of the falsity of the statement and of the fact the statement was made.

E.   OTHER ASPECTS OF LIABILITY FOR THE ACTS OF ANOTHER

1.   VICARIOUS LIABILITY

COMMONWEALTH v. KOCZWARA

Supreme Court of Pennsylvania, 1959.
397 Pa. 575, 155 A.2d 825, certiorari denied 363 U.S. 848,
80 S.Ct. 1624, 4 L.Ed.2d 1731.

COHEN, Justice.   This is an appeal from the judgment of the Court of Quarter Sessions of Lackawanna County sentencing the defendant to three months in the Lackawanna County Jail, a fine of five hundred dollars and the costs of prosecution, in a case involving violations of the Pennsylvania Liquor Code.

John Koczwara, the defendant, is the licensee and operator of an establishment on Jackson Street in the City of Scranton known as J. K.'s Tavern.   At that place he had a restaurant liquor license issued by the Pennsylvania Liquor Control Board.   The Lackawanna County Grand Jury indicted the defendant on five counts for violations of the Liquor Code.   The first and second counts averred that the defendant permitted minors, unaccompanied by parents, guardians or other supervisors, to frequent the tavern on February 1st and 8th, 1958; the third count charged the defendant with selling beer to minors on February 8th, 1958; the fourth charged the defendant with permitting beer to be sold to minors on February 8th, 1958, and the fifth or final count was an averment of a prior conviction for violations of the Liquor Code.

Prior to trial, the averment of prior convictions was removed from the consideration of the jury upon motion of counsel that submission of the same would deprive the defendant of his fundamental right to exclude evidence of former convictions.

At the conclusion of the Commonwealth's evidence, count three of the indictment, charging the sale by the defendant personally to the minors, was removed from the jury's consideration by the trial judge on the ground that there was no evidence that the defendant had personally participated in the sale or was present in the tavern when sales to the minors took place.   Defense counsel then demurred to the evidence as to the other three counts.   The demurrer was overruled.   Defendant thereupon rested without introducing any evidence and moved for a directed verdict of acquittal.   The motion was denied, the case went to the jury and the jury returned a verdict of guilty as to each of the remaining three counts: two counts of permitting minors to frequent the licensed premises without parental or other supervision, and the count of permitting sales to minors.

Upon the conclusion of the trial, defendant filed a motion in arrest of judgment. After argument before the court *en banc*, the motion was overruled by Judge Hoban, who sentenced the defendant to pay the costs of prosecution, a fine of five hundred dollars and to undergo imprisonment in the Lackawanna County Jail for three months.

The defendant took an appeal to the Superior Court, which, in an opinion by Judge Hirt, affirmed the judgment and sentence of the lower court. A petition for an allowance of an appeal was filed by the defendant. Because of the importance of the issues raised, the petition was allowed and an appeal granted.

Defendant raises two contentions, both of which, in effect, question whether the undisputed facts of this case support the judgment and sentence imposed by the Quarter Sessions Court. Judge Hoban found as fact that "in every instance the purchase [by minors] was made from a bartender, not identified by name, and service to the boys was made by the bartender. There was *no* evidence that the defendant was present on any one of the occasions testified to by these witnesses, nor that he had any personal knowledge of the sales to them or to other persons on the premises." We, therefore, must determine the criminal responsibility of a licensee of the Liquor Control Board for acts committed by his employees upon his premises, without his personal knowledge, participation, or presence, which acts violate a valid regulatory statute passed under the Commonwealth's police power.

While an employer in almost all cases is not criminally responsible for the unlawful acts of his employees, unless he consents to, approves, or participates in such acts, courts all over the nation have struggled for years in applying this rule within the framework of "controlling the sale of intoxicating liquor." See Annotation, 139 A.L.R. 306 (1942). At common law, any attempt to invoke the doctrine of *respondeat superior* in a criminal case would have run afoul of our deeply ingrained notions of criminal jurisprudence that guilt must be personal and individual.[1] In recent decades, however, many states have enacted detailed regulatory provisions in fields which are essentially noncriminal, e. g., pure food and drug acts, speeding ordinances, build-

---

1. The distinction between *respondeat superior* in tort law and its application to the criminal law is obvious. In tort law, the doctrine is employed for the purpose of settling the incidence of loss upon the party who can best bear such loss. But the criminal law is supported by totally different concepts. We impose penal treatment upon those who injure or menace social interests, partly in order to reform, partly to prevent the continuation of the anti-social activity and partly to deter others. If a defendant has personally lived up to the social standards of the criminal law and has not menaced or injured anyone, why impose penal treatment?

ing regulations, and child labor, minimum wage and maximum hour legislation. Such statutes are generally enforceable by light penalties, and although violations are labelled crimes, the considerations applicable to them are totally different from those applicable to true crimes, which involve moral delinquency and which are punishable by imprisonment or another serious penalty. Such so-called statutory crimes are in reality an attempt to utilize the machinery of criminal administration as an enforcing arm for social regulations of a purely civil nature, with the punishment totally unrelated to questions of moral wrongdoing or guilt. It is here that the social interest in the general well-being and security of the populace has been held to outweigh the individual interest of the particular defendant. The penalty is imposed despite the defendant's lack of a criminal intent or mens rea.

Not the least of the legitimate police power areas of the legislature is the control of intoxicating liquor. As Mr. Justice B. R. Jones recently stated in In re Tahiti Bar, Inc., 1959, 395 Pa. 355, 360, 150 A.2d 112, 115, "There is perhaps no other area of permissible state action within which the exercise of the police power of a state is more plenary than in the regulation and control of the use and sale of alcoholic beverages." [2] It is abundantly clear that the conduct of the liquor business is lawful only to the extent and manner permitted by statute. Individuals who embark on such an enterprise do so with knowledge of considerable peril, since their actions are rigidly circumscribed by the Liquor Code.

Because of the peculiar nature of this business, one who applies for and receives permission from the Commonwealth to carry on the liquor trade assumes the highest degree of responsibility to his fellow citizens. As the licensee of the Board, he is under a duty not only to regulate his own personal conduct in a manner consistent with the permit he has received, but also to control the acts and conduct of any employee to whom he entrusts the sale of liquor. Such fealty is the *quid pro quo* which the Commonwealth demands in return for the privilege of entering the highly restricted and, what is more important, the highly *dangerous* business of selling intoxicating liquor.

In the instant case, the defendant has sought to surround himself with all the safeguards provided to those within the pale of criminal sanctions. He has argued that a statute imposing criminal responsibility should be construed strictly, with all doubts resolved in his favor. While the defendant's position is entirely correct, we must remember that we are dealing with a statutory crime within the state's plenary police power. In the field of liquor regulation, the legislature

2. See also Cavanaugh v. Gelder, 1950, 364 Pa. 361, 72 A.2d 85, wherein this Court went to great lengths to establish the legal and constitutional bases for the state's control of the liquor trade. Such regulation is now embodied in the Liquor Code, Act of April 12, 1951, P.L. 90, 47 P.S. § 1–101 et seq.

has enacted a comprehensive Code aimed at regulating and controlling the use and sale of alcoholic beverages. The question here raised is whether the legislature *intended* to impose vicarious criminal liability on the licensee-principal for acts committed on his premises without his presence, participation or knowledge.

This Court has stated, as long ago as Commonwealth v. Weiss, 1891, 139 Pa. 247, 251, 21 A. 10, 11 L.R.A. 530, that "whether a criminal intent, or a guilty knowledge, is a necessary ingredient of a statutory offense * * * is a matter of construction. It is for the legislature to determine whether the public injury, threatened in any particular matter, is such, and so great as to justify an absolute and indiscriminate prohibition." In the Weiss case, and in Commonwealth v. Miller, 1890, 131 Pa. 118, 18 A. 938, 6 L.R.A. 633, this Court construed the statute in question in the light of its letter and spirit and its manifest purpose. See also Commonwealth v. Jackson, 146 Pa. Super. 328, 22 A.2d 299, affirmed per curiam by this Court in 1942, 345 Pa. 456, 28 A.2d 894.[3]

In the Liquor Code, Section 493, the legislature has set forth twenty-five specific acts which are condemned as unlawful, and for which penalties are provided in Section 494. Subsections (1) and (14) of Section 493 contain the two offenses charged here. In neither of these subsections is there any language which would require the prohibited acts to have been done either knowingly, wilfully or intentionally, there being a significant absence of such words as "knowingly, wilfully, etc." That the legislature intended such a requirement in other related sections of the same Code is shown by examining Section 492(15), wherein it is made unlawful to *knowingly* sell any malt beverages to a person engaged in the business of illegally selling such beverages. The omission of any such word in the subsections of Section 494 is highly significant. It indicates a legislative intent to eliminate both knowledge and criminal intent as necessary ingredients of such offenses. To bolster this conclusion, we refer back to Section 491 wherein the Code states, "It shall be unlawful (1) For any person, by himself *or by an employe or agent*, to expose or keep for sale, or

---

3. This case is not governed by Carlson's License, 1889, 127 Pa. 330, 18 A. 8; Commonwealth v. Sellers, 1889, 130 Pa. 32, 18 A. 541, 542; Commonwealth v. Holstine, 1890, 132 Pa. 357, 19 A. 273; or Commonwealth v. Zelt, 1891, 138 Pa. 615, 21 A. 7, 11 L.R.A. 602. Those cases hold persons answerable for sales made by *themselves*, and prevent them from pleading ignorance of the nonage or intemperate habits of those to whom they sell. Nor is this case governed by Commonwealth v. Junkin, 1895, 170 Pa. 194, 32 A. 617, 31 L.R.A. 124, which refused to hold a principal criminally liable for the wrongful act of his agent, where the act was in positive disobedience of the principal's instructions. The Junkin case did *not* involve a comprehensive regulatory scheme which clearly evidenced a legislative purpose to hold a licensee responsible for all illegal acts conducted on the licensed premises. The Liquor Code of Pennsylvania in effect makes the act of the employee the act of the licensee for the purpose of enforcing the rigid restrictions on the sale of liquor.

directly or *indirectly* * * * to sell or offer to sell any liquor within this Commonwealth, except in accordance with the provisions of this act and the regulations of the board." The Superior Court has long placed such an interpretation on the statute. Commonwealth v. Speer, 1945, 157 Pa.Super. 197, 42 A.2d 94.[4]

As the defendant has pointed out, there is a distinction between the requirement of a mens rea and the imposition of vicarious absolute liability for the acts of another. It may be that the courts below, in relying on prior authority, have failed to make such a distinction.[5] In any case, we fully recognize it.[6] Moreover, we find that the intent of the legislature in enacting this Code was not only to eliminate the common law requirement of a mens rea, but also to place a very high degree of responsibility upon the holder of a liquor license to make certain that neither he nor anyone in his employ commit any of the prohibited acts upon the licensed premises. Such a burden of care is imposed upon the licensee in order to protect the public from the potentially noxious effects of an inherently dangerous business. We, of course, express no opinion as to the *wisdom* of the legislature's imposing vicarious responsibility under certain sections of the Liquor Code. There may or may not be an economic-sociological justification for such liability on a theory of deterrence. Such determination is for the legislature to make, so long as the constitutional requirements are met.

Can the legislature, consistent with the requirements of due process, thus establish absolute criminal liability? Were this the defendant's first violation of the Code, and the penalty solely a minor fine of from $100–$300, we would have no hesitation in upholding such a judgment. Defendant, by accepting a liquor license, must bear this financial risk. Because of a prior conviction for violations of the Code, however, the trial judge felt compelled under the mandatory

4. It is established that a liquor license may be legally suspended or revoked for violations of the Code committed by employees of the licensee even though there is no evidence that the licensee knew of such violations. McGrath v. Pennsylvania Liquor Control Board, 1958, 185 Pa.Super. 187, 137 A.2d 812; Southern Outing Club of Pittsburgh Liquor License Case, 1950, 166 Pa.Super. 555, 72 A.2d 600.

5. We must also be extremely careful to distinguish the present situation from the question of *corporate* criminal liability, such as was involved in Commonwealth v. Liberty Products Company, 1925, 84 Pa.Super. 473. For a penetrating inquiry into this latter subject, see Mens Rea And The Corporation, 19 U.Pitt.L.Rev. 21 (1957).

6. For an extremely interesting and incisive analysis of the mens rea requirement in criminal offenses, see Mueller, On Common Law Mens Rea, 42 Minn.L.Rev. 1043 (1958). While we sympathize fully with the author's eloquent plea for a return to the moral implications of criminal guilt, we await further determinations by the Supreme Court of the United States as to whether the rationale of Lambert v. People of State of California, 1957, 355 U.S. 225, 78 S.Ct. 240, 2 L.Ed.2d 228, will be extended to all statutory offenses which have been interpreted as not requiring a criminal mens rea. See also Allen, Book Review, 66 Yale L.J. 1120 (1957); Mueller, Mens Rea And The Law Without It, 58 W.Va. L.Rev. 34 (1955).

language of the statute, Section 494(a), to impose not only an increased fine of five hundred dollars, but also a three month sentence of imprisonment. Such sentence of imprisonment in a case where liability is imposed vicariously cannot be sanctioned by this Court consistently with the law of the land clause of Section 9, Article I of the Constitution of the Commonwealth of Pennsylvania., P.S.[7]

The Courts of the Commonwealth have already strained to permit the legislature to carry over the civil doctrine of *respondeat superior* and to apply it as a means of enforcing the regulatory scheme that covers the liquor trade. We have done so on the theory that the Code established petty misdemeanors involving only light monetary fines. It would be unthinkable to impose vicarious criminal responsibility in cases involving true crimes. Although to hold a principal criminally liable might possibly be an effective means of enforcing law and order, it would do violence to our more sophisticated modern-day concepts of justice. Liability for all true crimes, wherein an offense carries with it a jail sentence, must be based exclusively upon personal causation. It can be readily imagined that even a licensee who is meticulously careful in the choice of his employees cannot supervise every single act of the subordinates. A man's liberty cannot rest on so frail a reed as whether his employee will commit a mistake in judgment. See Sayre, Criminal Responsibility For Acts of Another, 43 Harv.L.Rev. 689 (1930).

This Court is ever mindful of its duty to maintain and establish the proper safeguards in a criminal trial. To sanction the imposition of imprisonment here would make a serious change in the substantive criminal law of the Commonwealth, one for which we find no justification. We have found *no* case in any jurisdiction which has permitted a *prison term* for a vicarious offense. The Supreme Court of the United States has had occasion only recently to impose due process limitations upon the actions of a state legislature in making unknowing conduct criminal. Lambert v. People of State of California, 1957, 355 U.S. 225, 78 S.Ct. 240, 2 L.Ed.2d 228. Our own courts have stepped in time and again to protect a defendant from being held criminally responsible for acts about which he had no knowledge and over which he had little control. Commonwealth v. Unkrich, 1940, 142 Pa.Super. 591, 16 A.2d 737; Commonwealth v. Schambers, 1932, 105 Pa.Super. 467, 161 A. 624; Commonwealth v. Rovnianek, 1889, 12 Pa.Super. 86. We would be utterly remiss were we not to so act under these facts.

In holding that the punishment of imprisonment deprives the defendant of due process of law under these facts, we are not declaring that Koczwara must be treated as a first offender under the Code. He has clearly violated the law for a second time and must be pun-

7. Sec. 9. " * * * nor can he be deprived of his life, liberty or property, unless by the judgment of his peers or the law of the land."

ished accordingly. Therefore, we are only holding that so much of the judgment as calls for imprisonment is invalid, and we are leaving intact the five hundred dollar fine imposed by Judge Hoban under the subsequent offense section.

* * *

Judgment, as modified, is affirmed.

BELL, MUSMANNO and McBRIDE, JJ., file separate dissenting opinions.

* * *

MUSMANNO, Justice (dissenting).

The Court in this case is doing what it has absolutely no right to do. It is laying aside its judicial robes and officiating as members of the General Assembly. It is declaring a crime which has no existence in the statute books, it is imposing a penalty which is not authorized by the criminal code.

* * *

The Majority introduces into its discussion a proposition which is shocking to contemplate. It speaks of "vicarious criminal liability". Such a concept is as alien to American soil as the upas tree. There was a time in China when a convicted felon sentenced to death could offer his brother or other close relative in his stead for decapitation. The Chinese law allowed such "vicarious criminal liability". I never thought that Pennsylvania would look with favor on anything approaching so revolting a barbarity.

* * *

The Majority Opinion attempts to give authority to its legislative usurpation by referring to twenty-five specific acts which are designated as unlawful in Section 494 of the Liquor Code. It is true that the General Assembly has enumerated certain proscribed situations, but nowhere has the Legislature said that a person may be tried and convicted for a personal act committed in the darkness of his absence and in the night of his utter lack of knowledge thereof.

Battling for some solid terrain upon which to stand to uphold its unstable position, the Majority points to an invisible phantom. It seeks to fortify its argument not by what it finds in the Code, but by what it does *not* find in the Code. It asserts that the *omission* of the word "knowingly" from Section 494 "indicates a legislative intent to eliminate both knowledge and criminal intent as necessary ingredients of such offenses." But a person's liberties should not hang on so thin a thread as "indicates." Where the sovereign body of the Commonwealth, the General Assembly, decides that a citizen is to be deprived of his life, liberty, or good name upon the commission of a certain act, it does not merely "indicate" the drastic penalty awaiting the person who violates the specific legislative provision. It specifically and in mandatory language orders the penalty. If the Legislature intended to punish a person for acts committed by another, (assuming it had the constitutional power to do so), it would have declared that for certain acts committed within a liquor-dispensing establishment the proprietor will be criminally responsible "whether present or not." But the Legislature did not see fit to add such words. This Court is now adding those words and in doing so, it is usurping the functions of the Legislature which, I repeat, it has no authority to do.

* * *.

If it is wrong to send a person to jail for acts committed by another, is it not wrong to convict him at all? There are those who value their good names to the extent that they see as much harm in a degrading criminal conviction as in a jail sentence. The laceration of a man's reputation, the blemishing of his good name, the wrecking of his prestige by a criminal court conviction may blast a person's chances for honorable success in life to such an extent that a jail sentence can hardly add much to the ruin already wrought to him by the conviction alone.

* * *

COMMONWEALTH v. ALI

Supreme Court of Pennsylvania, 1970.
438 Pa. 463, 265 A.2d 796.

POMEROY, Justice. At a non-jury trial, appellant was convicted of having issued a worthless check in violation of § 854 of the Penal Code of June 24, 1939, P.L. 872, 18 P.S. § 4854. His motions in arrest of judgment and for a new trial were denied and he was sentenced to imprisonment for a term of 60 days to 23 months. On appeal to the Superior Court, his judgment of sentence was affirmed in a per curiam decision to which Judge Spaulding filed a dissenting opinion which Judge Hoffman joined. 214 Pa.Super. 512, 257 A.2d 370 (1969). We granted allocatur.

The worthless check upon which the prosecution was based was issued to the Totem Lumber Company in the amount of $349.95. The basic facts surrounding presentation of the check were not disputed. They are that on September 9, 1966, appellant signed a blank check and gave it to his employee, one Garmusa; that Mr. Garmusa took the check to the Totem Lumber Company for the purpose of purchasing supplies for appellant; that at the Lumber Company, the amount of the check was filled in by or at the direction of Garmusa, and accepted by the Lumber Company for materials delivered to Garmusa; and that the materials delivered to Garmusa were itemized on a sales slip, which showed a total cost of $349.95. The check was twice returned by the drawee bank for insufficient funds and was never paid.

Appellant testified that on the preceding day, September 8, he had ordered paint, lumber and nails by telephone from one Nick Grande, an employee of Totem Lumber Co.; that Grande told him that the total cost of the materials would be about $80 but that as Grande could not determine the exact amount, appellant could send a signed, blank check with the man who would pick up the materials, and the check could be completed at the time the materials were called for; and that he had signed a blank check and given it to Garmusa for this purpose. Appellant denied ordering or receiving any materials other than paint, lumber and nails costing about $80. Called by the Commonwealth in rebuttal, Grande denied requesting appellant to send a blank check, and stated that he could not recall whether appellant had personally placed an order over the telephone. Garmusa did not testify.

Upon this evidence, the trial court found that all elements of the crime had been established by the Commonwealth and found appellant guilty. We do not agree.

Under § 854 of the Penal Code the three essential elements of the crime of issuing a worthless check are: (1) making, drawing, uttering or delivering a check; (2) intent to defraud; and (3) knowledge at the time of making the check that the maker or drawer has insufficient funds for the payment thereof in, or credit with, the bank or other entity upon which the check is drawn. Under the second paragraph of § 854, the making, drawing, uttering or delivering of a check, payment of which is refused by the drawee,[1] "shall be prima facie evidence of intent to defraud and of knowledge of insufficient funds in, or credit with" the drawee, unless the check (together with any interest or protest fees) is made good within ten days after the maker receives notice that the check has not been paid. Thus the Commonwealth may establish a prima facie case of guilt of this crime by introducing evidence that (1) the defendant was the maker of a worthless check, and (2) that he did not make it good within ten days of receipt of notice that it had not been paid. It seems likely that the trial court relied upon this statutory scheme of proof in finding appellant guilty, since there was no direct evidence either of his intent to defraud or of his knowledge of insufficient funds.[2]

In our opinion, however, the Commonwealth did not sustain its burden of proving that appellant made or drew a worthless check. While appellant signed the instrument, he did not himself complete it by filling in the amount of $349.95. Making a check or other nego-

1. Although "drawee" is used in § 854 to refer both to the entity or person upon whom the check is drawn and the person to whom it is payable, the term "drawee" technically refers only to the former while the latter is properly the "payee". Drawee is used in this opinion only in its technical sense.

2. Under our view of this case we need not determine whether the effect of the second paragraph of § 854 is merely to enable the Commonwealth to withstand a demurrer to the evidence where it produces no direct evidence of intent or knowledge, or whether it is to create an issue for the finder of fact on these two elements even in the face of contrary evidence, and we express no opinion on this question.

tiable instrument is more than merely signing it; it is issuing a completed instrument, or an incomplete instrument with authority in another to complete it. In order for the finder of fact to determine that appellant made the check in the amount of $349.95, evidence was required that he authorized the check to be so completed. No such evidence was introduced; the only testimony on the subject was that of appellant himself that he intended and expected the check to be made out for approximately $80. It may be folly and negligent to sign a blank check or other negotiable instrument and entrust it to another for completion, and doing so may very well entail liability to a holder in due course,[3] but it does not per se render the maker guilty of a crime. The prima facie evidence provision of the second paragraph of § 854 does not help the Commonwealth here, and direct evidence of authority was therefore necessary. Since it was not adduced, and the only evidence was that there was no authority, the elements of the crime were not made out.

The order of the Superior Court is reversed, the judgment of sentence is vacated, and the motion in arrest of judgment is granted and the defendant is discharged.

BELL, C. J., did not participate in the decision of this case.

NOTES

1. If Koczwara himself had made the sale would the court have had difficulty in affirming the conviction and sentence? Even if the minors appeared to be of age and presented apparently valid evidence in proof thereof?

2. Is there any question as to Koczwara's liability if he had known of his agent's practice of selling to minors? Cf. Commonwealth v. Feinberg, 433 Pa. 558, 253 A.2d 636 (1969) (convictions for involuntary manslaughter arising from death of thirty-one skid-row denizens due to drinking industrial Sterno sold, in some cases, by appellant's agent in his absence, upheld given finding that appellant stocked the same for sale knowing that purchasers would ingest it).

3. Does the statute in *Koczwara*, like that in *Ali*, require for conviction a finding that the defendant acted with knowledge of wrong-doing? If not, and if Koczwara would have been held responsible if he had made the sale, albeit in good faith reliance on the appearance, assertions and identification of the minor customers, what values are served by limiting his liability where he acts through an agent? To what extent, if any, are legitimate objectives of the criminal law sacrificed by such a limitation? Is the problem here that the liability is vicarious or that it is strict?

4. A Pennsylvania statute requires, in absolute terms, that every judicial officer who collects fines for violations of the motor vehicle code

---

3. See, e. g., §§ 3–115, 3–406 and 3–407 of the Uniform Commercial Code, 12A P.S. §§ 3–115, 3–406 and 3–407. Section 3–115 places the burden on the maker to prove that the terms of the instrument as completed by another were unauthorized, but this civil standard of proof is not governing in a criminal prosecution.

make a sworn report of these to the state Department of Revenue. Failure to do so may be punished by a fine of $500 plus costs, imprisonment for up to 60 days, or both. Is the prosecution required to prove a mens rea despite any reference to such in the statute? Does the fact that this is a crime of omission affect your analysis? Does the *Koczwara* discussion of "police regulations" aid the resolution of the question? See Commonwealth v. Bready, 220 Pa.Super. 157, 286 A.2d 654 (1971).

2. CRIMINAL LIABILITY OF ORGANIZATIONS AND THEIR AGENTS

Among the problems presented by use of traditional concepts of criminal liability in an increasingly organized society are those concerning the criminal liability of a corporation or other organization and the criminal liability of members of such organizations for crimes involving the organization. These materials raise questions regarding the extent to which criminal liability in this context serves traditional (or other) functions of imposing such liability, and the extent to which imposing it may run counter to traditional limitations upon the imposition of criminal liability.

COMMONWEALTH v. BENEFICIAL FINANCE CO.

Supreme Judicial Court of Massachusetts, 1971.
— Mass. —, 275 N.E.2d 33.

SPIEGEL, Justice. We have before us appeals emanating from 2 separate series of indictments and 2 separate jury trials of various individual and corporate defendants.

* * *

All of these appeals are before us because of the convictions of a number of individuals and corporations. The corporations convicted in the first trial were Beneficial Finance Company (Beneficial), Household Finance Corporation (Household) and Liberty Loan Corporation (Liberty). The individuals convicted in the first trial were John M. Farrell, Francis T. Glynn, Nathaniel W. Barber, James S. Pratt, Lyle S. Woodcock, Morris Garfinkle and Martin J. Hanley. In the second trial the corporate defendants convicted were Beneficial, Household and Local Finance Corporation (Local). The individuals convicted in the second trial were Hanley, Farrell, Glynn, Barber, Pratt and Edward R. Newhall.

These cases have become generally known as the "small loans" cases. In each case the defendants were charged with various offences under numerous indictments returned in 1964 by a special grand jury. The offences charged were offering or paying, or soliciting or receiving, bribes, or conspiring to do so. * * *

Some insight into the sheer detail involved in reviewing the proceedings may be gleaned from the fact that "[p]retrial motions on these indictments were heard for sixty-five court days ending May 9, 1966. The transcript of the pre-trial proceedings covers 4,730 pages. The decisions disposing of the various motions cover almost 700 pages. * * * [After hearing the judge made extensive findings and rulings on the pre-trial motions.] Forty-nine of the indictments were grouped for [the first] trial which began on July 18, 1966. The trial lasted about five months and generated a voluminous record." See Barber v. Commonwealth, 353 Mass. 236, 237–238, 230 N.E.2d 817. The transcript of evidence consists of 103 volumes containing more that 7,500 pages.

The evidence in the first trial, pertinent portions of which we summarize in detail later in this opinion, is here synopsized. This evidence tends to show that during the year 1962, several licensed small loans companies (corporate defendants), together with certain of their officers and employees (some of whom are defendants), conspired to bribe Hanley and Garfinkle in their capacities as public officials. The purpose of the alleged conspiracy and the payment of the bribe money was to insure the maintenance of a maximum interest rate which companies licensed to do business in the Commonwealth were permitted to charge. Hearings on this matter were conducted by the Small Loans Regulatory Board (Rate Board) in 1962 and the bribe money allegedly paid to Hanley was intended to "fix" the results of these hearings.

The second trial began on July 17, 1967, and required 222 trial days (over a period of about 12 months). Twenty-one of the indictments were grouped for the trial. The transcript of this trial consists of 223 volumes containing more than 11,800 pages. Collectively (pretrial and both cases), the defendants took more than 5,400 exceptions and assign about 700 numbered multiple assignments of error. The findings, rulings and decisions of the judge (covering all proceedings) contain more than 1,400 printed pages.

The evidence in the second trial, set out in detail in the subsequent portion of this opinion, tends to show that over a period of some 7 years (1957–1963) a number of small loans companies (including the corporate defendants), together with a number of their officers and employees (including the individual defendants named in the conspiracy indictment), allegedly conspired to bribe Hanley. His office as a public official clothed him with extensive powers to approve or disapprove the activities of small loans companies doing business in the Commonwealth. The bribes were alleged to have been paid to Hanley over this period to induce Hanley (1) to approve various requests pertaining to routine matters; (2) to refrain from taking action adverse to certain of the defendants and co-conspirators at rate hearings held during 1957; and (3) to obtain approval of various changes in small loans regulations.

Although these cases were argued consecutively, some of the issues involved necessarily overlapped. The pre-trial issues in both cases were argued jointly. In the interest of lucidity and conciseness this opinion consists of 3 parts.

First, we treat with the pre-trial issues raised by all or some of the defendants whether in the first or second trials. Subsequently we deal with specific issues raised in the first trial and finally with issues raised during the second trial.

* * *

PART II.

THE FIRST TRIAL.

A. THE EVIDENCE.

We summarize pertinent portions of the evidence most favorable to the Commonwealth. In 1962, the small loans industry in Massachusetts was regulated by the Commissioner of Banks (Commissioner) who was head of the division of banks and loan agencies within the Department of Banking and Insurance. G.L. c. 26, §§ 1, 2. At that time, the law of this Commonwealth provided that any person who sought to engage in the business of making small loans had first to obtain a license from the Commissioner. The Commissioner was also authorized to appoint a deputy to serve as supervisor of loan agencies. In 1962, and at all times material to this case, the supervisor of loan agencies and Deputy Commissioner of Banks was Martin J. Hanley.

The permissible interest rate on small loans was regulated by the Rate Board which was within the division of banks and loan agencies.
* * *

Among the corporations actively engaged in making "small loans" at interest rates established by the Rate Board were the following: Beneficial, Household, Liberty, American Investment Company of Illinois (American), Family Finance Corporation (Family) and State Loan and Finance Corporation (State).

* * *

[The remainder of the opinion's lengthy recitation of the evidence is omitted but is recommended as illustrating the detailed reconstruction of facts that is necessary in conspiracy cases of this nature. In brief, the evidence revealed that Glynn (Beneficial's "Director of Industry Relations"), his superior, Farrell, Pratt (Household's New England "Regional Director of Public Relations"), his superior, Barber, Woodcock (Liberty's executive vice-president) and Heath (American's New England regional director) were the central figures in the effort to put together a "program" under which $25,000, contributed by the various loan companies, would be given to Hanley to insure that the Rate Board would maintain the same maximum permissible interest rate on loans of $1,501 to $3,000 as applied to loans below $1,500.   Heath, the prosecution's principal witness, testified to numerous meetings with other loan companies' representatives at which the "program" was thrashed out.   The crucial meeting was held in New York on October 17, 1962.   The Rate Board hearings began on November 13th and were terminated, without changing the existing interest rate, on December 27th "on the basis of the record, and particularly the request of Mr. Hanley".[51]   Payment to Hanley was allegedly made on January 22, 1963 in Washington, D.C.]

C. THE SUFFICIENCY OF THE EVIDENCE.

The Corporate Defendants.

Having concluded that the evidence was sufficient to establish that the defendants Pratt and Woodcock were part of a conspiracy joined in by Farrell, Glynn and Barber to bribe Hanley and Garfinkle, we turn to the question of whether there was sufficient evidence to support a finding that Beneficial, Household, and Liberty were parties to the conspiracy.   Each of the corporate defendants raised this issue by means of a motion for a directed verdict.   In view of the fact that this issue is discussed extensively in the briefs of the respective corporate defendants as well as in the Commonwealth's brief, and because the legal principles involved permeate these cases, in this part of the opinion we discuss at length the applicable legal standards concerning the extent to which a corporation may be held criminally responsible for the acts of its directors, officers and agents.   We then summarize the evidence admitted against the respective corporations and apply the appropriate legal standard to the evidence.   * * *

With this in mind, perhaps it would be helpful at this point to briefly summarize the relationships between the various corporate defendants and individual defendants: (1) Household was held criminally responsible, in part, for the criminal conduct of Barber and Pratt.   Barber and Pratt were employees of Household, but were neither directors nor officers.   (2) Liberty was held liable, in part, for the criminal acts of Woodcock, who was 1 of Liberty's 2 executive vice-presidents and 1 of its 11 directors.   (3) Beneficial was held

---

51. Hanley's "request" was embodied in a statement which reads as follows: "[T]he Department [of Banking] wishes to indicate with reluctance that due to the absence of these vital figures in the figures reported by the industry for the year 1961 that it is utterly impossible for anyone to determine at this time the precise amount of a book asset base and, therefore, the Department has absolutely no alternative but to suggest that this Board take no action upon the matter * * * until the 1962 figures have been received and processed by the Banking Department, which should occur to the best of the Department's knowledge and prediction some time in July or September of next year."

criminally responsible, in part, for the conduct of Farrell and Glynn who were neither directors, officers nor employees of that corporation. Farrell was a vice-president and Glynn was an employee of Beneficial Management, a wholly owned subsidiary of the defendant, Beneficial. Other evidence pertaining to the criminal responsibility of the corporate defendants will be summarized as we treat with each of them.

1. *Standards of Criminal Responsibility*—The defendants and the Commonwealth have proposed differing standards upon which the criminal responsibility of a corporation should be predicated. The defendants argue that a corporation should not be held criminally liable for the conduct of its servants or agents unless such conduct was performed, authorized, ratified, adopted or tolerated by the corporations' directors, officers or other "high managerial agents" who are sufficiently high in the corporate hierarchy to warrant the assumption that their acts in some substantial sense reflect corporate policy. This standard is that adopted by the American Law Institute Model Penal Code, approved in May 1962. Section 2:07 of the Code provides that, except in the case of regulatory offences and offences consisting of the omission of a duty imposed on corporations by law, a corporation may be convicted of a crime if "the commission of the offence was authorized, requested, commanded, performed or recklessly tolerated by the board of directors or by a high managerial agent acting in behalf of the corporation within the scope of his office or employment." The section proceeds to define "high managerial agent" as "an officer of a corporation * * * or any other agent * * * having duties of such responsibility that his conduct may fairly be assumed to represent the policy of the corporation." [55]

The Commonwealth, on the other hand, argues that the standard applied by the judge in his instructions to the jury was correct. These instructions, which prescribe a somewhat more flexible standard than that delineated in the Model Penal Code, state in part, as follows: "[T]he Commonwealth must prove beyond a reasonable doubt that there existed between the guilty individual or individuals and the corporation which is being charged with the conduct of the individuals, such *a relationship that the acts and the intent of the individuals were*

---

55. Section 2.07 of the Model Penal Code was materially amended between 1955 (Tentative Draft No. 4, p. 22; see pp. 146–155, for the comments on the unamended section) and its adoption in 1962 (Proposed Final Draft, pp. 35, 38) by adding the italicized words "or recklessly tolerated." These words seem to expand corporate criminal liability to include at least cases where high managerial officers shut their eyes to (or try to remain aloof from and apparently unaware of) criminal activity by subordinates undertaken for the corporation's benefit. Cf. Restatement 2d: Agency, § 217D, comment d (1957): "Apart from statute, an employer is not subject to a penalty for an unauthorized act constituting a crime committed by an ordinary servant in the scope of employment if the basis for liability is a specific criminal intent. However, * * * an employer may be penalized for the act of an advisory or managerial person acting in the scope of employment."

the acts and intent of the corporation. Or, to put it differently, the Commonwealth must prove beyond a reasonable doubt that when the individuals were acting criminally in committing the acts which constitute the crime, and in having the intent required for the crime, *the corporation was actually so acting and intending,* and therefore is criminally liable. The Commonwealth must prove that.

"How is that to be shown? How is the jury to determine whether the Commonwealth has proved that? First let me say that the Commonwealth does not have to prove that the individual who acted criminally was expressly requested or authorized in advance by the corporation to do so, nor must the Commonwealth prove that the corporation expressly ratified or adopted that criminal conduct on the part of that individual or those individuals. *It does not mean that the Commonwealth must prove that the individual who acted criminally was a member of the corporation's board of directors, or that he was a high officer in the corporation, or that he held any office at all.* If the Commonwealth did prove that an individual for whose act it seeks to hold a corporation criminally liable was an officer of the corporation, the jury should consider that. *But more important than that, it should consider what the authority of that person was as such officer in relation to the corporation.* The mere fact that he has a title is not enough to make the corporation liable for his criminal conduct. The Commonwealth must prove that the individual for whose conduct it seeks to charge *the corporation criminally was placed in a position by the corporation where he had enough power, duty, responsibility and authority to act for and in behalf of the corporation to handle the particular business or operation or project of the corporation in which he was engaged at the time that he committed the criminal act, with power of decision as to what he would or would not do while acting for the corporation, and that he was acting for and in behalf of the corporation in the accomplishment of that particular business or operation or project, and that he committed a criminal act while so acting.*

"The Commonwealth must prove all that beyond a reasonable doubt before you can hold a corporation criminally liable or guilty by reason of the criminal acts or conduct of an individual.

"You will note from what I said that it is not necessary that the Commonwealth prove that an individual had any particular office or any office at all or that he had any particular title or any title at all. It isn't the title that counts. *It isn't the name of the office that counts, but it's the position in which the corporation placed that person with relation to its business, with regard to the powers and duties and responsibilities and authority which it gave to him which counts.* If it placed him in a position with such power, duty, authority, and responsibility that it can be found by you that, when he acted in the corporation's business, the corporation was acting, then you may find the corporation equally guilty of the criminal acts which he commits and of the intent which he holds, if you first find that the individual was guilty of the crime.

"Now, this test doesn't depend upon the power, duty, the responsibility, or the authority which the individual has with reference to the entire corporation business. The test should be applied to his position with relation to the particular operation or project in which he is serving the corporation." (emphasis supplied).

The difference between the judge's instructions to the jury and the Model Penal Code lies largely in the latter's reference to a "high managerial agent" and in the Code requirement that to impose corporate criminal liability, it at least must appear that its directors or high managerial agent "authorized * * * or recklessly tolerated" the allegedly criminal acts. The judge's instructions focus on the authority of the corporate agent in relation to the *particular* corporate business in which the agent was engaged. The Code seems to require that there be authorization or reckless inaction by a corporate representative having some relation to framing corporate policy, or one "having duties of such responsibility that his conduct may fairly be assumed to represent the policy of the corporation." Close examination of the judge's instructions reveals that they preserve the underlying "corporate policy rationale of the Code by allowing the jury to infer "corporate policy" from the *position* in which the corporation placed the agent in commissioning him to handle the particular corporate affairs in which he was engaged at the time of the criminal act. We need not deal with the Model Penal Code in greater detail. Although we give it careful consideration as a scholarly proposal, it has not been enacted in Massachusetts and does not purport to be a restatement of existing law. It is not clear that if the Code had been in effect in Massachusetts, when the acts alleged and proved were committed, the corporate defendants would have been in a better situation, in view of the proof here of concerted criminal conduct (in a "program" designed to be of benefit to finance companies) by plainly significant representatives of three or more competing financing companies and the sums involved. We do not consider whether the circumstances would permit inferences of facts constituting a violation of the Code. The judge correctly charged the jury on the basis of decided cases, rather than on the basis of a proposed model code.

It may also be observed that the judge's standard is somewhat similar to the traditional common law rule of respondeat superior. However, in applying this rule to a criminal case, the judge added certain requirements not generally associated with that common law doctrine. He further qualified the rule of respondeat superior by requiring that the conduct for which the corporation is being held accountable be performed *on behalf of the corporation*. This factor is noted as important in the commentary to § 2.07(1) of the Model

Penal Code. It may well be that there is often little distinction between an act done *on behalf of a principal* and an act done *within the scope of employment,* which is the traditional requirement of the doctrine of respondeat superior. Nevertheless, in the circumstances of this case it might reasonably be concluded that the explicit instruction of the judge that the jury look to the authority vested in the agent by the corporation to act within the particular sphere of corporate affairs relating to the criminal act, together with the explicit instruction that such act be performed on behalf of the corporation, required in effect, the type of evidence which would support an inference that the criminal act was done as a matter of corporate policy. We deem this to be a valid conclusion, especially in view of the quantum of proof required in a criminal case in order to prove guilt beyond a reasonable doubt.

The defendants seek to make the question of corporate criminal responsibility one of first impression in this Commonwealth. They argue that there is "no Massachusetts case" dispositive of the question as to when a corporation may be held criminally liable for the acts of its servants or agents *where the offence is one which involves specific intent.* Conversely, the Commonwealth contends that the standard applied by the judge was expressed long ago in the case of Telegram Newspaper Co. v. Commonwealth, 172 Mass. 294, 299, 52 N.E. 445. This case, it is argued, serves as precedent for the rule that corporate criminal responsibility can be predicated on the acts of an agent who is neither a director nor an officer of the corporation.

* * *

[The court's review of the four Massachusetts' cases involving prosecution of a corporation for a crime with an intent requirement (none being a prosecution for bribery or conspiracy) is omitted]

The thrust of each of the cases cited above involving a human principal is that it is fundamental to our criminal jurisprudence that for more serious offences guilt is personal and not vicarious. "One is punished for his own blameworthy conduct, not that of others." Commonwealth v. Stasiun, 349 Mass. 38, 48, 206 N.E.2d 672, 679, citing Perkins, Criminal Law, 550, and Sayre, Criminal Responsibility for the Acts of Another, 43 Harv.L.Rev. 689. Professor Sayre's article is heavily relied on by Beneficial for the proposition that the considerations proposed by Sayre apply with equal weight to corporations. However, we do not think that the Sayre article, or the rule in the master-servant cases, is helpful to these corporations. The essence of Sayre's discussion is that, as to certain crimes, a theory of vicarious liability is an inadequate basis for imposing criminal liability on a natural person who can suffer imprisonment or ignominy for the acts of his agents. *Id.* at 722–723. (We, too, have recently rejected the concept of individual guilt by mere association. Commonwealth v. Pina, Mass., 273 N.E.2d 806.) In fact, Professor Sayre explicitly refrains from dealing with the problem of imposing corporate criminal liability when he states: "The problem of the criminal liability of a corporation for the acts of corporate agents depends upon a consideration of two quite distinct problems, one a problem of agency, and the other a problem of the law of corporations. The first involves the general question of criminal responsibility for the acts of another. Would the principal be criminally liable for the acts of the agent if the principal were a natural person instead of a corporation? The second problem involves the entirely distinct question of when the acts and intent of a natural person, for example of a vice-president or general manager, are to be treated as those of the corporation itself. In * * * [this article], only the first of these two problems is considered." Sayre, Criminal Responsibility for the Acts of Another, 43 Harv.L.Rev. at 689.

As alluded to by Professor Sayre, and pointed out by the Commonwealth in its brief, the very nature of a corporation as a "person" before the law renders it impossible to equate the imposition of vicarious liability on a human principal with the imposition of vicarious liability on a corporate principal. "A corporation can act only through its agents. * * * [C]orporate criminal liability is necessarily vicarious." Note, Criminal Liability of Corporations for Acts of Their Agents, 60 Harv.L.Rev. 283. See Francis, Criminal Responsibility of the Corporation, 18 Ill.L.Rev. 305, 308; Lee, Corporate Criminal Liability, 28 Col.L.Rev. 1, 13. Since a corporation is a legal fiction, comprised only of individuals, it has no existence separate and distinct from those whom it has clothed with authority and commissioned to act for it whether such individuals are directors, officers, shareholders or employees. Thus, the issue is not whether vicarious liability should be imposed on a corporation under the "direct participation and assent rule" of the master-servant cases cited above, but rather, whether the acts and intent of natural persons, be they officers, directors or employees, can be treated as the acts and intent of the corporation itself. For the foregoing reasons, despite the strenuous urging of the defendants, we are unconvinced that the standard for imposing criminal responsibility on a human principal adequately deals with the evidentiary problems which are inherent in ascribing the acts of individuals to a corporate entity.

* * *

[The court then examines cases from other jurisdictions involving mala in se offenses. It concludes that three in particular, C.I.T. Corp. v. United States, 150 F.2d 85 (9th Cir. 1945), Egan v. United States, 137 F.2d 369 (8th Cir. 1943) and United States v. Nearing, 252 Fed. 223 (S.D.N.Y.1918), are] strong precedent for the rule that a corporation is criminally liable for the acts of an agent who has been vested with the authority to act on behalf of the corporation in the sphere of corporate business in which he commits the criminal act. Numerous other Federal cases have been brought to our attention which also support this rule. * * *.

Household, Beneficial and Liberty all vigorously attack these cases in an attempt to distinguish them from the cases before us. The thrust of their argument is that all of these cases fall into 1 of 2 categories; either they involve public welfare and regulatory statute crimes in which intent was not an element, or if the crimes did include intent as a necessary element, then they assert that the corporations were only held liable if one high in the corporate hierarchy directed, approved or acquiesced in the agent's criminal act. In support of this argument, Household cites several law review articles in which their authors have attempted to categorize these cases in a similar manner.[57]

We think that the answer to these contentions is twofold. First, the defendants' attempted categorization of the above cases into two neat little groups greatly oversimplifies the complex and multifaceted issues which confronted the various courts in the cases we have cited. The principal cases of *Egan, C.I.T.* and *Nearing* all entail prosecutions for the crimes of conspiracy, a crime requiring specific intent. In addition, the object of the conspiracies in those cases involved a wide scope of serious criminal activity, usually in matters tending to be of benefit to the corporation, extending from violations of the Espionage Act in the *Nearing* case, through the making of illegal political contributions in the *Egan* case, various types of fraudulent acquisitive crimes * * * and conspiracy to violate the Sherman Act through price fixing * * *. Furthermore, as we previously noted, even if the statute in the *New York Central* [212 U.S. 481, 29 S.Ct. 304, 53 L.Ed. 613 (1909)] case dispensed with the necessity of proving corporate intent, the *Egan* case and other Federal cases specifically expanded the rule of that case to cases involving crimes requiring specific intent. Secondly, the argument that only high corporate officers were involved has no basis in fact. In the *C.I.T.* case, a minor branch

---

57. The defendants appear to principally rely on the Note, Criminal Liability of Corporations for Acts of Their Agents, 60 Harv.L.Rev. 283, 289, and on the Note, Corporate Criminal Liability for Acts in Violation of Company Policy, 50 Georgetown L.J. 547, 549, to substantiate the categorizations made above. The question of corporate criminal responsibility has of course been discussed extensively by text writers and in law reviews. See Anderson, Wharton's Criminal Law & Procedure, § 52, p. 120; Fletcher, Cyc. Corporations (Rev.Ed.) § 4959; Lee, Corporate Criminal Liability, 28 Col. L.Rev. 1; Edgerton, Corporate Criminal Responsibility, 26 Yale L.J. 827;

Mueller, Mens Rea and the Corporation, A Study of the Model Code Position on Corporate Criminal Liability, 19 U. of Pittsburgh L.Rev. 21. The Mueller article, which is also heavily relied on in support of the defendants' view of the Model Penal Code standard, does, however, make the following statement in referring to "high managerial agents." "Not the mode of acquisition of a corporate office but the scope of trust and power is the proper criterion." Mueller, supra, at 40. We think this test is easily equated to the "scope of authority" or "kinship of authority to the act" test employed by the judge.

manager was involved, and in the *Zito* case [64 F.2d 772 (7th Cir. 1933)], a salesman. In addition, although the criminal acts in the *Egan* case were performed by an officer of the corporation, the court consistently stressed, as is shown from the language previously quoted that the corporation could be held responsible for the acts of either officers or agents. Indeed, the court emphatically stated that the focal point of inquiry is not whether corporate authorization or participation was shown in the upper echelon of the corporate ranks, but whether the agent or officer in doing the criminal act "was engaged in 'employing the corporate powers actually authorized' for the benefit of the corporation 'while acting within the scope of his employment in the business of the principal.'" P. 379 of 137 F.2d.

Household argues that in applying the foregoing standard of corporate criminal responsibility, we are merely applying the rule of respondeat superior as it is applied in civil cases and that we are "reaching out to state a completely new rule of law." We agree that the above cases, as well as the judge's instructions to the jury, essentially employ the rationale underlying the doctrine of respondeat superior. However, we do not agree that application of this doctrine to a criminal case involving specific intent is a "completely new rule of law." The courts in the *New York Central* case and the other Federal cases cited above, especially in the *Egan* case, unequivocally focus their inquiry on the scope of authority which the corporation has conferred upon its agents to act on behalf of the corporation in managing the particular activities in which the agents were engaged when they committed the criminal act. P. 379.

It may be held that the theoretical principles underlying this standard are, in general, the same as embodied in the rule of respondeat superior. Nevertheless, as we observed at the outset, the judge's instructions, as a whole and in context, required a greater quantum of proof in the practical application of this standard than is required in a civil case. In focusing on the "kinship" between the authority of an individual and the act he committed, the judge emphasized that the jury must be satisfied "beyond a reasonable doubt" that the act of the individual *"constituted"* the act of the corporation. Juxtaposition of the traditional criminal law requirement of ascertaining guilt beyond a reasonable doubt (as opposed to the civil law standard of the preponderance of the evidence), with the rule of respondeat superior, fully justifies application of the standard enunciated by the judge to a criminal prosecution against a corporation for a crime requiring specific intent.

The foregoing is especially true in view of the particular circumstances of this case. In order to commit the crimes charged in these indictments, the defendant corporations either had to offer to pay money to a public official or conspire to do so. The disbursal of funds is an act peculiarly within the ambit of corporate activity. These corporations by the very nature of their business are constantly dealing with the expenditure and collection of moneys. It could hardly be expected that any of the individual defendants would conspire to pay, or would pay, the substantial amount of money here involved, namely $25,000, out of his own pocket. The jury would be warranted in finding that the disbursal of such an amount of money would come from the corporate treasury. A reasonable inference could therefore be drawn that the payment of such money by the corporations was done as a matter of corporate policy and as a reflection of corporate intent, thus comporting with the underlying rationale of the Model Penal Code, and probably with its specific requirements.

Moreover, we do not think that the Model Penal Code standard really purports to deal with the evidentiary problems which are inherent in establishing the quantum of proof necessary to show that the directors or officers of a corporation authorize, ratify, tolerate, or participate in the criminal acts of an agent when such acts are apparently performed on behalf of the corporation. Evidence of such authorization or ratification is too easily susceptible of concealment. As is so trenchantly stated by the judge: "Criminal acts are not usually made the subject of votes of authorization or ratification by corporate Boards of Directors; and the lack of such votes does not prevent the act from being the act of the corporation."

It is obvious that criminal conspiratorial acts are not performed within the glare of publicity, nor would we expect a board of directors to meet officially and record on the corporate records a delegation of authority to initiate, conduct or conclude proceedings for the purpose of bribing a public official. Of necessity, the proof authority to so act must rest on all the circumstances and conduct in a given situation and the reasonable inferences to be drawn therefrom.

Additional factors of importance are the size and complexity of many large modern corporations which necessitate the delegation of more authority to lesser corporate agents and employees. As the judge pointed out: "There are not enough seats on the Board of Directors, nor enough offices in a corporation, to permit the corporation engaged in widespread operations to give such a title or office to every person in whom it places the power, authority, and responsibility for decision and action." This latter consideration lends credence to the view that the title or position of an individual in a corporation should not be conclusively determinative in ascribing criminal responsibility. In a large corporation, with many numerous and distinct departments, a high ranking corporate officer or agent may have no authority or involvement in a particular sphere of corporate activity, whereas a lower ranking corporate executive might have much broader power in dealing with a matter peculiarly within the scope of his authority. Employees who are in the lower echelon of the corporate hierarchy often exercise more responsibility in the *everyday operations* of the corporation than the directors or officers. Assuredly, the title or office that the person holds may be considered, but it should not be the decisive criterion upon which to predicate corporate responsibility.

The validity and soundness of these considerations are especially reflected in the activities of public relations men in the employ of many large corporations. This is graphically illustrated in the *Egan* case, 137 F.2d 369, *supra*. That case is particularly applicable to the ones before us because of its inquiry into the type of authority exercised by the officers and agents who made the political contributions for which their corporations were held responsible. The court characterized the activities of these agents as being "authorized public relations activities * * * within the defendant corporation's powers." In reviewing the evidence relating to this type of authority, the court highlighted the following factors: "The evidence shows that the corporation in the exercise of this power regards its public relations and its good will as matters of great importance. It has a right to do so and it does send its officers to appear before legislative committees to influence those legislatures and to persuade them to pass laws advantageous to the company's interest and to reject proposed laws inimical to its interest. In the exercise of its powers, it has a right to do so and it does send its officers to state capitals to influence the individual members of the legislatures to be friendly to its interests. It sends its officers to appear before state and municipal boards and officers having power to impose taxes upon its property for the purpose of presenting arguments and data in its interest. To cultivate and develop the friendship of its patrons, prospective patrons, legislators and taxing authorities the company gives entertainments for invited guests including legislators, members of tax boards, patrons and others whose friendship it deems important. It maintains a 'lodge' at the lake above its dam in the Ozark Mountains to which it invites for free entertainment state officers and candidates for office."

The similarity between the kinship of authority and the acts of the agents in the *Egan* case with the kinship between the acts and authority of the individuals in the present cases is striking. It approaches the incredible for us to conclude from the evidence in the instant case that the public relations men, in their constant and prolonged communications with Hanley, were engaging in independent endeavors. The inference is obvious that their concerted activities along the lines outlined in our summary of the facts could not have been carried on without the knowledge or at least the reckless toleration of highly placed corporate executives.

To permit corporations to conceal the nefarious acts of their underlings by using the shield of corporate armor to deflect corporate responsibility, and to separate the subordinate from the executive, would be to permit "endocratic" corporations to inflict widespread public harm without hope of redress. It would merely serve to ignore the scramble and realities of the market place.[58] This we decline to do. We believe that stringent standards must be adopted to discourage any attempt by "endocratic" corporations' executives to place the sole responsibility for criminal acts on the shoulders of their subordinates.

We believe that our decision is supported by basic considerations of public policy. The President's Commission on Law Enforcement and Administration of Justice, Task Force Report—Crime and Its Impact—An Assessment (1967) provides a sound rationale for imputing criminal responsibility to the corporation for the acts of lower echelon corporate officials who have the authority to act on behalf of the corporation. The report states at p. 104 that "[w]hite collar crime also does serious damage to social and economic institutions. * * * Thus, crimes such as bribery and violation of conflict of interest statutes strike deeply at responsible, impartial government." The report further points out at p. 108 that: "A pervasive problem affecting enforcement is the fact that white collar crime is often business crime and business crime is often corporate crime. Where corporate defendants are involved, the only criminal sanction available is the fine. As noted previously, fines may be inadequate as deterrents for a variety of reasons. There are also serious practical problems in imposing sanctions upon corporate employees. It is very difficult to obtain the conviction of the true policy formulators in large, complex corporations. The top executives do not ordinarily carry out the overt criminal acts—it is the lower or middle management officials who, for example, attend price-fixing meetings." The President's Commission concluded, at p. 108, that: "where corporate misconduct is involved, the offenders—and particularly the offenders against whom evidence of guilt can be obtained—act as part of a corporate hierarchy and, ordinarily, follow a pattern of corporate behavior. Individual responsibility is therefore reduced—the offenders are often following orders from above, either explicit or implicit. Moreover, the fact that acts are performed to further the interests of the corporation, and not merely the offenders' personal interests, helps to rationalize misconduct. Thus in the *Electrical Equipment* cases, personal explanations for the acts were, for the most part, sought in the structure of corporate pressures. The defendants almost invariably testified that they came new to a job, found price-fixing an established way of life, and simply entered into it as they did into other aspects of their job." [59]

58. The term "endocratic" was coined by Dean Rostow and means a "large, publicly-held corporation, whose stock is scattered in small fractions among thousands of stockholders." Note, Increasing Community Control Over Corporate Crime—A Problem in the Law of Sanctions, 71 Yale L.J. 280, 281, n. 3.

59. The public policy rationale underlying our decision is also illustrated in a recent article by Professor Alan M. Dershowitz. He discusses the effect of criminal sanctions on the treasuries of large "endocratic" corporations. He states that "[t]he criminal fine as presently administered against the endocratic corporation guilty of acquisitive crime is thus

The above considerations seem to us to support the principles stated in the judge's charge for adjudicating the criminal responsibility of these corporate principles. We are aware that *some* jurisdictions and legal writers have approved the Model Penal Code,[60] even as contained in the 1955 draft. Indeed, the 1955 comments on the Code (prior to the addition of the significant words "or recklessly tolerated") merely say that the limitations on corporate liability there set out are "generally consistent with the position of the English courts and those of *some* American States" (emphasis supplied). Model Penal Code, § 2.07, comment p. 151 (Tent. Draft No. 4, 1955). This may mean that the majority of jurisdictions in this country do not adhere to the standard proposed in 1955.

* * *

Cases relied upon by the defendants which apparently support what they conceive as the Model Penal Code principle are Grant Bros. Constr. Co. v. United States, 13 Ariz. 388, 114 P. 955, and People v. Canadian Fur Trappers' Corp., 248 N.Y. 159, 161 N.E. 455. Particular emphasis is placed on the *Canadian Fur Trappers'* case for the proposition that a corporation can be held criminally responsible "only for acts which it authorizes through action of its officers or which * * * [are] done with the acquiescence of its officers." 248 N.Y. at 164, 161 N.E. at 456. It should be noted, however, that the *Canadian Fur Trappers'* case involved a closely held corporation in which four brothers "constituted the corporation and were its only officers."

---

little more than 'a reasonable license fee' for engaging in such conduct and may be practically ignored as *de minimis* in an analysis of the profit diminishing effect of present sanctions." Note, Increasing Community Control Over Corporate Crime—A Problem in the Law of Sanctions. 71 Yale L.J. 280, 287. The article goes on to refer to "the presently insubstantial nature of the criminal fine" and "the difficulty of pinpointing guilt above the level of overt actors, the real formulators of endocratic corporate policy have little cause to fear corporate penalties. These phenomena help to explain why, in the area in which effective criminal sanctions *should* achieve the highest degree of over-all deterrence, they are essentially ineffective, as evidenced by the startling rate of acquisitive crime recidivism among endocratic corporations." Id. at 293, citing Sutherland, White Collar Crime, 25. After analyzing criminal anti-trust cases in which the scope of authority test is well established, Dershowitz concludes that greater penalties are necessary in or-

der to obtain adequate deterrence. We, of course, have no occasion to express an opinion concerning any administrative action which may follow as a consequence of convictions in these cases.

60. Statutes recently enacted in New York, Georgia and Illinois have adopted similar standards. See New York Penal Law, c. 40 of Consolidated Laws, Title B, art. 20, § 20.20, Amendment, Laws of 1965, c. 1030. Illinois Crim. Code, c. 38, Title II, art. 5, § 5-4. Georgia Code Anno. Title 26, § 26-803 (1969). Legal writers indorsing the Model Penal Code standard or something analogous thereto are Mueller, Mens Rea and the Corporation, A Study of the Model Code Position on Corporate Criminal Liability," 19 U. of Pittsburgh L.Rev. 21, 41 (high managerial agents or "inner circle"), Winn, The Criminal Responsibility of Corporations, 3 Cambridge L.J. 398, 414 ("primary representatives"), and Welsh, The Criminal Liability of Corporations, 62 L.Q.Rev. 345, 362 ("governing body"). See fn. 57, supra.

P. 165, 161 N.E. p. 457. Thus, the court in that case had only to confine its opinion to the acts of individuals who were, in fact, the corporation. See fn. 62, infra. It seems appropriate to distinguish a situation of that kind from large, endocratic corporations such as are involved in the present case.

Considering everything we have said above, we are of opinion that the quantum of proof necessary to sustain the conviction of a corporation for the acts of its agents is sufficiently met if it is shown that the corporation has placed the agent in a position where he has enough authority and responsibility to act for and in behalf of the corporation in handling the *particular* corporate business, operation or project in which he was engaged at the time he committed the criminal act. The judge properly instructed the jury to this effect and correctly stated that this standard does not depend upon the responsibility or authority which the agent has with respect to the entire corporate business, but only to his position with relation to the particular business in which he was serving the corporation. Some of the factors that the jury were entitled to consider in applying the above test, although perhaps not in themselves decisive, are the following: (1) the extent of control and authority exercised by the individual over and within the corporation; [62] (2) the extent and manner to which corporate funds were used in the crime; (3) a repeated pattern of criminal conduct tending to indicate corporate toleration or ratification of the agent's acts. Applying these criteria within the "kinship of the act to authority" test to the present case we next consider the evidence admitted against Household, then Liberty, and lastly, Beneficial.

[The court's discussion of the responsibility of Household and Liberty for the acts of their employees is omitted. The court found little difficulty in holding that the evidence was sufficient to permit the conclusion that the employees acting within the authority conferred on them conspired to bribe Hanley and Garfinkle.] * * *

4. *Beneficial*—The conviction of Beneficial presents a more involved situation regarding the sufficiency of evidence than that of the other loan companies. This is due to the interlocking corporate structure of the "Beneficial Finance System" (a term used by Beneficial to describe itself and its wholly owned subsidiaries), rather than the sufficiency of the evidence against Farrell and Glynn, both of whom were employees of the "System." Indeed, Farrell and Glynn emerge as 2 of the major proponents of the plot to bribe Hanley and Garfinkle,

---

62. With regard to a small closely held corporation, in which the individual *is* the corporation, this factor may be considered somewhat decisive. Cf. Mininsohn v. United States, 101 F.2d 477 (3d Cir.); Old Monastery Co. v. United States, 147 F.2d 905, 908 (4th Cir.); United States v. Empire Packing Co., 174 F.2d 16, 19 (7th Cir.); People v. Canadian Fur Trappers' Corp., 248 N.Y. 159, 164, 161 N.E. 455; State v. Graziani, 60 N.J.Super. 1, 158 A.2d 375, cert. den. 363 U.S. 830, 80 S.Ct. 1001, 4 L.Ed.2d 1524.

there being an overwhelming amount of evidence relative to the participation of each.

The evidence discloses that Farrell and Glynn were not formally the employees of the defendant Beneficial. Farrell was vice-president and director of Beneficial Management. Similarly, Glynn was employed by Beneficial Management and was formally on the payroll of Industrial Bankers, a Massachusetts business trust completely owned and controlled by Beneficial. In addition to Industrial Bankers, Beneficial fully owns and operates 2 other Massachusetts business trusts—New England Equity and Workingmen's Loan Association. These 3 trusts engage in the consumer loan business within the Commonwealth and operate a total of 58 licensed small loans offices. The parent, Beneficial, controls the appointment of the trustees and officers of the 3 trusts and provides them with the funds necessary for continued operation.

Beneficial Management also is a wholly owned subsidiary of Beneficial. * * * It is apparent that many of the officers and directors of Beneficial are also officers and directors of Beneficial Management.[66] In fact, Beneficial refers to the officers and key exec-

66. The following chart compiled by the Commonwealth discloses a network of interlocking directorates and officeholders within the Beneficial Finance "System."

	Beneficial	Beneficial Management	Industrial Bankers	New England Equity	Workingmen's Loan Ass'n	58 Individual Licensees
T. A. McGrath	President	Director				
R A. Tucker	Vice-President	Director				
W. C. Thompson	Vice-President		Trustee	Trustee	Trustee	
A. H. Strothman	Secretary		Secretary	Secretary	Secretary	Secretary
O. W. Casperson	Director	Director				
R. G. Dorr	Director			President		
D. H. Finck	Director	Director				
D. E. McMichael	Director	President				
Frank J. McCann		Vice-President	Trustee	Trustee	Trustee	
D. J. Paul	Director	Senior Vice-President	Trustee			

utives of Beneficial Management as "the men behind Beneficial." As a vice-president and director of Beneficial Management, the defendant Farrell is so listed.

The public relations area was handled for all of the individual Beneficial loan offices and business trusts in Massachusetts by the defendant, Glynn, Beneficial's director of industry relations. Although Glynn was on the payroll of Industrial Bankers, he was not assigned to any particular office or department of Industrial Bankers; nor was he the subordinate of any employee of that trust. He did public relations work and reported principally to Farrell.

Glynn's activities included ingratiating himself with legislators and members of the small loans division. He entertained Hanley extensively. Glynn expedited the procurement of an additional license for Beneficial for the movement of one of its offices. His primary function was to "sell Beneficial's position on any policies, matters of legislation, anything affecting regulations with the Department [of Banking], anything affecting annual and monthly reports with the Department, anything affecting the increase in license fees of the Department."

It is clear from the above evidence concerning Glynn's duties and Farrell's position within the Beneficial Finance "System," that Farrell and Glynn possessed sufficient authority to at least act on behalf of Beneficial Management in dealing with Hanley particularly in connection with Rate Board hearings. * * * Farrell's position and authority as vice-president and director of Beneficial Management raises the inference that he was sufficiently highly placed in the corporate hierarchy of Beneficial Management to permit the jury to find that he was a "high managerial agent" whose "conduct may fairly be assumed to represent the policy of the corporation." Model Penal Code, § 2.07(2)(c) (Proposed Official Draft). * * *

However, the principal issue confronting us here is whether the evidence was sufficient as matter of law to warrant a finding that Farrell and Glynn *acted within the authority granted to them by Beneficial*. Beneficial vigorously argues that this court should not disregard Beneficial Management as a corporate entity, should adopt its view of the Model Penal Code standard, and therefore should conclude that Farrell was not a high managerial agent of the parent, Beneficial. On the other hand, the Commonwealth argues that the pervasive control of Beneficial Management by Beneficial and the "use of the former entity by Beneficial solely for its own ends within the 'Beneficial Finance System' while representing to the public at large that such 'System' was a unitary, centrally controlled whole, and the delegation by Beneficial to Beneficial Management of the powers, duties, authority, and responsibilities for dealing with the Massachusetts small loans regulatory authorities," warrants looking through the corporate structure to the parent, Beneficial. The Commonwealth concludes that Farrell should be regarded as a "high managerial agent" of Beneficial whose actions bind that corporation.

Essentially, we are in agreement with the position of the Commonwealth. We concede that the law is well settled that the parent's ownership of the entire stock of its subsidiary as well as control over the latter's affairs do not, without more, warrant treating 2 separate and distinct corporate entities identically. * * * But it is also clear that "courts look through the corporate form to the individuals in order to protect the public, prevent a fraud, or to accomplish some other essential justice." Hallett v. Moore, 282 Mass. 380, 399, 185

N.E. 474, 482, citing J. J. McCaskill Co. v. United States, 216 U.S. 504, 515, 30 S.Ct. 386, 54 L.Ed. 590; * * *

In the recent decision of My Bread Baking Co. v. Cumberland Farms, Inc., 353 Mass. 614, 233 N.E.2d 748, we held a corporation liable for the torts of various satellite corporations even though the principal corporation did not own stock in any of the affiliates. The evidence in that case revealed that one Haseotes was the secretary, treasurer and a stockholder of Cumberland Farms, Inc. The Haseotes family also owned all of the stock in numerous other corporations operating retail stores which sold the dairy products of Cumberland Farms, Inc. Although the satellite corporations were not the subsidiaries of Cumberland Farms, Inc., they all had the same officers, operated as a single enterprise from a single headquarters and used the name of Cumberland Farms, Inc. as a trade name. From this evidence we inferred that Haseotes was a dominant figure in the enterprise, and that the store managers of the various retail outlets followed his orders and acted as agents of the principal corporation. With reference to the question of when employees of 1 corporation may be treated as the agents of another, we said:

"A corporation or other person controlling a corporation and directing, or participating actively in * * * its operations may become subject to civil or criminal liability on principles of agency or of causation. * * * This may sometimes occur where corporations are formed, or availed of, to carry out the objectives and purposes of the corporations or persons controlling them. * * * The circumstances in which one corporation, or a person controlling it, may become liable for the acts or torts of an affiliate or a subsidiary under common control have been frequently discussed. Although common ownership of the stock of two or more corporations together with common management, standing alone, will not give rise to liability on the part of one corporation for the acts of another corporation or its employees, additional facts may be such as to permit the conclusion that an agency or similar relationship exists between the entities. Particularly is this true (a) when there is active and direct participation by the representatives of one corporation, apparently exercising some form of pervasive control, in the activities of another and there is some fraudulent or injurious consequence of the intercorporate relationship, or (b) when there is a confused intermingling of activity of two or more corporations engaged in a common enterprise with substantial disregard of the separate nature of the corporate entities, or serious ambiguity about the manner and capacity in which the various corporations and their respective representatives are acting." Pp. 618–619, 233 N.E.2d p. 751.

We are of opinion that the standards enunciated above apply with equal validity to the case before us. Here, there is a clear interpenetration of corporate officers and directors between Beneficial and

Beneficial Management. Beneficial's president, 2 vice-presidents, and 2 directors were all directors of Beneficial Management. One of the directors of Beneficial was the president and another was the senior vice-president, and a third was a vice-president of Beneficial Management. The duality of corporate authority in these top executives reflects the extent of control and participation exercised by Beneficial over Beneficial Management.

Also of significance is the fact that Beneficial owned all of the stock of Beneficial Management and supplied operating funds to it. Additionally, the business services furnished by Beneficial Management were provided essentially as a part of the business operations of Beneficial. In this regard, Beneficial Management emerges as but a division of the Beneficial Finance "System" and an adjunct to Beneficial.

*   *   *

We also consider noteworthy the fact that the entire consumer finance business of Beneficial was operated under the name of Beneficial Finance Company. It seems obvious that Beneficial derives a substantial amount of publicity and good will by representing to the public and its shareholders that it operates as a single, integral, mutually supporting entity. The *My Bread* case also noted this factor in ascertaining an agency relationship between many apparently distinct corporations. Supra, at 620, 233 N.E.2d 748.

Beneficial argues that the standards enunciated in the *My Bread* case "may be justifiable in a civil suit for damages" but that they "should not apply in a criminal case" where a defendant "is entitled to a presumption of innocence and the burden [is] on the prosecution to prove the defendant's guilt beyond a reasonable doubt."

The fact that this is a criminal case does not alter our view nor does it warrant adopting a rule different from that in the *My Bread* case. The traditional protection afforded a criminal defendant by placing the burden on the prosecution to prove guilt beyond a reasonable doubt and by clothing the defendant with a presumption of innocence is not undermined by subjecting a parent corporation to criminal responsibility on the grounds that it fully controls and participates in the operations of its subsidiary which commits the criminal act. This is the rule of our cases and it was so cited in the *My Bread* case. In the *My Bread* case, citing Commonwealth v. Abbott Engr. Inc., 351 Mass. 568, 579–580, 222 N.E.2d 862 (a criminal case concerning larceny by false pretenses), we said that "[a] corporation * * * controlling a corporation and directing, or participating actively in * * its operations may become subject to *civil or criminal liability* on principles of agency or of causation" (emphasis supplied). *My Bread,* supra, at 618, 233 N.E.2d at 751.

Thus, we discern no valid reason for not applying the standards of the *My Bread* case in looking behind the corporate structure of the defendant Beneficial. The interest of the Commonwealth in protecting itself and its citizens from the criminal acts of foreign corporations is of much greater importance than the right of 1 person to pursue a civil remedy against a foreign corporate defendant. The inherent power of the Commonwealth to prosecute those who violate the law, whether they be individuals or corporations dictates that such offenders should not be permitted to insulate themselves from criminal prosecution by shielding themselves behind instrumentalities which they promulgate to conceal their criminal acts. This is especially true of large endocratic corporations which are structured to enable them to create a flow of authority from the upper echelons of directors and officers to lower ranks of corporate executives. Such a structure makes the responsibility for a criminal act more easily susceptible of concealment. Even greater beclouding of responsibility by a corporate principal takes place where a corporation such as Beneficial creates subsidiaries and business trusts to carry out its everyday administration and business operations. We find it appalling to allow such a corporate structure to shield those corporate entities which directly or indirectly receive the monetary benefits of criminal activity and at the same time avoid the sanctions which may be imposed upon those corporate employees who commit the actual criminal act.

In view of everything we have said above, we hold that there is sufficient evidence to support a finding that there existed between the defendants Farrell and Glynn and the corporation Beneficial Management a relationship of agency with the corporation Beneficial which empowered Farrell and Glynn to act on behalf of Beneficial in dealing with Hanley in his official capacity and also in connection with the Rate Board proceedings. Beneficial's motion for a directed verdict on the conspiracy indictment was properly denied.

[The remainder of this 109 page opinion is omitted. It concerns claimed errors in the conduct of the first and second trials, and the sufficiency of the evidence in the second trial for the conviction of the individual and corporate defendants. All judgments were affirmed. Fines of an unstated amount were imposed on the corporate defendants and sentences of unstated duration to the house of correction were imposed on the individual defendants. Commonwealth v. Beneficial Finance Co., 355 Mass. 373, 37 n. 2, 244 N.E.2d 586, 587 n. 2 (1969)].

McCOLLUM v. STATE

Court of Criminal Appeals of Texas, 1957.
165 Tex.Cr.R. 241, 305 S.W.2d 612.

DAVIDSON, Judge. In view of appellant's argument and citation of additional authorities in his motion for rehearing, we now withdraw our original opinion and substitute therefor the following:

This is a conviction for the pollution of public waters, which is prohibited by Art. 698b, Vernon's P.C., with punishment assessed at a fine of $110.

The Hess Terminal was a tank storage depot for the loading of ships, barges, and tank cars adjacent to and along the Houston Ship Channel. Appellant was the vice-president of the company and in complete charge of its operation.

According to the testimony of the state's witness who reported the fact to appellant, oil was found escaping from Hess Terminal into the Ship Channel, thereby polluting those public waters. Appellant promised, then, to take all necessary steps to prevent further pollution. Shortly thereafter, oil was again found in the channel of such nature and in such amount as to constitute pollution of public waters, under the statute, and to warrant the conclusion that the operation of boats thereon was endangered.

While there was some dispute in the evidence, the conclusion is reached that the evidence is sufficient to warrant the trial court's ruling that the oil actually escaped into the channel from Hess Terminal because of defective or improper operation of a separator designed to prevent such escape.

Appellant did not testify as a witness in his own behalf.

James, who was the superintendent of the Hess Terminal and appellant's subordinate, testified as to the prior efforts of the company not only to salvage escaping oil but to prevent pollution of the channel waters by the installation and operation of the separator. He denied any knowledge of the escaped oil, involved in this prosecution, from the separator or premises of Hess Terminal.

It will be noted that there is an absence of any testimony showing that appellant was actually in charge of the operation or maintenance of the separator or that he was in any manner personally connected with the oil escaping from the premises of the company and the resultant pollution of the channel or that he knowingly permitted such pollution.

On the other hand, it is established that appellant was the head of the company and, as such, was responsible for its operation and maintenance by and through delegated subordinates or employees.

This conviction is against appellant, personally. It is not a proceeding against Hess Terminal.

The question for determination, then, turns upon whether—under the facts stated—appellant may be adjudged guilty of the pollution of the channel waters.

In support of his contention that the facts do not warrant the conclusion of guilt, he poses this question:

Suppose the pollution here shown had caused damage to the person or property of another, who, as a result thereof, sues both Hess Terminal and him to recover the damage, would the instant facts authorize a judgment against him, personally, for the damage sustained?

The position taken is that the question should be answered in the negative because the undisputed facts show that appellant was the general manager in charge of the Hess Terminal plant and had delegated the operations of the plant to subordinates who, in turn, delegated their functions to other employees.

Appellant insists that he could not be personally liable for the defective operation of the sump or separator causing the pollution and, since he had delegated the operation of the separator to subordinates, he could not be held criminally responsible for his subordinates' failure to act.

In support of the position taken, appellant cites the case of S. H. Kress & Co. v. Selph, Tex.Civ.App., 250 S.W.2d 883, writ refused, n. r. e. That case appears to be directly in point and covers a very similar state of facts. It sustains this appellant's contention that a civil suit for damages could not be successfully maintained against him for damages that might have been sustained by another because of the pollution here shown.

We have reached the conclusion, here, that inasmuch as the facts fail to show any personal connection on the part of the appellant with the pollution or the maintenance or operation of the separator, he cannot be held liable, criminally, for the acts of his subordinates or employees in the absence of a showing that he was connected therewith in some manner recognized by law, whereby one may be criminally liable for the acts of another or others. Myers v. State, 148 Tex.Cr.R. 77, 184 S.W.2d 924, is deemed also in point, and supports our holding here.

The statute under which this prosecution was conducted prohibits pollution of public waters by corporations and companies. The conclusion here reached does not foreclose the right of the state to proceed against the Hess Terminal.

It is now determined that the facts do not warrant the conviction in the instant case.

Accordingly, appellant's motion for rehearing is granted, the judgment of affirmance is set aside, and the judgment of the trial court is now reversed and the cause remanded.

NOTES

1. Employees of defendant corporation entered a scheme with one Thompson, the owner of an oil lease, whereby Thompson would be credited by the defendant for oil produced in violation of production limitations imposed by state law and thus "hot oil" within the meaning of the Connolly Act, 15 U.S.C.A. § 715. In some cases records were falsified so that oil produced by other leases, some owned in part by defendant, was attributed to Thompson's wells. The question was whether the defendant could be held liable for a knowing violation of the statute on the basis of the acts of its employees even though not performed for the defendant's benefit and, indeed, sometimes involving a theft of the defendant's property. Is there any reason why the knowledge of subordinate employees should not be deemed knowledge of the corporation? Should it matter whether the acts knowingly performed by these employees did not benefit the corporation or even resulted in adverse consequences? Should the answer turn on the employee's intent rather than the results of his conduct? Standard Oil Co. of Tex. v. United States, 307 F.2d 120 (5th Cir. 1962).

2. The president of defendant corporation gave $4,500 of corporate funds to the president of the local union representing some of defendant's employees. The Government charged this transaction violated the Taft-Hartley Act, 29 U.S.C.A. § 186(a) & (b), which makes it a crime for an employer to pay any money to an official of a union representing its employees. The two individuals claimed that they were social friends, that the money was a loan for the purchase of a new home and that the corporation received a note in exchange for the loan. No effort was made to collect the note. May the corporation be convicted of "wilfully" violating the law? Was the president acting within the scope of his employment. How should that phrase be defined for this purpose? United States v. Carter, 311 F.2d 934 (6th Cir. 1963).

3. What goals of the criminal law are furthered by the imposition of criminal liability on a corporation given the fact that the only possible punishment is a fine which may be passed on to either the stockholders or customers, both of which groups are likely to be innocent of any wrongdoing?

4. If financial penalties are seen as efficacious, why wouldn't civil suits for damages resulting from the "criminal" conduct of the corporation serve the same purpose as well or better than the generally small—relative to the assets of many corporations—fines, which can be imposed?

5. Would not punishment of the responsible individual more effectively achieve legitimate goals of the criminal law without raising the problems incident to vicarious liability? Who would be the appropriate individual in a situation such as that presented in *McCollum*?

6. The Proposed Federal Criminal Code (1971) contains the following resolution of the major issues illustrated by the preceding cases.

§ 402. Corporate Criminal Liability

(1) Liability Defined. A corporation may be convicted of:

(a) any offense committed by an agent of the corporation within the scope of his employment on the basis of conduct authorized, requested or commanded, by any of the following or a combination of them:

[(a) any offense committed in furtherance of its affairs on the basis of conduct done, authorized, requested, commanded, ratified or recklessly tolerated in violation of a duty to maintain effective supervision of corporate affairs, by any of the following or a combination of them:]

(i) the board of directors;

(ii) an executive officer or any other agent in a position of comparable authority with respect to the formulation of corporate policy or the supervision in a managerial capacity of subordinate employees;

(iii) any person, whether or not an officer of the corporation, who controls the corporation or is responsibly involved in forming its policy;

(iv) any other person for whose act or omission the statute defining the offense provides corporate responsibility for offenses;

(b) any offense consisting of an omission to discharge a specific duty of affirmative conduct imposed on corporations by law;

(c) any misdemeanor committed by an agent of the corporation within the scope of his employment; or

(d) any offense for which an individual may be convicted without proof of culpability, committed by an agent of the corporation within the scope of his employment.

(2) Defense Precluded. It is no defense that an individual upon whose conduct liability of the corporation for an offense is based has been acquitted, has not been prosecuted or convicted or has been convicted of a different offense, or is immune from prosecution, or is otherwise not subject to justice.

§ 403. Individual Accountability for Conduct on Behalf of Organizations

(1) Conduct on Behalf of Organization. A person is legally accountable for any conduct he performs or causes to be performed in the name of an organization or in its behalf to the same extent as if the conduct were performed in his own name or behalf.

(2) Omission. Except as otherwise expressly provided, whenever a duty to act is imposed upon an organization by a statute or regulation thereunder, any agent of the organization having primary responsibility for the subject matter of the duty is legally accounta-

ble for an omission to perform the required act to the same extent as if the duty were imposed directly upon himself.

(3) Accomplice of Organization. When an individual is convicted of an offense as an accomplice of an organization, he is subject to the sentence authorized when a natural person is convicted of that offense.

(4) Default in Supervision. A person responsible for supervising relevant activities of an organization is guilty of an offense if he manifests his assent to the commission of an offense for which the organization may be convicted by his willful default in supervision within the range of that responsibility which contributes to the occurrence of that offense. Conviction under this subsection shall be of an offense of the same class as the offense for which the organization may be convicted, except that if the latter offense is a felony, conviction under this subsection shall be for a Class A misdemeanor.

§ 409. General Provisions for Chapter 4

(1) Definitions. In this Chapter:

(a) "organization" means any legal entity, whether or not organized as a corporation or unincorporated association, but does not include an entity organized as or by a governmental agency for the execution of a governmental program;

(b) "agent" means any partner, director, officer, servant, employee, or other person authorized to act in behalf of an organization.

(2) Unincorporated Associations. Nothing in this Chapter shall limit or extend the criminal liability of an unincorporated association.

It is interesting to note that the bracketed provision in § 402(1)(a) was the one recommended in the 1970 Study Draft. What do you see as the merits of the alternative formulations? Recognition of the unusual problems involved in devising effective sanctions for organizations was reflected in the Study Draft's section 405 which provided, in part:

(1) Organization. When an organization is convicted of an offense, the court may, in addition to or in lieu of imposing other authorized sanctions, do either or both of the following:

(a) require the organization to give appropriate publicity to the conviction by notice to the class or classes of persons or sector of the public interested in or affected by the conviction, by advertising in designated areas or by designated media, or otherwise;

(b) direct the Attorney General, United States Attorney, or other attorney designated by the court to institute supplementary proceedings in the case in which the organization was convicted of the offense to determine, collect and distribute damages to persons in the class which the statute was designed to protect who suffered injuries by reason of the offense, if the court finds that the multiplicity of small claims or other circumstances make restitution by individual suit impractical.

The Final Report retreats somewhat from this position. It omits (1)(b) because of separate congressional consideration of class actions by consumers, and offers (1)(a) only as a bracketed alternative to the following provision:

§ 3007. Special Sanction for Organizations

When an organization is convicted of an offense, the court may require the organization to give notice of its conviction to the persons or class of persons ostensibly harmed by the offense, by mail or by advertising in designated areas or by designated media or otherwise.

The Report comment explains that a "broader sanction envisioning 'publicity,' rather than 'notice,' was rejected as inappropriate with respect either to organizations or to individuals, despite its possible deterrent effect, since it came too close to the adoption of a policy approving social ridicule as a sanction."

IV. THE INCHOATE CRIMES

The offenses of attempt, solicitation, and conspiracy are all "inchoate" in that they consist of incompleted activity related to other acts, usually criminal acts. Part IV deals with these three offenses and defenses to them. Conspiracy raises a number of special problems, largely because in addition to serving as an inchoate offense conspiracy may (when conviction is sought for conspiracy as well as completed offenses) serve as a means of aggravating the actual or potential punishment for other crimes or may be used to attach liability to one individual for crimes committed by others.

MODEL PENAL CODE COMMENT TO ARTICLE 5, 24–26

(Tent. Draft No. 10, 1960).

Introduction

This Article undertakes to deal systematically with attempt, solicitation and conspiracy to commit crimes, conduct which has in common that it is designed to culminate in the commission of a substantive offense but either has failed to do so in the discrete case or has not yet achieved its culmination because there is something that the actor or another still must do. The offenses are inchoate in this sense.

These, to be sure, are not the only crimes which are so defined that their commission does not rest on proof of the occurrence of the evil that it is the object of the law to prevent; many specific, substantive offenses also have a large inchoate aspect. This is true not only with respect to crimes of risk-creation, such as reckless driving, or specific crimes of preparation, like those of possession with unlawful purpose. It is also true, at least in part, of crimes like larceny, forgery, kidnaping and even arson, not to speak of burglary, where a purpose to cause greater harm than that which is implicit in the actor's conduct is an element of the offense. It may be thought, indeed, that murder is the only crime which by its definition calls for proof that the full evil that the law endeavors to prevent has come to pass. This reservation notwithstanding, attempt, solicitation and conspiracy have such generality of definition and of application as inchoate crimes that it is useful to bring them together in the Code and to confront the common problems they present.

Since these offenses always presuppose a purpose to commit another crime, it is doubtful that the threat of punishment for their commission can significantly add to the deterrent efficacy of the sanction—which the actor by hypothesis ignores—that is threatened for the crime that is his object. There may be cases where this does occur, as when the actor thinks the chance of apprehension low if he succeeds but high if he should fail in his attempt, or when reflection is promoted at an early stage that otherwise would be postponed until too late, which may be true in some conspiracies. These are, however, special situations. Viewed generally, it seems clear that general deterrence is at most a minor function to be served in fashioning provisions of the penal law addressed to these inchoate crimes; that burden is discharged upon the whole by the law dealing with the substantive offenses.

Other and major functions of the penal law remain, however, to be served. They may be summarized as follows:

First: When a person is seriously dedicated to commission of a crime, there is obviously need for a firm legal basis for the intervention of the agencies of law enforcement to prevent its consummation. In determining that basis, there must be attention to the danger of abuse; equivocal behavior may be misconstrued by an unfriendly eye as preparation to commit a crime. It is no less important, on the other side, that lines should not be drawn so rigidly that the police confront insoluble dilemmas in deciding when to intervene, facing the risk that if they wait the crime may be committed while if they act they may not yet have any valid charge.

Second: Conduct designed to cause or culminate in the commission of a crime obviously yields an indication that the actor is disposed towards such activity, not alone on this occasion but on others. There is a need, therefore, subject again to proper safeguards, for a legal basis upon which the special danger that such individuals present may be assessed and dealt with. They must be made amenable to the corrective process that the law provides.

Third: Finally, and quite apart from these considerations of prevention, when the actor's failure to commit the substantive offense is due to a fortuity, as when the bullet misses in attempted murder or when the expected response to solicitation is withheld, his exculpation on that ground would involve inequality of treatment that would shock the common sense of justice. Such a situation is unthinkable in any mature system, designed to serve the proper goals of penal law. See Section 1.02, Tentative Draft No. 4 (1955).

These are the main considerations in the light of which the draft has been prepared. Insofar as they have different weight in the three areas involved, attempt, solicitation and conspiracy, the differences are dealt with in the comments in the settings in which they arise. So, too, the other special values that may be involved in dealing with these different types of conduct—such as the fact that solicitation involves speech and that conspiracy implies group crime—are discussed in the later comments. The bearing of the inchoate character of these offenses on their proper grading for the purposes of sentence also is discussed hereafter in the comment on the grading system here proposed (§ 5.05). It should suffice, therefore, to indicate at this stage what we deem to be the major results of the draft. They are:

(a) to extend the criminality of attempts by sweeping aside the defense of impossibility (including the distinction between so-called factual and legal impossibility) and by drawing the line between attempt and non-criminal preparation further away from the final act; the crime becomes essentially one of criminal purpose implemented by an overt act strongly corroborative of such purpose;

(b) to establish criminal solicitation as a general offense;

(c) to limit the unity and scope of criminal conspiracy by emphasizing the primordial element of individual agreement, while preserving, so far as possible, the procedural advantage of joint prosecution of related segments of an organized criminal enterprise;

(d) to eliminate as objectives which may make conspiracy a crime such vague determinants as "oppression," "public morals," and the like;

(e) to establish in attempt, solicitation and conspiracy a limited defense in cases of renunciation of the criminal objective; and

(f) to establish these inchoate crimes as offenses of comparable magnitude to the completed crimes which are their object.

A. ATTEMPTS

According to Sayre, Criminal Attempts, 41 Harv.L.Rev. 821 (1928), until quite recently there was no generalized doctrine that attempts to commit crime were, in themselves, criminal. Although some few early convictions for unsuccessful efforts to commit especially heinous crimes are reported, these, according to Professor Sayre, were based on an earlier doctrine that the intention is to be taken for the deed (*voluntas reputabitur pro facto*). The danger of imposing liability upon mere intent was too great to permit resort to this maxim often. Professor Sayre dates the modern doctrine of attempts from Rex v. Scofield, Cald. 397 (1784) where it was declared that "[t]he *intent* may make an act, innocent in itself, criminal; nor is the *com-*

pletion of an act, criminal in itself, necessary to constitute criminality." Id. at 400. Many issues vital to the law of attempts seem unsettled and resistant to ready resolution. Perhaps the relative youth of the doctrine explains this; perhaps the difficulties are inherent in efforts to criminalize in the absence of a prohibited result.

Model Penal Code, Comment to § 5.01, 26 (Tent. Draft No. 10, 1960):

1. *The Definition of Attempt.* The literature and decisions dealing with the definition of a criminal attempt reflect ambivalence as to how far the governing criterion should be found in the dangerousness of the actor's conduct, measured by objective standards, and how far in the dangerousness of the actor, as a person manifesting a firm disposition to commit a crime. Both criteria may lead, of course, to the same disposition of a concrete case. When they do not, we think, for reasons stated in the *Introduction,* that the proper focus of attention is the actor's disposition, and the draft is framed with this in mind. Needless to say, we are in full agreement that the law must be concerned with conduct, not with evil thoughts alone. The question is what conduct, when engaged in with a purpose to commit a crime or to advance towards the attainment of a criminal objective, should suffice to constitute a criminal attempt?

In fashioning an answer we must keep in mind that in attempt, as distinct from solicitation and conspiracy, it is not intrinsic to the actor's conduct that he has disclosed his criminal design to someone else; nor is there any natural line that is suggested by the situation—like utterance or agreement. The law must deal with the problem presented by a single individual and must address itself to conduct that may fall anywhere upon a graded scale from early preparation to the final effort to commit the crime.

We think, therefore, that it is useful to begin with any conduct designed to effect or to advance towards the attainment of the criminal objective and to ask when it ought *not* to be regarded as a crime, either because it does not adequately manifest the dangerousness of the actor or on other overriding grounds of social policy. The formulations in this section are intended as responses to this question.

1. THE ACT: BEYOND MERE PREPARATION

MODEL PENAL CODE

(Proposed Official Draft, 1962).

Section 5.01.   Criminal Attempt

(1) *Definition of Attempt.*   A person is guilty of an attempt to commit a crime if, acting with the kind of culpability otherwise required for commission of the crime, he:

(a) purposely engages in conduct which would constitute the crime if the attendant circumstances were as he believes them to be; or

(b) when causing a particular result is an element of the crime, does or omits to do anything with the purpose of causing or with the belief that it will cause such result without further conduct on his part; or

(c) purposely does or omits to do anything which, under the circumstances as he believes them to be, is an act or omission constituting a substantial step in a course of conduct planned to culminate in his commission of the crime.

(2) *Conduct Which May Be Held Substantial Step Under Subsection (1) (c).*   Conduct shall not be held to constitute a substantial step under Subsection (1) (c) of this Section unless it is strongly corroborative of the actor's criminal purpose.   Without negativing the sufficiency of other conduct, the following, if strongly corroborative of the actor's criminal purpose, shall not be held insufficient as a matter of law:

(a) lying in wait, searching for or following the contemplated victim of the crime;

(b) enticing or seeking to entice the contemplated victim of the crime to go to the place contemplated for its commission;

(c) reconnoitering the place contemplated for the commission of the crime;

(d) unlawful entry of a structure, vehicle or enclosure in which it is contemplated that the crime will be committed;

(e) possession of materials to be employed in the commission of the crime, which are specially designed for such unlawful use or which can serve no lawful purpose of the actor under the circumstances;

(f) possession, collection or fabrication of materials to be employed in the commission of the crime, at or near the place contemplated for its commission, where such possession, collection or fabrication serves no lawful purpose of the actor under the circumstances;

(g) soliciting an innocent agent to engage in conduct constituting an element of the crime.

(3) *Conduct Designed to Aid Another in Commission of a Crime.* A person who engages in conduct designed to aid another to commit a crime which would establish his complicity under Section 2.06 if the crime were committed by such other person, is guilty of an attempt to commit the crime, although the crime is not committed or attempted by such other person.

(4) *Renunciation of Criminal Purpose.* When the actor's conduct would otherwise constitute an attempt under Subsection (1) (b) or (1) (c) of this Section, it is an affirmative defense that he abandoned his effort to commit the crime or otherwise prevented its commission, under circumstances manifesting a complete and voluntary renunciation of his criminal purpose. The establishment of such defense does not, however, affect the liability of an accomplice who did not join in such abandonment or prevention.

Within the meaning of this Article, renunciation of criminal purpose is not voluntary if it is motivated, in whole or in part, by circumstances, not present or apparent at the inception of the actor's course of conduct, which increase the probability of detection or apprehension or which make more difficult the accomplishment of the criminal purpose. Renunciation is not complete if it is motivated by a decision to postpone the criminal conduct until a more advantageous time or to transfer the criminal effort to another but similar objective or victim.

Section 5.05. Grading of Criminal Attempt, Solicitation and Conspiracy; Mitigation in Cases of Lesser Danger; Multiple Convictions Barred

(1) *Grading.* Except as otherwise provided in this Section, attempt, solicitation and conspiracy are crimes of the same grade and degree as the most serious offense which is attempted or solicited or is an object of the conspiracy. An attempt, solicitation or conspiracy to commit a [capital crime or a] felony of the first degree is a felony of the second degree.

(2) *Mitigation.* If the particular conduct charged to constitute a criminal attempt, solicitation or conspiracy is so inherently unlikely to result or culminate in the commission of a crime that neither such conduct nor the actor presents a public danger warranting the grading of such offense under this Section, the Court shall exercise its power under Section 6.12 to enter judgment and impose sentence for a crime of lower grade or degree or, in extreme cases, may dismiss the prosecution.

(3) *Multiple Convictions*.   A person may not be convicted of more than one offense defined by this Article for conduct designed to commit or to culminate in the commission of the same crime.

MODEL PENAL CODE, COMMENT TO § 5.01(1), 39–48

(Tent. Draft No. 10, 1960).

The General Distinction between Preparation and Attempt.   Paragraph (c) deals with the most difficult problem in defining attempt liability: the formulation of a general standard for distinguishing acts of preparation from acts constituting the attempt.   If the "last proximate act" is not required in order for there to be an attempt, and if—as is generally assumed—every act done with intent to commit a crime is not to be made criminal, it becomes necessary to establish a means of inclusion and exclusion.   Some of the approaches which have been tried or suggested are as follows:

(a) *The physical proximity doctrine*.   Some courts purport to be guided by principles which state in general terms that the overt act required for an attempt must be proximate to the completed crime, or that the act must be one directly tending toward the completion of the crime, or that the act must amount to the commencement of the consummation.   Such opinions often admit that each case must be decided on its own facts and examine in detail the act's remoteness from the completed crime, emphasizing time, distance and the number of necessary acts as yet undone.   A stringent view of the physical proximity test holds that the actor's conduct does not proceed beyond preparation until the actor has the power—or at least the apparent power—to complete the crime forthwith.   The physical proximity test is not in itself inconsistent with principles of attempt liability: other things being equal, the further the actor progresses toward completion of the offense, the greater is the dangerousness of character manifested and the need for preventative arrest.   But the standard is a vague one and emphasizes only one aspect of the actor's behavior.   The physical proximity test does not provide much guidance in answering the crucial problem of how close is close enough for attempt liability.

(b) *The dangerous proximity doctrine*.   A test which incorporates the physical proximity approach within it, but which proceeds beyond it, is the doctrine given impetus by the writings and opinions of Mr. Justice Holmes.   In order to determine whether a given act constitutes an attempt the following factors are considered: the gravity of the offense intended, the nearness of the act to completion of the crime, and the probability that the conduct will result in the offense intended.   The greater the gravity and probability, and the nearer the act to the crime, the stronger is the case for calling the act an attempt.   The test is based on the assumption that the purpose of punishing attempts is to deter undesirable behavior and that until the actor's conduct becomes sufficiently dangerous there is not adequate reason for deterring it. The assumption, as it relates to the law of attempts, is not, in our view, the right foundation for the liability. The primary purpose of punishing attempts is to neutralize dangerous individuals and not to deter dangerous acts. Since the dangerousness of the actor's conduct has some relation to the dangerousness of the actor's personality, and to the need for preventative arrest, the test is not entirely irrelevant. But the basic orientation of the dangerous proximity doctrine is so at odds with the principles of attempt liability on which the draft is based that we cannot embrace it as a working *rationale*. The shortcomings of the physical proximity test are also applicable.

(c) *The indispensable element approach.* One variation of the several proximity tests emphasizes any indispensable aspect of the criminal endeavor over which the actor has not yet acquired control. Some decisions seem to stand for the proposition that, if the successful completion of a crime requires the assent or action of some third person, that assent or action must be forthcoming before the actor can be guilty of an attempt. Thus if *A* and *B* plan to defraud a life insurance company by pretending that *A*, the insured, is dead, and if *C*, the beneficiary, must file a formal claim before any proceeds can be paid, it has been held that the acts of *A* and *B* cannot amount to an attempt to defraud the insurance company until *C* files a claim or agrees to file a claim. And one court has held that giving counterfeit matter to another, in order that he may "pass" it, does not constitute an attempt to "pass" on the giver's part until the other makes an effort to pass the counterfeit matter to an innocent third party. If the actor seeks to influence a juror by asking a third party to approach the juror, the cases split on whether the actor has attempted to corrupt a juror. The reasoning of the courts which refuse to find an attempt here because of the need for the third party's cooperation is similar to that applied in cases which hold that solicitation does not constitute an attempt because completion of the crime requires action by the party solicited.

An analogous group of cases supports the view that a person cannot be guilty of an attempt if he lacks a means essential to completion of the offense. Thus it has been held that one cannot be guilty of an attempt to introduce whiskey into a forbidden territory until he acquires the whiskey; that a person cannot attempt an assault with a dangerous weapon until he acquires the weapon; that one cannot attempt to illegally manufacture whiskey until he acquires the necessary apparatus; and that one cannot attempt to vote illegally until he obtains a ballot.

This approach is subject to the same general objections as the proximity tests of which it is a variation.

(d) *The probable desistance test.* Oriented largely toward the dangerousness of the actor's conduct but giving slightly more emphasis to the actor's personality is the rule which provides that the actor's conduct constitutes an attempt if, in the ordinary and natural course of events, without interruption from an outside source, it will result in the crime intended. Apart from any question as to the suitability of the means employed for achieving the criminal end contemplated (considered in connection with "impossibility")¦, this test seems to require, in order for there to be an attempt, a judgment in each case that the actor had reached a point where it was unlikely that he would have voluntarily desisted from his efforts to commit the crime. But in cases applying this test no inquiry is made into the personality of the particular offender before the court. The question is whether *anyone* who went so far would stop short of the final step.

The recently enacted Wisconsin Criminal Code adopts a variation of the probable desistance test in classifying as an attempt "acts toward the commission of the crime which demonstrate unequivocally, under all the circumstances, that [the actor formed an intent to commit the crime] and would commit the crime except for the intervention of another person or some other extraneous factor."

Accepting for the time being the underlying assumption that probability of desistance (or actual abandonment of the criminal endeavor) sufficiently negatives dangerousness as to warrant immunity from attempt liability, still this test does not appear to provide a workable standard. Is there a sufficient empirical basis for making predictions in various types of cases as to whether desistance is probable at various points along the way? The opinion has been voiced that one who undertakes a criminal endeavor and performs an act pursuant to that purpose is not likely to stop short of the final step. And in actual operation the probable desistance test is linked entirely to the nearness of the actor's conduct to completion, this being the sole basis of unsubstantiated judicial appraisals of the probabilities of desistance. The test as applied appears to be little more than the physical proximity approach.

(e) *The abnormal step approach.* One commentator, recognizing the role of attempts in revealing dangerous personalities, defines an attempt as a step toward crime which goes beyond the point where the normal citizen would think better of his conduct and desist. Despite its proper orientation, this approach has several serious deficiencies. First, with respect to some crimes—and probably with respect to most crimes—any step toward the crime is a departure from the conduct of the normal citizen. Thus as to these crimes the approach would effect a major revolution in attempt liability—making it an attempt to do any act for the purpose of committing such crimes. Second, there may be some offenses where the normal citizen does not stop at all. To tie attempt liability to the normal citizen in this

case is to raise the whole problem of unpopular laws and their enforcement. It seems untenable that normalcy in violation or near-
violation should constitute a defense to an attempt charge. Finally,
who is to judge where the normal citizen will stop and what kind of
proof will be appropriate for such a determination? The test is
oriented toward singling out dangerous personalities but it is virtually
impossible of application.

(f) *The res ipsa loquitur test.* Taking an entirely different approach to the preparation-attempt problem is the view which holds
that an attempt is committed when the actor's conduct manifests an
intent to commit a crime. The conduct would be considered in relation to all the surrounding circumstances exclusive of representations made by the actor about his intentions; but presumably representations of the actor which negative a criminal intent would be
admissible to disprove the intention imputed. The object of this
approach is to subject to attempt liability conduct which unequivocally
demonstrates that the actor is being guided by a criminal purpose.
There are two lines of thought upon which this view can be sustained.

The first goes to the problem of proof. Assuming that any act
done for the purpose of committing a crime is an act which demonstrates dangerousness, why not make all such acts attempts? One
answer is that such a law would allow prosecutions for acts which are
externally equivocal and would create a risk that innocent persons
would be convicted. It is assumed that the conduct involved is non-
causal, so at the outset there is the opportunity to charge a crime
where nothing is amiss. There is no corpus delicti to verify the fact
that somebody has caused some sort of trouble. Moreover, there is
a further difference between the conduct involved in an attempt case
and the conduct questioned in a case involving the completed crime.
In the latter the last proximate act must be proved. For an attempt
conviction this is not necessary; if immunity for preparation is eliminated almost any act would do. Thus, with respect to any substantive
crime, the chances are that more steps will have to be proved if the
completed crime is involved than if it is the attempt which is charged.
Finally, there is the problem, if preliminary acts toward the crime are
externally equivocal, of establishing the necessary purpose. Recourse
must be had to statements made by the actor before, during, and after
the acts in question. The first two kinds of statements are not reliable
because the actor may have been bluffing or he may have entertained
an idea or inclination without really acting upon it, the act in question
being motivated by a noncriminal purpose. Statements made after the
act, usually in the form of a confession, are not always considered
reliable.

The *res ipsa* rule on preparation-attempt may be viewed entirely
as a matter of procedure, as a device to prevent liability based solely
on confessions and other representations of purpose because of the

risks they raise when considered with the other probative weaknesses incident to attempt liability. And whether the requirement of unequivocality is considered part of the substantive definition of attempt or as a separate rule of evidence, it can be realistically administered only by means of a procedural mechanism—*i.e.*, by excluding from the jury, in whole or in part, the actor's incriminating representations of purpose. If it is problems of proof which are the basis of the preparation-attempt distinction, then the *res ipsa* approach has considerable merit.

There is considerable support in the cases for the proposition that the preparation-attempt distinction is the result of difficulty in proving purpose. There are cases which make explicit reference to the necessity for unequivocal behavior. And it has been said, with some frequency, that the overt act must manifest the intent to commit the crime. Moreover, many courts which adopt a stringent view as to what constitutes an attempt reveal their actual motivation by openly expressing concern over the inadequate proof of criminal intent.

A second point of departure in considering the *res ipsa* test is its relation to the manifested dangerousness of the actor. If an act unequivocally demonstrates a criminal purpose, does this show something more about the dangerousness of the actor's personality than an act done with a criminal purpose which must be established "independently"? The assumption underlying an affirmative answer is that there is some relationship between the actor's state of mind and the external appearance of his acts. While the actor's behavior is externally equivocal the criminal purpose in his mind is likely to be unfixed—a subjective equivocality. But once the actor must desist or perform acts which he realizes would incriminate him if all external facts were known, then in all probability a firmer state of mind exists. Subjective equivocality seems inconsistent with an act which unequivocally demonstrates a criminal purpose. A hunter might buy extra supplies to facilitate an escape in the event he resolves to kill his companion, a question as yet unsettled in his mind. But when he buys poison which has no reasonable use under the circumstances other than the murder of his companion, the chances are that the debate has been resolved and the actor's purpose is fixed on murder.

The basis for our rejection of the *res ipsa* or unequivocality test can best be explained in connection with a consideration of the test proposed in the instant paragraph.

(g) *Substantiality and corroboration.* In addition to criminal purpose, the proposed paragraph, together with Subsection 5.01(2), sets forth two requirements which distinguish attempt from preparation: (1) the act must be "a *substantial* step in a course of conduct" planned to accomplish the criminal result, and (2) the act must be "strongly corroborative" of criminal purpose in order for it to constitute such a "substantial step."

Whether a particular act is a substantial step is obviously a matter of degree. To this extent the present paragraph retains the element of imprecision found in most of the other approaches to the preparation-attempt problem. There are, however, several differences to be noted:

First, this formulation shifts the emphasis from what remains to be done—the chief concern of the proximity tests—to what the actor *has already done*. The fact that further major steps must be taken before the crime can be completed does not preclude a finding that the steps already undertaken are substantial. It is expected, in the normal case, that this approach will broaden the scope of attempt liability.

Second, although it is intended that the requirement of a substantial step will result in the imposition of attempt liability only in those instances in which some firmness of criminal purpose is shown, no finding is required as to whether the actor would probably have desisted prior to completing the crime. Potentially the probable desistance test could reach very early steps toward crime—depending upon how one assesses the probabilities of desistance—but since in practice this test follows closely the proximity approaches, rejection of probable desistance will not narrow the scope of attempt liability.

Finally, the requirement of proving a substantial step generally will prove less of a hurdle for the prosecution than the *res ipsa loquitur* approach, which requires that the actor's conduct must itself manifest the criminal purpose. The difference will be illustrated in connection with the present section's requirement of corroboration. Here it should be noted that, in the present formulation, the two purposes to be served by the *res ipsa loquitur* test are, to a large extent, treated separately. Firmness of criminal purpose is intended to be shown by requiring a substantial step, while problems of proof are dealt with by the requirement of corroboration (although, under the reasoning previously expressed, the latter will also tend to establish firmness of purpose).

In addition to assuring firmness of purpose, the requirement of a substantial step will remove very remote preparatory acts from the ambit of attempt liability and the relatively stringent sanctions imposed for attempts. On the other hand, by broadening liability to the extent suggested, apprehension of dangerous persons will be facilitated and law enforcement officials and others will be able to stop the criminal effort at an earlier stage—thereby minimizing the risk of substantive harm—without providing immunity for the offender.

PROPOSED FEDERAL CRIMINAL CODE (1971)

§ 1001.   Criminal Attempt

(1) Offense.   A person is guilty of criminal attempt if, acting with the kind of culpability otherwise required for commission of a crime, he intentionally engages in conduct which, in fact, constitutes a substantial step toward commission of the crime.   A substantial step is any conduct which is strongly corroborative of the firmness of the actor's intent to complete the commission of the crime. Factual or legal impossibility of committing the crime is not a defense if the crime could have been committed had the attendant circumstances been as the actor believed them to be.

(2) Complicity.   A person who engages in conduct intending to aid another to commit a crime is guilty of criminal attempt if the conduct would establish his complicity under section 401 were the crime committed by the other person, even if the other is not guilty of committing or attempting the crime, for example, because he has a defense of justification or entrapment.

(3) Grading.   Criminal attempt is an offense of the same class as the offense attempted, except that (a) an attempt to commit a Class A felony shall be a Class B felony, and (b) whenever it is established by a preponderance of the evidence at sentencing that the conduct constituting the attempt did not come dangerously close to commission of the crime, an attempt to commit a Class B felony shall be a Class C felony and an attempt to commit a Class C felony shall be a Class A misdemeanor.

UNITED STATES v. COPLON

United States Court of Appeals for the Second Circuit, 1950.
158 F.2d 629, certiorari denied 342 U.S. 920, 72 S.Ct. 362, 96 L.Ed. 688.

L. HAND, Chief Judge.   *   *   *   A neat doctrine by which to test when a person, intending to commit a crime which he fails to carry out, has "attempted" to commit it, would be that he has done all that it is within his power to do, but has been prevented by intervention from outside; in short, that he has passed beyond any *locus poenitentiae*.   Apparently that was the original notion, and may still be law in England; but it is certainly not now generally the law in the United States, for there are many decisions which hold that the accused has passed beyond "preparation," although he has been interrupted before he has taken the last of his intended steps. The decisions are too numerous to cite, and would not help much anyway, for there is, and obviously can be, no definite line; but Judge

Cullen's discussion in People v. Sullivan,[1] and Mr. Justice Holmes' in two Massachusetts decisions,[2] are particularly enlightening. In the second of the Massachusetts opinions Holmes, J., said: "Preparation is not an attempt. But some preparations may amount to an attempt. It is a question of degree. If the preparation comes very near to the accomplishment of the act, the intent to complete it renders the crime so probable that the act will be a misdemeanor, although there is still a locus poenitentiae, in the need of a further exertion of the will to complete the crime." We have found scarcely any decisions of federal courts, but, so far as they go, they are in accord.

* * *

PEOPLE v. BOWEN

Court of Appeals of Michigan, 1968.
10 Mich.App. 1, 158 N.W.2d 794.

LEVIN, Judge. Defendants, Sherrel Bowen and William Rouse, appeal their convictions of attempted larceny in a building.

On January 19, 1965, at approximately eight o'clock p. m., the defendants and two female companions were admitted to the home of one Matilda Gatzmeyer, an 80 year old woman. The defendants' car was observed parked in front of Miss Gatzmeyer's residence and a neighbor, believing the defendants to have designs upon her property, called the police. Two police officers arrived and entered the home along with the neighbor. The defendants were found in the rear of the house near or on the basement steps. The two female companions were seated on either side of Miss Gatzmeyer, apparently engaged with her in conversation. The bedroom of the house was in a state of disarray.

* * *

Bowen had been to the Gatzmeyer home on a number of prior occasions, ostensibly as a handy man, the same reason he gave Miss Gatzmeyer for appearing on the night in question. Miss Gatzmeyer testified that on this occasion the defendants sought to hire themselves out to clean and to do some masonry work on the chimney. She complained about the high prices charged by Bowen and his failure to do work as agreed, and that Bowen's helper (the role allegedly filled by Rouse at the time of the incident) generally helped himself to things that belonged to her.

The neighbor testified that she had met Bowen on three occasions prior to the one in question and that on one occasion Bowen had induced Miss Gatzmeyer to go with him to the bank, but it was

1. 173 N.Y. 122, 133–136, 65 N.E. 989, 63 L.R.A. 353.

2. Commonwealth v. Kennedy, 170 Mass. 18, 20, 22, 48 N.E. 770; Commonwealth v. Peaslee, 177 Mass. 267, 272, 59 N.E. 55, 56.

not clear whether the visit to the bank was to withdraw money to pay Bowen that which was due him or unlawfully to separate Miss Gatzmeyer from her money.

The neighbor testified that she visited with Miss Gatzmeyer daily and assisted her in various chores and generally in getting around. She stated that when she and the police officers arrived on the night in question the dresser drawers in the bedroom were all pulled out and everything thrown all over the bed. This was not the way Miss Gatzmeyer generally kept the house according to the neighbor: "she has a very neat house, everything is in its place."

* * *

At the beginning of his charge to the jury, the trial judge stated that because he doubted whether the case properly could be submitted to the jury on the original charge of larceny in a building he had decided to submit it to the jury solely on the included offense of attempt to commit larceny in a building.

There was sufficient evidence to support the defendants' conviction of attempt to commit larceny. * * *

We do find error in the judge's failure properly to charge the jury on the necessity of finding an overt act. It has been said that the overt act "is the essence of the offense" or the "gravamen of the offense." Not only did the trial judge fail to charge the jury at all concerning the necessity of finding an overt act, but he also incorrectly charged that the jury could convict if it found that the defendants came to or entered Miss Gatzmeyer's house with the intention of committing larceny.

* * *

There was ample evidence from which the jury could have found felonious intent. * * *

In the absence of a request * * * the trial judge's failure to charge the jury on the necessity of finding commission of an overt act, as a separate ingredient or element, might not be error if he were correct in charging the jury that if it found defendants "came" to or "entered" Miss Gatzmeyer's house with intent to commit larceny it could bring in a verdict of guilty. If defendants' coming to, or entering, Miss Gatzmeyer's house with felonious intent was an "overt act", the jury verdict of guilty could be viewed as a finding of the requisite overt act.

Thus, the narrow question before us is whether the defendants when they came to or entered Miss Gatzmeyer's house with the intent to commit larceny committed an overt act that would support their conviction of attempted larceny. In our opinion, their mere coming to or entry of Miss Gatzmeyer's house was not an overt act, under the circumstances that Mr. Bowen and other helpers had rightfully been in the house on prior occasions and were admitted to the house by Miss Gatzmeyer on the night in question.

* * *

In People v. Coleman [350 Mich. 268, 86 N.W.2d 281 (1957)] the Supreme Court stated that a defendant may not be convicted of an attempt unless he has "gone beyond acts of an ambiguous nature" or those that are "equivocal",[7] and that a "thoughtful test for the resolution of the equivocal act has been phrased by Turner in his article, 'Attempts to Commit Crimes' in 5 Camb.LJ, 230, 237 [238,] in these words:

'If the acts of the accused, taken by themselves, are unambiguous, and cannot in reason, be regarded as pointing to any other end than the commission of the specific crime in question, then they constitute a sufficient *actus reus*. In other words, his acts must be *unequivocally referable* to the commission of the specific crime. They must, as the late Sir John Salmond said, 'speak for themselves.' If the example may be permitted, it is as though a cinematograph film, which has so far depicted merely the accused person's acts without stating what was his intention, had been suddenly stopped, and the audience were asked to say to what end those acts were directed. If there is only one reasonable answer to this question then the accused has done what amounts to an 'attempt' to attain that end. If there is more than one reasonably possible answer, then the accused has not yet done enough.' " (350 Mich. p. 278, 86 N.W.2d p. 286)

* * *

It has been suggested that the basic function of the overt act is corroboration of the felonious intent.[9] However, that analysis can

7. Accord: State v. Mandel (1954), 78 Ariz. 226, 278 P.2d 413; People v. Miller (1935), 2 Cal.2d 527, 42 P.2d 308, 98 A.L.R. 913; "* * * so long as the equivocal quality remains, no one can say with certainty what the intent of the defendant is"; Groves v. State (1902), 116 Ga. 516, 42 S.E. 755, 59 L.R.A. 598: "In general, the act must be inexplicable as a lawful act, and must be more than mere preparation."

Other courts have said much the same thing in describing the overt act as one that can have "no other purpose" or "apparent result" than the commisson of the principal crime—the "natural and probable" effect test is of the same genre; and then there are the judicial and text statements which speak of the overt act as an act that "commences" or has a "direct tendency"

or "sufficient proximity" or "sufficient nearness" to the commission of the principal offense that (some add, having in mind the seriousness and enormity of the principal offense), in the opinion of the court, the actor's purpose is clear. See Keedy, Criminal Attempts At Common Law (1954) 102 Univ. of Penn LR 464, 474. Whether the differences in language used by the courts bring about different results or merely permit the courts that speak in terms of proximity or nearness or the like to explain their results with greater ease is beyond the scope of this opinion. On the question before us, we found substantial uniformity in results, if not in their explanation.

9. "The basic function of the 'act requirement' in the area of attempts is to corroborate clearly the presence of *mens rea* by indicating the earnest-

become somewhat circular if we permit intent to be gleaned from the overt act itself.

The testimony in this case was that defendant Bowen had, on a number of prior occasions, been in Miss Gatzmeyer's house with helpers. With that in mind and even if it be assumed (on the basis of the jury finding) that the defendants entered her house with a felonious intent, their mere presence there did not indicate, let alone "corroborate", that intention. The defendants did not break into Miss Gatzmeyer's house—they were voluntarily admitted by her. At the time of defendants' admission to Miss Gatzmeyer's house their *acts* were entirely "ambiguous" and "equivocal".

Our analysis of the authorities convinces us that the function of the overt act is not to "corroborate", but rather to demonstrate that the defendant has converted resolution into action. Man being what he is, evil thoughts and intentions are easily formed. Fortunately, for society, most felonious thoughts are not fulfilled. The law does not punish evil intent or even every act done with the intent to commit a crime. The requirement that the jury find an overt act proceeds on the assumption that the devil may lose the contest, albeit late in the hour.

The overt act is not any act. In this connection "overt" is used in the sense of "manifest" or symbolic. The act must manifest, or be symbolic of, the crime. Considering that Bowen and helpers had been in Miss Gatzmeyer's house on previous occasions (and, whatever her differences with Bowen may have been, she nevertheless again admitted him on the night in question), the fact that the defendants came to and entered Miss Gatzmeyer's house would not manifest or symbolize the crime of which they were convicted of attempting to commit. * * *

Where entry or attempted entry upon the victim's premises has been held, in itself, sufficient to constitute an overt act, such entry or attempted entry has been without permission, or the defendant came armed or with burglary tools or other means of committing the crime.

ness of the actor's intent to commit the offense involved [see Model Penal Code Commentary, Tentative Draft No. 10, pp. 39–73]." From the proposed Michigan Revised Criminal Code-Final Draft, September, 1967, p. 83. The chief reporter and special consultants on the model penal code collaborated on a comprehensive article which reviews both the common law and the proposed code. Wechsler, The Treatment of Inchoate Crimes in the Model Penal Code of the American Law Institute: Attempt, Solicitation and Conspiracy, Part 1 (1961) 61 Col LR 571.

DAVEY v. LEE

Queens Bench Division, 1967.
[1968] 1 Q.B. 366.

The defendants, Michael John Davey, Michael John Rigler and Robert Rigler, appealed to Devon Quarter Sessions from their conviction on March 2, 1966, by Woodbury justices sitting at Exmouth, on a charge that they at Sowton on February 10, 1966, jointly attempted to steal a quantity of metal, the property of the South Western Electricity Board.

Quarter sessions heard the appeals on April 15 and 18, 1966, and found the following facts: (a) At about 6.30 p. m. on February 10, 1966, Motor Patrol Constable Jane went to the east side of the South Western Electricity Board's compound at Sowton. When the officer was about 100 yards from the compound he heard, coming from the vicinity of the perimeter of the compound, a snipping sound and when he was about 75 yards from the compound he heard a scrambling sound. The officer saw two men by the edge of the perimeter fence of the compound; the officer shone his torch and was able to identify one of the two men as being the defendant Michael John Rigler; the officer was unable to identify the second man. (b) At about 6.50 p. m. on the same day Wilfred Seldon saw a motor van, registered number 21 NYA, parked without lights on a piece of private ground about half-a-mile from the compound. Shortly afterwards he saw the van driven off and it travelled 30 or 40 yards before its lights were switched on. He saw two men, one of whom was driving the van and the other running alongside the van at the passenger's door. (c) At about 9.55 p. m. on the same day the same motor van was stopped by Motor Patrol Constable Manley at Barnstaple Cross, which was approximately 14 miles from the place at which Mr. Seldon had seen the van. The defendants were in the motor van, which was being driven by the defendant Robert Rigler. In the pockets of the driver's door was found a pair of wire-cutters. (d) When the wire-cutters were found, the defendant Robert Rigler said, "They are wire-cutters, we've been pigeon-shooting." When asked to go to Crediton police station, Robert Rigler said, "Yes, its better to get it cleared up now." (e) The motor van moved off and after it had travelled eight to ten yards something was thrown from the van. On the following day police officers found a pair of bolt-croppers in a hedge near Barnstaple Cross at about the place at which something had been thrown from the van on the previous night. The bolt-croppers were produced to and inspected by the justices. (f) On February 11, 1966, at Exmouth police station all the defendants gave as an explanation that they had been pigeon-shooting on the evening of February 10, 1966. (g) An album of photographs with a descriptive index was proved in evidence. (h) The eastern end of the South Western Electricity Board compound at

Sowton was the copper store; at that point the compound was en-closed by an outer single-strand wire fence and a number of cypress trees, a fence consisting of six strands of heavy barbed wire, a fence consisting of four strands of insulated wire and finally a chain-link fence. (i) On February 11, 1966, when Detective Constable Medland inspected the fences, the outer single-strand wire fence had been cut, the barbed-wire and insulated-wire fences had been cut, and the chain-link fence had been cut to within a height of two feet from its top. (j) It was proved by forensic evidence which was accepted that all four types of wire could have been cut by the bolt-croppers and that only the insulated wire could have been cut by the wire-cutters. (k) The compound contained drums of copper, other stores, an office building and dwelling-houses. One member of the court knew that the bolt-croppers were fit to be used for the purpose of cutting into manageable lengths the copper on the drums.

The defendants did not give evidence.

Quarter sessions were satisfied by the evidence that the defend-ants intended to break and enter the compound and to steal therein in the vicinity of the place where the fences had been attacked such copper as was removable, with or without the use of bolt-croppers, but that they were interrupted by Motor Patrol Constable Jane when they had very nearly completed the last of the steps necessary to break into the compound for the purpose of carrying out their in-tention.

It was contended by the defendants that there was insufficient evi-dence to justify convictions on the information for the following reasons: (a) that the act of cutting through the fences was insuffi-ciently proximate to the offence of stealing metal to constitute an attempt; and (b) that as the compound contained other stores, an office building and dwelling-houses as well as the copper store, the act of cutting through the fences, even if it was rightly found to be an attempt to commit some other offence, could not be held beyond reasonable doubt to be an attempt to commit the offence charged as opposed to an attempt to commit some other offence.

It was contended by the prosecutor that the defendants were rightly convicted, as the act of cutting through the fences being one in which it was open to quarter sessions to find that they had been interrupted could amount to an attempt and that as the fences cut were near the copper store it was open to them to find that the defendants had attempted to steal metal. Quarter sessions were of the opinion that the act of cutting the fences was immediately con-nected with the larceny of metal and dismissed the appeals.

The defendants appealed.

A. *Whitfield* for the defendants. The authorities show that when a defendant is charged with an attempt, he is not convicted unless he is found to have perpetrated some action connected with the offence charged.

In Carey v. Martin there was no evidence that the defendant ever did anything towards committing the larceny which was charged, so on appeal his conviction for attempted larceny was quashed. The test set out in Reg. v. Eagleton is, if there is anything to be done further by the defendant before the crime is complete, then no charge of attempt will lie.

In Reg. v. Roberts however, a wider test was used, namely whether the act done was directly approximate to the commission of an offence. But later authorities rely on the test in Reg. v. Eagleton.

Thus, in Rex v. Robinson, where a jeweller pretended to be robbed, but confessed before he made a claim, it was held, applying Reg. v. Eagleton, that to be convicted of attempted fraud, the jeweller would have had to have made a claim. So in this case the defendants would, at least, have had to handle copper, whereas in fact they did not touch it. Although there may have been a proposed scheme, the merely preparatory acts had not ceased and the defendants had not yet unequivocally associated themselves with the copper, the object of the attempted larceny here charged.

* * *

The cutting of the wire cannot be connected with the copper in any way; it may have been a preparatory act, but was not sufficiently proximate to the offence to stand as an attempt.

* * *

LORD PARKER, C. J. * * * [I]t seems to me abundantly clear when one looks at the photographs proved in evidence that, granted an intention to break in and steal, it was clearly an intention to steal metal. The real point taken by Mr. Whitfield is that of course an intention to steal is not sufficient to constitute an attempt, but there must be acts which have moved further than being merely preparatory acts. What amounts to an attempt has been described variously in the authorities, and for my part I prefer to adopt the definition given in Stephen's Digest of the Criminal Law, 5th ed. (1894), art. 50, where it says that:

> "An attempt to commit a crime is an act done with intent to commit that crime, and forming part of a series of acts which would constitute its actual commission if it were not interrupted."

As a general statement that seems to me to be right, although it does not help to define the point of time at which the series of acts begins. That, as Stephen said, depends upon the facts of each case.

A helpful definition is given in paragraph 4104 in the current (36th) edition (1966) of Archbold's Criminal Pleading, Evidence and Practice, where it is stated in this form:

> "It is submitted that the actus reus necessary to constitute an attempt is complete if the prisoner does an act which is a step towards the commission of the specific crime, which is immediately and not merely remotely connected with the commission of it, and the doing of which cannot reasonably be regarded as having any other purpose than the commission of the specific crime."

It seems to me that the facts of this case fully come within that test, and that quarter sessions were undoubtedly right in the view they formed. I would dismiss this appeal.

DIPLOCK, L. J. I agree. There are some branches of the criminal law in which it is permitted for justices and juries to use their common sense. I am glad to find that I am not constrained by the authorities to say that the law of attempt is excluded from those branches. I accept the definition which my Lord has taken from the current edition of Archbold as a correct definition of the test to be applied, and the facts of this case fall amply within that definition.

ASHWORTH, J. I agree.

Appeal dismissed.

NOTE

Both the *Bowen* and *Davey* courts voice approval of what has been called the *res ipsa loquitur* test for identifying a sufficient actus reus to constitute an attempt. What advantages do you believe this test offers, and to whom? Did Lord Parker properly apply the test in *Davey*? Can cutting the fence be reasonably regarded as having no other purpose than the theft of "a quantity of metal"? If, as is suggested in the Turner article quoted in *Bowen*, we are to evaluate the defendant's acts as though we were watching them recorded on film what would be the appropriate result where the film shows the defendant trying a key in the door of another's car and is charged with attempting to take and drive away a car without consent? Jones v. Brooks, [1968] Crim.L.Rev. 498 (Q.B.). Assume the film shows a woman alone in a laundromat, her purse on a chair near her. The defendant enters with a knife, says something to her, they struggle, he stabs her, she flees and he disappears. There is no movement by the defendant towards the purse but he is charged with attempted robbery. State v. Thompson, 414 S.W.2d 261 (Mo.Sup.1967). If the act, without more, should unequivocally demonstrate the intent should not the film be silent? What if Thompson had said to the woman "this is a robbery"? What if Brooks had confessed that his intention was to steal the car? In *Brooks* the lower court, in accord with the *Davey* opinion, had dismissed the charge and the prosecution appealed. The High Court, Lord Parker presiding, allowed the appeal, holding that where the acts are equivocal the defendant's expressed intention should be taken into account and here the defendants should be convicted. In *Thompson* the court simply took defendant at his word: "We do no violence to logic when we attribute to defendant's actions and words exactly the meaning and character with which defendant himself described them at the moment they were performed". 414 S.W.2d at 264.

DUPUY v. STATE

Supreme Court of Tennessee, 1959.
204 Tenn. 624, 325 S.W.2d 238.

PREWITT, Justice. The defendant below, James Russell Dupuy, was convicted under an indictment charging him with attempt to procure a miscarriage on a young woman named June Harris. This appeal in error resulted.

* * *

The facts appearing in the record are that the defendant, Dupuy, was a druggist and pharmacist in the City of Memphis, and his business establishment was located on Linden Circle.

It seems that Dupuy had a good reputation as an individual and as a pharmacist.

The police of Memphis suspected him of violating the law as to abortion and that they anonymously heard that he was producing miscarriages.

In furtherance of the plan of the police to apprehend the defendant they selected a young woman to get in the confidence of the defendant and set up a situation to find him guilty of violating the law.

This young woman, June Harris, was selected by the officers but she was not pregnant at the time. It seems that this young woman went into the place of business of the defendant two or three times, and finally solicited his help; that the defendant finally agreed to come to her assistance and that they went to a room taking along various instruments owned by the defendant. When they got into the room the officers, who were waiting close by, came upon the defendant and arrested him.

It appears that the defendant had all of his instruments ready on the table and that the woman left the room before any attempt was made to touch her body, or it seems that the defendant never got within five feet of her. About this time the officers came upon the scene and arrested the defendant.

* * *

It appears that in this case this young woman never allowed the man to touch her either with his hands or his instruments. While his conduct is very reprehensible and he would no doubt have carried out this attempt had he not been thwarted in his efforts by the arrival of the police.

It has been suggested that since the female here was not in fact pregnant that the commission of the attempt was impossible.

The State relies upon the case of Rafferty v. State, 91 Tenn. 655, 659, 16 S.W. 728, 729, in which the Court said:

> "Hayes v. State [15 Lea 64] was approved and followed in the late case of Clark v. State, 86 Tenn. 511, 8 S.W. 145, wherein it was decided that one who feloniously opened the cash-drawer of another, believing it to contain money or other valuables, and intending to steal the same, was guilty of an attempt to commit larceny, and punishable as for a felony, though the drawer proved to be entirely empty."

The holding in the above case is a complete answer to this proposition. The intent was there and the overt act was there.

We have no such case here. While the defendant had completed his plan to do this crime the element of attempt does not appear in this record. The proof shows that he did not use any of the instruments and did not touch the body of the girl in question. Under such facts we do not think that the defendant is guilty under the statute.

We seem to have no Tennessee case directly in point. We quote the following from 14 Am.Jur. Sec. 68, page 816:

> "In a general way, however, it may be said that preparation consists in devising or arranging the means or measures necessary for the commission of the offense and that the attempt is the direct movement toward the commission after the preparations are made. Even though a person actually intends to commit a crime, his procurement of the instrumentalities adapted to that end will not constitute an attempt to commit the crime in the absence of some overt act."

For example the procurement by a prisoner of tools adapted to breaking jail does not render him guilty of an attempt to break jail.

* * *

It follows that we find a full preparation to do the act with the criminal intent but the overt act is wholly lacking.

It results that the judgment of the conviction must be reversed and remanded.[a]

---

a. Compare People v. Berger, 131 Cal. App.2d 127, 280 P.2d 136 (Dist.Ct.App. 1955) where the facts appear to be identical to those in *Dupuy* except that the accused's accomplice who was to perform the abortion admitted that this was her intention upon her arrest. The court held that while the sterilization of instruments might be too equivocal an act to constitute an attempt, when the intent with which the act was performed was established it became sufficient to support a conviction for an attempt to commit an abortion.

NOTE

Is the lesson of *Dupuy* that police officers should wait until the last possible moment before making the arrest? Would that be the insertion of an instrument? Is such forbearance a desirable guideline for law enforcement? Would it be preferable to criminalize conduct preparatory to crime, and, if so, how could this be done?

In the recent past vagrancy statutes would commonly be employed to justify the arrest and punishment of persons apprehended in circumstances in which a conviction for "attempt" would be difficult to obtain: if, for example, the defendants in *Davey* had been arrested at the fence but before a single wire had been cut. In Papachristou v. Jacksonville, reprinted at page 192, Mr. Justice Douglas acknowledged the usefulness of such statutes to the police and, in footnote 15, offered the following table as evidence of the frequency with which they were invoked.

The table below contains nationwide data on arrests for "vagrancy" and for "suspicion" in the three-year period 1968–1970.

Year*	Vagrancy		Suspicion		Combined Offenses	
	Total rptd. arrests	Rate per 100,000	Total rptd. arrests	Rate per 100,000	Total rptd. arrests	Rate per 100,000
1968	99,147	68.2	89,986	61.9	189,133	130.1
1969	106,269	73.9	88,265	61.4	194,534	135.3
1970	101,093	66.1	70,173	46.3	171,266	113.0
3 year averages	102,170	69.6	82,808	56.5	184,978	126.1

*Reporting agencies represent population of: 1968—145,306,000; 1969—143,815,000; 1970—151,604,000.

Source: FBI Annual Crime Reports, 1968–1970.

Despite, or perhaps because of, heavy police reliance on such statutes, the city ordinance challenged in *Papachristou* was unanimously held void for vagueness in language which sounds a death knell for all similar statutory provisions.

If traditional vagrancy statutes are not to be available to police efforts to "nip crime in the bud," should laws making it criminal to possess tools commonly employed in, or capable of being used for, burglary be enacted? Given the commonplace nature of many instruments which can be and are employed in burglaries such a statute would, to withstand challenge, have to contain some further element of criminality. One that is commonly employed is that they be possessed with intent to commit burglary but that possession is to be deemed presumptive evidence of such intent. E. g., Iowa Code Ann. § 708.7 (1950), which was upheld in State v. Von Voltenburg, 260 Iowa 200, 147 N.W.2d 869 (1967). There the defendant, upon being interrogated by a watchman who stopped him in an alley at 2:15 A.M., dropped a paper bag containing a pry bar and a screwdriver. When arrested he was found to have a butter knife on his person. His conviction under the statute was affirmed, the court holding that since the presumption was not conclusive no unconstitutional burden was placed on the accused. Another technique is to make possession a crime if it is without lawful excuse and to require the defendant to carry the burden of proving lawful excuse. E. g., Conn.Gen.Stat. Ann. § 53–71 (1968), which was held unconstitutional in State v. Nales, 28 Conn.Supp. 28, 248 A.2d 242 (1968). The court held that placing the burden on the accused violated his Fifth Amendment privilege against self-incrimination, and that the presumption from mere possession in the night was irrational. In 1969 Connecticut adopted a new penal code and provided that possession would be a misdemeanor if "under circumstances manifesting an intent to use * * * in the commission of an offense of such character". Conn.Gen.Stat.Ann. § 53a–106. Still another technique is that selected by Texas which makes possession of such instruments "under circumstances evincing an intent to use * * * in the commission of burglary" a felony if the possessor has been convicted of a felony—a one bite at the apple notion. Vernon's Ann.Tex.P.C. art. 1402(b) (Penal Code) (1953). This was upheld against a vagueness challenge in Logan v. State, 448 S.W.2d 462 (Tex.Crim.App.1970).

Without some such statute are not the police and prosecutors at a serious disadvantage in their efforts to prevent the commission of crimes? Even if the authority to "stop and frisk", Terry v. Ohio, 392 U.S. 1, 88 S.Ct. 1868, 20 L.Ed.2d 889 (1968), permits early intervention in such situations and thereby the probable prevention of the specific burglary, what of the accused's future activities? Is not a major objective of the criminal law the identification of persons who are appropriate subjects for correction and/or restraint?

Both the Model Penal Code and the Proposed Federal Criminal Code have a general provision prohibiting an attempt to commit any other enumerated offense? It has generally been assumed without significant discussion that this is desirable. Glazebrook, Should We Have a Law of Attempted Crime?, 85 L.Q.Rev. 28 (1969) has recently challenged this view. Rather than including a catch-all attempt provision, he suggests, draftsmen should select those offenses in regard to which a situation short of the completed offense should give rise to liability and then include this within the definitions of those crimes.

The primary defect in a general attempt statute, as Glazebrook sees the situation, is the inherent vagueness of the preparation/attempt distinction. This, he feels, has permitted courts to impose liability for preparation far beyond the initial legislative intent, as, for example, when an attempt statute is used as the basis for holding a defendant liable for an attempt to solicit. Moreover, the awareness that many of those not coming within the definition of the completed crime will nevertheless come within the definition of attempt causes draftsmen to take less care than is desirable in drafting the definition of the completed crime. Abolition of the general attempt rule would require that statutory crimes be more carefully drafted and thus improve the quality of criminal codes.

Glazebrook also argues that the propriety of distinguishing between acts directed towards the completion of a crime and those amounting to the completed crime differs among the various crimes. Whether or not one who "attempts" but fails should be treated differently than one who achieves success should be decided on a crime-to-crime basis rather than by a generally applicable statute which assumes the appropriateness of such a distinction in all cases. For example, Glazebrook admits the desirability of distinguishing between those who kill and those who merely attempt to kill, but he suggests that there is little to be gained in forceful sexual attack cases by extended inquiries into whether or not penetration was achieved.

One may inquire whether in practice the distinctions which Glazebrook thinks desirable are not in fact made. In the absence of a general statutory attempt provision courts will apply some common law formulation to measure whether or not an attempt has been made. Thus, in State v. Woodmansee, 124 Vt. 387, 205 A.2d 407 (1964), the defendant appealed his conviction of attempted arson. The evidence showed the defendant, at about two o'clock in the morning, in company with another, carrying a jug of some kind from an automobile into an empty second-floor apartment of which he was neither owner nor tenant. Seconds later he was discovered there, kneeling in the middle of the kitchen floor, matches in hand, together with a cone-shaped roll of newspaper, with a jar of paint thinner beside him and in the presence of a strong odor of gasoline, while the apartment was in darkness. The court held that the appropriate rule was that "the preparation must be such that, if not extraneously interrupted it would be likely to end in the consummation of the crime intended." "Here", said the court, "the striking of a match would have * * * consummated the crime. That evidence, therefore, amply supported the submission of the charged attempt to the jury."

Compare this with the case of R. v. N. & B., [1952] 4 S.Afr.L.R. 210 where appellants, a European man and a native woman, appealed their conviction of attempting to violate the South African Immorality Act which criminalized illicit inter-racial sexual intercourse. The evidence accepted by the appellate court was that when apprehended the woman "was seated on the ground, probably with her bloomers down, and ready for the act of intercourse" while the man had "his jacket and waistcoat off, his trousers probably down or unbuttoned, and about to put on a contraceptive with a view to having intercourse." The question, of course, was whether "their conduct when interrupted had reached the stage of an attempt at intercourse, or was mere preparation. The court adopted as its rule the "commencement of the consummation" test, quoting with approval from an earlier case, R. v. Schoombie, [1945] A.D. 540, in which the court said "if a wrongdoer has finally made up his mind to commit a crime and has taken steps to carry out his resolution, the exact moment at which he is interrupted and prevented from fulfilling his intention should not be the sole determining factor in deciding whether or not his morally wrongful act should be regarded as a crime." If, according to the *Schoombie* court, "his acts have reached such a stage that it can properly be inferred that his mind was finally made up to carry through his evil purpose he deserves to be punished * * *. Consequently the Courts should lean towards giving a wide interpretation to the phrase 'commencement of the consummation' by including in such consummation all the last series of acts which would constitute a continuous operation, unbroken by intervals of time which might give an opportunity for reconsideration." However, the *N. & B.* court noted, this test, which seems quite similar to that announced in *Woodmansee*, must be applied with an eye to the particular crime and case. *Schoombie* was a case of attempted arson whereas this was a sexual offense. In cases of such a nature the question of whether the accused has "finally made up his mind" must be considered in light of "the possibility of a sudden revulsion of feeling or recession of the sexual impulse * * *. [T]he interval of time which would give an opportunity for reconsideration would not necessarily be more than momentary". The court then concluded:

> In the present case, * * * the bodies of the two accused were not yet in juxtaposition and the male accused had not yet drawn on the contraceptive, and that being so, not only was there an opportunity in point of time for reconsideration before the consummation of the act, but several possible causes for reconsideration can easily be imagined; I need only mention as an illustration the possible discovery that the woman was menstruating, as the evidence in fact showed that she was. I do not consider therefore that it is established beyond reasonable doubt that the act of intercourse would have been consummated but for the intervention of the policemen.

> The offence created by the statute in secs. 1 and 2 is sexual intercourse between a European male and a native female, or *vice versa*, and intercourse only takes place by penetration. An attempt to have intercourse is therefore an attempt to penetrate, and though there was preparation for the act of intercourse, there was, in the ordinary meaning of the language, no attempt to penetrate. Nor can it in my opinion be said that the accused were interrupted when they were on the point of committing the act of intercourse. * * * In my view the conduct of the two accused had not passed beyond the stage of preparation, and the convictions and sentences must accordingly be set aside.

Assume that the charge is attempted rape and the accused's conduct, aside from the assertion of his intention to have intercourse, forcibly if necessary, had proceeded no further than that of the male defendant in *N. & B.* Do you think that the result would be the same even though rape is also an offense of a sexual nature? See Le Barron v. State, page 742 infra. Look again at Dupuy v. State, page 705 supra and the standard there announced for distinguishing between preparation and attempt. It would appear that merely to require that some "direct movement toward the commission after the preparations have been made" is, if anything, a less stringent standard then that in *Woodmansee*. Would it have strained the language of the *Dupuy* test to have held that the agreement to meet to perform the abortion was the preparation and that actually appearing at the site with the instruments was the requisite "direct movement". Indeed, the court in *Dupuy* notes that the defendant "would no doubt have carried out this attempt had he not been thwarted in his efforts by the arrival of the police." Can the differing results in *Woodmansee, Le Barron, N. & B.* and *Dupuy* be explained except in terms of the gravity with which the courts viewed the substantive offenses involved? Would the results be necessarily altered under MPC § 5.01? Would that be desirable? Does the problem lie in the definition of attempt or in that of the substantive offense?

Glazebrook argues that the definition of each substantive offense should be expanded so as to cover only those unsuccessful efforts to achieve the offense which the underlying rationale of the offense dictates should be criminalized. Is the problem of encompassing the variety of ways in which men may fail to produce a harmful result as amenable to solution as the problem of defining the offense itself? Is the difficulty of anticipating the diversity of failure a good reason for not attempting it? See Stuart, The Actus Reus in Attempts, [1970] Crim.L.Rev. 505, 513.

In connection with this controversy consider the following statement by Sir James Fitzjames Stephen: "I pass now towards those imperfect crimes which constitute the first steps, so to speak, in criminality. These are—incitement to a crime, conspiracy to commit a crime, and attempts to commit crimes which are not in fact committed. All such preliminary steps towards crime are * * * themselves criminal. The exact point at which they become criminal cannot, in the nature of things, be precisely ascertained, nor is it desirable that such a matter should be made the subject of great precision. There is more harm than good in telling people precisely how far they may go without risking punishment in the pursuit of an unlawful object." A General View of the Criminal Law of England 83 (1890). If Stephen is correct as to the inherent vagueness of the law of attempt why is it not subject to constitutional challenge on that basis? Can this difficulty be resolved by adopting Glazebrook's approach and carefully defining with respect to each substantive offense, those acts which will be penalized even though they fall short of success? Alternatively, or by way of supplementation, we might have statutes criminalizing certain specific forms of preparatory conduct such as those concerning the possession of burglar's tools previously discussed, or prohibiting the use, manufacture, or distribution of combustible or explosive substances with intent to burn property. E. g. Mich.Comp.Laws Ann. § 750.77 (1968) applied in People v. Davis, 24 Mich.App. 304, 180 N.W.2d 285 (1970) (defendant properly convicted where, with intent to burn, he aided others in the manufacture of Molotov cocktails although he did not participate in their use).[b]

To what extent is the desirability of a general attempt statute affected by a decision as to the role of attempt prosecutions in general deterrence? It has been suggested that deterrence is of minor or no consequence in the law of attempts inasmuch as the fact of the attempt establishes that the actor was not deterred by the sanction attached to the substantive offense which it was his object to commit. Nevertheless, it seems reasonable to

---

[b]. Another and rather more dramatic example of penalizing conduct well removed from an actual attempt is 18 U.S.C.A. § 871 (1970) which provides for a fine of $1,000 and/or not more than five years imprisonment for any person who "knowingly and willfully" makes any threat of bodily harm against the President or any officer in the order of succession to the President. Then Judge Burger has written, in the course of affirming a conviction under this statute—the defendant had publically stated that if required to carry a gun (be drafted) "the first person I want in my sights is LBJ"—that its ultimate purpose was to deter the killing or injuring of the President by deterring such threats, and that there is no requirement that the threat be made with intent to execute it. Watts v. United States, 402 F.2d 676 (D.C.Cir.) rev'd on other grounds, per curiam, 394 U.S. 705, 89 S.Ct. 1399, 22 L.Ed.2d 664 (1968). The Supreme Court's reversal was grounded on the view that the statement was mere "political hyperbole". The opinion announces, without discussion, that the statute is facially constitutional, but questions the validity of the Court of Appeals position on the intent required.

assume that the more frequently criminal conduct is punished the more likely it is that the rest of us will be conscious of the reality of the existence of the sanction and the greater its deterrent effect. If so, is this a reason to spread the net of attempt as widely as possible consistent with other values in the criminal justice system?

---

2. THE STATE OF MIND REQUIRED

MODEL PENAL CODE, COMMENT TO § 5.01, 27–30

(Tent. Draft No. 10, 1960).

3. *5.01(1). The Requirement of Purpose.* As previously stated, the proposed definition of attempt follows the conventional pattern of limiting this inchoate crime to purposive conduct. In the language of the courts, there must be "intent in fact" or "specific intent" to commit the crime allegedly attempted. Nonetheless a problem of drafting is presented in endeavoring to explain the nature of the requisite purpose.

This section adopts the view that the actor must have for his purpose to engage in the criminal conduct or accomplish the criminal result which is an element of the substantive crime but that his purpose need not encompass all the surrounding circumstances included in the formal definition of the substantive offense. As to them, it is sufficient that he acts with the culpability that is required for commission of the crime. Suppose, for example, that it is a federal offense to kill or injure an FBI agent and that recklessness or even negligence with respect to the identity of the victim as an agent suffices for commission of the crime. There would be an attempt to kill or injure such an agent under the present formulation if the actor with recklessness or negligence as to the official position of the victim attempts to kill or injure him. Under paragraph (b) the killing or injuring would be the required purpose; the fact that the victim is an agent would be only a circumstance as to which the actor had "the kind of culpability otherwise required for commission of the crime."

It is difficult to say what the result would be in this kind of case under prevailing principles of attempt liability. However, the proposed formulation imposes attempt liability in a group of cases where the normal basis of such liability is present—purposive conduct manifesting dangerousness—and allows the policy of the substantive crime, respecting recklessness or negligence as to surrounding circumstances, to be applied to the attempt to commit that crime.

With rare exceptions, the necessity for showing intent has not given rise to many difficulties in applying prevailing attempt principles. * * *

Under paragraph (b), liability for an attempt may be founded upon the actor's belief that his conduct will cause a particular result which is an element of the crime. If, for example, the actor's purpose were to demolish a building and, knowing and believing that persons in the building would be killed by the explosion, the actor nonetheless detonated a bomb, there would be an attempt to kill even though it was no part of the actor's purpose—i. e., he did not consciously desire—that the building's inhabitants should be killed. Again, it is difficult to say what the decision would be under prevailing attempt principles in a case of this kind. It might be held that the actor did not specifically intend to kill the inhabitants of the building; on the other hand, the concept of "intent" has always been an ambiguous one and might be thought to include results which are believed by the actor to be the inevitable consequences of his conduct.

The inclusion of such conduct as a basis for liability under paragraph (b) is based on the conclusion that the manifestation of dangerousness is as great—or very nearly as great—as in the case of purposive conduct. In both instances a deliberate choice is made to bring about the consequence forbidden by the criminal laws, and the actor has done all within his power to cause this result to occur. The absence in one instance of any desire for the forbidden result is not, under these circumstances, a sufficient basis for differentiating between the two types of conduct involved.

It should be emphasized that this extension of paragraph (b) beyond the area of purposive behavior does *not* result in the inclusion of reckless conduct. Indeed, as previously noted, the additional ground of liability may well be within the common law concept of intentional behavior. Certain types of non-causal reckless conduct are encompassed by § 201.11 of the Code, Tentative Draft No. 9 (1959).

THACKER v. COMMONWEALTH

Supreme Court of Appeals of Virginia, 1922.
134 Va. 767, 114 S.E. 504.

WEST, J. This writ of error is to a judgment upon the verdict of a jury finding John Thacker, the accused, guilty of attempting to murder Mrs. J. A. Ratrie, and fixing his punishment at two years in the penitentiary.

The only assignment of error is the refusal of the trial court to set aside the verdict as contrary to the law and the evidence.

The accused, in company with two other young men, Doc Campbell and Paul Kelly, was attending a church festival in Alleghany county, at which all three became intoxicated. They left the church between 10 and 11 o'clock at night, and walked down the county road about 1½ miles, when they came to a sharp curve. Located in this curve was a tent in which the said Mrs. J. A. Ratrie, her husband, four children, and a servant were camping for the summer. The husband, though absent, was expected home that night, and Mrs. Ratrie, upon retiring, had placed a lighted lamp on a trunk by the head of her bed. After 11 o'clock she was awakened by the shots of a pistol and loud talking in the road near by, and heard a man say, "I am going to shoot that God-damned light out;" and another voice said, "Don't shoot the light out." The accused and his friends then appeared at the back of the tent, where the flaps of the tent were open, and said they were from Bath county and had lost their way, and asked Mrs. Ratrie if she could take care of them all night. She informed them she was camping for the summer, and had no room for them. One of the three thanked her, and they turned away, but after passing around the tent the accused used some vulgar language and did some cursing and singing. When they got back in the road, the accused said again he was going to shoot the light out, and fired three shots, two of which went through the tent, one passing through the head of the bed in which Mrs. Ratrie was lying, just missing her head and the head of her baby, who was sleeping with her. The accused did not know Mrs. Ratrie, and had never seen her before. He testified he did not know any of the parties in the tent, and had no ill will against either of them; that he simply shot at the light, without any intent to harm Mrs. Ratrie or any one else; that he would not have shot had he been sober, and regretted his action.

The foregoing are the admitted facts in the case.

An attempt to commit a crime is composed of two elements: (1) The intent to commit it; and (2) a direct, ineffectual act done towards its commission. The act must reach far enough towards the accomplishment of the desired result to amount to the commencement of the consummation.

The law can presume the intention so far as realized in the act, but not an intention beyond what was so realized. The law does not presume, because an assault was made with a weapon likely to produce death, that it was an assault with the intent to murder. And where it takes a particular intent to constitute a crime, that particular intent must be proved either by direct or circumstantial evidence, which would warrant the inference of the intent with which the act was done.

When a statute makes an offense to consist of an act combined with a particular intent, that intent is just as necessary to be proved as the act itself, and must be found as a matter of fact before a conviction can be had; and no intent in law or mere legal presumption, differing from the intent in fact, can be allowed to supply the place of the latter.

In discussing the law of attempts, Mr. Clark in his work on Criminal Law says, at page 111:

> "The act must be done with the specific intent to commit a particular crime. This specific intent at the time the act is done is essential. To do an act from general malevolence is not an attempt to commit a crime, because there is no specific intent, though the act according to its consequences may amount to a substantive crime. To do an act with intent to commit one crime cannot be an attempt to commit another crime, though it might result in such other crime. To set fire to a house and burn a human being who is in it, but not to the offender's knowledge, would be murder, though the intent was to burn the house only; but to attempt to set fire to the house under such circumstances would be an attempt to commit arson only and not an attempt to murder. A man actuated by general malevolence may commit murder, though there is no actual intention to kill; to be guilty of an attempt to murder there must be a specific intent to kill."

Mr. Bishop, in his Criminal Law, vol. 1 (8th Ed.), at section 729, says:

> "When the law makes an act, whether more or less evil in itself, punishable, though done simply from general malevolence, if one takes what, were all accomplished, would be a step towards it, yet if he does not mean to do the whole, no court can justly hold him answerable for more than he does. And when the thing done does not constitute a substantive crime, there is no ground for treating it as an attempt. So that necessarily an act prompted by general malevolence, or by a specific design to do something else, is not an attempt to commit a crime not intended. * * * When we say that a man attempted to do a given wrong, we mean that he intended to do specifically it, and proceeded a certain way in the doing. The intent in the mind covers the thing in full; the act covers it only in part. Thus (section 730) to commit murder, one need not intend to take life, but to be guilty of an attempt to murder, he must so intend. It is not sufficient that his act, had it proved fatal, would have been murder. Section 736. We have seen that the unintended taking of life may be murder, yet there can be no attempt to murder without the specific intent to commit it—a rule the latter branch whereof appears probably in a few of the states to have been interfered with by statutes (citing Texas cases). For example, if one from a housetop recklessly throws down a billet of wood upon the sidewalk where persons are constantly passing, and it falls upon a

person passing by and kills him, this would be the common-law murder, but if, instead of killing, it inflicts only a slight injury, the party could not be convicted of an assault with attempt to commit murder, since, in fact, the murder was not intended."

The application of the foregoing principles to the facts of the instant case shows clearly, as we think, that the judgment complained of is erroneous. While it might possibly be said that the firing of the shot into the head of Mrs. Ratrie's bed was an act done towards the commission of the offense charged, the evidence falls far short of proving that it was fired with the intent to murder her.

However averse we may be to disturb the verict of the jury, our obligation to the law compels us to do so.

The judgment complained of will be reversed, the verdict of the jury set aside, and the case remanded for a new trial therein, if the commonwealth shall be so advised.

Reversed.

NOTES

1. Does a defendant charged with attempted first degree murder have a right to have the jury instructed on: attempted second degree murder—causing death "by conduct imminently dangerous to another and evincing a depraved mind, regardless of human life"; attempted third degree murder—causing death "as a natural and probable consequence of the commission of or attempt to commit" a felony; and/or attempted manslaughter? State v. Carter, 44 Wis.2d 151, 170 N.W.2d 681 (1969).

2. Can one be convicted of an attempt to commit a strict liability offense without proof of intent to commit the offense? Cf. Gardner v. Akeroyd, [1952] 2 Q.B. 743 (although a butcher may be held strictly and vicariously liable for the sale of meat at prices in excess of the regulatory maxima, he cannot be held liable for "any act preparatory to the commission" of that offense (prepared but undelivered parcels of meat were found in the shop with tickets showing overcharges) in the absence of mens rea).

3. Is there any doubt that Thacker had identified himself as a dangerous person and a proper subject for correction? If so, is it desirable to make the assessment of his punishment so dependent upon the fortuity of the result of his conduct? For an argument in favor of permitting verdicts of attempted manslaughter where the defendant has acted recklessly or with gross negligence see Stuart, Mens Rea, Negligence and Attempts [1968] Crim.L.Rev. 647.

3. ATTEMPT TO COMMIT "ATTEMPT-LIKE" CRIMES

STATE v. WILSON

Supreme Court of Oregon, 1959.
218 Or. 575, 346 P.2d 115.

O'CONNELL, Justice. The defendant appeals from a judgment of the circuit court for Multnomah county entered on a verdict pronouncing him guilty of the crime of attempted assault with a dangerous weapon * * *.

The following statement of facts set out in plaintiff's brief adequately describes the circumstances under which the alleged crimes were committed. "On the afternoon of September 12, 1957, the defendant, Harvey Raymond Wilson, went unarmed to the laundry room of the New Heathman Hotel in Portland, Oregon, where his wife, Frances Ora Wilson, from whom he was separated, was employed. At that time a half dozen or more women, including defendant's wife and a Vivian Smith, were working in the laundry room. Defendant approached his wife. (He had been in the same laundry room the previous Saturday and had called her a "yellow bellied son of a bitch" and in addition had said to her, "I'll give you just twenty-four hours to live.") This time he stated to his wife: 'This is it.' Whereupon she ran from the room to an adjoining office where she started to call the police on a telephone. However, the defendant, who had followed her into the room, took the phone from her, tore it loose from the wall and threw it at her. She ducked and the phone hit another woman named Goldie Reed, a co-worker of defendant's wife. Defendant's wife then ran out of that office into another room where she did call the police on another phone.

"Meanwhile the defendant went outside the hotel to where his car was parked nearby and got from it a 12-gauge shotgun which was loaded with three shells. He then returned to the laundry room, having only been gone approximately three or four minutes. As he approached the laundry room, with the loaded gun held in a position to shoot directly in front of him, he was walking down a hall which had an open doorway on his right approximately ten feet ahead of him. Almost directly across the hall from this open doorway into the laundry room was another doorway which led into the office where his wife was. At this very time as the defendant was approximately ten feet up the hall from this doorway to the office, his wife started to come out of that doorway into the hall. She then saw the defendant who was also seen at the same time by a Grace Scebeta, another co-worker of defendant's wife. Miss Scebeta immediately pushed defendant's wife back into the office. The door was quickly shut as was another door leading into the office which now had in it defendant's wife, Grace Scebeta and Goldie Reed.

"Defendant meanwhile continued walking down the hall until he came to the doorway of the laundry room. He then entered the laundry room still carrying the loaded shotgun, where he confronted Vivian Smith and Helen Robbins, who also worked in the laundry room. Miss Robbins is a deaf mute. While standing not more than a couple of feet away from these two women, the defendant said to them, 'Don't move anyone or I'll shoot you.' Shortly after that the defendant turned around and walked away. As he was leaving the building he was apprehended by a police officer who was sent to the hotel as the result of the phone call to the police made by defendant's wife."

The crime of assault with a dangerous weapon is defined in ORS 163.250 as follows:

"Any person, who is armed with a dangerous weapon and assaults another with such weapon, shall be punished upon conviction by imprisonment in the penitentiary for not more than 10 years, or by imprisonment in the county jail not less than one month nor more than one year, or by a fine of not less than $100 nor more than $1,000."

There is no statute dealing specifically with an attempt to commit assault with a dangerous weapon. The state relies upon the general attempt statute, ORS 161.090, which reads in part as follows:

"Any person who attempts to commit a crime, and in the attempt does any act towards the commission of the crime but fails or is prevented or intercepted in the perpetration thereof, shall be punished upon conviction, when no other provision is made by law for the punishment of such attempt, as follows: * * * "

The defendant attacks Count I of the indictment on the ground that it does not state a crime under the laws of this state. Defendant argues that there is no such crime as an attempted assault with a dangerous weapon. In stating his grounds for objecting to the introduction of evidence in proof of the first count counsel for defendant said " * * * it is the contention of the defendant that there is no such thing as an attempted assault; it is no more than an attempt to inflict an injury or battery, so if a person attempts to assault one then he lacks the attempt to commit the battery." His reasoning is further spelled out in his brief as follows: "An assault is an attempt within itself and there must be some act done towards the commission of battery which is intercepted and prevented * *. An attempt must include, except for consummation, all essential elements of the crime intended * * *. Thereby, one committing an assault must have intent to commit a battery. If then, there is such a crime as attempted assault, the one so attempting must have intent to commit an assault. Does he then intend to commit a battery?"

* * *

The charge that an attempt to attempt to do an act is beyond understanding, seems at first blush to be justified. It could be interpreted to be the equivalent of a statement that one is guilty of a crime if he proceeds to act in such a way that, if not interrupted, his conduct would result in the commission of an act which if not interrupted would result in a substantive crime.

If we should view criminal assault as a separate substantive crime and not as an attempted battery, the foregoing objection would disappear. If we use the words "assault" and "battery" to express distinct ideas, then criminal assault can mean either (1) an act which causes another to be put in reasonable apprehension of corporal injury and the act is done with the intent of causing either the apprehension or the corporal injury, or (2) an act intended to cause corporal injury by one who has the present ability to carry out such intent. Under the first meaning of assault a crime is committed if the victim is put in apprehension of injury whether there is any actual intent to injure or not. Thus, if the defendant should point an unloaded gun intending only to subject his victim to the apprehension of corporal injury a crime would be committed. The crime is not defined in terms of an attempted battery but as a crime complete in itself. So viewed, there is no logical difficulty in describing as a criminal attempt the acts leading up to the conduct by which the defendant actually places his victim in apprehension. As pointed out earlier, attempt to commit an assault as defined under the second definition given above has, however, been regarded in some circles as involving the absurdity of recognizing an attempt to commit an attempt to commit a crime.

Before dealing with this criticism we shall first consider the nature of the crime of assault as it has been defined in Oregon.

* * *

The manner in which our cases have defined assault, describing conduct which is designed to produce a criminal battery but for some reason falls short of the final harm, lends support to the idea that the crime is no more than an attempt to commit a crime and that it is not a crime standing upon its own separate ground. At this point two questions present themselves. First, is it accurate to regard criminal assault as an attempt in the sense that the concept is used in the law of criminal attempt, or to put it differently, does the word "attempt" as used in the definition of assault convey the same meaning as the word attempt in the law of criminal attempt generally? The second question is: Assume that we are forced to deal with an attempt to attempt to commit a battery, is there any reason why we cannot and should not bring such conduct within the law of criminal attempt generally?

Considering now the first question, it seems evident that a definition which describes conduct in terms of "present ability" to consummate a further act adds something to the idea of attempt as it is used to describe the steps leading up to a final substantive crime. One may be guilty of an attempt to commit a crime under circumstances where there is no *present* ability to consummate the crime attempted. This suggests that the word "attempt" as used to describe assault is not meant to describe the preparatory stages pointing toward a battery but to contrast assault with battery by speaking of the former as something less than the latter.

When assault is defined in terms of the victim's apprehension of injury, as many courts do, assault is viewed as a self-contained criminal act rather than as an attempted battery, and yet the definition carries with it the idea that the conduct which causes the apprehension may be, and often is, a step toward the ultimate act of inflicting corporal injury. The fact that the preliminary conduct is described with reference to an act which ordinarily follows, or which is intended to follow, does not preclude us from considering the preliminary conduct as a separate crime distinct from criminal battery, and this is true whether we define assault in terms of the purpose and ability to commit a battery or in terms of putting the victim in fear of corporal injury. Defined either way, the conduct of the actor has advanced to such a stage that his propinquity to the victim's person is in itself a harm either because it generates fear in the victim under one definition, or exposes him to imminent danger of physical injury under the other. That distinct harm can be differentiated from the harm which the law sees at the point where the actor has not yet come upon the scene but has gone far enough to move past the mere preparation phase and into the stage of attempt. Cf. Hall, Principles of Criminal Law (1947), ch. 4. See Note: Is Criminal Assault A Separate Substantive Crime Or Is it An Attempted Battery?, 33 Ky.L.J. 189 (1945). We are of the opinion that criminal assault, even as defined by this court, should be regarded as a distinct crime rather than as an uncompleted battery.

If we should regard assault as an attempted battery, is it reasonable to recognize the crime of attempted assault? It has been categorically asserted that there can be no attempt to commit a crime which is itself merely an attempt. 1 Wharton, Criminal Law & Procedure (Anderson ed.)

* * * Upon the basis of this premise it is said that there can be no such offense as an attempted assault. 1 Wharton, op. cit. supra, § 72 at 154, states that "as an assault is an attempt to commit a battery there can be no attempt to commit an assault." * * * In none of these sources is it explained why this conclusion is inevitable. It appears to be assumed that logic permits no other conclusion. But is that so? Thurman Arnold, in an article in 40 Yale L.J. 53, 65 (1930) answers as follows:

> " * * * [It is said that] there can be no attempt at a direct attempt. But the query immediately arises, Why not?

We do not punish attempts at ordinary assaults which carry light penalties. But suppose the accused is guilty of conduct tending toward an aggravated assault but which does not seem to require the heavier penalty. The court is confronted with the alternative of either discharging the accused or modifying the penalty to make it more nearly fit his conduct. An easy way to accomplish this is by making attempts at aggravated assaults punishable, and this is frequently done. It is academic to call such cases 'wrong' because assault is in the nature of an attempt and hence cannot be attempted, particularly when a common sense result is reached. In short the generalization that there can be no attempt at a crime in the nature of an attempt tells us nothing and tends merely to divert the court's mind from the real issue."

We agree with the foregoing analysis. The mere fact that assault is viewed as preceding a battery should not preclude us from drawing a line on one side of which we require the present ability to inflict corporal injury, denominating this an assault, and on the other side conduct which falls short of a present ability, yet so advanced toward the assault that it is more than mere preparation and which we denominate an attempt. * * *

The acts of the defendant after obtaining the gun from his automobile may not have been sufficient to establish that he had the present ability to inflict corporal injury upon his wife who was behind a locked door, but he had proceeded far beyond the stage of preparation and it is reasonable to treat his conduct as an attempt.

* * *

Defendant contends that if [the statute prohibiting attempts] embraces an attempt to commit an assault the statute is unconstitutional in that it does not sufficiently define the criminal acts which would constitute a violation of the statute. But this is no more than a criticism of the entire law of criminal attempt which admittedly is vague in that each case must be decided upon its own facts in determining whether the defendant's conduct has proceeded far enough toward the consummation of the crime to warrant punishment. The problem confronting the courts in drawing the line in an attempted assault case is no more difficult than it is where other attempted crimes are involved.

* * *

The judgment of the lower court is affirmed.

NOTE

Compare Allen v. People, 485 P.2d 886 (Colo.1971), reaching the opposite result under a statute which defined assault in terms of an attempt to injure another or an attempt to commit a battery.

4. THE "DEFENSE" OF IMPOSSIBILITY

BOOTH v. STATE

Court of Criminal Appeals of Oklahoma, 1964.
398 P.2d 863.

NIX, Judge. John Fletcher Booth, Jr., was charged by information by information in the District Court of Oklahoma County with the crime of Receiving Stolen Property, and was found guilty of the lesser crime of Attempt to Receive Stolen Property. The jury assessed his penalty at Two Years in the Oklahoma State Penitentiary, and to pay a fine in the amount of $150.00. From said judgment and sentence the defendant appeals.

The record before this Court reveals that this case arose out of a circumstance as testified to by a self-admitted, well-known thief bearing the name of Charley Stanford, whose FBI "rap sheet" covers 8 pages of arrests extending over a period of 15 years. He was obviously braggadocio about his convictions and related from the witness stand that he had been arrested approximately 300 times on everything in the book, short of murder and rape. He admitted serving 4 terms in the penitentiary, and having been committed to a mental institution twice. He testified, in substance, that in the early morning hours he was walking in the parking lot at the YMCA in Oklahoma City and sighted a topcoat in a parked automobile. That he jimmied the window and removed the coat, took it to his home at 308 N.E. 8th Street, where he retired until about 7:00 at which time he proceeded down to a pay telephone where he called his attorney (the defendant herein). He testified that he advised him he had the coat he had ordered, and agreed to let him have the coat for $20.00. Arrangements were made for the defendant to meet him at the thief's home at approximately 11:00 A.M. where the transfer was to be made. He returned home, and a friend came by and invited him to go get a drink. He started from his house to his friend's car and was arrested by Lt. Anthony of the Oklahoma City Police Department. He was wearing the stolen coat at the time of his arrest. Lt. Anthony took Stanford to the police station, and asked him where he had gotten the coat and he confessed getting it from the car in the YMCA parking lot.

Lt. Anthony testified, in substance, that he received an anonymous telephone call at approximately 7:00 A.M. on the morning of the day in question, and proceeded to the YMCA and located the owner of the vehicle that had been burglarized. They went then to the vehicle and observed the wing glass had been broken, pried open, and a gray cashmere coat and some shirts were missing. Officer Anthony proceeded to the 300 block on N.E. 8th and saw an ex-convict by the name Charley Stanford leaving his house wearing a gray cashmere coat. Anthony then and there arrested Stanford for Burglary and took him to the police station. He then called Mr. Gothard to the police station, where he identified the coat as his and asked Lt. Anthony for the coat, but was advised that they needed it as evidence. Officer Anthony, Officer Reading and Stanford proceeded to 308 N.E. 8th taking the recovered coat with them. After arriving, they took their position behind a closet door containing "peep-holes" and waited for the arrival of defendant Booth. According to the testimony of Anthony, the following transpired:

* * *

"A.   Booth entered the house, and   *   *   *   I heard Charlie Stanford say, 'John, I got the coat which you wanted.' 'I need the twenty dollars right away.' And Mr. Booth said, 'This is child support month, Charlie, come to my office later and I will give you a check.'

* * *

well, Booth picked up the coat in his arms and there was conversation of and he warned him that the thing was 'hot'.

"Q.   Who warned who?

"A.   Charlie Stanford warned John Booth that the thing was 'hot'.

"Q.   That the coat was 'hot'?

"A.   Yes, that's the way he termed it.

"Q.   What did Mr. Booth say?

"A.   He said, 'well, I know how to handle things like this, don't worry about it, Charlie.'

* * *

"Q.   Then what happened?

"A.   At this point they went into a rest-room and what went on in there, I didn't hear. Then they came back out, and Booth went to his car and put the coat in the turtle-back of his car and then returned to the house and that is about all that occurred.

After taking Stanford to the police station, Anthony obtained a search warrant and then maintained a surveillance of Booth's house until he arrived. He then entered the premises, arrested Booth, and again recovered the coat.

Though defendant Booth was charged with Receiving Stolen Property, at the conclusion of the evidence and after the state and defendant had rested their case, the trial judge gave the following instruction:

"You are instructed that under the law of this case you are at liberty to consider only the included offense of whether the defendant John Fletcher Booth may be guilty of the crime of Attempt to Receive Stolen Property. In this regard you are instructed, an attempt to commit a crime is defined as being the compound of two elements.

"(1) The intent to commit a crime. (2) A direct ineffectual act done towards its commission.

"Preparation alone to an attempt to commit a crime is not sufficient. * * * "

No doubt this instruction was given based upon the theory that once stolen property has been recovered by the police it loses its character as stolen property.

* * *

The general rule evidently adopted by the trial court is stated in 76 C.J.S. Receiving Stolen Goods § 5, pg. 7, as follows:

"In order to convict of receiving stolen goods, the goods in question must have retained their stolen character at the time they were received by accused; if they were stolen, they continue to be stolen goods until they are recovered by their owner or some one for him. Hence, where the actual physical possession of stolen goods has been recovered by the owner or his agent and afterwards carried to the receiver either by the original thief or the instrumentality through which the thief originally intended to convey it, at the express direction of the owner or his agent, for the purpose of entrapping the receiver, his receiving of the goods is not a receiving of stolen goods."

* * *

The law seems to be clear on this point, leaving the only question to be decided as whether or not the defendant could be convicted of an attempt to receive stolen property in such cases. It is the defendant's contention that if he could not be convicted of the substantive charge, because the coat had lost its character as stolen property; neither could he be convicted of an attempt because the coat was not in the category of stolen property at the time he received it.

The briefs filed in the case, and extensive research has revealed that two states have passed squarely on the question—New York and California. It is definitely one of first impression in Oklahoma.

The New York Court, in passing upon the question, laid down the following rule in the case of People v. Jaffe, 185 N.Y. 497, 78 N.E. 169, 6 L.R.A.,N.S., 263, on the following facts:

"A clerk stole goods from his employer under an agreement to sell them to accused, but before delivery of the goods the theft was discovered and the goods were recovered. Later the employer redelivered the goods to the clerk to sell to accused, who purchased them for about one-half of their value, believing them to have been stolen.

> "Held that the goods had lost their character as stolen goods at the time defendant purchased them, and that his criminal intent was insufficient to sustain a conviction for an attempt to receive stolen property, knowing it to have been stolen."

The Jaffe case, supra, was handed down in 1906, and has prevailed as the law in New York state 58 years without modification * * *

The State of California has passed upon the question several times and up until 1959, they followed the rule laid down in the Jaffe case, supra.

In 1959, in the case of People v. Camodeca, 52 Cal.2d 142, 338 P.2d 903, the California Court abandoned the Jaffe rationale that a person accepting goods which he believes to have been stolen, but which was not in fact stolen goods, is not guilty of an attempt to receive stolen goods, and imposed a liability for the attempt, overruling its previous holding to the contrary in the above cited cases. The Camodeca case, supra, was affirmed in People v. Rojas, 55 Cal.2d 252, 10 Cal.Rptr. 465, 358 P.2d 921, 85 A.L.R.2d 252, 1961.

Though the instant case, insofar as it pertains to the specific crime of attempting to receive stolen property is one of first impression in Oklahoma. This Court held in the Nemecek v. State, 72 Okl.Cr. 195, 114 P.2d 492, 135 A.L.R. 1149, involving attempting to receive money by false pretenses:

> "An accused cannot be convicted of an attempt to commit a crime unless he could have been convicted of the crime itself if his attempt had been successful. Where the act, if accomplished, would not constitute the crime intended, there is no indictable attempt."

In the Nemecek case, supra, the Court quotes with approval, In re Schurman, 40 Kan. 533, 20 P. 277; wherein the Kansas Court said:

> "With reference to attempt, it has also been said that 'if all which the accused person intended would, had it been done, constitute no substantive crime, it cannot be a crime, under the name "attempt," to do, with the same purpose, a part of this thing.'"

The two paramount cases of latest date; Rojas of Calif.1961, supra, and [People v.] Rollino, [37 Misc.2d 14, 233 N.Y.S.2d 580 (1962)]; present two rationales directly contrary to each other relative to an attempt to receive stolen property after it had been recovered by the police.

Before adhering too closely to either rationale, it is deemed advisable to briefly discuss the development of the "attempt to commit crimes" and the complexity pertaining thereto.

* * *

That attempts were indictable as such was restated and definitively determined in Rex. v. Higgins, 2 East 5 (1801). Fifty-six years later, the question of "impossibility" was raised for the first time in Regina v. McPherson, Dears. & B. 197, 201, (1857), when Baron Bramwell said:

> " * * * The argument that a man putting his hand into an empty pocket might be convicted of an attempt to steal appeared to me at first plausible; but suppose a man, believing a block of wood to be a man who was his deadly enemy, struck it a blow intending to murder, could he be convicted of attempting to murder the man he took it to be?"

Subsequently, in Regina v. Collins, 9 Cox C.C. 497, 169 Eng.Rep. 1477 (1864), the Court expressly held that attempted larceny was not made out by proof that the defendant pickpocket actually inserted his hand into the victim's pocket with intent to steal. Chief Justice Cockburn, declaring, at page 499:

> "We think that an attempt to commit a felony can only be made out when, if no interruption had taken place, the attempt could have been carried out successfully, and the felony completed of the attempt to commit which the party is charged."

This very broad language, encompassing as it did all forms of "impossibility", was subsequently rejected by the English courts and it was held that the inability of the pickpocket to steal from an empty pocket did not preclude his conviction of an attempted larceny. Regina v. Ring, 17 Cox C.C. 491, 66 L.T. (N.S.) 306 (1892).

In this country it is generally held that a defendant may be charged with an attempt where the crime was not completed because of "physical or factual impossibility", whereas a "legal impossibility" in the completion of the crime precludes prosecution for an attempt. (Smith, "Two Problems in Criminal Attempts", 70 Harvard Law Review, 422.)

What is a "legal impossibility" as distinguished from a "physical or factual impossibility" has over a long period of time perplexed our courts and has resulted in many irreconcilable decisions and much philosophical discussion by legal scholars in numerous articles and papers in law school publications and by text-writers. See, for example: * * * [Arnold, Criminal Attempts—the Rise and Fall of an Abstraction, 40 Yale L.J. 53 (1930); Curren, Criminal and Non-Criminal Attempts, 19 Geo.L.J. 185, 316 (1931); Keedy, Criminal Attempts at Common Law, 102 U.Pa.L.Rev. 464 (1954); Ryu, Contemporary Problems of Criminal Attempts, 32 N.Y.U.L.Rev. 1170 (1957); Sayre, Criminal Attempts, 41 Harv.L.Rev. 821 (1928); Strahorn, The Effect of Impossibility on Criminal Attempts, 78 U.Pa.L.Rev. 962 (1930).]

The reason for the "impossibility" of completing the substantive crime ordinarily falls into one of two categories: (1) Where the act if completed would not be criminal, a situation which is usually described as a "legal impossibility", and (2) where the basic or substantive crime is impossible of completion, simply because of some physical or factual condition unknown to the defendant, a situation which is usually described as a "factual impossibility".

The authorities in the various states and the text-writers are in general agreement that where there is a "legal impossibility" of completing the substantive crime, the accused cannot be successfully charged with an attempt, whereas in those cases in which the "factual impossibility" situation is involved, the accused may be convicted of an attempt. Detailed discussion of the subject is unnecessary to make it clear that it is frequently most difficult to compartmentalize a particular set of facts as coming within one of the categories rather than the other. Examples of the so-called "legal impossibility" situations are:

(a) A person accepting goods which he believes to have been stolen, but which were not in fact stolen goods, is not guilty of an attempt to receive stolen goods. (People v. Jaffe, 185 N.Y. 497, 78 N.E. 169, 9 L.R.A.,N.S., 263).

(b) It is not an attempt to commit subornation of perjury where the false testimony solicited, if given, would have been immaterial to the case at hand and hence not perjurious. (People v. Teal, 196 N.Y. 372, 89 N.E. 1086, 25 L.R.A.,N.S., 120).

(c) An accused who offers a bribe to a person believed to be a juror, but who is not a juror, is not guilty of an attempt to bribe a juror. (State v. Taylor, 345 Mo. 325, 133 S.W.2d 336).

(d) An official who contracts a debt which is unauthorized and a nullity, but which he believes to be valid, is not guilty of an attempt to illegally contract a valid debt. (Marley v. State, 58 N.J.L. 207, 33 A. 208).

(e) A hunter who shoots a stuffed deer believing it to be alive is not guilty of an attempt to shoot a deer out of season. (State v. Guffey, 262 S.W.2d 152 (Mo.App.)).

Examples of cases in which attempt convictions have been sustained on the theory that all that prevented the consummation of the completed crime was a "factual impossibility" are:

(a) The picking of an empty pocket. (People v. Moran, 123 N.Y. 254, 25 N.E. 412, 10 L.R.A. 109; Commonwealth v. Mc-Donald, 5 Cush. 365 (Mass.); People v. Jones, 46 Mich. 441, 9 N.W. 486).

(b) An attempt to steal from an empty receptacle. (Clark v. State, 86 Tenn. 511, 8 S.W. 145) or an empty house (State v. Utley, 82 N.C. 556).

(c) Where defendant shoots into the intended victim's bed, believing he is there, when in fact he is elsewhere. (State v. Mitchell, 170 Mo. 633, 71 S.W. 175).

(d) Where the defendant erroneously believing that the gun is loaded points it at his wife's head and pulls the trigger. (State v. Damms, 9 Wis.2d 183, 100 N.W.2d 592, 79 A.L.R.2d 1402).

(e) Where the woman upon whom the abortion operation is performed is not in fact pregnant. (Commonwealth v. Tibbetts, 157 Mass. 519, 32 N.E. 910; People v. Huff, 339 Ill. 328, 171 N.E. 261; and Peckham v. United States, 96 U.S. App.D.C. 312, 266 F.2d 34).

Your writer is of the opinion that the confusion that exists as a result of the two diverse rationales laid down in the Rollino case (NY) supra, and the Rojas case (Calif) supra, was brought about by the failure to recognize the distinction between a factual and a legal impossibility to accomplish the crime. In the Camodeca case (Calif) supra, the facts revealed a prevention of the crime because of a factual situation as stated on page 906, 338 P.2d:

"In the present case there was not a legal but only a factual impossibility of consummating the intended offense * * *."

In the Rojas case, supra, wherein was adopted the departure from the Jaffe case, by saying:

"The situation here is materially like those considered in People v. Camodeca."

The Rojas case was definitely not materially the same. In the Rojas case the facts reveal a legal and not factual impossibility.

In the case at bar the stolen coat had been recovered by the police for the owner and consequently had, according to the well-established law in this country, lost its character as stolen property. Therefore, a legal impossibility precluded defendant from being prosecuted for the crime of Knowingly Receiving Stolen Property.

It would strain reasoning beyond a logical conclusion to hold contrary to the rule previously stated herein, that,

"If all which the accused person intended would, had it been done, constituted no substantive crime, it cannot be a crime under the name 'attempt' to do, with the same purpose, a part of this thing."

If a series of acts together will not constitute an offense, how can it be said that one of the acts alone will constitute an indictable offense? Bishop Crim.Law § 747.

The rule is well stated by the English Court in the case of R. v. Percy, Ltd., 33 Crim.App.R. 102 (1949):

> "Steps on the way to the commission of what would be a crime, if the acts were completed, may amount to attempts to commit that crime, to which, unless interrupted, they would have led; but steps on the way to the doing of something, which is thereafter done, and which is no crime, cannot be regarded as attempts to commit a crime."

The defendant in the instant case leaves little doubt as to his moral guilt. The evidence, as related by the self-admitted and perpetual law violator indicates defendant fully intended to do the act with which he was charged. However, it is fundamental to our law that a man is not punished merely because he has a criminal mind. It must be shown that he has, with that criminal mind, done an act which is forbidden by the criminal law.

Adhering to this principle, the following example would further illustrate the point.

A fine horse is offered to A at a ridiculously low price by B, who is a known horse thief. A, believing the horse to be stolen, buys the same without inquiry. In fact, the horse had been raised from a colt by B and was not stolen. It would be bordering on absurdity to suggest that A's frame of mind, if proven, would support a conviction of an attempt. It would be a "legal impossibility".

Our statute provides that defendant must attempt to *Knowingly* Receive Stolen Property before a conviction will stand. How could one know property to be stolen when it was not? The statute needs to be changed so it would be less favorable to the criminal.

J. C. Smith, a Reader in Law, University of Nottingham, B.A., Cambridge, 1949, LL. B1, 1950, M. A., 1954, said in an article (70 Harvard Law Review 422) supporting the Jaffe case, supra, and the above reasoning:

> "If it appears wrong that the accused should escape unpunished in the particular circumstances, then it may be that there is something wrong with the substantive law and his act ought to be criminal. But the remedy then is to alter the substantive crime. Otherwise "there is no ACTUS REUS because 'the accident has turned up in his favour' " and the accused ought to be acquitted. When a man has achieved all the consequences which he set out to achieve and those consequences do not, in the existing circumstances, amount to an ACTUS REUS it is in accordance both with principle and authority that that man should be held not guilty of any crime."

We earnestly suggest that the Legislature revise the law on Attempts in accordance with The * * * "Model Penal Code", * * * Article 5.01 * * *.

In view of our statutory law, and the decisions herein related, it is our duty to Reverse this case, with orders to Dismiss, and it is so ordered.   However, there are other avenues open to the County Attorney which should be explored.

JOHNSON, P. J., and BUSSEY, J., concur.

UNITED STATES v. THOMAS

United States Court of Military Appeals, 1962.
13 U.S.C.M.A. 278, 32 C.M.R. 278.

KILDAY, Judge.   The accused herein, Thomas and McClellan, were tried in common by general court martial.   Separate charges against the pair alleged the offenses of rape * * *.   Each was acquitted of rape, but the court martial found them guilty of attempted rape [and conspiracy to commit rape]. * * *

The evidence adduced at the trial presents a sordid and revolting picture which need not be discussed in detail other than as necessary to decide the certified issues.   In brief, both these young accused— Thomas being twenty years of age, and McClellan only nineteen, at the time of the instant offenses—started their fateful evening on a "bar hopping" spree.   They were accompanied by an eighteen-year-old companion, Abruzzese, who, like both accused, held the grade of airman in the Navy.   The latter was a co-actor in these offenses, but was granted immunity from prosecution for his criminality in the incidents, and testified as a witness for the Government.

After several stops the trio entered a tavern known as "Taylor's Place" where McClellan began dancing with a girl.   Almost at once she collapsed in McClellan's arms.   Thereafter, he, with his two companions, volunteered to take her home.   They placed the apparently unconscious female in McClellan's car and left.   Abruzzese was seated beside McClellan, who drove; Thomas was in the left rear seat next to the girl.   Before they had proceeded very far McClellan, in frank, expressive language, suggested that this was a good chance for sexual intercourse as apparently this woman was just drunk and would never know the difference.   Each of the three subsequently did or attempted to consummate this act and then started their return to town.   The three became concerned as the woman had not regained consciousness.

In the meantime they dropped Abruzzese off at the USO.   The accused, unable to find the female's home and becoming more concerned about her condition, stopped at a service station seeking help.   The attendant called the police who, upon arriving at the service station, examined the girl and determined she was dead.   An ambulance was called and she was taken to a hospital for further examination.   An autopsy, later performed, revealed that she apparently died of "acute interstitial myocarditis." In general terms this is a weakening of the heart muscles with edema and inflammation which occurs more in young people without its presence being suspected. It was the general undisputed opinion that her death probably occurred at the time she collapsed on the dance floor at Taylor's Place or very shortly thereafter. Apparently, in deaths of this type, rigor mortis does not usually begin for some time and as a result the accused were unaware of the fact she was dead.

Despite the fact that defense counsel at trial vigorously urged to the law officer that the offenses of attempt and conspiracy could not be found validly if the victim's death occurred prior to the commission of the alleged acts, the law officer ruled otherwise.

* * *

We hold * * * in accordance with the * * * authorities, that in this instance the fact that the female, upon whom these detestable acts were performed, was already dead at the time of their commission, is no bar to conviction for attempted rape.

However, for purposes of clarity, we should make mention of that portion of paragraph 159, Manual for Courts-Martial, supra, which reads:

> "It is not an attempt when every act intended by the accused could be completed without committing an offense, even though the accused may at the time believe he is committing an offense."

That provision has no reference to questions we have here discussed. Such language says no more than that if what an accused believed to be a substantive crime was actually no crime at all, he cannot be guilty of an attempt to commit such crime. That is, when the intended action, even if completed, is not an offense despite the fact accused believed otherwise, he cannot be held for a criminal attempt. Under those circumstances a substantive offense is nonexistent, and an accused's acts, whether carried to fruition or not, constitute wholly lawful conduct. It is interesting to observe that the same situation will exist under the Model Penal Code. * * *

Chief Judge QUINN concurs.

FERGUSON, Judge (concurring in part and dissenting in part):

* * *

As it is, therefore, an utter impossibility for the consummated offense of rape to be committed upon the body of a dead person, may the accused who commits all the acts necessary to such offense upon a dead body, with the requisite *mens rea*, be convicted of an attempt to rape? * * *

Charges of attempted rape seem uniformly to have allowed legal impossibility as a defense when a juridical impediment was found to prevent the consummation of the crime. Thus, in Frazier v. State, 48 Tex.Crim. 142, 86 S.W. 754 (1905), it was concluded to be legally impossible for a husband to be convicted of the attempted criminal violation of his wife's person. And in Foster v. Commonwealth, 96 Va. 306, 31 S.E. 503 (1898), a jurisdiction applying the common-law's conclusive presumption of legal incapacity of a boy under the age of fourteen to commit rape determined that, because of such presumption, he could not be convicted of attempted rape. * * *

Where, however, a jurisdiction holds to the view that a boy's age as less than fourteen years creates only a *rebuttable factual* presumption of noncapacity, it also is concluded that there may be a conviction of attempted rape by such an individual. Davidson v. Commonwealth, 20 Ky.Law Rep. 540, 47 S.W. 213 (1898). So, also, is the defense of legal impossibility unavailable in the case of individuals above the common-law age of legal capacity who, for physical reasons, are impotent and thus unable to consummate the crime of rape. Preddy v. Commonwealth, 184 Va. 765, 36 S.E.2d 549 (1946).

In contrast to * * * cases upholding convictions of attempts wherein, but for the fact of absence, disbelief, poor aim, and physical inability to accomplish the result sought, are those in which there is, so to speak, no "victim in being." Thus, we find that one cannot attempt to influence a juror who is not a juror. One cannot attempt to pursue a deer which is nothing more than a stuffed hide. One cannot attempt to kill by firing into a corpse or commit rape upon a mannequin. Nor can one attempt to receive stolen goods which are not in fact stolen, or attempt rape where he legally has no capacity so to act.

It seems to me that * * * accused's conviction of attempted rape must be vitiated on the basis of legal impossibility. * * *

In each of these instances, there is simply no "victim" or thing which the particular law intended to be broken is designed to protect. Thus, embracery statutes are designed to protect jurors rather than those whom an accused believes to be jurors. Only *stolen* goods are within the proscription against attempts to receive. Only a deer can be the subject of an attempt to hunt deer. In short, the subject matter of accused's acts must be one within the prohibition of the particular statute which he is alleged to have violated, no matter what his personal belief may be, so that he could have been convicted of the consummated crime had he been entirely successful.

* * *

* * * [A]ccused did everything they set out to do, but they admittedly could not commit the actual crime of rape because their victim was dead * * *. In brief, this is not the case of an empty pocket but one in which there was no pocket to pick. * * *

Despite my position with respect to the charge of attempted rape, I would affirm the conviction of conspiracy to commit rape. * * * My objection is simply to the action of my brothers in transferring the subjective approach in conspiracy to the objective questions involved in attempts. * * *

MODEL PENAL CODE, COMMENT TO § 5.01, 30–32

(Tent. Draft No. 10, 1960).

Rejection of the "Impossibility" Defense. The purpose of this paragraph is to reverse the results in cases where attempt convictions have been set aside on the ground that it was legally impossible for the actor to have committed the crime contemplated. * * *

The basic rationale of these decisions is that, judging the actor's conduct in the light of the actual facts, what he intended to do did not amount to a crime. This approach, however, is unsound in that it seeks to evaluate a mental attitude—"intent" or "purpose"—not by looking to the actor's mental frame of reference, but to a situation wholly at variance with the actor's beliefs. In so doing, the courts exonerate defendants in situations where attempt liability most certainly should be imposed. In all of these cases (1) criminal purpose has been clearly demonstrated, (2) the actor has gone as far as he could in implementing that purpose, and (3) as a result, the actor's "dangerousness" is plainly manifested.

* * *

Of course, it is still necessary that the result desired or intended by the actor constitute a crime. If, according to his beliefs as to facts and legal relationships, the result desired or intended is not a crime, the actor will not be guilty of an attempt even though he firmly belives that his goal is criminal.[22]

The basic premise here is that the actor's mind is the best proving ground of his dangerousness. In connection with the discussion which follows of the general application of the impossibility doctrine in the law of criminal attempts, consideration will be given to the proposition that the nature of the actor's mistaken beliefs may negative dangerousness. This factor has not played any role in the impossibility cases discussed above.

NOTE

For a recent critique of the Model Penal Code, or "orthodox", position on impossibility, see Hughes, One Further Footnote on Attempting the Impossible, 42 N.Y.U.L.Rev. 1005 (1967). Professor Hughes claims that there can be no simple rule whereby Jaffe or Booth, for example, would always be guilty or always innocent. He argues that the test of whether or not

---

22. Thus it has been held that there is no attempt to suborn a witness if the testimony sought is immaterial and would not, if given, constitute perjury. People v. Teal, 196 N.Y. 372, 89 N.E. 1086 (1909) * * *.

the accused has attempted to receive stolen goods when the goods in question have lost their stolen quality should be whether the "conduct of the accused * * * conjures up for us the complete act of receiving stolen goods and therefore can be seen as *trying* to receive stolen goods." The accused's conduct should be matched "against model versions of the offense implicit in the statutory description of the actus reus." Id. at 1030–31.

---

5. THE "DEFENSE" OF ABANDONMENT

STEWART v. STATE

Supreme Court of Nevada, 1969.
85 Nev. 388, 455 P.2d 914.

MOWBRAY, Justice. A jury found Ernest Stewart guilty of attempted robbery. He has appealed to this court, seeking a reversal, on the sole ground that the evidence received during his trial was insufficient to support the jury's verdict.

Marvin Luedtke, who was the victim of the crime, and two police officers appeared for the State. Their testimony stands uncontroverted. It shows that the appellant, Stewart, approached Luedtke, a service station operator, and after brandishing a loaded .32 caliber automatic pistol, said, "I want all of your money." When Luedtke told him that the money was kept in a cash box located near the fuel pumps in front of the station, Stewart demanded the contents of Luedtke's wallet, which Luedtke promptly produced. It was at this juncture that the two police officers drove into the station. One of the officers actually saw the pistol in Stewart's hand. When Stewart saw the officers, he directed Luedtke to bring him two cans of oil and to act as though he, Stewart, were purchasing the oil. Luedtke gave him the oil. Stewart took one can, put his pistol in Luedtke's desk drawer, and attempted to leave the station. He was immediately apprehended by the officers.

Stewart argues that the attempted robbery was not proved because the evidence shows that he had abandoned his intent to commit the crime when he put down the pistol and left the station. We do not agree. The attempted robbery of Luedtke was completed when Stewart produced his pistol and demanded the money. The fact that Luedtke was apprehended on the spot does not lessen his guilt. As the court said in People v. Robinson, 180 Cal.App.2d 745, 4 Cal.Rptr. 679, 682 (1960), " * * * once an intent to commit a crime has been formed and overt acts toward the commission of that crime have been committed by a defendant he is then guilty of an attempt, whether he abandoned that attempt because of the approach of other persons or because of a change in his intentions due to a stricken conscience."

Affirmed.

COLLINS, ZENOFF, BATJER and THOMPSON, JJ., concur.

PEOPLE v. STAPLES

California Court of Appeal, 1970.
6 Cal.App.3d 61, 85 Cal.Rptr. 589.

REPPY, Associate Justice. Defendant was charged in an information with attempted burglary (Pen.Code, §§ 664, 459). Trial by jury was waived, and the matter submitted on the testimony contained in the transcript of the preliminary hearing together with exhibits. Defendant was found guilty. Proceedings were suspended before pronouncement of sentence, and an order was made granting defendant probation. The appeal is from the order which is deemed a final judgment. (Pen.Code, § 1237.)

In October 1967, while his wife was away on a trip, defendant, a mathematician, under an assumed name, rented an office on the second floor of a building in Hollywood which was over the mezzanine of a bank. Directly below the mezzanine was the vault of the bank. Defendant was aware of the layout of the building, specifically of the relation of the office he rented to the bank vault. Defendant paid rent for the period from October 23 to November 23. The landlord had 10 days before commencement of the rental period within which to finish some interior repairs and painting. During this prerental period defendant brought into the office certain equipment. This included drilling tools, two acetylene gas tanks, a blow torch, a blanket, and a linoleum rug. The landlord observed these items when he came in from time to time to see how the repair work was progressing. Defendant learned from a custodian that no one was in the building on Saturdays. On Saturday, October 14, defendant drilled two groups of holes into the floor of the office above the mezzanine room. He stopped drilling before the holes went through the floor. He came back to the office several times thinking he might slowly drill down, covering the holes with the linoleum rug. At some point in time he installed a hasp lock on a closet, and planned to, or did, place his tools in it. However, he left the closet keys on the premises. Around the end of November, apparently after November 23, the landlord notified the police and turned the tools and equipment over to them. Defendant did not pay any more rent. It is not clear when he last entered the office, but it could have been after November 23, and even after the landlord had removed the equipment. On February 22, 1968, the police arrested defendant. After receiving advice as to his constitutional rights, defendant voluntarily made an oral statement which he reduced to writing.

Among other things which defendant wrote down were these:

"Saturday, the 14th * * * I drilled some small holes in the floor of the room. Because of tiredness, fear, and the implications of what I was doing, I stopped and went to sleep.

"At this point I think my motives began to change. The actutal [sic] commencement of my plan made me begin to realize that even if I were to succeed a fugitive life of living off of stolen money would not give the enjoyment of the life of a mathematician however humble a job I might have.

"I still had not given up my plan however. I felt I had made a certain investment of time, money, effort and a certain pschological [sic] commitment to the concept.

"I came back several times thinking I might store the tools in the closet and slowly drill down (covering the hole with a rug of linoleum square). As time went on (after two weeks or so). My wife came back and my life as bank robber seemed more and more absurd."

* * *

There was definitely substantial evidence entitling the trial judge to find that defendant's acts had gone beyond the preparation stage.

The instant case provides an out-of-the-ordinary factual situation * * * Usually the actors in cases falling within that category of attempts are intercepted or caught in the act. Here, there was no direct proof of any actual interception. But it was clearly inferable by the trial judge that defendant became aware that the landlord had resumed control over the office and had turned defendant's equipment and tools over to the police. This was the equivalent of interception.

The inference of this nonvoluntary character of defendant's abandonment was a proper one for the trial judge to draw. However, it would seem that the character of the abandonment in situations of this type, whether it be voluntary (prompted by pangs of conscience or a change of heart) or nonvoluntary (established by inference in the instant case), is not controlling. The relevant factor is the determination of whether the acts of the perpetrator have reached such a stage of advancement that they can be classified as an attempt. Once that attempt is found there can be no exculpatory abandonment. "One of the purposes of the criminal law is to protect society from those who intend to injure it. When it is established that the defendant intended to commit a specific crime and that in carrying out his intention he committed an act that caused harm or sufficient danger of harm, it is immaterial that for some collateral reason he could not complete the intended crime." (People v. Camodeca, 52 Cal.2d 142, 147, 338 P.2d 903, 906.)

The order is affirmed.

NOTES

1. If the decision in *Stewart* is proper, is the same result required in *Staples?* Compare the case of People v. Von Hecht, 133 Cal.App.2d 25, 283 P.2d 764 (1955) where the defendant had been convicted of attempted grand

theft based on his ordering certain automotive equipment offering, as a basis for his order, another's credit card. The order required that the defendant leave his car at the garage. When the defendant returned to pick up the car and was arrested he did not have the card on his person and claimed he had abandoned his plan to use it but instead intended to pay cash. The court announced as its principle of law:

> "Abandonment is a defense if the attempt to commit a crime is freely and voluntarily abandoned before the act is put in process of final execution and *where there is no outside cause* prompting such abandonment."

133 Cal.App.2d at 36, 283 P.2d at 771. However, it found that here the trial court could properly find that the defendant had abandoned his scheme because he saw police at the garage. Should the law as announced in *Von Hecht* have been applied in *Staples?* in *Stewart?* Consider the following from Model Penal Code, Comments to § 5.01(4) (reprinted at page 689) 69–74 (Tent.Draft No. 10, 1960):

> *Renunciation of Criminal Purpose.* There is uncertainty under the present law whether abandonment of a criminal effort, after the bounds of preparation have been surpassed, will constitute a defense to a charge of attempt. In passing on this issue it is customary to distinguish between "voluntary" and "involuntary" abandonments.
>
> An "involuntary" abandonment occurs where the actor ceases his criminal endeavor because he fears detection or apprehension, or because he decides he will wait for a better opportunity, or because his powers or instruments are inadequate for completing the crime. There is no doubt that such an abandonment does not exculpate the actor from attempt liability otherwise incurred.
>
> By a "voluntary" abandonment is meant a change in the actor's purpose not influenced by outside circumstances, what may be termed repentance or change of heart. Lack of resolution or timidity may suffice. A reappraisal by the actor of the criminal sanctions hanging over his conduct would presumably be a motivation of the voluntary type as long as the actor's fear of the law is not related to a particular threat of apprehension or detection. Whether voluntary abandonments constitute a defense to an attempt charge is far from clear, there being few decisions squarely facing the issue.
>
> If assault cases are not considered, the prevailing view—contrary to the general conceptions of the commentators—is in favor of allowing voluntary desistance as a defense.[c] Supplementing these "express" statements are opinions which impliedly accept this view by emphasizing the fact that desistance in the particular case was involuntary or by giving effect to voluntary desistance

c. Lest prospective defense attorneys take too much comfort from this assertion it should be noted that the authors of the Comment cite four cases in direct support. Three are from American jurisdictions; only one is a decision of the jurisdiction's highest appellate court. One is from South Africa. The most recent is a 1922 Georgia Court of Appeals decision in which the supporting statement is dictum uttered in the course of affirming the conviction. Parker v. State, 29 Ga.App. 26, 113 S.E. 218 (1922).

in classifying the actor's discontinued conduct as "preparation". Also supporting this position is the widespread statutory definition of attempt—one who "does any act toward the commission of such crime, but fails or is prevented or intercepted in the perpetration thereof"—which, by enumerating involuntary causes of failure, may be taken to exclude voluntary desistance. A similar implication is present in the oft-quoted judicial doctrine that an attempt requires an act which would, in the natural course of things, if not interrupted by an intervening cause independent of the will of the actor, consummate the offense. The bulk of the decisions squarely denying the defense are cases involving assaults, and these are distinguishable. Whether they are correct need not be decided here; it is enough to note that something in the way of a substantive offense had been committed and immunity was accordingly withheld.

It must be noted that even where voluntary desistance is not itself a defense, an abandonment by the actor may result in exoneration if the abandonment negatives a criminal intent. Where the charge is assault with intent to rape and the evidence shows that the accused apparently had it within his power to complete the offense, proof of a voluntary abandonment will weigh heavily in favor of the accused. One state makes it conclusive evidence that defendant did not intend to rape.

The present subsection does not utilize the "voluntary-involuntary" terminology of the prior cases but reaches much the same result by allowing abandonment as a defense only where the circumstances manifest "renunciation of [the actor's] criminal purpose." The requirement of "renunciation" of purpose involves two elements: (1) that the abandonment of the criminal effort originate with the actor and not be forced upon him by some external circumstance such as police intervention; and (2) that the abandonment be permanent and complete rather than temporary or contingent—e. g., a decision by the actor to wait for a better opportunity to commit the crime would not manifest renunciation of criminal purpose.

The basis for allowing the defense involves two related considerations.

First, renunciation of criminal purpose tends to negative dangerousness. As previously indicated, much of the effort devoted to excluding early "preparatory" conduct from criminal attempt liability is based on the desire not to punish where there is an insufficient showing that the actor has a firm purpose to commit the crime contemplated. In cases where the actor has gone beyond the line drawn for preparation, indicating *prima facie* sufficient firmness of purpose, he should be allowed to rebut such a conclusion by showing that he has plainly demonstrated his lack of firm purpose by completely renouncing his purpose to commit the crime.

This line of reasoning, however, may prove unsatisfactory where the actor has proceeded far toward the commission of the contemplated crime, or has perhaps committed the "last proximate act." It may be argued that, whatever the inference to be drawn where the actor's conduct was in the area near the preparation-attempt line, in cases of further progress the inference of dangerousness from such an advanced criminal effort outweighs the countervailing inference arising from abandonment of the effort. However, it is in this latter class of cases that the second of the two policy considerations comes most strongly into play.

A second reason for allowing renunciation of criminal purpose as a defense to an attempt charge is to encourage actors to desist from pressing forward with their criminal designs, thereby diminishing the risk that the substantive crime will be committed. While, under the proposed subsection, such encouragement is held out at all stages of the criminal effort, its significance becomes greatest as the actor nears his criminal objective and the risk that the crime will be completed is correspondingly high. At the very point where abandonment least influences a judgment as to the dangerousness of the actor—where the last proximate act has been committed but the resulting crime can still be avoided—the inducement to desist stemming from the abandonment defense achieves its greatest value.

It is possible, of course, that the defense of renunciation of criminal purpose may add to the incentives to take the *first* steps toward crime. Knowledge that criminal endeavors can be undone with impunity may encourage preliminary steps that would not be undertaken if liability inevitably attached to every abortive criminal undertaking that proceeded beyond preparation. But this is not a serious problem. First, any consolation the actor might draw from the abandonment defense would have to be tempered with the knowledge that the defense would be unavailable if the actor's purposes were frustrated by external forces before he had an opportunity to abandon his effort. Second, the encouragement this defense might lend to the actor taking preliminary steps would be a factor only where the actor was dubious of his plans and where, consequently, the probability of continuance was not great.

On balance, it is concluded that renunciation of criminal purpose should be a defense to a criminal attempt charge because, as to the early stages of an attempt, it significantly negatives dangerousness of character, and, as to later stages, the value of encouraging desistance outweighs the net dangerousness shown by the abandoned criminal effort. And, because of the importance of encouraging desistance in the final stages of the attempt, the defense is allowed even where the last proximate act has occurred but the criminal result can be avoided—e. g., where the fuse has been lit but can still be stamped out. If, however, the actor has gone so far that he has put in motion forces which he is powerless to stop, then the attempt has been completed and cannot be abandoned. In accord with existing law, the actor can gain no immunity for this completed effort (e. g., firing at the intended victim and missing); all he can do is desist from making a second attempt.

*   *   *

In considering the significance to be attached to abandonment of a criminal attempt, one solution which was rejected was provision for reduction of penalty in the event of such abandonment. Insofar as encouragement of desistance is concerned, reductions in sanction would have to be very great in order to have a substantial impact on those already engrossed in a criminal attempt; indeed it is unlikely that anything short of complete immunity would suffice. And in dealing with the question of dangerousness, it seems that, once liability is established, sanctions should be linked to neutralizing the actor's dangerousness and determined on a broad basis with reference to the requirements of the particular offender. An automatic reduction in the case of abandonment would be inconsistent with this approach.

2.   What result on the following facts:

[A]bout 2:30 or 3 a. m., appellant and Pust drove into the pump area of the service station. At that time Thorne [the service station attendant and victim of the alleged attempted robbery] was busy waiting on a customer. He finished with the customer and returned the money to the till inside the station. When he came out the door appellant and Pust drove up in front of him, got out of the car and offered Thorne a pair of pliers in exchange for some money to buy gasoline. Thorne refused the offer. However, he noticed a gun partially covered by a shirt on the back seat of the car and asked if it was a .22. Appellant opened the car door, sat on the edge of the back seat, picked up the gun and pointed it at Thorne's chest. Appellant mumbled something which sounded to Thorne like "this is a stickup" or "this is a holdup." Then when Thorne asked if it was a holdup appellant replied, "That's what it means. That's what it looks like."

Thorne tried to talk the boys out of the holdup. He told them, "Boys, let's just talk this all over and think twice before you do it. I am talking to you father's advice." However, Pust told Thorne that they had "some girls" and needed the money to get out of town. Pust also suggested that Thorne claim colored people had held him up. Thorne answered, "The girls ain't worth going through this. As far as that, I'll put the gas, I'll give you some gas." Then Thorne took $2 from his pocket and said he would put $2 worth of gasoline in the car and make up the shortage with the $2. A woman drove into the station just as Thorne was finishing putting the gasoline in the car. Pust gave Thorne the pliers and he and appellant drove away.

Would further information be of value? If so, what information? See People v. Crary, 265 Cal.App.2d 534, 71 Cal.Rptr. 457 (1968).

STATE v. MILLER

Court of Appeals of Oregon, 1971.
6 Or.App. 366, 487 P.2d 1387.

LANGTRY, Judge. Defendant appeals from conviction of first degree murder. ORS 163.010. He was jointly indicted with Homer Lee Denniston and Dennis H. Cole for the murder of a storekeeper during an armed robbery. He asserts that the trial court erred * * * in its refusal to give certain requested instructions on attempt to commit murder and abandonment of the crime.

The defendant testified that he and the two other men planned the armed robbery of the grocery store. During the robbery the store owner was shot several times and killed. Defendant said he had gone with Denniston to the store, went in alone and bought some gum, and came back out, telling Denniston he had decided that he didn't want to go ahead with the holdup. Denniston said "okay" and that he would do it alone. Defendant testified he stayed outside when Denniston went inside. He said that he saw Denniston strike the storekeeper and shoot him; that Denniston took money, ran out of the store, grabbed the defendant and told him to "come on." Defendant said that after seeing Denniston shoot the storekeeper he just didn't know what to do. He testified that Denniston did not give him any money taken in the robbery, but that he bought "stuff," including beer, for him.

* * *

The defendant excepted to the court's refusal of his request that the jury be instructed that if it found he had abandoned "an attempt to commit this crime" he should be acquitted.

Defendant's testimony was that after he had gone into the store and came back out, he told his accomplice that he wasn't going to go through with the robbery. He stated he remained outside the store and left with his companion after the robbery and murder were completed, and later had, at least, beer as a fruit of the robbery.

Speaking of withdrawal from and abandonment of a crime as a defense, Clark and Marshall says:

> "The withdrawal must be something more than an expression of an intent to withdraw, made to his accomplices. *It must be accompanied by some affirmative effective action* * * *." Clark and Marshall, Crimes 537, 538, § 8.11 (7th ed. 1967). (Emphasis supplied.)

Taking defendant's story as a whole, if it is believed, his words and acts did not measure up to the standard of affirmative effective action.

Affirmed.

LE BARRON v. STATE

Supreme Court of Wisconsin, 1966.
32 Wis.2d 294, 145 N.W.2d 79.

Plaintiff in error David Le Barron (hereinafter the "defendant") was charged with [and convicted of] attempted rape.

* * *

CURRIE, Chief Justice. The appeal raises [this issue]: Was the evidence adduced sufficient to prove the finding of defendant guilty beyond a reasonable doubt of the crime of attempted rape?

* * *

In order to resolve the first issue it is necessary to set forth a résumé of the material facts adduced in evidence.

On March 3, 1965 at 6:55 p. m., the complaining witness, Jodean Randen, a housewife, was walking home across a fairly well-traveled railroad bridge in Eau Claire. She is a slight woman whose normal weight is 95 to 100 pounds. As she approached the opposite side of the bridge she passed a man who was walking in the opposite direction. The man turned and followed her, grabbed her arm and demanded her purse. She surrendered her purse and at the command of the man began walking away as fast as she could. Upon discovering that the purse was empty, he caught up with her again, grabbed her arm and told her that if she did not scream he would not hurt her. He then led her—willingly, she testified, so as to avoid being hurt by him—to the end of the bridge. While walking he shoved her head down and warned her not to look up or do anything and he would not hurt her.

On the other side of the bridge along the railroad tracks there is a coal shack. As they approached the coal shack he grabbed her, put one hand over her mouth, and an arm around her shoulder and told her not to scream or he would kill her. At this time Mrs. Randen thought he had a knife in his hand. He then forced her into the shack and up against the wall. As she struggled for her breath he said, "You know what else I want," unzipped his pants and started pulling up her skirt. She finally succeeded in removing his hand from her mouth, and after reassuring him that she would not scream, told him she was pregnant and pleaded with him to desist or he would hurt her baby. He then felt of her stomach and took her over to the door of the shack, where in the better light he was able to ascertain that, under her coat, she was wearing maternity clothes. He thereafter let her alone and left after warning her not to scream or call the police, or he would kill her.

After he had left, she proceeded to a nearby restaurant, had a cup of coffee, and kept calling home by phone until she reached her husband. He came to the restaurant for her and upon reaching home he called the police to report the incident. Based on a description given by Mrs. Randen to city police, defendant was determined to be a suspect. Subsequently, he was arrested by the sheriff's department. At the police station Mrs. Randen identified the defendant as the man who accosted her.

* * *

The material portions of the controlling statutes provide:

Sec. 944.01(1), Stats. "Any male who has sexual intercourse with a female he knows is not his wife, by force and against her will, may be imprisoned not more than 30 years."

Sec. 939.32(2), Stats. "An attempt to commit a crime requires that the actor have an intent to perform acts and attain a result which, if accomplished, would constitute such crime and that he does acts toward the commission of the crime which demonstrate unequivocally, under all the circumstances, that he formed that intent and would commit the crime except for the intervention of another person *or some other extraneous factor.*" (Italics supplied.)

* * *

We conclude that a jury could infer beyond a reasonable doubt from these overt acts of defendant that he intended to have sexual intercourse with defendant by force and against her will. The fact, that he desisted from his attempt to have sexual intercourse as a result of the plea of complainant that she was pregnant, would permit of the opposite inference. However, such desistance did not compel the drawing of such inference nor compel, as a matter of law, the raising of a reasonable doubt to a finding that defendant had previously intended to carry through with having intercourse by force and against complainant's will.

Defendant relies strongly on Oakley v. State [22 Wis.2d 298, 125 N.W.2d 657 (1964)] where this court held that defendant Oakley's acts were so equivocal as to prevent a finding of intent beyond a reasonable doubt to have sexual intercourse by force and against the will of the complainant. The evidence in the case disclosed neither physical violence nor threat of physical violence up to the time Oakley desisted from his attempt to have sexual intercourse with the complainant. He did put his arm around her and attempted to kiss her while entreating her to have intercourse, and also attempted to put his hand in her blouse and to lift up her skirt but did not attempt to renew this endeavor when she brushed his hand away. Thus the facts in *Oakley* are readily distinguishable from those of the case at bar. To argue that the two cases are analogous because, in the one instance the accused desisted because the complainant was menstruating and in the other because of pregnancy, is an oversimplification. Such an argument overlooks the radical difference in the nature of the overt acts relied upon to prove intent.

The argument, that the pregnancy of the instant complainant which caused defendant's desistance does not qualify as an "extraneous factor" within the meaning of sec. 939.32, Stats., is in conflict with our holding in State v. Damms [9 Wis.2d 183, 100 N.W.2d 592 (1960)]. There we upheld a conviction of attempt to commit murder where the accused pulled the trigger of an unloaded pistol intending to kill his estranged wife thinking the pistol was loaded. It was held that the impossibility of accomplishment due to the gun being unloaded fell within the statutory words, "except for the intervention of * * * some other extraneous factor." Particularly significant is this statement in the opinion:

> "An unequivocal act accompanied by intent should be sufficient to constitute a criminal attempt. Insofar as the actor knows, he has done everything necessary to insure the commission of the crime intended, and he should not escape punishment because of the fortuitous circumstance that by reason of some fact unknown to him it was impossible to effectuate the intended result."

The unloaded condition of the gun was every bit as much a part of the intrinsic fact situation in the *Damms* Case as was complainant's pregnancy in the instant case. We determine that such pregnancy constituted the intervention of an "extraneous factor" within the meaning of sec. 939.32(2), Stats.

PROPOSED FEDERAL CRIMINAL CODE (1971)

§ 1005. General Provisions Regarding Sections 1001 to 1004

* * *

(3) Renunciation Defense.

(a) Attempt. In a prosecution under section 1001 it is an affirmative defense that, under circumstances manifesting a voluntary and complete renunciation of his criminal intent, the defendant avoided the commission of the crime attempted by abandoning his criminal effort and, if mere abandonment was insufficient to accomplish such avoidance, by taking further and affirmative steps which prevented the commission thereof.

B. SOLICITATION

GERVIN v. STATE

Supreme Court of Tennessee, 1963.
212 Tenn. 653, 371 S.W.2d 449.

DYER, Judge. This appeal in error is from a verdict and judgment convicting Gervin, the appellant here and defendant below, of an attempt to commit murder * * *.

The question to be decided is whether or not an indictment which alleges criminal solicitation is sufficient in law to aver an attempt to commit a felony * * *. This question necessarily involves the primary consideration of common law, criminal solicitation as an attempt.

We hold that such an indictment is not legally sufficient, and that mere criminal solicitation does not constitute an attempt to commit murder * * *.

Robert George Gervin was arraigned and convicted under an indictment, the pertinent parts of which read:

"The Grand Jurors * * * present that Robert George Gervin * * * unlawfully and feloniously did commit and otherwise attempt to commit a felony * * * that is to say, the defendant with intent to feloniously and with malice aforethought commit murder in the first degree, did hire, persuade, try to persuade, and otherwise procure another to attempt to kill and murder another * * * contrary to the statute and against the peace and dignity of the State."

The defendant moved to quash the indictment, challenging the sufficiency of the averments. The motion to quash was overruled by the trial court, and this is assigned as error on appeal. Numerous other assignments of error are made which we do not reach as the one question is determinative.

The terms "attempt" and "solicitation" as used in criminal law are often confused and frequently these terms are merged. Nevertheless attempts and solicitation are distinct by definition. 25 L.R.A. 434 (1894).

"An attempt is an act done with the intent of committing a crime, but which fails of completion. To constitute an attempt, the defendant must, (1) with the intent to commit a specific crime, (2) do an overt act directed to its commission, which goes beyond mere preparation, and is apparently suitable for that purpose, but (3) which fails to result in the commission of the intended crime. 1 Wharton, Criminal Law and Procedure, Sec. 71 at 151–2 (1957)."

Common law, criminal solicitation is defined to include any words or devices by which a person is "requested, urged, advised, counseled, tempted, commanded or otherwise enticed to commit a crime." Perkins, Criminal Law 505 (1957).

It is evident from the above definitions that the indictment in question is couched in terms of criminal solicitation while averring an attempt to commit a felony. This, we hold, is not permissable in Tennessee.

The weight of American authority holds, as a general proposition, that mere criminal solicitation of another to commit a crime does not constitute an attempt.

The weight of authority is, of course, not determinative, but the reasons for that position are compelling.

The definitions of attempts and solicitation are not only different, but these offenses are analytically distinct. The gist of criminal solicitation is incitement. The body of the crime is the act of solicitation, and any additional conduct is incidental and collateral. Curran, Solicitations: A Substantive Crime, 17 Minn.L.Rev. 499, 503 (1932–33).

An attempt, on the other hand, requires three elements; (1) an intent to commit a specific crime; (2) an overt act; and (3) failure to consummate the crime. 1 Wharton, op. cit. supra Sec. 71 at 151–152. In attempts, the intent must be to commit the contemplated crime. The intent required in solicitation is the intent to have the crime committed with the purpose of communicating that intent to another. Blackburn, Solicitation to Crimes, 40 W.Va.L.Q. 135 (1933–34). But in relation to attempts, solicitation only supplies a wrongful intent. Solicitation to Commit Murder as an Attempt to Commit, 40 U.Mo.Bull.L.Ser. 45 (1928). Consequently, if the solicitor does not plan to take an active part in effecting the crime, and the solicitation is held an attempt, the requirement of a specific intent may be violated. See Perkins, op. cit. supra at 509.

To constitute an attempt there must also be an act of perpetration, that is, an overt act. However solicitation is preparation rather than perpetration. This being true, to call solicitation an attempt is to delete the element of an overt act. The element of an overt act is, however, necessary and serves a useful purpose as pointed out in State v. Mandel, 78 Ariz. 226, 278 P.2d 413 (1954).

The fundamental reason for an overt act is that until such act occurs, there is too much uncertainty that a design is to be apparently carried out. Until that time the situation is equivocal. 278 P.2d at 415–416.

We are reluctant to hold, and indeed our cases indicate we cannot, that at the stage of preparation the attempt will be carried out and that the situation is unequivocal. At this point there are too many contingencies, such as the willingness of the solicitant to carry out the design, to say the dye [sic] is cast. But to hold solicitation an attempt this would be necessary.

Not only would the merging of attempts and solicitations do violence to the respective concepts, but there are other reasons which are grounded in policy. There is not the same degree of heinousness in solicitation as in attempts, nor is solicitation as likely to result in a completed crime, there not being the same dangerous proximity to success as found in attempts.

In most areas of the law degrees of culpability and fault are recognized and different penalties are prescribed. We can see no good reason why there should be an exception made here. * * *

The latest decision in point is Valley v. State, 203 Tenn. 80, 309 S.W.2d 374 (1958). The defendant was indicted under T.C.A. § 39–603 for an assault with the intent to commit a felony, that is, have unnatural relations with a 14 year old boy. The testimony of the victim tended to prove that the defendant actually had made propositions to the boy and on one occasion had tried unsuccessfully to touch the boy.

This court said that although a technical assault was not made out the defendant was still guilty as the statute under which he was prosecuted also covered attempts. The court held this was at least an attempt.

Chief Justice Neil dissented upon the basis that since no overt act was shown the evidence was insufficient to sustain a conviction for an attempt.

We do not think this case stands for the proposition that solicitation is an attempt. At most the case indicates that solicitation in addition to some other conduct which transcends preparation may constitute an attempt. Interpreting this case as we do, we are cognizant of the contrary interpretation in Miller, Criminal Law and Procedure—1958 Tennessee Survey, 11 Vand.L.Rev. 1226, 1228–1229 (1958).

A reading of the decision in the Valley case indicates that the court was impressed that the defendant had tried to touch the victim. This is strengthened by the fact that the court quoted only that part of the testimony which dealt with the attempted touching. Further, we think it significant that the dissent was based on no overt act being shown. Therefore any difference of opinion within the court appears to have been grounded on whether there was or was not an overt act, and not over the question of whether or not solicitation is an attempt.

* * *

In reaching our conclusion in this case, we are mindful of the formidable opposition to making any distinction between attempts and criminal solicitation. One authority takes the position that the policy of attempt statutes should be expanded to cover solicitation, because solicitation involves the same consideration attempts do, and any distinction is artificial. Arnold, Criminal Attempts—The Rise and Fall of an Abstraction, 40 Yale L.J. 53, 76–77 (1931–32).

* * *

The appellee's contention implies that if solicitation cannot be punished as an attempt the solicitor may go free though guilty of reprehensible conduct. If this was the case we would be inclined to agree with the appellee. However, we think the crime of solicitation may be punished as an independent crime although we find no evidence of it ever having been done in this state. We therefore must turn to our statutes or to the common law.

* * *

At common law, solicitation to commit a crime, which by statute or common law is a felony, is a substantive crime. Furthermore so much of the common law as has not been abrogated or repealed by statute is in full force and effect in Tennessee. Finding no local statute which abrogates the offense of common law solicitation, we must conclude it is an indictable offense in Tennessee. And being an indictable offense, solicitation to commit a felony is treated as a misdemeanor. * * *

The trial court, therefore, erred in failing to sustain the defendant's motion to quash the indictment.

The cause is reversed and remanded.

MODEL PENAL CODE (PROPOSED OFFICIAL DRAFT, 1962)

Section 5.02. Criminal Solicitation

(1) *Definition of Solicitation.* A person is guilty of solicitation to commit a crime if with the purpose of promoting or facilitating its commission he commands, encourages or requests another person to engage in specific conduct which would constitute such crime or an attempt to commit such crime or which would establish his complicity in its commission or attempted commission.

(2) *Uncommunicated Solicitation.* It is immaterial under Subsection (1) of this Section that the actor fails to communicate with the person he solicits to commit a crime if his conduct was designed to effect such communication.

(3) *Renunciation of Criminal Purpose.* It is an affirmative defense that the actor, after soliciting another person to commit a crime persuaded him not to do so or otherwise prevented the commission of the crime, under circumstances manifesting a complete and voluntary renunciation of his criminal purpose.

PROPOSED FEDERAL CRIMINAL CODE
(STUDY DRAFT 1970)

§ 1003. Criminal Solicitation

(1) Offense. A person is guilty of criminal solicitation if he commands, induces, entreats, or otherwise attempts to persuade another person to commit a particular crime which is, in fact, a felony, whether as principal or accomplice, with intent to promote or facilitate the commission of that crime, and under circumstances strongly corroborative of that intent.

(2) Defense. It is a defense to a prosecution under this section that, if the criminal object were achieved, the defendant would be a victim of the offense or the offense is so defined that his conduct would be inevitably incident to its commission or he otherwise would not be guilty under the statute defining the offense or as an accomplice * * *.

(3) Defense Precluded. It is no defense to a prosecution under this section that the person solicited could not be guilty of the offense because of lack of responsibility or culpability, or other incapacity or defense.

(4) Renunciation and Withdrawal. It is an affirmative defense to a prosecution under this section that the defendant, after soliciting another person to commit a felony, persuaded him not to do so or otherwise prevented the commission of the felony, under circumstances manifesting a complete and voluntary renunciation of the defendant's criminal intent. A renunciation is not "voluntary and complete" if it is motivated in whole or in part by (a) a belief that a circumstance exists which increases the probability of detection or apprehension of the defendant or another or which makes more difficult the consummation of the crime or (b) a decision to postpone the crime until another time or to substitute another victim or another but similar objective.

(5) Grading. Criminal solicitation shall be subject to the penalties provided for attempt in section 1001(4).

* * *

Comment

While a few statutes prohibit specific solicitations as substantive offenses, existing federal law has no general prohibition against solicitation of crimes. If the solicitation is successful, the solicitor is criminally liable as an accomplice; if the solicitation does not result in commission of the crime, but the solicitee agrees and an overt act is committed, the solicitor is criminally liable for conspiracy. Thus, solicitation may be viewed as an attempt to form a conspiracy. This section would expand federal law to cover unsuccessful solicitations of felonies, so as to permit earlier intervention against a criminal enterprise which has moved well beyond mere talk. It should be noted that some other modern criminal code revisions would make solicitation of any crime an offense. In this Code solicitations of crimes which are not felonies are proscribed in a few particular instances rather than by general provision here. See § 1346, dealing with solicitation of offenses obstructing justice.

Instigation is required; mere encouragement is not enough. "Particular" crimes must be solicited because to prohibit general exhortations would raise free speech problems. The circumstances under which the solicitation is made must strongly corroborate that the solicitor is serious about having the person solicited act upon the solicitation. An alternative would be to penalize solicitation only if the person solicited was so far persuaded as to commit an overt act in compliance with the solicitation. Such a rule would preclude prosecution based on solicitation allegedly addressed to a law enforcement official or undercover agent.

NOTES

1. The drafters of the Model Penal Code and the Draft of the New Federal Criminal Code take a rather more serious view of those who solicit crime than does the Tennessee Supreme Court in *Gervin*. The Comments to § 5.02, Model Penal Code, Tent.Draft No. 10 at 82 (1960), acknowledge the existence of views such as those expressed in *Gervin* but continue: "Against this is the view that a solicitation is, if anything, more dangerous than a direct attempt, since it may give rise to that cooperation among criminals that is a special hazard. Solicitation may, indeed, be thought of as an attempt to conspire. Moreover, the solicitor, working his will through one or more agents, manifests an approach to crime more intelligent and masterful than the efforts of his hireling." It goes on to note that " * * * the imposition of liability for criminal solicitation may be an important means by which the leadership of a movement deemed criminal may be suppressed." [4] The citations offered in support of this statement illustrate the major concern that civil libertarians have with the criminalization of solicitation.

How great is the danger that such statutes will be employed to stifle First Amendment rights either directly or by its "chilling effect"? Cf. *Speiser v. Randall*, 357 U.S. 513, 78 S.Ct. 1332, 2 L.Ed.2d 1460 (1958). Is either MPC § 5.02 or Proposed Federal Criminal Code § 1003 consistent with the "clear and present danger" doctrine? Need they be?

4. Political agitation. Masses Pub. Co. v. Patten, 246 Fed. 24 (2d Cir. 1917); United States v. Nearing, 252 Fed. 223 (S.D.N.Y.1918); United States v. Galleanni, 245 Fed. 977 (D.Mass.1917); People v. Most, 171 N.Y. 423, 64 N.E. 175 (1902) (based on breach of peace statute); Rex v. Bowman, 76 J.P. 271 (Central Crim.Ct.1912); Rex v. Antonelli & Barberi, 70 J.P. 4 (Central Crim.Ct.1905); The Queen v. Most, 7 Q.B.D. 244 (C.C.R.1881); R. v. M'Carthy, Holland, and O'Dwyer, [1903] 2 Irish Rep. 146 (1902).

Labor agitation. State v. Schleifer, 99 Conn. 432, 121 Atl. 805 (1923); State v. Quinlan, 86 N.J.L. 120, 91 Atl. 111 (Sup.Ct.1914), aff'd per curiam, 87 N.J.L. 333, 93 Atl. 1086 (Ct.Err. & App. 1915); State v. Boyd, 86 N.J.L. 75, 91 Atl. 586 (1914), rev'd on other grounds, 87 N.J.L. 560, 94 Atl. 807 (Ct.Err. & App.1915); Rex v. O'Brien, [1914] So. Afr.L.R. (Trans.Prov.Div.) 287.

2. If a general solicitation statute poses serious dangers to First Amendment rights, would it be preferable to have statutes aimed at more specific evils. An example of such is N.J.Stat.Ann. 2A:148–10 which reads as follows:

> Any person who, in public or private, by speech, writing, printing or otherwise, advocates, encourages, justifies, praises or incites:
>
> a. The unlawful burning or destruction of public or private property; or
>
> b. Assaults upon any of the armed forces of the United States, the national guard, or the police force of this or any other state or of any municipality; or
>
> c. The killing or injuring of any class or body of persons or of any individual—
>
> Is guilty of a high misdemeanor.

See State v. Cappon, 118 N.J.Super. 9, 285 A.2d 287 (1971) (at the end of a Puerto Rican Day parade in Newark defendant cried "get those motherfuckers" and bottles began to be hurled at nearby police officers) and State v. Hopson, 109 N.J.Super. 382, 263 A.2d 205 (1970) (in the course of a demonstration concerning grievances at a local high school defendant's son was arrested, whereupon she uttered words "of the general purport of, 'get the cops,' and 'Free the black boy.'"). Turner v. La Belle, 251 F.Supp. 443 (D.C.Conn.1966) involved a prosecution under a virtually identical Connecticut statute. There, four leaders of civil rights groups in Hartford sought to restrain enforcement of the statute against them. They had led a demonstration of support in the Hartford Ghetto shortly after the Watts riots. One defendant allegedly said " * * * treat every cop as your enemy * * * until America wakes up." Another was alleged to have told the small crowd: "If I can't be imported back, then kill me, kill me, or I'll kill you" and "anyone that's black is so very angry that he wants to fight, that he wants to shoot, well then, only look to the left, to the blue shirts."

3. Another way of limiting the reach of solicitation statutes is that adopted by the Proposed Federal Criminal Code which, in its Final Draft, adds the following clause at the end of § 1003(1)

> "and the person solicited commits an overt act in response to the solicitation."

The Comment explains:

> "the solicitee either has not yet agreed (although he has committed an overt act, such as coming back for further discussions) or he has agreed but no overt act has been committed sufficient to make the crime a conspiracy. * * * An overt act is required so that criminality depends on something besides speech."

In what way does the commission by the solicitee of a possibly trivial overt act affect the culpability of the solicitor?

4. Consider the following comments by the New York Court of Appeals concerning the recently-enacted New York solicitation statute:

> There are * * * potential difficulties inherent in this penal provision which should be looked at, even though all of them

are not decisive in this present case.   One, of course, is the absence of any need for corroboration.   *   *   *   [T]here are types of criminal conduct which might be solicited where there would be a heavy thrust placed on the credibility of a single witness testifying to a conversation.   Extraordinary care might be required in deciding when to prosecute; in determining the truth; and in appellate review of the factual decision.

One example would be the suggestion of one person to another that he commit a sexual offense; another is the suggestion that he commit perjury.   The Model Penal Code did not require corroboration; but aside from the need for corroboration which is traditional in some sexual offenses, there are dangers in the misinterpretation of innuendos or remarks which could be taken as invitations to commit sexual offenses.   *   *   *

Another potential problem with the statute is that it includes an attempt to commit unlawful solicitation, i. e., solicits, etc., "or otherwise attempts to cause" the conduct.   This has the same effect as the Model Penal Code, but the language there is different.   The code spells the purpose out more specifically that: "It is immaterial   *   *   *   that the actor fails to communicate with the person he solicits to commit a crime if his conduct was designed to effect such communication" (Model Penal Code, § 5.02, subd. [2], Tent. Draft No. 10   *   *   *).   This could be an attempt in the classic sense and might be committed by a telephone message initiated but never delivered.   The present Penal Law, stated in different language, has the same effect.

People v. Lubow, 29 N.Y.2d 58, 272 N.E.2d 331, 334–35 (1971).   Are these really "potential problems?"   If so, how should they be dealt with?

5.   Assume MPC § 5.02 is enacted.

a.   A, whose daughter is pregnant, asks B to arrange for an illegal abortion.   C overhears the request and, before B takes any action, reports it to the local District Attorney.   Cf. Comments to § 5.02, Model Penal Code, Tent.Draft No. 10 at 87 (1960).

b.   A writes B urging him not to report for induction into the armed services because of the alleged immorality of the Viet Nam War.   C, B's mother, intercepts the letter before it reaches B and reports it to the United States Attorney.   What if A merely publishes a general appeal for resistance to the war and condemns the draft and the telephone surtax?   Cf. Spock v. United States, 416 F.2d 165 (1st Cir. 1969), reprinted at page 884, and People v. Quentin, 58 Misc.2d 601, 296 N.Y.S.2d 443 (Dist.Ct., Nassau County, 1968).

c.   A, an attorney specializing in adoption, advises B who claims to be uncertain as to the paternity of her fetus, that he will obviate this problem if she has a friend.   B introduces C to A who proposes that C swear B's husband could not be the father and coaches her as to proposed testimony.   In fact B and C are welfare department investigators; B is not pregnant and so there could be no custody proceedings. Bensen v. Superior Court, 57 Cal.2d 240, 368 P.2d 116, 18 Cal.Rptr. 516 (1962).

    d. A, an undercover police agent, asks B, a suspected marijuana dealer, to sell him some. B refuses and reports A to the local district attorney. Cf. Howard v. Felton, 85 Idaho 286, 379 P.2d 414 (1963) (dissenting opinion).

Is there any reason why A in each of the above situations should not be considered a fit subject for the criminal sanction? If so, does your reason have anything to do with the propriety of criminalizing solicitation?

C. CONSPIRACY

---

1. MODEL STATUTORY FORMULATIONS

MODEL PENAL CODE (PROPOSED OFFICIAL DRAFT, 1962)

Section 5.03. Criminal Conspiracy

(1) *Definition of Conspiracy.* A person is guilty of conspiracy with another person or persons to commit a crime if with the purpose of promoting or facilitating its commission he:

    (a) agrees with such other person or persons that they or one or more of them will engage in conduct which constitutes such crime or an attempt or solicitation to commit such crime; or

    (b) agrees to aid such other person or persons in the planning or commission of such crime or of an attempt or solicitation to commit such crime.

(2) *Scope of Conspiratorial Relationship.* If a person guilty of conspiracy, as defined by Subsection (1) of this Section, knows that a person with whom he conspires to commit a crime has conspired with another person or persons to commit the same crime, he is guilty of conspiring with such other person or persons, whether or not he knows their identity, to commit such crime.

(3) *Conspiracy With Multiple Criminal Objectives.* If a person conspires to commit a number of crimes, he is guilty of only one conspiracy so long as such multiple crimes are the object of the same agreement or continuous conspiratorial relationship.

* * *

(5) *Overt Act.* No person may be convicted of conspiracy to commit a crime, other than a felony of the first or second degree,

unless an overt act in pursuance of such conspiracy is alleged and proved to have been done by him or by a person with whom he conspired.

(6) *Renunciation of Criminal Purpose.* It is an affirmative defense that the actor, after conspiring to commit a crime, thwarted the success of the conspiracy, under circumstances manifesting a complete and voluntary renunciation of his criminal purpose.

(7) *Duration of Conspiracy.* For purposes of Section 1.06(4):

(a) conspiracy is a continuing course of conduct which terminates when the crime or crimes which are its object are committed or the agreement that they be committed is abandoned by the defendant and by those with whom he conspired; and

(b) such abandonment is presumed if neither the defendant nor anyone with whom he conspired does any overt act in pursuance of the conspiracy during the applicable period of limitation; and

(c) if an individual abandons the agreement, the conspiracy is terminated as to him only if and when he advises those with whom he conspired of his abandonment or he informs the law enforcement authorities of the existence of the conspiracy and of his participation therein.

Section 5.04. Incapacity, Irresponsibility or Immunity of Party to Solicitation or Conspiracy

(1) Except as provided in Subsection (2) of this Section, it is immaterial to the liability of a person who solicits or conspires with another to commit a crime that:

(a) he or the person whom he solicits or with whom he conspires does not occupy a particular position or have a particular characteristic which is an element of such crime, if he believes that one of them does; or

(b) the person whom he solicits or with whom he conspires is irresponsible or has an immunity to prosecution or conviction for the commission of the crime.

(2) It is a defense to a charge of solicitation or conspiracy to commit a crime that if the criminal object were achieved, the actor would not be guilty of a crime under the law defining the offense or as an accomplice under Section 2.06(5) or 2.06(6)(a) or (b).

PROPOSED FEDERAL CRIMINAL CODE (1971)

§ 1004.   Criminal Conspiracy

(1) Offense.   A person is guilty of conspiracy if he agrees with one or more persons to engage in or cause the performance of conduct which, in fact, constitutes a crime or crimes, and any one or more of such persons does an act to effect the objective of the conspiracy.   The agreement need not be explicit but may be implicit in the fact of collaboration or existence of other circumstances.

(2) Parties to Conspiracy.   If a person knows that one with whom he agrees has agreed or will agree with another to effect the same objective, he shall be deemed to have agreed with the other, whether or not he knows the other's identity.

(3) Duration of Conspiracy.   A conspiracy shall be deemed to continue until its objectives are accomplished, frustrated or abandoned.   "Objectives" includes escape from the scene of the crime, distribution of booty, and measures, other than silence, for concealing the crime or obstructing justice in relation to it.   A conspiracy shall be deemed to have been abandoned if no overt act to effect its objectives has been committed by any conspirator during the applicable period of limitations.

(4) Defense Precluded.   It is no defense to a prosecution under this section that the person with whom such person is alleged to have conspired has been acquitted, has not been prosecuted or convicted, has been convicted of a different offense, is immune from prosecution, or is otherwise not subject to justice.

(5) Liability as Accomplice.   Accomplice liability for offenses committed in furtherance of the conspiracy is to be determined as provided in section 401.

(6) Grading.   Conspiracy shall be subject to the penalties provided for attempt in section 1001(3).

(7) Jurisdiction.   There is federal jurisdiction over an offense defined in this section as prescribed in section 203.

Comment

* * *

4. *Grading and Sentencing.*   Existing law (18 U.S.C.A. § 371) establishes a maximum term of five years' imprisonment for conspiracy to commit any felony, regardless of whether the felony itself carries a penalty of 2 or 20 years;   many existing statutes defining specific offenses therefore do not rely upon the general conspiracy statute and repeat the conspiracy provision in order to correlate the sentencing provisions.   Subsection (6) of this section relates the penalty to the class of the offense which is the objective of the conspiracy.   The Code treats conspiracy, however, as a species of multi-party

attempt; the grading is comparable to that provided for attempt and, as is provided for attempt, under § 3204 one cannot be sentenced consecutively for conspiracy and the substantive crime. Although, under the general rule of § 1001, the grading of a conspiracy offense would be lower where the conspiracy had not come dangerously close to accomplishing its goals, conspiracy is punishable equally with the completed offense in the case of certain offenses in the Code, where explicit provision is made for such grading. See, e. g., § 1112 (espionage).

* * *

8. *Alternative Treatment of Conspiracy.* A substantial body of opinion in the Commission favors an alternative to subsection (6) which would read as follows: "Grading. Conspiracy shall be graded at the same level as the highest crime conduct constituting which was agreed to be performed or caused." This would reflect the view that conspiracy should be treated not only as an inchoate offense, but also as a separate crime. See Model Penal Code, Tent. Draft No. 10, p. 96 (1960); Callanan v. United States, 364 U.S. 587, 593–94 (1961). In the opinion of these Commissioners, there is insufficient justification, either in theory or experience, to warrant the approach of the text, which would narrow the scope of present conspiracy law. These same Commissioners wish to express concern that the Code would not permit the imposition of a consecutive sentence for conspiracy and the commission of the contemplated offense (see § 3204(2)(b); *cf.* Clune v. United States, 159 U.S. 590 (1895)), and that subsection (5) of this section overrules the Supreme Court's decision in Pinkerton v. United States, 328 U.S. 640 (1946). Finally, these Commissioners wish to alert the Congress to the need to give special attention to procedural and evidentiary aspects of conspiracy law when it undertakes substantive reform. See Working Papers, pp. 395–400.

See Working Papers, pp. 155–57, 381–82, 383–402, 431, 434, 1106–07.

2. ELEMENTS OF THE OFFENSE

a. AGREEMENT

(1) GENERAL REQUIREMENT OF AGREEMENT

BENDER v. STATE

Supreme Court of Delaware, 1969.
253 A.2d 686.

WOLCOTT, Chief Justice. This is an appeal from a conviction of robbery and conspiracy to commit robbery. William L. Bender, Frank Lightcap and Kenneth Lloyd were jointly indicted, tried and convicted on the two charges. All three appeal. Basically, the question raised is the sufficiency of the State's evidence to support the convictions.

The State's case was as follows:

On June 28, 1967, at about 6:30 p. m., Eli Byler was walking with David Detweiler at Ninth and Shipley Streets in Wilmington. Byler was approached by Lloyd who asked for a cigarette and for money. Byler refused and started to walk away. At this point, Bender and Lightcap came up. Lloyd then threatened Byler with a glass bottle he had in his hand.

Byler began to run and was chased by the three defendants. He was caught from behind by Lightcap and was held from behind by more than one person. His wallet was taken from his pocket and money removed from it by Lloyd. Thereupon, all three defendants, Lightcap, Lloyd and Bender, fled the scene.

Appellants argue that there was insufficient evidence of robbery as to Bender to submit to the jury, and that there was no evidence as to conspiracy to commit robbery as to any of the appellants. Accordingly, they seek a reversal and a remand for new trial as to Lloyd and Lightcap on the robbery charge, and a judgment of acquittal as to Bender on the robbery charge, and as to all three on the conspiracy charge.

We think, however, that under the evidence, the State proved without question that Byler was the victim of a robbery and that all three of the defendants participated in it. No other conclusion seems credible when it is considered that all were present when Byler was threatened by Lloyd. When Byler sought to flee, all three defendants pursued him. At least two of them held him from behind while, presumably, Lloyd removed his wallet. All three defendants then ran off together.

* * *

With respect to the conspiracy charge, the State, of course, produced no evidence of a prior agreement among the defendants to commit this robbery. The State contends that the presence of the three defendants on the scene and their concerted action in committing the crime justify the conclusion that they had agreed among themselves.

A conspiracy is the combination of two or more persons to commit a crime. It is not necessary that there be a formal agreement in advance of the crime. The basic requirement is that there be an unlawful combination, and that the parties have a common design or purpose. If a person understands the unlawful nature of the acts taking place, and nevertheless assists in any manner in the carrying out of the common scheme, he thereupon becomes a conspirator to commit the offense.

We think there is sufficient evidence of the joint participation in this crime of these defendants to warrant the inference that they had the common design or purpose of robbing Byler. The matter was therefore properly submitted to the jury which found them guilty.

The judgments below are affirmed.

ZIATZ v. PEOPLE

Supreme Court of Colorado, 1970.
171 Colo. 58, 465 P.2d 406.

LEE, Justice. Plaintiff in error, Ronald Arthur Ziatz, was convicted in the Denver District Court of making a false statement and order for Dilaudid, a narcotic drug, in violation of C.R.S.1963, 48–5–17(3) and (5), and of conspiracy to commit that offense in violation of C.R.S.1963, 40–7–35. Ziatz was sentenced to consecutive terms in the penitentiary of four to five years on the drug count and of eight to ten years on the conspiracy count.

On the evening of April 4, 1966, a man and woman entered a pharmacy on West Colfax Avenue in Denver, Colorado. The man remained in the front portion of the store and the woman proceeded to the rear and presented a prescription for Dilaudid to the druggist in charge, requesting that it be filled. The druggist described Dilaudid as "an unusual drug in not too much use today." Because of the nature of the drug and the handwriting which he suspected not to be genuine, the druggist called the doctor whose name appeared on the prescription blank. As he commenced this telephone inquiry, the woman and man proceeded rapidly from the store. The doctor advised that the prescription was false and the druggist immediately notified the police. Investigating officers presented photographs to the druggist and to a clerk, who each identified the man and the woman, respectively, as Ronald Arthur Ziatz and Lorraine Irene Valdez. Both Valdez and Ziatz were thereafter apprehended and placed under arrest. Miss Valdez was charged jointly with Ziatz in this case, but was tried separately and is not a party to this writ of error.

The People's evidence showed that the handwriting on the prescription was that of Ziatz. He did not testify and presented only one witness, whose testimony related to his employment prior to the time of the transaction under consideration.

* * *

THE CONSPIRACY COUNT

4. Ziatz asserts several errors in relation to his conviction on the conspiracy count. We find it unnecessary to consider such specifications in view of what we consider a complete absence of substantial evidence to support the conspiracy conviction.

Ziatz' motion for an acquittal at the conclusion of the People's case was denied. The motion for judgment of acquittal should have been granted as to the conspiracy count. We have searched the record for any evidence that Ziatz conspired with Valdez or any other person to commit the substantive offense charged in count 1 of the information, which was that of making a false statement and order for Dilaudid under C.R.S.1963, 48–5–17(3) and (5). We note that Ziatz was not charged under subsection 1 of section 17 with obtaining a narcotic drug by use of a false name or the giving of a false address. Although he was charged under subsection 5 of section 17 with making a false statement and order for Dilaudid, he was not charged with the alternative offense described in subsection 5—that of "uttering" a false prescription and order. This is of significance, since the conspiracy count relates only to the first count of the information and not to other criminal conduct.

The evidence at the trial was directed to two phases of the transaction. The first phase related to the activities at the pharmacy where Valdez and Ziatz attempted to obtain the narcotic drug by uttering the false prescription, a crime of which they were not here charged. The second phase related to the fabrication of the false prescription. There was no direct evidence whatsoever as to the fabrication of the false prescription. Neither Ziatz nor Valdez testified, nor did any other witness, concerning this phase of the case. The only evidence that Ziatz fabricated the prescription was that of the handwriting expert. There was a complete lack of any proof that Ziatz and Valdez were acquainted with each other or had any association at or prior to the time when the prescription was fabricated, nor were there any circumstances shown from which it could reasonably be inferred that they illegally agreed, conspired or cooperated to fabricate the prescription. Thus, the conclusion that Ziatz and Valdez illegally conspired to make the false statement and order is based solely upon one circumstance, that they jointly attempted to obtain the narcotic drug by means and use of the false prescription.

In order to convict one on circumstantial evidence alone, the facts and circumstances must be such as are inconsistent, upon any reasonable hypothesis, with the innocence of the defendant, and incapable of explanation upon any reasonable hypothesis other than that of the guilt of the defendant. It is not necessarily to be inferred from the act alone of uttering or passing a false prescription that the actor fabricated or was an accomplice to the fabrication of the false prescription. Such is the situation here. No doubt that Ziatz and Valdez could have been charged under the circumstances of this case with the commission of conspiracy to commit some other offense, e. g., conspiracy to utter a false prescription, and have been successfully convicted on the evidence presented in this case. However, such does not justify a conviction of conspiracy to commit the offense with which they were here charged. The judgment of conviction for conspiracy must therefore be set aside.

NOTE

Conspiracy doctrine permits the state to intervene long before the defendants have taken any action which brings them close to the achievement of their criminal purpose. It permits this intervention on the basis of conduct, other than the agreement, which may be extremely equivocal as an expression of criminal purpose. Therefore, it is clear that the establishment of an agreement is essential to the rationale for conspiracy prosecutions. The existence of the agreement presumably allays any concerns we might have about possible misidentification of the accused. It has been asserted that:

> " * * * The act of agreeing with another to commit a crime * * * is concrete and unambiguous; it does not present the infinite degrees and variations possible in the general category of attempts. The danger that truly equivocal behavior may be misinterpreted as preparation to commit a crime is minimized; purpose must be relatively firm before the commitment involved in agreement is assumed."

Wechsler, Jones, & Korn, The Treatment of Inchoate Crimes in the Model Penal Code of The American Law Institute: Attempt, Solicitation, and Conspiracy, 61 Colum.L.Rev. 957, 958 (1961). How consistent is this position with that of the Arkansas Supreme Court:

> "Appellant seems to take the position that there must be direct evidence of a conspiracy, common design or purpose, and of the intent of the conspirators or joint actors to engage therein. In this he is mistaken. We have long recognized * * * that it is not necessary that an unlawful combination, conspiracy or concert of action to commit an unlawful act be shown by direct evidence, and that it may be proved by circumstances. * * * It may be inferred, even though no actual meeting among the parties is proved, if it be shown that two or more persons pursued by their acts the same unlawful object, each doing a part, so that their acts, though apparently independent, were in fact connected."

Griffin v. State, 248 Ark. 1223, 1225, 455 S.W.2d 882, 884 (1970).

Would this formulation be acceptable unless the criminal object has been achieved as in Bender v. State, supra? Should the presence of a substantive offense permit a more relaxed view of what will satisfy the agreement requirement?

Given the obvious difficulties of proving an agreement for criminal purposes isn't it necessary that the state be permitted considerable leeway in how it may establish this element? This view has clearly been expressed in Interstate Circuit v. United States, 306 U.S. 208, 59 S.Ct. 467, 83 L.Ed. 610 (1939). There, defendant motion picture distributors and exhibitors were charged with conspiring, in violation of the Sherman Antitrust Act, to restrain trade by restricting the minimum prices that could be charged by exhibitors. The appellants argued, inter alia, that the finding of conspiracy was not supported by the evidence because all that had been shown was separate agreements between each of the exhibitor defendants and each of the distributor defendants, not acting in concert with any other distributors, to impose restrictions necessary to the protection of their mutual interests in copyright rewards. Mr. Justice Stone, writing for the Court responded.

As is usual in cases of alleged unlawful agreements to restrain commerce, the Government is without the aid of direct testimony that the distributors entered into any agreement with each other to impose the restrictions upon subsequent-run exhibitors. In order to establish agreement it is compelled to rely on inferences drawn from the course of conduct of the alleged conspirators.

The trial court drew the inference of agreement from the nature of the proposals made on behalf of Interstate and Consolidated; from the manner in which they were made; from the substantial unanimity of action taken upon them by the distributors; and from the fact that appellants did not call as witnesses any of the superior officials who negotiated the contracts with Interstate or any official who, in the normal course of business, would have had knowledge of the existence or non-existence of such an agreement among the distributors. This conclusion is challenged by appellants because not supported by subsidiary findings or by the evidence. We think this inference of the trial court was rightly drawn from the evidence. * * * from the beginning each of the distributors knew that the proposals were under consideration by the others. Each was aware that all were in active competition and that without substantially unanimous action with respect to the restrictions for any given territory there was risk of a substantial loss of the business and good will of the subsequent-run and independent exhibitors, but that with it there was the prospect of increased profits. There was, therefore, strong motive for concerted action, full advantage of which was taken by Interstate and Consolidated in presenting their demands to all in a single document.

There was risk, too, that without agreement diversity of action would follow. * * * It taxes credulity to believe that the several distributors would, in the circumstances, have accepted and put into operation with substantial unanimity such far-reaching changes in their business methods without some understanding that all were to join, and we reject as beyond the range of probability that it was the result of mere chance.

* * *

While the District Court's finding of an agreement of the distributors among themselves is supported by the evidence, we think that in the circumstances of this case such agreement for the imposition of the restrictions upon subsequent-run exhibitors was not a prerequisite to an unlawful conspiracy. It was enough that, knowing that concerted action was contemplated and invited, the distributors gave their adherence to the scheme and participated in it. Each distributor was advised that the others were asked to participate; each knew that coöperation was essential to successful operation of the plan. They knew that the plan, if carried out, would result in a restraint of commerce, which, we will presently point out, was unreasonable within the meaning of the Sherman Act, and knowing it, all participated in the plan. The evidence is persuasive that each distributor early became aware that the others had joined. With that knowledge they renewed the arrangement and carried it into effect for the two successive years.

It is elementary that an unlawful conspiracy may be and often is formed without simultaneous action or agreement on the part of the conspirators. Acceptance by competitors, without previous agreement, of an invitation to participate in a plan, the necessary consequence of which, if carried out, is restraint of interstate commerce, is sufficient to establish an unlawful conspiracy under the Sherman Act.

Is there any reason why these principles should not be equally applicable to conspiracies to commit traditional crimes?

UNITED STATES v. KNIGHT

United States Court of Appeals for the Ninth Circuit, 1969.
416 F.2d 1181.

JAMES M. CARTER, Circuit Judge. Appellants were charged with a conspiracy under 18 U.S.C.A. § 371 to (1) wilfully and knowingly encourage and induce Mexican aliens to enter the United States illegally, a violation of 8 U.S.C.A. § 1324(a) (4); (2) to wilfully and knowingly [shield from detection] * * * Mexican aliens, then illegally within the United States, a violation of § 1324(a) (3); and (3) to wilfully and knowingly transport, Mexican aliens, then illegally within the United States, a violation of 8 U.S.C.A. § 1324(a) (2).

Co-conspirators John Besse and Vicente Ruiz-Tellez were named but not indicted. Appellants were convicted at a jury trial and sentenced to imprisonment for a period of two years.

Each appellant was represented by separate counsel in the trial court, and they filed separate briefs. We will consider the appeals together.

THE QUESTIONS PRESENTED

Appellant Herman Knight contends:

(1) The evidence was insufficient to support the verdict;

* * *

(1) *Sufficiency of the Evidence.*

Counsel for appellant Herman Knight conceded at the argument in this court, that the record showed that Herman Knight knew of the conspiracy; but he contends that the evidence was insufficient to connect Herman Knight with it, or show his participation therein.

We have examined the transcript, and viewed the evidence, as we must, in the light most favorable to the government. We find that there was sufficient evidence to show Herman Knight's participation in the conspiracy.

Ruiz-Tellez, a Mexican alien and a named co-conspirator, was one of the chief witnesses against the appellants. In late May 1967, Ruiz-Tellez had been transporting four aliens north from Nogales, Arizona, when his Pontiac car broke down. The four aliens hid in the desert. Besse, (a co-conspirator) and appellant Ralph Knight offered Ruiz-Tellez assistance, and gave him a ride back to the Pontiac with gas and oil. When the Pontiac still wouldn't start, Besse and Ralph Knight pushed the Pontiac to Besse's house in Tucson. Besse then sold his used Buick to Ruiz-Tellez for $250.00. Besse drove Ruiz-Tellez back toward Nogales to get the money. Ruiz-Tellez had him stop the car, went into the brush covered desert, collected $210.00 from the four hidden aliens and gave it to Besse. Ruiz-Tellez then transported the aliens to Idaho.

The foregoing led to Herman and Ralph Knight's entry into the conspiracy. This modern enactment of the old saying, "There's gold in them thar hills" inspired Herman and Ralph Knight.

The evidence showed that shortly thereafter, on at least four occasions, Herman and Ralph Knight went to Nogales, Sonora, the area from which the illegal Mexicans were coming, looking for, and to talk to Ruiz-Tellez. Ruiz-Tellez had not returned from Idaho. Ralph Knight and Besse finally contacted Ruiz-Tellez. They asked him where he got "the money in the desert." He told them of the smuggling and transportation venture. Ralph Knight and Besse then cut themselves into the illegal conspiracy.

Thereafter three smuggling trips to Idaho were completed and one attempted. The three trips were as follows: (1) about July 3, 1967, involving eleven aliens; (2) July 12–16, involving 17 aliens; (3) July 19, involving 12 aliens. The fourth trip started August 3, 1967, and as we shall see hereafter, resulted in the arrest of Besse.

We come to Herman Knight's participation in the conspiracy. Prior to the July 12–16 trip, Ruiz-Tellez and Ralph Knight were at Herman Knight's home. Ruiz-Tellez testified "we collected the money from the boys * * * Ralph received all the money and then gave it to Herman" in the presence of Ruiz-Tellez.

Prior to August 3, 1967, the date of the last trip, Ruiz-Tellez testified he met Herman and Ralph Knight and Besse at the Regis bar in Nogales, Sonora, Mexico. Ruiz stated at this meeting that he would take "the boys that were going to cross" to the border and asked that "they" give him the pick-up. He further testified "as soon as I took them over there, then I came back and delivered the pick-up to them," "to Ralph." He further testified he met the aliens on the American side and that he was in the Falcon station wagon with Herman Knight and went with Herman to "see if he could pick up the boys." The Falcon station wagon belonged to Herman Knight.

Herman Knight's gasoline credit cards were used to pay for gasoline for the transportation of the aliens on some of the trips from the southern part of Arizona to Idaho, and for the return trip of the vehicle. The original slips were sent to Herman Knight, along with each billing. Herman Knight's white Falcon station wagon was used in at least one of the trips.

The foregoing is sufficient to connect Herman Knight with the conspiracy. "Once the existence of a conspiracy is clearly established, slight evidence may be sufficient to connect a defendant with it." United States v. Cohen, 197 F.2d 26 (3 Cir. 1952), quoting from our decision in Nye & Nissen v. United States, 168 F.2d 846, 852 (9 Cir. 1948), affirmed 336 U.S. 613, 69 S.Ct. 766, 93 L.Ed. 919 (1949).

It is sufficient if the acts and conduct of a defendant were of such character that the minds of reasonable men could conclude therefrom that an unlawful agreement or understanding existed, and that the defendant, with knowledge of the existence of the unlawful enterprise, acted to further it. It was the province of the jury to determine if a conspiracy existed and if appellant Herman Knight was part of it.

One may join a conspiracy already formed and in existence, and be bound by all that has gone on before in the conspiracy, even if unknown to him. "[T]he new member is as guilty as though he was an original conspirator," Marino v. United States, 91 F.2d 691, 113 A.L.R. 975 (9 Cir. 1937), cert. denied sub nom. Gullo v. United States, 302 U.S. 764, 58 S.Ct. 410, 82 L.Ed. 593 (1938).

Herman Knight puts great weight upon the fact that at an early meeting some time in May or June of 1967, Ruiz-Tellez testified that he, Herman, and Ralph Knight started to make a deal concerning the transportation of a particular group of aliens, but that Herman said he would see if he would make a deal or not. Herman then said, in the presence of appellant Ralph Knight and Ruiz-Tellez, apparently speaking to Ralph Knight, "It's up to you * * * it's up to you if you want to, go ahead if you want to." This is certainly no statement that Herman had still to make up his mind. A possible interpretation, and one which the jury apparently believed, was that Herman was telling Ralph, that Ralph could make the particular deal or not.

There was a well organized conspiracy of transporting many aliens to the Idaho area, at about $200.00 an alien. The evidence is sufficient to show Herman's participation and his assignment of error is without merit.

NOTES

1. A and B burglarize a post office on December 16, 1968. $17,000 in unused postage is taken. They then meet F who arranges for the sale of these stamps for 35% of their face value. F requests that A obtain some blank money orders. On January 18, 1969, A, B and C burglarize another

post office and obtain $87,000 worth of postage. A calls F who is not at home but whose wife arranges for the sale of the stamps to G. On March 27, 1969, A, B and C burglarize a third post office and obtain $40,000 worth of postage and some money orders. They immediately repair to F's home and another sale is arranged.

Is F guilty of conspiring to burglarize post offices and to receive, possess and sell property stolen from the United States? Why? See United States v. Cook, 461 F.2d 906 (5th Cir. 1972).

2. A and B kidnap V in Minnesota and take him to Illinois. They release him unharmed after receipt of a $200,000 ransom. Four months later C, a resident of Michigan, agrees to arrange for the exchange of the ransom money for unmarked bills and does so in Havana, Cuba.

Is C guilty of conspiracy to kidnap, transport in interstate commerce, and hold for ransom? See McDonald v. United States, 89 F.2d 128 (8th Cir.), cert. denied 301 U.S. 697, 57 S.Ct. 925, 81 L.Ed. 1352 (1937).

3. In *Knight* the court says "one may join a conspiracy already formed and in existence, and be bound by all that has gone on before in the conspiracy, even if unknown to him." Does this mean Knight could be convicted of the substantive offenses committed prior to his entry? that F, in note 1 supra, is guilty of the three burglaries? of the last two? that C, in note 2 supra, is guilty of the kidnapping? If V, in note 2 supra, had been killed by A and B, would C be guilty of murder?

---

(2) NUMBER OF AGREEMENTS

LIEVERS v. STATE

Court of Special Appeals of Maryland, 1968.
3 Md.App. 597, 241 A.2d 147.

ANDERSON, Judge. Appellants Steven Richard Lievers, Jr. and James McLean, together with Ernest Cherry, John E. Bell, and Samuel Terry, were charged in the Circuit Court for Howard County under a three-count Criminal Information (No. 3458), substantially as follows:

(1) That on March 19, 1965, in Howard County, Maryland, they did unlawfully conspire to cause and procure to be falsely made, forged and counterfeited a certain check made payable to Steven Thompson, dated March 18, 1965, in the amount of $104.87, with intent to defraud.

(2) That on the same day, in the same county, they did unlawfully conspire to utter and publish as true a false, forged, altered and counterfeited check, being the same check as above described in count one, with intent to defraud.

(3) That on the same day, in the same county, they did unlawfully conspire by a certain false pretense to obtain from Rock Hill Corporation cash in the amount of $104.87, with intent to defraud.

Appellants, together with the above named co-defendants, were also charged under Criminal Information No. 3459, as follows:

(1) That on the same day, in the same county, they did unlawfully conspire to hold and use a forged and counterfeited Maryland chauffeur's license issued to Steven Thompson, knowing such license to have been altered, forged and falsified, with intent to defraud.

(2) That on the same day, in the same county, they did unlawfully conspire to utter and publish as true, a false, forged, altered and counterfeited Maryland chauffeur's license issued to Steven Thompson, with intent to defraud.

Tried before the Circuit Court for Howard County (Macgill, J., presiding without a jury), appellants were convicted on each count of Criminal Information No. 3458, and on the first count of Criminal Information No. 3459. * * *

From these judgments, appellants have appealed, contending * * *

(d) that they were improperly convicted of four conspiracies when, at most, only one conspiracy was shown by the State's evidence.

The evidence adduced at the trial showed that William Wilson and James Jason, while awaiting trial on certain criminal charges, had agreed to aid the police in breaking up a bogus check ring; that Wilson advised Corporal Armond Elliott of the Baltimore County Rackets Squad that he had been invited by appellant Lievers to participate on March 19, 1965 in the activities of the ring and was to meet with Lievers and the others at noon at the Twelve and A Half Club in Baltimore City; that Corporal Elliott went to this location at the appointed time and, through binoculars, observed appellant Lievers and John Ellis Bell, sitting together in a 1963 Pontiac in front of the Club; that he observed Bell pass a small brown paper bag to Lievers, who opened it, pulled out some green pieces of paper which appeared to be checks, look at them, and return them to the bag; that Lievers then left the Pontiac and joined appellant McLean, Cherry, Terry, Jason and Wilson, in a 1959 brown and white Oldsmobile; that the Oldsmobile and its six passengers—appellants Lievers and McLean, Terry, Cherry, Jason, and Wilson—thereafter drove away, shortly after which Elliott arrested Bell and notified Lt. Michael Kradz of the Howard County Police Department by phone to be on the lookout for the Oldsmobile and its six passengers.

The evidence further discloses that Lt. Kradz had been investigating the activities of appellant Lievers and John Bell since January of 1965 and that with Corporal Elliott, had arranged for the assistance of Wilson and Jason in breaking up the operations of the bogus check ring; that after Kradz had talked with Elliott by phone on March 19, he received a call from Wilson who informed him, in effect, that the

1959 Oldsmobile, which he described, together with its six occupants, was proceeding in a designated direction toward Howard County to cash bogus checks; that as a result of the call from Wilson, Kradz stationed men along the route of the Oldsmobile's travel and first observed it as it parked at Gabriel's liquor store in Baltimore County; that Kradz saw three of the occupants of the Oldsmobile, one of whom was appellant McLean, enter the store; that after they departed from the store, the Oldsmobile picked them up and proceeded into Ellicott City in Howard County, where they parked on a parking lot and the same three persons entered the Rock Hill liquor store; that Lt. Kradz then went over to the Oldsmobile and told appellant Lievers that he was under arrest, immediately after which he went into the Rock Hill liquor store where he learned from the proprietor that a tall Negro with a mustache, wearing an Army field jacket and a green sweat shirt and a hood had attempted to cash a check; that Kradz left the store and arrested appellant McLean, who answered the description provided by the liquor store proprietor; and that McLean turned over to Kradz a brown envelope containing a Robert C. Herd & Co. check made payable to Steven Thompson for $104.87, a voter's card, Social Security card, and chauffeur's license, all of which were in the name of Steven Thompson, and all of which proved to be forgeries and counterfeits.

Following the arrests, the Oldsmobile was taken to the Howard County police station where a search of its interior revealed a brown paper bag containing a number of checks, identification cards, and chauffeurs' licenses made out in the name of various individuals, all of which also proved to be forgeries and counterfeits. The documents taken from McLean and seized from the Oldsmobile in which Lievers was a passenger at the time of his arrest were introduced into evidence over objection.

It was shown at the trial through the testimony of Wilson, Jason, Cherry, and Terry that appellant Lievers provided appellant McLean and the other occupants of the Oldsmobile with forged checks and identification cards, including forged and counterfeited Maryland chauffeurs' licenses, for the purpose of having the checks negotiated, and that this mode of operation was pursued, *albeit* unsuccessfully, both at Gabriel's liquor store in Baltimore County and at the Rock Hill liquor store in Howard County on March 19.

*   *   *

Appellants' fourth and final contention is that the lower court erred in finding them guilty of four crimes when, in fact, only one crime existed according to the State's evidence. They argue that the State's testimony related exclusively to an alleged meeting of the minds in Baltimore City to pass bogus checks in Howard County and that each of the elements forming the subject matter of the conspiracy was listed in separate counts and even separate informations, when, in substance, they were all elements which made up only one conspiracy, namely, to defraud through the use of bogus checks; and that therefore the finding of guilt as to separate offenses of conspiracy was in error.

As indicated, appellants were convicted of (a) conspiracy to forge a designated check in the amount of $104.87, (b) conspiracy to utter said forged check, (c) conspiracy to obtain $104.87 from a designated corporation by a "certain" false pretense, and (d) conspiracy to hold and use a designated forged and counterfeited Maryland chauffeur's license. In Tender v. State, 2 Md.App. 692, 237 A.2d 65, we held that a person should not be twice punished for the same acts whether the offenses charged by reason of such acts be deemed to be inconsistent, duplicitous, or to have merged. The true test of merger of offenses is whether one crime necessarily involves the other. Green v. State, 243 Md. 75, 220 A.2d 131. Thus in Sutton v. State, 2 Md.App. 639, 236 A.2d 301, we held, on the facts of that case, that the substantive offense of uttering merged into the offense of false pretenses where the false representation consisted only of the uttering. It appears to us from the evidence in this case that the conspiracy to utter merged into the conspiracy to obtain money by false pretenses since no false representation independent of the uttering of the forged check itself is shown by the evidence.

Holding and using a forged Maryland chauffeur's license with fraudulent intent is a felony under Section 77(a) (4) of Article 66½ of the Maryland Code (1967 Repl.Vol.). We think it clear that appellant's conviction for conspiring to hold and use such a document clearly charges an act separate and distinct from any of the conspiracies charged under Criminal Information No. 3458 and is indeed broader in scope than the other conspiracies since it is not limited to an agreement to hold and use such forged license solely in connection with an illegal effort to negotiate a forged check made payable to Steven Thompson in the amount of $104.87, dated March 18, 1965.

As to each appellant under Criminal Information No. 3458:
Judgments affirmed as to the first and third counts; judgments vacated as to the second count as merging with the third count.

As to each appellant under Criminal Information No. 3459:
Judgments affirmed.

BLUMENTHAL v. UNITED STATES

Supreme Court of the United States, 1947.
332 U.S. 539, 68 S.Ct. 248, 92 L.Ed. 154, rehearing denied
332 U.S. 856, 68 S.Ct. 385, 92 L.Ed. 425.

Mr. Justice RUTLEDGE delivered the opinion of the Court.

The four petitioners and Abel, another defendant, were convicted of conspiring to sell whiskey at prices above the ceiling set by regulations of the Office of Price Administration, in violation of the Emergency Price Control Act. 50 U.S.C.Appendix, §§ 902(a), 904(a) and 925(b), 50 U.S.C.A.Appendix, §§ 902(a), 904(a), 925(b). The charge was made pursuant to the general conspiracy statute, § 37 of the Criminal Code, 18 U.S.C.A. § 88. The convictions were affirmed by the Circuit Court of Appeals, one judge dissenting. 158 F.2d 883, dissenting opinion at 158 F.2d 762. Abel has not sought review in this Court. Certiorari was granted, 331 U.S. 799, 67 S.Ct. 1306, as to the other four defendants because we thought important questions were presented concerning the applicability of our recent decision in Kotteakos v. United States, 328 U.S. 750, 66 S.Ct. 1239, 90 L.Ed. 1557.

We did not limit our grant of certiorari to that question, however, and on the record it is inseparably connected with the other issues, which relate to the admissibility and sufficiency of the evidence. Accordingly we have considered all of petitioners' contentions. The competent proof was clearly sufficient to show that each petitioner had aided in the whiskey's illegal sale and had conspired with others to do so. The only phase of the case meriting further attention is whether, because of a difference in the state of the proof affecting two groups of defendants, the proof, in variance from the indictment, shows that there was more than one conspiracy.

I.

The indictment charges a single conspiracy in a single count. Ten overt acts are specified. The Government alleged and sought to establish that all of the defendants and other unidentified persons conspired together to dispose of two carloads, each consisting of about 2,000 cases, of Old Mr. Boston Rocking Chair Whiskey at over the ceiling wholesale prices.

This whiskey was shipped by rail from the distiller or his agent to the Francisco Distributing Company, in San Francisco, in December, 1943. Goldsmith was the individual and sole owner of that business and held a wholesale liquor dealer's basic permit as required by federal law. Weiss, his former partner, was sales manager for the business. Feigenbaum operated the Sunset Drugstore in San Francisco. Blumenthal owned and operated the Sportorium, a sporting goods and pawn shop in the same city. Abel either owned or worked in a jewelry store in Vallejo, California. The evidence does not show that any of these last three was connected with Francisco in any way except that each had part in arranging sales and deliveries of portions of these two shipments to purchasers. These were tavern owners in San Francisco and near-by towns such as Vallejo, Santa Rosa, Livermore, Cottonwood and El Cerrito. Proof of the activities of Feigenbaum, Blumenthal and Abel was made largely by the testimony of the various tavernkeepers with whom they respectively dealt.

The evidence showed that on arrival of the whiskey in San Francisco legal title was taken in Francisco's name, in which the shipping

documents were made out; that it honored sight drafts for both shipments, upon Goldsmith's directions to Francisco's bank to pay them
out of Francisco's account; that some of the whiskey was delivered
ex car directly to tavernkeepers who previously had arranged for purchases in lots varying from 25 to 200 cases; that the remainder was
placed in storage with the San Francisco Warehouse Company, pursuant to arrangements made by Weiss, and thereafter was delivered by
the warehouse to various purchasers holding invoices issued by Francisco [1] on orders given by Weiss. The *ex car* deliveries also were made
pursuant to similar invoices and orders.

It further appeared that the cost of the whiskey to Francisco
was $21.97 a case,[2] the wholesale ceiling price was $25.27, and Francisco received, by check of the purchasing tavernkeepers, $24.50 for
each case sold. There was thus left to it a margin above cost of $2.53
on each case, out of which were to come storage charges, if any, and
legitimate net profit.

Thus far no illegal act, transaction, intent or agreement appears.
But by the testimony of purchasing tavernkeepers the Government
proved that in connection with each sale the purchaser had paid to the
selling intermediary, in addition to the $24.50 per case remitted by
check to Francisco, an additional sum in cash amounting roughly to
from $30 to $40 per case. Thus the actual cost to the retailer was
from $55 to $65 per case.

In some instances the identity of the person arranging the transaction for the seller and receiving the cash payment was not established or known to the witness testifying to the sale and its details. In
others, however, Blumenthal, Feigenbaum or Abel was identified as
the salesman or intermediary. It was not brought out with what person or persons Abel, Feigenbaum, Blumenthal or the other salesmen
dealt in securing the whiskey from Francisco.[3] In two sales, Figone,
a tavernkeeper of El Cerrito, testified he arranged for the purchases
in Francisco's offices, but could not identify the person with whom
he dealt.

In all instances, however, whether involving sales to San Francisco or to out-of-town dealers and whether through identified or un-

---

1. Of the more than 4,000 cases received
by Francisco, proof concerning disposition at over-ceiling prices related to
less than half, or some 1,500-plus cases.

2. Consisting of $19.24 per case to the
distiller, 81¢ for freight, and $1.92 for
state taxes.

3. The witnesses identifying Feigenbaum testified they sought him out at
the Sunset Drugstore in San Francisco and made the arrangements with
him for their purchases there. Similar testimony was given by those iden-

tifying Blumenthal with the arrangements taking place in the Sportorium.

In some instances the out-of town purchasing witnesses testified that they
went to San Francisco in search of
whiskey to buy and by one means or
another, usually through inquiry of
persons frequenting bars where the
witnesses stopped, were directed to the
selling agent. In other instances the
intermediary sought out the tavernkeeper as a prospective purchaser at
his place of business.

identified selling intermediaries, the sales followed the general pattern described above. That is, once the understanding had been reached, the purchaser made out his check at the price of $24.50 per case, to the order of "Francisco Distributing Co.," at the direction of the selling intermediary, to whom the check was delivered; at the same time or later the purchaser also paid in cash to the intermediary the difference between the amount of the check and the agreed overceiling purchase price; then or later the purchaser received invoices in the name of Francisco for the number of cases of Old Mr. Boston Rocking Chair Whiskey bought showing only the legal price of $24.50 per case; and thereafter the purchaser received delivery of the whiskey from the warehouse company, by freight in the case of out-of-town buyers. Weiss gave the warehouse company instructions for shipments or local deliveries. Francisco collected the checks by endorsing and sending them through its bank for collection. Slight variations in detail of the pattern appear in some instances but they are insignificant for our purposes.

The foregoing is substantially the evidence used, not only in part to show the conspiracy, but also to connect Blumenthal, Feigenbaum and Abel with it. In addition to the evidence already related as it affects Goldsmith and Weiss, the court received as to them alone the testimony of Harkins, a special investigator for the Alcohol Tax Unit of the Treasury Department. He related conversations had with Goldsmith and Weiss, during which important admissions were made by one or the other or both. Those admissions give rise to the crucial problems in the case.

At the initial conference "early in January," 1944, attended by both Goldsmith and Weiss, the latter "did most of the talking." Questioned concerning who purchased the two carloads and how they were handled, Weiss said "that his firm received $2.00 a case for clearing it through their books." Goldsmith concurred in this and both stated that they divided the $2.00, each taking a dollar. "They both stated, agreed, that they did not sell any of the whiskey. It was sold by others, and they received the check generally for the payment for the whiskey in advance of the date that they had to take up the sight draft bills of lading. At that time they did not tell us who actually sold the whiskey."

Later conferences held separately with Goldsmith and Weiss simply confirmed the substance of the first to the effect that Francisco was not the actual owner, but that Goldsmith and Weiss were acting for an unidentified person in handling the shipments in Francisco's name.[4] The identity of the owner was not established. But Goldsmith added the admission that he wrote most of the invoices.

4. At an interview with Goldsmith "early in September," Goldsmith was asked "who actually bought him the whiskey, who owned it." In reply "he said that Blumenthal brought it in, and when asked if he knew of his own knowledge, he said, 'No.'" He again stated that Francisco received

Shortly after the trial began the court announced that it would save time and be fairer to all for the evidence to be received initially only as against the particular defendant or defendants to whom it appeared expressly related, reserving to the Government, however, the right to move for its admission as against any or all of the other defendants whenever in the Government's opinion sufficient facts had been introduced to show such defendants to have been connected with the conspiracy charged.

This course was followed. At the close of the Government's case, the court granted its motion to admit all of the evidence as against all of the defendants, except that it declined to allow Harkins' testimony concerning his conversations with Goldsmith and Weiss to be admitted as against the defendants Blumenthal, Feigenbaum and Abel. That testimony however was allowed to stand against both Goldsmith and Weiss insofar as it related the conversation had in the presence of both, and as to each of them respectively to the extent that the other interviews took place in his presence.

The court overruled numerous objections to these rulings by each defendant. None offered evidence in his own behalf.

Following its rulings on admissibility, the trial court concluded as against various objections that the evidence was sufficient to go to the jury on the issues whether the conspiracy charged had been made out and concerning each defendant's connection with it. Accordingly, it overruled the defendants' motions for directed verdicts and submitted the case to the jury. In the instructions the court expressly stated, in accordance with the previous rulings on admissibility, that Harkins' testimony was to be considered only as against Goldsmith and Weiss, not as against the other three defendants.

II.

In the Kotteakos case, supra, the Government conceded that, under the charge of a single, all-inclusive conspiracy, the proof showed distinct and separate ones connected only by the fact that one man, Brown, was a participant and key figure in all. But it urged that under the ruling in Berger v. United States, 295 U.S. 78, 55 S.Ct. 629,

---

$2 per case, of which he gave Weiss half.

A still further questioning of Goldsmith took place on September 13. Harkins showed Goldsmith several invoices given to purchasers in fhe name of Francisco. Goldsmith admitted that he wrote most of the invoices and identified his own handwriting, stating however that a few were written by his bookkeeper.

Harkins testified also regarding a conversation with Weiss on May 14, 1944.

In this Weiss stated "it was true that he received half of the $2 commission paid to the Francisco Distributing Company for clearing this whiskey through their books, and he finally refused to answer who actually owned the whiskey. He said 'I don't want to involve myself.'" Weiss also admitted knowing Blumenthal, but "refused to state, to the best of my [the witness'] recollection, positively, whether Mr. Blumenthal was the owner of the whiskey or not."

79 L.Ed. 1314, the variance was at the most harmless error, a contention we rejected. Here the situation is the reverse. The Government has conceded, in effect, that prejudice has resulted if more than one conspiracy has been proved. But it insists that the evidence establishes a single conspiracy and no more, an issue not presented or determined in the Kotteakos case.

The proof, in relation to whether one or more conspiracies were shown as well as relative to whether any was made out, requires somewhat different treatment concerning the two groups of defendants, Weiss and Goldsmith, on the one hand, and Blumenthal, Feigenbaum and Abel, on the other. This is by reason of the court's exclusion of the admissions of Goldsmith and Weiss from consideration as to the other three defendants.

The Government does not maintain that Francisco, or Goldsmith (or therefore Weiss), was the owner of the whiskey. It accepts the view that another or others unidentified, were the real owner or owners and that Francisco (and thus Goldsmith and Weiss) was merely a channel for distributing the liquor and giving that unlawful process a legal facade. Indeed the "innocent appearing actions" of Weiss and Goldsmith in their use of Francisco, the brief asserts, "were the crux of the conspiracy * * * since the color of legitimacy was an essential part of the plan to dispose of the liquor to tavern owners at over-ceiling prices."

The evidence including the admissions was clearly sufficient to establish that the owner devised a plan which contemplated the entire chain of events from the original purchase in Francisco's name to the ultimate black market sales and deliveries. This includes the obvious inference that he made the arrangements for clearance through Francisco's books. Since Goldsmith and Weiss were the owner and sales manager respectively of Francisco and had active parts personally in carrying out those arrangements, there hardly can be any question that they knew the owner, had part in making the arrangements with him and, by virtue of those facts and their parts in facilitating the sales and deliveries to the tavernkeepers, knew also of his intention to resell the whiskey and of his plan for doing so in every material respect except that he intended to sell at over-ceiling prices.

The showing on that crucial question was entirely circumstantial. It was nonetheless substantial. Goldsmith and Weiss knew that there was a margin of only about 77¢ between the legal price ceiling and the $24.50 per case they received by check in payment for the whiskey. They knew that the invoices sent by Francisco to each purchaser gave no room for even that slender margin but represented only the owner's cost figure. They knew further that by using Francisco's name, services and facilities the owner was concealing his identity from the purchasers in the sales, making Francisco appear as the owner on the paper records; that sales were being made to numerous and widely scattered tavernkeepers; and that in every sale remittance was made to them uniformly not only by check, usually of the purchaser, but also in the exact amount of $24.50 per case.

The inference that the unknown owner [was] giving away the liquor is scarcely conceivable. The most likely inferences to be drawn were two, namely, that the owner was selling for a legal margin of not more than 77¢ or that he was selling at over-ceiling prices. The first inference is hardly tenable, especially in view of the prevailing and wide-spread shortage and demand, with accompanying black market activity, of which the most meticulous wholesale liquor dealer hardly could have been ignorant. The inference was not only justified, it was almost inescapable, that Goldsmith and Weiss knew of the owner's intent and purpose to sell above the lawful price, as well as most of the detail of his plan for doing so. With that knowledge their active aid toward executing his design made them co-conspirators with him, and he with them, toward accomplishing it.

III.

It remains however to consider whether, without the admissions, Blumenthal, Feigenbaum and Abel have been shown to have conspired together and with Goldsmith and Weiss in the scheme proved against the latter two.

The admissions alone disclosed the unknown owner's existence; that Goldsmith and Weiss were acting for him, not for themselves; received from the transactions, and divided equally, the $2 per case; and gave the use of Francisco's name to cover up the unknown owner's existence, identity and part in the scheme.

Whether or not the evidence stripped of those facts was sufficient to sustain the charge, a preliminary question arises upon the trial court's disposition of the admissions. They supplied strong confirmatory or supplementing proof to show, not only the connections of Goldsmith and Weiss with the scheme, but also its existence and illegal character. If therefore it were shown, or even were doubtful, that the admissions had been improperly received as against Blumenthal, Feigenbaum and Abel, reversal would be required as to them.

But the trial court's rulings, both upon admissibility and in the instructions, leave no room for doubt that the admissions were adequately excluded, insofar as this could be done in a joint trial, from consideration on the question of their guilt. The rulings told the jury plainly to disregard the admissions entirely, in every phase of the case, in determining that question. The direction was a total exclusion, not simply a partial one as the Government's argument seems to imply. The court might have been more emphatic. But we cannot say its unambiguous direction was inadequate. Nor can we assume that the jury misunderstood or disobeyed it.

With the admissions thus entirely excluded, we think nevertheless that the remaining evidence was sufficient to show, in accordance with the charge, that the five defendants joined in a single conspiracy to sell the whiskey at over-ceiling prices in the guise of legal sales. We set forth in the margin the remaining evidence, in part, which justifies this conclusion both as to Goldsmith and Weiss and as to the other three defendants.

The main difference comes with the elimination of the unknown owner from view, and Francisco's consequent appearance as both actual and legal owner. This changes the detail of the facade, but does not remove either the facade itself or the essence of the unlawful scheme. That still was to sell the whiskey illegally in the guise of legal sales, to the knowledge of each defendant. The gist of the conspiracy lay not in who actually owned the whiskey, but in the agreement to sell it in this unlawful fashion, regardless of who might own it.

With the case thus posited, it is true the salesmen did not know of the unknown owner's existence or part in the plan. And in a hypertechnical aspect the case as a whole might be regarded as showing in one phase an agreement among Goldsmith, Weiss and the unknown owner, X, and in the other an agreement among the five defendants to which X was not a party. Thus in the most meticulous sense it might be regarded as disclosing two agreements, with Goldsmith and Weiss as figures common to both.

Indeed that may be what took place chronologically, for conspiracies involving such elaborate arrangements generally are not born full grown. Rather they mature by successive stages which are necessary to bring in the essential parties. And not all of those joining in the earlier ones make known their participation to others later coming in.

The law does not demand proof of so much. For it is most often true, especially in broad schemes calling for the aid of many persons, that after discovery of enough to show clearly the essence of the scheme and the identity of a number participating, the identity and the fact of participation of others remain undiscovered and undiscoverable. Secrecy and concealment are essential features of successful conspiracy. The more completely they are achieved, the more successful the crime. Hence the law rightly gives room for allowing the conviction of those discovered upon showing sufficiently the essential nature of the plan and their connections with it, without requiring evidence of knowledge of all its details or of the participation of others. Otherwise the difficulties, not only of discovery, but of certainty in proof and of correlating proof with pleading would become insuperable, and conspirators would go free by their very ingenuity.

Here, apart from the weight which the proof of the unknown owner's existence and participation added to the convictions of Weiss and Goldsmith, it added no essential feature to the charge against the five defendants. The whiskey was the same. The agreements related alike to its disposition. They comprehended illegal sales in the guise of legal ones. Who owned the whiskey was irrelevant to the basic plan and its essential illegality. It was a matter of indifferent detail to the salesmen, as by the same token was the fact that Goldsmith and Weiss were receiving and splitting only the $2 per case. It mattered nothing to the others whether those two received only that amount or the larger illegal sums.

We think that in the special circumstances of this case the two agreements were merely steps in the formation of the larger and ultimate more general conspiracy. In that view it would be a perversion of justice to regard the salesmen's ignorance of the unknown owner's participation as furnishing adequate ground for reversal of their convictions. Nor does anything in the Kotteakos decision require this. The scheme was in fact the same scheme; the salesmen knew or must have known that others unknown to them were sharing in so large a project; and it hardly can be sufficient to relieve them that they did not know, when they joined the scheme, who those people were or exactly the parts they were playing in carrying out the common design and object of all. By their separate agreements, if such they were, they became parties to the larger common plan, joined together by their knowledge of its essential features and broad scope, though not of its exact limits, and by their common single goal. * * * All knew of and joined in the overriding scheme. All intended to aid the owner, whether Francisco or another, to sell the whiskey unlawfully, though the two groups of defendants differed on the proof in knowledge and belief concerning the owner's identity. All by reason of their knowledge of the plan's general scope, if not its exact limits, sought a common end, to aid in disposing of the whiskey. True, each salesman aided in selling only his part. But he knew the lot to be sold was larger and thus that he was aiding in a larger plan. He thus became a party to it and not merely to the integrating agreement with Weiss and Goldsmith.

We think therefore that in every practical sense the unique facts of this case reveal a single conspiracy of which the several agreements were essential and integral steps, and accordingly that the judgments should be affirmed.

MODEL PENAL CODE, COMMENT TO § 5.03(1), 119–24

(Tent. Draft No. 10, 1960).

The Draft relies upon the combined operation of Subsections (1), (2) and (3) to delineate the identity and scope of a conspiracy. All three provisions focus upon the culpability of the individual actor. Subsections (1) and (2) limit the scope of his conspiracy (a) in terms of its criminal objects, to those crimes which he had the purpose of promoting or facilitating and (b) in terms of parties, to those with whom he agreed, except where the same crime that he conspired to commit is, to his knowledge, also the object of a conspiracy between one of his co-conspirators and another person or persons. Subsection (3) provides that his conspiracy is a single one despite a multiplicity of criminal objectives so long as such crimes are the object of the same agreement or continuous conspiratorial relationship.

2. *Party and Object Dimensions.* The operation of these provisions may be illustrated by considering some of the typical cases of complex criminal networks that have caused difficulty in the courts. The relationships in these networks are sometimes analogized to a wheel (or circle) and a chain. In the former, communication and cooperation exist primarily between a central figure (the "hub") and each individual member (the "spokes"), and not between the spokes themselves. In the chain relationship, there is successive communication and cooperation between A and B, B and C, C and D, and so on, frequently with regard to the distribution from manufacturer to ultimate consumer of such contraband commodities as narcotics, illicit whiskey or counterfeit money.

United States v. Bruno [98] involved both types of relationships. In that case, 88 defendants were indicted for a conspiracy to import, sell and possess narcotics. The proof showed a vast operation extending over a long period of time, which included smugglers who brought narcotics into New York City, middlemen who paid the smugglers and distributed to retailers, and two groups of retailers selling to addicts—one in New York and the other in Texas and Louisiana. There was no evidence of cooperation or communication between the smugglers and either group of retailers or between the two widely separated groups of retailers. The relationship between the smugglers, the middlemen and each group of retailers consequently was a typical chain, with communication as well as narcotics passing from smuggler to middleman to retailer. The two groups of retailers, on the other hand, may be considered separate spokes of a wheel whose hub was the middlemen, since they communicated and cooperated only with the middlemen and not with each other.

The appellants argued that the evidence may have established several separate conspiracies but not the single one alleged. The court held that the jury could have found a single large conspiracy "whose object was to smuggle narcotics into the Port of New York and distribute them to addicts both in [New York] and in Texas and Louisiana." This required, the court reasoned, the cooperation of all the various groups—smugglers, middlemen and the two groups of retailers.

98. 105 F.2d 921 (2d Cir. 1939).

"[T]he smugglers knew that the middlemen must sell to retailers, and the retailers knew that the middlemen must
buy of importers of one sort or another. Thus the conspirators at one end of the chain knew that the unlawful business
would not, and could not, stop with their buyers; and those
at the other end knew that it had not begun with their sellers. That being true, a jury might have found that all the
accused were embarked upon a venture, in all parts of which
each was a participant, and an abettor in the sense that
the success of that part with which he was immediately
concerned, was dependent upon the success of the whole." [99]

The only possible basis mentioned in the opinion for a finding
of separate conspiracies was the fact that there was apparently "no
privity" between the two separate groups of retailers. To the argument that there were consequently two conspiracies—one including the smugglers, the middlemen and the New York retailers, and
the other the smugglers, the middlemen and the Texas and Louisiana retailers—the court replied:

"Clearly, quoad the smugglers, there was but one conspiracy, for it was of no moment to them whether the middlemen sold to one or more groups of retailers, provided they
had a market somewhere. So too of any retailer; he knew
that he was a necessary link in a scheme of distribution,
and the others, whom he knew to be convenient to its execution, were as much parts of a single undertaking or enterprise as two salesmen in the same shop." [100]

The Draft would require a different approach to a case such as
Bruno and might produce different results.

Since the overall operation involved separate crimes of importing by the smugglers and possession and sale by each group—smugglers, distributors and retailers—the question as to each defendant
would be whether and with whom he conspired to commit *each* of
these crimes, under the criteria set forth in Subsections (1) and
(2). The conspiratorial objective for the purpose of this inquiry
could not be characterized in the manner of the *Bruno* court, as
"to smuggle narcotics into the Port of New York and distribute
them to addicts both in [New York] and in Texas and Louisiana."
This is indeed the overall objective of the entire operation. It may
also be true of *some* of the participants that they conspired to commit all of the crimes involved in the operation: under Subsection
(3) of the Draft as under prevailing law they would be guilty of
only one conspiracy if all these crimes were the object of the same
agreement or continuing conspiratorial relationship (see pp. 126–130,
infra), and the objective of *that* conspiracy or relationship could

99. Id. at 922.   100. Id. at 923.

fairly be phrased in terms of the overall operation. But this multiplicity of criminal objectives affords a poor referent for testing the culpability of each individual who is in any manner involved in the operation.

With the conspiratorial objectives characterized as the particular crimes and the culpability of each participant tested separately, it would be possible to find in a case such as *Bruno*—considering for the moment only each separate chain of distribution—that the smugglers conspired to commit the illegal sales of the retailers but that the retailers did not conspire to commit the importing of the smugglers. Factual situations warranting such a finding may easily be conceived: the smugglers might depend upon and seek to foster their retail markets while the retailers might have many suppliers and be indifferent to the success of any single source. The court's approach in *Bruno* does not admit of such a finding, for in treating the conspiratorial objective as the entire series of crimes involved in smuggling, distributing and retailing it requires either a finding of no conspiracy or a single conspiracy in which all three links in the chain conspired to commit all of each other's crimes.

It would also be possible to find, with the inquiry focused upon each individual's culpability as to each criminal objective, that some of the parties in a chain conspired to commit the entire series of crimes while others conspired only to commit some of these crimes. Thus the smugglers and the middlemen in *Bruno* may have conspired to commit, promote or facilitate the importing and the possession and sales of all of the parties down to the final retail sale; the retailers might have conspired with them as to their own possession and sales but might be indifferent to all the steps prior to their receipt of the narcotics. In this situation, a smuggler or a middleman might have conspired with all three groups to commit the entire series of crimes, while a retailer might have conspired with the same parties but to commit fewer criminal objectives. Such results are conceptually difficult to reach under existing doctrine not only because of the frequent failure to focus separately upon the different criminal objectives, but because of the traditional view of the agreement as a bilateral relationship between each of the parties, congruent in scope both as to its party and its objective dimensions.

Of course, the major difficulty in finding any conspiracy which includes as parties both the smugglers and the retailers is the absence of direct communication or cooperation between them. Despite such absence an agreement may be inferred from mutual facilitation and evidence of a mutual purpose. Subsection (1) of the Draft would not preclude the inference, though it is more specific than the present law on the purpose requirement. But the present concept of agreement and even the more specific criteria embodied in Subsection (1) tend to become somewhat ambiguous when applied to a relationship that involves no direct communication or cooperation. Consequently,

Subsection (2) of the Draft has been designed to facilitate the inquiry in such cases.

Subsection (2) extends the party dimension of a defendant's conspiracy beyond those with whom he agreed but at the same time preserves the basic limitation that the defendant must have conspired with someone to pursue the particular objective within the meaning of Subsection (1). He must have agreed with someone with the purpose of promoting or facilitating the commission of a particular crime; if to his knowledge others have conspired with his coconspirator to commit the *same* crime he is also guilty of conspiring with them to commit that crime. In each chain of the *Bruno* case, for example, where actual cooperation and communication were established only between the smugglers and the middlemen and between the middlemen and the retailers, separate conspiracies might easily be found under Subsection (1) between each of these pairs of groups; and the objectives of each such conspiracy might consist of any or all of the crimes directly committed by its members. The smugglers and the retailers could then be drawn into a single conspiracy under Subsection (2) only as to objectives common to both such conspiracies, if each had knowledge of the other's conspiracy with the middlemen to commit these crimes. Absent such knowledge on the part of, say, the retailers, it would be possible for the smugglers to have conspired with the retailers through the middlemen to commit these crimes while the retailers conspired only with the middlemen. In this case there would be separate conspiracies congruent as to objective but differing as to parties.

The Draft also affords more helpful and precise criteria than existing doctrine in considering the wheel aspect of the *Bruno* case —the relationship between the two separate groups of retailers. The court recognized that these groups presented the greatest obstacle to a finding of a comprehensive conspiracy including all of the parties and all of the criminal objectives. The preceding discussion has indicated the possible conclusions regarding the guilt of a member of one group of retailers for a conspiracy not involving the other retailing group—i. e., a conspiracy with the smugglers or the middlemen to commit any or all of the series of crimes involved in funneling the narcotics to him and his sales. It would generally be more difficult to connect him with any conspiracy that includes the other retailing group as parties or that includes the other group's possession and sales as objectives.

As to any conspiracy including the other group as parties, there is the difficulty of lack of direct communication or cooperation between the two groups. A finding that they were both parties to a single conspiracy to commit any crime would have to rest on the communication and concert of each of them with the middlemen. They could be connected under Subsection (2) in a conspiracy to commit any objective that they each conspired with the middlemen to commit, to the knowledge of the other. With regard to the crimes involved in the middlemen's and the smugglers' operations—assuming each so conspired with the middlemen to the others' knowledge— the problems would be similar to those in the simple chain relationship; the smugglers and the retailers would probably have to be connected under Subsection (2). With regard to a conspiracy including the other retailing group's possession and sales as objectives, however, there would be the additional difficulty of proving the requisite purpose to promote or facilitate such crimes; since those crimes are not a part of the series that funnels the narcotics to him, his interest in promoting them will, as a general matter, probably be more difficult to prove than his interest in the crimes of the smugglers and middlemen.

NOTES

1. In Braverman v. United States, 317 U.S. 49, 63 S.Ct. 99, 87 L.Ed. 23 (1942), the defendants were charged with seven conspiracies each having as its objective the violation of a different provision of the Internal Revenue laws. The evidence revealed a long-standing collaboration among the defendants to manufacture, transport and distribute distilled spirits. The defense moved, at the beginning and end of the trial, to require the Government to elect one of the seven counts of the indictment upon which to proceed, contending that the proof could not establish more than one agreement. The Government and the lower courts were of the view that a single conspiracy to commit several offenses permitted conviction and punishment of the defendants for conspiracy as to each contemplated offense. The Supreme Court reversed. Mr. Chief Justice Stone wrote: "the precise nature and extent of the conspiracy must be determined by reference to the agreement which embraces and defines its objects. Whether the object of a single agreement is to commit one or many crimes, it is in either case that agreement which constitutes the conspiracy which the statute punishes. The one agreement cannot be taken to be several agreements and hence several conspiracies because it envisages the violation of several statutes rather than one." 317 U.S. at 53, 63 S.Ct. at 102, 87 L.Ed. at 28.

Is *Lievers* consistent with this view?

2. What are the potential benefits, if any, to defendants under a single conspiracy, multiple objectives, theory? under a multiple conspiracy theory? Which theory is more likely to result in accurate identification of the relative levels of culpability of the individual conspirators? Is that a very significant objective given pre-sentence reports and the wide range of sentencing alternatives available to judges?

3. Was there evidence that Abel, Blumenthal and Feigenbaum knew each other, knew that any of the others obtained whiskey from Goldsmith and Weiss, knew that any of the others were selling whiskey and at what price? Should that matter? See Judge Denman's dissent in Blumenthal v. United States, 158 F.2d 762 (9th Cir. 1947).

4. Assume that in Blumenthal the owner of the whiskey had been identified and charged as a conspirator in the single "chain" conspiracy. Would he have been able to defend himself on the grounds that he had sold the

whiskey, albeit at an unlawful price, to Francisco, that he did not know or care what Francisco did with it, and that he did not know the ultimate sellers and had no interest in their activity? Compare United States v. Bruno, 105 F.2d 921 (2d Cir. 1939) with United States v. Peoni, 100 F.2d 401 (2d Cir. 1938). What if the prosecution proved that Weiss and Goldsmith thought that the owner would provide more whiskey if, after selling this load, they were to request it? See United States v. Spanos, 462 F.2d 1012 (9th Cir. 1972).

5.   United States v. Griffin, 464 F.2d 1352 (9th Cir. 1972), involved an alleged conspiracy to import heroin. Although the government charged a single conspiracy its evidence could be seen a revealing five with a single source selling to several purchasers who didn't know of each others existence. Defendants argued that this prejudiced them because having the jury hear all the evidence might result in "guilt transference". The Court of Appeals, however, was satisfied that any prejudice flowing from the variance was largely eliminated by the following cautionary instruction to the jury:

> "Now, suppose—just because I don't know what your findings are going to be—but suppose that you do not find that the government has proven beyond a reasonable doubt the defendants Montano and Griffin were a part of the same single overall conspiracy. I don't know whether you can find that or not. That, of course, is your determination. There is an alternate area of the law that I wish to call to your attention, and that has to do with the individual conspiracies that may be found in this indictment.

> "If you do not find beyond a reasonable doubt that the defendant Montano conspired with defendant Griffin—that is they were in the same and single conspiracy—but find that the defendant Montano did conspire with Lorenzo Rodriguez and or Maria Bueno and or with others you may, if the evidence so convinces you beyond a reasonable doubt, find defendant Montano guilty of the conspiracy. However, under this circumstance—to which I'm just making reference—you cannot consider any evidence except that which was admitted against defendant Montano. Likewise if you do not find beyond a reasonable doubt that defendant Griffin conspired with defendant Montano in one single overall conspiracy, but find that the defendant Griffin did conspire with Lorenzo Rodriguez and/or Maria Bueno or with others you may, if the evidence so convinces you beyond a reasonable doubt, find the defendant Griffin guilty of conspiracy."

6.   The government charges twenty-two persons with violation of 18 U.S.C.A. § 241 which prohibits conspiring "to injure * * * any citizen in the free exercise or enjoyment of any right * * * secured to him by the Constitution or laws of the United States". The conspiracy in question allegedly resulted in the dilution of the votes of Starr County, Texas voters through the casting of unlawful ballots. The indictment charged the defendants, mainly county officials and employees, with six counts. The first count charged a single, broad conspiracy involving all the defendants. The remaining five counts charged five separate conspiracies involving different combinations of defendants. The government explained that this was done to allow the jury to conclude that there were separate conspiracies

as to particular precincts or ballot boxes. Does this indictment threaten the defendants, as they argued, with double jeopardy?

If the government, in response to defendants' objections, elects to proceed on a single conspiracy theory may the defendants argue on appeal that the evidence in fact showed multiple conspiracies?

If defendants may raise this issue on appeal how should the court resolve the question if the evidence shows that although some of the defendants were involved in many of the separate efforts to obtain absentee ballots from voters unlawfully, none was involved in every such acquisition. See United States v. Morado, 454 F.2d 167 (5th Cir. 1972).

----

(3) OBJECTIVE OF THE AGREEMENT

STATE v. BOWLING

Court of Appeals of Arizona, 1967.
5 Ariz.App. 436, 427 P.2d 928.

MOLLOY, Judge. The defendants in this action appeal from convictions upon two counts of an indictment rendered against them by a grand jury. Both were charged in count one of this indictment with conspiracy to commit an act " * * * injurious to the public morals or unlawfully perverting or obstructing justice or due administration of the laws * * * " and in count two of receiving a bribe, while a member of the Arizona State Legislature, " * * * upon an understanding that their official opinions, judgments and actions should be influenced thereby * * * ".

The facts giving rise to these charges are substantially without dispute. A resident of Pima county by the name of Jerry Hanson, the co-proprietor of a tavern, was desirous of obtaining a new liquor license for his business, which would permit the sale of additional types of liquor. He had a conversation with Bowling, one of the defendants, who was at the time a member of the House of Representatives of the Arizona State Legislature, about assistance in obtaining such license. Bowling informed Hanson that he might be able to assist him, and arranged a meeting between Hanson, himself, and the other defendant, Cook, who was also a member of the Arizona House of Representatives. Hanson testified that Cook was introduced to him only as a legislator, while Bowling testified that Cook was introduced as a real estate broker. At this meeting, Hanson was informed that it would cost approximately $5,000 for the license over and above regular license fees and at a subsequent meeting, it was agreed that Hanson would pay $4,200, over and above the normal license fees, if the liquor license was obtained for him.

An application for such a license was duly submitted and a personal conference with Mr. John Duncan, Superintendent of Liquor Licenses and Control for the State of Arizona, followed, with Hanson, Bowling and Cook all speaking in behalf of the issuance of the license.

The statements made in support of issuing the license were in the nature of character references for Hanson and his father, who was a partner in the tavern, and included the argument that such a license was needed because two families were to be supported from this one business. There was no showing in the evidence of any inducements being offered to Mr. Duncan to issue the license nor of any improper persuasions advanced. The testimony is undisputed that Hanson was fully qualified under applicable law for the issuance of the license and that the location as to which the license application pertained fulfilled all of the legal requirements for such a license.

About a month after the conversation with Duncan, Cook contacted Hanson to inform him that the license had been issued, and Cook together with Bowling, brought the license to Hanson's home, where Hanson gave them $4,200 in cash. Bowling testified that all of this money was received and retained by Cook; Cook did not take the stand during the trial.

Numerous questions are raised on appeal, but it is our judgment that this proceeding must be disposed of on the basis of the contention that the trial court erred in refusing to direct a verdict of acquittal at the close of the State's case as to both counts of the indictment.

Count one of the indictment charges a crime under A.R.S. § 13–331. This statute, insofar as pertinent here, reads as follows:

"A. It is unlawful for two or more persons to conspire to:

*   *   *   *   *   *   *   *   *   *

"5. Commit any act injurious to the public health or public morals.

"6. Pervert or obstruct justice or due administration of laws.

"B. A person who violates any provision of this section shall be punished by imprisonment in the state prison for not to exceed one year, or by a fine not exceeding one thousand dollars.

"C. No conspiracies other than those enumerated in this section are punishable criminally."

From this statute, the following language was selected to charge that the defendants: " *   *   * did unlawfully conspire with each other to obtain a Series No. 6 Arizona State Liquor License for one JERRY HANSON from JOHN A. DUNCAN, the Superintendent of the Arizona State Department of Liquor Licenses and Control, *   *   * such act being injurious to the public morals or unlawfully perverting or obstructing justice or due administration of the laws *   *   *."

Initially, the appellants challenge the language charged in the indictment—-that they conspired to commit an act "injurious to public morals"—on the grounds that it is unconstitutionally indefinite. * *

In considering a Utah statute with similar wording, the Supreme Court of the United States said:

"Standing by itself, it would seem to be warrant for conviction for agreement to do almost any act which a judge and jury might find at the moment contrary to his or its notions of what was good for health, morals, trade, commerce, justice or order."

Musser v. State of Utah, 333 U.S. 95, 68 S.Ct. 397, 398, 92 L.Ed. 562 (1948).

The Supreme Court of the United States remanded the *Musser* case to the Utah Supreme Court to consider whether the language of this statute was unconstitutionally vague. The United States Supreme Court suggested that there was a possibility that under Utah statutory or case law the broad language of the statute might have been limited so as to give the required degree of specificity thereto.

The Supreme Court of Utah, however, was unable to point to any limitations upon the subject language and came to the conclusion that this statute, making it a crime to conspire to commit an act " * * * injurious * * * to public morals * * * " was unconstitutional:

"No language in this or any other statute of this state or other law thereof or any historical fact or surrounding circumstance connected with the enactment of this statute has been pointed to as indicating that the legislature intended any limitation thereon other than that expressed on the face of the words used. We are therefore unable to place a construction on these words which limits their meaning beyond their general meaning. The conviction of the defendants thereunder cannot be upheld. This part of the statute is therefore void for vagueness and uncertainty under the Fourteenth Amendment to the Federal Constitution."

State v. Musser, 118 Utah 537, 223 P.2d 193, 194 (1950).

Likewise, we know of no statutory or case law in this state which limits the broad sweep of that which is encompassed within the words " * * * injurious to * * * public morals * * * ". Common-law crimes have not survived in this state, and unless certain conduct is singled out by criminal statute, conduct is not a crime no matter how reprehensible.

We are aware that if a criminal statute refers by name to a common-law crime, the elements of that common-law crime may give sufficient definiteness to statutory language. However, we know of no common-law crime which bears analogy to the committing of an act "injurious to public morals."

In our view, these key words are even more vague and indefinite than the language "obscene or indecent," which was struck down by our Supreme Court in State v. Locks [97 Ariz. 148, 397 P.2d 949 (1964)]. We follow the specific holding of State v. Musser, supra, in declaring that this language is not sufficiently definite to satisfy due process requirements.

The State has contended that California, from whence our state adopted the statutory language under which these defendants were charged, has upheld the statute as to constitutionality. The cases cited are: Lorenson v. Superior Court, 35 Cal.2d 49, 216 P.2d 859 (1950); People v. Sullivan, 113 Cal.App.2d 510, 248 P.2d 520 (1952); Calhoun v. Superior Court, 46 Cal.2d 18, 291 P.2d 474 (1955); and Davis v. Superior Court, 175 Cal.App.2d 8, 345 P.2d 513 (1959). An examination of these decisions, however, will disclose no reliance upon that portion of the statute pertaining to acts injurious to the "public morals." These decisions all lean upon the words "to pervert or to obstruct justice or the due administration of the laws", as illustrated in the following language in *Lorenson:*

> "Considering the well-settled meaning at common law of the words 'to pervert or obstruct justice, or the due administration of the laws', the other and more specific provisions in the Penal Code concerning 'Crimes Against Public Justice', and the relative certainty of words employed in statutes which have been held valid, it cannot be said that subsection 5 of section 182 of the Penal Code is unconstitutional."

216 P.2d at 866.

In each of the four California cases, there was at least one specific criminal statute as to which the charges of conspiracy related. Here the State points to no criminal statute which the defendants are charged to have conspired to violate. Hence, under these California decisions, this charge can be sufficiently specific only if it charges a conspiracy to commit an act which would constitute the common-law crime "to pervert or obstruct justice, or the due administration of laws." *Lorenson* undertakes to define this common-law misdemeanor in this language:

> "Section 182 defines as criminal conspiracy acts committed with the purpose ' * * * to pervert or obstruct justice, or the due administration of the laws.' [G]enerally speaking, conduct which constitutes an offense against public justice, or the administration of law includes *both malfeasance and nonfeasance by an officer in connection with the administration of his public duties,* and also *any-*

*thing done by a person in hindering or obstructing an offi-
cer in the performance of his official obligations.* Such an
offense was recognized at common law and generally punishable as a misdemeanor. Now, quite generally, it has
been made a statutory crime, and, under some circumstances, a felony. Burdick, Law of Crimes [1946], vol. 1,
p. 382, et seq.; 20 Cal.Jur. 347–354." (Emphasis added)
216 P.2d at 865.

In *Davis*, in rejecting the contention that the "obstruction of
justice" statute was unconstitutional on its face, the court said:

"The constitutionality of the California statute, however, rests upon the fact that three cases have charted
boundaries to its otherwise limitless sea of criminality."
345 P.2d at 517.

These California decisions leave open the possibility that the
remaining language in count one of the subject indictment—"unlawfully perverting or obstructing justice or due administration of
the laws"—properly charges a criminal offense. In this regard,
the appellants do not directly attack this charging language upon
constitutional grounds, but rather on the basis of lack of proof. In
considering this argument, we have concluded that unless the acceptance of $4,200 by the defendants constituted a violation of this
law, there was no proof submitted to the jury meriting a conviction
on the conspiracy charge.

* * *

It seems clear that these defendants, Bowling and Cook, or
any other person, could have recommended to Mr. Duncan the issuance of a license to any particular applicant, for any legitimate
reason, without violating criminal law, and, in fact, this is not disputed by the State in this action. But the State contends that the
acceptance of the $4,200 renders that which would otherwise be
legal conduct into a perversion or obstruction of justice and/or due
administration of laws. No pertinent authority is cited.

We see no justification for characterizing the defendants' conduct as a perversion or obstruction of "justice or due administration
of laws," assuming that these concepts are made sufficiently definite by reference to the common law. The act charged as to which
there was alleged to have been a conspiracy was the obtaining of the
license for Hanson. The selection of Hanson by Duncan for the receipt of one of the quota licenses was not, in and of itself, a "mal-
feasance" or a "nonfeasance" nor a failure to perform "official obligations." (In the language of *Lorenson*.) The conduct of the defendants simply does not fit the charging language in count one of
the indictment. Any conspiratorial conduct of the defendants, if
criminal at all under the then existing law, most closely approached

being a conspiracy to violate a bribery statute, a charge not made, nor, as we shall see, supportable in the evidence. The fact that conduct may be highly reprehensible in the eyes of the courts does not justify the court in distorting language of a criminal statute to fit the conduct. A verdict should have been directed for the defendants on count one.

McKINNIE v. STATE

Supreme Court of Tennessee, 1964.
214 Tenn. 195, 379 S.W.2d 214.

BURNETT, Chief Justice. The plaintiffs in error were convicted of conspiring to injure the business of the B & W Cafeteria by blocking the entrance thereto in the event they were denied entrance to and service in said cafeteria. The jury recommended a fine of less than $50.00. The trial judge sentenced each of these defendants to ninety days in the Davidson County workhouse and fined each of them $50.00. An appeal was seasonably perfected, able briefs filed, and oral arguments were heard, and, after a thorough study of the record and applicable authorities, we now have the matter for disposition.

The indictment alleges a violation of two sections of the Tennessee Code, § 39–1101(7), T.C.A., and § 62–711, T.C.A. The pertinent part of § 39–1101, T.C.A., is as follows:

"The crime of conspiracy may be committed by any two (2) or more persons conspiring: * * * (7) to commit any act injurious to public health, public morals, trade, or commerce * * *."

Section 62–711, T.C.A., provides, in part, that "any person guilty of turbulent or riotous conduct within or about" any hotel, inn, restaurant, etc., is subject to indictment and a fine of not less than $100.00. Section 62–710, T.C.A.[d], was also mentioned in the indictment and the trial court's charge, but the defendants were not charged with violating this Section of the Code; nor could they

---

d. Right of owners to exclude persons from places of public accommodation. —The rule of the common law giving a right of action to any person excluded from any hotel, or public means of transportation, or place of amusement, is abrogated; and no keeper of any hotel, or public house, or carrier of passengers for hire (except railways, street, interurban, and commercial) or conductors, drivers, or employees of such carrier or keeper, shall be bound, or under any obligation to entertain, carry, or admit any person whom he shall, for any reason whatever, choose not to entertain, carry, or admit to his house, hotel, vehicle, or means of transportation, or place of amusement; nor shall any right exist in favor of any such person so refused admission; the right of such keepers of hotels and public houses, carriers of passengers, and keepers of places of amusement and their employees to control the access and admission or exclusion of persons to or from their public houses, means of transportation, and places of amusement, to be as complete as that of any private person over his private house, vehicle, or private theater, or places of amusement for his family.

have been so charged since this Section does not purport to define an indictable offense. It was mentioned merely to indicate that the B & W Cafeteria was permitted, by statute, to refuse admittance to any person whom it did not desire to serve.

* * *

At about 12:20, P.M., Sunday, October 21, 1962, just after many church services had ended, and at a time when the patrons of the B & W Cafeteria were arriving for lunch, the defendants appeared at the entrance of the cafeteria which is located on Sixth Avenue, in the heart of Nashville, Tennessee. When they arrived, they were informed by the doorman that the cafeteria did not serve colored people and that they could not enter. Despite this, the defendants remained at the entrance to the cafeteria and insisted that, "We are coming in and are going to eat when we git in."

The defendants were asked in a polite way to move along and to refrain from making any trouble. At this time, they had entered a vestibule to the cafeteria, the size of which is estimated as being from four feet by four feet to six feet by six feet and four inches. The defendants were in the vestibule, but were not permitted to enter the main part of the restaurant. After the defendants refused to remove themselves from the vestibule and after the acts hereinafter set forth had been committed, the police were called and they escorted the defendants away.

* * *

The record clearly shows that these defendants physically blocked the entrance to the B & W Cafeteria by placing themselves in this small vestibule so as to prevent people from entering or leaving; and that entrance to and exit from the restaurant was not possible without squeezing and worming through the wall of flesh created by the defendants' presence and position. The evidence likewise shows that in blocking this entrance, the defendants were pushing and shoving to some extent in an effort to enter this restaurant, but were prevented from doing so because the doorman kept the inner door closed to them.

* * *

Section 39–1101, T.C.A., makes it a misdemeanor for two or more persons to conspire to do an unlawful act. In order for the offense to be indictable, it must be committed *manu forti*— in a manner which amounts to a breach of the peace or in a manner which would necessarily lead to a breach of the peace. The charge here, as it is clearly set forth in the indictment, is that the defendants crowded into this small vestibule and through their actions, as detailed above, committed an act injurious to trade and commerce. When two or more persons conspire to commit an act such as this, § 39–1101, T.C.A., provides that they shall be guilty of a conspiracy. Section 62–711, T.C.A., in part provides that when a person is guilty of turbulent or riotous conduct within or about restaurants, hotels, etc., he may be indicted and fined not less than $100.00. * * *

The defendants through various motions and throughout the trial attempted to say that this prosecution was brought for the purpose of enforcing a rule of segregation or racial exclusion in facilities licensed by the State, open to the public, and vested with public interest; and that such a prosecution is contrary to the due process and equal protection clauses of the 14th Amendment to the Constitution of the United States. From a very careful examination and reading of the record, the indictment, and the charge of the court, we certainly feel that such questions are not determinative of this prosecution. We can assume for the sake of argument that discrimination based on race by a facility such as this cafeteria does violate the due process and equal protection clauses, but these questions are not presented here. A careful reading of this record shows that the only question is whether or not these defendants were attempting, in an illegal manner, to correct what they deemed to be an unconstitutional practice on the part of this cafeteria; and, if the method which these defendants adopted was illegal, whether it constitutes a misdemeanor under the Sections of the Code under which they were indicted.

This Court long ago in State v. Lasater, 68 Tenn. 584 (1877), held that an indictment under § 62–711, T.C.A., was good and that the act was constitutional. In that case, a judgment quashing the indictment was reversed where the indictment alleged that the defendant had been guilty of turbulent and riotous conduct within and about a hotel by quarreling, committing assaults and batteries, breaches of the peace, loud noises, and trespass upon a hotel. It seems to us that there is sufficient proof in the instant case, which the jury apparently believed, to warrant the conviction under this Section. The word "riotous" is defined by Webster's New World Dictionary as "having the nature of a riot or disturbance of the peace." The conduct of the defendants certainly meets this definition. Nowhere in this record is it insisted that there was not a prior agreement to engage in such conduct if entrance to this restaurant was denied. In Smith and Reynolds v. State, [205 Tenn. 502, 327 S.W.2d 308 (1959), cert. denied, 361 U.S. 930, 80 S.Ct. 372, 4 L.Ed.2d 354 (1960)], this Court had occasion to define a criminal conspiracy. This definition seems to meet the situation here. We likewise held in the Smith and Reynolds case that a conspiracy may be inferred from the nature of the acts done, the relation of the parties, the interest of the alleged conspirators, and other circumstances; and that such a conspiracy consists of a combination between two or more persons for the purpose of accomplishing a criminal or unlawful act, or an object, which although not criminal or unlawful in itself, is pursued by unlawful means, or the combination of two or more persons to do something unlawful, either as a means or as an ultimate end. While the request for admittance by the defendants was not criminal in the first instance, and while for the sake of argument, we may even assume that they had a right to go on the premises of the restaurant, the method they employed to effect their admittance was clearly unlawful.

* * *

Had this been a labor dispute, the actions of the defendants would clearly be beyond that of peaceful picketing, which does not include in its definition any form of physical obstruction or interference with business. It is well established that labor has the right to peacefully picket and thereby express its views on the subjects involved in a labor dispute. But the picketing must be peaceful. When it goes beyond the peaceful stage and involves force, violence, threats, terror, intimidation, coercion and other things of like kind, it cannot be tolerated and those persons guilty of such acts are subject to state and federal laws. By analogy, if the conduct of the defendants here transcended the bounds of peaceful picketing, they would, under the evidence in this record, be guilty of acts injurious to trade. We think that their conduct clearly goes beyond the bounds of peaceful demonstration and picketing.

It is very forcefully insisted that the two Sections of the Code under which this indictment was laid should have been declared unconstitutional because they do not clearly and sufficiently define the offense charged against the defendants. In all the years that these Code Sections have been the law in this State, this question has not been raised as far as we can determine. As far as we know, there is no criminal statute which describes every specific kind of violation that might be indictable under it; but so long as the statute generally states, as these statutes do, what is prohibited, their constitutionality cannot be challenged for indefiniteness. We think that the statutes now under consideration clearly set forth the offense intended and that the indictment framed thereunder clearly sets forth the way in which these defendants allegedly violated their provisions.

* * *

It would not have been an unlawful conspiracy for the defendants to agree to seek entry into this cafeteria for the purpose of being served food coupled with an overt act in furtherance of this agreement; but any agreement to obstruct the entrance of a place of business and thus injure their business does constitute an unlawful conspiracy.[e]

NOTES

1. Modern criminal codes, proposed and adopted, require that the objective of a conspiracy be a crime specifically defined in the code. See, e. g.,

e. The judgment was reversed, per curiam, on grounds unrelated to the legitimacy of the conspiracy charge, in 380 U.S. 449, 85 S.Ct. 1101, 14 L.Ed.2d 151 (1965).

Smith-Hurd Ill.Ann.Stat. ch. 38, § 8–2(a); McKinney Consol.Laws of N.Y. (Penal Law) §§ 105.00, 105.05, 105.10 & 105.15; Proposed New Federal Criminal Code § 1004(1); and MPC § 5.03 (1).

2. How should conspiracy be graded for purposes of punishment? Would it be improper to punish as a felony a conspiracy to commit a misdemeanor? Does the answer depend on whether the inchoate crime aspect of conspiracy is viewed as more important than its character as a substantive offense? In the *McKinnie* case, supra, does the danger of group criminality far exceed the danger of individual acts of "riotous conduct"? How do the Model Penal Code and the Proposed New Federal Criminal Code deal with this issue? Would it be desirable to limit conspiracy to agreemnts to commit a felony as is required by Vernon's Ann.Tex.P.C. art. 1622 (Penal Code)?

----

(4) DEFENSES BASED ON THE REQUIREMENT OF AN AGREEMENT

REGLE v. STATE

Court of Special Appeals of Maryland, 1970.
9 Md.App. 346, 264 A.2d 119.

MURPHY, Chief Judge.   On September 28, 1968, Sergeant Frank Mazzone, a Maryland State Police officer working under cover, was advised by other police officers that Michael Isele, a police informer, had informed them that he had been invited by the appellant Regle to participate in a robbery.   Mazzone immediately contacted Isele, whom he previously knew, and together they went to see the appellant. Isele introduced Mazzone to the appellant as a prospective participant in the planned robbery.   After some discussion, the appellant invited Mazzone to participate in the robbery.   While appellant did not then specify the place to be robbed, he indicated to Mazzone that Richard Fields had been involved with him in planning the robbery, and that he would also participate in the crime.   Appellant, Mazzone, and Isele then met with Fields and the robbery plan was outlined by appellant and Fields.   The need for guns was discussed and appellant and Fields spoke of the necessity of killing two employees at O'Donnell's restaurant, the situs of the proposed robbery.   The four men then drove in Isele's car to appellant's home where appellant phoned Kent Chamblee for the purpose of purchasing a shotgun.   Thereafter, the men drove to Chamblee's home, purchased the gun from him, and tested it in his presence.   While Chamblee knew that the shotgun was to be used "for a job," he did not accompany the others when they then drove to the restaurant to perpetrate the robbery.   Upon arriving there, Mazzone told appellant that he first wanted to "case" the restaurant.   This being agreed, Mazzone and Isele went into the restaurant while appellant and Fields went to a nearby bar to await their return.   Once inside the restaurant, Mazzone contacted police headquarters and requested assistance.   Thereafter, he and Isele left the restaurant and rejoined appellant and Fields. While several police cars promptly responded to the scene, Mazzone found it necessary, in the interim, to reveal his identity as a police officer and to arrest appellant and Fields at gunpoint. At the same time he also arrested Isele in order "to cover him." After the arrest, appellant made an incriminating statement to the effect that he and Fields had planned the robbery and that he had invited Isele to participate in the crime.

Appellant, Fields, and Chamblee were thereafter jointly indicted for conspiracy to rob with a dangerous and deadly weapon and for carrying a deadly weapon openly with intent to injure. Appellant was separately tried by a jury, found guilty on both counts, and sentenced to twenty years on the conspiracy charge, and two years, concurrent, on the weapons offense.

The docket entries indicate that the conspiracy indictment against Chamblee was *nol prossed* prior to appellant's trial. It also appears that at his trial appellant established through the testimony of a police officer that Fields had been examined by State psychiatrists at the Clifton Perkins State Hospital and found "not guilty by reason of being insane at the time of the alleged crime." The State did not rebut the officer's testimony, although the record indicates that two of the State psychiatrists who had examined Fields were then present in court.

Against this background, appellant contends that since the indictment against Chamblee was *nol prossed*, only he and Fields were charged as conspirators; and that because Fields was found insane at the time of the commission of the crime and thus was not a person legally capable of engaging in a criminal conspiracy, his own conviction cannot stand since one person alone cannot be guilty of the crime of conspiracy.

Conspiracy—a common law misdemeanor in Maryland—is defined as a combination by two or more persons to accomplish a criminal or unlawful act, or to do a lawful act by criminal or unlawful means. Jones v. State, 8 Md.App. 370, 259 A.2d 807. The gist of the offense is the unlawful combination resulting from the agreement, rather than the mere agreement itself, and no overt act is required to constitute the crime. Wilson v. State, 8 Md.App. 653, 262 A.2d 91. In other words, as succinctly stated by the Supreme Court of New Jersey in State v. Carbone, 10 N.J. 329, 91 A.2d 571, 574, the "gist of the offense of conspiracy lies, not in doing the act, nor effecting the purpose for which the conspiracy is formed, nor in attempting to do them, nor in inciting others to do them, but in the forming of the scheme or agreement between the parties." Concert in criminal purpose, it is said, is the salient factor in criminal conspiracy. Criminal conspiracy is a partnership in crime—"It is the coalition of manpower and human minds enhancing possibilities of achievement aimed at the objective that present a greater threat to society than does a lone offender." Clark and Marshall Crimes (6th Edition) Section

9.00. In short, it is *the existence* of the conspiracy which creates the danger. Dennis v. United States, 341 U.S. 494, 511, 71 S.Ct. 857, 95 L.Ed. 1137.

As one person cannot conspire or form a combination with himself, it is essential in proving the existence of a criminal conspiracy to show "the consent of two or more minds," Bloomer v. State, 48 Md. 521, 536, viz., it must be shown that at least two persons had a meeting of the minds—a unity of design and purpose—to have an agreement. Wilson v. State, supra; Jones v. State, supra. A formal agreement need not, however, be established; it is sufficient if the minds of the parties meet understandingly, so as to bring about an intelligent and deliberate agreement to do the acts contemplated. As the crime of conspiracy is one requiring a specific intent, and necessarily involves at the least two guilty parties, the required criminal intent must exist in the minds of two or more parties to the conspiracy.

In view of these principles, it is the well settled general rule that one defendant in a prosecution for conspiracy cannot be convicted where all of his alleged coconspirators, be they one or more, have been acquitted or discharged under circumstances that amount to an acquittal. The validity of the general rule has been consistently recognized by the Court of Appeals. See State v. Buchanan, 5 H & J 317; Bloomer v. State, supra; Hurwitz v. State, 200 Md. 578, 92 A.2d 575. We recognized the rule in Wilson v. State, supra (footnote 9). The rationale underlying the rule appears clear: that it is illogical to acquit all but one of a purported partnership in crime; that acquittal of all persons with whom a defendant is alleged to have conspired is repugnant to the existence of the requisite corrupt agreement; and that regardless of the criminal animus of the one defendant, there must be someone with whom he confected his corrupt agreement, and where all his alleged coconspirators are not guilty, a like finding as to him must be made. See 91 A.L.R.2d, at p. 703. But "It is only where one is convicted and another or others are acquitted, resulting in a repugnancy upon the record, that the convicted conspirator may be discharged." Berry v. State, 202 Ind. 294, 173 N.E. 705 cited with approval in Hurwitz v. State, supra.

Generally speaking, it would appear that so long as the disposition of the case against a coconspirator does not remove the basis for the charge of conspiracy, a single defendant may be prosecuted and convicted of the offense, even though for one reason or another his coconspirator is either not tried or not convicted. See the exhaustive collection of cases at 72 A.L.R. 1180–1192 and 91 A.L.R.2d 700–733. Consistent with this rule, the authorities all agree that the death of one conspirator does not of itself prevent the conviction of the other, where the conspiracy between them is shown by the evidence. In Hurwitz v. State, supra, a case in which all but one of the conspirators were granted immunity from prosecution on a ground not inconsistent with their participation in the conspiracy, the court held that such grant of immunity was not equivalent to acquittal and would not require reversal of the conviction of the one remaining conspirator. The same rule has been applied where one of two conspirators enjoyed diplomatic immunity and therefore could not be prosecuted for the conspiracy. Farnsworth v. Zerbst, 98 F.2d 541 (5th Cir.). In Adams v. State, 202 Md. 455, 97 A.2d 281, it was held that conviction of one defendant in a conspiracy case was proper despite failure to convict any of the other conspirators where it was alleged and shown that there were persons unknown to the prosecution with whom the convicted defendant had conspired. And while the cases are generally divided on the question whether the entry of a *nolle prosequi* as to one of two alleged conspirators compels an acquittal of the remaining conspirator, the better reasoned view would appear to support the proposition that it does not, at least where the *nolle prosequi* was not entered without the coconspirator's consent after the trial had begun (which then would have amounted to an acquittal and precluded reindictment). See Greathouse v. State, 5 Md.App. 675, 249 A.2d 207. In *Hurwitz*, it was held that the entry of a "stet" to a coconspirator's indictment was not tantamount to an acquittal and did not compel the discharge of the only remaining conspirator.[1]

Some cases suggest that the rule that acquittal of all save one of the alleged conspirators results in the acquittal of all applies only to acquittals on the merits. See Farnsworth v. Zerbst, supra. Other cases—while recognizing that acquittals are not always tantamount to a declaration of innocence—nevertheless conclude that an acquittal is in effect a judicial determination, binding on the State, that the acquitted defendant was not a participant in a criminal conspiracy. See United States v. Fox, 130 F.2d 56 (3rd Cir.); State v. Smith, 117 Ark. 384, 175 S.W. 392. The State urges that where the acquittal of one of the alleged conspirators is based solely on the fact that he was insane at the time of the crime, the remaining conspirator should nonetheless be held responsible for the offense. The State relies on Jones v. State, 31 Ala.App. 504, 19 So.2d 81, a case in which the defendant, convicted of murder, maintained that the actual killing was done by his brother and that because his brother was insane at the time of the crime, and hence innocent of the offense, he (the defendant) must likewise be exonerated. The court, after characterizing the defendant as "a co-conspirator and an aider and abettor in the homicide," said (p. 83):

> " * * * the insanity [of appellant's brother] would not exculpate the appellant if he conspired with the principal or aided or abetted him in the killing of deceased * * *. If appellant so conspired or aided or abetted in the homicide,

1. By the Maryland stet procedure, the prosecutor indicates that he does not choose *at that time* to further prosecute the indictment.

the mental irresponsibility of [his brother] could not be invoked to exonerate said appellant. One may or could use an insane person as the agent of destruction—or conspire with such person to accomplish the homicide—just as guilty as with a person of sound mind. The fact, if true, that the coconspirator or principal in the crime is not amenable to justice because of mental irresponsibility does not exempt the other from prosecution. Pruitt v. State, 91 Tex.Cr.R. 189, 237 S.W. 572; People v. Armstrong, 299 Ill. 349, 132 N.E. 547; Conley v. People, 170 Ill. 587, 48 N.E. 911; 22 C.J.S. Criminal Law §§ 85, 101."

We think the cases relied upon by the *Jones* court to support its conclusion stand for the proposition that it is no defense to one who participates either as a principal or aider or abettor in the actual commission of the substantive criminal offense that the principal offender was insane at the time of the crime. The principle would appear similar to the rule that a coconspirator may be convicted of any crime committed by any member of a conspiracy to do an illegal act if the act is done in furtherance of the purpose of the conspiracy. The conspiracy being established, the fact that the member who committed the crime was insane at the time would thus not exonerate the others from complicity in the commission of the substantive offense. See State v. Alton, 139 Mont. 479, 365 P.2d 527.

We do not find these cases controlling of the primary question before us, namely, whether *under an indictment for conspiracy*, one conspirator may be convicted of the offense where the only other conspirator was shown to be insane at the time the agreement between them was concluded. Conspiracy to commit a crime is a different offense from the crime that is the object of the conspiracy. One necessarily involves joint action; the other does not. By its nature, conspiracy is a joint or group offense requiring a concert of free wills, and the union of the minds of at least two persons is a prerequisite to the commission of the offense. The essence of conspiracy is, therefore, a mental confederation involving at least two persons; the crime is indivisible in the sense that it requires more than one guilty person; and where the joint intent does not exist, the basis of the charge of conspiracy is necessarily swept away. See Feder v. United States, 257 F. 694 (2nd Cir.). In short, the guilt of both persons must concur to constitute that of either. It is upon this premise that the authorities all agree that if two persons are charged as conspirators and one is an entrapper, or merely feigns acquiescence in the criminal intent, there is no punishable conspiracy because there was no agreement on the part of the one to engage in a criminal conspiracy.[2] Delaney v. State, 164 Tenn. 432, 51 S.W.2d 485; Woo Wai v. United States, 223 F. 412 (9th Cir.); State v. Dougherty, 88

2. This would not be true, however, if after elimination of the alleged entrapper, there are at least two other parties to the conspiracy.

N.J.L. 209, 96 A. 56; Solomon v. State, 168 Tenn. 180, 76 S.W.2d 331; Odneal v. State, 117 Tex.Cr.R. 97, 34 S.W.2d 595. For like reasons, we hold that where only two persons are implicated in a conspiracy, and one is shown to have been insane at the time the agreement was concluded, and hence totally incapable of committing any crime, there is no punishable criminal conspiracy, the requisite joint criminal intent being absent.

The evidence in the record before us plainly shows that appellant and Fields planned to commit a robbery at O'Donnell's restaurant. There is some evidence in the record to suggest that Chamblee may also have been a conspirator, although the State made little effort at the trial to establish his involvement in the conspiracy. Since an insane person is mentally incapable of forming a criminal intent, Bradford v. State, 234 Md. 505, 514, 200 A.2d 150, it is clear that if Fields was actually insane at the time of the offense, he could not be found guilty of engaging in a criminal conspiracy. It does not appear however, that Fields was ever tried and acquitted of the conspiracy charge. But the only evidence in the record—the testimony of the police officer—is that Fields was found by State psychiatrists upon examination to have been insane at the time of the commission of the offense. While such testimony is hardly the equivalent of the expert medical evidence required to prove insanity, see Millard v. State, 8 Md.App. 119, 261 A.2d 227, the trial judge, in his charge to the jury, stated as a fact that Fields "was found to be insane." Assuming this to be the true situation, it is unlikely that Fields will ever be brought to trial on the conspiracy charge.

As to Chamblee, the docket entries indicate the entry of a *nolle prosequi* to his conspiracy indictment. We cannot ascertain, therefore, whether, in the circumstances in which it was entered, the *nolle prosequi* operated as an acquittal or not. See Greathouse v. State, supra. It appears, however, from colloquy between counsel and with the court that Chamblee was permitted to plead to a lesser offense than conspiracy, possibly with the understanding that he would not thereafter be charged with that offense.

In his advisory instructions to the jury, the trial judge, after fully defining the crime of conspiracy, stated that under Maryland law where only two parties are involved in the alleged conspiracy, and one is found not guilty, "the other could not be tried because one person cannot conspire except with another to commit a crime." He further advised the jury that there has to be "an outright finding of not guilty" but such was not the case with Fields who was merely found to be insane and for that reason not brought to trial. With reference to Chamblee, the trial judge instructed that he had not been found not guilty of conspiracy; that he did not believe that Chamblee had been prosecuted for that offense.

While appellant made no objection to the court's instructions, on the state of the record before us we think they constituted "plain

error * * * material to the rights of the accused" under Maryland
Rule 756 g. See Parker v. State, 4 Md.App. 62, 241 A.2d 185. We
thus deem it essential in the interest of justice that appellant's conspiracy conviction be reversed and that the State be afforded the opportunity to retry the case in light of the principles of law which we
consider relevant and controlling. If, upon retrial, the State intends
to charge only Fields and appellant as conspirators, and the evidence
properly shows that Fields was legally insane at the time the agreement to perpetrate the robbery was concluded, then even though
Fields has not been acquitted of the offense of conspiracy by a judicial
determination that he was insane, nevertheless the requisite *joint*
criminal intent being absent, appellant cannot properly be convicted of
engaging with Fields in a criminal conspiracy. If Fields is shown so
to be insane, but the facts show that the conspiracy indictment against
Chamblee was not *nol prossed* under circumstances amounting to an
acquittal (see Greathouse v. State, supra), then the State may undertake to adduce evidence showing that Chamblee was a conspirator,
with appellant, in the plan to commit the robbery.

KING v. STATE

Supreme Court of Florida, 1958.
104 So.2d 730.

Certiorari denied without opinion.

On Rehearing Granted

PER CURIAM. By an information filed in the Court of Crimes
of Dade County, the petitioner King and two other persons, Carberry
and Monroe, were charged with conspiring with one another and with
one Moscovitz to violate §§ 849.01 and 849.25 of the Florida statutes,
F.S.A., relating to the unlawful keeping or maintaining of a place for
the purpose of gambling and to bookmaking, respectively. * * *

The information further alleged that the defendants and Moscovitz
did plan to set up and establish Moscovitz in the business of illegal
bookmaking in a certain hotel room, therein described, and that the
defendants would receive from Moscovitz pecuniary remuneration for
so planning and conspiring with Moscovitz. It was alleged that, as a
part of the conspiracy, the defendants King and Carberry, who were
police officers of the City of Miami, would not arrest Moscovitz for
keeping and maintaining the gambling room and would allow him to
continue such illegal keeping and maintaining of the gambling room.

The evidence of the State's witness, Moscovitz, revealed that
Moscovitz, acting pursuant to a plan of and as the agent of the Miami
Crime Commission and the County Solicitor, established himself as
bookmaker in the hotel room in question for the laudable purpose of
ferreting out corruption in the police force of the City. From funds
of the Crime Commission and the Dade County Commission, Mosco-

vitz was paid a weekly salary and provided with expense money for the hotel room and his bookmaking activities. After he had been in operation about two weeks in the hotel room, Moscovitz made a telephone call under an assumed name to the police station, complaining of gambling going on in the hotel room. This call brought King and Carberry to the hotel room, where Moscovitz had planted a scratch sheet, racing form, and other bookmaking paraphernalia. According to Moscovitz, the arrangement whereby he would pay a weekly sum to the defendants for protection was thereafter agreed upon and several such payments were made by him during the next three or four weeks to the defendant Monroe, a taxicab driver, pursuant to instructions received from the defendant King. The "pay-off" money was, of course, also supplied from public funds. Moscovitz' testimony as to the "protection" agreement was denied by defendants.

The jury returned a verdict finding the defendants King and Monroe, guilty, and the defendant Carberry not guilty. On appeal to the circuit court of Dade County, the judgment of conviction as to the defendants King and Monroe was affirmed. Upon the petition of King, certiorari to review the judgment of affirmance was denied by this court without opinion, and is now before the court on King's petition for rehearing.

On the petition for rehearing we have reconsidered the question of whether the defendants King and Monroe could legally be found guilty of the conspiracy charged against them under the evidence adduced by the State. We have concluded that there was no legal justification for the judgment of conviction under the evidence.

Our statute, § 833.01, Fla.Stat.1955, F.S.A., makes it a crime for two or more persons to conspire to commit—that is, themselves commit—"any offense". Here, the defendants King and Carberry were not charged with a conspiracy to accept unauthorized compensation for the performance or nonperformance of their duty as officers of the law, as denounced by § 838.06, Fla.Stat.1955, F.S.A.; in fact, * * * these defendants had been previously informed against and tried for the substantive offense described in § 838.06 and acquitted by the jury. Thereafter, by the information filed against them in the instant case, they were charged with a conspiracy to commit the offenses denounced by § 849.01 and § 849.25. * * *

Sec. 849.01 denounces the keeping of a house or other place for any manner of gaming or gambling. Sec. 849.25 defines "bookmaking" as "the taking or receiving of any bet or wager upon the result of any trial or contest of skill, speed, power, or endurance of man, beast, fowl or motor vehicle" and provides that "whoever engages in bookmaking shall be guilty of a misdemeanor * * *". Although the information in the instant case charged that the defendants conspired "one with the other" (as well as with Moscovitz) to commit the offenses described in § 849.01 and § 849.25, the evidence does not support the charge.

Both an agreement and an intention to commit an offense are necessary components of the substantive offense of conspiracy. Here, the agreement and the intention proved by the State was that Moscovitz would commit the offenses denounced by § 849.01 and § 849.25. The hotel room was to be kept and maintained by Moscovitz, not by the defendants; it was, in fact, so kept and paid for with public funds pursuant to the plan conceived by government officials for ensnaring, if not entrapping, corrupt police officers. It was Moscovitz, not the defendants, who was to "make book." Clearly, the participation of Moscovitz was an integral part of the plan, as proved by the State; without his complicity, the conspiracy—that is, the agreement and the intention—to commit the offenses charged is not proved.

But Moscovitz, in the circumstances here, is not criminally liable as a co-conspirator; nor can it be seriously contended that a government agent can be prosecuted for a violation of a criminal statute committed in the performance of his duty as such agent. We are cognizant of the fact that a punishable conspiracy may exist whether or not the crime intended to be accomplished by it was committed. But it is equally well settled that where one of two persons who conspire to do an illegal act is an officer acting in the discharge of his duty, the other person cannot be convicted on a charge of conspiracy. And counsel for the State has cited no case, and our independent research has revealed none, in which a conspiracy conviction against two or more persons has been upheld where the proof showed that some act *essential* to the crime charged as the object of the conspiracy was performed by a government agent, acting in the line of duty. There are, however, decisions striking down such convictions. See Woo Wai v. United States, 9 Cir., 1915, 223 F. 412.

In United States v. Wray, D.C.Ga.1925, 8 F.2d 429, 430, relied upon by counsel for the State, Wray and another were accused of conspiracy to violate the Prohibition Act. The proof showed that one Russell, a revenue agent, by pretending to be a dealer in illicit whiskey, induced defendants to make sales to him. In holding that a verdict of not guilty could not properly be directed for the defendants and that the issue of conspiracy should be submitted to the jury, the court said: "If a purchaser and seller of liquor, both knowing the sale to be illegal, can be considered conspirators, still where the purchaser is an officer in the discharge of his duty, there is no indictable conspiracy. But here the indictment charges, also, that the two defendants conspired with one another, and there is evidence in support of this view of the case." Since the evidence is not set out in the opinion, it is impossible to tell whether the revenue agent's purchase of the illicit whiskey was an essential element of the violation of the Prohibition Act charged to be the object of the conspiracy. So this case is not authoritative here.

We hold, therefore, with what appears to be the weight of, if not the only, authority, that where two or more persons conspire with another who is, unknown to them, a government agent acting in the line of duty, to commit an offense under an agreement and an intention that an essential ingredient of the offense is to be performed by, and only by, such government agent, such persons may not legally be convicted of a conspiracy. As stated in Woo Wai v. United States, supra, 223 F. 412, 415, where a conviction of two persons who conspired with a government agent was reversed, "If no violation of the law was to be accomplished by the act of the defendants, it follows that they could not be held for conspiracy to do that act." Or, as stated in State v. Dougherty, supra, 96 A. 56, 57, "It [the State] cannot be permitted by splitting the single conspiracy in two to say one was criminal and the other meritorious; that in one the councilmen [defendants] alone were involved, in the other 'Harris' was also a party, when the fact is that 'Harris' was a necessary party throughout. As the Supreme Court of the United States has recently said: 'The character and effect of a conspiracy is not to be judged by dismembering it and viewing its separate parts, but only by looking at it as a whole.' United States v. Patten, 226 U.S. 525, 544, 33 S.Ct. 141, 145, 57 L.Ed. 333." * * *

Since all of the evidence adduced by the State in support of the charge of conspiracy made against the defendants, when given full face value, formed no legal basis for a conviction of such charge, an affirmance of such conviction by the Circuit Court was fundamental error amounting to a departure from the essential requirements of law reachable on a petition for certiorari.

MODEL PENAL CODE, COMMENT TO § 5.03(1), 102

(Tent. Draft No. 10, 1960).

2. *The Conspiratorial Relationship.*

Unilateral Approach of the Draft. The definition of the Draft departs from the traditional view of conspiracy as an entirely bilateral or multilateral relationship, the view inherent in the standard formulation cast in terms of "two or more persons" agreeing or combining to commit a crime. Attention is directed instead to each individual's culpability by framing the definition in terms of the conduct which suffices to establish the liability of any given actor, rather than the conduct of a group of which he is charged to be a part—an approach which in this comment we have designated "unilateral."

One consequence of this approach is to make it immaterial to the guilt of a conspirator whose culpability has been established that the person or all of the persons with whom he conspired have not been or cannot be convicted. Present law frequently holds otherwise, reasoning from the definition of conspiracy as an agreement between two or more persons that there must be at least two guilty conspirators or none.

———

ROBINSON v. STATE

Court of Appeals of Maryland, 1962.
229 Md. 503, 184 A.2d 814.

BRUNE, Chief Judge. The defendant, Robinson, was indicted separately (a) for several substantive offenses under the lottery laws and (b) for conspiracy to violate these laws. Under the substantive offense indictment he was found not guilty on a charge of selling lottery tickets, but he was found guilty of keeping a "place"—an automobile—for the sale of lottery tickets, of permitting an automobile to be used as a place for such sale, of possession of lottery tickets and of possession of lottery paraphernalia. He was also charged and found guilty as a second offender on the last two charges. The conspiracy indictment, on which he was also found guilty, charged him with conspiracy with one Charles George Vain, and other persons unknown, to violate the lottery laws. He was tried under both indictments together and was sentenced to five years' imprisonment under the first indictment and to one year under the second, the sentences to run concurrently. He appeals. By the direction of this Court the case has been reargued as to matters pertaining mainly to the conspiracy charge.

* * *

Under the second indictment, the defendant claims that the evidence was insufficient to warrant his conviction (a) because of the so called "concert of action rule" (sometimes known as "Wharton's rule"), and (b) because (even if the agreement of a writer and player could constitute a conspiracy), necessary corroboration of the testimony of accomplices was lacking.

* * *

When we turn to the conspiracy charge, the case comes before us on a record which is not so complete and explicit as we might wish. Though the indictment is sufficient, it is not highly informative. The defendant sought further information with regard to the charge of conspiracy through an interrogatory, which the State claimed it was not obliged to answer. As a result of a discussion immediately prior to the trial the State furnished information which apparently satisfied this demand of the defendant. The Assistant State's Attorney said that the State's "position is that the co-conspirators are players and not writers." He then specifically stated that this was true as to Charles G. Vain, the defendant's named co-conspirator (referred to below for brevity as "Vain, Sr."); but as to Charles J. Vain (son of

Charles G., and referred to below, for brevity, as "Vain, Jr.") he went on to say in part: "We do not stipulate that he is engaged in lottery in any capacity, even as a player"; and as to Hagner, who, like Vain, Jr., was employed at Vain, Sr.'s service station, he said that this man was "[s]imply a witness, not a participant."

As to Hagner, the evidence is that he did not engage in playing numbers. On one occasion, in response to a telephone call from Robinson, he gave the latter a list of numbers which Vain, Sr. had left in his desk; and on another occasion he received a package of money from Robinson for Vain (apparently a pay-off on a number that "hit"). Vain, Jr. according to his own testimony, gave his father's lists of numbers to Robinson over the telephone on a number of occasions when Vain, Sr. was not at the service station; and Vain, Jr. also played about $6.00 a week himself. There was further testimony to the effect that for a period of about two months prior to the arrest of Robinson, Robinson would call Vain, Sr. by telephone each day and would accept numbers from him and that once or possibly twice a week Robinson would call to make collections or pay-offs, crediting the amount of his purchases of gasoline against amounts owed him by Vain, Sr. All of the testimony relating to the above transactions came from Vain, Sr., Vain, Jr. and Hagner.

It is on this evidence that we take up the defendant's contentions based upon the concert of action rule in conspiracy cases and upon the requirement for corroboration of the testimony of accomplices. This requires consideration of the nature of the agreement constituting the alleged conspiracy and of the parties thereto—as to the latter, specifically the position of Vain, Jr. and that of Hagner.

The indictment, as already noted, is not very informative. The testimony indicates that the original and basic agreement to violate the lottery laws upon which the conspiracy charge rests was an agreement between Robinson and Vain, Sr. that Robinson would write and Vain, Sr. would play numbers. The testimony also shows a course of dealing between Robinson and Vain, Jr. from which it might be inferred that there was a similar agreement between them under which Robinson was to write numbers for Vain, Jr. The State's contention on reargument in this Court is that Vain, Jr. was a co-conspirator and that Hagner was neither a conspirator nor an accomplice. With regard to Vain, Jr. there does not, however, appear to be any evidence to show that the defendant's writings for the father and his writings for the son were pursuant to any single agreement either as an original proposition or as the result of the original agreement between Robinson and Vain, Sr. being extended so as to include Vain, Jr. On the contrary, there would appear to have been two separate agreements— one to write for Vain, Sr., the other for Vain, Jr.

If there were two separate agreements and if there were only one party on each side—a writer and a player—the conspiracy charge would fall within the concert of action rule. Under that rule (sometimes known as "Wharton's rule"), as stated in the now current edition of Wharton's Criminal Law and Procedure (Anderson Ed., 1957) § 89 (differing somewhat from the statement of the rule in the 1932 edition): "An agreement by two persons to commit a particular crime cannot be prosecuted as a conspiracy when the crime is of such a nature as to necessarily require the participation of two persons for its commission." (P. 191). The rule was thus stated by Mr. Justice Stone in Gebardi v. United States, 287 U.S. 112, 122, 53 S.Ct. 35, 77 L.Ed. 206 (which, however, was decided upon a different theory): "[W]here it is impossible under any circumstances to commit the substantive offense without co-operative action, the preliminary agreement between the same parties to commit the offense is not an indictable conspiracy either at common law [citing cases, including Shannon and Nugent v. Commonwealth, 14 Pa.St. 226 (1850), apparently the original authority for Wharton's first statement of the rule], or under the federal statute." See also * * * Developments in the Law—Criminal Conspiracy, 72 Harv.L.Rev. 920, 953–56 (1959). In the article just cited, it is stated (p. 954): "Briefly, the Wharton rule states that when by definition the intended substantive offense requires a plurality of actors, a conspiracy prosecution cannot be maintained if only the minimum number of parties logically necessary for the commission of the substantive offense agree to commit it. The courts seem to justify this rule on the basis that when two parties conspire to commit such an offense there is no danger involved beyond that inherent in the offense itself." The article then proceeds to criticize the rule and certain of its applications (one of which was in a case of the giving and receiving of a bribe, United States v. Dietrich, C.C., 126 F. 664).

The American Law Institute also criticizes Wharton's rule. See Model Penal Code, Tentative Draft No. 10 (1960), particularly the Commentary on § 5.04, pp. 172–174. This Section is not substantially changed in the Proposed Official Draft of 1962, and the Commentary in Draft No. 10 is, in effect, incorporated by reference. That Commentary states, *inter alia*: "That an offense inevitably requires concert is no reason to immunize criminal preparation to commit it." The Institute's solution of the problem is thus summarized (pp. 173–174): "The Draft * goes no further than to provide that a person who may not be convicted of the substantive offense under the complicity provision may not be convicted of the inchoate crime under the general conspiracy and solicitation sections. On the other hand, the party who would be guilty of the substantive offense if it should be committed, may equally be convicted of soliciting or conspiring for its commission, since the immunity of the other party gives him no defense under Subsection (1) (b)." See §§ 5.04 and 2.06(6) (a) and (b) of the 1962 Draft and their predecessors in the 10th and 4th Tentative Drafts, respectively. The A.L.I. Drafts, of course, present a proposed statute, and we are dealing with the common law of this State.

Hurwitz v. State, [200 Md. 578, 92 A.2d 575] considered the concert of action rule at some length. There are well recognized limitations upon that rule which Hurwitz applied. Chief Judge Markell there said (200 Md. at 590, 92 A.2d at 580): "A sufficient answer to appellant's contention is that the indictment does not charge—and the evidence does not show—as an object of the conspiracy, and the lottery laws do not prohibit, as a substantive offense, any concert of action or plurality of agents which is essential to commission of a substantive offense. Unless by implication the lottery laws prohibit the purchase of a lottery ticket (by prohibition of sale or otherwise) there seems to be no violation of these laws which could not be committed by one person; this is notably true of possession, the broadest of all such offenses. The indictment does not charge, and the evidence does not show, that any of the conspirators were mere 'players', i. e., purchasers."

In Hurwitz the appellant and his co-conspirators were writers, not players of numbers. That is not the situation in the instant case, and the passage quoted carries a rather clear intimation that at least in the case of an agreement between one writer and one player for the writing of numbers the rule would apply, even though only the seller would be guilty of an offense. In such a case concert of action between the writer-seller and the player-buyer appears logically necessary to the commission of the offense.

Where more parties participate in the conspiracy than are logically necessary to the commission of the substantive offense contemplated by the conspiracy, the rule does not apply.

A further limitation upon the rule is that the substantive offense must have been committed.   *   *   *   That seems to have been the fact here.

Conversely to the more-parties-than necessary limitation, as was recognized in Hurwitz, the fact that logically action by only one person may be essential to the commission of the offense which is the object of the conspiracy bars the application of the concert of action rule. Lisansky v. United States, 31 F.2d 846, 67 A.L.R. 67 (C.C.A., 4th), cert. den. 279 U.S. 873, 49 S.Ct. 514, 73 L.Ed. 1008 (conspiracy to defraud the United States by filing a false partnership income tax return).

On the other hand, the fact that there may be several parties on each "side" of the offense has been said or held not to prevent the application of the rule so as to bar a conspiracy charge.

The concert of action rule has sometimes been supported or the same result has been reached on other grounds than the usual one of there being no greater danger from the same number of participants, which is mentioned in the article on Criminal Conspiracy in 72 Harv.

L.Rev. above cited. Sometimes it is reached on a theory of merger of offenses or double jeopardy (see 11 Am.Jur., Conspiracy, § 20) and sometimes, in the case of statutes manifesting an intent that one party shall not be punished for the substantive offense, a further legislative intent that the same act shall not serve as a basis for a prosecution for conspiracy.

Following the Hurwitz case, the concert of action rule was asserted as a defense to a charge of conspiracy to violate the lottery laws in Rouse v. State, 202 Md. 481, 97 A.2d 285, cert. den. 346 U.S. 865, 74 S.Ct. 104, 98 L.Ed. 376, but this defense was abandoned. Rouse, like Hurwitz, involved a conspiracy between several writers. So did McGuire, in which one writer "laid off" some of his bets with another writer (the appellant) and so did Scarlett. This last case rejected a plea based upon double jeopardy and *res judicata* and held that an acquittal on certain charges of lottery did not bar a subsequent prosecution for conspiracy to violate the lottery laws or prevent the use therein of some of the evidence offered in the earlier substantive offense case. Rouse, too, involved and rejected a defense of *res judicata* (under a defense of former jeopardy). None of the cases just cited involved a writer-player conspiracy, as does the instant case.

The rule adopted by the Model Penal Code has much to recommend it as against the concert of action rule and its refinements and limitations or exceptions as they have been developed. However that is only a proposed statute, and the concert of action rule has, we think, been recognized by this Court in the Hurwitz case. We do not undertake to depart from it.

We turn then to the status of Vain, Jr. and Hagner and a consideration of the effect of their presence in the case. At this point the State encounters this dilemma: if Vain, Jr. and Hagner were co-conspirators or accomplices, corroboration of their testimony and that of Vain, Sr. would be required in order to sustain the conviction of the defendant * * *; if they were not, then the only conspirators were the seller-writer, Robinson, and the buyer-player, Vain, Sr., and the conspiracy charge would fail under the concert of action rule above discussed.

Without the evidence seized as a result of the illegal search of the defendant's automobile, we think that the necessary corroboration of the testimony of co-conspirators or accomplices is lacking. Much the same considerations are applicable here as those which led us to conclude that the officers did not have a sufficient basis to arrest the defendant and search his car, and we shall not repeat them.

The State cannot, we think, escape the horns of this dilemma through its contentions that Vain, Jr. was a conspirator and that Hagner was neither a conspirator nor an accomplice. If Vain, Jr. was a party to a conspiracy between Vain, Sr. and Robinson (and this does not appear to have been the State's contention at the trial), the evidence, we think, shows no more than that Vain, Jr., with knowledge of the arrangement between Vain, Sr. and Robinson, telephoned in numbers for Vain, Sr. (His own playing of numbers with Robinson appears, as we have already said, to have been under an arrangement of his own.) If this activity of Vain, Jr. as agent for Vain, Sr. was enough to make him a co-conspirator, we see no reason why like reasoning, applied to Hagner's lesser activity as agent for Vain, Sr., but with knowledge of the nature of the arrangement between Vain, Sr. and the defendant, would not also make Hagner a party to the conspiracy or at least an accomplice. We think it unnecessary to decide whether Hagner was or was not an accomplice. We think, however, that if Vain, Jr. was one, so was Hagner.

This brings us back to the point that the conviction on the conspiracy charge must be reversed because, if Vain, Jr. and Hagner were conspirators or accomplices, there was not sufficient corroboration of their testimony and that of Vain, Sr., or if they were not parties to the alleged conspiracy, it was not punishable as such under the concert of action rule.

Judgments reversed and cases remanded for new trials; the costs of this appeal to be paid by the Mayor and City Council of Baltimore.

NOTES

1. A and B are charged with conspiracy to commit grand theft. A pleads guilty. B stands trial and is acquitted. A is then sentenced. Are A's conviction and sentence void? Is the answer dictated by *Regle*? Is judicial responsibility for overseeing the plea bargaining process a basis for intervention? See Eyman v. Deutsch, 92 Ariz. 82, 373 P.2d 716 (1962). Should the answer be different if B's acquittal came after A's guilty plea and sentence? See United States v. Strother, 458 F.2d 424 (5th Cir. 1972).

2. Does the decision in *Regle* comport with your view of the rationales for the crime of conspiracy? How does the insanity of an alleged co-conspirator lessen the dangers which conspiracy doctrine is designed to avoid?

3. Is the *King* decision better understood as a reaction to "entrapment"? What reason is there, if any, to bar conspiracy prosecutions based upon an "agreement" between a law enforcement officer or agent and one other person?

4. Given its rationale, should the Wharton rule be applied where, as in *Robinson*, only one of the two participants would be guilty of the substantive offense? Is there then an identity in the danger posed by the conspiracy and that inherent in the crime intended? If Vain, Sr. could not be convicted for purchasing a number is there any reason why he and Robinson should not be convicted for conspiring to violate the lottery laws? See United States v. Holte, 236 U.S. 140 (1915) (although the transported woman arguably cannot be convicted of violating the White Slave Act, she may be convicted of conspiring to commit that offense). If conviction of Vain, Sr. of conspiracy might be seen as violative of legislative intent is there any reason why Robinson should not be convicted?

5. Could the prosecution in any of the preceding cases have avoided these adverse decisions by alleging that the conspiracy involved other, unknown persons? How much evidence of the existence of such unknown conspirators should be required? See United States v. Hernandez-Carreras, 451 F.2d 1315 (9th Cir. 1971).

----

b. OVERT ACT REQUIREMENT

PEOPLE EX REL. CONTE v. FLOOD

Supreme Court of New York, 1966.
53 Misc.2d 109, 277 N.Y.S.2d 697.

MEMORANDUM

MARIO PITTONI, Justice. Relator, Dino Conte, has petitioned to be released pursuant to a Writ of Habeas Corpus on the ground that he has been illegally incarcerated since September 4, 1966. The reason given for such release is that pursuant to Section 250 of the Correction Law, as amended, he was entitled to 10 days per month for "good time". Relator Conte says that the pertinent part of Section 250 of the Correction Law became effective as to crimes committed after June 1, 1964 and his crime of conspiracy was consummated after June 1, 1964.

Count One of the indictment, to which Relator Conte pleaded guilty, charges him with violating Section 580–a of the Penal Law which reads as follows:

> "If two or more persons conspire to commit the crime of * * * extortion, and if some act besides the agreement to commit such crime be done to effect the object of the agreement by one or more of such persons, each of them is guilty of a felony."

Count One of the indictment, to which he pleaded guilty, alleges that Relator Conte and others "between the 1st day of May, 1964 to the 15th day of July, 1964 did * * * combine * * * conspire and agree together to extort money * * * from Irving Holzman", and that they committed certain overt acts in pursuance and furtherance of the conspiracy.

The first alleged overt act is no overt act at all. It merely states that during the 2½ month period involved the conspirators threatened Irving Holzman and members of his family with physical harm. This is not an overt act required under Sections 580–a and 583 of the Penal Law. It must be a specific, affirmative, independent, identified overt act done to further the object of the conspiracy.

The second overt act is that the conspirators "did on or about the 8th day of June, 1964 assault one Ruth Holzman * * * by * * * striking her with a * * * pistol * * *".

The third overt act is that the conspirators "did on or about the 2nd day of July, 1964 have a telephone conversation with Irving Holzman * * *".

The fourth overt act is that the conspirators "on or about the 30th day of June, 1964 * * * did make a telephone call to Dolores Billing * * *".

The fifth alleged overt act is a general statement of conversations among the conspirators within the 2½ month period of the conspiracy. But it is "hornbook" law that conversations among co-conspirators in forming and planning the conspiracy are not overt acts in furtherance of the conspiracy, as meant by "overt acts" in Sections 580-a and 583 of the Penal Law.

As one can see, the only valid overt acts alleged in the indictment took place on three dates: June 8, 1964, June 30, 1964 and July 2, 1964, all after the important or key date involved in this proceeding, June 1, 1964. It is well established that the crime of conspiracy is not complete until the commission of an overt act. Clearly, therefore, the conspiracy in our case was not completed or consummated till after June 1, 1964.

Assuming, arguendo, that an overt act were not necessary to complete or consummate the crime of conspiracy, we would be bound to interpret or construe the statutes involved herein "according to the fair import of their terms, to promote justice and effect the objects of the law" (Section 21 of Penal Law). A crime which starts before June 1, 1964 and ends after June 1, 1964 is committed after June 1, 1964.

Be that as it may, as previously pointed out, a conspiracy under Sections 580-a and 583 of the Penal Law is not completed and is no crime until an overt act in furtherance of that conspiracy has been committed.

It follows that the benefit of Section 250 of the Correction Law effective June 1, 1964 applies to Relator Conte, who was sentenced on December 10, 1965, and his legal period of incarceration has already run its course.

The writ is *sustained*.

UNITED STATES v. ARMONE

United States Court of Appeals, Second Circuit, 1966.
363 F.2d 385, certiorari denied 385 U.S. 957, 87 S.Ct. 391, 17 L.Ed.2d 303
and 87 S.Ct. 392 and 87 S.Ct. 398.

FEINBERG, Circuit Judge. Four defendants appeal from convictions of violating the conspiracy provision of the federal narcotics laws, 21 U.S.C.A. §§ 173, 174. * * *

Since the main arguments in this court are not directed to the sufficiency of the evidence, the facts developed at the seven-week trial will not be outlined in detail. Viewing the government's case after a jury verdict of guilty in the light most favorable to the prosecution, as we must, it was, briefly, that appellants, together with the co-defendants and co-conspirators, conspired from 1956 through 1960 to import and distribute heroin in the United States. The drugs originated in France, and would be smuggled into this country with the aid of couriers, who usually travelled as part of their occupations. * * *

The next asserted error is the treatment of an overt act, number 10 in the indictment. * * *

Of the eleven acts alleged in the indictment, only two were submitted to the jury; the trial judge held that the statute of limitations barred consideration of the other nine. The indictment alleged as overt act 10 that "in or about March of 1960," Joseph Armone was "in the vicinity of 122 Second Avenue, New York, New York." Thereafter, the government in a bill of particulars specified the act as taking place "during March or April of 1960, approximately between 1:00 P. M., and 5:00 P. M., inside 207 Second Avenue, New York City." 207 Second Avenue was, of course, a different address from that specified in the indictment—122 Second Avenue.

At the trial, there was evidence that in April or May 1960, Hedges had a conversation with Armone in Lulu's Bar (conceded here to be located at 207 Second Avenue) during which Hedges complained about the amount of his payments. There was also testimony of a conversation between the same persons at the same place and some time in the same months concerning a counterfeit $100 bill passed by Godwin, Hedges's cousin and one of the co-conspirators. Hedges testified that in Lulu's Bar Joseph Armone told him that a counterfeit $100 bill given "them" by Godwin would cause trouble in the form of an investigation. Godwin gave testimony corroborating this conversation.

* * *

Appellants have three further major thrusts based on overt act 10: * * * (2) the conversation, in any event, was not an act in furtherance of the conspiracy * * *

As to the second contention, an overt act is an act "committed in pursuance of the agreement." United States v. Agueci, 310 F.2d 817, 828, 99 A.L.R.2d 478 (2d Cir. 1962), cert. denied, Guippone v. United States, 372 U.S. 959, 83 S.Ct. 1013, 10 L.Ed.2d 11 (1963). Appellants seem to argue that conversation cannot be an "act," and that, in any event, this conversation was not in furtherance of the conspiracy. However, much talk is "action" with direct legal consequences; e. g., people "decide," "promise," and "reject." Cf. decisions holding telephone conversations to be overt acts, Singer v. United States, 208 F.2d 477, 480 (6th Cir. 1953); Bartoli v. United States, 192 F.2d 130, 132 (4th Cir. 1951); Smith v. United States, 92 F.2d 460, 461 (9th Cir. 1937). Here we have a warning to co-conspirator Hedges by defendant Armone, after the conspirators had gone to the trouble of tracing the source of the counterfeit bill. We hold that this conversation qualified as an "act." Moreover, the jury could find that Armone was attempting to stave off investigation of the conspiracy by warning Hedges of the dangers of passing counterfeit money among the conspirators. The trial court left the issue of furtherance to the jury. We cannot say as a matter of law that the jury could not reasonably have concluded that this conversation, viewed in the context of the other evidence, was in furtherance of the conspiracy.

NOTES

1. People v. Olson, 232 Cal.App.2d 480, 42 Cal.Rptr. 760, 767 (1965):

But, by definition, the overt act must be one to effect the object of the conspiracy or which, at least, has a tendency to forward the purpose of the conspiracy. In this country, evil thoughts alone cannot constitute a criminal offense; unless and until something objective is done toward the effectuation of the illegal plan, no prosecution is justified; if there is no overt or open act there can be no conviction, and the overt act must be such as furthers the object of the conspiracy.

In United States v. German-American Vocational League, 3 Cir., 153 F.2d 860, 863, it is said:

"'An overt act is one which manifests the intention of the doer to commit the offense.'"

It has been reiterated more than once in apposite legal opinions that an overt act must " * * * at least start to carry the conspiracy into effect" (People v. Moran, 166 Cal.App.2d 410, 414, 333 P.2d 243, 245; People v. George, 74 Cal.App. 440, 241 P. 97). Chavez v. United States, 9 Cir., 275 F.2d 813, 817, says:

"In criminal law an overt act is an outward act done in pursuance of the crime and in manifestation of an intent or design, looking toward the accomplishment of the crime."

One reason for requiring the allegation and proof of an overt act in connection with a conspiracy is to allow an opportunity to the conspirators to repent and to terminate the unlawful agreement before any decisive act is done in furtherance of it. The requirement of the allegation and proof of such an overt act " * * * affords a *locus poenitentiae*, so that before the act done either one or all of the parties may abandon their design, and thus avoid the penalty prescribed by the statute." (United States v. Britton, 108 U.S. 199, 2 S.Ct. 531–534, 27 L.Ed. 698.)

In light of the above how do you explain section 5.03(5) of the Model Penal Code? Is the approach of the Proposed Federal Criminal Code preferable? Why?

2. A and B are charged with a conspiracy to have an illegal abortion performed on C. Is the conversation of A and B and their agreement to pursue this objective a sufficient overt act? Is A's arranging to have C meet B such an act? Is A's arranging to have C pay money to B such an act? See People v. Wolff, 42 Misc.2d 166, 247 N.Y.S.2d 829 (1964).

c. THE STATE OF MIND REQUIRED

CLEAVER v. UNITED STATES

United States Court of Appeals for the Tenth Circuit, 1956.
238 F.2d 766.

LEWIS, Circuit Judge. * * *

Defendants next challenge the conviction upon the ground that the trial court did not adequately charge the jury relative to the law pertaining to the testimony of accomplices; specific complaint is made that the court did not inform the jury that two of the government's witnesses, Thomas Sullivan and James Webster, were accomplices. Sullivan admitted and testified to his participation in the crime from its inception to his arrest in Tulsa, Oklahoma, where he passed some of the stolen money orders. He, of course, was an accomplice. Webster, however, did not participate in the planning or the commission of the burglary, although he was present during a number of the conversations among the various conspirators. Mere knowledge, approval of or acquiescence in the object or the purpose of the conspiracy, without an intention and agreement to cooperate in the crime is insufficient to constitute one a conspirator.

PEOPLE v. LAURIA

California Court of Appeal, 1967.
251 Cal.App.2d 471, 59 Cal.Rptr. 628.

FLEMING, Associate Justice. In an investigation of call-girl activity the police focused their attention on three prostitutes actively plying their trade on call, each of whom was using Lauria's telephone answering service, presumably for business purposes.

On January 8, 1965, Stella Weeks, a policewoman, signed up for telephone service with Lauria's answering service. Mrs. Weeks, in the course of her conversation with Lauria's office manager, hinted broadly that she was a prostitute concerned with the secrecy of her activities and their concealment from the police. She was assured that the operation of the service was discreet and "about as safe as you can get." It was arranged that Mrs. Weeks need not leave her address with the answering service, but could pick up her calls and pay her bills in person.

On February 11, Mrs. Weeks talked to Lauria on the telephone and told him her business was modelling and she had been referred to the answering service by Terry, one of the three prostitutes under investigation. She complained that because of the operation of the service she had lost two valuable customers, referred to as tricks. Lauria defended his service and said that her friends had probably lied to her about having left calls for her. But he did not respond to Mrs.

Weeks' hints that she needed customers in order to make money, other than to invite her to his house for a personal visit in order to get better acquainted. In the course of his talk he said "his business was taking messages."

On February 15, Mrs. Weeks talked on the telephone to Lauria's office manager and again complained of two lost calls, which she described as a $50 and a $100 trick. On investigation the office manager could find nothing wrong, but she said she would alert the switchboard operators about slip-ups on calls.

On April 1 Lauria and the three prostitutes were arrested. Lauria complained to the police that this attention was undeserved, stating that Hollywood Call Board had 60 to 70 prostitutes on its board while his own service had only 9 or 10, that he kept separate records for known or suspected prostitutes for the convenience of himself and the police. When asked if his records were available to police who might come to the office to investigate call girls, Lauria replied that they were whenever the police had a specific name. However, his service didn't "arbitrarily tell the police about prostitutes on our board. As long as they pay their bills we tolerate them." In a subsequent voluntary appearance before the Grand Jury Lauria testified he had always cooperated with the police. But he admitted he knew some of his customers were prostitutes, and he knew Terry was a prostitute because he had personally used her services, and he knew she was paying for 500 calls a month.

Lauria and the three prostitutes were indicted for conspiracy to commit prostitution, and nine overt acts were specified. Subsequently the trial court set aside the indictment as having been brought without reasonable or probable cause. (Pen.Code, § 995.) The People have appealed, claiming that a sufficient showing of an unlawful agreement to further prostitution was made.

To establish agreement, the People need show no more than a tacit, mutual understanding between coconspirators to accomplish an unlawful act. Here the People attempted to establish a conspiracy by showing that Lauria, well aware that his codefendants were prostitutes who received business calls from customers through his telephone answering service, continued to furnish them with such service. This approach attempts to equate knowledge of another's criminal activity with conspiracy to further such criminal activity, and poses the question of the criminal responsibility of a furnisher of goods or services who knows his product is being used to assist the operation of an illegal business. Under what circumstances does a supplier become a part of a conspiracy to further an illegal enterprise by furnishing goods or services which he knows are to be used by the buyer for criminal purposes?

The two leading cases on this point face in opposite directions. In United States v. Falcone, 311 U.S. 205, 61 S.Ct. 204, 85 L.Ed. 128,

the sellers of large quantities of sugar, yeast, and cans were absolved
from participation in a moonshining conspiracy among distillers who
bought from them, while in Direct Sales Co. v. United States, 319
U.S. 703, 63 S.Ct. 1265, 87 L.Ed. 1674, a wholesaler of drugs was convicted of conspiracy to violate the federal narcotic laws by selling
drugs in quantity to a codefendant physician who was supplying them
to addicts. The distinction between these two cases appears primarily
based on the proposition that distributors of such dangerous products
as drugs are required to exercise greater discrimination in the conduct
of their business than are distributors of innocuous substances like
sugar and yeast.

In the earlier case, *Falcone,* the sellers' knowledge of the illegal
use of the goods was insufficient by itself to make the sellers participants in a conspiracy with the distillers who bought from them. Such
knowledge fell short of proof of a conspiracy, and evidence on the
volume of sales was too vague to support a jury finding that respond-
ents knew of the conspiracy from the size of the sales alone.

In the later case of *Direct Sales,* the conviction of a drug wholesaler for conspiracy to violate federal narcotic laws was affirmed on a
showing that it had actively promoted the sale of morphine sulphate
in quantity and had sold codefendant physician, who practiced in a
small town in South Carolina, more than 300 times his normal requirements of the drug, even though it had been repeatedly warned
of the dangers of unrestricted sales of the drug. The court contrasted
the restricted goods involved in *Direct Sales* with the articles of free
commerce involved in *Falcone:* "All articles of commerce may be put
to illegal ends," said the court. "But all do not have inherently the
same susceptibility to harmful and illegal use. * * * This difference is important for two purposes. One is for making certain that
the seller knows the buyer's intended illegal use. The other is to show
that by the sale he intends to further, promote and cooperate in it.
This intent, when given effect by overt act, is the gist of conspiracy.
While it is not identical with mere knowledge that another purposes
unlawful action, it is not unrelated to such knowledge. * * * The
step from knowledge to intent and agreement may be taken. There
is more than suspicion, more than knowledge, acquiescence, careless-
ness, indifference, lack of concern. There is informed and interested
cooperation, stimulation, instigation. And there is also a 'stake in the
venture' which, even if it may not be essential, is not irrelevant to the
question of conspiracy." (319 U.S. at 710–713, 63 S.Ct. at 1269–1270.)

While *Falcone* and *Direct Sales* may not be entirely consistent
with each other in their full implications, they do provide us with a
framework for the criminal liability of a supplier of lawful goods or
services put to unlawful use. Both the element of *knowledge* of the
illegal use of the goods or services and the element of *intent* to further
that use must be present in order to make the supplier a participant
in a criminal conspiracy.

Proof of *knowledge* is ordinarily a question of fact and requires no extended discussion in the present case. The knowledge of the supplier was sufficiently established when Lauria admitted he knew some of his customers were prostitutes and admitted he knew that Terry, an active subscriber to his service, was a prostitute. In the face of these admissions he could scarcely claim to have relied on the normal assumption an operator of a business or service is entitled to make, that his customers are behaving themselves in the eyes of the law. Because Lauria knew in fact that some of his customers were prostitutes, it is a legitimate inference he knew they were subscribing to his answering service for illegal business purposes and were using his service to make assignations for prostitution. On this record we think the prosecution is entitled to claim positive knowledge by Lauria of the use of his service to facilitate the business of prostitution.

The more perplexing issue in the case is the sufficiency of proof of *intent* to further the criminal enterprise. The element of intent may be proved either by direct evidence, or by evidence of circumstances from which an intent to further a criminal enterprise by supplying lawful goods or services may be inferred. Direct evidence of participation, such as advice from the supplier of legal goods or services to the user of those goods or services on their use for illegal purposes, such evidence as appeared in a companion case we decide today, People v. Roy, 59 Cal.Rptr. 636, provides the simplest case. When the intent to further and promote the criminal enterprise comes from the lips of the supplier himself, ambiguities of inference from circumstance need not trouble us. But in cases where direct proof of complicity is lacking, intent to further the conspiracy must be derived from the sale itself and its surrounding circumstances in order to establish the supplier's express or tacit agreement to join the conspiracy.

In the case at bench the prosecution argues that since Lauria knew his customers were using his service for illegal purposes but nevertheless continued to furnish it to them, he must have intended to assist them in carrying out their illegal activities. Thus through a union of knowledge and intent he became a participant in a criminal conspiracy. Essentially, the People argue that knowledge alone of the continuing use of his telephone facilities for criminal purposes provided a sufficient basis from which his intent to participate in those criminal activities could be inferred.

In examining precedents in this field we find that sometimes, but not always, the criminal intent of the supplier may be inferred from his knowledge of the unlawful use made of the product he supplies. Some consideration of characteristic patterns may be helpful.

1. Intent may be inferred from knowledge, when the purveyor of legal goods for illegal use has acquired a stake in the venture. (United States v. Falcone, 2 Cir., 109 F.2d 579, 581.) For example, in Regina

v. Thomas, (1957), 2 All.E.R. 181, 342, a prosecution for living off the earnings of prostitution, the evidence showed that the accused, knowing the woman to be a convicted prostitute, agreed to let her have the use of his room between the hours of 9 p. m. and 2 a. m. for a charge of £3 a night. The Court of Criminal Appeal refused an appeal from the conviction, holding that when the accused rented a room at a grossly inflated rent to a prostitute for the purpose of carrying on her trade, a jury could find he was living on the earnings of prostitution.

In the present case, no proof was offered of inflated charges for the telephone answering services furnished the codefendants.

2.   Intent may be inferred from knowledge, when no legitimate use for the goods or services exists. The leading California case is People v. McLaughlin, 111 Cal.App.2d 781, 245 P.2d 1076, in which the court upheld a conviction of the suppliers of horse-racing information by wire for conspiracy to promote bookmaking, when it had been established that wire-service information had no other use than to supply information needed by bookmakers to conduct illegal gambling operations.

In Rex v. Delaval (1763) 3 Burr. 1434, 97 E.R. 913, the charge was unlawful conspiracy to remove a girl from the control of Bates, a musician to whom she was bound as an apprentice, and place her in the hands of Sir Francis Delaval for the purpose of prostitution. Lord Mansfield not only upheld the charges against Bates and Sir Francis, but also against Fraine, the attorney who drew up the indentures of apprenticeship transferring custody of the girl from Bates to Sir Francis. Fraine, said Lord Mansfield, must have known that Sir Francis had no facilities for teaching music to apprentices so that it was impossible for him to have been ignorant of the real intent of the transaction.

In Shaw v. Director of Public Prosecutions, [1962] A.C. 220, the defendant was convicted of conspiracy to corrupt public morals and of living on the earnings of prostitution, when he published a directory consisting almost entirely of advertisements of the names, addresses, and specialized talents of prostitutes. Publication of such a directory, said the court, could have no legitimate use and serve no other purpose than to advertise the professional services of the prostitutes whose advertisements appeared in the directory. The publisher could be deemed a participant in the profits from the business activities of his principal advertisers.

Other services of a comparable nature come to mind: the manufacturer of crooked dice and marked cards who sells his product to gambling casinos; the tipster who furnishes information on the movement of law enforcement officers to known lawbreakers. (Cf. Jackson v. State of Texas, 164 Tex.Cr.R. 276, 298 S.W.2d 837 (1957), where the furnisher of signaling equipment used to warn gamblers of the police was convicted of aiding the equipping of a gambling place.)

In such cases the supplier must necessarily have an intent to further the illegal enterprise since there is no known honest use for his goods.

However, there is nothing in the furnishing of telephone answering service which would necessarily imply assistance in the performance of illegal activities. Nor is any inference to be derived from the use of an answering service by women, either in any particular volume of calls, or outside normal working hours. Night-club entertainers, registered nurses, faith healers, public stenographers, photographic models, and free lance substitute employees, provide examples of women in legitimate occupations whose employment might cause them to receive a volume of telephone calls at irregular hours.

3. Intent may be inferred from knowledge, when the volume of business with the buyer is grossly disproportionate to any legitimate demand, or when sales for illegal use amount to a high proportion of the seller's total business. In such cases an intent to participate in the illegal enterprise may be inferred from the quantity of the business done. For example, in *Direct Sales,* supra, the sale of narcotics to a rural physician in quantities 300 times greater than he would have normal use for provided potent evidence of an intent to further the illegal activity. In the same case the court also found significant the fact that the wholesaler had attracted as customers a disproportionately large group of physicians who had been convicted of violating the Harrison Act. In Shaw v. Director of Public Prosecutions, [1962] A.C. 220, almost the entire business of the directory came from prostitutes.

No evidence of any unusual volume of business with prostitutes was presented by the prosecution against Lauria.

Inflated charges, the sale of goods with no legitimate use, sales in inflated amounts, each may provide a fact of sufficient moment from which the intent of the seller to participate in the criminal enterprise may be inferred. In such instances participation by the supplier of legal goods to the illegal enterprise may be inferred because in one way or another the supplier has acquired a special interest in the operation of the illegal enterprise. His intent to participate in the crime of which he has knowledge may be inferred from the existence of his special interest.

Yet there are cases in which it cannot reasonably be said that the supplier has a stake in the venture or has acquired a special interest in the enterprise, but in which he has been held liable as a participant on the basis of knowledge alone. Some suggestion of this appears in *Direct Sales,* supra, where both the knowledge of the illegal use of the drugs and the intent of the supplier to aid that use were inferred. In Regina v. Bainbridge (1959), 3 W.L.R. 656 (CCA 6), a supplier of oxygen-cutting equipment to one known to intend to use it to break into a bank was convicted as an accessory to the crime. In Sykes v. Director of Public Prosecutions [1962] A.C. 528, one having knowledge of the theft of 100 pistols, 4 submachine guns, and 1960 rounds of ammunition was convicted of misprision of felony for failure to disclose the theft to the public authorities. It seems apparent from these cases that a supplier who furnishes equipment which he *knows* will be used to commit a serious crime may be deemed from that knowledge alone to have intended to produce the result. Such proof may justify an inference that the furnisher intended to aid the execution of the crime and that he thereby became a participant. For instance, we think the operator of a telephone answering service with positive knowledge that his service was being used to facilitate the extortion of ransom, the distribution of heroin, or the passing of counterfeit money who continued to furnish the service with knowledge of its use, might be chargeable on knowledge alone with participation in a scheme to extort money, to distribute narcotics, or to pass counterfeit money. The same result would follow the seller of gasoline who knew the buyer was using his product to make Molotov cocktails for terroristic use.

Logically, the same reasoning could be extended to crimes of every description. Yet we do not believe an inference of intent drawn from knowledge of criminal use properly applies to the less serious crimes classified as misdemeanors. The duty to take positive action to dissociate oneself from activities helpful to violations of the criminal law is far stronger and more compelling for felonies than it is for misdemeanors or petty offenses. In this respect, as in others, the distinction between felonies and misdemeanors, between more serious and less serious crime, retains continuing vitality. In historically the most serious felony, treason, an individual with knowledge of the treason can be prosecuted for concealing and failing to disclose it. (Pen.Code, § 38; 18 U.S.Code, § 2382.) In other felonies, both at common law and under the criminal laws of the United States, an individual knowing of the commission of a felony is criminally liable for concealing it and failing to make it known to proper authority. (4 Blackstone 121; Sykes v. Director of Public Prosecutions [1962] A.C. 528; 18 U.S.Code, § 4.) But this crime, known as misprision of felony, has always been limited to knowledge and concealment of felony and has never extended to misdemeanor. A similar limitation is found in the criminal liability of an accessory, which is restricted to aid in the escape of a principal who has committed or been charged with a *felony*. (Pen.Code, § 32.) We believe the distinction between the obligations arising from knowledge of a felony and those arising from knowledge of a misdemeanor continues to reflect basic human feelings about the duties owed by individuals to society. Heinous crime must be stamped out, and its suppression is the responsibility of all. Backun v. United States, 4 Cir., 112 F.2d 635, 636, 637. Venial crime and crime not evil in itself present less of a danger to society, and perhaps the benefits of their suppression through the modern equivalent of the posse, the hue and cry, the informant, and the citizen's arrest, are outweighed by the disruption to everyday life brought about by amateur law enforcement and private officiousness in relatively inconsequential delicts which do not threaten our basic security. The subject has been summarized in an English text on the criminal law: "Failure to reveal a felony to the authorities is now authoritatively determined to be misprision of felony, which is a common-law misdemeanor; misprision of treason is punishable with imprisonment for life. * * * No offence is committed in failing to disclose a misdemeanour. * * *

" 'To require everyone, without distinction, as to the nature and degree of the offence, to become an accuser, would be productive of inconvenience in exposing numbers to penal prosecutions, multiplying criminal charges, and engendering private dissension. It may sometimes be more convenient that offences should be passed over, than that all should indiscriminately be made the subject of prosecution; and a law would be considered to be harsh and impolitic, if not unjust, which compelled every party injured by a criminal act, and, still more so, to compel everyone who happened to know that another had been so injured, to make a public disclosure of the circumstances. Here, therefore, there is reason for limiting the law against mere misprisions to the concealment of such crimes as are of an aggravated complexion.' " (Criminal Law, Glanville Williams (2d ed.) p. 423.)

With respect to misdemeanors, we conclude that positive knowledge of the supplier that his products or services are being used for criminal purposes does not, without more, establish an intent of the supplier to participate in the misdemeanors. With respect to felonies, we do not decide the converse, viz. that in all cases of felony knowledge of criminal use alone may justify an inference of the supplier's intent to participate in the crime. The implications of *Falcone* make the matter uncertain with respect to those felonies which are merely prohibited wrongs. See also Holman v. Johnson, 98 E.R. 1120, (1775) (sale and delivery of tea at Dunkirk known to be destined for smuggling into England not an illegal contract). But decision on this point is not compelled, and we leave the matter open.

From this analysis of precedent we deduce the following rule: the intent of a supplier who knows of the criminal use to which his supplies are put to participate in the criminal activity connected with the use of his supplies may be established by (1) direct evidence that he intends to participate, or (2) through an inference that he intends to participate based on, (a) his special interest in the activity, or (b) the aggravated nature of the crime itself.

When we review Lauria's activities in the light of this analysis, we find no proof that Lauria took any direct action to further, encourage, or direct the call-girl activities of his codefendants and we find an absence of circumstances from which his special interest in their activities could be inferred. Neither excessive charges for standardized services, or the furnishing of services without a legitimate use, nor an unusual quantity of business with call girls, are present. The offense which he is charged with furthering is a misdemeanor, a category of crime which has never been made a required subject of positive disclosure to public authority. Under these circumstances, although proof of Lauria's knowledge of the criminal activities of his patrons was sufficient to charge him with that fact, there was insufficient evidence that he intended to further their criminal activities, and hence insufficient proof of his participation in a criminal conspiracy with his codefendants to further prostitution. Since the conspiracy centered around the activities of Lauria's telephone answering service, the charges against his codefendants likewise fail for want of proof.

In absolving Lauria of complicity in a criminal conspiracy we do not wish to imply that the public authorities are without remedies to combat modern manifestations of the world's oldest profession. Licensing of telephone answering services under the police power, together with the revocation of licenses for the toleration of prostitution, is a possible civil remedy. The furnishing of telephone answering service in aid of prostitution could be made a crime. (Cf. Pen.Code, § 316, which makes it a misdemeanor to let an apartment with knowledge of its use for prostitution.) Other solutions will doubtless occur to vigilant public authorities if the problem of call-girl activity needs further suppression.

The order is affirmed.

MODEL PENAL CODE, COMMENT TO 5.03, 107–10

(Tent. Draft No. 10, 1960).

The Requirement of Purpose. The purpose requirement is crucial to the resolution of the difficult problems presented when a charge of conspiracy is leveled against a person whose relationship to a criminal plan is essentially peripheral. Typical is the case of the person who sells sugar to the producers of illicit whiskey. He may have little interest in the success of the distilling operation and be motivated mainly by the desire to make the normal profit of an otherwise lawful sale. To be criminally liable, of course, he must at least have knowledge of the use to which the materials are being put, but the difficult issue presented is whether knowingly facilitating the commission of a crime ought to be sufficient, absent a true purpose to advance the criminal end. In the case of vendors conflicting interests are also involved: that of the vendors in freedom to engage in gainful and otherwise lawful activities without policing their vendees, and that of the community in preventing behavior that facilitates the commission of crimes. The decisions are in conflict, although many of those requiring purpose properly emphasize that it can be inferred from such circumstances as, for example, quantity sales, the seller's initiative or encouragement, continuity of the relationship, and the contraband nature of the materials sold. The considerations are the same whether the charge be conspiracy or complicity in the substantive crime, and the Institute has resolved them, in the complicity provisions of the Code, in favor of requiring a purpose to advance the criminal end. Under the proposed Draft, the same purpose requirement that governs complicity is essential for conspiracy: the actor must have "the purpose of promoting or facilitating" the commission of the crime.

The requirement of purpose would also play a crucial role in the case where a charge of conspiracy is based on membership in an organization having both lawful and criminal objectives, as in the Communist cases. The defendant's membership and dues may encourage and assist the organization in pursuing all its objects, legal and illegal. He would not be guilty of conspiracy, however, unless he had the purpose of promoting or facilitating the attainment of a criminal objective. Of course, knowledge of that objective and conscious assistance may justify an inference of such purpose, but they would not be independently sufficient to establish liability.

* * *

It is worth noting, futher, that as related to those elements of substantive crimes that consist of proscribed conduct or undesirable results of conduct, the Draft requires purposeful behavior for guilt of conspiracy, regardless of the state of mind required by the definition of the substantive crime. If the crime is defined in terms of prohibited conduct, such as the sale of narcotics, the actor's purpose must be to promote or facilitate the engaging in such conduct by himself or another. If it is defined in terms of a result of conduct, such as homicide, his purpose must be to promote or facilitate the production of that result.

Thus, it would not be sufficient, as it is under the attempt draft, if the actor only believed that the result would be produced but did not consciously plan or desire to produce it. For example—to use the same illustration as the comments on attempt—if two persons plan to destroy a building by detonating a bomb, though they know and believe that there are inhabitants in the building who will be killed by the explosion, they are nevertheless guilty only of a conspiracy to destroy the building and not of a conspiracy to kill the inhabitants. While this result may seem unduly restrictive from the viewpoint of the completed crime, it is necessitated by the extremely preparatory behavior that may be involved in conspiracy. Had the crime been completed or had the preparation progressed even to the stage of an attempt, the result would be otherwise. As to the attempt, knowledge or belief that the inhabitants would be killed would suffice. As to the completed crime, the complicity draft covers the matter, despite its general requirement of a purpose to promote or facilitate the commission of the crime, by the special provision of Section 2.06(4). This provides that where causing a particular result is an element of a crime, a person is an accomplice in the crime if he was an accomplice in the behavior that caused the result and shared the same purpose or knowledge with respect to the result that is required by the definition of the crime.

A fortiori, where recklessness or negligence suffices for the actor's culpability with respect to a result element of a substantive crime —where, for example, homicide through negligence is made criminal —there could not be a conspiracy to commit that crime. This should be distinguished, however, from a crime defined in terms of conduct that creates a risk of harm, such as reckless driving or driving above a certain speed limit. In this situation the conduct rather than any result it may produce is the element of the crime, and it would suffice for guilt of conspiracy that the actor's purpose is to promote or facilitate such conduct—for example, if he urged the driver of the car to go faster and faster.

UNITED STATES v. ROSELLI

United States Court of Appeals for the Ninth Circuit, 1970.
432 F.2d 879, certiorari denied 401 U.S. 924, 91 S.Ct. 883, 27 L.Ed.2d 828, and
91 S.Ct. 884, rehearing denied 402 U.S. 924, 91 S.Ct. 1366, 28 L.Ed.2d 665.

BROWNING, Circuit Judge. Appellants participated in an organized scheme to cheat for profit in card games played at the Friars Club, a private social club in Beverly Hills, California. Victims were induced to join high stake gin rummy games. Observers stationed at ceiling peekholes transmitted playing instructions to confederates in the game via electronic signaling devices.

The activity continued from the summer of 1962 to the summer of 1966. Games were "peeked" almost daily during a portion of this period. Appellants and other participants in the scheme made large profits. George Seach, an unindicted coconspirator who acted as "peekman" from late June 1962 to early April 1963, estimated the "take" during this period at $400,000.

After a long and complex trial appellants were convicted of conspiracy to violate 18 U.S.C.A. § 1952 (interstate travel and use of interstate facilities in aid of racketeering enterprises) and § 2314 (interstate transportation of fraudulently taken securities), and substantive violations of these sections [1] and of 26 U.S.C.A. § 7206 (false statements in income tax returns).

* * *

---

1. 18 U.S.C.A. § 1952 provides:

"(a) Whoever travels in interstate or foreign commerce or uses any facility

in interstate or foreign commerce, including the mail, with intent to—
"(1) distribute the proceeds of any unlawful activity; or

Each appellant challenges the sufficiency of the evidence.

A few additional background facts are necessary to an understanding of the issues raised.

Count 1 of the indictment charged a conspiracy to violate 18 U.S.C.A. §§ 1952 and 2314; * * * The section 1952 charges required proof that appellants used interstate facilities and traveled in interstate commerce to promote the unlawful gambling enterprise; the section 2314 charges required proof that appellants transported in interstate commerce securities that they knew had been taken by fraud. See note 1.

The general theory of the Government's case was as follows.

Friedman, the prime mover in the scheme, lived in Las Vegas, Nevada, as did George Seach, who "peeked" the earlier games. Edwin Gebhard, who replaced Seach as "peekman," lived in Miami, Florida. When a rigged game was planned, Friedman telephoned Seach in Las Vegas and asked him to come to Beverly Hills. Seach then traveled to Beverly Hills and "peeked" the game. When Seach went to prison and was no longer available, appellant Jacobs telephoned Gebhard in Miami, and Gebhard traveled to Beverly Hills for the same purpose. Friedman carried checks obtained from victims in payment of losses in the peeked games back to Las Vegas and deposited them in his Las Vegas bank account.

* * *

Teitelbaum. Teitelbaum argues that the evidence was insufficient to support his conviction of conspiracy to violate sections 1952 and 2314 because it failed to establish that he agreed to the use of the interstate facilities and to the interstate travel and transportation, which are essential elements of the substantive offenses. We reject the argument on alternate grounds. First, the knowing use of interstate facilities is not an essential element of either the substantive offenses or the conspiracy to commit them; and, second, if it were, the evi-

"(2) commit any crime of violence to further any unlawful activity; or

"(3) otherwise promote, manage, establish, carry on, or facilitate the promotion, management, establishment, or carrying on, of any unlawful activity,

and thereafter performs or attempts to perform any of the acts specified in subparagraphs (1), (2), and (3), shall be fined not more than $10,000 or imprisoned for not more than five years, or both.

"(b) As used in this section 'unlawful activity' means (1) any business enterprise involving gambling, liquor on which the Federal excise tax has not been paid, narcotics, or prostitution offenses in violation of the laws of the State in which they are committed or of the United States, or (2) extortion, bribery, or arson in violation of the laws of the State in which committed or of the United States.

"(c) Investigations of violations under this section involving liquor or narcotics shall be conducted under the supervision of the Secretary of the Treasury."

18 U.S.C.A. § 2314 provides in part:

"Whoever transports in interstate commerce any * * * securities or money, of the value of $5,000 or more, knowing the same to have been * * taken by fraud; * * * shall be fined not more than $10,000 or imprisoned not more than ten years, or both."

dence was sufficient to establish that Teitelbaum acted with the requisite knowledge.

The words of sections 1952 and 2314 do not suggest that Congress intended to condition liability upon knowing use of interstate facilities; their natural import is to the contrary. In both sections the requisite mental state is identified, and in neither does it include knowledge of the interstate element of the offense. See note; United States v. Bash, 258 F.Supp. 807, 809–813 (N.D.Ind.1966), aff'd sub nom. United States v. Miller, 379 F.2d 483 (7th Cir. 1967). Compare 18 U.S.C.A. §§ 1084, 1958, 2421.

We have found nothing in the legislative history that indicates a purpose to limit sections 1952 and 2314 to violators who specifically intend to utilize interstate facilities. It is quite clear that in enacting section 1952 Congress was not concerned with regulating interstate travel or the use of interstate facilities, but rather with directly suppressing unlawful local activities from which organized crime drew its sustenance. Similarly, section 2314 is aimed at the evils of theft, fraud, and counterfeiting and not at the regulation of interstate transportation. Suppression of movement of the fruits of theft and fraud is only the means to the end of suppressing theft and fraud themselves. The sole reason for conditioning the statutes' prohibitions upon use of interstate commerce is to provide a constitutional basis for the exercise of federal power.

As the Second Circuit recently pointed out in discussing the same issue in connection with 18 U.S.C.A. § 1343, the purpose of statutes of this kind argues against a construction making a specific "anti-federal" intent an element of the offense:

> "The statute does not condition guilt upon knowledge that interstate communication is used. The use of interstate communication is logically no part of the crime itself. It is included in the statute merely as a ground for federal jurisdiction. The essence of the crime is the fraudulent scheme itself. Nothing is added to the guilt of the violator of the statute by reason of his having used an interstate telephone to further his scheme. There is consequently no reason at all why guilt under the statute should hinge upon knowledge that interstate communication is used. If the wire employed is an interstate wire the requirements for federal jurisdiction are satisfied. It is wholly irrelevant to any purpose of the statute that the perpetrator of the fraud knows about the use of interstate communication." United States v. Blassingame, 427 F.2d 329 (2d Cir. 1970).

Accordingly, knowing interstate travel or knowing use of an interstate facility is not an essential element of a violation of section 1952 and knowing interstate transportation is not an essential element of a violation of section 2314.

There is therefore no rational basis for holding that such knowledge is an essential element of a conspiracy to commit the offenses created by the substantive sections. The essence of the offense under the general conspiracy statute, 18 U.S.C.A. § 371, is an agreement by two or more persons to commit the substantive crime. In virtually all cases the meeting of minds is established simply by inference from a concert of action that produces the forbidden result. There is no apparent reason for requiring not only proof of a concert of action that includes all elements of the substantive offense, but also proof of knowledge of the jurisdictional element that is not required for conviction of the substantive offense. Such knowledge is as irrelevant to the purposes of the general conspiracy statute [18] as it is to the purposes of the substantive statutes. See Developments in the Law—Criminal Conspiracy, 72 Har.L.Rev. 920, 938–939 (1959).[19]

Teitlebaum's argument is that conspiracy to commit a federal substantive offense necessarily includes an agreement upon all elements of that offense. We think it sufficient that the agreement contemplates the commission of a crime and that the crime contemplated is in fact and law a federal offense.

It is an element of the offenses created by the first paragraph of section 2314 that the value of the stolen securities exceeds $5,000. It would not be a defense to a charge of the substantive offense that the accused *thought* the securities worth only $2,000, if in fact their value exceeded the statutory minimum. Can it be that a lack of knowledge of this jurisdictional element would nonetheless afford a defense to a charge of conspiracy to violate section 2314?

It may be argued that because a conspiracy to commit a substantive offense may exist without actual commission of the substantive offense, conspiracies to commit state crimes might be charged under the federal conspiracy laws if there were no need to prove agreement about the aspects of the crime that confer federal jurisdiction. The simple answer is that absent the presence of the jurisdictional element, no charge can be made. The point is not that the jurisdictional ele-

---

18. The reasons for condemning conspiracies were stated in United States v. Rabinowich, 238 U.S. 78, 88, 35 S.Ct. 682, 685, 59 L.Ed. 1211 (1915): "For two or more to confederate and combine together to commit or cause to be committed a breach of the criminal laws, is an offense of the gravest character, sometimes quite outweighing, in injury to the public, the mere commission of the contemplated crime. It involves deliberate plotting to subvert the laws, educating and preparing the conspirators for further and habitual criminal practices. And it is characterized by secrecy, rendering it diffi-cult of detection, requiring more time for its discovery, and adding to the importance of punishing it when discovered."

These evils of conspiracy are present whether or not the conspirators are aware of the jurisdictional aspects of their crime.

19. Several opinions have assumed the need for such proof, but apparently without consideration of the problem. See, e. g., Pereira v. United States, 347 U.S. 1, 12–13, 74 S.Ct. 358, 98 L.Ed. 435 (1954) (conspiracy to violate § 2314).

ment need not exist, but merely that there need be no proof that the defendants were aware of its existence.

In the second place, as we have said, Teitelbaum's conviction of conspiracy was proper even if knowledge of the interstate aspects of the illegal scheme is an essential element of the offense.

In Twitchell v. United States, 313 F.2d 425 (9th Cir. 1963), we construed the Mann Act, 18 U.S.C.A. §§ 2421–2422, as requiring knowledge of the illegal transportation of females in interstate commerce for immoral purposes.[21] We held, however, that possession of the requisite knowledge by one charged with conspiracy to violate the Act could be established by circumstantial proof that he agreed to a scheme "in which it was known that the likelihood of illegal interstate transportation was great." (429)

At Teitelbaum's request, the jury was instructed in accordance with the *Twitchell* formulation,[22] in a manner that completely satisfied his definition of the elements of the present offenses; and we are satisfied that the evidence was sufficient to justify the jury's conclusion that the proof of his guilt met the *Twitchell* standard.

21. Our construction of the Mann Act in *Twitchell* is not inconsistent with the interpretation we have given to sections 1951 and 2813.

The words of the Mann Act ("Whoever *knowingly* transports in interstate or foreign commerce," etc.) strongly suggest that knowledge of the interstate transportation is an element of the offense.

Moreover, the Act's legislative history establishes that Congress' purpose was not to control local immorality but rather to deny the use of interstate facilities to a traffic viewed as evil.

Opposition to the bill that became the Mann Act was based largely on the thesis that, although cast in the form of a regulation of interstate commerce, the statute was in reality an attempt to regulate prostitution and other immoral practices exclusively within the states' police power. Proponents of the bill repeatedly assured Congress that the statute's intent was to deal solely with the evil of transportation of women and girls in interstate and foreign commerce for immoral purposes. Thus, the Report of the House Committee on Interstate and Foreign Commerce denies any purpose to interfere with state control of local immorality, insists repeatedly that the evil at which the statute is directed is the movement of women and girls in commerce—the importation of women and girls and their transportation from one state to another—and points out that the Act's prohibitions "have been so drawn that they are limited to cases in which there is an act of transportation in interstate commerce of women for purposes of prostitution." H.R.Rep.No.47, 61st Cong., 2d Sess., pp. 1, 2, 3, 4, 5, 9, 10, 11. * * *.

22. The full formulation in *Twitchell* is as follows:

"We think that, in a case of this kind, the evidence must show in relation to Twitchell that either:

"1. he *directly* agreed to the illegal interstate transportation, or *directly* agreed to a scheme which could not be consummated without illegal interstate transportation, or *directly* agreed to a scheme in which it was known that the likelihood of illegal interstate transportation was *great* (it being understood that such agreement need not be overt, and may be inferred from circumstantial evidence; and that directness refers not to face-to-face dealings, but to the extent of his knowledge of the purpose and scope of the conspiracy); *or*

"2. he evidenced his indirect agreement by substantial participation in the scheme *with actual knowledge* of the proposed, or completed, illegal interstate transportation." 313 F.2d at 429.

There was direct testimony by Seach that Teitlebaum joined the conspiracy in September 1962, and participated actively in it until at least April 1963. He set up at least one rigged game, played in such games, received signals from the hidden "peekman," and shared in the spoils. As we have noted, the evidence also established, as an integral part of the scheme, a pattern of interstate phone calls, interstate travel, and interstate transportation. The jury was entirely warranted in concluding, as we do, that it is inconceivable that one so intimately connected with the conspiracy over so long a period could have been unaware of these interstate activities.

* * *

NOTES

1. The *Blassingame* case, quoted with approval in *Roselli*, involved a prosecution for a substantive offense. Should that make any difference? In United States v. Crimmins, 123 F.2d 271 (2d Cir. 1941) the defendant had been convicted of a conspiracy to transport stolen securities in interstate commerce in violation of 18 U.S.C.A. 415. He was the receiver of the securities and although the evidence was sufficient to permit a finding that he knew they were stolen there was no evidence that he knew of any movement in interstate commerce. Does the absence of evidence of such knowledge require reversal? Judge Learned Hand conceded that proof of specific intent to move the securities in interstate commerce would not be required for conviction of the substantive offense, but held that "there can be no conspiracy to 'cause' stolen securities 'to be transported interstate' * * * unless it is understood to be part of the project that they shall cross state lines." In the course of his opinion Judge Hand struck off the following memorable analogy:

> "While one may, for instance, be guilty of running past a traffic light of whose existence one is ignorant, one cannot be guilty of conspiring to run past such a light, for one cannot agree to run past a light unless one supposes that there is a light to run past." Id. at 273.

2. Should a different result obtain where the charge is conspiracy to buy, receive or possess chattels stolen from an interstate shipment in violation of 18 U.S.C.A. § 659? Then, it might be argued, Judge Hand's stop light is already past; the reference to interstate commerce merely describing the nature the chattel must possess for the defendant's act to be a crime rather than an objective he must be shown to have sought. See United States v. Vilhotti, 452 F.2d 1186 (2d Cir. 1971).

3. Are there any policy arguments for favoring either the *Crimmins* or the *Roselli* analysis? Does your position depend on the importance you attach to a federal form of government?

4. The problem underlying the conflict between *Roselli* and *Crimmins* would be resolved by the Proposed New Federal Criminal Code. Section 201 of the Code recites twelve jurisdictional bases commonly used for offenses defined by the Code. Sections 204 and 302(3)(c) then specifically provide that: "Except as otherwise expressly provided, culpability is not required with respect to any fact which is solely a basis for federal jurisdiction."

3. IMPOSSIBILITY

STATE v. MORETTI

Supreme Court of New Jersey, 1968.
52 N.J. 182, 244 A.2d 499, certiorari denied 393 U.S. 952,
89 S.Ct. 376, 21 L.Ed.2d 363.

PROCTOR, J. Defendants John J. Moretti, Marietta Schmidt, and Lawrence Gianettino were convicted in the Essex County Court of conspiracy to commit an unlawful abortion on Sylvia Swidler. N.J.S. 2A:98–1, 2, N.J.S.A.; N.J.S. 2A:87–1, N.J.S.A.[1] Gianettino died shortly after the trial. On the appeal of Moretti and Schmidt, the Appellate Division affirmed the conviction with one judge dissenting. 97 N.J.Super. 418, 235 A.2d 226 (App.Div.1967). Moretti and Schmidt appealed to this Court * * *.

On the evidence the jury could find that Mrs. Schmidt arranged with Moretti, a physician, to have an abortion performed on Mrs. Swidler. The abortion was to be performed by Gianettino, an inspector for the New Jersey State Board of Barber Examiners. Unknown to the defendants, Mrs. Swidler was a special investigator for the Essex County Prosecutor's Office. Gianettino appeared at about eleven o'clock one evening at the Swidler home pursuant to an appointment with Mrs. Swidler. She paid him $600 in marked money and they went upstairs to her bedroom where the abortion was to be performed. As Gianettino removed instruments to perform the abortion from a bag he had brought with him, the police who had been secreted in the house arrested him. The State concedes that Mrs. Swidler was not pregnant.

It has been held that under our statute an essential element of the crime of abortion is that the woman be pregnant. The defendants contend that since it was impossible to commit an abortion upon Mrs. Swidler because she was not pregnant, they cannot be convicted of a criminal conspiracy to commit an abortion. The argument runs that if no violation of the law was to be accomplished by the act of the defendants, they cannot be held for conspiracy to do that act. The majority of the Appellate Division rejected this argument, while the dissenting judge found it to be ground for reversing the convictions.

The crime of conspiracy is distinct from the substantive offense which the conspirators plotted to commit. The essence of the stat-

---

1. The pertinent provisions of these statutes are:
  * * *
N.J.S. 2A:87–1, N.J.S.A.:
  "Any person who, maliciously or without lawful justification, with intent to cause or procure the miscarriage of a pregnant woman, administers or prescribes or advises or directs her to take or swallow any poison, drug, medicine or noxious thing, or uses any instrument or means whatever, is guilty of a high misdemeanor.
  * * *."

utory crime of conspiracy is the joining together of the conspirators with an unlawful intent. It is this unlawful purpose upon which they agreed which makes a conspiracy punishable once any overt act is committed in furtherance of it. As Justice Heher said for this Court in State v. Carbone, 10 N.J. 329, 338, 91 A.2d 571, 575 (1952): "The union is invested with a potentiality for evil that renders the plan criminal in itself, and punishable as such if an act be done to effect its object." Here, there can be no doubt that if, as the jury found, there was an agreement among the defendants, its purpose was to commit an unlawful abortion and the conspirators took substantial steps in an endeavor to accomplish this end. That, unknown to them, Mrs. Swidler was not in a condition to be aborted in no way negates their clearly manifested intent to commit a criminal act. Such concerted intent, coupled with an overt act, is punishable whether or not the contemplated crime is consummated. That a factor unknown to the conspirators makes it impossible for them to complete their intended crime in no way lessens the degree of culpability involved in the criminal combination. People v. Nathanson, 389 Ill. 311, 318, 59 N.E.2d 677, 680, certiorari denied, 325 U.S. 872, 65 S.Ct. 1412, 89 L.Ed. 1990 (1945) (holding that in a prosecution for conspiracy to commit an abortion it was not necessary to prove the woman's pregnancy); Craven v. United States, 22 F.2d 605 (1st Cir. 1927), certiorari denied 276 U.S. 627, 48 S.Ct. 321, 72 L.Ed. 729 (1928) (holding that the defendant could be convicted of conspiring with others to smuggle imported liquor even though he had been deceived by the substitution of liquor of domestic origin).

The case has been argued as though, for purposes of the defense of impossibility, a conspiracy charge is the same as a charge of attempting to commit a crime. It seems that such an equation could not be sustained, however, because, as discussed above, a conspiracy charge focuses primarily on the *intent* of the defendants, while in an attempt case the primary inquiry centers on the defendants' *conduct* tending toward the commission of the substantive crime. The crime of conspiracy is complete once the conspirators, having formed the intent to commit a crime, take any step in preparation; mere preparation, however, is an inadequate basis for an attempt conviction regardless of the intent. Thus, the impossibility that the defendants' conduct will result in the consummation of the contemplated crime is not as pertinent in a conspiracy case as it might be in an attempt prosecution. However, we need not pursue this point since we are satisfied that even if we treat the present appeal as an attempt case the defense of impossibility does not shield the defendants.

*　　*　　*

[The court's review of impossibility in the law of attempt is omitted.]

In the present case, the defendants' intent to commit an abortion on Mrs. Swidler is clear; believing her to be pregnant, they did all that was in their power to bring about the criminal result they desired. That, had the police not intervened, they would have been thwarted in attaining this end by the unknown fact that Mrs. Swidler was not pregnant does not in one whit diminish the criminal quality of their agreement. The consequence the defendants intended was a result which, if successful, would have been a crime. We hold that when the consequences sought by a defendant are forbidden by the law as criminal, it is no defense that the defendant could not succeed in reaching his goal because of circumstances unknown to him. See Marley v. State, 58 N.J.L. 207, 212, 33 A. 208 (1895) where our former Supreme Court recognized that criminal liability would attach to a person "designing to perpetrate a crime, when he cannot effect it by reason of the existence of some fact unknown to him at the time." Accordingly, we conclude that the defendants could be convicted of conspiracy to perform an abortion on Mrs. Swidler notwithstanding the absence of pregnancy.

VENTIMIGLIA v. UNITED STATES

United States Court of Appeals, Fourth Circuit, 1957.
242 F.2d 620.

SOBELOFF, Circuit Judge. The Taft-Hartley Act forbids the payment of money by an employer subject to its provisions to "any representative of any of his employees." 29 U.S.C.A. § 186(a). The defendants were indicted for three substantive violations of this law and for conspiracy to violate it. At a trial before the District Judge, sitting without a jury, the defendants were acquitted of the substantive offenses, but convicted of the conspiracy. The sufficiency of the evidence to sustain the conviction is the question raised by this appeal.

Weather-Mastic, Inc., is a non-unionized contractor engaged in the insulating and weather-proofing business. Parran is its general manager and Ventimiglia its labor relations adviser. In the prevailing industry practice, workers are required to have in their possession some evidence of union membership, if in fact affiliated with a union, or "working cards," which the union customarily issues to a limited number of non-union men seeking work on union jobs. Having been accepted as a sub-contractor for a job in Alexandria on which Stone and Webster, a unionized company, was general contractor, Weather-Mastic faced the need of obtaining working cards for its men. Joseph Martin, business agent of Local No. 80 of United Slate, Tile and Composition Roofers, Damp and Water Proof Workers, complained to Weather-Mastic that its workmen were carrying "working cards" issued, not by him, but by Ventimiglia, who was then in the service of Weather-Mastic, Inc., but had earlier been the business agent of the union. After discussion, Martin was persuaded by the defendants to issue working cards to Weather-Mastic's employees, for which the defendants agreed to pay Martin One Hundred Dollars each month.

Martin's duties as business agent for Local No. 80 are said to be of the usual type: negotiating wage contracts and working conditions, representing the union members and acting as peacemaker between employers and union members in respect to disputes or grievances. Martin never represented any of Weather-Mastic's employees in any of these respects. He did issue working cards signed by him, which he delivered to Ventimiglia. For this he received several monthly payments from the defendants.

An additional duty of union business agents is to check on the union credentials of men engaged on a union job who are not members of his union. The evidence is that if another business agent was skeptical of an employee's working card, the usual procedure would be to make inquiry of the agent who had issued the card, and if he verified its validity, that ordinarily would be enough to satisfy the inquirer. While Weather-Mastic's men were never asked to show their cards, except by the Federal Bureau of Investigation (to whom Martin had reported his agreement with the defendants), the significance sought to be attached to this fact is that Martin, it is said, was prepared to stand behind and vouch for Weather-Mastic's employees if questions as to their status should ever arise.

It is, of course, beyond dispute that a punishable conspiracy may exist independent of the actual commission of the substantive offense which was the object of the conspiracy. This need not be labored. However, there can be no conviction for conspiracy to commit an offense against the United States if the act that the alleged conspirators agree to do has not been made unlawful, and is not planned to be accomplished in an unlawful manner.

According to the Court's findings, the testimony affirmatively established that the corporate defendant's employees were not at any time members of Martin's union, and that there is no evidence that they authorized or subsequently ratified Martin's representing them; and the Court added—correctly, we think—that there is here no representation by operation of law. If Martin was no representative of the employees, Section 186(a) did not apply to him. The Court concluded, as we think was required in these circumstances, that the section was not violated, and he entered the not guilty verdict as to the three substantive counts.

In considering the conspiracy count, however, the Court predicated a verdict of guilty upon the theory that while the defendants did not desire Martin to represent the employees in *all* respects, they did intend to deal with him as their employees' representative in issuing cards evidencing the union's willingness to permit them to work on union jobs. The opinion says: [145 F.Supp. 43] "He [Martin] was to furnish the necessary indicia of union membership, and if questions arose, handle the matter so that there would be no interruption to work. * * * He was not to organize them, or to negotiate on their behalf with the employer as to wages. But there can be no doubt that the defendants intended Martin to do acts which a representative of employees would be expected to do—insure the availability and continuity of work. Likewise, Martin could have become the formal representative of the employees had they initiated the issuance of cards, or accepted or used them knowing the reasons for which, and the circumstances under which the cards were issued."

Thereupon, the Court concluded that, for a period at least, defendants intended to deal with and dealt with Martin as a representative of their employees. He added that "the defendants cannot avoid the natural consequences of their conduct by a simple denial that Martin was such a representative when the evidence is that they intended him to be and dealt with him in that capacity; nor does the fact that they did not want him to be (and indeed forbade him to be) the employees' representative in certain respects, prevent him from being such representative in the limited field in which he was to, and did, act."

In analyzing the evidence in connection with the conspiracy count, the District Judge, we think fell into error. The testimony, it seems to us, does not lend itself to the treatment given it. Plainly enough, the defendants did not deal with Martin as their employees' representative, and never intended to deal with him as such. They did not want him to approach their employees or organize them, or represent them, and he did not do so. As the Court declared in a subsidiary finding of fact, the defendants induced Martin *not* to organize or represent the employees. The cards he issued were not "indicia of union membership;" on the contrary, they were working cards such as are customarily issued to non-members, to workers *not* represented by the union. Employees represented by the union or by its business agent require no such cards. The purpose of the cards is to sanction work by *non*-union men, who are unrepresented. So, far from treating them as union members and thus under representation by Martin, he treated them as the only class of workers who could carry such cards, namely, persons not in the union or represented by it or by its officers. * * *

The Government contends that a conspiracy may be punished even if the objective of the conspirators cannot be achieved, but the conspirators mistakenly think it can be. Even assuming that the defendants intended to treat Martin as their employees' representative, though in fact he was not, such a theory cannot avail to sustain the prosecution. The Government has referred us to cases in which conviction for conspiracy has been upheld despite the fact that, unknown to the conspirators, the object of the conspiracy was impossible of accomplishment, as where pickpockets conspired to rob an intended victim, but were frustrated by the fact that his pocket was empty.

Such unexpected physical impossibility would not prevent successful prosecution for conspiracy.

But the present case is not comparable to the attempt to pick an empty pocket. The analogy to the present case would be closer if we assumed an attempt or conspiracy to pick the pocket of what is merely a wooden dummy. Criminal liability in such a case would seem highly implausible, and it would not save the prosecution to prove that the defendants thought that the object of their design and effort was human. A like distinction is that between an unsuccessful murder attempt due to a faulty gun or a blank cartridge, and a failure due to the fact that the intended victim was merely a block of wood, or a shadow. In the former, there would be a criminal attempt, while in the latter there would not. The distinction in these pairs of cases is readily discernible. It lies in the difference between, on the one hand, a physical impediment to completion of the crime due merely to miscalculation or to the choice of ineffective means which would normally be effective, and, on the other hand, a failure due to an inherent impossibility of completing the crime.

* * *   See also O'Kelley v. U. S., 8 Cir., 116 F.2d 966, where it was held that there could be no conspiracy to commit larceny of an interstate shipment, because there could be no substantive violation inasmuch as the goods had lost their interstate character. Similarly, if one thinks that a uniformed doorman is a police officer and bribes him not to tag his car, it is no crime, and neither the attempt nor the conspiracy can be, for there is an inherent or legal impossibility of consummating the offense, although the act itself was completed. Likewise, where one mistakenly believes a certain individual is the union representative of his employees, the misconception cannot sufficiently negative the impossibility of committing the substantive offense so as to provide the basis for a conspiracy conviction. But where the object of a bribe is a draft board official of the United States who, but for the defendant's mistake of registering with the wrong board, would have had no jurisdiction over the defendant, the impossibility was not inherent but was due simply to a prior mistaken course of action. See United States v. Schanerman, 3 Cir., 150 F.2d 941.

* * *

Even were we to doubt the foregoing propositions and their application here, the present case is on the facts of an even more extreme variety, for it is said merely that the defendants *intended* to deal with Martin as their employees' representative. The previous example of the doorman will suffice to show the fallacy of basing a conviction on such a fact. Had the defendant in that hypothetical case, knowing that the doorman was not a police officer, nevertheless intended to deal with him as such, it could certainly not be said that he attempted to bribe a police officer.

* * *

We conclude, therefore, that there could be no conviction under this indictment even if the defendants mistakenly thought that Martin was a representative of Weather-Mastic's employees. Even less can a conviction be sustained when it is clear beyond dispute, not only that he was not the employees' representative, but that no one concerned thought or pretended that he was.

Reversed.

---

4. THE DEFENSE OF ABANDONMENT

ELDREDGE v. UNITED STATES

United States Court of Appeals, Second Circuit, 1932.
62 F.2d 449.

McDERMOTT, Circuit Judge. Eldredge and three fellow-employees of the Utah State National Bank commenced embezzling the funds of the bank in 1919, concealing the embezzlements by falsification of the books. He left the bank in 1921, but the embezzlements continued, Eldredge participating therein and assisting in the concealment by opening a spurious account in another bank. In 1924 he became a bookkeeper for the Western Loan and Building Company, and aided in concealing the continuing abstractions by approving false reconcilement statements for that company. His last affirmative act, in aid of the conspiracy, was the making of a false reconcilement statement on August 15, 1927, by which the then shortage of $69,000 was effectively concealed. In March, 1928, Eldredge told his associates that he was about to be promoted. He testified as to a conversation with one of his fellow-conspirators:

"I told him I would be unable further to help him shield or conceal the shortage at the Utah State National Bank as I was due for a promotion with the Western Loan and Building Company; further, that I was absolutely through and would have nothing further to do with the shortage at the Utah State National Bank. I had helped Mr. Johnson cover up the shortage up to August 15, 1927, and I knew there was a shortage at the Utah State National Bank in about $69,000.00 and was alarmed at the amount of it."

The embezzlements continued until October, 1931, when the inevitable dénouement revealed a shortage of $108,200. The indictment, filed November 7, 1931, charged Eldredge and his associates with conspiring to embezzle moneys of the bank, and with conspiring to make false entries to conceal the embezzlements. Nineteen overt acts of embezzlements and of false entries are alleged.

The defense is that the prosecution is barred by the statute of limitations (18 U.S.C.A. § 582). The indictment was filed more than three years after Eldredge's last affirmative act in aid of the conspiracy, and more than three years after the conversation quoted above, which Eldridge claims effected his withdrawal from the conspiracy. The trial court denied a motion for an instructed verdict; he submitted to the jury the question of whether Eldredge had withdrawn from the conspiracy as far as participation in further embezzlements was concerned, but declined to submit the question of withdrawal from the conspiracy to falsify the books in order to conceal embezzlements then accomplished. Error is assigned on such rulings. The only evidence of withdrawal is that above quoted. The question presented, then, is whether that is evidence from which a jury might find that Eldredge had effectively withdrawn from the conspiracy to falsify the records prior to the statutory period.

The legal haze arising from the original concept that a conspiracy begins and ends with the unlawful agreement, and that the requirement of an overt act is to afford the conspirator a locus poenitentiae, was dispelled in United States v. Kissel, 218 U.S. 601, 31 S.Ct. 124, 54 L.Ed. 1168, and in Hyde v. United States, 225 U.S. 347, 32 S.Ct. 793, 803, 56 L.Ed. 1114, Ann.Cas.1914A, 614. The overt act is an essential ingredient of the crime; a conspiracy which contemplates a series of overt acts is a continuing conspiracy, and the statute does not commence to run until the last overt act, performed in compliance with the original agreement, has been accomplished. Brown v. Elliott, 225 U.S. 392, 32 S.Ct. 812, 56 L.Ed. 1136; Ware v. United States (C.C.A.8) 154 F. 577, 12 L.R.A.(N.S.) 1053, 12 Ann.Cas. 233; Breese v. United States (C.C.A.4) 203 F. 824; Miller v. United States (C.C.A. 4) 277 F. 721, 725. In the case at bar, overt acts, in furtherance of the conspiracy charged, were proven to have been committed within a few months of the indictment. That such overt acts were those of members of the conspiracy other than Eldredge is of no moment, if he had not theretofore withdrawn from the conspiracy.

If a member effectively withdraws from a conspiracy, he is not liable for acts of his former associates after his withdrawal; and the statute of limitations commences to run, as to him, upon his withdrawal. But withdrawal must be accomplished by some affirmative and effective act. Boyle v. United States (C.C.A.7) 259 F. 803. In Hyde v. United States, supra, the Supreme Court said:

"Nor does it take from a conspirator the power to withdraw from the execution of the offense or to avert a continuing criminality. It requires affirmative action, but certainly that is no hardship. Having joined in an unlawful scheme, having constituted agents for its performance, scheme and agency to be continuous until full fruition be secured, until he does some act to disavow or defeat the purpose he is in no situation to claim the delay of the law. As the offense has not been terminated or accomplished, he is still offending. And we think, consciously offending—offending as certainly, as we have said, as at the first moment of his confederation, and continuously through every moment of its existence."

What sort of an affirmative act is necessary to accomplish withdrawal depends upon the nature of the crime contemplated. If the object of the conspiracy is the doing of a single act, withdrawal may be effected by a notification to his associates, seasonably in advance of the time set, that a member will not carry on. In the case at bar, a part of the conspiracy was the embezzlement of funds; a notification to his associates that he would no longer participate in their plans to abstract further funds from the bank, is an affirmative and effective withdrawal from that part of the conspiracy.

But an essential part of the conspiracy planned was to conceal the shortage by a falsification of the books. If the embezzlement had stopped with the first sum abstracted in 1919, it would have been necessary to have falsified the books each succeeding month of each succeeding year until the money was repaid. This was what was planned, and this was what was successfully accomplished for 12 years. As was said by the Circuit Court of Appeals of the Fourth Circuit concerning the identical offense here charged, "A conspiracy such as is charged here continues until its purpose has been fully effected or until it has been abandoned." Breese v. United States, 203 F. 824, 830.

Conceding that the conversation of March, 1928, was notice to his associates that he would no longer participate in or consent to the embezzlement of further sums from the bank, can it fairly be interpreted as a request to his associates that they cease their efforts to conceal the shortage? Could the jury find, from this conversation, that Eldredge would no longer assent to the further concealment of sums theretofore embezzled, and in which he had shared? For, as Judge Walter H. Sanborn aptly said, the test is one of assent. Ware v. United States (C.C.A.8) 154 F. 577, 580, 12 L.R.A. (N.S.) 1053, 12 Ann.Cas. 233. We cannot so construe this conversation. Eldredge knew that the defalcations would be immediately discovered, and the object of the conspiracy defeated, if his associates ceased to falsify the books. Failure to falsify a single statement would result in immediate disclosure of the crime; if Eldredge intended to confess his participation in the embezzlements of the past, some more conventional and effective method would have been employed. Eldredge, in this conversation, did not instruct his associates no longer to conceal their crime. Rather, he advised them that he was not in position longer to assist in the concealment, and that he would participate in no further abstractions. What he said, at the outset, was that he would be unable further to "help him shield or conceal the shortage." The conversation cannot be twisted into a withdrawal of the authority, theretofore expressly conferred, to continue to conceal the existing shortage.

We are not persuaded that Eldredge intended to withdraw his assent to continued concealment by his associates. But even if he did, it is not enough. A withdrawal from a conspiracy cannot be effected by intent alone; it must be accompanied by some affirmative action which is effective. A declared intent to withdraw from a conspiracy to dynamite a building is not enough, if the fuse has been set; he must step on the fuse. The first abstraction from this bank set in motion a chain of inescapable consequences, if the conspiracy was to succeed. To withdraw, that chain must be interrupted; and that is not done by advising his associates to confess. Eldredge must have known that his associates must continue to conceal the shortage unless they, too, were willing to confess and take the consequences. If he had admonished them no longer to falsify the records, which he did not, such admonition would have amounted to no more than a suggestion that all confess their crime; if his associates were not in the mood so to do, such a declaration to them could have been no more than an ineffective gesture.

We hold, therefore, that Eldredge did not manifest an intent, in the conversation with his confederate, that the shortage should be revealed and their crime confessed; but if he did so intend, a manifestation of that laudable purpose to his co-conspirator was not an effective method of disclosure or an adequate confession of guilt.

The judgment is, therefore, affirmed.

COTTERAL, Circuit Judge, dissents.

PEOPLE v. BROWN

Supreme Court of Illinois, 1962.
26 Ill.2d 308, 186 N.E.2d 321.

DAILY, Justice. An indictment returned to the criminal court of Cook County jointly charged Fred Brown, Leonard McGarry, James Washington and Charles Gunn with the murder of Richard Hunter, who was shot to death in the course of an attempted robbery. Washington and McGarry pleaded guilty to the crime, whereas Brown and Gunn, who waived a jury, were found guilty after a bench trial and each was sentenced to the penitentiary for a term of 14 years. This writ of error is prosecuted by Brown, to whom we shall refer as defendant, and as grounds for reversal he contends that he was not proved guilty beyond a reasonable doubt, that he had withdrawn from the robbery plan in such a manner as to avoid liability for its consequences, and that he was denied a fair and impartial trial due to the incompetency of his appointed counsel and to the admission of evidence relating to another crime.

The victim of the homicide was among those present on July 12, 1959, at a party being held in a basement apartment of a building located at 4601 S. Michigan Avenue in Chicago. Gambling seems to have been the principal activity at the "party," while the "apartment" appears to have been in the nature of an unlicensed tavern. Around 3:30 A.M. four men, later identified as defendant and those indicted

with him, entered the premises. Washington and McGarry produced
guns, under circumstances later to be detailed, announced that it was
a stickup and ordered those present to lie on the floor. Decedent, however, jumped on McGarry's back and was shot by Washington, the
fatal bullet first passing through McGarry's body. In the confusion
the robbers were able to flee from the premises.

Defendant and Washington were apprehended in Nashville,
Tennessee, and were delivered into the custody of Chicago police on
August 17, 1959. At this time defendant made several oral statements
and signed a written statement wherein he consistently acknowledged
that he and his codefendants had first met in a tavern in South Chicago
on the night in question and that they had driven to the Michigan Avenue address in furtherance of an express plan to rob those at the party.
In addition, he consistently stated at all times prior to trial that he had
looked through a window when they arrived at the apartment, that
he then advised his companions he was not going in because there were
too many people, and that he then took a taxi back to South Chicago.
In his written statement he said he next saw his co-defendants an
hour later in South Chicago, that McGarry was then suffering from
a gunshot wound in the back, and that McGarry had been taken to
defendant's room and ministered to.

At the trial, however, defendant deviated materially from his
prior statements and testified there had been no plan or conversation
relating to a robbery and that he had gotten into the car with the
others merely for the purpose of going to the party. He stated that
just as they reached the entrance of the building McGarry announced
he was "going to make him some money," whereupon defendant said
he didn't want any part of it and took a taxi back to South Chicago.

The chief witness for the prosecution was defendant's co-conspirator, Leonard McGarry. Although completely irreconcilable with
his subsequent testimony, McGarry also testified there had been no
preconceived plan or intention of committing a robbery and stated he
and his companions had set out for the apartment solely for the purpose of gambling. Gunn, it was stated, had lost money at the party
earlier and wanted to win it back. According to McGarry, he and
his three companions went into the apartment and found about 25
persons present. He said that Gunn walked in first and went to the
bar, that Washington remained behind at the door, and that he and
the defendant walked to the middle of the room at a point four to five
feet equidistant from Gunn and Washington. One Jimmy Jones, who
had driven the men to the apartment, remained outside in the car.

McGarry said that after looking around for a moment he remarked there were "too many people," and that defendant thereupon
replied: "Yes, forget it, let's go." At this, to use McGarry's words
"most of us turned to go," but defendant asked him to wait and walked
across the floor to a washroom. Immediately after defendant went
into the other room, still according to McGarry, Washington pulled his

gun, shouting as he did so, and when people started running about McGarry drew his pistol, fired a shot into the ceiling and announced that it was a "stickup." The witness said he then vaulted over the bar and demanded the money there and that defendant, "looking surprised," came out of the rest room at this time. Several patrons attempted to seize defendant but, McGarry testified, defendant fought them off and ran out the front door shouting that "one had got away." It was following this that Hunter was fatally shot as he grappled with McGarry. Concluding his testimony, McGarry stated that he staggered to the car, that he lost consciousness, and that his next recollection was being taken to defendant's house.

Fletcher Henderson, who was present at the party, appeared as a witness for the prosecution and pointed out defendant as one of the robbers. However, it appears he had been unable to identify defendant when called upon to do so on two occasions before the trial. Another prosecution witness, Helen Wilson, who was tending bar in the apartment, testified that defendant had had a drink at the bar, prior to the shooting, and that she had not seen him after the melee occurred. Gunn, who was jointly tried with defendant, testified on cross-examination that he was the last to arrive at the apartment where the murder took place, that defendant, Washington and McGarry were already present in the front room, and that he, the witness, had protested when Washington pulled a gun.

Defendant's initial contention that he is not guilty of murder because he had abandoned and withdrawn from the criminal enterprise of his companions must fail in two respects. We held in People v. Rybka, 16 Ill.2d 394, 406, 158 N.E.2d 17, 23, that it is "the communication of intent to withdraw and not the naked fact of withdrawal that determines whether one who advised, encouraged or incited another to commit a crime is to be released from liability as an accessory before the fact." To this need may be added the further requirement that the withdrawal must be timely, that is to say it must be "such as to give his coconspirators a reasonable opportunity, if they desire, to follow his example and refrain from further action before the act is committed," and it must be possible for the trier of fact "to say that the accused had wholly and effectively detached himself from the criminal enterprise before the act with which he is charged is in the process of consummation or has become so inevitable that it cannot reasonably be stayed." * * *

Stated otherwise, withdrawal may not be effectively made from a felony murder when the "transaction which immediately begets it has actually been commenced." People v. Nichols, 230 N.Y. 221, 129 N.E. 883, 886.

In the instant case, while there may have been "communication" by defendant to McGarry, the evidence in the record does not satisfactorily show communication to Washington and Gunn who were admittedly four to five feet away in a noisy crowded room. Indeed,

Washington was standing behind defendant and McGarry and his conduct in drawing a gun when he did strongly militates against the argument that he had been apprised of the alleged abandonment by defendant. However, even if it could be said that communication to Washington and Gunn is a matter in which reasonable doubt should be resolved for defendant, we are of the opinion the attempt at withdrawal came too late. Not only was there insufficient time given to provide the co-conspirators a reasonable opportunity to withdraw, but the criminal enterprise which begot the murder had already commenced. When defendant and his companions, at least two of whom were armed, entered the apartment they passed beyond mere preparation in their common plan to rob those present, and defendant, by his presence, was efficiently encouraging and aiding the others. Cf. People v. Chapman, 224 N.Y. 463, 121 N.E. 381.

Nor is it of any consequence that defendant had fled the premises before the murder of Hunter took place. Defendant knew his companions were armed and is deemed to have known they would use their weapons if resistance was met. Where conspirators contemplate that violence may be necessary to enable them to carry out their conspiracy or common purpose, all are liable for the acts done in furtherance of the common object, and where death results from the prosecution of the common object, all are equally guilty of murder, whether or not each is actually present. People v. Rybka, 16 Ill.2d 394, 158 N. E.2d 17; People v. Suddeth, 374 Ill. 132, 28 N.E.2d 268.

UNITED STATES v. CHESTER

United States Court of Appeals, Third Circuit, 1969.
407 F.2d 53, certiorari denied 394 U.S. 1020, 89 S.Ct. 1642, 23 L.Ed.2d 45.

FREEDMAN, Circuit Judge. James Cames Chester appeals from his conviction by a jury of conspiring to violate the bank robbery statute (18 U.S.C.A. § 2113(a), (b), (d)) and of violating the substantive sections of the statute as an aider and abettor under 18 U.S. C.A. § 2.

An armed robbery of the Lyons Avenue Branch of the Fidelity Union Trust Company in Newark, New Jersey, was committed on July 12, 1966. The participants at the time were Chester's co-defendants, Murray and Lewis, together with a man called Willie, who was not apprehended. Murray and Lewis confessed to the crime and the involvement of their accomplice, Willie. They later told the authorities of Chester's participation in the planning of the robbery and the division of the spoils.

Murray and Lewis pleaded guilty and their testimony was the cornerstone of the case against Chester, who pleaded not guilty.

Appellant's court-appointed counsel asserts that the government's evidence shows that Chester effectively withdrew from the conspiracy before the robbery. Hence he argues that testimony regarding events and conversations which occurred among the conspirators after Chester withdrew was inadmissible against him and also that the trial judge should have instructed the jury on what constitutes a withdrawal from the conspiracy and the effect of withdrawal before the conspiracy is executed. No mention was made of the theory of withdrawal at the trial, but it is urged that this omission in the charge was plain error under Rule 52(b) of the Federal Rules of Criminal Procedure.

The difficulty with these contentions is that there is nothing in the government's case which required submission to the jury of the factual issue on which they rest. Viewed in the light most favorable to the defendant the government's evidence does not furnish a basis for a finding of withdrawal by Chester from the conspiracy. Chester initiated the conspiracy, he planned the robbery, prepared and provided a sketch of the bank, brought the participants together, assigned various responsibilities to them, and supplied some of the tools for the robbery, including a car which he stole for that specific purpose, and a gun.

Appellant lays stress upon a telephone call which Chester received from his wife when all the confederates were together as they were about to execute the robbery. The testimony is that he told them that his wife had received a message from his lawyer that he was to appear in court immediately and, therefore, could not participate in the robbery which was planned to go forward at that time. The evidence indicates at the most, however, that Chester was willing that the other three men either wait until he returned when he would join them, or that they should go on without him, but there is nothing in it which would justify the conclusion that he was removing himself from the conspiracy. A more sinister interpretation is that he was seeking to avoid the risk involved in the actual robbery while at the same time remaining in the conspiracy and sharing in its fruits. In fact, shortly after the robbery was committed Chester met Murray and expressed his anger and disappointment that the loot amounted only to $21,000. He then agreed with Murray to tell the others that a smaller amount had been obtained so that he and Murray could deprive them of their full share. Chester himself took $6,000.

In these circumstances there was no fundamental error in the trial judge's failure to charge the jury on the law relating to withdrawal from a conspiracy. Nor was it error to admit the declarations of Chester's co-conspirators after he left them to go to court.

The law is clear that in order to sustain a claim of withdrawal from a conspiracy a defendant must prove an "affirmative action * * * to disavow or defeat the purpose [of the conspiracy]" (Hyde v. United States, 225 U.S. 347, 369, 32 S.Ct. 793, 803, 56 L.Ed. 1114 (1911)), or some "definite, decisive and positive step" which shows that his disassociation is "full, decisive and complete." Deacon v. United States, 124 F.2d 352, 357, 359 (1 Cir. 1941).

NOTE

The Final Draft of the Proposed New Federal Criminal Code would provide in section 1005(3)(b) for an affirmative defense of renunciation to a conspiracy charge "that, under circumstances manifesting a voluntary and complete renunciation of his criminal intent, the defendant prevented the commission of * * * the crime or crimes contemplated by the conspiracy." Such a defense is consistent with the view of conspiracy as an inchoate crime. Is it consistent with the view that it is inherently dangerous? See Orear v. United States, 261 F. 257, 259 (5th Cir. 1919):

> Section 6 of the Penal Code does not base conspiracy on the doing of an overt act, as does section 37 of the Penal Code. It is, in this respect, like the Sherman Anti-Trust Act (Act July 2, 1890, c. 647, 26 Stat. 209 [Comp.St. §§ 8820–8823, 8827–8830]). Under that act the Supreme Court held that common-law conspiracies were made punishable, and that it did not make "the doing of any act other than the act of conspiring a condition of liability." Nash v. United States, 229 U.S. 373, 33 S.Ct. 780, 57 L.Ed. 1232. Withdrawal from the conspiracy after its formation would not exculpate from guilt * * *.

Should the standard proposed in 1005(3)(b) be applied where the claim of abandonment is offered not as a defense to the charge of conspiracy but to avoid liability for the substantive offenses of co-conspirators committed after some " 'definite, decisive and positive step' which shows that his disassociation is 'full, decisive and complete.' "? Where it is offered to show, as in *Eldredge*, that the statute of limitations has run as to him, or, as in *Chester*, to bar the admission against him of his co-conspirators declarations? Should communication of withdrawal, however forceful, be sufficient for any of these purposes?

---

5. USE OF THE CONSPIRACY DOCTRINE

---

a. LIABILITY FOR CRIMES OF CO–CONSPIRATORS

PINKERTON v. UNITED STATES

Supreme Court of the United States, 1946.
328 U.S. 640, 66 S.Ct. 1180, 90 L.Ed. 1489, rehearing denied
329 U.S. 818, 67 S.Ct. 26, 91 L.Ed. 697.

Mr. Justice DOUGLAS delivered the opinion of the Court.

Walter and Daniel Pinkerton are brothers who live a short distance from each other on Daniel's farm. They were indicted for violations of the Internal Revenue Code. The indictment contained ten substantive counts and one conspiracy count. The jury found Walter guilty on nine of the substantive counts and on the conspiracy count. It found Daniel guilty on six of the substantive counts and on the conspiracy count. Walter was fined $500 and sentenced generally on the substantive counts to imprisonment for thirty months. On the conspiracy count he was given a two year sentence to run concurrently with the other sentence. Daniel was fined $1,000 and sentenced generally on the substantive counts to imprisonment for thirty months. On the conspiracy count he was fined $500 and given a two year sentence to run concurrently with the other sentence. The judgments of conviction were affirmed by the Circuit Court of Appeals. 151 F.2d 499.

* * *

A single conspiracy was charged and proved. Some of the overt acts charged in the conspiracy count were the same acts charged in the substantive counts. Each of the substantive offenses found was committed pursuant to the conspiracy. Petitioners therefore contend that the substantive counts became merged in the conspiracy count, and that only a single sentence not exceeding the maximum two-year penalty provided by the conspiracy statute (Criminal Code § 37, 18 U.S.C. § 88, 18 U.S.C.A. § 88) could be imposed. Or to state the matter differently, they contend that each of the substantive counts became a separate conspiracy count but since only a single conspiracy was charged and proved, only a single sentence for conspiracy could be imposed. They rely on Braverman v. United States, 317 U.S. 49, 63 S.Ct. 99, 87 L.Ed. 23.

In the Braverman case the indictment charged no substantive offense. Each of the several counts charged a conspiracy to violate a different statute. But only one conspiracy was proved. We held that a single conspiracy, charged under the general conspiracy statute, however diverse its objects may be, violates but a single statute and no penalty greater than the maximum provided for one conspiracy may be imposed. That case is not apposite here. For the offenses charged and proved were not only a conspiracy but substantive offenses as well.

Nor can we accept the proposition that the substantive offenses were merged in the conspiracy. There are, of course, instances where a conspiracy charge may not be added to the substantive charge. One is where the agreement of two persons is necessary for the completion of the substantive crime and there is no ingredient in the conspiracy which is not present in the completed crime. See United States v. Katz, 271 U.S. 354, 355, 356, 46 S.Ct. 513, 514, 70 L.Ed. 986; Gebardi v. United States, 287 U.S. 112, 121, 122, 53 S.Ct. 35, 37, 77 L.Ed. 206, 84 A.L.R. 370. Another is where the definition of the substantive offense excludes from punishment for conspiracy one who voluntarily participates in another's crime. Gebardi v. United States, supra. But those exceptions are of a limited character. The common law rule that the substantive offense, if a felony, was merged in the conspiracy, has little vitality in this country. It has been long and consistently recognized by the Court that the commission of the substantive offense and a conspiracy to commit it are separate and distinct offenses. The power of Congress to separate the two and to affix to each a different penalty is well established. Clune v. United States, 159 U.S. 590, 594, 595, 16 S.Ct. 125, 126, 40 L.Ed. 269. A conviction for the conspiracy may be had though the substantive offense was completed. See Heike v. United States, 227 U.S. 131, 144, 33 S.Ct. 226, 228, 57 L.Ed. 450, Ann.Cas.1914C, 128. And the plea of double jeopardy is no defense to a conviction for both offenses. Carter v. McClaughry, 183 U.S. 365, 395, 22 S.Ct. 181, 193, 46 L.Ed. 236. It is only an identity of offenses which is fatal. See Gavieres v. United States, 220 U.S. 338, 342, 31 S.Ct. 421, 422, 55 L.Ed. 489. Cf. Freeman v. United States, 6 Cir., 146 F.2d 978. A conspiracy is a partnership in crime. United States v. Socony-Vacuum Oil Co., 310 U.S. 150, 253, 60 S.Ct. 811, 858, 84 L.Ed. 1129. It has ingredients, as well as implications, distinct from the completion of the unlawful project. As stated in United States v. Rabinowich, 238 U.S. 78, 88, 35 S.Ct. 682, 684, 685, 59 L.Ed. 1211:

"For two or more to confederate and combine together to commit or cause to be committed a breach of the criminal laws is an offense of the gravest character, sometimes quite outweighing, in injury to the public, the mere commission of the contemplated crime. It involves deliberate plotting to subvert the laws, educating and preparing the conspirators for further and habitual criminal practices. And it is characterized by secrecy, rendering it difficult of detection, requiring more time for its discovery, and adding to the importance of punishing it when discovered."

And see Sneed v. United States, 5 Cir., 298 F. 911, 912, 913; Banghart v. United States, 4 Cir., 148 F.2d 521.

Moreover, it is not material that overt acts charged in the conspiracy counts were also charged and proved as substantive offenses. As stated in Sneed v. United States, supra, 298 F. at page 913, "If the overt act be the offense which was the object of the conspiracy, and is also punished, there is not a double punishment of it." The agreement to do an unlawful act is even then distinct from the doing of the act.

It is contended that there was insufficient evidence to implicate Daniel in the conspiracy. But we think there was enough evidence for submission of the issue to the jury.

There is, however, no evidence to show that Daniel participated directly in the commission of the substantive offenses on which his conviction has been sustained, although there was evidence to show that these substantive offenses were in fact committed by Walter in furtherance of the unlawful agreement or conspiracy existing between the brothers. The question was submitted to the jury on the theory that each petitioner could be found guilty of the substantive offenses, if it was found at the time those offenses were committed petitioners were parties to an unlawful conspiracy and the substantive offenses charged were in fact committed in furtherance of it.

Daniel relies on United States v. Sall [116 F.2d 745 (3rd Cir. 1940)]. That case held that participation in the conspiracy was not itself enough to sustain a conviction for the substantive offense even though it was committed in furtherance of the conspiracy. The court held that, in addition to evidence that the offense was in fact committed in furtherance of the conspiracy, evidence of direct participation in the commission of the substantive offense or other evidence from which participation might fairly be inferred was necessary.

We take a different view. We have here a continuous conspiracy. There is here no evidence of the affirmative action on the part of Daniel which is necessary to establish his withdrawal from it. Hyde v. United States, 225 U.S. 347, 369, 32 S.Ct. 793, 803, 56 L.Ed. 1114, Ann.Cas.1914A, 614. As stated in that case, "Having joined in an unlawful scheme, having constituted agents for its performance, scheme and agency to be continuous until full fruition be secured, until he does some act to disavow or defeat the purpose he is in no situation to claim the delay of the law. As the offense has not been terminated or accomplished, he is still offending. And we think consciously offending,—offending as certainly, as we have said, as at the first moment of his confederation, and consciously, through every moment of its existence." Id., 225 U.S. at page 369, 32 S.Ct. at page 803. And so long as the partnership in crime continues, the partners act for each other in carrying it forward. It is settled that "an overt act of one partner may be the act of all without any new agreement specifically directed to that act." United States v. Kissel, 218 U.S. 601, 608, 31 S.Ct. 124, 126, 54 L.Ed. 1168. Motive or intent may be proved by the acts or declarations of some of the conspirators in furtherance of the common objective. Wiborg v. United States, 163 U.S. 632, 657, 658, 16 S.Ct. 1127, 1137, 1197, 46 L.Ed. 289. A scheme to use the mails to defraud, which is joined in by more than one person, is a conspiracy. Yet all members are responsible, though only one did the mailing. The governing principle is the same when the substantive offense is committed by one of the conspirators in furtherance of the unlawful project. The criminal intent to do the act is established by the formation of the conspiracy. Each conspirator instigated the commission of the crime. The unlawful agreement contemplated precisely what was done. It was formed for the purpose. The act done was in execution of the enterprise. The rule which holds responsible one who counsels, procures, or commands another to commit a crime is founded on the same principle. That principle is recognized in the law of conspiracy when the overt act of one partner in crime is attributable to all. An overt act is an essential ingredient of the crime of conspiracy under § 37 of the Criminal Code, 18 U.S.C. § 88, 18 U.S.C.A. § 88. If that can be supplied by the act of one conspirator, we fail to see why the same or other acts in furtherance of the conspiracy are likewise not attributable to the others for the purpose of holding them responsible for the substantive offense.

A different case would arise if the substantive offense committed by one of the conspirators was not in fact done in furtherance of the conspiracy, did not fall within the scope of the unlawful project, or was merely a part of the ramifications of the plan which could not be reasonably foreseen as a necessary or natural consequence of the unlawful agreement. But as we read this record, that is not this case.

Affirmed.

Mr. Justice JACKSON took no part in the consideration or decision of this case.

Mr. Justice RUTLEDGE, dissenting in part.

The judgment concerning Daniel Pinkerton should be reversed. In my opinion it is without precedent here and is a dangerous precedent to establish.

Daniel and Walter, who were brothers living near each other, were charged in several counts with substantive offenses, and then a conspiracy count was added naming those offenses as overt acts. The proof showed that Walter alone committed the substantive crimes. There was none to establish that Daniel participated in them, aided and abetted Walter in committing them, or knew that he had done so. Daniel in fact was in the penitentiary, under sentence for other crimes, when some of Walter's crimes were done.

There was evidence, however, to show that over several years Daniel and Walter had confederated to commit similar crimes concerned with unlawful possession, transportation, and dealing in whiskey, in fraud of the federal revenues. On this evidence both were convicted of conspiracy. Walter also was convicted on the substantive counts on the proof of his committing the crimes charged. Then, on that evidence without more than the proof of Daniel's criminal agreement with Walter and the latter's overt acts, which were also the substantive offenses charged, the court told the jury they could find Daniel guilty of those substantive offenses. They did so.

I think this ruling violates both the letter and the spirit of what Congress did when it separately defined the three classes of crime, namely, (1) completed substantive offenses; (2) aiding, abetting or counseling another to commit them; and (3) conspiracy to commit them. Not only does this ignore the distinctions Congress has prescribed shall be observed. It either convicts one man for another's crime or punishes the man convicted twice for the same offense.

* * *

The court's theory seems to be that Daniel and Walter became general partners in crime by virtue of their agreement and because of that agreement without more on his part Daniel became criminally responsible as a principal for everything Walter did thereafter in the nature of a criminal offense of the general sort the agreement contemplated, so long as there was not clear evidence that Daniel had withdrawn from or revoked the agreement. Whether or not his commitment to the penitentiary had that effect, the result is a vicarious criminal responsibility as broad as, or broader than, the vicarious civil liability of a partner for acts done by a co-partner in the course of the firm's business.

Such analogies from private commercial law and the law of torts are dangerous, in my judgment, for transfer to the criminal field. Guilt there with us remains personal, not vicarious, for the more serious offenses. It should be kept so. The effect of Daniel's conviction in this case, to repeat, is either to attribute to him Walter's guilt or to punish him twice for the same offense, namely, agreeing with Walter to engage in crime. Without the agreement Daniel was guilty of no crime on this record. With it and no more, so far as his own conduct is concerned, he was guilty of two.

COMMONWEALTH v. STASIUN

Supreme Judicial Court of Massachusetts, 1965.
349 Mass. 38, 206 N.E.2d 672.

SPALDING, Justice.   *   *   *   We turn now to assignments relating to the charge. The judge in effect instructed the jury that if they found that Manning, Stasiun and Rymszewicz had entered into a conspiracy to solicit a bribe, then, by virtue of their agreement, all could be found guilty of the substantive offence of solicitation on proof that only one committed that offence and without proof that the others participated in any way in the solicitation.

The rule in this jurisdiction is to the contrary. To be liable for the substantive offence, a coconspirator must participate or aid in the commission of it. See Commonwealth v. Knapp, 9 Pick. 495, 518; Commonwealth v. Lucas, 2 Allen 170; Commonwealth v. Clune, 162 Mass. 206, 214, 38 N.E. 435; Commonwealth v. Lavery, 255 Mass. 327, 333, 151 N.E. 466. Long ago this court cautioned that the proof of conspiracy, without more, did not justify a finding that a conspirator had committed the offence which was the object of the conspiracy. In Commonwealth v. Knapp, 9 Pick. 495, 518–519, it was said by Putnam, J., "We do not however assent to the position which has been taken by the counsel for the government, that if it should be proved that the prisoner conspired with others to procure the murder to be committed, it follows as a legal presumption, that the prisoner aided in the actual perpetration of the crime unless he can show the contrary to the jury. The fact of the conspiracy being proved against the prisoner is to be weighed as evidence in the case having a tendency to prove that the prisoner aided, but it is not *in itself* to be taken as a legal presumption of his having aided unless disproved by him."

If the rule were otherwise, the fundamental distinction between a substantive offence and a conspiracy to commit that offence would be ignored. Each is a separate and distinct offence and each may be separately punished. Fox v. Commonwealth, 264 Mass. 51, 53, 161 N.E. 803. Commonwealth v. Stuart, 207 Mass. 563, 571, 93 N.E. 825. See Clune v. United States, 159 U.S. 590, 16 S.Ct. 125, 40 L.Ed. 269. "The combination for the illegal purpose or for the use of illegal means is the essence of conspiracy." Attorney Gen. v. Tufts, 239 Mass. 458, 493, 131 N.E. 573, 132 N.E. 322, 328, 17 A.L.R. 274. Punishment is imposed for entering into the combination. This is not the same thing as participating in the substantive offence which was the object of the conspiracy. While it has been said that a conspiracy is a "partnership in crime" (United States v. Socony-Vacuum Oil Co. Inc., 310 U.S. 150, 253, 60 S.Ct. 811, 84 L.Ed. 1129), that metaphor should not be pressed too far. It does not follow that such a partnership is governed by the same principles of vicarious liability as would apply in civil cases. Our criminal law is founded on the principle that guilt, for the more serious offences, is personal, not vicarious. One is punished for his own blameworthy conduct, not that of others. Perkins on Criminal Law, 550. Sayre, Criminal Responsibility for the Acts of Another, 43 Harv.L.Rev. 689. Compare Gurney v. Tenney, 197 Mass. 457, 466, 84 N.E. 428 (civil liability of a conspirator for the misrepresentation of another). To ignore the distinction between the crime of conspiracy and the substantive offence would enable "the government through the use of the conspiracy dragnet to convict a conspirator of every substantive offense committed by any other member of the group even though he had no part in it or even knowledge of it" United States v. Sall, 116 F.2d 745, 748 (3d Cir.).

* * *

We are mindful that a different rule now prevails in the Federal courts as a result of the decision in Pinkerton v. United States, 328 U.S. 640, 66 S.Ct. 1180, although prior to that decision the views of the lower Federal courts were conflicting. See United States v. Sall, 116 F.2d 745 (3d Cir.), and compare Johnson v. United States, 62 F.2d 32 (9th Cir.). With deference, we are not persuaded to follow the Pinkerton case. The reasoning of Rutledge, J., in his dissenting opinion (concurred in by Frankfurter, J.), seems to us more convincing. It follows that the instruction of the trial judge was error.

MABRY v. STATE

Court of Appeals of Alabama, 1959.
40 Ala.App. 129, 110 So.2d 250, certiorari dismissed
268 Ala. 660, 110 So.2d 260.

HARWOOD, Presiding Judge. This appellant has been adjudged guilty of mayhem, an offense denounced by Section 359, Title 14, Code of Alabama 1940. Punishment was fixed at imprisonment in the penitentiary for a term of twenty years, the maximum permissible under said section.

The victim of the mayhem was Judge Edward Aaron, who suffered castration.

The evidence presented below depicts conduct shocking in its foulness, viciousness, and savage brutality.

Without dispute the evidence shows that late on the afternoon of 2 September 1957, a group gathered in the yard of appellant's home. Included in this group were the appellant, Joe Pritchett, Bart Floyd, John Griffin, Bill Miller, and Grover McCullough.

Among the things discussed was the election of a "captain" for the group. Bart Floyd was a prospect for this office. However, it was thought that Floyd should "prove" his leadership before being elected.

To enable Floyd to establish his qualifications it was decided that the group would go out and "grab a negro," or "grab a negro and scare hell out of him."

The group set out on this mission in two automobiles. Appellant was in a car driven by John Griffin, in which Bill Miller was also a passenger.

At one point a stop was made by the two cars and Bart Floyd went into a drug store and emerged with a small package. While appellant denied he knew the contents of the package, other evidence shows that it contained razor blades and turpentine.

Driving around, apparently at random, the group came upon Aaron walking along the Huffman-Tarrant City road, accompanied by Cora Parker.

Aaron was forced into one of the cars and made to lie upon the rear floor.

Although at this point the appellant took over as driver of the car into which Aaron had been forced, he claimed in his testimony that he did not know what force had been used to get Aaron into the car as he had kept his face to the front in order to avoid any later identification. He did however admit furnishing his handkerchief to be used to blindfold Aaron.

With appellant driving the lead car, the two cars proceeded to a concrete block house, on the outskirts of Birmingham, used as a meeting hall for the group. Hoods were procured for the group to put on. Aaron was made to crawl into the house, guided by Pritchett and followed by appellant.

Inside the house Aaron was questioned, and during the process was kicked in the face by Pritchett. Eventually he was asked if he "wanted his life or his testicles." Appellant testified he heard this part of the questioning.

Aaron was forced to remove his trousers and shorts, some scuffling ensuing at this junction. According to Aaron he was struck on the head with a pistol by the appellant, and also hit by someone else. According to other evidence introduced by the State, he was hit on the head with a tire tool by another of the group and knocked unconscious. Pritchett then commanded Floyd to do his duty.

Floyd proceeded to castrate Aaron with a razor blade, excising the entire scrotum and contents in the process.

After about five minutes Aaron was assisted to one of the cars and put in the trunk compartment. The appellant left the meeting hall in this car. Driving to a remote area, Aaron was removed from the car and left on the road. A few hours later he was discovered by two police officers of the City of Birmingham and taken to a hospital. After lingering between life and death for some two weeks Aaron eventually recovered.

In general, the State's case was presented on the theory of appellant's guilt as a conspirator.

The defense was directed toward an attempt to show that if a conspiracy ever existed, it was merely to "scare a negro," and that Floyd's act was his own independent act, beyond the scope of any original conspiracy entered into by the appellant, and therefore an act for which the appellant should not be held responsible.

* * *

As pointed out in [Martin v. State, 89 Ala. 115, 8 So. 23 (1890)]: "It should be observed however, that while the parties are responsible for consequent acts growing out of the general design, they are not for independent acts growing out of the particular acts of individuals."

Counsel for appellant argues that the castration of Aaron must be considered as the malicious independent act of Floyd, for which appellant was not responsible, because not within the scope of the agreement to "scare a negro."

Such argument overlooks the undisputed facts that after Aaron was in the meeting house he was asked by Pritchett if he wanted his life or his testicles. Appellant admits hearing this question propounded, and that he heard a scuffle. That he had been up to his neck in this unlawful enterprise up to this point cannot be denied.

The purpose of the conspiracy from this point on became crystal clear. The appellant made no objections to its execution, and no effort towards its prevention. He would seek to escape responsibility by saying that he turned his head and did not see the actual overt act.

NOTE

In People v. Weiss, 50 Cal.2d 535, 327 P.2d 527, 544–545 (1958) the court stated:

As we read CALJIC Instruction 932 (Calif. Jury Instructions, Criminal, 1946 ed.), it is susceptible, as defendants urge, of the interpretation that one who "becomes a party to a conspiracy after the formation thereof, and who adopts the said conspiracy and its purposes and objects, becomes *liable* for every act * * * of each and all the other conspirators done in pursuance and furtherance of the conspiracy" (italics added), including criminal acts done before the person joining the conspiracy became a party thereto. This is not the law and we are not disposed to adopt such a rule as the substantive law of the state. At oral argument the People commendably disavowed any purpose of contending for such a rule of substantive law and urged only the rule that where a person joins a conspiracy after its formation and actively participates in it, he adopts the prior acts and declarations of his fellow conspirators pursuant to the conspiracy *to the extent that evidence of those acts and declarations is admissible against him.*[f] * * *

We recognize that it is said in 1 Wharton's Criminal Law and Procedure (1957), § 90, p. 198, and 11 Am.Jur., Conspiracy, § 8, p. 549, that "The rule of responsibility for the acts of co-conspirators includes acts done before the defendant joined the conspiracy, as well as the acts subsequent to his participation," and in 15 C.J.S. Conspiracy § 75, p. 1108, that persons who come into a conspiracy after its formation and assist in the furtherance of its execution with knowledge of its purpose "are deemed in law parties to all acts done by any of the other parties, either before or after, in furtherance of the common design."[1] But the cases cited in those

f. An example of the purposes for which admission of such prior acts might be sought is offered by United States v. Bletterman, 279 F.2d 320 (2d Cir. 1960). The charge was conspiracy to possess and sell property stolen from interstate commerce. Defendant, a "fence", entered the scheme after the thieves had made two separate thefts. The jury was instructed, over the defendant's objection, that defendant might be found guilty if they were satisfied that he had participated in the conspiracy and that at least one of six overt acts, including these prior thefts, were committed in furtherance of the conspiracy. On appeal the court concluded: "While we need not now decide whether a new party may be subjected to additional liability for crimes committed by the original parties prior to his entry, we hold that previous acts of coconspirators suffice to satisfy the overt-act requirement."

1. In the latter work it is added that "some authorities have held that a person joining in a conspiracy after its formation is not responsible for acts done by other members of a combination before he became a member," citing State v. Duncan (1876), 64 Mo. 262, 266, where it is said, "The second instruction given for the State is erroneous in telling the jury that if

works for the quoted propositions are not cases where a defendant was convicted of a substantive offense committed by his co-conspirators before he became a member of the conspiracy.

Nor do the California cases which contain language in seeming accord with those propositions uphold conviction of a substantive offense committed by conspirators before the defendant joined the conspiracy.

---

b. CONVICTION FOR CONSPIRACY IN ADDITION TO COMPLETED OFFENSES

BENDER v. STATE

[This case appears at page 756, supra.]

JIMENEZ v. STATE

District Court of Appeal of Florida, 1968.
208 So.2d 124.

PER CURIAM. These combined appeals were by the defendants below whose convictions stemmed from the same transaction.

The appellants were found guilty of conspiring to commit abortion (Count I) and of an attempt to commit abortion (Count II). Appellants Maria Luisa Moreno and Israel Alfonso were convicted also of aggravated assault (Count III). A not guilty verdict was directed against all defendants on a charge of resisting arrest with violence, and in favor of the defendant Alieda Jimenez on the charge of aggravated assault.

The record discloses that Virginia Jimenez, hereinafter referred to as Virginia, an employee of the state's attorney's office who had been deputized by the sheriff of Dade County, made arrangements by telephone for an abortion. By prearrangement she was picked up by the appellant Maria Luisa Moreno and transported by automobile to a designated residence at 13201 Southwest 62nd Avenue. There Virginia undressed as directed and was examined by appellants Maria Luisa Moreno and Alieda Jimenez. The latter then requested $500 which Virginia paid. Thereupon Virginia identified herself as a

---

there was a party of persons combined for the purpose of stealing horses, etc., and sharing the proceeds, and defendant at any time, at or after the formation of said company became a member, he was criminally liable for all the acts done by any other person belonging to the combination, before and afterwards, in furtherance of the common design. In other words, if the defendant joined a company of horse thieves, he was liable for all the thefts they or any of them may have committed before he became a member, whether he received any part of the property so stolen, or its proceeds or not; his joining the company had relation back, and implicated him in every theft they had committed, even years before. The statement of the proposition is its own refutation."

police officer and announced to the persons present that they were under arrest. Appellants Maria Luisa Moreno, and Israel Alfonso and a man referred to as "doctor" who also were present, knocked Virginia down and held her on the floor, at which point she fainted. When Virginia regained consciousness Alieda Jimenez and the "doctor" had departed, and Maria Luisa Moreno was holding her down. They stood her up and dressed her and then bound her. Maria Luisa Moreno produced a gun with which she threatened Virginia. Thereupon they placed Virginia in an automobile where she again was threatened with the gun. Virginia was transported some distance and was put out and left in a vacant lot.

* * *

The remaining contentions of appellants are as to the sufficiency of the evidence to support the convictions * * *. An examination of the record leads us to the conclusion that the evidence amply supports the convictions of the appellants. * * *

---

c. PROSECUTORIAL ADVANTAGES IN THE USE OF CONSPIRACY

KRULEWITCH v. UNITED STATES

Supreme Court of the United States, 1949.
336 U.S. 440, 69 S.Ct. 716, 93 L.Ed. 790.

[Petitioner's conviction for violation of the Mann Act was reversed because the trial court's admission of a co-conspirator's hearsay declaration made more than six weeks after the alleged conspiracy's termination was held to be error on the grounds that a statement made at that time could not properly be viewed as made in furtherance of the conspiracy or in furtherance of an implied subsidiary conspiracy to avoid detection and punishment.]

Mr. Justice JACKSON, concurring in the judgment and opinion of the Court.

This case illustrates a present drift in the federal law of conspiracy which warrants some further comment because it is characteristic of the long evolution of that elastic, sprawling and pervasive offense. Its history exemplifies the "tendency of a principle to expand itself to the limit of its logic." [1] The unavailing protest of courts against the growing habit to indict for conspiracy in lieu of prosecuting for the substantive offense itself, or in addition thereto,[2] suggests

---

1. The phrase is Judge Cardozo's—The Nature of the Judicial Process, p. 51.

2. The Conference of Senior Circuit Judges, presided over by Chief Justice Taft, in 1925 reported:

"We note the prevalent use of conspiracy indictments for converting a joint misdemeanor into a felony; and we express our conviction that both for this purpose and for the purpose—or at least with the effect—of bringing

that loose practice as to this offense constitutes a serious threat to fairness in our administration of justice.

The modern crime of conspiracy is so vague that it almost defies definition.[3] Despite certain elementary and essential elements,[4] it also, chameleon-like, takes on a special coloration from each of the many independent offenses on which it may be overlaid.[5] It is always

in much improper evidence, the conspiracy statute is being much abused. "Although in a particular case there may be no preconcert of plan, excepting that necessarily inherent in mere joint action, it is difficult to exclude that situation from the established definitions of conspiracy; yet the theory which permits us to call the aborted plan a greater offense than the completed crime supposes a serious and substantially continued group scheme for cooperative law breaking. We observe so many conspiracy prosecutions which do not have this substantial base that we fear the creation of a general impression, very harmful to law enforcement, that this method of prosecution is used arbitrarily and harshly. Further the rules of evidence in conspiracy cases make them most difficult to try without prejudice to an innocent defendant." Annual Report of the Attorney General for 1925, pp. 5–6.

Fifteen years later Judge Learned Hand observed: " * * * so many prosecutors seek to sweep within the drag-net of conspiracy all those who have been associated in any degree whatever with the main offenders. That there are opportunities of great oppression in such a doctrine is very plain, and it is only by circumscribing the scope of such all comprehensive indictments that they can be avoided." United States v. Falcone, 109 F.2d 579, 581.

3. Harno, Intent in Criminal Conspiracy, 89 U. of Pa.L.Rev. 624: "In the long category of crimes there is none, not excepting criminal attempt, more difficult to confine within the boundaries of definitive statement than conspiracy."

An English author—Wright, The Law of Criminal Conspiracies and Agreements, p. 11—gives up with the remark: "but no intelligible definition of 'conspiracy' has yet been established."

4. Justice Holmes supplied an oversimplified working definition in United

States v. Kissel, 218 U.S. 601, 608: "A conspiracy is a partnership in criminal purposes." This was recently restated "A conspiracy is a partnership in crime." Pinkerton v. United States, 328 U.S. 640, 644. The latter is inaccurate, since concert in criminal purposes, rather than concert in crime, establishes the conspiracy.

Carson offers the following résumé of American cases: "It would appear that a conspiracy must be a combination of two or more persons by some concerted action to accomplish some criminal object; or some object not criminal by criminal means; or, some object not criminal by means which are not criminal, but where mischief to the public is involved; or, where neither the object nor the means are criminal, or even unlawful, but where injury and oppression to individuals are the result." The Law of Criminal Conspiracies and Agreements, as Found in The American Cases, p. 123.

5. See, for example:

8 U.S.C.A. § 47, Conspiracy to interfere with civil rights; (1) Preventing officer from performing duties; (2) Obstructing justice, intimidating party, witness or juror; (3) Depriving persons of rights or privileges. 10 U.S. C.A. § 1566, Conspiracy by persons in military service to defraud the U. S. 12 U.S.C.A. § 1138d(f), Conspiracy involving Farm Credit Banks, Administration, etc. 15 U.S.C.A.: §§ 1–3, Conspiracy in restraint of trade; § 8, Conspiracy in restraint of import trade. 18 U.S.C.A. as revised by the Act of June 25, 1948, 62 Stat. 928 et seq., effective September 1, 1948: § 2384, Seditious conspiracy; §§ 2385, 2387, Conspiracy to impair loyalty of armed forces or advocate overthrow of U. S. Government by force; § 241, Conspiracy to injure person in exercise of civil rights; § 372, Conspiracy to prevent officer from performing duties; § 286, Conspiracy to defraud the Government by obtaining payment of a false claim; § 371, Conspiracy to de-

"predominantly mental in composition" because it consists primarily of a meeting of minds and an intent.

The crime comes down to us wrapped in vague but unpleasant connotations. It sounds historical undertones of treachery, secret plotting and violence on a scale that menaces social stability and the security of the state itself. "Privy conspiracy" ranks with sedition and rebellion in the Litany's prayer for deliverance. Conspiratorial movements do indeed lie back of the political assassination, the *coup d'état*, the *putsch*, the revolution, and seizures of power in modern times, as they have in all history.[7]

But the conspiracy concept also is superimposed upon many concerted crimes having no political motivation. It is not intended to question that the basic conspiracy principle has some place in modern criminal law, because to unite, back of a criminal purpose, the strength, opportunities and resources of many is obviously more dangerous and more difficult to police than the efforts of a lone wrongdoer. It also may be trivialized, as here, where the conspiracy consists of the concert of a loathsome panderer and a prostitute to go from New York to Florida to ply their trade (see 145 F.2d 76 for details) and it would appear that a simple Mann Act prosecution would vindicate the majesty of federal law. However, even when appropriately invoked, the looseness and pliability of the doctrine present inherent dangers which should be in the background of judicial thought wherever it is sought to extend the doctrine to meet the exigencies of a particular case.

Conspiracy in federal law aggravates the degree of crime over that of unconcerted offending. The act of confederating to commit a misdemeanor, followed by even an innocent overt act in its execution, is a felony and is such even if the misdemeanor is never consummated.[9] The more radical proposition also is well-established

---

fraud the United States; §§ 1501–1506, Conspiracy to obstruct justice; §§ 752, 1792, Conspiracy to cause riots at federal penal institutions; § 1201, Conspiracy to transport kidnapped person in interstate commerce; § 2314, Conspiracy to transport stolen property and counterfeiting instruments in interstate commerce; § 1951, Conspiracy to violate Anti-Racketeering Act; § 2192, Conspiracy to incite mutiny on shipboard; § 2271, Conspiracy to cast away vessel. 22 U.S.C.A. § 234, Conspiracy to injure property of foreign government. 31 U.S.C.A. § 231, Conspiracy to obtain payment of false claims. 34 U.S.C.A. § 749a, Conspiracy to bid collusively on construction of naval aircraft. 38 U.S.C.A. § 715, Conspiracy to falsify pension claims. 50 U.S.C.A. § 34, Conspiracy to disclose national defense information or commit espionage. 50 U.S.C.App. § 311, Conspiracy to violate Selective Service Act.

7. See Senturia, Conspiracy, Political, IV Encyc.Soc.Sci. 238 (1931).

On conspiracy principles German courts, on May 30, 1924, adjudged the Nazi Party to be a criminal organization. It also held in 1928 that the Leadership Corps of the Communist Party was a criminal organization and in 1930 entered judgment of criminality against the Union of Red Front Fighters of the Communist Party. See note 15.

9. 18 U.S.C.A. § 371. Until recently, the punishment for such a felony could

that at common law and under some statutes a combination may be a criminal conspiracy even if it contemplates only acts which are not crimes at all when perpetrated by an individual or by many acting severally.[10]

Thus the conspiracy doctrine will incriminate persons on the fringe of offending who would not be guilty of aiding and abetting or of becoming an accessory, for those charges only lie when an act which is a crime has actually been committed.

Attribution of criminality to a confederation which contemplates no act that would be criminal if carried out by any one of the conspirators is a practice peculiar to Anglo-American law. "There can be little doubt that this wide definition of the crime of conspiracy originates in the criminal equity administered in the Star Chamber." In fact, we are advised that "The modern crime of conspiracy is almost entirely the result of the manner in which conspiracy was treated by the court of Star Chamber." The doctrine does not commend itself to jurists of civil-law countries,[14] despite universal recognition that an organized society must have legal weapons for combatting organized criminality. Most other countries have devised what they consider more discriminating principles upon which to prosecute criminal gangs, secret associations and subversive syndicates.[15]

A recent tendency has appeared in this Court to expand this elastic offense and to facilitate its proof. In Pinkerton v. United States, 328 U.S. 640, it sustained a conviction of a substantive crime where there was no proof of participation in or knowledge of it, upon the novel and dubious theory that conspiracy is equivalent in law to aiding and abetting.

have been far in excess of that provided for the substantive offense. However, the Act of June 25, 1948, c. 645, 62 Stat. 683, 701, provides that in such a case the punishment for the conspiracy shall not exceed the maximum provided for such misdemeanor.

10. This is the federal law applicable to antitrust prosecutions. For the history of this conception and its perversion, particularly in labor cases, see Sayre, Criminal Conspiracy, 35 Harv. L.Rev. 393. On the abuse of conspiracy see O'Brian, Loyalty Tests and Guilt by Association, 61 Harv.L.Rev. 592, and Note, The Conspiracy Dilemma: Prosecution of Group Crime or Protection of Individual Defendants, 62 Harv.L.Rev. 276.

14. "It is utterly unknown to the Roman law; it is not found in modern Continental codes; few Continental lawyers ever heard of it. It is a fortunate circumstance that it is not encrusted so deep in our jurisprudence by past decisions of our courts that we are unable to slough it off altogether. It is a doctrine which has proved itself the evil genius of our law wherever it has touched it." Sayre, Criminal Conspiracy, 35 Harv.L.Rev. 393, 427.

15. Counsel representing the United States, the United Kingdom, the French Republic, and the Soviet Union, and German defendants, indulged in some comparisons of the relevant laws of several nations before the International Military Tribunal at Nürnberg in connection with organizations there accused as criminal. 8 Trial of Major War Criminals (GPO 1947), pp. 353, et seq.; 2 Nazi Conspiracy and Aggression (GPO 1946), p. 1; Jackson, The Nürnberg Case, p. 95.

Doctrines of conspiracy are not only invoked for criminal prosecution, but also in civil proceedings for damages or for injunction, and in administrative proceedings to apply regulatory statutes. This conspiracy concept was employed to prosecute laborers for combining to raise their wages and formed the basis for abuse of the labor injunction. The National Labor Relations Act found it necessary to provide that concerted labor activities otherwise lawful were not rendered unlawful by mere concert. But in other fields concert may still be a crime though it contemplates only acts which each could do lawfully on his own.

The interchangeable use of conspiracy doctrine in civil as well as penal proceedings opens it to the danger, absent in the case of many crimes, that a court having in mind only the civil sanctions will approve lax practices which later are imported into criminal proceedings. In civil proceedings this Court frankly has made the end a test of the means, saying, "To require a greater showing would cripple the Act," United States v. Griffith, 334 U.S. 100, in dispensing with the necessity for specific intent to produce a result violative of the statute. Further, the Court has dispensed with even the necessity to infer any definite agreement, although that is the gist of the offense. "It is elementary that an unlawful conspiracy may be and often is formed without simultaneous action or agreement on the part of the conspirators. * * *" United States v. Masonite Corp., 316 U.S. 265, 275. One might go on from the reports of this and lower courts and put together their decisions condoning absence of proof to demonstrate that the minimum of proof required to establish conspiracy is extremely low, and we may expect our pronouncements in civil cases to be followed in criminal ones also.

Of course, it is for prosecutors rather than courts to determine when to use a scatter-gun to bring down the defendant, but there are procedural advantages from using it which add to the danger of unguarded extension of the concept.

An accused, under the Sixth Amendment, has the right to trial "by an impartial jury of the State and district wherein the crime shall have been committed." The leverage of a conspiracy charge lifts this limitation from the prosecution and reduces its protection to a phantom, for the crime is considered so vagrant as to have been committed in any district where any one of the conspirators did any one of the acts, however, innocent, intended to accomplish its object.[19] The Government may, and often does, compel one to defend at a great distance from any place he ever did any act because some accused confederate did some trivial and by itself innocent act in the chosen

19. Hyde v. United States, 225 U.S. 347. Mr. Justice Holmes, on behalf of himself and Justice Hughes, Lurton and Lamar, wrote a vigorous protest which did not hesitate to brand the doctrine as oppressive and as "one of the wrongs that our forefathers meant to prevent." 225 U.S. 347, 387.

district. Circumstances may even enable the prosecution to fix the place of trial in Washington, D. C., where a defendant may lawfully be put to trial before a jury partly or even wholly made up of employees of the Government that accuses him. Cf. Frazier v. United States, 335 U.S. 497.

When the trial starts, the accused feels the full impact of the conspiracy strategy. Strictly, the prosecution should first establish *prima facie* the conspiracy and identify the conspirators, after which evidence of acts and declarations of each in the course of its execution are admissible against all. But the order of proof of so sprawling a charge is difficult for a judge to control. As a practical matter, the accused often is confronted with a hodgepodge of acts and statements by others which he may never have authorized or intended or even known about, but which help to persuade the jury of existence of the conspiracy itself. In other words, a conspiracy often is proved by evidence that is admissible only upon assumption that conspiracy existed. The naive assumption that prejudicial effects can be overcome by instructions to the jury, cf. Blumenthal v. United States, 332 U.S. 539, 559, all practicing lawyers know to be unmitigated fiction. See Skidmore v. Baltimore & Ohio R. Co., 167 F.2d 54.

The trial of a conspiracy charge doubtless imposes a heavy burden on the prosecution, but it is an especially difficult situation for the defendant. The hazard from loose application of rules of evidence is aggravated where the Government institutes mass trials.[20] Moreover, in federal practice there is no rule preventing conviction on uncorroborated testimony of accomplices, as there are in many jurisdictions, and the most comfort a defendant can expect is that the court can be induced to follow the "better practice" and caution the jury against "too much reliance upon the testimony of accomplices." Caminetti v. United States, 242 U.S. 470, 495.

A co-defendant in a conspiracy trial occupies an uneasy seat. There generally will be evidence of wrongdoing by somebody. It is difficult for the individual to make his own case stand on its own merits in the minds of jurors who are ready to believe that birds of a feather are flocked together. If he is silent, he is taken to admit it and if, as often happens, co-defendants can be prodded into accusing or contradicting each other, they convict each other. There are many practical difficulties in defending against a charge of conspiracy which I will not enumerate.

---

20. An example is afforded by Allen v. United States, 4 F.2d 688. At the height of the prohibition frenzy, seventy-five defendants were tried on charges of conspiracy. A newspaper reporter testified to going to a drinking place where he talked with a woman, behind the bar, whose name he could not give. There was not the slightest identification of her nor showing that she knew or was known by any defendant. But it was held that being back of the bar showed her to be a co-conspirator and, hence, her statements were admissible against all. He was allowed to relate incriminating statements made by her.

Against this inadequately sketched background, I think the decision of this case in the court below introduced an ominous expansion of the accepted law of conspiracy. The prosecution was allowed to incriminate the defendant by means of the prostitute's recital of a conversation with defendant's alleged co-conspirator, who was not on trial. The conversation was said to have taken place after the substantive offense was accomplished, after the defendant, the co-conspirator and the witness had all been arrested, and after the witness and the other two had a falling out.

* * *

It is difficult to see any logical limit to the "implied conspiracy," either as to duration or means, nor does it appear that one could overcome the implication by express and credible evidence that no such understanding existed, nor any way in which an accused against whom the presumption is once raised can terminate the imputed agency of his associates to incriminate him. Conspirators, long after the contemplated offense is complete, after perhaps they have fallen out and become enemies, may still incriminate each other by deliberately harmful, but unsworn declarations, or unintentionally by casual conversations out of court. On the theory that the law will impute to the confederates a continuing conspiracy to defeat justice, one conceivably could be bound by another's unauthorized and unknown commission of perjury, bribery of a juror or witness, or even putting an incorrigible witness with damaging information out of the way.[g]

Moreover, the assumption of an indefinitely continuing offense would result in an indeterminate extension of the statute of limitations. If the law implies an agreement to cooperate in defeating prosecution, it must imply that it continues as long as prosecution is a possibility, and prosecution is a possibility as long as the conspiracy to defeat it is implied to continue.

I do not see the slightest warrant for judicially introducing a doctrine of implied crimes or constructive conspiracies. It either adds a new crime or extends an old one.

* * *

There is, of course, strong temptation to relax rigid standards when it seems the only way to sustain convictions of evildoers. But statutes authorize prosecution for substantive crimes for most evildoing without the dangers to the liberty of the individual and the

g. In Dutton v. Evans, 400 U.S. 74, 91 S.Ct. 210, 27 L.Ed.2d 213 (1970), the Court was presented with the issue of whether a state evidentiary rule permitting the use of declarations made during the concealment phase of a conspiracy violated the right to confrontation guaranteed by the Sixth Amendment. Mr. Justice Stewart writing for himself and three other justices held that although *Krulewitch* remained the position of the federal courts this limitation on the use of co-conspirators' declarations was not constitutionally compelled. Mr. Justice Harlan concurred in the judgment on the grounds that the state statute did not offend the Due Process Clause.

integrity of the judicial process that are inherent in conspiracy charges. We should disapprove the doctrine of implied or constructive crime in its entirety and in every manifestation. And I think there should be no straining to uphold any conspiracy conviction where prosecution for the substantive offense is adequate and the purpose served by adding the conspiracy charge seems chiefly to get procedural advantages to ease the way to conviction.

* * *

---

(1) CONSPIRACY AS A WEAPON AGAINST ORGANIZED CRIME

BLAKEY, ASPECTS OF THE EVIDENCE GATHERING PROCESS IN ORGANIZED CRIME CASES: A PRELIMINARY ANALYSIS, IN TASK FORCE REPORT: ORGANIZED CRIME

80, 81–83 (1967).

The utility of conspiracy theory in the prosecution of organized crime is manifest. No other single substantive legal tool has been as effective in bringing organized crime to book. Nevertheless, a dispassionate examination and analysis of its origin, development and use today leaves a feeling of uneasiness. An almost direct relation seems to exist between its present efficiency and its potential threat to individual liberty.

The exact origin of conspiracy theory in the common law apparently is not known. While it first received legislative recognition as early as 1305,[4] it did not reach full maturity until the 17th century when the criminal law experienced perhaps its greatest growth largely at the hands of the infamous Star Chamber. In 1611, the Star Chamber in the *Poulterers Case*[5] held for the first time that an unexecuted agreement was itself punishable. Emphasis was thus shifted from the substantive crime to the agreement which preceded it. Thereafter, the history of conspiracy theory aptly illustrated, as Mr. Justice Jackson has pointed out, "the tendency of a principle to expand itself to the limit of its logic."

Writing in 1842, Chief Justice Shaw in the leading case of Commonwealth v. Hunt[7] summed up the historical development of conspiracy law and gave to the concept its classic definition: "a combination of two or more persons, by some concerted action, to accomplish some criminal or unlawful purpose, or to accomplish some purpose, not in itself criminal or unlawful, by criminal or unlawful means."

---

4. Ordinance of Conspirators, 1305, 33 Edw. 1.

5. 9 Co.Rep. 55b, 77 Eng.Rep. 813 (Star Chamber 1611).

7. 45 Mass. (4 Met.) 111, 123 (1842).

The development of conspiracy theory in the law constituted an acute recognition by society of the special danger presented by group crime. Division of labor, specialization, anonymity, complexity of organization, continuity of operation, insulation from the normal investigative techniques of law enforcement, enhanced ability to corrupt the processes of law enforcement, and the accumulation of capital and skills are all made possible. There is no question that multiple-party, conspiratorial organized crime presents to society a challenge materially different from incident crime. Conspiracy theory is the attempt of the law to take the measure of that difference.

* * *

Conspiracy theory itself differs little from jurisdiction to jurisdiction. A conspiracy is thought to constitute a continuing crime. Criminal liability thus remains viable during the entire life of any organized criminal activity. While each co-conspirator must be aware of the existence of con-conspirators, he need not know their identity or the exact outlines of the criminal organization. Indeed, it is not necessary that any expressed communication take place between the conspirators. Criminal liability attaches to those on the periphery and reaches into the center of the conspiracy touching the chief figures no matter how hard they might seek to insulate thmselves from overt criminal activity. All members of a criminal organization are thus equally liable for the crime of conspiracy. In addition, concerted criminal activity carries with it vicarious substantive criminal liability. Every party to a conspiracy is liable for any offense committed by a co-conspirator reasonably contemplated by the conspiracy and committed in furtherance of it. Management-level members of a criminal combine may thus be held responsible not only for the crime of conspiracy but also for substantive offenses committed by others in furtherance of it.

All of this may be concretely illustrated by the investigation, prosecution and conviction for compulsory prostitution of Charles "Lucky" Luciano, the head of a criminal syndicate in New York City in the late 1930's. Over a period of years, Luciano gained monopoly control over prostitution in New York. Luciano himself did not take an active part in the daily operation of the business. His organization included such diverse functionaries as "strong arm enforcers," "protection collectors," "booking agents," "keepers of the houses" and the prostitutes themselves. Indeed, Luciano's combine was so large and well set up that it is clear that he did not know all of the people in his organization. In addition, the organization's activities were not limited solely to vice aspects of the business. If arrested, the girls were supplied bail, counsel, and other help in escaping punishment. Ultimately, Luciano's substantive conviction for compulsory prostitution rested on evidence which established his role in the overall conspiracy.

The list of major and minor organized crime figures convicted by utilizing conspiracy theory is long. Indeed, there is no question that existing conspiracy theory is equal to the challenge of organized crime. The failure of the criminal law to meet the challenge of organized crime must be sought elsewhere.

We began this section with the observation that modern conspiracy law poses a danger to individual liberty. The danger does not lie in the theory itself. It lies instead in what is often necessary to do to bring a successful conspiracy prosecution today. Typically, the organized crime conspiracy case must be built largely on circumstantial evidence. Direct evidence or confessions are seldom available. Consequently, trial courts have had to give the prosecution wide latitude in the introduction of evidence if convictions are ever to be obtained. Testimony has been admitted relating to the events occurring prior to the earliest date in the indictment; it has even been admitted when it relates to events occurring prior to the date of the enactment of the statute prohibiting the substantive offense. The only test has been one of remoteness and relevancy. Reviewing courts, moreover, have accorded great discretion to trial courts in admitting such evidence, and once the unlawful agreement has been established, only slight evidence has been held necessary to connect a co-conspirator with the conspiracy. Usually, of course, hearsay testimony cannot be used to show guilt, and an individual can be held criminally responsible only for his own acts. Establish a conspiracy, however, and connect a party with it by such slight independent evidence, and "any act or declaration by one co-conspirator committed in furtherance of the conspiracy and during its pendency is admissible against each co-conspirator."

Again, an individual usually stands trial alone. Fifteen to twenty defendants, however, are not uncommon in the typical conspiracy trial. A great quantity of evidence of wrong-doing is introduced. Little of it in reference to time, place and person deals directly with any single individual. Most of it must be introduced initially under instructions limiting its admissibility until the conspiracy itself has been prima facie established. The danger that an individual will get caught up in an indiscriminate general finding of guilt is real. It is here that the danger to individual liberty lies.

Recognizing this danger, the law has developed a number of devices to minimize or eliminate it. Initially, of course, the decision to bring a multiple-defendant conspiracy prosecution lies with the prosecutor. Today, however, on the Federal level and in New York, Illinois and California, it is possible to move the trial court for a severance and a separate trial. Denying the motion lies in the discretion of the court. Nevertheless, the motion is seldom granted. Indeed, after New York abolished its old rule according a defendant an absolute right to severance in 1926, it was fourteen years before the Court of Appeals reversed a trial court's denial.

Granting a severance seldom works substantial justice. Too often the limited resources of the government dictate the unwisdom of trying each defendant separately. This is particularly true in the case of parties on the periphery of the organization, who should nonetheless be held responsible for their conduct. In addition, the added burden on prosecution witnesses is formidable. It is extremely difficult to secure cooperation in organized crime cases. The prospect of multiple trials virtually guarantees that it will not be secured. A severance also gives to all, save those first tried, virtually complete pretrial criminal discovery, a serious problem in the area of organized crime. Further, multiple trials increase the prospect of inconsistent verdicts, a specter which no system of justice whose impact is significantly didactic can easily ignore.

In addition to severance, other devices are available. Defense counsel, for example, can identify themselves and their client when they participate actively in the trial. A seating chart of the defendants can be given to the jury. It is possible to allow the jury to take notes. Pre-trial stipulations on non-essential matters can be worked out. It is thus not possible to say that the range of techniques is unduly limited.

While it is possible, although difficult, to conduct the multiple defendant conspiracy trial fairly, there is, however, one large area where major improvement could be made: the evidence gathering process itself. Most of the crucial problems now associated with the conspiracy trial—ambiguous circumstantial evidence, possibly suspect accomplice testimony, prejudicial variance where multiple conspiracies are proven, termination of the conspiracy and the issues of the statute of limitations or the co-conspirator declaration rule—are basically evidentiary questions. Defendant and prosecution alike suffer when there are deficiencies in the evidence available. If we can significantly raise the quantity and quality of the evidence available to the prosecution in the types of situations best handled through the device of the conspiracy charge, we can reasonably expect materially to reduce the significance and re-occurrence of these questions. More convictions could not only be secured, but fairly secured. Evaluation of subsequent proposals in this paper in the area of the evidence gathering process, particularly immunity grants and electronic surveillance techniques, should take this into account: the tools have positive civil liberties implications.

NOTE

The special problems posed by mass conspiracy trials is examined at greater length in Wessel, the Conspiracy Charge as a Weapon Against Organized Crime, 38 Notre Dame Lawyer 689 (1963).

(2) An Alternative

STUDY DRAFT OF A PROPOSED FEDERAL CRIMINAL CODE (1970)

§ 1005. Organized Crime Leadership. (Alternative I)

(1) Offense. A person is guilty of leading organized crime if he knowingly organizes, manages, directs, supervises, or finances a criminal syndicate, or knowingly employs violence or intimidation to promote or facilitate its criminal objectives, or with intent to promote or facilitate its criminal objectives furnishes legal, accounting, or other managerial assistance, or intentionally promotes or facilitates its criminal objectives by any act or omission of a public servant in violation of his official duty. No person shall be convicted under this section on the basis of accomplice liability unless he aids or participates in one of the ways herein specified.

(2) Definitions. A criminal syndicate is an association of ten or more persons for engaging on a continuing basis in crimes of the following character: illicit trafficking in narcotics or other dangerous substances, liquor, weapon, or stolen goods; gambling; prostitution; extortion; engaging in a criminal usury business; counterfeiting; bankruptcy or insurance frauds by arson or otherwise; and smuggling. If more than ten persons are so associated, any group of ten or more associates is a "criminal syndicate" although it is or was only a part of a larger association. Association, within the meaning of this section, exists among persons who collaborate in carrying on the criminal operation although:

(a) associates may not know each other's identity;

(b) membership in the association may change from time to time; and

(c) associates may stand in a wholesaler-retailer or other arm's length relationship in an illicit distribution operation.

(3) Grading. The offense is a Class A felony if the number of associates exceeds twenty-five or if the activity of the association embraces Class A or B felonies. Otherwise the offense is a Class B felony.

(4) Attorney General's Certification. No prosecution shall be instituted under this section unless the Attorney General certifies that the nature and scope of the criminal association is of national concern and warrants invocation of the extraordinary sanctions herein provided.

(5) Jurisdiction. There is federal jurisdiction over an offense defined in this section when any crime engaged in by the association is a federal crime.[h]

---

h. This section was deleted from the final draft.

Comment

Traditional conspiracy notions of an agreement of two or more to commit a crime seem outdated when applied to an organized criminal business characterized by specialization of function, continuity of operation with changing personnel and a system of internal laws. Obviously, provisions such as this section which make for severe penalties against leaders of criminal syndicates will not alone solve the problem of organized crime; but it may be a significant step forward. An alternative approach is to provide extended sentences for ordinary crimes committed through large criminal syndicates, as in proposed § 3203. A current Senate bill, The Organized Crime Control Act of 1969 (S. 30), adopts the sentencing procedure. Arguments favoring that alternative include: the factors which warrant imposition of more severe penalties than in the case of an ordinary offender relate more to issues involved in treatment than issues involved in the determination of criminal liability; the sentencing process permits greater flexibility with respect to proof and to changing circumstances, i. e., organized crime moves, from time-to-time, into new fields of operation; consideration of some of these factors at the trial may unduly prejudice determination of guilt as to the underlying crime.
* * *

Arguments favoring this section include: circumstances which warrant imposition of the severe penalties prescribed should be specifically defined by the Congress, and their availability should result from jury findings made in the usual manner and under traditional standards; definition as a specific crime may raise the level of deterrence.

A possible middle ground is the establishment of a two-stage trial, analogous to that proposed for imposition of the death penalty. See provisional Chapter 36 and comment thereto, infra.

It should be noted that none of the several methods for enhancement of penalties for organized crime leadership is warranted if the maximum authorized for the underlying offense is set at an exceptionally high level in order to reach such conduct upon conviction of that offense alone.

Note that the culpability required in subsection (1) differs for different kinds of activity: for the organizers, enforcers and others who run the syndicate the required culpability is knowledge of the scope and criminal objectives; for the lawyers and other managerial assistants, the corrupted public servants and those who corrupt them, the required culpability is intent to promote the business. The last sentence of subsection (1) is designed to preclude criminal liability as full accomplices of the leaders for those who work for the business as underlings.

To provide greater flexibility "criminal syndicate" could be defined, in subsection (2), without reference to specific crimes; but, without such specification, many business crimes without organized crime connections would be covered, e. g., housing code violations, truck overloading.

The federal jurisdictional base proposed in the draft is the fact that the association commits a federal crime. Jurisdiction therefore depends upon the jurisdictional base or bases provided for that crime. This offense could also have any or all of the bases listed in § 201, e. g., use of interstate facilities, affecting commerce, etc.; or, upon appropriate findings by the Congress, e. g., that such syndicates do have an effect on interstate or foreign commerce, even when their operations are essentially local, jurisdiction could be plenary.

---

d. VALUES AND DANGERS OF USE OF THE CONSPIRACY DOCTRINES

UNITED STATES v. BUFALINO

United States Court of Appeals for the Second Circuit, 1960.
285 F.2d 408.

LUMBARD, Chief Judge. Russell Bufalino and nineteen co-defendants appeal from judgments of conviction in the Southern District of New York for conspiring to obstruct justice and commit perjury (18 U.S.C.A. §§ 371, 1503, 1621) by giving, before federal grand juries, false and evasive testimony regarding a gathering attended by them and at least 39 others at the home of Joseph Barbara, Sr., in Apalachin, New York, on November 14, 1957. Named as members of the conspiracy were seven other co-defendants and 36 co-conspirators. The appellants were all sentenced to prison terms running from three to five years, and in addition thirteen of them were each fined $10,-000.

The indictment, the charging part of which is set forth in the margin, alleged a conspiracy from November 14, 1957, the date of the Apalachin gathering, to the filing of the indictment on May 13, 1959. The 29 overt acts of the indictment which the court submitted to the jury charged that pursuant to the conspiracy various conspirators made statements and gave testimony under oath at different stated places and times from November 14, 1957 to May 11, 1959, including testimony on eleven occasions before federal grand juries in the Southern District of New York.

The indictment did not allege what the November 14, 1957 gathering at Apalachin was about, and the government stated at the beginning of the trial that it could present no evidence of its purpose. There is nothing in the record of the trial to show that any violation of federal or state law took place or was planned at the gathering, although federal grand juries in the Southern and Western Districts of New York on twenty occasions over the following year and one-half, and a variety of other federal and state officials on numerous other occasions, questioned many of those present about the Apalachin gathering and the surrounding circumstances.

* * *

I

The government contends that the November 14 gathering was planned in advance; that when those present became aware that law-enforcement officers had discovered the assemblage they thought there might be an investigation and immediately agreed to give false, fictitious and evasive accounts of the circumstances of the gathering to official inquiries, including formal proceedings calling for sworn testimony; and that when some were summoned before federal grand juries inquiring into the nature of the gathering, they testified falsely pursuant to the agreement. The government's claim was that "the participants gave false and evasive accounts as to the planning and purpose of the meeting and the circumstances and reasons for their presence, all of which were basically similar in that they were calculated to explain away the meeting as a mere coincidental gathering."

The government's proof of the agreement consisted entirely of testimony by state and federal officers regarding unsworn statements made by the conspirators on November 14 and on numerous occasions thereafter and of excerpts from official records of sworn statements made after November 14. The defendants did not take the stand and offered no evidence to counter the government's contention that they had conspired. The government's theory is that the similarity of the statements, insofar as "they all deny planning and seek to concoct a picture of accidental and coincidental presence at Barbara's," and insofar as most of them explain the visits as motivated by concern for Barbara's illness, can be accounted for only if there was an agreement on November 14, 1957.

The government claimed that the conspiracy was formed between 12:40 P.M. on November 14, when Barbara's wife saw the officers' unmarked car in the driveway, and 1:20 P.M. when a mass exodus from Barbara's home began. The court charged the jury that in order to find that any defendant was a member of the conspiracy it would have to conclude that he "willingly entered" the conspiracy sometime before midnight on November 14, at which time the officers completed their questioning of the alleged conspirators at the state police barracks at Vestal.

A. The Events on November 14

At 12:40 P.M. on November 14, Sergeant Edgar Croswell of the New York State Police, accompanied by another state trooper and two agents of the Alcohol and Tobacco Tax Unit of the U. S. Treasury

Department, drove from a public road into the parking lot in front of Barbara's garage. Barbara's home was an estate of 130 acres in a rural section, and his house and garage were on a dead-end dirt road. After recording the license numbers of some of the eight or ten cars in the lot and observing several unidentified men, they drove away. Before leaving, however, Croswell noticed four or five men walking or running toward the house and saw at least 20 other cars parked away from the house. At 12:50, Croswell and his companions parked their car half a mile from Barbara's home and set up what amounted to a roadblock.

When Croswell backed out of the Barbara driveway Mrs. Barbara saw his car and exclaimed, in the hearing of her maid, "There's the state troopers." A few minutes later Ignatius Cannone drove past the roadblock on his way to Barbara's. At about 1:15, Bartolo Guccia, in his pick-up truck, drove down from Barbara's past the parked police car and returned five minutes later. The jury could have concluded that Cannone and Guccia reported what they had seen, and that Guccia had been sent down the road to investigate.

During the next few hours, 58 men were stopped and asked to identify themselves. Of these, 35 were more or less perfunctorily questioned by state troopers, occasionally assisted by federal officers. At 1:20 P.M. Emanuel Zicari and Dominic Alaimo drove past the roadblock and were stopped, on radioed instructions from Croswell, by other officers and asked to identify themselves. Next came Russell Bufalino in his Chrysler Imperial with Joseph Ida, Gerardo Catena, Dominick Oliveto and Vito Genovese. Upon being stopped at the roadblock, they all identified themselves. Bufalino said that he had come to visit his sick friend, Barbara. Vito Genovese remarked that he understood that he did not have to say anything and he said nothing. Ida, Catena, and Oliveto said nothing about the meeting and apparently were not asked about it. Other cars, driven by Joseph Magliocco, John Ormento, Pasquale Turrigiano, Anthony Riela, Pasquale Monachino, Joseph Falcone, Vincent Rao, Joseph Barbara, Jr., Cannone and Guccia, were stopped in the next few minutes. Passengers in these cars were Joseph Profaci, Sam Monachino, Pasquale Sciortino, Anthony Guarnieri, Salvatore Falcone, Rosario Mancuso, Dominick D'Agostino and Sam Lagattuta.

After it began to rain, at about 2:30 P.M., the officers took those stopped at the roadblock to the Vestal barracks located about seven miles away. So treated were Santo Trafficante, James Osticco, Frank DeSimone, Joseph Civello, Simone Scozzari, Joseph Rosato, Natale Evola, Frank Cucchiara, Carmine Lombardozzi, Joseph Riccobono, Paul Castellano, Carlo Gambino, Michele Miranda, Armand Rava, Constanza Valenti, Frank Valenti, Angelo Sciandra, Charles Chiri, Mike Genovese, Gabriel Mannarino, and Salvatore Tornabe.

At about 1:45 P.M., A.T.U. agent Brown had seen eight or ten men walking in single file toward some woods and pastures behind

Barbara's house, and A.T.U. agent Ruston had seen three or four running in the open away from the house. Four of these men were apprehended in the fields—John Montana, Antonio Magaddino, Joseph Bonanno and Giovanni Bonventre. Between 2 and 2:30 P.M., a villager named Glen Craig saw Frank Majuri and Louis Larasso hitch-hiking about three quarters of a mile from Barbara's and he gave them a ride. Agent Brown stopped Craig's car at about 3:00 P.M. and took Majuri and Larasso to the barracks. A New York State trooper found Frank Zito on the stoop of a house about a mile from Barbara's, and James Colletti was found nearby. These eight and Roy Carlisi, John DeMarco, James LaDuca and John Scalish, on whom the record is not clear as to where they were apprehended, were also taken to the Vestal barracks for questioning.

B.   The Statements Made on November 14
and Thereafter

Of the 58 men who were stopped by the officers on November 14, only 36 were then questioned beyond mere identification, and of these only 27 then gave some explanation for their presence in the area. None of them suggested that they had been invited to a gathering for other than social purposes and only three said that they had been invited at all. The most common explanation, given in one form or another by ten was that the purpose of the visit was to call upon Barbara, a sick friend. Eleven gave other explanations for their visit to Barbara's. Of these, three said they were invited to a party by Bufalino; three gave personal business reasons; two claimed that they came along with others for the trip; one, Profaci, said that he was visiting an old friend; one, Magaddino, stated that his companion's car had broken down nearby; and one, Guarnieri, insisted that he came for a good meal. Six denied being at Barbara's, and gave some other reason for their presence in the area.

Of the 58 men identified on November 14, forty-three were questioned after that date and of these 35 then gave some explanation for their presence in the Apalachin area. Most of the Apalachin visitors were questioned both on November 14 and on later occasions, many of them several times.

As on November 14, none stated that he had been invited for other than social purposes. Again, the most common explanation, given by fourteen, was that the purpose of the visit was to call upon a sick friend or to accompany someone doing so. A related explanation was given by one, Castellano, who said he had accompanied a relative who wanted to see Barbara to discuss a similar heart condition. Nineteen gave other explanations for their visit to Barbara's. Of these, seven said that they had a personal business reason for coming; three said that they had been invited to a party; two that they had accompanied friends on business trips; two that their car had broken down; one, Zicari, that he came to see a friend; one,

Riccobono, that he went for a ride; and one, Lombardozzi, that he came to hunt. Three denied being at Barbara's and gave some other reason for their presence in the area.

C. The Insufficiency of the Evidence

The government introduced enough evidence to justify a finding that Barbara had made preparations for a large gathering for other than social purposes and that some, if not most, of these present had been invited to attend. The government contends that the common thread which can be traced through all the alleged conspirators' stories is their concealment of the fact that a meeting was planned in advance. From this the government argues that in the 40 minutes from 12:40 to 1:20 P.M. there must have been an agreement on the part of some to obstruct justice by giving false and evasive testimony to the effect the meeting was not planned and that before midnight of the same day the other alleged conspirators associated themselves with the venture. We disagree.

The fact that none of those present admitted that he was asked to attend a meeting for other than social purposes and that at least some of those present must have lied, does not warrant a jury's conclusion that any or all lies were told pursuant to an agreement made on November 14. There is nothing in the record or in common experience to suggest that it is not just as likely that each one present decided for himself that it would be wiser not to discuss all that he knew.

* * *

If a precisely similar explanation in support of a claim of casual attendance had been given by those present, rather than statements similar only in that they denied that presence was planned, this would be some evidence of agreement. But in our view the similarity of the stories told is insignificant under all the circumstances. Only a minority relied to any degree on Barbara's illness but even this is of little weight since Joseph Barbara, Sr., had in fact been suffering from a severe heart ailment from which he died before the trial.

* * *

II

We conclude also that there was not sufficient evidence for the jury to find that the defendants knew or should have known on November 14 that they would be called to testify under oath concerning the Apalachin gathering.

* * *

III

Although the insufficiencies of proof dispose of these appeals, we feel it appropriate to comment on several other features of the prosecution and trial of this case. Since the jury was instructed that it would have had to find, as to each defendant, that he did, in fact, lie, in order to number him among the conspirators, it had to consider the truth of each defendant's story separately. There was ample basis for the jury to conclude that some, if not most, of the stories were false since it is extremely unlikely that such a number of men would convene uninvited, some from distant places, on a weekday, in a secluded country town. It is fallacious, however, to reason that the falsity of most stories establishes the falsity of each; and improper to permit the jury to substitute a feeling of collective culpability for a finding of individual guilt.

As appears from our discussion, the government's case rested on the jury's consideration of the many statements made by those present at Barbara's on November 14. The jury had to evaluate what 59 (Joseph Barbara, Sr. and the 58 who were identified) men did on November 14, and, in addition, had to analyze the testimony of 84 witnesses, many of whom testified to statements of the alleged conspirators. In addition the jury had before it sworn testimony in question-and-answer form taken before various governmental bodies including the New York State Liquor Authority, the United States Immigration and Naturalization Service, and grand juries both state and federal. We have found the analysis and the comparison of these statements most difficult; it is virtually impossible to keep them separately in mind and to weigh them without considerable study and without voluminous notes and indices.[24] Courts have long indulged in the somewhat naive supposition that jurors can properly assess such evidence and determine from it the individual guilt of each of many defendants, even when aided by a careful summary of the evidence such as Judge Kaufman gave here. This makes it especially important for trial and appellate courts to determine the sufficiency of the evidence as to each defendant in mass conspiracy trials. Cf. Developments in the Law: Criminal Conspiracy, 72 Harv.L.Rev. 920, 980–83 (1953); Note, The Conspiracy Dilemma: Prosecution of Group Crime or Protection of Individual Defendants, 62 Harv.L.Rev. 276, 284 (1948).

The flimsiness of the evidence against appellant Cannone and co-conspirator Guccia demonstrates the danger of a shotgun conspiracy charge aimed at everyone who gave an explanation inconsistent with the government's suspicion of the purpose of the gathering. Both Cannone and Guccia were residents of Apalachin. According to undisputed evidence, both were old friends of Barbara and frequently visited him. The explanations they gave were in no way implausible and did not refer to a visit to a sick friend. Cannone, who arrived at 12:55 P.M., after the police had set up their roadblock, stated that he had come to get advice about the purchase of equip-

---

24. The jury's request for the testimony of Ormento at Vestal, when there was no evidence that he had ever been there, is a striking example of these difficulties. * * *

ment for his bar. He concededly managed a tavern nearby and Barbara's business interests were along similar lines. Guccia said that he had come to sell some fish. There was no testimony given by anyone else which even suggested that these explanations were false. Indeed there was not a shred of evidence, even giving weight to the hearsay aspect of the numerous statements before the jury, to show that Cannone and Guccia did not visit for the reasons given; there was no possible basis for concluding that they conspired with anyone to give false explanations about their visit or that they had any motive for falsifying.

We must suppose that the jury convicted a defendant such as Cannone, and that the government named individuals such as Guccia as co-conspirators, only on the theory that everyone at Barbara's was a participant in some illegal activity and that all had an interest in concealing what could not be proven. The danger of sweeping within the net of such a conspiracy an innocent visitor whose honestly told story may in its omissions have coincided with some falsehold told by others calls for special precautions in this type of case.

Moreover, the government here charges the defendants with a conspiracy to commit perjury proved solely by evidence of lying without attempting to prove that the underlying substantive crime has been committed. It should not be forgotten that where the government charges the crime of perjury the law requires the testimony of two witnesses, or at least evidence stronger than the mere word of one man against another.

In this case the government circumvents the salutary requirements of proof in perjury cases in two respects. In the first place, with respect to all the November 14 statements, and most of the statements made thereafter, the alleged lies were not told under oath or under circumstances where the truth was required. Secondly, the government was not required to prove, and did not prove, by the traditional perjury standard that any single witness before a grand jury lied as any material matter. Moreover, the government has not even been required to make a specification of what the claimed perjury was as to any particular witness.

We doubt the advisability of requiring that the government meet any absolute standards in conspiracy cases. At the same time we cannot state too strongly our view that it is incumbent on trial judges, in deciding whether the government has made out a sufficient case to go to the jury, to analyze with meticulous care the evidence as to each defendant. When this is not done, it is the duty of the appellate courts to act. Cases such as this prove all too well the need for the caution which from time to time has been articulated by the Supreme Court with respect to the indiscriminate indictment of numerous defendants in conspiracy cases. What Mr. Justice Jackson, joined by Justices Frankfurter and Murphy, warned against in his concurrence in Krulewitch v. United States, 1949, 336 U.S. 440, 449–454, 69 S.Ct.

716, 93 L.Ed. 790, anticipates the disturbing features of this case. See also Yates v. United States, 1957, 354 U.S. 298, 330 n. 36, 77 S.Ct. 1064, 1 L.Ed.2d 1356.

The government is not without resources to make inquiry about matters of possible public concern. If false testimony is given under oath a prosecution for perjury may be brought. Even those who block the road by asserting their rights under the Fifth Amendment may, under many statutes, be compelled to answer as they thereby become immune from prosecution regarding the matters concerning which they are forced to talk. If, after having received immunity, such witnesses testify falsely they may still be prosecuted for perjury. If they refuse to testify they may be committed for contempt.

The administration of our system of criminal justice and our basic concepts of fair dealing are centered on the requirement that in each case we reach a result based solely on the charges made in the particular indictment and on the evidence which appears on the record with regard to those charges. Doubtless many of Barbara's visitors are bad people, and it is surely a matter of public concern that more is not known of their activities. But bad as many of these alleged conspirators may be, their conviction for a crime which the government could not prove, on inferences no more valid than others equally supported by reason and experience, and on evidence which a jury could not properly assess, cannot be permitted to stand.

Reversed and remanded with directions to dismiss the conspiracy count of the indictment.

UNITED STATES v. COLASURDO

United States Court of Appeals for the Second Circuit, 1971.
453 F.2d 585.

OAKES, Circuit Judge:

* * *

[This case involved an extraordinarily complex scheme to gain control of Crescent Corporation's assets. In essence, the defendants, charged with conspiracy to defraud the government and the Securities and Exchange Commission, borrowed the money of Crescent in order to purchase control of it. This was achieved by the sale of an asset— a blueberry plantation—owned by Pakco Companies, Inc., which was controlled by defendants, to Crescent through four, rapid-fire sham transactions. It was the prosecution's theory that the scheme could not succeed without concealing the true nature of the transactions from the SEC and the stockholders and creditors and that the defendants conspired to this end.]

Appellants further contend that there was insufficient evidence to support a conviction under the conspiracy count in that there was no direct evidence of an agreement to conspire to defraud the SEC. They rely upon Grunewald v. United States [353 U.S. 391, 77 S.Ct. 963, 1 L.Ed.2d 931 (1957)]; Krulewitch v. United States, 336 U.S. 440, 69 S.Ct. 716, 93 L.Ed. 790 (1949), and United States v. Bufalino, 285 F.2d 408 (2d Cir. 1960). These cases stand for the proposition that "[a]cts of covering up, even though done in the context of a mutually understood need for secrecy, cannot themselves constitute proof that concealment of the crime after its commission was part of the initial agreement among the conspirators." *Grunewald*, supra, 353 U.S. at 402, 77 S.Ct. at 972. But here of course the concealment was the essence of the object of the conspiracy—concealment from the SEC of the use of a Pakco asset to accomplish the Crescent takeover was the very aim of the sham transactions in which the conspirators engaged. Filing false statements with, and submitting false testimony to, the SEC were means of furthering that aim, since both Pakco and Crescent were publicly owned and required to disclose to the SEC transactions such as were engaged in here.

After examining the evidence concerning the series of transfers of the blueberry plantation and the reports thereon, the court rejected the defendants' contentions.

In other words, there was direct evidence of acts of concealment of a continuing conspiracy in which concealment was not only essential to the success of the scheme but was the very heart and object of it. Forman v. United States, 361 U.S. 416, 421–422 n. 5, 80 S.Ct. 481, 4 L.Ed.2d 412 (1960). We read *Grunewald*, supra, Lutwak v. United States, 344 U.S. 604, 73 S.Ct. 481, 97 L.Ed. 593 (1953), and *Krulewitch*, supra, as did the Supreme Court in Ingram v. United States, 360 U.S. 672, 679 n. 10, 79 S.Ct. 1314, 1319, 3 L.Ed.2d 1503 (1959):

> The Court's decisions in Grunewald v. United States, Lutwak v. United States, and Krulewitch v. United States, do not, as petitioners appear to contend, prevent the jury from treating this subsidiary objective [secrecy] as an element of the conspiracy. Those cases hold only that the life of the conspiracy cannot be extended by evidence of concealment after the conspiracy's criminal objectives have been fully accomplished. (Citations omitted.)

Here, unlike United States v. Bufalino, 285 F.2d 408 (2d Cir. 1960), the statements and acts of the appellants were similar in that they each attempted to convey to the SEC that Pakco-Crescent acquisition transactions were in each instance at arm's length and good faith business dealings, not shams to keep the SEC from discovery of the true acquirer, the true means of acquisition and the true facts surrounding the acquisition. In the Form 8–k and 10–k Crescent reports, Colasurdo and Whorl disclosed enough to mislead the SEC with half-truths and concealed the key facts underlying the transactions (Colasurdo's ownership of ALCA, BLCB's purchase, involvement of the Pakco blueberry plantation, the purchase of the blueberry plantation from Pakco and Colasurdo's interest in the transaction).

UNITED STATES v. CALARCO

United States Court of Appeals for the Second Circuit, 1970.
424 F.2d 657.

ANDERSON, Circuit Judge. John Calarco, Frank Gilfone and Teddia Riviello appeal from their convictions upon jury verdicts of guilty of conspiring to steal a truck containing an interstate shipment of merchandise and of the substantive offense of stealing the truck, in violation of 18 U.S.C.A. §§ 371, 659 and 2. We affirm.

There were eight co-conspirators named in the indictment, among whom there was a confessed hijacker of wide experience, named Roland Warren, who was the chief witness for the Government. Of the others, three entered guilty pleas before trial, and the appeal of a fourth, who was convicted with the appellants Calarco, Gilfone and Riviello, has been dismissed.

There was evidence from which the jury could find the following facts: On December 14, 1966, Warren met with David Tronco and Philip Garretson in a bar in Newark to discuss hijacking a truck which made a regular journey from a New Jersey railroad yard into Manhattan, loaded with television sets and phonographs. Tronco said he knew "people in Jersey City" who would be interested in buying the shipment; and he telephoned the appellant Calarco, who joined the other three at the bar. Calarco then asked the others to accompany him across town to talk to "the people that was going to get the load of televisions."

Calarco, Warren, Tronco and Garretson joined James Matthews, who had been waiting outside the bar in Tronco's Thunderbird automobile, and drove to the Democrat Club, another bar. Calarco went inside alone, explaining that he was going to talk to "the buyer." After about an hour, Tronco went to get Calarco, who came out and told the other four in the car that he and they would follow "these people"—indicating two individuals emerging from the Democrat Club. Calarco told the others he "wanted to show [them] where to bring the truck" after the hijacking.

Those in the Thunderbird then followed a Buick, driven by the appellant Riviello, who was accompanied by an unidentified man, to a location on the McCarter Highway, near Fourth Avenue in Newark. Both cars stopped there and turned off their lights, with the Thunderbird directly behind the Buick. Calarco got out, went over to the Buick, and spoke with Riviello for about fifteen minutes. As Calarco was returning, a police patrol car was approaching, but he got back into the Thunderbird and said, "When you get the truck this is where you are going to bring it, bring it here." At that point, the police arrived and required the occupants of both cars to identify themselves. Riviello explained to an officer that he was just giving the people in the other car directions to Jersey City, and he departed. Tronco and

Warren were arrested when it was discovered that traffic warrants were outstanding against them. They were shortly released on bail provided by Calarco, who told Warren that the money had come from Riviello.

Notwithstanding this unforeseen interruption, members of the group reassembled early on the morning of December 16, at Calarco's apartment in Jersey City, to make detailed plans for the hijacking. Those present were Calarco, Warren, Garretson, Matthews, Tronco, and a new addition to the group, John Orangio. It was here agreed that Tronco would approach the driver of the target truck when he boarded the ferry to Manhattan sometime around 5 a. m. that same day and ask for a ride. He was further instructed to draw a gun, provided by Calarco, when the truck had disembarked and reached a point some five blocks away from the ferry in Manhattan, and at that time to order the driver out of the cab. The plan then called for another member of the group to pull alongside the truck in a car, stolen for this purpose, and to take the driver in it to some suitably distant point before releasing him. In the meantime, Warren was to arrive in still another car alongside the stolen truck and drive it to the Tunnel Diner outside the Holland Tunnel in Jersey City, where Calarco would meet him and give further instructions. Calarco gave one of the members. of the group the phone number of a motel room in which he, Calarco, would be waiting for notification that Warren was on his way to the diner with the truck.

Tronco succeeded in hitching a ride with the truck driver, one Calanders Cherry; but from that point on, everything went wrong for the hijackers. Matthews was left behind in the washroom of a New Jersey diner when his companions and the ferry suddenly departed. Tronco then pulled the gun on Cherry when the truck was barely out of sight of the Manhattan ferry slip. Rather than surrender the truck, Cherry put up a fight, which delayed things until Garretson arrived in the stolen car and helped to subdue him. While Tronco and Garretson drove Cherry to Yonkers, members of the group following in another car approached the truck. They decided, however, that completion of the robbery had become impossible because several construction workers were standing near the prematurely-seized truck. They, therefore, simply left it standing on West Street, with its engine running. One of them called Calarco to tell him the news, and they returned to New Jersey.

When Warren got back to the diner, he found Calarco, the appellant Gilfone, and an unidentified man waiting outside. The four of them and Orangio drove back to Manhattan to see if the truck might yet be driven away; but when they found a number of people milling around it, they gave up.

Calarco and Warren went back to the Democrat Club in Newark, and Calarco went inside for a few moments. When he came out, he told Warren that Tronco, following his abduction of Cherry, got in touch with Riviello and learned that his premature action had frustrated the attempt to get the truck back to New Jersey. Tronco then said to Riviello that he would finish the job himself, and meet "those two guys" at a new rendezvous point on Route 46. Calarco told Warren that the two of them must go to the unloading place on Route 46 to warn Gilfone, and the unidentified person with him, that a police trap was now suspected. Meanwhile, Tronco and Garretson had returned from Yonkers to the truck, which, after several hours, was still parked on West Street with its engine running.

The police, whom Cherry had called from Yonkers, found the truck and staked out the area around it. They apparently saw Tronco approach the truck around 9 a. m., but when a detective went after him, he fled. Garretson came to Tronco's rescue in the stolen automobile, and the two of them made their escape down the street as the detective fired five shots into the car. But they were not destined to drive very far. No sooner had they eluded the detective than Garretson crashed the getaway car into another automobile while attempting to avoid a double-parked truck a block and one-half away. Both Garretson and Tronco were arrested as they attempted to flee on foot.

Riviello and Calarco, after their arrest, both waived their rights to remain silent. They were shown photographs of some of the others who were being held in connection with the offense, but Riviello denied knowing Calarco, and Calarco denied knowing either Riviello, Warren, Garretson or Gilfone.

All of those indicted who did not plead guilty were convicted after being tried; and Calarco and Riviello were each sentenced to concurrent terms of five years for conspiracy and ten years on conviction of the substantive theft offense. Gilfone received concurrent prison terms of four years on each of the two counts.

Riviello argues in his appeal that the evidence was insufficient to establish either his participation in the conspiracy or that he aided and abetted the theft itself. The only connection shown between these events and him, he alleges, was his "mere presence" with the others at the McCarter Highway site. He claims that all the other testimony involving him consisted only of hearsay statements by various conspirators.

As has been many times stated, the rule is that before the jury may be permitted to consider other conspirators' hearsay utterances in furtherance of the conspiracy as a means of determining a particular defendant's guilt beyond a reasonable doubt, the trial judge must first conclude from all the evidence that the defendant in question has been shown to be a member of that conspiracy "by a fair preponderance of the evidence independent of the hearsay utterances." United States v. Geaney, 417 F.2d 1116 (2 Cir. Nov. 6, 1969). The non-hearsay evidence linking Riviello to the conspiracy in this case included not just his "mere presence" at a certain site, but also his acts of leading the others from the Democrat Club to that location and there relaying instructions to them through Calarco.[1] This was sufficient for the trial judge to conclude that Riviello was a participant in the conspiracy and that hearsay statements of his co-conspirators in furtherance of the conspiracy were admissible against him. United States v. Nuccio, 373 F.2d 168, 173–174 (2 Cir.), cert. denied, 387 U.S. 906, 87 S.Ct. 1688, 18 L.Ed.2d 623 (1967).

* * *

The judgments are affirmed.

DOOLING, District Judge (dissenting in part).

It would appear that Riviello is entitled to a new trial.

When the Government rested, Riviello strenuously argued for acquittal on the ground that the evidence *aliunde* and independent of hearsay declarations about him made in his absence was insufficient to warrant submission of the case to the jury. The trial judge ruled that under the doctrine of United States v. Nuccio, 373 F.2d 168 (2 Cir.), the evidence sufficed. When all parties rested Riviello again moved for acquittal, the trial judge reserved decision, and then charged the jury.

After defining conspiracy as including the element of the defendants' knowingly associating themselves with the conspiracy, the Court charged that if the jury concluded that the conspiracy did exist, it had then to determine separately for each defendant whether he participated in it and did so with knowledge of its unlawful purpose. The court then charged

> "In determining whether or not the defendant knowingly joined the conspiracy you should examine and consider all the evidence in the case, including the acts *and statements* of the defendant under consideration as well as the acts *and statements* of other persons with whom that defendant is alleged to have conspired" (italics supplied)

---

1. Warren testified that Calarco walked back to the Thunderbird after holding a conversation with Riviello, in Warren's sight and only a few feet away, and that Calarco then said "this is where you are going to bring [the truck]." This testimony was not hearsay as to Riviello, because Warren's testimony about Calarco's statement was not offered in this context to show the truth of either Calarco's suggestion that the McCarter Highway location was a suitable one for de-livery of the truck or Warren's own assertion that Calarco's statement concerned delivery of a truck. The fact that Riviello gave an instruction relayed to the other conspirators at this point in their planning of the hijacking was relevant and admissible independent of its contents, as a nonhearsay "verbal act." See United States v. Lopez, 420 F.2d 313, 318 (2 Cir. Dec. 1, 1969); United States v. Geaney, supra, 417 F.2d p. 1120, fn. 3 and 4.

and the Court then went on to other parts of the charge. Before the jury retired, Riviello's counsel excepted in the following language

> "I think, your Honor, whether the request is made or not, failed to charge this jury that where a person is sought to become a member of a conspiracy he should be adjudged by his own independent acts or statements that he makes. It is not enough to limit it to only those cases where he knowingly and wilfully joins a conspiracy with knowledge of it. The cases hold that in order to seek one to become a member of a conspiracy it must be done by what he himself says or does aliunde or independent of any declarations or admissions or statements made by an alleged co-conspirator. I spent a great deal of time on that in my summation to the jury and I think, and I think in fairness to Riviello and Gilfone that should be charged."

The Court, however, stated "I believe I have charged exactly in accordance with the prevailing rule in the Second Circuit." The Court, plainly, bowed to the line of cases, given their evidently definitive expression in United States v. Geaney, 1969, 417 F.2d 1116, 1119–1121 * * * The Court did not give Riviello's belated request No. 39: it posed an opposite view: that the jury must review the adequacy of the "independent" evidence to implicate a defendant in the conspiracy separately, and may not consider evidence of verbal acts ("hearsay declarations") attributed to and implicating him that took place out of his presence in deciding whether or not the Government has proved the conspiracy and his complicity beyond a reasonable doubt. The requested charge was based on a charge of Judge Weinfeld in United States v. Galgano, that if the jury found a conspiracy, it had then to determine whether each defendant joined it by evaluating the evidence "without regard to, and independently of, the statements, acts or declarations of others." The requested charge told the jury that out-of-court declarations or admissions received against the persons who made them were received "on a conditional or tentative basis" with respect to absent defendants "subject to independent proof of the existence of the conspiracy, and such absent defendants' knowing participation in the conspiracy." The requested charge continued:

> "In other words, the alleged participation by a defendant in the conspiracy cannot be established against him by the acts and declarations of any of his alleged co-conspirators done or made *in his absence*. A defendant's connection with the conspiracy must be established by independent proof based upon the reasonable inferences to be drawn from such defendant's own actions, his own conduct, his own testimony or declarations, his own connection with the actions and conduct of the other alleged co-conspirators.

"Each defendant's acts and declarations may be evidence of his own connection with the conspiracy and the conspiracy may be proved by the sum total of the independent acts and declarations of all the alleged participants.

"However, once you are satisfied beyond a reasonable doubt that a conspiracy existed and that a defendant on trial was a member of the conspiracy, using the test of independent proof, I have described, then the acts and declarations of any one of the other persons whom you may find was also a member of the conspiracy, made during the pendency of the conspiracy and in furtherance of its objectives are considered the acts of all of the others, even though they were not present."

As to Judge Weinfeld's charge see United States v. Carminati, 2d Cir. 1957, 247 F.2d 640, 644-645. See in the general context United States v. Elgisser, 2d Cir. 1964, 334 F.2d 103, 107.

The view of the cases from *VanRiper* through *Lopez* is now so deeply rooted in Second Circuit law, that to note a dissent may be futile; indeed, the contrary doctrine has been criticized by some commentators,[1] and the Second Circuit's decisions have been followed elsewhere (see, e. g., Carbo v. United States, 9th Cir. 1963, 314 F.2d 718, 735-738). Although the practice of giving the conditional form of instruction may be fairly widespread, appellate support for the propriety and necessity of the practice is uncertain and to an extent of a negative cast.

The admissibility against absent defendants of evidence of "declarations of co-conspirators in furtherance of the conspiracy" depends on whether the words themselves were tools used to effectuate a criminal act. They are not admissible for their narrative content but for their constitutive role—as "verbal acts." The merely narrative utterance is inadmissible, and evidence of a "verbal act" is not received for its spurious value as narrative implicating an absent de-

---

1. Cf. Maguire and Epstein Preliminary Questions of Fact in Determining the Admissibility of Evidence, 1927, 40 Harv.L.Rev. 392, 397, fn. 19, 415–424 (condemning theory that court should rule only preliminarily on admissibility and then "pass the question of admissibility along to the jury for their determination," pages 420–421); Morgan, Functions of Judge and Jury in the Determination of Questions of Fact, 1929, 43 Harv.L.Rev. 165, 176 (to believe jurors will reject heard evidence if unable to find a fact which determines its relevancy "requires a credulity impossible to achieve"; such approach furnishes "the defendant an opportunity to entrap an unwary trial judge"); cf. Developments in the Law, Criminal Conspiracy, 1959, 72 Harv.L.Rev. 920, 987 (noting that if declarations are thought logically admissible only if independent evidence connects defendant with the conspiracy, yet the evidence is conditionally admitted and the issue passed to the jury, the provisionally admitted evidence may in fact be used to support the *prima facie* case, hearsay thus lifting itself by its own boot straps to the level of competency, and that where that practice prevails, "the requirement of independent evidence is virtually meaningless").

fendant. If an utterance is a verbal act, its evidentiary significance depends not on its truth or falsity—that is beside the point—but upon its function in the commission of the crime. In some circumstances —and may not the present case be one?—a black lie about the absent defendant's role and orders would be the most efficacious utterance to advance the crime (cf. *Geaney*, supra, 417 F.2d at 1121, fn. 4) and the most damning if treated as competent evidence of the complicity of the absent defendant.

The cases which have evolved to climax in *Geaney*, have not suggested that the declarations are competent evidence of the absent defendant's complicity.[2] They explicitly preserve the idea that the Court must keep the case from the jury unless satisfied that the prosecution has proved participation "by a fair preponderance of the evidence independent of the hearsay utterances." United States v. Geaney, supra, 417 F.2d at 1120. *Geaney* is, none the less, pellucid that the jury is not only not to be instructed that it must find from the "independent" evidence beyond a reasonable doubt that the defendant was implicated in the crime before considering the hearsay declarations as part of the total proofs, but that the jury is to be freed affirmatively to consider the hearsay on the issue of the absent defendant's guilt beyond a reasonable doubt (417 F.2d at 1120), to the point, indeed, of using it to "tip the scale" in a case in which the independent evidence might not convince the jury of guilt (ibid). See, e. g., United States v. Bless, 2d Cir. 1970, 422 F.2d 210 at pp. 212–213; United States v. Eskow, 2d Cir. 1970, 422 F.2d 1060 at pp. 1069–1070. The threshold of admissibility is designedly set low enough to accord that advantage to the prosecution.

2. The "multiple hearsay" exception (American Law Institute, Model Code of Evidence, 1942, Rule 530; Uniform Rules of Evidence, 1953, Rule 66; McCormack, Evidence, 1954, § 225, p. 461) would not embrace so much of Warren's testimony that Calarco had stated to him that Riviello had stated fact "X" to Calarco as sought to put in evidence against Riviello his asserted statement of "X" to Calarco as an "admission" of Riviello's. Warren can testify to what the defendant Calarco said to him because the words of Calarco made up a verbal act in furtherance of the conspiracy. If it were of moment to show that *Calarco* thought that Riviello was a party to the burgeoning crime, Warren's testimony that Calarco's words to him also implicated Riviello would be admissible, not to show that Riviello *was* implicated, but to show as against Calarco that *if* Riviello really was involved, *then* Calarco knew it. Uniform Rule 66 illustrates the "multiple hearsay" exception by saying that a hospital record (true "hearsay" and within an exception) would be admissible under the business entry exception to the hearsay rule [(Rule 63(13))], and, if it contained a history of the accident as given by an accident-case plaintiff, that history could be put into evidence against the plaintiff as his "admission" under the Rule 63(7) exception.

The scope of Preliminary Draft of Proposed Rules of Evidence for United States District Courts and Magistrates, 1969, Rule 8–01(c)(3)(v) (comment at p. 169) is uncertain; proposed Rule 8–05 is similar to Uniform Rule 66 and illustrates its sense by use of a hospital record example.

The present case may now seem at several removes from the context of Bruton v. United States, 1968, 391 U.S. 123, 88 S.Ct. 1620, 20 L.Ed.2d 476, but underlying *Bruton* is the value put on the defendant's right to confront and to cross-examine his accuser. Riviello could not because Calarco was his accuser; he could not call Calarco to the witness stand, nor meet Calarco's out-of-court imputation without himself testifying. Cf. Douglas v. Alabama, 1965, 380 U.S. 415, 418–419, 85 S.Ct. 1074, 13 L.Ed.2d 934. And in the frame of reference in which *Geaney* fixes the matter, the aim and effect of the procedure are to dilute the reasonable doubt requirement—a due process exaction, Matter of Winship, 1970, 397 U.S. 358, 90 S.Ct. 1068, 25 L.Ed. 2d 368 at the point at which, in a large class of prosecutions, the evidence of the prosecution is frequently most suspect, the informer or accomplice testifying to what a silent co-defendant said the absent defendant had said. If the words had a place in the record because they functioned in executing the crime or forming the criminal plan, they were admissible. But does not basic fairness require that the jury be told at once that the declaration is not evidence that the absent defendant was a participant in the crime and will never become such evidence no matter what other evidence is brought in? The declaration as a verbal act may become, perhaps, the *responsibility* of the absent defendant as a proved participant in the offense, but in an evaluation of the proofs in the legal perspective, it can not contribute to a finding that he was a party to the corrupt program.

If there be truth in the idea of jury incompetency to winnow evidence in pursuance of instructions (contrast United States v. Bless, supra, 422 F.2d at pp. 213–214), the consequence would not be the admission of such evidence for all purposes upon the judge's impression that a preponderance of the evidence, if believed, would indicate that the absent defendant was associated in the venture, but the exclusion of the evidence for every purpose on the ground that its prejudicial effect as spurious evidence of participation outweighs its utility as evidence of a constitutive act. Mr. Justice Jackson's vivid portrayal of the pitfalls of conspiracy practice in the courts (Krulewitch v. United States, 1949, 336 U.S. 440, 453–455, 69 S.Ct. 716, 93 L.Ed. 790) surely argues for the due-process importance of precision in jury instructions. See as questioning the view that juries were less capable than judges of making the required analyses, Morgan, supra, 43 Harv.L.Rev. at 188, 191.

NOTES

1. It should be noted that the problem involved in *Calarco* is not the rule of substantive law that makes one co-conspirator liable for the acts—including words—of another in furtherance of the conspiracy. Thus, if A and B conspire to extort money from V, A's threats to V are attributable to B just as would be his act of beating V. Rather the issue is whether and under what restrictions may A's out of court statements be used as evidence

to establish as to B the elements of the conspiracy and his involvement therein.

2.   If the charge requested by Riviello were employed, what purpose would be served by the declarations admitted under the co-conspirator exception to the hearsay rule? As is noted by Judge Dowling in *Calarco,* the commonly accepted position expressed by the majority offers the prosecution a substantial advantage. Given the secrecy inherent in almost all conspiracies isn't it necessary to relax evidentiary rules to facilitate their successful prosecution? Is the use of one conspirator's hearsay statement as evidence against another distinguishable from the use of a business agent's authorized statement concerning the business against his principal? Isn't a conspiracy, according to Justices Holmes and Douglas, "a partnership in criminal purposes"?   United States v. Kissel, 218 U.S. 601, 608, 31 S.Ct. 124, 126, 54 L.Ed. 1168 (1910), Pinkerton v. United States, 328 U.S. 640, 644, 66 S.Ct. 1180, 1182, 90 L.Ed. 1489 (1946).

3.   Judge Dowling suggests that the majority view in *Calarco* raises serious constitutional problems. First, that Riviello's Sixth Amendment right to confront the witnesses against him has been violated. In Bruton v. United States, 391 U.S. 123, 88 S.Ct. 1620, 20 L.Ed.2d 476 (1968), the court held that the admission in evidence of the confession of a co-defendant, A, inculpating defendant B violated B's right to confrontation where A never took the stand, despite an explicit instruction to the jury that the evidence was not to be considered as to B's guilt. Is the use of a co-conspirator's out of court statement distinguishable on the grounds that, given the necessary preliminary finding by the trial judge that a conspiracy involving the defendant existed, such a statement made during and in furtherance of a conspiracy can be viewed as having been authorized by the defendant? As noted previously, note g, page 859, supra, the Supreme Court has held that the co-conspirator exception to the hearsay rule does not violate the right to confrontation. Dutton v. Evans, 400 U.S. 74, 91 S.Ct. 210, 27 L. Ed.2d 213 (1970). See Davenport, The Confrontation Clause and the Co-Conspirator Exception in Criminal Prosecutions: A Functional Analysis, 85 Harv.L.Rev. 1378 (1972).

Judge Dowling also implies that where such evidence is offered the defendant may be forced to waive his Fifth Amendment right not to testify in order to challenge the statement effectively. This, of course, is not involved in the case of an admission by an agent or a partner offered in civil litigation. However, is this choice any harder than that faced by a criminal defendant whose personal admissions are offered in evidence?

Finally, Judge Dowling argues that the lesser standard for the admissibility of the co-conspirator's statements dilutes the due process requirement that the prosecution prove its case beyond a reasonable doubt. However, the Supreme Court has now decided that a preponderance of the evidence standard is sufficient for the determination of the admissibility of a confession challenged as involuntary. Lego v. Twomey, 404 U.S. 553, 92 S. Ct. 619, 30 L.Ed.2d 618 (1972). Could any argument be made that a higher standard be required for the admission of the probably less damaging evidence of a co-conspirator's statement?

UNITED STATES v. SPOCK

United States Court of Appeals for the First Circuit, 1969.
416 F.2d 165.

ALDRICH, Chief Judge. These are appeals by four defendants convicted under a single count indictment for conspiracy. We reverse.

As is well known, the war in Vietnam and the draft to support it have engendered considerable animosity and frustration. In August 1967 a number of academic, clerical, and professional persons discussed the need of more vigorous opposition to governmental policies. From their eventually consolidated efforts came a document entitled "A Call to Resist Illegitimate Authority" (hereinafter the Call) and a cover letter requesting signatures and support. The letter was signed by defendant Dr. Benjamin Spock and defendant Rev. William Sloane Coffin, Jr., and two other persons. The Call was originally signed by them, numerous others, and eventually by hundreds. The defendant Mitchell Goodman had been preparing a somewhat similar statement against the war and the draft. In mid-September he learned of the Call, which he also signed. He, Coffin, Spock and others spoke on October 2 at a press conference in New York City to launch the Call. It was there announced by Goodman that further activities were contemplated, including a nationwide collection of draft cards and a ceremonial surrender thereof to the Attorney General. On October 16 a draft card burning and turn-in took place at the Arlington Street Church in Boston, arranged by the defendant Michael Ferber, and participated in by Coffin. Four days afterwards all four defendants attended a demonstration in Washington, in the course of which an unsuccessful attempt was made to present the fruits of that collection and similar gatherings to the Attorney General.[2] The details of these matters will be discussed later.

The indictment was framed under section 12 of the Military Selective Service Act of 1967, 50 App. U.S.C.A. § 462(a). It charged that defendants, and others known and unknown, conspired to "counsel, aid and abet diverse Selective Service registrants to * * * neglect, fail, refuse and evade service in the armed forces of the United States and all other duties required of registrants under the

2. In addition, considerable evidence was introduced of Spock's participation in a sit-in in front of the Whitehall induction center in New York City. We will assume with the defendants and now, apparently, the government as well, that this was token activity and protected political expression. See Brown v. Louisiana, 1966, 383 U.S. 131, 141–142, 86 S.Ct. 719, 15 L.Ed.2d 637; but cf. Adderley v. Florida, 1966, 385 U.S. 39, 87 S.Ct. 242, 17 L.Ed.2d 149; Cox v. Louisiana, 1965, 379 U.S. 559, 85 S.Ct. 476, 13 L.Ed.2d 487. Because of our resolution of the case on other grounds we need not pursue this matter, or explore the possibility of prejudice arising from the introduction of this evidence.

Universal Military Training and Service Act * * * and the rules, regulations and directions duly made pursuant to said Act * * * to * * * fail and refuse to have in their personal possession at all times their registration certificates [and] * * * valid notices of classification [3] [and conspired to] * * * unlawfully, willfully and knowingly hinder and interfere, by any means, with the administration of the Universal Military Training and Service Act." The case was tried to a jury, which answered special questions framed by the court, most answers being unfavorable to the defendants, and returned general verdicts of guilty. On this appeal defendants raise a number of issues, the most basic of which is their asserted right to directed acquittals, either because of constitutional immunity or because the government failed in its proof. We consider these contentions in that order.

I

Inseparable from the question of the sufficiency of the evidence to convict are the rights of the defendants, and others, under the First Amendment. We approach the constitutional problem on the assumption, which we will later support, that the ultimate objective of defendants' alleged agreement, viz., the expression of opposition to the war and the draft, was legal, but that the means or intermediate objectives encompassed both legal and illegal activity without any clear indication, initially, as to who intended what. This intertwining of legal and illegal aspects, the public setting of the agreement and its political purposes, and the loose confederation of possibly innocent and possibly guilty participants raise the most serious First Amendment problems. Indeed our Brother Coffin, in dissent, admits to a temptation "to say that the law should recognize no overt conspiracy in the sensitive area of public opinion." This temptation leads him down paths that we cannot follow, but which, nevertheless, we must consider.

As the defendants point out, most conspiracies are secret. To argue from this, however, that illegality presupposes secrecy is to confuse means with ends. Illegality normally seeks cover, but conspirators may act openly or not, as best suits their purpose. Here the defendants' primary object was publicity, and their conduct was designedly open. No one before has suggested that this fact, or the concomitant warning to the government of impending danger, requires that the government's hand be stayed until the substantive offense is committed.[7] Contrary to the defendants' position, many

---

3. Hereinafter, without distinction, draft cards.

7. In Direct Sales Co. v. United States, 1943, 319 U.S. 703, 63 S.Ct. 1265, 87 L.Ed. 1674, for example, the agreement was embodied in catalogues widely distributed through the mails, and in order blanks the form of which was prescribed by the Secretary of the Treasury and which were, by law, retained for government inspection. Indeed, periodic reports, some monthly, some weekly, were made by Direct

"public" conspiracies have been successfully prosecuted. A case remarkably similar is Fraina v. United States, 2 Cir., 1918, 255 F. 28. There two defendants were charged with conspiring, together with persons unknown, to aid, abet and counsel divers unknown persons to evade and neglect the requirements of the then Selective Service Act. The overt acts alleged were the organizing of a mass meeting and the distribution of pamphlets entitled "Conscientious Objectors" (who proved to be "nonreligious conscientious objectors" whose "idealism compels them to decline all forms of military service.") The opinion affirming the convictions touches many aspects of the case at bar in addition to the matter of publicity.[8]

That openness does not immunize an agreement may be demonstrated by an example. A group of vigilantes agreeing in the town square to solicit cohorts to call out a lynch mob would not be absolved because their agreement was open. Nor should their agreement be protected by the First Amendment if, at the same time, they were engaging in free speech on the evils of their victim's alleged offense; nor, indeed, because their principal object was the proper one of deterring such offenses. The dissent's finding the present agreement pasteurized because it was exposed to the light is in effect granting a right to public association which is not given free speech itself. Cox v. Louisiana, 1965, 379 U.S. 559, 563–564, 85 S.Ct. 476, 13 L.Ed.2d 487; Giboney v. Empire Storage & Ice Co., 1949, 336 U.S. 490, 501–502, 69 S.Ct. 684, 93 L.Ed. 834. Lack of arcana cannot be determinative.[9]

Sales to the government disclosing the names of purchasers and the amounts of purchases. The dissent supports its attachment to overtness with a dictum by Mr. Justice Harlan in Grunewald v. United States, 1957, 353 U.S. 391, 402, 77 S.Ct. 963, 972, 1 L.Ed.2d 931 ("every conspiracy is by its very nature secret"). With great respect to the Justice, this was a somewhat casual remark in a case dealing with a plainly illegal conspiracy, and is erroneous, as even the dissent's citations demonstrate. We may be pardoned for observing that more affection seems to be exhibited for this dictum than for some of the Justice's holdings in connection with agreements that are partly legal and partly not.

8. Other cases in which the conspiracy itself was to a large degree public include Wells v. United States, 9 Cir., 1919, 257 F. 605 (meetings, apparently public, and circulars widely distributed demanding "Resist! Refuse!"); Haywood v. United States, 7 Cir., 1920, 268 F. 795, cert. denied 256 U.S. 689, 41 S.Ct. 449, 65 L.Ed. 1172; Anderson v. United States, 8 Cir., 1921, 273 F. 20, cert. denied 257 U.S. 647, 42 S.Ct. 56, 66 L.Ed. 415; United States v. Gordon, 7 Cir., 1943, 138 F.2d 174, cert. denied 320 U.S. 798, 64 S.Ct. 266, 88 L.Ed. 481.

9. Neither can the claim that the conspiracy was "non-cohesive." If any cohesive motive be thought necessary where there already was a written document, cf. Interstate Circuit, Inc. v. United States, 1939, 306 U.S. 208, 222, 59 S.Ct. 467, 83 L.Ed. 610, there was ample common purpose here. The dissent's emphasis upon "discipline" again confuses means and result. Discipline may be needed for a secret conspiracy in order to keep it secret. The thrust of conspiracy, however, is in the agreement for joint action, not in the method of accomplishing it.

Admittedly, the First Amendment rights of free speech and free association, see, e. g., Elfbrandt v. Russell, 1966, 384 U.S. 11, 86 S.Ct. 1238, 16 L.Ed.2d 321; NAACP v. Alabama, 1958, 357 U.S. 449, 460, 78 S.Ct. 1163, 2 L.Ed.2d 1488, are of such importance that they must prevail if the government's interest in deterring substantive crimes before they take place [10] is insubstantial, or there is a "less restrictive alternative" by which the substantive evil may be prevented. United States v. Robel, 1967, 389 U.S. 258, 265–268, 88 S.Ct. 419, 19 L.Ed.2d 508; Aptheker v. Secretary of State, 1964, 378 U.S. 500, 512–514, 84 S.Ct. 1659, 12 L.Ed.2d 992; Shelton v. Tucker, 1960, 364 U.S. 479, 488–489, 81 S.Ct. 247, 5 L.Ed.2d 231. This calls for a weighing. In *Aptheker* the Court struck down the broad Congressional proscription against issuing passports to Communists only after considering the availability and adequacy of other security measures, one actually proposed by the President. In defendants' much emphasized case of New York Times Co. v. Sullivan, 1964, 376 U.S. 254, 279–283, 84 S.Ct. 710, 11 L.Ed.2d 686, not all public discussion was held protected; immunity was denied speakers motivated by "actual malice."

In comparing the present private and public interests we start with the assumption that the defendants were not to be prevented from vigorous criticism of the government's program merely because the natural consequences might be to interfere with it, or even to lead to unlawful action. Thus Bond v. Floyd, 1966, 385 U.S. 116, 87 S.Ct. 339, 17 L.Ed.2d 235, held that the First Amendment protected an expression of "sympathy * * * and support [for] the men in this country who are unwilling to respond to a military draft." The Court said, with specific reference to section 462(a), "[T]his statement alone cannot be interpreted as a call to unlawful refusal to be drafted." Id. at 133, 87 S.Ct. at 348. The defendants here are not charged, however, with expressions of sympathy and moral support, but with conspiring to counsel, aid and abet Selective Service registrants to disobey various duties imposed by the Selective Service Act. The maintenance of an army in peacetime is a valid, in fact vital, governmental function. United States v. O'Brien, 1968, 391 U.S. 367, 377–378, 88 S.Ct. 1673, 20 L.Ed.2d 672. If a registrant may be convicted for violation of the draft laws, surely "[a] man may be punished for encouraging the commission of [the] crime." Cox v. Louisiana, supra, at 563, 85 S.Ct. at 480; Fox v. Washington, 1915, 236 U.S. 273, 35 S.Ct. 383, 59 L.Ed. 573.

The government's ability to deter and punish those who increase the likelihood of crime by concerted action has long been established. See Developments in the Law—Criminal Conspiracy, 72 Harv.L.Rev.

---

10. The "general principle [is] that society, having the power to punish dangerous behavior, cannot be powerless against those who work to bring about that behavior." Scales v. United States, 1961, 367 U.S. 203, 225, 81 S.Ct. 1469, 1484, 6 L.Ed.2d 782.

920, 923–25 (1959). Restricting it to punishment of substantive violations ignores the potency of conspiratorial conduct;[12] to wait for the substantive offense may be to wait too long. Congress has a right to prefer registrants to felons. However attractive the dissent's conclusion may be to those of liberal First Amendment views, it sets its own stage by asking "whether there is reason or authority which *compels* the application [here] of the conspiracy sanction." (emphasis in orig.) The authority is an act of Congress. We do not read the "less restrictive alternative" cases as placing such a burden upon the government.[13]

* * *

In the early Smith Act cases, in considering the defendants' conduct in teaching the doctrines of revolution and advocacy of violence, substantial questions arose as to imminency of accomplishment. Dennis v. United States, 1951, 341 U.S. 494, 71 S.Ct. 857, 95 L.Ed. 1137; Yates v. United States, 1957, 354 U.S. 298, 77 S.Ct. 1064, 1 L.Ed.2d 1356. In the case at bar the defendants were concerned with the present. Their objective did not relate to some future war, but was a call for immediate action to thwart the one at hand. See Thomas v. Collins, 1945, 323 U.S. 516, 529–538, 65 S.Ct. 315, 89 L.Ed. 430. See also De Jonge v. Oregon, 1937, 299 U.S. 353, 365, 57 S.Ct. 255, 81 L.Ed. 278. What is effective persuasion must depend on the circumstances. The existence of a large number of young men, perhaps impressionable, and in any event oriented in defendants' direction by natural self-interest, adequately distinguishes this case from Wood v. Georgia, 1962, 370 U.S. 375, 82 S.Ct. 1364, 8 L.Ed.2d 569, and Bridges v. California, 1941, 314 U.S. 252, 62 S.Ct. 190, 86 L.Ed. 192. In this context the "soft sell" may be the most telling.[16]

Despite the validity of the government's present interest, the defendants were entitled under the cases to certain protections before they could be convicted of conspiracy in what we might call a bifarious undertaking, involving both legal and illegal conduct. This

---

12. The occasionally asserted judicial hostility to conspiracy prosecutions, Krulewitch v. United States, 1949, 336 U.S. 440, 445, 69 S.Ct. 716, 93 L.Ed. 790 (Jackson, J., concurring); United States v. Falcone, 2 Cir., 1940, 109 F.2d 579, 581, aff'd, 311 U.S. 205, 61 S.Ct. 204, 85 L.Ed. 128, springs largely from the government's overenthusiastic use of some of the procedures of conspiracy law rather than from a rejection of the public interest served by that law. Indeed, Justice Jackson, author of the *Krulewitch* concurrence, noted in Dennis v. United States, 341 U.S. at 577, 71 S.Ct. at 901: "There is no constitutional right to 'gang up' on the Government."

13. The issue may perhaps be more objectively considered if we approach it in terms other than the present case where it may be easy to sympathize with many of the defendants' aims and be tempted to overlook, as incidental and peripheral, the illegal aspects of some of the means. It is not difficult to visualize conspirators whose basic ends are plainly illegal but who color them in order to obtain needed support of others, innocent and well intentioned, by adding lawful and popular objects.

16. We note Spock's candid statement that direct urging of draft violations would in his opinion be "poor psychological practice."

matter was considered by Mr. Justice Harlan, speaking for the Court in Scales v. United States, 1961, 367 U.S. 203, 81 S.Ct. 1469, 6 L.Ed.2d 782. The question there was whether convicting "active" members of the Communist party would interfere with the freedom of inactive, or legal, members. In the course of discussing this question he spoke of such groups as not being a "technical conspiracy" because of their mixed motives, and recognized the impropriety of a "blanket prohibition of association with a group having both legal and illegal aims." It did not follow, however, that distinction could not be effected. Indeed, this is the substantive purpose of all conspiracy law, which is directed only at those who have intentionally agreed to further the illegal object.[17] The First Amendment cases merely present a more difficult problem of insuring that the government does not use its procedural advantages to expand the strict elements of the offense.

In *Scales* the Court held that protection for the innocent could be adequately accomplished by requiring that the defendants' specific illegal intent be proved to the degree demanded in Noto v. United States, 1961, 367 U.S. 290, 81 S.Ct. 1517, 6 L.Ed.2d 836. "[C]riminal intent * * * must be judged *strictissimi juris*, for otherwise there is a danger that one in sympathy with the legitimate aims of such an organization, but not specifically intending to accomplish them by resort to violence, might be punished for his adherence to lawful and constitutionally protected purposes, because of other and unprotected purposes which he does not necessarily share." Noto v. United States, at 299–300, 81 S.Ct. at 1522. When the alleged agreement is both bifarious and political within the shadow of the First Amendment, we hold that an individual's specific intent to adhere to the illegal portions may be shown in one of three ways: by the individual defendant's prior or subsequent unambiguous statements; by the individual defendant's subsequent commission of the very illegal act contemplated by the agreement; or by the individual defendant's subsequent legal act if that act is "clearly undertaken for the specific purpose of rendering effective the later illegal activity which is advocated." Scales v. United States, 367 U.S. at 234, 81 S.Ct. at 1488.

Application of such a standard should forcefully answer the defendants' protests that conviction of any of them would establish criminal responsibility of all of the many hundreds of persons who signed the Call. Even if the Call included illegal objectives, there is a wide gap between signing a document such as the Call and demonstrating one's personal attachment to illegality. Of greater import-

---

17. Justice Harlan noted in *Scales*, 367 U.S. at 229, 81 S.Ct. at 1486, "[A] technical conspiracy * * * is defined by its criminal purpose, so that *all* knowing association with the con-spiracy is a proper subject for criminal proscription as far as First Amendment liberties are concerned." (emphasis in the original).

ance, it responds to the legitimate apprehension of the amicus that the evil must be separable from the good without inhibiting legitimate association in an orderly society.

At the same time, this principle demonstrates a fundamental error in the government's approach. Adopting the panoply of rules applicable to a conspiracy having purely illegal purposes, the government introduced numerous statements of third parties alleged to be co-conspirators. This was improper. The specific intent of one defendant in a case such as this is not ascertained by reference to the conduct or statements of another even though he has knowledge thereof. Cf. United States v. Silverman, 2 Cir., 1957, 248 F.2d 671; Enfield v. United States, 8 Cir., 1919, 261 F. 141, 143–144. The metastatic rules of ordinary conspiracy are at direct variance with the principle of *strictissimi juris*.[20] We need not determine, however, to what extent, because of a failure to recognize this principle, there may have been prejudicial error requiring a new trial. For reasons that we will come to, (Point III, infra,) a new trial is required in any event. What we do determine is that the First Amendment does not, per se, require acquittal.

II

In this section we consider whether, on the review of the record which is required by Yates v. United States, supra, and Dennis v. United States, supra, the evidence was sufficient to take the defendants to the jury. We divide this consideration into three parts. First, whether there was evidence of an agreement; second, whether the agreement contemplated or included illegal activity; third, whether the defendants individually adhered to that illegality.

The Evidence of Agreement

The government's claim of agreement looks basically to the Call, the cover letter, and the subsequent press conference. Spock participated in drafting the Call and, as has been stated, he and Coffin were two of the four persons who signed the cover letter. Goodman signed the Call, and was an active participant in the launch-

---

20. We do not believe that section 462 (a) is overbroad or vague. A special obligation exists as to federal statutes to construe them so to avoid unconstitutionality, Scales v. United States, supra, so long as such does not result in substantial re-writing. See Aptheker v. Secretary of State, 1964, 378 U.S. 500, 515–516, 84 S.Ct. 1659, 12 L.Ed.2d 992. The fact that a seemingly normal criminal statute, by virtue of its prohibition of conspiracy and crime counselling, may in some instances apply to affect freedom of association or freedom of speech does not invalidate the statute. See United States v. O'Brien, 1968, 391 U.S. 367, 88 S.Ct. 1673, 20 L.Ed.2d 672. The court's obligation is, rather, to make sure that such a statute does not improperly infringe upon speech in any particular instance. See, e. g., Street v. New York, U. S., April 21, 1969, 394 U.S. 576, 89 S.Ct. 1354, 22 L.Ed.2d 572. Nor do we believe the indictment failed in its function of informing the defendants of the crime with which they were charged.

ing press conference which was chaired by Coffin and at which Spock appeared. Ferber did not sign the Call. The Call was addressed "To the young men of America, to the whole of the American people, and to all men of good will everywhere." It observed there was a "growing number of young American men" who, because of their moral and religious beliefs could not contribute to the war in Vietnam in any way. After setting forth at some length the signers' belief that the war was unconstitutional and illegal, it stated, "[W]e believe on all these grounds that every free man has a legal right and a moral duty to exert every effort to end this war, to avoid collusion with it, and to encourage others to do the same." There followed a recital of the forms of resistance that young men were exercising, the detail of which we will return to, and an assertion of the signers' belief that "each of these forms of resistance * * * is courageous and justified. * * * We will continue to lend our support to those who undertake resistance to this war. We will raise funds to organize draft resistance unions, to supply legal defense and bail, to support families and otherwise aid resistance to the war in whatever ways may seem appropriate. * * * We call upon all men of good will to join us in this confrontation with immoral authority. * * * Now is the time to resist."

The cover letter, requesting signatures and other response to the Call, stated that the signers of the Call "have pledged themselves to extend material and moral support to young men who are directly resisting the war." There followed a "box" containing requests for further signatures of "endorsement," contributions of "$_____ to support the work of RESIST. (Please make checks payable to RESIST.)," and volunteers interested in organizing or joining local groups "to support young men directly resisting the war." A similar "box" appeared in the Call itself, when printed.

At the press conference, in addition to discussing the Call, Goodman advanced his own paper, signed also by Coffin, along strikingly similar lines, entitled "Civil Disobedience Against the War" (hereinafter Civil Disobedience). It announced that the purpose of the signers was to "take away from the government the support and bodies it needs" and contained the following:

> "The draft law commands that we shall not aid, abet or counsel men to refuse the draft. But as a group of the clergy has recently said, * * * when young men refuse to allow their conscience to be violated by an unjust law and a criminal war, then it is necessary for their elders —their teachers, ministers, friends—to make clear their commitment, in conscience, to *aid, abet and counsel* them against conscription. Most of us have already done this privately. Now publicly we will demonstrate, side by side with

these young men, our determination to continue to do so."
(emphasis in orig.)

Goodman described the Call as a first step, and said that further
activity was to follow. He announced a demonstration to be held
in Washington on October 20, as an act of "direct creative resistance," at which time draft cards surrendered at turn-ins that had
been planned for October 16 would be delivered to the Attorney General. This announcement, as both conceded, was the result of a prearrangement with Coffin.

Spock argues that there was no "agreement among leaders of an
integrated political group * * *. [T]his case presents no more
than the publicly expressed coincidence of views on public affairs."
No merit, however, lies in the suggestion that there must be a cohesiveness in the group beyond the confines of the agreement itself.
See Direct Sales Co. v. United States, supra n. 7, at 713, 63 S.Ct. 1265;
cf. United States v. Falcone, 1940, 311 U.S. 205, 61 S.Ct. 204, 85
L.Ed. 128.[23] In the light of all the circumstances the jury was not
obliged, in considering the question of agreement, to find a mere
coincidence in the appearance of several speakers on the same platform. See Fraina v. United States, [2 Cir., 1918, 255 F. 28]. Cf.
United States v. Kompinski, 2 Cir., 1967, 373 F.2d 429, 434.[24]

The Call was not what is known in law as an integrated document, limited to the four corners of the instrument. The jury could
properly infer that it could not occur in the abstract, with no parents, and no active participants in a joint undertaking. We hold that
they could look to Spock as one of the drafters, and to Spock and
Coffin as two of the four signers of the solicitation letter, and in the
light of the press conference held to publicize the Call in which
Goodman took a prominent part, they could find that Goodman included himself as an active member. The evidence disclosed more
than parallel conduct, see United States v. Bufalino, 2 Cir., 1960,
285 F.2d 408, 414–415; rather there are several instances of concerted activity from which the jury could infer an agreement.
Whether the defendants' intended participation was unlawful is another matter.

---

23. See also n. 9, supra. By the same
token, nothing is taught by the frequently stressed fact that the signa-
tories were in many instances persons
of prominence, or that, apart from
their common opposition to the war
and to the draft, they were of dispar-
ate backgrounds and interests.

24. In *Fraina* the court said, 255 F. at
34, "This case is one of the simplest
instances of proper proof in limine of
combination ever brought to a court's
attention. If, as per advertisement,
an audience is gathered before a platform containing intending speakers,

and is called to order by a chairman,
who announces the object of the gathering again, as per advertisement, it is
impossible not to infer a combination
in thought among the platform occupiers and their helpers." The rule of
strictissimi juris may well require
greater proof today of a defendant's
specific intent, but in distinguishing
Fraina on this ground the dissent confuses consensual principles with the
ascertainment of what was consented
to. The principles remain. See Yates
v. United States, supra, 354 U.S. at
333, 77 S.Ct. 1064.

The Evidence of Illegal Purpose

The defendants contend that nothing in the record would justify a finding of unlawful purpose in their agreement. Spock puts this succinctly: "There is nothing in the Call to Resist * * * which suggests the objective of counseling, aiding and abetting anyone to resist induction." Rather, he contends the only action contemplated was "simply moral support and financial aid for young men and their families who in good conscience are unable to participate in the war." Coffin argues further, "[D]raft 'resistance' is not a crime; the statute forbids only 'evasion' and 'refusal.' "

Examination of the Call shows nothing suggesting it sought to distinguish between "resistance" and "refusal." It was addressed to laymen, and is to be given a common sense and not a legalistic interpretation. We look, as indeed with any document, to its own clues as to what its subscribers may have intended the words to mean. So doing, we believe a jury would be amply justified in finding that "resist" included that type of resistance which the signers recognized, to use the words of Bond v. Floyd, supra, as "a call to unlawful refusal." Hence the whole concept of "illegitimate" authority. "[R]efusing to be inducted" must imply an order of induction to be refused. Hence the "heavy penalty" for "resisting openly." Hence the "need to support families," since families would not need support if the registrants' conduct met legal standards. "[S]anctuary in other countries" scarcely suggests travel authorized by the registrant's draft board.

Nor was this a mere factual recital of what others were doing. "Now is the time to resist." It was at least open to the jury to find that these illicit actions were within what the Call, to use its own word, sought to "encourage;" and that the Call was, to repeat, in the words of the Court in Bond, "a call to unlawful refusal to be drafted."

This is not to deny that the Call contained many lawful criticisms of the war, lawful adjurations and expressions of sympathy and support for persons who acted illegally, and contemplated conduct of an entirely lawful character. It is also true, as Spock points out, that the Call stated that funds would be used "in whatever ways may seem appropriate." From this he argues that the persons signing the Call "reserve to themselves the determination of 'what ways may seem appropriate.' " While this may be so, nonetheless the Call on its face indicated that some signers considered the illegal to be the appropriate. Cf. Truax v. Corrigan, 1921, 257 U.S. 312, 327–328, 42 S.Ct. 124, 66 L.Ed. 254. We adopt the description given in the perceptive brief of the Unitarian Universalist Association, amicus on behalf of Ferber. The Call had "a double aspect: in part it was a denunciation of governmental policy and, in part, it involved a public call to resist the duties imposed by the Act."

The Evidence of Specific Intent

There remains the question whether it could have been found, within the strict test laid down by the cases supra, that the individual defendants personally agreed to employ the illegal means contemplated by the agreement including counselling unlawful refusal to be drafted or other violations of the Selective Service Act. We will begin with Goodman and his affirmative statement regarding counselling contained in "Civil Disobedience," written by him and signed by Coffin, quoted supra. In describing this paper, Coffin argues, as he did with the Call, that it "cannot be interpreted as a call to unlawful *refusal* to be drafted." "One may counsel *against* conscription by urging the claiming of exemption or deferment * * *. [O]nly counselling of *evasion* or *refusal* is unlawful, not counselling of *avoidance*. Avoidance may be entirely lawful—as by claiming lawful exemption or deferment." (Emphasis in orig.) This appraisal seems divorced from the realities. No defendant either here or at any time, used the word "avoidance." There is not even a reference in Civil Disobedience to "exemption or deferment," except for an expression of approval of those who voluntarily waive such. Nor does anyone explain the reference to long jail sentences, if "refusing * * * to serve when called" means lawful refusal.[27]

In addition, Goodman's remarks at the Washington demonstration were pari passu. There, after referring to the continuing activities of the Resistance in their successful solicitation of "draft resisters," Goodman stated that those of the older generation were present "because *we* want specifically to form an alliance with these young men which *we* will persist in, at least as long as the war lasts, in which *we* will encourage them and aid and abet and counsel them in every way we know how." (emphasis suppl.) The ambiguity in the original agreement was clarified, as to Goodman, by his own statements. Because a properly instructed jury could have found Goodman had the requisite specific intent he was not entitled to an acquittal.[28]

Coffin also signed Civil Disobedience, but if it could be thought that in some manner he is not to be personally charged therewith

---

27. Additionally, we note that defendant Goodman's printed statement at the October 2 press conference contained the following: "The activity of the Resistance groups will be continuing beyond October 16, as more *draft refusers* come forward. It is our intention to parallel that development with continuing private and public activity in support of them." (Emphasis suppl.).

28. Were it necessary to go any further, the Washington demonstration, planned by Goodman and Coffin, completed the surrender of draft cards; those who "surrendered" them at the Arlington Street Church having been told that they had a right of recall. This act, of course, was not mere speech, and could be found to satisfy the requirement of a "course of conduct clearly undertaken for the specific purpose of rendering effective" the illegal objects of the agreement. Scales v. United States, 367 U.S. at 234, 81 S.Ct. 1469.

we quote his remarks at Washington, when it was sought to present turned-in cards to the Attorney General, again, like Goodman, speaking in terms of a joint undertaking.

"The law of the land is clear. Section 12 of the National Selective Service Act declares that anyone 'who knowingly counsels, aids, or abets another to refuse or evade registration or service in the armed forces * * * shall be liable to imprisonment for not more than five years or a fine of ten thousand dollars or both.'

"We hereby publicly counsel these young men to continue in their refusal to serve in the armed forces as long as the war in Vietnam continues, and we pledge ourselves to aid and abet them in all the ways we can. This means that if they are now arrested for failing to comply with a law that violates their consciences, we too must be arrested, for in the sight of that law we are now as guilty as they.

"It is a longstanding tradition, sanctioned by American democracy, that the dictates of government must be tested on the anvil of individual conscience. This is what we now undertake to do—not as a first but as a last resort. And in accepting the legal punishment we are, in fact, supporting, not subverting, the legal order.

"Still, to stand in this fashion against the law and before our fellow Americans is a difficult and even fearful thing. But in the face of what to us is insane and inhuman we can fall neither silent nor servile. Nor can we educate young men to be conscientious only to desert them in their hour of conscience. So we are resolved, as they are resolved, to speak out clearly and to pay up personally." [29]

Finally, at the Arlington Street Church ceremony on October 16 Coffin not only spoke but assisted in the collection of draft cards. This participation and assistance could well have been found to be

---

29. In spite of this final remark, made then and at other times, by both Coffin and Goodman, they argue now that they were not guilty if they believed that their actions were legal and that any conviction would be unconstitutional. For this they cite Keegan v. United States, 1945, 325 U.S. 478, 65 S.Ct. 1203, 89 L.Ed. 1745. The opinions there, however, are far from clear as to the extent of such a principle; nor have other courts reached a consensus. Compare Holdridge v. United States, 8 Cir., 1960, 282 F.2d 302, 310–311, and Kiyoshi Okamoto v. United States, 10 Cir., 1945, 152 F.2d 905, with Lantis v. United States, 9 Cir., 1950, 186 F.2d 91, 92–93, and Warren v. United States, 10 Cir., 1949, 177 F.2d 596, 600, cert. denied 338 U.S. 947, 70 S.Ct. 485, 94 L.Ed. 584. A defendant's motive in testing an act might properly go to sentence, but these defendants are contending that, having violated the statute, they should, in effect, be subject only to a riskless declaratory judgment. No such purpose was made known until the defendants reached the courtroom. Before that time, they publicly asserted that they were placing their own necks on the block. They should not now be heard to say that no axe was involved.

aiding and abetting nonpossession.[30] Because it was this very type
of resistance that the agreement might have been found to contemplate, a properly instructed jury could find that Coffin had the
requisite specific intent. The jury was not obliged to view his conduct as he would have it on appeal. Before us he argues, "It is no
crime * * * to *agree* to deliver turned-in draft cards to the Attorney General * * *. [T]his action was completely law-abiding—Rev. Coffin accurately viewed it as the delivery to the law of
evidence of a crime." (emphasis suppl.) We do not think of Coffin
as one to run with the hare and hold with the hounds. In any event,
he was not entitled to an acquittal.

The principle of *strictissimi juris* requires the acquittal of Spock.
It is true that he was one of the drafters of the Call, but this does
not evidence the necessary intent to adhere to its illegal aspects.
Nor does his admission to a government agent that he was willing
to do "anything" asked to further opposition to the war. Specific
intent is not established by such a generalization. Whatever the
reason[31] the fact is that his speech was limited to condemnation of
the war and the draft, and lacked any words or content of counselling.
The jury could not find proscribed advocacy from the mere fact,
which he freely admitted, that he hoped the frequent stating of his
views might give young men "courage to take active steps in draft
resistance." This is a natural consequence of vigorous speech.

Similarly, Spock's actions lacked the clear character necessary
to imply specific intent under the First Amendment standard. He
was not at the Arlington Street Church meeting; in fact he knew
nothing of it until afterwards. Although he was at the Washington
demonstration he had, unlike Goodman and Coffin, no part in its
planning. He contributed nothing, even by his presence, to the turning in of cards. Nor, finally, did his statements in the course of
the Washington demonstration extend at all beyond the general anti-
war, anti-draft remarks he had made before. His attendance is as
consistent with a desire to repeat this speech as it is to aid a violation of the act.

The dissent would fault us for drawing such distinctions, but it
forgets the teaching of Bond v. Floyd and other cases that expressing
one's views in broad areas is not foreclosed by knowledge of the con-

---

30. Willful nonpossession of a draft
card is criminal. O'Brien v. United
States, 1 Cir., 1967, 376 F.2d 538, rev'd
on other grounds, 391 U.S. 367, 88 S.Ct.
1673, 20 L.Ed.2d 672. One "who contributed consciously to furthering that
illicit enterprise aided and abetted its
commission." United States v. Johnson, 1943, 319 U.S. 503, 515, 63 S.Ct.
1233, 1239, 87 L.Ed. 1546. Coffin was
not merely present in the church,

Hicks v. United States, 1893, 150 U.S.
442, 449–450, 14 S.Ct. 144, 37 L.Ed.
1137; Long v. United States, 1966, 124
U.S.App.D.C. 14, 360 F.2d 829, 835, he
was an active, knowing participant.
Wyatt v. United States, 10 Cir., 1968,
388 F.2d 395; Moore v. United States,
5 Cir., 1966, 356 F.2d 39.

31. See n. 16, supra.

sequences, and the important lesson of *Noto, Scales* and *Yates* that one may belong to a group, knowing of its illegal aspects, and still not be found to adhere thereto. Viewing the record as a whole we feel we would be doing poor service to the rule of *strictissimi juris*, and to the principle that there must be substantial evidence, Yoffe v. United States, 1 Cir., 1946, 153 F.2d 570, and not a mere scintilla, Magnat Corp. v. B & B Electroplating Co., 1 Cir., 1966, 358 F.2d 794, to warrant submitting a case to the jury if we failed to hold Spock entitled to an acquittal.[32] Cf. Hellman v. United States, 9 Cir., 1961, 298 F.2d 810.[33]

The defendant Michael Ferber presents a different situation. Ferber was a draft-age student. His activities were limited to assisting in the burning and surrender of draft cards. Although he made an address at the Arlington Street Church, it was not counselling draft resistance, or even the surrendering of cards. Not only did he not sign the Call, or the cover letter, or attend the press conference, but the evidence did not warrant a finding that through other statements or conduct he joined the larger conspiracy for which the other defendants were prosecuted. The fact that he made incidental use of the services of some of the other defendants for his own purposes does not mean that he evidenced an attachment to all of theirs. It may be that Ferber engaged in a smaller conspiracy. This does not mean that he should be convicted for the larger one. Daily v. United States, 9 Cir., 1960, 282 F.2d 818. He must be acquitted.

III

As already stated, we have not fully pursued the question of prejudicial error in the course of trial because, in the exercise of our supervisory power, we feel obliged to consider another question, the answer to which occasions no doubt. The district court, sua sponte,

---

32. This, too, dissatisfies the dissent, which is unhappy whatever we do. Viz., because we recognize the necessity of special protection, thereby letting some defendants go free, we should not punish conspiracies in the field of speech at all; it is improper to apply the *Scales* and *Noto* safeguard because it is not strict enough; here we have applied it too strictly. Continuing with Ferber, infra, this conspiracy is too broad, it might have been proper to prosecute Ferber for a conspiracy limited to the Arlington Street Church matter; it is over-generous not to regard Arlington Street as a joining of the larger conspiracy. Basically, all this means is that the dissent refuses to draw distinctions.

33. A similar situation involving a demonstrably active, as opposed to passive, participant in a bifarious organization, was faced in Hellman v. United States, [9 Cir., 1962, 298 F.2d 810]. While "Hellman was an exceedingly active member of the Party," 298 F.2d at 813, the court found that there was insufficient proof, given a *strictissimi juris* standard, to show specific intent to further the Party's illegal, as opposed to legal, methods. "[T]he activity portrayed is explainable on the basis that he intended to bring about the Party's ultimate goals through peaceable means."

put to the jury, in addition to the general issue of guilty or not guilty, ten special questions to be answered "Yes" or "No."

* * *

The submission of questions to the jury in civil cases is an everyday occurrence. In criminal cases, outside of a special, narrow area, the government is not only without precedent, but faces a formidable array of objections. The simplest is that the Federal Rules of Criminal Procedure contain no provision complementing F.R.Civ.P. 49 covering the civil practice. Indeed, as emphasizing this difference, we note that F.R.Crim.P. 23(c) provides for special findings by the judge. While the absence of a rule is not necessarily determinative, particularly in the light of F.R.Crim.P. 57(b), it is highly suggestive.

Of more substantive importance is the fundamental difference in the jury's functions in civil and criminal cases. In civil trials the judge, if the evidence is sufficiently one-sided, may direct the jury to find against the defendant even though the plaintiff entered the case bearing the burden of proof. F.R.Civ.P. 50. In a criminal case a court may not order the jury to return a verdict of guilty, no matter how overwhelming the evidence of guilt. This principle is so well established that its basis is not normally a matter of discussion. There is, however, a deep undercurrent of reasons. Put simply, the right to be tried by a jury of one's peers finally exacted from the king would be meaningless if the king's judges could call the turn. Bushel's Case, 124 Eng.Rep. 1006 (C.P.1670). In the exercise of its functions not only must the jury be free from direct control in its verdict, but it must be free from judicial pressure, both contemporaneous and subsequent. Both have been said to result from the submission of special questions.

> "It is one of the most essential features of the right of trial by jury that no jury should be compelled to find any but a general verdict in criminal cases, and the removal of this safeguard would violate its design and destroy its spirit."

G. Clementson, Special Verdicts and Special Findings by Juries, 49 (1905).

* * *

This merges into a more basic reason which the court noted but, because of special circumstances, did not accept, in United States v. Ogull, S.D.N.Y., 1957, 149 F.Supp. 272, 276, affirmed without discussion of this point, sub nom. United States v. Gernie, 2 Cir., 1958, 252 F.2d 664, cert. denied, 356 U.S. 968, 78 S.Ct. 1006, 2 L.Ed.2d 1073,

> "To ask the jury special questions might be said to infringe on its power to deliberate free from legal fetters; on its power to arrive at a general verdict without having to support it by reasons or by a report of its deliberations; and on its power to follow or not to follow the instructions of the

court. Moreover, any abridgement or modification of this institution would partly restrict its historic function, that of tempering rules of law by common sense brought to bear upon the facts of a specific case."

* * *

Uppermost of these considerations is the principle that the jury, as the conscience of the community, must be permitted to look at more than logic. Indeed, this is the principle upon which we began our discussion. If it were otherwise there would be no more reason why a verdict should not be directed against a defendant in a criminal case than in a civil one. The constitutional guarantees of due process and trial by jury require that a criminal defendant be afforded the full protection of a jury unfettered, directly or indirectly. See Morris v. United States, 9 Cir., 1946, 156 F.2d 525.

In this circumstance, the government makes two answers. The first is that in a small number of criminal cases special findings have been permitted. No useful purpose would be served by discussing these cases; they are distinguishable.[41]

* * *

We are not necessarily opposed to new procedures just because they are new, but they should be adopted with great hesitation. Cf. Gray v. United States, [174 F.2d 919, 924 (8th Cir. 1949), cert. denied 338 U.S. 848, 70 S.Ct. 90, 94 L.Ed. 519] ("It is not the function of the courts subordinate to the Supreme Court to introduce innovations of criminal procedure."). It takes but little imagination to see that the present case should be the last, rather than the first, to embark upon a practice of submitting special jury findings in a criminal case along with the general issue for no significant reason. Here, whereas, as we have pointed out, some defendants could be found to have exceeded the bounds of free speech, the issue was peculiarly one to which a community standard or conscience was, in the jury's discretion, to be applied. Cf. Wigmore, A Program for the Trial of Jury Trial, 12 Am.Jud.Soc.J. 166, 170–71 (1929). Whether we agree with defendants' position or not, this was not a case to be subjected to special limitations not sanctioned by general practice. We must hold the court's action to be prejudicial error.

The verdicts are set aside, and the judgments vacated. Judgments are to be entered for the defendants Spock and Ferber, and a new trial is ordered for the defendants Goodman and Coffin.

41. There are only two classes of cases in which such findings have been used. First, in certain cases the determination of a particular fact will be crucial to sentencing the defendants, as, for example, which of the several objects of a conspiracy, some felonies, some misdemeanors, the defendant agreed to, or the duration of a defendant's participation in a conspiracy. Gernie, 2 Cir., 1958, 252 F.2d 664, cert. denied, 356 U.S. 968, 78 S.Ct. 1006, 2 L.Ed.2d 1073. Second, in treason cases the finding of an overt act is specifically required by the federal constitution. U.S.Const. art. III, § 3.

COFFIN, Circuit Judge (dissenting in part).

I concur in that part of the court's opinion dealing with the submission of special questions to the jury. However, I would grant acquittals to all appellants, since, in my view, whatever substantive crimes of aiding, abetting, and counselling, or whatever more specific conspiracies may have been committed, the crime of conspiracy, as charged in the indictment, was not. To apply conspiracy doctrine to these cases is, in my view, not compelled by conspiracy precedents, not consistent with First Amendment principles, not required to deal effectively with the hazard to public security, and not capable of discriminating application as between the culpable and the innocent.

* * *

Historically, the doctrine of conspiracy was concerned with only a secret enterprise. Indeed, the word conspiracy devolves from the Latin "conspirare" meaning "to breathe together". If a group, having illegal designs, desired to achieve its ends through surprise, thus depriving society of open confrontation, assessment, and preparation, it was both fair and necessary to give society the means to deal with it effectively, i. e., the ability to prosecute individuals who may never commit a substantive offense or never be caught in committing one, but whose responsibility for and participation in the enterprise are established. Effective response also meant the ability of the state to act in timely fashion—to forestall a serious threat to its safety and welfare before a debacle occurred. Finally, the core idea underlying the conspiracy theory is that disciplined, concerted action poses a greater threat to society than does individual or uncoordinated group effort in that larger numbers permit a division of labor, and discipline makes withdrawal from the enterprise less likely.[1]

* * *

In the case of public "conspiracies" in the field of opinion, however, the historic rationale for prosecuting the instigators of a group effort loses much of its force. The fact that the group initially places itself at the mercy of the public marketplace of ideas, risking disapproval, recommends that it have the protection of the First Amendment in its effort to gain approval. That a public "agreement" has been arrived at is not so much the genesis of the undertaking or a key to identifying masterminds as it is the manifestation of common concern. There is no possibility of taking society by surprise. There is no difficulty in ascertaining the activists who bear watching.

1. The court, in its footnote 9, criticizes my reference to discipline as a traditional component of conspiracy, citing Interstate Circuit, Inc. v. United States, 306 U.S. 208, 59 S.Ct. 467, 83 L.Ed. 610 (1939). In that case cohesiveness was effectively assured by the presence of substantial economic factors which impelled near unanimity of action. To derive sanction from what was in effect a monopoly power play for the proposition that cohesiveness and discipline are unimportant in conspiracy law, particularly in the public expression area, seems to me an unjustified leap in the wrong direction.

One is tempted to say that the law should recognize no overt conspiracy in the sensitive area of public discussion and opinion. But this would be to go too far. Were this so, "going public" would confer an immunity both on nefarious joint undertakings and an absolute protection to criminal enterprise not vouchsafed by the First Amendment even for individual speech.

Do the cases indicate where the line should be drawn? Of course, closely-knit groups directed at the execution of orthodox criminal enterprises are clearly punishable as conspiracies. Although there are not many conspiracy cases in the field of opinion, I think it is possible to locate the outer limits of the reach of the conspiracy weapon. The cases closest to the traditional criminal conspiracy are those in which a disciplined, cohesive organization—perhaps more covert than overt—devotes itself with singleness of mind to one illegal purpose.[3] Then there are cases where a disciplined organization strives to accomplish a number of purposes, some legal and some illegal. In both types of cases the conspiracy cannot really be said to be open; and in both the combination is bound together by strict party-like discipline.

Moving along the spectrum to associations which are at once more adventitious and amorphous in structure and wholly overt in their functioning, we find little authority. When such a combination has as its objective a specific enterprise devoted to a single illegal purpose, it is possible to concede that a culpable conspiracy has been formed. The planning and execution of the Arlington Street Church draft card turn-in might have been such a conspiracy, assuming that the timing, publicity, and foreseeable impact provided a sufficient basis for finding a high probability of substantial harm. In such a case the participants would have been a discrete group; the objective of the affair would have been illegal (abetting turn-ins); and it

---

3. See, e. g., Dennis v. United States, 341 U.S. 494, 71 S.Ct. 587, 95 L.Ed. 1137 (1951); Pierce v. United States, 252 U.S. 239, 40 S.Ct. 205, 64 L.Ed. 542 (1920); Schenck v. United States, 249 U.S. 47, 39 S.Ct. 247, 63 L.Ed. 470 (1919).

The "public" conspiracy cases cited by the court would appear to fall within this category in that in each case the efforts of a cohesive group were aimed at a single illegal goal—the frustration of conscription. See, e. g., Wells v. United States, 257 F. 605 (9th Cir., 1919) (No Conscription League); Haywood v. United States, 268 F. 795 (7th Cir.), cert. denied, 256 U.S. 689, 41 S.Ct. 449, 65 L.Ed. 1172 (1920). (Industrial Workers of the World); Anderson v. United States, 273 F. 20 (8th Cir.), cert. denied, 257 U.S. 647,

42 S.Ct. 56, 66 L.Ed. 415 (1921) (Industrial Workers of the World); United States v. Gordon, 138 F.2d 174 (7th Cir.), cert. denied, 320 U.S. 798, 64 S.Ct. 266, 88 L.Ed. 481 (1943) (Peace Movement of Ethiopia).

Even within the limits of a cohesive group and a single illegal purpose I question whether the above cases would be sound authority today—not because age carries a presumption of invalidity, but because in none of the cases did the court demonstrate an appreciation of First Amendment issues. Indeed, in *Gordon*, supra, and *Wells*, supra, the First Amendment was discussed only in passing, and in *Haywood*, supra, and *Anderson*, supra, not at all. See also Fraina v. United States, 255 F. 28 (2d Cir. 1918), discussed infra.

might well be that one who planned but did not participate (and thus did not commit a substantive offense of aiding or abetting or counselling) would be indictable as a conspirator.

Such is the hypothetical case put by the court of a lynching-bent group of vigilantes. Openness of course could not pasteurize the illegality of purpose. The example, however, suffers in the limited and subordinate extent to which speech is involved. More apposite to the sharply defined open conspiracy in the free speech area is *Fraina v. United States*, 255 F. 28 (2d Cir. 1918). The factual situation is close to that which would have been presented by a conspiracy indictment against those responsible for the Arlington Church affair. Even this authority for this narrow proposition is less than robust.[5] And we have found no other.

But we face here something quite different from an indictment for an overt promotion of a specific event for an overriding illegal purpose. Here we confront a "conspiracy" where (1) the effort was completely public; (2) the issues were all in the public domain; (3) the group was ill-defined, shifting, with many affiliations; (4) the purposes in the "agreement" are both legal and illegal; and (5) the need for additional evidence to inculpate—notwithstanding the absence of a statutory requirement for an overt act—is recognized.

There is no legal precedent for applying the conspiracy theory to such an effort. This is, to my knowledge, the first attempt to use conspiracy as a prosecutorial device in such circumstances. The attempt to distill the several individual lessons taught by prior cases, mostly old, and combine them in such a case as this is not to apply precedents but to extend them. I would not—for the first time—grant this weapon to the government in this kind of case without the alternative assurance that hazards to individual rights would not be increased or that the interest in the nation's well-being and security cannot be as well served in less repressive ways. So viewing conspiracy law, I ask whether there are hazards to free expression of opinion in extending conspiracy to the cases at bar. The court has attempted to be scrupulously fair and sensitive to the possibility of abuse of the conspiracy weapon. It carefully rejects the use of "the

---

5. While a half century's age is not necessarily fatal, *Fraina* would not appear to have outlived its time. Two men addressed a meeting each detailing why he was a conscientious objector. A pamphlet describing the philosophy and proper response of the conscientious objector was distributed. The court, blessedly oblivious of contemporary meetings where a goodly part of the audience come to heckle, was able to say that if a meeting is called to hear certain speakers on a certain subject, "[I]t is impossible not to infer a combination in thought among the platform occupiers and their helpers." 255 F. at 34. The court drew sustenance from the principle that the standards by which to judge whether speech should be proscribed are "the common-law rules in force when the constitutional guaranties were established." In my view the court's comments on both conspiracy law and the First Amendment demonstrate that the opinion is only of antiquarian interest.

Call" to jeopardize its signers without the proof of specific intent. And equally carefully it delimits the ways in which specific intent can be established: (1) proof of prior or subsequent unambiguous statements; (2) proof of commission of illegal acts; (3) proof of subsequent legal acts clearly undertaken for rendering effective the advocated illegal action.

By so proceeding, the court goes far to depriving the "agreement" of significance. Indeed, it upholds the indictment as to only one of the original four signers of the "Call" and acquits another original signer. But the evil is that such a document is pregnant with any significance at all.

What are the implications of the three methods of activating one's signature to the "Call" to status as a full-fledged conspirator? To say that prior or subsequent unambiguous statements change the color of the litmus is to say that while one exercise of First Amendment rights is protected, two are not.[8] To say that actual commission of illegal acts (i. e., encouraging turning in or burning draft cards—not specifically described in the "Call") renders culpable the more opaque original "agreement" is to say simply that the subsequent commission of one crime becomes suddenly the commission of two crimes. To say that "subsequent *legal* acts clearly undertaken for rendering effective the advocated illegal action" [my emphasis] renders retrospectively conspiratorial the earlier protected ambiguous advocacy is to say that two rights make a wrong. For example, were the janitor of Arlington Church to have signed the "Call" and subsequently to have volunteered his services to tidy the pews for the turn-in, he would have metamorphosed into a conspirator.

* * *

To summarize, the hazards to free speech from the sequential open-endedness of the specific intent formulas and the lateral open-endedness of overbreadth and vagueness are not lightly to be tolerated. We should be slow to grant grudgingly today what may become license tomorrow. This leads to the question whether the danger to society justifies such circumscribing of First Amendment rights.

In addressing this question, both the court and I make reciprocal concessions. I concede that there is a need to maintain a peace time army, that a registrant may be convicted for violation of the draft laws, that one may be punished for encouraging such violation, that there exists a danger of widespread disaffection and resistance to the draft laws, and that the government is entitled to take all reason-

8. I assume that if X were to say unambiguously, before or after signing the "Call", "What I would really like to see is every local draft board deluged with turn-ins," he becomes a conspirator on the happening of the later event although each statement is, by itself, protected. Moreover, the period of time between the two statements is apparently subject to no statute of limitations.

able steps to protect itself before such disaffection becomes epidemic. The court concedes that speech need not be forbidden because it bears a causal relation to ultimate unlawful acts, and that the First Amendment rights of free speech and association are to prevail unless the government's interest in preventing substantive crimes is substantial or unless there is a "less restrictive alternative" to deal with the problem, citing United States v. Robel, 389 U.S. 258, 88 S.Ct. 419, 19 L.Ed.2d 508 (1967); Aptheker v. Secretary of State, 378 U.S. 500, 84 S.Ct. 1659, 12 L.Ed.2d 992 (1964); and Shelton v. Tucker, 364 U.S. 479, 81 S.Ct. 247, 5 L.Ed.2d 231 (1960). It concedes that this principle calls for a weighing.

Here we part company, for the court attends only to one side of the balance. Into that scale it puts four weights: (1) the nation's interest in raising an army; (2) the right of government, in view of "the potency of conspiratorial conduct", not to await the commission of substantive offenses; (3) the effectiveness as "incitement" of appellants' call for immediate action on a large number of sympathetic young men; and (4) the fact that Congress has authorized the conspiracy sanction.

Congressional authorization of the conspiracy sanction cannot, in my view, weigh heavily on the scales once a genuine issue is raised as to the availability of a less restrictive alternative. When, however, such a threat appears substantial, courts must ask if there are other approaches which "more precisely and narrowly" serve the same governmental interest. See United States v. O'Brien, 391 U.S. 367, 381, 88 S.Ct. 1673, 20 L.Ed.2d 672 (1968). The fact that Congress has prescribed one approach presents the occasion for weighing; it cannot additionally predetermine the result, or the less restrictive alternative doctrine, as applied, for example, in *Robel* and *Aptheker* would have no meaning.

Indeed, the question here is not really one of Congress' authority. In § 462(a) Congress has provided for the use of the conspiracy sanction, and I do not quarrel with its application in a proper case. All that can be drawn from the statute is that Congress authorized the use of conspiracy where appropriate to protect the nation's interest in raising an army. If it could be imagined that Congress intended to apply conspiracy to the facts of this case, my answer is that the First Amendment denies it the power to do so.

The unexplored question is whether these interests can be as well served without resort to the conspiracy weapon. Here the "agreement" itself was an insufficient predicate. Something more was required. Neither Coffin nor Goodman, under the court's rationale, became culpable until he made a statement or executed an act which constituted the substantive offense of aiding, abetting, or counselling draft evasion.

Had the appellants individually or collectively been indicted or tried for their separate offenses, the task would have been much simpler, as a reading of the transcript convincingly illustrates. The government would not have been delayed in time. It could have chosen whoever seemed most significant for psychological impact. Its proof against each would have been narrowly confined. It would not have faced the difficulties of special instructions on the occasion of the admission of evidence and on the occasion of the charge. I observe also that the penalty for conspiracy under § 462(a) is not greater than that for the substantive offenses. Moreover, the government could have chosen a specific incident for the focus of a conspiracy— as, for an arguable example, the Arlington Church turn-in or the Department of Justice card collection ceremony.

Nowhere does the court indicate why either approach could not have served the societal interest equally well. If "less restrictive alternative" is to have any real meaning, courts should examine with specificity the utility of the rifle before resort is had to the shotgun.

In short, the court's lack of emphasis on the "agreement" element results in its applying a form of substantive offense prosecution. The difference is—and it is a critical one—that a defendant may be punished not only for illegal acts but also on the basis of protected speech and legal acts. I conclude that prosecution for substantive offenses or for a narrow, discrete conspiracy, would fully serve the government's interest—perhaps even more than the court's sweeping conspiracy theory—without delivering such a serious blow to First Amendment freedoms.

To the extent that the court's acquittal of the defendants Spock and Ferber is thought to illustrate the discriminating capacity of its rationale to separate the sheep from the goats, I respectfully take issue. In my view the acquittals are not justified by the court's own guidelines.

* * *

In my view the court's acquittal of Spock and Ferber is the product of its own generosity rather than the inevitable result of its rationale. Were this only a disagreement over the application of legal principles, perhaps there would not be so much cause for concern. But this is a landmark case and no one, I take it, supposes that this will be the last attempt by the government to use the conspiracy weapon. The government has cast a wide net and caught only two fish. My objection is not that more were not caught but that the government can try again on another day in another court and the court's rationale provides no meaningful basis for predicting who will find themselves within the net. Finally, there is the greater danger that the casting of the net has scared away many whom the government had no right to catch.

APPENDIX

A Call to Resist Illegitimate Authority

———

To the young men of America, to the whole of the American people, and to all men of good will everywhere:

1.   An ever growing number of young American men are finding that the American war in Vietnam so outrages their deepest moral and religious sense that they cannot contribute to it in any way.   We share their moral outrage.

2.   We further believe that the war is unconstitutional and illegal.   Congress has not declared a war as required by the Constitution.   Moreover, under the Constitution, treaties signed by the President and ratified by the Senate have the same force as the Constitution itself.   The Charter of the United Nations is such a treaty.   The Charter specifically obligates the United States to refrain from force or the threat of force in international relations.   It requires member states to exhaust every peaceful means of settling disputes and to submit disputes which cannot be settled peacefully to the Security Council.   The United States has systematically violated all of these Charter provisions for thirteen years.

3.   Moreover, this war violates international agreements, treaties and principles of law which the United States Government has solemnly endorsed.   The combat role of the United States troops in Vietnam violates the Geneva Accords of 1954 which our government pledged to support but has since subverted.   The destruction of rice, crops and livestock; the burning and bulldozing of entire villages consisting exclusively of civilian structures; the interning of civilian non-combatants in concentration camps; the summary executions of civilians in captured villages who could not produce satisfactory evidence of their loyalties or did not wish to be removed to concentration camps; the slaughter of peasants who dared to stand up in their fields and shake their fists at American helicopters;—these are all actions of the kind which the United States and the other victorious powers of World War II declared to be crimes against humanity for which individuals were to be held personally responsible even when acting under the orders of their governments and for which Germans were sentenced at Nuremberg to long prison terms and death.   The prohibition of such acts as war crimes was incorporated in treaty law by the Geneva Conventions

of 1949, ratified by the United States. These are commitments to other countries and to Mankind, and they would claim our allegiance even if Congress should declare war.

4. We also believe it is an unconstitutional denial of religious liberty and equal protection of the laws to withhold draft exemption from men whose religious or profound philosophical beliefs are opposed to what in the Western religious tradition have been long known as unjust wars.

5. Therefore, we believe on all these grounds that every free man has a legal right and a moral duty to exert every effort to end this war, to avoid collusion with it, and to encourage others to do the same. Young men in the armed forces or threatened with the draft face the most excruciating choices. For them various forms of resistance risk separation from their families and their country, destruction of their careers, loss of their freedom and loss of their lives. Each must choose the course of resistance dictated by his conscience and circumstances. Among those already in the armed forces some are refusing to obey specific illegal and immoral orders, some are attempting to educate their fellow servicemen on the murderous and barbarous nature of the war, some are absenting themselves without official leave. Among those not in the armed forces some are applying for status as conscientious objectors to American aggression in Vietnam, some are refusing to be inducted. Among both groups some are resisting openly and paying a heavy penalty, some are organizing more resistance within the United States and some have sought sanctuary in other countries.

6. We believe that each of these forms of resistance against illegitimate authority is courageous and justified. Many of us believe that open resistance to the war and the draft is the course of action most likely to strengthen the moral resolve with which all of us can oppose the war and most likely to bring an end to the war.

7. We will continue to lend our support to those who undertake resistance to this war. We will raise funds to organize draft resistance unions, to supply legal defense and bail, to support families and otherwise aid resistance to the war in whatever ways may seem appropriate.

8. We firmly believe that our statement is the sort of speech that under the First Amendment must be free, and that the actions we will undertake are as legal as is the war resistance of the young men themselves. But we recognize that the courts may find otherwise, and that if so we might all be liable to prosecution and severe punishment. In any case, we feel that we cannot shrink from fulfilling our re-

sponsibilities to the youth whom many of us teach, to the country whose freedom we cherish, and to the ancient traditions of religion and philosophy which we strive to preserve in this generation.

9.   We call upon all men of good will to join us in this confrontation with immoral authority. Especially we call upon the universities to fulfill their mission of enlightenment and religious organizations to honor their heritage of brotherhood. Now is the time to resist.

For further information contact

RESIST, 166–5th Ave., NYC
10010/675–2270

* Printed by volunteer labor

Resist

Room 210, 166 Fifth Avenue, New York

August 1967

Dear Friend:

The time has come to resist the war in Vietnam.

The enclosed statement, "A Call to Resist Illegitimate Authority," constitutes a first step toward the more vigorous response to the war which the time requires of us. Those who have signed, including ourselves, have pledged themselves to extend material and moral support to young men who are directly resisting the war. Many of us are further committed to joining those young men in acts of civil disobedience.

Over 200 persons have already signed the statement. The statement and the names of the signers will be made public at the end of September through a press conference held by a committee of prominent signers and through ads in *The New York Review of Books* and *The New Republic*.

We ask you to join us by signing "A Call to Resist Illegitimate Authority." More than that, we ask you to commit yourself to the fullest possible extent to the tasks of resisting the war and bringing it to a halt.

There is an urgent need for funds to bring assistance to draft resisters and to those in the armed forces who refuse to fight in Vietnam. Will you help as generously as you can?

There is an equally urgent need to organize local groups of academics, clergymen, professionals and other adults for the purpose of directly supporting those who resist the draft and the armed forces. Are you willing to organize or join such a group in your community?

We *can* all do something to end this war. And we must.

Sincerely,

(s) Noam Chomsky
Noam Chomsky

(s) Dwight Macdonald
Dwight Macdonald

(s) William S. Coffin, Jr.
William S. Coffin, Jr.

(s) Benjamin Spock
Benjamin Spock

----

clip and send to: RESIST / Rm. 510 / 166 5th Ave. / NYC 10010

...... I wish to sign "A Call to Resist Illegitimate Authority" and am willing to have my endorsement made public.

...... I enclose a contribution of $....... to support the work of RESIST. (Please make checks payable to RESIST.)

...... I am interested in organizing or joining a group in my community to support young men directly resisting the war.

name ....

profession and title ....

address ....

city .... state ....

phone .... (office) .... (home)

V. THE HOMICIDE OFFENSES

WOLFGANG, A SOCIOLOGICAL ANALYSIS OF CRIMINAL HOMICIDE

Federal Probation, Vol. 25, No. 4 (March, 1961) pages 48, 49, 53.

[R]esearch was conducted in Philadelphia, using all criminal homicides recorded by the Philadelphia Homicide Squad from January 1, 1948 through December 31, 1952. Excusable and justifiable homicides were excluded from the study and concentration was only on criminal cases listed by the police. * * *

During the period from 1948 through 1952 there were 588 cases of criminal homicide in Philadelphia; i.e., there were 588 victims. Because several people were sometimes involved in killing one person, there were 621 offenders arrested by the police and taken into custody. In terms of a mean annual rate per 100,000 population in the city, the victim rate was 5.7 and the offender rate 6.0. This is neither high nor low. Compared with 18 other cities across the country, each of which had a population of a quarter of a million or more in 1950, Philadelphia ranks ninth, with the range between Miami having a victim rate of 15.1 and Milwaukee having a low of 2.3. * * *

Some Basic Findings: Race, Sex, and Age

Research has shown that although criminal homicide is largely an unplanned act, there are nonetheless in the act regular uniformities and patterns. We have found, as previous research has noted, that there is a statistically significant association between criminal homicide and the race and sex of both victim and offender. Negroes and males involved in homicide far exceed their proportions in the general population and rates for these two groups are many times greater than for whites and females. The rate per 100,000 by race and sex of offenders reveals the following rank order of magnitude: Negro males (41.7), Negro females (9.3), white males (3.4), and white females (.4). Although Negroes of either sex, and males of either race, are positively related to criminal slayings, the association between race and homicide is statistically more significant than that between sex and homicide. * * *

Among offenders, the age group 20–24 predominates with a rate of 12.6 per 100,000, while the highest rate for victims is in the age group 25–34. In short, victims are generally older than their offenders; the median age of the former being 35.1 years and of the latter 31.9 years. The importance of the race factor here is striking in view of the fact that the *lowest* 5-year age-specific rates for Negro males and females are similar to, or higher than the *highest* of such

910

rates for white males and females, respectively. Although males of both races more frequently commit criminal homicide during their twenties than during any other period of life, Negro males in their early sixties kill as frequently as do white males in their early twenties.

* * *

Place Where Crimes Occur

The place where the crime occurred is also important. The most dangerous single place is the highway (public street, alley, or field), although more slayings occur in the home than outside the home. Men kill and are killed most frequently in the street, while women kill most often in the kitchen but are killed in the bedroom. For victims and offenders of each race and sex group significant differences have been noted. Most cases of Negro males who kill Negro males involve a stabbing in a public street; most cases of white males who kill white males involve a beating in a public street. * * *

Presence of Alcohol

Either or both the victim and offender had been drinking immediately prior to the slaying in nearly two-thirds of the cases. The presence of alcohol in the homicide situation appears to be significantly associated with Negroes—either as victims or as offenders—and, separately, with Negro male and female victims. Particular caution must be exercised in evaluating the presence of alcohol in these homicides, since drinking—particularly on Saturday night, the time of highest incidence of homicide—is an integral part of the mores of most groups involved in this crime. A significantly higher proportion of weekend homicides than of homicides occurring during the remainder of the week had alcohol present (in either the victim, the offender, or both). An association between alcohol, weekend slayings, and the payment of wages on Friday was indicated and crudely confirmed by the available data. We have, therefore, suggested that when the socioeconomic group most likely to commit homicide almost simultaneously receives its weekly wages, purchases alcohol, and meets together socially, it is not unlikely that the incidence of homicide should also rise.

Previous Police Record and Victim-Offender Relationships

Contrary to many past impressions, an analysis of offenders in criminal homicide reveals a relatively high proportion who have a previous police or arrest record. Of total offenders, nearly two-thirds have a previous arrest record, and of total victims, almost half have such a record. Having a previous record is also associated with males both among victims and offenders, and is obvious from the fact that more *male victims* have such a record than do *female offenders*. Moreover, when an offender has a previous record, he is more likely to have a record of offenses against the person than against property; and when he has a record of offenses against the person, he is more likely than not to have a record of having committed a serious assault offense, such as aggravated assault or assault with intent to kill. A greater proportion of Negro male and female victims have a previous arrest record than do white male and female offenders, respectively.

* * *

Criminal homicide usually results from a vaguely defined altercation, domestic quarrel, jealousy, argument over money, and robbery. These five police-recorded "motives" are involved in 8 out of 10 cases. Most of the identified victim-offender relationships may be classified as "primary group" relations, or those that include intimate, close, frequent contacts. Close friends and relatives accounted for over half of the contacts, and the combined categories which involve primary group contacts constitute 59 percent of all victim-offender relationships among males, but significantly as much as 84 percent among females. Because white males were killed more frequently than Negro males during the commission of a robbery, the former were also more frequently strangers to their slayers than the latter.

Mate slayings have been given special attention. Of the 100 husband-wife homicides, 53 victims were wives and 47 were husbands. The number of wives killed by their husbands constitutes 41 percent of all women killed, whereas husbands slain by their wives make up only 11 percent of all men killed. Thus, when a woman commits homicide, she is more likely than a man to kill her mate; and when a man is killed by a woman, he is most likely to be killed by his wife. Husbands are often killed by their wives in the kitchen with a butcher knife, but nearly half of the wives are slain in the bedroom. More male than female offenders in these spouse slayings were found guilty, were convicted of more serious degrees of homicide, and committed suicide.

In 94 percent of the cases, the victim and offender were members of the same race, but in only 64 percent they were of the same sex. Thus, the ratio of intra- to interracial homicide is 15.2 to 1; but the ratio of intra- to intersex homicide is only 1.8 to 1. In general, it may be said that victims were homicidally assaulted most frequently by males of their own race, and least frequently by females of another race.

In 32 cases involving 57 offenders and 6 victims, a felony, in addition to the killing, was perpetrated at the time of the slaying. In most cases the other felony was robbery, and white males accounted for a larger proportion of these felony-murders than they did among all homicides in general.

Victim-Precipitated Homicide

The term *victim-precipitated* homicide has been introduced to refer to those cases in which the victim is a direct, positive precipitator in the crime—the first to use physical force in the homicide drama. After establishing a theoretical and legal basis for analysis, the Philadelphia data reveal several factors significantly associated with the 150 victim-precipitated homicides, which is 26 percent of all homicides. These factors are: Negro victims and offenders, male victims, female offenders, stabbings, victim-offender relationships involving male victims and female offenders, mate slayings, husbands who were victims in mate slayings, alcohol, victims with a previous arrest record, particularly an arrest record of assault. Thus, in most of these cases, the role and characteristics of the victim and offender are reversed, the victim assumes the role of determinant, and the victim makes a definite contribution to the genesis of his own victimization.

Recently, I have extended the meaning of victim precipitated homicide to include a sociological and psychoanalytic discussion of these 150 victims as being bent on suicide. Although it is impossible to verify an assumption of subconscious suicide wishes among these victims, empirical data from broad social factors combine with psychological and sociological data suggesting that victims in many cases present themselves as willing targets for violent aggression leading to homicide.

*   *   *

Court Dispositions

Finally, analysis has been made of the tempo of legal procedures, of court disposition, designation of the degree of homicide, insanity, and sentences imposed by the court. Two-thirds of the offenders were arrested on the same day that the crime was committed, and over half appeared in court for trial within 6 months after the crime. Two-thirds of those taken into police custody, and over three-quarters of those who experienced a court trial were declared guilty. Proportionately, Negroes and males were convicted more frequently than whites and females; but previous analysis of the nature of these cases reveals that Negroes and males had in fact committed more serious offenses   *   *   *[.]

Of the 387 offenders convicted and sentenced, 30 percent were guilty of murder in the first degree, 29 percent of murder in the second degree, 36 percent of voluntary manslaughter, and 15 percent of involuntary manslaughter. Less than 3 percent of the offenders were declared insane by the courts   *   *   *[.]

NOTE

Of what, if any, value is this type of information in formulating or working with the substantive law of homicide? Should an effort be made to differentiate for legal purposes any of the categories of offenders described by Wolfgang? To what extent do the categories created by the statutes in the next section do this? Is the Wolfgang material helpful in determining the extent to which reliance should be placed upon severity of penalty—or upon criminal penalties at all—in preventing killings?

A. STATUTORY FORMULATIONS

PENN. STAT. ANN. TITLE 18 (1963)

§ 4701. Murder of the first and second degree

All murder which shall be perpetrated by means of poison, or by lying in wait, or by any other kind of willful, deliberate and premeditated killing, or which shall be committed in the perpetration of, or attempting to perpetrate any arson, rape, robbery, burglary, or kidnapping, shall be murder in the first degree. All other kinds of murder shall be murder in the second degree. * * *

Whoever is convicted of the crime of murder of the first degree is guilty of a felony and shall be sentenced to suffer death in the manner provided by law, or to undergo imprisonment for life, at the discretion of the jury trying the case, which shall, in the manner hereinafter provided, fix the penalty. * * *

Whoever is convicted of the crime of murder of the second degree is guilty of a felony, and shall, for the first offense, be sentenced to undergo imprisonment by separate or solitary confinement not exceeding twenty (20) years, or fined not exceeding ten thousand dollars, or both, and for the second offense, shall undergo imprisonment for the period of his natural life.

§ 4703. Voluntary and involuntary manslaughter

Whoever is convicted of voluntary manslaughter is guilty of a felony, and shall be sentenced to pay a fine not exceeding six thousand dollars ($6,000), and to undergo imprisonment, by separate or solitary confinement at labor or simple imprisonment, not exceeding twelve (12) years, and in the discretion of the court, to give security for good behavior during life, or for any less time, according to the nature and enormity of the offense.

Whoever is convicted of involuntary manslaughter, happening in consequence of an unlawful act, or the doing of a lawful act in an unlawful way, is guilty of a misdemeanor, and shall be sentenced to pay a fine not exceeding two thousand dollars ($2,000), or to undergo imprisonment not exceeding three (3) years, or both.

CALIFORNIA PENAL CODE (1970)

§ 187. Murder defined

MURDER DEFINED. Murder is the unlawful killing of a human being, with malice aforethought.

§ 188. Malice, express malice, and implied malice defined

MALICE DEFINED. Such malice may be express or implied. It is express when there is manifested a deliberate intention unlawfully to take away the life of a fellow creature. It is implied, when no considerable provocation appears, or when the circumstances attending the killing show an abandoned and malignant heart.

§ 189. Murder; degrees

All murder which is perpetrated by means of a bomb, poison, lying in wait, torture, or by any other kind of willful, deliberate, and premeditated killing, or which is committed in the perpetration of, or attempt to perpetrate, arson, rape, robbery, burglary, mayhem, or any act punishable under Section 288 [prohibiting "any lewd or lascivious act * * * upon or with the body, or any part or member thereof, of a child under the age of fourteen years, with the intent of arousing, appealing to, or gratifying the lust or passions or sexual desires of such person or of such child * * *"], is murder of the first degree; and all other kinds of murders are of the second degree.

As used in this section, "bomb" includes any device, substance, or preparation, other than fixed ammunition or fireworks regulated under * * * the Health and Safety Code, which is designed to cause an explosion and is capable of causing death or serious bodily injury.

§ 190. Murder; punishment; discretion of jury

Every person guilty of murder in the first degree shall suffer death, or confinement in the state prison for life, at the discretion of the court or jury trying the same, and the matter of punishment shall be determined [in a separate proceeding before the court or a jury], and every person guilty of murder in the second degree is punishable by imprisonment in the state prison from five years to life.

§ 192. Manslaughter; voluntary, involuntary, and in driving a vehicle defined; construction of section

Manslaughter is the unlawful killing of a human being, without malice. It is of three kinds:

1. Voluntary—upon a sudden quarrel or heat of passion.

2. Involuntary—in the commission of an unlawful act, not amounting to felony; or in the commission of a lawful act which

might produce death, in an unlawful manner, or without due caution and circumspection; provided that this subdivision shall not apply to acts committed in the driving of a vehicle.

3. In the driving of a vehicle—

(a) In the commission of an unlawful act, not amounting to felony, with gross negligence; or in the commission of a lawful act which might produce death, in an unlawful manner, and with gross negligence.

(b) In the commission of an unlawful act, not amounting to felony, without gross negligence; or in the commission of a lawful act which might produce death, in an unlawful manner, but without gross negligence.

This section shall not be construed as making any homicide in the driving of a vehicle punishable which is not a proximate result of the commission of an unlawful act, not amounting to felony, or of the commission of a lawful act which might produce death, in an unlawful manner.

§ 193. Manslaughter; punishment

Manslaughter is punishable by imprisonment in the state prison for not exceeding 15 years, except that a violation of subsection 3 of Section 192 of this code is punishable as follows: In the case of a violation of subdivision (a) of said subsection 3 the punishment shall be either by imprisonment in the county jail for not more than one year or in the state prison for not more than five years, and in such case the jury may recommend by their verdict that the punishment shall be by imprisonment in the county jail; in the case of a violation of subdivision (b) of said subsection 3, the punishment shall be by imprisonment in the county jail for not more than one year. In cases where, as authorized in this section, the jury recommends by their verdict that the punishment shall be by imprisonment in the county jail, the court shall not have authority to sentence the defendant to imprisonment in the state prison, but may nevertheless place the defendant on probation as provided in this code.

PROPOSED FEDERAL CRIMINAL CODE (1971)

Homicide

§ 1601. Murder

A person is guilty of murder, a Class A felony, if he:

(a) intentionally or knowingly causes the death of another human being;

(b) causes the death of another human being under circumstances manifesting extreme indifference to the value of human life; or

(c) acting either alone or with one or more other persons, commits or attempts to commit treason, offenses defined in sections 1102 [Participating in or Facilitating War Against the United States Within Its Territory] or 1103 [Armed Insurrection] espionage, sabotage, robbery, burglary, kidnapping, felonious restraint, arson, rape, aggravated involuntary sodomy, or escape and, in the course of and in furtherance of such crime or of immediate flight therefrom, he, or another participant, if there be any, causes the death of a person other than one of the participants; except that in any prosecution under this paragraph in which the defendant was not the only participant in the underlying crime, it is an affirmative defense that the defendant:

(i) did not commit the homicidal act or in any way solicit, command, induce, procure, counsel or aid the commission thereof; and

(ii) was not armed with a firearm, destructive device, dangerous weapon or other weapon which under the circumstances indicated a readiness to inflict serious bodily injury; and

(iii) reasonably believed that no other participant was armed with such a weapon; and

(iv) reasonably believed that no other participant intended to engage in conduct likely to result in death or serious bodily injury.

Paragraphs (a) and (b) shall be inapplicable in the circumstances covered by paragraph (b) of section 1602.

§ 1602. Manslaughter

A person is guilty of a Class B felony if he:

(a) recklessly causes the death of another human being; or

(b) causes the death of another human being under circumstances which would be murder, except that he causes the death under the influence of extreme emotional disturbance for which there is reasonable excuse. The reasonableness of the excuse shall be determined from the viewpoint of a person in his situation under the circumstances as he believes them to be. An emotional disturbance is excusable, within the meaning of this paragraph, if it is occasioned by any provocation, event or situation for which the offender was not culpably responsible.

§ 1603. Negligent Homicide

A person is guilty of a Class C felony if with criminal negligence he causes the death of another human being.

NOTES

1. As an alternative to what became § 1601(c) in the Proposed Federal Criminal Code, the Study Draft proposed the following expansion of what became § 1601(b):

> (b) causes the death of another human being under circumstances manifesting extreme indifference to the value of human life. Such indifference is presumed if the actor is engaged in the commission of, or an attempt to commit, or flight after committing or attempting to commit, a Class A or B felony or a felony involving force or danger to human life. An accomplice of such actor in the commission of or attempt to commit such felony is deemed an accomplice in the conduct causing the death. A participant in such felony is deemed to have caused a death resulting from resistance to the commission of the felony or from prevention or an attempt to prevent flight of a participant, whether or not the killing is committed by a participant.

2. The California statute and the Proposed Federal Criminal Code define murder as the killing of a "human being." In Keeler v. Superior Court, 2 Cal.3d 619, 87 Cal.Rptr. 481, 470 P.2d 617 (1970), the California Supreme Court held, over dissent, that "human being" did not include an unborn but viable foetus. In the case before it, there was little doubt that the defendant had assaulted a woman with the intention of aborting the foetus. Is this appropriate? Why, or why not?

The California statutes were amended to provide as follows:

§ 187. Murder defined; death of fetus

(a) Murder is the unlawful killing of a human being, or a fetus, with malice aforethought.

(b) This section shall not apply to any person who commits an act which results in the death of a fetus if any of the following apply:

(1) The act complied with the Therapeutic Abortion Act, Chapter 11 (commencing with Section 25950) of Division 20 of the Health and Safety Code.

(2) The act was committed by a holder of a physician's and surgeon's certificate, as defined in the Business and Professions Code, in a case where, to a medical certainty, the result of childbirth would be death of the mother of the fetus or where her death from childbirth, although not medically certain, would be substantially certain or more likely than not.

(3) The act was solicited, aided, abetted, or consented to by the mother of the fetus.

(c) Subdivision (b) shall not be construed to prohibit the prosecution of any person under any other provision of law.

Cal.Penal Code § 187 (1972 Supp.). Is this an appropriate resolution of the problem? See Comment, Is The Intentional Killing of An Unborn Child Homicide? California's Law to Punish The Willful Killing of a Fetus, 2 Pac.L.J. 170 (1971). Is the matter at all affected by the United States Supreme Court's decisions severely restricting the extent to which abortions may be prohibited? See Roe v. Wade, —— U.S. ——, 93 S.Ct. 705, 35 L.Ed. 2d 147 (1973); Doe v. Bolton, —— U.S. ——, 93 S.Ct. 755, 35 L.Ed.2d 201 (1973).

3. For general treatments of the law of homicide, see R. Moreland, Law of Homicide (1952); Danforth, The Model Penal Code and Degrees of Homicide, 11 Am.U.L.Rev. 147 (1962); Parker, The Evolution of Criminal Responsibility, 9 Alberta L.Rev. 47 (1970); Perkins, The Law of Homicide, 36 J.Crim.L. & C. 391 (1946); Wechsler and Michael, A Rationale of the Law of Homicide, 37 Colum.L.Rev. 701, 1261 (1937). For a discussion emphasizing Canadian law, see Hooper, Some Anomalies and Developments in the Law of Homicide, 3 U.B.C.L.Rev. 55 (1967). English law is covered in Royal Commission on Capital Punishment 1949–1953, Report 25 72 (1953).

B. THE STATE OF MIND REQUIRED FOR MURDER: MALICE AFORETHOUGHT

PEOPLE v. MORRIN

Michigan Court of Appeals, 1971.
31 Mich.App. 301, 187 N.W.2d 434.

LEVIN, Judge. Leslie Taylor Morrin was convicted of first-degree murder by a jury in Monroe County Circuit Court. At the trial he testified that he killed the victim in self-defense. His evidence, coupled with the jury's unquestioned right to reject the claim of self-defense, provided sufficient evidence to sustain a verdict finding that he committed the crime of second-degree murder by killing another human being with malice aforethought.

* * *

I.

Morrin killed William Abell, a 53-year-old unmarried male. Abell died from some combination of eight blows to the head inflicted by Morrin with a large pair of tongs.

There were no witnesses to the killing or the events that preceded it. Morrin's testimony is the only affirmative evidence concerning the circumstances of the killing.

Morrin was 37 years old at the time of the killing. He was a millwright by trade. On March 27, 1967, at approximately 8:30 A.M., he completed seventeen hours of work in Oregon, Ohio. He testified that after eating breakfast he went to a union hall in nearby Toledo, Ohio, to talk to the union's business agent. Finding that the agent was not there, he stopped at a nearby bar, where he periodically phoned the union hall to see if the business agent had returned. Morrin drank seven or eight glasses of beer before 1:00 P.M., when he learned the agent was gone for the day.

While sitting in the bar, Morrin was approached by Abell, a complete stranger. Abell asked for a ride to Erie, Michigan, which was near Morrin's home in Monroe, Michigan. After Morrin learned that the business agent was unavailable, he and Abell left together.

When they reached Erie, Abell asked to be taken to a specific location. Morrin agreed, and proceeded at Abell's direction to traverse a number of quite remote, unpaved roads. Ultimately the car became mired in a mudhole. Abell alighted to push while Morrin attempted to extricate the vehicle by rocking the wheels. Their joint efforts succeeded, and the car was freed, whereupon Abell reentered the car.

At this point, Morrin testified, Abell pulled out a knife. Grabbing Morrin by the hair, he held the knife to his throat. Morrin offered to let Abell have all the money in his possession. Abell said that Morrin would first have to commit an oral sexual act upon him.

With Abell still holding the knife at Morrin's throat, they slid out of the car, whereupon Morrin was forced to assume a kneeling position, facing Abell. Abell directed Morrin to remove his (Abell's) trousers, but when Morrin did not move Abell partially removed them himself. Abell then commanded Morrin to commit the sexual act. When Morrin still did not move, Abell grasped him by the back of the head to pull him forward.

Morrin testified that he then struck Abell in the testicles. Rising to his feet, Morrin started to flee before he saw Abell advancing on him with the knife. Morrin then grabbed a large pair of tongs from the back seat of the car. (The tongs apparently were one of the tools of his trade and he customarily took them on trips to and from work.) A struggle then ensued and the two men exchanged blows. Finally, as Morrin swung the tongs, they entered Abell's rectum. Abell fell forward slightly and Morrin struck him several more times with the tongs. When Abell fell to the ground, Morrin seized Abell's knife and threw it away. (The knife was not found.) Morrin then ran to his car and drove away. He drove straight home, stopping once at a gasoline station. He told the attendant that he had been in a scuffle.

Upon reaching home, he was in a distraught and hysterical state. His wife called his sister who immediately came over. Morrin said that he had hurt someone, perhaps killed him. He was crying and somewhat incoherent. He kept repeating the words, "if he hadn't disgusted me so." He took his sister out to the car to convince her he was telling the truth. His sister washed the blood off the car and also washed the tongs which were in the back seat.

Morrin and his sister drove back to the place of the fight to see whether Abell was alive. The sister drove. It took them some time to find the exact place. Morrin alone got out of the car and found that Abell was, indeed, dead. They then returned home. It was agreed that they would do nothing immediately but would take some action the next morning.

The sister then returned to her home and phoned an attorney who then phoned the police. The police picked up the sister who took them to Abell's body. Morrin said that the next morning, without having heard from his sister, he decided to turn himself in. He met the police on the way to his sister's home.

This was substantially the evidence upon which the case went to the jury. The prosecution introduced numerous photographs of the deceased taken at the scene. Morrin produced two character witnesses. Throughout the trial, the prosecutor repeatedly emphasized the bizarre rectal wound suffered by Abell; he claimed that the wound was inflicted after Abell was already dead.

The jury was instructed on the elements of first-degree murder, second-degree murder, and manslaughter, as well as self-defense.

II.

Homicide, the killing of one human being by another, may be innocent or criminal. There are two categories of innocent homicide; they are called justifiable homicide and excusable homicide. Homicide is "justifiable" if it is authorized (*e.g.*, self-defense) or commanded (*e.g.*, execution of a death sentence) by law. Homicide is "excusable" if the death is the result of an accident and the actor was not criminally negligent.

A person who kills another is guilty of the crime of murder if the homicide is committed with malice aforethought. Malice aforethought is the intention to kill, actual or implied, under circumstances which do not constitute excuse or justification or mitigate the degree of the offense to manslaughter. The intent to kill may be implied where the actor actually intends to inflict great bodily harm or the natural tendency of his behavior is to cause death or great bodily harm. (The common-law felony-murder rule is an example of implied intent or implied malice aforethought.)

Thus, as "malice aforethought" is now defined, a killing may be murder even though the actor harbored no hatred or ill will against the victim and even though he "acted on the spur of the moment." Whatever may be the philological origin of the words "malice aforethought," today "each word has a different significance in legal usage than in ordinary conversation."

The nature of malice aforethought is the source of much of the confusion that attends the law of homicide. The cause of this confusion has been the evolution of malice aforethought from an independently significant element of murder to a "term of art" whose significance is largely historical and procedural.

The precise roots of malice aforethought are uncertain. Common-law courts spoke of "malice prepense" as early as the 13th century. The requirement that malice aforethought be established in all murder prosecutions represented the common law's recognition that a rational legal system will punish certain homicides (for example, those that are intentional) while excusing others (accidental homicides, for example).

From the beginning malice aforethought was defined principally in functional terms. We know what it did; it both distinguished criminal from innocent homicide and murder from manslaughter. Yet what it was, the precise state of mind which it described, eluded symmetrical definition.

The common-law courts were faced with a difficult problem: malice aforethought was a requisite element of murder, but one so elusive that in many cases it resisted direct proof. Their solution was to create a presumption of malice. As early as the 16th century proof that the accused person killed the victim gave rise to a "presumption" that the act was done with malice aforethought. Once it was established that the accused killed the victim, the burden was upon the accused to prove circumstances of justification, excuse, or mitigation.

This rule, firmly rooted in English law, has taken hold in a great many American jurisdictions, including Michigan * * *.

The merits of the rule are that it relieves the prosecution from the necessity of proving the nonexistence of circumstances of excuse, justification, and mitigation—frequently an impossible burden—and instead allocates the burden of proving such circumstances to the defendant, who, arguably, has greater ability to do so than the prosecution.

*　　*　　*

There is also, however, a grave drawback to this presumptive device. This defect arises in connection with jury instructions, to instruct a jury that malice is presumed from the fact of killing is to invite confusion concerning the ultimate burden of proof in the trial. The prosecution must always prove the defendant guilty beyond a reasonable doubt; a rule of law that shifts the burden of proof with respect to "malice" tends to cloud the dimensions of the prosecution's ultimate burden.

It was this danger which led the House of Lords in 1935 to repudiate instructions that charged jurors that they are to presume malice from the mere fact of killing.[21] Speaking of the presumption of innocence as a "golden thread" running through the common law, the Court rejected a formulation that required the jurors to find a defendant guilty unless he discharged his burden of rebutting the presumption of malice.

The Court did not rule that malice must be proved by evidence independent of the killing itself. The fact of homicide still *permits* the jury to find malice aforethought. But it in no sense *compels* such a finding, even absent any evidence of excuse, justification or mitigation on the part of the defendant.

> "All that is meant is that if it is proved that the conscious act of the prisoner killed a man and nothing else appears in the case, there is evidence upon which the jury may, not must, find him guilty of murder." Woolmington v. The Director of Public Prosecutions, [1935] AC 462, 480.

The Michigan Supreme Court recognized at an early date the importance of categorizing malice aforethought as a permissible inference rather than a presumption.

* * *

Consider that the term "malice aforethought" is supposed to signify both what murder is: the presence of an essential element of the offense (intent to kill, actual or implied), and what it isn't: the absence of certain defenses (excuse and justification)—but not other defenses [24]—and, as well, the absence of circumstances which would mitigate the seriousness of the offense reducing it to manslaughter. Add that the term "malice aforethought" does not mean malice as used in ordinary speech,[25] and forethought is not required, and it becomes clear that it is well-nigh impossible to communicate to jurors in the arcane jargon of malice aforethought the mental state required. No doubt many jurors are confused, and many, in error but under-

21. Woolmington v. The Director of Public Prosecutions, [1935] A.C. 462, 472. * * *

24. Coercion, mistake, insanity, among others are possible defenses, but they would not necessarily negative malice aforethought taken to mean intent to kill, actual or implied, neither excused nor justified.

25. Since "malice," as that word is used in ordinary speech, is not an issue, it is misleading to continue to speak to juries of ill will, corruption or malignancy of heart and depravity of the soul. It is, of course, arguable that where the issue is first-degree or second-degree murder, a court might describe one who premeditates and deliberates and decides to kill as being corrupt, malignant or depraved. But the issue is whether the actor deliberated or premeditated, not whether he was corrupt, malignant or depraved. Similarly, those words can be used to distinguish the "non-malignant" conduct of a person who accidentally kills his victim or who acted in self-defense or under circumstances of mitigation; however, again, the true issue would not be whether the actor was corrupt, malignant or depraved but whether he was justified in acting as he did in self-defense or whether it was an accident or there were circumstances of mitigation.

standably, make up their own working definition out of their own appreciation of what malice aforethought "must" mean.

* * *

The new penal codes, in defining the crime of murder, eliminate the word "malice." Although Michigan has not remolded its penal code along these lines, a restatement of the common law need not wait upon legislative action. Murder is a common-law crime: "Neither murder nor manslaughter is defined by our statutes, and the definition of murder remains the same as at common law." 3 Gillespie, Michigan Criminal Law and Practice, § 1637, p. 1969. If the language of the common law is misleading it should be clarified. It is the duty of the common-law courts to speak clearly in language that jurors can understand, not to persist in the lazy repetition of words which have lost all capacity to convey relevant thoughts and which are frequently misleading.

The problem of formulating suitable instructions on malice aforethought does not lend itself to ready solution. Although the formulation of jury instructions is outside the scope of this opinion, defendants charged with murder will either deny that they killed the victim or direct their defense toward the proof of facts inconsistent with malice aforethought, claiming either that they did not intend to kill or, even if it is found that they did, that the homicide was justified, excusable, or committed under circumstances of mitigation.

In People v. Dunn (1925), 233 Mich. 185, 197, 206 N.W. 568, 572, the Supreme Court of Michigan observed:

"In practical application legal refinements of definition over which those learned in the law often differ are of scant aid to a jury.

" 'If the jurors are told what constitutes legal justification or excuse, and what circumstances will reduce the killing to manslaughter, they have all the law they need to determine whether the particular homicide is murder or not, without the mention of the word malice.' 13 R.C.L. 773."

Courts might well emphasize that juries can convict of murder only when they are convinced beyond a reasonable doubt that (1) the defendant intended (actually or impliedly) to kill and (2) circumstances of justification, excuse or mitigation do *not* exist. A judge could, for example, charge that the defendant is guilty of the crime of murder if the jurors find, beyond a reasonable doubt, that he killed the victim and that he actually intended to kill the victim or (where relevant), although he did not actually intend to kill, he actually intended to inflict great bodily harm or engaged in behavior the natural tendency of which is to cause death or great bodily harm, unless (where relevant) the jurors have a reasonable doubt whether

(i) circumstances of mitigation are present, in which event the offense is reduced from murder to manslaughter, or (ii) the killing was accidental, or (iii) the defendant justifiably acted in self-defense.

We have addressed ourselves to this perplexing question in order to make clear the nature of the presumption of malice aforethought, to caution against misdirection of jurors regarding the "presumption", and to show why in the instant case there was adequate evidence to sustain a conviction for common-law, *i. e.,* second-degree, murder. The fact that Morrin killed his victim was not in dispute. From this fact, the jury was permitted to infer that the killing was committed with malice aforethought. Morrin's testimony concerning self-defense sought to nourish a reasonable doubt in the minds of the jurors as to the existence of this inferential fact. The jury, nevertheless, chose to draw the requisite inference and exercised its prerogative to disbelieve Morrin's exculpatory testimony.

NOTES

1. The United States Supreme Court has held that a conviction under a statute authorizing the inference of one fact from another must be scrutinized to prevent conviction upon insufficient proof. Reliance upon such an inference violates the due process clause of the Fifth and Fourteenth Amendments "unless it can be said with substantial assurance that the presumed fact is more likely than not to flow from the proved fact on which it is made to depend." Leary v. United States, 395 U.S. 6, 37, 89 S.Ct. 1532, 23 L.Ed.2d 57 (1969). See also, e. g., Turner v. United States, 396 U.S. 398, 90 S.Ct. 642, 24 L.Ed.2d 610 (1970). Does this cast any doubt upon the appropriateness of the approach of the court in the instant case? Is the approach consistent with the presumption of innocence? See State v. Cuevas, 53 Hawaii 110, 488 P.2d 322 (1971) striking down an instruction placing upon the defendant the burden of proving the absence of "malice aforethought" once the act of killing has been proved.

2. Is the approach of the court in the instant case to the problem of how to instruct the jury satisfactory? Consider the various statutory formulations of homicide offenses and the material in the following sections in evaluating the comment, relied upon in the instant case, that "in practical application legal refinements of definition over which those learned in the law often differ are of scant aid to a jury."

3. To what extent may—or should—a showing that a "deadly" weapon was used suffice to support a determination of guilt of murder? See Ober-er, The Deadly Weapon Doctrine—Common Law Origin, 75 Harv.L.Rev. 1565 (1962).

4. See Perkins, A Re-examination of Malice Aforethought, 43 Yale L.J. 537 (1934); Ross and Williams, The Law Commission: Imputed Criminal Intent, 30 Mod.L.Rev. 431 (1967).

1. GROSS RECKLESSNESS

COMMONWEALTH v. MALONE

Supreme Court of Pennsylvania, 1948.
354 Pa. 180, 47 A.2d 445.

MAXEY, Chief Justice. This is an appeal from the judgment and sentence under a conviction of murder in the second degree. William H. Long, age 13 years, was killed by a shot from a 32-caliber revolver held against his right side by the defendant, then aged 17 years. These youths were on friendly terms at the time of the homicide. The defendant and his mother while his father and brother were in the U. S. Armed Forces, were residing in Lancaster, Pa., with the family of William H. Long, whose son was the victim of the shooting.

On the evening of February 26th, 1945, when the defendant went to a moving picture theater, he carried in the pocket of his raincoat a revolver which he had obtained at the home of his uncle on the preceding day. In the afternoon preceding the shooting, the decedent procured a cartridge from his father's room and he and the defendant placed it in the revolver.

After leaving the theater, the defendant went to a dairy store and there met the decedent. Both youths sat in the rear of the store ten minutes, during which period the defendant took the gun out of his pocket and loaded the chamber to the right of the firing pin and then closed the gun. A few minutes later, both youths sat on stools in front of the lunch counter and ate some food. The defendant suggested to the decedent that they play "Russian Poker." Long replied: "I don't care; go ahead." The defendant then placed the revolver against the right side of Long and pulled the trigger three times. The third pull resulted in a fatal wound to Long. The latter jumped off the stool and cried: "Oh! Oh! Oh!" and Malone said: "Did I hit you, Billy? Gee, Kid, I'm sorry." Long died from the wounds two days later.

The defendant testified that the gun chamber he loaded was the first one to the right of the firing chamber and that when he pulled the trigger he did not "expect to have the gun go off." He declared he had no intention of harming Long, who was his friend and companion. The defendant was indicted for murder, tried and found guilty of murder in the second degree and sentenced to a term in the penitentiary for a period not less than five years and not exceeding ten years. A new trial was refused and after sentence was imposed, an appeal was taken.

* * *

The killing of William H. Long by this defendant resulted from an act intentionally done by the latter, in reckless and wanton disregard of the consequences which were at least sixty per cent certain from his thrice attempted discharge of a gun known to contain one bullet and aimed at a vital part of Long's body. This killing was, therefore, murder, for malice in the sense of a wicked disposition is evidenced by the intentional doing of an uncalled-for act in callous disregard of its likely harmful effects on others. The fact that there was no motive for this homicide does not exculpate the accused. In a trial for murder proof of motive is always relevant but never necessary.

STATE v. CHALMERS

Supreme Court of Arizona, 1966.
100 Ariz. 70, 411 P.2d 448.

LOCKWOOD, Justice. * * * The facts of the case are as follows: The defendant was driving his Chevrolet automobile at approximately 12:30 a. m. on April 24, 1963 in a northerly direction on Oracle Road near the intersection of Wetmore Road which is located in Pima County, Arizona. Oracle Road is a two lane highway at and near the location where the collision shortly thereafter occurred.

The Chevrolet car was traveling at a speed estimated between eighty and one hundred miles per hour. It passed several other cars moving in the same direction, and in order to do so crossed into the left or southbound lane. Two vehicles which were moving in a southerly direction were forced to leave the roadway because the Chevrolet car was in the southbound lane. The first southbound vehicle was a pickup truck with a camper body, and the second was a Pima County Sheriff's patrol car. The Chevrolet car swerved back into the right lane after forcing the patrol car off the road, and again into the left lane where it shortly thereafter collided with two vehicles moving in a southerly direction in the southbound or left lane.

As a result of the collision two passengers in one of the cars involved in the collision were killed, the driver and one other passenger were injured. The driver of the second car involved was also injured. [Defendant was convicted on two counts charging second degree murder based upon the deaths of the two passengers. He appealed from these convictions.] * * * At the time the appeal was taken, this Court was committed to the proposition that wanton and reckless conduct, in utter disregard of the safety of others and of himself, on the part of a person driving a motor vehicle, was sufficient to supply the willful and unlawful intention to inflict bodily injury upon another if such occurred. Brimhall v. State, 31 Ariz. 522, 255 P. 165, 53 A.L.R. 231 (1927). However, in State v. Balderrama, 97 Ariz. 134, 397 P.2d 632 (1964) we expressly overruled Brimhall so far as it held that evidence of negligent conduct may be sufficient to prove the criminal intent with which an act is done. This being so, in a prosecution for murder, the element of malicious intent may not be shown by a proof of gross negligence in the operation of a motor vehicle which produces the death of another person.

In view of the fact that the crime of manslaughter in the driving of a vehicle may occur by the commission of an unlawful act not amounting to a felony and *without gross negligence,* it is obvious that a mere showing that there was no considerable provocation for the killing of a human being under such circumstances cannot supply the implied malicious intent to constitute murder.

There remains the Legislative provision that in the crime of murder malice may be implied "when the circumstances attending the killing show an abandoned and malignant heart." This term also occurs in many other jurisdictions in defining the offense of murder. However, we have found no case which would indicate that gross negligence alone would constitute such conduct as appears to be contemplated when referring to *"an abandoned and malignant heart."* The latter phrase seems to mean conduct by the use of a weapon or other appliance likely to produce death, and by the brutal and blood-thirsty use of such instrumentality. Daniels v. State, 197 Ga. 754, 30 S.E.2d 625 (1944); People v. Endner, 73 Cal.App.2d 20, 165 P.2d 712 (1946), (evidence of a long course of physical abuse of the victim, defendant's mother, and evidence of a severe beating which caused her death); People v. Lamothe, 222 Cal.App.2d 314, 35 Cal.Rptr. 122 (1963), (evidence that defendant had slapped and beat his stepdaughter, a sixteen-month old baby, to such an extent that she died from a brain injury, and that defendant had frequently struck and thrown the child on the floor, rendering her unconscious.)

* * *

In the instant case, there is sufficient evidence for the jury to find gross negligence and utter disregard of the safety or welfare of any persons who might have been in the vicinity of defendant's car at the time of the collision. There was no evidence in the record tending to show that defendant had by the use of any weapon indulged in vicious or brutal conduct which might support a finding of "an abandoned and malignant heart." There was no evidence that defendant deliberately used his Chevrolet car for the purpose of a weapon to inflict injury upon another. Nor is there evidence tending to show that defendant had used any other instrumentality as a weapon for indulging in vicious or brutal conduct, which could support a finding of "an abandoned and malignant heart." As stated in Balderrama, supra, criminal neglect can supply the place of intent only where the legislative power has expressly so provided. It therefore follows that under all the facts the defendant was not guilty of murder. Nor, under the holding in Balderrama, supra, could he be guilty of an assault with a deadly weapon. Even though defendant failed to raise this issue on appeal, it is such fundamental error as to require a reversal in any event. It may be that because of the utter disregard of the defendant for the consequences of his operation of an automobile which could and did cause a senseless tragedy in loss of life and in personal injuries, he should be subject to severe criminal responsibilities. However, as stated in Balderrama, supra, if there is an inadequacy of the present laws dealing with criminal responsibility in cases of this kind the remedy lies with the Legislature.

Judgment of the lower court is reversed and the case remanded for further proceedings in accordance with this opinion.

UDALL, Justice (specially concurring).

I concur in the majority opinion as to the law set forth but disagree with the application of the facts of this matter to that law. Because of the complete agreement by other members of this Court, I do not desire to file a dissent in this matter but would like to express my views as to why the jury verdict should be upheld.

* * *

The majority opinion concludes that "[t]here was no evidence in the record tending to show that defendant had by the use of any weapon indulged in vicious or brutal conduct which might support a finding of 'an abandoned and malignant heart.'" This conclusion supplants the determination of the jury which, after hearing the evidence, rendered a verdict convicting defendant of second degree murder. The jury was instructed and found that defendant's conduct distinctly manifested "an abandoned and malignant heart" necessary to convict him of murder.

* * *

The facts would indicate the accident was not the typical automobile accident where a driver makes a gross error of judgment and is thus tried for manslaughter. Rather, the conduct surpasses the usual vehicle manslaughter case and demonstrates characteristics of wanton conduct and an abandoned and malignant heart. The jury found that the accused should have known of the plain and obvious likelihood that death or great bodily injury could have resulted from driving his automobile in such a manner.

NOTES

1. Compare Gibson v. State, 476 P.2d 362 (Okl.Cr.App.1970) in which the defendant, while being transported to jail in a car driven by a police officer, lunged across the front seat of the car and grabbed the steering wheel. This caused the vehicle to veer across the center line of the highway, where it struck another vehicle killing the driver of the police car. Defendant's conviction for murder was upheld on the ground that his actions could have been found to come within the statutory definition of murder which included "an act imminently dangerous to others and evincing a depraved mind, regardless of human life."

2. In attempting to reconcile Malone and Chalmers, is it relevant that the instrument used in Chalmers was a motor vehicle? In evaluating whether the statistical risk of death created by the defendant (and of which he was aware) was sufficient to give rise to liability for murder, is it proper to consider the general social utility of the instrument? Thus, in order to commit murder by use of a motor vehicle might one have to create a greater risk of death by one's use of the car than would be necessary if the instrument used was a firearm, because of the general greater social utility assigned to motor vehicles?

------

2. INTENT TO DO PHYSICAL HARM

PEOPLE v. GEIGER

Court of Appeals of Michigan, 1968.
10 Mich.App. 339, 159 N.W.2d 383.

BURNS, Judge. Defendant appeals from a circuit court jury conviction of manslaughter.

Sometime after 11 p. m., May 6, 1965, defendant confronted his estranged wife, Sharon Geiger, in the parking lot of a bar in Prudenville, Michigan, as she was about to enter the bar with Joan Greening. Joan Greening testified that she and Mrs. Geiger had had only one drink at another bar prior to meeting the defendant, that Mrs. Geiger's health appeared normal and that she observed no black and blue marks or abrasions upon Mrs. Geiger that evening. Joan Greening further testified that she was told by the defendant to wait for Mrs. Geiger in the bar, but that she waited in the parking lot and observed the defendant talking to his wife and trying to force her into the car; he then "threw" her into the car and drove away.

State police officers who had interrogated the defendant after the alleged offense testified that defendant told them the couple drove to the Prudenville elementary school playing field. They argued and got out of the car. Defendant struck his wife "two or three times" with his open hand and pushed her to the ground in such a manner that she bumped her head against the car. When Mrs. Geiger failed to get up and appeared unconscious, defendant picked her up and placed her in his car. He then allegedly attempted to clean her after driving a short distance to a house trailer which the Geigers had rented until May 1, 1965.

Early in the morning on May 7, defendant left his wife in the trailer and drove to James Meigs' house where defendant had been residing while he and his wife were separated. Meigs was awakened around 3:15 a. m., at which time defendant persuaded Meigs to help move the automobile which Mrs. Geiger had driven to the bar. After taking the vehicle to Mrs. Geiger's parents' home, defendant finally replied to Meigs' inquiries as to what was going on; defendant stated that he might be "facing a murder rap."

Between 3:30 a. m. and 4:30 a. m., May 7, defendant aroused his employer, asked for $100 and was given $50 in order to get away for a few days.

Defendant apparently returned to the house trailer, placed his wife in the front seat of his car and put a blanket over her. He drove south for approximately 186 miles and at 7:30 a. m. or 8 a. m., stopped at the Addison Community Hospital, Addison, Michigan, where his wife was pronounced dead.

* * *

Defendant was charged with first-degree murder, but the jury was instructed only as to second-degree murder and manslaughter. Defendant contends that the instructions regarding second-degree murder should not have been submitted to the jury because there were no proofs showing malice.

Malice has been defined as "an intent to cause the very harm that results *or some harm of the same general nature, or an act done in wanton or wilful disregard of the plain and strong likelihood that some such harm will result.*" (Emphasis supplied.) People v. Hansen (1962), 368 Mich. 344, 350, 118 N.W.2d 422, 425. Consistent with this definition, it follows that an assault by blows without a weapon may, under certain circumstances, permit a jury to infer an intent to kill. Wellar v. People (1874), 30 Mich. 16; People v. Collins (1942), 303 Mich. 34, 5 N.W.2d 556; also, see 22 A.L.R.2d 854.

On pages 19 and 20 of 30 Mich. of the *Wellar* Case, supra, Justice Campbell said:

> "In determining whether a person who has killed another without meaning to kill him is guilty of murder or manslaughter, the nature and extent of the injury or wrong which was actually intended, must usually be of controlling importance.

> "It is not necessary in all cases that one held for murder must have intended to take the life of the person he slays by his wrongful act. It is not always necessary that he must have intended a personal injury to such person. But it is necessary that *the intent with which he acted shall be equivalent in legal character to a criminal purpose aimed against life.* Generally the intent must have been to commit either a specific felony, or at least an act involving all the wickedness of a felony. And if the intent be directly to produce a bodily injury, it must be such an injury as may be expected to involve serious consequences, either periling life or leading to great bodily harm. There is no rule recognized as authority which will allow a conviction of murder where a fatal result was not intended, *unless the injury intended was one of a very serious character which might naturally*

and commonly involve loss of life, or grievous mischief." (Emphasis supplied.)

 "The intent to kill must undoubtedly be established, as an inference of fact, to the satisfaction of the jury; but they may draw that inference, as they draw all other inferences, from any fact in evidence which, to their minds, fairly proves its existence. Intentions can only be proved by acts, as juries cannot look into the breast of the criminal. And where any act is knowingly committed which naturally and usually leads to certain consequences, a jury certainly has the right, in the exercise of ordinary sagacity, to draw the inference that such results are intended." People v. Scott (1859), 6 Mich. 287, 296.

The question before this Court is: was there evidence from which a jury could infer defendant's alleged intent to produce great bodily injury with the attendant likelihood that death would result therefrom?

 It was legally possible for the jury in this case to find that the nature and extent of Sharon Geiger's injuries were reflective of an intent equivalent to a criminal purpose aimed against life. This consideration standing alone would be insufficient to establish malice, but the extent and nature of the injuries is not set against a solitary backdrop. Defendant "forced" or "pushed" the deceased into his car shortly before he severely beat her. After the beating decedent's unconsciousness and general physical appearance, as revealed to the jury from photographs and the autopsy report, showed a need for medical attention. Notwithstanding this need, defendant failed to immediately take his wife to a local hospital; instead he waited approximately 6 to 8 hours, during which time he travelled over 180 miles. Although by no means conclusive, defendant's statement to James Meigs that he "might be facing a murder rap" would give a jury additional insight into defendant's intent. An inference of intent to kill could be drawn from these and other facts presented in this case.

NOTES

1. May a trier of fact convict a defendant of murder simply upon a finding that the defendant intentionally inflicted "great bodily injury" upon the victim? Or is it necessary that it infer from this that the defendant intended to cause the victim's death? In what sort of cases, if any, would this make any difference?

2. What type of injury meets the requirement of "great bodily injury?" Is it necessary that the injury be of a type which more often than not causes death? If so, was the injury inflicted in the instant case of that type? Suppose the defendant in the instant case had inflicted the same injury upon his brother, who was similar to the defendant in size and age. Would the result have been the same? Explain. See State v. Sallie, 13 N.C.App. 499, 186 S.E.2d 667, certiorari denied 281 N.C. 316, 188 S.E.2d 900 (1972); Annot., 22 A.L.R.2d 854 (1952).

C. FIRST DEGREE MURDER: THE PREMEDITATED KILLING

STATE v. SNOWDEN

Supreme Court of Idaho, 1957.
79 Idaho 266, 313 P.2d 706.

McQUADE, Justice. This is an appeal by the defendant, who had entered a plea of guilty to an information charging him with the crime of murder in the first degree. At all times during the proceedings the defendant was represented by counsel. The district court, after hearing evidence to determine the degree of the crime and mitigating circumstances, if any, held the offense was murder in the first degree, and entered judgment sentencing the defendant to death.

The victim, Cora Lucyle Dean, was stabbed to death September 22, 1956, in Garden City, Idaho. The evidence showed the following sequence of events:

Defendant Snowden had been playing pool and drinking in a Boise pool room early in the evening. With a companion, one Carrier, he visited a club near Boise, then went to nearby Garden City. There the two men visited a number of bars, and defendant had several drinks. Their last stop was the HiHo Club.

Witnesses related that while defendant was in the HiHo Club he met and talked to Cora Lucyle Dean. The defendant himself said he hadn't been acquainted with Mrs. Dean prior to that time, but he had "seen her in a couple of the joints up town." He danced with Mrs. Dean while at the HiHo Club. Upon departing from the tavern, the two left together.

In statements to police officers, that were admitted in evidence, defendant Snowden said after they left the club Mrs. Dean wanted him to find a cab and take her back to Boise, and he refused because he didn't feel he should pay her fare. After some words, he related:

"* * * she got mad at me so I got pretty hot and I don't know whether I back handed her there or not. And, we got calmed down and decided to walk across to the gas station and call a cab. * * *"

They crossed the street, and began arguing again. Defendant said:

"* * * She swung and at the same time she kneed me again. I blew my top."

Defendant said he pushed the woman over beside a pickup truck which was standing near a business building. There he pulled his knife—a pocket knife with a two-inch blade—and cut her throat.

The body, which was found the next morning, was viciously and sadistically cut and mutilated. An autopsy surgeon testified the voice box had been cut, and that this would have prevented the victim from making any intelligible outcry. There were other wounds inflicted while she was still alive—one in her neck, one in her abdomen, two in the face, and two on the back of the neck. The second neck wound severed the spinal cord and caused death. There were other wounds all over her body, and her clothing had been cut away. The nipple of the right breast was missing. There was no evidence of a sexual attack on the victim; however, some of the lacerations were around the breasts and vagina of the deceased. A blood test showed Mrs. Dean was intoxicated at the time of her death.

Defendant took the dead woman's wallet. He hailed a passing motorist and rode back to Boise with him. There he went to a bowling alley and changed clothes. He dropped his knife into a sewer, and threw the wallet away. Then he went to his hotel and cleaned up again. He put the clothes he had worn that evening into a trash barrel.

After hearing the testimony of police officers and other witnesses, the trial court determined the killing was murder in the first degree and there were no circumstances in mitigation of the offense or of the punishment to be inflicted. The defendant was sentenced to death. This appeal is from that judgment.

* * *

The second assignment of error of the defendant is based upon the finding of the court that the defendant's acts in taking the life of Cora Lucyle Dean were willful, deliberate, and premeditated. I. C. § 18–4003 requires first degree homicide to be perpetrated by any kind of willful, deliberate, and premeditated killing * * *[.] The test to determine if the killing was willful, deliberate, and premeditated has been set out in State v. Shuff, 9 Idaho 115, 72 P. 664, 668, wherein the court stated:

"* * * The unlawful killing must be accompanied with a deliberate and clear intent to take life, in order to constitute murder of the first degree. The intent to kill must be the result of deliberate premeditation. It must be formed upon the pre-existing reflection, and not upon a sudden heat of passion sufficient to preclude the idea of deliberation. * * *"

The court further stated in this case while approving an instruction:

"* * * That instruction reads as follows, to wit: 'From these definitions the jury will see that any unlawful killing of a human being, with malice aforethought, is murder; but if nothing further characterizes the offense it is murder of the second degree. To constitute the higher offense there must be superadded, to the general definition above given, willfulness, deliberation, and premeditation. By willfulness is meant that it was of purpose, with the intent that, by the given act, the life of the party should be taken. It must be deliberate and premeditated. By this it is not meant that the killing must have been conceived or intended for any particular length of time. It is sufficient if it was done with reflection and conceived beforehand. And in this view, as I have said before, the deliberate purpose to kill and the killing may follow each other as rapidly as successive impulses or thoughts of the mind. It is enough that the party deliberate before the act—premeditate—the purpose to slay before he gave the fatal blow. But while the purpose, the intent, and its execution may follow thus rapidly upon each other, it is proper for the jury to take into consideration the shortness of such interval in considering whether such sudden and speedy execution may not be attributed to sudden passion and anger, rather than to deliberation and premeditation, which must characterize the higher offense. * * *."

[handwritten margin note: 1st degree murder is premeditated & deliberate. Beyond malice aforethought it REQ. willfulness, deliberation premeditation of the fatal blow. But intent (premed) & the act may still follow in Rapid succession though speed of Execut. in may indicate sudden passion rather than deliberation]

The Supreme Court of Arizona held in the case of Macias v. State, 283 P. 711, 715:

> "* * * There need be no appreciable space of time between the intention to kill and the act of killing. They may be as instantaneous as successive thoughts of the mind. It is only necessary that the act of killing be preceded by a concurrence of will, deliberation, and premeditation on the part of the slayer, and, if such is the case, the killing is murder in the first degree * * *."

In the present case, the trial court had no other alternative than to find the defendant guilty of willful, deliberate, and premeditated killing with malice aforethought in view of the defendant's acts in deliberately opening up a pocket knife, next cutting the victim's throat, and then hacking and cutting until he had killed Cora Lucyle Dean and expended himself. The full purpose and design of defendant's conduct was to take the life of the deceased.

The fourth assignment of error is directed at the imposition of the penalty of death upon the defendant. * * * It is abuse of discretion we are dealing with, and in particular the alleged abuse of discretion in prescribing the punishment for murder in the first degree as committed by the defendant. To choose between the punishments of life imprisonment and death there must be some distinction between one homicide and another. This case exemplifies an abandoned and malignant heart and sadistic mind, bent upon taking human life. It is our considered conclusion, from all the facts and circumstances, the imposition of the death sentence was not an abuse of discretion by the trial court.

The judgment is affirmed.

NOTES

1. Does the factual situation in the instant case really provide a basis from which it can be inferred "beyond a reasonable doubt" that Snowden "premeditated" the killing within any reasonable definition of that phrase? Consider the following:

> The most striking phase of the development of the English law was the reduction of "malice aforethought" to a term of art signifying neither "malice" nor "forethought" in the popular sense. Strikingly analogous in the judicial development of the American law of homicide is the narrow interpretation of "deliberation" and "premeditation" to exclude the two elements which the words normally signify: a determination to kill reached (1) calmly and (2) some appreciable time prior to the homicide. The elimination of these elements leaves, as Judge Cardozo pointed out,[24] nothing precise as the crucial state of mind but intention to kill. Such a result creates peculiar difficulty in a jurisdiction like New York where "design" to kill is, by statute, the distinguishing feature of second-degree murder. The trial judge must solemnly distinguish in his charge between the two degrees in terms which frequently render them quite indistinguishable,[27] a procedure which obviously confers on the jury a discretion to follow one aspect of the charge or the other, if not a valid excuse for neglecting the charge entirely.

Wechsler and Michael, A Rationale of the Law of Homicide, 37 Colum.L.Rev. 701, 707–09 (1937).

24. What Medicine Can Do for Law (1928) in Law and Literature (1930) 70, 96 et seq.

27. Since People v. Guadagnino, 233 N.Y. 344, 135 N.E. 594 (1922) it has been settled that it is error to charge in the language of People v. Clark, 7 N.Y. 385, 394 (1852) and of People v. Leighton, 88 N.Y. 117 (1882) that it "is enough if the intention precedes the act although the act follows instantly." However, the jury may apparently be told, in the language of People v. Majone, 91 N.Y. 211 (1883), that the "design must precede the killing by some appreciable space of time. But the time need not be long. It must be sufficient for some reflection and consideration upon the matter, for choice to kill or not to kill, and for the formation of a definite purpose to kill." It may also be told, in the language of People v. Guadagnino, supra: "A design to kill formed at the instant of the killing where there is no deliberation and premeditation preceding the act is murder in the second degree, not murder in the first degree. * * * There must be some appreciable space of time for such deliberation, or circumstances showing such deliberation preceding the act." It may also be told, in the language of People v. Barberi, 149 N.Y. 256, 267, 43 N.E. 635, 638 (1896): "Deliberation and premeditation imply the capacity at the time to think and reflect, sufficient volition to make a choice, and by the use of these powers to refrain from doing a wrongful act." And People v. Caruso, 246 N.Y. 437, 445, 159 N.E. 390, 392 (1927), warrants a charge that time "to make a choice whether to kill or not to kill—to overcome hesitation and doubt—to form a definite purpose" is not decisive.

2. What "causes" the result in the instant case and the often-seen result described by Wechsler and Michael above? Do the results suggest that courts do not regard "premeditation" (defined in a meaningful way) as an appropriate basis for distinguishing those killers who should be dealt with most severely?

3. What is the relationship, if any, between the premeditation formula and the death penalty? In McGautha v. California, 402 U.S. 183, 91 S.Ct. 1454, 28 L.Ed.2d 711 (1971) the petitioners had been convicted of first degree murder in California and Ohio and sentenced to death. Petitioner McGautha was convicted under the California statute, reprinted at page 915, supra, of a death caused by a shooting during the commission of a robbery by McGautha; McGautha apparently fired the fatal shot. Petitioner Crampton was convicted under Ohio law of killing his wife "purposely, and * * * of deliberate and premeditated malice." Ohio Rev. Code § 2901.01 (1954). Both statutes permitted, but did not require, the trial jury to impose a death sentence upon a defendant convicted of first degree murder. Neither statute authorized the death penalty upon the conviction of any other homicide crime. Both petitioners argued that by granting the jury this broad discretion without providing guidelines or limitations upon the ability of the jury to impose the death penalty, the statutes deprived them of life without due process of law. Rejecting this argument, the Court reasoned as follows:

> In order to see petitioners' claim in perspective, it is useful to call to mind the salient features of the history of capital punishment for homicides under the common law in England, and subsequent statutory developments in this country. This history reveals continual efforts, uniformly unsuccessful, to identify before the fact those homicides for which the slayer should die. Thus, the laws of Alfred, echoing Exodus 21:12–13, provided: "Let the man who slayeth another wilfully perish by death. Let him who slayeth another of necessity or unwillingly, or unwilfully, as God may have sent him into his hands, and for whom he has not lain in wait be worthy of his life and of lawful bot if he seek an asylum." Quoted in 3 J. Stephen, History of the Criminal Law of England 24 (1883). In the 13th century, Bracton set it down that a man was responsible for all homicides except those which happened by pure accident or inevitably necessity, although he did not explain the consequences of such responsibility. Id., at 35. The Statute of Gloucester, 6 Edw. 1, c. 9 (1278), provided that in cases of self-defense or misadventure the jury should neither convict nor acquit, but should find the fact specially, so that the King could decide whether to pardon the accused. It appears that in time such pardons—which may not have prevented forfeiture of goods—came to issue as of course. 3 Stephen, supra, at 36–42.

> During all this time there was no clear distinction in terminology or consequences among the various kinds of criminal homicide. All were *prima facie* capital, but all were subject to the benefit of clergy, which after 1350 came to be available to almost any man who could read. Although originally those entitled to benefit of clergy were simply delivered to the bishop for ecclesiastical proceedings, with the possibility of degradation from orders, incarcera-

tion, and corporal punishment for those found guilty, during the 15th and 16th centuries the maximum penalty for clergyable offenses became branding on the thumb, imprisonment for not more than one year, and forfeiture of goods. 1 Stephen, supra, at 459–464. By the statutes of 23 Hen. 8, c. 1, §§ 3, 4 (1531), and 1 Edw. 6, c. 12, § 10 (1547), benefit of clergy was taken away in all cases of "murder of malice prepensed." 1 Stephen, supra, at 464–465; 3 id., at 44. During the next century and a half, however, "malice prepense" or "malice aforethought" came to be divorced from actual ill will and inferred without more from the act of killing. Correspondingly, manslaughter, which was initially restricted to cases of "chance medley," came to include homicides where the existence of adequate provocation rebutted the inference of malice. 3 id., at 46–73.

The growth of the law continued in this country, where there was rebellion against the common-law rule imposing a mandatory death sentence on all convicted murderers. Thus, in 1794, Pennsylvania attempted to reduce the rigors of the law by abolishing capital punishment except for "murder of the first degree," defined to include all "willful, deliberate and premeditated" killings, for which the death penalty remained mandatory. Pa.Laws 1794, c. 1777. This reform was soon copied by Virginia and thereafter by many other States.

This new legislative criterion for isolating crimes appropriately punishable by death soon proved as unsuccessful as the concept of "malice aforethought." Within a year the distinction between the degrees of murder was practically obliterated in Pennsylvania. Other States had similar experiences. The result was characterized in this way by Chief Judge Cardozo, as he then was:

> "What we have is merely a privilege offered to the jury to find the lesser degree when the suddenness of the intent, the vehemence of the passion, seems to call irresistibly for the exercise of mercy. I have no objection to giving them this dispensing power, but it should be given to them directly and not in a mystifying cloud of words." What Medicine Can Do For Law, in Law and Literature 70, 100 (1931).

At the same time, jurors on occasion took the law into their own hands in cases which were "willful, deliberate, and premeditated" in any view of that phrase, but which nevertheless were clearly inappropriate for the death penalty. In such cases they simply refused to convict of the capital offense. * * *

In order to meet the problem of jury nullification, legislatures did not try, as before, to refine further the definition of capital homicides. Instead they adopted the method of forthrightly granting juries the discretion which they had been exercising in fact. * * * Tennessee was the first State to give juries sentencing discretion in capital cases, but other States followed suit, as did the Federal Government in 1897. * * *

In recent years academic and professional sources have suggested that jury sentencing discretion should be controlled by standards of some sort. The American Law Institute first published such a recommendation in 1959. Several States have enacted new criminal codes in the intervening 12 years, some adopting features of the Model Penal Code. Other States have modified their laws with respect to murder and the death penalty in other ways. None of these States have followed the Model Penal Code and adopted statutory criteria for imposition of the death penalty. In recent years, challenges to standardless jury sentencing have been presented to many state and federal appellate courts. No court has held the challenge good. As petitioners recognize, it requires a strong showing to upset this settled practice of the Nation on constitutional grounds. * * *

Petitioners seek to avoid the impact of this history by the observation that jury sentencing discretion in capital cases was introduced as a mechanism for dispensing mercy—a means for dealing with the rare case in which the death penalty was thought to be unjustified. Now, they assert, the death penalty is imposed on far fewer than half the defendants found guilty of capital crimes. The state and federal legislatures which provide for jury discretion in capital sentencing have, it is said, implicitly determined that some— indeed, the greater portion—of those guilty of capital crimes should be permitted to live. But having made that determination, petitioners argue, they have stopped short—the legislatures have not only failed to provide a rational basis for distinguishing the one group from the other, * * * but they have failed even to suggest any basis at all. Whatever the merits of providing such a mechanism to take account of the unforeseeable case calling for mercy, as was the original purpose, petitioners contend the mechanism is constitutionally intolerable as a means of selecting the extraordinary cases calling for the death penalty, which is its present-day function.

In our view, such force as this argument has derives largely from its generality. Those who have come to grips with the hard task of actually attempting to draft means of channeling capital sentencing discretion have confirmed the lesson taught by the history recounted above. To identify before the fact those characteristics of criminal homicides and their perpetrators which call for the death penalty, and to express these characteristics in language which can be fairly understood and applied by the sentencing authority, appear to be tasks which are beyond present human ability. * * *

In light of history, experience, and the present limitations of human knowledge, we find it quite impossible to say that committing to the untrammeled discretion of the jury the power to pronounce life or death in capital cases is offensive to anything in the Constitution. The States are entitled to assume that jurors confronted with the truly awesome responsibility of decreeing death for a fellow human will act with due regard for the consequences of their decision and will consider a variety of factors, many of which will have been suggested by the evidence or by the arguments of defense counsel. For a court to attempt to catalog the appropriate factors in this elusive area could inhibit rather than expand the scope of consideration, for no list of circumstances would ever be really complete. The infinite variety of cases and facets to each case would make general standards either meaningless "boiler-plate" or a statement of the obvious that no jury would need.

Are the Court's conclusions sound? In light of Furman v. Georgia, 408 U.S. 238, 92 S.Ct. 2726, 33 L.Ed.2d 346 (1972) (reprinted at page 71), would it be possible to define an offense of "first degree murder" for which a mandatory death penalty would be appropriate? If so, how? If Furman v. Georgia means that as a practical matter the death penalty may no longer be imposed for any homicide offenses, is there any longer a need to differentiate between "first" and "second degree" murders?

4. Is premeditation, under any definition, an appropriate criterion with which to select those cases in which the maximum penalty—whatever it is—may be imposed? Consider the following:

The Significance of Deliberation and Impulse

Whether and to what extent homicidal behavior was preceded by deliberation is plainly of evidential value in determining what the actor knew and intended when he acted. The more extensive the deliberation, the more probable it is that at least the more palpable risks created by the homicidal act were clearly perceived, and at least its more immediate consequences intended. From this point of view, however, gradations in homicidal behavior from the purely impulsive to the completely deliberate bear directly upon the question whether the actor created the homicidal risk inadvertently or advertently and, if advertently, whether or not he intended to kill, and only indirectly upon his character. The difficult question is whether the impulsiveness or deliberateness of his behavior has direct and independent significance in relation to his character. Assuming that other factors indicative of his character, such as knowledge, intent and motive are the same, of what additional importance is it that his act was the product of or was preceded by more or less deliberation? It may be argued that the more carefully considered and the less impulsive the act is, the more it indicates basic perversion of the actor's conceptions of good and evil. But it is surely not self-evident that the man who acts on wrong principles is a more dangerous man than one who acts without considering what is good. There are, moreover other objections to this view of the significance of deliberation. In the first place, it ignores that passion may influence deliberation as well as lead to action without deliberation, so that deliberate as well as impulsive action may be contrary to the actor's real notions of good and evil. In the second place, it does not embrace either deliberation about means rather than ends or acts which are preceded by but are not in accord with the results of deliberation. And yet it is extremely difficult in most cases to discover in what terms the actor deliberated or what was the relationship between deliberation and act. These objections are not avoided by stating the significance of deliberation in another way. Thus it may be said that reflection prior to action indicates that the actor lacks the sort of desires that will prevent such an act, since reflection is the opportunity to bring such desires into play, an opportunity which, by hypothesis, is not afforded by impulsive action; whereas action without reflection does not permit of that inference because if the actor had deliberated he might not have acted as he did. But in order to draw from these premises the conclusion that the man who acts deliberately is more dangerous than the man who acts impulsively, it must be asserted that the probability that the former's deliberations will result in wrong judgments is greater than the probability that the latter will not reflect before acting. This proposition also requires proof. The truth is, we think, that deliberation has no independent significance in relation to character and that the importance usually accorded it properly belongs to other factors which are its concomitants such, for example, as lapse of time, or to still other factors which it evidences, such as knowledge and intent. When the matter is viewed in that way, no difficulty is experienced in dealing with cases in which deliberation itself results in the intensification of passion, as it may when the enormity of an injury done the actor or the value of an end to be served by a homicidal act becomes apparent only after thought.

Wechsler and Michael, A Rationale of the Law of Homicide, 37 Colum.L. Rev. 701, 1261, 1282–84 (1937).

PEOPLE v. ANDERSON

Supreme Court of California, 1968.
70 Cal.2d 15, 73 Cal.Rptr. 550, 447 P.2d 942.

TOBRINER, Justice. Defendant was indicted for the murder of Victoria Hammond, a 10-year-old girl, in 1962. The jury found defendant guilty of first degree murder, found that he was sane, and fixed the penalty at death.

The Facts.

Defendant, a San Jose cab driver, had been living for about eight months with a Mrs. Hammond and her three children, Cynthia, aged 17, Kenneth, aged 13, and the victim, Victoria, aged 10. On the morning of the day of the murder, December 7, 1962, Mrs. Hammond left for work at 7:30 a. m., leaving only Victoria at home with the defendant. Defendant was still in bed. He had been home from work for the previous two days, during which time he had been drinking heavily, and apparently he did not go to work on the day of the murder.

The owner of a nearby liquor store testified that defendant purchased a quart of whisky from him sometime between 1 and 2 p. m. on December 7, 1962. The only other witness who testified as to defendant's whereabouts that day prior to the discovery of the murder was the victim's 13-year-old brother Kenneth.

Kenneth testified that he arrived home from school at 3:30 p. m. on December 7. He found the front door locked, which was not unusual, so he went around to the back of the house and down to the basement. Kenneth stayed there awhile working with his microscope. In a short time he heard noise coming from upstairs in the house which sounded like boxes and other things being moved around, like someone was cleaning up. He then heard the shower water running. A police officer later verified that a person in the basement could hear water running in the shower and movement in Victoria's bedroom.

Kenneth testified further that he then came up from the basement and went to the back porch screen door. The screen door was locked, which also was not unusual, so Kenneth jerked on it so the hook would pop out. Kenneth then went from the back porch directly into his bedroom to change his clothes. He then returned through the back porch to the kitchen door which was also locked. Kenneth knocked on the door and the defendant opened it. Kenneth testified that the defendant was wearing slacks only. Kenneth went into the kitchen and asked defendant for $1.00 for a teen club dance he intended to attend that evening. Defendant obtained a dollar for him out of the pocket of another pair of slacks hanging on the knob of a bedroom door. When Kenneth noticed the blood on the kitchen floor and asked defendant about it, the defendant told Kenneth that he had cut himself. This explanation apparently satisfied Kenneth, as he finished dressing and left the house sometime before 4 p. m.

Kenneth testified that no one else was at his house when he was there between 3:30 and 4 p. m. He further testified that about 6:30 he realized that he had forgotten his wallet and returned home. As he approached the front door, his mother came out and asked to see the cut on his arm, and Kenneth explained that he had no cut. His mother then asked defendant about the blood she had noticed and defendant told her that Victoria had cut herself, but that the mother should not worry, as the cut was not serious. After defendant told her that Victoria was at a friend's for dinner, the mother wanted to take Kenneth with her to get Victoria. Kenneth went back to his room to get a jacket. Because he had a "weird" feeling, he looked into Victoria's room. He found her nude, bloody body under some boxes and blankets on the floor near her bed. Kenneth ran out of the room screaming that defendant had killed her. Mrs. Hammond, after seeing Victoria's body, went next door to phone the police.

Mrs. Hammond testified that she returned home from work at 4:45 p. m. The front door was locked, she rang the doorbell, and defendant answered. Mrs. Hammond noticed blood on the couch in the living room, and when she asked defendant about it, he told her that Kenneth had cut himself playing with a knife and that he was at a teenage dance. Mrs. Hammond then went to the grocery store and returned about 5:30 p. m. She testified that at both times she arrived home defendant was drinking a highball. She also testified as to examining Kenneth's arm for a cut when he returned home for his wallet and as to defendant's subsequent explanation that Victoria had been cut, but not seriously. Mrs. Hammond discovered Victoria's body after Kenneth came out of Victoria's room.

A classmate of Victoria, who was the last person to see Victoria alive, testified that she left Victoria in front of the Hammond house about 3:45 p. m. after the two of them had walked home from school.

When the police arrived at 7 p. m. the shades were down on all the windows and the doors were locked. Defendant finally opened the front door for one of the officers who arrested and handcuffed defendant. The arresting officer testified that defendant was wearing slacks, no shirt or shoes, and that there was no blood on him.

The arresting officer found Victoria's body on the floor near her bed. He found defendant's blood-spotted shorts on a chair in the living room, and a knife and defendant's socks, with blood encrusted on the soles, in the master bedroom. The evidence established that the victim's torn and bloodstained dress had been ripped from her, that her clothes, including her panties out of which the crotch had been ripped, were found in various rooms of the house, that there were bloody footprints matching the size of the victim's leading from the master bedroom to Victoria's room, and that there was blood in almost every room including the kitchen, the floor of which appeared to have been mopped.

The TV cameraman who covered the murder story for channel 11, the officer who drove defendant to the police station, and the officer who "observed" defendant for four hours at the station the night of December 7, 1962, all testified that defendant did not appear intoxicated. The officers who talked to defendant testified, however, that they smelled alcohol on his breath; a blood test taken at 7:45 p. m. indicated that the alcohol content in defendant's blood was .34 percent, which was more than necessary for an automobile driver to be classified as "under the influence."

Over 60 wounds, both severe and superficial, were found on Victoria's body. The cuts extended over her entire body, including one extending from the rectum through the vagina, and the partial cutting off of her tongue. Several of the wounds, including the vaginal lacerations, were post mortem. No evidence of spermatozoa was found in the victim, on her panties, or on the bed next to which she was found.

The prosecution contended that the murder was sexually motivated. The defendant, who pleaded not guilty and not guilty by reason of insanity, presented no defense whatsoever.

(a) *The evidence is insufficient to support a finding of premeditation and deliberation.*

It is well established that the brutality of a killing cannot in itself support a finding that the killer acted with premeditation and deliberation. "If the evidence showed no more than the infliction of multiple acts of violence on the victim, it would not be sufficient to show that the killing was the result of careful thought and weighing of considerations."

Given the presumption that an unjustified killing of a human being constitutes murder of the second, rather than of the first, degree, and the clear legislative intention to differentiate between first and second degree murder, we must determine in any case of circumstantial evidence whether the proof is such as will furnish a *reasonable foundation* for an inference of premeditation and deliberation * * * or whether it "leaves only to *conjecture and surmise* the conclusion that defendant either arrived at or carried out the intention to kill as the result of a concurrence of deliberation and premeditation." (Italics added.) * * *

As we noted in People v. Bender, supra, 27 Cal.2d 164, 183, 163 P.2d 8, we find no indication that the Legislature intended to give the words "deliberate" and "premeditated" other than their ordinary dictionary meanings. Moreover, we have repeatedly pointed out that the legislative classification of murder into two degrees would be meaningless if "deliberation" and "premeditation" were construed as requiring no more reflection than may be involved in the mere formation of a specific intent to kill. * * *

Thus we have held that in order for a killing with malice aforethought to be first rather than second degree murder, " '[t]he intent to kill must be * * * formed upon a *pre-existing* reflection' * * * [and have] been the subject of actual deliberation or *forethought.* * * *'" (People v. Thomas, supra, 25 Cal.2d at pp. 900–901, 156 P. 2d 7, at p. 18.) (Italics added.) We have therefore held that "a verdict of murder in the first degree * * * [on a theory of a wilful, deliberate, and premeditated killing] is proper only if the slayer killed 'as a result of careful thought and weighing of considerations; as a *deliberate* judgment or plan; carried on coolly and steadily, [especially] according to a *preconceived design.*' * * *"

The type of evidence which this court has found sufficient to sustain a finding of premeditation and deliberation falls into three basic categories: (1) facts about how and what defendant did *prior* to the actual killing which show that the defendant was engaged in activity directed toward, and explicable as intended to result in, the killing—what may be characterized as "planning" activity; (2) facts about the defendant's *prior* relationship and/or conduct with the victim from which the jury could reasonably infer a "motive" to kill the victim, which inference of motive, together with facts of type (1) or (3), would in turn support an inference that the killing was the result of "a pre-existing reflection" and "careful thought and weighing of considerations" rather than "mere unconsidered or rash impulse hastily executed" (People v. Thomas, supra, 25 Cal.2d 880, at pp. 898,

900, 901, 156 P.2d 7, at p. 14); (3) facts about the nature of the killing from which the jury could infer that the *manner of killing was so particular and exacting* that the defendant must have intentionally killed according to a "preconceived design" to take his victim's life in a particular way for a "reason" which the jury can reasonably infer from facts of type (1) or (2).

Analysis of the cases will show that this court sustains verdicts of first degree murder typically when there is evidence of all three types and otherwise requires at least extremely strong evidence of (1) or evidence of (2) in conjunction with either (1) or (3). As will become clear from the following analysis of representative cases, the present case lacks evidence of any of the three types.

In People v. Hillery, supra, 62 Cal.2d 692, 44 Cal.Rptr. 30, 401 P.2d 382, the jury could reasonably infer that the defendant engaged in the following "extended course of conduct": defendant parked his car near the victim's (a 15-year-old girl's) house, entered the house surreptitiously, seized the victim while she was sewing and covered her head with a towel and slip to prevent outcry or identification, cut a length of cord in another room to secure her hands behind her, took the victim's scissors, dragged her to a nearby irrigation ditch where her body was subsequently found, engaged in a struggle with the victim, and then plunged the scissors directly into her chest. (Id. at p. 704, 44 Cal.Rptr. 30, 401 P.2d 382.)

Hillery represents a case of very strong type (1) evidence: the defendant's surreptitious conduct, subjection of his victim to his complete control, and carrying off of his victim to a place where others were unlikely to intrude, can be described as "planning" activity directly related to the killing. Moreover, there is also strong evidence of type (3): directly plunging a lethal weapon into the chest evidences a deliberate intention to kill as opposed to the type of "indiscriminate" multiple attack of both severe and superficial wounds which defendant engaged in in the instant case.

In People v. Kemp (1961) 55 Cal.2d 458, 11 Cal.Rptr. 361, 359 P.2d 913, the defendant entered his victim's apartment through a window after removing the screen, found the victim alone in bed, tied stockings around her neck and hands, gagged her with a washcloth, and then raped and strangled her. In *Kemp*, as in *Hillery*, defendant's surreptitious coming upon the victim and calculated efforts to prevent her from identifying her assailant or crying out for help, together with the deliberate manner of killing—evidence of types (1) and (3) —point to a killing which is the result of "preconceived design" as opposed to "an explosion of violence." People v. Anderson, supra, 63 Cal.2d at p. 360, 46 Cal.Rptr. 763, at p. 768, 406 P.2d 43, at p. 48.)

The present case is strikingly similar to People v. Granados, supra, 49 Cal.2d 490, 319 P.2d 346, in which this court reduced a verdict of first degree murder to second degree murder on the ground that the evidence was insufficient to show either premeditation and deliberation or that the killing occurred in the course of an attempted violation of section 288 of the Penal Code. The evidence of premeditation and deliberation in *Granados,* while clearly insufficient to sustain the verdict of first degree murder on that theory, was stronger than in the present case in which we find no evidence from which the jury could *reasonably* infer that defendant acted " *'with a deliberate and clear intent to take life.'* " * * *

In *Granados,* defendant lived in a common law relationship with the mother of his victim, a 13-year-old girl. After taking the deceased and her brother to a real estate office, defendant gave the brother a note requesting money to take to his mother who worked nearby. When the brother returned home with the requested money he saw defendant at the rear of the house. As he started to enter the house, defendant came running to him and asked him to get some alcohol for his sister (decedent) who had fainted. The brother noticed blood on one of defendant's hands and that defendant had the other hand behind his back.

The brother unsuccessfully looked for some alcohol. Defendant then suggested they get a doctor and an ambulance. The brother then noticed that defendant's hand had been washed. Defendant then drove the brother to a drugstore, gave him 50 cents for some alcohol, and told him he would wait for him. The defendant drove away and did not return for the brother.

Defendant then called the mother and told her the victim had poisoned herself. The mother returned to the house with a friend who found the victim's body in the bedroom lying on the floor. Her skirt was pulled up exposing her private parts, there were bloodstains on the wall, floor, and decedent's head, and a machete covered with blood was lying in a corner of the living room behind a small heater.

Defendant testified that on the day of the killing the girl was helping him clean the house and that he asked her if she was a virgin, to which she replied that it was none of his business. Defendant said that she had never answered him in that way and that he therefore struck her with his hand, but did not remember striking her with the machete.

Decedent's mother testified that she had warned defendant that the next time he bothered her daughter, she would tell the police, and that defendant in reply threatened to kill her and both her children if she did.

The prosecution argued that the murder was sexually motivated. This court, per Justice McComb, held that the evidence was insufficient as a matter of law to support a verdict of first degree murder. (49 Cal.2d at p. 497, 319 P.2d 346.)

Applying the standards developed above to *Granados,* we find that the only evidence of (1) defendant's behavior prior to the killing which could be described as "planning" activity related to a killing purpose was defendant's sending the victim's brother on an errand and apparently returning home alone with the decedent. Such evidence is highly ambiguous in terms of the various inferences it could support as to defendant's purpose in so behaving. The evidence of (2) defendant's prior behavior with the victim (alleged sexual molestation and his question as to her virginity) is insufficient to support a reasonable inference that defendant had a "motive" to kill the girl, which could in turn support an inference that the striking with the machete was the result of a "preconceived design" and "forethought." Finally, the evidence of (3) the manner of killing (brutal hacking) does not support a reasonable inference of deliberately placed blows, which could in turn support an inference that the act of killing was premeditated rather than "hasty and impetuous."

Justice Carter dissented in *Granados* on the ground that the following evidence was sufficient to sustain a finding of premeditation and deliberation: the nature of the instrument, the condition of the body, defendant's sending the brother on an errand immediately prior to the time of the killing, and defendant's prior threats against the girl and her family. (49 Cal.2d at pp. 498–499, 319 P.2d 346.) Justice Carter's dissent demonstrates that there was some evidence of premeditation and deliberation in *Granados,* albeit insufficient. Here, on the other hand, we do not have any evidence of either (1) any conduct by defendant prior to the killing which would indicate that he was planning anything, felonious or otherwise, or (2) any behavior towards Victoria from which the jury could reasonably infer that defendant had a "motive" or desire to sexually attack and/or kill her. The evidence of (3), the manner of killing and the condition of the body, is the same in both cases: the only inference which the evidence reasonably supports in either case is that the killing resulted from a "random," violent, indiscriminate attack rather than from deliberately placed wounds inflicted according to a preconceived design. * * *

Finally, the defendant in *Granados,* as here, attempted to "cover up" the crime by lying to the brother and the mother of the victim. Although this type of evidence may possibly bear on defendant's state of mind *after* the killing, it is irrelevant to ascertaining defendant's state of mind immediately prior to, or during, the killing. Evasive conduct shows fear: it cannot support the double inference that defendant planned to hide his crime at the time he committed it and that therefore defendant committed the crime with premeditation and deliberation.

The judgment is modified by reducing the degree of the crime to murder of the second degree and, as so modified, is affirmed. The cause is remanded to the trial court with directions to arraign and pronounce judgment on defendant in accordance with the foregoing ruling.

TRAYNOR, C. J., and PETERS and PEEK, JJ., concur.

BURKE, Justice (dissenting). * * * I believe there is credible evidence from which the jury could find a premeditated homicide, e. g. the locking of the doors (whether before or after the actual killing is a matter of conjecture), the duration of the assault, the pursuit through many rooms with a quantity of blood being left in each room, the extensive stabbings many of which would have sufficed as fatal, the removal of the murder weapon from one room and the apparent repeated use of it in other rooms.

NOTES

1. Contrast the analysis in the instant case with that in Davis v. State, 251 Ark. 771, 475 S.W.2d 155 (1972). In Davis, the defendant, a black youth of seventeen, struck the deceased, a young white medical technician, as the deceased left a basketball game. There was no evidence that the two had ever had a confrontation of any kind or that they had met. In upholding a verdict of guilty of premeditated murder, the court explained:

> There is not one scintilla of evidence to show that the deceased did anything to arouse the appellant's anger. The weapon selected by appellant is significant. It is a hardwood post about three feet long and tapered on one end. It weighs approximately nine pounds. Appellant pushed one of his friends aside, apparently to enable appellant to get a full swing. The situs on the body which appellant chose to strike is also significant, being the head. The viciousness of the swing of the club was revealed by the physician's testimony. Appellant struck with such force that the brain was lacerated on both sides. The brain was extensively lacerated, with hemorrhages both in the brain substance and on the cover thereof. The brain disintegrated. After striking the fatal blow appellant threw the post at the friend of the deceased and with such force as to knock him down. Whereupon the appellant fled the scene. The next day appellant went to school. There he was found reading a newspaper "to see if he had killed that man." We are unable to say that the jury was wrong in inferring premeditation and deliberation.

2. Does the approach of the California Supreme Court in the instant case create a satisfactory criterion for distinguishing those killers that should be dealt with most severely? For example, the court cites People v. Hillery and People v. Kemp as examples of adequate proof of premeditation. Were the defendants in those cases sufficiently different from the defendants in the instant case and People v. Granados (also discussed in the instant case) to justify treating them more severely? Does it matter that the most important aspect of this increased severity might be the possibility of the death penalty? How might the answers to these questions differ if the death penalty were abolished in the jurisdiction?

3. To what extent might dissatisfaction with the premeditation criterion be based upon its perceived unsatisfactoriness when applied to

"psychologically abnormal" offenders? If this is important, should the distinction between the degrees of homicide be tailored to distinguish among psychologically abnormal offenders, or should they be premised upon "normal" offenders and some other doctrine (see section VII of this text) be developed to permit consideration of psychological abnormality? Does the answer depend upon how many "psychologically normal" people commit killings that the law might want to classify as the most serious offense? If so, how many are there? See generally, Brenner, The Impulsive Murder and the Degree Device, 22 Fordham L.Rev. 274 (1953); 21 Md.L.Rev. 349 (1961).

4. Does premeditation have to occur prior to forming the intent to kill? Prior to deciding to act on it? See State v. Stewart, 176 Ohio St. 156, 198 N.E.2d 439, 443 (1964): "It makes no difference whether the deliberation was in forming the design maliciously to kill, or, in the continuance of such design after being formed, until the same was executed." Does this mean that a finder of fact could conclude that a defendant premeditated and deliberated between blows? In *Anderson*, could the defendant have premeditated during the course of the killing?

5. The attraction with which American law has regarded premeditation and deliberation as a criterion for distinguishing capital homicides is evidenced in the Delaware court's interpretation of express malice aforethought (which under the Delaware statutory scheme differentiates first degree murder from second degree murder) as requiring an intent to kill or do great bodily harm formed by "a sedate and deliberate mind." See Seeney v. State, 277 A.2d 670 (Del.1971).

6. Does premeditation require an intent to kill? If one carefully considers the legal and moral implications of engaging in an act creating an extremely high risk of death of others, could he be guilty of first degree murder under a scheme defining first degree murder as a "deliberate and premeditated killing"?

D. FELONY MURDER

PROBLEM

Consider the liability of Mayfield, Brown and Dennis for the death of Ricard given the following facts:

> During the early morning hours of June 10, 1962, Ronald Mayfield and Charles Brown, appellants, together with one Sammy Dennis, met at a bar in Los Angeles, California. In a conversation which ensued the three men decided to pool their funds and purchase a supply of narcotics (heroin) for their own use from an individual known to Brown. The three men in search of the source of supply proceeded to the corner of Adams and Normandie Streets in Los Angeles,

where they met the deceased, Willie Ricard. Ricard was also interested in the purchase of narcotics and offered to chip in his pro-rata.

The record shows that two balloons containing heroin were purchased at $10.00 apiece from one Billy Reid at or about the place where the three men met Ricard, but it is uncertain as to who made the purchase. After the heroin had been obtained, the four men proceeded in Ricard's car to Brown's apartment. Each balloon was divided for use between two men. The contents of the first balloon were divided between the deceased and Mayfield. The contents of the second balloon were then divided between Sammy Dennis and Appellant Brown. The deceased applied his own tourniquet and injected the heroin compound into himself. Appellant Mayfield said the deceased tied and fixed himself and Brown confirmed the fact that each of the four men had injected himself with heroin. Mayfield wasn't sure who supplied the kit. Brown testified he furnished the spoon. Brown also supplied a necktie (used as a tourniquet) but it was only for himself, Dennis and Mayfield. The deceased used his own handkerchief. Brown, too, did not know who supplied the kit. According to Appellant Mayfield, after the deceased injected himself, there was an argument over the money. Brown testified he had chipped in $2.00. Brown didn't have the $5.00 he had promised to contribute. The deceased had contributed his $5.00. There was a discussion as to the balance.

Almost immediately after Ricard had injected the heroin into his veins, he walked slowly out of the room and disappeared from view. A few minutes later Mayfield noticed Ricard's absence and looked into the bathroom, where he found Ricard lying unconscious on the floor. Attempts were made to revive Ricard by shaking him and applying cold towels to his face, but to no avail. Some thought was given to placing Ricard in a cold bath, but Dennis noticed that Ricard's heart and pulse had ceased beating. Further attempts to revive Ricard were abandoned. Appellant Mayfield and Sammy Dennis then left the premises.

When Mayfield and Dennis left, Brown pulled Ricard to the couch, covered him with a blanket, and went to look for help. He located his brother at a hot dog stand and both men returned to Brown's house. Ricard was carried to his car and driven to the corner of 24th and Normandie Streets, where he was left lying in the back seat of the car. Brown testified that he thought that Ricard might revive by exposure to the fresh air and that he wasn't aware of the fact that Ricard was dying or already dead.

Appellant Brown had a girl friend call the police and advise them where Ricard's body was. She did, but didn't indicate that Brown in any way was connected to the body. Brown was subsequently arrested due to information furnished by an informer. Mayfield departed from his home in Bakersfield on the morning in which the above events took place.

Assume a homicide statutory scheme such as that of California (see page 915, supra) and the following statutes:

Sec. 11501. "Except as otherwise provided in this division, every person who transports, imports into this State, sells, furnishes, administers or gives away, or offers to transport, import into this State, sell, furnish, administer, or give away, * * * except upon the written prescription of a physician, * * * shall be punished by imprisonment, * * * in the state prison from five years to life."

Sec. 11721. "No person shall use, or be under the influence of, or be addicted to the use of narcotics, excepting when administered by or under the direction of a person licensed by the State to prescribe and administer narcotics. * * * Any person convicted of violating any provision of this section is guilty of a misdemeanor and shall be sentenced to serve a term of not less than 90 days nor more than one year in the county jail. * * *"

Violation of section 11501 is classified as a felony; a violation of section 11721 is a misdemeanor. For one court's answer to the problem, see People v. Mayfield, 225 Cal.App.2d 263, 37 Cal.Rptr. 340 (1964). See also People v. Cruciani, 70 Misc.2d 528, 334 N.Y.S. 2d 515 (County Ct. 1972); Annot., 32 A.L.R.2d 589 (1970).

---

1. THE BASIC DOCTRINE

PEOPLE v. PHILLIPS

Supreme Court of California, 1966.
64 Cal.2d 574, 51 Cal.Rptr. 225, 414 P.2d 353.

TOBRINER, Justice. [Defendant, a doctor of chiropractic, had been convicted of second degree murder. The prosecution relied in part upon the theory that the death of the victim, one of defendant's patients, had been caused by defendant's commission of the felony of grand theft by obtaining money falsely representing his ability to cure cancer. The California statutes defining the homicide offenses appear at page 915, supra.]

Defendant challenges the propriety of the trial court's instructions to the jury. The court gave the following * * * instruction on murder in the second degree:

> [T]he unlawful killing of a human being with malice aforethought, but without a deliberately formed and premeditated intent to kill is murder of the second degree:
>
> * * *
>
> (3) If the killing is done in the perpetration of or attempt to perpetrate a felony such as Grand Theft. If death occurs in the perpetration in a course of conduct amounting to Grand Theft, which course of conduct is a proximate cause of the unlawful killing of a human being, such course of conduct constitutes murder in the second degree, even though the death was not intended.

Despite defendant's contention that the Penal Code does not expressly set forth any provision for second degree felony murder and that, therefore, we should not follow any such doctrine here, the concept lies embodied in our law. * * * [T]he cases hold that the perpetration of some felonies, exclusive of those enumerated in [the Penal Code section defining first degree murder] may provide the basis for a murder conviction under the felony murder rule.

NOTES

1. The traditional semantic framework for felony murder has been that the intent necessary for the underlying felony supplies the malice aforethought necessary for murder. Of course, where a statute makes a felony murder first degree murder, the underlying felony must be regarded as not only supplying malice aforethought but also as an adequate alternative to whatever other factors might raise a killing from second to first degree murder.

2. Throughout the materials dealing with felony murder (and its manslaughter equivalent), keep in mind the following queries: To what extent does the felony murder doctrine make a real difference, i. e., to what extent could the results achieved by use of the felony murder doctrine also be achieved by other methods? What, if any, constitutional attacks might be made upon the felony murder doctrine or its application to a specific set of facts? What should be the appropriate attitude of a court in interpreting statutes dealing with felony murder? For example, could the court in Phillips have read the statute as not applying the felony murder doctrine? If so, should it have done so? Why, or why not?

PEOPLE v. STAMP

California Court of Appeals, 1969.
2 Cal.App.3d 203, 82 Cal.Rptr. 598, certiorari denied
400 U.S. 819, 91 S.Ct. 36, 27 L.Ed.2d 46.

COBEY, Associate Justice. These are appeals by Jonathan Earl Stamp, Michael John Koory and Billy Dean Lehman, following jury verdicts of guilty of robbery and murder, both in the first degree. Each man was given a life sentence on the murder charge together with the time prescribed by law on the robbery count.

Defendants appeal their conviction of the murder of Carl Honeyman who, suffering from a heart disease, died between 15 and 20 minutes after Koory and Stamp held up his business, the General Amusement Company, on October 26, 1965, at 10:45 a. m. Lehman, the driver of the getaway car, was apprehended a few minutes after the robbery; several weeks later Stamp was arrested in Ohio and Koory in Nebraska.

* * *

On this appeal appellants primarily rely upon their position that the felony-murder doctrine should not have been applied in this case due to the unforeseeability of Honeyman's death.

THE FACTS

Defendants Koory and Stamp, armed with a gun and a blackjack, entered the rear of the building housing the offices of General Amusement Company, ordered the employees they found there to go to the front of the premises, where the two secretaries were working. Stamp, the one with the gun, then went into the office of Carl Honeyman, the owner and manager. Thereupon Honeyman, looking very frightened and pale, emerged from the office in a "kind of hurry." He was apparently propelled by Stamp who had hold of him by an elbow.

The robbery victims were required to lie down on the floor while the robbers took the money and fled out the back door. As the robbers, who had been on the premises 10 to 15 minutes, were leaving, they told the victims to remain on the floor for five minutes so that no one would "get hurt."

Honeyman, who had been lying next to the counter, had to use it to steady himself in getting up off the floor. Still pale, he was short of breath, sucking air, and pounding and rubbing his chest. As he walked down the hall, in an unsteady manner, still breathing hard and rubbing his chest, he said he was having trouble "keeping the pounding down inside" and that his heart was "pumping too fast for him." A few minutes later, although still looking very upset, shaking, wiping his forehead and rubbing his chest, he was able to walk in a steady manner into an employee's office. When the police arrived, almost immediately thereafter, he told them he was not feeling very well and that he had a pain in his chest. About two minutes later, which was 15 to 20 minutes after the robbery had occurred, he collapsed on the floor. At 11:25 he was pronounced dead on arrival at the hospital. The coroner's report listed the immediate cause of death as heart attack.

The employees noted that during the hours before the robbery Honeyman had appeared to be in normal health and good spirits. The victim was an obese, sixty-year-old man, with a history of heart disease, who was under a great deal of pressure due to the intensely competitive nature of his business. Additionally, he did not take good care of his heart.

Three doctors, including the autopsy surgeon, Honeyman's physician, and a professor of cardiology from U.C.L.A., testified that although Honeyman had an advanced case of atherosclerosis, a progressive and ultimately fatal disease, there must have been some immediate upset to his system which precipitated the attack. It was their conclusion in response to a hypothetical question that but for the robbery there would have been no fatal seizure at that time. The fright induced by the robbery was too much of a shock to Honeyman's system. There was opposing expert testimony to the effect that it could not be said with reasonable medical certainty that fright could ever be fatal.

SUFFICIENCY OF THE EVIDENCE RE CAUSATION

* * *

A review of the facts as outlined above shows that there was substantial evidence of the robbery itself, that appellants were the robbers, and that but for the robbery the victim would not have experienced the fright which brought on the fatal heart attack.

APPLICATION OF THE FELONY-MURDER RULE

* * *

There is no requirement that the killing occur, "while committing" or "while engaged in" the felony, or that the killing be "a part of" the felony, other than that the few acts be a part of one continuous transaction. Thus the homicide need not have been committed "to perpetrate" the felony. There need be no technical inquiry as to whether there has been a completion or abandonment of or desistence from the robbery before the homicide itself was completed.

The doctrine is not limited to those deaths which are foreseeable. Rather a felon is held strictly liable for *all* killings committed by him or his accomplices in the course of the felony. As long as the homicide is the direct causal result of the robbery the felony-murder rule applies whether or not the death was a natural or probable consequence of the robbery. So long as a victim's predisposing physical condition, regardless of its cause, is not the *only* substantial factor bringing about his death, that condition, and the robber's ignorance of it, in no way destroys the robber's criminal responsibility for the death. So long as life is shortened as a result of the felonious act, it does not matter that the victim might have died soon anyway. In this respect, the robber takes his victim as he finds him.

REX v. LUMLEY

Central Criminal Court, 1911.
22 Cox Crim.C. 635.

[Charles Lumley, a physician, was charged with the murder of Mabel Gorringe. The evidence tended to show that the defendant had performed an illegal abortion upon the victim, and that she had died as a result of this operation. The following is a portion of the trial court's instruction on the felony murder doctrine.]

AVORY, J. (in the course of his summing up) directed the jury as follows: If the evidence satisfies you beyond reasonable doubt that the prisoner did, in fact, either use an instrument or other means, for the purpose and with the intention of procuring abortion, and that death resulted from that act, then you must ask yourselves the further question: When he did the act, did he contemplate, or must he as a reasonable man have contemplated, that death was likely to result, or must he as a reasonable man have contemplated that grievous bodily harm was likely to result? If, in your opinion, he must as a reasonable man have contemplated either of those consequences, then your duty is to find him guilty of murder. If you are of the opinion, and are driven to the conclusion by the evidence, that he did the act which is charged against him, but that he had not at the time in contemplation, and would not as a reasonable man have contemplated, that either death or grievous bodily harm would result, but thought that by his own skill as a medical man he could perform this operation without any risk of either death or grievous bodily harm, then you would be justified in convicting him of manslaughter.

[margin handwritten note: FORESEEABLE—murder / NOT " —Manslaughter]

NOTES

1. Although it is frequently said that a felon is not liable for murder if during the felony he causes a death in an unforeseeable manner because the felonious activity is not the "proximate cause" of the death, e. g., W. La-Fave and A. Scott, Criminal Law 264 (1972), American case law support for this proposition is sparse. Most of the support is dicta in cases holding defendants liable for what is determined to have been a foreseeable death. E. g., State v. Glover, 330 Mo. 709, 50 S.W.2d 1049 (1932) (defendant who set fire to drug store to collect insurance liable for felony-murder of fireman killed fighting the blaze on the ground that he had reason to anticipate that members of the fire department would endanger themselves fighting the fire). See Ward v. State, 109 S.W.2d 207 (Tex.Crim.App.1937) in which the defendant caused fire to be set to a building; a person in an upper

room was killed in the fire. "The testimony," concluded the court, "excludes the idea that the principals knew, or should have known, that any person was in the building at the time the arson was consummated." Defendant also denied any knowledge of this fact. He was charged with murder under a statute in the arson section of the penal code providing that "Where death is occasioned by any offense described in this * * * chapter the offender is guilty of murder." The conviction was upheld, although the court commented that in the absence of the statute it would have grave doubt that the defendant would be liable for murder "unless the death in question was the natural and reasonable consequence of [the] arson * * *." Should the existence of such a statute preclude application of a "proximate cause" requirement of foreseeability?

2. What is the purpose of the felony-murder rule? Consider the following statement by Chief Justice Traynor of the California Supreme Court:

> The purpose of the felony-murder rule is to deter felons from killing negligently or accidentally by holding them strictly liable for killings they commit. * * *
>
> It is contended * * * that another purpose of the felony-murder rule is to prevent the commission of robberies [and other felonies]. Neither the common-law rationale of the rule nor the Penal Code supports this contention. In every robbery there is a possibility that the victim will resist and kill. The robber has little control over such a killing once the robbery is undertaken * * *. To impose an additional penalty for the killing would discriminate between robbers, not on the basis of any difference in their own conduct, but solely on the basis of the response by others that the robber's conduct happened to induce. An additional penalty for a homicide * * * [caused in this manner] would deter robbery haphazardly at best. To "prevent stealing, the law would do better to hang one thief in every thousand by lot." (Holmes, The Common Law, p. 58.)

People v. Washington, 62 Cal.2d 777, 44 Cal.Rptr. 442, 402 P.2d 130, 133 (1965).

3. The President's Commission on Crime in the District of Columbia examined the circumstances of selected samples of serious crimes committed in the District of Columbia. Consider the following conclusions as they may relate to the appropriateness of a felony-murder rule, or as to the selection of offenses as to which any such rule should apply:

> Of the 172 murders committed between 1963 and 1964, twenty-four (or 14 percent) were felony murders. Seventeen (10 percent) were incidental to robberies, and seven (4 percent) were incidental to rapes.

President's Commission on Crime in the District of Columbia, Report 45 (1966)

> Of 151 rapes committed during 1964, thirty-eight (25 percent) involved assailants armed with dangerous weapons. Twenty-seven of these were armed with knives.

Id. at 54.

> Of 297 robberies committed in December, 1965, 120 (40 percent) involved armed perpetrators. 86 were armed with guns and 16 with

knives. Seventy-five (25 percent) of the victims were injured; no figure as to the number killed was given. Injuries occurred in ten (11 percent) of 91 holdups or armed robberies; injuries occurred in thirty (45 percent) of the "yokings" (strong-arm robbery, usually involving assault from the back).

Id. at 64.

4. Must the death be caused by the felonious aspect of the defendant's conduct for the felony-murder doctrine to take effect? See Moynahan v. State, 140 Tex.Crim. 540, 146 S.W.2d 376 (1941) in which the defendant was charged with felony-murder for a death arising out of an automobile accident which occurred while the defendant allegedly was intoxicated. Driving while intoxicated was a felony under state law. The conviction was reversed on the basis of the prosecutor's following argument to the jury: "It makes no difference how carefully the defendant was driving his car; he could have been driving it five miles an hour, and if he was drunk at the time of the collision he is guilty of murder." The "correct statement of the settled law of the state," the court held, was embodied in the trial court's instruction that the defendant "would not be guilty of murder if he was operating the same in the manner that it would be operated by one not under the influence of intoxicating liquor." Suppose at the time the accident occurred the defendant was driving at five miles an hour because he realized he was intoxicated and wanted to be especially careful. Would he be liable for murder on the theory that if he had not been intoxicated he would have driven faster and not been at the intersection at the same time as the deceased? Compare Ross v. State, 314 S.W.2d 592 (Tex.Crim.App.1958) affirming a conviction for felony-murder arising out of a motor vehicle accident occurring when the defendant was allegedly intoxicated despite what a dissenting judge described as "not the least suggestion in [the] record that the intoxication of the appellant caused him to run into the motorcycle [upon which the deceased was riding]."

5. People v. Stamp is critically discussed in 24 Ark.L.Rev. 342 (1970). For other discussions of the felony murder doctrine, see Ludwig, Foreseeable Death in Felony Murder, 18 U.Pitt.L.Rev. 51 (1956); Ritz, Felony Murder, Transferred Intent, and the *Palsgraf* Doctrine in the Criminal Law, 16 Wash. & Lee L.Rev. 169 (1959); Note, Imputing Act and Intent in Felony Murder Cases: An Elaborate Fiction, 40 Conn.B.J. 107 (1966). California developments are treated in Recent Development, California Rewrites Felony Murder, 18 Stan.L.Rev. 690 (1966).

6. The felony-murder rule has been specifically abolished in England by statute. See Homicide Act, 1957, 5 & 6 Eliz. II, c. 11, § 1. The Supreme Court of Iowa has interpreted its statute to require "a purpose or intent to kill," even where the killing is caused in the perpetration of felonies enumerated in the statute. Robbins v. State, 8 Ohio St. 131 (1857); State v. Farmer, 156 Ohio St. 214, 102 N.E.2d 11 (1951). But cf. State v. Salter, 149 Ohio St. 264, 78 N.E.2d 575 (1948).

IN RE ALLEN

Court of Appeals of New York, 1912.
205 N.Y. 158, 98 N.E. 470.

WILLARD BARTLETT, J. Some time in November, 1910, one Jacob Kuhn and the appellant, Ralph Friedman, entered into a conspiracy to obtain money feloniously and by force, in the nighttime, from the person or custody of George A. Schuchart, a grocer in the city of Rochester. The conspiracy was carried into effect between half past 9 and half past 10 o'clock in the evening of November 15, 1910. One of the conspirators waited in the street outside the store; the other entered the store to perform the more active part of the contemplated robbery or larceny. A struggle ensued within between the grocer and his assailant during which three revolver shots were fired, one of which inflicted a mortal wound upon Mr. Schuchart. The appellant, Friedman, who claims to have been the one who waited outside, testified that he entered the door upon hearing the three shots and found Kuhn and Mr. Schuchart there engaged in a personal encounter. He states that he reached his arm over to knock the revolver up, when a fourth shot was fired which penetrated his left wrist. The conspirators then fled, leaving Mr. Schuchart dying upon the floor of his grocery. * * * The proof * * * suffices to uphold the conviction even if the killing was unintentional, on the ground that the homicide was committed by persons engaged in a common attempt to commit a felony.

At the close of the charge, counsel for the defendant asked the court to instruct the jury as follows: "If the jury believe that the defendant, Friedman, and Kuhn did confederate and agree together to enter the store of Schuchart and take money from it by stealth, and that the scope and plan of execution of their unlawful enterprise did not involve the use of force or violence which might result in the taking of human life, then the defendant is not responsible for the act of Kuhn in taking human life if they find that the defendant did not shoot and kill Schuchart."

It is contended that the refusal to charge this request was error. I think not. The learned trial judge had previously charged the jury correctly on this subject, as follows: "If they [Friedman and Kuhn] went to the store of Schuchart merely to steal his money, that would not necessarily mean that their errand was of a dangerous, homicidal character, or that it necessarily involved the use of violence which might result in the taking of human life unlawfully. But if they confederated together to commit a felony at Schuchart's store, then it is left to you to say whether or not they intended the natural and probable consequence of their act, and each one would be responsible for the acts of the other in carrying out their joint enterprise."

If the natural and probable consequence of the common enterprise was the killing of Mr. Schuchart in case of resistance on his part, the defendant was liable for murder in the first degree, although he did not do the actual killing. The request assumes that, if the appellant did not fire the fatal shot, he could escape liability unless the conspiracy expressly contemplated the use of such force or violence as might cause death. This is an erroneous view of the law. An express agreement by intending robbers not to kill in carrying out a plan of robbery would not save any of the conspirators from responsibility for a homicide by one of them in committing or attempting to commit the robbery, if such killing was the natural and probable result of the robbery or attempt to rob in such a contingency as actually occurred in this case.

A stood outside
A tried to stop shooting

1st deg M if Nat'l & Prob. Conseq.

* * *

Judgment of conviction affirmed.

NOTES

1. Is the result in the instant case consistent with general principles of complicity? If not, how can the difference be justified? Is the felony murder rule an exception to the "act" requirement as well as to the "state of mind" requirement of murder?

2. Suppose that A and B agree to assault C with their fists. During the affray, B, upon an "impulse," pulls a gun and shoots C. C dies. Is this sufficient to convict A of the death of C on a felony-murder theory? Cf. People v. Raybourn, 72 Ill.App.2d 379, 219 N.E.2d 711 (1966). Would it be relevant that A did or did not know that B had a gun? Would the result differ if B had planned all along to shoot C during the fight, but did not reveal this to A? Would it differ if B had not intended to kill C when the fight began and had assured A of this, but formed the intent to kill when, during the fight, C revealed to B that he was the person who had earlier stolen certain property belonging to B?

2. LIMITATIONS UPON FELONIES THAT INVOKE THE DOCTRINE

PEOPLE v. SEARS

Supreme Court of California, 1970.
2 Cal.3d 180, 465 P.2d 847, 84 Cal.Rptr. 711.

PETERS, Justice. [A] jury found defendant guilty of the first degree murder of his stepdaughter Elizabeth Olives, the attempted murder of his wife Clara Sears, and the attempted murder of his mother-in-law Frances Montijo. The penalty for the murder was fixed as death. * * *

[Defendant had entered his estranged wife's cottage and, after an apparent attempt to discuss a reconciliation with her, assaulted her, her daughter, and her mother. His wife's daughter died as a result of the assault.]

In his argument to the jury, the prosecutor urged at some length that the first degree felony-murder doctrine was applicable, urging that defendant committed a burglary in entering the cottage. He emphasized repeatedly that burglary included an entry with an intent to commit any felony, not merely theft, and he repeatedly asserted that defendant entered with intent to assault.

[After beginning deliberations,] the jury returned to the courtroom and asked the judge the following question. "Does assault on wife constitute a felony regardless of intent upon entering and if so, does felony murder doctrine dictating first degree murder apply?" The court * * * stated: "In answer to the specific inquiry, the court would advise that the specific intent to commit the assault must exist at the time of entry, otherwise the felony-murder rule does not apply. Does that answer your question?" Whereupon the foreman of the jury stated that he believed it did.

The jurors continued their deliberations for six hours after the above instruction before retiring for the night. The jury returned its verdict the following morning, apparently one and a half hours after resuming deliberations.

In People v. Ireland, 70 A.C. 557, 573 et seq., 75 Cal.Rptr. 188, 450 P.2d 580, we considered the applicability of the second degree felony-murder rule to a situation where the claimed felony in the course of which the homicide occurred was an assault with a deadly weapon. * * *

We * * * stated: "We have concluded that the utilization of the felony-murder rule in circumstances such as those before us extends the operation of that rule 'beyond any rational function that it is designed to serve.' (People v. Washington (1965) 62 Cal.2d 777, 783, 44 Cal.Rptr. 442, 446, 402 P.2d 130, 134.) To allow such use of the felony-murder rule would effectively preclude the jury from considering the issue of malice aforethought in all cases wherein homicide has been committed as a result of a felonious assault—a category which includes the great majority of all homicides. This kind of bootstrapping finds support neither in logic nor in law. We therefore hold that a second degree felony-murder instruction may not properly be given when it is based upon a felony which is an integral part of the homicide and which the evidence produced by the prosecution shows to be an offense included in fact within the offense charged." (Footnote omitted.)

We also pointed out that other jurisdictions, through a so-called "merger" doctrine, had applied similar limitations on the felony-murder doctrine and that, although it was not clear whether we would adopt the entire doctrine, "we believe that the reasoning underlying that doctrine is basically sound and should be applied to the extent that it is consistent with the laws and policies of this state."

Ireland was followed in our recent decision of People v. Wilson, 1 Cal.3d 431, 82 Cal.Rptr. 494, 462 P.2d 22, where the jury was instructed on the first degree felony-murder rule on the theory that the homicide was committed in the course of a burglary because the defendant entered the premises with intent to commit a felonious assault. In *Wilson,* the defendant forcibly entered his estranged wife's apartment carrying a shotgun. He shot one man on the stairs of the apartment, shot William Washington in the living room of the apartment, broke into the bathroom, and killed Mrs. Wilson. The defendant was convicted of the second degree murder of Washington and the first degree murder of his wife. We held that there was error in instructing the jury on both the second degree and the first degree felony-murder rules.

In reversing the judgment convicting defendant of first and second degree murder, we stated with respect to the first degree felony-murder instruction: "Here the prosecution sought to apply the felony-murder rule on the theory that the homicide occurred in the course of a burglary, but the only basis for finding a felonious entry is the intent to commit an assault with a deadly weapon. When, as here, the entry would be nonfelonious but for the intent to commit the assault, and the assault is an integral part of the homicide and is included in fact in the offense charged, utilization of the felony-murder rule extends that doctrine 'beyond any rational function that it is designed to serve.' We have heretofore emphasized 'that the felony-murder doctrine expresses a highly artificial concept that deserves no extension beyond its required application.' * * * Where a person enters a building with an intent to assault his victim with a deadly weapon, he is not deterred by the felony-murder rule. That doctrine can serve its purpose only when applied to a felony independent of the homicide. In *Ireland,* we reasoned that a man assaulting another with a deadly weapon could not be deterred by the second degree felony-murder rule, since the assault was an integral part of the homicide. Here, the only distinction is that the assault and homicide occurred inside a dwelling so that the underlying felony is burglary based on an intention to assault with a deadly weapon, rather than simple assault with a deadly weapon.

"We do not suggest that no relevant differences exist between crimes committed inside and outside dwellings. We have often recognized that persons within dwellings are in greater peril from intruders bent on stealing or engaging in other felonious conduct. Persons within dwellings are more likely to resist and less likely to be able to avoid the consequences of crimes committed inside their homes. However, this rationale does not justify application of the felony-murder rule to the case at bar. Where the intended felony of the burglar is an assault with a deadly weapon, the likelihood of homicide from the lethal weapon is not significantly increased by the site of the assault. Furthermore, the burglary statute in this state includes within its definition numerous structures other than dwellings as to which there can be no conceivable basis for distinguishing between an assault with a deadly weapon outdoors and a burglary in which the felonious intent is solely to assault with a deadly weapon.

* * *

We conclude that the same bootstrapping is involved [here as in *Ireland*] in instructing a jury that the intent to assault makes the entry burglary and that the burglary raises the homicide resulting from the assault to first degree murder without proof of malice aforethought and premeditation. * * *

Under *Ireland* and *Wilson,* the instructions of the court on the court on the first degree felony-murder rule and the court's answer to the question asked by the jury must be held erroneous. Those instructions and the answer could reasonably be understood to mean that if defendant entered with intent to assault his wife and stepdaughter he was guilty of burglary and that the first degree felony-murder rule was applicable. To apply the felony-murder rule to such a situation would extend the doctrine "beyond any rational function that it is designed to serve." As pointed out in *Wilson,* that doctrine can serve its purpose only when applied to a felony independent of the homicide, and where a person enters a building with intent to assault his victims with a deadly weapon, he is not deterred by the felony-murder rule.

The Attorney General, pointing out that there is evidence from which the jury might have concluded that defendant entered with intent to assault his wife with a deadly weapon but not his stepdaughter, urges that the felony-murder rule is applicable on the theory that the burglary based on the intent to assault the wife was independent of and collateral to the killing of the stepdaughter. It may be noted in this connection that in New York it has been held that, although the felony-murder rule does not apply where a defendant intentionally assaults each of his two victims who die as a result of the assaults, the rule is applicable if the defendant assaulted one person but killed another who came to the first's defense. (People v. Moran, 246 N.Y. 100, 158 N.E. 35, 36–37 (1927); People v. Wagner (1927) 245 N.Y. 143, 156 N.E. 644, 646.)

However, the instructions given to the jury did not posit the applicability of the felony-murder rule upon any such theory. Moreover, we are satisfied that the distinction made by the New York cases is untenable in the light of ordinary principles of culpability. It would be anomalous to place the person who intends to attack one person and in the course of the assault kills another inadvertently or in the heat of battle in a worse position than the person who from the outset intended to attack both persons and killed one or both.

Where a defendant assaults one or more persons killing one, his criminal responsibility for the homicide should not depend upon which of the victims died but should be the greatest crime committed viewing each victim of the attack individually and without regard to which in fact died. This result is reached in application of existing principles of transferred intent, and it is unnecessary to resort to the felony-murder rule. Thus if a person purposely and of his deliberate and premediated malice attempts to kill one person but by mistake and inadvertence kills another instead, the law transfers the intent and the homicide so committed is murder of the first degree. * * *

The error in instructing on the felony-murder rule must be held prejudicial. Although there is substantial evidence of premeditation and malice aforethought in the record, the evidence is not overwhelming, and there is conflicting evidence. The question asked of the court by the jury during its lengthy deliberations indicates that the felony-murder instruction played a decisive role in the jury's verdict.

PEOPLE v. TAYLOR

California Court of Appeals, 1970.
11 Cal.App.3d 57, 89 Cal.Rptr. 697.

KAUS, Presiding Justice. After a court trial defendant was convicted of second degree murder.

The facts revealed that the victim died as a result of an overdose of heroin which had been furnished to her by the defendant [in violation of section 11501 of the Health and Safety Code]. In finding the defendant guilty the trial court expressed a reasonable doubt that, on the evidence before it, defendant had actually injected the heroin into the victim. * * * [Defendant argues that] the Supreme Court's decision in People v. Ireland, 70 Cal.2d 522, 538–540, 75 Cal.Rptr. 188, 450 P.2d 580, precludes the application of the felony-murder rule in the case at bar.

* * *

Whether or not, under the *Ireland* doctrine, the violation of section 11501 of the Health and Safety Code merged into the homicide so that defendant's conviction cannot stand unless the record contains substantial evidence of actual malice, express or implied, is not easy to answer, for neither *Ireland* nor *Ireland's* progeny, are explicit with respect to the rationale of the doctrine of merger as it is to be applied in California.

The difficulty arises from the fact that * * * the language of *Ireland* * * * applies to all felonies which are "an integral part of the homicide and which the evidence produced by the prosecution shows to be an offense included *in fact* within the offense charged." * * * While the felony-murder rule can hardly be much of a deterrent to a defendant who has decided to assault his victim with a deadly weapon, it seems obvious that in the situation presented in the case at bar, it does serve a rational purpose: knowledge that the death of a person to whom heroin is furnished may result in a conviction for murder should have some effect on the defendant's readiness to do the furnishing. * * *

Just how broadly the *Ireland* language concerning felonies which are an integral part of the homicide and are included in fact within the offense charged will be interpreted is not for us to say. The perimeter of the connection between the underlying felony and the death of the victim is that the homicide must be the direct causal result of the commission of the felony. Unless the Supreme Court intended to abolish second degree felony-murder, we must assume that there are situations where a felony inherently dangerous to human life can be the direct cause of a homicide without, at the same time, being an integral part thereof and included in fact therein. We hold that the case at bar presents such a situation.

The judgment is affirmed.

PEOPLE v. SATCHELL

Supreme Court of California, 1971.
6 Cal.3d 28, 98 Cal.Rptr. 33, 489 P.2d 1361.

SULLIVAN, Justice. In a two count indictment defendant John M. Satchell was charged respectively with murder (Pen.Code, § 187) and assault with a deadly weapon upon a peace officer * * *. The jury acquitted him of the aggravated assault charged in the second count of the indictment but found him guilty of murder of the second degree. Defendant appeals from the judgment of conviction.

For the reasons set forth below we have concluded that it was prejudicial error for the trial court to instruct the jury on the theory of second degree felony murder. Accordingly we reverse the judgment.

The facts relevant to our determination can be briefly stated. On July 2, 1969, defendant and the victim Jordan became engaged in a heated argument on a public street in San Francisco. The argument progressed beyond mere harsh language when defendant shoved Jordan. The latter then withdrew some distance down the street; defendant went to his automobile, which was parked nearby and got in. A few minutes later Jordan returned and walked over to defendant's car. The argument then resumed, but it was abruptly terminated when defendant emerged from the car holding a sawed-off shotgun, shot Jordan once in the chest, and then drove off. Jordan died of the shotgun wound.

At trial defendant took the stand and testified that he had shot Jordan, with whom he had had no prior acquaintance, in self-defense when the latter threatened him and made movements which defendant interpreted as efforts to draw a weapon. A defense witness testified that Jordan had a gun in his hand at the time of the shooting, which gun was taken from the victim after defendant had departed.[1]

The trial court instructed the jury on the definition of murder and malice and the degrees of murder, but it eliminated first degree murder from the consideration of the jury by indicating that none of the felonies enumerated in section 189 of the Penal Code was here involved and by not instructing on premeditation. The jury was fully instructed on second degree murder, however, and the following instruction on second degree felony murder was given: "The unlawful killing of a human being, whether intentional, unintentional or accidental, which occurs as a direct causal result of the commission of or attempt to commit a felony inherently dangerous to human life, namely, the crime of *possession of a concealable firearm by a felon,* and where there was in the mind of the perpetrator the specific intent to commit such crime, is murder of the second degree. The specific intent to commit *the crime of possession of a concealable firearm by a felon* and the commission of or attempt to commit such crime must be proved beyond a reasonable doubt."

The trial court went on to give a series of instructions defining and explaining the crime of possession of a concealable firearm by a felon. (Pen.Code, § 12021; see Pen.Code, § 12001.)[5]

Finally, the court gave instructions concerning manslaughter, heat of passion, and provocation, and instructions concerning justifiable homicide and self-defense. * * *

1. The charge of aggravated assault upon a police officer, of which defendant was acquitted, arose out of circumstances surrounding defendant's arrest later in the day.

5. Section 12021 of the Penal Code at the time here pertinent provided: "Any person who is not a citizen of the United States and any person who has been convicted of a felony under the laws of the United States, of the State of California, or any other state, government, or country, or who is addicted to the use of any narcotic drug, who owns or has in his possession or under his custody or control any pistol, revolver, or other firearm capable of being concealed upon the person is guilty of a public offense, and shall be punishable by imprison-ment in the state prison not exceeding 15 years, or in a county jail not exceeding one year or by a fine not exceeding five hundred dollars ($500), or by both."

Section 12001 of the Penal Code at the time here pertinent provided in relevant part: " 'Pistol,' 'revolver,' and 'firearm capable of being concealed upon the person' as used in this chapter shall apply to and include any device, designed to be used as a weapon, from which is expelled a projectile by the force of any explosion, or any other form of combustion, and which has a barrel less than 12 inches in length. * * *" The sawed-off shotgun involved in this case had a barrel 11¾ inches in length.

Defendant moved for a new trial on the ground that the second degree felony-murder instruction should not have been given, but the motion was denied. He appeals from the judgment of conviction on the same ground among others. We have concluded that his contention must be sustained.

In the case of People v. Washington (1965) 62 Cal.2d 777, at page 783, 44 Cal.Rptr. 442, 446, 402 P.2d 130, 134, this court struck the keynote which has guided all our subsequent consideration of cases involving the felony-murder doctrine. Acknowledging the substantial body of legal scholarship which has concluded that the doctrine not only "erodes the relation between criminal liability and moral culpability" but also is usually unnecessary for conviction, we went on to say of it: "Although it is the law in this state (Pen.Code, § 189), *it should not be extended beyond any rational function that it is designed to serve.*" (Italics added.)

Applying this principle to various concrete factual circumstances, we have sought to insure that the "highly artificial concept" (People v. Phillips (1966) 64 Cal.2d 574, 582, 51 Cal.Rptr. 225, 414 P.2d 353) of strict criminal liability incorporate in the felony-murder doctrine be given the narrowest possible application consistent with its ostensible purpose—which is to deter those engaged in felonies from killing negligently or accidentally * * *.[12]

In the instant case it is clear that the victim was killed by defendant while he was engaged in the commission of a felony other than the six enumerated in section 189 of the Penal Code. Thus, in determining whether the felony-murder doctrine is properly applicable the threshold inquiry is whether the felony in which defendant was engaged was a "felony inherently dangerous to human life" within the meaning of People v. Phillips, *supra*, 64 Cal.2d 574, 51 Cal.Rptr. 225, 414 P.2d 353, and People v. Williams [(1965), 63 Cal.2d 452, 47 Cal.Rptr. 7, 406 P.2d 647]. If the felony in question was not such an inherently dangerous felony, the felony-murder instruction given was without legal foundation and the judgment must be reversed if the giving of that instruction was prejudicial.[14]

At the outset it is clear that this court has unequivocally held on more than one occasion that the offense set forth in section 12021

---

12. In *Williams* we stated that the ostensible purpose of the felony-murder rule "may be well served with respect to felonies such as robbery or burglary, but it has little relevance to a felony which is not inherently dangerous. If the felony is not inherently dangerous it is highly improbable that the potential felon will be deterred; he will not anticipate that any injury or death might arise solely from the fact that he will commit the felony." (63 Cal.2d at pp. 457–458, fn. 4, 47 Cal.Rptr. at p. 10, 406 P.2d at p. 650.)

14. Clearly the question whether the underlying felony is inherently dangerous and therefore capable of supporting a second degree felony-murder instruction logically precedes the question whether such a felony merges with the charged homicide crime and is therefore not subject to utilization as the basis of such an instruction.

is a felony capable of supporting a second degree felony-murder instruction. * * * It is equally clear, however—in light of our continuing concern that the felony-murder doctrine not be extended beyond its rational function—that those decisions cannot be invested with a vitality independent from the developing concept of inherent danger * * *. Rather, our task today is to assess the cited decisions as they relate to that concept and determine whether or not the conclusion announced by them is consistent therewith and should endure. "[T]he branch cannot bear fruit by itself, except it abides in the vine." (John XV, 4.)

It is useful to consider the subject decisions within the chronological development of the principle of inherent danger. That principle * * * was first stated as positive law in People v. Ford, *supra* (1964), 60 Cal.2d 772, at page 795, 36 Cal.Rptr. 620 at page 635, 388 P.2d 892 at page 907: "A homicide that is a direct causal result of the commission of *a felony inherently dangerous to human life* (other than the six felonies enumerated in Pen.Code, § 189) constitutes at least second degree murder." (Italics added.) That case itself involved a violation of section 12021, and this court, looking to the facts of the particular case and relying on the prior (i. e., pre-*Ford*) decision in People v. Robillard (1960), 55 Cal.2d 88, 98, 10 Cal.Rptr. 167, 358 P.2d 295, concluded that that offense was inherently dangerous to human life and could properly support a second degree felony-murder instruction. This conclusion was followed in People v. Schader (1965), 62 Cal.2d 716, 732, 44 Cal.Rptr. 193, 401 P.2d 665, * * * again looking to the facts of the particular case which involved the armed holdup of a store by a previously convicted felon.

However, in 1965 we held that, in assessing whether a felony was inherently dangerous within the meaning of *Ford*, "we look to the elements of the felony in the abstract, not the particular 'facts' of the case." (People v. Williams, supra (1965), 63 Cal.2d 452, 458, fn. 5, 47 Cal.Rptr. 7, 10, 406 P.2d 647, 650.) There the victim, an illegal supplier of methedrine, was killed with a knife during an affray which resulted after defendants demanded that he pay a debt either in methedrine or in money. The jury was given a second degree felony-murder instruction based upon the crime of conspiracy to possess methedrine without a prescription. We held that the instruction was erroneous because the subject felony, viewed in the abstract "is surely not, as such, inherently dangerous." (63 Cal.2d at p. 458, 47 Cal.Rptr. at p. 10, 406 P.2d at p. 650.)[16]

[handwritten margin note: BUT LOOK TO ELEMENTS IN ABSTRACT NOT PARTICULAR FACTS OF CASE E.G]

16. In holding that the felony must be viewed in the abstract we disapproved any contrary implications in People v. Pulley (1964) 225 Cal.App.2d 366, 373, 37 Cal.Rptr. 376. There it was held that a second degree felony-murder instruction was properly based on a violation of section 10851 of the Ve-hicle Code, automobile theft, because the theft in question led to a high speed chase and a collision which took the life of the victim. The Court of Appeal stated in that case: "By any reasonable standard, stealing and driving a stolen car and endeavoring to escape pursuing officers with the

The teaching of *Williams* was applied and explained in People v. Phillips, supra (1966) 64 Cal.2d 574, 51 Cal.Rptr. 225, 414 P.2d 353. There the defendant, a chiropractor, was tried for murder following the death from cancer of a patient whom he dissuaded from surgery and purported to treat through chiropractic methods. The jury was given a second degree felony-murder instruction based upon the crime of grand theft by false pretenses. (Pen.Code, §§ 484, 487.) Holding that the crime of grand theft, viewed in the abstract, was not inherently dangerous to human life, we went on to reject the contention of the prosecution that the subject felony should be characterized in light of the defendant's actual conduct as "grand theft medical fraud," assertedly an inherently dangerous offense. ["To fragmentize the 'course of conduct' of defendant so that the felony-murder rule applies if any segment of that conduct may be considered dangerous to life would widen the rule beyond calculation. It would then apply not only to the commission of specific felonies, which are themselves dangerous to life, but to the perpetration of *any* felony during which defendant may have acted in such a manner as to endanger life.] [Par.] The proposed approach would entail the rejection of our holding in *Williams*. That case limited the felony murder doctrine to such felonies as were themselves inherently dangerous to life. That decision eschews the prosecution's present sweeping concept because, once the Legislature's own definition is discarded, the number or nature of the contextual elements which could be incorporated into an expanded felony terminology would be limitless. We have been, and remain, unwilling to embark upon such an uncharted sea of felony murder." (64 Cal.2d at pp. 583–584, 51 Cal.Rptr. at p. 233, 414 P.2d at p. 361.)

*   *   *

The foregoing chronological review clearly shows that the prior decisions of this court concerning violation of Penal Code section 12021 as a basis for felony murder have applied a standard different from that required by our *Williams* and *Phillips* cases in that they have not undertaken to view that felony in the abstract when assessing the danger to human life inherent in its commission. Accordingly, in addressing ourselves to that task for the first time today, we decide what is in effect a question of novel impression in this court: *Viewed in the abstract*, is the possession of a concealable firearm by a person who has previously been convicted of a felony an offense inherently dangerous to human life?

We first consider two decisions of the Court of Appeal which have treated this question. In People v. Lovato (1968) 258 Cal.App.2d

stolen car, entering an intersection against all rules of the road at 70 to 80 miles per hour and crashing with other cars lawfully proceeding therein, is highly dangerous." (225 Cal. App.2d at p. 373, 37 Cal.Rptr. at p.

380.) Our insistence in *Williams* that the felony be viewed in the abstract necessarily precludes a determination of inherent danger based upon this kind of reasoning.

290, 65 Cal.Rptr. 638, the specific issue before the court was whether the possession of a concealable firearm by an *alien* (which is also proscribed by section 12021 of the Penal Code) was an offense inherently dangerous to human life capable of supporting a second degree felony-murder instruction. The Court of Appeal, over the dissent of one of the three justices, held that it was not. Viewing the crime in the abstract as required by the *Williams-Phillips* principle, the court concluded: "It is common knowledge that several million aliens are living in this country and that the vast majority are peaceful and law-abiding. Undoubtedly, many are serving or have children serving in the armed forces. Consequently, to categorically hold that every alien who is intentionally in possession of a concealable weapon, regardless of the reason, is guilty of an offense inherently dangerous to human life, and hence is guilty of murder in the second degree if the offense results in a homicide, under every possible circumstance we can visualize, would manifestly lead to unjust and even absurd results. Moreover, to in effect state that a person's citizenship is the controlling factor as to whether a homicide was committed with malice is not only illogical but would constitute an affront to the judiciary which through the years has constantly striven to find compelling reasons rather than arbitrary distinctions before making rules which result in differing treatment of people." (258 Cal.App.2d at p. 293, 65 Cal.Rptr. at p. 641.)

It was urged upon the court, however, that in light of the line of cases holding that possession of a concealable firearm by a *felon* was inherently dangerous to life * * *, the same result should follow in cases involving aliens. In answering this contention the court, still applying the *Williams-Phillips* principle of considering the felony in the abstract, stated: "[W]e conclude that there is a clear, rational and logical distinction between the nature of the offense when committed by an ex-felon and when committed by an alien. *An ex-felon by his felony conviction has demonstrated instability and a propensity for crime. Thus, there is a core of logic in the assumption that if such a person arms himself with a concealable weapon he commits a crime* per se *dangerous to human life.* However, a person does not demonstrate instability, nor does he show a tendency toward crime, simply because he is not a citizen of this country. Consequently, although it may be reasonable for the Legislature to include aliens within the ambit of section 12021 for regulatory purposes, it would be illogical and unreasonable for a court to hold that every alien who violates the section necessarily commits a crime inherently dangerous to human life." (Italics added.) (258 Cal.App. 2d at pp. 295–296, 65 Cal.Rptr. at p. 642.)

* * *

While we agree with the approach and reasoning of the *Lovato* court in assessing the danger inherent in the crime of possession of a concealable firearm by an *alien*, we believe that its dictum concerning such possession by an *ex-felon* departs from that approach and reasoning and reaches an incorrect conclusion. Thus, we cannot agree that, whereas on the one hand it would be "illogical" and "arbitrary" to conclude "that a person's citizenship is the controlling factor as to whether a homicide was committed with malice", yet on the other hand "there is a core of logic" in the conclusion that the presence or absence of a felony conviction on a person's past record should have such a controlling effect. The logical process by which this conclusion is reached fails to proceed beyond its own major premise: granting that "[a]n ex-felon by his felony conviction has demonstrated instability and a propensity for crime", one cannot logically achieve the conclusion that such a person, when he arms himself, commits a crime inherently dangerous to human life, unless it also be shown that one who so demonstrates instability and a propensity for crime is inherently disposed toward acts dangerous to human life. We do not think that this has been shown. To borrow the phrasing of the *Lovato* court, we have concluded that "to in effect state that [the presence or absence of a felony conviction on a person's past record] is the controlling factor as to whether a homicide was committed with malice is not only illogical but would constitute an affront to the judiciary which through the years has constantly striven to find compelling reasons rather than arbitrary distinctions before making rules which result in differing treatment of people."

It bears emphasis that, in determining whether a felony is inherently dangerous for purposes of the felony-murder rule we assess that felony *in the abstract*. The felony here in question is possession of a concealable firearm by one who has previously been convicted of a (i. e., another) felony. We do *not* look to the specific facts of the case before us in order to determine whether, in light of the nature of the particular felony of which defendant was previously convicted, his possession of a concealable firearm was inherently dangerous. Rather, we direct our attention to the genus of crimes known as felonies and determine whether the possession of a concealable firearm by one who has been convicted of *any crime within that genus* is an act inherently dangerous to human life which, as such, justifies the extreme consequence (i. e., imputed malice) which the felony-murder doctrine demands.

It is manifest that the range of antisocial activities which are criminally punishable as felonies in this state is very wide indeed. Some of these felonies, such as certain well-known crimes against the person of another, distinctly manifest a propensity for acts dangerous to human life on the part of the perpetrator. Others, just as distinctly fail to manifest such a propensity. Surely it cannot be said that a person who has committed a crime in this latter category, when he arms himself with a concealable weapon, presents a danger to human life so significantly more extreme than that presented by a non-felon similarly armed as to justify the imputation of malice to him if a homicide should result. Accordingly, because we can conceive of such a vast number of situations wherein it would be grossly illogical to impute malice, we must conclude that the violation of section 12021 by one previously convicted of a felony is not itself a felony *inherently* dangerous to human life which will support a second degree felony-murder instruction.

Thus, it was error in this case to give a second degree felony-murder instruction based upon defendant's violation of section 12021 of the Penal Code. * * *

Our consideration of an issue which may arise upon retrial reveals an even more fundamental reason why the felony-murder instruction was erroneous in this case.

Although the jury was given a second degree felony-murder instruction based upon section 12021 of the Penal Code, it was not given such an instruction based upon section 12020 of the same code. That section * * * provides in substance as here relevant that *any person* who possesses a sawed-off shotgun is guilty of a felony. Because a second degree felony-murder instruction based on section 12020 may be offered on retrial, we deem it incumbent to determine whether the offense proscribed by that section, viewed in the abstract, is inherently dangerous to human life. We conclude that it is not, and that therefore a violation of section 12020 may not properly support a second degree felony-murder instruction.

This court has stated that the purpose of the Legislature in enacting section 12020 was to outlaw the possession of "weapons common to the criminal's arsenal. * * *"

* * *

This purpose proceeds from the recognition that persons who possess the specialized instruments of violence listed in the section are ordinarily persons who intend to use them in violent and dangerous enterprises. Thus, rather than simply proscribing the *use* of such instruments, the Legislature has sought to prevent such use by proscribing their mere *possession*. In order to insure the intended prophylactic effect, the intent or propensity for violence of the possessor has been rendered irrelevant.

While we have no doubt that * * * the proscription of the mere possession of articles of this sort lies within the constitutional competency of the Legislature, we decline to hold that such a statute, which makes no distinction between the innocent "collector" and the hardened criminal, can be utilized to posit malice aforethought in a prosecution for murder. Looking at the subject felony in the abstract, as we are required to do, it appears that to permit the application of the felony-murder doctrine on the ground of violation of section 12020 would "erode [   ] the relation between criminal liability and moral culpability" beyond all recognition and would extend the operation of that doctrine "beyond any rational function that it is designed to serve." (People v. Washington, supra, 62 Cal.2d 777, 783, 44 Cal.Rptr. 442, 446, 402 P.2d 130, 134.)

Viewing the matter from the standpoint of inherent danger, we find it difficult to understand how any offense of mere passive possession can be considered to supply the element of malice in a murder prosecution. To be sure, if such possession is of an extremely reckless nature manifesting a conscious disregard for human life, malice may be imputed by means of basic murder principles. Moreover, if passive possession ripens into a felonious *act* in which danger to human life is inherent, the purpose of the felony murder rule is served by its application—for it is the deterrence of such acts by felons which the rule is designed to accomplish. However, mere possession *in itself*—ignoring the propensities and conduct of the possessor—is essentially neutral in its intentional aspect and should not serve as the basis for the imputation of malice.

* * *

The judgment is reversed.

NOTES

1. Under the approach of the California Supreme Court in the instant case, could the offense of escape from state or local penal facilities support a second degree murder instruction?

We answer this question in the negative. * * * [T]he crime of escape * * * comprehends a multitude of sins. It applies to the man who is tardy in returning from a work furlough as well as to the man who obtains a contraband weapon and decides to shoot his way out of jail. It applies to the committed inebriate who wanders off from a county road job in search of drink as well as to the desperate felon who seizes a hostage in order to bargain for his freedom. It applies to those who, like this defendant, fashion a rope from blankets, climb down it, and steal into the woods as well as to those who strangle a guard to obtain his key. We cannot conclude that those who commit nonviolent escapes such as those here suggested thereby perpetrate an offense which should logically serve as the basis for the imputation of malice aforethought in a murder prosecution. Because [the statute] draws no relevant distinction between such escapes and the more violent variety, it proscribes an offense which, considered in the abstract, is not *inherently* dangerous to human life and cannot properly support a second degree felony-murder instruction.

We reject the argument that all escapes, however nonviolent, are inherently dangerous because they invite efforts of prevention and apprehension by custodial and law enforcement officers. The possibility of violence during an escape can become an actuality only when, under the facts of the particular case, the escapee attempts violent resistance or, in his efforts to elude capture, conducts himself in a reckless manner. We cannot conclude that such a reaction on the part of escapees is so common as to be considered intrinsic to the crime of escape. The fact that such reactions do occur in some cases is not sufficient to support the conclusion that one who escapes from legal confinement thereby creates a situation inherently dangerous to human life.

People v. Lopez, 6 Cal.3d 45, 98 Cal.Rptr. 44, 489 P.2d 1372, 1376–77 (1971).

2. Upon what, if any, policy grounds can the approach of the California Supreme Court be defended? Does it represent only a desire to limit the felony murder rule at every available opportunity?

3. Compare the analysis in Jenkins v. State, 230 A.2d 262, 268–69 (Del.1967):

> The only rational function of the felony-murder rule is to furnish an added deterrent to the perpetration of felonies which, by their nature or by the attendant circumstances, create a foreseeable risk of death. This function is not served by application of the rule to felonies not foreseeably dangerous. The rule should not be extended beyond its rational function. Moreover, application of the rule to felonies not foreseeably dangerous would be unsound analytically because there is no logical basis for imputing malice from the intent to commit a felony not dangerous to human life.

> * * *

> Whether the commission of a particular felony in a given instance was foreseeably dangerous is for the court and jury to decide. In that determination, both the nature of the felony and the circumstances of its commission are relevant factors. Burglary * * * may, or may not, be foreseeably dangerous to human life, depending upon whether someone may be reasonably expected to be present in the building, and upon other circumstances of the case.

3. DURATION OF THE UNDERLYING FELONY

PROBLEM

Defendant commits an armed robbery. Police are called by a bystander and arrive just as defendant leaves the premises. They pursue him and he surrenders. As he is being taken to police headquarters, he suddenly jumps from the police car. The officer pursues him and in the scuffle the officer is shot with his own gun. Assuming a jurisdiction with the California statutory provisions (see page 915, supra), is the defendant guilty of first degree murder on a felony murder theory? Cf. People v. Goree, 30 Mich.App. 490, 186 N.W.2d 872 (1971).

PEOPLE v. LOPEZ

California Court of Appeal, 1971.
16 Cal.App.3d 346, 93 Cal.Rptr. 885, affirmed 6 Cal.3d 45,
98 Cal.Rptr. 44, 489 P.2d 1372.

DEVINE, Presiding Justice. Appellant was convicted by jury of second degree murder and robbery. (Pen.Code, §§ 187, 211.) Although the notice of appeal would include the robbery, no argument is made on the subject of that crime; wherefore, the appeal is deemed abandoned as to that crime.

On Tuesday, June 17, 1969, appellant, Lopez, and three other prisoners escaped without the use of force, from the San Francisco Jail at San Bruno. Appellant and another, Galindo, parting from the others, made their way beyond the fence at the jail's boundary and headed for the hills. Their departure was discovered at midnight. On Wednesday and Thursday, they remained at large, eating only wild berries. Lopez testified that on five occasions they came close to being discovered. This testimony, of course, need not have been believed, and besides, was conclusionary; but there were at least two episodes which brought the fugitives close to apprehension. One was testified to by two high school girls, and corroborated by Lopez. The girls met Lopez and another man (Galindo) who was sick and nervous. Lopez was agreeable. The men were sitting on a fence near a schoolyard. Lopez told the girls of the escape and asked them to fetch food and clothing. The girls refused. The other episode, testified to by appellant and not contradicted, was that police officers had entered the Pedersen home, where the homicide later occurred, looked around and departed, while the fugitives were in the shed behind the house. So, the men reached several successive points of temporary safety.

On Friday morning, a vicious attack was made on both of the Pedersens, as a result of which Mr. Pedersen died and his wife was severely injured. She was unable to testify, perhaps by reason of her age and perhaps because of the injuries. Galindo was not on trial with Lopez. He was called as a defense witness, but he refused to testify on the ground of self-incrimination. Lopez' testimony is that Galindo, who was ill, probably from lack of food, decided to enter the Pedersen home and that he, Lopez, after trying to dissuade Galindo from this project on the ground that it was dangerous from the standpoint of capture, parted company with his companion and walked away from the home. He had not gone far before he heard a woman's cries and he returned to find that Galindo had gone beserk and was striking both of the Pedersens with metal shears. Lopez then shielded Mrs. Pedersen, he testified, and applied a cloth to her wounds, while her husband lay on the bed. The two men had something to eat and changed their clothes, taking Mr. Pedersen's, took some money (the robbery charge is based on this taking), called a cab, and prepared to leave for San Francisco. Neighbors, having suspected that something was wrong, called the police and the two men were found while trying to hide under the house.

The principal point on this appeal is that of the application of the second degree felony-murder rule. The jury was instructed as follows:

"The unlawful killing of a human being, whether intentional, unintentional or accidental, which occurs as a direct causal result of the commission of or attempt to commit a felony inherently dangerous to human life, namely, the crime of escape, and where there was in the mind of the perpetrator the specific intent to commit such a crime, is murder of the second degree.

"The specific intent to commit escape and the commission of or attempt to commit such crime must be proved beyond a reasonable doubt."

The crime of escape was not defined to the jury, nor was anything more said on the subject of escape.

* * *

Appellant's * * * contention is that even if escape be regarded an inherently dangerous offense, the second degree murder concept does not apply to the instant case because the crime of escape had terminated. It is necessary to consider whether escape is such a crime as to be completed when the fugitive has arrived at a place of temporary safety, or is one which continues beyond that point. We conclude that the crime of escape, like that of robbery, does come to such termination. In cases in which a homicide became murder in the first degree because it was committed in the perpetration of robbery, although the culprit had left the immediate scene of the encounter with the victim, it has been pointed out carefully that the robber had not reached a place of temporary safety. * * *

In People v. Ford, 65 Cal.2d 41, 56–57, 52 Cal.Rptr. 228, 416 P.2d 132, many hours had elapsed between the time of the robbery and the shooting of an officer. The officer was not in pursuit of the robber and did not even know of the robbery, although he knew of a subsequent crime of assault which had been committed by the robber during his flight. It was held that the first degree felony rule did not apply. In People v. Schnittspan, 250 Cal.App.2d 951, 953, 59 Cal.Rptr. 93, appellants, who had fled from a prison camp, committed a burglary, robbery, car theft and grand theft more than 48 hours after their departure from the camp and more than twenty miles away, argued that these actions were all part of the single crime of escape, but it was held that escape was complete when the prisoners departed from the limits of their custody and that, therefore, there were not multiple charges of the same offense.

There are crimes which, by their nature, are continuous and which are inherently dangerous to life, such as kidnapping. Wherefore, it was held in People v. Ford, that although first degree murder did not result automatically from the shooting of the officer, as explained above, second degree murder did result automatically from

the commission of continuing kidnappings. But escape, we conclude, is not of the same nature as kidnapping. Kidnapping may be
terminated by the felon by the releasing of his captive, but the guilty
person himself is the sole subject of escape. In a certain sense, he
is escaping custody until he turns himself in or is caught, even if his
liberty were to endure for years as with Jean Valjean of "Les Misera-
bles," but the *crime* of escape ends, upon the violation of lawful custody. In People v. Herrera, 255 Cal.App.2d 469, 63 Cal.Rptr. 96;
and People v. Temple, 203 Cal.App.2d 654, 21 Cal.Rptr. 633, the prisoners had not left the grounds of the penitentiary, but the crime of
escape had been completed by their exit from the places where they
were supposed to be. We take it, however, that if escaping prisoners commit a crime which is a result of their escape, during what
has been called immediate pursuit or fresh pursuit (in common law
it was known as hot pursuit), the crime would be second degree murder, by application of the reasoning in People v. Ford, supra.

We consider, therefore, what the result must be by reason of
the facts in the present case. The trial judge came to the conclusion that, as a matter of law, the escape was continuing at the time
of the homicide. Appellant contends, first, that, as a matter of law,
the crime of escape had terminated and second, that if this be not
so, at least the question whether the fugitives had arrived at a place
of temporary safety should have been submitted to the jury. In
People v. Ford, it was held that, as a matter of law, the robbery had
terminated prior to the homicide (65 Cal.2d at p. 56, 52 Cal.Rptr. 228,
416 P.2d 132). We make the same holding. The fugitives had been
away from custody for two full days and nights, and for part of the
first night. Although they were still being hunted, they had reached
a place of temporary safety. On the night before their entry to the
Pedersen home they had slept within a tool shed. At one point in
their flight they had engaged in a rather amiable conversation with
two high school girls in an open place. The fact that the officers
apprehended the two men at the Pedersen home does not show (as
respondent argues) that they had not yet reached a point of *temporary* safety. Nor does the fact that the officers were engaged in a
continuing search do so. The fugitive from such a crime as robbery,
having reached a place of refuge, may still be hunted and be the
object of an all-points search, but the robbery no longer is being
committed. The officers did not discover the presence of the fugitives by their own efforts, but only by information given by the
Pedersens' neighbors. Nor is continuance of the *crime* of escape
shown by the fact that it would have been helpful to flight if the men
could obtain food and a change of clothing. A multitude of other
acts during whatever time they remained at large would do so,
and so would such acts be helpful to the fugitive from arrest for
crimes other than escape.

* * *

In each of the cases cited by respondent, State v. Holloway, 355 Mo. 217, 195 S.W.2d 662; State v. Lindsey, 333 Mo. 139, 62 S.W.2d 420, and Schockley v. United States (9 Cir.) 166 F.2d 704, the homicide occurred within the prison walls during attempted escape.

* * *

The judgment of conviction of robbery is affirmed. The judgment of conviction of second degree murder is reversed.

NOTES

1. Does the instant case provide a rationale for determining which deaths caused after the commission of a felony will be murder by virtue of the felony-murder rule; does that rationale bear a reasonable relationship to the purported function of the felony-murder rule? If not, could such a standard be articulated? If the function of the rule is to provide additional deterrence to the commission of offenses that are viewed as posing especially grave dangers to human life, why not provide that any death caused following a felony shall be murder if the activity causing death would not have been engaged in had the defendant not committed the felony? If the function is viewed as encouraging felons to use maximum care in the commission of felonies likely to pose a danger to human life, why not provide that any death caused following the commission of a felony shall be murder if, at the time the death was caused, the defendant's activity was still of the type that posed a high risk to human life similar to that posed during actual commission of the felony?

2. If A stabs B during a fight and, after B drops to the pavement, A decides to take any money B has on his person, is A guilty of felony murder? See People v. Joyner, 26 N.Y.2d 106, 257 N.E.2d 26 (1970).

---

4. DEATHS CAUSED WITHOUT THE "DIRECT" INVOLVEMENT OF THE DEFENDANT: THE OUTER LIMITS OF FELONY MURDER

COMMONWEALTH v. ALMEIDA

Supreme Court of Pennsylvania, 1949.
362 Pa. 596, 68 A.2d 595, certiorari denied 339 U.S. 924, 70 S.Ct. 614,
94 L.Ed. 1346, rehearing denied 339 U.S. 950, 70 S.Ct. 798, 94 L.Ed. 1364,
certiorari denied 340 U.S. 867, 71 S.Ct. 83, 95 L.Ed. 633.

MAXEY, Chief Justice. This is an appeal from a judgment of guilty of murder in the first degree, with the death penalty. The crime's locale was Philadelphia; its victim, Cecil Ingling, a 42 year old patrolman off duty. On January 30, 1947, David Almeida, Edward Hough and James Smith imbibed freely of liquor at a Philadelphia taproom, and in another taproom at 22d and Fitzwater Street Smith gave a .45 automatic type revolver to Hough and "a large pistol" to Almeida. Hough had a smaller pistol. Carrying out a "hold-up" plan they then went to a garage, pointed their pistols at the attendant, stole a blue car and motored to the Acme Market, 29th and Fairmount Avenue. There Smith said: "This looks like a good place." Almeida and Hough entered the market. The former had a handkerchief tied around the lower part of his face, and the latter wore black glasses. They entered the market with drawn guns. Hough emptied a cash register, saying: "This is a hold-up." He also took $3 from the cashier's wallet. He then robbed another cash register. Almeida, with gun in hand, approached the store manager. The latter yelled, "Hold-up," and grabbed two cans of corn, whereupon Almeida cursed him, and said: "I'll get you" and started firing. The manager was not hit. The total amount stolen was $262. Almeida also grabbed some bills from a one-armed customer.

Upon leaving the Acme Market they went to the blue car, which Smith was backing away from the curb. Patrolman Ingling was off duty at the time and when the bandits were backing their car Ingling returned to his car in which his wife, his son Leon and his daughter Jean, age 16 and 15 respectively, were sitting. The cries of "hold-up" brought three policemen and two police cars to the scene. Officer Waters and Officer Fox, in one of the police cars, came almost abreast of the blue car when Hough fired a bullet in their direction at a distance of about 30 feet. Policeman Waters then fired a shot at him.

Mrs. Ingling testified that as Hough attempted to get into the blue car her husband grabbed Hough by the back of the neck and that Smith then deliberately fired three consecutive shots at her husband, and that the first shot hit him. Her children also testified that it was Smith who fired the fatal shot.

Hough was at once apprehended. Smith and Almeida were arrested several months later for participating in a bank hold-up in New Orleans.

Hough at his trial pleaded guilty to the murder of Ingling and was sentenced to death in the electric chair. After the Almeida trial Smith was tried, convicted of first degree murder and sentenced to life imprisonment. In behalf of Almeida his counsel cite certain facts which they contend "raise the very strong inference that the fatal shot was fired mistakenly by a policeman." Almeida did not take the stand.

The Commonwealth contends that the jury was justified in finding that the bullet which killed Ingling was fired by one of the three confederates and further that it is immaterial whether the bullet was fired by one of them or whether it was fired by one of the policemen in repelling the assault of the bandits and in attempting to frustrate their escape.

The defendant's first assignment of error is that the court charged the jury as follows: " * * * it makes no difference who fired the shot, even if a shot was fired by Mrs. Ingling it was murder." Defendant's second assignment of error is based on the court's refusal to affirm defendant's thirteenth point for charge, which reads as follows: "If you find that the bullet which was fired and killed the deceased was not fired by any one of the three men charged with perpetrating the robbery in question, you cannot convict the defendant of murder in the first degree."

* * *

The defendant's thirteenth point for charge which the trial judge correctly rejected was in effect a request that the court instruct the jury that in order to convict the defendant of the death of Officer Ingling, the jury would have to find that the fatal shot was fired by one of the three robbers. Such an instruction would have been in defiance of this court's decision in Commonwealth v. Moyer and Commonwealth v. Byron, 357 Pa. 181, 53 A.2d 736, 741, which decision the trial judge dutifully followed. In that decision handed down on June 30, 1947, this court held in an opinion concurred in by the six judges who heard the argument on appeal, that: "A man or men engaged in the commission of such a felony as robbery can be convicted of murder in the first degree if the bullet which causes death was fired not by the felon but by the intended victim in repelling the aggressions of the felon or felons. * * * when a felon's attempt to commit robbery or burglary sets in motion a chain of events which were or should have been within his contemplation when the motion was initiated, he should be held responsible for any death which by direct and almost inevitable sequence results from the initial criminal act. For any individual forcibly to defend himself or his family or his property from criminal aggression is a primal human instinct. It is the right and duty of both individuals and nations to meet criminal aggression with effective countermeasures. Every robber or burglar knows when he attempts to commit his crime that he is inviting dangerous resistance. * * *

Our decision in the Moyer-Byron case was an application of the long established principle that he whose felonious act is the *proximate cause* of another's death is *criminally* responsible for that death and must answer to society for it exactly as he who is *negligently* the *proximate cause* of another's death is *civilly* responsible for that death and must answer in damages for it. Wharton on *Homicide,* Third Edition, p. 30, says under the heading of "Causal Connections" that: " * * * one whose wrongful act hastens or accelerates the death of another, or contributes to its cause, is guilty of homicide, though other causes co-operate. And he is guilty *if his act was the cause of the cause of death, if the relation was causal,* and the injured condition was not merely the occasion upon which another cause intervened not produced by the first injury, or related to it in any other than a causal way, then the person inflicting the injury is guilty of homicide."

* * *

Courts in the United States, England and Canada have applied the foregoing principles of "proximate cause" in murder cases * *.

* * *

Applying the aforegoing principles to the instant case, we have a band of robbers engaged in an exchange of shots with city police-men *whose duty it is to subdue the bandits if possible.* In the course of the exchange of deadly bullets Officer Ingling is slain. The po-licemen cannot be charged with any wrongdoing because their par-ticipation in the exchange of bullets with the bandits was both in justifiable self-defense and *in the performance of their duty.* The felonious acts of the robbers in firing shots at the policemen, well knowing that their fire would be returned, as it should have been, was the proximate cause of Officer Ingling's death.

* * *

The judgment is affirmed and the record is remitted to the court below so that the sentence imposed may be carried out.

LINN, Justice (Concurring).

I am convinced by the record that appellant was not harmed by the challenged instructions to the jury and therefore concur in the order of this court affirming the judgment.

JONES, Justice (dissenting).

I would reverse the judgment and remand the case for a retrial because of fundamental error in the trial court's charge to the jury. The case was submitted on the felony murder theory; yet the trial judge charged in effect that, even though the fatal shot was not fired by one of the felons but by someone attempting to frustrate the robbery, all the jury would need find in order to hold the de-fendant guilty of murder was that he was engaged in a robbery at the time of the killing. That instruction inadequately stated the law applicable to the circumstances.

On proof of no more than the perpetration of a felony and an incidental killing, liability for murder can be visited upon the par-ticipating felons *only* where the causation of the homicide is direct, i. e., where one of the felons or one acting in furtherance of the felonious design inflicted the fatal wound. The so-called shield cases do not derogate from this principle. There, the causation require-ment for liability is met by instructions to the jury to determine whether the offenders placed their victim in mortal jeopardy for their felonious purpose, e. g., to absorb antagonistic fire or to dis-suade antagonists from firing. On the other hand, as the majority opinion points out, even though a felon or one acting in his aid does not fire the fatal bullet, his conduct may have initiated such a causative chain of events as to render him legally chargeable with having been the causa causans of the homicide, and indictable for murder accordingly. In such circumstances, the felony murder theory supplies the malice necessary to make the killing murder while the proximate (although indirect) causation of the death is capable of fastening on the felon responsibility for the homicide. Sufficiency of the evidence to support a finding of the "chain of events" is, of course, a question of law for a court, but whether the "chain of events" existed unbroken and was the proximate cause of the homicide are questions of fact that only *a jury* can properly resolve. Those important factual inquiries were not submitted in the instant case. Causation was assumed by the learned trial judge and all that was left to the jury to determine, in order to hold the defendant guilty of murder, was that he was engaged in a "holdup" at the time of the killing notwithstanding there was evidence that someone other than the felons had fired the fatal bullet.

* * *

The jury should have been instructed that, in order to find the defendant guilty of murder, it was not only necessary for them to find the killing to have been coincidental with the perpetration of a felony in which the defendant was at the time participating but that they would also have to find that the fatal shot was fired by one of the felons or, if not fired by one of them, that the conduct of the defendant or his accomplices set in motion a chain of events among whose reasonably foreseeable consequences was a killing such as actually occurred. * * *

COMMONWEALTH v. THOMAS

Supreme Court of Pennsylvania, 1955.
382 Pa. 639, 117 A.2d 204.

ARNOLD, Justice. The Commonwealth appeals from the judgment of the court below sustaining the defendant's demurrer to the Commonwealth's evidence in the trial of defendant upon an indictment for murder.

For the purposes of this appeal, the following are the pertinent agreed facts: Defendant and one Henry Jackson, Jr., the deceased, entered the grocery store of one Cecchini and ordered him to open the cash drawer. Jackson was armed with a revolver which he displayed to Cecchini. The defendant removed the money, and he and Jackson ran from the store,—Jackson running one way and defendant the other. Cecchini secured his own pistol and chased Jackson. In the exchange of shots Cecchini killed Jackson. Defendant escaped, but was later apprehended.

The sole question is whether defendant can be convicted of murder under this state of facts. That is, can a co-felon be found guilty of murder where the victim of an armed robbery justifiably kills the other felon as they flee from the scene of the crime?

* * *

In applying the felony-murder statute, we have held that the malice of the initial offense attaches to whatever else the criminal may do in connection therewith. "It makes no difference that [the defendant] * * * and the other conspirators could not know in advance the precise course of events that would follow when they attempted to complete their evil designs". Commonwealth v. Guida, 341 Pa. 305, 310, 19 A.2d 98, 100.

* * *

If the defendant sets in motion the physical power of another, he is liable for its results. * * * Commonwealth v. Almeida, 362 Pa. 596, 605, 629, 68 A.2d 595, 600, 611, 12 A.L.R.2d 183.

As has been said many times, such a rule is equally consistent with reason and sound public policy, and is essential to the protection of human life. * * *

In Commonwealth v. Bolish, 381 Pa. 500, 113 A.2d 464, 474, (reversed on other grounds) we held a conviction of murder in the first degree to be proper even though defendant's accomplice (in arson) actually set the fire which caused his own death. The defendant there contended that the accomplice's act was an intervening and superseding force relieving the defendant of the killing. We there said: "Courts have a duty, especially in these days when crime has become so prevalent, to see that the lives, the property and the rights of law-abiding people are protected and consequently must delicately balance the scales of justice so that the rights of the public are protected equally with those of persons accused of crime. An arsonist is bound to know the perils and natural results of a fire which are reasonably foreseeable according to the common experience of mankind, and in particular to know that an occupant of the building set on fire, *an accomplice*, a fireman and the public who are likely to come to watch the fire, may die in or as a natural proximate result of the fire. The attempt of an officer or person to put out the fire, or to rescue people or property therein, or the attempt of any person to escape from the burning building does not constitute in legal contemplation a superseding cause which is sufficient to relieve the arsonist from murder in the first degree. In reason, logic and principle we can see no valid distinction between those cases and a case where an accomplice is killed while setting fire to a house (or building) or attempting to escape therefrom,—the latter's death is just as readily foreseeable as is the death of an owner who attempts to escape or to rescue lives or property from the building." (Italics supplied.) In the Bolish case the co-felon's death was the unintentional result of his own acts (of arson), without the intervention of a third person or of the defendant.

So, too, in the instant case. That the victim, or any third person such as an officer, would attempt to prevent the robbery or to prevent the escape of the felons, and would shoot and kill one of the felons was "as readily foreseeable" as the cases where an innocent bystander is killed, even unintentionally, by the defendant's accomplice, or where the victim of the robbery is slain, or where a pursuing officer is killed. The killing of the co-felon is the natural foreseeable result of the initial act. The robbery was the proximate cause of the death. We can see no sound reason for distinction merely because the one killed was a co-felon. It was a killing in the perpetration of a robbery which was "unquestionably contemplated and callously ignored by the defendant, who most certainly intended to commit a crime which he knew might well give rise to it". Commonwealth v. Sterling, 314 Pa. 76, 80, 170 A. 258, 260.

[margin note: Crim. Liable NATURAL FORESEEABLE CAUSES.]

So far as this defendant is concerned, the justification or excuse of the actual slayer, for the killing under consideration, is no different than for the killings in the cases hereinbefore cited.

Judgment reversed and new trial ordered.

JONES, Justice (dissenting).

I am at a loss to understand how anyone can be found guilty of murder at common law for a killing that, unquestionably, was a justifiable homicide. Yet, that is precisely the eventuality which the court's decision in this case portends.

[margin note: No crim. because killing justifiable Homicide]

* * *

It would seem to be clear beyond cavil that the ruling in the Almeida case was a judicial extension of the felony-murder doctrine. Such being its status, application of the ruling should be restricted to facts similar to those to which it was applied, viz., the killing of an innocent person by another innocent person as a result of indiscriminate gun fire on a busy public thoroughfare incidental to the attempted frustration and apprehension of armed robbers seeking to flee the scene of their felony.

* * *

The ruling of the majority in the instant case goes far beyond the holding in the Almeida case. Here, Jackson, the deceased, forfeited any right to the law's protection when he entered upon his armed aggression against a peaceful citizen who, in killing Jackson, acted throughout with the permission, if not at the command, of the law. Observe the absurd situation brought about by constructively making Thomas the killer. If such he be, then he performed a justifiable act. He cut down in his tracks a felon who, at the very moment of his death, was murderously assaulting a blameless citizen who was protecting his life and property. On the basis of the majority's constructive-killer theory, Thomas should be commended, and not condemned, for the lawful dispatch of the armed robber, Jackson, by way of a justifiable homicide.

I would affirm the order of the court below sustaining the defendant's demurrer.

NOTE

Should the result in such cases depend simply on the identity of the victim? Consider the following:

[T]he [felony murder] statute is primarily designed to protect the innocent public; and it would be incongruous to reach a conclusion having the effect of placing the perpetrators [of the felony] themselves beneath its mantle. * * * So really, in these cases, the inquiry should be simply whether an innocent person was killed.

State v. Williams, 254 So.2d 548, 551 (Fla.App.1971).

COMMONWEALTH v. REDLINE

Supreme Court of Pennsylvania, 1958.
391 Pa. 486, 137 A.2d 472.

CHARLES ALVIN JONES, Chief Justice. The defendant was convicted of murder in the first degree with penalty fixed at life imprisonment for the death of his co-felon from a gunshot wound inflicted by a police officer endeavoring to apprehend the two culprits who were attempting to flee the scene of their armed robbery.

* * *

Around midnight of April 11, 1956, Redline, the present defendant, and his companion, Erbor Worseck, perpetrated at gun point a robbery of certain persons in the Midway Restaurant in Reading. During the course of the crime, two police officers were disarmed and held captive in the establishment. The defendant and his accomplice Worseck, fleeing the scene, compelled one Raymond R. Herschman to accompany them. Redline was the first to leave the building, behind him was Herschman and behind Herschman was Worseck. As they were departing, uniformed police officers outside bore down upon them. Redline, seeing one of the officers, shouted to him, "The man you want is in there [apparently meaning the building he had just left]." With that, Redline aimed a 45-caliber revolver at the policeman, who was then approximately fifteen to twenty feet distant, and fired point-blank but failed to hit his intended victim. Prior to this shot by Redline, there had been no shooting whatever. The policeman immediately returned the fire, and there then ensued a gun battle involving several policemen and the defendant and Worseck. During the course of the shooting, two policemen were seriously wounded, the defendant himself was wounded and so was Worseck. The latter's wound, which admittedly was inflicted by a bullet from a policeman's gun, proved fatal. It was Worseck's death for which Redline was indicted, tried and convicted for murder. As stipulated of record at trial, no bullet from the defendant's gun ever touched Worseck.

The above recited circumstances would, of course, support a serious criminal charge against Redline but *not for murder*. He was a willing participant in an armed robbery for which he could be indicted and found guilty at common law and, more lately in this State, under a pertinent statute. But, he is not chargeable under any known relevant rule of law, save for the decision in the Thomas case, with murder for the death of his co-felon. The question here involved calls for a complete review of the felony-murder theory.

* * *

In adjudging a felony-murder, it is to be remembered at all times that the thing which is imputed to a felon for a killing incidental to his felony is *malice* and *not the act of killing*. The mere coincidence of homicide and felony is not enough to satisfy the requirements of the felony-murder doctrine. "It is necessary * * * to show that the conduct causing death was done in furtherance of the design to commit the felony. Death must be a consequence of the felony * * and not merely coincidence": Hitchler, [The Killer and His Victim in Felony-Murder Cases, 53 Dick.L.Rev. 3 (1948)] citing Perkins, Malice Aforethought, 43 Yale L.J. 537 (1934).

[margin handwritten notes: F-M imputes malice Not the act of killing. But for malice to be imputed death must be a CONSEQ not just coincidence of Felony]

* * *

The instant appeal affords an appropriate occasion for the repudiation of Commonwealth v. Thomas, which we now expressly overrule as an unwarranted judicial extension of the felony-murder rule. Fortunately, no one has suffered any penalty as a result of the holding in that case. Following our remand of the record in the Thomas case, the district attorney moved the trial court for leave to *nol pros* the murder indictment. The court approved the motion, and a *nolle prosequi* was duly entered. At the same time, the court accepted the defendant's plea of guilty to an indictment charging him with armed robbery of which he was unquestionably guilty and for which he was immediately sentenced and committed to the penitentiary where he is now serving his sentence. Since we herewith overrule Commonwealth v. Thomas, it follows that the present appellant's conviction of murder cannot be sustained on the basis of the decision in that case.

[margin handwritten note: overrule THOMAS]

The Commonwealth contends, however, that, entirely apart from the Thomas case, the appellant's conviction of murder can be upheld on the rationale of Commonwealth v. Almeida. As already indicated, Almeida was, itself, an extension of the felony-murder doctrine by judicial decision and is not to be extended in its application beyond facts such as those to which it was applied. In short, the Almeida case was concerned with the killing, during the perpetration of a felony, of an innocent and law-abiding person by someone other than the felons or ones acting in aid of their criminal conspiracy. The evidence warranted a finding that it was an accidental killing by an officer of the law, but the felons were held accountable nonetheless on the basis of proximate causation regardless of who fired the fatal shot. In the present instance, the victim of the homicide was one of the robbers who, while resisting apprehension in his effort to escape, was shot and killed by a policeman in the performance of his duty. Thus, the homicide was justifiable and, obviously, could not be availed of, on any rational legal theory, to support a charge of murder. How can anyone, no matter how much of an outlaw he may be, have a criminal charge lodged against him for the consequences of the lawful conduct of another person? The mere statement of the question carries with it its own answer.

[Here Homicide Justified]

It is, of course, true that the distinction thus drawn between Almeida and the instant case on the basis of the difference in the character of the victims of the homicide is more incidental than legally significant so far as relevancy to the felony-murder rule is concerned * * *[.] In other words, if a felon can be held for murder for a killing occurring during the course of a felony, even though the death was not inflicted by one of the felons but by someone acting in hostility to them, it should make no difference to the crime of murder who the victim of the homicide happened to be. However, the factual difference, so noted, admits of a recognizable distinction with respect to a felon's responsibility for an incidental killing (which another has committed), depending upon whether the homicide was justifiable or excusable, and such distinction serves the useful purpose of thwarting further extension of the rule enunciated in Commonwealth v. Almeida that it is immaterial who fires the fatal shot so long as the accused was engaged in a felony.

[Admits to hair-splitting on distinction from Almeida]

The limitation which we thus place on the decision in the Almeida case renders unnecessary any present reconsideration of the extended holding in that case. * * *

Judgment of sentence reversed and record remanded with directions that the defendant's motion in arrest of judgment be reinstated and thereupon granted.

COMMONWEALTH EX REL. SMITH v. MYERS

Supreme Court of Pennsylvania, 1970.
438 Pa. 218, 261 A.2d 550.

OPINION OF THE COURT

O'BRIEN, Justice. This is an appeal from the order of the Court of Common Pleas of Philadelphia County, denying James Smith's petition for a writ of habeas corpus. The facts upon which the convictions of appellant and his co-felons, Almeida and Hough, rest are well known to this Court and to the federal courts. In addition to vexing the courts, these cases have perplexed a generation of law students, both within and without the Commonwealth, and along with their progeny, have spawned reams of critical commentary.

Briefly, the facts of the crime are these. On January 30, 1947, Smith, along with Edward Hough and David Almeida, engaged in an armed robbery of a supermarket in the City of Philadelphia. An off-duty policeman, who happened to be in the area, was shot and killed while attempting to thwart the escape of the felons. Although the evidence as to who fired the fatal shot was conflicting in appellant's 1948 trial, the court charged the jury that it was irrelevant who fired the fatal bullet * * *. To this part of the charge appellant took a specific exception.

The jury convicted Smith of first degree murder, with punishment fixed at life imprisonment. * * *

Appellant urges that he was denied due process by virtue of the trial court's charge that it was irrelevant who fired the fatal bullet. * * *

The common law felony-murder rule * * * has been subjected to some harsh criticism, most of it thoroughly warranted. * * *

[One] * * * commentator suggests that the rule should be modified, so that a killing committed during the perpetration of a felony would create merely a *rebuttable* presumption of intention, rather than the *conclusive* presumption now created.[8] Other opponents of the felony-murder rule point out that it is hardly an essential weapon in the Commonwealth's arsenal. Our neighboring state of Ohio has managed quite well without a felony-murder rule since abolishing it over a century ago. See Robbins v. State, 8 Ohio St. 131 (1857).

In fact, not only is the felony-murder rule non-essential, but it is very doubtful that it has the deterrent effect its proponents assert. * * *

We have gone into this lengthy discussion of the felony-murder rule not for the purpose of hereby abolishing it. That is hardly necessary in the instant case. But we do want to make clear how shaky are the basic premises on which it rests. With so weak a foundation, it behooves us not to extend it further and indeed, to restrain it within the bounds it has always known. * * * *Redline* rejected the proximate cause tort analogy which *Almeida* found so appealing

8. Crum, Causal Relations and the Felony-Murder Rule, 1952 Wash.U. Law Q., 191, 205.

* * *. [T]he uninitiated might be surprised to learn that *Redline* did not specifically overrule *Almeida*. This Court did overrule *Thomas*, holding that no conviction was possible for a *justifiable* homicide, where a policeman shot a felon, but "distinguished" *Almeida* on the ground that the homicide there, where an innocent third party was killed by a policeman, was only *excusable*. This distinction was rather remarkable in view of the cases relied upon by the Court—almost all cases in which the victim was an innocent third party rather than a felon. * * *

In fact, even the majority in *Redline* seemed to realize that they were seizing upon a will of the wisp in attempting to refrain from *then* overruling Almeida: "It is, of course, true that the distinction thus drawn between Almeida and the instant case on the basis of the difference in the character of the victims of the homicide is more incidental than legally significant so far as relevancy to the felony-murder rule is concerned: * * *. In other words, if a felon can be held for murder for a killing occurring during the course of a felony, even though the death was not inflicted by one of the felons but by someone acting in hostility to them, it should make no difference to the crime of murder who the victim of the homicide happened to be." *Redline*, 391 Pa. at page 509, 137 A.2d at page 483.

The "distinction" *Redline* half-heartedly tries to draw has not escaped criticism from the commentators. While the result reached in *Redline* and most of its reasoning have met with almost unanimous approval, the *deus ex machina* ending has been condemned. One learned journal has commented:

> "It seems, however, that Almeida cannot validly be distinguished from [Redline]. The probability that a felon will be killed seems at least as great as the probability that the victim will be an innocent bystander. Any distinction based on the fact that the killing of a felon by a policeman is sanctioned by the law and therefore justifiable, while the killing of an innocent bystander is merely excusable, seems unwarranted. No criminal sanctions now attach to either in other areas of criminal law, and any distinction here would seem anomalous. Indeed, to make the result hinge on the character of the victim is, in many instances, to make it hinge on the marksmanship of resisters. Any attempt to distinguish between the cases on the theory that the cofelon assumes the risk of being killed would also be improper since this tort doctrine has no place in the criminal law in which the wrong to be redressed is a public one—a killing with the victim's consent is nevertheless murder. It is very doubtful that public desire for vengeance should alone justify a conviction of felony murder for the death of an innocent bystander

when no criminal responsibility will attach for the death of a cofelon." [16]

Redline concluded, at page 510, 137 A.2d at page 483, in this manner: "The limitation which we thus place on the decision in the Almeida case renders unnecessary any present reconsideration of the extended holding of that case. It will be time enough for action in such regard if and when a conviction for murder based on facts similar to those presented by the Almeida case (both as to the performer of the lethal act and the status of its victim) should again come before this court." The time is now. The facts are not merely similar to those of *Almeida*; they are identical, Smith and Almeida being cofelons. The case law of centuries and the force of reason, both dealt with in great detail in *Redline* and above, require us to overrule *Almeida*.

The order of the court below is reversed, an appeal is allowed *nunc pro tunc*, and a new trial is granted.

NOTES

1. How can situations like those in *Almeida, Thomas,* and *Redline* be distinguished from situations in which the felony murder rule should be applied? Can this be done in a manner consistent with the purported function of the felony murder rule? In People v. Washington, 62 Cal.2d 777, 44 Cal.Rptr. 442, 402 P.2d 130 (1965) Chief Justice Traynor argued that the sole purpose of the felony-murder rule is to deter felons from killing negligently or accidentally. He then suggested that holding a defendant guilty of murder where the act of killing was not committed by him or an accomplice acting in furtherance of their common design would extend the rule beyond the function it is designed to serve. Does this explanation stand up under analysis? For example, could it reasonably be expected that the existence of a felony-murder rule might deter felons from creating dangerous situations during the commission of a felony that might cause others to kill? For example, might other felons in Almeida's situation be expected to surrender when confronted by approaching police officers rather than begin a combined gun battle and chase? In any case, would any such expectation be less reasonable than the expectation that imposing liability upon a co-felon will somehow deter felons from killing negligently or accidentally?

2. In People v. Morris, 1 Ill.App.3d 566, 274 N.E.2d 898 (1971) the Illinois Appellate Court considered whether a surviving member of a three-man robbery team could be convicted of the death of another robber on a felony-murder theory. The co-felon had been killed by the discharge of his own gun during a struggle with one Phelps who had walked into the restaurant while the robbery was in progress. The deceased robber had approached Phelps and demanded his wrist watch. Phelps refused and a struggle ensued during which shots were fired that killed both Phelps and the deceased robber. After noting that "the great majority of those jurisdictions which faced the same issue have followed the *Redline* decision," the

16. 71 Harv.L.Rev. [1565,] 1566 [(1958)];
See, to similar effect, 106 U.Pa.L.Rev.
[1176,] 1178 [(1958)].

court reversed the conviction on the ground that felony-murder requires that the conduct causing death be an act done in furtherance of the common design to commit a forcible felony and the struggle with Phelps was not such an act. Is this reasonable? Suppose Morris had been charged with murder based upon the death of Phelps?

But compare State v. Kress, 105 N.J.Super. 514, 253 A.2d 481 (Law Div. 1969) in which bank robbers used an innocent bystander as a shield, and the bystander was killed by police bullets. Holding that despite the apparent trend in the case law the New Jersey statute "seem[ed] to justify" a felony-murder charge, the court emphasized that the statute provides that one committing or attempting enumerated felonies is guilty of murder "if the death of anyone ensues from the committing or attempting to commit any such crime." The case is noted in 24 Rutgers L.Rev. 591 (1970). See also Johnson v. State, 482 S.W.2d 600 (Ark.1972).

3. The matters in issue in the Pennsylvania and California cases above have given rise to extensive commentary. For an early analysis, see Morris, the Felon's Responsibility for the Lethal Acts of Others, 105 U.Pa. L.Rev. 50 (1956). For more recent comments, see Note, The California Supreme Court Assails the Felony-Murder Rule, 22 Stan.L.Rev. 1059 (1970); Note, Criminal Liability of a Participant in Crime for the Death of a Fellow Participant, 22 Syracuse L.Rev. 1065 (1971); Note, Criminal Responsibility for the Death of a Co-Felon: Taylor v. Superior Court of Alameda County, 7 Cal.West.L.Rev. 522 (1971); Note, Limitations on the Applicability of the Felony-Murder Rule in California, 22 Hastings L.Rev. 1327 (1971).

4. The doctrine of "proximate" cause provides some potential for limiting applicability of the felony-murder rule. Consider the matter after covering the causation material at pages 573–608, infra. See generally, Crum, Causal Relations and the Felony-Murder Rule, 1952 Wash.U.L.Q. 191. Insofar as *Redline* and *Smith* are rejections of tort concepts of "proximate cause" when offered to expand the felony-murder doctrine, do they suggest or portend an unwillingness to use similar concepts to limit application of the same doctrine? In other words, if a felon is not liable for all foreseeable deaths resulting from his felony does this affect his liability for unforeseeable deaths caused by the felony?

TAYLOR v. SUPERIOR COURT

Supreme Court of California, 1970.
3 Cal.3d 578, 91 Cal.Rptr. 275, 477 P.2d 131.

BURKE, Justice. Petitioner and his codefendant Daniels were charged by information with the murder of John H. Smith, robbery, assault with a deadly weapon against Linda West, and assault with a deadly weapon against Jack West. The superior court denied petitioner's motion to set aside the information as to the murder count, and we issued an alternative writ of prohibition.

At the preliminary hearing, the following facts were adduced regarding the murder count: On the evening of January 12, 1969, two men attempted to rob Jax Liquor Store which was operated by Mrs. Linda Lee West and her husband Jack. Mrs. West testified that James Daniels entered the store first and asked Mr. West, who was behind the counter, for a package of cigarettes. While Mr. West was getting the cigarettes, John Smith entered the store and approached the counter. Mrs. West, who was on a ladder at the time the two men entered the store, then heard her husband say something about money. Turning her attention to the counter, she heard Daniels repeatedly saying, "Put the money in the bag," and observed her husband complying with the order.

While Mr. West was putting the money from the register in the bag, Daniels repeatedly referred to the fact that he and Smith were armed. According to Mrs. West, Daniels "chattered insanely" during this time, telling Mr. West "Put the money in the bag. Put the money in the bag. Put the money in the bag. Don't move or I'll blow your head off. He's got a gun. He's got a gun. Don't move or we'll have an execution right here. Get down on the floor. I said on your stomach, on your stomach." Throughout this period, Smith's gun was pointed at Mr. West. Mrs. West testified that Smith looked "intent" and "apprehensive" as if "waiting for something big to happen." She indicated that Smith's apparent apprehension and nervousness was manifested by the way he was staring at Mr. West.

While Daniels was forcing Mr. West to the floor, Mrs. West drew a pistol from under her clothing and fired at Smith, who was standing closest to her. Smith was struck on the right side of the chest. Mrs. West fired four more shots in rapid succession, and observed "sparks" coming from Smith's gun, which was pointed in her direction. A bullet hole was subsequently discovered in the wall behind the place Mrs. West had been standing, approximately eight or nine feet above the floor. During this period, Mr. West had seized a pistol and fired two shots at Smith. Mrs. West's last shot was fired at Daniels as he was going out of the door. He "lurched violently and almost went down, [but] picked himself up and kept going." Smith died as the result of multiple gunshot wounds.

The evidence at the preliminary examination indicated that petitioner was waiting outside the liquor store in a getaway car. He was apprehended later and connected with the crime through bills in his possession and through the automobile which was seen by a witness leaving the scene of the robbery.

Under Penal Code section 995, an information must be set aside if the defendant has been committed without "reasonable or probable cause." * * *

The information herein charged petitioner with the crime of murder. * * * Petitioner correctly contends that he cannot be convicted under the felony-murder doctrine * * *. (People v. Washington, 62 Cal.2d 777, 780, 44 Cal.Rptr. 442, 445, 402 P.2d 130, 133.)

However, apart from the felony-murder doctrine, petitioner could be found guilty of murder on a theory of vicarious liability.

As stated in People v. Gilbert, 63 Cal.2d 690, 704–705, 47 Cal. Rptr. 909, 917, 408 P.2d 365, 373, rev. on other grounds, 388 U.S. 263, 87 S.Ct. 1951, 18 L.Ed.2d 1178, "When the defendant or his accomplice, with a conscious disregard for life, intentionally commits an act that is likely to cause death, and his victim or a police officer kills in reasonable response to such act, the defendant is guilty of murder. In such a case, the killing is attributable, not merely to the commission of a felony, but to the intentional act of the defendant or his accomplice committed with conscious disregard for life. [Para.] Thus the victim's self-defensive killing or the police officer's killing in the performance of his duty cannot be considered an independent intervening cause for which the defendant is not liable, for it is a reasonable response to the dilemma thrust upon the victim or the policeman by the intentional act of the defendant or his accomplice. [Citations.]" * * *

Therefore, if petitioner were an accomplice to the robbery, he would be vicariously responsible for any killing attributable to the intentional acts of his associates committed with conscious disregard for life, and likely to result in death. We must determine whether the committing magistrate had any rational ground for believing that Smith's death was attributable to intentional acts of Smith and Daniels meeting those criteria.

Petitioner relies upon the following language in *Washington*, wherein defendant's accomplice merely pointed a gun at the robbery victim who, without further provocation, shot and killed him: "In every robbery there is a possibility that the victim will resist and kill. The robber has little control over such a killing once the robbery is undertaken as this case demonstrates. To impose an additional penalty for the killing would discriminate between robbers, *not on the basis of any difference in their own conduct,* but solely on the basis of the response by others that the robber's conduct happened to induce."

As indicated by the italicized words in the foregoing quotation, the central inquiry in determining criminal liability for a killing committed by a resisting victim or police officer is whether the *conduct* of a defendant or his accomplices was sufficiently provocative of lethal resistance to support a finding of implied malice. If the trier of fact concludes that under the particular circumstances of the instant case Smith's death proximately resulted from acts of petitioner's accomplices done with conscious disregard for human life, the natural consequences of which were dangerous to life, then petitioner may be convicted of first degree murder.

For example, we pointed out in *Washington* that "Defendants who initiate gun battles may also be found guilty of murder if their victims resist and kill. Under such circumstances, 'the defendant for a base, anti-social motive and with wanton disregard for human life, does an act that involves a high degree of probability that it will result in death' [citation], and it is unnecessary to imply malice by invoking the felony-murder doctrine."

Petitioner contends that since neither Daniels nor Smith fired the first shot, they did not "initiate" the gun battle which led to Smith's death. However, depending upon the circumstances, a gun battle can be initiated by acts of provocation falling short of firing the first shot. Thus, in People v. Reed, 270 Cal.App.2d 37, 75 Cal.Rptr. 430 (hg. den.), defendant resisted the officers' commands to "put up your hands," and pointed his gun toward the officers and toward the kidnap-robbery victim. The officers commenced firing, wounding defendant and killing the victim. Although defendant did not fire a single shot, his murder conviction was upheld on the theory that his "aggressive actions" were sufficient evidence of implied malice, and that "under these circumstances it may be said that defendant initiated the gunplay. * * *"

Similarly, in Brooks v. Superior Court, 239 Cal.App.2d 538, 48 Cal.Rptr. 762 (hg. den.), petitioner had directed "opprobrious language" to the arresting officer and had grasped the officer's shotgun. The officer, being startled and thinking that petitioner was trying to disarm him, yanked backwards and fired the gun, mortally wounding a fellow officer. In upholding an indictment for murder, the court concluded that under the circumstances, the petitioner's act of reaching for and grasping the officer's shotgun was "fraught with grave and inherent danger to human life," and therefore sufficient to raise an inference of malice.

In the instant case, the evidence at the preliminary hearing set forth above discloses acts of provocation on the part of Daniels and Smith from which the trier of fact could infer malice, including Daniels' coercive conduct toward Mr. West and his repeated threats of "execution," and Smith's intent and nervous apprehension as he held Mr. West at gunpoint. The foregoing conduct was sufficiently provocative of lethal resistance to lead a man of ordinary caution and prudence to conclude that Daniels and Smith "initiated" the gun battle, or that such conduct was done with conscious disregard for human life and with natural consequences dangerous to life.[3] Accordingly, we

3. Petitioner contends that we should ignore evidence regarding Smith's conduct, on the theory that Smith could not have been held responsible for his own death. We rejected a similar contention in *Washington*, stating that "A distinction based on the person killed, however, would make the defendant's criminal liability turn upon the marksmanship of vic-tims and policemen. A rule of law cannot reasonably be based on such a fortuitous circumstance. The basic issue therefore is whether a robber can be convicted of murder for the killing of *any* person by another who is resisting the robbery." (62 Cal.2d at p. 780, 44 Cal.Rptr. at p. 444, 402 P.2d at p. 132, italics added.) Therefore, the trier of fact may find that

conclude that the evidence supported the magistrate's finding that reasonable and probable cause existed to charge petitioner with first degree murder.

The alternative writ heretofore issued is discharged and the peremptory writ is denied.

WRIGHT, C. J., and McCOMB and SULLIVAN, JJ., concur.

PETERS, Justice (dissenting).

I dissent.

* * * To hold, as do the majority, that petitioner can be convicted of murder for acts which constitute a first degree robbery solely because the victims killed one of the robbers is in effect to reinstate the felony-murder rule in cases where the victim resists and kills.

* * * The majority are making the incredible statement that because the robber in *Washington* did not articulate his obvious threat—because, in the majority's words, he "merely" pointed a gun at the victim—it cannot be said that he committed an act with conscious disregard for life and likely to result in death, whereas if he articulated his threat—as did the robbers in the instant case—his act could be found to have met such criteria.

* * *

Moreover, the robbers in *Gilbert* expressly threatened to kill one of the robbery victims and in fact did kill a policeman, but we stated that they could be convicted of murder of Weaver only if it was found that they initiated the shooting which resulted in Weaver's death. Obviously, if this court in *Gilbert* was of the opinion that the act of threatening victims at gunpoint—which act was clearly involved in that case—could constitute a "malicious act," it would have sent the case back for retrial on the charge of Weaver's murder on that theory as well as on the theory that the shooting of Weaver was in response to shooting initiated by the robbers.

* * *

Not only is the majority's holding contrary to the holdings and language of *Washington* and *Gilbert,* it is also contrary to the fundamental rationale of those cases—that the culpability of criminal de-

Smith set into motion, through the intentional commission of acts constituting implied malice and in furtherance of the robbery, a gun battle resulting in his own death. Since petitioner may be held vicariously responsible for *any* killing legally attributable to his accomplices, he may be charged with Smith's death.

The cases of People v. Ferlin, 203 Cal. 587, 597, 265 P. 230; Woodruff v. Superior Court, 237 Cal.App.2d 749, 750–751, 47 Cal.Rptr. 291, and People v. Jennings, 243 Cal.App.2d 324, 328–329, 52 Cal.Rptr. 329, are not apposite for they simply held that an accomplice cannot be charged with murder when his confederate accidentally kills himself while committing a felony. The courts in those cases were not faced with a situation involving the intentional commission of acts provoking lethal resistance by victims or police officers.

fendants should be determined by their own acts, not by the fortuitous acts of their victims which are beyond the defendants' control and thus logically irrelevant to the defendants' culpability. * * *

In the instant case as in *Washington,* the robbers committed acts constituting a first degree robbery; they committed no additional acts—such as initiating a gun battle—that would reflect a culpability beyond that of any other first degree robbers and that would justify the additional charge of murder. * * * To convert such acts—i. e., to convert a first degree robbery—into murder solely because the victim killed one of the robbers is in effect to reinstitute the felony-murder doctrine in such a situation—contrary to the basic *Washington* holding that a defendant cannot be convicted of murder simply because he and his accomplices committed a felony in which a death resulted. In the instant case as in *Washington,* to impose an additional penalty on the defendant, not because of any independently malicious act (such as initiating a gun battle) by him or his accomplices, but because of the uncontrollable act of the victim who resists and kills is to "deter robbery haphazardly at best."

* * *

MOSK, Justice (dissenting).

I dissent.

* * *

Fundamental principles of criminal responsibility dictate that the defendant be subject to a greater penalty only when he has demonstrated a greater degree of culpability. To ignore that rule is at best to frustrate the deterrent purpose of punishment, and at worst to risk constitutional invalidation on the ground of invidious discrimination. * * * In my view, a robber who simply articulates one of the foregoing conditional threats is in no way more culpable than one who remains silent while brandishing a gun in his victim's face. The reason for this is apparent: every such conditional threat—whether express or implied—is inherent in the commission of the robbery itself. * * *

This is not to maintain that no conduct short of actually pulling the trigger first will support a finding of implied malice aforethought. Thus the true distinction to be drawn in robbery cases is not between an express and an implied *conditional* threat, but between a conditional threat—whether express or implied—and an *unconditional* threat to kill. For example, after seizing the property the robber might voice an intent to shoot his victims on the spot to prevent their giving an alarm or later identifying him; or, being surprised by the police and having no hope of escape, a desperate criminal might announce that rather than surrender he will take his own life and that of his hostages as well. Manifestly such a threat greatly increases the risk of harm over and above that which is present in the usual robbery situation, and hence demonstrates a greater degree of culpability on the part of the wrongdoer. The consequences of creating this risk are likewise predictable: if one of the victims has access to a hidden weapon, he will be driven to use it in a last-ditch attempt to prevent his assailant from carrying out his unconditional threat to kill. Such a threat, accordingly, may fairly be said to "initiate" the ensuing gun battle just as surely as if the robber had been the first to fire.

* * *

E. MANSLAUGHTER

1. VOLUNTARY MANSLAUGHTER

LANG v. STATE

Court of Special Appeals of Maryland, 1969.
6 Md.App. 128, 250 A.2d 276, certiorari denied 396 U.S. 971,
90 S.Ct. 457, 24 L.Ed.2d 438.

PER CURIAM. The appellant, John Frederick Lang, was convicted of assault with intent to murder by a jury in the Criminal Court of Baltimore, Judge Meyer M. Cardin presiding. He was sentenced to ten years under the jurisdiction of the Department of Correction.

In this appeal the following questions are properly before us:

(1) Did the lower court err in failing to instruct the jury that a homicide, if committed in the "heat of passion", is reduced from murder to manslaughter; thereby reducing the crime charged, assault with intent to murder, to assault?

* * *

The exact point of dispute is whether there was sufficient evidence adduced at trial to support an instruction on the heat of passion doctrine. * * *

The relevant elements of the heat of passion doctrine are (a) that there must be passion actually aroused in the actor, (b) that such passion must be an intensity sufficient to obscure the reason of the actor, and, (c) that such passion must be due to a legally adequate provocation. Thus, in order for instruction regarding heat of passion to be required, evidence must be introduced from which the jury could have found each of the above mentioned elements. We shall consider the elements seriatim.

Evidence was introduced which could support a finding that appellant was in passionate anger or, what is more likely, that he was in passionate terror. As we mentioned above, this element involves the appellant's subjective state of mind. One witness testified that the appellant "must have been awfully scared because he looked * * * like animals * * * he was all shakey * * * his face was sort of distorted * * * how you get when when you're real mad or something." Another witness testified that appellant "looked pretty scared * * * his face didn't seem contorted." The appellant himself testified as follows:

"Q. Why did you shoot him?

"A. I was scared. I didn't know what he was going to do.

"Q. What were you scared of?

"A. I was scared of him, what he was going to do. I didn't know if he had a gun or what."

This testimony might also have been sufficient to support a finding that the anger or terror was sufficiently intense to obscure the appellant's reason, again a subjective inquiry.

With respect to the element of adequate provocation, the evidence showed that immediately before the shooting the victim called the appellant "a chump" and "a chicken," dared the appellant to fight, shouted obscenities at the appellant, pointed his finger at the appellant, and shook his fist at the appellant, all of this occurring at distances variously ranging from five to thirty feet. The victim was approximately fifteen feet from the appellant when shot. During the entire incident the victim was on the lawn outside of the appellant's apartment and the appellant was inside the apartment. During the latter part of the incident the appellant was standing at his window. The window sill was approximately four feet from the ground level and under the window was a window well six to seven feet in length and three to four feet in depth, with no figure given at trial as to width.

At this point our inquiry becomes an objective one, namely, whether the above facts constitute such provocation as would drive a reasonable and ordinary man into passionate anger or terror. It is generally held that mere words, threats, menaces or gestures, however offensive and insulting, do not constitute adequate provocation. However, there is authority that sufficient provocation may consist of words accompanied by conduct indicating a present intention and ability to cause the appellant bodily harm. In the instant case we understand the provocation to be merely words and gestures. The record shows no indication that the victim had a present *intention* to cause the appellant bodily harm; he (the victim) certainly made no attempt to enter the apartment through the door, and he showed no inclination to try to climb through the window. Without entering the apartment he had no present *ability* to harm the appellant, as he was unarmed during the entire incident.

We hold, therefore, that merely shouting epithets such as "chump" and "chicken," or shouting obscene words, or shaking finger or hand at the appellant, where there is no evidence of a present intent or ability to cause the appellant bodily harm will not constitute legally sufficient provocation for purposes of requiring an instruction on heat of passion. Thus it was not error for the trial court to refuse such an instruction.

NOTES

1. Concerning the effect which the provocation must have upon the killer, consider the following passage from State v. Davis, 50 S.C. 405, 27 S.E. 905, 911–12 (1897):

It is contended that there was error in the following charge: "Now, as I said before, if the testimony in this case (and you are the sole judges of that) satisfies you that the defendant here took the life of the deceased in sudden heat and passion, and upon sufficient legal provocation, and the deceased said anything or did anything to the defendant which was calculated to highly exasperate and inflame and arouse his passion, so that he had an uncontrollable impulse, and he was so inflamed with passion that he hardly knew what he was doing, and in that heat and passion he took the life of the deceased, without malice, then you can find him guilty of manslaughter." It is objected that this charge (1) prescribed a stricter rule than that required by law as to the degree of heat and passion necessary to reduce the killing from murder to manslaughter; * * The circuit judge correctly defined "manslaughter" as the killing of any human being, without malice, in sudden heat and passion, and upon sufficient legal provocation. It is contended, however, that he was not authorized to go further, and add words indicating that the heat and passion should amount to an "uncontrollable impulse," and that passion should so inflame that "he hardly knew what he was doing." In Desty, Cr.Law, § 128d, it is stated that adequate provocation and ungovernable passion must concur; that, to reduce murder to manslaughter, a provocation must be established sufficient to render the passion irresistible. In Clark, Cr.Law, p. 165, the doctrine is laid down "that the provocation must be such as the law deems adequate to excite uncontrollable passion in the mind of a reasonable man." Mr. Bishop, in his Criminal Law (volume 2, p. 386, § 697), says: "The sufficiency of the passion to take away malice, and reduce what would be murder to manslaughter, is so much a question of law that it is difficult to say, on the authorities, how intense, in fact, it must be. * * * The passion must be such as is sometimes called irresistible, yet it is too strong to say that the reason of the party should be dethroned, or he should act in a whirlwind of passion." So, in Clark, Cr.Law, p. 167, it is said: "The provocation must deprive one of the power of self-control, but it need not entirely dethrone reason." * * * In the case of State v. Hill, 4 Dev. & B. 491 relied on by appellant, Gaston, J., said: "We nowhere find that the passion which in law rebuts the imputation of malice must be so overpowering as for the time to shut out knowledge and destroy volition. All the writers concur in representing this indulgence of the law to be a condescension to the frailty of the human frame, which, during the furor brevis, renders a man deaf to the voice of reason, so that, although the act done was intentional of death, it was not the result of malignity of heart, but imputable to human infirmity." "The provocation by the deceased must be the direct and controlling cause of the passion, and it must be such as naturally and instantly to produce in the minds of persons ordinarily constituted the highest degree of exasperation, rage, anger, sudden resentment, or terror, rendering the mind incapable of cool reflection." 9 Am. & Eng.Enc.Law, p. 579. In State v. Smith, 10 Rich.Law, 347, the passion which reduces a felonious killing to manslaughter is characterized as a "temporary phrensy excited by sufficient legal provocation"; and in State v. McCants, 1 Speer, *390, Judge Wardlaw speaks of this passion as "the violent impulse of anger, outstripping the tardier operations of reason, provoked by sufficient cause." It may be concluded, therefore, that "the sudden heat and passion, upon sufficient legal provocation," which mitigates a felonious killing to manslaughter, while it need not dethrone reason entirely, or shut out knowledge and volition, must be such as would naturally disturb the sway of reason, and render the mind of an ordinary person incapable of cool reflection, and produce what, according to human experience, may be called an "uncontrollable impulse to do violence." We do not think the charge of the judge went beyond the limits above prescribed, and it was therefore not error, in so far as his charge relates to acts which the law deems adequate to provoke such passion.

See generally, Note, Manslaughter and the Adequacy of Provocation: The Reasonableness of the Reasonable Man, 106 U.Pa.L.Rev. 1021 (1958).

2. Why, as a matter of policy, should the fact that a killing was in response to adequate provocation reduce the grade of the offense for which the defendant is liable? Reconsider the material at pages 940–41, supra, concerning the significance of deliberation and impulse in grading liability.

3. Brett, The Physiology of Provocation, [1970] Crim.L.Rev. 634 suggests that individuals vary significantly in their physiological response to stress. "Fight or flight" reactions, caused by a complex relationship between the hypothalamus (a small area at the base of the brain), hormones, and the brain, include changes in pulse rate, blood pressure, level of blood glucose, and sensory perception. If this evidence that some persons are highly vulnerable to stress and others strikingly resistant to it is credited, "it at once becomes clear that the reasonable man of provocation law is a figment of the imagination." Id. at 637. An objective standard might still be justified, Brett notices, on the possibility that an individual can learn to modify and to some extent control the degree of intensity of his "fight or flight" reactions:

> [T]hat argument must stand or fall on the proposition that learning of the convictions of others for murder will act as a stimulus

to people to start learning to control their reactions. There is not the slightest evidence to suppose that this educative or deterrent effect will occur, and, I would think, every reason to suppose that it will not.

Id. at 638. If the reasonable person standard is not—or cannot be— abolished, Brett recommends the use of evidence of the accused's physiological reactions under experimentally-induced conditions of stress to establish that he is close to the sensitive end of the range of "normal" reaction to stress. But he then observes:

> [A]ny attempt to * * * allow production of evidence as to ordinary behavior emanating from psychiatrists, psychologists, and sociologists, is likely to be met with the justifiable observation that much of what is currently bandied around as established scientific fact is in truth largely speculation, lacking in any scientific foundation * * *.

Id. at 640. Would it be reasonable to modify the objective provocation standard by permitting defendants to establish that they were physiologically abnormal but to deny them the opportunity to show psychological abnormality?

4. The cases frequently speak of "mutual combat" as adequate provocation to reduce a killing from murder to manslaughter. Mutual combat arises where the victim and the defendant intend to fight and are ready to do so, and the defendant acts in the "heat of blood" engendered by the situation. It is not necessary that blows have actually been struck for mutual combat to exist, but if any blows have been struck it is not material which participant struck the first blow or that the deceased may have struck no blows at all. See Whitehead v. State, 9 Md.App. 7, 262 A.2d 316 (1970). But see also United States v. Hardin, 443 F.2d 735, 738 n. 6 (D.C.Cir. 1970): "[M]utual combat alone is not a true alternative ground for mitigating a murder to manslaughter; it is merely one of the circumstances from which the jury could find adequate provocation." If this is accurate, under what circumstances should mutual combat constitute adequate provocation? The court in Whitehead v. State, supra, noted that in that case "the [trial] court did not find that an unfair advantage was taken by appellant at the outset of the combat or that at the commencement of the contest they did not start on equal terms." Is this relevant? controlling?

THE QUEEN v. McGREGOR

New Zealand Court of Appeal, 1962.
[1962] N.Z.L.R. 1069.

APPEAL against conviction for murder on the ground of misdirection.

The appellant was convicted at Auckland on 22 February 1962 of the murder of one Wallace Bernard Whiteford on 9 January 1962. The circumstances were these: The appellant—a married man aged 28 years—and Whiteford were neighbours who in recent months had quarrelled, largely over relatively trivial matters concerning the

boundary between the two properties. Each on occasion had acted in
a way likely to cause the other some irritation. It was also said that
Whiteford had on one occasion used a rude word to the appellant's
wife, and on occasions had "wolf-whistled" her when she appeared in
shorts. On the other hand, the appellant's father, who was the previous owner of the house and had known Whiteford for some years,
seems to have held aloof from the quarrel, and had remained on
neighbourly terms with Whiteford. On 9 January 1962 the appellant spent a considerable period of the afternoon in a hotel at Papa-
toetoe drinking with friends; one of whom, Neville-White, drove him
home and was invited to stay for tea. The appellant was to some
extent under the influence of liquor when he arrived home, but was in
good humour. However, when his father arrived home shortly afterwards, and on being questioned, acknowledged that he had joined
Whiteford in a glass of beer, the appellant became very angry, and
accused him of acting disloyally in associating with Whiteford. His
father resented this and said he was not involved in the quarrel and
he was entitled to live his own life. The appellant and his father
normally were on very good terms, and before long the appellant
quietened down and apologised for the way he had spoken. However,
not very long afterwords, the appellant became very upset, and apparently experienced something in the nature of an emotional crisis.
He commenced to sob and suddenly shouted to his father: "Go over
there and get the bastard and bring him over here so that we can
have it out." His father replied: "Not tonight, Jack, some other
time." The appellant's wife then intervened and encouraged her husband to go to his bedroom and lie down, which he did for a time.
Later he came out of the bedroom and passed swiftly through the
kitchen where his wife, his father, and Neville-White were seated,
leaving the house by the kitchen door. He was observed by one or
more of them to be carrying a rifle, and his wife immediately ran
after him begging him to come back. By mischance, it so happened
that at this time, Whiteford, who was having a meal with his wife,
was asked by her to go and get some ice cream from their deep-freeze
in a nearby shed. This he proceeded to do, carrying a plate and a
spoon with him. Shortly after he emerged from the house he was
seen by the appellant, who raised his rifle to his shoulder, and a shot
was fired which entered Whiteford's chest, killing him almost immediately. According to Neville-White, whom the Judge described as a
reluctant witness for the prosecution, the appellant, as he passed
through the kitchen, had said: "I'll blow the bastard's brains out."
According to another neighbour, Mrs. Buckley, who was in her garden,
the appellant, as he raised his rifle to his shoulder, called out: "I'll get
you, you bastard," or words to that effect. There was ample evidence called by the prosecution, to raise a *prima facie* case of murder.

One of the defences offered at the trial was that the charge of
murder should be reduced to manslaughter on the ground that the

appellant had acted under provocation, and the case is reported on this point only.

The judgment of the Court was delivered by

NORTH, J. [after stating the facts as above]:

* * *

The principal ground of appeal related to the defence of provocation. The crime was committed only nine days after the Crimes Act 1961 came into force, replacing the Crimes Act 1908. Thus it became necessary for the learned trial Judge, unaided by previous decisions, to interpret the new definition of the circumstances in which provocation might be raised as a defence to a charge of murder. This is contained in s. 169 which reads:

(1) Culpable homicide that would otherwise be murder may be reduced to manslaughter if the person who caused the death did so under provocation.

(2) Anything done or said may be provocation if—

(a) In the circumstances of the case it was sufficient to deprive a person having the power of self-control of an ordinary person, but otherwise having the characteristics of the offender, of the power of self-control; and

(b) It did in fact deprive the offender of the power of self-control and thereby induced him to commit the act of homicide.

(3) Whether there is any evidence of provocation is a question of law.

(4) Whether, if there is evidence of provocation, the provocation was sufficient as aforesaid, and whether it did in fact deprive the offender of the power of self-control and thereby induced him to commit the act of homicide, are questions of fact.

(5) No one shall be held to give provocation to another by lawfully exercising any power conferred by law, or by doing anything which the offender incited him to do in order to provide the offender with an excuse for killing or doing bodily harm to any person.

(6) This section shall apply in any case where the provocation was given by the person killed, and also in any case where the offender, under provocation given by one person, by accident or mistake killed another person.

(7) The fact that by virtue of this section one party to a homicide has not been or is not liable to be convicted of murder shall not affect the question whether the homicide amounted to murder in the case of any other party to it.

Comparing the provisions of the new section with s. 184 of the Crimes Act 1908, it will be noticed not only that there are differences in language and arrangement, but that a new test for determining the sufficiency of the provocation is prescribed. Subsection (1) no longer speaks of persons who cause the death of another "in the heat of passion caused by sudden provocation" but of persons who do so "under provocation". Nor does subs. (2) in terms require that the offender should act "on the sudden and before there has been time for his passion to cool". Instead subs. (2)(b) merely makes it a requirement that the provocation did in fact deprive the offender of the power of self-control and thereby induced him to commit the act of homicide. A good deal of the argument we heard from Mr. Finlay for the appellant, turned on the omission of the words to which we have just referred. Mr. Finlay's broad submission was that "the cornerstone of the common law had been dropped from the new section with the consequence that the tests, which juries in the past have been directed to apply in their deliberations, have been swept away, and that now there is really only one test, though twofold in character, namely, was the provocation sufficient to measure up to certain standards, and did it, in fact, deprive the accused of his self-control? In his submission the learned trial Judge misdirected the jury in three main respects: (1) as to the time element in provocation: (a) in telling the jury that it was still necessary that the acts or words which constituted the alleged provocation must induce a lack or absence of self-control that was sudden and temporary in character, and (b) in telling them that the time element was still important and by implication a necessary ingredient, and that the acts or words complained of could only be regarded as constituting provocation in law if they occurred immediately before the killing: (2) as to the relationship between the act of provocation and the act causing death: in telling the jury that they should consider whether the mode of resentment bore some proper and reasonable relationship to the sort of provocation that had been given: (3) as to the true meaning of s. 169: in failing to instruct the jury correctly as to the meaning of the requirement that the provocation must be sufficient to deprive a person having the power of self-control of an ordinary person, but otherwise having the characteristics of the offender, of the power of self-control".

Before considering these submissions it is, we think, necessary to refer to the history of the development of the common law relating to provocation and to the course of events in England which led to the adoption of the new test to be found in s. 169. Provocation does not render an unlawful homicide excusable or justifiable. If established, it reduces the crime from murder to manslaughter. In this respect it differs from self-defence, which, if established, provides a complete answer to the charge of murder; this distinction, however, has not always been clearly recognised. Provocation, as distinct from chance-medley, emerged during the 17th century as a ground for differentiating manslaughter from murder. As society progressed, it came to be recognised that manslaughter would be the proper verdict where the circumstances disclosed that the accused had acted under serious provocation and when passion for the time being had dethroned his reason. Hale in his Pleas of the Crown written in the 17th century but not published until 1736, was the first writer to elaborate on the topic of provocation, and in R. v. Mawgridge (1706) Kelyng 119; 84 E.R. 1107, Holt C.J. considered the law on the matter as it was then. Speaking of this judgment, Sir James Fitzjames Stephen said in 3 History of the Criminal Law 71, that the former view had been superseded

> "by the broader and deeper view that the moral character of homicide must be judged principally by the extent to which the circumstances of the case show, on the one hand, brutal ferocity, whether called into action suddenly or otherwise, or on the other, inability to control natural anger excited by a serious cause."

The learned editor of the 11th edition of Russell on Crime, in discussing the history of provocation in relation to murder, states that from the examples discussed by *Hale* it would appear that what was prominent in the law in his day was that an intentional homicide would be reduced from murder to manslaughter if the prisoner had really acted in a passion and if it was clear that the killing was done with sudden heat and was not premeditated in cold blood. Throughout the development of the doctrine it was emphasised both in the cases and by the institutional writers that there must be a close relationship in point of time between the provocative act and the retaliatory act, and more often than not the word "sudden" was used to describe this relationship.

For a time the Judges treated provocation as a matter of law and it was not until the 19th century that a definite rule was established that the question was one for the jury to decide as a matter of fact. When this rule began to be recognised, in the early part of the 19th century, juries were directed to apply what would seem to be largely a subjective test. Nevertheless, the nature of the provocation, the time element, the weapon used and the presence or absence of brutality, were put forward as matters of great importance for the consideration of the jury as may be seen from the directions given in such cases as R. v. Lynch (1832) 5 Car. & P. 324; 172 E.R. 995; R. v. Hayward (1833) 6 Car. & P. 157; 172 E.R. 1188 and R. v. Thomas (1837) 7 Car. & P. 817; 173 E.R. 356. Later it was recognised that juries might fail to give sufficient consideration to the necessity that the acts of provocation should be grave and weighty; that they were required to consider whether the acts relied on would have been sufficient to deprive a "reasonable man" of his power of self-control; and only if they did reach that standard should the crime be reduced from murder to manslaughter.   R. v. Welsh (1869) 11 Cox 336 is usually regarded as having established this objective test.

By the time our Criminal Code Act 1893 was enacted, the principle that the provocation must be of such a nature as to be sufficient to deprive a reasonable man of the power of self-control was firmly established as part of the common law of England.   Therefore, this test was incorporated into s. 165 of the Criminal Code Act 1893, and later into s. 184 of the Crimes Act 1908, save that those responsible for the legislation apparently preferred to speak of an "ordinary person" rather than of a "reasonable man".   For the sake of completeness, it should perhaps be added that the section made one alteration to the common law by providing that an insult without a blow could be sufficient to constitute provocation in law.

All attempts to persuade English Courts to modify the full rigour of the "reasonable man" test have failed.   Thus, in R. v. Lesbini [1914] 3 K.B. 1116, the Court of Criminal Appeal refused to accept an argument that provocation should be judged on the mental ability of the prisoner rather than on the effect of the provocation on the mind of a "reasonable man".   When in 1942 the House of Lords in Mancini's case [1942] A.C. 1; [1941] 3 All E.R. 272 expressly approved R. v. Lesbini (supra) that door was finally shut.   Next, in R. v. McCarthy [1954] 2 Q.B. 105; [1954] 2 All E.R. 262 the contention that drunkenness which might lead a person to attack another in a manner which no reasonably sober man would do was likewise rejected by the Court of Criminal Appeal, Lord Goddard saying: "We see no distinction between a person who by temperament is unusually excitable or pugnacious and one who is temporarily made excitable or pugnacious by self-induced intoxication.   It may be that an excitable, pugnacious or intoxicated person may be more easily provoked than a man of quiet or phlegmatic disposition, but the former cannot rely on his excitable state of mind if the violence used is beyond that which a reasonable, or, as we may perhaps say, an average person would use to repel an act which can in law be regarded as provocation.   No court has ever given, nor do we think ever can give, a definition of what constitutes a reasonable or an average man.   That must be left to the collective good sense of the jury, and what, no doubt, would govern their opinion would be the nature of the retaliation used by the provoked person" (ibid., 112; 265).

Finally, and perhaps the most controversial case of all was *Bedder's* case [1954] 1 W.L.R. 1119; (1954) 2 All E.R. 801.   This was the case of a sexually impotent person who killed a prostitute who jeered, hit and kicked him when he attempted in vain to have intercourse with her.   All the Lords concurred in the judgment delivered by Lord Simonds L.C., who expressed his concurrence with what was said in R. v. McCarthy (supra).   He rejected the argument that in considering the reaction of the hypothetical reasonable man to the acts of provocation, the jury should not only place him in the circumstances in which the accused was placed, but also invest him with the personal physical peculiarities of the accused. He said: "For that proposition I know of no authority; nor can I see any reason in it. It would be plainly illogical not to recognise an unusually excitable or pugnacious temperament in the accused as a matter to be taken into account but yet to recognise for that purpose some unusual physical characteristic, be it impotence or another. Moreover the proposed distinction appears to me to ignore the fundamental fact that the temper of a man which leads him to react in such and such a way to provocation is, or may be itself conditioned by some physical defect. It is too subtle a refinement for my mind or, I think, for that of a jury to grasp that the temper may be ignored but the physical defect taken into account. * * * It was urged on your Lordships that the hypothetical reasonable man must be confronted with all the same circumstances as the accused, and that this could not be fairly done unless he was also invested with the peculiar characteristics of the accused. But this makes nonsense of the test. Its purpose is to invite the jury to consider the act of the accused by reference to a certain standard or norm of conduct and with this object the 'reasonable' or the 'average' or the 'normal' man is invoked. If the reasonable man is then deprived in whole or in part of his reason, or the normal man endowed with abnormal characteristics, the test ceases to have any value. This is precisely the consideration which led this House in *Mancini's* case to say that an unusually excitable or pugnacious person is not entitled to rely on provocation which would not have led an ordinary person to act as he did. In my opinion, then, the Court of Criminal Appeal was right in approving the direction given to the jury by the learned judge and this appeal must fail" (ibid., 1123; 803).

This last door of escape having been firmly shut, and the common law of England on the subject of the defence of provocation having been finally laid down by the House of Lords, it is not surprising that when the Royal Commission on Capital Punishment was constituted in 1949, the opportunity was taken to make representations that the present scope of legally recognised provocation should be enlarged. It was suggested that in considering whether there existed sufficient provocation the sole test should be whether the accused was in fact deprived of self-control and the jury should not be required to consider the reactions of a "reasonable man". However, the Commission did not recommend any change in the law, expressing the opinion that the adoption of the proposal was likely to offend a fundamental principle of the criminal law that it should be based on a generally accepted standard of conduct applicable to all citizens alike; that idiosyncracies of individual temperament or mentality that might make a man more easily provoked or more violent in his response to provocation, ought not therefore to affect his liability to conviction. At the same time the Commission said that it felt sympathy with the view which prompted the proposal and added that it had no doubt that if the criterion of the reasonable man was strictly applied, it would be too harsh in its operation.

Following upon the presentation of the report of the Royal Commission, the Homicide Act 1957, 37 Halsbury's Statutes of England, 2nd ed. 172 was enacted. Section 3 of that Act reads thus:

> Where on a charge of murder there is evidence on which the jury can find that the person charged was provoked (whether by things done or by things said or by both together) to lose his self-control, the question whether the provocation was enough to make a reasonable man do as he did shall be left to be determined by the jury; and in determining that question the jury shall take into account everything both done and said according to the effect which, in their opinion, it would have on a reasonable man.

It will be observed that, when for the first time the common law defence of provocation was made the subject of a statutory provision, no attempt was made to introduce into the section the words which appeared in our own Acts of 1893 and 1908 and which have been omitted from s. 169 of the present Act. It was left for the common law to supply the rules and principles which had been evolved over the years as guides in determining whether the person charged was so provoked as to lose his self-control.

With this review of the history of the matter, we pass on to consider the provisions of s. 169 of our own statute. Notwithstanding the observations of their Lordships in *Bedder's* case (supra), to the effect that it was well-nigh impossible to invest a reasonable man with the peculiar characteristics of the accused without making nonsense of the test, it is apparent, even from a cursory examination of the new section, that those who were entrusted with the drafting and approving of the provisions of the Crimes Act 1961 have attempted that task. Therefore it is plainly the duty of this Court to endeavour to see that their efforts are not rendered unavailing notwithstanding the manifold difficulties that arise in defining what is meant by the somewhat vague words "the characteristics of the offender".

Turning to the first ground of appeal relied on by Mr. Finlay, it may be said at once that in our opinion, there is no validity in his submission that the changed language of s. 169 has resulted in what he described as the "corner stone of the common law in relation to provocation being dropped". But for the fact that he was able to point to the more detailed provisions of the earlier section, clearly there would have been no justification for concluding merely as a matter of construction, that the language of the new section required the Court to hold that the common law rules for ascertaining whether an offender had acted under provocation were no longer applicable, any more than it could be said that the English section has that effect. The omission from the new section of references to "heat of passion", "sudden provocation", and "before there has been time for his passion to cool", do not abrogate the rule always emphasised in the common law that a defence of provocation can only avail when the homicide has been committed in hot blood and while the accused is still in the throes of passion. It was said in the judgment of the Privy Council in Attorney-General for Ceylon v. Perera [1953] A.C. 200, 207 that "in the opinion of their Lordships it is quite wrong to say that because the code does not in so many words say that the retaliation must bear some relation to the provocation, it is true to say that the contrary is the case". In the same way, it cannot be said that the omission from the new section of the references to suddenness and the heat of passion, means in any way that these matters have become irrelevant. The argument for the appellant gives insufficient weight to the fact that s. 169 provides that before murder may be reduced to manslaughter, the killing must have taken place "under provocation" and while the offender has been deprived of the power of self-control. The trial Judge must instruct the jury what is meant by these words. The deprivation of self-control implies a sudden transition to a state, necessarily temporary, during which the power of self-control is absent. In the nature of things, it would not be possible for the Judge to direct the jury on this topic without explaining that it is of the essence of the defence of provocation that the acts or words of the dead man have caused the accused a sudden and temporary loss of self-control, rendering him so subject to passion as to make him for the moment not master of his mind. Without some such direction, the jury would be left with the impression that circumstances which merely predisposed to a violent act or caused a person to become extremely angry would be enough. Reasons may readily be suggested which would account for the omission from the new section of the references to suddenness and the like. It was said in The Attorney-General of Ceylon v. Perera (supra) that the word "sudden" is a relative term, and having regard to what was said by this Court in R. v. Noel [1960] N.Z.L.R. 212, on a closely related topic, it may have been thought preferable to deal with provocation in general terms and so ensure that none of the common law guides for determining whether provocation had been established was elevated into a matter of law. The Solicitor-General advanced another reason. He submitted that in applying this relative term to the circumstances of any particular case, it may have been thought desirable to ensure that juries might properly allow for the fact that reaction periods may vary with different persons. It is unnecessary, and perhaps undesirable that we should express any concluded opinion on this submission, though we would point out that if he be right, caution would be called for at this point because the longer the lapse of time the greater the probability that the accused acted from feelings of vengeance and not while still suffering from a loss of self-control. But whatever the reasons may have been for the omission of the words we have referred to, we agree with the Solicitor-General that the language of the new section itself clearly recognises the importance of the time element as the offender must act while still "under provocation".

In our opinion, then, the learned trial Judge was fully entitled to tell the jury, as he did, that it was of the essence of provocation that it should cause a sudden and temporary loss of self-control rendering the accused so subject to passion as to make him for the moment not master of his mind. This being so, it necessarily followed that the Judge was quite right in telling the jury that the time element was of importance. We agree that it would have been wrong if he had told the jury that as a matter of law it was necessary that the provocation should occur immediately before the killing, but contrary to the way Mr. Finlay's submission was framed, the Judge said no such thing.

* * *

Mr. Finlay's second ground of appeal may be dealt with quite shortly. We see no reason to question the direction given by the Judge that the jury should consider whether the mode of resentment—namely the killing—bore any proper or reasonable relationship to the sort of provocation which Whiteford was said to have given to the appellant. This is in conformity with what was decided by this Court in R. v. Noel (supra) where it was pointed out that the notion of the relationship between the provocation and the retaliation was long ago recognised in the common law. For much the same reasons as have been referred to in dealing with the relevance of the time element, despite the omission of any express reference thereto in the section, we think the absence of any reference to the relationship of the provocative and retaliatory acts is immaterial.

This being the view we take, it seems to us necessarily to follow that Mr. Finlay is placed in some difficulty in supporting the appellant's third ground of appeal. The acts and words of Whiteford which are relied on as providing a basis for the defence of provocation are in no way related in point of time to the killing, and whatever meaning is to be given to the words "but otherwise having the characteristics of "the offender" it is plain that the appellant, though no doubt angered by Whiteford's conduct and words, did not, in the course of these unneighbourly disputes, lose his power of self-control. On each occasion he was able to restrain any temptation he may have experienced to injure Whiteford. In these circumstances, we think there was no foundation for the contention that the appellant caused the death of Whiteford under provocation. In truth, what happened was that in his somewhat alcoholic condition he got matters out of perspective, quarrelled with his father, and then became very angry and emotional about past wrongs, and after an interval, went out and shot

Whiteford. Unless Mr. Finlay can point to some other provision in s. 169 which helps him, it would seem to us that there was no evidence of provocation to go to the jury, though we fully understand the learned Judge's reluctance in so ruling, faced as he was with a new section which had not yet been the subject of judicial interpretation. Mr. Finlay endeavoured to meet this difficulty by submitting that the deeds or words referred to in s. 169(2) could emanate from any source, and there was nothing in the section limiting them to the deeds and words of the victim. When his attention was drawn to the provisions of subs. (6) he submitted that the language of this subsection was ambiguous. We cannot agree. In our opinion the subsection makes quite plain what in any event is inherent in the use of the word "provocation", namely that the law shows a measure of indulgence to a person who kills another who has provoked him. It may well be that earlier happenings between the appellant and Whiteford could be taken into account in determining whether a subsequent comparatively trivial act of provocation on the part of Whiteford could cause slumbering fires of passion to burst into flame, but in the present case, Whiteford did or said nothing to arouse the passion of the appellant and all that can really be said is that the circumstances surrounding his father's visit to Whiteford induced in him a sudden passion of anger which clearly is not enough: R. v. Duffy [1949] 1 All E.R. 932.

If we are right in the view we have expressed, that there was no evidence of provocation, then it is no longer material whether the learned trial Judge correctly instructed the jury with reference to the test they were required to apply in determining whether the evidence was sufficient to constitute provocation and whether it did in fact deprive the appellant of the power of self-control, and thereby induced him to commit the act of homicide. But, as it is of some importance that trial Judges should know the view of this Court when it becomes necessary for them to instruct juries on the defence of provocation in murder cases, we think that as we have had the advantage of hearing a full argument from counsel, we should go on and indicate the way we interpret this very difficult section.

The earlier statutes contemplated "an ordinary person". Now there has been appended this qualification—"an ordinary person but otherwise having the characteristics of the offender". If the phrase "but otherwise" were construed to mean "in other respects" then the test of the power of self-control of an ordinary person would remain unaffected. Upon this interpretation, the section would constitute as provocation anything which in the circumstances of the case would have led to the loss of control of an ordinary person, being one who in other respects (i. e. other than the power of self-control) had his own personal characteristics. Such a construction would make the characteristics of the offender relevant, but not in regard to self-control; the added words would therefore have effected little, for it would still be the reaction of the ordinary person in regard to the exercise of control (which is what matters) that would govern the consideration of the matter as hitherto. This could not have been the intention of the Legislature, for the purpose of adopting the new provision must have been to give some relief from the rigidity of the purely objective test of the reactions of a reasonable man. The Legislature must be regarded as having in contemplation a person with the power of self-control of an ordinary person, but having nevertheless some personal characteristics of his own, which are proper to be taken into account, so that his reaction to provocation is to be judged on the basis whether the provocation was sufficient to bring about loss of self-control in an ordinary person who nevertheless possessed as well the special characteristics of the offender.

If the characteristics of the offender are thus to be integrated with the concept of the ordinary man, then the ordinary man test becomes displaced, at any rate in cases where the offender has attributes which can be regarded as sufficiently distinctive to constitute characteristics. No difficulty is occasioned in grasping the objective test of the "ordinary man", and in giving an appropriate direction to a jury thereon. Likewise, no difficulty would be occasioned in the comprehension of a wholly subjective test, and in directing a jury on such a test. The section, however, now requires a fusion of these two discordant notions, and this immediately gives rise to difficulties of the nature which were referred to by Lord Simonds in *Bedder's* case (supra). In these circumstances, in order to make the section capable of application, while preserving the ordinary man test, there must be some limitation of the term "the characteristics".

The Legislature has given no guide as to what limitations might be imposed, but perforce there must be adopted a construction which will ensure regard being had to the characteristics of the offender without wholly extinguishing the ordinary man. The offender must be presumed to possess in general the power of self-control of the ordinary man, save insofar as his power of self-control is weakened because of some particular characteristic possessed by him. It is not every trait or disposition of the offender that can be invoked to modify the concept of the ordinary man. The characteristic must be something definite and of sufficient significance to make the offender a different person from the ordinary run of mankind, and have also a sufficient degree of permanence to warrant its being regarded as something constituting part of the individual's character or personality. A disposition to be unduly suspicious or to lose one's temper readily will not suffice, nor will a temporary or transitory state of mind such as a mood of depression, excitability or irascibility. These matters are either not of sufficient significance or not of sufficient permanency to be regarded as "characteristics" which would enable the offender to be distinguished from the ordinary man. The "unusually excitable or pugnacious individual" spoken of in R. v. Lesbini (supra) is no more entitled to special consideration under the new section than he was when that case was decided. Still less can a self-induced transitory state be relied upon, as where it arises from the consumption of liquor. The word "characteristics" in the context of this section is wide enough to apply not only to physical qualities but also to mental qualities and such more indeterminate attributes as colour, race and creed. It is to be emphasised that of whatever nature the characteristic may be, it must be such that it can fairly be said that the offender is thereby marked off or distinguished from the ordinary man of the community. Moreover, it is to be equally emphasised that there must be some real connection between the nature of the provocation and the particular characteristic of the offender by which it is sought to modify the ordinary man test. The words or conduct must have been exclusively or particularly provocative to the individual because, and only because, of the characteristic. In short, there must be some direct connection between the provocative words or conduct and the characteristic sought to be invoked as warranting some departure from the ordinary man test. Such a connection may be seen readily enough where the offender possesses some unusual physical peculiarity. Though he might in all other respects be an ordinary man, provocative words alluding for example to some infirmity or deformity from which he was suffering might well bring about a loss of self-control. So too, if the colour, race or creed of the offender be relied on as constituting a characteristic, it is to be repeated that the provocative words or conduct must be related to the particular characteristic relied upon. Thus, it would not be sufficient, for instance, for the offender to claim merely that he belongs to an excitable race, or that members of his nationality are accustomed to resort readily to the use of some lethal weapon. Here again, the provocative act or words require to be directed at the particular characteristic before it can be relied upon.

Special difficulties, however, arise when it becomes necessary to consider what purely mental peculiarities may be allowed as characteristics. In our opinion it is not enough to constitute a characteristic that the offender should merely in some general way be mentally deficient or weak-minded. To allow this to be said would, as we have earlier indicated, deny any real operation to the reference made in the section to the ordinary man, and it would, moreover, go far towards the admission of a defence of diminished responsibility without any statutory authority in this country to sanction it. There must be something more, such as provocative words or acts directed to a particular phobia from which the offender suffers. Beyond that, we do not think it is advisable that we should attempt to go.

We have necessarily been obliged to speak on this matter in somewhat general terms, in the hope that what has been said may afford some guidance to trial Judges in the application of this section. Although we have referred to a number of the more obvious matters that may or may not be regarded as characteristics, it is manifestly impossible to attempt to be exhaustive, and though it may be said that generally the characteristic must be such as substantially to make him different from the ordinary man and to impair his power of self-control when provoked, cases will no doubt arise where the particular circumstances may give rise to further problems in the application of the section. So far as the present case is concerned, none of the matters relied upon by Mr. Finlay could be regarded as characteristics which under the section were to be engrafted upon "the ordinary man" and nothing that was said by the learned trial Judge to the jury in dealing for the first time, as he was required to do, with the new section, really conflicts with the views we have expressed.

* * *

For the reasons we have given the appeal is dismissed.

Appeal dismissed.

NOTES

1. For an instruction following the directives of the instant case, see R. v. Smith, (1964) N.Z.L.R. 834.

2. Does the Court of Appeal's interpretation of the statute provide a theoretically satisfactory standard for distinguishing those killings that should be reduced to manslaughter? Is it a standard that juries could be expected to apply with reasonable accuracy? See generally, Milligan, Provocation and the Subjective Test, 1967 N.Z.L.J. 19.

3. Defendant stabbed decedent. One witness testifies that he saw defendant on top of decedent and that defendant threatened to cut decedent's head off and "to kill this honkey." Another witness testifies that before defendant and decedent fell to the floor in the altercation, "he heard the decedent call defendant a "black son-of-a bitch" and saw him slap defendant a couple of times." Is defendant entitled to an instruction on voluntary manslaughter in a prosecution for second degree murder? See State v. Fulford, 290 Minn. 236, 187 N.W.2d 270, 274 (1971): "Such provocation would, as a matter of law, be insufficient to cause the reasonably induced 'heat of passion' reducing the crime to manslaughter." Compare the concurring opinion, describing such a dismissal of the matter as "cavalier." 187 N.W.2d at 276. In resolving the matter, is the race of the defendant relevant? The race of the decedent? The cultural background of the defendant? His political and social beliefs and experience? Should any of these matters be relevant?

Consider Howard, What Colour is the "Reasonable Man"? [1961] Crim. L.Rev. 41, describing the application of the English provocation standard in the Northern Territory of Australia in cases wherein the defendant is an aborigine. In practice, Howard observes, the reasonable person standard is modified, so that the jury is asked to determine whether an ordinary reasonable aborigine in the specific vicinity would have been adequately provoked by the situation. This, he concludes, is adequate and just. But he emphasizes that the white and aborigine populations are relatively even in size, live apart and have room to do so, and as a result it is not difficult to distinguish between the different influences at work on members of the two racial groups:

> The case is very different where members of one community voluntarily join another, perhaps altogether strange in background and customs, for some economic advantage. In this situation it is reasonable that the new comers should take their adopted country as they find it, even if, as often happens, they tend to preserve their own customs and language in a separate sub-community. The law would be over-complicated if a Jamaican who killed another Jamaican in London were entitled to an inquiry by the jury whether at the time of the killing he was more under the influence of Jamaican than of English customs.

Id. at 47. Are these conclusions correct? What, if any, relevance do they have for the issues posed by State v. Fulford? For a discussion of similar difficulties in defining the term "ordinary person" in a provocation formula in Papua and New Guina, see O'Regan, Provocation and Homicide in Papua and New Guinea, 10 West.Aust.L.Rev. 1, 8–12 (1971). See generally, Brown, The "Ordinary Man" in Provocation: Anglo-Saxon Attitudes and "Unreasonable Non-Englishmen," 13 Int. & Comp.L.Q. 203 (1964).

4. In People v. Pecora, 107 Ill.App.2d 283, 246 N.E.2d 865 (1969), appellant was charged with the murder of his ex-wife. The following evidence was offered:

(1) In a custody battle concerning the children of the marriage, the ex-wife had been "cited" for immoral conduct before the children.

(2) Defendant was a member of St. Mary's Roman Catholic Church.

(3) On the evening before the killing, the deceased told the defendant that he did not know how to make love, that she had been intimate with five men, and that she had had an abortion before she married the defendant.

(4) On the evening of the killing, defendant begged the deceased to "stop her immoral conduct and to get together with him again," but "she said that she did not want any part of it because she was having too good a time."

(5) Defendant had been diagnosed as a "schizoid personality" with a "paranoid reaction," had exhibited anger and hostility towards his ex-wife, and had been hospitalized for his emotional problems.

(6) The killing occurred after the deceased made a "flip" response to defendant's plea that she give them another chance.

(7) The deceased's body contained twenty-one stab wounds.

Which of these items should be admitted as evidence? Should the jury be instructed on voluntary manslaughter? In the case cited, all of the information was received, apparently without objection, but the trial court refused to instruct on manslaughter and this was affirmed on appeal.

5. To what extent does the English Homicide Act of 1957, quoted in the instant case, permit or compel a subjective test? The matter has given rise to a great deal of discussion on the part of commentators. See English,

What Did Section Three Do To the Law of Provocation (1970) Crim.L.Rev. 249; Samuels, Excusable Loss of Self-Control in Homicide, 34 Mod.L.Rev. 163 (1971); White, A Note on Provocation (1970) Crim.L.Rev. 446.

6. To what extent would § 1602(b) of the Proposed Federal Criminal Code permit or require the same result as in the instant case? Consider the following comment to the provision in the Model Penal Code which uses identical language (except that the Model Penal Code does not include the last sentence of § 1602(b)):

> Though it is difficult to state a middle ground between a standard which ignores all individual peculiarities and one which makes emotional distress decisive regardless of the nature of its cause, we think that such a statement is essential. For surely if the actor had just suffered a traumatic injury, if he were blind or were distraught with grief, if he were experiencing an unanticipated reaction to a therapeutic drug, it would be deemed atrocious to appraise his crime for purposes of sentence without reference to any of these matters. They are material because they bear upon the inference as to the actor's character that it is fair to draw upon the basis of his act. * * *

> We submit that the formulation in the draft affords sufficient flexibility to differentiate between those special factors in the actor's situation which should be deemed material * * * and those which properly should be ignored. * * * The question in the end will be whether the actor's loss of self-control can be understood in terms that arouse sympathy enough to call for mitigation. That seems to us to be the issue to be faced.

Model Penal Code § 201.3, comment (Tent.Draft No. 9, 1959). But does the formulation provide any assistance in determining how to differentiate between those factors to be considered and those to be ignored? Is any further assistance possible?

---

2. INVOLUNTARY MANSLAUGHTER

PROBLEM

Consider the liability of the defendant, Isabel L. Rodriguez, for the death of her son, Carlos, under the following facts:

> In November 1959 defendant was living with her four children in a single-family residence at 130 South Clarence Street, Los Angeles. The oldest child was 6 years of age. Carlos Quinones was the youngest, either 2 or 3 years of age.

> Olive Faison lived across the street from defendant. About 10:45 p. m. on November 8, 1959 Miss Faison heard some children calling, "Mommy, mommy." For about 15 or 20 minutes she did not "pay too much attention." She

noticed the cries became more shrill. She went to the front window and saw smoke coming from defendant's house. She "ran across the street and commenced to knock the door in and started pulling the children out." There was a screen door on the outside and a wooden door inside the screen door. The screen door was padlocked on the outside. The other door was open. She broke the screen door and with the help of neighbors pulled three of the children out of the house. She tried to get into the house through the front door but could not because of the flames. A neighbor entered through the back door but could not go far because of the flames. Miss Faison took the three children to her apartment and shortly thereafter returned to the scene of the fire. She remained "until after the little boy was brought out and revived and sent to the hospital." Miss Faison did not see defendant around the house or the neighborhood at the time of the fire.

Firemen arrived at the scene some time after 10 p. m. The front door was open; there was no obstruction. Fireman Hansen went inside and found a baby boy in the back bedroom near the bed. The fire was about 3 feet away from the boy. Hansen took the boy out of the house. "He appeared to be dead at the time." The child was Carlos Quinones.

Around 4 or 4:30 p. m. on November 8, 1959 defendant was in "Johnny's Place." She was at the bar drinking "coke." She stayed about an hour. As John Powers, one of the bartenders, was closing the place about 2:30 a. m. on the morning of November 9, he saw the defendant outside the building. He had not seen her inside before that time.

Maria Lucero, defendant's sister, went to defendant's home about 12 p. m. on November 8, 1959. She went looking for defendant. She found her about 2 or 2:30 a. m. in the same block as "Johnny's Place." Defendant was nervous and frightened, said she knew about the fire and that she went over to tell Johnny Powers about it. Defendant had not been drinking.

Carlos Quinones died from "thermal burns, second and third degree involving 50 to 60 percent of the body surface." Defendant did not testify.

The jurisdiction's statutes contain the following:

"Any person who willfully causes or permits any child to suffer, or who inflicts thereon unjustifiable physical pain or mental suffering, and whoever, having the care or custody of any child, causes or permits the life or limb of such child to be endangered, or the health of such child to be injured, and any person who willfully causes or permits such child to be placed in such situation that its life or limb may be endangered, or its health likely to be injured, is guilty of a misdemeanor."

For one court's analysis, see People v. Rodriguez, 186 Cal.App.2d 433, 8 Cal.Rptr. 863 (1961).

---

a. NEGLIGENT OMISSION

COMMONWEALTH v. WELANSKY

Supreme Judicial Court of Massachusetts, 1944.
316 Mass. 383, 55 N.E.2d 902.

LUMMUS, Justice. On November 28, 1942, and for about nine years before that day, a corporation named New Cocoanut Grove, Inc., maintained and operated a "night club" in Boston, having an entrance at 17 Piedmont Street, for the furnishing to the public for compensation of food, drink and entertainment, consisting of orchestra and band music, singing and dancing. It employed about eighty persons. The corporation, its officers and employees, and its business, were completely dominated by the defendant Barnett Welansky, who is called in this opinion simply the defendant, since his co-defendants were acquitted by the jury. He owned, and held in his own name or in the names of others, all the capital stock. He leased some of the land on which the corporate business was carried on, and owned the rest, although title was held for him by his sister. He was entitled to, and took, all the profits. Internally, the corporation was operated without regard to corporate forms, as though the business were that of the defendant as an individual. It was not shown that responsibility for the number or condition of safety exits had been delegated by the defendant to any employee or other person.

The defendant was accustomed to spend his evenings at the night club, inspecting the premises and superintending the business. On November 16, 1942, he became suddenly ill, and was carried to a hospital, where he was in bed for three weeks and remained until discharged on December 11, 1942. During his stay at the hospital, although employees visited him there, he did not concern himself with the night club, because, as he testified, he "knew it would be all right" and that "the same system * * * [he] had would continue" during his absence. There is no evidence of any act, omission or condition at the night club on November 28, 1942 (apart from the lighting of a match hereinafter described), that was not within the usual and regular practice during the time before the defendant was taken ill when he was at the night club nearly every evening. While the defendant was at the hospital, his brother James

Welansky and an employee named Jacob Goldfine, who were made codefendants, assumed some of the defendant's duties at the night club, but made no change in methods.   *   *   *

A little after ten o'clock on the evening of Saturday, November 28, 1942, the night club was well filled with a crowd of patrons. It was during the busiest season of the year. An important football game in the afternoon had attracted many visitors to Boston. Witnesses were rightly permitted to testify that the dance floor had from eighty to one hundred persons on it, and that it was "very crowded." Witnesses were rightly permitted to give their estimates, derived from their observations, of the number of patrons in various parts of the night club. Upon the evidence it could have been found that at that time there were from two hundred fifty to four hundred persons in the Melody Lounge, from four hundred to five hundred in the main dining room and the Caricature Bar, and two hundred fifty in the Cocktail Lounge. Yet it could have been found that the crowd was no larger than it had been on other Saturday evenings before the defendant was taken ill, and that there had been larger crowds at earlier times. There were about seventy tables in the dining room, each seating from two to eight persons. There was testimony that all but two were taken. Many persons were standing in various rooms. The defendant testified that the reasonable capacity of the night club, exclusive of the new Cocktail Lounge, was six hundred fifty patrons. He never saw the new Cocktail Lounge with the furniture installed, but it was planned to accommodate from one hundred to one hundred twenty-five patrons.

A bartender in the Melody Lounge noticed that an electric light bulb which was in or near the cocoanut husks of an artificial palm tree in the corner had been turned off and that the corner was dark. He directed a sixteen year old bar boy who was waiting on customers at the tables to cause the bulb to be lighted. A soldier sitting with other persons near the light told the bar boy to leave it unlighted. But the bar boy got a stool, lighted a match in order to see the bulb, turned the bulb in its socket, and thus lighted it. The bar boy blew the match out, and started to walk away. Apparently the flame of the match had ignited the palm tree and that had speedily ignited the low cloth ceiling near it, for both flamed up almost instantly. The fire spread with great rapidity across the upper part of the room, causing much heat. The crowd in the Melody Lounge rushed up the stairs, but the fire preceded them. People got on fire while on the stairway. The fire spread with great speed across the foyer and into the Caricature Bar and the main dining room, and thence into the Cocktail Lounge. Soon after the fire started the lights in the night club went out. The smoke had a peculiar odor. The crowd were panic stricken, and rushed and pushed in every direction through the night club, screaming, and overturning tables and chairs in their attempts to escape.

The door at the head of the Melody Lounge stairway was not opened until firemen broke it down from outside with an axe and found it locked by a key lock, so that the panic bar could not operate. Two dead bodies were found close to it, and a pile of bodies about seven feet from it. The door in the vestibule of the office did not become open, and was barred by the clothing rack. The revolving door soon jammed, but was burst out by the pressure of the crowd. The head waiter and another waiter tried to get open the panic doors from the main dining room to Shawmut Street, and succeeded after some difficulty. The other two doors to Shawmut Street were locked, and were opened by force from outside by firemen and others. Some patrons escaped through them, but many dead bodies were piled up inside them. A considerable number of patrons escaped through the Broadway door, but many died just inside that door. Some employees, and a great number of patrons died in the fire. Others were taken out of the building with fatal burns and injuries from smoke, and died within a few days.

* * *

The defendant, his brother James Welansky, and Jacob Goldfine, were indicted for manslaughter in sixteen counts of an indictment * * *[.] Voluntarily the Commonwealth filed specifications as to those counts, by which it specified among other things that the alleged misconduct of the defendant consisted in causing or permitting or failing reasonably to prevent defective wiring, the installation of inflammable decorations, the absence of fire doors, the absence of "proper means of egress properly maintained" and "sufficient proper" exits, and overcrowding.

The defendant was found guilty * * *[.] He was sentenced to imprisonment in the State prison upon each count for a term of not less than twelve years and not more than fifteen years, the first day of said term to be in solitary confinement and the residue at hard labor * * *, the sentences to run concurrently.

The Commonwealth disclaimed any contention that the defendant intentionally killed or injured the persons named in the indictments as victims. It based its case on involuntary manslaughter through wanton or reckless conduct. The judge instructed the jury correctly with respect to the nature of such conduct.

Usually wanton or reckless conduct consists of an affirmative act, like driving an automobile or discharging a firearm, in disregard of probable harmful consequences to another. But where as in the present case there is a duty of care for the safety of business visitors invited to premises which the defendant controls, wanton or reckless conduct may consist of intentional failure to take such care in disregard of the probable harmful consequences to them or of their right to care. * * *

To define wanton or reckless conduct so as to distinguish it clearly from negligence and gross negligence is not easy.   *   *   * Sometimes the word "wilful" is prefaced to the words "wanton" and "reckless" in expressing the concept.   That only blurs it.   Wilful means intentional.   In the phrase "wilful, wanton or reckless conduct," if "wilful" modifies "conduct" it introduces something different from wanton or reckless conduct, even though the legal result is the same.   Wilfully causing harm is a wrong, but a different wrong from wantonly or recklessly causing harm.   If "wilful" modifies "wanton or reckless conduct" its use is accurate.   What must be intended is the conduct, not the resulting harm.   *   *   *   The words "wanton" and "reckless" are practically synonymous in this connection, although the word "wanton" may contain a suggestion of arrogance or insolence or heartlessness that is lacking in the word "reckless." But intentional conduct to which either word applies is followed by the same legal consequences as though both words applied.

The standard of wanton or reckless conduct is at once subjective and objective   *   *   *[.]   Knowing facts that would cause a reasonable man to know the danger is equivalent to knowing the danger. *   *   *   The judge charged the jury correctly when he said, "To constitute wanton or reckless conduct, as distinguished from mere negligence, grave danger to others must have been apparent and the defendant must have chosen to run the risk rather than alter his conduct so as to avoid the act or omission which caused the harm. If the grave danger was in fact realized by the defendant, his subsequent voluntary act or omission which caused the harm amounts to wanton or reckless conduct, no matter whether the ordinary man would have realized the gravity of the danger or not.   But even if a particular defendant is so stupid [or] so heedless   *   *   *   that in fact he did not realize the grave danger, he cannot escape the imputation of wanton or reckless conduct in his dangerous act or omission, if an ordinary normal man under the same circumstances would have realized the gravity of the danger.   A man may be reckless within the meaning of the law although he himself thought he was careful."

The essence of wanton or reckless conduct is intentional conduct, by way either of commission or of omission where there is a duty to act, which conduct involves a high degree of likelihood that substantial harm will result to another.   Wanton or reckless conduct amounts to what has been variously described as indifference to or disregard of probable consequences to that other   *   *   *   or the rights of that other.   *   *   *   But we are not prepared to give unqualified approval to a further statement found in some of our reported decisions, for example in Query v. Howe, 273 Mass. 92, 96, 172 N.E. 887, that to constitute wanton or reckless conduct, disregard of the rights of another must be as complete or utter as though such rights did not exist.   If taken literally, that statement would permit a trifling regard for the rights of another to exonerate a defendant from the criminal consequences of flagrant wrongdoing.

The words "wanton" and "reckless" are thus not merely rhetorical or vituperative expressions used instead of negligent or grossly negligent. They express a difference in the degree of risk and in the voluntary taking of risk so marked, as compared with negligence, as to amount substantially and in the eyes of the law to a difference in kind. * * * For many years this court has been careful to preserve the distinction between negligence and gross negligence, on the one hand, and wanton or reckless conduct on the other. * * *

Notwithstanding language used commonly in earlier cases, and occasionally in later ones,[3] it is now clear in this Commonwealth that at common law conduct does not become criminal until it passes the borders of negligence and gross negligence and enters into the domain of wanton or reckless conduct. There is in Massachusetts at common law no such thing as "criminal negligence." * * *

If by wanton or reckless conduct bodily injury is caused to another, the person guilty of such conduct is guilty of assault and battery. * * * And since manslaughter is simply a battery that causes death * * *, if death results he is guilty of manslaughter. * * *

To convict the defendant of manslaughter, the Commonwealth was not required to prove that he caused the fire by some wanton or reckless conduct. Fire in a place of public resort is an ever present danger. It was enough to prove that death resulted from his wanton or reckless disregard of the safety of patrons in the event of fire from any cause.

* * *

Judgments affirmed.

NOTES

1. What factors are relevant in determining whether a defendant's actions justify a conviction of involuntary manslaughter? Consider United States v. Escamilla, 467 F.2d 341 (4th Cir. 1972) (en banc). Escamilla and the deceased were members of a research team on T—3, "an island of glacial ice * * * which meanders slowly about the general area of the Arctic Ocean." During the summer months, it was virtually impossible to reach the island from the outside. There was no organized law enforcement, and "discipline and order on the island depended upon the cooperation of all of the

3. In early cases what is now known as wanton or reckless conduct was variously described as wilful negligence, wanton negligence, gross negligence, and culpable negligence * * *. So in criminal cases what was necessary to make conduct criminal was often so described. The expression "criminal negligence" was often used. But it seems that what we now know as wanton or reckless conduct was in fact required. The terminology, not the law, is what has changed. * * *

In other jurisdictions a variety of similar expressions has been used in describing conduct that will create criminal liability. But in many of them the substantial equivalent of wanton or reckless conduct is required. * *

men and the effectiveness of the group leader." Escamilla caused the death of the deceased on July 16 during a dispute concerning whether another member of the party, whose drinking and resultant violent behavior had become a problem, should be given some of Escamilla's wine. Escamilla had been waving a loaded gun at the deceased, and at trial he claimed it discharged accidentally; there was evidence that the gun was defective in that it tended to discharge without having the trigger pulled. The prosecution contended that Escamilla's actions in waiving a loaded gun at the deceased constituted gross negligence for purposes of liability for manslaughter. Escamilla requested that the jury be instructed as follows:

> In determining whether or not the defendant is guilty of involuntary manslaughter, the jury must measure his conduct against all of the existing circumstances and determine therefrom whether what he did was in its nature dangerous to life or grossly negligent. Some of the circumstances you may consider in this case are the location of the alleged act, and its lack of law enforcement and medical facilities * * *.

Should such an instruction have been given? Why, or why not? If the circumstances mentioned are relevant, does the offered instruction make clear how they are to be considered? Could this be made clearer? How?

2. For discussions of the English law, see Turpin, Mens Rea in Manslaughter, 1962 Cambridge L.J. 200; Walker, Mens Rea in Manslaughter, 117 New.L.J. 950 (1967). Canadian law is emphasized in O'Hearn, Criminal Negligence: An Analysis in Depth, 7 Crim.L.Q. 27 (1964), 7 Crim.L.Q. 407 (1965). The development of American manslaughter law is dealt with in Coldiron, Historical Development of Manslaughter, 38 Ky.L.J. 527 (1950).

---

b. · THE "UNLAWFUL ACT" DOCTRINE

STATE v. GIBSON

Court of Special Appeals of Maryland, 1968.
4 Md.App. 236, 242 A.2d 575, affirmed 254 Md. 399, 254 A.2d 691.

MURPHY, Chief Judge. A six-count indictment was returned against appellee Gibson by the Grand Jury of Baltimore County as a result of the death on September 10, 1966 of Diane Grempler by reason of appellee's alleged illegal and improper operation of a motor vehicle. Each of the first three counts of the indictment charged that appellee "did feloniously kill and slay" the deceased as a direct result of his commission of certain statutory misdemeanors, viz., that he operated his motor vehicle in violation of the motor vehicle laws of Maryland, Maryland Code (1967 Repl.Vol.) Article 66½, and more specifically:

1. *As to the first count*—that appellee, in violation of Sections 233 and 242, did fail to stop his motor vehicle in obedience to a stop sign and grant the right of way to a vehicle traveling on a paved highway.

2. *As to the second count*—that appellee, in violation of Section 209, recklessly operated his motor vehicle upon a public highway.

3. *As to the third count*—that appellee, in violation of Section 206, operated his motor vehicle under the influence of intoxicating liquors.

The fourth count of the indictment charged that appellee "did feloniously kill and slay" the deceased as a direct result of his commission of a misdemeanor, *viz.*, that he violated the provisions of Section 19.2 of the Baltimore County Code in that he bought, consumed, and possessed an alcoholic beverage on a public highway, he then being a minor.

Each of the first four counts of the indictment expressly characterized the offenses therein charged as constituting a "common law misdemeanor—manslaughter."

The fifth count of the indictment charged that appellee, while operating a motor vehicle "unlawfully in a grossly negligent manner" caused the death of the decedent. This count of the indictment was expressly based upon Section 388 of Article 27 of the Maryland Code (1967 Repl.Vol.), which provides, in pertinent part, as follows:

> "Every person causing the death of another as the result of the driving, operation or control of an automobile, motor vehicle, motorboat, locomotive, engine, car, streetcar, train or other vehicle in a grossly negligent manner, shall be guilty of a misdemeanor to be known as 'manslaughter by automobile, motor vehicle, motorboat, locomotive, engine, car, streetcar, train or other vehicle,' and the person so convicted shall be sentenced to jail or the house of correction for not more than three years, or be fined not more than $1,000.-00 or be both fined and imprisoned. * * * "

* * *

On June 28, 1967, Judge W. Albert Menchine in the Circuit Court for Baltimore County, granted appellee's motion to dismiss [the first four counts of the indictment] stating in a brief opinion accompanying his order that under the common law, a showing of gross negligence was the main requirement for conviction of involuntary manslaughter; and that as none of the four counts alleged either an intention or purpose to harm in the operation of a motor vehicle, or the existence of gross negligence, such counts were not legally sufficient to charge a common law offense. The State has appealed from that order.

The State contends that involuntary manslaughter at common law consisted of an unintentional killing while doing some unlawful act not amounting to a felony, nor naturally tending to cause death or great bodily harm, or in negligently doing some act lawful in itself.

More particularly, it differentiates the two classes of involuntary manslaughter by characterizing the first class as comprising all those cases wherein the defendant has caused the death of another as a direct and proximate result of doing an unlawful act not amounting to a felony, i.e., a misdemeanor (misdemeanor-manslaughter). As to this category of involuntary manslaughter, the State urges that the existence of negligence is not an element of the offense; that the doing of an unlawful act, which is *malum in se* or which if *malum prohibitum*, was in violation of a statute provided to prevent injury to the person, constitutes involuntary manslaughter irrespective of the existence of negligence. The State identifies the second distinct class of involuntary manslaughter as comprising those cases where the defendant, while doing a lawful act in a grossly negligent manner, kills.

It is the State's position that the common law misdemeanor-manslaughter rule is applicable in Maryland and has not been revised, amended or repealed by the manslaughter by automobile statute (Section 388), which it contends applies only to a case where the defendant is charged with an unintentional killing in the course of doing a lawful act in an unlawful manner, i.e., driving a motor vehicle in a grossly negligent manner. It is upon this premise that the State maintains that the first four counts of the indictment properly charged the offense of common law manslaughter in that the appellee operated his vehicle in violation of the law in the four particulars set forth in counts one through four of the indictment; that the first three of these are *mala in se*, but even if *mala prohibita*, they were violations of statutes calculated to prevent injury to the person.

The appellee, on the other hand, urges that the common law crime of involuntary manslaughter where homicide was the unintentional result of an automobile accident has been repealed by Section 388, and that all cases involving the unintentional killing of a person by an automobile can only be prosecuted under the manslaughter by automobile statute; and that in such prosecutions the State carries the burden of proving gross negligence in order to obtain a conviction.

Manslaughter is a common law offense and a felony in Maryland; it may be voluntary or involuntary, depending upon the requisite intent, and since the crime is not defined by statute, it is afforded its common law meaning in this State. * * * By Section 387 of Article 27 of the Maryland Code, manslaughter, whether voluntary or involuntary, is punishable by a term of imprisonment not exceeding ten years. The crime of manslaughter by automobile created by Section 388 is a separate statutory misdemeanor, unknown to the common law, and is punishable under the statute by a designated fine and/or imprisonment in jail or the house of correction for a term not to exceed three years.

Involuntary manslaughter at common law has been generally defined as the killing of another unintentionally and without malice (1) in doing some unlawful act not amounting to a felony, or (2) in negligently doing some act lawful in itself, or (3) by the negligent omission to perform a legal duty. * * *

It is well settled in this State that where a charge of involuntary manslaughter is predicated on negligently doing some act lawful in itself, or by negligently failing to perform a legal duty (the second and third classes of involuntary manslaughter above delineated), the negligence necessary to support a conviction must be gross or criminal, *viz.*, such as manifests a wanton or reckless disregard of human life. * * * It is equally well settled that the Legislature, in enacting Section 388, making it a misdemeanor to cause the death of another as a result of operating an automobile "in a grossly negligent manner," intended to adopt this same standard of gross negligence (a wanton or reckless disregard of human life) as the minimum requirement to support a conviction for this statutory offense. * * *

It is likewise clear that the Maryland cases have generally recognized that a charge of involuntary manslaughter at common law could in some circumstances at least be based on the doing of an unlawful act. * * * [The cases] * * * seemingly share a common thread—that where a prosecution for involuntary manslaughter is based on the commission of an unlawful act causing death, the act must itself be dangerous to life. * * *

It is against this background that we examine whether the first four counts of the indictment returned against the appellee—which are expressly bottomed upon the applicability of the so called misdemeanor-manslaughter rule (an unintended homicide committed in the course of doing an unlawful act, i.e., committing a misdemeanor)—properly charge an existing offense in this State, when considered in light of the provisions of Section 388 and of the legislative intention in enacting that statute.

We note at the outset that the manner of operating a motor vehicle is commonly regulated in detail by statute or ordinance and that it is an unlawful act in itself to drive a vehicle in violation of such laws. It is not, however, a generally accepted rule that the fact alone that the operator of an automobile was violating the motor vehicle laws when his car struck and killed a person renders him, without more, guilty of involuntary manslaughter at common law. The authorities are divided on the question, some holding, as in State v. Hupf, 9 Terry 254, 101 A.2d 355 (Del.), that where a person violates a traffic statute which proximately results in the death of another, he is guilty of involuntary manslaughter, without regard to whether the violation was *malum prohibitum* or *malum in se*, and irrespective of whether there was any proof that the motorist's conduct evidenced a wanton or reckless disregard for the lives and safety of others. Other authorities support the view as articulated in State v. Strobel, 130 Mont. 442, 304 P.2d 606, that such violations of law proximately resulting in the death of another, whether the violation was *malum in se*, or *malum prohibitum*, do not constitute involuntary manslaughter, unless the element of criminal negligence is also present. Still other authorities distinguish between unlawful acts *mala prohibita* and *mala in se*, and conclude in effect, that where the violation was merely *malum prohibitum*, no criminal homicide results, unless the violation was dangerous to life and constituted a reckless disregard for the safety of others; but that where the unlawful act underlying death was *malum in se* the violator would be guilty of involuntary manslaughter, even though the unlawful act was not calculated to cause death. * * *

While [the] cases might be construed to place Maryland among those authorities which hold that an unintentional killing committed in the course of doing some non-felonious unlawful act dangerous to life or *malum in se*, constitutes involuntary manslaughter at common law, irrespective of the existence of criminal negligence, we are persuaded that if such was ever the law of this State, it no longer has any application to those cases where the homicide results unintentionally from the operation of a motor vehicle—it being our view that such cases can only be prosecuted under Section 388.

There is no legislative history to which we may turn to ascertain the exact reach of Section 388, or of the effect of that statute upon the common law felony of involuntary manslaughter. We think it plain, however, that when Section 388 was enacted by Chapter 414 of the Acts of 1941, there then existed much confusion and little enlightenment among the authorities with respect to which of the several theories underlying application of the misdemeanor-manslaughter rule was the correct one. Quite clearly, where such unintentional homicides proximately resulted from driving an automobile in violation of laws designed to regulate and control the operation of motor vehicles in the interest of public safety there was an overlapping and blurring between and among the different theories of criminal responsibility, since in most instances such a violation constituted not only an unlawful act, but one dangerous to the lives and safety of others and such as manifested a wanton and reckless disregard of human life. We believe that the Legislature in enacting Section 388 to punish persons who cause the death of another "as the result of the driving, operation or control of an automobile * * * in a grossly negligent manner," intended to treat all unintended homicides thereby resulting in the same way, without regard to whether the homicide occurred in the course of doing a lawful or an unlawful act, or whether such act was *malum in se* or merely *malum prohibitum*. To otherwise conclude would be to attribute an intention to the Legislature to permit the prosecution of offenders either for the felony of common law manslaughter, with its ten-year penalty, or for the statutory misdemeanor of manslaughter by automobile, with its three-year penalty, even though, where the prosecution is based upon gross negligence, the proof necessary to justify a conviction in either case would be precisely the same (a wanton or reckless disregard of human life). A similarly incongruous result would follow from attributing an intention to the Legislature to permit a felony conviction and ten-year sentence upon simple proof that the accidental homicide occurred in the commission of an unlawful act (a misdemeanor), while requiring a greater degree of proof under the statute to support a conviction for a lesser grade of homicide, a misdemeanor punishable by a maximum of three years imprisonment. In construing statutes, results that are unreasonable or inconsistent with common sense should be avoided, whenever possible. We conclude, therefore, that in enacting Section 388, the Legislature intended to deal with an entire subject matter-unintended homicides resulting from the operation of a motor vehicle—and that the common law crime of involuntary manslaughter, when based on homicides so occurring, is in conflict with the statute and must yield to it to the extent of the inconsistency. * * *

Order affirmed.

NOTES

1. Is not the result of the court's decision to cause one who kills by means of a gun used with gross negligence to be guilty of manslaughter but one who kills with a motor vehicle used with the same disregard of risk to be guilty of a significantly lesser offense? If so, is this not as incongruous a result as that avoided by the court's holding? What factors might have caused the legislature to rationally conclude that the potential penalty for grossly negligent killing should be reduced where the means used to accomplish the result was a "vehicle"? Could the same—or a similar—result be accomplished within the framework of the common law concept of criminal negligence? For example, in determining whether the appellant in the instant case would be liable for manslaughter as the common law defined the crime, would it be appropriate to consider the social utility of the motor vehicle and the extent to which Americans have apparently reconciled themselves to the fact that widespread use of the motor vehicle as a means of transportation (and entertainment) will involve loss of life? See Comment, The Fallacy and Fortuity of Motor Vehicle Homicide, 41 Neb. L.Rev. 793 (1962).

2. If the court in the instant case had come to the opposite conclusion, which, if any, of the offenses alleged in the first four counts of the indictment would have justified a finding of guilty of manslaughter? Explain.

3. See generally, Wilner, Unintentional Homicide in the Commission of an Unlawful Act, 87 U.Pa.L.Rev. 811 (1939).

PEOPLE v. STUART

Supreme Court of California, 1956.
47 Cal.2d 167, 302 P.2d 5.

TRAYNOR, Justice. [Defendant, a licensed pharmacist, was convicted of manslaughter. In the course of his employment as a pharmacist, he had filled a prescription for the eight day old Sills infant. Unknown to him, the bottle from which he took the sodium citrate used in the medication also contained traces of sodium nitrite, a poison. As a result, the prescription contained the poisonous sodium nitrite which caused the death of the infant. Evidence showed that the bottle had been used only for sodium citrate at all times since the pharmacy had been purchased from its former owner; the bottle was part of the inventory. Only laboratory analysis could have determined the presence of sodium nitrite in the bottle.]

No evidence whatever was introduced that would justify an inference that defendant knew or should have known that the bottle labeled sodium citrate contained sodium nitrite. On the contrary, the undisputed evidence shows conclusively that defendant was morally entirely innocent and that only because of a reasonable mistake or unavoidable accident was the prescription filled with a substance containing sodium nitrite. Section 20 of the Penal Code makes the union of act and intent or criminal negligence an invariable element of every crime unless it is excluded expressly or by necessary implication. Moreover, section 26 of the Penal Code lists among the persons incapable of committing crimes "[p]ersons who committed the act or made the omission charged under an ignorance or mistake of fact, which disproves any criminal intent", subd. 4, and "[p]ersons who committed the act or made the omission charged through misfortune or by accident, when it appears that there was no evil design, intention, or culpable negligence." Subd. 6; see also Pen.Code, §§ 195, 199. The question is thus presented whether a person can be convicted of manslaughter or a violation of section 380 of the Penal Code in the absence of any evidence of criminal intent or criminal negligence.

The answer to this question as it relates to the conviction of manslaughter depends on whether or not defendant committed an "unlawful act" within the meaning of section 192 of the Penal Code when he filled the prescription. The Attorney General contends that even if he had no criminal intent and was not criminally negligent, defendant violated section 26280 of the Health and Safety Code and therefore committed an unlawful act within the meaning of section 192 of the Penal Code.

Section 26280 of the Health and Safety Code provides: "The manufacture, production, preparation, compounding, packing, selling, offering for sale, advertising or keeping for sale within the State of California * * * of any drug or device which is adulterated or misbranded is prohibited." In view of the analyses of the contents of the prescription bottle and the bottle labeled sodium citrate and defendant's stipulation, there can be no doubt that he prepared, compounded, and sold an adulterated and misbranded drug.

Because of the great danger to the public health and safety that the preparation, compounding, or sale of adulterated or misbranded drugs entails, the public interest in demanding that those who prepare, compound, or sell drugs make certain that they are not adulterated or misbranded, and the belief that although an occasional nonculpable offender may be punished, it is necessary to incur that risk by imposing strict liability to prevent the escape of great numbers of culpable offenders, public welfare statutes like section 26280 are not ordinarily governed by section 20 of the Penal Code and therefore call for the sanctions imposed even though the prohibited acts are committed without criminal intent or criminal negligence. * * *

It does not follow, however, that such acts, committed without criminal intent or criminal negligence, are unlawful acts within the meaning of section 192 of the Penal Code, for it is settled that this section is governed by section 20 of the Penal Code. * * * Since section 20 also applies to the phrase "unlawful act," the act in question must be committed with criminal intent or criminal negligence to be an unlawful act within the meaning of section 192. By virtue of its application to both phrases, section 20 precludes the incongruity of imposing on the morally innocent the same penalty, Pen.Code, § 193, appropriate only for the culpable. Words such as "unlawful act, not amounting to felony" have been included in most definitions of manslaughter since the time of Blackstone * * * and even since the time of Lord Hale, "unlawful act" as it pertains to manslaughter has been interpreted as meaning an act that aside from its unlawfulness was of such a dangerous nature as to justify a conviction of manslaughter if done intentionally or without due caution. * * * To be an unlawful act within the meaning of section 192, therefore, the act in question must be dangerous to human life or safety and meet the conditions of section 20. * * *

It follows, therefore, that only if defendant had intentionally or through criminal negligence prepared, compounded, or sold an adulterated or misbranded drug, would his violation of section 26280 of the Health and Safety Code be an unlawful act within the meaning of section 192 of the Penal Code. Thus, in People v. Penny, [44 Cal.2d 861, 285 P.2d 926 (1955)] in discussing section 7415 of the Business and Professions Code, which prohibits the use by licensed cosmetologists of a solution of more than 10% phenol on a human being, we said that had the defendant been a licensed cosmetologist, she would have been guilty of violating section 7415 and therefore of an unlawful act within the meaning of section 192 of the Penal Code. The defendant in that case knew that she was using such a solution. The intentional or criminally negligent use of such a solution on a human being by a licensed cosmetologist in violation of section 7415 of the Business and Professions Code would clearly meet the conditions of section 20 of the Penal Code and would therefore be an unlawful act within the meaning of section 192. When, as in this case, however, the defendant did not know, and could not reasonably be expected to know, that the sodium citrate bottle contained nitrite, those conditions are not met and there is therefore lacking the culpability necessary to make the act an unlawful act within the meaning of section 192.

* * *

The judgment and order are reversed.

---

3. KILLINGS REDUCED TO MANSLAUGHTER BY "IMPERFECT" DEFENSES

SANCHEZ v. PEOPLE

Supreme Court of Colorado, 1970.
470 P.2d 857.

LEE, Justice. Plaintiff in error, Richard Bernard Sanchez, was convicted in the District Court of Mesa County of murder in the second degree and was sentenced to the penitentiary for a term of ten to forty years. By this writ of error, he seeks reversal of the judgment of conviction, and a new trial.

Sanchez asserts three grounds for reversal. We need to consider only the one proposition—that the trial court committed prejudicial error in refusing to instruct the jury on the lesser included offense of involuntary manslaughter. From a review of the record, we have concluded that Sanchez was entitled to such an instruction. Accordingly, the judgment of conviction must be reversed and the cause remanded for a new trial.

The events out of which the murder charge arose occurred in the early morning hours of October 13, 1966. At approximately 3 a.m. Felix Martinez was found dead in his apartment across the street from the Grand Junction police station. Medical evidence showed that death was caused by a puncture type stab wound which pierced the heart, allowing massive hemorrhaging. Sanchez, who had been observed earlier in the vicinity of the apartment house where Martinez was found, was arrested at his home at approximately 4:35 a.m. He was found sleeping in bed, fully clothed, and when aroused appeared to be in a drunken condition. He was taken to the police station and fully advised of his rights. Because of his obvious condition of intoxication, questioning was discontinued and later that day he was released from custody without any charges being filed against him.

Sanchez' intoxicated condition was the result of an extended drinking spree which commenced during the early afternoon hours of the preceding day and continued sporadically into the early morning hours of October 13. He and one Lucy Vigil, Mrs. Martinez' sister, were visiting in the Martinez apartment with Mrs. Martinez, awaiting Felix who finally arrived between 1 and 2 a.m. Felix had also been drinking and was described by his wife as being drunk when he arrived at the apartment. The men resumed their drinking. Eventually Martinez and his wife became involved in a violent argument, in which blows were exchanged. Sanchez sought to intervene and presumably it was in the course of his peace-making effort that Martinez was stabbed.

The evidence was far from clear as to the course of events. Although both were present in the same room, neither Mrs. Martinez nor Lucy Vigil would admit they saw Sanchez stab Felix.

After things had presumably quieted down, Sanchez and Lucy Vigil left for their home. Mrs. Martinez testified that she observed Martinez lying on the floor. Thinking he was asleep she did not bother him; but when she saw blood on his clothing she became alarmed and notified the police. Oddly enough, the investigating officer testified that he found Martinez seated at the kitchen table in a slumped-over position. The officer, not knowing whether Martinez was still alive, put him on the floor to administer first aid and then discovered that he was dead.

Three weeks later Sanchez contacted the Grand Junction police and requested to talk concerning the Martinez death. On November 11 he gave an extensive written statement in which he admitted stabbing Martinez twice during their argument. This statement was admitted into evidence. The voluntariness of this statement is not here challenged, nor is Sanchez' waiver of his right to have an attorney present at the time it was taken. At the trial Sanchez testified in his own behalf. He repudiated the statement and denied the stabbing.

Among other things the statement contains the following questions and answers:

"Q. Is my understanding correct, then, up to the point that you stabbed him when he lunged at you, this had been mostly argument, then, between the two of you, it was verbal?

"A. Yes, and threatening, more or less, like he said, 'I will kill you, you little son-of-a-bitch, who do you think you are?' It was just stuff like that."

*   *   *

"Q. Now, Richard, is there anything else concerning what happened on this night in question that you would like to tell us or that you would like to include in this statement?

"A. Well, yes, I guess, and that is, hell, I was just afraid of getting hurt, otherwise I wouldn't have used a knife on him. I was afraid, if you got somebody to call you names and say, 'I will kill you, you little son-of-a-bitch,' or something like that—you know, you get pretty mad, and then if he was intoxicated or something, you just don't know what he might do or anything, and look what it got me."

The trial court instructed the jury on second degree murder and voluntary manslaughter only; it refused to give the instruction on involuntary manslaughter, although such was specifically requested and tendered by Sanchez.

It is well-established that a defendant in a homicide case is entitled to an instruction on lesser included offenses when there is evidence, however manifested, whether presented by the people or by the defense, to indicate the commission of the lesser offense. * * *

It was the defendant's theory—and there was evidence to support it—that he was threatened with harm from Martinez; that he was only acting in self-defense at the time of the stabbing; and that he did not intend to kill Martinez, but only to protect himself. In other words, if in the act of defending himself he overreacted to a belief that he was in danger from Martinez and the killing resulted from the application of excessive force, then the exercise of his right of self-defense, lawful in the first instance, became unlawful by reason of the manner in which he defended himself. Under these circumstances the killing would not be legally justified. However, the criminal culpability, assuming the evidence was believed by the jury, would be limited to involuntary manslaughter—"* * * the killing of a human being without any intent so to do; in the commission of an unlawful act or a lawful act which probably might produce such a consequence, in an unlawful manner; * * *." C.R.S.1963, 40–2–7.

Thus it was the jury's function to determine in the first instance whether Sanchez did in fact administer the fatal blow, he having repudiated the incriminating admission in his written statement. It was also within the jury's province to disbelieve his testimony of repudiation and to ascribe truth to the written statement from which the jury could conclude that his actions were within the realm of self-defense and were thus justifiable; or the jury could conclude his actions were beyond the scope of legitimate self-defense by reason of the application of excessive force; or the jury could conclude that Sanchez did in fact intentionally kill as a result of a serious provocation, but without malice; or, finally, that he killed maliciously, but without deliberation or premeditation. Under the evidence the jury was entitled to consider each and all of these alternatives. That we may concur in the belief of the trial court that the evidence is "improbable, unreasonable or slight," is of no moment, as such determination is in the exclusive province of the jury.

* * *

NOTES

1. See generally, Parker, A Plea of Self-Defense Resulting in Manslaughter, 3 Alberta L.Rev. 16 (1963).

2. Why is involuntary rather than voluntary manslaughter the appropriate category for those who kill under circumstances giving rise to an "imperfect" defense? W. LaFave and A. Scott, Criminal Law 584 n. 7 (1972) observe that in the cases such killings are generally described as manslaughter without any modifying adjective. They then conclude, without explanation, that voluntary manslaughter "is the proper classification." Section 608 of the Proposed Federal Criminal Code (reprinted at page 1083) provides that a defendant's reckless or negligent belief that circumstances are such that his conduct would, if the circumstances were as he believed, be within one of the generally applicable defenses, "is not excuse in a prosecution for an offense for which negligence or recklessness, as the case may be, suffices to establish culpability." If this is—or were to be—the law, why should not "imperfect defense" cases be involuntary manslaughter on the theory that the culpable act consists of negligently creating circumstances which make it necessary to kill?

VI. DEFENSES NOT DIRECTLY RELATED TO THE BASIC REQUIREMENTS FOR LIABILITY

A number of so-called "defenses" to criminal liability are really only a challenge to the prosecution's case in the sense that they amount to either questioning whether the prosecution has proved one element of the offense or offering proof that tends to show that one element did not exist. This is most common in regard to those matters such as mistake of fact which merely "disprove" the existence of the requisite state of mind required for liability. These matters were covered in Part III. B. 6. Part VI deals with those matters which generally do not involve challenging the prosecution's proof of the elements of the offense, but rather involve the establishment of facts which establish that the defendant is entitled to acquittal despite the adequacy of proof of all elements of the offense. These are the true "defenses" to criminal liability.

A. THE GENERAL PRINCIPLE OF JUSTIFICATION

PROPOSED FEDERAL CRIMINAL CODE (STUDY DRAFT, 1970)

§ 608. Conduct Which Avoids Greater Harm

Conduct is justified if it is necessary and appropriate to avoid harm clearly greater than the harm which might result from such conduct and the situation developed through no fault of the actor. The necessity and justifiability of such conduct may not rest upon considerations pertaining only to the morality and advisability of the penal statute defining the offense, either in its general application or with respect to its application to a particular class of cases arising thereunder.

NOTE

This statement of the doctrine of "necessity" was deleted from the final draft. Similar formulations may be found in Smith-Hurd Ill.Ann.Stat. ch. 38, § 7.13 and McKinney Consol.Laws of N.Y. (Penal) § 35.05(2).

PEOPLE v. RICHARDS

California Court of Appeal, 1969.
269 Cal.App.2d 768, 75 Cal.Rptr. 597.

SIMS, Associate Justice. Defendant has appealed from a judgment of conviction rendered on jury verdicts which found him guilty of escape from a state prison without force or violence in violation of subdivision (b) of section 4530 of the Penal Code, and sane at the time of the commission of the offense. He contends that the trial court committed prejudicial error in refusing to receive evidence, embodied in an offer of proof, on a proposed defense of coercion and duress as justification for the offense charged, and in refusing to give proffered instructions on the same issue. These points are examined and found wanting. The judgment must be affirmed.

On July 19, 1967, defendant was assigned to a farm crew as an inmate of the California Correctional Training Facility, Soledad, Monterey County. Sometime after 2:30 p. m. defendant left the work area without permission and hid in a corn field until dark. Defendant then proceeded to the main road, and caught a ride to King City. He was apprehended by the California Highway Patrol on July 20, 1967 at 2:30 a. m. at a service station in King City. Defendant was still in prison dress, and he made no attempt to resist arrest.

On his return to the prison on July 20th, defendant was admonished as to his constitutional rights and questioned by a correctional officer as to his motive for escape. Defendant stated that he left prison without permission because "he felt he was doing too much time, that he was proceeding to Los Angeles to his mother's place to engage a lawyer to see if something couldn't be done."

The prison records officer authenticated the "Summary of Sentence Data" which indicated defendant's commitment and his movement in and through the state prison system. On cross-examination the defendant brought out, over objection, that while at a conservation center camp between November 10, 1966 and March 28, 1967 he had complained that there was pressure from other inmates to engage in homosexual activity. The court sustained an objection to a question propounded to determine if the records indicated whether or not the authorities at the center had checked into the defendant's complaint. According to the summary, the complaints, coupled with a very poor camp record, resulted in defendant's retransfer to Soledad in March.

In his opening statement the attorney for the defendant stated: "Ladies and gentlemen of the jury, you heard what is called a prima facie case of escape. The law provides that in certain circumstances there are defenses to crimes * * *. The law as to the various defenses will be stated to you by the Court. I will not attempt to state it. But the defense we are raising is called duress. Coercion. And we are going to present a series of witnesses, including the defendant himself, and these witnesses and the defendant will tell you of the threats made to his life and the reason that he ran away in order to save his own life, at least in his own mind he was doing this. And this will be the nature of our defense * * *."

The training officer in charge of defendant's work detail was called as a witness for the defendant. He testified that he had worked in the prison system for approximately 20 years and was familiar with the expression used by prisoners around the prison; that "a snitch" was someone who tells on someone else; and that if one prisoner disclosed that another prisoner was forcing him to commit homosexual acts it would be considered one of the more serious, if not the most serious, form of snitching. An objection to the relevancy and materiality of the next question—"What in your experience usually happens to inmates who snitch?"—was sustained.[2]

The court, at the request of the defendant, thereupon heard argument outside the presence of the jury. In the course of this argument the defendant adverted to the provisions of subdivision Eight of section 26 of the Penal Code.[3] He represented to the court that acts of sodomy had been inflicted on the defendant, that the defendant did snitch, that threats were made upon his life, that the guards would do nothing, and that defendant had exhausted every possible remedy short of escape to avoid the threat of death. The court adhered to the view that the threat, in order to be a justification, would have to be a threat designed to directly induce the act with which the defendant was charged. In response to the court's invitation to make an offer of proof, the defendant represented that inmate Joel Blume would testify "that inmates told him to remain away from the defendant * * * because Wayne Richards was going * * * to be killed * * * so keep his distance away from him or he would be killed too." Defendant himself would testify that "he was told by Mr. Blume who confided in him that he was marked to be killed or seriously injured and that the defendant understood this was going to be imminent, immediate, or as soon as possible and he felt that he had two possibilities, one to go to the guards, something that he's tried in the past and the guards have only responded by telling him to punch someone in the mouth or to commit probably a worse crime than escape, and, number two, to remove himself from the threat; and the

2. No review has been sought of the propriety of the court's ruling on this question, which merely initiated the discussion which followed. In any event, it would appear that the defendant's, not the officer's knowledge and experience would be the only relevant evidence on the defendant's motivation if it in fact were a proper issue.

3. Section 26 of the Penal Code provides in part: "All persons are capable of committing crimes except those belonging to the following classes: * * Eight—Persons (unless the crime be punishable with death) who committed the act or made the omission charged under threats or menaces sufficient to show that they had reasonable cause to and did believe their lives would be endangered if they refused."

only other way to remove himself from the threat is to remove himself from the imprisonment, the prison itself; and for this reason the defendant took the only alternative that he saw."

The court sustained the prosecution's objection to the testimony which had been offered. Thereupon, the defendant rested without presenting any further evidence.[4]

The instructions offered by the defendant included the following subjects: the effect of threats and menace as set forth in CALJIC Instruction No. 71–F (Revised) as found in 1967 Cumulative pocket part;[5] considerations governing the determination of whether a danger should be considered as imminent and immediate, predicated on People v. Villegas (1938) 29 Cal.App.2d 658, 85 P.2d 480 (see infra);[6] and an instruction on necessity as a defense.[7] The court in fact in-

4. At the sanity trial inmate Blume testified, "I was told that I had best stay away from him because there was a couple of knives waiting to be stuck in him and if I was around him at the time I would be stuck also." He further averred that he passed this information on to defendant three or four days prior to the time of the escape. The defendant testified that "near to just prior" to his escape he had been forced with violence to submit to homosexual acts at Soledad; that he had told on some inmates at the conservation center (who presumably had engaged in similar attacks); that he learned that word of his having done so had reached Soledad; that five inmates showed him a piece of steel like a knife and told him " * * * you told on our friends up there * * *. Before this week is over we're going to [shank (stab) you]"; that three nights later he was jumped from behind by two inmates who got him in position on a lawn and had him by the neck; that they told him he had a choice; that they said "You snitched. You're dead" but that he could avoid trouble by submitting to acts of sodomy; that on his refusal they said, "You don't have any choice" and "We'll see you before the week is over, we'll see what you're going to be or not"; that he reported his fears to a correctional lieutenant and was told to settle down and to find himself an old man to take care of him; that on the Sunday (July 16th, three days) prior to his escape on July 19th he reported his trouble to the chaplain and was advised to try to defend himself and fight his persecutors; that he did not seek further psychiatric

help because consultations at the camp with a nurse, a doctor, the head counselor and a psychologist had produced only advice to grow up and fight back; that he never voluntarily submitted to any homosexual acts or had any desire to engage in them; that he found them revolting; that he did not know how to fight and could not bring himself to fight; and that he thought the threats were serious, that he would be dead, and he just wanted to get away.

5. This instruction read: "A person is not guilty of crime when he commits an act or engages in conduct, otherwise criminal, when acting under threats and menaces under the following circumstances: 1. Where the threats and menaces are such that they would create in the mind of a reasonable person the fear that his life would be in imminent and immediate danger if he did not commit the act or engage in the conduct charged, and 2. If such person then believed that his life would be so endangered. This rule does not apply to threats, menaces, and fear of future danger to his life."

6. This instruction read: "Whether a danger should be considered an imminent and immediate danger as opposed to a future danger is a question of fact to be determined by you the jury. Whether a danger is imminent or immediate will depend on all the surrounding circumstances, including the defendant's ability to withdraw and avoid the danger."

7. This instruction read: "Necessity is a defense to criminal prosecution un-

structed the jury, "The reasons, if any, given for the alleged escape are immaterial and not to be considered by you as in any way justifying or excusing, if there was such. The only requirement for the commission of the crime of escape is that the defendant intentionally, wilfully, and unlawfully, departed from the limits of his custody." Since the defendant's offer of proof had been rejected, there was no evidence to show any legal justification, and the instructions were properly refused. They are only material insofar as they highlight the respective contentions of the parties on the question of what type of coercion, compulsion or necessity may relieve a person of responsibility for what would otherwise be a criminal act.

In the argument concerning the admission of evidence there was a failure to articulate the distinction between the compulsion or duress recognized in the code (see fns. 3, 5 and 6, supra), and the principle of necessity (fn. 7, supra) which recognizes a defense of justification because of the duress occasioned by extrinsic circumstances. This distinction has been generally recognized by text writers in the field of criminal law.

The court properly rejected the evidence insofar as it was offered to show the defendant's lack of capacity to commit the offense under provisions of Penal Code section 26 (see fn. 3, supra). The statute, since it refers to the option to refuse or accept, contemplates that the threat or menace be accompanied by a direct or implied demand or request that the actor commit the criminal act. In his case there was no offer to show that anyone demanded or requested that the defendant escape. * * *

In People v. Sanders (1927) 82 Cal.App. 778, 256 P. 251, the court approved an instruction reading as follows: " ' * * * a person who commits an act under threats or menaces sufficient to show that he

der certain circumstances. As a defense to escape from a penal institution the defense is necessarily limited to those cases where the remedy to the situation producing the necessity lies beyond the control of the prison authorities and personnel. For example, if a prison caught fire the inmates would probably not be guilty of the crime of escape if they fled to save themselves from the conflagration. On the other hand if an inmate escaped because he felt escape necessary to save himself from treatment at the hands of the imprisoners [sic] authority then this would not be a valid defense, since by being imprisoned it is expected that an inmate should accept the policies, actions, and treatment of the imprisoning authorities as part of his punishment. Your task is to determine first, whether correction of the conditions producing the necessity was within or beyond the control of the imprisoning authorities. If correction of the conditions producing the necessity was beyond the control of the imprisoning authorities then necessity is no defense to any type of escape. If correction of the conditions producing the necessity was beyond the control of the imprisoning and [sic] authorities, as in the case of a fire out of control then necessity may be a defense to an escape accomplished without force or violence. Whether the correction of conditions giving rise to a necessity was or was not within the control of the imprisoning authorities in this is a question of fact for you the jury to determine."

had reasonable cause to believe and did believe that his life would be endangered if he refused, is incapable of committing a crime.

" 'In order for duress or fear produced by threats or menace to be a valid, legal excuse for doing anything, which otherwise would be criminal, the act must have been done under such threats or menaces as show that the life of the person threatened or menaced was in danger, or that there was reasonable cause to believe and actual belief that there was such danger. The danger must not be one of future violence, but of present and immediate violence at the time of the commission of the forbidden act. The danger of death at some future time in the absence of danger of death at the time of the commission of the offense will not excuse. A person who aids and assists in the commission of the crime, or who commits a crime, is not relieved from criminality on account of fears excited by threats or menaces unless the danger be to life, nor unless that danger be present and immediate.' " (82 Cal.App. at p. 785, 256 P. at p. 254. Accord: People v. Villegas, supra, 29 Cal.App.2d 658, 661, 85 P.2d 480, and see Annotation, Criminal Law—Defense—Coercion (1955) 40 A.L.R.2d 908.) If the statutory test of capability were deemed to be applicable to the evidence contained in the offer of proof, it still falls short of establishing that there was a present and immediate danger to defendant's life on the afternoon he secreted himself and left the confines of the prison. It may further be noted that his subsequent testimony reflected that he was given alternative courses of action. The submission to sodomy, abhorrent as it may be, falls short of loss of life. The commission of that offense, in response to the threat to his life, accompanied by requests or directions to submit, would fall within the statutory pattern.

There remains for consideration the question of whether the evidence offered by the defendant should have been received to show justification on the grounds of necessity. The principle has been phrased as follows: "An act which would otherwise be a crime may be excused if the person accused can show that it was done only in order to avoid consequences which could not otherwise be avoided, and which, if they had followed, would have inflicted upon him, or upon others whom he was bound to protect, inevitable and irreparable evil; that no more was done than was reasonably necessary for that purpose; and that the evil inflicted by it was not disproportionate to the evil avoided." (Clark & Marshall, Law of Crimes (6th Ed., Wingersky, 1958) p. 322, quoting from Stephen, Digest of the Criminal Law, art. 32. See also American Law Institute, Model Penal Code (Proposed Official Draft 1962) § 3.02.)

In People v. Whipple (1929) 100 Cal.App. 261, 279 P. 1008, the court stated, "In this state the common law is of no effect so far as the specification of what acts or conduct shall constitute a crime is concerned * * * likewise with excuses or justifications—if no

statutory excuse or justification apply as to the commission of the
particular offense, neither the common law nor the so-called 'unwritten law' may legally supply it." The court noted "if the facts
were as stated by the defendant, he was subjected to brutal treatment
of extreme atrocity." The defendant contended that the brutal and
inhumane treatment he received made his imprisonment intolerable
and justified the escape. The court, nevertheless, upheld the action
of the trial court " * * * in instructing the jury that an excuse for
the escape of defendant, founded upon any alleged unsanitary conditions, or alleged harsh, brutal or inhumane treatment received by him
at the hands of his custodian, would constitute no defense in the law
for the commission of the offense." From the foregoing it would
appear that the principle of justification by necessity is not recognized
under the law of this state, except as it is embodied in the Penal Code.

Nevertheless in *Whipple* the court, as an alternative ground of
decision, did recognize the existence of the principle, and found that it
did not apply to the facts to which the defendant had testified. The
opinion recites, "Although authority exists to the effect that, generally speaking, absolute necessity will excuse the commission of a criminal offense [citations]; so far as the crime of escaping from a jail is
concerned, the authorities are in practical accord in holding that
ordinary adverse circumstances will not present such a condition as
will support a legal excuse for effectng an escape. In 1 Hale, P.C.,
611 (1736), it is said that 'if a prison be fired by accident, and there
be a necessity to break prison to save his life, this excuseth the felony.'
* * * But whatever may be the common law with reference to
escape, where either '*se defendendo*,' misfortune, or 'first offense' is or
may be invoked as a defense to the accusation for which imprisonment
has resulted, so far as the decisions by the courts of sister states are
concerned, neither the unsanitary condition of the jail [citation], fear
of violence from third persons [citation], nor unmerited punishment
at the hands of the custodian [citation], will present a situation which
in the law may be accepted as an excuse for violation of the statute."
(Id., 100 Cal.App. pp. 263–264, 279 P. at 1009.) The court concluded,
"It is manifest that to allow a prisoner to decide whether the conditions justify him in attempting to escape would be destructive of the
necessary discipline which must be maintained in any well-ordered
prison. * * * Generally speaking, when a man has been lawfully
convicted of a crime, and a judgment of imprisonment has been regularly entered against him, it becomes his duty to submit to the
penalty. Unquestionably, it is the duty of the state and of its officers
to accord to the prisoner such safety and humane treatment as may
be consistent with the safekeeping of the prisoner. It is, unfortunately, possible for the conditions of imprisonment to be so unwholesome
as to seriously imperil the health and life of the prisoner by exposure
to infection and disease, and unhappily it is possible for prison guards
to subject prisoners to abuses and serious physical injury unjustified

by any disciplinary need.   However, a prisoner who escapes for any such reason does so at his peril."

Defendant seeks to avoid the effect of this controlling precedent on the theory that *Whipple* recognized that the improper treatment might constitute a justification for escape if the defendant had exhausted all other alternatives.   The court did observe, " * * * the record fails to disclose any attempt on the part of defendant to show that, before escaping, he had, in good faith or at all, endeavored to be relieved by lawful means from any alleged improper irregularities or practices which he claimed were present in the matter of his confinement."   Nevertheless immediately thereafter the court acknowledged, "In a remote mountain camp, far from the sheriff's office, what relief could he obtain by telling his custodian that he wanted to see the sheriff?   If the defense could be admitted at all, it should not be conditioned upon the making of a plainly useless request."   It is, therefore, apparent that the court's decision would not have been altered had *Whipple* shown, as the defendant alleges here, that he had reported his complaints to the authorities and had been denied relief.

In *Whipple*, and as well this case, the reviewing court was struck by the enormity of the pressure to which the defendant was subjected if his allegations were true.   The court observed, " * * * it is with very great reluctance that we admit that, under practically all of the authorities, the foregoing opinion states the established law. * * * The function of the court is to declare the law as it is, and we are not authorized to usurp the place of the Legislature, which has the power to make laws, and the duty to make just laws."

The Legislature has in fact adopted many statutes regulating the treatment of prisoners.   The courts of this state have extended the use of the writ of habeas corpus to protect the fundamental basic rights of prisoners.   The principle of justification by necessity, if applicable, involves a determination that "the harm or evil sought to be avoided by such conduct is greater than that sought to be prevented by the law defining the offense charged."   The compulsion from the harm or evil which the actor seeks to avoid, should be present and impending, as in the case of the threat or menace contemplated by the Penal Code.   This is not a case where the prisoner departed from the limits of his custody while pursued by those who would take his life because he "snitched," or by those who sought by force and violence to have him submit to sodomy.   Moreover, any and all alternative courses should be considered, and it must be determined that the threatened consequences could not otherwise be avoided.   The evil sought to be prevented is not only the escape of the prisoner in question, but also, as noted in *Whipple*, supra, the destruction of the general discipline of the prison.

The balancing of all of these factors leads to the conclusion that the principles set forth in *Whipple* should be adhered to and applied in this case. The prisoner should be denied self-help by escape, and should be relegated to relief through established administrative channels, or, that failing, through the courts. The trial court properly rejected defendant's offer of proof and the instructions which depended upon that evidence.

The judgment is affirmed.

NOTES

1. The same result was reached in State v. Green, 470 S.W.2d 565 (Mo. Sup.Ct.1971) (En Banc) which involved factual allegations remarkably similar to those in *Richards*. A possibly relevant distinction is that Green alleged that he had not only been subjected to multiple homosexual rape on two occasions and had unsuccessfully sought aid from prison authorities by injuring or feigning to injure himself, but that on the day of his escape he was told by five inmates of their plans to so assault him that evening. Does the alleged prevalence of coerced homosexuality in American jails and prisons (State v. Green, supra, at 569 n. 1 (dissenting opinion of Judge Seiler)) suggest the practical wisdom of the judgments in *Richards* and *Green*? In People v. Noble, 18 Mich.App. 300, 170 N.W.2d 916 (1969), Chief Judge Lesinski wrote: "Finally, defendant protests that he only fled the prison work camp in desperation to avoid homosexual attacks by other prisoners. The problem of homosexuality in the prisons is serious and perplexing, and never more so than in a case such as this where such activity is forced upon a young man against his will. However, the answer to the problem is not the judicial sanctioning of escapes. While we have no reason to doubt the sincerity of this defendant, it is easy to visualize a rash of escapes, all rationalized by unverifiable tales of sexual assault. The solution must rather come from some kind of penological reform." Comments on this problem may be found in 45 S.Cal.L.Rev. 1062 (1972) and 6 U.San.Fran.L.Rev. 430 (1972).

2. Missouri has recognized that a homicide may be justified if necessary to prevent sodemy. State v. Robinson, 328 S.W.2d 667, 670–671 (Mo. Sup.Ct.1959). If Green had killed an inmate-assailant to prevent a forcible act of sodomy would it be a denial of due process to refuse to allow him to offer this defense? Is it consistent with due process to deny Richards and Green the opportunity to convince a jury that escape was a necessary and lesser evil than submission to further sexual assault?

3. The principle of justification is, as is illustrated by this section, expressed in a number of well-recognized defenses. In all but one of these criminal liability is sought to be avoided because the defendant's conduct is alleged to have been a justifiable or excusable response to the conduct of another person. The exception is the defense of necessity which involves the defendant's response to the pressures of natural rather than human forces. Although seldom employed it has been involved in some of the most dramatic cases in the annals of Anglo-American jurisprudence. These are cases in which the rules of positive law and their rationales, which normally operate quite satisfactorily, seem inadequate to deal with the harsh conflict between the urge for self preservation and our commitment to the sanctity of life. A brilliant exposition of this philosophical and jurisprudential thicket is Fuller, "The Case of the Speluncean Explorers," 62 Harv.L.Rev. 616 (1949).

Also of interest is Brody, "Son of the Speluncean Explorer," 55 Iowa L.Rev. 1233 (1970) and Glazebrook, "The Necessity Plea in English Criminal Law," 30 Camb.L.J. 88 (1972).

4. In April 1841 an American vessel carrying emigrants struck an iceberg and had to be abandoned. Nine crew members and thirty-two passengers got into the ship's longboat commanded by the first mate; the captain and others were in another boat. Before the two boats separated the captain advised the crew members to obey the mate's orders as though they were his own. After a day a storm arose and the overladen and leaky longboat seemed to the mate destined to sink. He directed the seamen, including one Holmes, to throw overboard all unmarried, adult, male passengers. Sixteen passengers were thus lost. The next day, the boat, still afloat, was sighted by a ship and all aboard were saved. On arrival in port Holmes was tried for manslaughter. What defenses would you offer? What result would be appropriate? United States v. Holmes, 26 F.Cas. 360 (No. 15,383) (C.C.E.D.Pa.1842). Much of counsels' arguments in the case, of the charge and opinion, together with some fascinating facts and questions concerning these events is found in Weinreb, CRIMINAL LAW 199–209 (Foundation Press 1969).

5. In 1884 three English seamen and a cabin boy, the victims of a shipwreck, were adrift in an open boat 1,600 miles from the Cape of Good Hope. After twenty days, the last nine without food, two of the seamen over the dissent of the third killed the weakened boy. The three men fed upon the body and blood of the boy for four days until they were rescued. It was agreed that had they not so fed they would probably not have survived to be rescued. On their return to England the two instigators were tried for murder. What is the proper verdict and, if it is guilty, what is the proper penalty? Regina v. Dudley & Stephens, 14 Q.B.D. 273 (1884). The facts surrounding the prosecution are to be found in Mallin, "In Warm Blood: Some Historical and Procedural Aspects of Regina v. Dudley and Stephens, 34 U.Chi.L.Rev. 387 (1967).

6. The difficulty of balancing evils where human life is placed in both trays of the scale is reduced where qualitative distinctions may be made. Thus, in almost all American anti-abortion statutes an exception was made by legislative judgment for cases in which the abortion was deemed necessary for the preservation of the woman's life. In prosecutions under statutes which did not contain such an exception the necessity plea would presumably have been available as a common law defense. See, e. g., La.Rev. Stat. § 14:87 (1964) which contains no exception but had been interpreted, in conjunction with La.Rev.Stat. § 37:1285(6) (dealing with revocation of physicians' certificate), as excepting abortions done by a physician "for the relief of a woman whose life appears in peril". Rosen v. Louisiana State Board of Medical Examiners, 318 F.Supp. 1217, 1225 (D.C.E.D.La.1970). Where the legislature has made the decision the burden is on the prosecution to plead and prove that the abortion was not necessary, United States v. Vuitch, 402 U.S. 62, 91 S.Ct. 1294, 28 L.Ed.2d 601 (1971). Otherwise, the defense of necessity must be raised by the defendant. Of course, under modern "abortion on request" statutes and the Roe v. Wade decision (reprinted at page 275), at least as to abortions during the first two trimesters, no necessity issue would be involved inasmuch as the legislative and judicial judgment is to assign the embryo or fetus a zero value.

7. If the defendant is involved in an automobile accident resulting in injuries to the driver of the other car and to himself, should the necessity of obtaining medical care for himself be a defense to a charge of failure to stop and render aid? What factors would influence your judgment? The relative severity of the injuries; the presence of negligence by one or the other drivers? What if the defendant's child was injured? Cf. Woods v. State, 121 S.W.2d 604 (Tex.Crim.App.1938). Should it be a defense to a charge of driving while intoxicated that the defendant who had no telephone was in search of medical aid for a severe cut suffered when he fell on his whiskey bottle? That he was taking his wife to the hospital for treatment of injuries suffered when he struck her in a drunken rage? That he was taking her because she had begun labor prematurely? Cf. Butterfield v. State, 317 S.W.2d 943 (Tex.Ct.Crim.App.1958).

8. May an alien charged with illegal presence in the United States after having been deported defend on the grounds that he re-entered only because his American attorney urged him "that he must enter and give a deposition in a civil suit or face 'financial ruin'"? United States v. Palmer, 458 F. 2d 663 (9th Cir. 1972). Should necessity be permitted as a defense for defendants charged with grand larceny arising when a group of unemployed persons in the depths of the great depression seized groceries after the local public relief chairman had refused them an increase in their flour allowance? State v. Moe, 174 Wash. 303, 24 P.2d 638 (1933).

B. DURESS

STATE v. ELLIS

Supreme Court of Oregon, 1962.
232 Or. 70, 374 P.2d 461.

ROSSMAN, Justice. This is an appeal by the defendant, Arlie Day Ellis, from a judgment of the circuit court which adjudged him guilty of the crime of kidnapping and imposed sentence. The defendant was one of three persons indicted for the crime. Since the other participants pleaded guilty, our only concern on this appeal is with Ellis.

* * *

On the evening of February 20, 1961, the defendant Ellis and his co-defendants, Lawrence Morrow and Darlene Wood (an 18 year-old girl) were riding in an automobile operated by Morrow. They stopped at a service station in Salem where Morrow intended to purchase gasoline. When he noticed a state police car pull up directly behind him he drove out of the station without refueling and headed southerly at a high rate of speed. For some reason which is not divulged by the record Morrow preferred to avoid the police. Officer Hedgecoke, the driver of the police car, followed closely behind Morrow

A few miles south of Salem Morrow, realizing that he was almost out of fuel, stopped his car at the side of the road. Officer Hedgecoke stopped behind the Morrow car and ordered its occupants to get out. They complied. After having ordered Morrow and the girl to stand in front of the car, Hedgecoke proceeded to frisk Ellis for weapons. While Hedgecoke was thus occupied the girl produced a pistol and pointed it directly at him telling him to "hold it right there." A few moments later Morrow took Darlene's pistol and trained it on the officer. Then Morrow relieved the officer of his pistol and handed it to the defendant Ellis, who immediately held it on the officer, apparently at Morrow's request. At that juncture Morrow ordered Officer Hedgecoke into the driver's seat of his (Morrow's) car. The defendant Ellis took a seat immediately behind the officer and for a while at least kept a gun pointed at him. Morrow and the girl sat in the front seat with the officer. Officer Hedgecoke, obedient to Morrow's order, put the car into movement. About this time the three alleged kidnappers spoke of driving into California. Whatever may have been their plans as to their ultimate destination the officer drove the car at the command of Morrow, if not that of all three, along the country roads south of Salem until he was forced to slow down by a police barricade some twenty minutes later. Although the officer was ordered by Morrow to circumvent the road block, he stopped the car and, after jumping out, made a dash for cover.

* * *

The second and third assignments of error contest the trial court's denial of both the defendant's motion to dismiss and his later motion for a directed verdict. Both motions were based on the contention that, in taking part in the kidnapping, Ellis acted under duress and compulsion and that therefore the element of intent was lacking. The defendant concludes that in the absence of a showing of intent the state has failed to prove that he is guilty of the crime with which he has been charged.

To sustain his contention the defendant attempts to cast himself in the role of an unsuspecting and unwilling participant in the events which led up to the kidnapping. He claims that he assisted in the actual crime only because he was forced at gunpoint to do so. The following excerpt is taken from page 17 of his brief:

> " * * * When the defendant Ellis stepped out of the
> car in which he was riding as a passenger, the police officer
> ordered him to place his hands upon the top of the car. At
> this point the defendant Wood pulled out a pistol and was
> pointing it both at the officer and at defendant Ellis. The
> defendant Morrow took the police officer's pistol and for a
> time had both guns in his hands pointing at the officer and
> in the direction of defendant Ellis. At this point he handed
> the police's revolver to defendant Ellis * * * and told

him to hold it on the officer while he went back to the police car. The defendant's statement * * * was, 'And I looked, and she was pointing a gun at the officer and at myself, the way it looked.' * * *

"It is submitted to the Court that Ellis was functioning under fear of injury, not knowing what would happen next if he attempted to resist * * *."

In stating the applicable rule in State v. Patterson, 117 Or. 153, 241 P. 977 (1926), the Court quoted from 16 C.J. 91 as follows:

"An act which would otherwise constitute a crime may also be excused on the ground that it was done under compulsion or duress. The compulsion which will excuse a criminal act, however, must be present, imminent, and impending, and of such a nature as to induce a well-grounded apprehension of death or serious bodily harm if the act is not done. A threat of future injury is not enough. Such compulsion must have arisen without the fault of the person who insists upon it as a defense." See also, 22 C.J.S. Criminal Law § 44, p. 135.

Fear of death or of bodily injury is not, of itself, enough. The fear must be a well grounded one. In order to determine whether the fear which defendant claims he experienced was well grounded it is again necessary to take into consideration the entire circumstances.

Both the defendant and Morrow swore that nobody compelled Ellis to accompany Morrow and Wood in Morrow's car on the evening the crime was committed. The testimony reveals that Morrow's attitude as to whether Ellis joined them was one of total indifference. There is nothing in the record which indicates that Ellis was in the car for any reason other than that he chose to be there.

The defendant places great emphasis on the fact that while Morrow was pointing the gun at Officer Hedgecoke he was also pointing in the general direction of the defendant. He concludes that this gunwaving, with the defendant in the general line of fire, engendered in the latter fear sufficient to cause him to assist in the kidnapping although he inwardly rebelled at the idea. The uncertainty and hesitancy of defendant's testimony affords but a weak basis for such a conclusion. We quote from his words:

"The revolver, the gun he had was pointed at me the bigger share of the time. This was going on until Larry [Morrow] took the—Larry took the revolver from the officer. It was pointed toward me—at least it looked like that and I am pretty sure it was pointed in my direction—until he took the revolver from the officer and handed it to me. I am pretty sure, the nozzle first, the way it looked. I don't remember now, and he handed it to me and told me to hold it on the officer."

It is evident that he was not sure that the gun was at any time pointed in his direction.

Nor did Morrow's behaviour at that time or at any time during the course of the evening give the defendant cause to fear that he would resort to physical violence if the defendant did not comply with his requests. To the contrary, it has been shown that Morrow's attitude as to the defendant's participation was one of indifference. The defendant had no reason to believe that that attitude had changed. He had no reason to believe that his life was endangered.

In this connection it is significant that there is not the slightest indication in the record that Ellis at any time or in any way indicated a desire to escape from the dilemma into which he claims he had been thrust. The following is taken from the testimony of Officer Hedgecoke:

"Q Can you tell the jury, Officer, at any time from the time you came upon this trio, did the defendant Ellis ever ask them to stop what they were doing?

"A No, he did not. As a matter of fact, before they ever put me in the car I tried to talk them out of it. I told them they were getting in further trouble, to give up while they could. In fact I tried several times to talk them out of it, but to no avail. Nobody said a word. They were right and that was it.

"Q At any time, from the time you came upon the car and saw the defendant, until you eventually jumped out of the car at the road block, did the defendant Ellis ever ask them to stop and desist from what they were doing?

"A No, he didn't.

*　　*　　*　　*　　*　　*　　*　　*　　*　　*

"Q * * * from the time you came on this car until you left the car, did the defendant Ellis manifest or evidence any desire or wish on his part to leave the car, to get out of the car, to get out of the situation?

"A None whatsoever."

Far from disputing that evidence, the defendant's own testimony corroborates it. With all of his protestations of unwillingness to participate, and of duress and of threats, the defendant never once gave an indication, verbal or otherwise, of this state of mind to anyone until he testified at the trial.

The evidence points only to the conclusion that the defendant acted at all times as a free agent, and that any fears which he may have had as to Morrow's intentions were not well grounded. It indicates that the defendant Ellis, as well as his companions, consciously chose this court of action because they at that time believed it to be the most effective means of evading arrest. We conclude that the jury was entitled to find in the actions of the defendant the element of intent to commit the crime of kidnapping. The motions to dismiss were properly denied.

PROPOSED FEDERAL CRIMINAL CODE (1971)

§ 610. Duress

(1) Affirmative Defense. In a prosecution for any offense it is an affirmative defense that the actor engaged in the proscribed conduct because he was compelled to do so by threat of imminent death or serious bodily injury to himself or another. In a prosecution for an offense which does not constitute a felony, it is an affirmative defense that the actor engaged in the proscribed conduct because he was compelled to do so by force or threat of force. Compulsion within the meaning of this section exists only if the force, threat or circumstances are such as would render a person of reasonable firmness incapable of resisting the pressure.

(2) Defense Precluded. The defense defined in this section is not available to a person who, by voluntarily entering into a criminal enterprise, or otherwise, willfully placed himself in a situation in which it was foreseeable that he would be subjected to duress. The defense is also unavailable if he was negligent in placing himself in such a situation, whenever negligence suffices to establish culpability for the offense charged.

Comment

This section excuses from criminal liability conduct which is engaged in because of certain compelling circumstances which would have caused even a person of reasonable firmness to succumb. Present federal law recognizes the defense only where the apprehension of immediate death or serious injury is created by another person. The section affords a broader protection covering such apprehension regardless of the source of the threat or the identity of the victim. For misdemeanors, any force or threat of force which compels the conduct is sufficient to excuse it. Two factors constrict the availability of what may seem to be a very liberal excuse; the burden of proof is imposed upon the defendant and a jury finding that a person of reasonable firmness would not have been able to resist the pressure is required.

Among the alternatives are: (1) to provide that the offense should not be available in the case of certain exceptionally grave offenses, e. g., murder; and (2) to provide that compulsion should reduce the grade of the offense rather than constitute a full defense.

C. ENTRAPMENT

SHERMAN v. UNITED STATES

United States Supreme Court, 1958.
356 U.S. 369, 78 S.Ct. 819, 2 L.Ed.2d 848.

Mr. Chief Justice WARREN delivered the opinion of the Court.

The issue before us is whether petitioner's conviction should be set aside on the ground that as a matter of law the defense of entrapment was established. Petitioner was convicted under an indictment charging three sales of narcotics in violation of 21 U.S.C. § 174, 21 U.S.C.A. § 174. A previous conviction had been reversed on account of improper instructions as to the issue of entrapment. 2 Cir., 200 F.2d 880. In the second trial, as in the first, petitioner's defense was a claim of entrapment: an agent of the Federal Government induced him to take part in illegal transactions when otherwise he would not have done so.

In late August 1951, Kalchinian, a government informer, first met petitioner at a doctor's office where apparently both were being treated to be cured of narcotics addiction. Several accidental meetings followed, either at the doctor's office or at the pharmacy where both filled their prescriptions from the doctor. From mere greetings, conversation progressed to a discussion of mutual experiences and problems, including their attempts to overcome addiction to narcotics. Finally Kalchinian asked petitioner if he knew of a good source of narcotics. He asked petitioner to supply him with a source because he was not responding to treatment. From the first, petitioner tried to avoid the issue. Not until after a number of repetitions of the request, predicated on Kalchinian's presumed suffering, did petitioner finally acquiesce. Several times thereafter he obtained a quantity of narcotics which he shared with Kalchinian. Each time petitioner told Kalchinian that the total cost of narcotics he obtained was twenty-five dollars and that Kalchinian owed him fifteen dollars. The informer thus bore the cost of his share of the narcotics plus the taxi and other expenses necessary to obtain the drug. After several such sales Kalchinian informed agents of the Bureau of Narcotics that he had another seller for them. On three occasions during November 1951, government agents observed petitioner give narcotics to Kalchinian in return for money supplied by the Government.

At the trial the factual issue was whether the informer had convinced an otherwise unwilling person to commit a criminal act or whether petitioner was already predisposed to commit the act and exhibited only the natural hesitancy of one acquainted with the narcotics trade. The issue of entrapment went to the jury, and a conviction resulted. Petitioner was sentenced to imprisonment for ten years. The Court of Appeals for the Second Circuit affirmed. 240 F.2d 949. We granted certiorari. 353 U.S. 935, 77 S.Ct. 812, 1 L.Ed.2d 758.

In Sorrells v. United States, 287 U.S. 435, 53 S.Ct. 210, 77 L.Ed. 413, this Court firmly recognized the defense of entrapment in the federal courts. The intervening years have in no way detracted from the principles underlying that decision. The function of law enforcement is the prevention of crime and the apprehension of criminals. Manifestly, that function does not include the manufacturing of crime. Criminal activity is such that stealth and strategy are necessary weapons in the arsenal of the police officer. However, "A different question is presented when the criminal design originates with the officials of the government, and they implant in the mind of an innocent person the disposition to commit the alleged offense and induce its commission in order that they may prosecute." 287 U.S. at page 442, 53 S.Ct. at page 212. Then stealth and strategy become as objectionable police methods as the coerced confession and the unlawful search. Congress could not have intended that its statutes were to be enforced by tempting innocent persons into violations.

However, the fact that government agents "merely afford opportunities or facilities for the commission of the offense does not" constitute entrapment. Entrapment occurs only when the criminal conduct was "the product of the *creative* activity" of law-enforcement officials. (Emphasis supplied.) See 287 U.S. at pages 441, 451, 53 S.Ct. at pages 212, 216. To determine whether entrapment has been established, a line must be drawn between the trap for the unwary innocent and the trap for the unwary criminal. The principles by which the courts are to make this determination were outlined in Sorrells. On the one hand, at trial the accused may examine the conduct of the government agent; and on the other hand, the accused will be subjected to an "appropriate and searching inquiry into his own conduct and predisposition" as bearing on his claim of innocence. See 287 U.S. at page 451, 53 S.Ct. at page 216.

We conclude from the evidence that entrapment was established as a matter of law. In so holding, we are not choosing between conflicting witnesses, nor judging credibility. Aside from recalling Kalchinian, who was the Government's witness, the defense called no witnesses. We reach our conclusion from the undisputed testimony of the prosecution's witnesses.

It is patently clear that petitioner was induced by Kalchinian. The informer himself testified that, believing petitioner to be undergoing a cure for narcotics addiction, he nonetheless sought to persuade petitioner to obtain for him a source of narcotics. In Kalchinian's own words we are told of the accidental, yet recurring, meetings, the ensuing conversations concerning mutual experiences in regard to narcotics addiction, and then of Kalchinian's resort to sympathy. One request was not enough, for Kalchinian tells us that additional ones were necessary to overcome, first, petitioner's refusal, then his evasiveness, and then his hesitancy in order to achieve capitulation. Kalchinian not only procured a source of narcotics but apparently also induced petitioner to return to the habit. Finally, assured of a catch, Kalchinian informed the authorities so that they could close the net. The Government cannot disown Kalchinian and insist it is not responsible for his actions. Although he was not being paid, Kalchinian was an active government informer who had but recently been the instigator of at least two other prosecutions.[2] Undoubtedly the impetus for such achievements was the fact that in 1951 Kalchinian was himself under criminal charges for illegally selling narcotics and had not yet been sentenced.[3] It makes no difference that the sales for which petitioner was convicted occurred after a series of sales. They were not independent acts subsequent to the inducement but part of a course of conduct which was the product of the inducement. In his testimony the federal agent in charge of the case admitted that he never bothered to question Kalchinian about the way he had made contact with petitioner. The Government cannot make such use of an informer and then claim disassociation through ignorance.

The Government sought to overcome the defense of entrapment by claiming that petitioner evinced a "ready complaisance" to accede to Kalchinian's request. Aside from a record of past convictions, which we discuss in the following paragraph, the Government's case is unsupported. There is no evidence that petitioner himself was in the trade. When his apartment was searched after arrest, no narcotics were found. There is no significant evidence that petitioner

---

2. "Q. And it was your [Kalchinian's] job, was it not, while you were working with these agents to go out and try and induce somebody to sell you narcotics, isn't that true?

* * * * *

"A. No, it wasn't my job at all to do anything of the kind.
"Q. Do you remember this question [asked at the first trial]—. . .
'Q. And it was your job while working with these agents to go out and try and induce a person to sell narcotics to you, isn't that correct? A. I would say yes to that.' Do you remember that?
"A. If that is what I said, let it stand just that way.

* * * * *

"Q. So when you testify now that it was not your job you are not telling the truth?

"A. I mean by job that nobody hired me for that. That is what I inferred, otherwise I meant the same thing in my answer to your question." R. 100.

3. "Q. But you had made a promise, an agreement, though, to cooperate with the Federal Bureau of Narcotics before you received a suspended sentence from the court?
"A. [Kalchinian]. I had promised to cooperate in 1951.
"Q. And that was before your sentence?
"A. Yes, that was before my sentence." R. 99.

Kalchinian received a suspended sentence in 1952 after a statement by the United States Attorney to the Judge that he had been cooperative with the Government. R. 89, 98.

even made a profit on any sale to Kalchinian. The Government's characterization of petitioner's hesitancy to Kalchinian's request as the natural wariness of the criminal cannot fill the evidentiary void.

The Government's additional evidence in the second trial to show that petitioner was ready and willing to sell narcotics should the opportunity present itself was petitioner's record of two past narcotics convictions. In 1942 petitioner was convicted of illegally selling narcotics; in 1946 he was convicted of illegally possessing them. However, a nine-year-old sales conviction and a five-year-old possession conviction are insufficient to prove petitioner had a readiness to sell narcotics at the time Kalchinian approached him, particularly when we must assume from the record he was trying to overcome the narcotics habit at the time.

The case at bar illustrates an evil which the defense of entrapment is designed to overcome. The government informer entices someone attempting to avoid narcotics not only into carrying out an illegal sale but also into returning to the habit of use. Selecting the proper time, the informer then tells the government agent. The set-up is accepted by the agent without even a question as to the manner in which the informer encountered the seller. Thus the Government plays on the weaknesses of an innocent party and beguiles him into committing crimes which he otherwise would not have attempted. Law enforcement does not require methods such as this.

It has been suggested that in overturning this conviction we should reassess the doctrine of entrapment according to principles announced in the separate opinion of Mr. Justice Roberts in Sorrells v. United States, 287 U.S. 435, 453, 53 S.Ct. 210, 217, 77 L.Ed. 413. To do so would be to decide the case on grounds rejected by the majority in Sorrells and, so far as the record shows, not raised here or below by the parties before us. We do not ordinarily decide issues not presented by the parties and there is good reason not to vary that practice in this case.

At least two important issues of law enforcement and trial procedure would have to be decided without the benefit of argument by the parties, one party being the Government. Mr. Justice Roberts asserted that although the defendant could claim that the Government had induced him to commit the crime, the Government could not reply by showing that the defendant's criminal conduct was due to his own readiness and not to the persuasion of government agents. The handicap thus placed on the prosecution is obvious.[7] Furthermore, it was the position of Mr. Justice Roberts that the factual issue of entrapment—now limited to the question of what the govern-

7. In the first appeal of this case Judge Learned Hand stated: "Indeed, it would seem probable that, if there were no reply [to the claim of inducement], it would be impossible ever to secure convictions of any offences which consist of transactions that are carried on in secret." United States v. Sherman, 2 Cir., 200 F.2d 880, 882.

ment agents did—should be decided by the judge, not the jury. Not only was this rejected by the Court in Sorrells, but where the issue has been presented to them, the Courts of Appeals have since Sorrells unanimously concluded that unless it can be decided as a matter of law, the issue of whether a defendant has been entrapped is for the jury as part of its function of determining the guilt or innocence of the accused.

To dispose of this case on the ground suggested would entail both overruling a leading decision of this Court and brushing aside the possibility that we would be creating more problems than we would supposedly be solving.

The judgment of the Court of Appeals is reversed and the case is remanded to the District Court with instructions to dismiss the indictment.

Reversed and remanded.

Mr. Justice FRANKFURTER, whom Mr. Justice DOUGLAS, Mr. Justice HARLAN, and Mr. Justice BRENNAN join, concurring in the result.

Although agreeing with the Court that the undisputed facts show entrapment as a matter of law, I reach this result by a route different from the Court's.

The first case in which a federal court clearly recognized and sustained a claim of entrapment by government officers as a defense to an indictment was, apparently, Woo Wai v. United States, 9 Cir., 223 F. 412. Yet the basis of this defense, affording guidance for its application in particular circumstances, is as much in doubt today as it was when the defense was first recognized over forty years ago, although entrapment has been the decisive issue in many prosecutions. The lower courts have continued gropingly to express the feeling of outrage at conduct of law enforcers that brought recognition of the defense in the first instance, but without the formulated basis in reason that it is the first duty of courts to construct for justifying and guiding emotion and instinct.

Today's opinion does not promote this judicial desideratum, and fails to give the doctrine of entrapment the solid foundation that the decisions of the lower courts and criticism of learned writers have clearly shown is needed. Instead it accepts without re-examination the theory espoused in Sorrells v. United States, 287 U.S. 435, 53 S.Ct. 210, 77 L.Ed. 413, over strong protest by Mr. Justice Roberts, speaking for Brandeis and Stone, JJ., as well as himself. The fact that since the Sorrells case the lower courts have either ignored its theory and continued to rest decision on the narrow facts of each case, or have failed after penetrating effort to define a satisfactory generalization, see, e. g., United States v. Becker, 2 Cir., 62 F.2d 1007 (L. Hand, J.), is proof that the prevailing theory of the Sorrells case ought not to be deemed the last word. In a matter of this kind the Court should not rest on the first attempt at an explanation for what sound instinct counsels. It should not forego re-examination to achieve clarity of thought, because confused and inadequate analysis is too apt gradually to lead to a course of decisions that diverges from the true ends to be pursued.

It is surely sheer fiction to suggest that a conviction cannot be had when a defendant has been entrapped by government officers or informers because "Congress could not have intended that its statutes were to be enforced by tempting innocent persons into violations." In these cases raising claims of entrapment, the only legislative intention that can with any show of reason be extracted from the statute is the intention to make criminal precisely the conduct in which the defendant has engaged. That conduct includes all the elements necessary to constitute criminality. Without compulsion and "knowingly," where that is requisite, the defendant has violated the statutory command. If he is to be relieved from the usual punitive consequences, it is on no account because he is innocent of the offense described. In these circumstances, conduct is not less criminal because the result of temptation, whether the tempter is a private person or a government agent or informer.

The courts refuse to convict an entrapped defendant, not because his conduct falls outside the proscription of the statute, but because, even if his guilt be admitted, the methods employed on behalf of the Government to bring about conviction cannot be countenanced. As Mr. Justice Holmes said in Olmstead v. United States, 277 U.S. 438, 470, 48 S.Ct. 564, 575, 72 L.Ed. 944 (dissenting), in another connection, "It is desirable that criminals should be detected, and to that end that all available evidence should be used. It also is desirable that the government should not itself foster and pay for other crimes, when they are the means by which the evidence is to be obtained. * * * [F]or my part I think it a less evil that some criminals should escape than that the government should play an ignoble part." Insofar as they are used as instrumentalites in the administration of criminal justice, the federal courts have an obligation to set their face against enforcement of the law by lawless means or means that violate rationally vindicated standards of justice, and to refuse to sustain such methods by effectuating them. They do this in the exercise of a recognized jurisdiction to formulate and apply "proper standards for the enforcement of the federal criminal law in the federal courts," McNabb v. United States, 318 U.S. 332, 341, 63 S.Ct. 608, 613, 87 L.Ed. 819, an obligation that goes beyond the conviction of the particular defendant before the court. Public confidence in the fair and honorable administration of justice, upon which ultimately depends the rule of law, is the transcending value at stake.

The formulation of these standards does not in any way conflict with the statute the defendant has violated, or involve the initiation of a judicial policy disregarding or qualifying that framed by Congress. A false choice is put when it is said that either the defendant's conduct does not fall within the statute or he must be convicted. The statute is wholly directed to defining and prohibiting the substantive offense concerned and expresses no purpose, either permissive or prohibitory, regarding the police conduct that will be tolerated in the detection of crime. A statute prohibiting the sale of narcotics is as silent on the question of entrapment as it is on the admissibility of illegally obtained evidence. It is enacted, however, on the basis of certain presuppositions concerning the established legal order and the role of the courts within that system in formulating standards for the administration of criminal justice when Congress itself has not specifically legislated to that end. Specific statutes are to be fitted into an antecedent legal system.

It might be thought that it is largely an academic question whether the court's finding a bar to conviction derives from the statute or from a supervisory jurisdiction over the administration of criminal justice; under either theory substantially the same considerations will determine whether the defense of entrapment is sustained. But to look to a statute for guidance in the application of a policy not remotely within the contemplation of Congress at the time of its enactment is to distort analysis. It is to run the risk, furthermore, that the court will shirk the responsibility that is necessarily in its keeping, if Congress is truly silent, to accommodate the dangers of overzealous law enforcement and civilized methods adequate to counter the ingenuity of modern criminals. The reasons that actually underlie the defense of entrapment can too easily be lost sight of in the pursuit of a wholly fictitious congressional intent.

The crucial question, not easy of answer, to which the court must direct itself is whether the police conduct revealed in the particular case falls below standards, to which common feelings respond, for the proper use of governmental power. For answer it is wholly irrelevant to ask if the "intention" to commit the crime originated with the defendant or government officers, or if the criminal conduct was the product of "the creative activity" of law-enforcement officials. Yet in the present case the Court repeats and purports to apply these unrevealing tests. Of course in every case of this kind the intention that the particular crime be committed originates with the police, and without their inducement the crime would not have occurred. But it is perfectly clear from such decisions as the decoy letter cases in this Court, e. g., Grimm v. United States, 156 U.S. 604, 15 S.Ct. 470, 39 L.Ed. 550, where the police in effect simply furnished the opportunity for the commission of the crime, that this is not enough to enable the defendant to escape conviction.

The intention referred to, therefore, must be a general intention or predisposition to commit, whenever the opportunity should arise, crimes of the kind solicited, and in proof of such a predisposition evidence has often been admitted to show the defendant's reputation, criminal activities, and prior disposition. The danger of prejudice in such a situation, particularly if the issue of entrapment must be submitted to the jury and disposed of by a general verdict of guilty or innocent, is evident. The defendant must either forego the claim of entrapment or run the substantial risk that, in spite of instructions, the jury will allow a criminal record or bad reputation to weigh in its determination of guilt of the specific offense of which he stands charged. Furthermore, a test that looks to the character and predisposition of the defendant rather than the conduct of the police loses sight of the underlying reason for the defense of entrapment. No matter what the defendant's past record and present inclinations to criminality, or the depths to which he has sunk in the estimation of society, certain police conduct to ensnare him into further crime is not to be tolerated by an advanced society. And in the present case it is clear that the Court in fact reverses the conviction because of the conduct of the informer Kalchinian, and not because the Government has failed to draw a convincing picture of petitioner's past criminal conduct. Permissible police activity does not vary according to the particular defendant concerned; surely if two suspects have been solicited at the same time in the same manner, one should not go to jail simply because he has been convicted before and is said to have a criminal disposition. No more does it vary according to the suspicions, reasonable or unreasonable, of the police concerning the defendant's activities. Appeals to sympathy, friendship, the possibility of exorbitant gain, and so forth, can no more be tolerated when directed against a past offender than against an ordinary law-abiding citizen. A contrary view runs afoul of fundamental principles of equality under law, and would espouse the notion that when dealing with the criminal classes anything goes. The possibility that no matter what his past crimes and general disposition the defendant might not have committed the particular crime unless confronted with inordinate inducements, must not be ignored. Past crimes do not forever outlaw the criminal and open him to police practices, aimed at securing his repeated conviction, from which the ordinary citizen is protected. The whole ameliorative hopes of modern penology and prison administration strongly counsel against such a view.

This does not mean that the police may not act so as to detect those engaged in criminal conduct and ready and willing to commit further crimes should the occasion arise. Such indeed is their obligation. It does mean that in holding out inducements they should act in such a manner as is likely to induce to the commission of crime only these persons and not others who would normally avoid crime and through self-struggle resist ordinary temptations. This test shifts attention from the record and predisposition of the particular defendant to the conduct of the police and the likelihood, objectively considered, that it would entrap only those ready and willing to commit crime. It is as objective a test as the subject matter permits, and will give guidance in regulating police conduct that is lacking when the reasonableness of police suspicions must be judged or the criminal disposition of the defendant retrospectively appraised. It draws directly on the fundamental intuition that led in the first instance to the outlawing of "entrapment" as a prosecutorial instrument. The power of government is abused and directed to an end for which it was not constituted when employed to promote rather than detect crime and to bring about the downfall of those who left to themselves, might well have obeyed the law. Human nature is weak enough and sufficiently beset by temptations without government adding to them and generating crime.

What police conduct is to be condemned, because likely to induce those not otherwise ready and willing to commit crime, must be picked out from case to case as new situations arise involving different crimes and new methods of detection. The Sorrells case involved persistent solicitation in the face of obvious reluctance, and appeals to sentiments aroused by reminiscences of experiences as companions in arms in the World War. Particularly reprehensible in the present case was the use of repeated requests to overcome petitioner's hesitancy, coupled with appeals to sympathy based on mutual experiences with narcotics addiction. Evidence of the setting in which the inducement took place is of course highly relevant in judging its likely effect, and the court should also consider the nature of the crime involved, its secrecy and difficulty of detection, and the manner in which the particular criminal business is usually carried on.

As Mr. Justice Roberts convincingly urged in the Sorrells case, such a judgment, aimed at blocking off areas of impermissible police conduct, is appropriate for the court and not the jury. "The protection of its own functions and the preservation of the purity of its own temple belongs only to the court. It is the province of the court and of the court alone to protect itself and the government from such prostitution of the criminal law. The violation of the principles of justice by the entrapment of the unwary into crime should be dealt with by the court no matter by whom or at what stage of the proceedings the facts are brought to its attention." 287 U.S. at page 457, 53 S.Ct. at page 218 (separate opinion). Equally important is the consideration that a jury verdict, although it may settle the issue of entrapment in the particular case, cannot give significant guidance for official conduct for the future. Only the court, through the gradual evolution of explicit standards in accumulated precedents, can do this with the degree of certainty that the wise administration of criminal justice demands.

GROSSMAN v. STATE

Supreme Court of Alaska, 1969.
457 P.2d 226.

CONNOR, Justice. This appeal raises the question of whether the evidence before the court below required a finding of entrapment as a matter of law.

Appellant was indicted for selling morphine to an undercover agent of the Alaska State Police. She pleaded not guilty, was tried by a jury, and was convicted and sentenced upon a verdict of guilty. At the close of the prosecution's case, her counsel moved for a judgment of acquittal on the ground that the evidence required a finding of entrapment as a matter of law. The motion was denied and the issue of entrapment was submitted to the jury, which found against appellant. * * *

It is plain enough that the underlying basis of entrapment is found in public policy, as discerned and announced by the courts. As Judge Learned Hand perceptively observed in United States v. Becker, 62 F.2d 1007, 1009 (2d Cir. 1933),

"The whole doctrine derives from a spontaneous moral revulsion against using the powers of government to beguile innocent, though ductile, persons into lapses which they might otherwise resist."

* * *

[The court's review of the "subjective" test of the *Sorrells* and *Sherman* majority and the "objective" test expounded by Mr. Justice Roberts and Mr. Justice Frankfurter is omitted.]

The scholarly examinations of the defense of entrapment have * * * revealed the inadequacies of the subjective test.[8] To speak of entrapment as an implied statutory condition, and then to focus inquiry on the origin of intent, the implantation of criminal design, and the predisposition of the defendant does not make much sense. If entrapment is a substantive condition of guilt, then it ought to apply when private persons induce the commission of an offense. But no court has ever been willing to make such an application of the

8. Cowen, The Entrapment Doctrine in the Federal Courts, and Some State Court Comparisons, 49 Northwestern L.Rev. 447 (1959); Donnelly, Judicial Control of Informants, Spies, Stool Pigeons, and Agent Provocateurs, 60 Yale L.J. 1091 (1951); Mikkell, The Doctrine of Entrapment in the Federal Courts, 90 U.Pa.L.Rev. 245 (1942); Senneff, Entrapment in the Federal Courts, 1 U.S.F.L.Rev. 177 (1966); Williams, The Defense of Entrapment and Related Problems in Criminal Prosecution, 28 Fordham L.Rev. 399 (1959); Comment, 33 N.Y.U.L.Rev. 1033 (1958). The American Law Institute in its proposed Model Penal Code has recommended that an objective test should be employed. Model Penal Code § 2.13 (Proposed Official Draft, 1962).

Sorrells doctrine. An external standard, if it can be achieved, is certainly preferable to a doctrine founded in theoretical riddles.

* * *

We feel that the proper solution is the objective test which focuses the determination upon the particular conduct of the police in the case presented. Inducements should be limited to those measures which, objectively considered, are likely to provoke to the commission of crime only those persons, and not others, who are ready and willing to commit a criminal offense.

The objective test can be stated as follows: unlawful entrapment occurs when a public law enforcement official, or a person working in cooperation with him, in order to obtain evidence of the commission of an offense, induces another person to commit such an offense by persuasion or inducement which would be effective to persuade an average person, other than one who is ready and willing, to commit such an offense. Conversely, instigations which would induce only a person engaged in an habitual course of unlawful conduct for gain or profit do not constitute entrapment.[9]

Examples of what might constitute prohibited activity, depending upon an evaluation of the facts in each case, are extreme pleas of desperate illness, appeals based primarily on sympathy, pity, or close personal friendship, and offers of inordinate sums of money. While the line between what is permitted and not must be drawn somewhat as a matter of degree, this is no different from many determinations which the courts must make in the cases before them. For example, an officer should be able to offer money in reasonable amounts at a prevailing price level in an unlawful traffic. But offers of profit which are grossly disproportionate to what is reasonably expectable in that traffic should not be permitted when those offers would have the effect of overwhelming the self-control of a normal person.

In applying the objective test we do not mean that the course of conduct between the officer and the defendant should be ignored. The transactions leading up to the offense, the interaction between the officer and the defendant, and the defendant's response to the inducements of the officer are all to be considered in judging what the effect of the officer's conduct would be on a normal person.

In short, we do not intend that entrapment should become a ready escape hatch for those who are engaged in a course of criminal enter-

9. DeFeo, Entrapment As A Defense To Criminal Responsibility: Its History, Theory and Application, 1 U.S.F.L.Rev. 243 (1967), at 275, criticizes the objective test because he believes that it permits only police activity which would tempt a chronic violator, but would require that a number of situational offenders be set free who commit consensual offenses. We do not intend such a result, nor do we state the test of entrapment in those terms.

prise. But, under standards of civilized justice, there must be some control on the kind of police conduct which can be permitted in the manufacture of crime.

* * *

We now turn to the case before us.

At her trial appellant presented no evidence on her own behalf. The state's evidence consisted largely of the testimony of Joseph P. Turner about the events leading up to the sale of morphine and the circumstances of the sale itself. His testimony was along the following lines:

Officer Turner was assigned to the Anchorage area during November of 1967 to investigate and report on criminal activities in Anchorage. On December 2, 1967, at about 5:30 a. m., he went to the Woods' Barbecue, an establishment run by the appellant. On that occasion he had a conversation with her during which she said that she was using pills to stay awake and that if he needed any she could get him some. He declined this offer but said that he could use some "pot." They discussed the price and he ordered a matchbox of it. He returned at about 10:30 a. m. that day, at which time she said she would get the marijuana. Subsequently she did get the marijuana for him.

Officer Turner throughout his dealings with the appellant made it his policy to gain her confidence and attempt to befriend her. He saw her almost daily from the date of their first meeting until December 18, 1967, the date of the offense charged. On one occasion, the night of December 4, he took appellant to various bars in the Anchorage area. At another time he helped her with her grocery shopping. His policy of friendship toward appellant was so successful that she asked Turner to help her run the bar on December 8. The officer testified to other dealings with the appellant leading up to the sale of morphine. On December 3, while at the Woods' Barbecue, he asked the appellant about the possibilities of getting "dexies" (amphetamines). She said that she would take care of it for him, and he ordered about a dozen. On December 8 he delivered some pills for her and collected payment from the recipient for her. In the early morning of December 12 she told him that when the "squares" left the premises of the Woods' Barbecue there would be a party. Apparently he did not stay for the party. On December 16 appellant asked Turner to watch the bar for her while she took someone home. She said that if anyone came by for pills while she was gone to tell them she would have some on Monday.

On December 13 officer Turner again went to the bar, and on this occasion he asked appellant about the possibility of getting some "hard stuff" for a friend in Fairbanks who needed a new contact. By "hard stuff" the officer said that he meant heroin or morphine. Officer Turner stated that between the time of this initial request and the sale, he repeated his request a number of times. He specifically mentioned a telephone call he made to the appellant on December 15 when he asked if she had received the morphine yet. On December 18 she told the officer that she had received the shipment. She then took him to her trailer and sold him part of the shipment amounting to ten "fixes." She told him also that she had given some of the shipment to a friend to dispose of on her behalf. It was for the sale to officer Turner that appellant was arrested and prosecuted.

Although, in the present case, Turner dated the defendant on one occasion, there is no evidence of a romantic relationship between them. Nor does it appear that the brief friendship between them was close. After appellant evinced an interest in supplying marijuana and dexedrine pills to Turner, he was justified in continuing his contacts with her and in asking to purchase morphine.

Under the objective test we have announced today, the issue of entrapment is to be ruled on by the trial court. Therefore, it was error for the court below to submit the question to the jury. Although on the face of the record appellant's claim seems rather weak, we feel that the trial judge who heard and saw the witness would be better able to weigh the evidence. Accordingly, the case is remanded to the superior court for determination of the issue of entrapment by the trial judge. If the trial judge should conclude, as the jury was allowed to conclude, that the claim of entrapment was not sustained, the conviction shall stand. If the trial judge reaches a different result, the indictment should be dismissed.

Reversed and remanded.

NOTES

1. Where the origin-of-intent test enunciated by the majority in *Sherman* is employed, the defendant's predisposition becomes a crucial issue. Evidence, ordinarily inadmissible, such as the defendant's criminal record or even testimony as to alleged criminal conduct for which the defendant was never prosecuted, will be permitted on this point. For examples of judicial efforts to limit the use of such evidence see United States v. Johnston, 426 F.2d 112 (7th Cir. 1970) commented upon in 71 Columb.L.Rev. 157 (1971), and Hansford v. United States, 112 U.S.App.D.C. 359, 303 F.2d 219 (1962).

2. If a court determines as a matter of law that the defendant was entrapped into the sale of two marijuana cigarettes may he nevertheless be tried and convicted for possession? Does your conclusion turn on whether the jurisdiction in question follows the view of the majority or of the minority in *Sherman*? People v. Sinclair, 194 N.W.2d 878, 887–891 (Mich.Sup. Ct.1972).

3. Should the issue of entrapment be decided by the judge or the jury? Consider the views of Chief Justice Traynor dissenting in People v. Moran, 1 Cal.3d 755, 83 Cal.Rptr. 411, 463 P.2d 763 (1970):

[S]ubmission of the issue to the jury cannot be justified on the ground that it goes to the defendant's guilt or innocence. The crucial issue is whether the court or the jury can best achieve the purpose of the defense: the deterrence of impermissible police conduct. A jury verdict of guilty or not guilty tells the police nothing about the jury's evaluation of the police conduct. A verdict of guilty may mean that the jury did not believe the defendant's testimony that would have established entrapment. It may also mean that the jury did not believe that the conduct created a substantial risk of inducing one not ready to commit the offense into doing so. Since the defendant may assert entrapment and also deny that he committed the crime a "not guilty" verdict may also shed no light on the jury's assessment of police conduct. Moreover, even when the verdict settles the issue of entrapment in the particular case, it "cannot give significant guidance for official conduct for the future. Only the court, through the gradual evolution of explicit standards in accumulated precedents, can do this with the degree of certainty that wise administration of criminal justice demands." (Sherman v. United States, supra, 356 U.S. 369, 385, 78 S.Ct. 819, 827. (Frankfurter, J., concurring). In other areas involving police conduct, we have recognized the paramount importance of committing the assessment of such conduct to the court. Thus, the trial court, subject to appropriate appellate review, determines the admissibility of confessions and other evidence claimed to have been illegally obtained. It should also determine the issue of entrapment.

UNITED STATES v. BRAVER

United States Court of Appeals for the Second Circuit, 1971.
450 F.2d 799.

FEINBERG, Circuit Judge. Irving Braver and Morton Lehrer appeal from a judgment of conviction, entered after a trial in the United States District Court for the Southern District of New York before Lloyd F. MacMahon, J., and a jury. Both were convicted on two counts, bribing a government official in violation of 18 U.S.C.A. § 201(b), and conspiracy to bribe in violation of 18 U.S.C.A. § 371. Each was sentenced on the conspiracy count to six months imprisonment and a $10,000 fine and on the substantive count to a concurrent six month sentence and a $20,000 fine. Appellants are presently at liberty on their own recognizance. On appeal, they challenge the charge given by the trial judge on entrapment * * *.

The facts of this case, as could have been found by the jury, arose from the activities of Harold Wenig, an undercover agent of the Internal Revenue Service (IRS). At the time in question, Wenig had posed as a corruptible IRS inspector. In June 1967, Wenig told an IRS agent, Sidney Romanoff,[3] that the IRS was investigating the de-

---

3. Before the June 1967 meeting, Romanoff had paid Wenig $200 for information concerning an IRS investigation of Romanoff. In 1968, he resigned from the IRS and subsequently pleaded guilty to an indictment charging conspiracy to bribe. At the time of trial, Romanoff had not yet been sentenced.

fendants' accounting firm and inquired whether Romanoff knew Braver or Lehrer. Romanoff, who had "moonlighted" for the firm, said that he did. Wenig then informed him that information concerning the investigation of the firm would be available for a price. During the early part of July, Romanoff relayed the message to the defendants and, after some hesitation, Braver indicated that they would purchase the information for $500 although they were not sure it would have any value to them.

On July 13, Romanoff met Wenig in Manhattan where Romanoff copied information pertaining to the investigation of defendants' firm that Wenig read to him. Romanoff paid Wenig $500 in cash for this information and explained that he was advancing the money for the defendants. Wenig then offered to sell for $1,000 additional information about proposed grand jury questions. Immediately after this meeting, Romanoff delivered the information to Lehrer and asked if the defendants would be interested in the grand jury questions. Lehrer said that he would think about it. Approximately one week later Braver visited Romanoff at his home and reimbursed him for the $500 paid to Wenig.

On July 20, Wenig informed Romanoff that he would be interviewing clients of defendants' firm and Romanoff requested the list of the taxpayers. When questioned by Romanoff, Lehrer expressed no interest in the grand jury questions but told Romanoff that, as part of the $500 already paid, he and Braver were entitled to the list of the taxpayers. Romanoff again requested the list as a personal favor from Wenig and, on August 4, Wenig delivered it. A few days later Romanoff gave the list to Braver. There was no further exchange of money and the defendants never met Wenig.

I

Appellants' central argument concerns the district court's charge on entrapment. That charge, quoted in the margin,[4] bifurcated the defense of entrapment into two elements, inducement and propensity. The judge instructed the jury that the defendants had the burden of proving inducement by a fair preponderance of the evidence and that

4. The question of entrapment involves two issues. The first issue is whether the defendant was led or induced to commit the crime by anyone acting for the government. That is, did the government initiate the criminal transaction? On this issue the defendant has the burden of proof. He does not have to prove it beyond a reasonable doubt but he must prove it by a fair preponderance of the evidence. That is, he must satisfy you that it is more likely than not that the government initiated the criminal transaction involved in this case. If you do not find such inducement then there was no entrapment, but if you do find such inducement then you must consider the second issue.

The second issue is whether the defendant was ready and willing to commit the crime without persuasion. This is sometimes expressed as an issue of whether he had a propensity to commit the crime. On this issue the government has the burden of proof and it must prove it beyond a reasonable doubt. * * *

the Government had to prove propensity beyond a reasonable doubt. * * * Essentially, appellants argue that dividing entrapment into two issues and placing the burden on the defendant to prove inducement is error because it conflicts with the constitutionally mandated presumption of innocence and because it is unduly prejudicial.

* * *

As to the former, the claim is that placing upon the defendant the burden of proving inducement denies him due process. In re Winship, 397 U.S. 358, 364, 90 S.Ct. 1068, 1073, 25 L.Ed.2d 368 (1970), relied upon by appellants, held that:

> [T]he Due Process Clause protects the accused against conviction except upon proof beyond a reasonable doubt of every fact necessary to constitute the crime with which he is charged.

Without discussing the various rationales for the entrapment defense, it is enough to say that the law of this circuit is that the defense "does not negative any of the essential elements of the crime." United States v. Greenberg, 444 F.2d 369, 372 (2d Cir. 1971).

As to the alleged confusion created by the *Sherman* instructions, appellants have a number of arguments. First, they claim that a lay jury cannot really distinguish in the same case between proof beyond a reasonable doubt and proof by a preponderance of the evidence. Second, they say that the central issue in entrapment cases is "whether the crime was the product of government activity—or the response of a ready and willing individual merely awaiting an opportunity to commit the crime" and that considering "the initiation of the criminal activity apart from the defendants' willingness to engage" in it is "an unrealistic separation." Finally, they claim that on the facts of this case, where the evidence of government initiation was both sufficient under United States v. Riley, 363 F.2d 955 (2d Cir. 1966), and uncontradicted, submitting the issue to the jury was error because this gave the jury the impression that the evidence before it was insufficient to prove inducement.

Taking the last of these arguments first, we do not agree that because the evidence was so overwhelmingly against the Government on the issue of inducement, it was prejudicial error to submit the issue to the jury at all. The basic premise that the submission itself indicated to the jury that there was not enough evidence to prove inducement is logically unsound. One might argue with equal force that submission to the jury implies just the opposite. Moreover, no clear request was made to the judge to withdraw the issue from jury consideration, nor can we conceive that the jury on this record found that defendants had not established initiation. While the judge might properly have told the jury that government initiation of the crime had been proved, his failure to do so was not reversible error.

The claim that the true focus should be on a single issue is more substantial. This was the emphasis of the First Circuit in Kadis v. United States, 373 F.2d 370, at 373–374 (1967), where the court said:

> We will no longer bifurcate entrapment into sub-issues of inducement and predisposition. * * * [W]e will look, singly, at the ultimate question of entrapment. If the defendant shows, through government witnesses or otherwise, some indication that a government agent corrupted him, the burden of disproving entrapment will be on the government; but such a showing is not made simply by evidence of a solicitation. There must be some evidence tending to show unreadiness.

However, as this formulation indicates, sub-issues still remain. Evidence of "solicitation" is not enough; there must also be evidence "tending to show unreadiness." Presumably evidence of the latter without the former would also not suffice for a defendant. We realize that under the *Kadis* opinion the analysis of these sub-issues apparently remains only for the court, with the jury getting a general instruction to decide whether the Government had met its burden "to show that the defendant was not in fact corrupted by the government agent." [10] 373 F.2d at 374. But, as will be seen below, we think that an alternative formulation will provide enough of the unitary emphasis without departing too far from our precedents.

Finally, we do not agree that there is prejudicial error because the jury must use two different tests of burden of proof. Issues upon which the Government's burden of proof is by a preponderance of evidence only or on which the defendant has the burden of proof are not unknown in the criminal law. If defendants' proposition were sound, there could be no valid convictions in such instances. Indeed, the specific suggestion of § 702 of the Proposed Federal Criminal Code, is to place upon the defendant the burden of proof as to entrapment by a preponderance of the evidence, and the notes to the section indicate the possibility of jury trial of the issue. While nothing in this opinion should be viewed as approval of that proposal, it at least suggests that one scholarly group does not regard the use of two burdens of proof in the same criminal case as hopelessly confusing to a jury.

---

10. It should be noted that this is still a subjective test of entrapment because it focuses not only on the governmental activities but also on the state of mind of the accused. An objective test, focusing solely on the governmental activities and based primarily on the concurring opinions of Justice Roberts in Sorrells * * * and of Justice Frankfurter in Sherman * * * has been suggested in the Proposed Federal Criminal Code. Under that proposal, objective entrapment would be an affirmative defense with the defendant having the burden of proof by a preponderance of the evidence, but proof of prior criminal record to show propensity would apparently be eliminated. Proposed Federal Criminal Code § 702; 1 Working Papers 303–28. Whatever the merits of this approach, we have not been asked to reconsider our use of a subjective test.

This does not mean that we are averse to changing the entrapment charge if there are good reasons for doing so. In * * * [United States v. Berger, 433 F.2d 680 (2d Cir. 1970), cert. denied, 401 U.S. 962, 91 S.Ct. 970, 28 L.Ed.2d 246 (1971)] we noted approval of a charge that defendant had to:

> [A]dduce some evidence that a government agent by initiating the illegal conduct himself induced the defendant to commit the offense. If you find that the defendant * * * has adduced such evidence then the government must prove beyond a reasonable doubt that the inducement was not the cause of the crime, that is, that the defendant * * * was ready and willing to commit the offense.

* * * [W]e suggest that it would be preferable for the district courts of this circuit to use an entrapment charge that does not give to the jury two ultimate factual issues to decide on two different burdens of persuasion imposed upon two different parties. * * * The language quoted from United States v. Berger, supra, would obviously be appropriate.

* * *

The convictions are affirmed.

NOTES

1. N.Y.Penal Law § 40.05 provides:

> "In any prosecution for an offense, it is an affirmative defense that the defendant engaged in the proscribed conduct because he was induced or encouraged to do so by a public servant, or by a person acting in cooperation with a public servant, seeking to obtain evidence against him for purpose of criminal prosecution, and when the methods used to obtain such evidence were such as to create a substantial risk that the offense would be committed by a person not otherwise disposed to commit it. Inducement or encouragement to commit an offense means active inducement or encouragement. Conduct merely affording a person an opportunity to commit an offense does not constitute entrapment."

Subdivision two of N.Y.Penal Law § 25.00 explains the meaning of "affirmative defense" as follows:

> "When a defense declared by statute to be an 'affirmative defense' is raised at a trial, the defendant has the burden of establishing such defense by a preponderance of the evidence."

The constitutionality of thus placing on the defendant the burden of producing evidence and of ultimate persuasion by a preponderance was challenged in People v. Laietta, 30 N.Y.2d 168, 281 N.E.2d 157 (1972). In unanimously upholding the statute the court relied, in part, on Leland v. Oregon, 343 U.S. 790, 72 S.Ct. 1002, 96 L.Ed. 1302 (1952) in which an Oregon statute placing the burden on the defendant to prove his legal insanity beyond a reasonable doubt was sustained and distinguished the problem posed when the burden of pursuasion is placed on a defendant with respect to the defense of alibi. The latter has been held to violate due process, in part because the defense negates an essential element of the crime (Stump v. Bennett, 398 F.2d 111 (8th Cir. 1967) cert. denied 393 U.S. 1001, 89 S.Ct. 483, 21 L.Ed. 466 (1968) (reprinted at page 30, supra); a similar result was reached with respect to the Georgia alibi defense in Smith v. Smith, 454 F.2d 572 (5th Cir. 1972)). Entrapment, in contrast, "is not a defense which negatives an essential element of the crime, but rather constitutes a defense in the nature of confession and avoidance." 281 N.E.2d at 161.

2. Even if reliance on *Leland* may be misplaced in light of In re Winship, 397 U.S. 358, 90 S.Ct. 1068, 25 L.Ed.2d 368 (1970), may it not still be appropriate to place on defendants the burden of producing evidence with respect to a defense such as entrapment which may lie peculiarly within his knowledge? If so, should the defendant also bear the burden of persuasion? Does your answer depend on whether or not you accept the view of the *Sherman* majority that the entrapped defendant is not guilty because of an implied exception in the criminal statute? If a defense goes to the defendant's guilt should the presumption of innocence be seen as requiring that the prosecution carry the burden of persuasion once the defendant has produced evidence raising a reasonable doubt?

3. May a defendant simultaneously deny participation in the alleged illegal act and offer the defense of entrapment? See Ortega v. United States, 348 F.2d 874 (9th Cir. 1965).

Inconsistency of defenses, which disturbed the *Ortega* court, has been found to be present even where the defendant admits possession of the prohibited substance but denies knowledge of its nature or illegal origin. United States v. Barrios, 457 F.2d 680 (9th Cir. 1972). Although it is commonly held that the defense of entrapment cannot be asserted in the absence of an admission of the acts constituting the crime the reason for this position, other than the assertion that entrapment and denial are inconsistent, is difficult to fathom. In Rodriguez-Gastelum v. United States, 429 F.2d 536 (9th Cir. 1970), the court in affirming a refusal to instruct on entrapment explained: " * * * the appellant denied either bringing heroin into the United States or selling heroin to Agent Jordan. With this evidence before the jury, how could the district court instruct the jury that the appellant claimed he was *induced* by the government agents to sell them heroin, without in effect telling the jury appellant was a liar?". (Emphasis in original). Is there any reason why the defendant should be protected against the danger of the jury drawing such an inference? Is it constitutional to require a defendant to surrender his Fifth Amendment privilege against self-incrimination as a condition for assertion of the defense of entrapment? See Comment, The Assertion of Inconsistent Defenses in Entrapment Cases, 56 Iowa L.Rev. 686 (1971).

STATE v. DAVIS

Supreme Court of Iowa, 1970.
175 N.W.2d 407.

MOORE, Chief Justice.   [On September 29, 1968 at 10:00 P.M., two juveniles, defendant and one Pilkington, were apprehended in an attempt to break and enter a garage by deputy sheriffs Slycord and Allgood who had the premises under surveillance.   Defendant was waived to the criminal courts where he was convicted and sentenced to five years.   He claims error in the judge's refusal to instruct as requested on the issue of entrapment.]

* * *

On cross-examination deputy Slycord stated he was acquainted with Pilkington, he was in the area of 1712 Williams in the afternoon or early evening of September 29 and had a conversation with Pilkington.   Slycord's cross-examination includes:

"Q.   Yes.   And at that time, Mr. Pilkington advised you that he was going to enter into that garage, isn't that true?   A.   That's true.

"Q.   Yes.   And he said that this defendant, did not want him to go into that garage, isn't that true?   A.   That's not true.

"Q.   Isn't it true, Mr. Slycord, that you advised Mr. Pilkington to make the robbery or to proceed with the robbery?   Isn't that true, sir?   A.   That's true, yes.

"The information that I received from Mr. Pilkington was the fact that he told me that he was going to rob the rear of the garage and break into the place that night.   * * *

"Q.   Well, in the afternoon or early evening of September 29, you did talk to Pilkington and you did tell him to perform the robbery is that right?   A.   I didn't tell him to, he told me he was going to.

"Q.   And you told him to go ahead and do it, isn't that right?   A.   I told him to use his own judgment, because he was going to be the one that was in trouble."

On redirect examination Slycord stated: "When I had occasion to talk to Mr. Pilkington, earlier that day, I did not suggest the B. & E. to him or to break and enter, and I informed this person at that time that they would be arrested if they attempted to do this.   There was no suggestion by me of continuing with this crime."

On recross-examination Slycord stated: "I did not do anything to prevent this minor from perpetrating the crime.   All I told him was that I would put him under arrest for B. & E. if he did that."

His redirect examination included: "On the Direct Examination, I was asked whether or not I advised Mr. Pilkington to make the robbery or proceed with the robbery. What I meant by that was that if he went ahead with the robbery, he was going to get arrested for B. & E. I did not ever actually tell this individual to attempt to rob or break into this garage."

After the State rested its case in chief and defendant's motion for a directed verdict had been overruled the State made a motion in limine out of the presence of the jury. It sought to avoid any inquiry by defense counsel of the outcome of any charges in juvenile court against Pilkington.

During discussion of the motion in limine the trial court asked what is "the situation with Carl Pilkington?" to which the assistant county attorney responded: "Apparently, Mr. Pilkington has been an informer for the sheriff's department and there has been a series of breakings and enterings in which Mr. Pilkington had been involved. Mr. Pilkington has given information on a series of these matters and action has been taken in some of these matters, but in this particular instance no action has been taken against Mr. Pilkington to the best of my knowledge.

"The only purpose that this would serve then in bringing this out before this jury at this time would be to prejudice the case against the State and leaving the inference that one person is being punished and the other is not, which is not the case in this particular situation."

The trial court overruled the State's motion in limine. Trial in the presence of the jury was then resumed. No mention of the assistant county attorney's remarks was made in the presence of the jury.

Defendant testified he had known Carl Pilkington for approximately two years before the incident, a couple of days before September 29 Pilkington told him he was in trouble, he needed the tools in Mrs. Edwards' garage so he could get money to go to California and he said "no" to Pilkington's suggestion they break into the garage. Defendant further testified that during the morning of September 29 Pilkington "kept pressuring me to go with him that night" but he told Pilkington he would not go and Pilkington left. He stated that evening while riding around Pilkington again mentioned the tools and after again refusing he did go to the garage with Pilkington. He described how they surveyed the area before going to the rear of the garage and how a window was removed. He admitted running from the scene and later being arrested at his nearby home. He stated he was induced by Pilkington to go to the garage.

Defendant filed this requested instruction: "You are further instructed that in this case the theory of the defense of the Defendant is the principle of entrapment. Entrapment is a complete, legal and proper defense and means that where the criminal design does not originate in the mind of the accused, but was the design originated in the mind of the entrapping officer or other person who lured the defendant into the commission of a crime in order to secure his conviction therefor, the State is estopped from prosecuting therefor and a defendant should not be convicted, under such circumstances.

* * *

The trial court gave an instruction on entrapment by a police officer substantially the same as the above requested instruction but omitted "or other person" where used in the requested instruction.

* * *

In his brief defendant * * * argues deputy sheriff Slycord was acting through an informant, namely Carl Pilkington, and therefore the claimed inducement conduct of Pilkington was that of the officer. Some of the cited authorities lend support to such a theory if the facts are sufficiently clear. We need not and do not decide this question of law. Defendant's factual contentions are not supported by the record. The dialogue which took place during the motion in limine discussion was not made in the presence of or called to the attention of the jury. The plan to break and enter the garage was conceived in the mind of the apparently boastful teenager Pilkington at least one day before he talked to the deputy. The criminal design was not that of the deputy sheriff.

* * *

The evidence introduced does not establish a jury question on defendant's theory of entrapment by the use of an informant. His assignment of error is without merit.

* * *

Affirmed.

NOTE

Informers used in law enforcement must normally be compensated in some way. Often this involves agreements not to prosecute the informer for his own criminal activity. Sometimes cash payments are made. See, e. g., Donnelly, "Judicial Control of Informants, Spies, Stool Pigeons and Agent Provocateurs", 60 Yale L.J. 1091 (1951); "Informers in Federal Narcotics Prosecutions," 2 Colum.J.L. & Soc.Prob. 47 (1966); and "Entrapment by Federal Officers", 33 N.Y.U.L.Rev. 1033 (1958). If Pilkington in the *Davis* case had been "employed" on a contingent fee basis, that is, he was to receive a certain amount for each conviction achieved through his efforts, should the evaluation of the entrapment defense be different? In what way? What if he were specifically employed to produce evidence against Davis? See United States v. Grimes, 438 F.2d 391 (6th Cir. 1971).

UNITED STATES v. RUSSELL

United States Supreme Court, 1973.
— U.S. —, 93 S.Ct. 1637, — L.Ed.2d —.

Mr. Justice REHNQUIST delivered the opinion of the Court.

Respondent Richard Russell was charged in three counts of a five count indictment returned against him and codefendants John and Patrick Connolly. After a jury trial in the District Court, in which his sole defense was entrapment, respondent was convicted on all three counts of having unlawfully manufactured and processed methamphetamine ("speed") and of having unlawfully sold and delivered that drug in violation of 21 U.S.C. §§ 331(q)(1), (2), 360a(a), (b) (Supp. V, 1964). He was sentenced to concurrent terms of two years in prison for each offense, the terms to be suspended on the condition that he spend six months in prison and be placed on probation for the following three years. On appeal the United States Court of Appeals for the Ninth Circuit, one judge dissenting, reversed the conviction solely for the reason that an undercover agent supplied an essential chemical for manufacturing the methamphetamine which formed the basis of respondent's conviction. The court concluded that as a matter of law "a defense to a criminal charge may be founded upon an intolerable degree of governmental participation in the criminal enterprise." United States v. Russell, 459 F.2d 671, 673 (CA9 1972). We granted certiorari, 409 U.S. 911 (1972), and now reverse that judgment.

There is little dispute concerning the essential facts in this case. On December 7, 1969, Joe Shapiro, an undercover agent for the Federal Bureau of Narcotics and Dangerous Drugs, went to respondent's home on Whidbey Island in the State of Washington where he met with respondent and his two codefendants, John and Patrick Connolly. Shapiro's assignment was to locate a laboratory where it was believed that methamphetamine was being manufactured illicitly. He told the respondent and the Connollys that he represented an organization in the Pacific Northwest that was interested in controlling the manufacture and distribution of methamphetamine. He then made an offer to supply the defendants with the chemical phenyl-2-propanone, an essential ingredient in the manufacture of methamphetamine, in return for one-half of the drug produced. This offer was made on the condition that Agent Shapiro be shown a sample of the drug which they were making and the laboratory where it was being produced.

During the conversation Patrick Connolly revealed that he had been making the drug since May 1969 and since then had produced three pounds of it.[2] John Connolly gave the agent a bag containing a quantity of methamphetamine that he represented as being from "the last batch that we made." Shortly thereafter, Shapiro and Patrick

---

2. At trial Patrick Connolly admitted making this statement to Agent Shapiro but asserted that the statement was not true.

Connolly left respondent's house to view the laboratory which was located in the Connolly house on Whidbey Island. At the house Shapiro observed an empty bottle bearing the chemical label phenyl-2-propanone.

By prearrangement Shapiro returned to the Connolly house on December 9, 1969, to supply 100 grams of propanone and observe the chemical reaction. When he arrived he observed Patrick Connolly and the respondent cutting up pieces of aluminum foil and placing them in a large flask. There was testimony that some of the foil pieces accidentally fell on the floor and were picked up by the respondent and Shapiro and put into the flask.[3] Thereafter Patrick Connolly added all of the necessary chemicals, including the propanone brought by Shapiro, to make two batches of methamphetamine. The manufacturing process having been completed the following morning, Shapiro was given one-half of the drug and respondent kept the remainder. Shapiro offered to buy, and the respondent agreed to sell, part of the remainder for $60.

About a month later Shapiro returned to the Connolly house and met with Patrick Connolly to ask if he was still interested in their "business arrangement." Connolly replied that he was interested but that he had recently obtained two additional bottles of phenyl-2-propanone and would not be finished with them for a couple of days. He provided some additional methamphetamine to Shapiro at that time. Three days later Shapiro returned to the Connolly house with a search warrant and, among other items, seized an empty 500-gram bottle of propanone and a 100-gram bottle, not the one he had provided, that was partially filled with the chemical.

There was testimony at the trial of respondent and Patrick Connolly that phenyl-2-propanone was generally difficult to obtain. At the request of the Bureau of Narcotics and Dangerous Drugs, some chemical supply firms had voluntarily ceased selling the chemical.

At the close of the evidence, and after receiving the District Judge's standard entrapment instruction, the jury found the respondent guilty on all counts charged. On appeal the respondent conceded that the jury could have found him predisposed to commit the offenses, 459 F.2d at 672, but argued that on the facts presented there was entrapment as a matter of law. The Court of Appeals agreed, although it did not find the District Court had misconstrued or misapplied the traditional standards governing the entrapment defense. Rather, the court in effect expanded the traditional notion of entrapment, which focuses on the predisposition of the defendant, to mandate dismissal of a criminal prosecution whenever the court determines that there has been "an intolerable degree of governmental

3. Agent Shapiro did not otherwise participate in the manufacture of the drug or direct any of the work.

participation in the criminal enterprise." In this case the court decided that the conduct of the agent in supplying a scarce ingredient essential for the manufacture of a controlled substance established that defense.

This new defense was held to rest on either of two alternative theories. One theory is based on two lower court decisions which have found entrapment, regardless of predisposition, whenever the government supplies contraband to the defendants. United States v. Bueno, 447 F.2d 903 (C.A.5 1971); United States v. Chisum, 312 F.Supp. 1307 (C.D.Cal.1970). The second theory, a nonentrapment rationale, is based on a recent Ninth Circuit decision that reversed a conviction because a government investigator was so enmeshed in the criminal activity that the prosecution of the defendants was held to be repugnant to the American criminal justice system. Greene v. United States, 454 F.2d 783 (C.A.9 1971). The court below held that these two rationales constitute the same defense, and that only the label distinguishes them. In any event, it held that "[b]oth theories are premised on fundamental concepts of due process and evince the reluctance of the judiciary to countenance 'overzealous law enforcement.'" 459 F.2d, at 674, quoting Sherman v. United States, 356 U.S. 369, 381 (1958). (Frankfurter, J., concurring).

* * *

In the instant case respondent asks us to reconsider the theory of the entrapment defense as it is set forth in the majority opinions in *Sorrells* and *Sherman*. His principal contention is that the defense should rest on constitutional grounds. He argues that the level of Shapiro's involvement in the manufacture of the methamphetamine was so high that a criminal prosecution for the drug's manufacture violates the fundamental principles of due process. The respondent contends that the same factors that led this Court to apply the exclusionary rule to illegal searches and seizures, Weeks v. United States, 232 U.S. 383 (1914); Mapp v. Ohio, 367 U.S. 643 (1961), and confessions, Miranda v. Arizona, 384 U.S. 436 (1966), should be considered here. But he would have the Court go further in deterring undesirable official conduct by requiring that any prosecution be barred absolutely because of the police involvement in criminal activity. The analogy is imperfect in any event, for the principal reason behind the adoption of the exclusionary rule was the government's "failure to observe its own laws." Mapp v. Ohio, supra, 367 U.S., at 659. Unlike the situations giving rise to the holdings in *Mapp* and *Miranda,* the government's conduct here violated no independent constitutional right of the respondent. Nor did Shapiro violate any federal statute or rule or commit any crime in infiltrating the respondent's drug enterprise.

Respondent would overcome this basic weakness in his analogy to the exclusionary rule cases by having the Court adopt a rigid constitutional rule that would preclude any prosecution when it is shown that the criminal product would not have been possible had not an undercover agent "supplied an indispensable means to the commission of the crime that could not have been obtained otherwise, through legal or illegal channels." * * *

The record discloses that although the propanone was difficult to obtain it was by no means impossible. The defendants admitted making the drug both before and after those batches made with the propanone supplied by Shapiro. Shapiro testified that he saw an empty bottle labeled phenyl-2-propanone on his first visit to the laboratory on December 7, 1969. And when the laboratory was searched pursuant to a search warrant on January 10, 1970, two additional bottles labeled phenyl-2-propanone were seized. Thus, the facts in the record amply demonstrate that the propanone used in the illicit manufacture of methamphetamine not only *could* have been obtained without the intervention of Shapiro but was in fact obtained by these defendants.

While we may some day be presented with a situation in which the conduct of law enforcement agents is so outrageous that due process principles would absolutely bar the government from invoking judicial processes to obtain a conviction, cf. Rochin v. California, 342 U.S. 165 (1952), the instant case is distinctly not of that breed. Shapiro's contribution of propanone to the criminal enterprise already in process was scarcely objectionable. The chemical is by itself a harmless substance and its possession is legal. While the government may have been seeking to make it more difficult for drug rings, such as that of which respondent was a member, to obtain the chemical, the evidence described above shows that it nonetheless was obtainable. The law enforcement conduct here stops far short of violating that "fundamental fairness, shocking to the universal sense of justice," mandated by the Due Process Clause of the Fifth Amendment. Kinsella v. United States ex rel. Singleton, 361 U.S. 234, 246 (1960).

The illicit manufacture of drugs is not a sporadic, isolated criminal incident, but a continuing, though illegal, business enterprise. In order to obtain convictions for illegally manufacturing drugs, the gathering of evidence of past unlawful conduct frequently proves to be an all but impossible task. Thus in drug-related offenses law enforcement personnel have turned to one of the only practicable means of detection: the infiltration of drug rings and a limited participation in their unlawful present practices. Such infiltration is a recognized and permissible means of apprehension; if that be so, then the supply of some item of value that the drug ring requires must, as a general rule, also be permissible. For an agent will not be taken into the confidence of the illegal entrepreneurs unless he has something of value to offer them. Law enforcement tactics such as this can hardly be said to violate "fundamental fairness" or "shocking to the universal sense of justice," *Kinsella*, supra.

Respondent also urges as an alternative to his constitutional argument, that * * * the views of Justices Roberts and Frankfurter, concurring in *Sorrells* and *Sherman*, respectively, which make the essential element of the defense turn on the type and degree of governmental conduct, be adopted as the law.

We decline to overrule these cases. *Sorrells* is a precedent of long standing that has already been once reexamined in *Sherman* and implicitly there reaffirmed. Since the defense is not of a constitutional dimension, Congress may address itself to the question and adopt any substantive definition of the defense that it may find desirable.

* * *

* * * [I]t [does not] seem particularly desirable for the law to grant complete immunity from prosecution to one who himself planned to commit a crime, and then committed it, simply because government undercover agents subjected him to inducements which might have seduced a hypothetical individual who was not so predisposed. We are content to leave the matter where it was left by the Court in *Sherman* * * *[.]

Several decisions of the United States district courts and courts of appeals have undoubtedly gone beyond this Court's opinions in *Sorrells* and *Sherman* in order to bar prosecutions because of what they thought to be for want of a better term "overzealous law enforcement." But the defense of entrapment enunciated in those opinions was not intended to give the federal judiciary a "chancellor's foot" veto over law enforcement practices of which it did not approve. The execution of the federal laws under our Constitution is confided primarily to the Executive Branch of the Government, subject to applicable constitutional and statutory limitations and to judicially fashioned rules to enforce those limitations. We think that the decision of the Court of Appeals in this case quite unnecessarily introduces an unmanageably subjective standard which is contrary to the holdings of this Court in *Sorrells* and *Sherman*.

Those cases establish that entrapment is a relatively limited defense. It is rooted not in any authority of the Judicial Branch to dismiss prosecutions for what it feels to have been "overzealous law enforcement," but instead in the notion that Congress could not have intended criminal punishment for a defendant who has committed all the elements of a prescribed offense, but who was induced to commit them by the government.

* * * It is only when the government's deception actually implants the criminal design in the mind of the defendant that the defense of entrapment comes into play.

Respondent's concession in the Court of Appeals that the jury finding as to predisposition was supported by the evidence is, therefore, fatal to his claim of entrapment. He was an active participant in an illegal drug manufacturing enterprise which began before the government agent appeared on the scene, and continued after the government agent had left the scene. He was, in the words of *Sher-*

man, supra, not an "unwary innocent" but an "unwary criminal." The Court of Appeals was wrong, we believe, when it sought to broaden the principle laid down in *Sorrells* and *Sherman*. Its judgment is therefore

Reversed.

[The dissenting opinion of Mr. Justice Douglas, with Mr. Justice Brennan concurring, is omitted.]

Mr. Justice STEWART, with whom Mr. Justice BRENNAN and Mr. Justice MARSHALL join, dissenting.

* * *

In my view [the] objective approach to entrapment advanced by the concurring opinions in *Sorrells* and *Sherman* is the only one truly consistent with the underlying rationale of the defense.

In the case before us, I think that the District Court erred in submitting the issue of entrapment to the jury, with instructions to acquit only if it had a reasonable doubt as to the respondent's predisposition to committing the crime. Since, under the objective test of entrapment, predisposition is irrelevant and the issue is to be decided by the trial judge, the Court of Appeals, I believe, would have been justified in reversing the conviction on this basis alone. But since the appellate court did not remand for consideration of the issue by the District Judge under an objective standard, but rather found entrapment as a matter of law and directed that the indictment be dismissed, we must reach the merits of the respondent's entrapment defense.

Since, in my view, it does not matter whether the respondent was predisposed to commit the offense of which he was convicted, the focus must be, rather, on the conduct of the undercover government agent. What the agent did here was to meet with a group of suspected producers of methamphetamine, including the respondent; to request the drug; to offer to supply the chemical phenyl-2-propanone in exchange for one-half of the methamphetamine to be manufactured therewith; and, when that offer was accepted, to provide the needed chemical ingredient, and to purchase some of the drug from the respondent.

It is undisputed that phenyl-2-propanone is an essential ingredient in the manufacture of methamphetamine; that it is not used for any other purpose; and that, while its sale is not illegal, it is difficult to obtain, because a manufacturer's license is needed to purchase it, and because many suppliers, at the request of the Federal Bureau of Narcotics and Dangerous Drugs, do not sell it at all. It is also undisputed that the methamphetamine which the respondent was prosecuted for manufacturing and selling was all produced on December 10, 1969, and that all the phenyl-2-propanone used in the manufacture of that batch of the drug was provided by the government agent. In these circumstances, the agent's undertaking to supply this ingredient to the respondent, thus making it possible for the Government to prosecute him for manufacturing an illicit drug with it, was, I think, precisely the type of governmental conduct that the entrapment defense is meant to prevent.

Although the Court of Appeals found that the phenyl-2-propanone could not have been obtained without the agent's intervention—that "there could not have been the manufacture, delivery, or sale of the illicit drug had it not been for the Government's supply of one of the essential ingredients," 459 F.2d 671, 672—the Court today rejects this finding as contradicted by the facts revealed at trial. The record, as the Court states, discloses that one of the respondent's accomplices, though not the respondent himself, had obtained phenyl-2-propanone from independent sources both before and after receiving the agent's supply, and had used it in the production of methamphetamine. This demonstrates, it is said, that the chemical was obtainable other than through the government agent; and hence the agent's furnishing it for the production of the methamphatamine involved in this prosecution did no more than afford an opportunity for its production to one ready and willing to produce it. Thus, the argument seems to be, there was no entrapment here, any more than there would have been if the agent had furnished common table salt, had that been necessary to the drug's production.

In cannot be doubted that if phenyl-2-propanone had been wholly unobtainable from other sources, the agent's undercover offer to supply it to the respondent in return for part of the illicit methamphetamine produced therewith—an offer initiated and carried out by the agent for the purpose of prosecuting the respondent for producing methamphetamine—would be precisely the type of governmental conduct that constitutes entrapment under any definition. For the agent's conduct in that situation would make possible the commission of an otherwise totally impossible crime, and, I should suppose, would thus be a textbook example of instigating the commission of a criminal offense in order to prosecute someone for committing it.

But assuming in this case that the phenyl-2-propanone was obtainable through independent sources, the fact remains that that used for the particular batch of methamphetamine involved in all three counts of the indictment with which the respondent was charged— i. e., that produced on December 10, 1969—was supplied by the Government. This essential ingredient was indisputably difficult to obtain, and yet that used in committing the offenses of which the respondent was convicted was offered to the respondent by the government agent, on the agent's own initiative, and was readily supplied to the respondent in needed amounts. If the chemical was so easily available elsewhere, then why did not the agent simply wait until the respondent had himself obtained the ingredients and produced the drug, and then buy it from him? The very fact that the agent felt it incumbent upon him to offer to supply phenyl-2-propanone in return for the drug casts considerable doubt on the theory that the chemical could easily have been procured without the agent's intervention, and that therefore the agent merely afforded an opportunity for the commission of a criminal offense.

In this case, the chemical ingredient was available only to licensed persons, and the Government itself had requested suppliers not to sell that ingredient even to people with a license. Yet the government agent readily offered and supplied that ingredient to an unlicensed person and asked him to make a certain illegal drug with it. The Government then prosecuted that person for making the drug produced *with the very ingredient* which its agent had so helpfully supplied. This strikes me as the very pattern of conduct that should be held to constitute entrapment as a matter of law.

It is the Government's duty to prevent crime, not to promote it. Here, the Government's agent asked that the illegal drug be produced for him, solved his quarry's practical problems with the assurance that he could provide the one essential ingredient that was difficult to obtain, furnished that element as he had promised, and bought the finished product from the respondent—all so that the respondent could be prosecuted for producing and selling the very drug for which the agent had asked and for which he had provided the necessary component. Under the objective approach that I would follow, this respondent was entrapped, regardless of his predisposition or "innocence."

In the words of Mr. Justice ROBERTS:

> "The applicable principle is that courts must be closed to the trial of a crime instigated by the government's own agents. No other issue, no comparison of equities as between the guilty official and the guilty defendant, has any place in the enforcement of this overruling principle of public policy." Sorrells v. United States, supra, at 459.

I would affirm the judgment of the Court of Appeals.

NOTES

1. State Bar Committee on Revision of the Penal Code, Final Draft Texas Penal Code (1970):

§ 8.05. Entrapment

(a) It is a defense to prosecution that a peace officer, or a person directed by a peace officer, induced the commission of an offense, in order to obtain evidence of the commission for prosecution, by methods creating a substantial risk that the offense would be committed by one not otherwise ready to commit it. However, there is no defense under this section if the peace officer, or person directed by him, merely afforded the actor an opportunity to commit the offense.

(b) The defense provided by this section is available even though the actor denies commission of the conduct charged to constitute the offense.

(c) On written motion of the defendant, the court shall determine as a matter of fact and law, after a hearing without the jury, whether the defendant was entrapped to commit the offense. The defendant shall file the motion with the court at least 10 days before the trial begins, or if the court sets a pretrial hearing, the defendant shall file the motion during the hearing. However, the court for good cause shown may permit filing the motion at a later time determined by the court.

(d) If the court determines the defendant was entrapped to commit the offense, it shall acquit him if the state has concluded its case, or dismiss the offense with prejudice if the state has not concluded its case. If the court determines the defendant was not entrapped, but believes reasonable minds could differ over the issue, the court shall submit the entrapment defense to the jury.

To what extent would this alter the defense of entrapment as presently employed in most jurisdictions? Compare this formulation with the following proposal made by the American Civil Liberties Union in its Report of its testimony before the Senate Subcommittee on Criminal Law and Procedures on the Final Report of the National Commission on Reform of the Federal Criminal Laws. 37–38 (March 21, 1972).

§ 702. Entrapment

(1) Defense. It is a defense that the defendant was entrapped into committing the offense.

(2) Entrapment Defined. Entrapment occurs (i) when a law enforcement agent induces the commission of an offense, using persuasion or other means likely to cause normally law abiding persons to commit the offense; or (ii) when the criminal design originates with a law enforcement agent and he implants in the mind of an innocent person the disposition to commit an offense and induce its commission in order that the government may prosecute; or (iii) when the law enforcement agent induces the criminal act without reasonable suspicion [probable cause] that the person being solicited to commit an offense or with whom an illegal transaction is initiated is engaged in or prepared to engage in such offense or transaction. Conduct merely affording a person an opportunity to commit an offense does not constitute entrapment.

(3) The defense afforded by this section may be raised under a plea of not guilty. The defendant shall be entitled to have the issue of entrapment decided by the court and to have the fact that the defense has been raised and evidence introduced in support thereof kept from the attention of the jury. Evidence of the defendant's past criminal conduct is inadmissible on the entrapment issue.

(4) Law Enforcement Agent Defined. In this section "law enforcement agent" includes personnel of state and local law en-

forcement agencies as well as of the United States, and any person cooperating with such an agency.

2. To what extent can the problems of official misconduct inherent in entrapment situations be ameliorated by making such conduct a defense to prosecution? Is our national experience with the exclusionary rule with respect to searches and seizures and confessions relevant? Should the misbehaving officer be subject to direct sanctions? Reconsider these problems in connection with section "G. Participation in Offense for Purposes of Aiding Law Enforcement", infra p. 1137.

3. Would an alternative solution be to change the substantive criminal law with respect to the crimes which appear to engender such activity? How much weight should this consideration be given in evaluating the present drug laws?

D. DEFENSE OF PERSONS OR PROPERTY

PROPOSED FEDERAL CRIMINAL CODE (1971)

§ 601. Justification

(1) Defense. Except as otherwise expressly provided, justification or excuse under this Chapter is a defense.

(2) Danger to Other Persons. If a person is justified or excused in using force against another, but he recklessly or negligently injures or creates a risk of injury to innocent persons, the justifications afforded by this Chapter are unavailable in a prosecution for such recklessness or negligence, as the case may be.

*   *   *

§ 603. Self-Defense

A person is justified in using force upon another person in order to defend himself against danger of imminent unlawful bodily injury, sexual assault or detention by such other person, except that:

(a) a person is not justified in using force for the purpose of resisting arrest, execution of process, or other performance of duty by a public servant under color of law, but excessive force may be resisted; and

(b) a person is not justified in using force if (i) he intentionally provokes unlawful action by another person in order to cause bodily injury or death to such other person, or (ii) he has entered into a mutual combat with another person or is the initial aggressor. A person's use of defensive force after he withdraws from an encounter and indicates to the other person that he has done so is justified if the latter nevertheless continues or menaces unlawful action.

§ 604.   Defense of Others

A person is justified in using force upon another person in order to defend anyone else if (a) the person defended would be justified in defending himself, and (b) the person coming to the defense has not, by provocation or otherwise, forfeited the right of self-defense.

§ 606.   Use of Force in Defense of Premises and Property

Force is justified if it is used to prevent or terminate an unlawful entry or other trespass in or upon premises, or to prevent an unlawful carrying away or damaging of property, if the person using such force first requests the person against whom such force is to be used to desist from his interference with the premises or property, except that:

>   (a) request is not necessary if (i) it would be useless to make the request, or (ii) it would be dangerous to make the request, or (iii) substantial damage would be done to the property sought to be protected before the request could effectively be made;

>   (b) the use of force is not justified to prevent or terminate a trespass if it will expose the trespasser to substantial danger of serious bodily injury.

§ 607.   Limits on the Use of Force: Excessive Force; Deadly Force

(1) Excessive Force.   A person is not justified in using more force than is necessary and appropriate under the circumstances.

(2) Deadly Force.   Deadly force is justified in the following instances:

>   (a) when it is expressly authorized by a federal statute or occurs in the lawful conduct of war;

>   [(a) when it is authorized by a federal law or occurs in the necessary and appropriate conduct of war;]

>   (b) when used in lawful self-defense, or in lawful defense of others, if such force is necessary to protect the actor or anyone else against death, serious bodily injury, or the commission of a felony involving violence, except that the use of deadly force is not justified if it can be avoided, with safety to the actor and others, by retreat or other conduct involving minimal interference with the freedom of the person menaced.   A person seeking to protect someone else must, before using deadly force, try to cause that person to retreat, or otherwise comply with the requirements of this provision, if safety can be obtained thereby; but (i) a public servant or an officer of a ship or aircraft justified in using force in the performance of his duties or a person justified in using force in his assistance need not desist from his efforts be-

cause of resistance or threatened resistance by or on behalf of the person against whom his action is directed, and (ii) no person is required to retreat from his dwelling, or place of work, unless he was the original aggressor or is assailed by a person who he knows also dwells or works there;

(c) when used by a person in possession or control of a dwelling or place of work, or a person who is licensed or privileged to be thereon, if such force is necessary to prevent commission of arson, burglary, robbery or a felony involving violence upon or in the dwelling or place of work or to prevent a person in flight immediately after committing a robbery or burglary from taking the fruits thereof from the dwelling or place of work, and the use of force other than deadly force for such purposes would expose anyone to substantial danger of serious bodily injury;

(d) when used by a public servant authorized to effect arrests or prevent escapes, if such force is necessary to effect an arrest or to prevent the escape from custody of a person who has committed or attempted to commit a felony involving violence, or is attempting to escape by the use of a deadly weapon, or has otherwise indicated that he is likely to endanger human life or to inflict serious bodily injury unless apprehended without delay;

(e) when used by a guard or other public servant, if such force is necessary to prevent the escape of a prisoner from a detention facility unless he knows that the prisoner is not such a person as described in paragraph (d) above. A detention facility is any place used for the confinement, pursuant to a court order, of a person (i) charged with or convicted of an offense, or (ii) charged with being or adjudicated a youth offender or juvenile delinquent, or (iii) held for extradition, or (iv) otherwise confined pursuant to court order;

(f) when used by a public servant, if such force is necessary (i) to prevent overt and forceful acts of treason, insurrection or sabotage, or (ii) to prevent murder, manslaughter, aggravated assault, arson, robbery, burglary or kidnapping in the course of a riot if the deadly force is employed following reasonable notice of intent to employ deadly force, and does not carry with it an unreasonable danger to life of non-participants in the riot, and is employed pursuant to a decision or order of a public servant having supervisory authority over ten or more other public servants concerned in the suppression of the riot;

(g) when used by an officer of a ship or aircraft if such force is necessary to prevent overt and forceful acts of mutiny, after the participants in such acts against whom such

force is to be used have been ordered to cease and given reasonable notice of intent to employ deadly force;

(h) when used by a duly licensed physician, or a person
acting at his direction, if such force is necessary in order to
administer a recognized form of treatment to promote the
physical or mental health of a patient and if the treatment
is administered (i) in an emergency, or (ii) with the consent
of the patient or, if the patient is a minor or an incompetent
person, with the consent of his parent, guardian or other
person entrusted with his care and supervision, or (iii) by
order of a court of competent jurisdiction;

(i) when used by a person who is directed or authorized
to use deadly force by a public servant or an officer of a ship
or aircraft and who does not know that, if such is the case,
the public servant or such officer is himself not authorized to
use deadly force under the circumstances.

§ 608.   Excuse

(1) Mistake.   A person's conduct is excused if he believes that
the factual situation is such that his conduct is necessary and appropriate for any of the purposes which would establish a justification or excuse under this Chapter, even though his belief is mistaken,
except that, if his belief is negligently or recklessly held, it is not an
excuse in a prosecution for an offense for which negligence or recklessness, as the case may be, suffices to establish culpability.   Excuse
under this subsection is a defense or affirmative defense according
to which type of defense would be established had the facts been as
the person believed them to be.

(2) Marginal Transgression of Limit of Justification.   A person's conduct is excused if it would otherwise be justified or excused
under this Chapter but is marginally hasty or excessive because he
was confronted with an emergency precluding adequate appraisal or
measured reaction.

§ 619.   Definitions for Chapter 6

In this Chapter:

(a) "force" means physical action, threat or menace
against another, and includes confinement;

(b) "deadly force" means force which a person uses
with the intent of causing, or which he knows to create a
substantial risk of causing, death or serious bodily injury.
Intentionally firing a firearm or hurling a destructive device
in the direction of another person or at a moving vehicle in
which another person is believed to be constitutes deadly
force.   A threat to cause death or serious bodily injury, by the
production of a weapon or otherwise, so long as the actor's

intent is limited to creating an apprehension that he will use deadly force if necessary, does not constitute deadly force;

(c) "premises" means all or any part of a building or real property, or any structure, vehicle or watercraft used for overnight lodging of persons, or used by persons for carrying on business therein;

(d) "dwelling" means any building or structure, though movable or temporary, or a portion thereof, which is for the time being a person's home or place of lodging.

———

1. DEFENSE OF SELF

———

STATE v. ABBOTT

Supreme Court of New Jersey, 1961.
36 N.J. 63, 174 A.2d 881.

WEINTRAUB, C. J. Frank Abbott was convicted of atrocious assault and battery. The Appellate Division affirmed, 64 N.J.Super. 191, 165 A.2d 537 (1960), and we granted certification, 34 N.J. 176, 167 A.2d 676 (1961).

Abbott shared a common driveway with his neighbors, Michael and Mary Scarano. The Scaranos engaged a contractor to pave their portion. Abbott obtained some asphalt from the contractor and made a doorstop to keep his garage door from swinging onto the Scaranos' property. Nicholas Scarano, who was visiting with the Scaranos, his parents, objected to Abbott's innovation. After some words between them a fist fight ensued.

Although Abbott managed to land the first punch, with which he sent Nicholas to the ground, a jury could find Nicholas was the aggressor. At this point Michael Scarano came at Abbott with a hatchet. Michael said the tool had just been returned to him by the contractor, and denied he meant to use it as a weapon. According to Abbott, Mary Scarano followed, armed with a carving knife and large fork. The actors gave varying versions of what happened, but the end result was that all of the Scaranos were hit by the hatchet. Nicholas received severe head injuries. Abbott claimed he too suffered a laceration.

Abbott admitted he finally wrested the hatchet from Michael but denied he wielded it at all. Rather he insisted that the Scaranos were injured during a common struggle for the instrument. A jury could, however, find Abbott intentionally inflicted the blows.

Abbott was separately indicted for atrocious assault and battery upon each of the Scaranos. There was a common trial of these indictments.   The jury acquitted Abbott of the charges relating to Michael and Mary, but found him guilty as to Nicholas.

The principal question is whether the trial court properly instructed the jury upon the issue of self-defense.   The trial court charged upon the subject of excessive force, as to which Abbott does not complain.   It charged also upon the subject of retreat, and it is here that error is alleged.   Although the jury could have found Abbott used excessive force, we cannot know whether the jury found for him on that subject and convicted because he had failed to retreat in accordance with the trial court's instruction.

As to retreat, the trial court charged upon two hypotheses.   One was that the critical events occurred upon Abbott's property.   Upon that basis, the court said Abbott could stand his ground, and, of course, of this Abbott does not complain.   The second hypothesis was that the alleged offense occurred upon the common driveway. * * *   the trial court held that since all the principals were equally entitled to be on the driveway, Abbott could not claim immunity from the ordinary retreat rule.   Abbott does not question that thesis, but disputes the court's statement of the conditions under which an obligation to retreat would arise.

*   *   *

The subject of retreat usually arises in homicide matters.   We will first discuss it in that context, and then consider whether the principles apply to a charge of atrocious assault and battery, and if they do, whether the trial court correctly guided the jury in this difficult area.

We should make it clear that we are discussing the doctrine of retreat and not the subject of the use of excessive force.   If the force used was unnecessary in its intensity, the claim of self-defense may fall for that reason.   In the discussion which follows we assume a defendant used no more force than he believed necessary to protect himself in the circumstances as they reasonably appeared to him, and consider only whether the claim of self-defense should be denied because he could have avoided the use of that force by retreating.

The question whether one who is neither the aggressor nor a party to a mutual combat must retreat has divided the authorities.   Self-defense is measured against necessity.   From that premise one could readily say there was no necessity to kill in self-defense if the use of deadly force could have been avoided by retreat.   The critics of the retreat rule do not quarrel with the theoretical validity of this conclusion, but rather condemn it as unrealistic.   The law of course should not denounce conduct as criminal when it accords with the behavior of reasonable men.   Upon this level, the advocates of no-retreat say the manly thing is to hold one's ground, and hence society should not demand what smacks of cowardice.   Adherents of the retreat rule reply it is better that the assailed shall retreat than that the life of another be needlessly spent. They add that not only do right-thinking men agree, but further a rule so requiring may well induce others to adhere to that worthy standard of behavior. There is much dispute as to which view commands the support of ancient precedents, a question we think it would be profitless to explore.

* * * Our Court of Errors and Appeals deliberately adopted the retreat rule with an awareness of the contending views, * * * The Model Penal Code embraces the retreat rule while acknowledging that on numerical balance a majority of the precedents oppose it. Model Penal Code § 3.04, comment 3, at p. 24 (Tent.Draft No. 8, 1958).

We are not persuaded to depart from the principle of retreat. We think it salutary if reasonably limited. Much of the criticism goes not to its inherent validity but rather to unwarranted applications of the rule. For example, it is correctly observed that one can hardly retreat from a rifle shot at close range. But if the weapon were a knife, a lead of a city block might well be enough. Again, the rule cannot be stated baldly, with indifference to the excitement of the occasion. As Mr. Justice Holmes cryptically put it, "Detached reflection cannot be demanded in the presence of an uplifted knife." Brown v. United States, 256 U.S. 335, 343, 41 S.Ct. 501, 502, 65 L.Ed. 961, 963 (1921). Such considerations, however, do not demand that a man should have the absolute right to stand his ground and kill in any and all situations. Rather they call for a fair and guarded statement of appropriate principles.

In Brown, supra, the United States Supreme Court said (256 U.S., at p. 343, 41 S.Ct. at p. 502, 65 L.Ed., at p. 963):

"* * * Rationally the failure to retreat is a circumstance to be considered with all the others in order to determine whether the defendant went farther than he was justified in doing; not a categorical proof of guilt."

The comment to § 3.04 of the Model Penal Code (at p. 24) says the passage just quoted "seems to be a median position" and "would apparently remit the issue to the jury, without a legal mandate on the point." We are not sure we correctly understand these observations. We think it clear that Brown accepted the retreat doctrine, but we do not read the opinion of Mr. Justice Holmes to mean that the subject should be submitted without guidance, thus permitting each jury to decide whether the subject of retreat should be considered, and if so, what the ingredients of the doctrine should be. We know of no jurisdiction which leaves to a jury the task of devising the legal principles. Rather we read Brown to hold only that the particular "formula laid down by the [trial] court" was not "adequate to the protection of the defendant's rights" (256 U.S., at pp. 342–343, 41 S.Ct. at p. 502, 65 L. Ed., at pp. 962–63) in the factual pattern which the defendant there asserted.

We believe the following principles are sound:

1. The issue of retreat arises only if the defendant resorted to a deadly force. It is deadly force which is not justifiable when an opportunity to retreat is at hand. Model Penal Code § 3.04(2) (b) (iii). As defined in § 3.12(2) a deadly force means "force which the actor uses with the purpose of causing or which he knows to create a substantial risk of causing death or serious bodily harm."

Hence, it is not the nature of the force defended against which raises the issue of retreat, but rather the nature of the force which the accused employed in his defense. If he does not resort to a deadly force, one who is assailed may hold his ground whether the attack upon him be of a deadly or some lesser character. Although it might be argued that a safe retreat should be taken if thereby the use of *any* force could be avoided, yet, as the comment in the Model Penal Code observes (at p. 23), "The logic of this position never has been accepted when moderate force is used in self-defense; here all agree that the actor may stand his ground and estimate necessity upon that basis." Hence, in a case like the present one, the jury should be instructed that Abbott could hold his ground when Nicholas came at him with his fists, and also when Michael and Mary came at him with the several instruments mentioned, and that the question of retreat could arise only if Abbott intended to use a deadly force.

2. What constitutes an opportunity to retreat which will defeat the right of self-defense? As § 3.04(2) (b) (iii) of the Model Penal Code states, deadly force is not justifiable "if the actor *knows* that he can avoid the necessity of using such force *with complete safety* by retreating * * *." We emphasize "knows" and "with complete safety." One who is wrongfully attacked need not risk injury by retreating, even though he could escape with something less than serious bodily injury. It would be unreal to require nice calculations as to the amount of hurt, or to ask him to endure any at all. And the issue is not whether in retrospect it can be found the defendant could have retreated unharmed. Rather the question is whether he knew the opportunity was there, and of course in that inquiry the total circumstances including the attendant excitement must be considered. We add that upon a retrial the facts as developed in the light of this principle may be such that Abbott would be entitled to an instruction that if his version of the approach by Michael and Mary is accepted, the issue of retreat must be resolved in Abbott's favor.

3. There has been some uncertainty in the language of our cases upon the burden of proof with respect to self-defense. The decisions are treated in State v. Chiarello, N.J.Super., 174 A.2d 506 (1961) where the Appellate Division correctly said that although the burden is upon a defendant to adduce evidence to support the defense, yet if such evidence appears either in the State's case or upon the defendant's case, the issue must be left to the jury with this instruction: that the burden is upon the State to prove beyond a reasonable doubt that the de-

fense is untrue, and hence there must be an acquittal if there is a reasonable doubt as to whether defendant did act in self-defense within the definition of that defense. Accordingly, if the issue of retreat is raised in connection with the defense of self-defense, the jury should be instructed that the burden is also the State's to prove beyond a reasonable doubt that defendant knew he could have retreated with complete safety, and that if a reasonable doubt upon that question should exist, the issue of retreat must be resolved in defendant's favor.

As we have said, the subject of retreat arises most often in homicide cases. It is equally pertinent if the charge is assault with intent to kill. Here the charge is atrocious assault and battery, a crime which involves vicious or brutal conduct. An intent to kill is not an ingredient of that offense, but an intent to do serious bodily harm would seem to be implicit. The doctrine of retreat reflects a policy with respect to the use of deadly force, and the same policy considerations equally obtain if the end result is something less than murder. The Appellate Division held the doctrine applicable to atrocious assault and battery. The comment to Article 3 of the Model Penal Code (at p. 3) expresses the same view, saying, "If the particular force, for example, would be unjustifiable in a prosecution for homicide it should be equally unjustifiable if the victim survives and what is charged is an assault." This seems sound, and hence an instruction upon the subject is appropriate in a trial for atrocious assault and battery, but the instruction should be expressly centered about the use of deadly force.

We turn to the instruction of the trial court. It reads:

"* * * If you find the charges involved or either of them happened on the joint or common driveway and that the defendant had an available opportunity to retreat and you also find that he was or appeared to be threatened by assault and battery with imminent danger of life or serious bodily harm, again there is no duty to retreat. On the other hand, under the latter circumstances, if you find that he did not appear to be threatened by assault and battery with imminent danger of life or great bodily harm, he had a duty to retreat and if he failed to retreat the defense of self-defense would not avail him and would not constitute a defense to these charges or any of these charges if you find that he had a duty to retreat."

It is at once apparent that the charge consists of abstract propositions, unanchored to the factual setting. It will be recalled the encounter had two phases, although one quickly followed the other. The first phase was an unarmed attack by Nicholas which Abbott met in kind; the second involved, as the jury could find, an attack or apparent attack by hatchet in the hands of Michael and by kitchen utensils allegedly wielded by Mary, both aided by Nicholas who had arisen from the initial punch. We have no way of knowing whether the jury understood Abbott was required to retreat when first assailed by Nicholas alone. The jury may well have so gathered since the instruction excluded self-defense "if you find that he [Abbott] did *not* appear to be threatened by assault and battery with imminent danger of life or great bodily harm," and of course Nicholas's attack with his fists readily fitted within those terms.

The State asks us to assume the jury understood an unarticulated premise, i.e., that the court was referring solely to the hatchet affair. If we could so assume, still under the instruction the obligation to retreat would depend upon the nature of the attack upon Abbott rather than the amount of force Abbott intended to employ. In short, there was no reference to the use of a deadly force by Abbott. And if we should read the charge in still another way, to wit, that the court was merely defining its prior reference to "an available opportunity" to retreat and hence meant that the opportunity was not "available" if retreat would have subjected Abbott to imminent danger to his life or of great bodily harm but was "available" if he could get away with a hurt of lesser character, still the charge would be incorrect. This is so because there is no obligation to retreat unless retreat can be effected "with complete safety," and indeed with knowledge that retreat can be so effected. Further, upon that interpretation, the instruction would be devoid of any statement of the facts prerequisite for consideration of the subject, i.e., an intent by the defendant to use a deadly force.

We have said enough to indicate the insufficiency of the charge. Even upon study and restudy we are not sure we can extract the thesis the trial court held. A jury which listens to a single reading of an instruction cannot be expected to debate its meaning and reach a correct view of it. A charge should be a clear, unambiguous guide related to the evidence in the case. The conviction must be reversed.

GRAY v. STATE

Supreme Court of Alaska, 1970.
463 P.2d 897.

BONEY, Justice. On the evening of January 4, 1968, Benjamin F. Strong, an Anchorage city police officer, was on stake-out duty at a Brown Jug Liquor Store in Anchorage. He was not in uniform because he had volunteered for the assignment on his own time. Strong concealed himself in a storeroom in the store. One of the swinging doors to the room was off its hinges, and therefore, Strong stacked cardboard boxes on both sides of the door to support it. He remained on stake out for several hours. He was armed with his own .45 automatic and a .12 gauge shotgun loaded with .00 buck.

At approximately 11:00 p.m., Dewey Gray, brother of Willie Gray, entered the back of the store. When he entered, Dewey held a

.25 automatic in his hand and wore a ski mask. The clerk on duty was Ruth McCoy. There was no one else in the store (except, of course, for the hidden officer). Miss McCoy was told by Dewey to turn off the lights and lock the doors. She did not turn off all the lights. She stated "the lighting was—I cannot remember exactly which lights were on, I recall that the lighting was adequate to see, I had no difficulty in seeing either inside or outside the store." As she was walking to the front door to lock it, Willie Gray came in the front door. Willie went to the cash register and started removing the money. Willie was not armed and had little to do with Ruth McCoy. While Willie was emptying the cash register, Dewey took Miss McCoy to the bathroom near the rear of the store. There Dewey tied up Miss McCoy, who knelt on the floor. Willie stayed at the register. After Dewey had completed tying Miss McCoy, he picked up his gun and started to walk back to where Willie was, and Willie started to leave. Then "in one sequence or another I'm not exactly sure which", Miss McCoy heard boxes tumbling to the floor, heard unidentifiable shouts of more than one voice, but could not discern any words at all. She heard a shot or shots. At some time she turned around and saw Willie shot. She then kicked shut the door to the bathroom and got out of the way. Then she heard "Brown Jug Library hold up" and the phone clattering to the floor. After waiting a while she came out of the bathroom and called the police. The Grays were gone, and Officer Strong was dead.

At trial Dewey elected to testify and admitted that Miss McCoy's description was correct up to the point of being tied up. Dewey stated that after he finished tying up Miss McCoy he turned to leave; Willie was in front of him and was also leaving. Then Dewey heard the sound of boxes falling in the stockroom. As he turned he saw Officer Strong stumbling, crouched on his knees, and firing his .45. The shots were in rapid sequence. Dewey heard no one speak. He saw Willie shot and saw him fall to his knees; he then heard more shots, and at each shot Willie flinched as if hit. It was later stipulated that Willie was shot once in the back of the leg. While looking at Willie, Dewey was shot in the leg, which spun him around and dropped him to his knees. Then "out of reflex and fright" he "threw up a shot too", without aiming, and was immediately thereafter shot again in the shoulder. This second shot caused him to pass out momentarily. Dewey later stated that he did not know who Officer Strong was, that he thought Willie was dead and he would, himself, be killed. When he regained consciousness Dewey crawled to his car and drove home. Once home he told his wife to call the police because he had been shot; she evidently did this. Meanwhile, Willie had managed to escape on foot, and was found later at a friend's apartment.

Appellants at trial attempted to rely on the privilege of self-defense as a justification for the admitted shooting of Officer Strong. The trial court refused to instruct the jury on the elements of self-defense and the amount of force that may be used in effecting arrest. On appeal it is appellants' contention that a person may claim self-defense when he reasonably defends himself from the use of excessive force by an arresting officer.

The overwhelming weight of authority indicates that a person subjected to an unlawful arrest may use reasonable force to defend himself. In the case of Miller v. State, 462 P.2d 421 (Alaska December 15, 1969), we modified this rule by holding that there was no right to resist a peaceful arrest, even though the arrest was unlawful. The *Miller* case did not deal, however, with the circumstances of the present case, where it has been claimed that the arrest was unlawful because Officer Strong used unprivileged force to effect the arrest. An officer in making an arrest is privileged by statute to use only that force which is necessary to restrain the arrested person. To the use of necessary force the arrested person cannot claim the privilege of self-defense. If more than necessary force is used, then the officer commits an unprivileged assault on the arrested person. To an arresting officer's unprivileged use of force, the arrested person must have the right to use reasonable force to defend himself.

However, the state contends that one who provokes "the difficulty" may not claim self-defense and that appellants provoked the difficulty by committing the armed robbery. Authority clearly supports the contention in this respect and indicates that a person who provokes a difficulty thereby forfeits his right to self-defense. This doctrine has been extended to preclude a person who commits a felony from claiming self-defense not only to the intended victim of the felony, but also as to any person intervening in an attempt either to prevent the crime or to apprehend the criminal.

This court is faced, then, with two competing principles. On the one hand is the doctrine that a person has the right to use necessary force to protect himself against an unlawful arrest involving excessive force; on the other hand is the doctrine that a person provoking a difficulty forfeits his right to self-defense. We believe that, in the particular circumstances before us now, the latter doctrine must prevail. In our recent opinion in Miller v. State, we said in part:

> The control of man's destructive and aggressive impulses is one of the great unsolved problems of our society. Our rules of law should discourage the unnecessary use of physical force between man and man. Any rule which promotes rather than inhibits violence should be re-examined. Along with increased sensitivity to the rights of the criminally accused there should be a corresponding awareness of our need to develop rules which facilitate decent and peaceful behavior by all.

Here we are again presented with a situation which calls for further development and refinement in light of the guidelines which were articulated in *Miller*. Given the exigencies of the circumstances which flowed from appellants' still incomplete armed robbery, we can perceive of no persuasive policy reasons for according appellants the privilege of self-defense. We hold, therefore, that a person who commits an armed robbery forfeits his right to claim as a defense the necessity to protect himself against the use of excessive force by either the intended victim of the robbery or by any person intervening to prevent the crime or to apprehend the criminal, absent a factual showing that at the time the violence occurred, the dangerous situation created by the armed robbery no longer existed.

Accordingly, in the instant case, even if it is conceded that there is some evidence that Officer Strong used excessive force in attempting to arrest the Gray brothers, the perilous situation created by the armed robbery continued to exist at the time the shooting occurred. The uncontradicted evidence shows that Officer Strong was killed by Dewey Gray while the Grays were in the course of perpetrating an armed robbery. This is one of the most dangerous crimes known to man. Both Dewey and Willie Gray were still inside the robbed premises and in possession of the stolen money when surprised by Officer Strong, and the gun Dewey used in the robbery was still in his hand. It is no answer that the suddenness of Officer Strong's attempts to stop the commission of this crime prevented appellants from manifesting their intent to abandon the robbery or to surrender. Here appellants created the very situation which precluded any effective communication at the time in question.

Thus, on the facts of this case, we conclude that there is no room for difference of opinion among reasonable men that appellants were in fact engaging in and attempting to complete an armed robbery at the time they were intercepted by Officer Strong, and that they are thereby precluded from claiming self-defense. We believe this conclusion to be a sound one. Where, as in this case, the defendant commits a felony which includes an immediate threat of violence, he has created a situation so fraught with peril as to preclude his claim of self-defense to any act of violence arising therefrom. Our holding is limited to the situation where the armed robbery is still in progress and where there is grave danger of violence, injury, or loss of life because a weapon is being used to consummate the felony.

Before a self-defense instruction will be required, two evidentiary tests must be met. First there must be some evidence that excessive force was used to effect an arrest or stop the commission of a felony. Second, there must be some evidence from which a jury could conclude that the dangerous situation created by the felony no longer existed. In the case now before us the second requirement has not been met.

To permit appellants to justify their slaying of Officer Strong by claiming self-defense on the facts of this record would be to fashion a rule of law unresponsive to society's need for protection against just such extraordinarily dangerous conduct. This would not, in our view, tend to "facilitate decent and peaceful behaviour by all." To bestow such a privilege to slay would be manifestly unsound.

NOTES

1. If Abbott had killed one of the Scaranos in the honest but unreasonable belief that deadly force was necessary in self-defense, should he be held liable for any grade of criminal homicide? Why? If you believe that self-preservation is instinctual how can punishment of Abbott under the hypothetical facts be justified?

2. Does the requirement that the defendant's belief in the necessity for his use of deadly force be *reasonable* add anything to our analysis? Can the use of deadly force be necessary if it was *unreasonable* under the circumstances as they would have appeared to a reasonable man in the defendant's situation? Apparently both the legislature and Supreme Court of Nebraska thought so. In 1969 the legislature enacted Neb.Rev.Stat. § 29–114 (1969 Cum.Supp.) which provided:

> No person in this state shall be placed in legal jeopardy of any kind whatsoever for protecting, by any means necessary, himself, his family, or his real or personal property, or when coming to the aid of another who is in imminent danger of or the victim of aggravated assault, armed robbery, holdup, rape, murder, or any other heinous crime.

> When substantial question of self defense in such a case shall exist, which needs legal investigation or court action for the full determination of the facts, and the defendant's actions are subsequently found justified under the intent of this section, the State of Nebraska shall indemnify or reimburse such defendant for all loss of time, legal fees, court costs, or other expense involved in his defense.

In State v. Goodseal, 186 Neb. 359, 183 N.W.2d 258 (1971), the court, sua sponte, held that the statute was an unconstitutional attempt to delegate to those asserting the right of self-defense the power to decide the punishment of the aggressor. The court focused solely on the first paragraph of § 29–114 and relied heavily on the fact that efforts to amend the statute to make reference to "reasonable means" had been defeated. It did not refer to the second paragraph of the section, yet would not the process of determining the existence of justification there contemplated involve an evaluation of something more than the honesty of the defendant's belief in the necessity for his actions?

3. If, under the hypothetical facts of note 1 supra, Abbott is to be deemed culpable, what grade of homicide would be most appropriate? Is your analysis the same as in the provocation formula for manslaughter? Should there be any distinctions?

4. A invites B and C to his place of business. An altercation ensues between B and C. A requests B to leave. This causes a conflict between A and B which escalates to the point where A is in reasonable fear of imminent danger to his life from B. May A use deadly force even if he has a safe retreat by leaving his place of business? Commonwealth v. Johnston,

438 Pa. 485, 263 A.2d 376 (1970). If, as the *Johnston* court announces, "life is sacred," what reason can be offered for extending the "no retreat" rule to a defendant's place of business?

If our society believes that a man's home (and even, perhaps, his place of work) is a "sanctuary" from which flight is unnecessary as a precondition to the use of deadly force, should he be required to retreat into his home if that would offer safety or may he stand on his porch and use deadly force? State v. Bonano, 59 N.J. 515, 284 A.2d 345 (1971) (defendant armed with pistol need not retreat before assailant brother-in-law mounting porch steps armed with knife; "a porch or similar appurtenance" is deemed to come within the concept of being within one's dwelling house).

The *Bonano* decision reflects the special importance of the home as a place of safety. Under this view force, including deadly force, to prevent a forcible entry into a dwelling may be resorted to earlier than would otherwise be authorized under the rules pertaining to prevention of crime, defense of self or, of course, of property. Although the decisions are not entirely in agreement it seems clear that deadly force may not be employed merely to prevent trespass without more. Rather there must be a reasonable apprehension that the assailant intends to make forcible entry for the purpose of committing a felony or to inflict personal harm on the occupants. However, once entry has been made the normal standards for the rise of force, including the no-retreat rule, are employed for deciding the issue of justification. State v. Brookshire, 353 S.W.2d 681 (Mo.Sup.1962); State v. Couch, 52 N.M. 127, 193 P.2d 405 (1946).

5. If A in note 4 supra had initiated the aggression would he be required to retreat before being lawfully permitted to resort to deadly force in response to B? Even though he initiates the conflict with non-deadly force and it occurs on his own premises?

6. Is the *Gray* court saying that an armed robber may be executed if apprehended in the course of his crime? Would it be a desirable legal principle that there can be no claim of self-defense if the killing of the defendant would have been justifiable or excusable homicide? What if the deceased was employing deadly force in the honest and reasonable but erroneous belief that the defendant was engaged in a violent felony?

Under the written "unwritten law" of Texas it is justifiable homicide if a man kills his wife's lover if he does so "before the parties to the act have separated." Vernon's Ann.Tex.P.C. art. 1220 (Penal Code) (1967). If the adulterer caught in such a compromising situation resists the husband's efforts to commit justifiable homicide and kills him, can he plead self-defense? Does the answer depend on whether adultery is a felony or misdemeanor in Texas? Reed v. State, 11 Tex.App. 509, 40 Am.Rep. 795 (1882). See State v. Taylor, 15 N.C.App. 303, 190 S.E.2d 254 (1972) (living with another man's wife does not, in itself, deprive defendant of his right of self defense with respect to attack by irate husband).

7. One of the errors claimed by Abbott on appeal was the trial court's sustaining of an objection to the following portion of defense counsel's direct examination of the defendant.

"Q. How much do you weigh, Mr. Abbott? A. At the present time?

Q. At the present time. A. Just close to 200 pounds, right now.

Q. Now, on July 15, 1957 [the date of the alleged crime] do you know how much you weighed? About July 15, not necessarily on that day, say within a few pounds either way. A. About 135, 140 pounds, I guess.

Q. Why was your weight so low at that time?

Mr. Loftus: I object on the ground it is irrelevant. I don't see any relevancy to this situation.

The Court: I will sustain the objection."

174 A.2d at 887. Was the ruling of the trial judge correct? What if at the time of the altercation the defendant, as he claimed, was recovering from serious injuries and illness? To what extent, if at all, should the physical characteristics of the defendant be admissible on the issue of self-defense? His psychological characteristics? *Compare* Abbott *with* State v. Bess, 53 N.J. 10, 247 A.2d 669 (1968).

8. The court in *Abbott* approved the view that the burden of persuasion with respect to the defense of self-defense rests with the prosecution. In a minority of jurisdictions the defendant not only has the burden of producing evidence with respect to self-defense but also has the burden of persuasion, usually by a preponderance. See State v. Millett, 273 A.2d 504, 505–508 (Me.1971). Which view more fully expresses the belief that human life is the supreme value?

Should the rule against inconsistent defenses, mentioned in connection with entrapment, have any application to self-defense? Does a defendant who denies striking the fatal blow have a right to an instruction on self-defense? Commonwealth v. Gray, 441 Pa. 91, 271 A.2d 486 (1970).

---

2. DEFENSE OF OTHERS

PEOPLE v. YOUNG

New York Supreme Court, Appellate Division, 1961.
12 A.D.2d 262, 210 N.Y.S.2d 358.

BREITEL, Justice. The question is whether one is criminally liable for assault in the third degree if he goes to the aid of another who he mistakenly, but reasonably, believes is being unlawfully beaten, and thereby injures one of the apparent assaulters. In truth, the seeming victim was being lawfully arrested by two police officers in plain clothes. Defendant stands convicted of such a criminal assault, for which he received a sentence of 60 days in the workhouse, the execution of such sentence being suspended.

Defendant, aged 40, regularly employed, and with a clean record except for an $8 fine in connection with a disorderly conduct charge 19 years before in Birmingham, Alabama, observed two middle-aged men beating and struggling with a youth of 18. This was at 3:40 p. m. on October 17, 1958 in front of 64 West 64th Street in Manhattan. Defendant was acquainted with none of the persons involved; but believing that the youth was being unlawfully assaulted, and this is not disputed by the other participants, defendant went to his rescue, pulling on or punching at the seeming assailants. In the ensuing affray one of the older men got his leg locked with that of defendant and when defendant fell the man's leg was broken at the kneecap. The injured man then pulled out a revolver, announced to defendant that he was a police officer, and that defendant was under arrest. It appears that the youth in question had played some part in a street incident which resulted in the two men, who were detectives in plain clothes, seeking to arrest him for disorderly conduct. The youth had resisted, and it was in the midst of this resistance that defendant came upon the scene.

At the trial the defendant testified that he had known nothing about what had happened before he came upon the scene; that he had gone to his aid because the youth was crying and trying to pull away from the middle-aged men; and that the older men had almost pulled the trousers off the youth. The only detective who testified stated, in response to a question from the court, that defendant did not know and had no way of knowing, so far as he knew, that they were police officers or that they were making an arrest.

Two things are to be kept sharply in mind in considering the problem at hand. The first is that all that is involved here is a criminal prosecution for simple assault (Penal Law, § 244), and that the court is not concerned with the incidence of civil liability in the law of torts as a result of what happened on the street. Second, there is not here involved any question of criminal responsibility for interfering with an arrest where it is known to the actor that police officers are making an arrest, but he mistakenly believes that the arrest is unlawful.

In this State there are no discoverable precedents involving mistake of fact when one intervenes on behalf of another person and the prosecution has been for assault, rather than homicide. (The absence of precedents in this state and many others may simply mean that no enforcement agency would prosecute in the situations that must have occurred.) No one would dispute, however, that a mistake of fact would provide a defense if the prosecution were for homicide. This divided approach is sometimes based on the untenable distinction that mistake of fact may negative a "specific" intent required in the degrees of homicide but is irrelevant to the general intent required in simple assault, or, on the even less likely distinction, that the only intent involved in assault is the intent to touch without consent or legal justification (omitting the qualification of unlawfulness). The last, of course, is a partial confusion of tort law with criminal law, and even then is not quite correct (Restatement, Torts, §§ 63–75).

There have been precedents elsewhere among the states. There is a split among the cases and in the jurisdictions. Most hold that the rescuer intervenes at his own peril, but others hold that he is excused if he acts under mistaken but reasonable belief that he is protecting a victim from unlawful attack. Many of the cases which hold that the actor proceeds at his peril involve situations where the actor was present throughout, or through most, or through enough of the transaction and, therefore, was in no position to claim a mistake of fact. Others arise in rough situations in which the feud or enmity generally to the peace officer is a significant factor. Almost all apply unanalytically the rubric that the right to intervene on behalf of another is no greater than the other's right to self-defense, a phrasing of ancient but questionable lineage going back to when crime and tort were not yet divided in the common law—indeed, when the right to private redress was not easily distinguishable from the sanction for the public wrong.

It would protract the discussion and be bootless to detail all the cases, or even to make further illustrative selection. In England, however, it is interesting to observe, a defendant who intervened mistakenly in a proper arrest by peace officers has been held liable, not for assault, but under a specific statute related to police officers acting in the execution of their duty, and which, the courts construed, did not require knowledge on the part of the third party in order to make him responsible. Of course, in this state, too, there is an express crime for interfering with a lawful arrest. It is a felony and requires a "specific" intent to resist the lawful apprehension. So that here we have rejected the policy adopted in England expressly making innocent interference with a lawful arrest a crime.

The modern view, as already noted, is not to impose criminal responsibility in connection with intent crimes for those who act with good motivation, in mistaken but reasonable misapprehension of the facts. Indeed, Prosser would not even hold such a person responsible in tort (Torts [2d Ed.] pp. 91–92). He makes the added argument that "if an honest mistake is to relieve the defendant of liability when he thinks that he must defend himself, his meritorious defense of another should receive the same consideration." (Restatement, Torts, supra, § 76, also exculpates an actor for intervention on behalf of a third person where the actor has a reasonable belief that the third person is privileged and that such intervention is necessary. Notably, the Restatement sharply limits the persons on whose behalf the actor may intervene, but this, of course, is in the area of civil liability and, as already noted, there are those who would extend the privilege.)

More recently in the field of criminal law the American Law Institute in drafting a model penal code has concerned itself with the question in this case. Under section 3.05 of the Model Penal Code the use of force for the protection of others is excused if the actor behaves under a mistaken belief (Model Penal Code, Tent.Draft No. 8, May 9, 1958.)

The comments by the reporters on the Model Penal Code are quite appropriate. After stating that the defense of strangers should be assimilated to the defense of oneself the following is said:

> "In support of such a ruling, it may perhaps be said that the potentiality for deterring the actor from the use of force is greater where he is protecting a stranger than where he is protecting himself or a loved one, because in the former case the interest protected is of relatively less importance to him; moreover the potential incidence of mistake in estimating fault or the need for action on his part is increased where the defendant is protecting a stranger, because in such circumstances he is less likely to know which party to the quarrel is in the right. These arguments may be said to lead to the conclusion that, in order to minimize the area for error or mistake, the defendant should act at his peril when he is protecting a stranger. This emasculates the privilege of protection of much of its content, introducing a liability without fault which is indefensible in principle. The cautious potential actor who knows the law will, in the vast majority of cases, refrain from acting at all. The result may well be that an innocent person is injured without receiving assistance from bystanders. It seems far preferable, therefore, to predicate the justification upon the actor's belief, safeguarding if thought necessary against abuse of the privilege by the imposition of a requirement of proper care in evolving the belief. Here, as elsewhere, the latter problem is dealt with by the general provision in Section 3.09." (Model Penal Code, Tent.Draft No. 8, supra, at p. 32.)

Apart from history, precedents, and the language distinctions that may be found in the statutes, it stands to reason that a man should not be punished criminally for an intent crime unless he, indeed, has the intent. Where a mistake of relevant facts is involved the premises for such intent are absent. True, there are occasions in public policy and its implementation for dispensing with intent and making one responsible for one's act even without immediate or intentional fault. This is generally accomplished by statute, and generally by statute which expressly dispenses with the presence of intent. Thus, it may well be that a Legislature will determine that in order to protect the police in their activities and to make it difficult to promote false defenses one may proceed against a police officer while acting in the line of duty only at one's peril, as do the English, *vide* supra. But this is not a part of the intent crime of assault as it existed under common law or as it exists today under the statutes.

Indeed, if the analysis were otherwise, then the conductor who mistakenly ejects a passenger for not having paid his fare would be guilty of assault, which is hardly the case. So, too, a police officer who came to the assistance of a brother police officer would be guilty of assault if it should turn out that the brother police officer was engaged in making an unlawful arrest or was embarked upon an assault of his own private motivation.

It is a sterile and desolate legal system that would exact punishment for an intentional assault from one like this defendant, who acted from the most commendable motives and without excessive force. Had the facts been as he thought them, he would have been a hero and not condemned as a criminal actor. The dearth of applicable precedents—as distinguished from theoretical generalizations never, or rarely, applied—in England and in most of the states demonstrates that the benevolent intervenor has not been cast as a pariah. It is no answer to say that the policeman should be called when one sees an injustice. Even in the most populous centers, policemen are not that common or that available. Also, it ignores the peremptory response to injustice that the good man has ingrained. Again, it is to be noted, in a criminal proceeding one is concerned with the act against society, not with the wrong between individuals and the right to reparation, which is the province of tort.

Accordingly, the judgment of conviction should be reversed, on the law, and the information dismissed.

VALENTE, Justice (dissenting).

I dissent and would affirm the conviction because the intent to commit a battery was unquestionably proven; and, since there was no relationship between defendant and the person whom the police officers were arresting, defendant acted at his peril in intervening and striking the officer. Under well-established law, defendant's rights were no greater than those of the person whom he sought to protect; and since the arrest was lawful, defendant was no more privileged to assault the police officer than the person being arrested.

The conclusion that defendant was properly convicted in this case comports with sound public policy. It would be a dangerous precedent for courts to announce that plain-clothes police officers attempting lawful arrests over wrongful resistance are subject to violent interference by strangers ignorant of the facts, who may attack the officers with impunity so long as their ignorance forms a reasonable basis for a snap judgment of the situation unfavorable to the officers. Although the actions of such a defendant, who acts on appearances, may eliminate the specific intent required to convict him of a felony assault, it should not exculpate him from the act of aggressive assistance to a law breaker in the process of wrongfully resisting a proper arrest.

I do not detract from the majority's views regarding commendation of the acts of a good Samaritan, although it may be difficult in some cases to distinguish such activities from those of an officious intermeddler. But opposed to the encouragement of the "benevolent intervenor" is the conflicting and more compelling interest of protection of police officers. In a city like New York, where it becomes necessary to utilize the services of a great number of plain-clothes officers, the efficacy of their continuing struggle against crime should not be impaired by the possibility of interference by citizens who may be acting from commendable motives. It is more desirable—and evidently up to this point the Legislature has so deemed it—that in such cases the intervening citizen be held to act at his peril when he assaults a stranger, who unknown to him is a police officer legally performing his duty. In this conflict of interests, the balance preponderates in favor of the protection of the police rather than the misguided intervenor.

PEOPLE v. YOUNG

Court of Appeals of New York, 1962.
11 N.Y.2d 274, 229 N.Y.S.2d 1, 183 N.E.2d 319.

PER CURIAM. Whether one, who in good faith aggressively intervenes in a struggle between another person and a police officer in civilian dress attempting to effect the lawful arrest of the third person, may be properly convicted of assault in the third degree is a question of law of first impression here.

The opinions in the court below in the absence of precedents in this State carefully expound the opposing views found in other jurisdictions. The majority in the Appellate Division have adopted the minority rule in the other States that one who intervenes in a struggle between strangers under the mistaken but reasonable belief that he is protecting another who he assumes is being unlawfully beaten is thereby exonerated from criminal liability. The weight of authority holds with the dissenters below that one who goes to the aid of a third person does so at his own peril.

While the doctrine espoused by the majority of the court below may have support in some States, we feel that such a policy would not be conducive to an orderly society. We agree with the settled policy of law in most jurisdictions that the right of a person to defend another ordinarily should not be greater than such person's right to defend himself. Subdivision 3 of section 246 of the Penal Law, Consol.Laws, c. 40, does not apply as no offense was being committed on the person of the one resisting the lawful arrest. Whatever may be the public policy where the felony charged requires proof of a specific intent and the issue is justifiable homicide (cf. People v. Maine, 166 N.Y. 50, 59 N.E. 696), it is not relevant in a prosecution for assault in the third degree where it is only necessary to show that the defendant knowingly struck a blow.

In this case there can be no doubt that the defendant intended to assault the police officer in civilian dress. The resulting assault was forceful. Hence motive or mistake of fact is of no significance as the defendant was not charged with a crime requiring such intent or knowledge. To be guilty of third degree assault "It is sufficient that the defendant voluntarily intended to commit the unlawful act of touching" (1 Wharton's Criminal Law and Procedure [1957], § 338, p. 685). Since in these circumstances the aggression was inexcusable the defendant was properly convicted.

Accordingly, the order of the Appellate Division should be reversed and the information reinstated.

NOTE

Does the "alter ego" rule for evaluating the scope of one's right to defend another which is embraced by the Court of Appeals in *Young* abandon moral culpability as a prerequisite to criminal liability? If so, under what rationale can punishment of Young be justified? Will we have a more "orderly society" if people are discouraged from intervening to protect others from physical violence? *Compare* State v. Fair, 45 N.J. 77, 211 A.2d 359 (1965). The *Young* decision is critically examined in 63 Colum.L.Rev. 160 (1963) and 111 U.Pa.L.Rev. 506 (1963).

---

3. DEFENSE OF PROPERTY

RUSSELL v. STATE

Supreme Court of Alabama, 1929.
219 Ala. 567, 122 So. 683.

Robert Russell was convicted of murder in the first degree, and he appeals.

FOSTER, J. According to defendant's evidence, decedent and two others went to defendant's home to repossess a cooking stove, upon which it was claimed one of them had acquired by transfer a conditional (or lease) sale contract, from the alleged seller to defendant; that defendant informed them that if they had a writ of detinue it was perfectly all right, but otherwise not to get the stove; that they said they did not need any law, that law cost money, etc., and went on in the kitchen to take it; that defendant had no gun, but picked up a pick handle and followed them to the kitchen, and they went to the stove; that defendant told them they had to get out and leave his home, and he was not going to give up the stove without the proper means. One of them said to defendant that he must put that stick down, or he would give defendant a "stick fit," and made a motion for his hip and pointed his finger at defendant, and said, "I will shoot you in two, boy." Defendant threw down the pick handle and ran out to where his wife was in the yard, and told her to go in there and tell them to get out of there and leave his house; that defendant then went to a neighbor's next door and procured a gun (pistol) and came back home, and went to the front porch where one of the men was, and told him to stay out of his house; defendant then heard his wife and little kids crying out, and he ran back in the house, and heard her begging them to stop taking out the stove and leave; that as defendant came to the door, deceased said, "didn't we put you out once"; defendant said, "yes, you put me out once, but I am back here again"; that defendant went up to him and caught him by the right arm, and would not let him go with the stove, and told him to put the stove down and get out; that one of the party, not deceased, said "set it down, and I will put that son of a bitch out of here to stay this time," and when he said that defendant shot as the men were putting down the stove, and the bullet, after going through the warming closet, hit the companion of deceased who had made the remark, but he was not killed, and defendant shot again as deceased at the same time kicked defendant, and deceased was hit by that shot, which killed him. Defendant then ran, and went off to another mine some 12 or 15 miles away, where he was later arrested. Neither deceased nor any of his companions displayed a weapon, and if they had one it was not shown.

The testimony for the state was that no threats were made, no anger displayed; that when defendant returned with the weapon he placed it against deceased and shot and killed him without warning or provocation, after having shot and wounded his companion.

* * *

We think that charges 6, 27, and 28, refused appellant, conflict with the rules of law which we have found to be generally accepted as authoritative. The portion of the general charge attacked in brief seems correctly to assert the same principle. It is the following statements: "This defendant would not be justified under the laws of Alabama in shooting the deceased, to prevent the removal from his house of a stove or range. The law would not justify a homicide to prevent the commission of a trespass upon the doctrine of self-defense." * * *

We think the charges were properly refused, and the excerpt from the general charge now argued by appellant as being erroneous was also without error, for the reasons which we will now discuss.

It is well understood that deceased and his companions did not have the right to take possession of the stove, if, in doing so, it was necessary to commit a breach of the peace, or to use violence. Street v. Sinclair, 71 Ala. 110. It is stated in Street v. Sinclair, supra: "But he proceeds at his own peril if he commits the slightest assault, or other breach of the public peace, for, if individuals were thus allowed to redress their own private injuries, the peace of society and good order of government would cease." In another case it is said: "It is a settled principle of our law, that every one has the right to defend his person and property against unlawful violence, and may employ as much force as is necessary to prevent its invasion. Property would be of little value, if the owner was bound to stand with folded arms and suffer it taken by him who is bold and unscrupulous enough to seize it. But when it is said a man may rightfully use as much force as is necessary for the protection of his person and property, it must be recollected the principle is subject to this most important qualification, that he shall not, except in extreme cases, inflict great bodily harm, or endanger human life. State v. Morgan [25 N.C.] 3 Ired. 186 [38 Am. Dec. 714]. The preservation of human life, and of limb and member from grievous harm, is of more importance to society than the protection of property. Compensation may be made for injuries to, or the destruction of, property; but for the deprivation of life there is no recompense; and for grievous bodily harm, at most, but a poor equivalent. It is an inflexible principle of the criminal law of this State, and we believe of all the states, as it is of the common law, that for the prevention of a bare trespass upon property, not the dwelling-house, human life can not be taken, nor grievous bodily harm inflicted. If in the defense of property, not the dwelling-house, life is taken with a deadly weapon, it is murder, though the killing may be actually necessary to prevent the trespass." Simpson v. State, 59 Ala. 1, 14, 31 Am.Rep. 1; * * *

The rule at common law is that one may prevent an aggressor from entering his home, when the door is closed, even to the taking of life. But once inside peaceably, even though misbehaving, the owner cannot intentionally take his life for his refusal to leave, though he may use reasonable force to exclude him.

A felonious homicide is committed by one who inflicts death merely in opposing an unlawful endeavor to carry away his property. He has the right to resist, but not to the taking of life.

Our conclusion is that the charges refused appellant conflict with these well-established principles.

Charges 14 and 17 justify defendant in killing deceased if the latter were committing a felony in defendant's home. It is sometimes said that "the law will justify the taking of life when it is done from necessity to prevent the commission of a felony." But this rule has limitations not now material.

Decedent and his companions were attempting to repossess property under a claim of right, by virtue of a conditional sale contract. We do not think a jury would be justified in finding a felonious intent under those circumstances. That intent is a necessary element of such a felony as may be claimed against the parties on that occasion. There is no claim here that they were acting under a mere dishonest pretense of right to the stove. There was therefore no felony, and the charges were abstract, if not bad for other reasons.

The doctrine of want of necessity to retreat when defendant is attacked in his own home as embraced in some of the refused charges has no application when, as here, there does not seem to have been a just cause to believe that an attack was about to be made on defendant such as would justify him in his claim of self-defense.

Affirmed.

STATE v. CHILDERS

Supreme Court of Ohio, 1938.
133 Ohio St. 508, 14 N.E.2d 767.

On December 3, 1935, an indictment was returned charging that on or about September 1, 1935, Arn Childers "unlawfully shot one Daniel Earl Wagoner, with intent to wound him, the said Daniel Earl Wagoner."

* * *

Childers owned a farm which was some distance from the house in which he resided. On the farm was a field of watermelons planted by a tenant, but which were at the time in question under the control of Childers.

A few days before September 1, 1935, considerable damage was done to the watermelon crop, apparently by some boys in the neighborhood. The evidence shows that one of these boys was Daniel Earl Wagoner [who lived on an adjoining farm].

After the damage was done to his melons, Childers set six spring guns, one concealed at each end of the melon patch. Attached to the triggers were small wires which went all around the patch. The guns so placed and set were single-barrel shotguns loaded with ordinary type of shells. The wires were so arranged that if anyone came in contact with them, the guns would be discharged. The defendant claimed there were two notices written on pieces of paper, saying "Dangerous, don't go in this patch. Go back out," which were placed one at each end of the patch.

On or about September 1, 1935, when young Wagoner entered the patch, one of the guns was discharged and he received about 150 shot, principally in his right side, arm and leg. He was seriously wounded, and remained in the hospital 18 days. Upon these facts in brief, an indictment was returned against Childers. At the trial, Childers admitted setting the guns, after his melon patch had been destroyed, for the purpose of preventing anyone from again coming on that part of his premises. Young Wagoner testified that while he had been in

the patch on the Sunday before the shooting, he did not see any notices on September 1st, and that he thought the watermelons belonged
to members of his family.

Upon this evidence, the jury found the defendant, Childers, guilty.

* * *

The principal question involved is whether the facts proven warrant a conviction of Childers of the offense of shooting with intent
to wound. This is the first time in its history that this court has been
called upon to pass upon the legality of spring guns, although there
is no dearth of such cases in other jurisdictions.

Counsel for defendant claims that, since there is no specific statute in Ohio making it unlawful to set a spring gun on one's own property, no crime was committed by Childers. If, however, the proof
adduced brings the acts of the defendant within the provisions of section 12420, General Code, a specific statute would be unnecessary.

At early common law, the setting of a spring gun was not in itself unlawful, and if a person was killed by it while attempting to commit a felony no criminal liability ensued. This rule in England has
now been changed by statute to cover acts such as this. In this country, at least one State has adopted a statute making spring guns
unlawful. Schmidt v. State, 159 Wis. 15, 149 N.W. 388, Ann.Cas.
1916E, 107.

However, the early common law of England has never been followed in this country. The right to set a trap in defense of one's own
dwelling has sometimes found approval in our courts as well as in
England under its statute. Some early cases have indicated that protection of property is also a justification.

In 1832, in the case of Gray v. Combs, 7 J.J.Marsh., Ky., 478, 23
Am.Dec. 431, when a slave attempted to break into a warehouse and
was shot and killed by a trap gun, the slave owner was not permitted
to recover, on the ground that the shooting was done in prevention of
a felony.

In Aldrich v. Wright, 53 N.H. 398, 16 Am.Rep. 339, it was held not
to be unlawful to set a gun which killed four fur-bearing mink which
were damaging the owner's property.

Both of these cases, under the peculiar circumstances of the law,
involved property rights solely, and the questions arose in civil actions.

In State v. Moore, 31 Conn. 479, 83 Am.Dec. 159, the court said
that the mere setting of a spring gun on one's own premises for their
protection is not unlawful in itself. If it would become a public nuisance, however, the court said a person so setting it could be prosecuted.

The rules set out in these three cases are somewhat broader than
the one generally adhered to in this country. By the overwhelming

weight of authority, a person is not justified in taking human life or inflicting bodily harm upon the person of another by means of traps, spring guns, or other instruments of destruction, unless, as a matter of law, he would have been justified had he been personally present and had taken the life or inflicted the bodily harm with his own hands.

 Tested by these principles, one might set a spring gun in his own home, and if its discharge prevented the ingress of a burglar, he might be justified because if he had been present he could have fired the the shot. Has he the right, however, to set such a gun in an open field to prevent trespassers from entering his melon patch?

A criminal act may be committed through an innocent agent as well as in person. There are many instances where the defendant is deemed to have committed a crime although not personally present at the time the act was performed.

No one should be permitted to do indirectly what he may not do directly. Defendant's absence from the scene of the shooting should not enlarge his rights.

In this case, the facts are to be considered just as if Childers, himself, was in the melon patch and fired the shot, or as if he had stationed another there to fire a shot in case trespassers entered the patch. Childers knew that if anyone came in contact with the wires the gun would be discharged. It was not only the natural and probable consequence that bodily injuries would be received in that event, but it was also his intention that they should be inflicted.

Daniel Earl Wagoner was a boy 14 years of age. He was a mere trespasser entering upon Childers' land to commit at most a petit larceny by eating his melons. While a person has a right to protect his property from a trespass, and, after warning or notice to the trespasser, use such force as is reasonably necessary so to do, he cannot unlawfully use firearms to expel the intruder where he has no reasonable ground to fear the trespasser will do him great bodily harm.

The jury found that no warning was given Wagoner and that the force used was unnecessary to prevent the trespass. Had Wagoner been killed, a homicide charge could have been instituted. Not having lost his life but having received a great bodily injury, a charge of shooting with intent to wound was fully sustained by the evidence.

* * *

The setting of the gun created a menace and a nuisance, calculated to impose great bodily harm on those who entered the melon patch. If Wagoner saw Childers in the patch with a shotgun, he could not enter and take the gun away from him. If, however, Childers, without just cause, fired the shotgun and hit Wagoner in order to prevent a mere trespass, a crime was committed. The unlawful act is the shooting itself. One may shoot in self-defense, but if he shoots another maliciously and intentionally without justification the law is violated.

In accordance with the great weight of authority, one who sets a ⚡ spring gun or trap does so at his peril. If it is set in a dwelling house and prevents the entrance of a felon, the justification may be sufficient to acquit the owner. If on the other hand it inflicts death or great bodily harm on an innocent person, or one who is a mere trespasser, the one who set the trap must suffer the consequences. He is presumed to intend the natural and probable results of his voluntary act. It becomes as much of an assault on another as if he was personally present and pulled the trigger.

If Childers was vexed by secret trespassers or marauders, he could have found protection by his own vigilance within lawful limits. He could have provided a stronger inclosure or kept a more constant watch. If these had failed, an appeal to the agencies of the law would no doubt have given him adequate protection. His reckless disregard for the value of human life can find neither sanction within the law, nor sympathy without, from this court.

By setting the trap, Childers, must be held responsible for that which happened just as if he had been personally present. The boy, Wagoner, was a mere trespasser and unarmed. Childers could not maintain a claim of self-defense or that the shooting was accidental. * * *

[A]ffirmed.

STATE v. DOOLEY

Supreme Court of Missouri, 1894.
121 Mo. 591, 26 S.W. 558.

GANTT, P. J. On the 15th of June, 1892, Mrs. Gus Price was the owner of two horses, which were in the possession of the defendants, at Sweet Springs. Mrs. Price * * * had offered a reward for these horses. On the 15th of June, 1892, Gus Price was engaged in driving [his wife's horses for the defendants' bus line] * * *. On this day, Marshal Bennett and Constable Evans arrived at Sweet Springs, and made known to defendants that they had a warrant for the arrest of Gus Price for stealing these horses; and they arrested Price, and told Dooley they would start with Price and the horses that night. In the mean time, Price proposed to sell the horses to W. H. Dooley, and Dooley agreed to give him $150, and stand good for all the expenses. There was no evidence that Dooley paid Price anything for the horses, in pursuance of this agreement. It does appear, in a general way, that the defendants had hired the horses, and Price to drive the bus * * *. Next morning the team was hitched to the bus, and placed in charge of a driver named Taylor, and was driven into the city, to the station, to meet a train. Defendant Harvey Dooley accompanied the bus. * * * While the team was standing at the station, awaiting the train, Bennett, Evans, and Gus Price suddenly appeared, and at once began to unhitch the horses from the bus. Harvey Dooley wanted to know if they had a warrant for the horses, and they said "No;" that Price had told them to take them. And, when asked, Price said he gave them authority to take them. They placed the extra halters on the two horses, and left in the carriage, leading the Price horses. Harvey Dooley at once notified his father and co-defendant. Harvey armed himself with a Winchester rifle, and William H. Dooley took a revolver, and, mounting their horses, they pursued Bennett and Evans. They overtook them * * *, rode up on either side of Bennett's carriage, ordered the driver to stop, which he did; and they pointed their weapons at Bennett and Evans, ordered them to throw up their hands, and turn the horses loose, or they would shoot their heads off. Bennett and Evans made no resistance, but at once released the horses * * *. The defendants were indicted for an assault with intent to kill Bennett, with malice aforethought, and were convicted of an assault to kill, without malice, and a fine of $75 each assessed against them by the jury, which the court increased to the minimum fine of $100 each, and from these fines they appeal.

* * *

The ninth instruction for the state told the jury that "even though they should believe that Richard T. Bennett and George C. Evans irregularly or improperly obtained possession of the horses in controversy, yet such fact would not justify defendants in retaking the same by force, nor by the use of a deadly weapon," whereas defendants, in their sixth instruction, which was refused by the court, prayed the court to instruct the jury "that if the defendants had possession of said horses, and George C. Evans, Richard Bennett, and Gus Price took said team from defendants, without defendants' authority, and drove away with said horses, and that immediately thereafter the defendants followed said parties, and demanded and took said horses away from said Bennett, Evans, and Price, and used no more force than was necessary to do so, then defendants are guilty of no crime." The propriety of the giving of the said instruction for the state, and refusal of said instruction for defendants, will determine the merits of this appeal. That the evidence sustains the claim that the defendants were in the actual possession of the horses, claiming a property or possessory right in or to them, must be, we think, conceded. Their conduct must be measured, so far as this charge is concerned, by the facts as they existed that morning, or reasonably appeared to exist. Now, Bennett and Evans had no writ or authority to take the horses. Conceding they had a warrant for Price, that did not authorize them to seize the horses in the possession of a third person. Admitting that they were without lawful authority to take the horses, but that they did so, two questions arise: First, could defendants lawfully recapture them without resorting to the process of the courts? And, secondly, how much force could they lawfully use in affecting a recapture?

The first question must be answered in the affirmative. If the jury found, as we think there was evidence from which they could so find, that the defendants were in possession of these horses, in good faith claiming said possession, and Bennett and Evans, without authority, forcibly, in their presence, took them from their driver, the defendants had the right to retake them from Bennett and Evans.

And this brings us to the second, and important, inquiry in this case: How much force might defendants exert in reclaiming the horses? The power to retake is incident to the right to defend, but it is sometimes said that the right to recapture property is more limited than its defense, when in actual possession; and, while it is allowed, the courts have been cautious in defining the right, and justly so, on account of the danger usually attending the recapture, both to the owner and the peace of the community. When one's property is taken with a felonious intent, the urgency of the recapture is vastly greater than when there is a simple conflict in the claim of title to the property. In the case of felony great force may be resorted to with propriety; but where there is, clearly, no felony, but a mere dispute as to the legal ownership, a resort to violence disproportionate to the value of the property, and where peaceful remedies would prove equally efficacious, should not be sustained. It is asserted by Bishop that "while a man may use all reasonable and necessary force to defend his real or personal estate, of which he is in the actual possession, against another, who comes to dispossess him without right, he cannot innocently carry this defense to the extent of killing the aggressor." 1 Bish.Cr.Law (New) § 857; Bish.Cr.Law (6th Ed.) § 861. And the same learned authority also says: "Yet, consistent with this proposition, is another,—that one in the defense of his property (as distinguished from the defense of his person) should not resort to means reasonably calculated to endanger life." Bish.Cr.Law, § 862. * * * In State v. Morgan, 3 Ired. 186, a constable had seized the defendant's gun, which was his "arms for muster," and was privileged by law from seizure. The defendant drew his axe on the constable, and said "Give up the gun, or I'll split you down." After some further parley, the matter was arranged, and the gun released. On an indictment for an assault with intent to kill, the question was whether the conditional threat, coupled with the act of holding the axe in a position to strike, constituted an assault with intent to kill. Judge Gaston said: "Assuming, then, that the constable had wrongfully taken the gun, and that the defendant had a right to require its return, and that exertion of force, nothing short of that which was begun on the part of the defendant, would have availed to compel its return, in our opinion, the assault is not justified. It was made with a deadly weapon, which, if used, would have probably occasioned death, and made without any previous resistance on the part of the officer. It was therefore an assault with intent to kill. If this intent were lawful, the assault with that intent was lawful. If the intent was unlawful, the assault cannot be justified. Now, when it is said that a man may rightfully use as much force as is necessary for the protection of his person or property, it should be recollected that this rule is subject to this most important modification: that he shall not, except in extreme cases, endanger human life, or great bodily harm. * * * The purpose is, indeed, rightful, but it is not one of such paramount necessity as to justify a resort to such desperate means." The case at bar is strikingly similar to the case of State v. Morgan, supra. In this case, as in that, the act of the defendants in presenting two deadly weapons at Bennett and Evans was apparently a most dangerous assault, accompanied with a present purpose to do great bodily harm, or kill them; and the only declaration by which the character of the assault is mitigated, or attempted to be changed, is that their purpose was not unconditional, but having commenced the assault, and proceeded far enough to put Evans and Bennett in extreme danger, they suspended long enough to permit them to comply unconditionally with their demands to loose the horses.

* * *

Several witnesses in this case testified that the defendant William H. Dooley had his pistol drawn, and his son Harvey, to use his own expression, "covered Bennett with his rifle" before they demanded the horses. In his testimony, defendant W. H. Dooley, when asked, if they had not given him the horses, if it was not his purpose to use his pistol, answered, "I was after those horses. If I had to use them, I would have scuffled with them awhile, first. If they had attempted to shoot, we would have drawed there, and might have got them." In other words, not only his conduct, but his own testimony, indicated that he had a settled and determined purpose to shoot Bennett and Evans unless they complied with his demands. The pistol and rifle were both in position to shoot before the demand was made. If the defendants did effect the recapture of the horses by presenting the loaded revolver and rifle at Bennett and his party, then they exceeded the force authorized by law, and the unlawful taking of the horses by Bennett is no justification for such an assault.

* * * Had the court, in the ninth instruction for the state, only said that defendants would not be justified in retaking said horses by the use of a deadly weapon, that instruction would have been correct; but it went further, and said they would not be justified in retaking "by force." Now, we have seen that defendants were authorized to regain their lawful possession by force, provided that force did not consist of "means reasonably calculated to endanger life, or great bodily harm;" and hence the instruction, in this respect, denied de-

fendants a right vouchsafed them by the law. The defendants' sixth instruction should have been modified so as to restrict their right to recapture to such force as was reasonably necessary to effect that purpose, provided it did not extend to the use of a deadly weapon or to an assault likely to produce death or great bodily harm. Subject to this qualification, it is a question of fact for the jury, in each case, how much force is reasonable and necessary.

* * * This eighth instruction was also erroneous in that it denies, as does the second instruction for the defendant, the right to pursue and take the property. If, as we understand these two instructions, they limit the right of defendants to retake to the immediate time and place of taking, and deny it if the horses were temporarily taken out of their sight, in the flight to Higginsville, although the pursuit was immediate, we think they restrict the right of recaption too narrowly. With these modifications, the instructions will fairly present the case to the jury on a new trial. The judgment is reversed, and the cause remanded for a new trial. All of this division concur.

NOTES

1. An extensive review of both civil and criminal cases involving the use of mechanical devices for the protection of property may be found in Katko v. Briney, 183 N.W.2d 657 (Iowa 1971). There the court affirmed a verdict of $20,000 actual and $10,000 punitive damages for injuries caused to the trespassing plaintiff by a spring gun set by the defendant in his abandoned farmhouse.

2. Aside from situations such as the spring gun in *Childers* the defense of property will usually be raised as only one of several forms of justification: self-defense, defense of habitation, and prevention of crime.

Although the right to use force in defense of property has been the subject of rather ringing rhetoric, see State v. Lee, 258 N.C. 44, 127 S.E.2d 774 (1962), it is clear that, in general, our law values property far below life and limb. Compare the view expressed by Tex.Penal Code Ann. arts. 1224 and 1227 (1961):

"1224. Homicide is justifiable also in the protection of the person or property against any other unlawful and violent attack besides those mentioned, [art. 1222 announces that homicide is justifiable for preventing murder, rape, robbery, maiming, disfiguring, castration, arson, burglary and theft at night, or upon persons found armed with deadly weapons and in disguise in the night time on premises not their own] and in such cases all other means must be resorted to for the prevention of the injury, and the killing must take place while the person killed is in the very act of making such unlawful and violent attack * * *.

"1227. When under article 1224 a homicide is committed in the protection of property, it must be done under the following circumstances:

1. The possession must be of corporeal property, and not of a mere right, and the possession must be actual and not merely constructive.

2. The possession must be legal, though the right of the property may not be in the possessor.

3. If possession be once lost, it is not lawful to regain it by such means as result in homicide.

4. Every other effort in his power must have been made by the possessor to repel the aggression before he will be justified in killing."

Lilly v. State, 20 Tex.App. 1 (1885) made clear that these statutes represent an exception to the general rule that deadly force is not justified to prevent the forcible taking or removal of one's property, and that the right to so defend property was not dependent on whether injury to it is or is not accompanied by violence to the person. Would this statute have led to Russell's acquittal? Would that have been undesirable?

3. How would the *Dooley* case be resolved under the proposed Federal Criminal Code? If there is a difference in result, how can it be justified?

E.   RESISTANCE TO UNLAWFUL ARREST

BAD ELK v. UNITED STATES

Supreme Court of the United States, 1900.
177 U.S. 529, 20 S.Ct. 729, 44 L.Ed. 874.

[The defendant had been convicted of the murder of John Kills Back, a policeman, and sentenced to hang. The facts adduced were that one Gleason, angered at the defendant's discharge of his gun in the air, had, without authority, directed several policemen to arrest defendant and take him to the Indian Agency some 25 miles away. Although the prosecution claimed that the defendant shot without provocation, the latter testified that after he had agreed to go to the agency the following morning the deceased seemed to move for his gun and that he shot for fear that the others would.]

Mr. Justice PECKHAM delivered the opinion of the court.

* * *

Counsel for plaintiff in error asked the court to charge as follows:

"From the evidence as it appears in this action, none of the policemen who sought to arrest the defendant in this action prior to the killing of the deceased, John Kills Back, were justified in arresting the defendant, and he had a right to use such force as a reasonably prudent person might do in resisting such arrest by them."

The court denied the request, and counsel excepted.

The court charged the jury, among other things, as follows:

"The deceased, John Kills Back, had been ordered to arrest the defendant; hence he had a right to go and make the attempt to arrest the defendant. The defendant had no right to resist him. It is claimed on the part of the defendant that he made no resistance, and he was willing to go with the officer in the morning. I charge you, of course, that the officer, John Kills Back, had a right to determine for himself when this man should go to the agency with him.

*   *   *

"In this connection I desire to say to you, gentlemen of the jury, that the deceased, being an officer of the law, had a right to be armed, and for the purpose of arresting the defendant he would have had the right to show his revolver. He would have had the right to use only so much force as was necessary to take his prisoner, and the fact that he was using no more force than was necessary to take his prisoner would not be sufficient justification for the defendant to shoot him and kill him. The defendant would only be justified in killing the deceased when you should find that the circumstances showed that the deceased had so far forgotten his duties as an officer and had gone beyond the force necessary to arrest defendant, and was about to kill him or to inflict great bodily injury upon him, which was not necessary for the purpose of making the arrest."

This charge was duly excepted to.

We think the court clearly erred in charging that the policeman had the right to arrest the plaintiff in error, and to use such force as was necessary to accomplish the arrest, and that the plaintiff in error had no right to resist it.

The evidence as to the facts immediately preceding the killing was contradictory; the prosecution showing a killing when no active effort was at that very moment made to arrest, and the defendant showing an intended arrest and a determination to take him at that time at all events, and a move made by the deceased towards him with his pistol in sight and a seeming intention to use it against the defendant for the purpose of overcoming all resistance. Under these circumstances the error of the charge was material and prejudicial.

At common law, if a party resisted arrest by an officer without warrant, and who had no right to arrest him, and if in the course of that resistance the officer was killed, the offence of the party resisting arrest would be reduced from what would have been murder, if the officer had had the right to arrest, to manslaughter. What would be murder, if the officer had the right to arrest, might be reduced to manslaughter by the very fact that he had no such right. So an officer, at common law, was not authorized to make an arrest without a warrant, for a mere misdemeanor not committed in his presence. If the officer have no right to arrest, the other party might resist the illegal attempt to arrest him, using no more force than was absolutely necessary to repel the assault constituting the attempt to arrest.

We do not find any statute of the United States or of the State of South Dakota giving any right to these men to arrest an individual without a warrant on a charge of misdemeanor not committed in their presence.

* * *

No rule or regulation for the government of Indians upon a reservation has been cited, nor have we found any, which prohibits the firing of a gun there, "for fun," nor do we find any law, rule or regulation which authorizes an arrest, without warrant, of an Indian not charged even with the commission of a misdemeanor, nor does it anywhere appear that Gleason had authority to issue a warrant for an alleged violation of the rules or regulations.

It is plain from this review of the subject that the charge of the court below, that the policemen had the right to arrest this plaintiff in error, without warrant, and that, in order to accomplish such arrest, they had the right to show and use their pistols so far as was necessary for that purpose, and that the plaintiff in error had no right to resist such arrest, was erroneous. That it was a material error, it seems to us, is equally plain. It placed the transaction in a false light before the jury, and denied to the plaintiff in error those rights which he clearly had. The occasion of the trouble originated in Gleason's orders to arrest him, and in the announced intention on the part of the policemen, which they endeavored to accomplish, to arrest the plaintiff in error that night and take him to the agency, and all that followed that announcement ought to be viewed in the light of such proclaimed intention. And yet the charge presented the plaintiff in error to the jury as one having no right to make any resistance to an arrest by these officers, although he had been guilty of no offence, and it gave the jury to understand that the officers, in making the attempt, had the right to use all necessary force to overcome any and all opposition that might be made to the arrest, even to the extent of killing the individual whom they desired to take into their custody. Instead of saying that plaintiff in error had the right to use such force as was absolutely necessary to resist an attempted illegal arrest, the jury were informed that the policemen had the right to use all necessary force to arrest him, and that he had no right to resist. He, of course, had no right to unnecessarily injure, much less to kill, his assailant; but where the officer is killed in the course of the disorder which naturally accompanies an attempted arrest that is resisted, the law looks with very different eyes upon the transaction, when the officer had the right to make the arrest, from what it does if the officer had no such right. What might be murder in the first case might be nothing more than manslaughter in the other, or the facts might show that no offence had been committed.

The plaintiff in error was undoubtedly prejudiced by this error in the charge, and the judgment of the court below must therefore be

Reversed, and the case remanded with instructions to grant a new trial.

STATE v. KOONCE

Superior Court of New Jersey, Appellate Division, 1965.
89 N.J.Super. 169, 214 A.2d 428.

CONFORD, S. J. A. D. Certain charges against the defendants arising out of an arrest of defendant Kurt Koonce ("Kurt," hereinafter) by Newark police officers for selling liquor to a minor were tried before the Municipal Court of the City of Newark. The charge against Kurt of unlawful sale to a minor was, according to the docket record, "dismissed for lack of evidence." A complaint against Kurt for assault and battery on Police Officer Costanzo resulted in a conviction and a 90-day jail term in the county penitentiary. Both Kurt and Florence Koonce ("Florence," hereinafter) were convicted on a complaint of assault and battery on Police Captain Zizza; Kurt was sentenced to time spent in jail and Florence to a $25 fine.

On appeal to the Essex County Court, and after a trial *de novo* Kurt was found guilty of the assault on Costanzo but acquitted of the charge as to Zizza. He was sentenced to a 90-day jail term. Florence was found guilty of the assault on Zizza and fined $25.

* * *

The events which here concern us occurred in the early morning of May 30, 1964 at a tavern on Springfield Avenue in Newark known as the Glitter Club. Washington Koonce was president of the corporate alcoholic beverage control licensee. He was father of Kurt and husband of Florence. At approximately 1:30 A.M. uniformed patrolmen of the Newark Police Department arrived in response to a call from the club that a patron was brandishing a knife. By the time, shortly thereafter, that Captain Zizza and other officers arrived, the police were in process of removing the offender. However, they noticed that some of the patrons present seemed to be minors, whereas R.S. 33:1–77, N.J.S.A., makes the sale of any alcoholic beverage to a minor a misdemeanor (subject to certain provisos). Testimony offered at the trial *de novo* fairly permitted the following findings of fact as to the events thereafter. Zizza had observed an apparent patron, one Carol Gray, standing at the bar with a glass of amber-colored fluid in her hand. He questioned her about her age and she told him it was 24 and that she was born in 1942. She then corrected the birth year to 1940. At that point he turned the interrogation over to Detective Thomas to whom she admitted she was 17. Zizza asked her who had served her, and her response was,

"I can't tell you nothing." Zizza noticed a strong smell of alcohol on her breath. Behind the bar were three men and a woman. Zizza asked them who served the girl, whereupon Kurt handed Zizza a slip of paper containing Miss Gray's signature to a statement that she was over 21, which he said she had given him three weeks previously. But he said no one had served her liquor.

In addition to the Koonces there was another bartender on duty at the time. There was defense testimony that Kurt was not then on bartending duty, having completed that stint at 6 P.M. the previous evening, but that he was washing glasses and cleaning tables just before the incident in question. Zizza testified that when he entered the premises Kurt was "the bartender working" the end of the bar where Miss Gray was. Another officer, however, testified Kurt had been "outside the bar," "fixing something."

Zizza told Kurt that he was under arrest for serving a minor. Kurt at first came from behind the bar, "apparently resigned to the fact that he was coming with us" (Zizza's testimony). However, he then returned to a position behind the bar, ostensibly to get his cigarettes, but ultimately refused to go with the officers. Zizza then ordered Costanzo to "go and take Kurt Koonce." Zizza's testimony was to the effect that as Costanzo reached out to take Koonce "he was met with a flailing of arms, punching." Zizza jumped over the bar to assist Costanzo who was being punched by Kurt. But Zizza was punched from the rear by Florence. He was struck repeatedly "all around my body." The defendants were then subdued and removed. Zizza's testimony was corroborated by that of Costanzo, who added the detail that he was hit by Kurt when he put a handcuff on his right wrist. There was also corroboration of Zizza's account of the events by the testimony of Officers Thomas and McParland.

For the defense, Carol Gray testified that she had gone into the bar to make a phone call. Although she had been drinking before she went to the bar, she did not order anything or have anything to drink while she was there. She was stopped by the policemen as she was on her way out, after having made the call. She lied about her age because she was scared. Washington Koonce testified that at the time in question he was tending bar with another man other than Kurt. He denied that anyone had served Miss Gray and he had orally protested to the police the arrest of his son. At the time, his wife had been working at the cash register. Washington stated that the officers shoved his wife aside and seized his son. At no time did either of them physically resist or strike the officers. The officers also forcibly seized his wife. This version was substantiated by the testimony of Florence and Kurt. Kurt added that prior to the incident he had been clearing tables in the bar. He denied serving Miss Gray. Jimmy Weems, a patron of the bar, corroborated the stories of the three defendants.

The trial judge in the Essex County Court found the testimony of the police witnesses basically credible and that of the defense witnesses not, in relation to the respective factual versions as to the assaults charged against the defendants, with the dispositions stated hereinabove.

Defendants' second appellate point is that "defendants' alleged conduct, in repelling an unlawful arrest, was legally justified." Here defendants invoke the common-law rule that a citizen may use such force as may be reasonably necessary to repel or prevent an illegal arrest. They contend that since the statutory offense of selling liquor to a minor, though denominated a "misdemeanor," is punishable by imprisonment for not more than 90 days, it is in the category of common-law misdemeanor rather than felony for purposes of applying the general common-law rule that a peace officer may arrest without a warrant (there was no warrant here) for a misdemeanor only if the offense was committed in his presence.

* * *

We turn, then, to the first premise of the thesis advanced: Kurt Koonce did not violate R.S. 33:1–77, N.J.S.A., in the presence of the arresting police; therefore, his arrest for that offense was unlawful. We have little difficulty in agreeing with defendants to this extent, i. e., that assuming a violation of the statutory proscription of *sale* to a minor by some person connected with the operation of the Glitter Club on the occasion in question in the presence of the officers, the officers had insufficient basis for a determination that Kurt was the offender to justify his arrest.

* * *

We are thus finally brought to the determinative issue in the case. Is the so-called common-law rule of right of a citizen to physical resistance to an illegal arrest by a police officer to be taken to be the law of New Jersey in present-day society? We have concluded to the contrary.

While, as indicated above, there is no doubt that the common-law rule is that a citizen has the right of reasonable resistance, even to the extent of force, to an illegal arrest by a police officer, and American jurisdictions, generally, continued to adhere thereto, no New Jersey court of highest jurisdiction has expressly applied or approved that rule, to our knowledge, nor is it declared by legislative enactment, and we are therefore free to examine the question of its continued justification as a part of our non-statutory law in contemporary civilization.

* * *

In Brown v. State, 62 N.J.L. 666, 42 A. 811 (E. & A.1899), defendant was convicted of murder when he shot a plainclothes policeman in escaping after an arrest by the latter on suspicion of a felony or attempted felony.   The opinion of Mr. Justice Dixon, dissenting from an affirmance, states that the issues involved the question of the lawfulness of the arrest, since failure of the State to prove such lawfulness should have caused the arrest to be "treated as any other unlawful interference with personal liberty,—as an act which may be lawfully resisted".   In the course of its determination that the portions of the trial court's charge under attack contained nothing prejudicially injurious to defendant's rights, the opinion of the majority had no occasion to express agreement or disagreement with Justice Dixon's thus stated view, the charge containing nothing in derogation of defendant's supposed common-law rights in the respect noted.

Both the Uniform Arrest Act and the Model Penal Code recommend abolition of the common-law rule.   Section 5 of the former provides:

> "If a person has reasonable ground to believe that he is being arrested by a peace officer, it is his duty to refrain from using force or any weapon in resisting arrest regardless of whether or not there is a legal basis for the arrest."

Professor Warner, Reporter to the Interstate Commission on Crime, which formulated the Uniform Arrest Act, explained the background of the law of arrest preceding organization of regular metropolitan police forces in early 19th Century England as follows:

> "[It] was developed largely during a period when most arrests were made by private citizens, when bail for felonies was usually unattainable, and when years might pass before the royal judges arrived for a jail delivery.   Further, conditions in the English jails were then such that a prisoner had an excellent chance of dying of disease before trial."   Warner, "The Uniform Arrest Act," 28 Va.L.Rev. 315 (1942).

See also Hall, "Legal and Social Aspects of Arrest," 49 Harv.L.Rev. 566, 578–92 (1936).

In the Warner article cited above the author goes on to discuss the rule here at issue:

> "It has always been illegal to resist a lawful arrest. But [contra] if the arrest is unlawful * * *.   The rule developed when long imprisonment, often without the opportunity of bail, 'goal [sic] fever,' physical torture, and other great dangers were to be apprehended from arrest, whether legal or illegal. * * *
>
> When the law of arrest developed, resistance to an arrest by a peace officer did not involve the serious dangers it does today.   Constables and watchmen were armed only

with staves and swords, and the person to be apprehended might successfully hold them off with his own weapon and thus escape."   (28 Va.L.Rev., at p. 330)

The new rule of the Uniform Act was justified in the same article on two grounds: first, that the fate of today's arrestee is usually a few hours in a reasonably clean place of detention rather than the probable consequences awaiting the arrestee of yore.   (Id., at p. 315); second, and more important:

> "Today, every [American] police officer is armed with a pistol and has orders not to desist from making an arrest though there is forceful resistance. Accordingly, successful resistance is usually possible only by shooting the officer to prevent him from shooting first." (Id., at p. 330)

Section 5 of the Uniform Arrest Act, or the equivalent thereof, is statute law in New Hampshire, Rhode Island, California and Delaware.

There is much discussion in the literature of arrest law as to the *quantum* of force which should be permitted the officer in a legal arrest and an arrestee in an unlawful arrest. See, inter alia, Moreland, "The Use of Force in Effecting or Resisting Arrest," 33 Neb.L. Rev. 408 (1954); "Justification for the Use of Force in the Criminal Law," 13 Stan.L.Rev. 566 (1961). These writings indicate a consensus that a line must be drawn beyond which the fracas resulting from an arrest may not go. The two works just cited submit that the officer's force must be tailored to the crime, i. e., that an officer may not kill to apprehend a driver whose hour has expired on the parking meter, but may use great force to subdue a murderer. Another commentator puts forth the tentative generalization that the victim of an unlawful arrest should be permitted to resist only if less than serious bodily harm will be inflicted upon the arrester. "Criminal Law: Force That May be Used to Resist an Illegal Arrest," 9 Okla.L. Rev. 60, 65 (1956).

But it seems to us that an appropriate accommodation of society's interests in securing the right of individual liberty, maintenance of law enforcement, and prevention of death or serious injury not only of the participants in an arrest fracas but of innocent third persons, precludes tolerance of any formulation which validates an arrestee's resistance of a police officer with force merely because the arrest is ultimately adjudged to have been illegal. Force begets force, and escalation into bloodshed is a frequent probability. The right or wrong of an arrest is often a matter of close debate as to which even lawyers and judges may differ. In this era of constantly expanding legal protections of the rights of the accused in criminal proceedings, one deeming himself illegally arrested can reasonably be asked to submit peaceably to arrest by a police officer, and to take recourse in his legal remedies for regaining his liberty and defending the ensuing prosecution against him. At the same time, police officers attempting in good faith, although mistakenly, to perform their duties in effecting an arrest should be relieved of the threat of physical harm at the hands of the arrestee.

The principles expressed herein were adumbrated by this court in State v. Hayes, 52 N.J.Super. 178, 145 A.2d 28 (App.Div.1958), where we held that the detention of a 17-year-old boy in a "bull pen" with adults, contrary to N.J.S. 2A:4–33, did not justify the boy's escape from detention even though the penal escape statute, N.J.S. 2A:104–6, speaks to persons "in lawful custody or control." Judge Goldmann there said:

> "The great weight of authority, and reason, militate against defendant's claim that he had the right to break jail in the circumstances here present. The Legislature, presumably, sought to deter prisoners from attempting escape because of the great danger of violence such an attempt would involve, and the unquestioned disruption of discipline that would almost inevitably follow. If defendant prevails in this case, that deterrent effect would be weakened. * * *

> To uphold defendant's contention would be to give prisoners the right of self-judgment and self-help. A minor and unintentional infraction of some legislative command would mean that escaping prisoners could hope to go entirely unpunished. This could only breed disrespect for the law." (at p. 187, 145 A.2d at p. 33)

The concept of self-help is in decline. It is antisocial in an urbanized society. It is potentially dangerous to all involved. It is no longer necessary because of the legal remedies available.

Being confident that the Supreme Court of New Jersey would approve the foregoing views, we declare it to be the law of this State that a private citizen may not use force to resist arrest by one he knows or has good reason to believe is an authorized police officer engaged in the performance of his duties, whether or not the arrest is illegal under the circumstances obtaining.

So much decided, shall these defendants as a consequence stand rightfully convicted of assault? It must be remembered that when the inculpated conduct occurred it was undoubtedly the general understanding that the common-law rule of right of resistance to an illegal arrest applied in this State * * *

In the foregoing circumstances, the judicial evocation of an altered rule of criminal law should have prospective application only. It is uniformly recognized that it would be fundamentally unjust to render criminal, by an overruling decision, conduct which was not criminal when it occurred. This would be equivalent in effect on the accused of an *ex post facto* statute.

* * *

For the foregoing reasons, the conduct of the defendants having been free from criminality when it transpired it will not be rendered criminal by our present declaration that hereafter, as more specifically stated hereinabove, it shall not be lawful to resist a police officer undertaking to effect an arrest notwithstanding the illegality of the arrest.

Judgments reversed.

STATE v. MULVIHILL

Supreme Court of New Jersey, 1970.
57 N.J. 151, 270 A.2d 277.

FRANCIS, J. Defendant Mulvihill was charged by indictment with violating N.J.S.A. 2A:90–4 in that he allegedly committed an assault and battery upon a Somerville policeman who was in uniform and acting in the performance of his duty at the time. He was convicted at a jury trial in which the court refused to allow him to defend by asserting self-defense and declined to submit that issue to the jury for determination. On appeal, the conviction was reversed and a new trial ordered. This Court granted the State's petition for certification.

The testimony reveals that Officer Dowling was operating a patrol car along a public street in Somerville, N. J. While doing so, he observed the defendant Mulvihill, a 20-year-old youth, and two other persons standing in front of a pizzeria. He noticed Mulvihill pouring something from a bottle into a paper cup held by one of the other two persons. Since there was a local ordinance prohibiting the drinking of alcoholic beverages on a public street, the officer stopped the car, got out and called to the young men to come over to him. As they did so, Mulvihill threw the paper cup on the sidewalk. Dowling asked him what was in the cup and defendant did not answer.

The testimony as to the events which immediately followed is in conflict. However, for the purpose of determining whether the legal issue of self-defense was available for jury consideration, it is necessary to consider the facts in the light most favorable to the defendant. According to Mulvihill, when he failed to disclose what he had been drinking the officer grabbed him and asked to smell his breath. He held his breath and remained silent, whereupon Dowling shook him "back and forth" by the shoulders, and said "I should arrest you, you punk." Mulvihill tried to pull away and Dowling "jerked him back around" with the result that both men fell. They arose with Dowling still holding him. When he tried to pull free, Dowling struck defendant on the side of the head with his gun lacerating his scalp. Mulvihill then fell toward Dowling and they both went down again. The officer's right hand was being held by Mulvihill who was trying to keep the gun pointing away from himself, while the officer was endeavoring to direct it at him and saying "Stop or I'll shoot." Mulvihill testified that at this time he was trying to avoid being shot. Then the gun went off, harmlessly, and with his right hand Mulvihill punched the officer in the left side of the face. It was for this blow that he was indicted. In the meantime, other officers appeared and defendant was immobilized.

On the assumption *as a matter of law* that Mulvihill had been arrested before he struck the allegedly criminal blow, the trial court informed defense counsel that no discussion of or reliance upon self-defense would be permitted in summation, nor would that issue be submitted in the charge for consideration by the jury. The action was taken because the court believed * * * it was required by State v. Koonce. That belief, of course, was incorrect.

Koonce held that "a private citizen may not use force to resist arrest by one he knows or has good reason to believe is an authorized police officer engaged in the performance of his duties, whether or not the arrest is illegal under the circumstances obtaining." 89 N.J. Super. at 184, 214 A.2d at 436. The opinion put to rest the notion that the common law rule existing in some jurisdictions, which permits a citizen to resist, even with reasonable force, an unlawful arrest by a police officer, was applicable in New Jersey. Instead, the Appellate Division adopted the above quoted contrary doctrine, and we think rightly so. Accordingly, in our State when an officer makes an arrest, legal or illegal, it is the duty of the citizen to submit and, in the event the seizure is illegal, to seek recourse in the courts for the invasion of his right of freedom.

However, as the Appellate Division said in reversing the conviction here, it went no further in *Koonce* than to hold that the citizen must submit peaceably to an apparently authorized arrest or other apparently lawful restraint by a police officer, even if it later proves to have been illegal. If the citizen resists the arrest, the officer is not only justified in but has the duty of employing such force as is reasonably necessary to overcome the resistance and accomplish the arrest. But, as the Appellate Division noted, that principle is not dispositive in all cases of an arrestee's right to claim self-defense to a charge of assault and battery on the officer. If, in effectuating the arrest or the temporary detention, the officer employs excessive and unnecessary force, the citizen may respond or counter with the use of reasonable force to protect himself, and if in so doing the officer is injured no criminal offense has been committed.

There is sound reason for a difference in the rights and duties of the citizen in the two situations. Despite his duty to submit quietly without physical resistance to an arrest made by an officer acting in the course of his duty, even though the arrest is illegal, his right to freedom from unreasonable seizure and confinement can be protected, restored and vindicated through legal processes. However, the rule permitting reasonable resistance to excessive force of the officer, whether the arrest is lawful or unlawful, is designed to protect a person's bodily integrity and health and so permits resort to self-defense. Simply stated, the law recognizes that liberty can be restored through legal processes but life or limb cannot be repaired in a courtroom. And so it holds that the reason for outlawing resistance to an unlawful arrest and requiring disputes over its legality to be resolved in the courts has no controlling application on the right to resist an officer's excessive force.

Two qualifications on the citizen's right to defend against and to repel an officer's excessive force must be noticed. He cannot use greater force in protecting himself against the officer's unlawful force than reasonably appears to be necessary. If he employs such greater force, then he becomes the aggressor and forfeits the right to claim self-defense to a charge of assault and battery on the officer. Furthermore, if he knows that if he desists from his physically defensive measures and submits to arrest the officer's unlawfully excessive force would cease, the arrestee must desist or lose his privilege of self-defense.

It has been suggested that the latter qualification is not reasonable because it would require a citizen being subjected to excessive force or attack and defending against it to make a split second determination, amounting to a gamble, as to whether if he terminates his defensive measures, he will suffer further beyond arrest. But application of the rule does not require such action as should follow opportunity for detached reflection. It merely commands that the citizen's conduct be reasonable in the light of all the circumstances apparent to him at the moment. And thus it is a counter-protective measure for the original aggressor officer. Administration of the rule should be no more difficult than those dealing with the duty of an assaulted person to retreat to avoid the attack or the duty not to continue the affray after the original aggressor ceases the assault; once the danger is past, the original victim cannot continue measures that were originally defensive. *Cf.* State v. Abbott, 36 N.J. 63, 69–73, 174 A.2d 881 (1961).

Applying the stated principles to the present case, it is plain that the trial court erred in eliminating self-defense from the case as a matter of law. Two bases exist for that conclusion. The jury could have found on the disputed facts that Dowling had informed Mulvihill expressly, or by his course of conduct, that he was under arrest for an ordinance violation offense. If such a finding were made, it would follow that Dowling was justified in using such force in overcoming Mulvihill's resistance as was reasonably necessary to make the arrest effective. But it was open to the jury to find also that the resistance was such that the officer, in attempting to overcome it, employed unnecessary and excessive force when he drew his gun and struck Mulvihill in the head with it so as to cause a lacerated scalp. They could have found further that this caused Mulvihill reasonably to feel and to fear that an effort was being made to point the gun at him and to fire it. Assuming a finding of such facts and that they preexisted the charged assault and battery on the officer, defendant was entitled to have the issue of self-defense passed upon by the jury.

The second and more crucial basis for accepting self-defense as a legitimate contention in the case was not considered at all at the trial level. The court assumed as a matter of law that Mulvihill had been arrested before the alleged assault and battery was committed. But there was a clear factual dispute on that point. According to defendant, Officer Dowling simply said: "I should arrest you, you punk." Obviously that statement did not constitute an arrest nor did it, in conjunction with the circumstances existing when the statement was made (as the jury could have found them), constitute a temporary detainer by an officer in the pursuit of his official duty for purposes of investigation. If Mulvihill was believed on this aspect of the case, then the fracas between the two men took on the character of a combat between two private individuals. In such situation he was entitled to have the jury decide whether in striking Dowling with his fists he was defending himself against the officer's onslaught with a gun.

Accordingly, we agree with the Appellate Division that the conviction must be reversed and the case remanded for retrial. Assuming substantially the same factual controversy on the retrial, the jury must be called upon to decide whether Mulvihill was arrested before the physical combat arose. Then they should be instructed that once that issue has been decided they should consider the matter of self-defense in accordance with the controlling principles outlined above.

As explained earlier, we have outlined the disputed facts most favorably to the defendant. That was done in order to deal with his contention that the claim of self-defense was an issue which the trial court was obliged to submit to the jury for determination. In holding that the evidence was sufficient to require such submission, we are not indicating a view that defendant's version of the facts should be accepted. The problem of credibility between defendant and the State's witnesses is a matter for resolution by the jury. Officer Dowling's account of the affair, as noted by the Appellate Division, was that he placed defendant Mulvihill under arrest for drinking on a public street. Then "[a]s he told defendant to get into the police car, the latter struck him on the left side of the face. He was knocked to the ground by the blow and immediately got up and grabbed defendant. Defendant and the officer 'tussled' and again both fell to the ground. The officer again got up from the ground and told defendant that he was going to handcuff him and put him into the police car, whereupon defendant kicked the officer in the groin and grabbed him around the waist with one hand on the officer's gun, causing both of them to fall to the sidewalk a third time. As they were on the ground, the officer and defendant struggled for the officer's gun and it discharged against the side of the adjoining building." 105 N.J.Super. at 460–461, 253 A.2d at 176. If that version of the fracas is believed by the jury, the defendant would be guilty of the offense charged against him, and accordingly the jury would not reach the question whether the officer used excessive force in overcoming defendant's resistance to his removal to police headquarters.

The judgment of the Appellate Division is affirmed and the cause remanded for new trial.

NOTES

1. The *Koonce* decision and that of the Alaska Supreme Court in *Miller v. State*, 462 P.2d 421 (1969), appear to be the only state judicial abrogations of the right to resist arrest. A similar movement is taking place in the Federal courts. *United States v. Ferrone*, 438 F.2d 381 (3rd Cir. 1971) (no right to forcibly resist execution of search warrant); *United States v. Beyer*, 426 F.2d 773 (2nd Cir. 1970) (no right to resist unlawful arrest); *United States v. Simon*, 409 F.2d 474 (7th Cir. 1969) (no right to resist lawful arrest or, as dictum, unlawful arrest). The same result has been achieved by statute in California, Delaware, Illinois, New Hampshire, New York, and Rhode Island. West's Ann.Cal.Penal Code § 834 (1970); 11 Del.Code Ann. § 1905 (1953); Smith-Hurd Ill.Ann.Stat. ch. 38, § 7–7 (1972); N.H.Rev.Stat.Ann. 594.5 (1955); McKinney Consol.Laws of N.Y. (Penal Law) § 35.27; R.I.Gen.Laws 1956, § 12–7–10.

It has been argued that eliminating self-help facilitates unlawful arrests and thus violates the Fourth Amendment's prohibition against unreasonable seizures and the due process clause of the Fourteenth Amendment. Two courts which have addressed these contentions have rejected them on the grounds that inasmuch as reasonable force in the exercise of self-help is unlikely to be effective in escaping an armed and technologically sophisticated police force these statutes do not, in fact, contribute to the deprivation of liberty. *State v. Ramsdell*, 109 R.I. 320, 285 A.2d 399 (1971) and *People v. Curtis*, 70 Cal.2d 347, 74 Cal.Rptr. 713, 450 P.2d 33 (1969).

2. One of the few pieces criticizing the trend illustrated by the preceding cases is Chevigny, The Right to Resist an Unlawful Arrest, 78 Yale L.Rev. 1128 (1969). The author argues that the premises concerning alternative resolutions, such as civil damage actions, are to a great extent illusory and, moreover, beside the point. The crucial question for Mr. Chevigny is whether a citizen who impulsively resists the arbitrary and

unlawful exercise of police power should be punished. Since the Chevigny article many successful actions have been brought under the Civil Rights Act of 1871, Rev.Stat. § 1979, 42 U.S.C.A. § 1983, for damages due to unlawful arrest, imprisonment and mistreatment by police and other public officials. E. g., McDaniel v. Carroll, 457 F.2d 968 (6th Cir. 1972) (award of compensatory and punitive damages against sheriff, deputy sheriff and surety on sheriff's bond for injuries sustained by plaintiffs when shot by deputy in course of effort to arrest affirmed; amount not stated); Roberts v. Williams, 456 F.2d 819 (5th Cir. 1972) (award of $85,000 against superintendent of Mississippi county prison farm for damages resulting from accidental discharge of shotgun held by trusty guard remanded for consideration of other possible elements of damages); Jenkins v. Averett, 424 F.2d 1228 (4th Cir. 1970) (award of $448 for out-of-pocket expenses resulting from defendant police officer's shooting of plaintiff in course of chase rejected as inadequate and remanded for consideration of other elements of compensatory and punitive damages); Sexton v. Gibbs, 327 F.Supp. 134 (N.D.Tex.1970) aff'd per curiam 446 F.2d 904 (5th Cir. 1971) (awards of $500 and $250 made against two police officers for unlawful arrest and search of plaintiff's car). Nevertheless, it seems probable that the great majority of those subject to unlawful treatment by the police, particularly when it is only an unlawful arrest, are unlikely to recover lost employment or wages much less any compensation for the indignity experienced. If so, does it not seem inequitable that such persons should also be liable for criminal sanctions if they initially resisted such mistreatment?

Can the new "no sock" rule be justified by its possible effect on the conduct of the police? That is, by possibly reducing police anticipation of physical conflict might it make them less apt to interpret verbal remonstrance or passive reluctance as signals for the exercise of force on their part with its potential for escalation? If the net effect of the new rule is a reduction in physical injuries to police and public would that be a satisfactory answer to Chevigny's argument?

Given the realities of our society, is the risk of unlawful arrest experienced equally by all segments of our population? Are the possibilities for rapid and meaningful relief? Is the no-resistance rule a form of "class-legislation"?

F. PREVENTION OF CRIME

VILIBORGHI v. STATE

Supreme Court of Arizona, 1935.
45 Ariz. 275, 43 P.2d 210.

LOCKWOOD, Chief Justice. Jeff Viliborghi, hereinafter called defendant, was informed against by the county attorney of Maricopa county for the crime of murder. He was tried before a jury, which returned a verdict of manslaughter, and after judgment on the verdict had been returned, this appeal was taken.

The evidence introduced by the state in its case in chief tended to show the following facts: Deceased, one Alfredo Carrion, a Mexican boy about sixteen years old, and two companions of about the same age had attended a moving picture show the evening of the homicide. On their way home they decided to run a race, and did so, finishing the race in front of a store owned by defendant. While standing there talking together, a shot was fired from the interior of the store, and deceased fell to the ground. His companions ran home and informed deceased's parents and notified the police, thereafter returning to the store, where they found the body of deceased, the cause of death being a gunshot wound in the brain. Defendant was arrested, and while he was under arrest admitted to various witnesses that he fired the shot which killed the deceased. This, of course, under the statute, was sufficient to make a prima facie case of second-degree murder, and put upon defendant the burden of proving circumstances of mitigation, or that justified or excused the killing. Section 5050, R.C.1928.

Defendant claimed the killing to be justifiable under subdivisions 1 and 2 of section 4590, R.C.1928, which section reads in part as follows:

"4590. Justifiable homicide; bare fear as justification: Homicide is also justifiable when committed by any person: 1. When resisting any attempt to murder any person, or to commit a felony, or to do some great bodily injury upon any person; or, 2. when committed in defense of habitation, or property, against one who manifestly intends or endeavors, by violence or surprise, to commit a felony, or manifestly intends and endeavors, in a violent, riotous, or tumultuous manner, to enter the habitation of another for the purpose of offering violence to any person therein; * * *

"A bare fear of the commission of any of the offenses mentioned in subdivisions two and three hereof, is not sufficient to justify a homicide. But the circumstances must be sufficient to excite the fears of a reasonable person, and the party killing must have acted under the influence of such fears alone."

In order to sustain this defense, he offered evidence which tended to show the following facts:

Defendant had been engaged in the grocery business at the location where the killing occurred since 1925. The premises occupied by him as a store were also used for his residence, and he lived there alone. Three times between 1925 and the date of the killing his premises had been burglarized, or an attempt at burglary made, and on one occasion some unknown person had attempted to shoot him while he was in the building. The night of the killing defendant closed his store and retired about 10 p. m., but some time shortly thereafter he was awakened by hearing a noise in the front part of the building. Believing that some one was about to again rob the premises, he was afraid to turn on any light or expose himself before the windows. He arose from his bed, secured a revolver, and crept into the store part of the building to determine what the situation was, and, if it could be done safely, to go out through the front door to call for help. He continued to hear various noises around the building, and as he progressed toward the front he saw a human hand reaching in the front window and apparently trying to unhook the fastenings thereof. Believing that burglars were trying to break into the building, and that his life and property were in danger, he fired his revolver through the window and immediately heard the footfalls of persons running away. He went back to his bedroom, partially dressed, and the noises having ceased, went through the front door and turned on the electric light and saw a body lying on the sidewalk. Beside it he saw a jar of preserves and a bottle of pickles which had evidently been taken from a shelf adjacent to the broken window through which he saw the hand entering. On examining the body he discovered it was that of a sixteen year old boy. He had known the boy before, but had had no previous difficulties with him or any of his family. He thereupon notified the police and was arrested and placed in the city jail. * * *

The seventh, eighth, ninth, and tenth assignments of error discuss certain instructions given by the court, and we consider them together. As we have said, the vital issue was whether the defendant was justified in firing the fatal shot. In order for the jury to determine this it was necessary that the court should instruct them under what circumstances the law considers a homicide justifiable or excusable, and it is contended by defendant that the instructions objected to necessarily gave the jury an entirely wrong understanding of the law.

The defendant asked for the following instruction as to the law of justifiable homicide, which was given:

"You are instructed, gentlemen, that any citizen of this state has a right to defend his habitation, his home, against any unlawful or violent intrusion by another, without his consent, for a felonious purpose, and his right to defend his home is governed by the same rule which governs a man's right to defend his person. Now, if at the time the defendant Viliborghi shot and killed the deceased, the latter was attempting to, or the defendant had reasonable ground to believe that the deceased was attempting to, make an unlawful and forcible intrusion upon the habitation of the defendant against the will of the defendant, and that the defendant believed at the time that it was necessary for the protection of his home or his person against an unlawful and violent intrusion by the deceased, and you further find that the belief and fear on the part of the defendant was reasonable, viewing the same from the standpoint of a reasonable man at the time, then the defendant had a right under our law to protect his person or his home, even to the extent of taking the life of the deceased. And if you so find from the evidence in this case, you will find the defendant not guilty, or, if after considering all the evidence in this case, you have a reasonable doubt on this question, you will give the defendant the benefit of that doubt and render a verdict of not guilty."

This we think is a correct general statement of the law as applicable to the evidence in this case, and if no further instructions on the subject of justifiable homicide had been given, the jury could not have been misled. The court, however, in addition thereto, gave the following instructions at the request of the state:

"Gentlemen, if you believe from the evidence in this case beyond a reasonable doubt that the deceased, together with others, was passing the store or standing in front of the store of the defendant, and did not attempt to burglarize defendant's store, then I charge you that the defendant was not justified in taking the life of the deceased, and in that event he would be guilty of either murder or manslaughter—that is, if you believe from the evidence beyond a reasonable doubt that the defendant fired the shot which resulted in the death of the deceased."

"I instruct you, gentlemen of the jury, that the right to kill to protect one's habitation, or to prevent the commission of a felony, is based upon the law of necessity or apparent necessity; the right is limited to prevention and does not extend to punishment for an act already committed."

"I instruct you in this regard that if you find from the evidence beyond a reasonable doubt that the defendant shot the deceased for the purpose of punishment and not to prevent the commission of a felony, then I instruct you that he was not justified in shooting the deceased, unless you further find from the evidence that defendant was in actual or apparent danger of losing his life, or sustaining great bodily injury."

"I instruct you that the owner may resist an entry into his store or house but he has no right to kill unless it be necessary, or apparently necessary, to prevent a felonious stealing or destruction of his property, or to defend himself against loss of life, or great bodily harm, and if you find from the evidence in this case beyond a reasonable doubt that defendant did not shoot the deceased until after the entry or taking of the merchandise in question, if you find that deceased did enter and take the merchandise of defendant, then I instruct you that the defendant would not be justified in taking the life of the deceased, except to defend his own life, or save himself from great bodily injury."

"You are instructed, gentlemen of the jury, that the law does not give one the right to take the life of another merely to prevent the theft of property and in this respect, I charge you that if you believe from the evidence beyond a reasonable doubt that this defendant shot and killed the deceased merely to prevent the theft or loss of the canned goods, even though you find that the deceased was in the act of stealing the said canned goods, but if the defendant had no reasonable cause to believe that his life was in imminent danger, then I instruct you that you should return a verdict of guilty."

On comparing these instructions with the one given at the request of the defendant, it is obvious that they do not agree as to the law, and cannot in any reasonable manner be reconciled.

It was the contention of defendant, sustained by evidence offered in his behalf, that the deceased was, at the time the fatal shot was fired, actually engaged in a first-degree burglary, with the intent to commit petit larceny. * * * This offense of itself is merely a misdemeanor, and the killing of a thief who is engaged merely in a misdemeanor is not justifiable. It may be urged that, since under our statute the burglary is completed as soon as the felonious entry is made, the actual taking of property as a result of and immediately after the entry is not burglary, but merely petit larceny, and therefore the owner of the premises can only resist such taking in the manner allowed for the prevention of a misdemeanor. We think this is a most unreasonable limitation of the law of justifiable homicide. If this be the law, all a burglar needs to do is to complete his entry, and he may then with impunity continue his burglarious purpose without fear of being shot by the justly incensed home owner, so long as he tells the latter that he has no intention of taking more than $50 worth of property. We cannot conceive such to be the law, and hold that so far as the question of justifiable homicide is concerned, when goods are stolen during the commission of a burglary, the entire act from beginning to end is a felony, and any one who may kill the perpetrator before he has fully completed his purpose is to be tried by the rules applying to homicides committed to prevent felonies, and not those which govern misdemeanors. It therefore follows that the owner of the premises burglarized may, at any stage of a burglary, kill the burglar if it be reasonably necessary to prevent the final completion of his felonious purpose, regardless at what stage of the crime the shooting occurs. He may, even after the burglary has been completed, and the burglar is withdrawing from the scene of his crime, if the latter attempts to resist or flee from arrest, use such force as is reasonably necessary for the apprehension of the offender, even to the taking of life. And in all of such cases the question of the necessity of the killing depends upon the reasonable apprehension and belief of the defendant, and not whether such apprehension and belief was justified by the facts as they actually existed. With these tests it clearly appears that the instructions complained of were erroneous in several respects.

The first one states positively that, regardless of what the circumstances would lead the defendant, as a reasonable man, to believe, if as a matter of fact the deceased was not actually engaged in an attempt to burglarize the defendant's store, the latter would be guilty of either murder or manslaughter in killing him. It omits entirely the test of reasonable grounds for belief, and directs the jury to return their verdict on the facts as they actually existed, and not as they appeared to the reasonable apprehension of the defendant.

The second instruction is correct, for under no circumstance may one person shoot another as a punishment for a crime which has been committed.

The third instruction is somewhat ambiguous in that it might be construed to mean that, after the entry had been completed, even though the burglary is still in progress, the owner of the premises may not kill to prevent the completion of the attempted crime. This, as we have said, is not the law. This instruction alone, however, in view of the general instructions, would probably not be reversible error, for the ambiguity is hardly of such a serious nature that, taking the instructions as a whole, it would mislead the jury.

The fourth instruction, however is fatally erroneous. It states flatly that if the defendant killed the deceased to prevent the loss of the canned goods which are referred to in the evidence, even though the deceased was in the act of stealing them, he would be guilty of manslaughter. As we have stated, had the stealing been a simple misdemeanor, the instruction would have been correct, but the whole evidence shows beyond doubt that if the deceased did steal the canned goods referred to, it must have been done in the perpetration of a burglary, and the stealing was therefore part of a felony and the defendant was justified in killing the deceased if it was reasonably necessary to prevent its completion. In no possible way can this instruction be reconciled with the law, and it is obvious that it, considered with the evidence which appears in the record, was in the highest degree prejudicial, and could not be cured by a reference to the general instructions.

Because of the various errors which we have discussed, we are of the opinion that the defendant did not have that fair and impartial trial guaranteed him by the law, and the judgment of the superior court is therefore reversed, and the case remanded for a new trial.

SAULS v. HUTTO

United States District Court, E.D.La., 1969.
304 F.Supp. 124.

RUBIN, District Judge. A police officer who shot and killed a fleeing seventeen-year-old suspected of committing a felony is here sued for damages. The suit raises the question of justification for the use of deadly force in contemporary society.

On March 21, 1965, at about 10:00 p. m., two police officers, James Hutto and Frederick C. Ruppert, Jr., were operating Patrol Car 54. They drove to an ice cream parlor to investigate a complaint. While they were there, a Mustang automobile was driven recklessly past them at a high rate of speed. They jumped in the patrol car and, with Hutto driving, pursued the Mustang. Hutto turned on the blue police warning light and sounded the siren. But the driver of the Mustang continued to flee, driving through the streets of New Orleans at a high rate of speed. The defendants therefore suspected the speeding car was stolen.

There were four young men in the car. Philip Paul Bartlett, also known as Philip Sauls, was driving. According to the testimony of the three passengers, he had invited them for a ride. They also testified that Bartlett had told them the automobile belonged to his brother. In fact Bartlett had stolen the car by putting a jumper wire on the ignition circuit.

Four pistol shots were fired by Officer Ruppert at the racing car in an effort to bring it to a halt. One shot missed completely; two struck the car but did not penetrate it; and the last shot, which was fired at the car as it careened to its right around a corner on Esplanade Street, penetrated the right front door, ricocheted off the dashboard and fell spent inside the vehicle.

When the passengers heard Ruppert's shots and realized that the police were after them, one of them urged Bartlett to stop. Bartlett, however, said that the car was stolen, and that he could not afford to stop.

Bartlett lost control of the Mustang, and it crashed into a parked car. The police car also stopped, and the two policemen ran up, guns in hand. Three of the juveniles surrendered and Ruppert took them into custody. Bartlett, however, tried to escape, crouching as he ran away. Officer Hutto ran after him. He shot once at the fleeing boy, and his shot struck Bartlett in the back. Because Bartlett was bent over, the bullet went through his body at an angle, penetrated his liver, spleen, stomach and heart, and he fell dead in the street.

Shortly thereafter, Hutto said that he had not intended to kill Bartlett, but being excited, he was not entirely certain what had happened. One of the other occupants of the car was later found to be carrying a weapon. Some also had prior police records. All of them were hardened youths, and all later were convicted and sentenced for theft.

Defendants contend they had probable cause to arrest Bartlett for theft, and they are correct.

Suit is brought by the natural mother of the deceased (an illegitimate child) for damages under the Civil Rights Act, 42 U.S.C.A. § 1983, and other Louisiana law, LSA–C.C. Arts. 2315, 2316, under the doctrine of pendent jurisdiction. The police officers are no longer with the New Orleans police force and are presently unemployed. Therefore, should the plaintiff prevail, there is scant likelihood that any recovery can be effected, but the plaintiff seeks vindication for her son.

* * *

Officer Hutto had probable cause to arrest Bartlett for theft, a felony not involving danger to life or person, and he reasonably believed that the suspect could not be immediately apprehended without the use of deadly force. In these circumstances, was he legally justified in shooting at the deceased? There has been a spate of literature dealing with this problem,[9] and various state legislatures have recently been reconsidering their laws to reflect current attitudes on it.

At common law, any person, whether policeman or private citizen, was privileged to use *any* force necessary, albeit deadly, to apprehend a fleeing felon if he had cause to believe a felony had been committed. Deadly force, however, was never permissible to apprehend misdemeanants. To a great extent, this view was based on the fact that, at common law, felonies were punishable by death.

Louisiana has not followed the common law approach. The provisions of the Louisiana Criminal Code and Code of Criminal Procedure when read together limit the use of deadly force even by police officers to situations involving danger to life or person.

Article 220 of the Code of Criminal Procedure provides:

"A person shall submit peaceably to a lawful arrest. The person making a lawful arrest may use reasonable force to effect the arrest and detention, and also to overcome any resistance or threatened resistance of the person being arrested or detained."

The draftsmen of the Code pointed out in the Official Comment to Article 220 that the "requirement of reasonableness would preclude the use of clearly inappropriate force." More significant assistance in determining what is reasonable force on the part of police officers is provided by the definition of justifiable homicide in the Louisiana Criminal Code:

"A homicide is justifiable:

(1) When committed in self-defense * * *

(2) When committed, for the purpose of preventing a violent or forcible felony involving danger to life or of great

9. See, e. g., Note, "The Use of Deadly Force in the Apprehension of Fugitives from Arrest," 14 McGill L.J. 293 (1968); Tsimbinos, "The Justified Use of Deadly Force," 4 Criminal Law Bulletin 3 (1968); McDonald, "Use of Force by Police to Effect Lawful Arrest," 9 Criminal Law Quarterly 435 (1966–67); Robin, "Justifiable Homicide by Police Officers," 54 Journal of Criminal Law, Criminology, and Police Science, 225 (1963); Comment, "Justification for the Use of Force in the Criminal Law," 13 Stan.L.Rev. 566 (1961); Comment, "The Use of Deadly Force in the Protection of Property Under the Model Penal Code," 59 Col. L.Rev. 1212 (1959).

bodily harm, by one who reasonably believes that such an offense is about to be committed and that such action is necessary for its prevention.   *   *   * " LSA–R.S. 14:20.

Thus, deadly force may not be used to prevent the commission of a felony involving only property, a marked departure from the common law rule.

Since it is illegal for one to use deadly force to *prevent* the commission of a felony involving only property, it is unreasonable (and inappropriate) for a policeman to use deadly force to *arrest* a man suspected of committing such a crime.

The current Regulations on Firearms of the New Orleans Police Department also limit the use of deadly force in felony cases.   They provide:

> "The use of deadly force shall be restricted to the apprehension of perpetrators, who in the course of their criminal actions threaten the use of deadly force or apprehensions when officers believe that the person whose arrest is sought will cause death or serious bodily harm if his apprehension is delayed."

The use of deadly force in apprehending persons suspected of committing felonies not involving danger to life or person has never been specifically considered by Louisiana's appellate courts.   However, three cases have held that deadly force may not lawfully be used to arrest a misdemeanant or prevent the commission of a misdemeanor. State v. Turner, 1938, 190 La. 198, 182 So. 325; State v. Plumlee, 1933, 177 La. 687, 149 So. 425; Graham v. Ogden, 3d La.App., 1963, 157 So.2d 365.   And two of them, State v. Turner, supra, and State v. Plumlee, supra, indicate that deadly force can be used only to prevent "a great crime."   Both LSA–R.S. 14:20, which does not permit the use of deadly force in crimes not involving danger to life or person and LSA–R.S. 14:67, which provides for a 10 year maximum sentence for theft, suggest that Bartlett had not committed "a great crime," and that Officer Hutto acted unlawfully in using deadly force in an attempt to apprehend him.

The Model Penal Code [16] of the American Law Institute has followed the same approach as Louisiana and does not permit the use of deadly force to make an arrest for a crime involving only prop-

16.   The Model Penal Code provides: "The use of deadly force is not justifiable under this Section, unless:
   (i) the arrest is for a felony * *;
   (iv) the [police officer] believes that: (1) the crime for which the arrest is made involved conduct including the use or threatened use of deadly force; or

(2) there is a substantial risk that the person to be arrested will cause death or serious bodily harm if his apprehension is delayed."
American Law Institute, Model Penal Code, Section 3.07(2) (b) (i), (iv), pp. 56–57 (1962).

erty.[18] The various interests at stake have been balanced; the felon's life may be taken only if his escape would provide a threat to the life or personal safety of his fellow citizens.

Our society does not lightly forfeit human life. No longer is there a host of felonies punishable by death. Indeed, since June, 1967, no one has been executed in the United States for a criminal offense. Fifteen states have entirely eliminated the death penalty. Elsewhere capital punishment may be decreed only after due process of law has been afforded.

Hence a man's life may not be take on the spot by a police officer without substantial justification. Bartlett, a theft suspect and reckless driver, was not killed by Officer Hutto in self defense; nor was he slain to prevent a crime involving danger to life or person, or even to property, from being completed. The theft of the automobile had been completed and its reckless course through New Orleans streets was at an end. The automobile and three of its passengers were in custody. There was no longer any danger to pedestrians or other drivers, as there had been, of course, while Bartlett was driving with the police in hot pursuit. Bartlett's death was not the result of the bullets fired at the fleeing automobile. He was shot only to prevent his escape.

If Bartlett had been arrested, fairly tried, and convicted for theft, he could have been sentenced to "not more than 10 years with or without hard labor." He would have been eligible for parole after serving one-third of his sentence. If he had in addition been tried and convicted of resisting arrest, his maximum sentence on that charge would have been six months and a $500 fine.

Professor Mikell [sic] puts the question bluntly:

"It has been said, 'Why should not the man be shot down, the man who is running away with an automobile? * * *' May I ask what are we killing him for * * *. Are we killing him for stealing the automobile? If we catch him and try him we throw every protection around him. We say he cannot be tried until 12 men of the grand jury indict him, and then he cannot be convicted until 12 men of the petit jury have proved him guilty beyond a reasonable doubt, and then when we have done all that, what do we do to him? Put him before a policeman and have a policeman shoot him? Of course not. We give him three years in a penitentiary. It cannot be then that we allow the officer to

---

18. Professor Wechsler eloquently stated the basis for the Model Penal Code's (and Louisiana's) position: "The preservation of life has such moral and ethical standing in our culture and society, that the deliberate sacrifice of life merely for the protection of property ought not to be sanctioned by law." American Law Institute Proceedings, 1958, pp. 285–286.

kill him because he stole the automobile, because the statute provides only three years in a penitentiary for that.

* * * Is it for fleeing that we kill him? Fleeing from arrest is also a common-law offense and is punishable by a light penalty * * *. If we are not killing him for stealing the automobile and not killing him for fleeing, what are we killing him for?" Michael & Wechsler, Criminal Law and Its Administration, p. 82, n. 3 (1940).[24]

Louisiana's courts likely would take this view: a police officer is not justified in shooting at a man who is suspected of stealing an automobile in order to apprehend him. A bullet in the back is not Louisiana's penalty for fleeing to escape arrest. Deadly force may be used only when life itself is endangered or great bodily harm is threatened.

Under LSA–C.C. Art. 2315, plaintiff is entitled to recover damages from Officer Hutto for the wrongful death of her son. A hearing will be held to determine damages. Officer Ruppert did not participate in Bartlett's killing, and judgment is rendered dismissing the suit as to him.

NOTES

1. Compare the instant case with Cunningham v. Ellington, 323 F. Supp. 1072 (D.C.W.D.Tenn.1971) (3 jg.), a wrongful death action and a suit to have a Tennessee statute authorizing the use of deadly force to effect the arrest of a suspected felon declared unconstitutional. The plaintiffs contended that insofar as the statute authorized the use of such force where unnecessary to the protection of the life or safety of the officer or other person it violated the Eighth Amendment's prohibition against cruel and unusual punishment.

2. Normally, the use of deadly force to prevent crime is limited to the prevention or termination of "dangerous" or "atrocious" felonies. See the recitation of crimes in Vernon's Ann.Tex.P.C. art. 1222 (Penal Code) (1961) note 2, page 1111 supra. However, it has been held that the language of that statute extends to the prevention of statutory rape. Moore v. State, 91 Tex.Cr.R. 118, 237 S.W. 931 (1922). More representative of the premises and application of this defense is Commonwealth v. Emmons, 157 Pa. Super. 495, 43 A.2d 568 (1945), where the court held that deadly force may

---

24. Nor is the need to deter resistance to arrest a sufficient justification for the use of deadly force. If this be society's concern, then resisting arrest itself should be made a serious felony. The limited statistical evidence available indicates that there has been no significant increase in felonies in those states that have forbidden the use of deadly force in preventing the commission of crimes not involving danger to life or person. See F.B.I. Uniform Crime Report (1961); New York City Police Department Statistical Reports, June–October, 1967, p. 1. Police Commissioner Howard Leary of New York has stated:

"It is a step forward to have a clear statement that irresponsible teenagers whose actions happen to amount to felonies against property are not for that reason alone subject to death at the hands of a police officer attempting to arrest them."

not be employed to prevent the apparent theft of defendant's automobile when there was no danger to her person or threatened intrusion into her home.

3. Should there be any distinction made between private citizens and the police with respect to the use of deadly force to prevent crime? If so, why? What distinctions should be drawn? Should the same conclusions be reached with respect to the use of such force in making an arrest? See Commonwealth v. Chermansky, 430 Pa. 170, 242 A.2d 237, 32 A.L.R.3d 1072 (1968) and Note, Justifiable Use of Deadly Force by the Police: A Statutory Survey, 12 Wm. & Mary L.Rev. 67 (1970).

4. Even with respect to crimes that normally threaten serious personal injury should the use of deadly force be conditioned on the existence of a reasonable belief in its necessity—as to the existence of such danger and the futility of lesser measures—on the particular occasion? Does the fact that capital punishment may be unconstitutional affect your decision?

5. Would the analysis in the *Hutto* opinion be different if the death had occurred as a result of a shot aimed at the car's tires during the chase? Should it be? Compare People v. Klein, 305 Ill. 141, 137 N.E. 145 (1922) with Burt v. State, 138 Tex.Cr.R. 540, 137 S.W.2d 1045 (1945).

6. In Pennsylvania, one employing deadly force to effect the arrest of a person whom he reasonably believes to have committed a felony will be held criminally liable if, despite his belief and the necessity for the use of such force, the person killed or injured is, in fact, innocent. Commonwealth v. Duerr, 158 Pa.Super. 484, 45 A.2d 235 (1946). Is this rule a desirable device for assuring extreme caution by the police and others in the use of deadly force?

G. PARTICIPATION IN OFFENSE FOR PURPOSES OF AIDING LAW ENFORCEMENT

LILLY v. WEST VIRGINIA

United States Court of Appeals for the Fourth Circuit, 1928.
29 F.2d 61.

WADDILL, Circuit Judge. Plaintiff in error, hereinafter called defendant, is a prohibition agent in the service of the federal government. While chasing an automobile which he had reasonable cause to believe was engaged in transporting intoxicating liquor in violation of the National Prohibition Act, the automobile which he was driving struck and killed a pedestrian at a street intersection in the outskirts of Huntington, W. Va. He was indicted for involuntary manslaughter, and the case was removed to the federal court. He was there convicted of the charge, and in this writ of error he asks that the conviction be reversed, particularly because of errors in the charge of the court and in the refusal to give certain instructions prayed as to the law governing the case.

There was evidence that, at the time the car driven by defendant struck the deceased, it was being driven at a speed of around 35 or 40 miles an hour. Defendant was trying to overtake a car, which from information received and observations made he had reasons to believe, and did believe, was the car of a notorious violator of the liquor laws, and was loaded with liquor at the time. This car was fleeing from him down Piedmont road in the outskirts of the city of Huntington. As defendant approached the intersection of Piedmont road and Vinson street, deceased, with his wife, attempted to cross Piedmont road. Defendant testified that he was sounding the siren attached to his car, and was keeping a careful lookout. Shortly before he reached the intersection he had to pass a furniture truck, which put him on the left side of the street. About this time he observed the deceased and his wife crossing the street, and applied his brakes, but it was impossible to stop the car in time to avoid striking deceased. There was testimony that the wife of the deceased went on across the street in safety and that deceased was struck because he became confused, and stopped, and then stepped forward in front of the car. Defendant testified that in the emergency created he attempted to drive between deceased and his wife so as to avoid striking either of them, and that he would have succeeded in doing so if deceased had not stepped forward after having stopped.

If defendant's evidence is believed, therefore, while driving rapidly in an effort to overtake an automobile loaded with liquor, he was sounding a siren as a warning of his approach, was keeping a careful lookout, and in a moment of unexpected danger did everything that he could to stop his car and avoid striking deceased.

Defendant requested the court to give the jury the following instructions, which were refused, viz.:

"The court instructs the jury that if they believe from the evidence in this case that Mack B. Lilly was a federal prohibition officer at the time and occasion mentioned in the evidence, and that he was honestly and in good faith executing and attempting to perform a duty imposed upon him by the laws of the United States at the time of the accident, and in so doing, used reasonable care and diligence commensurate with his duty and the apparent danger, if any, then you will find him not guilty."

* * *

After refusing these instructions, the court, in the course of his charge, gave the jury the following instructions to which exception was duly taken, viz.:

"Now there is no question of the fact but what Lilly had a right, based on information he had, to catch that car if he could; but, as

I said a while ago, that did not give him a right to break any law of the state of West Virginia or the city of Huntington to do it."

In refusing to instruct the jury substantially as requested in the requests made by defendant from which we have quoted, and in charging the jury as thus set forth, we think that the learned District Judge committed error prejudicial to the defendant. Prohibition agents are, of course, not above the law. It is their duty, in attempting to apprehend criminals, as it is the duty of other officers of the law, having regard to existing ordinances and the circumstances in which they are placed, to exercise reasonable care and caution for the safety of the public; and, if they fail to do so, and such failure results in the death of any one, they are undoubtedly guilty of manslaughter. But we think that the court went too far in charging the jury that it was the duty of defendant, while chasing a suspected criminal, to have his car under such control in approaching a street intersection that he could avoid any possibility of hurting any one; that deceased had the right of way, if crossing at an intersection not controlled by an officer or traffic device; that the sounding of the whistle and acts relied upon as exercise of care by defendant made no difference, if deceased had the right of way; and, in effect, that the defendant should be convicted, if the death of deceased resulted from defendant's being unable to stop because of excessive speed, and that what was excessive should be determined, not by the circumstances of the case, but by the speed ordinances of the city of Huntington.

In this charge of the court, sight was apparently lost of the fact that the city's speed ordinances should be interpreted, not alone in the interest of the pedestrian, but for the protection of the public, having due regard to the rights of others, lawfully having to use the streets and highways, and this is especially true as to those engaged in the execution and enforcement of the criminal laws of the land. The failure to recognize speed ordinances under such circumstances must be viewed in the light of the rights of others to be affected, and a contrary view would operate unreasonably and be highly prejudicial to the public. The officer in this case was warranted in attempting to make the arrest under the circumstances, and he is by reason thereof excepted from the limitations of the speed prescribed by the city ordinance in issue, provided the jury believed that he acted in good faith in what he did, and with the prudence, care, and caution that an ordinarily prudent person would have exercised under the circumstances in which he was placed; the degree of care required being commensurate with the dangers existing, and to be increased in proportion to such dangers should there be an increase thereof.

The traffic ordinances of a city prescribing who shall have the right of way at crossings and fixing speed limits for vehicles are ordinarily binding upon officials of the federal government as upon all other citizens. Such ordinances, however, are not to be construed as applying to public officials engaged in the performance of a public duty where speed and the right of way are a necessity. The ordinance of Huntington makes no exemption in favor of firemen going to a fire or peace officers pursuing criminals, but it certainly could not have been intended that pedestrians at street intersections should have the right of way over such firemen or officers, or that firemen or officers under such circumstances should be limited to a speed of 25 miles, or required to slow down at intersections so as to have their vehicles under control. Such a construction would render the ordinances void for unreasonableness in so far as they applied to firemen or officers engaged in duties, in the performance of which speed is necessary; and we think that they should be construed as not applicable to such officers, either state or federal, under such circumstances. State v. Gorham, 110 Wash. 330, 188 P. 457, 9 A.L.R. 365.

In the Gorham Case, supra, the court well said:

"That the enforcement of statutory or ordinance provisions limiting the speed at which a motor-propelled vehicle shall be driven over a public highway, against a peace officer, would have a tendency to hamper him in the performance of his official duties, can hardly be doubted. The case in hand affords an illustration. Here the felon was fleeing with a stolen automobile. Naturally he would pay but little regard to the minor offense of exceeding the speed limit. And, if the sheriff must confine himself to that limit, pursuit in the manner adopted would have been useless, since the felon could not have been overtaken. The rule contended for would also hinder the public peace officer in enforcing the statutes regulating traffic upon the state highways. These statutes contain somewhat stringent regulations as to the speed a motor-propelled vehicle may be driven over them, and contain no exception in favor of the peace officers whose duty it is made to enforce them. If these officers may not pursue and overtake one violating the regulations without themselves becoming amenable to the penalties imposed by them, the old remedy of hue and cry is not available in such instances, and many offenders who are now brought to answer will escape."

For the reasons stated, we think that the action of the trial court should be reversed, and a new trial awarded.

Reversed.

NOTE

Green v. United States, 454 F.2d 783 (9th Cir. 1972), involved a rather common scheme whereby a Treasury Department agent, Courtney, posing as a "syndicate" member encouraged the defendants in a plan to produce and distribute moonshine whiskey. The court upheld the entrapment defense despite a finding that the defendants, Thomas and Becker, had a predisposition to make and sell bootleg whiskey. It explained that

The facts presented by this unique record do reveal circumstances which, in combination, require reversal of these convictions.

First, it was Courtney who, after the 1962 raid and arrest, re-initiated telephone contact with Becker. This re-establishment of contact occurred at a time when Courtney would ordinarily have had no reason to re-contact the defendants, because his earlier undercover work had been successfully completed.

Second, the course of events which led to the 1966 arrests was of extremely long duration, lasting approximately two and one-half years if measured from the defendants' 1963 release from jail, or three and one-half years if measured from Courtney's reinitiation of contact.

Third, Courtney's involvement in the bootlegging activities was not only extended in duration, but also substantial in nature. He treated Thomas and Becker as partners. He offered to provide a still, a still site, still equipment, and an operator. He actually provided two thousand pounds of sugar at wholesale.[5]

Fourth, Courtney applied pressure to prod Becker and Thomas into production of bootleg alcohol. The Government concedes that Courtney made the statement, "the boss is on my back." And we believe that in the context of criminal "syndicate" operations, of which Courtney was ostensibly a part, this statement could only be construed as a veiled threat.

Fifth, the Goverment, through its agent Courtney, did not simply attach itself to an on-going bootlegging operation for the purpose of closing it down and prosecuting the operators. Any continuing operation had been terminated with the 1962 raid and arrest. We think, rather, that the procedure followed by Courtney in this case helped first to reestablish, and then to sustain, criminal operations which had ceased with the first convictions.

Finally, throughout the entire period involved, the government agent was the only customer of the illegal operation he had helped to create. It is undisputed that the only alcohol sold went to Courtney, who paid for it with government funds.

Footnote five to the opinion reads:

5. Courtney, we note, was not just a government informer. He was a regularly-employed special investigator of the federal Alcohol and Tobacco Tax Division. Had he been acting in a private capacity, the facts stated above would label him an aider and abettor, and a co-conspirator with Thomas and Becker.

Why should Courtney's status as a law enforcement officer preclude his prosecution? Is the answer that under the implied-exception rationale of the entrapment defense no crime has been committed? Even if that were true would it bar a prosecution for solicitation? Or does the answer lie in the defense examined in this section? It has been argued that if our interest is in eliminating the practice of entrapment such prosecutions rather than the exoneration of the "entrapped" would be more effective. Mikell, The Doctrine of Entrapment in the Federal Courts, 90 U.Pa.L.Rev. 245, 264–65 (1942). Dean Mikell cites no cases in support of his view but some seven years after he wrote the Colorado Supreme Court quoted with approval from an earlier Colorado case: " "* * * when, in their zeal, or under a mistaken sense of duty, detectives suggest the commission of a crime, and instigate others to take part in its commission in order to arrest them while in the act, although the purpose may be to capture old offenders, their conduct is not only reprehensible, but criminal, and ought to be rebuked, rather than encouraged, by the courts.'" Reigan v. People, 120 Colo. 472, 210 P.2d 991, 993–94 (1949). In *Reigan* the court affirmed the convictions (with fines of $300) of two game wardens as accessories before the fact to the crime of unlawfully trapping beaver because they had entrapped two young men into this conduct. Can this position be squared with the defense of aiding law enforcement? If you were a legal advisor to a police department could you readily draft instructions which would guide officers as to the distinction between entrapment, for which they might be held criminally liable, and merely affording, through the necessary police tactics of stealth and strategy, opportunities for the commission of an offense? Would your task be eased if the following statute, proposed by the American Civil Liberties Union, were adopted?

Entrapment

(1) Offense. A law enforcement agent is guilty of an offense if he entraps another to commit a crime.

(2) Entrapment Defined. Entrapment as used in this statute occurs when a law enforcement agent induces the commission of an offense without probable cause [reasonable suspicion] to believe that the person being solicited to commit an offense or with whom an illegal transaction is initiated is engaged in or prepared to engage in such offense or transaction and when the persuasion or other means used to induce the commission of the offense would be likely to cause normally law abiding persons to commit the offense.

(3) Law Enforcement Agent Defined. In this section "law enforcement agent" includes personnel of state and local law enforcement agencies as well as of the United States, and any persons cooperating with such an agency.

ACLU REPORTS, Testimony Before the Senate Subcommittee on Criminal Law and Procedures on the Final Report of the National Commission on Reform of Federal Criminal Laws, pp. 38–39 (March 21, 1972).

H.   CONSENT OF THE VICTIM AND CONDONATION

PEOPLE v. SAMUELS

Court of Appeals of California, 1967.
250 Cal.App.2d 501, 58 Cal.Rptr. 439, certiorari denied 390 U.S. 1024,
88 S.Ct. 1404, 20 L.Ed.2d 281.

SHOEMAKER, Presiding Justice.   Defendant Marvin Samuels was charged by indictment with two counts of conspiracy to violate Penal Code, section 311.2 (preparing and distributing obscene matter); two counts of assault by means of force likely to cause great bodily injury; and a final count of sodomy. Defendant pleaded not guilty to all charges.

The jury acquitted defendant of sodomy but found him guilty on both charges of conspiracy, one charge of aggravated assault and the offense of simple assault included in the other charge of aggravated assault. The simple assault conviction was subsequently dismissed. The court suspended the imposition of sentence, fined defendant $3,000 and placed him on probation for a period of 10 years.

* * *

Defendant Samuels, an ophthalmologist, testified that he recognized the symptoms of sadomasochism in himself, and his primary concern became to control and release his sadomasochistic urges in ways which were harmless. Through his hobby of photography, he participated in the production of several films on the east coast. Three of these films depicted bound individuals being whipped. Defendant wielded the whip in two of the films and acted as the cameraman, producer and director for the third film. He testified that the apparent force of the whippings was "faked" and that cosmetics were used to supply the marks of the apparent beating. Defendant produced one of these films at the trial.

* * *

Defendant testified on his own behalf and admitted making both films in his home. The man who had been strung up in the "vertical" film had telephoned defendant after he had let it be known in the San Francisco "underground" that he wanted volunteers for sadomasochistic films to be sent to the Kinsey Institute. Defendant arranged to meet him at the San Jose bus depot and drove him to his Sunnyvale home. After the filming had been completed, defendant drove him back to the bus depot in the "same condition he came in." During the course of the filming, which took some four hours, defendant strung the man up with hospital restraints and struck him lightly with a riding crop, pulling his punches just before striking the man's body. He stopped the camera periodically and applied cosmetics. Defendant had coached the man to move violently so as to make the film seem realistic.

* * *

Defendant also contends that the consent of the victim is an absolute defense to the charge of aggravated assault and that the trial court erred in instructing the jury to the contrary. This argument cannot be sustained.

Although both parties concede that they were unable to find any California case directly in point, consent of the victim is not generally a defense to assault or battery, except in a situation involving ordinary physical contact or blows incident to sports such as football, boxing or wrestling. It is also the rule that the apparent consent of a person without legal capacity to give consent, such as a child or insane person, is ineffective.

It is a matter of common knowledge that a normal person in full possession of his mental faculties does not freely consent to the use, upon himself, of force likely to produce great bodily injury. Even if it be assumed that the victim in the "vertical" film did in fact suffer from some form of mental aberration which compelled him to submit to a beating which was so severe as to constitute an aggravated assault, defendant's conduct in inflicting that beating was no less violative of a penal statute obviously designed to prohibit one human being from severely or mortally injuring another. It follows that the trial court was correct in instructing the jury that consent was not a defense to the aggravated assault charge.

STATE v. GAROUTTE

Supreme Court of Arizona, En Banc, 1964.
95 Ariz. 234, 388 P.2d 809.

BERNSTEIN, Justice. The defendant, Wayne Garoutte, was charged by direct information in the Superior Court of Maricopa County, Arizona, with the crime of manslaughter in the driving of a motor vehicle, a misdemeanor, said crime happening on or about May 21, 1961. The defendant filed a motion to dismiss on the basis of A.R.S. § 13–1591 [1] which was granted. The order of the trial judge dismissing the charge was as follows:

"The misdemeanor with which defendant herein is charged arises as an alleged law violation based upon defendant's negligence and which negligence is defined under the manslaughter statute (13–456 ARS) as a necessary element of the offense charged. In such respect, therefore, and unlike the usual criminal charge where criminal intent is a necessary element of the crime, the elements of negli-

---

[1] "A. When a defendant is accused of a misdemeanor for which the person injured by the act constituting the offense has a remedy by a civil action, the offense may be compromised as provided in this section, except when the offense is committed by or upon any officer of justice while in the execution of the duties of his office, or when the offense is committed riotously, or with intent to commit a felony.

"B. If the party injured appears before the court in which the action is pend-

ing at any time before trial, and acknowledges that he has received satisfaction for the injury, the court may, on payment of the costs incurred, order the prosecution dismissed, and the defendant discharged. The reasons for the order shall be set forth and entered of record on the minutes and the order shall be a bar to another prosecution for the same offense.

"C. No public offense shall be compromised or the prosecution or punishment upon a compromise dismissed or stayed except as provided by law.

gence under civil and common law principals [sic] appear to enter into a determination of this particular type of offense.

"The statute in question (13–1591 ARS) can not be considered as an isolated fragment of our legal system. The manslaughter statute involving operation of motor vehicles (13–456 ARS) passed by the legislature in 1957 must necessarily be considered and construed in the light of the whole body of the law on this subject matter as it existed when that 1957 act was enacted into law, and the legislature is presumed to know of long established laws and procedures when passing new legislation. This is in accordance with well established rules of statutory construction.

"The statute in question (13–1591 ARS), which has been in effect since 1901 and applied by the courts for sixty years, specifically recognizes civil satisfaction in a misdemeanor charge based upon compromise of the civil rights and causes of action growing out of the same alleged negligent act of the defendant which forms the basis for the criminal charge. If such satisfaction is accomplished according to the provisions of this statute, then the action appropriately may be dismissed.

"The Court, upon the evidence and stipulation of facts entered into between the County Attorney and counsel for defendant, FINDS:

"That the widow and legal representative of the minor children of the decedent appeared before the court and acknowledged receipt of financial satisfaction and payment of damages for the injuries sustained and in compromise and settlement of all civil causes of action arising from the act in question; that the satisfaction and damages paid, as aforesaid, were fair and substantial in amount; that there was no criminal intent on the part of defendant in committing the act in question; that the death in question resulted solely from negligence on the part of defendant; and that the widow and said decedent requested that defendant not be prosecuted under the pending charge.

"IT IS ORDERED, therefore, that for the foregoing reasons the complaint against defendant herein be and the same is hereby dismissed, pursuant to defendant's motion.

"DONE IN OPEN COURT this 10 day of August, 1961."

* * *

In principle, civil suits and criminal prosecutions should be kept separate. The law should treat rich and poor alike, and the fact that a man might be able to pay for damages due to his negligence should not save him from criminal prosecution. But in practice, this principle is not always applied in misdemeanors, and some states, Arizona among them, have adopted statutes similar to A.R.S. § 13–1591, supra, authorizing the dismissal of misdemeanor cases where the injured party has been compensated. Miller, "The Compromise of Criminal Cases," 1 Southern California L.Rev. 1.

New York was among the first states to adopt this policy. In 1817, under the predecessor of the present New York and Arizona statutes, a prosecution for assault and battery by throwing vitriol on two women was permitted to proceed although payment had been made in a manner customary under the statute for the damage to their clothes. In re Gilmore (John Gilmore's Case), 2 N.Y. City Hall Recorder 29. In those days cases were reported, at times, by a reporter who was present, and not in a written opinion by the court. In this case the reporter summarized the case as follows: "To cast spirits of vitriol, aqua fortis, or any other powerful acid substance, on the person or clothes of another, wantonly and maliciously, is *at least, an infamous crime—and ought to be made* felony by statute." (Emphasis in original). In 1830 the New York Supreme Court, the then court of last resort, in People v. Bishop, 5 Wend. 111, said: "An offence for an assault and battery or other misdemeanor, except in certain cases, may be compromised either before or after an indictment." The exceptions, however, were not enumerated by the court. At that time the New York statute had an exception for "infamous crimes". The exception was dropped in the later revisions, and has never appeared in the Arizona statute.

In 1849, the New York Commissioners on Practice and Pleading, in explaining the policy of the statute, said:

> " 'There are many cases, which are technically public of-fences, but which are in reality rather of a private than a public nature, and where the public interests are better pro-moted by checking than by encouraging criminal prosecu-tions. Of this class are libels, and simple assaults and bat-teries; or those which according to section 731 [enacted as section 663], are not committed by or upon an officer of justice, while in the execution of the duties of his office, or riotously, or with an intent to commit a felony. With these exceptions, cases of this nature have by the policy of our statutes, always been considered fit subjects of compro-mise: 2 R.S. 3d ed. 815, 816, sec. 68–71; 1 R.L. of 1813, p. 499, sec. 19; a policy which has been carried by the courts, still further than the terms of the statute.' See Report of Commissioners on Practice and Pleadings, p. 339, submitted December 31, 1849." Historical Note, N.Y.Code of Criminal Procedure, § 663.

The California Act, now California Penal Code, §§ 1377–1379, from which the Arizona statute was derived, was first adopted in

1850. The Arizona compromise statute was adopted in 1864. Other states with similar legislation include Alaska, Georgia, Louisiana, Montana, Oregon, Pennsylvania, Virginia and Wisconsin.

Until modern traffic problems arose, manslaughter, as the lowest degree of homicide, was a felony in Arizona. It was never thought that the taking of a human life could be paid for and forgotten.

"Misdemeanor Manslaughter" made its appearance in Arizona law * * * in 1950. * * * On both occasions where the statute was before this court, the crime created was described as a "high misdemeanor", State v. Morf, [80 Ariz. 220, 295 P.2d 842]; State v. Gordon, 79 Ariz. 184, 285 P.2d 758.

In the light of this history the problem presented to us here is whether the compromise statute, A.R.S. § 13–1712, includes "high misdemeanors". The statute, A.R.S. § 13–103, divides crimes only into felonies and misdemeanors, and bases its classification on the term and place of imprisonment. The classification of misdemeanors as "high misdemeanors" or "misdemeanors" is a common law judicial classification. It is based on the seriousness of the crime and has nothing to do with the term or place of confinement or judgment. Arizona statutes make no distinction between high misdemeanors and mere misdemeanors. The legislature is presumed to have known of the compromise statute when it created misdemeanor manslaughter.

After the adoption of the Arizona compromise statute, courts in other states warned against the public evils of extending the compromise statute to all crimes which might be classed by statute as misdemeanors. See e. g. Commonwealth v. Heckman, 114 Pa.Super. 70, 172 A. 28 (1934).

The situation calls for clarification by the legislature. A bill which would specifically exclude misdemeanor manslaughter from the compromise statute is now pending before it. The present state of the law has this incongruous result. If a drunk or reckless driver does not hit anyone, he may go to jail (A.R.S. §§ 28–692, 28–693). If guilty, he cannot escape punishment. There is no "injured person" or "injured party" or possible "remedy by civil action," and the compromise statute may not be invoked. But if he damages property, hits someone, or even kills them, under the compromise statute he may completely escape criminal punishment by paying civil damages.

We hold that the compromise statute includes "high misdemeanors" and is applicable in misdemeanor manslaughter cases, and the judgment below must be affirmed.

PROPOSED FEDERAL CRIMINAL CODE (1971)

§ 1619. Consent as a Defense

(1) When a Defense. When conduct is an offense because it causes or threatens bodily injury, consent to such conduct or to the infliction of such injury by all persons injured or threatened by the conduct is a defense if:

(a) neither the injury inflicted nor the injury threatened is such as to jeopardize life or seriously impair health;

(b) the conduct and the injury are reasonably foreseeable hazards of joint participation in a lawful athletic contest or competitive sport; or

(c) the conduct and the injury are reasonably foreseeable hazards of an occupation or profession or of medical or scientific experimentation conducted by recognized methods, and the persons subjected to such conduct or injury, having been made aware of the risks involved, consent to the performance of the conduct or the infliction of the injury.

(2) Ineffective Consent. Assent does not constitute consent, within the meaning of this section, if:

(a) it is given by a person who is legally incompetent to authorize the conduct charged to constitute the offense and such incompetence is manifest or known to the actor;

(b) it is given by a person who by reason of youth, mental disease or defect, or intoxication is manifestly unable or known by the actor to be unable to make a reasonable judgment as to the nature or harmfulness of the conduct charged to constitute the offense; or

(c) it is induced by force, duress or deception.

Comment

Often the effect of consent is specified in the definition of an offense, e. g., rape, theft. But an explicit consent provision for crimes of assault and endangerment is necessary because they are crimes of infliction of bodily injury upon others, and even intentional infliction of injury may be consented to, as in surgery. The defense provided here serves to explicate matters which would, absent the statute, probably be resolved by prosecutorial discretion.

NOTES

1. Why should a distinction be drawn between Dr. Samuels' diversion and professional football or boxing? Is it a question of how many people enjoy the activity or are entertained by it? See the comment on the *Samuels* case in 81 Harv.L.Rev. 1339 (1968).

2. Should the deceased's consent, or indeed request, be a defense to a charge of murder where the defendant merely placed poison within the reach of his incurably-ill wife? People v. Roberts, 211 Mich. 187, 178 N.W. 690 (1920). Does your answer depend on whether you accept the *Samuels* court's assertion that consent to possible serious injury equals impaired mental faculties and therefore cannot be deemed consent? Is your answer different if the defendant is a doctor who, at the request of his terminally-ill patient "permits" death by ending or not initiating "extraordinary" medical procedures? What if he hastens death by administering fatal amounts of sedation. See generally Myers, The Human Body and the Law 139–59 (1970) and Morris, Voluntary Euthanasia, 45 Wash.L.Rev. 239 (1970).

3. Is the notion of compensation in lieu of punishment, embodied in compromise statutes such as that involved in *Garoutte*, repugnant? If, as is posited in *Garoutte*, there was no criminal intent why isn't tort law a more desirable model for resolution of the problems caused by the defendant? Are there any differences, other than the recipient of the payment, between the approach embodied in these compromise statutes and the pattern of enforcement of "public welfare" offenses?

In primitive societies, including that of the Saxons, such payments to the victim or his family were the norm even as to conduct that we would readily designate criminal. See Wolfgang, Victim Compensation in Crimes of Personal Violence, 50 Minn.L.Rev. 223 (1965). Although we distinguish compensation from punishment, which, if any, of the appropriate goals of the criminal law are sacrificed by such schemes? (Distinguish here between programs requiring restitution or compensation by the offender and those in which the state makes payments to the victims of crime as a form of social insurance. See, e. g., Note, New York Crime Victims Compensation Board Act: Four Years Later, 7 Colum.J.L. & Soc.Prob. 25 (1971).

I. DOMESTIC AUTHORITY

STATE v. ENGLAND

Supreme Court of Oregon, 1960.
220 Or. 395, 349 P.2d 668, 89 A.L.R.2d 392.

PERRY, Justice. The grand jury returned an indictment against the defendant David C. England seeking to charge him with the crime of involuntary manslaughter. The charging part of the indictment is as follows:

"* * * then and there being, did then and there unlawfully, feloniously and in the commission of a lawful act, to-wit: while disciplining his son Charles Edwin England, age 12, act without due caution and circumspection in that said defendant then and there having a duty to use reasonable force in said disciplining, did strike said Charles Edwin

England about the head and face with defendant's hand with force and violence thereby inflicting injuries upon the said Charles Edwin England, and did thereby and in the manner and by the means aforesaid proximately cause and produce the death of him, the said Charles Edwin England, who by reason of said injuries so inflicted, caused and produced, did die in Multnomah County, Oregon on the 8th day of February, 1959."

The trial court sustained the defendant's demurrer thereto on the grounds that the indictment failed to state facts sufficient to constitute a crime and the state has appealed.

ORS 163.040(2) defines the crime of involuntary manslaughter as follows:

"Any person who, in the commission of any unlawful act, or a lawful act without due caution or circumspection, involuntarily kills another, is guilty of manslaughter. The provisions of this subsection shall not apply to the killing of any person where the proximate cause of such killing is an act or omission defined as negligent homicide in ORS 163.091."

Under certain circumstances the law recognizes a homicide as excusable:

ORS 163.110(1): "The killing of a human being is excusable when committed:

"(1) By accident or misfortune in lawfully correcting a child or servant, or in doing any other lawful act, by lawful means, with usual and ordinary caution and without any unlawful intent."

The parties agree that these statutes are in pari materia and must be construed together.

It is the contention of the state that, having alleged the doing of a lawful act in a negligent manner which resulted in a homicide, the indictment fully and sufficiently charges the defendant with the crime of involuntary manslaughter. The difficulty, however, lies in the fact that the indictment alleges that the homicide was the result of a parent lawfully correcting his child "without due caution or circumspection,"—in other words, in a negligent manner.

Since time immemorial organized society has recognized that the duty of training children while under parental care rests with the parents and thus the law recognizes that parents have the right to "chastise their refractory and disobedient children." The law also requires, for the safety of the child, that the chastisement must not exceed the bounds of due moderation or the law will imply malice, thus making the parent criminally liable. State v. McDonie, 96 W.

Va. 219, 123 S.E. 405, 37 A.L.R. 699, and annotations following; State v. Spiegel, 39 Wyo. 309, 270 P. 1064, 64 A.L.R. 289.

Criminal malice or intent is not an element of the crime of involuntary manslaughter. In fact, it is this lack of intent that distinguishes manslaughter from murder.

The parties are agreed, and we agree with them, that ORS 163.110 deals with two distinct situations. The first portion deals with the correction of children and servants, the second portion with human relationships in general. The first portion of this act, which deals solely with the right of a parent to correct a child, or a master his servant, excuses a homicide through accident or misfortune. The second portion, which deals with all other human relationships, excuses a homicide where the act is lawful and performed not in a negligent manner. Had it been the intention of the legislature not to excuse the negligent homicide of a child while being lawfully corrected by a parent the legislature would have included in the first portion, the same as in the last, the words "with usual and ordinary caution." In excluding these words from the parent-child relationship the maxim of "expressio unius est exclusio alterius" is applicable in that, having applied the rule of due care in general to all homicides arising from human relationships, the legislative intent is clearly expressed to exclude the crime of involuntary manslaughter committed through negligence while lawfully correcting a child or servant.

Since the indictment in this case charges only that the defendant as a parent while lawfully correcting his child did so negligently and as a result of his negligence the child died, it states no criminal offense under the laws of this state and the trial court correctly sustained the demurrer to the indictment.

Affirmed.

STATE v. LUTZ

Court of Common Pleas of Ohio, 1953.
65 Ohio L.Abs. 402, 113 N.E.2d 757.

McLAUGHLIN, Judge. Defendant, Mervin R. Lutz, Canton grade school principal and teacher, appeals an assault and battery conviction for paddling a pupil. He with good reason believed the pupil, eleven year old Samuel Kafidies, had thrown a stone while on the way to school at a little girl schoolmate, and then fibbed about it. The stone knocked the little girl's glasses off and might have seriously injured her eyes. The paddle used was of normal proportions. He was severely spanked from six to fifteen times. His buttocks was vividly discolored, black and blue, which cleared up in about five days with some tenderness remaining longer. He was an epileptic since infancy, and this Court accepts his mother's story to the effect that he had three such fits after the paddling. The spanking was witnessed by Miss Evelyn Obermiller, his room teacher, on Thursday morning, October 23, 1952. The next day, Friday, the boy's parents and older brother took him to the office of Superintendent of Schools, Harold E. Eibling, who saw the bruises, listened to their complaint, but took no action. They then took him to the County Juvenile Court and had a talk with the Boy's Probation Officer there, Andrew Chlebeck, who took no action. They then went to Police Court and filed an affidavit. On the following Tuesday the boy returned to school and was then examined by the school doctor and the school nurse. By this time the discoloring was entirely gone.

Almost two months later on December 17, 1952, the case was tried to the Municipal Judge without a jury. The trial lasted about three days. On January 2, 1953, the Court entered a finding of guilty as charged, from which finding appeal is made to this Court.

* * *

When a teacher gives a pupil corporal punishment and is charged criminally therefor, certain fundamental propositions of law come to mind.

First, the teacher stands in loco parentis (i. e., in the place of a parent), and acts in a quasi judicial capacity and is not liable for an error in judgment in the matter of punishment.

Second, the teacher's responsibility attaches home to home (i. e., while the pupil is on the way to and from school).

Third, there is a presumption of correctness of the teacher's actions.

Fourth, there is a presumption that the teacher acts in good faith.

Fifth, mere, excessive or severe punishment on the part of the teacher does not constitute a crime unless it is of such a nature as to produce or threaten lasting or permanent injury, or unless the State has shown that it was administered with either express malice (i. e., spite, hatred or revenge), or implied malice (i. e., a wrongful act wantonly done without just cause or excuse), and beyond a reasonable doubt.

* * *

This rule is practically adopted by the Supreme and Appellate Courts of leading States throughout the country, particularly, Massachusetts, New York, Illinois and Alabama.

* * *

Three Ohio cases have come under our careful scrutiny; namely, Mohr v. State, 19 Ohio Cir.Ct.R.,N.S., 43; Martin v. State, 11 Ohio N.P,N.S., 183; and State v. Liggett, 84 Ohio App. 225, 83 N.E.2d 663.

* * * [T]he Mohr case * * * holds in effect that the parent is criminally liable for excessive or immoderate punishment, regardless of a parent's motives and all questions of malice.

* * * [T]he Martin case, 1910, * * * holds in effect that the teacher is not criminally liable for mere, excessive or immoderate punishment, but that malice, express or implied, and production or threatened production of lasting or permanent injuries must be shown; and, beyond a reasonable doubt.

In the Liggett case, 1947, a stepmother was charged with assault with intent to kill when she cruelly punished a nine year old stepson. The case holds [84 Ohio App. 225, 83 N.E.2d 664], "There was substantial evidence of these physical injuries, indicating punishment far in excess of that which the law authorizes one standing in loco parentis to inflict."

* * *

We note that in the Mohr case, the Circuit Court of Summit County did recognize "that the father is the judge of when he shall punish and for what" and the Court did further recognize the requirement of malice but stated that an instruction to the jury that they must find that defendant was prompted by malice and ill-will *towards his minor daughter Edith Mohr* in inflicting the punishment in question, "would have been improper since the severe punishment might have been inflicted because of ill-will that he had towards the parent's mother, sister or brother."

Parenthetically, we say that it is not too unusual for a parent or step-parent to bear ill-will towards another member of the family and not having an opportunity to vent their spleen upon him to "take their spite out on" some other innocent family member. Nevertheless, the ill-will or malice is still present in the mind and heart of the punisher. Such a situation does not exist in our school rooms, and a school teacher rarely punishes one pupil for the misdeeds of another. The quasi judicial capacity of the school teacher punisher is therefore more impersonal and more impartial than that of a parent or stepparent punisher.

* * *

Proper application of the rule in the Mohr and Liggett cases prompts us to ask the question, "Was the punishment in the case at Bar so severe, so excessive and so cruel as to be shocking to every right thinking man?" If so, then it was "punishment far in excess of what the law authorizes one standing in loco parentis to inflict," and malice will be implied.

This Court has examined the photographic exhibit of the boy's buttocks, and has carefully perused the record as to all bits of evidence concerning the severity of this paddling, and after weighing the evidence we find nothing that shocks the sensibilities of this

Court or points to any fact of excessive severity or cruelty. School day memories of the average individual, including this Court, will recall many experiences of corporal punishment more severe than this one properly given and of great benefit to the pupil and the school.

This corporal punishment came to the attention of a number of individuals without shocking their sensibilities.

First of all, the boy's room teacher watched the paddling; it did not shock her.

Second, * * * this whole matter came to the attention of the Superintendent of Schools who "seen the bruises on Sam" without having his sensibilities shocked into action, although he had ample authority under the law to discipline or remove the teacher.

Third, * * * [t]he authorities of the County Juvenile Court, at least, unofficially, had this entire matter before them without the shocking of sensibilities there, although they too had ample authority under the law to do something about it. The sensibilities of the school doctor and the school nurse were not shocked.

Next, what does the record show as to any production or threatened production of lasting or permanent injuries. The boy was examined by his family physician on the day following the paddling, and the record discloses that the doctor found the vivid discoloring of the boy's buttocks, black and blue, but nowhere does the record disclose that the injuries were such as to require any medical treatment. This boy had been an epileptic since infancy, and his mother did testify that after the paddling he had three such fits, but the record discloses no medical testimony indicating any causal connection between the paddling and the subsequent seizures, the only medical testimony thereon being the family doctor's statement (Record, Page 53), on December 18th, "To my knowledge he has been free from seizures this past year."

How then can it be said that there was any substantial evidence of either physical injuries or cruelty, indicating punishment in excess of that which the law authorizes one standing in loco parentis to inflict.

When the trial court called this punishment immoderate and excessive, the State's evidence was certainly given the benefit of most favorable interpretation. The defendant, and not the State, is entitled to such benefit when the law as to the presumption of innocence is properly applied.

* * *

Proper application of the rule of the Martin case and the rule of the Mohr and Liggett cases required the trial court to examine the State's evidence for a substantial showing of bad faith or malice or glaring injury.

This record discloses no evidence which would indicate that this teacher was actuated by any malice, express or implied, or of any serious physical injury or of any punishment in excess of that which the law authorizes one standing in loco parentis to inflict. Contrarily, there is ample evidence to indicate that this teacher acted in good faith with proper motives.

Since we are of the opinion that the trial court should have directed a verdict for the defendant at the conclusion of the State's evidence, this Court will enter such an order at this time and acquit the defendant.[a]

NOTES

1. Compare *England* with State v. Straight, 136 Mont. 255, 347 P.2d 482 (1959) which considers a domestic authority statute requiring that the force used be "reasonable in manner and moderate in degree".

2. Compare the *Lutz* view with the so-called "modern rule" stated in People v. Curtiss, 116 Cal.App. 771, 300 P. 801 (1931).

a. The policy of the Dallas, Texas School District authorizing corporal punishment was the subject of an unsuccessful challenge as violative of the Eighth Amendment and as a deprivation of due process is that corporal punishment is capricious and unrelated to any legitimate educational purpose. Ware v. Estes, 328 F.Supp. 657 (N.D.Tex.1971), aff'd per curiam, 458 F.2d 1360 (5th Cir. 1972).

VII. PSYCHOLOGICAL ABNORMALITY AND CRIMINAL LIABILITY

The substantive criminal law has traditionally attempted to provide for some consideration of the fact that some offenders are psychologically abnormal. The integration of formal substantive criminal law and developing knowledge concerning human behavior is one of the most challenging and difficult tasks of the law.

Despite the existence of a number of theoretical frameworks for considering human behavior, the law has, especially in recent years, dealt most extensively with psychodynamic psychology. This has been true for several reasons. First, psychodynamic theory has found favor with medical doctors, and the law has generally regarded physicians as the most desirable "experts" on psychological abnormality. Thus those whose expertise is most often offered to courts have been psychodynamically oriented.

But in addition psychodynamic theory appears, on the surface at least, to be that theoretical approach most easily integrated with the substantive criminal law. Criminal law assumes the existence of "free will" in most individuals, and consequently regards most crimes as the result of a "free" (and consequently "culpable") decision to do the prohibited act. Although there has been an increasing willingness to recognize exceptions, the law is likely to continue for the foreseeable future to insist upon assuming the existence of free will in most offenders. Criminal liability has, as the material on state of mind developed, been defined partially in terms of the potential offender's conscious mental processes. In the task of integrating criminal liability and psychological abnormality, it is clear that less difficulty exists (on a theoretical level, at least) if the framework used to explain the psychological abnormality is consistent (or at least is not inconsistent) with these two fundamental tenets of substantive criminal law: the existence of "free will" and the significance of conscious thought processes upon human behavior. Judged by this criterion, psychodynamic psychology seems well suited to the task. Although much emphasis has been upon unconscious processes, psychodynamic theory (in some forms) also recognizes that conscious thought processes have some effect upon human behavior.[a] More-

a. Dynamic psychology has been described as a completely deterministic approach which "rejects free will but replaces it with the libido." R. Caldwell, Criminology 191 (1956). This seems to be the substance of some statements by some dynamically-oriented psychologists. See, e. g., Zilboorg, Psychoanalysis and Criminology, in Encyclopedia of Criminology 402

over, by positing the possible existence of something ("mental illness" or "psychopathology") which exists in some but not all individuals and which may affect behavior, psychodynamic theory permits explanation of the exceptional case in terms that are not necessarily inconsistent with the existence of free will in other cases. Perhaps in part at least because of this compatibility with the assumptions of the criminal law, psychodynamic theory has become that theoretical approach most often involved in criminal litigation.[b]

This section, then, poses the issue of the integration of psychological abnormality (generally described in psychodynamic terms) and substantive criminal law. Emphasis is intended to be not only upon doctrine and theory, but also upon actual practice and the impact of practice upon either doctrine or theory or both. Because most of the limited empirical investigations of the impact in practice of substantive criminal law doctrine have been done in this area, it provides the best available vehicle for injecting into the consideration of what the law is and should be considerations of practical limitations imposed by the "real world" and possible undesirable "side ef-

(V. Branham & S. Kutask eds. 1949): "It is easily seen that criminal behavior is not a rational process. It has little to do with intellect * * *. Crime is deeply rooted in the instincts of man, and it is usually an act of the instinctual, impulsive life of the criminal individual." But a number of dynamically-oriented psychologists see no necessity for such a position, and postulate that in the absence of stress an individual does possess "free will" and his actions may be determined by intellectual deliberation and choice. P. Roche, The Criminal Mind 23–24 (1958). See Weiss, Determinism and Freedom in Psychoanalysis: Awareness and Responsibility, 28 Am.J. Psychoanalysis 59 (1968). This is logically consistent with the therapeutic approach of many dynamically-oriented mental health personnel. Therapy is designed, by providing insight into unconscious processes, to enable the patient to develop conscious control over his activity. Id. at 60. It is also consistent with the conclusions of many dynamic investigators who acknowledge an inability to demonstrate that personality malformation is "the cause" of all crime. See, e. g., W. Healy, Mental Conflicts and Misconduct 7–8 (1917), indicating that he was able to identify "mental conflict" as the cause of the delinquency in only about seven per cent of the cases studied.

b. See G. Shadoan, Law and Tactics in Federal Criminal Cases 243–44 (1964):
In order to pursuade the jury, the psychiatrist must do more than merely apply psychiatric labels to the defendant's condition. * * * He must explain the data upon which his conclusions are based and the reasoning process by which he reached those conclusions.

Only those psychiatrists of the "dynamic school" are equipped by both training and orientation to discern and describe the origin and development of the defendant's particular mental illness and its effect on his personality development, mental and emotional processes and behavior controls. Those trained in the "organic [or 'descriptive'] school," on the other hand, are concerned with mere diagnostic classification based on currently manifested symptoms rather than dynamic theories explaining the origin and development of personality or with the concepts of motivation and adaption of behavior.

* * * Unless the defendant's current symptomatology is so gross that a mere description and classification of his behavior will convince the jury of his lack of criminal responsibility, a psychiatrist of the "organic" school will not make an effective witness.

fects" of reform in the law-in-the-books. With this as its task, the section begins with a textual note concerning psychodynamic theory and its value in understanding the criminal act. Attention is then turned to the insanity defense, the major vehicle traditionally used to integrate law and psychology. Alternative vehicles are then explored: the "automatism" defense, diminished capacity, and diminished responsibility. Finally, an opportunity is provided to examine the efforts of a particular jurisdiction to better effectuate the integration in a limited area by modification of its substantive law of homicide.

A. DYNAMIC PSYCHOLOGY AND CRIMINAL ACTIVITY

Dynamic psychiatry has been defined as a system of psychiatry that is primarily concerned with internal, unconscious drives or energies that are presumed to determine behavior.[c] This can be contrasted with descriptive psychiatry, which refers to a system of psychiatry that is based primarily upon the study of observable symptoms and phenomena.[d] Psychiatry is the medical specialty concerned with

c. L. Hinsie and R. Campell, Psychiatric Dictionary 206 (4th Ed. 1970).

d. Id. See A. Hollingshead and F. Redlich, Social Class and Mental Illness 155–56 (1958):

Two distinctly different therapeutic orientations are represented by the 30 practitioners who live in the community. We divide these practitioners into those who have an analytic and psychological orientation (referred to as A–P group) and into those who have a directive and organic orientation (D–O group). At first, we referred to the D–O group—following common usage—as eclectics. However, most of these practitioners are not real eclectics. One psychiatrist who falls into the D–O group once declared, "To help a patient I would do anything, even stand on my head if necessary." He might do that, but he would not practice psychoanalytic therapy for two reasons: He is opposed to it, and he has never learned the technique. There are a few outstanding specialists, particularly in the psychosomatic field, who master all available methods, true eclectics— we prefer to call them individualists

—but today most practitioners, including psychiatrists in university centers and other institutions, fall into one group or the other. * * *

Our division is based on two criteria: the principal method of therapy and training for such therapy. We find that there is a definite division in theory and practice between the analytic-psychological approach and the directive-organic approach. The analytic approach consists essentially of analyzing behavior, relationships, and conscious and unconscious motivations according to psychoanalytic theories. The classical psychoanalytic approach consists of analyzing symptoms and defenses, transference and resistance, with the purpose of strengthening the ego through insight into unconscious forces, particularly into those which are apt to produce psychopathology. The so-called dynamic psychotherapeutic approach follows this general line with less rigor and greater flexibility. The emphasis is on gaining insight and applying insight and not on manipulation or direction unless this is absolutely necessary because of a weak ego; whenever directions are given they must at least be based

study, diagnosis, treatment, and prevention of mental illness. However, medically-trained personnel have no exclusive claim to the theoretical framework underlying dynamic psychiatry. Since the dynamic conceptualizations are used for diagnostic and therapeutic purposes by individuals without medical training, it is probably best to refer to this orientation as one of dynamic psychology. Such terminology makes clear that the dynamic approach relates to the entire science concerned with the mind and mental processes rather than only to one medical specialty.

Dynamic psychology postulates that physical action is one result of mental activity. Mental activity is of two kinds: conscious and unconscious. It is the emphasis upon the need to understand unconscious mental activity or processes that separates dynamic psychology from other psychological theoretical frameworks.[e] Mental

on analytic insights of the therapist. The approach is almost entirely psychological; organic methods of diagnosis and treatment are extraneous to it and are rarely employed by its practitioners.

The directive approach consists of changing attitudes, opinions, and behavior of the patient by means of directive and supportive methods such as assertion, suggestion, reassurance, advice, manipulation, and even coercion. It is usually not based on analytic insight but on the therapist's judgment and what is called clinical experience and evaluation of the patient's problems and situation. Depending on the therapist and the patient, the therapist may try to buck up the patient's low esteem, convert him to the therapist's own philosophy of life, give him a stern lecture, friendly advice, tell him to go to a resort, to take it easy or work harder, to treat his 'wife kindly or get a divorce. The success of any of these maneuvers, and they can be quite successful, depends on the wisdom and strength of the therapist rather than on his technical knowledge and also on the suggestibility and the ego strength of the patient. The directive approach requires, besides clinical experience, and even more urgently than technical knowledge, broad human experience and a willingness to assume authority.

Directive techniques are often combined with organic medical techniques, both diagnostic and therapeutic. D–O practitioners are likely to do medical and neurological examinations, carry out laboratory tests, prescribe drugs, administer shock treatments, and refer their patients to neurosurgeons or even carry out, themselves, "minor" neurosurgical procedures, like transorbital lobotomies. Many of their explanations, to themselves and to their patients, are couched in medical or pseudomedical terms. Although D–O practitioners have a general interest in psychology and the social sciences, their knowledge of these disciplines, is in practice and theory, weaker than that of the A–P group. What interest and knowledge they have are overshadowed by their stronger biological and medical interests. Hence, we refer to one as psychological and to the other as organic. Another basic difference is that the A–P group holds the expressed belief that the etiology of most mental illnesses, with the possible exception of a few organic disorders, is primarily psychological and that treatment, too, should be psychological.

See also A. Rogow, The Psychiatrists (1970).

e. The most obvious contrast is with the behavioral approach, which traditionally explains actions in terms of observable variables rather than in terms of unobservable "mental processes." See L. Ullman and L. Krasner, Introduction to Case Studies in Behavior Modification 1–39 (1965) for a discussion of the "medical model" of mental illness as contrasted with

processes, in turn, are caused by "psychic energy" or drives. Freud initially postulated only one "drive" or source of psychic energy, libido. Although often defined as "sexual energy," libido is used by dynamic psychologists in a broader sense than "sexual" usually suggests. In this specialized terminology, it refers to the drive for any sensual pleasure or pleasurable tension release connected with any part of the physical organism. It is now generally accepted that there is also an aggressive drive that along with libido serves as the motive force for mental activity. The function of the human personality is to satisfy these drives by seeking pleasure and avoiding pain. Thus the hypothesis that man is governed by the "pleasure principle."

Perhaps the most significant characteristic of the drives is the variety of ways in which they may be satisfied. They may be satisfied in a physical and direct manner, as by stimulation of various parts of the body. Satisfaction may also be physical and indirect or, in other words, symbolic; thus fondling (or mere possession) of a pencil may be an indirect method of satisfaction. Satisfaction may also be nonphysical as well as indirect. That is, to some extent mental processes may satisfy the drives. Thus a daydream of a sexual conquest may also satisfy the libido despite the lack of physical activity.

The various means of satisfaction differ in economy, i. e., in the amount of satisfaction returned for the effort required for the physical or mental processes. Generally speaking, direct and physical means are most economical in a short-term sense. Economy, however, must realistically be evaluated over a longer period of time.

the behavioralists' conception. Behavioralists are beginning, it has been asserted, to be concerned with hypothetical "processes" between stimulus and responsive behavior. U. Neisser, Cognative Psychology 5 (1967). Cognative psychology has taken as its field of concern the processes of sensation, perception, retention, recall, problem solving, and thinking, but at its present stage of development it is unlikely to be able to provide the basis for reliable explanations for such complex acts as are involved in much criminal activity. Cf. U. Neisser, Cognative Psychology (1967).

For the same reason, sociological analyses of crime causation are of minimal value to the resolution of questions concerning the legal guilt of a criminal defendant. While they focus on purported causal relationships between social conditions and criminal acts, most make little effort to investigate the human decision-making process. "Sociologists have not been much involved in the legal-psychiatric controversies about 'insanity' * * * Their involvement has been pretty much limited to criticism of the principal assumption that causes of crime are to be found 'in' individual offenders." D. Cressey and D. Ward, Introduction to Part X, in Delinquency, Crime, and Social Processes 1048 (D. Cressey & D. Ward eds. 1969). But see Cressey, The Differential Association Theory and Compulsive Crimes, 45 J.Crim.L., C. & P.S. 29 (1954).

Much the same can be said of attempts to relate physiological characteristics to criminal acts. See V. Mark and F. Ervin, Violence and the Brain (1970), suggesting that a significant amount of inter-personal violence is caused by brain malfunctioning often correctible by surgery. Although Mark and Ervin suggest that brain malfunctioning may lead to reduced impulse control, their discussion is not directed towards determining in particular cases such matters as whether—or when—the impulses became "uncontrollable."

That satisfaction is most economical which permits the most satisfaction for the least effort over a significant period of time. If a means that is immediately "economical" has side effects that make satisfaction more difficult later, it may turn out that this means is not nearly as "economical" in the long run as others.

Personality, then, consists of these drives plus the means developed to satisfy them. As a means of differentiating among the various aspects of the personality, dynamic psychologists use a structural analysis developed by Freud. This analysis postulates three "structures": The id, the ego, and the superego. These are not viewed as physically existing "things" but rather as conceptualizations of various differentiated functions performed by the personality. The id consists of the inborn, biological, drives that demand satisfaction. The superego, on the other hand, consists of internalized values assimilated primarily during early life from the parents or some symbolic substitute. The ego is posited as the mechanism for accommodating reality, the demands of the id, and the restrictions imposed by the superego. Essentially, then, the id demands gratifications, the ego ascertains the potential means of satisfaction and their comparative efficiency, and the superego "rules out" some because of their offensiveness to fundamental values. The id is viewed as operating entirely on an unconscious level, and the superego as primarily doing so. The ego, on the other hand, operates significantly in both the conscious and unconscious.

Anxiety is the device by which the interaction of the various aspects of the personality is accomplished. If id impulses become too strong (as if the methods being used to satisfy them are not sufficiently efficient) or if the superego is offended, as by an actual or anticipated course of action, the ego generates signal anxiety. This it finds so unpleasant that it immediately pursues other methods of satisfying the id's impulses, ones that will be more efficient or less offensive to the superego. This signal anxiety must be distinguished from the emotional reaction or "affect" of anxiety. Signal anxiety operates on an unconscious level; the individual is not consciously aware of its generation by the ego. The word anxiety is also, however, used to describe the consciously-experienced feeling or affect characterized by unreasonable apprehensiveness. This is described below as a symptom of mental illness; signal anxiety, of course, is a normal part of the personality's functioning.

Ideally, the personality would work simply: drives would demand satisfaction and the ego would be able to direct relatively efficient means of gratification that would not be unacceptable to the individual's appropriately developed superego. Deviations from the ideal, however, often mean that the personality does not function in such a manner. Under a variety of circumstances, the personality may be subjected to "stress," either external or internal. External stress may result relatively simply from an inability to find efficient means of satisfaction. Lack of food, for example, may interfere with the organism's ability to satisfy its drives. External stress may also be in the form of less direct restrictions. Unsatisfactory personal relationships may, for example, be extremely stressful because they render inefficient what is often an important means of gratification, meaningful interpersonal relationships.

Internal or "psychic" stresses, on the other hand, describe a situation in which the cause of the ego's anxiety is the superego. If the ego perceives no alternatives to means of satisfaction which offend the superego's values, or if the superego has developed too severe or rigid standards, the ego experiences anxiety. Under such circumstances, the individual may be said to be under internal or psychic stress.

The complexity of life means that individuals are with some frequency subjected to stress, either external or internal. The manner by which an individual responds to stress—and the resulting anxiety— is closely related to the potential for commission of a criminal act. In some cases, means of satisfaction are found or developed that neither stimulate harmful disapproval from society nor offend the individual's superego values. In such cases, the individual is said to have "sublimated" the underlying drives that gave rise to the anxiety. Other stressful situations, however, may be dealt with less satisfactorily by means of various "defense mechanisms."

Defense Mechanisms

If the ego is subjected to anxiety that it cannot avoid by realistic methods such as pursuing alternative direct means of gratification or sublimation, it turns to "defense mechanisms." These are generally less satisfactory because they are often relatively inefficient and involve some distortion of reality, thus reducing the person's ability to live efficiently in the real world. Numerations and categorizations of the defense mechanisms vary, but the following are universally regarded as among the most important: *Repression:* Repression consists of the unconscious process of putting out of conscious awareness those things which are offensive, such as the desire to do a given thing, the memory of having done it, or the awareness that a given situation exists. The device is obviously not economical, since it merely reduces the offensiveness of the situation. Because the superego is offended by unconscious as well as conscious mental processes, repression of, for example, a conscious wish offensive to the superego merely changes it to an unconscious wish which may be somewhat less offensive. The process of repression needs to be distinguished from that of suppression. The former occurs on an unconscious level, while suppression consists of the conscious and intentional putting of things out of conscious awareness.

Displacement: Displacement consists of shifting characteristics from one idea or object to another, often one with some symbolic resemblance to the original. Thus in the phobias, fear is displaced from one object to another, such as heights or uncleanliness. Projection is a special form of displacement in which the ego finds certain feelings or wishes unacceptable and in defense attributes them to another person. Thus a paranoid's unreasonable belief that others desire to harm him may be the result of the ego's projecting to others the individual's own aggressive wishes that were found offensive to his superego. Projection may be combined with fantasy, in which case the feelings or wishes are projected upon a nonexistent object which the person nevertheless perceives as real. A paranoid, for example, may believe others desire to harm him. He may also hear or see nonexistent persons threaten him with harm.

Rationalization: Inaccurate explanations for behavior may be asserted (and consciously believed) as a means of avoiding the necessity for conscious recognition of real—but offensive—motives. By thereby keeping the "real" motivation for actions from the conscious, the ego at least reduces the offensiveness of the action to the superego.

Dissociation: Dissociation consists of the process by which different personality functions are separated or "dissociated." This is done in order to isolate material that is perceived as objectionable on either a conscious or unconscious level. The description obviously covers a wide variety of divergent situations. One form, for example, involves the dissociation of mental processes or actions from affect or emotion. Thus an individual may not experience the "normal" emotional reaction to actions or thoughts because his affective reactions have been split off from his intellectual processes or behavior. Many—perhaps most—dissociations involve some impact upon the individual's consciousness. In the so-called "split personality" situation, for example, two aspects of a person's personality may govern behavior and thought at different times, although during the period when he is governed by one the person may be unaware of periods when he is governed by the other. The fugue state is another, which one authority describes as follows:

> There is a sudden change in state of consciousness during which the patient may be impelled by unconscious forces to perform complicated activities, perhaps traveling over long distances. Throughout this period the patient may appear quite normal to the casual observer. In some instances there is a loss of personal identity. In the fugue the patient indulges in acts of fantasies which are in conflict with his superego and the function of the fugue is to permit the carrying out of these acts or fantasies.[f]

f. A. Noyes, Modern Clinical Psychiatry 456 (1953).

Fantasy: When the actual environment proves too stressful for the ego to deal with as it exists, the ego may create a partial or entire fantasy environment in which the instincts are more readily gratified. Since instincts may be gratified by purely psychic processes, this may be an effective alternative to direct gratification, especially in the short run. Fantasy may involve only beliefs that, when held, tend to reduce stress. It may also involve false sensory perceptions, such as the apparent hearing or observation of nonexistent persons, or, in an extreme case, an entire nonexistent life situation. In the latter case, of course, during the fantasy the individual may withdraw completely from the real world and function entirely in his fantasy. But in most cases, the fantasy affects only part of the individual's life and he lives in—and responds to—a world partly real and partly composed of fantasy.

Identification: Identification consists of the unconscious process of developing the personality traits of another, thereby assuming attitudes or behavior traits of the other person. The implication of the close relationship following identification may provide a defense against fear of the person, and the individual who uses this defense mechanism may also vicariously experience the gratifications of the other person.

The defense mechanisms themselves are almost always potential causes of internal anxiety. Unlike sublimation, they do not necessarily involve adopting a substitute satisfaction that is inoffensive to either society or the superego. Thus the response to use of a defense mechanism may be social disapproval or worse, which may in turn reduce the individual's ability to function efficiently (i. e., in a manner which satisfies his drives) in the community. This, of course, results in anxiety, the very thing the defense mechanism was invoked to minimize. In addition, if the initial situation was offensive to the superego, the substitute defense mechanism adopted may be still offensive; the fact that a given activity is an indirect means of gratifying an offensive wish may be enough to render that activity offensive to the superego, although perhaps not as offensive as the direct gratification of the wish itself would be. The result, however, is a buildup of anxiety, this time from an internal source. Resort to defense mechanisms, then, is seldom a long-term satisfactory method of adapting to stress.

Personality Development

Dynamic theory holds that personality consists basically of the methods by which the individual has learned to satisfy his basic drives, including those defense mechanisms he has developed to respond to stressful situations. The formation of the personality occurs early in life and is greatly influenced by early experience; modification of an adult's personality is difficult or impossible without expert assistance.

The individual develops through a series of stages involving primarily the development of means of satisfying the pleasure instinct. During the oral stages, gratification is centered upon activity involving the mouth and lips. During the anal stage (from ages 2 to 4), gratification is centered upon activity involving the anal and rectal regions. Finally, gratification becomes centered in activity involving the genital organs. Various defense mechanisms tend to develop at various parts of this development, and a tendency (or predisposition) to rely upon a given mechanism is believed to be traceable to the individual's experiences during the corresponding period of development.

Since a primary unconscious determinant of behavior is hypothesized to be the superego, the development of this aspect of the personality is of special importance. In dynamic theory, the critical stage of personality development relating to the superego is the so-called Oedipus (in the case of a male) or Electra (in the case of a female) situation. In the case of a male, dynamic psychologists posit that during his third to fifth year the child develops a sexual attraction for his mother. He fears, however, his father's response to this attraction. The fear becomes so great that it is dealt with by means of a variation of the defense mechanism of identification pursuant to which the child identifies with the father and assumes his characteristics insofar as possible, including the values held by the father. The assimilation of the father's values becomes the basis for the superego. In the case of females, through a somewhat similar process the child turns to the father but subsequently identifies with the mother as a reaction to fear of the mother's disapproval.

This assimilation of the values of the parent of the same sex serves only as the basis for development of a normal superego. As the child matures, he assimilates additional values from his parents and symbolic substitutes for them, such as society and law. In addition, his values becomes moderated. Whereas initially they were held as absolutes, a normally developing superego tends to develop flexibility by recognizing the need for exceptions and some liberality in applying those values initially assimilated. Misdevelopment of the superego—with implications for later behavior—may occur in several ways. First, if there is no parent figure of the same sex available or if the identification is incomplete, the assimilation of values may be nonexistent or incomplete. With a faulty basis upon which to develop, this may mean that the mature superego will be nonexistent (the individual will be without unconsciously assimilated values) or incomplete. Second, if the assimilation is too complete (as if made under extreme fear), the superego may later be too inflexible to accommodate those compromises that daily life often makes necessary. As a result, performance of those things essential to gratification will often offend the superego with the result of a continual output of unconscious guilt, or the search for substitute means of gratification that may not be offensive to the superego. The implications for criminal behavior are relatively clear. In the first instance, the individual may lack the "normal" strong unconscious barriers to performance of many acts that may constitute crimes. In the second, the anxiety created by continual offensiveness to the superego in turn creates a need for defense mechanisms, some of which may involve factors leading towards criminal behavior.

"Mental Illness"

The concept of "illness" necessarily implies some disadvantage to the person being described. The definition of "mental illness," however, raises several important conceptual problems. The first is the focus of attention—is mental illness to be defined in terms of presently-observable "symptoms" or is it rather to be defined in terms of the underlying personality attributes that are believed to "cause" these symptoms? One approach focuses upon whether at the time at issue the person was exhibiting the symptoms; the other is less concerned with behavior at any particular time than with the tendency of the person to behave in a given manner under certain circumstances, whether or not those circumstances were present at the time in issue. The former approach has the advantage of avoiding assumptions—and thus dispute—concerning causation. The second, however, is more consistent with the approach of dynamic psychology and its emphasis upon the dynamics of behavior. Consequently, most dynamic psychologists would consider the question of whether a person is "mentally ill" in terms of what they consider to be his underlying personality structure.

The second major conceptual problem is that of distinguishing the mentally "healthy" from the mentally "ill." Since psychodynamic theory postulates that all behavior is "caused" through the same process, behavior that is labeled a symptom of mental illness cannot be distinguished by its nature. Nor can symptoms be viewed without regard to the context in which they are exhibited. Certain activities would have significantly different impacts upon a person depending upon the culture in which he lives, his place within that culture, and the occasions during which he engages in it. The only reasonable criterion can be the individual's efficient functioning—thus "symptoms" give rise to mental illness only if they interfere with the individual's functioning.

In terms of "symptoms," then, mental illness is best defined as a condition in which a person is exhibiting "symptoms" which, given the person's life situation, significantly reduce his ability to meet his needs with reasonable effectiveness. Defined in terms of personality structure, mental illness exists when the individual's personality structure is such that, given what can be predicted of his future life situation, his ability to meet his needs with reasonable effectiveness will be significantly reduced by symptoms, whether or not he is exhibiting those symptoms now. These definitions both make clear the relative nature of mental illness, and emphasize the extent to which the impact of a symptom depends upon the context in which it is exhibited. But they might result in different "labels" being used in particular situations. For example, two different analyses might be made of the subject of an examination who, at the time of the examination, was exhibiting no "symptoms." One examiner might conclude, "The subject was not mentally ill at the time of the examination because he was exhibiting no symptoms. This does not preclude the possibility that he might have been mentally ill at a previous time, of course." The other might assert, "Although the subject exhibited no symptoms during the interview, it is my conclusion that he would respond to certain stresses by exhibiting symptoms. Since there is a reasonable likelihood he will be subjected to such stresses, I believe he is presently mentally ill although his symptoms are presently in remission."

Descriptive Diagnosis of Mental Illness

Despite the disagreement among mental health professionals concerning the causation of "mental illness," there is relatively widespread agreement upon certain observable characteristics of an individual ("symptoms") which will be regarded as evidence of a condition which for convenience is called "mental illness" and certain classifications of these symptoms that are called specific mental illnesses. Use of such classifications is referred to as the task of descriptive diagnosis because, unlike dynamic psychology, it is concerned only with observable characteristics and not underlying causes. The following section discusses such symptoms in general, the categories of "mental illnesses," and the major mental illnesses.

Symptoms

The symptoms of mental illness are generally categorized into three groups: those of sensation and perception, those of thought and intelligence, and those of affect.

The symptoms in the first category include hallucinations and illusions. The former is a perception completely unjustified by reality; the latter is a mistaken and unreasonable interpretation of a real perception. Thus if A "observes" people watching him although no such persons are where he observes them, he is experiencing an hallucination. This category also includes other erroneous sensations, such as a lack of feeling in a part of the body or a sensation of something crawling on the skin.

The second category includes distortions of the sequence, manner and content of thinking. Distortions of sequence include those situations in which the person jumps rapidly during thought from one thought to another, or those in which thinking is slow and laborious. The manner of thinking may also become concrete, i. e., involving loss of the ability to generalize and think in the abstract, or autistic, involving a manner of reasoning unique to the person. Distortions of the content of thinking include delusions, false beliefs inconsistent with the individual's own knowledge and experiences. This includes delusions of reference, the belief that the remarks and behavior of others has reference to the person, and delusions of persecution, beliefs that others have singled the person out for harm or attention. Delusions may also involve unreasonable guilt, hopelessness or depersonalization, or the belief that one's identity has been lost. Other distortions of thought content are obsessions, the persistent intrusion into consciousness of an unwanted thought, and phobias, unreasonable fears not warranted by actual danger. This category of symptoms also includes disorientation, an inability to identify time, place or persons accurately, and generally below normal intellectual functioning as well as congenitally low intellectual capacity.

The final category of symptoms relates to consciously experienced emotional reactions, or "affects." The affects include elation, depression, anxiety (apprehensiveness and uneasiness, usually without the ability to identify the source), and anger. The distortion may involve an increase in the intensity of the affect, or it may involve a decrease (apathy). Normal variations may be increased, with the result that the person varies from "normalcy" to depression and back, or from elation to depression and back. Affect may also be inappropriate, as would be the case should an announcement of the death of a friend result in laughing (elation).

To some extent, behavior may also be regarded as symptomatic of mental illness. Thus, as will be discussed, the main features of the so-called personality disorders are behavior patterns. On the other hand, in most cases the behavior that might be regarded as itself a symptom can be traced back to a symptom in one of the three categories described above. Thus a person experiencing the affect of elation may engage in rapid, somewhat erratic behavior, and such behavior would be regarded as suggesting that the individual could be characterized as suffering from a manic-depressive illness. Conceptually, it is probably most helpful to regard anything "caused by" a symptom as evidence of that symptom rather than as an independent symptom itself. In most cases, therefore, behavior is best regarded as evidence of various symptoms but not as a symptom itself.

Classification of Symptom "Syndomes"

The classification of those who exhibit symptoms into diagnostic categories or "mental illnesses" is a difficult and perhaps hopeless task. Nevertheless, a number of specific illnesses have been defined, although the descriptions are to some extent vague and overlapping. These "mental illnesses" are generally divided into three main categories. The first are the "psychoses." "Psychosis" is a relatively vague term, often used simply to indicate the seriousness of the symptoms. The American Psychiatric Association's Diagnostic and Statistical Manual of Mental Disorders directs, however, that "patients are described as psychotic when their mental functioning is sufficiently impaired to interfere grossly with their capacity to meet the ordinary demands of life." [g] This impairment, of course, may be caused by symptoms related to perception, thought processes, or affect. The crucial factor is not the type of symptom but the effect upon the individual's ability to function in his own environment. The "neuroses" involve symptoms involving neither gross distortion or misinterpretation of reality nor extreme personality disorganization; the person usually is aware that his functioning is impaired. The "personality disorders" involve those cases in which the symptom takes the form of a long-term pattern of behavior, often recognizable by early adolescence or earlier and lasting for the individual's entire life. A personality disorder is less serious than a psychosis only in that the symptoms are less acute. Over a long span of time, a person with a character disorder may have no more success in coping with life's strains than has had the psychotic.

Specific Disorders [h]

(1) Schizophrenia: The major symptom is a thought disorder, altogether the person may also have distorted affect. Delusions and hallucinations are often present. The disorder may take the form of slow withdrawal and indifference to the outside world (simple type), shallow affect and unpredictable giggling (hebephrenic type) or either violent activity or excitement (catatonic type, excited) or stupor (catatonic type, withdrawn). The paranoid schizophrenic is characterized by persecutory or grandiose delusions, often with excessive religiosity and hostility and aggression. If the person's symptoms are not extreme but become part of his pattern of behavior, he may be diagnosed as "schizoid personality," a personality disorder.

(2) Manic-Depressive Illness: The primary feature of these disorders is extremes of affect, often occurring in swings. The person may experience only depressed moods (depressed type), only moods of elation (manic type), or both (circular or manic-depressive type). If the symptoms do not meet the criteria for psychosis and become ingrained into the person's life style, he may be classified as a cyclothymic or affective personality.

g. American Psychiatric Association, Diagnostic and Statistical Manual of Mental Disorders 23 (2nd ed. 1968).

h. The following definitions are taken from the American Psychiatric Association, Diagnostic and Statistical Manual of Mental Disorders (2nd ed. 1968).

(3) Paranoid states: In this relatively rare condition, the person's primary symptom is a delusion, usually persecutory or grandiose, although disturbances of mood, thinking and behavior may flow from this. The paranoid personality is the character disorder equivalent.

(4) Neuroses (or, in older terminology, the psychoneuroses): The neuroses are characterized by the type of symptom. Thus the individual may consciously feel the anxiety (anxiety neurosis), experience the loss of use of an organ (hysterical neurosis), develop an intense fear of an object or situation (phobic neurosis), or experience persistent but unwanted thoughts or urges which may be acted upon, as by going through complex but meaningless rituals (obsessive compulsive neurosis).

(5) Personality Disorders: In addition to those discussed above, the personality disorders include situations in which the person's behavior pattern is characerized by gross outbursts of rage or aggression different from his usual behavior (explosive personality) and generally ineffectual responses to the demands of living (inadequate personality). Also in this category is the antisocial personality (formerly designated the psychopath), generally characterized by a complete lack of loyalty to any groups or values, low frustration tolerance and impulsiveness, and an apparent inability to feel guilt or to learn from experience. "A mere history of repeated legal or social offenses," the Diagnostic Manual directs, "is not sufficient to justify this diagnosis."

Relationship Between "Mental Illness" and Criminal Behavior

Because of the ambiguity of the concept of mental illness, the matter of the relationship between such illness and crime is similarly clouded. In some cases, a traditional "symptom" bears an obvious causal relationship to a crime: A, entertaining the delusion that B is about to kill him, kills B when B makes an objectively harmless gesture. In these situations, it is reasonable to consider the matter in terms of the "mental illness" "causing" a "symptom" which in turn may have "caused" the crime. But in other cases, observable "symptoms" may not exist or, if they exist, their relationship to the crime may be much less obvious. In such cases it is necessary to consider the symptoms only as evidence of the underlying personality structure and to seek an explanation for the criminal activity in terms of that personality structure without any traditional symptom intervening between the personality structure and the criminal activity.[i]

i. Thus a non-dynamic psychologist, who sees no need to speculate about unconscious mental processes, may see the attempt to explain a relationship between "mental illness" and "crime" as a meaningless exercise:

Mental disease is a term referring to a class of behavior—hallucinations, delusions, anxieties, phobias, hysteria, antisocial acts. Crime is also behavior. Both crime and mental disease are dependent variables, and

The following are a number of ways in which "mental illness" might be related to criminal activity. Some are stated in terms of "mental illness—symptom—crime;" others are simply in terms of "personality structure—crime."

(1) Because of impairment of reasoning ability and the ability to conceptualize, an individual may lack the ability to understand a generalized value of right or wrong or the ability to apply it to a particular set of facts. Thus even if he would, by the exercise of conscious choice, avoid commission of those acts he recognized as inconsistent with legal or ethical standards, his impairment prevents the occurrence of the conscious mental process that must precede a conscious choice not to perform a given anticipated act.

(2) An individual's symptoms may provide an erroneous factual foundation for a rational (given the foundation) conclusion that an anticipated act is legally permissible, morally permissible, or economical as a means of gratification. Delusions or hallucinations may, for example, cause an individual to believe his life is endangered and immediate action in the form of an attack upon another is necessary to the preservation of his own life. The facts of United States v. Collier [j] presented such a case:

> The defendant signed on a crew member of a small fishing boat. When the boat was at sea, he experienced a number of delusions, including delusional beliefs that members of his family were aboard the boat and were being killed. He experienced hallucinations, including a scream he attributed to his mother. The next day, he believed he heard the captain say that he (the captain) was going to shoot the defendant off the rail in ten minutes. In the defendant's words, "I figured if he was going to knock me off in about ten minutes, I'd better do something so I went in and stabbed him."

(3) The value of the offense may be affected by the individual's dynamic response to the situation, so that the offense has greater value to him than is discernible without reference to his unconscious mental processes. For example, the crime may provide the oppor-

the statement "crime is a *product of* mental disease" contains no dependent variable. Behavior is what we are attempting to explain, and we cannot explain one class of behavior in terms of another class. Behavior cannot be used as an explanation of itself. When we relate crime to mental illness, we do not know whether the crime produced the mental illness, the mental illness produced the crime, or both were a product of a third factor.

C. Jeffery, Criminal Responsibility and Mental Illness 213 (1967). Of course, if some characteristic of the personality structure is viewed as "mental illness," it is not logically offensive to conclude that both the symptoms of mental illness and a particular crime were affected (or "caused") by the mental illness.

j.   453 F.2d 1173 (5th Cir. 1972).

tunity for symbolic gratification of an unconscious drive or a wish derived from the drive. Or, because of psychic pressures, the individual may have an unconscious striving for punishment; the likelihood of punishment following commission of the crime thus provides an additional element of attractiveness in the anticipated offense. Finally, the conscious or unconscious value of the anticipated offense may be increased because the individual's symptoms have minimized his alternatives. A schizophrenic's withdrawal makes satisfaction from "normal" activities more difficult, for example, so an anticipated crime may become—comparatively speaking—more attractive. Note that none of these possibilities *necessarily* mean that the value of the anticipated offense has become such that it is not capable of being prevented by conscious choice or by unconscious inhibitions. They merely suggest that a dynamic analysis may provide a means of better understanding the real value of the crime to the individual.

Probably the best known attempt to describe this process of causation is associated with Dr. Karl Menninger, who in several printed sources [k] has developed a description of a phenomena he refers to as "episodic dyscontrol." The underlying hypothesis is that aggressive behavior—especially assaultive behavior—is frequently an unconsciously caused reaction to stress, with the object often having some symbolic relationship to one or more of the major sources of stress. He proposes that the methods used by the ego to respond to stress (the defense mechanisms) fall into hierarchically successive groups, each representing greater degrees of failure to deal realistically with the stress and thus representing lower levels of "effective" functioning. The first "order," he suggests, consists of consciously experienced "nervousness" or anxiety. If this type of defense mechanism fails, devices of the Second Order are invoked, which include the traditional neurotic symptoms. Should these fail, the ego resorts to the Third Order of devices, which consists of outbreaks of aggressive actions. "The ego seems to 'give way'; some of the dangerous primitive impulses whose pressure is so largely responsible for the tension * * * elude its restraints. They escape; they are enacted; they go towards targets and they wreak their destructive purpose * * *. The internal tension has been relieved * * * " [l] Menninger distinguishes two types of these aggressive outbursts:

In the disorganized 'ideopathic' type, the break with reality is obvious in the chaotic nature of the outburst, even to

k. K. Menninger, The Vital Balance (1963); Menninger and Mayman, Episodic Dyscontrol: A Third Order of Stress Adaptation, 20 Bulletin of the Menninger Clinic 153 (1956); Satten, Menninger, Rosen and Mayman, Murder Without Apparent Motive: A Study in Personality Disorganization, 117 Am.J. Psychiatry 48 (1960).

l. Menninger and Mayman, supra note k, at 156.

the loss of consciousness and memory. In the more organized * * * aggressive outbursts, disturbances of consciousness are infrequent and the break with reality is apt
to be masked by rationalizations or misanthropic self-justi-
fications. But careful examination of the behavior and the
'reasons' given for the espousal of the anti-social behavior
reveals the presence of a definite and radical departure from
the concepts and rules of organized society and from the
dictates of sound judgment, reason and even 'common
sense.' [m]

Unless the sources of the stress are eliminated (by the outburst or
otherwise), the relief caused by the outburst is merely temporary.
When tension again builds up to a level unmanageable by First and
Second Order devices, the individual is likely again to respond by
aggressive outbursts. The episodes of "dyscontrol" are therefore
likely to be "episodic"; hence the descriptive name "episodic dyscontrol." Among the characteristics of those exhibiting episodic
dyscontrol Menninger found the following: exposure to extreme
parental violence during childhood, emotional deprivation during
childhood, poor general impulse control, self-images of themselves
as physically inferior, weak and inadequate, severe degrees of sexual
inhibition, shallow and cold relationships to others (and thus lone-
liness and isolation), and "bizarre, violent, and primitive" fantasy
lives.[n]

One example given by Menninger is as follows:

Adams: A 24-year-old corporal looking for a prostitute
near a French town, was approached by a 13-year-old boy
who persistently asked him to change Army script into
French currency; when refused, the boy seemed to mock or
make fun of him, whereupon he struck the boy. Adams insisted he had no intention of killing the victim and did not
recall the actual killing. When Adams 'found out' what he
was doing, the victim's body had been severely mutilated.[o]

Despite the existence of what might arguably be a "rational" conscious motive for the killing—the boy's taunting activity—Menninger argues that the killing was an episode of dyscontrol as described above. Moreover, the victim had an unconscious symbolic
significance for Adams: "[T]he murder appears to have been a deflected suicide * * * The victim represented * * * the murderer's own hated self-image; the young boy he killed was a camp
pet who ran errands for the soldiers, just as he himself had been a
mascot for the men in his father's lumber camp." [p]

m. Id. at 157.   o. Id. at 48.

n. Satten, Menninger, Rosen and May-   p. Id. at 52.
   man, supra note k.

Theories such as Menninger's episodic dyscontrol analysis focus on the failure of regularly used controls over aggressive behavior, and the resulting picture of the offender is one of an individual with pent up aggressive—or "criminal"—drives that occasionally defy control by available means. A significantly different approach is that which views criminal activity (or some of it, at least) as not the outburst of aggressive instinctual drives but as a means of adapting to life stress, and which offers psychoanalytic insights as a means of better understanding the value of crime as an adaptive mechanism. Dr. Seymour Halleck [q] has offered an explanation why criminal activity is often a more economical method of adapting to life stresses than the main alternatives, sublimation or the development of socially approved activities, and the development of symptoms of mental illness. All three are alternatives that can be explained in dynamic terms, and Halleck suggests that for some individuals criminal activity is reasonably regarded as the most practical of those methods of adaptation that are perceived as available. Viewing the effect of stress as the development of a feeling of "helplessness" in the face of oppression, Halleck suggests that criminal activity may have some or all of the following "advantages" to a person under stress:

1. Because crime is an active effort to change the environment, it causes the individual, while he is performing it, to feel less helpless. It also encourages the development of hope for relief from the oppression.

2. During the commission of the crime, the offender is generally free from outside restraints and thus experiences what may be only a brief but nevertheless important feeling of freedom.

3. Crime often offers excitement, especially when compared to the offender's everyday life.

4. The pursuit and response of the law to criminal activity provides the vehicle for excellent rationalizations for other problems. By creating a situation which he can blame for other life troubles, the offender may avoid the stressful experience of facing the real reasons for those troubles.

5. Criminal activity often provides the opportunity for an offender to form close and rewarding relationships with other offenders. Moreover, given the public's ambivalent attitude towards criminal activity, crime may provide a method of obtaining more widespread admiration or at least attention not adequately available from other sources.[r]

q. S. Halleck, Psychiatry and the Dilemmas of Crime (1967).   r. Id. at 76–80.

Some of these advantages might operate on a conscious level, so that by listing them Halleck may be doing little more than more fully explaining a free, conscious decision to engage in criminal activity. Others might operate only on an unconscious level. Most, however, even if operating on a conscious level could be significantly influenced by unconscious factors. The importance of the feeling of freedom during commission of the crime, for example, could be greatly affected by unconscious guilt feelings from an inflexible superego. Thus most provide at least the opportunity for more fully considering how the conscious or unconscious "choice" to commit a crime might operate and what factors might stimulate it. Halleck himself does not deny that many crimes provide immediate and important rewards, nor that the conscious desire for such rewards is a factor in the commission of crimes.

Halleck's approach is not inconsistent with that of Menninger, of course, and each can helpfully be viewed as explaining more effectively different types of criminal activity. Menninger's episodic dyscontrol is helpful in structuring an explanation for the generally law-abiding middle class individual who occasionally assaults members of his family; Halleck's approach is far less useful here. On the other hand, Halleck's approach is far more useful than Menninger's in understanding a Black ghetto resident who with relative frequency commits armed robberies. The extent to which either is useful in resolving legal issues is raised by the materials in the remainder of the chapter.

(4) The individual's response may be such as to explain why "normal" unconscious preventive devices (i. e., superego pressure) did not function effectively. There are a number of possibilities in this regard. Because of early life experiences (most likely an unsatisfactory relationship with the parent of the same sex), the individual may have developed no superego at all, thus rendering him essentially without internalized values. Or, he may have internalized "faulty" values—those he internalized were not coextensive with the values enforced by the law. For example, in certain American subcultures a violent physical response to some verbal insults is not only not condemned but is highly respected. An individual undergoing a "normal" development in a family belonging to such a subculture might well lack the internalized prohibition against certain actions the criminal law defines as serious assaults. Finally, despite the development of a normal superego, the ego may, by employing a relatively sophisticated defense mechanism, neutralize the impact of the superego in some circumstances. This is probably most frequently accomplished by means of the dissociative reactions, the defense mechanisms that in some manner render a situation less offensive to the superego than it would otherwise be. One source has described

the relationship between the dissociation reaction and criminal activity as follows:

> There is one particular psychopathologic condition among the many observed in connection with criminal behavior which is of particular interest. This is a mental state characterized by a splitting off of consciousness, better known as a "dissociative reaction." Dissociative reactions may appear in mild or severe forms. A few develop following the criminal act itself; more often, the criminal act is perpetrated in the course of the dissociative reaction. Often consciousness may be clouded to a varying degree * * *

> In the acute dissociative episode, powerful unconscious psychologic tensions split off from the rest of the personality and its controls, and temporarily gain ascendency as a conscious motivational force for a short period until the crisis is over. How exactly this may come about is not always discernible. The normal control mechanisms may be weakened by external environmental stresses, by internal psychic stresses or by chemical agents such as alcohol or certain drugs. Coincidentally certain present day life events may simulate certain traumatic early life situations, and activate primitive emotional reactions appropriate to that early time but now carried out with the savage strength of the more physically mature individual. Once the acute episode is over, the person will not know the reason behind his behavior and may attempt to rationalize his act. He may well have an amnesia for the events of the crime. It is particularly important where acts of violence occur, for it is here that it most often observed * * *

> Quite often one finds a passive, inhibited, innocuous looking offender, on the surface quite respectable and complaint, who has been involved in acts which include arson, sexual aggression and violence—acts which do not appear in keeping with his surface impression. In probing the personality of such an individual, one generally uncovers crucially significant etiologic factors which were masked from view. A good example of this is the case history of an attractive, conforming and intelligent young woman who killed her husband with a gun. As the amnesia cleared, she explained her act on the basis of fear, panic, and self defense. Her husband, who had been drinking, threatened to do her bodily harm. Exploring the deeper mental activity of this woman yielded a clearer understanding of what had actually occurred. Over a long period of time resentment and hostility for a very possessive and controlling mother had been built up in this woman. The resentment could

not be expressed because of an equally strong need to be protected and cared for by her mother. She entered into marriage as a means of escape, but found that her husband related to her the same castrating and controlling attitudes that the mother had previously expressed. During one particularly intense argument, she saw in him the image of her mother, and she killed him. Her real target was her mother; her husband was the helpless victim of displaced primitive infantile feelings.[s]

The dissociation reaction, then, tends less to explain the unconscious value of the criminal act than to explain how an act inconsistent with strongly held values can be rendered "commitable" by unconscious processes.

NOTES

1. For general presentations of dynamic psychology, see, e. g., Dynamic Psychiatry (F. Alexander and H. Ross eds. 1952); A. Watson, Psychiatry for Lawyers (1968); F. Alexander, Fundamentals of Psychoanalysis (1948). For an excellent discussion of crime causation embodying a broad dynamic view, see S. Halleck, Psychiatry and the Dilemmas of Crime 3–201 (1967). For other sources, see D. Abrahamsen, The Psychology of Crime (1960); F. Alexander and W. Healy, Roots of Crime (1935); F. Alexander and H. Staub, The Criminal, the Judge, and the Public (1956); W. Healy, Mental Conflicts and Misconduct (1917); W. Healy and A. Bronner, New Light on Delinquency and Its Treatment (1936); K. Friedlander, The Psychoanalytical Approach to Juvenile Delinquency (1945). See also Tanay, Psychiatric Study of Homicide, 125 Am.J.Psychiatry 146 (1969).

2. The dynamic analysis of behavior discussed above has been subjected to a significant amount of criticism. Some of this is probably irrelevant for legal purposes. For example, the learning behavior theorists have criticized the dynamic approach on the ground that it encourages undesirable emphasis in therapy upon the "underlying personality" rather than upon the specific symptoms that interfere with the individual's life. See Albee, Emerging Concepts of Mental Illness and Models of Treatment: The Psychological Point of View, 125 Am.J.Psychiatry 42 (1969). For purposes of legal analysis, it is probably unimportant whether the dynamic theory logically leads to the best therapeutic approaches. Rather, the law's concern should be with whether it enables the law to best analyze and understand particular acts so as to make most accurately those choices the law directs be made. Legal concern, then, should focus on those criticisms that relate to this demand upon dynamic psychology.

Perhaps the most significant criticism is that dynamic theory has not been adequately proved accurate. The mental processes which it postulates affect behavior are by definition not capable of direct observation. Most professionals with a dynamic orientation are therapists, whose function is not well-formulated research of the type that would test the validity of their

s. Brancale, More on McNaughten: A
Psychiatrist's View, 65 Dick.L.Rev.
277, 280–82 (1961).

assumptions in an impressive manner. Rather, the emphasis is upon therapy. Thus, much of the dynamic literature consists of "case histories" offered as illustrations of accepted theories rather than of broader studies offered to prove the theories. Moreover, it is argued that the need for proof of the theory's accuracy is especially important in view of the fact that it was formulated in work with the observably abnormal. A theoretical approach based upon the abnormal should not be accepted as a means of understanding "more normal" activity such as crime in the absence of significant proof of its accuracy.

Related to this is the criticism that dynamic theory is not sufficiently precise to justify using it as the basis for resolving legal issues. Discussion of this is best left until a discussion of the legal contexts in which such issues arise; only by first examining the issues posed by the law can the utility of dynamic analysis in resolving them be evaluated. But it is important to keep in mind the question of whether even if the basic dynamic approach is regarded as sufficiently supported by evidence, there is also sufficient evidence to support the accuracy of those sub-portions necessary to answer the law's questions.

Sociologically-oriented theorists have long argued that dynamic theory does not adequately consider the impact of social and cultural conditions upon the individual and his criminal acts. Somewhat oversimplified, their argument is that crime tends not to be the manifestation of a "sick" personality but rather the appropriate response of a well-structured personality to certain social and cultural conditions. This is significant legally, of course, only to the extent that the legal issues make relevant the degree to which social environment rather than the individual's personality structure contributed to a given criminal act. For legal purposes, the most relevant argument is basically that activity which dynamic psychologists explain as unconsciously-caused reactions to stress may well be the result of conscious choice that is "understandable" if one understands the values and expectations of the person acting:

> I suspect that the behavior that is commonly attributed to ego defect is actually determined by a number of different processes or mechanisms * * *. Take, for example, the inability to defer gratification, which is supposed to be one manifestation of ego defect. I suspect that much behavior explained in terms of such an inability may simply reflect a low valuation of the long-run payoffs of restraint and discipline, in comparison to a high valuation of the immediate pay-offs. Such an explanation would be compatible with a manifest ability to defer gratification where the payoffs are differently valued and thus would explain the observation that those people whose so-called impulsivity is explained by ego defect often exhibit other behavior that is controlled, disciplined, and rational. Or the apparent inability to defer gratification might reflect a low expectancy, based on experience or culturally transmitted cognitive beliefs, that restraint and discipline are likely to realize their goals * * *.

A. Cohen, A Sociologist's View of Psychiatric Criminology, in Psychiatric Aspects of Criminology 53, at 61–62 (S. Halleck and W. Bromberg eds. 1968).

This type of criticism is less appropriate when directed at modern dynamically-oriented theorists who clearly consider the stresses of the environment and "learned" responses to stress as legitimate factors in their analysis. See S. Halleck, Psychiatry and the Dilemmas of Crime (1967). Perhaps the difference is primarily one of emphasis. Therapists, concerned with the problems of a specific patient, naturally tend to focus upon the life experiences of that patient, and consider cultural and social factors only insofar as they can be shown to have had an impact upon that patient through his family life and other experiences. For those whose focus is upon the relationship of general social conditions and crime (rather than upon the causes or "cures" for particular persons' acts), focus is naturally placed upon general characteristics of the society rather than particular experiences of individuals.

Moreover, there is less likelihood of a necessary conflict between the two approaches if it is recognized that each might be most useful in particular situations. Sociological theory, for example, might well be most helpful in describing the "causation" of an assaultive crime committed by an individual who was reared in a culture in which assaultive responses to certain insults was not only not disapproved but was regarded as desirable. Dynamic theory, on the other hand, might well be most helpful in analyzing an assaultive offense committed by a person who rarely if ever had engaged in assaultive activity before and whose family and cultural background involved minimal exposure to favorably-regarded violence. Perhaps dynamic analysis is most useful if an effort is made to distinguish those cases in which it is especially likely to give satisfactory results.

The position has been taken, however, that dynamic psychology is so "unscientific" that expert testimony based upon it should not even be admissible in courts. Ziskin, Coping with Psychiatric and Psychological Testimony 74–75 (1970), after summarizing the attacks that may be leveled against dynamic (or, in his terminology, "psychoanalytic") psychology, concluded

> [P]sychoanalytic theory has not achieved scientific status nor has it even achieved that degree of acceptance among the scientific community as to justify its recognition as a science by the court. * * * [P]sychoanalytic theory is a highly controversial and speculative system, and * * * some courts would be willing to take the point of view that testimony based on it is simply too lacking in trustworthiness and probative value to be admitted. It cannot conceivably be stated for example, that psychoanalysis is in any higher state of scientific respectability than the polygraph, which at the present * * * is not admitted as evidence. If psychoanalytic theory is no more "reliable" or "accepted" than is the polygraph, does it necessarily follow that since the results of polygraph examinations are not admissible the observations and opinions of dynamically-oriented psychiatrists and psychologists should not be admitted? Consider the argument that the need for the polygraph results is much less, since there are always available the traditional methods of accessing the reliability of witnesses' testimony—observation of their demeanor and the like.

B. THE "INSANITY" DEFENSE

---

1. INTRODUCTION

---

a. THE THEORETICAL LEGAL FRAMEWORK

The "insanity" defense was offered to negate the required element of specific criminal intent by purporting to show that the defendant was not capable, because of his physical and psychological condition, of forming the necessary criminal intent. If his conduct was the product of a mental disease or defect, it was not the product of criminal intent as the law requires.

> United States v. Henry, 417 F.2d
> 267, 270 (2nd Cir. 1969)

[T]he court fails to recognize that there is no need for [an insanity] defense to remove criminal liability since it has concluded that no crime is established once mental illness * * * has cast doubt on *mens rea* * * *

[T]here emerges a purpose for the "insanity defense" which * * * has remained of extremely low visibility. That purpose seems to be obscured because thinking about [the relationship between insanity and *mens rea*] has generally been blocked by our collective conscience and our religious and moral traditions. Assuming the existence of [a] relationship between "insanity" and "*mens rea*," the defense is not to absolve of criminal responsibility "sick" persons who would otherwise be subject to criminal sanction. Rather, its real function is to authorize the state to hold those "who must be found not to possess the guilty *mens rea*," even though the criminal law demands that no person be held criminally responsible if doubt is cast on any material element of the offense charged * * *.

[T]he insanity defense is not designed * * * to define an exception to criminal liability, but rather to define for sanction an exception from among those who would be free of liability. It is as if the insanity defense were prompted by an affirmative answer to the silently posed question, "Does *mens rea* or any essential element of an offense exclude from liability a group of persons whom the community wishes to restrain? * * *" So conceived, the problem really facing the criminal process has been how to obtain authority to sanction the "insane" who would be excluded from liability by an overall application of the general principles of the criminal law.

> J. Goldstein and Katz, Abolish the "Insanity Defense"—Why Not? 72 Yale L.J. 853, 863–65 (1963)[t]

———

Mentally deranged persons can be separated from the mass of mankind by scientific tests, and can be given treatment instead of being subjected to punitive sanctions. Being a defined class, their segregation from punishment does not impair the efficacy of the sanction for people generally.

> G. Williams, Criminal Law, The General Part 347 (1st ed. 1953)

———

[I]t has been argued that insane offenders need not be punished because insane potential offenders cannot be deterred, and the exclusion from punishment of such offenders would not impair the general deterrent function of the criminal law on noninsane potential offenders. * * * It is obvious that all offenders are nondeterrable in the sense that they were not deterred by the existing system of criminal sanctions. It is similarly obvious that all offenders could be deterred by some set of circumstances. And it is far from obvious, although it may be true, that insane offenders can be deterred only by means far more immediate in application than necessary to deter noninsane offenders. * * * [T]he * * * argument [also] focuses only on the criminal law purpose of deterrence by intellectual balancing of pleasure and pain. The creation of the senses of abhorrence and responsibility might well be impaired by such an approach. And the community's respect for the justness of the criminal law, on which its utility must rest, would almost certainly be reduced. Finally, it is not at all clear that the existence of an insanity loophole would not diminish to some degree the general deterrent effect of the criminal law.

> Livermore and Meehl, The Virtues of M'Naghten, 51 Minn.L.Rev. 789, 798, 793–94, 799 (1967)

———

Modern penal law is founded on moral culpability. The law punishes a person for a criminal act only if he is morally responsible for it. To do otherwise would be both inhumane and unenlightened. As was said in Holloway v. United States, 80 U.S.App.D.C. 3, 5, 148 F.2d 665, 666, "Our collective conscience does not allow punishment where it

t. Reprinted by permission of The Yale Law Journal Company and Fred B. Rothman & Company from The Yale Law Journal, Vol. 52, p. 853.

cannot impose blame." It is this fundamental principle that exempts from punishment certain types of insane criminals.

> United States v. Fielding, 148
> F.Supp. 46, 49 (D.D.C.1957)
> (Holtzoff, J.)

[I]nsanity [may be] inconsistent with moral failure. A person may be morally blameless if under the circumstances it would be unreasonable to expect avoidance of the forbidden conduct. * * *

At least two difficulties arise in equating the reasonableness of expecting compliance with moral blameworthiness. First and most obvious is the absence of any standard by which to judge the reasonableness of expecting compliance. In addition, even in those cases where opinion is nearly unanimous that compliance cannot reasonably be expected, the criminal law has often imposed moral condemnation. Thus, in a nondefensive situation, one may not take another's life to save one's own even though it is known that the actor will almost certainly do so. That one acting reasonably is ignorant of the existence of a particular penal statute is no defense though one cannot be reasonably expected to comply with an unknown rule.

> Livermore and Meehl, The Virtues of M'Naghten,
> 51 Minn.L.Rev. 789, 794 (1967)

NOTE

For older general discussions of the insanity defense, see S. Glueck, Mental Disorder and the Criminal Law (1925); H. Weihofen, Mental Disorder as a Criminal Defense (1954); Keedy, Insanity and Criminal Responsibility, 30 Harv.L.Rev. 535 (1917). A. Goldstein, The Insanity Defense (1967) contains a thorough contemporary discussion. See also C. Jeffrey, Criminal Responsibility and Mental Disease (1967); Diamond, from M'Naghten to Currens, and Beyond, 50 Cal.L.Rev. 189 (1962); Hall, Mental Disease and Criminal Responsibility—M'Naghten Versus Durham and the American Law Institute's Tentative Draft, 33 Ind.L.J. 212 (1957); Hall, Psychiatry and Criminal Responsibility, 65 Yale L.J. 761 (1956); Insanity As a Defense (A Panel Discussion), 37 F.R.D. 365 (1965); Kuh, The Insanity Defense—An Effort to Combine Law and Reason, 110 U.Pa.L.Rev. 771 (1962); Overholser, Criminal Responsibility: A Psychiatrist's Viewpoint, 48 A.B.A.J. 527 (1962); Raab, A Moralist Looks at the Durham and M'Naghten Rules, 46 Minn.L.Rev. 327 (1961); Robitscher, Tests of Criminal Responsibility: New Rules and Old Problems, 3 Land & Water L.Rev. 153 (1968): Shaman, Responsibility and Insanity—Do They Exist?, 31 U.Pitt.L.Rev. 243 (1969); Silving, The Criminal Law of Mental Incapacity, 53 J.Crim.L., C. & P.S. 129 (1962); Slovenko, A History of Criminal Procedures As Related to Mental Disorders, 71 W.Va.L.Rev. 135 (1969); Symposium, 45 Marq.L.Rev. 477

(1962); Symposium, 22 U.Chi.L.Rev. 317 (1955); Waelder, Psychiatry and the Problem of Criminal Responsibility, 101 U.Pa.L.Rev. 378 (1952); Weintraub, Criminal Responsibility: Psychiatry Alone Cannot Determine It, 49 A.B.A.J. 1075 (1963).

---

b. INCIDENCE OF THE ISSUE

LEWIN, INCOMPETENCY TO STAND TRIAL: LEGAL AND ETHICAL ASPECTS OF AN ABUSED DOCTRINE, 1969 LAW AND THE SOCIAL ORDER

233, 234–35.

Judging from the experience of the state of Michigan, in which one of America's major criminal courts sits, the incidence of mental disease occurring in persons suspected of crime is not uncommon; indeed, it is frequently seen. The Detroit Recorder's Court, which handles over 6,000 felony cases annually, has a psychiatric clinic attached to it, and this clinic performs nearly 2,500 psychiatric examinations annually. * * * In a recent field survey of Michigan defense attorneys most active in the practice of criminal law, over 75 percent admitted having frequent contact with mentally ill defendants. Other jurisdictions report similar statistics, and the nation's mental institutions are overcrowded with mentally ill persons caught up in the criminal process.

A. MATTHEWS, MENTAL DISABILITY AND THE CRIMINAL LAW

26–30, 32, 34 (1970).[u]

Frequency of Criminal Responsibility Cases

* * *

Published criminal statistics do not record responsibility cases as we have defined that term. Just as state criminal statistics do not record whether the defense was one of alibi or self-defense, they do not report if the defense was based on insanity. Similarly, a successful defense of insanity is usually counted as an "acquittal" rather than an "acquittal on the grounds of insanity."

California comes closest to counting responsibility cases according to our definition. In California the defense of insanity cannot be presented at trial unless the defendant has entered a plea of not guilty by reason of insanity at the arraignment. The entry of the insanity plea is noted on the court record and reported to the California

u. Reprinted by permission of the American Bar Foundation, Chicago, Illinois.

Bureau of Criminal Statistics. * * * In 1965, of 36,643 felony dispositions, a plea of not guilty by reason of insanity was entered in 464 cases (1.3 percent of the total). Of this number, 213 pleas were withdrawn and an additional 56 cases were dismissed or placed off calendar, leaving a total of 195 cases tried in which a plea of insanity had not been withdrawn. (This figure represents 0.53 percent of the total felony dispositions in California during 1965.) Of this number, 109 defendants were acquitted and 86 convicted. How many of the 109 were acquitted "on account of insanity" is not known. Recorded admissions to Atascadero State Hospital in California show that during fiscal 1965, 66 persons were admitted after a finding of not guilty by reason of insanity; in 1966, 61 persons were admitted. These figures tend to indicate that roughly three-fifths of the total of 109 acquittals were on the grounds of insanity.

Nor is it known whether the defense of insanity was actually presented in these cases or in the 86 cases in which a conviction resulted. * * *

Unpublished data from New York, Illinois, and Michigan, consisting of recorded admissions to the maximum-security hospitals in these three states, reveal that only a handful of such admissions occur there each year. In New York, for the year ending March 31, 1963, two persons were admitted after a finding of not guilty by reason of insanity. Only seven persons in the hospital's whole inmate population were committed as the result of a finding of not guilty by reason of insanity. In Michigan, we were told that only "a few" admissions occur each year. As of November 1964, only fourteen persons were at the hospital as the result of an acquittal on grounds of insanity. During the fiscal year ending June 30, 1965, no persons were admitted to the comparable hospital in Illinois. Reports for other years indicate that only a few admissions of this kind occur each year.

Officials interviewed in Miami, Chicago, New York City, San Francisco, and Detroit told us that responsibility cases were "rare," "a few," "hardly ever occur," and the like. For example, the prosecuting attorneys, defense counsel, and judges with whom we talked in Detroit could recollect only one successful defense of insanity in the preceding five years. To test the actual frequency of dispositions based on lack of criminal responsibility in Detroit, and incidentally to test the recollection of the Detroit officials, the staff undertook a review of the homicide indictments over a five-year period in the city of Detroit. The results * * * were that one person in five years, a defendant charged with second degree murder, had been found not guilty by reason of insanity at trial. We can thus conclude that official recollection of such cases is quite accurate and that the actual frequency of responsibility cases is, as reported to us, in fact rare.

The criminal courts in the District of Columbia have been the subject of several special studies * * *. It is apparent that the volume of criminal responsibility cases in the District of Columbia is higher than in the other jurisdictions studied. The number of persons acquitted on grounds of insanity in Washington, D. C., rose steadily from 1954, when there were three such cases, until 1962 when sixty-six defendants were found not guilty by reason of insanity—5.1 percent of all felony cases terminated and 13.8 percent of all felony cases tried. Since 1962 acquittals because of insanity have declined to a total of twenty-six in 1966. One peculiarity of the District of Columbia system is the frequency of acquittals on grounds of insanity in misdemeanor cases—a pattern of disposition which is virtually unknown elsewhere * * *.

To summarize: in each jurisdiction criminal responsibility cases constitute a small percentage of all cases; in Illinois, New York, Michigan, and Florida only a handful of cases occur each year; there is a somewhat higher frequency in California and a still higher frequency in the District of Columbia.[11]

Characteristics of Responsibility Cases: "Traditional" and "Exceptional" Cases

It is sometimes stated in the literature that the defense of insanity is raised only in homicide or capital cases. This is *generally* true in the areas studied, except California and Washington, D. C., but it is not *literally* true anywhere. In Michigan, for example, where there is no capital punishment, five of the fourteen cases resulting in hospitalization were not homicide cases. In California and Washington, D. C. * * * the defense of insanity is raised in felonies other than homicide in larger number than in homicide cases. Elsewhere, however, the defense is limited largely to capital cases * * *.

What emerges is a rough distinction between "traditional" cases typified by the homicide cases observed during the field portion of this study, and "exceptional" cases typified by the cases we observed in the District of Columbia, none of which was a homicide case. The traditional cases have some common elements. Typically the charge is capital, frequently a case of homicide. Often the trial is attended by much publicity, and there is a positive identification of the accused as the perpetrator of the crime. More likely than not the crime

---

11. On the basis of population size—well over eighteen million in California and about three-quarters of a million in the District of Columbia—we would expect California to have twenty-four times as many cases as the District of Columbia; in fact, if the estimated 1965 totals of insanity acquittals in felonies in California (66) and Washington, D.C. (35) are compared on this basis, the District of Columbia had nearly thirteen times as many cases as California. Put differently, given the estimated number of acquittals on grounds of insanity in California in 1965, we would expect about three such acquittals in the District of Columbia. This was the actual number of acquittals in 1954, the year *Durham* was decided, and since then there have always been many more than three * * *[.]

will be a violent one and not one requiring deliberation such as murder by poisoning. Frequently there is no possible defense for the act except insanity. Finally, negotiated alternatives such as a plea of guilty are usually clearly excluded, often at the outset, because of a combination of the foregoing factors, or because negotiation is inhibited by a mandatory death penalty or the fact of attendant publicity or the viciousness of the crime. While such cases are serious, they are not necessarily the most bizarre ones. The truly bizarre case is more likely to be disposed of earlier in the proceedings, at the competency stage; for example, in New York State in 1964, 450 patients at Matteawan State Hospital had been sent there following a finding of incompetence to stand trial upon a charge of homicide, compared to a dozen patients committed there following an acquittal on grounds of insanity.

By "exceptional" cases we mean nothing more mysterious than cases in which we would not expect an insanity plea, the common elements characteristic of "traditional" cases being absent. * * *

"Exceptional" cases occur routinely in the District of Columbia, * * * but elsewhere the insanity defense is restricted largely to "traditional" cases and is in any event rarely used.

---

c. THE REQUIREMENT OF "MENTAL ILLNESS"

Although they vary in other aspects, all of the formulations of the insanity defense contain a basic requirement that the defendant have been "mentally ill" or its equivalent. Consider at this point whether this is an important or proper part of an insanity defense. Reconsider the matter in examining various alternative formulations of the defense.

T. SZASZ, THE MYTH OF MENTAL ILLNESS

15 American Psychologist 113, 114–15, 117 (1960).v

My aim * * * is to raise the question "Is there such a thing as mental illness?" and to argue that there is not. * * *

The term "mental illness" is widely used to describe something which is very different than a disease of the brain. * * *

The concept of illness, whether bodily or mental, implies deviation from some clearly defined norm. In the case of physical illness, the norm is the structural and functional integrity of the human body. Thus, although the desirability of physical health, as such, is an ethical value, what it is can be stated in anatomical and physiological terms. What is the norm deviation from which is regarded as mental illness? This question cannot be easily answered. But whatever this norm might be, we can be certain of only one thing: namely, that it must be stated in terms of psychosocial, ethical, and legal concepts. * * * [T]he widespread psychiatric opinion that only a mentally ill person would commit homicide illustrates the use of a legal concept as a norm of mental health. The norm from which deviation is measured whenever one speaks of a mental illness is a psychosocial and ethical one. * * *

[M]y aim in presenting this argument was expressly to criticise and counter a prevailing contemporary tendency to deny the moral aspects of psychiatry * * * and to substitute for them allegedly value free medical considerations. * * *

While I have argued that mental illnesses do not exist, I obviously did not imply that the social and psychological occurrences to which this label is currently being attached also do not exist. * * * They are real enough. It is the labels we give them that concerns us. * * *

NOTES

1. Consider the following attempts to define the term "mental illness" (or its equivalent) in formulations of the insanity test:

> Whenever the mental condition of a defendant is in issue, two basic questions are presented. One is whether he is afflicted with a mental illness or disease which acted to produce the conduct with which he is charged. This is entirely a medical, psychiatric question, in which the law has only incidental interest. It is answerable only by medical experts in the application of medical standards. The other, a fundamentally different and wholly legal question, is whether the defendant is to be charged with criminal responsibility for his conduct. Medical considerations play a part—but only a part—in its answer.
>
> State v. Crose, 88 Ariz. 389, 357 P.2d 136 (1960)

> In Hawaii, emotional insanity, unassociated with a disease of the brain, as defined below, is not an excuse for a crime. In order to constitute a defense * * *, the mental derangement under which the defendant acted at the time of the commission of the alleged offense must be caused by or be the effect of a disease of the brain rendering her incompetent to discern the nature and criminality of the act done by her. Territory v. Alcosiba, 36 Haw. 231. "Mental derangement, as indicated by the term itself, denotes a disordered or unsound mind. It is interchangeable in meaning with the word 'insanity.' Many authorities have referred to insanity as a disease of the mind. However, it is now generally conceded that insanity or mental derangement is rather the result or manifestation in the mind of a disease of the brain, and by disease is meant any underde-

velopment, pathological condition, lesion or malfunctioning of the brain or any morbid change or deterioration in the organic functions or structure thereof."

State v. Foster, 44 Hawaii 403, 354 P.2d 960, 972 (1960)

The statute * * * uses the term "mental disease or defect" in a generalized sense which * * * merely means a mind sufficiently disordered to cause the results indicated * * *. The term was not intended to designate any specific form or forms or medical classifications of mental disease.

State v. Garrett, 391 S.W.2d 235, 239 (Mo.1965)

We agree * * * that the law cannot "distinguish between psysiological, emotional, social and cultural sources of the impairment"—assuming, of course, requisite testimony establishing exculpation under the pertinent standard—and all such causes may be both referred to by the expert and considered by the trier of fact.

Breadth of input under the insanity defense is not to be confused with breadth of the doctrines establishing the defense. * * * [T]he latitude for salient evidence of, e. g., social and cultural factor pertinent to an abnormal condition of the mind significantly affecting capacity and controls, does not mean that such factors may be taken as establishing a separate defense for persons whose mental condition is such that blame can be imposed. We have rejected a broad "injustice" approach that would have opened the door to expositions of e. g., cultural deprivation, unrelated to any abnormal condition of the mind.

* * *

[W]e have not accepted suggestions to adopt a rule that disentangles the insanity defense from a medical model, and announces a standard for exculpating anyone whose capacity for control is insubstantial, for whatever cause or reason. There may be logic in these submissions, but we are not sufficiently certain of the nature, range, and implications of the conduct involved to attempt an all-embracing unified field theory. The applicable rule can be discerned as the cases arise in regard to other conditions—somnambulism or other automatism; blackouts due, e. g., to overdose of insulin; drug addiction. Whether these somatic conditions should be governed by a rule comparable to that herein set forth for mental disease would require, at a minimum, a judicial determination, which takes medical opinion into account, finding convincing evidence of an ascertainable condition characterized by "a broad consensus that free will does not exist."

United States v. Brawner, 471 F.2d 969 (D.C.Cir. 1972)

2. "The term [mental disease] was developed in the context of *legal* tests of criminal responsibility, but no *legal* definition evolved. Rather, since the courts and legislators were well aware of the analogy to physical disease, it was and has been generally assumed that "mental disease" is a medical term, more particularly a term within the special purview of those medical men charged with behavioral abnormalities—the psychiatrists.

Turning to the psychiatric literature to explore this general thesis reveals, however, that there is no authoritative or generally accepted medical definition of mental disease. Indeed, the single most impressive fact is a negative one: the phrase "mental disease" is notable by its absence in most of the vast theoretical, textbook, clinical, and dictionary literature. When the problem of defining mental disease is raised explicitly, it is resolved by psychiatric authorities in substantially the following very different ways: (1) There is no such medical entity as mental disease, or we would do well not to use the phrase. (2) Mental disease is psychosis but not neurosis. (3) Mental disease is any significant and substantial mental disturbance, or is any condition at all which is authoritatively dealt with by the psychiatrist or physician treating mental conditions. (4) Mental disease means substantial *social maladaptation* or incompetence or both as judged by legal criteria. (5) Mental disease is the failure to realize one's nature, capacities, or true self.

A review of the literature in psychology reveals similar results—there is neither a clear definition of mental disease nor agreement on how best to approach such a definition.

Turning briefly to the legal literature on the question, we again find inconsistency and no help toward providing an appropriate *medical* definition of mental disease. * * *

Since the law insists on "mental disease" as a central term but gives no clue as to its meaning except to say that it is a medical term, many psychiatrists, desirous of cooperating responsibly with the law, have felt compelled to decide the meaning of mental disease. Predictably, the course of reaching such decisions has required the psychiatrists to anticipate what the court will accept as a definition to excuse from criminal responsibility. As a result, psychiatrists have made a pragmatic judgment that the courts will not accept every disorder as a disease and a conscious attempt to utilize a psychiatric category which they suppose will roughly serve—at least serve better than any other single psychiatric category—to bring out the mental conditions relevant to criminal responsibility. Thus, the general tendency of the psychiatrists under both *Durham* and *M'Naghten* has been to equate mental disease with psychoses. Of course, in so doing the psychiatrist is making a judgment about criminal responsibility—a judgment which he explicitly is not authorized to make and with respect to which he is of course not expert. In effect, the courts have thus given the medical men a blank check in matters of vital importance to the court.

> Fingarette, The Concept of Mental Disease in Criminal Law Insanity Tests, 33 U.Chi.L.Rev. 229, 232–33, 240 (1966).[w]

3. Consider the following from Morris, Psychiatry and the Dangerous Criminal, 41 S.Cal.L.Rev. 514, 520 (1968):

> It too often is overlooked that one group's exculpation from criminal responsibility confirms the inculpation of other groups. Why not permit the defense of dwelling in a Negro ghetto? Such a defense

w. Professor Fingarette makes the same point in Fingarette, Herbert, The Meaning of Criminal Insanity, University of California Press, Berkeley & London, 1972, at pages 25–29, 31.

would not be morally indefensible. Adverse social and subcultural background is statistically *more* criminogenic than is psychosis; like insanity, it also severely circumscribes the freedom of choice which a non-deterministic criminal law (all present criminal law systems) attributes to accused persons. True, a defense of social adversity would politically be intolerable; but that does not vitiate the analogy for my purposes. You argue that insanity destroys, undermines, diminishes man's capacity to reject what is wrong and to adhere to what is right. So does the ghetto—more so. But surely, you reply, I would not have us punish the sick. Indeed I would, if you insist on punishing the grossly deprived. To the extent that criminal sanctions serve punitive purposes, I fail to see the difference between these two defenses. To the extent that they serve rehabilitative, treatment, and curative purposes I fail to see the need for the difference.

2. PRE–M'NAGHTEN STANDARD

REX v. ARNOLD

Court of Common Pleas, 1724.
16 How.St. Trials 695.

[The defendant had been charged with shooting at Lord Onslow with the intent of killing him. Evidence was introduced as to the insanity of the defendant, and the following is a portion of Justice Tracy's charge to the jury.]

Now I have laid it before you; and you must consider of it; and the shooting of my lord Onslow * * * is proved beyond all manner of contradiction; but whether this shooting was malicious, that depends upon the sanity of the man. That he shot, and that wilfully [is proved]: but whether maliciously, that is the thing: that is the question; whether this man hath the use of his reason and senses? If he was under the visitation of God, and could not distinguish between good and evil, and did not know what he did, though he committed the greatest offense, yet he could not be guilty of any offense against any law whatsoever; for guilt arises from the mind, and the wicked will and intention of the man. If a man be deprived of his reason, and consequently of his intention, he cannot be guilty; and if that be the case, though he had actually killed my lord Onslow, he is exempted from punishment: punishment is intended for example, and to deter other persons from wicked designs; but the punishment of a madman, a person that hath no design, can have no example. This is on one side. On the other side, we must be very cautious; it is not every frantic and idle humour of a man, that will exempt him from justice, and the punishment of the law. When a man is guilty of a great offense, it must be very plain and clear, before a man is allowed such an exemption; therefore it is not every kind of frantic humour or something unaccountable in a man's actions, that points him out to be such a madman as is to be exempted from punishment: it must be a man that is totally deprived of his understanding and memory, and doth not know what he is doing, no more than an infant, than a brute, or a wild beast, such a one is never the object of punishment; therefore I must leave it to your consideration, whether the condition this man was in, as it is represented to you on one side, or on the other, doth shew a man, who knew what he was doing, and was able to distinguish whether he was doing good or evil, and understood what he did: and it is to be observed, they admit he was a lunatic, and not an ideot. A man that is an ideot, that is born so, never recovers, but a lunatic may, and hath his intervals; and they admit he was a lunatic. You are to consider what he was at this day, when he committed this fact. There you have a great many circumstances about the buying the powder and the shot; his going backward and forward; and if you believe he was sensible, and the use of his reason, and understood what he did, then he is not within the exemptions of the law, but is as subject to punishment as any other person. Gentlemen, I must leave it to you.

---

3. THE M'NAGHTEN RULES

DANIEL M'NAGHTEN'S CASE

House of Lords, 1843.
10 Cl. & F. 200, 8 Eng.Rep. 718.

The prisoner had been indicted for that he, on the 20th day of January 1843, at the parish of Saint Martin in the Fields, in the county of Middlesex, and within the jurisdiction of the Central Criminal Court, in and upon one Edward Drummond, feloniously, wilfully, and of his malice aforethought, did make an assault; and that the said Daniel M'Naghten, a certain pistol of the value of 20s., loaded and charged with gunpowder and a leaden bullet (which pistol he in his right hand had and held), to, against and upon the said Edward Drummond, feloniously, wilfully, and of his malice aforethought, did shoot and discharge; and that the said Daniel M'Naghten, with the leaden bullet aforesaid, out of the pistol aforesaid, by force of the gunpowder, etc., the said Edward Drummond, in and upon the back of him the said Edward Drummond, feloniously, etc. did strike, penetrate and wound, giving to the said Edward Drummond, in and upon the back of the said Edward Drummond, one mortal wound, etc., of which mortal wound the said E. Drummond languished until the 25th of April and then died; and that by the means aforesaid, he the prisoner did kill and murder the said Edward Drummond. The prisoner pleaded Not guilty.

Evidence having been given of the fact of the shooting of Mr. Drummond, and of his death in consequence thereof, witnesses were called on the part of the prisoner, to prove that he was not, at the time of committing the act, in a sound state of mind. The medical evidence was in substance this: That persons of otherwise sound mind, might be affected by morbid delusions: that the prisoner was in that condition: that a person so labouring under a morbid delusion, might have a moral perception of right and wrong, but that in the case of the prisoner it was a delusion which carried him away beyond the power of his own control, and left him no such perception; and that he was not capable of exercising any control over acts which had connexion with his delusion: that it was of the nature of the disease with which the prisoner was affected, to go on gradually until it had reached a climax, when it burst forth with irresistible intensity: that a man might go on for years quietly, though at the same time under its influence, but would all at once break out into the most extravagant and violent paroxysms.

* * *

Verdict, Not guilty, on the ground of insanity.

This verdict, and the question of the nature and extent of the unsoundness of mind which would excuse the commission of a felony of this sort, having been made the subject of debate in the House of Lords * * *, it was determined to take the opinion of the Judges on the law governing such cases.

Lord Chief Justice Tindal: * * *

The first question proposed by your Lordships is this: "What is the law respecting alleged crimes committed by persons afflicted with insane delusion in respect of one or more particular subjects or persons: as, for instance, where at the time of the commission of the alleged crime the accused knew he was acting contrary to law, but did the act complained of with a view, under the influence of insane delusion, of redressing or revenging some supposed grievance or injury, or of producing some supposed public benefit?"

In answer to which question, assuming that your Lordships' inquiries are confined to those persons who labour under such partial delusions only, and are not in other respects insane, we are of opinion that, notwithstanding the party accused did the act complained of with a view, under the influence of insane delusion, of redressing or revenging some supposed grievance or injury, or of producing some public benefit, he is nevertheless punishable according to the nature of the crime committed, if he knew at the time of committing such crime that he was acting contrary to law; by which expression we understand your Lordships to mean the law of the land.

Your Lordships are pleased to inquire of us, secondly, "What are the proper questions to be submitted to the jury, where a person alleged to be afflicted with insane delusion respecting one or more particular subjects or persons, is charged with the commission of a crime (murder, for example), and insanity is set up as a defence?" And, thirdly, "In what terms ought the question to be left to the jury as to the prisoner's state of mind at the time when the act was committed?" And as these two questions appear to us to be more conveniently answered together, we have to submit our opinion to be, that the jurors ought to be told in all cases that every man is to be presumed to be sane, and to possess a sufficient degree of reason to be responsible for his crimes, until the contrary be proved to their satisfaction; and that to establish a defence on the ground of insanity, it must be clearly proved that, at the time of the committing of the act, the party accused was labouring under such a defect of reason, from disease of the mind, as not to know the nature and quality of the act he was doing; or, if he did know it, that he did not know he was doing what was wrong. The mode of putting the latter part of the question to the jury on these occasions has generally been, whether the accused at the time of doing the act knew the difference between right and wrong: which mode, though rarely, if ever, leading to any mistake with the jury, is not, as we conceive, so accurate when put generally and in the abstract, as when put with reference to the party's knowledge of right and wrong in respect to the very act with which he is charged. If the question were to be put as to the knowledge of the accused solely and exclusively with reference to the law of the land, it might tend to confound the jury, by inducing them to believe that an actual knowledge of the law of the land was essential in order to lead to a conviction; whereas the law is administered upon the principle that every one must be taken conclusively to know it, without proof that he does know it. If the accused was conscious that the act was one which he ought not to do, and if that act was at the same time contrary to the law of the land, he is punishable; and the usual course therefore has been to leave the question to the jury, whether the party accused had a sufficient degree of reason to know that he was doing an act that was wrong: and this course we think is correct, accompanied with such observations and explanations as the circumstances of each particular case may require.

The fourth question which your Lordships have proposed to us is this:—"If a person under an insane delusion as to existing facts, commits an offence in consequence thereof, is he thereby excused?" To which question the answer must of course depend on the nature of the delusion: but, making the same assumption as we did before, namely, that he labours under such partial delusion only, and is not in other respects insane, we think he must be considered in the same situation as to responsibility as if the facts with respect to which the delusion exists were real. For example, if under the influence of his delusion he supposes another man to be in the act of attempting to take away his life, and he kills that man, as he supposes, in self-defence, he would be exempt from punishment. If his delusion was that the deceased had inflicted a serious injury to his character and fortune, and he killed him in revenge for such supposed injury, he would be liable to punishment.

NOTES

1. Parsons v. State, 81 Ala. 577, 2 So. 854 (1887):

If the rule declared by the English judges be correct, it necessarily follows that the only possible instance of excusable homicide, in cases of delusional insanity, would be where the delusion, if real, would have been such as to create, in the mind of a reasonable man, a just apprehension of imminent peril to life or limb. The personal fear or timid cowardice of the insane man, although created by disease acting through a prostrated nervous organization, would not excuse undue precipitation of action on his part. Nothing would justify assailing his supposed adversary except an overt act, or demonstration on the part of the latter, such as, if the imaginary facts were real, would, under like circumstances, have justified a man perfectly sane in shooting or killing. If he dare fail to reason, on the supposed facts embodied in the delusion, as perfectly as a sane man could do on a like state of realities, he receives no mercy at the hands of the law. It exacts of him the last pound of flesh. It would follow also, under this rule, that the partially insane man, afflicted with delusions, would no more be excusable than a sane man would be, if, perchance, it was by his fault the difficulty was provoked, whether by word or deed; or if, in fine, he may have been so negligent as not to have declined combat when he could do so safely, without increasing his peril of life or limb. If this has been the law heretofore, it is time it should be so no longer. It is not only opposed to the known facts of modern medical science, but it is a hard and unjust rule to be applied to the unfortunate and providential victims of disease.

2. Consider the following analysis of M'Naghten from Livermore and Meehl, The Virtues of M'Naghten, 51 Minn.L.Rev. 789, 800–02, 804–08 (1967):

Before it is possible to assess whether *M'Naghten* is a satisfactory test of criminal responsibility, it is necessary to examine the meaning of the *M'Naghten* language. Although it is usually assumed that the meaning is obvious, as with most legal formulae, this is simply not the case. What follows is an attempt to put psychological meat on these legal bones.

From the psychologists' viewpoint, the noun "reason" refers to certain psychological functions, held together by virtue of a conceptual unity. This unity lies in the fact that, in carrying out any of these functions adequately, inference takes place. That is, some sort of mental transition occurs between one mental content and another where there is a rational or logical relation between the contents justifying the inferential step. The existence of this rational relation is a condition to a justifiable making of this trans-

ition. The adequacy of these inferential transitions usually tends
to be somewhat correlated in spite of differences in the particular
subject matter or logical form of the relation. That is, one would
expect that a person who reasons more ably than most people in
solving riddles will more likely than not reason more ably in other
domains. If a person's momentary state (e. g., sickness, fatigue, intoxication, rage) greatly impairs his ability to do arithmetic problems, it will also impair his working of crossword puzzles.

Identity of logical form and similarity of content will not, however, guarantee perfect correlation between reasoning abilities as
displayed in two reasoning tasks. If the tasks differ appreciably in
context or content (as they must if they are really two tasks), they
will involve specific (task-tied) abilities over and above the cognitive abilities they share. Further, especially in mentally abnormal
persons, they may arouse markedly different motivational or emotional states. Such noncognitive influences may aid, or may impede, the reasoning process. Fear, anger, shame, boredom, competing interests, bias, and all such we shall designate generically insofar as they exert an adverse influence, as "interfering factors."
In ordinary language, we do not usually attribute to defective reason those inferential errors caused by interfering factors. For example, if a man thinks rationally about everything except politics
(he is a zealous member of the Prohibition Party), we tend to describe him as "prejudiced" or "buggy about booze," rather than invoking a defect of reason. Ordinarily, we would not postulate a
defect of reason unless we had evidence of considerable generality
over diverse content domains, and, preferably, also lacked good evidence for exaggerated influence of interfering factors. In this
respect the psychologist proceeds rather closely in accord with the
usages of ordinary speech. A possible difference, however, is that
given a sufficiently extreme irrationality in a single domain (e. g.,
delusion of persecution), the psychologist is likely to invoke the notion of a defective ego, a concept that does imply at least the potential for defective reasoning over many or all domains. Whether
ordinary usage resembles "psychologese" here is hard to say, partly
because ordinary usage does not attempt these refinements for the
extreme case. We rather suspect, however, that the layman would
tend to question the financial judgment of a man who thought he
was Napoleon. It is probable that common usage actually inflates
the generality of reason.

In psychologese, then, a defect in reason would be a defect in
the class of mental functions involved in performing psychological transitions between mental contents on the basis of a logical
relation between them. In our view this is a sensible construction of these words and one which is wholly consistent with current psychological knowledge and practice. The argument often
advanced by *M'Naghten* detractors that this phrase involves an
outmoded conception of mental life is simply not so.

In addition to the process of reasoning, the phrase "defect of
reason" may also include the ability to perceive. The process
of perception and categorization, the subsuming of the perceived

item into its logical category, involves to some extent the ability to properly infer. Furthermore, when perceptions are demonstrably false, as when one hallucinates the voice of God speaking to him, the ability to reason is, usually, generally impaired. Accordingly, while a defect in perception does not always involve a defect in inferring, for purposes of *M'Naghten* such defects should be included in the concept defect in reason. This, in turn, changes the psychologese of defect in reason to defect in the cognitive ego functions—perceiving, remembering, inferring, classifying, judging, etc.—the meaning traditionally assigned to *M'Naghten*.

Defect of reason, of course, shares with the concept of mental abnormality the problem of degree. Inferential errors in the process of reasoning vary considerably in magnitude and depend on a variety of factors. It is impossible to say precisely how great a defect in reason is necessary to satisfy the *M'Naghten* rule. Words such as "substantial" or "gross" only mask the user's view. The substantial defects we have in mind, however, correspond roughly to the present distinction between psychosis and other mental abnormalities. * * *

With rare exceptions, the verb "know" in *M'Naghten* is used as a dispositional concept. Even though it is a verb grammatically, it usually refers to a state of potentiality rather than to an action or event. Dispositional concepts in psychology designate more or less enduring potentialities of the individual to react in a certain way given certain circumstances. If the circumstances rarely or never arise, the disposition remains unactivated, but it still has reality as a disposition. In this respect, dispositional concepts in psychology are not basically different from those attributed to inanimate objects. Thus, soluble is a dispositional concept, and we consider it literally correct to say that a particular sugarlump is soluble even though it happens never to be put into solution. It is obvious that most of the terms used to describe people, whether in psychologese or ordinary speech, are dispositional in nature. Skills, habits, abilities, and character traits are all dispositional; if it were otherwise we could never attribute any such trait to a person unless he was momentarily manifesting it. When we say, "Jones knows the date of the Norman Conquest," we do not require that he be saying or thinking it. His knowing is his disposition (power, potentiality, ability) to say, or think, or write "1066" under suitable eliciting circumstances. When we say that Jones knows the date of the Norman Conquest, we cannot predict for sure he will be able to come up with the correct response on each and every occasion. He may have a momentary blockage for any of a number of reasons. The only way to cover all such contingencies so as to formulate an accurate dispositional statement is to exclude the entire class of interfering factors among the pre-conditions. But since this list is, strictly speaking, unknown to us, the only way of referring to it is by saying "and other interfering factors being absent," which renders the dispositional statement tautologous and empirically applicable only after the fact.

What does it mean to "know * * * that his act was wrong"? If a psychologist were to employ this language, he would be intending either (or both) of two components. One of these components is of an ethical-cognition nature; the other is of a guilt-signal nature. For short, let us designate these components by notations "e_c" and "g_s" respectively.

The primarily cognitive component e_c consists of a whole family of dispositions to perceive, classify, expect, think, recognize, infer, and *talk* (especially internally) about actions with respect to their allowed or forbidden character. These dispositions are, of course, the product of life experiences of many kinds, including explicit instruction in moral rules, observation of and identification with significant figures, and the whole reward-punishment regime which the institutions of the family, peer-group and society have provided. We italicized "talk" because the ability to produce verbal responses in oneself, which in turn act as behavior controllers, is one of the most important dimensions in ethical choice. As we all know, a person can permit himself all sorts of inconsistent ethical behavior as long as he can avoid "talking to himself" about the real ethical nature of his actions. However, because the word talk has a social and out-loud implication, we shall employ the more neutral word "token," used by logicians and psycholinguists, as a generic term for the whole class of pyschological events that have a symbolic nature sufficient to justify treating them as essentially propositional.[48] Thus when we say "Jones tokened red," we mean that there occurred within Jones a psychological event of a symbolic, referential, representational character—that in some sense, however attenuated, he said to himself or thought or intended the English sign red. He may have spoken it aloud, or his vocal chords may have formed the word silently, but these are not necessary conditions for a tokening event.

The cognitive component e_c involves a family of dispositions including dispositions to token such statements as "this is forbidden," "I shall deserve punishment," "if I do that I am wicked," "I'll hate myself later," and the like. While philosophers dispute about what is the essential element of ethical tokenings, psychologically we cannot—at least presently—assign clearly privileged status to some of these over others. The main point is that a person's moral training (all kinds, from all sources, and largely inexplicit) results in his having a family of dispositions to token statements containing ethical concepts such as wrong, illicit, forbidden, duty, ought, bad, sinful, unfair, and the like. If we could make an exhaustive survey of these tokening dispositions, and could then sort out the common features of those actions he is disposed to categorize one way or the other, we would have arrived inductively at the content of his particular ethical system.

The noncognitive component g_s is a motivational-affective state or event which is normally elicited by the activation of the dispo-

48. A propositional mental event is one capable of being either true or false.

sitions e$_c$ and which in turn functions as a behavior inhibitor. It is called a signal because it warns of future consequences (punishment, disapproval, guilt feeling, loss of self-esteem). As Freud points out, we learn by experience how to turn off this internal anxiety signal aroused by our impulse to forbidden actions. Most of the time our forbidden impulses are suppressed so quickly and automatically that the anxiety signal consists only of the faintest, briefest "blip" of internal warning, and is often not reportable (consciously introspectable) by the individual.

When psychologists say, then, that a person knows something is wrong, they may mean two different things. First, an ethical-cognition signal may be meant. Thus, as we have indicated is only the tokening of the phrase "this act is forbidden." A guilt signal, on the other hand, involves some emotional response such as anticipatory anxiety. In ordinary language, the distinction may be illustrated by the speeding driver who knows (i. e., tokens an ethical-cognition signal that his act is illegal but does not feel that he is acting wrongly (i. e., does not adequately appreciate, in the sense of emotional-motivational overtones, that he may be imperilling the lives of himself and others). For *M'Naghten* purposes, it is obvious that the former meaning of "know" must be meant. That an offender has no conscious appreciation that he is presently acting dangerously, experiences no internalized inhibitory signal, and feels no guilt or remorse is irrelevant.

* * *

The *M'Naghten* rule can be restated in these terms: The defendant will be excused if at the time of the criminal act he had a mental disease or defect which included among its symptoms or consequences an impairment in one or more of the psychological functions requisite for reasoning (i. e., cognitive ego functions) which, in turn, reduced the strength of his disposition to token "this is wrong" to a negligibly low value and, as a result, he did not in fact token "this is wrong" though, if the impairment of reasoning had not been present, the probability of his so tokening would have been materially greater. We recognize that this formulation can hardly be said to improve on the surface clarity of *M'Naghten*. But, as we have observed, this surface clarity is delusive and, in dealing with the human mind, simple formulae cannot be expected.

The meaning we have given the *M'Naghten* language, while consistent with existing definitions, is not to our knowledge generally recognized.

PEOPLE v. WOOD

Court of Appeals of New York, 1962.
12 N.Y.2d 69, 236 N.Y.S.2d 44, 187 N.E.2d 116.

FROESSEL, Judge. On July 4, 1960 the bodies of John Rescigno and Frederick Sess, aged 62 and about 77 respectively, were discovered in the "little house" they shared in Astoria, Queens County. In addition to other wounds, Sess had sustained multiple skull fractures. On Rescigno's body were about 16 wounds; his jugular vein had been severed. Defendant, Frederick Charles Wood, aged 50, was convicted of murder first degree (two counts) and sentenced to death.

* * *

Defendant made no attempt to controvert the evidence which overwhelmingly established that he killed Rescigno and Sess. His sole defense was insanity. * * *

Defendant now merely urges that the People failed to establish beyond a reasonable doubt that he knew the acts were wrong. We now consider this contention. In substance, the expert testimony for the defense was that Wood had schizophrenic reaction, an illness from which he had suffered since about 1926, though "not probably an organic illness". In this connection, the defense psychiatrists stated that although defendant's memory was good, his sensorium clear, he was unaware of the full significance and consequences of his acts, though he knew their physical nature and quality, and that his judgment was impaired, his reasoning defective. Further, defendant told the psychiatrists at Bellevue that he considered himself to be "God's emissary" to take and to save life, and that he was presently charged with the duty of seeking out and killing those whom he believed were degenerates. Their cross-examination established beyond peradventure that Wood knew it was against the law to kill a human being.

One of the People's psychiatrists, Dr. Winkler, who first examined Wood in July, 1960 at Kings County Hospital and interviewed him in April, 1961, testified that defendant had a "highly pathological personality * * * a severe personality disorder", which manifested itself early in his life, but had not "deteriorated" since. Dr. Winkler noted that though defendant had been subjected to extensive hospital observation during the course of his lifetime, the diagnosis of schizophrenic reaction was made *for the first time* at Bellevue in the Fall of 1960. The witness further stated that Wood cannot be called "mentally ill or psychotic", and that his moral judgment was not distorted by illness or disease, but had "never developed". Another "peculiarity", Dr. Winkler testified, was defendant's "inability to control his impulses", a pathological sign but not "legal insanity". During three weeks' observation at the hospital in July, 1960, Wood had not shown any evidence of a psychotic condition.

Regarding the "God's emissary" delusion, Dr. Winkler entertained "definite doubts" that this was "a firm, fixed belief" and gave his reasons therefor. It is of some significance that Wood made this assertion for the *first* time in a psychiatric examination during the latter part of January or in February, 1961, seven months after the homicides with which he was charged, and following the administration of sodium amytal, a drug which, according to Dr. Winkler, might induce delusions. The Kings County Hospital report of July, 1960 does not contain a reference to this delusion. Most significant is the fact that Wood did not mention the delusion in his July 5th statement, but admitted he did something "wrong" on June 30th, namely, killed two men. Indeed, he stated then that *he* "always had a distaste" for degenerates, and had killed Rescigno partly "for the satisfaction of" killing a degenerate, and partly to steal money. It may also be noted that the "God's emissary" delusion and degeneracy had nothing to do with his previous three murders.

Moreover, he did not just kill Rescigno when he ascertained the latter was a degenerate, but first had to "figure out the angles", made sure his intended victim was drunk, and then distracted him by offering a cigarette. After the killings, defendant did not tarry long, being apprehensive that Sess' dying noises and the barking of a dog would alert neighbors to the fact "that something was *wrong*" (emphasis supplied). The People's psychiatrist, Dr. D'Angelo, supported Dr. Winkler in his view that defendant knew the nature and quality of his acts and that they were wrong.

In People v. Schmidt, 216 N.Y. 324, 339–340, 110 N.E. 945, 949, L.R.A.1916D, 519, Judge Cardozo, discussing the meaning of the word "wrong" as used in section 1120, Consol.Laws, c. 40 of the Penal Law, held that there are certain circumstances in which the word "ought not to be limited to legal wrong." Continuing: "Knowledge that an act is forbidden by law will in most cases permit the inference of knowledge that, according to the accepted standards of mankind, it is also condemned as an offense against good morals. Obedience to the law is itself a moral duty. If, however, there is an insane delusion that God has appeared to the defendant and ordained the commission of a crime, we think it cannot be said of the offender that he knows the act to be wrong. It is not enough, to relieve from criminal liability, that the prisoner is morally depraved [citation]. It is not enough that he has views of right and wrong at variance with those that find expression in the law. The variance must have its origin in some disease of the mind. People v. Carlin, 194 N.Y. 448, 455, 87 N.E. 805. * * * Cases will doubtless arise where criminals will take shelter behind a professed belief that their crime was ordained by God * * *. We can safely leave such fabrications to the common sense of juries."

As defendant concedes in his brief, the Trial Judge correctly charged the jury on the meaning of the word "wrong" when he stated: "When it speaks of the defendant's ignorance of his act as wrong, the law does not mean to permit the individual to be his own judge of what is right or wrong. It says that the individual has sufficient knowledge that an act was wrong if its perpetrator knows that his act is against the law and against the commonly accepted standards of morality and conduct which prevail in the community of mankind. He must know that his act was contrary to the laws of God and man."

STATE v. HARKNESS

Supreme Court of Iowa, 1968.
160 N.W.2d 324.

MASON, Justice. This is an appeal from judgment following a jury verdict convicting defendant Earl E. Harkness of second degree murder * * *.

The jury found, and there is no evidence upon the record submitted upon this appeal to dispute the fact, defendant shot and killed Dale Edgington April 18, 1966. He was sentenced to 40 years in the penitentiary at Fort Madison.

Defendant lived in a one-room cabin upon farm ground owned by one Arthur Stevenson. He was not employed by Stevenson, but was simply permitted to live there, from time to time picking up sticks and generally looking after the place. (There were a farm house and other buildings in the vicinity of defendant's cabin.)

Stevenson had hired Dale Edgington (deceased) to do some bulldozing and this involved clearing the land, part of which was proximal to defendant's cabin. Defendant complained to Stevenson that Edgington was running the bulldozer too close to his building, destroying the yard.

Doctor Truax, the psychiatrist who later examined defendant, testified defendant told him he had argued with Edgington about driving the bulldozer too close to the cabin, and asked him to keep it away. Further, Edgington had driven so close he broke the front sidewalk and almost pushed the cabin over.

Sunday, one week prior to April 18, deceased and some of his relatives were out looking over the farm and observed someone peering out a window in the farm house. Deceased explained it was probably "the old squatter who lived in the cabin." They proceeded to the farm house, walked in and were confronted by defendant who ordered them from the house.

Monday morning Edgington returned, attempted to start his bulldozer but apparently decided not to because it was too wet and then left.

Defendant grabbed one of his many rifles and walked to the creek to see how much it had rained. While there, he observed Edgington driving toward him rapidly in a pickup truck. Edgington stopped and apparently began kidding defendant about how much it had rained. Defendant felt that he was being ridiculed and told Edgington to move away. When Edgington did not, defendant "became very angry."

Defendant told Dr. Truax he remembered picking up his rifle, lifting it into a firing position, but did not remember moving the safety or pulling the trigger. The next thing he remembered was being in his cabin "with the vague feeling that he had killed something." He claimed a partial amnesia for the period of the shooting itself.

Defendant then drove to Mount Pleasant to the sheriff's office. Finding sheriff and deputy gone, he told the sheriff's wife he thought he was the man the sheriff was looking for, that he had just shot a man.

The defense relies almost wholly upon the testimony of Dr. Richard Allen Truax, a medical doctor who is presently a resident in psychiatry at the psychopathic hospital at the University of Iowa. Dr. Truax first met defendant June 8, 1966, when he was admitted to psychopathic hospital in Iowa City for purposes of evaluation.

The psychiatric evaluation is based upon the following. Data is compiled to construct a life history; then the patient is given a mental status evaluation to evaluate his intellectual function to see if there is any gross evidence of mental illness. He is observed in a series of interviews as to his emotional responses to the examiner and is given a physical examination. An electroencephalogram (a tracing or linear record of the electric currents generated by the brain) is given as well as a brain scan. Psychological and neurological tests are run. Dr. Truax personally had eight conversations with the patient over a period of approximately five weeks, each lasted 30 to 90 minutes. Finally, the patient is observed during his stay at the hospital to see what sort of person he is on the ward, partially stemming from his conversation and interrelationship with other people on the ward.

Basically, the life history is as follows. Early in life defendant engaged in farming, the junk business and later worked as a night watchman, as well as a part-time construction worker. He had a tendency to avoid people and lived by himself. His sister and brother more or less left him alone while he was working on the home farm. He preferred to work as a night watchman where he was alone, not around other people who disturbed him. After his mother died, he spent all of his free time in a shack out in the country away from people, avoiding people, seeming to question their motives and not wanting to get involved with them. Dr. Truax stated, "This aspect was part of an overall pattern permeating his life history. He learned to leave his brother alone as in doing so things would go pretty much okay. However, one time he did assault his brother with a hammer, and took an ax after a neighbor."

Defendant's brother Ival testified about the defendant's attempt to assault him with a hammer until his mother intervened and called the sheriff. Also, "as to Earl's disposition and temper, he don't bother nobody as long as nobody bothers him. When somebody bothers him, he gets pretty mad. I wouldn't know what all he would do when he gets mad."

* * *

Defendant was found to be in good physical health. His neurological examination revealed some early organic brain damage.

Observations of defendant's behavior at the hospital revealed the following. "He remained aloof from other people. He seemed to be suspicious of them. * * * Basically, he would tend to withdraw from activities. He would be friendly on approach, but he would withdraw from people as soon as he could. He stayed by himself."

Dr. Truax related the following from conversation had with defendant during interviews. "When he first arrived, I questioned him concerning the murder, and as he would relate the details of his encounter with the deceased, he became very angry, his face was flushed, his blood pressure went up. * * *. Mr. Harkness felt the deceased was ridiculing him and told him to move away. He didn't. Mr. Harkness said he became very angry. He does not remember exactly what the argument was about. * * * He has been consistent in his history as he has given it to me over quite a few hours of talking. This consistency, of course, is an indication that he is telling the truth."

Dr. Truax then stated the conclusions from the psychiatric evaluation and correlated them with facts already divulged in the life history. While Dr. Truax is himself not a board psychiatrist, he was at all times concerned during the evaluation under the supervision of Dr. Noyes, a board psychiatrist, and in conference with Dr. Paul Huston, director of the hospital. Also Dr. Truax testified his views represent substantially those of the medical staff at the hospital.

"Our medical findings and conclusions concerning Mr. Harkness were that we were dealing with an eccentric, suspicious, reclusive individual who easily felt other people were out to annoy him and that he would have to defend himself from them. * * *

"Our diagnosis of Mr. Harkness' condition is that he has a paranoid personality. Individuals who suffer from a paranoid personality have many of the traits of a schizoid personality coupled with an exquisite sensitivity in inter-personal relations, and with a conspicuous tendency to utilize a projection mechanism expressed by suspiciousness, envy, extreme jealousy and stubbornness. * * * When we speak of projection, this is a method where a person attributes his own thoughts and actions to sources outside of himself. For example, a man may be extremely angry, but he does not think in terms of the 'I' am angry. He thinks 'other people are angry at me, those people out there are angry at me.' This is not something that an individual can control himself, not to any significant degree. In this case, Mr. Harknesss' condition is not treatable to any significant degree. If he were to be placed in a similar situation again most likely the same thing would happen again. There is no medical treatment that will cure this paranoid personality that Mr. Harkness has.

"*   *   *   *   *   *   *   *   *   *

"We cannot say for certain whether or not Mr. Harkness was in the mental state that he was aware of the nature and consequences of his act or not.

"He has a suspicious personality. When stressed by somebody or something that would be a minor stress to somebody else, he could easily imagine that things were happening that were not happening, and then not be able to remember this episode, but we have no proof that this happened. You see, Mr. Harkness is a man that is not totally sane or totally insane. If he is stressed enough he loses control of his thought processes. *   *   *

"Q. Now, Dr. Truax, based on a reasonable medical certainty and concerning the mental illness or defect which you described Mr. Harkness as having did he lack substantial capacity either to appreciate the wrongfulness of his conduct or to conform his conduct to the requirements of law on April 16, 1966, at the time of the alleged crime? A. On this question I cannot honestly say if he had substantial capacity or not. *   *   * I could venture an opinion, but it would be an opinion only and it would not be an opinion that would be firm enough so that I think I should give it.

"*   *   *   *   *   *   *   *   *   *"

Cross-examination brought the following testimony.

"Q. Do you have any proof that Earl Harkness has not been malingering, proof, you may have an opinion or belief, but proof? A. I have proof to the reasonable medical certainty of 85–90%.

"Toward law and order, basically Mr. Harkness seems to be a man who believes in law and order and tries to comply with it, and it has been because he is so stressed by being around other people that he gets away from people. He cannot handle his hostility. He can't handle closeness with them. He gets away from them rather than get in trouble. In this case he felt surrounded apparently by this man. He was in around the shack, but the man was also around there, and it was just too much for him.

"*   *   *   *   *   *   *   *   *   *

"We suspect defendant has cerebral arteriosclerosis with reasonable medical certainty based upon the findings of the psychological test in the fact that his blood pressure would rise to such tremendous levels with only a little bit of stress being placed upon him. Now, just what the results of this impediment to the flow of blood to his brain are we really can't say. Certainly there are other people that have cerebral vascular disease that don't commit murder. I do not wish to make that connection here. *   *   *

" *   *   *   *   *   *   *   *   *   *

"Q. Doctor, do you know what the defendant's attitude is toward shooting another human being? A. He regards killing another human being as wrong. However, although he will say this, his emotions are confused to the point where he doesn't feel toward another human being like the rest of us feel. He was able at times for instance to laugh about the situation he was in and about what he had done. His way of feeling toward other people is distorted, but yet he knows that in a legal sense it is wrong to murder somebody. He knows now as he looks back on it he shouldn't have done it.

" *   *   *   *   *   *   *   *   *   *

"It is possible for a person to be legally sane at the instance of a shooting and then immediately thereafter by reason of the traumatic experience of having participated in such an event to become psychotic. *   *   *, but a paranoid personality itself is something that is more crystalized and something that is more developed. This is something that starts out in formative years of life, and it is possible that a person after commission of a crime may develop an acute psychotic episode but a person would not develop a crystalized disorder like a paranoid personality after the commission of a crime.

" *   *   *, now again this history that he gives of his past life is far too complex a thing, a person can't fake a paranoid personality over a period of years. This is just too big a thing to fake. I don't think I could do it or a psychiatrist would have a hard time doing it if such a thing could be faked. *   *   *

" *   *   *   *   *   *   *   *   *   *

"Q. Would you say the defendant is possessed of anti-social impulses? A. Well, Mr. Harkness has aggressive impulses that he has difficulty controlling. This isn't a voluntary thing that he wants to do, anti-social things as far as we can determine. He does not fall under the category of a sociopathic personality, but he has these urges and impulses within which he has a hard time controlling, and at times he can disrupt into anti-social acts if he is stressed to a sufficient degree.

"Q. By the same token you are also saying that he has and does intend control of these impulses at least to a point? A. To a point. It depends on how much he is stressed. Certainly not anywhere near the point where most of us can.

" *   *   *   *   *   *   *   *   *   *

"Q. Doctor, would the defendant have committed an act if a policeman were looking on? A. I suspect he would have. Again this is a speculative question, but I suspect he would have.

"Q. Do you feel that if he is released he might kill again? A. Yes. If he was given weapons and allowed to be in a situation where somebody could aggravate him, it certainly could happen again.

" *   *   *   *   *   *   *   *   *   *

"Q. Doctor, would you agree that every human being has a breaking point? A. Well, I would say every human being has a breaking point perhaps that would be absolute under sufficiently adverse circumstances, but not to the degree that every person has a breaking point in everyday life. * * * Given enough stress most people will break. Most normal people would not break under the stress that Mr. Harkness breaks under."

Dr. Truax was then asked why the defendant turned himself in to the sheriff after he had shot Dale Edgington.

"A. Well, I presume again here you are asking me for a judgmental answer. I presume he shot the man—at the time when he had little emotional control, perhaps wasn't quite aware of what he was doing. After he stopped for a minute he looked back and could see this is a mistake. This is something that is against the law perhaps more than that if I run away people will be after me, so he decided to do the thing most people would do if they find out they have made a tragic mistake of this type."

Instruction 21 stated * * * in substance the M'Naghten rule.

It is fair to assume the jury placed great emphasis upon Dr. Truax's testimony that defendant knew generally the difference between right and wrong and regarded killing another human being as wrong in the legal sense. Although defendant claimed partial amnesia at the time of the shooting, when he realized shortly thereafter he had killed something he turned himself in to the sheriff's office, and now looking back on the incident realizes what he did was wrong. This, coupled with the doctor's inability to say with any degree of certainty that at the time of the shooting defendant did not know what he was doing or that what he was doing was wrong, certainly enabled if not compelled this jury, under the instructions given, to find defendant at the moment of the shooting knew what he was doing, that it was wrong, was sane and guilty.

NOTES

1. Could a jury which was conscientiously trying to apply the M'Naghten test to the facts of Harkness reach any result other than conviction? If not, is this desirable? Consider the following criticism of M'Naghten by Judge Bazelon in Durham v. United States, 214 F.2d 862 (D.C.Cir. 1954):

> Medico-legal writers in large number, The Report of the Royal Commission on Capital Punishment 1949–1953, and The Preliminary Report by the Committee on Forensic Psychiatry of the Group for

the Advancement of Psychiatry present convincing evidence that the right-and-wrong test is "based on an entirely obsolete and misleading conception of the nature of insanity." The science of psychiatry now recognizes that a man is an integrated personality and that reason, which is only one element in that personality, is not the sole determinant of his conduct. The right-wrong test, which considers knowledge or reason alone, is therefore an inadequate guide to mental responsibility for criminal behavior. As Professor Sheldon Glueck of the Harvard Law School points out in discussing the right-wrong tests, which he calls the knowledge tests:

> "It is evident that the knowledge tests unscientifically abstract out of the mental make-up but one phase or element of mental life, the cognitive, which, in this era of dynamic psychology, is beginning to be regarded as not the most important factor in conduct and its disorders. In brief, these tests proceed upon the following questionable assumptions of an outworn era in psychiatry: (1) that lack of knowledge of the 'nature or quality' of an act (assuming the meaning of such terms to be clear), or incapacity to know right from wrong, is the sole or even the most important symptom of mental disorder; (2) that such knowledge is the sole instigator and guide of conduct, or at least the most important element therein, and consequently should be the sole criterion of responsibility when insanity is involved; and (3) that the capacity of knowing right from wrong can be completely intact and functioning perfectly even though a defendant is otherwise demonstrably of disordered mind." [29]

* * *

By its misleading emphasis on the cognitive, the right-wrong test requires court and jury to rely upon what is, scientifically speaking, inadequate, and most often, invalid and irrelevant testimony in determining criminal responsibility.

The fundamental objection to the right-wrong test, however, is not that criminal irresponsibility is made to rest upon an inadequate, invalid or indeterminable symptom or manifestation, but that it is made to rest upon *any* particular symptom. In attempting to define insanity in terms of a symptom, the courts have assumed an impossible role, not merely one for which they have no special competence. As the Royal Commission emphasizes, it is dangerous "to abstract particular mental faculties, and to lay it down that unless these particular faculties are destroyed or gravely impaired, an accused person, whatever the nature of his mental disease, must be held to be criminally responsible * * *." In this field of law as in others, the fact finder should be free to consider all information advanced by relevant scientific disciplines.

29. Glueck, Psychiatry and the Criminal Law, 12 Mental Hygiene 575, 580 (1928), as quoted in Deutsch, The Mentally Ill in America 396 (2d ed. 1949); and see, e. g., Menninger, The Human Mind 450 (1937); Guttmacher & Weihofen, Psychiatry and the Law 403–08 (1952).

2. In evaluating the criticism of M'Naghten, consider the following from Livermore and Meehl, The Virtues of M'Naghten, 51 Minn.L.Rev. 789, 810–11, 814–15 (1967):

The *M'Naghten* rule has been the subject of much criticism. Consider first the claim that since modern science has shown that the mind is an integrated whole, a rule such as *M'Naghten* which is formulated in terms of the rational or cognitive functions is counterscientific. The first thing to be clear about is what we mean by saying that the mind is an integrated whole. If this rather imprecise expression is taken to mean that modern medical and behavioral science does not recognize the existence and operation of part-functions in mental life and behavior, in the sense that the mind or the person-in-action is conceived of by psychologists and psychiatrists as a kind of undifferentiated blob, the generalization is simply false as a summary statement of the teachings of these sciences. We are unaware of any theoretical formulation, however many or few professional adherents it commands, which treats of mind or behavior as an undifferentiated unity of the sort which this phrase might seem to suggest to an uncritical reader. If we examine the conceptualizations of human behavior and experience arising from such different approaches as clinical psychiatry, the statistical analysis of performance on psychological tests (differential psychology), or the experimental study of human and animal learning, we find, in spite of the vast differences in methodology and in the resulting substantive content of such theories, that they all utilize a model of the mind which postulates the existence of distinguishable processes, state-variables, part-functions, factors, intrapsychic "structures," and the like.

* * *

A second frequently voiced objection to *M'Naghten* is that "reason" is not a psychological concept. With regard to the existence of a general reasoning factor, the statistical evidence is unclear. This may be attributable to the reliance most such studies place upon psychological tests (rather than clinical manifestations) as applied to samples of subjects drawn from the mentally healthy population. When abnormal individuals compose a large part of the sample, and the data subjected to factorization are ratings by skilled clinicians based on extensive diagnostic contact, a strong factor of cognitive slippage (ego weakness, thought disorder) emerges, being reflected in high factor loadings on such phenomena as disturbances of conceptualization, perceptual distortions, illogical or unrealistic thinking, altered states of consciousness, associative dyscontrol—in short, the group of abnormalities traditionally considered evidential of a psychotic process. Such a statistical finding, of course, should not be surprising to those versed in the psychodynamic system which measures ego strength in these terms.

Even assuming that there is no such thing as a general reasoning factor in psychology, it still would not follow that the *M'Naghten* reliance on that concept would be either unreasonable or counterscientific. It is important only that the concepts used in the law be compatible with existing scientific knowledge, not that the law utilizes scientific concepts. * * *

3. A. Goldstein, The Insanity Defense 53–56 (1967) states that "there is virtually no support in law for the view that *M'Naghten* is responsible for inhibiting the flow of testimony on the insanity issue." Evidence that "seems to fly in the very face of *M'Naghten*" is admitted in practice, and the language of some courts suggests that if insanity is in issue all evidence relating to the defendant's behavior is admissible. But see Grisson v. State, 237 So.2d 57 (Fla.App.1970): "The testimony of the psychiatrist which was offered was properly excluded. It would have presented as exculpatory a mental attitude of the defendant not adequate for defense under the *McNaughten* Rule." See also Campell v. State, 227 So. 2d 873 (Fla.1969), holding that the trial court did not err in refusing to let defense counsel elicit from a defense psychiatrist testimony that although the defendant could distinguish between right and wrong, he had little control over his behavior and might not have been able to conform his acts to the requirements of law. Similar testimony, however, had been elicited by defense counsel (over the objection from the state) from a prosecution psychiatrist during cross examination.

4. The defendant in Harkness had a long history of what was apparently a "mental illness." But how important is this to an "insanity" defense? There is apparently a significant amount of general concern over the reliance by criminal defendants upon "temporary insanity" as a defense.

Insofar as the phrase "temporary insanity" has any legal significance, it seems to refer to those situations in which it is asserted that the defendant was "mentally ill"— or exhibited symptoms of mental illness—only at the time of the offense. In fact, the substance of the expert testimony may be that the crime itself was the only gross observable symptom of mental illness. It is clear, then, that "temporary insanity' is not a separate defense to liability but merely one category of situations that may arise under any formulation of the generally-applicable insanity defense. See generally Block, Temporary Insanity—First Line of Defense, 15 U.Miami L. Rev. 392 (1961), who reports that "temporary insanity" was raised in forty per cent of the capital cases tried in Florida's Eleventh Circuit in 1957. Id. at 395. Probably the main difficulty of asserting the insanity defense in a "temporary insanity" situation is the task of convincing the finder of fact that despite the absence of long-term symptoms (or any symptoms other than the offense) the defendant was in fact "mentally ill" and that the "mental illness" had the impact upon him required by the applicable criterion. There are indications that although frequently raised, the "temporary insanity" case seldom is successful. See Block, supra.

5. For comparative discussion of the various formulations of the insanity defense that present arguments favorable to the M'Naghten Rules, see Mueller, M'Naghten Remains Irreplaceable: Recent Events in the Law of Incapacity, 50 Geo.L.J. 105 (1961); Weintraub, Criminal Responsibility: Psychiatry Alone Cannot Determine It, 49 A.B.A.J. 1075 (1963).

4. ALTERNATIVES TO THE M'NAGHTEN RULES: THE "CONTROL" TESTS

---

a. IRRESISTIBLE IMPULSE

PARSONS v. STATE

Supreme Court of Alabama, 1887.
81 Ala. 577, 2 So. 854.

Appeal from city court of Birmingham; SHARPE, Judge.

The indictment in this case charged that the defendants Nancy J. Parsons and Joe Parsons, unlawfully and with malice aforethought, killed Bennett Parsons, by shooting him with a gun. * * *

The court gave the following among other charges, at the request of the state, to which defendants duly excepted: * * * "(5) If the jury believe, from all the testimony, that the defendants at the time of the killing were in such a state of mind as to know that the act they were committing was unlawful and morally wrong, they are responsible as a sane person, if the jury believe they committed the act with which they are charged."

The defendants asked the following charges in writing, which the court refused to give, and to which rulings of the court exceptions were duly reserved: * * * "(8) If the jury believe from the evidence that the prisoners or either of them was moved to action by an insane impulse controlling their will or their judgment, then they are, or the one so affected is, not guilty of the crime charged."
* * *

The jury, on their retirement, found the defendants guilty of murder in the second degree, and this appeal is prosecuted from the judgment rendered on such finding.

SOMERVILLE, J. * * * We do not hesitate to say that we reopen the discussion of this subject with no little reluctance, having long hesitated to disturb our past decisions on this branch of the law. Nothing could induce us to do so except an imperious sense of duty, which has been excited by a protracted investigation and study, impressing our minds with the conviction that the law of insanity as declared by the courts on many points, and especially the rule of criminal accountability, and the assumed tests of disease, to that extent which confers legal irresponsibility, have not kept pace with the progress of thought and discovery in the present advanced stages of medical science. * * *

It is everywhere admitted, and as to this there can be no doubt, that an idiot, lunatic, or other person of diseased mind, who is afflicted to such extent as not to know whether he is doing right or wrong, is not punishable for any act which he may do while in that state. Can the courts justly say, however, that the only test or rule of responsibility in criminal cases is the power to distinguish right from wrong, whether in the abstract, or as applied to the particular case? Or may there not be insane persons, of a diseased brain, who, while capable of perceiving the difference between right and wrong, are, as matter of fact, so far under *the duress of such disease* as to destroy *the power to choose* between right and wrong? Will the courts assume as a fact, not to be rebutted by any amount of evidence, or any new discoveries of medical science, that there is and can be no such state of mind as that described by a writer on psychological medicine as one "in which the reason has lost its empire over the passions, and the actions by which they are manifested, to such a degree that the individual can neither repress the former, nor abstain from the latter?" Dean, Med.Jur. 497.

We first consider what is *the proper legal rule of responsibility in criminal cases.* No one can deny that there must be two constituent elements of legal responsibility in the commission of every crime, and no rule can be just and reasonable which fails to recognize either of them: (1) Capacity of intellectual discrimination; and (2) freedom of will. Mr. Wharton, after recognizing this fundamental and obvious principle, observes: "If there be either incapacity to distinguish between right and wrong as to the particular act, or delusion as to the act, or inability to refrain from doing the act, there is no responsibility." 1 Whart.Crim.Law. (9th Ed.) § 33. Says Mr. Bishop, in discussing this subject: "There cannot be, and there is not, in any locality or age, a law punishing men for what they cannot avoid." 1 Bish.Crim.Law, (7th Ed.) § 383b. If therefore, it be true, as matter of fact, that the disease of insanity can, in its action on the human brain through a shattered nervous organization, or in any other mode, so affect the mind as to subvert the freedom of the will, and thereby destroy the power of the victim *to choose* between the right and wrong, although he perceive it,—by which we mean the power of volition to adhere in action to the right and abstain from the wrong,—is such a one criminally responsible for an act done under the influence of such controlling disease? We clearly think not, and such we believe to be the just, reasonable, and humane rule, towards which all the modern authorities in this country, legislation in England, and the laws of other civilized countries of the world, are gradually but surely tending   *   *   *[.]

In the present state of our law, under the rule in *McNaghten's Case,* we are confronted with this practical difficulty, which itself demonstrates the defects of the rule. The courts, in effect, charge the juries, as matter of law, that no such mental disease exists as that often testified to by medical writers, superintendents of insane hospitals, and other experts; that there can be, as matter of scientific fact, no cerebral defect, cogenital or acquired, which destroys the patient's power of self control,—his liberty of will and action,—provided only he retains a mental consciousness of right and wrong. The experts are immediately put under oath, and tell the juries just the contrary, as matter of evidence; asserting that no one of ordinary intelligence can spend an hour in the wards of an insane asylum without discovering such cases, and in fact that "the whole management of such asylums presupposes a knowledge of right and wrong on the part of their inmates." Guy & F. Forensic Med. 220. The result in practice, we repeat, is that the courts charge one way, and the jury, following an alleged higher law of humanity, find another, in harmony with the evidence.

* * *

It is no satisfactory objection to say that the rule above announced by us is of difficult application. The rule in *McNaghten's Case* * * * is equally obnoxious to a like criticism. The difficulty does not lie in the rule, but is inherent in the subject of insanity itself. The practical trouble is for the courts to determine in what particular cases the party on trial is to be transferred from the category of sane to that of insane criminals; where, in other words, the border line of punishability is adjudged to be passed. But, as has been said in reference to an every-day fact of nature, no one can say where twilight ends or begins, but there is ample distinction nevertheless between *day* and *night*. We think we can safely rely in this matter upon the intelligence of our juries, guided by the testimony of men who have practically made a study of the disease of insanity; and enlightened by a conscientious desire, on the one hand, to enforce the criminal laws of the land, and, on the other, not to deal harshly with any unfortunate victim of a diseased mind, acting without the light of reason or the power of volition.

* * *

The judgment is reversed, and the cause remanded. In the meanwhile the prisoners will be held in custody until discharged by due process of law.

STATE v. HARRISON

Supreme Court of Appeals of West Virginia, 1892.
36 W.Va. 729, 15 S.E. 982.

BRANNON, J. * * *

This "irresistible impulse" test has been only recently presented, and, while it is supported by plausible arguments, yet it is rather refined, and introduces what seems to me a useless element of distinction for a test, and is misleading to juries, and fraught with great danger to human life, so much so that even its advocates have warningly said it should be very cautiously applied, and only in the clearest cases. What is this "irresistible impulse?" How shall we of the courts and juries know it? Does it exist when manifested in one single instance, as in the present case, or must it be shown to have been habitual, or at least to have evinced itself in more than a single instance * * * We have kleptomania and pyromania, which better works on medical jurisprudence tell us cannot excuse crime where there is capacity to know the character of the act. Shall we introduce homicidal mania, and allow him of the manslaying propensity to walk innocent through the land while yet not insane, but capable of knowing the nature and wrong of his murderous act? For myself I cannot see how a person who rationally comprehends the nature and quality of an act, and knows that it is wrong and criminal, can act through irresistible innocent impulse. Knowing the nature of the act well enough to make him otherwise liable for it under the law, can we say that he acts from irresistible impulse, and not criminal design and guilt?

NOTES

1. Is there such a phenomena as "irresistible impulse?" Consider the following views:

[T]he American law of several states remain[s] bound by old-fashioned individualism. This expresse[s] itself in the seemingly logical rule of the so-called "irresistible impulse."

There is with one exception no symptom in the whole field of psychopathology that would correspond to a really ungovernable or uncontrollable impulse. That exception is an obsessive-compulsive neurosis. Compulsions are felt by the individual as acts which he would much rather not do but which he subjectively feels impelled to do—the alternative being a most unpleasant and subjectively unbearable anxiety. Yet compulsions play no role in criminal acts. Psychiatry is not a vague science. It can be stated definitely and flatly that compulsions are always unimportant and harmless acts. A patient may have to count the windows of a room or of a building, he may have to wipe off the doorknob with his handkerchief (for fear of germs), he may have to avoid stepping on the cracks of a pavement, he may have to leave the elevator on the twelfth floor and walk up to the thirteenth; but he never has to commit a truly compulsive criminal act. Obsessions, often associated with compulsions, are not acts but ideas. They also come into the patient's mind against his will and judgment. They are usually of serious nature. For example, "What would happen if I use the table knife to slash my husband's throat?" "How can I help jumping out of the window?" "What if I'd yell out loudly an obscene word in the theater just at that moment when all is silent just before the curtain goes up?" These obsessions, although it is almost impossible for the patient (before he is cured) to believe it, are never acted out.

In the whole literature of psychiatry and psychoanalysis there is not a single case where a violent act, homicidal or suicidal, constituted a symptom in an obsessive-compulsive neurosis. It is therefore always bad psychopathology to speak of a compulsive murder or a compulsive suicide.

The medico-legal theory of the irresistible impulse is advocated only by laymen and by psychiatrists who are scientifically not sufficiently oriented. It lends an air of scientific literalness and accuracy to a purely legal definition without any foundation in the facts of life or science. On account of this basic obscurity the rule of the so-called "irresistible impulse" is socially backward.

Fredric Wertham, M.D., The Show of Violence 13–14 (1950)

[C]ompulsive-crime concepts are no less "wastebasket" categories than is the "psychopathic personality" concept. * * * [T]he application of the "compulsive crime" label often accompanies the inability of either the subject or the examiner to account for the behavior in question in terms of motives which are current, popular, and sanctioned in a particular culture or among the members of a particular group within a culture. For example, one criterion, usually overlooked, for designating behavior "kleptomania" rather than "theft" is apparent lack of economic need for the item on the part of the person exhibiting the behavior. This may be observed in at least two different ways. First, the probability that the term "kleptomania" will be applied to a destitute shoplifter is much lower than the probability that it will be applied to a wealthy person performing the same kind of act. "Kleptomania," then, often is simply a shorthand way of saying, as the layman does, "That woman is rich and can buy almost anything she desires. She does not need * * * to steal. She must be crazy." * * * The economic status of the observer probably is of great importance in determining whether he thinks a person is not in economic need and is consequently compulsive. * * * If all psychiatrists were poverty-stricken, the portion of shoplifters called "kleptomaniacs" probably would be much higher than it is. * * *

Second, the absence, from the observer's standpoint, of economic need is used as a criterion for designating persons as "kleptomaniacs" in cases in which the particular articles taken appear to be of no immediate use to the subject. For example, Alexander and Staub do not consider as kleptomanic the behavior of a physician (a "neurotic" criminal) who had been taking medical books and supplies, but his "theft of porcelain figures which were new and actually of no value is more in the nature of a kleptomaniac act," and Wallerstein has stated that a case "was hardly kleptomania in the usual sense because the articles were pawned or sold for money." [28]

Cressy, Role Theory, Differential Association, and Compulsive Crimes, in Delinquency, Crime, and Social Processes 1122 (D. Cressy & D. Ward eds. 1969).

28. Alexander and Staub, [The Criminal, The Judge, and the Public] 168 [(1931)]; James S. Wallerstein, "Roots of Delinquency, Nervous Child, Vol. 2 (October 1947), pp. 399–412.

2. Professor Wechsler has noted "impressive arguments" against broadening the insanity defense by abandoning the M'Naghten test:

> The purpose of the penal law is to express a formal social condemnation of forbidden conduct, buttressed by sanctions calculated to prevent it—not alone by incapacitating and so far as possible correcting the offending individual, but also by their impact on the general imagination, i. e., through the medium of general deterrence. Considerations of equality and of effectiveness conspire to demand that sanctions which are threatened generally be applied with generality upon conviction—not that the sentence disregard differences in circumstances or in individuals but that the sentence be imposed within the framework of such formal condemnation and conviction. Responsibility criteria define a broad exception. The theory of the exception is that it is futile thus to threaten and condemn persons who through no fault of their own are wholly beyond the range of influence of threatened sanctions of this kind. So long as there is any chance that the preventive influence may operate, it is essential to maintain the threat. If it is not maintained, the influence of the entire system is diminished upon those who have the requisite capacity, albeit that they sometimes may offend.
>
> On this analysis, the category of the irresponsible must be defined in extreme terms. The problem is to differentiate between the wholly non-deterrable and persons who are more or less susceptible to influence by law. The category must be so extreme that to the ordinary man, burdened by passion and beset by large temptations, the exculpation of the irresponsibles bespeaks no weakness in the law. He does not identify himself and them; they are a world apart. This will be found to be the case in every instance where *M'Naghten* operates; with tight administration that distinguishes with care between the irresistible and unresisted impulse, it is the case under this test as well, though doubts about the possibility of such administration surely have their point. Beyond such extreme incapacities, however, the exception cannot go. This, to be sure, is not poetic justice. It is public justice, which in the interest of the common good prescribes a standard all must strive to satisfy who can, those whose nature or nurture leads them to conform with difficulty no less than those who find compliance easy. Only so can the general effort be required and maintained. If finer distinctions are in order, let them be weighed with other factors that have bearing on the nature of the sentence and the mitigations that at that point may be made.

Wechsler, The Criteria of Criminal Responsibility, 22 U.Chi.L.Rev. 367, 374–75 (1955). How persuasive are they?

3. If those persons whose ability to control their actions was destroyed by mental illness can be identified, does the "irresistable impulse" test provide an adequate method for describing them? Consider the following comments by Judge Bazelon in Durham v. United States, 214 F.2d 862 (D.C.Cir. 1954):

> The term "irresistible impulse" * * * carries the misleading implication that "diseased mental condition[s]" produce only sud-

den, momentary or spontaneous inclinations to commit unlawful acts.[42]

As the Royal Commission found:

" * * * In many cases * * * this is not true at all. The sufferer from [melancholia, for example] experiences a change of mood which alters the whole of his existence. He may believe, for instance, that a future of such degradation and misery awaits both him and his family that death for all is a less dreadful alternative. Even the thought that the acts he contemplates are murder and suicide pales into insignificance in contrast with what he otherwise expects. The criminal act, in such circumstances, may be the reverse of impulsive. It may be coolly and carefully prepared; yet it is still the act of a madman. This is merely an illustration; similar states of mind are likely to lie behind the criminal act when murders are committed by persons suffering from schizophrenia or paranoid psychoses due to disease of the brain." [43]

* * * We find that the "irresistible impulse" test is also inadequate in that it gives no recognition to mental illness characterized by brooding and reflection and so relegates acts caused by such illness to the application of the inadequate right-wrong test.

4. In Leland v. Oregon, 343 U.S. 790, 72 S.Ct. 1002, 96 L.Ed. 1302 (1952), the United States Supreme Court held that legislative adoption of "the 'right and wrong' test of legal insanity in preference to the 'irresistable impulse' test" did not violate the Fourteenth Amendment's requirement of due process of law:

The science of psychiatry has made tremendous strides since the 'right and wrong' test was laid down in M'Naghten's Case, but the progress of science has not reached a point where its learning would compel us to require the states to eliminate the right and wrong test from their criminal law. Moreover, choice of a test of legal insanity involves not only scientific knowledge but questions of basic policy as to the extent to which that knowledge should determine criminal responsibility.

Would the Court reach the same result today? Reconsider whether the Federal Constitution requires any specific test of legal insanity—or whether it requires that there be an insanity defense—after coverage of the sections following.

42. Impulse, as defined by Webster's New International Dictionary (2d ed. 1950), is:
"1. Act of impelling, or driving onward with *sudden* force; impulsion, esp., force so communicated as to produce motion *suddenly*, or *immediately* * * *.
"2. An incitement of the mind or spirit, esp. in the form of an *abrupt* and vivid suggestion, prompting some *unpremeditated* action or leading to unforeseen knowledge or insight; a *spontaneous* inclination * * *.
"3. * * * motion produced by a *sudden* or *momentary* force * *." [Emphasis supplied.]

43. Royal Commission [on Capital Punishment 1949–53,] Report 110 * * * [(1953)] [.]

b. THE AMERICAN LAW INSTITUTE'S MODEL PENAL CODE FORMULATION

MODEL PENAL CODE (TENT. DRAFT NO. 4, 1955)

Article 4. Responsibility

Section 4.01. Mental Disease or Defect Excluding Responsibility

(1) A person is not responsible for criminal conduct if at the time of such conduct as a result of mental disease or defect he lacks substantial capacity either to appreciate the criminality of his conduct or to conform his conduct to the requirements of law.

(2) The terms "mental disease or defect" do not include an abnormality manifested only by repeated criminal or otherwise anti-social conduct.

* * *

Alternative formulations of paragraph (1).

(a) A person is not responsible for criminal conduct if at the time of such conduct as a result of mental disease or defect his capacity either to appreciate the criminality of his conduct or to conform his conduct to the requirements of law is so substantially impaired that he cannot justly be held responsible.

(b) A person is not responsible for criminal conduct if at the time of such conduct as a result of mental disease or defect he lacks substantial capacity to appreciate the criminality of his conduct or is in such state that the prospect of conviction and punishment cannot constitute a significant restraining influence upon him.

Comment
* * *

The draft accepts the view that any effort to exclude the non-deterrables from strictly penal sanctions must take account of the impairment of volitional capacity no less than of impairment of cognition; and that this result should be achieved directly in the formulation of the test, rather than left to mitigation in the application of *M'Naghten*. It also accepts the criticism of the "irresistible impulse" formulation as inept in so far as it may be impliedly restricted to sudden, spontaneous acts as distinguished from insane propulsions that are accompanied by brooding or reflection.

Both the main formulation recommended and alternative (a) deem the proper question on this branch of the inquiry to be whether the defendant was without capacity to conform his conduct to the requirements of law. * * * The application of the principle will call, of course, for a distinction between incapacity, upon the one hand, and mere indisposition on the other. Such a distinction is inevitable in the application of a standard addressed to impairment of volition. We believe that the distinction can be made.

Alternative (b) states the issue differently. Instead of asking whether the defendant had capacity to conform his conduct to the requirements of law, it asks whether, in consequence of mental disease or defect, the threat of punishment could not exercise a significant restraining influence upon him. To some extent, of course, these are the same inquiries. To the extent that they diverge, the latter asks a narrower and harder question, involving the assessment of capacity to respond to a single influence, the threat of punishment. Both Dr. Guttmacher and Dr. Overholser considered the assessment of responsiveness to this one influence too difficult for psychiatric judgment. Hence, though the issue framed by the alternative may well be thought to state the question that is most precisely relevant for legal purposes, the Reporter and the Council deemed the inquiry impolitic upon this ground. In so far as non-deterrability is the determination that is sought, it must be reached by probing general capacity to conform to the requirements of law. The validity of this conclusion is submitted, however, to the judgment of the Institute.

4. One further problem must be faced. In addressing itself to impairment of the cognitive capacity, *M'Naghten* demands that impairment be complete: the actor must *not* know. So, too, the irresistible impulse criterion presupposes a complete impairment of capacity for self-control. The extremity of these conceptions is, we think, the point that poses largest difficulty to psychiatrists when called upon to aid in their administration. The schizophrenic, for example, is disoriented from reality; the disorientation is extreme; but it is rarely total. Most psychotics will respond to a command of someone in authority within the mental hospital; they thus have some capacity to conform to a norm. But this is very different from the question whether they have the capacity to conform to requirements that are not thus immediately symbolized by an attendant or policeman at the elbow. Nothing makes the inquiry into responsibility more unreal for the psychiatrist than limitation of the issue to some ultimate extreme of total incapacity, when clinical experience reveals only a graded scale with marks along the way. * * *

We think this difficulty can and must be met. The law must recognize that when there is no black and white it must content itself with different shades of gray. The draft, accordingly, does not demand *complete* impairment of capacity. It asks instead for *substantial* impairment. This is all, we think, that candid witnesses, called on to infer the nature of the situation at a time that they did not observe, can ever confidently say, even when they know that a disorder was extreme.

If substantial impairment of capacity is to suffice, there remains the question whether this alone should be the test or whether the criterion should state the principle that measures how substantial it must be. To identify the degree of impairment with precision is, of course, impossible both verbally and logically. The recommended formulation is content to rest upon the term "substantial" to support the weight of judgment; if capacity is greatly impaired, that presumably should be sufficient. Alternative (a) proposes to submit the issue squarely to the jury's sense of justice, asking expressly whether the capacity of the defendant "was so substantially impaired that he can not justly be held responsible." Some members of the Council deemed it unwise to present questions of justice to the jury, preferring a submission that in form, at least, confines the inquiry to fact. The proponents of the alternative contend that since the jury normally will feel that it is only just to exculpate if the disorder was extreme, that otherwise conviction is demanded, it is safer to invoke the jury's sense of justice than to rest entirely on the single word "substantial", imputing no specific measure of degree. The issue is an important one and it is submitted for consideration by the Institute.

* * *

Paragraph (2) of section 4.01 is designed to exclude from the concept of "mental disease or defect" the case of so-called "psychopathic personality." The reason for the exclusion is that, as the Royal Commission put it, psychopathy "is a statistical abnormality; that is to say, the psychopath differs from a normal person only quantitatively or in degree, not qualitatively; and the diagnosis of psychopathic personality does not carry with it any explanation of the causes of the abnormality." While it may not be feasible to formulate a definition of "disease", there is much to be said for excluding a condition that is manifested only by the behavior phenomena that must, by hypothesis, be the result of disease for irresponsibility to be established. Although British psychiatrists have agreed, on the whole, that psychopathy should not be called "disease", there is considerable difference of opinion on the point in the United States. Yet it does not seem useful to contemplate the litigation of what is essentially a matter of terminology; nor is it right to have the legal result rest upon the resolution of a dispute of this kind.

MODEL PENAL CODE (P.O.D. 1962)

Article 4. Responsibility

Section 4.01. Mental Disease or Defect Excluding Responsibility

(1) A person is not responsible for criminal conduct if at the time of such conduct as a result of mental disease or defect he lacks

substantial capacity either to appreciate the criminality [wrongfulness] of his conduct or to conform his conduct to the requirements of law.

(2) As used in this Article, the terms "mental disease or defect" do not include an abnormality manifested only by repeated criminal or otherwise anti-social conduct.

---

c. THE FACTUAL INQUIRY INTO ABILITY TO CONTROL

UNITED STATES v. POLLARD

United States District Court for the Eastern District of Michigan, 1959.
171 F.Supp. 474, set aside 282 F.2d 450, mandate clarified 285 F.2d 81.

LEVIN, District Judge. The defendant, Marmion Pollard, having waived indictment, the Government instituted this prosecution on a three-count information charging him, under Section 2113(d), Title 18 U.S.C.A., with the attempted robbery of the Chene-Medbury Branch of the Bank of the Commonwealth and the 24th-Michigan Branch of the Detroit Bank & Trust Company on May 21, 1958, and the attempted robbery on June 3, 1958, of the Woodrow Wilson-Davison Branch of the Bank of the Commonwealth. These banks, members of the Federal Reserve System and insured by the Federal Deposit Insurance Corporation, are located in Detroit, Michigan.

On arraignment, the accused pleaded guilty before another judge of this Court. Subsequently, upon advice of counsel, he moved to set aside the guilty plea on the ground that he was insane at the time he committed the acts upon which the prosecution was based. The Court, with the acquiescence of the Government, permitted the defendant to withdraw his guilty plea, and a plea of not guilty was entered. The case was then assigned to me for trial.

Prior to trial, I was advised that a psychiatric report of a psychiatrist retained by the defendant indicated that the defendant was, at the time of the offenses, suffering from a diseased mind which produced an irresistible impulse to commit the criminal acts. Subsequently, a report was submitted to the Government by each of two psychiatrists who had examined the defendant at its request. These reports, which were made available to me, agreed with the conclusion of the defendant's psychiatrist. It then appeared to me that it would be in the interest of justice to secure a psychiatric evaluation of defendant's state of mind based upon more extensive study. I was particularly desirous of having such a study made inasmuch as the psychiatric reports submitted to me were based on interviews that did not exceed a maximum of two hours with each of the three psychiatrists. I, thereupon, on October 10, 1958, entered an order that the defendant be sent to the United States Medical Center at Springfield, Missouri. After a study of thirty days, the Medical Center submitted a report which was introduced in evidence. The gist of the report may be set out as follows:

During the period under inquiry, "a dissociative state may have existed and that his [defendant's] actions may not have been consciously motivated.

"It is, therefore, our opinion that during the period in question, Pollard, while intellectually capable of knowing right from wrong, may have been governed by unconscious drives which made it impossible for him to adhere to the right.

" * * * We readily acknowledge our inability either to marshal sufficient objective facts or formulate a completely satisfactory theory on which to base a solid opinion as to subject's responsibility during the period in question." [1]

The defendant elected to be tried by the Court without a jury. During the trial, the following facts appeared:

The defendant is an intelligent, twenty-nine year old man. In 1949, he married and, during the next four years, three sons and a daughter were born of this marriage. He was apparently a well-adjusted, happy, family man. In 1952, he became a member of the Police Department of the City of Detroit and continued to work as a policeman until he was apprehended for the acts for which he is now being prosecuted. In April, 1956, his wife and infant daughter were brutally killed in an unprovoked attack by a drunken neighbor.

On May 21, 1958, one day before he remarried, at about 11:00 A.M., defendant entered the 24th-Michigan Branch of the Detroit Bank & Trust Company. He paused for a few moments to look over the bank and then proceeded to an enclosure in which a bank official was at work. He told the official, whom he believed to be the manager, that he wanted to open a savings account. He then walked through a swinging gate into the enclosure, sat down at the desk, pulled out a gun and pointed it at the official. He ordered the official to call a teller. When the teller arrived, the defendant handed a brown paper grocery bag to him and told him to fill it with money. While it was being filled, defendant kept the bank official covered. The teller filled the bag with money as ordered and turned it over to the defendant. Thereupon, defendant ordered the bank official to accompany him to the exit. As both the defendant and bank official

1. Not only is this report, in the light most favorable to the defendant, inconclusive but in part is based upon facts which were not substantiated during the trial. The personal and social history section of the report states that after his wife's death "it was noted by his supervisors that he [defendant] became less efficient, less interested, more withdrawn and a noticeably less effective policeman". However, the police department records introduced in evidence reveal that the defendant's police work covering the period of inquiry, if anything, was more effective than his service prior to the death of his wife.

approached the exit, the official suddenly wrapped his arms around the defendant, who then dropped the bag and fled from the bank and escaped.

About 4:00 P.M., on the same day, he entered the Chene-Medbury Branch of the Bank of the Commonwealth and walked to a railing behind which a bank employee was sitting. He pointed his gun at the man and told him to sit quietly. The employee, however, did not obey this order but instead raised an alarm, whereupon the defendant ran from the bank and again escaped.

After the defendant was apprehended by the Detroit Police under circumstances which I shall later relate, he admitted to agents of the Federal Bureau of Investigation that after his abortive attempts to rob the two banks, he decided to rob a third bank and actually proceeded on the same day to an unnamed bank he had selected but decided not to make the attempt when he discovered that the bank was "too wide open"—had too much window area so that the possibility of apprehension was enhanced.

On June 3, at about 3:00 P.M., the defendant entered the Woodrow Wilson-Davison Branch of the Bank of the Commonwealth and went directly to an enclosure behind which a male and female employee were sitting at desks facing each other. Defendant held his gun under a jacket which he carried over his right arm. He ordered the woman employee to come out from behind the railing. In doing so, she grasped the edge of her desk. Defendant, in the belief that she may have pushed an alarm button, decided to leave but ordered the woman to accompany him out of the bank. When they reached the street, he told her to walk ahead of him, but not to attract attention. Defendant noticed a police car approaching the bank and waited until it passed him, then ran across an empty lot to his car and again escaped.

On June 11, 1958, he attempted to hold up a grocery market. He was thwarted in the attempt when the proprietor screamed and, becoming frightened, the defendant fled. In so doing, he abandoned his automobile in back of the market where he had parked it during the holdup attempt. Routinely, this car was placed under surveillance and later when the defendant, dressed in his Detroit Police Officer's uniform, attempted to get in it, he was arrested by detectives of the Detroit Police Force.

After his apprehension, the defendant confessed to eleven other robberies, or attempted robberies.

The three psychiatrists who submitted the written reports, all qualified and respected members of their profession, testified that in their opinion the defendant, at the time he committed the criminal acts, knew the difference between right and wrong and knew that the acts he committed were wrong but was suffering from a "traumatic neurosis" or "dissociative reaction", characterized by moods of depression and severe feelings of guilt, induced by the traumatic effect of the death of his wife and child and his belief that he was responsible for their deaths because by his absence from home he left them exposed to the actions of the crazed, drunken neighbor. They further stated that he had an unconscious desire to be punished by society to expiate these guilt feelings and that the governing power of his mind was so destroyed or impaired that he was unable to resist the commission of the criminal acts. In their opinion, however, the defendant was not then, nor is he now, psychotic or committable to a mental institution.

Three of defendant's fellow police officers, called as defense witnesses, testified that during the period in which the defendant committed the criminal acts he had a tendency to be late for work; that at times he was despondent; and that he occasionally seemed to be lost in thought and did not promptly respond to questions directed to him. One of the officers testified that on one occasion, he repeatedly beat the steering wheel of the police car in which they were riding, while at the same time reiterating the name of his murdered wife. However, none of them found his conduct or moods to be of such consequence that they believed it necessary to report the defendant to a superior officer.

Defendant's present wife, who impressed me as an intelligent person, testified that on two occasions defendant suddenly, and for no reason apparent to her, lapsed into crying spells and that he talked to her once or twice about committing suicide. She also testified that during one such period of depression he pointed a gun at himself; that she became frightened and called the police; that the police came, relieved him of his gun, and took him to the precinct police station; and that after his release he appeared jovial and acted as if nothing had happened. Defendant's brother-in-law stated that the defendant had always been a very happy person but that he became noticeably despondent after the death of his wife and child and expressed a desire to commit suicide because he now no longer had a reason for living.

A police lieutenant of the Detroit Police Department testified that the defendant's police work, during the period with which we are now concerned, as evidenced by his efficiency rating and his written duty reports, was, if anything, more effective than his service prior to the death of his wife.

Counsel for defendant contends that since all the medical testimony was to the effect that the defendant was suffering from an irresistible impulse at the time of the commission of the offenses, this Court must accept this uncontroverted expert testimony and find him not guilty by reason of insanity.

* * *

I have great respect for the profession of psychiatry. Vast areas of information have been made available through its efforts. I have found much comfort in having the assistance of psychiatrists in the disposition of many cases on sentence. Yet, there are compelling reasons for not blindly following the opinions of experts on controlling issues of fact. Expert testimony performs a valuable function in explaining complex and specialized data to the untutored lay mind. When the experts have made available their knowledge to aid the jury or the Court in reaching a conclusion, their function is completed. The opinions and judgments or inferences of experts, even when unanimous and uncontroverted, are not necessarily conclusive on the trier of the facts and may be disregarded when, in the light of the facts adduced, such judgments, opinions or inferences do not appear valid. The jury, in determining the probative effect to be given to expert testimony, is not to disregard its own experience and knowledge and its collective conscience. It follows that this is also true of the judge sitting without a jury.

The psychiatrists, as I hereinbefore related, testified that the defendant suffered from severe feelings of depression and guilt; and that in their opinion he had an irresistible impulse to commit criminal acts, an unconscious desire to be apprehended and punished; and that he geared his behavior to the accomplishment of this end. However, his entire pattern of conduct during the period of his criminal activities militates against this conclusion. His conscious desire not to be apprehended and punished was demonstrably greater than his unconscious desire to the contrary. After his apprehension, despite searching interrogation for over five hours by Detroit Police Officers and by agents of the Federal Bureau of Investigation, he denied any participation in criminal conduct of any kind. It was only after he was positively identified by bank personnel that he finally admitted that he did attempt to perpetrate the bank robberies. I asked one of the psychiatrists to explain this apparent inconsistency. In answer to my question, he stated that although the defendant had an unconscious desire to be apprehended and punished, when the possibility of apprehension became direct and immediate, the more dominating desire for self-preservation asserted itself. This explanation may have merit if applied to individual acts. However, the validity of a theory that attempts to explain the behavior of a person must be determined in light of that person's entire behavioral pattern and not with reference to isolated acts which are extracted from that pattern. The defendant's pattern of behavior of May 21, 1958, discloses that the desire for self-preservation was not fleeting and momentary but continuing, consistent and dominant. What, then, becomes of the theory of irresistible impulse? Looking to the events of that day, I am asked to believe, first, that the defendant, acting pursuant to an irresistible impulse, selected a bank site to rob, entered the bank to accomplish that end, purposely failed in the attempt and when the end he sought, apprehension, was in view, escaped because of the dominance, at the moment of ultimate accomplishment, of the stronger drive for self-preservation. I must then believe that when the defendant knew he was apparently free from detection, his compulsive state reasserted itself and that he again went through the steps of planning, abortive attempt and escape. And if I acquiesce in this theory, what other psychiatric theory explains his subsequent conduct—his plan to rob a third unnamed bank and the rejection of that plan because of his subjective belief that the possibility of apprehension would be too great? If the theory remains the same, then it appears that in the latter case, the fear of apprehension and punishment tipped "the scales enough to make resistible an impulse otherwise irresistible." Guttmacher and Weihofen, Psychiatry and the Law, 413. It is a logical inference that, in reality, the other robbery attempts were made as the result of impulses that the defendant did not chose voluntarily to resist because, to him, the possibility of success outweighed the likelihood of detection which is in essence a motivation for all criminal conduct. The impulse being resistible, the defendant is accountable for his criminal conduct.

Psychiatrists admit that the line between irresistible impulse and acts which are the result of impulses not resisted is not easy to trace. Guttmacher and Weihofen, Psychiatry and the Law. To the extent that the line may be traced, the distinguishing motivation of the action, whether the act is performed to satisfy an intrinsic need or is the result of extrinsic provocation, is a determining factor. Admittedly, motivations may be mixed. However, all the facts have clearly established that defendant's criminal activity was planned to satisfy an extrinsic need by a reasoned but anti-social method. The defendant had financial problems of varying degrees of intensity throughout his life. He had financial difficulties during his first marriage. He was now embarking upon a second marriage. He was about to undertake the responsibility of supporting not only a wife and himself, but also four children, three of them the product of his first marriage. In statements given to agents of the Federal Bureau of Investigation admitting his criminal activity, he stated: "Inasmuch as I was about to marry my second wife, I decided that I would not lead the same type of financially insecure life that I led with my first wife. I needed about $5,000 in order to buy a house. My only purpose in deciding to rob a bank was to obtain $5,000 and if I obtained the money, I did not intend to continue robbing." Defendant's entire pattern of conduct was consistent with this expressed motivation.

Life does not always proceed on an even keel. Periods of depression, feelings of guilt and inadequacy are experienced by many of us. Defendant was a devoted husband and loving father. His feelings of despondency and depression induced by the brutal killing of his wife and infant daughter were not unnatural. How else the defendant should have reacted to his tragic loss I am not told. His conduct throughout this crucial period did not cause any concern among his colleagues. All stated unequivocally that in their opinion he was sane. Significant also is the fact that his present wife married him on May 22, 1958, after a year of courtship. It is a permissible inference that defendant's conduct relative to his mental condition, as related by her, did not suggest to her that the defendant was insane.

I am satisfied beyond a reasonable doubt that the defendant committed the acts for which he is now charged and that when he committed them he was legally sane.

I, therefore, adjudge the defendant guilty of the three counts of the information.

———

POLLARD v. UNITED STATES

United States Court of Appeals for the Sixth Circuit, 1960.
282 F.2d 450, mandate clarified 285 F.2d 81.

McALLISTER, Chief Judge. * * * It is submitted by the government that whether appellant acted as a result of an irresistible impulse was a question of fact which was determinable by the trier of the facts—in this case, by the District Court, sitting without a jury, and that it properly found appellant guilty.

Appellant's counsel contends that the government did not prove appellant guilty beyond a reasonable doubt; and, further, that there was no evidence to sustain the trial court's finding that appellant was guilty beyond a reasonable doubt.

* * *

It is submitted by the government that, regardless of the unanimous testimony of six expert psychiatrists and a physician, appellant, in their opinion, acted under an irresistible impulse, and in spite of the fact that there was no evidence by experts or laymen to the contrary, the trial court was entitled to exercise its independent judgment "by weighing of the case in its entirety, as opposed to being bound by what might be considered to be uncontradicted expert opinion evidence," and to find, under the evidence in this case, that, beyond a reasonable doubt, appellant did not act under an irresistible impulse.

* * *

[A]cts that appear rational are not to be taken by the factfinder as evidence of sanity, where all of the other evidence in the case is proof of a defendant's mental unsoundness.

* * *

It is true, as the government suggests, that the Report of the Neuropsychiatric Staff Conference of the Medical Center was an opinion that Pollard, during the period in question, *may* have been governed by unconscious drives which made it impossible for him to adhere to the right, and that the staff "acknowledges [its] inability either to marshall sufficient objective facts or formulate a completely satisfactory theory on which to base a solid opinion as to [Pollard's] responsibility during the period in question." However, the staff did conclude that "the weight of objective historical evidence available to us tends to support the conclusion of previous examiners" and that the current findings indicated that during the period of the attempted robberies "a disassociative state may have existed and that his actions may not have been consciously activated."

* * *

From all of the evidence of the lay witnesses, * * * it cannot be affirmatively concluded that Pollard was sane. Obviously, as a result of the murder of his wife and child while he was absent from his home, he was suffering from some grave disorder, and that disorder was, in the opinion of all the psychiatric and medical experts, a disassociative reaction resulting in Pollard's commission of the acts charged because of an irresistible impulse.

* * *

It is emphasized by the government that Pollard was motivated to attempt the bank robberies because of his need for financial security. This, the government claims, is shown by the confession he signed, in which he stated:

> "On May 21, 1958, I was reflecting about the hard life that my first wife and I had led in attempting to achieve financial security. Inasmuch as I was about to marry my second wife, I decided that I would not lead the same type of financially insecure life that I led with my first wife. I needed about $5,000 in order to buy a house. My only purpose in deciding to rob a bank was to obtain $5,000 and, if I obtained the money, I did not intend to continue robbing."

The claimed motivation seems pointless. Pollard, during his first marriage, had been receiving the regular salary of a policeman with promotions, of approximately $450 a month. His first wife, at that time, was receiving about $300 a month as a clerk with the Michigan Unemployment Compensation Commission. Their joint income was almost twice what a regular policeman's salary would be. His second wife, at the time of her marriage to him, had money of her own—enough to pay her own bills, and take care of her daughter with the money which was paid for support by her former husband. She had previously held a position for six years with the Michigan Bell Telephone Company. She considered herself to be relatively comfortable financially. Between the time of Pollard's arrest on June 11, 1958, and his trial, she had, herself, paid off about $700 in bills that he had owed. Pollard's financial condition could not be considered a reasonable motivation for his attempted bank robberies. As far as income went, he was much better off than most other policemen and if such a financial condition could be considered a reasonable motivation for Pollard's attempted robberies, every other policeman in the department would have had twice the motivation to commit such crimes as Pollard had.

* * *

It is our conclusion from the record in this case that in the light of the unanimous testimony of the government's medical experts in psychiatry and appellant's expert witness, as well as the uncontradicted evidence of the lay witnesses, the presumption of sanity was overcome, and the government failed to sustain its burden of proving that appellant did not suffer from mental illness consequent upon the unprovoked murder of his wife and child while he was absent on police duty; and that it failed to prove that appellant did not act under irresistible impulse as a result of such mental illness.

In accordance with the foregoing, the judgment of the District Court is set aside and the case remanded for further proceedings consonant with this opinion.

SIMONS, Senior Judge (dissenting).

I greatly regret my inability to concur in the able, and thoroughly researched opinion of the Chief Judge reversing the conviction in the above case. I follow the fact findings of the District Judge and agree that they substantially sustain his conclusion that the Appellant was sane when he committed the crimes charged. Particularly am I unable to entertain the concept that the Appellant wished to be apprehended, while at the same time, yielding to an irresistible impulse to commit the crimes, and to escape detection and apprehension. I would sustain the conviction.

NOTES

1. In all cases in which a crime has been committed, the person committing it has failed to exercise control. Which failures to exercise control do—or should—have the legal effect of exculpating the defendant under the "control" tests? Is it possible to draw a reasonable line between those failures that will exculpate and those that will not? Livermore and Meehl, whose discussion of the ethical-cognition and guilt-signal components of the "knowing" process is reprinted at pages 1194–98, supra, argue that it is not:

It obviously will not do to exculpate the [defendant] simply because something impeded the activation of the e_c disposition, because that impeding something may be any of the motives and emotions which impel a man to commit wrong acts and concurrently impair his momentary ability to token a member of e_c. If nondisposition to token an e_c signal were enough in itself, then the plea 'my client didn't think his act was wrong at the time, because he hated the victim, and intensely wished him dead' would, if factually established, justify acquittal.

Livermore and Meehl, The Virtues of M'Naghten, 51 Minn.L.Rev. 789, 807 (1967). But do not the control tests assume that the definition of "mental illness" solves this problem? Is this a proper assumption? Reconsider the material on the definition of mental illness.

2. Assuming that factors other than conscious free choice may in some cases determine behavior, does the current state of knowledge of human behavior and clinical techniques make it practical to focus in particular criminal litigation upon whether a specific past act was one of those cases? Consider the following comments:

> [I]n a case where the abnormality of mind is one which affects the accused's self-control the step between "he did not resist his impulse" and "he could not resist his impulse" is, as the evidence in this case shows, one which is incapable of scientific proof. A fortiori there is no scientific measurement of the degree of difficulty which an abnormal person finds in controlling his impulses. These problems which in the present state of medical knowledge are scientifically insoluble, the jury can only approach in a broad, common-sense way.

Regina v. Bryne, [1960] 2 Q.B. 396, 404

> There is still lacking in the psychoanalytic, psychiatric or psychologic literature a simple and comprehensible statement of the problem of individual choice, decision, volition and moral responsibility which could be applied directly to the decision-making processes of the law. * * *

> About the most we feel able to agree upon—but we think it enough for practical interprofessional cooperation—is that there is ample evidence from psychoanalysis, psychiatry and the other behavioral sciences that the more free the individual is from the internal pressures of psychopathology and the less he is burdened with the detrimental forces of adverse social, economic and cultural conditions, the more he is able to make choices and decisions, to select among alternative patterns of behavior, in a manner which appears to approximate our traditional notion of free will.

Louisell and Diamond, Law and Psychiatry: Detente, Entenete, or Concomitance, 50 Cornell L.Q. 217, 220, 221 (1965).[x]

> Perhaps the earliest measure which psychiatrists utilized to assess responsibility was the degree of unreasonableness of the offender's behavior. A criminal act which seems totally alien to any goal that a rational man would pursue has traditionally been looked upon as a sign of illness. Both psychiatry and the culture as a whole are often willing to assume that the unreasonable man is a sick man and that a sick man is not responsible for his actions. De-

pending upon prevailing concepts of mental illness, a characterization of unreasonableness as sickness has often led to an assumption that unreasonable behavior is determined by external and mysterious agents. In eras when mental illness was approached from a more theological standpoint efforts were made to place the responsibility for sick behavior onto external "devils" such as incubi or succubi. With the advent of Kraepelinian psychiatry, responsibility for behavior was placed upon physical disease. Mental illness was thought of as being caused by hereditary or acquired organic impairment. It was the structural defect that was held responsible for such an individual's unreasonable behavior. Even today unreasonable behavior is often blandly described as mental illness, and that illness is characterized as a separate and pernicious external agent. We have repeatedly noted that such a demonological concept of mental illness has never been supported by scientific data and is antithetical to an adaptational or homeostatic viewpoint.

With the growth of psychoanalytic knowledge many psychiatrists have sought answers to the degree of man's responsibility in terms of the unconscious component in human behavior. They argue that if an individual behaves in an unreasonable manner because of motivations that are out of his awareness he cannot really help himself and should not be held responsible for his actions. Thus some psychoanalytic observers have argued that free will exists only to the extent that a person is aware of his motivations. According to this viewpoint, choice is available in inverse proportion to the amount of behavior or thinking which is dominated by unconscious processes.

While the author is deeply impressed with the role of the unconscious in determining behavior, he can see little value in utilizing this concept to clarify the problem of responsibility or free will. First of all, the degree to which motivation is unconscious is always relative. We have devised no means of measuring the degree to which a person is aware of his own motivations and must admit that every act carries with it a mixture of conscious and unconscious elements. We are therefore on highly tenuous grounds when we use this criterion to say that a man is responsible for one of his acts but not for another. Furthermore, the belief that out-of-awareness forces should mitigate responsibility subtly personifies the unconscious and relegates it to the role of a dangerous and unpredictable external agent. Used in this sense, it is as though the unconscious were a lurking shadow hidden somewhere in the soul of each individual, waiting only for the opportunity to commit some heinous act. This kind of thinking might lead to regrettable statements such as "It was not I who committed this offensive act but my unconscious mind." Such a notion assumes that a person's unconscious motivations are not a part of the individual in the same sense as his conscious motivations. It is in effect a denial of the existence of the person as an integrated unit.

Another way of looking at the psychoanalytic viewpoint is that an individual should not be held responsible for his actions if he is responding to internalized conflicts or misperceived oppression.

While this at first glance appears to be a humanitarian notion, it could in practice grossly discriminate against the offender who is responding to more readily observable stress. Actually, the person whose criminal behavior is primarily engendered by poverty or persecution may be motivated by forces which are just as powerful and unrelenting as those which motivate the emotionally disturbed offender. Crime may be necessary for survival in either case. If the psychiatrist can be persuaded to argue that an offender should not be held responsible for behavior which is largely determined by unconscious factors, then perhaps the sociologist should be required to argue that poverty, discrimination and delinquent associations would also make the offender nonresponsible. Either approach would be compatible with a deterministic viewpoint.

S. Halleck, Psychiatry and the Dilemmas of Crime 209–11 (1967).[y]

3. Compare the attitude of the Sixth Circuit in the instant case on the roles of juries and appellate courts in criminal "insanity" cases with that of Thurman Arnold (while a judge on the United States Court of Appeals for the District of Columbia Circuit) in Holloway v. United States, 148 F.2d 665 (D.C.Cir. 1945):

> [T]he issue of the criminal responsibility of a defendant suffering from mental disease is not an issue of fact in the same sense as the commission of the offense. The ordinary test of criminal responsibility is whether defendant could tell right from wrong. A slightly broader test is whether his reason had ceased to have dominion of his mind to such an extent that his will was controlled, not by rational thought, but by mental disease. The application of these tests, however they are phrased, to a borderline case can be nothing more than a moral judgment that it is just or unjust to blame the defendant for what he did. Legal tests of criminal insanity are not and cannot be the result of scientific analysis or objective judgment. There is no objective standard by which such a judgment of an admittedly abnormal offender can be measured. They must be based on the instinctive sense of justice of ordinary men.

> The institution which applies our inherited ideas of moral responsibility to individuals prosecuted for crime is a jury of ordinary men. These men must be told that in order to convict they should have no reasonable doubt of the defendant's sanity. After they have declared by their verdict that they have no such doubt their judgment should not be disturbed on the ground it is contrary to expert psychiatric opinion. Psychiatry offers us no standard for measuring the validity of the jury's moral judgment as to culpability. To justify a reversal circumstances must be such that the verdict shocks the conscience of the court.

4. To what extent should the law require that a verdict of guilty in a prosecution in which the defense of insanity has been raised be

y. From pp. 209–211 in Psychiatry and the Dilemmas of Crime by Seymour L. Halleck. Copyright © 1967 by Hoeber Medical Division, Harper & Row, Publishers, Inc. Reprinted by permission of the publishers.

supported by expert testimony? Consider the following comments by Judge Leo Brewster, a United States District Judge sitting as an appellate judge in Mims v. United States, 375 F.2d 135 (5th Cir. 1967):

> [W]hen evidence of insanity is received, * * * the prosecution has the burden of proving the mental capacity of the accused beyond a reasonable doubt. However, no case has been cited to us, and we have found none, laying down the arbitrary rule that an accused is entitled to a judgment of acquittal merely because he offers expert opinion evidence on the issue of his insanity and the prosecution attempts to rebut it without expert witnesses. On the other hand, one of the most generally accepted rules in all jurisprudence, state and federal, civil and criminal, is that the questions of the *credibility* and *weight* of expert opinion testimony are for the trier of facts, and that such testimony is ordinarily not conclusive even where it is uncontradicted.
>
> There is no good reason to make an exception for expert opinion evidence on insanity. It is just as subject to error as expert testimony on other matters. Psychiatry itself has progressed rapidly; but it is still a comparatively young profession dealing, not with an exact science, but with a controversial and rapidly developing one. In addition, the psychiatrist and the jury in a criminal case where insanity is an issue are concerned with entirely different questions. The psychiatrist deals with the question of the defendant's behavior problems from a clinical standpoint in an atmosphere of a physician-patient relationship. On the other hand, a jury is charged with the duty of determining from the evidence admitted in an adversary proceeding the broader question of the criminal responsibility of the accused. That issue includes the questions not only of whether the defendant had a mental defect or disease at the time of the alleged offense, but also of whether any such defect or disease, if found to exist, met the legal test of insanity, as an accused may have a mental disorder or deficiency and in some cases still be mentally competent to be held legally responsible for his crime. * * * However, even though expert opinion evidence is generally advisory in nature, it cannot be arbitrarily ignored.
>
> It has been recognized that expert opinion evidence may be rebutted by showing the incorrectness or inadequacy of the factual assumptions on which the opinion is based, "the reasoning by which he progresses from his material to his conclusion," the interest or bias of the expert, inconsistencies or contradictions in his testimony as to material matters, material variations between the experts themselves, and defendant's lack of cooperation with the expert. Also, in cases involving opinions of medical experts, the probative force of that character of testimony is lessened where it is predicated on subjective symptoms, or where it is based on narrative statements to the expert as to past events not in evidence at the trial. In some cases, the cross

examination of the expert may be such as to justify the trier of facts in not being convinced by him. One or more of these factors may, depending on the particular facts of each case, make a jury issue as to the credibility and weight to be given to the expert testimony; and in determining whether such issue is raised, due consideration must be given to the fact that the trier of facts has the opportunity to observe the witness if he testifies in person.

---

5. ALTERNATIVES TO THE M'NAGHTEN RULES: THE DURHAM EXPERIMENT

DURHAM v. UNITED STATES

United States Court of Appeals for the District of Columbia, 1954.
94 U.S.App.D.C. 228, 214 F.2d 862.

BAZELON, Circuit Judge.   Monte Durham was convicted of housebreaking, by the District Court sitting without a jury.   The only defense asserted at the trial was that Durham was of unsound mind at the time of the offense.   We are now urged to reverse the conviction (1) because the trial court did not correctly apply existing rules governing the burden of proof on the defense of insanity, and (2) because existing tests of criminal responsibility are obsolete and should be superseded.

I.

Durham has a long history of imprisonment and hospitalization. In 1945, at the age of 17, he was discharged from the Navy after a psychiatric examination had shown that he suffered "from a profound personality disorder which renders him unfit for Naval service."   In 1947 he pleaded guilty to violating the National Motor Theft Act and was placed on probation for one to three years.   He attempted suicide, was taken to Gallinger Hospital for observation, and was transferred to St. Elizabeths Hospital, from which he was discharged after two months.   In January of 1948, as a result of a conviction in the District of Columbia Municipal Court for passing bad checks, the District Court revoked his probation and he commenced service of his Motor Theft sentence.   His conduct within the first few days in jail led to a lunacy inquiry in the Municipal Court where a jury found him to be of unsound mind.   Upon commitment to St. Elizabeths, he was diagnosed as suffering from "psychosis with psychopathic personality."   After 15 months of treatment, he was discharged in July 1949 as "recovered" and was returned to jail to serve the balance of his sentence.   In June 1950 he was conditionally released.   He violated the conditions by leaving the District.   When he learned of a warrant for his arrest as a parole violator, he fled to the "South and Midwest obtaining money by passing a number of bad checks." After he was found and returned to the District, the Parole Board referred him to the District Court for a lunacy inquisition, wherein a jury again found him to be of unsound mind. He was readmitted to St. Elizabeths in February 1951. This time the diagnosis was "without mental disorder, psychopathic personality." He was discharged for the third time in May 1951. The housebreaking which is the subject of the present appeal took place two months later, on July 13, 1951.

According to his mother and the psychiatrist who examined him in September 1951, he suffered from hallucinations immediately after his May 1951 discharge from St. Elizabeths. Following the present indictment, in October 1951, he was adjudged of unsound mind in proceedings under § 4244 of Title 18 U.S.C.A., upon the affidavits of two psychiatrists that he suffered from "psychosis with psychopathic personality." He was committed to St. Elizabeths for the fourth time and given subshock insulin therapy. This commitment lasted 16 months—until February 1953—when he was released to the custody of the District Jail on the certificate of Dr. Silk, Acting Superintendent of St. Elizabeths, that he was "mentally competent to stand trial and * * * able to consult with counsel to properly assist in his own defense."

He was thereupon brought before the court on the charge involved here. * * *

His conviction followed the trial court's rejection of the defense of insanity in these words:

> "I don't think it has been established that the defendant was of unsound mind as of July 13, 1951, in the sense that he didn't know the difference between right and wrong or that even if he did, he was subject to an irresistible impulse by reason of the derangement of mind.

> "While, of course, the burden of proof on the issue of mental capacity to commit a crime is upon the Government, just as it is on every other issue, nevertheless, the Court finds that there is not sufficient to contradict the usual presumption of [sic] the usual inference of sanity.

* * *

We think this reflects error requiring reversal.

* * *

It has been ably argued by counsel for Durham that the existing tests in the District of Columbia for determining criminal responsibility, i. e., the so-called right-wrong test supplemented by the irresistible impulse test, are not satisfactory criteria for determining criminal responsibility.

[The court's discussion of the right-wrong test and the irresistible impulse test appear at pages 1206–07 and 1215–16, supra.]

We find that as an exclusive criterion the right-wrong test is inadequate in that (a) it does not take sufficient account of psychic realities and scientific knowledge, and (b) it is based upon one symptom and so cannot validly be applied in all circumstances. We find that the "irresistible impulse" test is also inadequate in that it gives no recognition to mental illness characterized by brooding and reflection and so relegates acts caused by such illness to the application of the inadequate right-wrong test. We conclude that a broader test should be adopted.

B. In the District of Columbia, the formulation of tests of criminal responsibility is entrusted to the courts and, in adopting a new test, we invoke our inherent power to make the change prospectively.

The rule we now hold must be applied on the retrial of this case and in future cases is not unlike that followed by the New Hampshire court since 1870. It is simply that an accused is not criminally responsible if his unlawful act was the product of mental disease or mental defect.

We use "disease" in the sense of a condition which is considered capable of either improving or deteriorating. We use "defect" in the sense of a condition which is not considered capable of either improving or deteriorating and which may be either congenital, or the result of injury, or the residual effect of a physical or mental disease.

Whenever there is "some evidence" that the accused suffered from a diseased or defective mental condition at the time the unlawful act was committed, the trial court must provide the jury with guides for determining whether the accused can be held criminally responsible. We do not, and indeed could not, formulate an instruction which would be either appropriate or binding in all cases. But under the rule now announced, any instruction should in some way convey to the jury the sense and substance of the following: If you the jury believe beyond a reasonable doubt that the accused was not suffering from a diseased or defective mental condition at the time he committed the criminal act charged, you may find him guilty. If you believe he was suffering from a diseased or defective mental condition when he committed the act, but believe beyond a reasonable doubt that the act was not the product of such mental abnormality, you may find him guilty. Unless you believe beyond a reasonable doubt either that he was not suffering from a diseased or defective mental condition, or that the act was not the product of such abnormality, you must find the accused not guilty by reason of insanity. Thus your task would not be completed upon finding, if you did find, that the accused suffered from a mental disease or defect. He would still be responsible for his unlawful act if there was no causal connection between such mental abnormality and the act. These questions must be determined by you from the facts which you find to be fairly deducible from the testimony and the evidence in this case.

The questions of fact under the test we now lay down are as capable of determination by the jury as, for example, the questions juries must determine upon a claim of total disability under a policy of insurance where the state of medical knowledge concerning the disease involved, and its effects, is obscure or in conflict. In such cases, the jury is not required to depend on arbitrarily selected "symptoms, phases or manifestations" of the disease as criteria for determining the ultimate questions of fact upon which the claim depends. Similarly, upon a claim of criminal irresponsibility, the jury will not be required to rely on such symptoms as criteria for determining the ultimate question of fact upon which such claim depends. Testimony as to such "symptoms, phases or manifestations," along with other relevant evidence, will go to the jury upon the ultimate questions of fact which it alone can finally determine. Whatever the state of psychiatry, the psychiatrist will be permitted to carry out his principal court function which, as we noted in Holloway v. U. S., "is to inform the jury of the character of [the accused's] mental disease [or defect]." [52] The jury's range of inquiry will not be limited to, but may include, for example, whether an accused, who suffered from a mental disease or defect did not know the difference between right and wrong, acted under the compulsion of an irresistible impulse, or had "been deprived of or lost the power of his will * * *."

Finally, in leaving the determination of the ultimate question of fact to the jury, we permit it to perform its traditional function which, as we said in Holloway, is to apply "our inherited ideas of moral responsibility to individuals prosecuted for crime * * *.' Juries will continue to make moral judgments, still operating under the fundamental precept that "Our collective conscience does not allow punishment where it cannot impose blame." But in making such judgments, they will be guided by wider horizons of knowledge concerning mental life. The question will be simply whether the accused acted because of a mental disorder, and not whether he displayed particular symptoms which medical science has long recognized do not necessarily, or even typically, accompany even the most serious mental disorder.

The legal and moral traditions of the western world require that those who, of their own free will and with evil intent (sometimes called *mens rea*), commit acts which violate the law, shall be criminally responsible for those acts. Our traditions also require that where such acts stem from and are the product of a mental disease or defect as those terms are used herein, moral blame shall not at-

---

52. 1945, 80 U.S.App.D.C. 3, 5, 148 F.2d 665, 667.

tach, and hence there will not be criminal responsibility. The rule we state in this opinion is designed to meet these requirements.

Reversed and remanded for a new trial.

NOTES

1. The initial reaction to Durham was quite favorable. See, e. g., Douglas, The Durham Rule: A Meeting Ground for Lawyers and Psychiatrists, 41 Iowa L.Rev. 485 (1956); Sobeloff, Insanity and the Criminal Law: From McNaghten to Durham, and Beyond, 41 A.B.A.J. 793 (1955); Symposium, 22 U.Chi.L.Rev. 317 (1955). A few voices were less enthusiastic. E. g., Roche, Durham and the Problem of Communication, 29 Temple L.Q. 264 (1956). For later discussions of the development of the Durham Rule, see Krash, The Durham Rule and Judicial Administration of the Insanity Defense in the District of Columbia, 70 Yale L.J. 904 (1961); Halleck, The Insanity Defense in the District of Columbia—A Legal Lorelei, 49 Geo.L.J. 294 (1960); Watson, Durham Plus Five Years: Development of the Law of Criminal Responsibility in the District of Columbia, 116 Am.J.Psy. 289 (1959). See also Symposium, Criminal Responsibility and Insanity—The Significance of Durham v. United States for Australian Courts, 3 U.W. Australia Am.L.Rev. 309 (1955). For a more recent discussion favoring the Durham Rule over the A.L.I. formulation, see Freedman, Guttmacher and Overholser, Mental Disease or Defect Excluding Responsibility, 1961 Wash.U.L.Q. 250.

2. Consider the following analysis:

[W]hat * * * is the basic significance of the *Durham case?* It is, I suggest, that the law has recognized modern psychiatry. It has taken notice of and acted upon the discoveries of psychiatry as to the enormous range, complexity, and variety of mental disorders and their profound effect upon behavior. It has repudiated, as too narrow and confined, a rule which in reality has no relation to the body of information, experience and techniques called psychiatry. This principle—the *M'Naghten* rule—that punishment should not be imposed upon one who as a result of mental disorder did not know he was doing wrong— is laudable, but it is not psychiatry. Under *M'Naghten*, psychiatry, so to speak, has made its way by stealth. It has been grudgingly admitted, for a price. The price was that it had to wear the garb of a restricted, ethical concept to which it had dubious claim and uncertain qualifications.

Under *Durham* this is changed: clearly, emphatically, cleanly and unmistakably. Psychiatry is given a card of admission on its own merits, and because of its own competence to aid in classifying those who should be held criminally responsible and those who should be treated as psychologically or emotionally disordered. It is not admitted to the courtroom merely as a handmaid of ethics, serving on the pretext that it can provide expert opinion as to whether the defendant knew the nature and quality of his act and whether it was right or wrong.

As the Court in *Durham* said, the psychiatrist will now be permitted to carry out his function which "is to inform the jury of the character of the accused's mental disease or defect." The law which previously, at best, had bootlegged psychiatric testimony of this general character, under *Durham* invites it to play a full part.

Under *Durham*, psychiatrists are not confronted with the necessity of choosing between conscience and justice. They are not faced with the unpalatable choice of prevaricating by testifying that an extreme paranoid did not know the difference between right and wrong—in which case he would probably be found insane —or of confessing that the defendant did know the difference, in which event he might be adjudged sane. They are at liberty to testify fully and honestly as to the defendant's mental condition and its meaning and implications.

Fortas, Implications of Durham's Case, 113 Am.J. Psychiatry 577, 581 (1957).[z]

CARTER v. UNITED STATES

United States Court of Appeals for the District of Columbia, 1957.
102 U.S.App.D.C. 227, 252 F.2d 608.

PRETTYMAN, Circuit Judge. Carter was indicted, tried, and sentenced to death for first degree murder. * * *

 * * * [W]ith respect to insanity the court instructed:

"As to the second requirement, that the act in question was the product of the mental abnormality, you may wonder what the Court means by the term 'product.'

"By this term 'product' or 'causal connection,' you are told that the criminal act must be the consequence, a growth, natural result or substantive end of a mental abnormality or unsoundness in order for the defendant to avail himself of the defense of insanity.

"The criminal act of the defendant, if you find he did the act, must have resulted or been produced by the unsoundness of his mental condition, not in a minor or nominal way, but in the sense of being in direct relation to and the consequence of the diseased or defective mental condition."

The foregoing instruction was not adequate or sufficiently accurate.

The phrases "product of" in Durham and "except for" in Douglas [9] were not attempts to phrase in a single expression a rule as to insanity in criminal cases. Such a single phrase would be an impossible task. The matter must be explained, not merely stated.

---

z. Reprinted from The American Journal of Psychiatry, volume 113, pages 577–582, 1957. Copyright 1957, the American Psychiatric Association.

9. Douglas v. United States, 99 U.S.App. D.C. 232, 239 F.2d 52 (1956).

The simple fact that a person has a mental disease or defect is not enough to relieve him of responsibility for a crime. There must be a relationship between the disease and the criminal act; and the relationship must be such as to justify a reasonable inference that the act would not have been committed if the person had not been suffering from the disease. There are two key factors in this defense, (1) a mental disease and (2) a critical relationship between that disease and the alleged criminal act.

* * *

When we say the defense of insanity requires that the act be a "product of" a disease, we do not mean that it must be a direct emission, or a proximate creation, or an immediate issue of the disease in the sense, for example, of Hadfield's delusion that the Almighty had directed him to shoot George III. We do not mean to restrict this defense to such cases; many mental diseases so affect areas of the mind that some or all of the mental elements requisite to criminal liability under the law are lacking. We mean to include such cases.

When we say the defense of insanity requires that the act be a "product of" a disease, we mean that the facts on the record are such that the trier of the facts is enabled to draw a reasonable inference that the accused would not have committed the act he did commit if he had not been diseased as he was. There must be a relationship between the disease and the act, and that relationship, whatever it may be in degree, must be, as we have already said, critical in its effect in respect to the act. By "critical" we mean decisive, determinative, causal; we mean to convey the idea inherent in the phrases "because of", "except for", "without which", "but for", "effect of", "result of", "causative factor"; the disease made the effective or decisive difference between doing and not doing the act. The short phrases "product of" and "causal connection" are not intended to be precise, as though they were chemical formulae. They mean that the facts concerning the disease and the facts concerning the act are such as to justify reasonably the conclusion that "But for this disease the act would not have been committed."

To the precise logician deduction of the foregoing inference involves a tacit assumption that if the disease had not existed the person would have been a law-abiding citizen. This latter is not necessarily factually true and can rarely, if ever, be proved, but in the ordinary conduct of these cases we make that tacit assumption. For ordinary purposes we make no mention of this logician's nicety.

FRIGILLANA v. UNITED STATES

United States Court of Appeals for the District of Columbia Circuit, 1962.
113 U.S.App.D.C. 328, 307 F.2d 665.

BERGER, Circuit Judge. [Defendant Helen Frigillana was convicted of murder.]

This case vividly illustrates the tangled web we have spun for ourselves under the ambiguous labels of Durham v. United States. Of seven expert witnesses who had observed the defendant, some for as much as eight years, not one could say that the mental disturbance "produced" the killing or that he could see any connection between the disturbed mental condition of the defendant and the act of killing. *But neither could they say categorically that the mental condition did not "produce" the act.*

* * *

As we see it the difficulty of the experts in this case arose in large part because they did not understand what "product" means as stated in our rule, for the term "product" has no special generally accepted meaning in medicine. And of course it has no special meaning in law. We believe this problem warrants continuing examination as our experience under the "product" test mounts.

* * * [O]nce a disease is shown to exist it is extraordinarily difficult for any psychiatrist to say or for the government to establish *beyond a reasonable doubt* that the act and the disease are unrelated. The present case eloquently illustrates that point. This is true partly because the psychiatrist, in his medical approach to the patient in the hospital, almost as a matter of course, assumes that every abnormal or antisocial act by a mentally ill person has a psychiatric explanation. As a tentative working hypothesis in the hospital, and as a diagnostic device that approach may well be valid. But our observation is that psychiatrists, when testifying *as expert witnesses*, tend to continue to *assume* that a causal connection exists whenever a mentally disturbed person commits an unlawful act.

If our objective is to excuse all mentally or emotionally disturbed persons from criminal responsibility we should frankly and honestly say that and proceed accordingly, for that is precisely where our rule, as applied, is taking us. * * *

It has sometimes been suggested that "product" is a good, solid, simple word which any layman can understand. We agree that this is true when that word is used in its usual and ordinary sense. It indeed has meaning when so used. For example, everyone knows what is meant by the statement that steel is a product of a steel mill, coal of a coal mine; that hens' eggs are a product of hens, a hangover of excessive imbibing. Our national folklore expresses this general idea in the aphorism "where there's smoke, there's fire." We understand and accept these propositions because ordinary experience in daily life has long demonstrated that they are true and we may safely act on them in forming judgments.

But does this kind of relationship exist between mental disease and crime? Are criminal acts generally and usually a "product" of mental disease or defect? If crime and disease are indeed related in the same sense that when we see smoke we can ordinarily act on the assumption that there is some kind of combustion nearby, then perhaps "product" is a safe word to rely upon. If that is not the case, "product" is not a safe word to use in this context.

McDONALD v. UNITED STATES

United States Court of Appeals for the District of Columbia, 1962.
114 U.S.App.D.C. 120, 312 F.2d 847.

PER CURIAM * * * Our eight-year experience under *Durham* suggests a *judicial* definition, however broad and general, of what is included in the terms "disease" and "defect." In *Durham*, rather than define either term, we simply sought to distinguish disease from defect. Our purpose now is to make it very clear that neither the court nor the jury is bound by *ad hoc* definitions or conclusions as to what experts state is a disease or defect. What psychiatrists may consider a "mental disease or defect" for clinical purposes, where their concern is treatment, may or may not be the same as mental disease or defect for the jury's purpose in determining criminal responsibility. Consequently, for that purpose the jury should be told that a mental disease or defect includes any abnormal condition of the mind which substantially affects mental or emotional processes and substantially impairs behavior controls. Thus the jury would consider testimony concerning the development, adaptation and functioning of these processes and controls.

We emphasize that, since the question of whether the defendant has a disease or defect is ultimately for the triers of fact, obviously its resolution cannot be controlled by expert opinion. The jury must determine for itself, from all the testimony, lay and expert, whether the nature and degree of the disability are sufficient to establish a mental disease or defect as we have now defined those terms. What we have said, however, should in no way be construed to limit the latitude of expert testimony.

NOTE

McDonald is discussed in Acheson, McDonald v. United States: The Durham Rules Redefined, 51 Geo.L.J. 580 (1963).

WASHINGTON v. UNITED STATES

United States Court of Appeals for the District of Columbia, 1967.
129 U.S.App.D.C. 29, 390 F.2d 444.

BAZELON, Chief Judge.   Appellant was convicted by a jury of rape, robbery, and assault with a deadly weapon.   His major defense was insanity.   * * *

We all agree that this court's limited role in supervising the verdict does not imply an equally limited role in supervising the evidence which is put before the jury.   To the contrary, the jury's wide latitude in deciding the issue of responsibility *requires* that trial judges and appellate judges ensure that the jury base its decision on the behavioral data which are relevant to a determination of blameworthiness.

The testimony of the defense psychiatrist, Dr. Adland, was based solely on a one hour and fifteen minute interview with defendant. Dr. Adland did not administer electroencephalogram, neurological, or physical tests, and did not have the benefit of reports of the tests given at Saint Elizabeths Hospital.   He requested permission to see them, but permission was denied.

Since the defendant was at Saint Elizabeths Hospital for two months, the two Government psychiatrists had an opportunity for more prolonged observation.   Yet both Dr. Owens and Dr. Hamman testified that they had seen Washington for approximately the same amount of time as Dr. Adland.   Of course, they did have the benefit of the testing and observations performed by others at the Hospital.   As Dr. Owens explained:

> When a patient is under constant observation, the examinations that were conducted in St. Elizabeth's by the psychiatrists, laboratory studies, psychological examinations, social service, interviews with relatives, all of this was part of the basis of my opinion that I rendered and the examination which I conducted at the medical staff conference on November 16, 1965.   * * *   By [constant observation] I mean 24 hours a day, and reports are submitted to the physicians as to their behavior, actions or activity while on the ward.

Unfortunately, except for brief references to a Rorschach test, none of this information was presented to the jury.   The Government psychiatrists claimed to have based their conclusions on these studies, but they told the jury only the conclusions without any explanation of the studies themselves, what facts the studies uncovered, and why these facts led to the conclusions.

There was other available information, as well, which the jury was not told about.   When Washington was twelve or thirteen, he was committed to Cedar Knolls, the District of Columbia School for Children. Apparently the records of that institution contained a lengthy history of Washington's childhood. At first, defense counsel moved them into evidence, but later he withdrew that request, perhaps because he thought it would be tactically unwise to make the jury read such a long report. Whatever the reason, the jury was forced to make its decision without any historical background on the defendant.

The omission of significant underlying information was one defect in the testimony. Another was that the jury was often subjected to a confusing mass of abstract philosophical discussion and fruitless disputation between lawyer and witness about legal and psychiatric labels and jargon. Dr. Hamman's entire testimony on direct examination was that Washington did not have a "passive-aggressive personality," did not suffer from any "personality trait disturbance," did not have "an irresistible impulse," was "not mentally ill," and was not "abnormal from the standpoint of psychiatric illness." A substantial part of Dr. Owens' testimony was similar.

These labels and definitions were not merely uninformative. Their persistent use served to distract the jury's attention from the few underlying facts which were mentioned. For example, the fact that Washington's difficulties "in relating adequately to other people are more severe or more extreme than the average [person's]" was immersed in a dispute about whether to classify these difficulties as a "personality defect," a "personality problem," a "personality disorder," a "disease," an "illness," or simply a "type of personality."

* * *

We all agree that more effort is needed in future cases to ensure that the issue of responsibility is decided upon sufficient information. * * *

Soon after *Durham* we found that, although the jury was being given more information, still too much emphasis was being placed upon the labels used by the psychiatrist, upon whether he concluded that the defendant did or did not have a "mental illness." * * * [S]o in McDonald v. United States we gave the terms "disease" and "defect" a *legal* definition independent of their medical meanings. We clearly separated the legal and moral question of culpability from the medical-clinical concept of illness. We hoped thereby to separate the roles of the psychiatrist and the jury, with the former stating medical-clinical facts and opinions and the latter making the judgments required by the legal and moral standard. Also, we hoped that the expert's conclusion, would not be so heavily weighted in the jury's minds if we made plain that the expert and the jury had different judgments to make.

Even after *McDonald*, though, we allowed the experts to state whether they thought the defendant had a mental disease or defect.

We assumed that the expert could separate the medical judgments which he was supposed to make from the legal and moral judgments which he was not supposed to make. It has become abundantly apparent that this theory has not worked out. Too often conclusory labels—both medical and legal—have substituted, albeit unwittingly, for the facts and analysis which underlie them. The transcript in this case illustrates that they may have served more to confuse the jury than to guide it. Also, testimony in terms of "mental disease or defect" seems to leave the psychiatrist too free to testify according to his judgment about the defendant's criminal responsibility.

The trial judge should limit the psychiatrists' use of medical labels—schizophrenia, neurosis, etc. It would be undesirable, as well as difficult, to eliminate completely all medical labels, since they sometimes provide a convenient and meaningful method of communication. But the trial judge should ensure that their meaning is explained to the jury and, as much as possible, that they are explained in a way which relates their meaning to the defendant.

The problem with labels, such as, "product" and "mental disease or defect," is even more difficult. Because these labels are employed in the legal test for responsibility, there is a danger that the psychiatric witness will view them as a legal-moral rather than a medical matter. There are two possible solutions. We could simply prohibit testimony in terms of "product" and "mental disease or defect." Or we could clearly instruct the expert to stick to medical judgments and leave legal-moral judgments to the jury.

A strong minority of this court has consistently advocated that psychiatrists be prohibited from testifying whether the alleged offense was the "product" of mental illness, since this is part of the ultimate issue to be decided by the jury. We now adopt that view. The term "product" has no clinical significance for psychiatrists. Thus there is no justification for permitting psychiatrists to testify on the ultimate issue. Psychiatrists should explain how defendant's disease or defect relates to his alleged offense, that is, how the development, adaptation and functioning of defendant's behavioral processes may have influenced his conduct. But psychiatrists should not speak directly in terms of "product," or even "result" or "cause."

It can be argued that psychiatrists should also be prohibited from testifying whether the defendant suffered from a "mental disease or defect," since this too is part of the ultimate issue. But unlike the term "product," the term "mental disease or defect" may have some clinical significance to the psychiatrist. Moreover, prohibition of testimony about "mental disease or defect" would not be a panacea. Other words and other concepts may similarly be transformed into labels. For example, in *McDonald* we spoke about "abnormal" conditions of the mind, about impairment of mental and emotional processes, and about control mechanisms. The transcript of this trial illustrates how easily these concepts can become slogans, hiding facts and representing nothing more than the witness's own conclusion about the defendant's criminal responsibility.

At least for now, rather than prohibit testimony on "mental disease or defect," we shall try to help the psychiatrists understand their role in court, and thus eliminate a fundamental cause of unsatisfactory expert testimony. A copy of the explanatory instruction to psychiatrists which we have set out in the Appendix should accompany all orders requiring mental examinations so that the psychiatrists will be advised of the kind of information they are expected to provide. To ensure that counsel and the jury are also so advised, the trial judge should give the explanatory instruction in open court to the first psychiatric witness immediately after he is qualified as an expert. It need not be repeated to later witnesses. Some of it will be repeated in the court's instruction to the jury at the end of the trial, but we think the jury should hear it in full and *before* the testimony. Although an instruction at this juncture is not usual, this court has required one in somewhat analogous circumstances.

Affirmed.

Appendix

Court's Instruction to Expert Witness in Cases
Involving the "Insanity Defense."

Dr. _____, this instruction is being given to you in advance of your testimony as an expert witness, in order to avoid confusion or misunderstanding. The instruction is not only for your guidance, but also for the guidance of counsel and the jury.

Because you have qualified as an expert witness your testimony is governed by special rules. Under ordinary rules, witnesses are allowed to testify about what they have seen and heard, but are not always allowed to express opinions and conclusions based on these observations. Due to your training and experience, you are allowed to draw conclusions and give opinions in the area of your special qualifications. However, you may not state conclusions or opinions as an expert unless you also tell the jury what investigations, observations, reasoning and medical theory led to your opinion.

As an expert witness, you may, if you wish and if you feel you can, give your opinion about whether the defendant suffered from a mental disease or defect. You may then explain how defendant's disease or defect relates to his alleged offense, that is, how the development, adaptation and functioning of defendant's behavioral processes may have influenced his conduct. This explanation should be so complete that the jury will have a basis for an informed judgment on whether the alleged crime was a "product" of his mental disease or defect. But it will not be necessary for you to express an opinion on whether the alleged crime was a "product" of a mental disease or defect and you will not be asked to do so.

It must be emphasized that you are to give your expert diagnosis of the defendant's mental condition. This word of caution is especially important if you give an opinion as to whether or not the defendant suffered from a "mental disease or defect" because the clinical diagnostic meaning of this term may be different from its legal meaning. You should not be concerned with its legal meaning. Neither should you consider whether you think this defendant should be found guilty or responsible for the alleged crime. These are questions for the court and jury. Further, there are considerations which may be relevant in other proceedings or in other contexts which are not relevant here; for example, how the defendant's condition might change, or whether he needs treatment, or is treatable, or dangerous, or whether there are adequate hospital facilities, or whether commitment would be best for him, or best for society. What is desired in this case is the kind of opinion you would give to a family which brought one if its members to your clinic and asked for your diagnosis of his mental condition and a description of how his condition would be likely to influence his conduct. Insofar as counsel's questions permit, you should testify in this manner.

When you are asked questions which fall within the scope of your special training and experience, you may answer them if you feel competent to do so; otherwise you should not answer them. If the answer depends upon knowledge and experience generally possessed by ordinary citizens, for example questions of morality as distinguished from medical knowledge, you should not answer. You should try to separate expert medical judgments from what we may call "lay judgments." If you cannot make a separation and if you do answer the question nonetheless, you should state clearly that your answer is not based solely upon your special knowledge. It would be misleading for the jury to think that your testimony is based on your special knowledge concerning the nature and diagnosis of mental conditions if in fact it is not.

In order that the jury may understand exactly what you mean, you should try to explain things in simple language. Avoid technical terms whenever possible. Where medical terms are useful or unavoidable, make sure you explain these terms clearly. If possible, the explanation should not be merely general or abstract but should be related to this defendant, his behavior and his condition. Where words or phrases used by counsel are unclear, or may have more than one meaning, you should ask for clarification before answering. You should then explain your answer so that your understanding of the question is clear. You need not give "yes or no" answers. In this way any confusion may be cleared up before the questioning goes on.

Some final words of caution. Because we have an adversary system, counsel may deem it is his duty to attack your testimony. You should not construe this as an attack upon your integrity. More specifically, counsel may try to undermine your opinions as lacking certainty or adequate basis. We recognize that an opinion may be merely a balance of probabilities and that we cannot demand absolute certainty. Thus you may testify to opinions that are within the zone of reasonable medical certainty. The crucial point is that the jury should know how your opinion may be affected by limitations of time or facilities in the examination of this defendant or by limitations in present psychiatric knowledge. The underlying facts you have obtained may be so scanty or the state of professional knowledge so unsure that you cannot fairly venture any opinion. If so, you should not hesitate to say so. And, again, if you do give an opinion, you should explain what you did to obtain the underlying facts, what these facts are, how they led to the opinion, and what, if any, are the uncertainties in the opinion.

* * *

STANFORD RESEARCH INSTITUTE, A DESCRIPTION OF ACTIVE JUVENILE OFFENDERS AND CONVICTED ADULT FELONS IN THE DISTRICT OF COLUMBIA 568, IN REPORT OF THE PRESIDENT'S COMMISSION ON CRIME IN THE DISTRICT OF COLUMBIA, APPENDIX (1966)

[Using a variety of sources, the study made an attempt to assess the mental condition of offenders convicted of criminal offenses (felonies) during fiscal 1965. These are offenders who either did not raise the insanity defense or who asserted it unsuccessfully. The results are presented in the following table.]

TABLE 62.—*Offender's mental/emotional disorder*

[Weighted composite of 932 convicted adult felons, District of Columbia, 1965]

	percent
None	63.4
Drug addiction	11.9
Nonaddicted drug user	3.1
Alcoholic	7.6
Been in mental institution	1.7
Had psychiatric treatment	2.7
History of homosexuality	3.2
Other sex deviate/offenses	1.1
Serious mental illness	1.4
Other mental problems	12.5

NOTE

This study prompted the President's Commission on Crime in the District of Columbia to comment, "Notwithstanding the *Durham* rule, many people with 'mental problems' are convicted and sent to correctional institutions rather than Saint Elizabeths Psychiatric Hospital." President's Commission on Crime in the District of Columbia 559 (1966). Of what, if, any, significance is this in assessing the *Durham* rule?

ARENS, THE DURHAM RULE IN ACTION, 1 LAW AND SOCIETY REVIEW

41, 47, 53, 47–49 (1967).[a]

This is a report on the response of government physicians, largely drawn from St. Elizabeths Hospital, to the Durham rule, particularly as reflected in the day to day development of the insanity defense.

* * *

FACILITIES

The poor of Washington depend on public psychiatric facilities for exploration of such questions as competency to stand trial and responsibility as affected by mental disease or defect.

Almost invariably an order for a mental examination entered by the District Court commits the criminal defendant to the diagnostic care and custody of St. Elizabeths Hospital. Even in the rare case in which the defendant has sufficient means to secure independent psychiatric examination, an order for his examination by the St. Elizabeths staff will usually be handed down by the court, and the defendant may be explicitly directed to cooperate with the St. Elizabeths physicians with the intimation that his lawyers may be cited for contempt if he does not.

Thus, St. Elizabeths is in all but the rarest of cases the ultimate arbiter of the existence of mental disease or defect for the people of the District of Columbia.

* * *

TESTIMONIAL PRACTICES

Most lawyers generally regard St. Elizabeths physicians as "good witnesses." These physicians gear their testimony to meet the psychological demands of the courtroom. In contrast to many private practitioners, they appear brief, succinct, and usually grammatical in courtroom testimony. Their testimony in fact often has the thrust of a good lawyer's argument on appeal. In this context, the striking fact is that St. Elizabeths physicians prefer to deliver their testimony in terms of the M'Naghten Rules, often with marked facility.

The conception of partisanship, entertained by some of the St. Elizabeths staff, has been expressed by Dr. Mauris M. Platkin, a senior physician at the John Howard Pavilion of St. Elizabeths Hospital, in these words: "Whatever the testimony of the psychiatrist, he will have previously determined in his own mind whether the defendant is suffering from a mental illness, and his testimony will inevitably be 'slanted' to lead the jury to the same conclusions as his own."

A major characteristic of such testimony is its conclusory form. Explanation of a given condition and how it arose, developed, and affected the mental and emotional processes of the defendant is minimal. Supporting data are predigested for the jury and the final conclusion of "with" or "without mental disorder" is stated with maximum emphasis.

Unlike most of the private psychiatrists encountered in the courtroom, St. Elizabeths physicians depend overtly and overwhelmingly upon the hospital record of the patient for their testimony. The hospital record is perused repeatedly in the course of their testimony both on direct and cross-examination. As one listens to their testimony one is clearly impressed with the legal virtuosity of the claim—usually of lack of mental disorder—which is propounded.

The flesh and blood individual who is asserted to be with or without mental disorder rarely emerges from such testimonial utterances. The testimony is nonetheless presented with an air of certitude which has an obvious appeal to the lay mind.

On most occasions, St. Elizabeths physicians will stress reliance upon what they describe as elaborate diagnostic studies but the quantitative character of diagnostic contacts will remain unstated except for those relatively rare occasions when opposing counsel will seek to exact specific answers on cross-examination.

Although background information as to the defendant will often be sketchy, the testimony of the typical testifying doctors drawn from the John Howard Pavilion (the maximum-security wing of St.

Elizabeths) will tend to dwell upon the various phases of a seemingly elaborate diagnostic work-up, even if the testifying witness has not participated in every such phase. It is not infrequent for such a witness to devote one-third of his testimony to describing his professional qualifications and the balance of his testimony, save for the conclusion of "with" or "without mental disorder," to describing each phase of the diagnostic work-up at St. Elizabeths Hospital—even to the mention of serology and X-rays.

The courtroom slant, as described by Dr. Platkin, is near hypnotic in impact. Hearing of X-ray studies in such a context, the average member of the courtroom audience thinks immediately of rationally relevant roentgenology—and assumes that skull X-rays have been taken. All too rarely does the bubble burst. When it does, impressive X-ray studies of the brain shrink to the standard chest X-ray of the routine "physical" on cross-examination.

The emerging legalistic virtuosity of St. Elizabeths psychiatrists' testimony is often coupled with unyielding and apparently irrational rigor. One example is provided by the Horton case. Disclosures by defense counsel of a suicidal attempt and the breaking of a window in the presence of police by the defendant—conceded to be a narcotics addict—in no way deflected a senior St. Elizabeths psychiatrist from his opinion that the defendant suffered from no mental disorder, and was in fact an "emotionally healthy" person.

A. MATTHEWS, MENTAL DISABILITY AND THE CRIMINAL LAW

55, 59–61 (1970).[b]

The insanity plea found favor with felony defendants in the District of Columbia as compared with other jurisdictions, for what seem to be three main reasons:

a) There is a better chance of succeeding with it than in other jurisdictions.

b) In comparison with other jurisdictions, the dispositional consequences of a successful defense of insanity in the District of Columbia have seemed to defendants and their counsel to be preferable to those of a criminal conviction.

b. Reprinted by permission of the American Bar Foundation, Chicago, Illinois.

c) Certain peculiarities about the civil commitment procedures in the District appear to have inhibited use of civil hospitalization as a means of diverting mentally ill persons from the criminal process.
* * *

The statutory provision that governed compulsory civil commitment in the District of Columbia in 1964 was characterized by procedural obstacles to commitment, especially the right of the proposed patient to demand and have a jury trial. The officials who interpreted these provisions in actual practice did so in the spirit in which they were enacted, so as to avoid unauthorized commitment at all cost—even to the point of keeping some severely ill persons from badly needed care.

* * *

As a result, it was difficult to get into a mental hospital at all.
* * *

[T]he Mental Health Commission has adopted in practice the standard that it perceives a jury of laymen would use in deciding such cases: committing only patients who show obvious and secondary symptoms—hallucinations and delusions. The Commission realizes that persons may be severely mentally ill and yet show no obvious symptomatology, but it believes a civil jury is unlikely to commit in these cases. Hence, it usually recommends against commitment to avoid what it considers to be the futile and bothersome task of presenting evidence it feels the jury will reject. However, even the presence of obvious secondary symptoms will not induce the Mental Health Commission to recommend commitment if a jury trial seems imminent. * * * We were also told that the Mental Health Commission had adopted an unwritten rule that "sociopaths," though definitely mentally ill, were persons who did not suffer from "secondary symptomatology" and consequently were ineligible for involuntary civil commitment in the District of Columbia.

* * *

R. SIMON, THE JURY AND THE DEFENSE OF INSANITY 203–04 (1967) [c]

The Durham rule in the District of Columbia

We compared the percentage of acquittals by reason of insanity in the District of Columbia for three years preceding *Durham* and for seven years following the *Durham* decision with the aim of an-

c. The Jury and the Defense of Insanity, Copyright © 1967, by Rita James Simon, reprinted with the permission of Little, Brown and Company (Inc.), Boston.

swering the question: Has the adoption of the *Durham* rule increased the proportion of acquittals on grounds of insanity? Table 61 lists

TABLE 61. PROPORTION OF CRIMINAL CASES IN THE DISTRICT OF COLUMBIA: PRE- AND POST-DURHAM

	Number of indictments	Per Cent of cases disposed of by pleas of guilty	Per Cent of cases disposed of by verdicts of guilty	Per Cent of cases disposed of by verdicts of not guilty	Per Cent of verdicts of not guilty by reason of insanity
		PRE-DURHAM			
1951	1400	68(956)	23(316)	9(128)	0 (0)
1952	1314	70(921)	21(279)	8(111)	.2 (3)
1953*	1446	48(696)	48(687)	4 (60)	.2 (3)
1954†	1345	64(864)	25(341)	10(133)	.6 (7)
		POST-DURHAM			
1955	1166	67(785)	23(265)	9(106)	1(10)
1956	1198	66(790)	26(305)	7 (88)	1(15)
1957	1048	65(686)	27(286)	7 (69)	1 (7)
1958	1176	64(756)	27(321)	7 (81)	2(18)
1959	1010	62(628)	28(276)	7 (73)	3(33)
1960	966	68(657)	24(236)	4 (39)	4(34)
1961‡	985	60(591)	29(286)	5 (52)	6(56)
Combined	13,054	64(8330)	28(3598)	7(940)	1(186)

* Anomalous as the figures for 1953 look, they have been checked and found to be correct.

† The year the Durham rule was adopted.

‡ We were unable to locate figures for the years following 1961.

the total number of indictments and compares them by the percentage of cases disposed of by pleas of guilty and by verdicts of guilty, not guilty, and not guilty by reason of insanity for each year.

Two facts are apparent from a first inspection of Table 61: the great majority of cases are disposed of before trial by pleas of guilty, and the number of not guilty by reason of insanity verdicts is small. In the three years preceding the adoption of the *Durham* rule, the rate of acquittals on grounds of insanity was .0016 (slightly more than one and one half per thousand). In 1954, the year of the *Durham* decision, the figure rose to .0058 (almost six per thousand). In the post-*Durham* era, between 1955 and 1961, the figure rose again to .025 (twenty-five per thousand).

By absolute standards, the number of cases resulting in acquittals on grounds of insanity compared to other verdicts is not large. But if we focus only on the magnitude of the *differences* between the pre- and post-*Durham* years, rather than on the numbers themselves, it turns out that the differences are significant; they cannot be attributed to chance. There has been a fifteen-fold increase in the proportion of defendants who were acquitted on grounds of insanity. The *Durham* rule has made a difference in the precentage of defendants who have gained acquittals on grounds of insanity in the District of Columbia. But we note also that the increase in the percentage of NGI verdicts took place at the expense of the acquittals and not at the expense of the guilty verdicts. There was no decrease in the percentage of pleas of guilty or guilty verdicts.

NOTE

The American Bar Foundation's study suggested a relationship between increasing acquittals under Durham in the District of Columbia and findings of incompetency to stand trial.

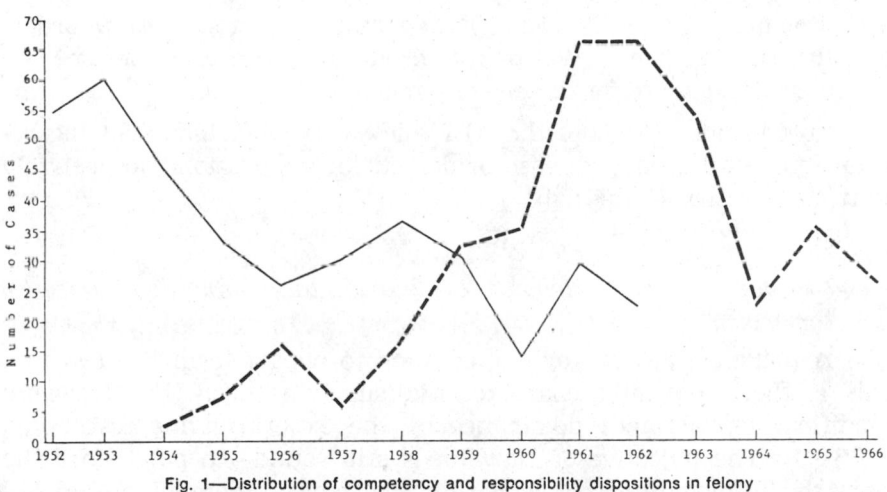

Fig. 1—Distribution of competency and responsibility dispositions in felony cases, District of Columbia, 1952–66. *Solid line,* number found incompetent; *dashed line,* number found not guilty by reason of insanity (from 1954 to 1962, includes persons previously found incompetent)

[A9019]

A. Matthews, Mental Disability, and the Criminal Law 53 (1970) (simplified).[d]

d. Reprinted by permission of the American Bar Foundation, Chicago, Illinois.

A. GOLDSTEIN, THE INSANITY DEFENSE 213 (1967) [e]

Durham's principal contribution has been less as a "solution" to the insanity problem than as a dramatic demonstration that there are no solutions. By giving the reformers their head, it has made apparent that a great deal of the criticism of the insanity defense is really misplaced—that their target is really the criminal law itself or the adversary process of trial or the complexities of modern life. The consequence has been highly beneficial. A retreat is at last beginning to be sounded from what had been almost exclusive preoccupation with the words of the insanity defense.

———

UNITED STATES v. BRAWNER

United States Court of Appeals for the District of Columbia Circuit, 1972.
471 F.2d 969.

LEVENTHAL, Circuit Judge. The principal issues raised on this appeal from a conviction for second degree murder and carrying a dangerous weapon relate to appellant's defense of insanity. After the case was argued to a division of the court, the court *sua sponte* ordered rehearing en banc. We identified our intention to reconsider the appropriate standard for the insanity defense * * *.

We have decided to adopt the ALI rule as the doctrine excluding responsibility for mental disease or defect, for application prospectively to trials begun after this date.

* * *

Need to depart from "product" formulation and undue dominance by experts

A principal reason for our decision to depart from the *Durham* rule is the undesirable characteristic, surviving even the *McDonald* modification, of undue dominance by the experts giving testimony. * * * The objective of *Durham* is still sound—to put before the jury the information that is within the expert's domain, to aid the jury in making a broad and comprehensive judgment. But when the instructions and appellate decisions define the "product" inquiry as the ultimate issue, it is like stopping the tides to try to halt the emergence of this term in the language of those with a central role in the trial— the lawyers who naturally seek to present testimony that will influence the jury who will be charged under the ultimate "product" standard, and the expert witnesses who have an awareness, gained from forensic psychiatry and related disciplines, of the ultimate "product" standard that dominates the proceeding.

* * * The more we have pondered the problem the more convinced we have become that the sound solution lies not in further shaping of the *Durham* "product" approach in more refined molds, but in adopting the ALI's formulation as the linchpin of our jurisprudence.

The ALI's formulation retains the core requirement of a meaningful relationship between the mental illness and the incident charged. The language in the ALI rule is sufficiently in the common ken that its use in the courtroom, or in preparation for trial, permits a reasonable three-way communication—between (a) the law-trained, judges and lawyers; (b) the experts and (c) the jurymen—without insisting on a vocabulary that is either stilted or stultified, or conducive to a testimonial mystique permitting expert dominance and encroachment on the jury's function. There is no indication in the available literature that any such untoward development has attended the reasonably widespread adoption of the ALI rule in the Federal courts and a substantial number of state courts.

* * *

Interest of uniformity of judicial approach and vocabulary, with room for variations and adjustments

Adoption of the ALI rule furthers uniformity of judicial approach —a feature eminently desirable, not as a mere glow of "togetherness," but as an appreciation of the need and value of judicial communication. In all likelihood, this court's approach under *Durham*, at least since *McDonald,* has differed from that of other courts in vocabulary more than substance. Uniformity of vocabulary has an important value, however, as is evidenced from the familiar experience of meanings that "get lost in translation." No one court can amass all the experience pertinent to the judicial administration of the insanity defense. It is helpful for courts to be able to learn from each other without any blockage due to jargon. It is an impressive virtue of the common law, that its distinctive reliance on judicial decisions to establish the corpus of the law furthers a multi-party conversation between men who have studied a problem in various places at various times.

* * *

ALI rule is contemplated as improving the process of adjudication, not as affecting number of insanity acquittals

Amicus Dempsey is concerned that a change by this court from *Durham-McDonald* to ALI will be taken as an indication that this court intends that the number and percentage of insanity acquittals be modified. That is not the intendment of the rule adopted today, nor do we have any basis for forecasting that effect.

We have no way of forecasting what will be the effect on verdicts, of juries or judges, from the reduction in influence of expert testimony on "productivity" that reflects judgments outside the domain of expertise. Whatever its effect, we are confident that the rule adopted today provides a sounder relationship in terms of the giving, comprehension and application of expert testimony. Our objective is not to steer the jury's verdict but to enhance its deliberation.

* * *

Broad presentation to the jury

Our adoption of the ALI rule does not depart from the doctrines this court has built up over the past twenty years to assure a broad presentation to the jury concerning the condition of defendant's mind and its consequences. Thus we adhere to our rulings admitting expert testimony of psychologists, as well as psychiatrists, and to our many decisions contemplating that expert testimony on this subject will be accompanied by presentation of the facts and premises underlying the opinions and conclusions of the experts, and that the Government and defense may present, in Judge Blackmun's words, "all possibly relevant evidence" bearing on cognition, volition and capacity.

* * *

Issue of Causality Testimony

We are urged to reverse appellant's conviction on the ground that the trial court erred in allowing Government experts to testify in terms of "causality."

The rule of Washington v. United States, 129 U.S.App.D.C. 29, 390 F.2d 444 (1967) that experts must not frame their testimony in terms of "product," was aimed at relieving a stubborn and recurring problem—that of experts using their facility with the esoteric and imprecise language of mental disease to exert an undue dominion over the jury's deliberations. The *Washington* opinion did not refer to the prior opinion in Harried v. United States, 128 U.S.App.D.C. 330, 389 F.2d 281 (1967), wherein the court stated that narrowly drawn, concrete questions addressed to the experts on the causal connection between the forbidden act and the alleged mental disease were permissible.

Since both *Washington* and *Harried* are superseded—on this point—by our change today of the ultimate rule, it would be bootless to consider to what extent *Washington* superseded *Harried*. It suffices for disposition of this case to say only: (1) Under the rule of *Harried* the questioning of Government experts on the question of the causal connection between appellant's crime and his mental disease or defect was proper. (2) Assuming, arguendo, that these questions were not consonant with *Washington* we are unable, on this record, to discern prejudice. We think the expert testimony in this case adequately and lucidly ventilated the issues, there was no use of the term "product," and we see no sign of overreaching.

The case is remanded for further consideration by the District Court in accordance with this opinion.

* * *

So ordered.

BAZELON, Chief Judge. We are unanimous in our decision today to abandon the formulation of criminal responsibility adopted eighteen year ago in Durham v. United States, 94 U.S.App.D.C. 228, 214 F.2d 862 (1954). * * * But the adoption of this new test is largely an anticlimax, for even though *Durham*'s language survived until today's decision, the significant differences between our approach and the approach of the ALI test vanished many years ago. As described in Judge Leventhal's scholarly opinion, the ALI test may make possible an improvement in the adjudication of the responsibility issue. But on the whole I fear that the change made by the Court today is primarily one of form rather than of substance.

Durham was designed to throw open the windows of the defense and ventilate a musty doctrine with all of the information acquired during a century's study of the intricacies of human behavior. It fueled a long and instructive debate which uncovered a vast range of perplexing and previously hidden questions. And the decision helped to move the question of responsibility from the realm of esoterica into the forefront of the critical issues of the criminal law. * * *

[T]he paramount cause of *Durham*'s failure is the cluster of practical obstacles that stand in the way of the full disclosure of information that *Durham* hoped to secure. Here too the Court's decision sheds no new light. For no matter how felicitous its phrasing, a responsibility test cannot, singlehanded, overcome these practical obstacles. Neither *Durham* nor *Brawner* lets slip our well-guarded secret that the great majority of responsibility cases concern indigents, not affluent defendants with easy access to legal and psychiatric assistance. In a long line of cases we have been asked to confront difficult questions concerning the right to an adequate psychiatric examination, the right to psychiatric assistance in the preparation of the defense, the right to counsel at various stages of the process, the role and responsibility of a government expert who testifies on behalf of an indigent defendant, the burden of proof, the right to treatment during postacquittal hospitalization, and many more. If the promise of *Durham* has not been fulfilled, the primary explanation lies in our answers, or lack of answers, to those questions. I fear that it can fairly be said of *Brawner*, just as it should be said of *Durham*, that while the generals are designing an inspiring new insignia for the standard, the battle is being lost in the trenches. In fact, our obligation to confront the practical problems now is greater than it was in 1954, if only because our efforts to implement *Durham* have brought many of these problems to first light.

[I]t is clear that *Durham* focused the jury's attention on the wrong question—on the relationship between the act and the impairment rather than on the blameworthiness of the defendant's action measured by prevailing community standards. If the ALI test is indeed an improvement, it is not because it focuses attention on the *right* question, but only because it makes the *wrong* question so obscure that jurors may abandon the effort to answer it literally.

Instead of asking the jury whether the act was caused by the impairment, our new test asks the jury to wrestle with such unfamiliar, if not incomprehensible, concepts as the capacity to appreciate the wrongfulness of one's action, and the capacity to conform one's conduct to the requirements of law. The best hope for our new test is that jurors will regularly conclude that no one—including the experts—can provide a meaningful answer to the questions posed by the ALI test. And in their search for some semblance of an intelligible standard, they may be forced to consider whether it would be just to hold the defendant responsible for his action. By that indirect approach our new test may lead juries to disregard (or at least depreciate) the conclusory testimony of the experts, and to make the "intertwining moral, legal, and medical judgments" on which the resolution of the responsibility question properly depends. The Court's own opinion hints at this approach, maintaining that "[t]here is wisdom in the view that a jury generally understands well enough that an instruction composed in flexible terms gives it sufficient latitude so that, without disregarding the instruction, it can provide that application of the instruction which harmonizes with its sense of justice. The ALI rule generally communicates that meaning."

The Court's approach may very well succeed and encourage jurors to look behind the testimony and recommendations of the experts. But * * * there is also a significant possibility that our new test will leave the power of the experts intact—or even make possible an enlargement of their influence. In my opinion, an instruction that tells the jurors candidly what their function is, is the instruction most likely to encourage the jurors to resist encroachments on that function. In itself, that might not be sufficient justification for adopting such a test if it were clear that its adoption would entail substantial costs as a necessary by-product. But I am unaware of any costs that compel us to adopt instead the ALI test, which offers so much less promise of dealing with the problems that initially brought this case to our attention.

Our instruction to the jury should provide that a defendant is not responsible *if at the time of his unlawful conduct his mental or emotional processes or behavior controls were impaired to such an extent that he cannot justly be held responsible for his act.* This test would ask the psychiatrist a single question: what is the nature of the impairment of the defendant's mental and emotional processes and behavior controls? It would leave for the jury the question whether that impairment is sufficient to relieve the defendant of responsibility for the particular act charged.

* * *

In a distressing number of recent cases this Court has been asked to consider questions unrelated to the substantive test of responsibility, but which have, as a practical matter, far greater impact on the operation of the defense than the language of the rule. The Court's decision to abandon *Durham-McDonald* in favor of ALI-*McDonald* does nothing to obsolete these questions or the Court's responses to them. If our paramount goal is an improvement of the process of adjudication of the responsibility issue, our attention should be focused on these questions rather than on the ultimate definition of the test. Obviously, these questions cannot all be resolved by one opinion. But the Court's approach to the disposition of this case offers some indication of the manner in which these questions will be handled in the future.

1. The one consistent note in the Court's analysis of our experience under *Durham* is the objection to domination by the experts accomplished through the productivity requirement. We attempted to deal with that problem in Washington v. United States by barring conclusory, expert testimony on the issue of productivity. Virtually all of the expert witnesses at Brawner's trial agreed that he was suffering from an abnormal condition of the mind. The issue in dispute was productivity—the ultimate issue for the jury. And the transcript is riddled with conclusory, expert testimony on that issue. It is hard to imagine a case which could make a stronger appeal for enforcement of the *Washington* rule.

The Court's unwillingness to reverse Brawner's conviction on this ground makes clear that this Court and the trial courts no longer have any weapons to combat the problem of conclusory testimony and the resulting domination by experts.

2. Since 1895 the federal courts have taken the position that if the defendant introduces "some evidence" of insanity, the issue will be submitted to the jury and the government will bear the burden of proving responsibility beyond a reasonable doubt. Davis v. United States, 160 U.S. 469, 484 (1895). Yet as the responsibility defense has developed under our case law, it has become increasingly clear that the defendant carries an overwhelming practical burden which is not acknowledged in the traditional rule. As a practical matter, the defendant often has very great difficulty obtaining adequate expert assistance to gather the information necessary for the presentation

of a significant defense. If he can obtain such information, his defense will often prove vulnerable to attack unrelated to the real merit of his responsibility claim. And even if the attack is very weak the defendant will rarely be entitled to a directed verdict.

With limited access to expert psychiatric assistance, indigent defendants normally rely on the government to provide an adequate psychiatric examination at the hospital to which the defendant is committed for observation. In a large number of cases the government's experts are called to testify on behalf of the defense, and their testimony has often proved inadequate. * * *

The practical burden on the defendant is greatly enhanced by the ease with which defense testimony can often be torn to pieces on cross-examination. Where a psychiatrist testifying for the government asserts that the defendant did not suffer from any abnormal condition which could impair his mental processes or behavior controls, defense counsel must have considerable expertise in psychiatry to pick out the weak points in the analysis. Yet "very few attorneys, if any, possess the requisite expertise, and we have no automatic procedure for enabling them to consult with psychiatric experts in the preparation and conduct of the defense." United States v. Leazer, No. 24,799 (D.C.Cir. Jan. 19, 1972), slip opinion at 14 (BAZELON, C. J., concurring). Even where the defendant has obvious symptoms of mental disorder, defense counsel is frequently helpless to rebut the suggestion by government psychiatrists that the defendant is malingering. If he produces testimony from a private psychiatrist that the defendant is not a malingerer, he is almost sure to find that the government and its expert witnesses will disparage that testimony on the grounds that it was based on an insufficient period of observation. * * *

There are other grounds on which the testimony of defense psychiatrists is extremely vulnerable. A psychiatrist or psychologist who testifies that the defendant suffered from some mental illness exposes himself to what the Court appropriately terms "know-nothing appeals to ignorance." For example, "by requiring the witness to describe in isolation the most minute 'symptoms' on which the diagnosis rests—the defendant's answer to a particular question or reaction to a particular ink-blot—the prosecution may succeed in making these symptoms seem trivial or commonplace." United States v. Leazer, No. 24,799 (D.C.Cir. Jan. 19, 1972), slip opinion at 14 (BAZELON, C. J., concurring). At Brawner's trial, the prosecutor ridiculed the testimony of a defense psychologist in his summation to the jury:

> Ladies and gentlemen, then we came to that ink blot, and the doctor said, well, the usual thing about that was those anatomical things, and how many of them were there. Well, let's see, and he counts, and there are four. How many responses? Fourteen of them. Fourteen responses and four

of them turn out to be anatomical things—hearts or whatever it happened to be. Is there something unusual about
that? Is a man crazy when he sees a heart or something else
four times, four different anatomical things or maybe the
same things in those little drawings, these little ink blots?
After all, they are just blots of ink. Is a man crazy when
he sees them?

Transcript of closing arguments at 36–37. We have seen almost identical efforts to ridicule defense experts in other cases. * * * The
difficulty of presenting credible expert testimony is a major part of
the burden on the defendant.

The defendant might be able to cope with these obstacles to the
successful use of the defense if we were willing to set aside jury verdicts unsupported by the evidence. In fact, we have been extremely
reluctant to overturn a jury verdict even in the face of substantial
evidence that the defendant's act was the product of a condition which
impaired his mental or emotional processes and behavior controls.
If the burden of proof does rest on the government, then acquittal
should be required not only when non-responsibility is proved, but also
when there is a reasonable doubt about responsibility.

---

6. ALTERNATIVES TO THE M'NAGHTEN RULES: LEAVING THE MATTER TO THE JURY'S SENSE OF JUSTICE

ROYAL COMMISSION ON CAPITAL PUNISHMENT 1949–53, REPORT (1953)

112–16 (1953).

321. This brings us to the alternative solution of dispensing
with a legal formula altogether. The assumption which underlies the
M'Naghten Rules, and would underlie any new criterion of criminal
responsibility, is that, since insanity [mental illness?] and irresponsibility cannot be taken as co-extensive, some formula must be provided
defining the relations between them. It is argued that, in the absence
of some such formula, the jury have no objective standard by which
to decide whether the degree of mental abnormality from which the
accused suffers (whether it is insanity, mental deficiency or some
other mental disease) is such that he ought not to be held criminally
responsible, and that this question cannot properly be left to their
decision without some such guidance. It is therefore the function of
the law to define the state or states of mind resulting from insanity
which justify exemption from responsibility; and the function of the

jury is limited to deciding a question of fact, namely, whether at the time of the offence the accused was in such a state of mind.

322. It seems clear from our evidence that this theory has largely broken down in practice. If the M'Naghten Rules were consistently applied, juries would be obliged to convict many persons who at the time of the offence were so insane that it would be wrong to hold them responsible. Sometimes they do, but usually such verdicts are not returned, because, unless the Judge charges them strictly in accordance with the M'Naghten Rules (and occasionally even when he does), juries exercise the discretion which the law in theory withholds from them. * * *

327. To abrogate the Rules would mean abandoning the assumption that it is necessary to have a rule of law defining the relation of insanity to criminal responsibility; the jury would be left free to decide, in the light of all the evidence given in each particular case, whether the accused was by reason of mental disease (or mental deficiency) not responsible for his actions at the time of the act or omission charged. The objection most strongly urged to this course is that it would lay on the jury a difficult, indeed an impossible, task. It was said that it would require them to decide a purely medical issue beyond their capacity, and that they could not be expected to come to a sound conclusion on technical matters, of which they had no expert knowledge, and which they could not fully understand unless they were able to apply a simple test and the problem was presented to them in terms which they could appreciate and assess as ordinary men and women. We think that this objection is put too high; that it rests on a misapprehension about the nature of the issue and on too low an estimate of the capacity and common sense of juries, which in other contexts were highly praised by many witnesses. The issue, as we have pointed out, is not a purely medical one, but is essentially an ethical question, in which both medicine and the law are closely involved. Juries have shown themselves capable of deciding extremely complicated and technical issues without the aid of definitions or formulae, for example in some civil actions in respect of technical or professional negligence, and should not be incapable of deciding the issue of responsibility in cases of insanity or mental abnormality.

* * *

Conclusions

333. Our conclusions on this part of our Terms of Reference are as follows:

> (i) (Mr. Fox-Andrews dissenting) that the test of responsibility laid down by the M'Naghten Rules is so defective that the law on the subject ought to be changed.

> (ii) That an addition to the Rules on the lines suggested in paragraph 317 [which cites a proposal that to the existing

tests should be added a provision for acquittal if the defendant, by reason of a "disorder of emotion," "did not possess sufficient power to prevent himself from committing" the offense] is the best that can be devised, consistently with their primary object, for improving them; and (Mr. Fox-Andrews dissenting) that it would be better to amend them in that way than to leave them as they are.

(iii) (Dame Florence Hancock, Mr. Macdonald and Mr. Radzinowicz dissenting) that a preferable amendment of the law would be to abrogate the Rules and to leave the jury to determine whether at the time of the act the accused was suffering from disease of the mind (or mental deficiency) to such a degree that he ought not to be held responsible.

NOTE

See Ehrenzweig, A Psychoanalysis of the Insanity Plea—Clues to the Problems of Criminal Responsibility and Insanity in the Death Cell, 73 Yale L.J. 425 (1964), who suggests that there can be no satisfactory single insanity formula or any rational criterion. Ultimately, the standard must be used to determine whether a defendant "ought" to be punished, an inquiry which differs depending on the crime being considered and which in any case is basically not a rational inquiry.

---

7. ALTERNATIVES TO THE M'NAGHTEN RULES: LIBERALIZATION OF THE M'NAGHTEN RULES BY INTERPRETATION

STATE v. ESSER

Supreme Court of Wisconsin, 1962.
16 Wis.2d 567, 115 N.W.2d 505.

FAIRCHILD, Justice. [Defendant was charged with murder. At trial, the defendant requested that the jury be instructed on insanity according to the Model Penal Code formulation. This was done, and the defendant was acquitted. Pursuant to state procedure, the trial court authorized the state to appeal on questions of law.]

Dr. Manfred S. Guttmacher, Chief Medical Officer of the Supreme Bench of Baltimore, calling attention to this problem, has stated:

"It seems to me that all that should be expected of the psychiatrist is the following:

"1. A statement as to whether the defendant is suffering from a definite and generally recognized mental disorder and why and how this conclusion was reached.

"2. If it has been asserted that the defendant suffered from a mental disorder, its name and its chief characteristics and symptoms, with particular emphasis on its effect on an individual's judgment, social behavior and self-control, should be given.

"3. There should then follow a statement of the way and degree in which the malady has affected the particular defendant's behavior, especially in regard to his judgment, social behavior, and self-control.

"4. He should then be asked whether the alleged criminal act was, in his opinion, a product of the mental disorder."

We agree that the psychiatrist should not be required to go further than as described in points 1, 2, and 3 just quoted. Point 4, it seems to us, is really a part of point 3. We do not say that a qualified expert should not be permitted to state his opinion of the effect of defendant's mental illness on his capacity to distinguish right from wrong. But neither should his opinion nor the observations on which he bases it, be excluded as of no probative value if he says he is unable to state it in terms of the accepted definition.

In State v. Carlson,[55] we said:

" * * * Even under the right-wrong test, no evidence should be excluded which reasonably tends to show the mental condition of the defendant at the time of the offense."

We reaffirm that statement. We are of the opinion that the jury will be best able to perform its function in dealing with this perplexing question if it is given all the information that qualified experts are able to give, even if such information does not fit nicely into the definition which the law has codified. For we are much impressed by the probability that no general standard can be devised that will satisfactorily fit all cases.

"Although the M'Naghten Rules are phrased in terms of cognition, they are generally interpreted broadly by the courts, with the result that all psychiatric evidence relevant to the defendant's mental condition is admitted. * * * "[56]

Courts have apparently considered that the requirement that defendant, to be excused, must be incapable of knowing the nature and quality of the act does not add anything to the requirement that he must be incapable of knowing right from wrong as to the act charged. This court so * * * stated in Jessner v. State [68] that

---

55. (1958), 5 Wis.2d 595, 607, 93 N.W.2d 354, 361.

56. Hall, [Psychiatry and Criminal Responsibility (1956), 65 Yale L.J. 761,] 774.

68. (1930), 202 Wis. 184, 196, 231 N.W. 634, 71 A.L.R. 1005.

"the two phrases express exactly the same thing, but in different language."

In a sense it may be true that one can not know that his act is right or wrong unless he can also know what the act is. If so it would follow that it would be superfluous to specify that one must be able to know the nature and quality of his act in order to be found sane in addition to stating that he must be able to distinguish between right and wrong with respect to it.

We think, however, that including the former element (nature and quality) gives important emphasis to one element of the realization of the wrongfulness of an act. Suppose that one vaguely realizes that particular conduct is forbidden, but lacks real insight into the conduct. He may be furtive about such conduct, but not really be able to make a normal moral judgment about it. Our study of the record in this case leads us to believe that this proposition is important. Although defendant Esser realized very soon after the fatal shot, first that it would be advisable to hide the victim's body, and later that he should report his act to the police, even referring to it as "murder," yet the expert testimony tends to create a reasonable doubt that he could appreciate and evaluate his act at the time he did it. Although Esser's conduct after the shooting suggests a knowledge that his acts had been wrong and therefore that he could distinguish right from wrong, the expert testimony describing his mental illness tends to show that at the time of the killing he did not understand the nature and quality of his acts and therefore could not distinguish right from wrong with respect to them.

We therefore approve the following definition of insanity for use by Wisconsin courts:

> "The term 'insanity' in the law means such an abnormal condition of the mind, from any cause, as to render the defendant incapable of understanding the nature and quality of the alleged wrongful act, or incapable of distinguishing between right and wrong with respect to such act."

The courts are not to instruct the jury * * * that the law does not recognize any form of insanity where there exists a capacity to distinguish right from wrong even though such insanity might render the afflicted one incapable of refraining from doing that which he recognizes as wrong. It seems to us that it is not wise, in view of the doubts in this perplexing field, to emphasize this negative proposition.

* * *

We conclude that it is improbable that the jury would have returned a different verdict if the court had defined insanity in the manner approved in this opinion.

Judgment affirmed.

DIETERICH, Justice (dissenting in part).

I agree with the majority of this court that no evidence should be excluded which reasonably tends to show the mental condition of the defendant at the time of the offense. The majority does not however, liberalize the M'Naghten rule sufficiently to allow instruction to the jury which would permit the jury to use the full range of evidence before it. This incongruity could, in large measure, be eliminated by the addition to the M'Naghten rule, as modified, an additional clause incorporating the irresistible impulse test. The rule as thus broadened would be more consistent with the admission of all relevant evidence of the defendant's mental condition at the time of the offense and would require instructions to the jury consistent with the evidence before it.

NOTES

1. Would Justice Dieterich's objection to the result reached by the majority be valid if the jury were carefully instructed concerning what is involved in "understanding the nature and quality of the alleged wrongful act?" Does the Wisconsin Supreme Court adopt that meaning of the word "understand" that Zilboorg gives to "know" in the following discussion:

> [The] fundamental difference between verbal or purely intellectual knowledge and the mysterious other kind of knowledge is familiar to every clinical psychiatrist; it is the difference between knowledge divorced from affect and knowledge so fused with affect that it becomes a human reality. The extreme cases of such divorcement between purely intellectual or verbal perception and full realistic perception present a clear-cut schizophrenic picture. But, not only the fully developed schizophrenic is affected with such a split between word-concept and fact. We know that compulsion neurotics, or obsessional neurotics, manifest the same clinical phenomenon, which in these cases is called *isolation*. The compulsion or obsessional neurotic 'knows' that it is foolish to keep on repeating by word of mouth or in his mind some incongruous and seemingly meaningless words or formulae which do not appear to have any value for the patient himself. Here the obsessional thought or the compulsive act are *isolated* affectively from the rest of the personality and become nonintegrated knowledge, or no knowledge at all. * * * To conceive that reason is an independent power, springing from reason only, and that it is fortified by nothing more than memory means to conceive of the human being as a combination of separate and autonomous mechanisms which act independently, all by themselves; it is almost as if we conceive of the individual as a phonograph record which may repeat time and again that it is wrong to kill and that killing means murdering. To accept this type of phonographic explanation as knowledge means to disregard everything that is human.
>
> Therefore, 'defect of reason' which the law stresses may not and, with the exception of cases of mental defectives, be within the field of reason at all, but within the field of emotional ap-

preciation. This emotional appreciation is a very complex phenomenon. It is based on a series of complex psychological mechanisms, the most potent of which is that of identification. What makes it possible for a civilized, mentally healthy human being to resist a murderous impulse is not the cold detached reasoning that it is wrong and dangerous but the automatic emotional, mostly unconscious identification with the prospective victim, an identification which automatically inhibits the impulse to kill and causes anxiety ("It is dangerous") which in turn produces the reflection: "It is wrong, the same may and should happen to me." Unless this identification is present the impulse breaks through and fear of the law and the sense of wrong is paled, devoid of its affective component; it becomes a verbal, coldly intellectual, formal, childish, infantile psychological presentation. It is not necessary to go into the number of psychological details which are not always clear and not universally accepted. What must be emphasized here is that understanding is not purely an intellectual process and that the word 'know' as it is used in the phrasing of the criminal law dealing with insanity is now used by psychiatrists in a sense totally different from that used a hundred or more years ago, that the meaning of the word 'know' was changed not suddenly but gradually, not by the arbitrary fantasies of psychiatrists but by invincible pressure of newly discovered facts about the working of the human psychic apparatus.

If such a definition of "know" or "understand" is accepted, what would be the effect in cases such as Harkness (reprinted at page 1201, supra) or (assuming the case to arise in a "control" jurisdiction) United States v. Pollard (reprinted at page 1220, supra)?

2. What, if anything, is wrong with defining the language of M'Naghten so broadly? Consider Royal Commission on Capital Punishment 1949–1953, Report 103–04 (1953):

[T]he burden of "stretching" the M'Naghten Rules, so as to avoid the unfortunate results of their strict application, falls largely and unfairly on medical witnesses. If a doctor is prepared to infer from his diagnosis of the nature and degree of the prisoner's insanity that at the moment when he committed his act of violence he was probably unconscious that it was wrong, the court will often be ready to accept that inference, although there may be no other evidence to support it, and even when the prisoner's acts or words seem to belie it. It is unfair to the medical witness to place him in a position where he is aware that his evidence as to the nature and degree of the prisoner's mental disease and its effect on his responsibility may be treated as irrelevant unless he is prepared to hazard the opinion that at the crucial moment the prisoner was probably unaware of the wrongfulness of his act. We are aware that medical evidence is sometimes unsatisfactory and open to justified criticism, but we have little doubt that its defects are often in large measure due to the impossible position in which medical witnesses are placed by what is to them the manifest absurdity of the M'Naghten test, and that amendment of the law, by relieving them of this embarrassment, would do much to improve the quality of psychiatric evidence.

8. ALTERNATIVES TO THE M'NAGHTEN RULES: ABOLITION OF THE DEFENSE OF INSANITY OR CHANGING THE DECISIONMAKER

WEINTRAUB, CRIMINAL RESPONSIBILITY: PSYCHIATRY ALONE CANNOT DETERMINE IT

49 A.B.A.J. 1075, 1078 (1963).

[T]he little we know suggests that insanity should have nothing to do with criminal accountability. Rather we should think of a conviction as simply a determination that the individual has demonstrated his capacity for antisocial behavior, and that having been proved, we ought then to draw upon medical knowledge for such help as it may offer in deciding what should be done with the offender.

MENTAL HEALTH ACT

1959, 7 & 8 Eliz. II, ch. 72, § 60.

(1) Where a person is convicted * * * and the following conditions are satisfied, that is to say—

(a) the court is satisfied, on the written or oral evidence of two medical practitioners * * *—

(i) that the offender is suffering from mental illness, psychopathic disorder, subnormality or severe subnormality; and

(ii) that the mental disorder is of a nature or degree which warrants the detention of the patient in a hospital for medical treatment * * *; and

(b) the court is of opinion, having regard to all the circumstances including the nature of the offense and the character and antecedents of the offender, and to the other available methods of dealing with him, that the most suitable method of disposing of the case is by means of an order under this section,

the court may by order authorise his admission to and detention in such hospital as may be specified in the order * * *.

A. GOLDSTEIN, THE INSANITY DEFENSE

223–25 (1967).[g]

[E]liminating the insanity defense would remove from the criminal law and the public conscience the vitally important distinction between illness and evil, or would tuck it away in an administrative process. The man who wished to contest his responsibility before the public and his peers would no longer be able to do so. Instead, he would be approached entirely in social engineering terms: How has the human mechanism gone awry? What stresses does it place upon the society? How can the stresses be minimized and the mechanism put right?

[The proposal to abolish the insanity defense] * * * overlooks entirely the place of the concept of responsibility itself in keeping the mechanism in proper running order. That concept is more seriously threatened today than ever before. This is a time of anomie —of men separated from their faiths, their tribes, and their villages —and trying to achieve in a single generation what could not previously be achieved in several. Many achieve all they expect, but huge numbers do not; these vent their frustration in anger, in violence, and in theft. In an effort to patch and mend the tearing social fabric, the state is playing an increasingly paternal role, trying to help as many as possible to realize their expectations and to soothe and heal those who cannot. As this effort gains momentum, there is a very real risk it will bring with it a culture which will not make the individuals within it feel it is important to learn the discipline of moderation and conformity to communal norms.

In such a time, the insanity defense can play a part in reinforcing the sense of obligation or responsibility. Its emphasis on whether an offender is sick or bad helps to keep alive the almost forgotten drama of individual responsibility. Its weight is felt through the tremendous appeal it holds for the popular imagination, as that imagination is gripped by a dramatic trial and as the public at large identifies with the man in the dock. In this way, it becomes part of a complex of cultural forces that keep alive the moral lessons, and the myths, which are essential to the continued order of society. In short, even if we have misgivings about blaming a particular individual, because he has been shaped long ago by forces he may no longer be able to resist, the concept of "blame" may be necessary.

However much we may concentrate our attention on the individual, we rely implicitly upon the existence of a culture, and a value system, which will enable us to move the individual toward conformity or to a reasonable nonconformity. That value system, if it is to be-

g. The Insanity Defense, Copyright ©, 1967, by Abraham S. Goldstein. Re-   printed with the permission of the publisher, Yale University Press.

come fixed early enough, must be absorbed from parents. And it, in turn, is a reflection of the larger culture, absorbed slowly and subtly over generations, transmitted by parent to child through the child-rearing devices extant in a given society. The concept of "blame," and insanity which is its other side, is one of the ways in which the culture marks out the extremes beyond which nonconformity may not go. It is one of the complex of elements which train people so that it becomes almost intuitive not to steal or rape or kill. A society which did not set such limits would probably, in time, become a less law-abiding society. This is not to say that there is not a good deal of room for humanizing the criminal law, or the insanity defense, but only that it is essential that "blame" be retained as a spur to individual responsibility.

Finally, the heart of the distinction between conviction and acquittal by reason of insanity lies in the fact that the former represents official condemnation. Yet the acquittal is itself a sanction, bringing with it comparable stigma and the prospect of indeterminate detention. If the choice between the two sanctions is to be made in a way that will not only be acceptable to the larger community but will also serve the symbolic function we have noted, it is important that the decision be made by a democratically selected jury rather than by experts—because the public can identify with the former but not with the latter. It does not follow, however, that the decision regarding the type of facility to which a particular offender is to be sent need also be made by the jury. Once the distinction between "blame" and compassion has been made, decisions as to disposition should be made by those who are professionally qualified.

NOTES

1. Consider the following comment upon the above passage:

I find statements like the above outrageous. Their inherent cynicism is incredible to me: The continued order of society rests upon the perpetuation of myths and popular dramas, upon rituals of blame and fictions of responsibility. We punish by blaming individuals irrespective of their blameworthiness. This is all right if it serves "as a spur to individual responsibility." I simply refuse to buy the theme, which Goldstein seems to be asserting, that a proper function of the criminal law is to provide sacrificial victims to support the mythologies of morality, responsibility, and justice. It is just such cynical disregard of the individual which has so frequently permitted the official institutions of the administration of criminal justice to become more immoral, more irresponsible, and more unjust than any single criminal would dare to be. So the law, through capital punishment, murders with impunity. The prison, supposedly a place for penitence and reform, becomes a cesspool of sadistic brutality and exploitation. And, as a psychiatrist I am sorry to admit, our hospitals for the criminally insane are only sham hospitals—prisons in disguise, where fake treatments are provided for imaginary ailments, perverting the healing spirit of medicine into an instrument of oppression and restraint.

Goldstein says: "The concept of 'blame,' and insanity which is its other side, is * * * one of the complex of elements which train people so that it becomes almost intuitive not to steal or rape or kill." Is it not painfully obvious that such "training" by the criminal law does not work effectively? And what lessons are trained into the minds of the people by the system of criminal justice which tolerates the penal farms of Arkansas, the mean, petty corruption of the urban municipal courts, police brutality in Selma and Oakland, and the Kafka nightmare of San Quentin's death row?

The conclusions in *The Insanity Defense* reflect the moral bankruptcy of the criminal law and the penal system. The hot issue today is "crime in the streets." The backlash of racism and bigotry reflected in this slogan have great political appeal. There is every indication that powerful political forces of reaction will not hesitate to turn the criminal law into a weapon of oppression and a device for the protection of vested power interests. What is this going to teach the black man about "the discipline of moderation and conformity to communal norms"? The unhappy truth is that the criminal law can never become an effective social force either as the embodiment of public moral values or as an educator of the individual conscience. The reason it cannot perform these tasks is that the criminal law easily becomes a tool of authoritarian control, an instrument of social oppression, and in the last analysis is only an expression of the corruption and hypocrisy of our society.

Diamond, Book Review, 56 Cal.L.Rev. 920, 922–23 (1968).[h]

2. Consider also the following commentary:

Criminal processes are, [it might be argued in support of retention of the insanity defense] public morality plays. They may also have deterrent purposes, but their primary aim is dramatically to affirm the minimum standards of conduct society will tolerate. By public ceremonial and defined liturgy, criminal trials stigmatize those who fail to conform to society's standards. In short, the criminal justice system is a name-calling, stigmatizing, community super-ego reinforcing system—a system which should not be used against the mentally ill. They are mad not bad, sick not wicked; it is important that we should not misclassify them.

The rebuttal to this defense of the defense of insanity is the fact of "double stigmatization." You will agree that some belief in the separateness and different roles of the prison and hospital systems infects the position of those who advocate retention or expansion of the defense of insanity. During the past three years I have been pursuing a sporadic unquantified, and impressionistic study of double stigmatization. This study was designed to answer the questions: Are psychologically disturbed criminals seen by prison authorities just as "criminal," and are the mentally ill who have committed or been charged with crime seen just as "mentally ill" by hospital authorities? Or are the former seen as "mentally ill criminals" and the latter as "criminal and mentally ill"? Are the systems separate or confused in the minds of the staff and of the inmates? The result of my study is that the null hypothesis is affirmed. Prison authorities regard their inmates in the facilities for the psychologically disturbed as both criminal and insane, bad and mad; mental hospital authorities regard their inmates who have been convicted—or only arrested and charged with crime—as both insane and criminal, mad and bad. While examining records in state mental hospitals I occasionally find notations in red ink to the effect that this person has been arrested for a crime. Discussion with the relevant authorities reveals that the red ink notation seriously influences the date of his likely discharge. Note that an arrest without a conviction has this effect.

Morris, Psychiatry and the Dangerous Criminal, 41 S.Cal.L.Rev. 514, 524–25 (1968).

3. To what extent does the following provide support for the argument that the insanity defense should be abolished:

I believe there has been gross failure, on the part of leading forensic psychiatrists as well as those responsible for the criminal justice system, sufficiently to mobilize psychiatric resources for the prevention and treatment of crime. Part of the fault lies with our monomania, our *folie à collective,* about criminal responsibility and the defense of insanity which has distracted us from many important tasks, two of which * * * [are] the task of defining the dangerous offender for sentencing and treatment purposes, and the mobilization of clinical resources for the treatment of such criminals.

Morris, Psychiatry and the Dangerous Criminal, 41 S.Cal.L.Rev. 514, 515 (1968).

4. Might not some reforms of less magnitude than abolition of the insanity defense meet some or many of the objections to the defense? Consider the following proposals:

I think [the issue of criminal responsibility] could be more satisfactorily determined by the judge than by the jury. * * * [W]hen the [American Law] Institute considered this * * * it was felt that the constitutional guarantee of jury trial required that the issue be submitted to the jury in a contested case since it was in effect an issue of guilt or innocence.

Wechsler, Insanity as a Defense, A Panel Discussion, 37 F.R.D. 365, 411 (1964).

[T]he [American Law] Institute proposals [1] would try to [achieve the advantages of taking the responsibility decision from the jury] without the disadvantages by fostering a system under

1. See Model Penal Code §§ 4.05, 4.07 (P.O.D.1962).

which, when this defense was interposed, the defendant would be examined by a court-designated psychiatrist rather than having the issue determined only in a battle of experts. The jury would be told that this man had been designated by the court and the expectation and hope would be that the jury would credit his disinterestedness proportionately. The defendant would still be permitted to offer [other proof], to call his own witnesses if he wanted to, but as a practical matter this would happen only rarely. If the court-appointed expert found mental disease excluding responsibility, the prosecution frequently would acquiesce in such a finding. If his findings were the other way, the defendant would still be able to contest it but would have a very up-hill fight to win before the jury.

Wechsler, Insanity as a Defense, A Panel Discussion, 37 F.R.D. 365, 411 (1964).j

It is possible to maintain the participation of the public in the responsibility decision through the use of the jury and still bring the psychiatric, scientific accuracy of the twentieth century into the courtroom. Both concepts would be served if a panel of psychiatrists would, before voir dire, in effect explain modern psychiatry to prospective jurors. This panel would present what could be called "instructions" to the laymen. * * * Since the panel would not be called by either side, there could be no challenges of immateriality and prejudice. One objection to such a panel might be expense. * * * Another objection would be the possibility of debate about what actually to tell the prospective jurors. Perhaps the American Medical Association, or some similar organization, could establish a pattern of instructions and standards for this panel. The composition of the panel and the selection of disciplines to be represented might also be the subject of debate * * *.

Comment, The Psychiatrist's Role in Determining Accountability For Crimes: The Public Anxiety and An Increasing Expertise, 52 Marq.L.Rev. 380, 391 (1969).

5. For a general discussion of abolishing the insanity defense and a specific proposal for doing so, see Shwedel and Roether, The Disposition Hearing: An Alternative to the Insanity Defense, 49 J.Urban L. 711 (1972).

PRESIDENT'S VERSION OF REVISED FEDERAL CRIMINAL CODE (1973)

13 Criminal Law Reporter 3001, 3002.

Sec. 502. *Insanity.*

It is a defense to a prosecution under any federal statute that the defendant, as a result of mental disease or defect, lacked the state of mind required as an element of the offense charged. Mental disease or defect does not otherwise constitute a defense.

NOTES

1. Is the Nixon Administration's proposal properly designated an abolition of the insanity defense? If enacted, would it be likely to increase or to decrease the percent of criminal defendants found not guilty by reason of insanity (or simply not guilty)? Consider the comment of Professors Goldstein and Katz, reprinted at pages 1180–81, supra. Revaluate the likely effect and desirability of this proposal after examining the material dealing with "diminished capacity" and "diminished responsibility" in Part VII (B), infra.

2. A similar proposal was made and defended in Robinson, Consultant's Report on Criminal Responsibility—Mental Illness: Section 503, in Working Papers of the National Commission on Reform of Federal Criminal Laws 229, 247–254 (1970). This position was also urged before the United States Court of Appeals for the District of Columbia Circuit by the National District Attorneys Association. Brawner v. United States, 471 F.2d 969, 985–986 (D.C.Cir. 1972).

----

9. XYY CHROMOSOMAL ABNORMALITY: A SPECIAL PROBLEM

MILLARD v. STATE

Court of Special Appeals of Maryland, 1970.
8 Md.App. 419, 261 A.2d 227.

MURPHY, Chief Judge. Charged with the offense of robbery with a deadly weapon, appellant filed a written plea that he was insane at the time of the commission of the crime under Maryland Code, Article 59, Section 9(a), which provides:

"A defendant is not responsible for criminal conduct and shall be found insane at the time of the commission of the alleged crime if, at the time of such conduct as a result of mental disease or defect, he lacks substantial capacity either to appreciate the criminality of his conduct or to conform his conduct to the requirements of law. As used in this section, the terms 'mental disease or defect' do not include an abnormality manifested only by repeated criminal or otherwise antisocial conduct."

The basis for appellant's insanity plea, as later unfolded at the trial, was that he had an extra Y chromosome in the brain and other cells of his body which constituted, within the meaning of Section 9(a), a mental defect resulting in his lacking substantial capacity either to appreciate the criminality of his conduct or to conform his conduct to the requirements of law.

At the trial before a jury in the Circuit Court for Prince George's County, the State established the *corpus delicti* adduced proof of appellant's criminal agency, and then rested its case. Thereafter, under the prescribed Maryland procedure, it became incumbent upon the appellant in undertaking to establish his insanity defense to first adduce sufficient competent proof in support thereof, out of the presence of the jury, from which the trial judge could properly find, as a preliminary matter of law, that the presumption of sanity had been rebutted and a doubt raised in the minds of reasonable men as to his sanity. * * * To this end, and in conformity with the approved procedure, appellant adduced evidence through the testimony of a Lieutenant at the Prince George's County Jail showing that while in confinement appellant was agitated, nervous, upset, and became so violent on occasions that he had to be handcuffed and shackled in leg irons; that appellant cut himself five or six times on his arm between the elbow and the wrist, resulting in severe bleeding, although no arteries were severed; that these cuts "ran the gamut from scratches to very severe cuts requiring quite a number of sutures"; and that as a result of his condition, appellant was sent to three different hospitals for treatment and evaluation.

Dr. Cecil Jacobson, the appellant's only medical witness, testified that he was an Assistant Professor in the Department of Obstetrics and Gynecology and Chief of the Reproduction Genetics Unit of the George Washington University School of Medicine * * * [.]

Dr. Jacobson testified that genetics was "a sub-speciality biology" having "quite a bit of inference in medicine," involving a specific diagnostic technique dealing with the "very basis of human development, the chromosome material"; that "chromosomes [in the cells of the body] are the way that all genetic machinery is passed from one generation to another"; that "all things that are passed on from parent to child must go through chromosomes"; and that 46 chromosomes constituted the normal complement per cell and a person who possessed 47 chromosomes was genetically abnormal.

Dr. Jacobson testified that on December 16, 1968, appellant was examined and his body cells found to contain an extra Y chromosome (XYY); that the presence of this extra chromosome constituted a "basic defect in the genetic complement of the cell" affecting not only the way the cells grow in the body, but also the physical growth of the body itself; that the presence of the extra Y chromosome caused "marked physical and mental problems" affecting the manner in which persons possessing the extra Y chromosome "will react to certain stimulus; certain physiological problems; certain behavioral characteristics." Dr. Jacobson then told of approximately 40 published reports indicating that persons possessed of an extra Y chromosome tended to be very tall, with limbs disproportionate to their body; that such persons had marked antisocial, aggressive and schizoid reactions and were in continual conflict with the law.

Dr. Jacobson stated that he had never previously testified in court. Asked whether he was familiar with the Maryland test of insanity, as defined in Section 9(a), he said that he had never read it, but believed it contained two parts—"One, whether there was a basic defect involved, and, secondly, whether or not the person is competent for his act." Section 9(a) was then read to Dr. Jacobson, and he was then asked whether appellant was insane. Dr. Jacobson responded with a professorial narrative of appellant's genetic make-up, after which he concluded that "if the definition of insanity has a mental defect, the answer is yes, he has a mental defect based upon his abnormal [chromosome] test." Asked whether the "defect" was such as to cause appellant to lack "substantial capacity either to appreciate the criminality of his conduct or to conform his conduct to the requirements of law," Dr. Jacobson answered:

"I cannot say that because I have not examined him as a psychiatrist. I have no competence in that area."

Appellant's counsel then told the court that he intended to show through "case histories" that individuals having the extra Y chromosome have extremely aggressive personalities, "to the extent that most of them end up in jail for one reason or another because of their aggressive reactions." Dr. Jacobson was then asked to examine appellant's arms to determine whether the cuts thereon were "suicidal or merely attention cuts." Dr. Jacobson did so briefly and stated that based on his experience as a medical doctor, he believed the cuts constituted an actual attempt at suicide; that based on this fact, and his brief questioning of appellant during a five-minute court recess, he felt appellant's "reactions" were not normal; that appellant had a fear of "forceful activity with an attempt at extension of this regression and a lack of adequately controlling this"; that although he was "greatly restricted" by not knowing the "developmental history" of appellant, he believed, based upon the testimony of the jail lieutenant concerning appellant's conduct while in confinement, including the suicide attempts, coupled with appellant's genetic defect, that "this does not fall within the realm of sanity, as I understand it." Dr. Jacobson then testified that the extra Y chromosome in appellant's genetic make-up affected his behavioral patterns, as reported in other cases of persons similarly possessed of the extra Y chromosome. He conceded that persons having the extra Y chromosome may differ among themselves depending upon "what other physical effects are found in the body of the XYY," environment also being a factor accounting for differences between XYY individuals.

Under further questioning by the trial judge, the prosecutor, and defense counsel, Dr. Jacobson stated that appellant's genetic defect—which he characterized as a mental defect—influenced "his competence or ability to recognize the area of his crime"; that appellant had a "propensity" toward crime because of his genetic abnormality; that based upon the medical literature, the appellant's conduct and behavioral patterns, and his genetic defect, he was insane and not even competent to stand trial. The doctor defined insanity in terms of the "ability to comprehend reality" or the "inability to judge one's action as far as consequence." Dr. Jacobson next testified that he had "insufficient evidence" upon which to base a conclusion whether appellant appreciated the consequences of his action, but that because he had attempted to commit suicide, such an act constituted "an inability to comprehend the consequences of his act, the act of suicide, being death"; and that appellant's actions were "not consistent with sanity."

At the conclusion of Dr. Jacobson's testimony, the trial judge indicated that he believed appellant had adduced sufficient evidence to rebut the presumption of sanity and permit the case to go to the jury. The prosecutor urged that the court withhold its ruling until it heard from the State's psychiatrist, Dr. Robert Sauer. There being no objection by appellant to this procedure, Dr. Sauer then testified that after extensive psychiatric examination of appellant, he had concluded, as did five other State psychiatrists, that appellant was not insane within the test prescribed in Section 9(a). He diagnosed appellant's condition as antisocial personality, severe, with schizoid trends, which indicated the likelihood of psychotic episodes in the future. Dr. Sauer testified that while he was aware of the literature pertaining to the extra Y chromosome, he made no study of appellant in this connection since he believed that if such genetic defect existed, it was not a "mental defect" within the contemplation of Section 9(a), but a physical defect, not affecting the mental functioning of the brain.

At the conclusion of Dr. Sauer's testimony, the trial judge ruled that he was not persuaded that reasonable minds could differ as to appellant's sanity; that the appellant's defect was physical and not mental; and that Dr. Jacobson's testimony did not, with reasonable medical certainty, overcome the presumption that appellant was sane. The trial judge thus declined to submit the issue of appellant's sanity to the jury. The jury subsequently found appellant guilty of robbery with a deadly weapon and he was sentenced to eighteen years under the jurisdiction of the Department of Correction.

We see no merit in appellant's contention on appeal that the trial judge erred in ruling that there had not been presented evidence of insanity under Article 59, Section 9(a) sufficient to overcome the presumption of sanity. Dr. Jacobson's testimony, if believed, clearly established that appellant possessed an extra Y chromosome

(XYY) and that he was therefore genetically abnormal. It also tended to show in a general way that appellant's possession of the extra Y chromosome caused him to be antisocial, aggressive, in continual conflict with the law, and to have a "propensity" toward the commission of crime. But * * * the test of responsibility for criminal conduct under Section 9(a) is predicated upon "mental disease or defect", the existence of which is "first and foremost a medical problem"; and that an opinion as to the ultimate fact whether an accused is insane under Section 9(a) should be reached "by a medical diagnosis," based on "reasonable medical certainty." The mere fact then that appellant had a genetic abnormality which Dr. Jacobson characterized as "a mental defect" would not, of itself, suffice to show that, under Section 9(a), he lacked, because of such defect, "substantial capacity either to appreciate the criminality of his conduct or to conform his conduct to the requirements of law." And to simply state that persons having the extra Y chromosome are prone to aggressiveness, are antisocial, and continually run afoul of the criminal laws, is hardly sufficient to rebut the presumption of sanity and show the requisite lack of "substantial capacity" under Section 9(a). Moreover, we think it entirely plain from the record that in testifying that appellant had a "mental defect," Dr. Jacobson did so only in a most general sense, without full appreciation for the meaning of the term as used in Section 9(a), and particularly without an understanding that such term expressly excludes "an abnormality manifested only by repeated criminal or otherwise antisocial conduct." But even if it were accepted that appellant had a "mental defect" within the contemplation of Section 9(a), Dr. Jacobson, by his own testimony, indicated an inability to meaningfully relate the effect of such defect to the "substantial capacity" requirements of the subsection. Not only did Dr. Jacobson candidly admit that he had "no competence" in the field of psychiatry, but he demonstrated that fact by showing that he had not theretofore familiarized himself with the substance of Section 9(a); indeed, his conception of the test of criminal responsibility in Maryland was shallow at best, at least until the test was read to him during his testimony. While Dr. Jacobson did ultimately testify in conclusory fashion that he thought appellant insane and even incompetent to stand trial, his testimony in this connection was obviously predicated on a definition of "insanity" different than that prescribed under Section 9(a) —a definition so general as to encompass as insane a person who would attempt suicide. At one point in his testimony Dr. Jacobson conceded that he had "insufficient evidence" upon which to conclude whether appellant appreciated the "consequences of his actions." Whether this concession was due to the fact that Dr. Jacobson had never subjected appellant to a psychiatric examination is unclear; what is clear is that Dr. Jacobson's testimony was too generalized and lacking in specifics to form the basis for an opinion, with reasonable medical certainty, that appellant was insane under Section 9(a). In so concluding, we do not intend to hold, as a matter of law, that a defense of insanity based upon the so-called XYY genetic defect is beyond the pale of proof under Section 9(a). We only conclude that on the record before us the trial judge properly declined to permit the case to go to the jury—a determination which, contrary to appellant's further contention, is not violative of any of his constitutional rights, state or federal. * * *

That Dr. Jacobson was a well qualified geneticist was clear beyond question. Equally clear is the fact that he was not a practicing physician, and his experience in mental illness was related essentially to his practice in the field of genetics. He conceded a lack of competence in the field of psychiatry, admitted having no prior familiarity with the provisions of Section 9(a), had not subjected appellant to any psychiatric examination, and defined "insanity" in terms different than those prescribed by the applicable law. * * * [T]o constitute proof of insanity sufficient to raise a doubt in the minds of reasonable men, competent medical evidence must be adduced to the positive effect that the accused, as a result of mental disease or defect, lacked substantial capacity either to appreciate the criminality of his conduct or to conform his conduct to the requirements of law; and evidence of some undefined mental disorder or instability is insufficient proof to overcome the presumption of sanity. On the record before us, we think Dr. Jacobson's opinion as to appellant's sanity under Section 9(a) was not competent in that it was not based on reasonable medical certainty, and that the trial judge, had he so concluded, would not have been in error.

Judgment affirmed.

NOTE

The relationship of chromosomal abnormalities to criminal liability has given rise to extensive commentary, See, e. g., Burke, The "XYY Syndrome": Genetics, Behavior and the Law, 46 Denver L.J. 261 (1969); Fox, the XYY Offender: A Modern Myth? 62 J.Crim.L., C. & P.S. 59 (1971); Kittrie, Will the XYY Syndrome Abolish Guilt?, 35 Federal Probation, No. 2 (June, 1971) at 26; Pitcher, Criminological Implications of Chromosomal Abnormalities, 121 New L.J. 1078 (1971); Note, the XYY Chromosomal Abnormality: Use and Misuse in the Legal Process, 9 Harv. J.Leg. 469 (1972); Note, the XYY Chromosome Defense, 57 Geo.L.J. 892 (1969); Note, The XYY Syndrome: A Challenge to Our System of Criminal Responsibility, 16 N.Y.L. Forum 232 (1970); Comment, the XYY Chromosome Complement: Brief Application to Criminal Insanity Tests, 14 St. L.U.L.J. 297 (1969).

10. SOME PRACTICAL CONSIDERATIONS: THE DOCTRINAL ISSUE IN PERSPECTIVE

---

a. THE IMPACT OF THE DOCTRINAL DECISION UPON THE DECISION AS TO GUILT

R. SIMON, THE JURY AND THE DEFENSE OF INSANITY

35–37, 50–53, 57–58, 66, 72–76, 84–85, 92–93, 217–18 (1967).[k]

[T]he experimental procedure consisted of the following steps.

*   *   *

1. A transcript of an actual case that had been decided by the court was obtained. The transcript was edited and condensed from a trial that lasted, generally, two or three days to one that could be heard in about 60 to 90 minutes. The experimental transcript contained the lawyers' opening and closing statements and the judge's instructions to the jury, as well as the testimony of all the witnesses.

2. The "experimental" trial was then recorded, with the parts of the attorneys, witnesses, principals in the case, and the judge performed by persons associated with the University of Chicago, largely members of the law school faculty.

3. With the cooperation of local bar associations and presiding judges in three jurisdictions, Chicago, St. Louis, and Minneapolis, subjects for the experiment were drawn by lot from the local jury pools. The jurors were assigned to these recorded trials by the court. A judge instructed them as to their duties by explaining the court's interest in this comprehensive study of the judicial process. He also told them that while their verdicts in the case could have no immediate practical consequences, the judges of this court were very much interested in the results of the study. A juror's service was not voluntary; it was part of his regular period of jury duty.

*   *   *

5. The jurors then listened to the recorded trial. The trial was interrupted once for lunch. Before leaving the court the jurors were instructed not to discuss the case among themselves.[5] After lunch the jurors reported back to the jury room and the trial was resumed.

*   *   *

---

5. The lunch break is supposed to simulate, in microcosm, the more extensive opportunities that jurors have to get to know one another during a real trial before they begin to deliberate.

7. The jury was then ready to deliberate. It had been told before the trial began that its deliberations would be recorded. Everyone (the bailiff, the experimenters, etc.) left the jury room except the twelve jurors, who had been instructed to select one of their members as foreman.

8. When the jury reached a verdict, the foreman reported it to the experimenter. * * *

9. The jury was then taken in front of the judge to report its verdict. The judge thanked the jurors for their service and either dismissed them or sent them back to the jury pool for further duty.

[After trying the above procedure with a housebreaking case modeled upon the facts of *Durham*, the experimenters concluded that it was not as effective a vehicle as had been hoped. Most of the defects in the housebreaking case were remedied in the second case, which is discussed in the following passages.]

Experiment II.   An incest trial

An exactly parallel process was followed in the development of the incest case.

In most cases in which a defense of insanity is introduced, the insanity issue is complicated by the issue of capital punishment, since the crime involved is usually murder, kidnapping, or rape. A charge of incest offers an interesting opportunity to examine jurors' reactions to a heinous offense without having to take into account public attitudes toward capital punishment. We also wanted to find out if the topic of incest could be adequately discussed by a group of men and women who were meeting for the first time. Our guess was that the institutional context of the court would provide enough structured impersonality so as to allow the jurors to participate in a discussion that under most conditions would be extremely threatening and anxiety provoking.

The basic facts of the case

In the original District of Columbia trial of *United States v. King*, the jury deliberated eight hours before it reported that it was hopelessly hung six to six. In a subsequent bench trial (the defendant waived his right to a jury trial), Judge Edward A. Tamm found the defendant not guilty by reason of insanity and ordered him committed to St. Elizabeth's Hospital. The facts of the renamed case are summarized below.

> Jason Lunt, a lieutenant in the Fire Department, lived with his wife, two sons, and two daughters, in a metropolitan city on the East Coast. The series of events leading to his arrest were initiated by his younger daughter who went to the police after she had been approached for sexual inter-

course two days in succession. His wife had been aware of
the incestuous relationships for some time and never reported the situation, nor did she testify during the trial. The
defendant had no history of criminal indictments or mental
illness.

A series of lay witnesses were called by the prosecution. They included the defendant's two daughters, who testified that they had had sexual intercourse with their father
for fourteen years. The Deputy Fire Chief and an old family
friend and associate at the Fire Department both testified
that until the incidents reported in this trial were made public it was their belief that the defendant was living a normal
life with the members of his family. In defense cross-examination, it came to light that the defendant had been erratic in his work and at the time of his arrest had been home
on sick leave ordered by the physician attached to the Fire
Department. The defendant did not take the stand; but
the statement he gave to the police officers at the time of his
arrest was offered in evidence by the prosecution. In his
statement, the defendant acknowledged further that these
acts had been committed over a period of fourteen years and
that during this time he sought to avoid pregnancy of his
daughters by instructing them in the use of contraceptive
devices.

The two psychiatrists, the only witnesses called by the
defense, testified that the defendant was suffering from
paraphiliac neurosis, which they claimed could be traced to
unresolved oedipal tensions. In addition they believed that
the defendant's total lack of affect of involvement with his
present situation was an indication of mental disorder. They
also reported that for ten to fifteen years the defendant had
been drinking heavily. But the doctors never indicated that
the defendant was suffering from a psychosis, and on cross-
examination they explicitly stated that he was not.

The final witness for the prosecution, called in rebuttal, was a psychiatrist who had neither examined nor seen
the patient before his appearance in the courtroom. He testified that "paraphiliac neurosis" was not a "mental" but an
"emotional" disturbance.

The recorded trial and the original trial were practically identical. We wish to stress that we did not "clean up" the experimental version by deleting accounts of violent or perverted sexual behavior. The facts heard in the courtroom of the original trial were
the same facts listened to by jurors who heard the recorded trial.

Design of the incest experiment

As in the housebreaking experiment, six versions of the incest trial were prepared. In this experiment the changes were a function of variations in the rules of law and in the testimonies of the medical experts.

Approximately one third of the juries heard the trial under the *M'Naghten* instructions, one third under the *Durham* instructions, and one third under the *uninstructed on responsibility* version. [In the "uninstructed" version, the juries were simply told to acquit the defendant if they found him "insane at the time he committed the act." No reference was made to any criterion for determining "sanity."]

In the incest case, the defense called only two witnesses; both were psychiatrists who examined the defendant between the time he was arrested and the time the trial began. Two versons of psychiatric testimony were prepared.

Half of the juries heard expert psychiatric testimony that followed closely the testimony actually heard in the real trial and that we think is typical of the kind of testimony usually heard in the courtroom. The typical testimony described the defendant's current symptoms and gave them psychiatric labels but offered almost no historical or developmental account of the origins of the defendant's behavior.

The other half of the juries heard testimony that we optimistically describe as model testimony. In the model version the psychiatrists offered a longer and more detailed clinical history of the defendant's illness from his infancy until his indictment. When medical labels were applied, they were defined in language that should have been understandable to the average layman. In the model version, the psychiatrists made more of an effort to tie together the defendant's clinical history and symptoms with his current behavior. The model testimony lasted almost twice as long as the typical testimony.

* * *

Concomitant changes in the script

The changes in psychiatric testimony necessitated by the variations in the rules of law are described below.

Under the *M'Naghten* rule, on cross examination the first doctor testified as follows:

Prosecuting Attorney: Doctor, from all your examinations of the defendant, would you say that he was able to distinguish right from wrong?

Witness: In the sense that he was probably aware of the fact that incest was socially and morally wrong, I would say that he could distinguish right from wrong.

The second doctor testified on cross examination:

Prosecuting Attorney: Let me ask you this, sir: From the examination that you made of him and the conclusion that you reached that he is a paraphiliac, would you say that this individual is able to distinguish between right and wrong?

Witness: In my opinion, he is.

In the *Durham* version on direct examination the first doctor testified as follows:

Defense Attorney: Doctor, I direct your attention to the fact that there is filed in this case a report which is signed by Dr. Hawley, who is the Director of Billington State Hospital, dated as of March 15, 1956, and that report is made in response to a direction of this court. In the report made to this court, Dr. Hawley states: We conclude that Jason Lunt is suffering from a mental illness of long standing, and that the crimes with which he is charged were the products of this mental disease. Now, Doctor, did you come to the conclusion that the offenses which are complained of here were the products of the defendant's disease?

Witness: It seems to me that the term "product" of a disease as the term is conventionally used, is not quite applicable here; in the sense that the defendant's behavior is really almost a symptom of an underlying illness; in other words, the behavior is so closely connected with the illness that one cannot think of it as being a result of the illness, but as a manifestation of hidden anxieties or fears, all of which have their roots in very early childhood.

The second doctor, on direct examination, said:

Defense Attorney: Doctor, one final question. Would you say that the offense with which the defendant is charged is a product of this mental illness?

Witness: I would say that the defendant's behavior and his illness are part and parcel of the same over-all picture; his behavior in this situation is an overt manifestation of his psychic problems.

In the *uninstructed* version neither doctor was asked whether the defendant could distinguish right from wrong or whether the act was a product of mental disease.

* * *

We turn now to an analysis of one of the basic questions in the study: What effect do legal rules have on the jury's verdict in defense of insanity cases?

* * *

TABLE 11. JURIES' VERDICTS BY RULES OF LAW
(INCEST)*

Rules of law	NGI	Hung	Guilty	Total Juries
Uninstructed	4	4	14	22
M'Naghten	0	1	19	20
Durham	5	6	15	26

* * *

The proportion of NGI verdicts under *M'Naghten* was significantly lower than under the *Durham* or the *uninstructed* versions.

Jurors who heard the *uninstructed* version behaved very much like the jurors who were exposed to the *Durham* rule. This is a surprising finding. When we talked with experienced lawyers and judges about the rules of thumb jurors were likely to use for assessing responsibility in the absence of instructions, most of them predicted that the jurors would fall back on the "right from wrong" formula. We had expected that verdicts in the *uninstructed* version would be much closer to the verdict reported by the juries deliberating under *M'Naghten*.

The findings in the incest experiment demonstrate that under the *M'Naghten* rule, jurors are less likely to acquit the defendant on grounds of insanity than they are under *Durham* and the *uninstructed* versions. When jurors are permitted to deliberate in the absence of a court-defined criterion of responsibility, they are more likely to find in favor of the defendant, but no more likely than when they are instructed under the *Durham* formula. Juries' verdicts in the *uninstructed* and *Durham* versions are almost identical. The *Durham* rule produces a powerful difference in jurors' verdicts, but it must be noted that it does not produce a monolithic response. Not all the juries that deliberated under *Durham* found the defendant not guilty by reason of insanity. Indeed most of them found the defendant guilty. Having observed how jurors in the incest trial reacted to the rules of law, it would be interesting to try a variety of crimes and see if the rule differences hold.

Any conclusions about the effects of rules of law on the jury should await further analysis. We have yet to examine how each of the rules fares under the two versions of psychiatric testimony. But before comparing verdicts by rules of law and type of expert

---

* Counting the hung juries as half acquittals, M'Naghten vs. Uninstructed, $X^2_{1d.f.}$ (.95) $= 3.8$; $X^2 = 4.9$; $p < .05$; M'Naghten vs. Durham, $X^2_{1d.f.}$ (.95) $= 3.8$; $X^2 = 6.0$; $p < .05$.

testimony, there is still another dimension of the impact of the rules of law on the jurors: length of deliberations under the three instruction versions.

Relative length of deliberations by instructions

[S]ome legal scholars opposed adoption of the *Durham* rule because they believed it would seriously limit the function of the jury, making it little more than a rubber stamp to the medical experts. We tested this belief empirically by comparing the amount of participation that the jurors engaged in before completing their task under the three instruction forms. If the fears about the influence of the *Durham* rule are valid, juries deliberating under *Durham*

TABLE 12.   MEAN BURSTS OF SPEECH PER JURY BY RULES OF LAW *

Uninstructed	496 (13)
M'Naghten	257 (12)
Durham	564 (14)

M'Naghten vs. Durham, $t = 4.3$; $p < .001$; M'Naghten vs. Uninstructed, $t = 3.7$; $p < .01$.

should have shorter deliberations. It seems reasonable to assume that the smaller the magnitude of the task, the less time it would take to complete.

Table 12 compares the lengths of the juries' deliberations under the three instruction versions. Juries deliberated significantly longer under *Durham* than they did under *M'Naghten*. They also deliberated longer under the *uninstructed* version than they did under *M'Naghten*.

But these differences that seem to be caused by rules of law could in fact have been caused by the differences in outcome of the verdicts. Table 13 compares the relative lengths of deliberations by verdicts and rules of law.

TABLE 13.   MEAN BURSTS OF SPEECH PER JURY BY RULES OF LAW AND JURY VERDICTS

	Uninstructed	*M'Naghten*	*Durham*
NGI	410 (4)	—	565 (5)
Guilty	470 (7)	239 (11)	486 (6)
Hung	768 (2)	454 (1)	721 (3)

Separating juries by verdicts did not change the rankings reported above. In each instruction version, hung juries deliberated longer than juries that reached consensus; and juries that found the defendant not guilty by reason of insanity deliberated longer than juries

* Counting the hung juries as half acquittals, M'Naghten vs. Uninstructed, $X^2_{1 d.f.} (.95) = 3.8$; $X^2 = 4.9$; $p < .05$; M'Naghten vs. Durham, $X^2_{1 d.f.} (.95) = 3.8$; $X^2 = 6.0$; $p < .05$.

that found the defendant guilty. But in each group the deliberation under *Durham* is considered longer than under *M'Naghten*. Again we are struck by the similarity of responses between *Durham* and *uninstructed* juries.

* * *

The data consistently indicate that deliberating under the *Durham* rule does not interfere with—but if anything increases—the involvement of the jury. Rather than lessen its responsibility, as many lawyers feared, the *Durham* rule causes the jury to assume greater responsibility.

* * *

Verdicts, psychiatric testimony, and rules of law

Of the 68 juries who heard the incest trial, 33 were exposed to the model version and 35 to the typical version. Tables 14 and 15 describe the jurors' pre-deliberation verdicts and the group verdict under the two versions of psychiatric testimony and the three rules of law.

TABLE 14.   PRE-DELIBERATION VERDICTS BY
PSYCHIATRIC TESTIMONY AND RULE OF LAW
(Per cent finding NGI)

	Uninstructed	M'Naghten	Durham
Model testimony	36% (264)	26% (240)	35% (312)
Typical testimony	33%	22%	37%

TABLE 15.   DISTRIBUTION OF JURIES' VERDICTS BY
PSYCHIATRIC TESTIMONY AND RULE OF LAW

	Uninstructed			M'Naghten			Durham		
	NGI	Hung	Guilty	NGI	Hung	Guilty	NGI	Hung	Guilty
Model testimony	2	2	7	—	—	9	2	4	7
Typical testimony	2	2	7	—	1	10	3	2	8

We had two expectations concerning the effects of the psychiatric testimony on the juries' verdicts. We thought that the model version would result in a greater proportion of NGI verdicts and that the *Durham* rule in contrast to the *M'Naghten* rule would have a greater impact on the jury under the model version. It is immediately apparent that both expectations were not realized. The faint suggestion that the model testimony increases the number of NGI verdicts as shown by the *uninstructed* and *M'Naghten* versions disappears when we note the opposite effect for the *Durham* version.

In any case, given such small differences we must conclude that our effort to vary psychiatric testimony had no impact on the jury.

It remains possible that a more dramatic variation in psychiatric testimony might have an effect on the jury. It must be remembered, however, that the particular variation we introduced was drafted with highly expert advice. It represents, therefore, a measure of difference in psychiatric testimony which the psychiatrists themselves thought to be interesting to test. And equally important, it represents the maximum improvement in quality of testimony which they thought was likely to occur in the actual administration of the criminal law.

* * *

[The experimenters informed half of the juries in the housebreaking case that the defendant, if acquitted by reason of insanity, would be committed to a mental institution. The other half were not so instructed.]

We have before us a question of practical concern to the administration of criminal law. Will the jury's verdict in an insanity case be affected by disclosure to the jury of information about commitment procedures? * * * The results are conclusive. The presence or absence of commitment information had no noticeable effect on the individuals' or the juries' verdicts. The absence of information did not increase, to any significant extent, the likelihood that a jury would find the defendant guilty; nor did the presence of information enhance the likelihood that the jury would acquit the defendant on grounds of insanity. We can only conclude from the data that information as to disposition of the defendant is *not* a crucial consideration in the jury's decision. The results, however, are surprising and sharply contrary to the expectations of the bench and bar.

* * *

On the * * * general question of the jurors' reactions to the psychiatric testimony, we found that jurors reviewed the testimony during the deliberations and seemed to understand its essence. But they were also very conscious of their responsibilities as jurors and adhered to the division of labor whereby the experts advised and they, the jurors, decided whether the defendant was responsible for his behavior. * * *

NOTES

1. What is the value of such research? How might the research design have been improved? What weight should the results of such research be given in legislative and judicial decisionmaking? What effect should a lack of any such empirical research have in legislative and judicial decisionmaking in other areas of substantive criminal law?

2. Diamond, Book Review, 56 Cal.L.Rev. 914, 916–19 (1968): [1]

In my opinion the so-called "model" psychiatric testimony utilized in this research is absurdly inappropriate, and I think the experimental jurors were quite right in rejecting it. * * *

I believe that the "model" psychiatric testimony created for the use of this research study demonstrates precisely what is wrong with modern psychiatric expert testimony in the criminal trial. The model testimony is an objective, impartial, calm and dispassionate presentation of the clinical facts of the defendant's life history replete with dynamic references to oedipus complex identity problems, exposure to sexual perversion as a child, infantile sexuality, and so on, the significance of which is all carefully explained to the jury.

But none of this testimony has any relevancy to the mysteries of the case with which the jurors had to struggle. These mysteries were: How was it possible for a man who appeared to be wholly rational in all other areas of his life to be so utterly irrational as to have repeated sexual relations with his own minor daughter; how was it possible for the wife to know that this was going on and yet stand by and say nothing to anyone; and finally, how can a man be so shrewd and deliberate as to procure contraceptives for his own daughter to use in this incestuous relationship and yet be so totally perverted as to violate the most fundamental of all sexual taboos? This case— like most cases involving violence, death, or sexual perversion— provides little with which the average person can identify. The facts were strange and bizarre, and the experimental juries struggled hard and long to understand what had happened. They received little help from the psychiatric experts. The psychiatrists either did not even mention the crucial issues of deviant behavior—which bewildered the jurors, yet which they had to understand in order to make a fair and just adjudication of the case—or discussed them in ways which simply did not shed any light on the difficult issues. For example:

> Answer: Well, it's always an extremely difficult task to predict or foresee from a person's childhood just what particular behavior patterns will result when he is an adult, but I would say that for this patient an incestuous relationship is not an unexpected result.

What exactly is a juror supposed to do with such a statement of equivocation?

Professor Rita Simon is a sociologist. Usually sociologists are not reticent in showing up the foibles and failures of psychiatry. So I am surprised that she does not place the emphasis where it belongs—on the failure of the psychiatric expert to provide the kind of information which the decisionmakers of the law need to make their decisions. It does not surprise me that her research showed that there was no difference in response of jurors to "model" as against "typical" expert testimony. Nor does it surprise me that the jurors of higher educational background did not appear to better understand or more readily accept the expert testimony. Rather, the hundreds of experimental jurors who rejected or ignored the expert testimony should have been congratulated for their astuteness. For they must have recognized that the clinical testimony, so carefully described and explained to them from the witness stand, was mumbo-jumbo, a hoax, a fraud. The testimony purported to be an explanation of the extraordinary behavioral deviancy of the defendant; it purported to provide the medical information which the jurors could utilize to reach a decision as to the sanity or insanity of the defendant. In truth, the expert testimony provided nothing useful. There was nothing in the detailed clinical history which explained in a really meaningful way why this man committed this particular series of crimes and why his wife stood by without interfering. The psychiatric experts related only a lot of psychiatric and psychoanalytic clichés and platitudes and a collection of isolated fragments of the defendant's life.

This reviewer, as a psychiatrist and psychoanalyst, could fill a good deal of space with a discussion of what was psychodynamically and theoretically deficient in the expert testimony of this experimental trial. But I shall confine this aspect of my discussion to just one point: I do not think the psychiatrists in this case actually had any idea of the cause of the defendant's incestuous criminal behavior. But for some reason or other they did not come right out and say they did not know— instead they filled up their testimony with clinical details and psychiatric jargon, leaving the jurors to correctly surmise that they did not have any real explanation of the defendant's outrageous behavior. * * *

I will simply list what I think are the reasons the model testimony in Professor Simon's experiment had so little impact on the jurors. (1) The psychiatrists believed that their job was to give the clinical facts in a wholly objective, impartial, and dispassioned manner. They felt they were not part of the adversary system and hence had no need to persuade the jury to accept their view of the defendant. (2) The psychiatrists believed that in order to maintain their objectivity and impartiality they should avoid all concrete references to the defendant's criminal behavior and confine their testimony to his background and psychology, leaving the decision about the criminal act itself to the jury. (3) The psychiatrists believed that they must say nothing about the ultimate issues which were to be decided by the jurors. (4) The psychiatrists must have assumed that they were not to comment on the obvious pathology of the family as a whole. Because neither the defendant, nor the wife, nor any of the children took the stand as witnesses, the psychiatrists confined their testimony to their clinical inferences about the defendant. Yet, it is obvious that in the crime of incest it is the entire family which is the psychopathological unit, and it is the entire family which must be explained and accounted for to the jury. (5) There is nothing in the testimony of the model experts which indicates that the experts themselves had any strong convictions, one way or other, about the issue of criminal responsibility of the defendant. From the testimony, one receives the impression that it really is not very clear whether the defendant is mentally sick or not; whether he should be punished or treated; or whether he should be sent to a prison or a hospital. There is a kind of wishy-washy quality to the testimony which, I suspect, was thought of as objectivity.

The type of testimony described above—impartial, nonadversary, nonpersuasive, "objective," and supposedly scientific, avoiding the ultimate issues of the criminal law—is precisely the sort of testimony which some important judges regard as most desirable from psychiatric experts. Judge David Bazelon, author of *Durham* and one of the foremost reformers of the law of criminal responsibility of the mentally ill, has recently written a long letter of instructions to the psychiatric expert. Bazelon provides, in effect, detailed information as to how the expert should behave on the witness stand. Most emphatically, he is to remain uninvolved in the outcome of the case—the final verdict should be of no concern to the expert. I am fearful that if the psychiatric expert remains as uninvolved in the adversary process and as unconcerned with the ultimate issues as Judge Bazelon (and the psychiatric advisors to the Simon research) would like, there will be only one result: The jury will be equally uninvolved and unconcerned with the expert's contribution to the administration of criminal justice.

3. Klein and Temerlin, On Expert Testimony in Insanity Cases, 119 J. Nervous and Mental Diseases 435 (1969) reports a study directed at jurors' evaluation of expert testimony and the defendant's apparent psychological condition. A professional actor portrayed the defendant during two tape recorded interviews; in one he portrayed the defendant as emotionally healthy and in the other as "psychotic." Eight mock juries were selected and were exposed to expert testimony concerning the defendant's responsibility. In some cases, both experts testified that the defendant was insane, in others both testified that he was sane. In others they split on the issue, and in some no expert testimony was provided. The jurors were then permitted to hear one of the recorded interviews, and were given a "standard" instruction on insanity. As might be expected, the study found that when the experts agreed the jurors tended to vote as the experts had testified, with little regard to the impression made by the defendant during the interview. But more surprisingly, when the experts disagreed or when there was no expert testimony, the jurors tended to regard the defendant as sane without regard to the interview. On 24 first ballots in such cases, the defendant psychotic during the interview was found sane in 18 cases. The "sane" defendant was found "sane" in 22 of 24 first ballots. "[T]here was," the study concluded, "a systematic tendency to consider the defendant

sane, regardless of his actual psychological state, when expert testimony was conflicting or absent." Another attempt to investigate jurors' response to insanity instructions is reported in Arens, Granfield, Susman, Jurors, Jury Charges and Insanity, 14 Cath.U.L.Rev. 1 (1956). Four versions of a Durham instruction were administered to groups of college students. The students were then given comprehension tests in an effort to ascertain the extent to which they remembered and understood the instructions. On the four major questions the percentage of students giving accurate responses varied from 11 to 69, but the overall percent of correct responses to the four questions varied (among the four instructions) from 31 to 40. If jurors' recollection and understanding is no better than that of the subjects of this study, the authors conclude, "in three out of four trials, only one-third of the jurors could be expected to recall the judge's charges with any significant accuracy during deliberations on the law of insanity." Id. at 22.

A. MATTHEWS, MENTAL DISABILITY AND THE CRIMINAL LAW

34, 36–43, 46–50 (1970).m

Criminal responsibility cases are rare because defendants, given the alternatives, choose not to plead insanity as a defense. The plea has drawbacks stemming both from the procedural difficulties it involves and from the consequences that follow if it is successful. This seems strange in view of the widespread belief—a belief that has colored procedural approaches to criminal responsibility in this century—that the defense is a great benefit to the defendant, who can readily purchase psychiatric testimony and thus have an easy way out of criminal liability.

Furthermore, since the prosecution must prove the defendant guilty beyond a reasonable doubt before the defendant is obliged in any way to offer a defense, the defense may even wait until the close of the prosecution's case at trial before presenting any evidence relating to the responsibility of the accused. Such an approach by a defendant would put the prosecution at the disadvantage of being surprised and might make it difficult for the prosecution to rebut expert psychiatric evidence of the lack of criminal responsibility. Many states have enacted legislation to circumvent this tactic, some statutes requiring the defense to furnish the prosecution and the court written notice of its intention to rely on the defense of insanity and others requiring the defense of insanity to be specially pleaded at an early stage in the criminal process or be conclusively waived. * * * [F]ew trial judges will hold the defense strictly to [such requirements]. Thus, in a case in which the defense actually waits until

m. Reprinted by permission of the American Bar Foundation, Chicago, Illinois.

the prosecution has finished its presentation before raising the defense of insanity, the prosecutor is in trouble. The best he can hope for is a temporary delay of the trial and it is not even clear that he can force a psychiatric examination of an unwilling defendant, even with the aid of a statute. Before the trial, also, while the prosecutor may suspect that the defendant is planning a defense of insanity, he has no effective means of discovering either what the mental condition of the defendant is in fact or what the defendant will claim it is, nor of preparing for such an eventuality.

How is it, then, that more defendants do not rely on this tactic if in a serious case in which trial may not occur for a year, or perhaps two, a defendant may have himself psychiatrically examined by experts of his own choosing and not raise the defense until the prosecution has put on its case at trial? In practice, this advantage belongs only to defendants who are well-off. The vast majority of persons charged with crime, including those who are mentally disabled, are indigent. Indigence means, as a practical matter, that the accused typically cannot hire his own psychiatric experts freely as he could if he had money, but must depend for psychiatric evidence on "impartial" experts appointed by the court. Indigence has other consequences which also adversely affect a defendant's chances of preparing and successfully presenting a defense of insanity in court (assuming that, in view of the consequences of success, he wants to do so). It is difficult for the defendant either to obtain, as a preliminary matter, expert advice on his chances for success should he raise the defense of insanity or to obtain psychiatric evidence that might be persuasive in court.

1. *Procedural Disadvantages of the Insanity Plea*

Indigence typically means, first of all, inability to make bond. This is a special disadvantage in the case of the mentally disabled. During the time he is in jail, the accused is under the eye of the prosecution; guards will be able to testify that he was "normal." Should a psychiatrist examine him, it cannot be kept secret from the prosecution. If the defendant were out on bail, he could go to the office of a private psychiatrist without the police or prosecution finding out; if not, however, the psychiatrist must visit him in jail, where records of visitors are kept. The prosecutor learning of the visit will probably assume that a defense of insanity is forthcoming. In this respect the wealthier defendant charged with a crime serious enough to be nonbailable is no better off than the indigent.

Second, the clinical conditions for psychiatric examination at a county jail leave much to be desired, so that it will be more difficult to persuade a psychiatrist to perform an examination if it must be carried out in jail than if the patient were able to come to the psychiatrist's office. It will thus be more difficult to resist an examination by doctors employed by the prosecution or by impartial experts. Finally, the accused cannot receive psychiatric treatment—which he may need badly—in the county jail. County jails do not have a psychiatric staff and private psychiatrists are unlikely to be willing to go to these jails to administer therapy. An accused who is on the borderline of mental stability may be pushed over the edge by having to stay in the county jail for months awaiting trial. The same accused out in the community and able to visit a psychiatric clinic might be able to stand trial. Even if the doctors at the clinic do not wish to testify at the trial, the fact of psychiatric treatment will be very much in the defendant's favor. If an insanity defense occurs, evidence of a treatment relationship will be brought to the attention of the jury. More importantly, however, the fact of an ongoing therapeutic relationship is a strong bargaining point for any defendant.

Most states have statutory provisions under which, once the defense of insanity has been formally raised, the court may appoint "impartial" experts to examine the mental condition of the defendant. In even raising the issue, therefore, the defendant must commit himself in advance to the opinion of impartial experts. Even the defendant who is reasonably confident that to raise the defense of insanity is the proper course of action is at a strategical disadvantage in that he is not permitted to choose the experts himself. (In some states an indigent defendant may obtain a psychiatric expert of his own choosing, but the appointment is made by the court on application, so that the fact of the request is known to the prosecution.)

These statutes also provide that a copy of the psychiatric report of the court-appointed experts be furnished to the prosecution and the court as well as to defense counsel. Because the defense ordinarily has little to say about the composition of the board of experts, because these "impartial" experts in fact tend to favor the prosecution, as will be seen later in this chapter, and because the prosecution receives a copy of the psychiatric report, the bargaining power of the indigent defendant is weakened, at least as compared to his well-to-do counterpart who has funds to hire his own experts in rebuttal —experts who do not have to furnish either the prosecution or the court with copies of their findings and who, naturally, will be selected for their presumed partiality toward the defense.

The defendant's bargaining position is also undermined by the fact that making the insanity plea is tantamount to a virtual confession that the defendant did the acts charged. If the state's case is less than conclusive, as it often is, a chance for acquittal is sacrificed.[20] Even where the state's evidence is strong, there is usually

20. The bifurcated trial, of course, obviates this particular difficulty, as is well illustrated in a recent case from the District of Columbia, holding that the trial judge may order a bifurcated trial in an appropriate case: Holmes v. United States, 363 F.2d 281 (D.C. Cir. 1966).

some doubt in the prosecutor's mind; when the state's case consists only of circumstantial evidence, even the most zealous prosecutor will have his doubts as to whether the defendant actually committed the crime charged. The plea of insanity dissipates these doubts, and they may be completely removed by the admission of guilt which the defendant almost invariably makes to the examining psychiatrists and which may very well be passed on to the prosecutor because the procedure for court-appointed experts makes no provisions restricting the use or distribution of information gathered by the experts during their interview with the defendant (although its use may be limited at trial). To whatever extent the prosecutor's doubts are relieved the bargaining power of the defendant is lessened, particularly if evidence in support of the insanity plea is not developed during the psychiatric examination. The defendant may be further disadvantaged in that the statutes calling for mental examination by impartial experts sometimes provide for inpatient hospitalization which may last for months. These disabilities could be removed if the defendant had access to confidential psychiatric opinion without having to plead the insanity issue as he must now do if he is indigent.

Even supposing that the defense and prosecution have both obtained experts, the defense of insanity presents additional complications for each side. Most prosecutors and defense counsel appear to be unfamiliar with psychiatry and with psychiatric testimony. Presenting such evidence requires much more extensive preparation than in the routine trial of criminal cases. Secondly, the trial of the issue will take more time in court than any other type of criminal case. In a case important enough to go to trial, both the defense and the prosecution will probably call more than one, usually several, experts, each of whom will give a rather long direct presentation and then be cross-examined at great length by opposing counsel. The testimony of other disciplines, such as psychology and social work, may be presented. Not infrequently a parade of lay witnesses may be brought to the stand to testify on the issue of the accused's sanity. Special instructions for the jury must be prepared. All of this is an investment of the lawyers' time which they are usually quite unwilling to make if some alternative course of proceeding is open to them. Many defense counsel are court-appointed and are not adequately compensated for their work, an additional reason for their desire to avoid a lengthy trial.

Operationally, the fact that an indigent defendant must depend for psychiatric evidence on "impartial experts" appointed by the court is important because the impartial expert has characteristic views about mental illness in general and in particular about the degree of mental disability that will excuse a defendant from criminal responsibility. Since nearly all criminal defendants are indigent, impartial experts are the witnesses in almost all cases, and to the extent that they agree among themselves, such agreement is in effect the accepted operational standard of criminal responsibility in that locale, for all but the occasional defendant who can retain experts of his own choosing.

In most cases the indigent defendant will have to submit himself to examination by a board of impartial experts in order to obtain any evidence at all for the defense of insanity. These impartial experts —at least in the opinion of the defense bar—are more likely to be favorable to the prosecution than to the defense. Furthermore, the issue of competency to stand trial may need to be raised in order to get a psychiatric examination. If so, the indigent defendant runs the risk of being found incompetent to stand trial in order to obtain evidence to be used for a defense of insanity. If the charge is serious enough, upon a showing most courts will appoint an independent expert chosen by the defense, but usually only one; in a contested trial, however, the number of experts may be as important as what the experts say. Hence, the popular conception of the defense of insanity, which assumes that defense counsel hire as many psychiatrists as they like, is not accurate in the case of the indigent defendant for whom "shopping around" is an economic impossibility.

* * *

Perhaps because the impartial expert is likely to be associated with the public mental hospital system, he tends to view mental illness from a different perspective than doctors in private practice. The major problem of doctors administering the state mental hospitals before the advent of the community mental health concept had been how to keep people out, given the great demand for admission to mental hospitals. The larger the demand, the more selective doctors had to be in their admission policies and only those persons were admitted who were unable to function on the outside— the grossly psychotic. Neurotics and psychopaths, being able to function (at least in a minimal sense) outside the hospital, were seldom seen and almost never admitted for treatment. These doctors tend to carry over these perceptions into the criminal law when they testify in the course of trials. To be "mental illness" in a legal sense, they testify, the illness must be a debilitating condition, must invade every aspect of the personality and completely immobilize it. This conclusion is expressed in the word "psychosis."

"Psychosis" also implies the classic disorders such as schizophrenia but excludes neurosis and character disorders, although clinically the latter may at times be indistinguishable from and more serious than the classical disorders. Many times doctors have testified (without objection from counsel) that "psychosis" is synonomous with "insanity," a legal word of art used to describe the degree of mental disability which in a particular case excuses one from criminal responsibility. Having performed a psychiatric examination and having reached the conclusion that a particular defendant ought not to be excused from criminal responsibility in a particular case, these doctors express that conclusion by stating on the stand that the accused is not psychotic.

In this context, the procedure from the point of view of those doctors who favor the defendant may be no more illuminating. Defense psychiatrists and defense counsel tend to accept the framework within which the prosecution presents its case, and to argue that the accused is indeed "psychotic." The issue presented in most of the cases is thus whether the accused at the time in question was "a psychotic" or "a sociopath." The doctors in private practice, perhaps because they treat a variety of mentally ill persons, tend to have a broader notion of mental disease than their counterparts in state mental hospitals. Their patients may resemble the person charged with crime more closely than do patients in a state hospital, who are more likely to be the victims of obvious and disabling mental illnesses. Since doctors in private practice have no need to fit patients into diagnostic categories for administrative or statistical purposes, they are less concerned with the importance of psychiatric systems of classification than with the individual dynamics of each patient. Their objective being treatment, their diagnostic procedures tend to be more thorough, more deeply probing, and more time-consuming than the diagnostic procedures of a typical state hospital. Psychiatrists in private practice are well aware of the limitations of a forty-five-minute interview with a person in the local county jail. In contrast, many institutional psychiatrists affirm that forty-five-minute interviews qualify them to render an opinion on the accused's mental condition, perhaps because such interviews are their routine hospital mode.

In many jurisdictions testimony, even in capital cases, is based on skimpy psychiatric examinations which seldom last more than an hour or two and in some cases may last even less. The brevity of the examinations is somewhat offset when past records and outside sources are available to the psychiatrists, but few experts make very much use of outside information. The fact that a defendant was referred for an inpatient examination over a period as long as thirty, sixty, or ninety days is no guarantee, either, that an adequate psychiatric examination has taken place. At the staff conferences we observed in one institution, the actual psychiatric examination— the interval when patient-accused is face to face with the doctor— lasted between five and twelve minutes. The doctors testify, accurately, that the "staff conference" lasted forty-five minutes or an hour, implying that patient and doctor were face to face for that time; but what the doctors do not say is that other patients may also have been presented at the staff conference during this time, and that the actual time spent with the accused may have been as short as five minutes. The result of hurried examinations is that the testifying psychiatrists actually know very little about the defendant. It is therefore not surprising that so much psychiatric testimony is in fact concerned with abstractions and with definitional arguments between witnesses about whether the patient is properly diagnosed as "psychotic" or "sociopathic." And the willingness of the legal professionals to allow doctors to testify in conclusional fashion about such things as psychosis, sociopathy, and the like has overemphasized the real disagreement among doctors on the validity of these classifications. It also underemphasizes how thin the evidence is, either way, in a typical case.

* * *

3. *Dispositional Consequences of the Insanity Defense*

A more subtle ground of dissatisfaction with the defense of insanity than some of its procedural disadvantages is the inflexible "either-or" characteristic of the defense viewed in terms of dispositional alternatives. It limits the discretion of the lawyers by taking control over the disposition of the case out of their hands and placing it in the hands of a judge or jury. In cases where this defense is not involved, negotiations over charge reduction and entry of guilty plea are conducted in terms pretty well assessable by both sides: the circumstances of the offense itself, and the defendant's prior record, attitude, and prospects for staying out of further trouble. The testimony relating to the insanity issue, on the other hand, is not equally subject to discovery and appraisal, and its significance is more dependent on the eventualities of the trial process. It is therefore of less help in providing either an early or a simple disposition of the charges. When the defense of insanity is raised, it is usually because the lawyers are unable to work out any other alternatives; it is, in short, a last resort.

Furthermore, aside from capital cases, the defense of insanity in New York, Chicago, and Detroit seemed to many lawyers and psychiatrists an empty undertaking since the dispositional consequences of the successful insanity plea did not look any better than those which follow upon conviction. While there is no single explanation of this aspect of the "last resort" quality of the insanity plea, the following were given to us: (1) the inevitability of indefinite commitment if the defense is successful and the defendant found "insane"; (2) the belief that psychiatric treatment at the maximum-security hospital "does not exist" or is likely to prove ineffective; (3) the reluctance of many defendants to label themselves "maniacs" or even fit candidates for mental treatment; and (4) fear that the prospects of release are dim even if the mental health of the offender improves.

The indigent defendant is particularly at a disadvantage when it comes to disposition after a successful defense of insanity, for his prospects at the maximum-security mental institution to which he will be committed are even less hopeful than those of the defendant with money.   Since these hospitals, by and large, are located far away from the major cities, the relatives of poor persons will not be able to visit them—at least not very frequently.   It will be more difficult for the indigent patient to obtain a promise of employment, which is the indispensable ingredient for release from psychiatric hospitals.   He will not be able to employ the legal counsel and independent psychiatric testimony which are often necessary to gain release and which, more importantly, are a means of prodding the maximum-security hospital to do something with a patient who otherwise may be "lost" among hundreds of persons similarly situated.   *   *   *

The situation in Illinois and Michigan in 1964 was much like that in New York.   The hospitals for the criminally insane did not compare favorably, even in terms of living conditions, with their counterparts within the criminal justice system, the state prisons.   The prospects of effective psychiatric treatment, and consequently the hope of ever seeing the outside world again, were bleak.   In Illinois if the accused is "schizophrenic," the commitment is literally for life.   *   *   *

The dispositional consequences in California are somewhat better.   This perhaps accounts for the defense being somewhat more popular there than in the three states just discussed.   The single responsibility case we observed in San Francisco, for example, resulted in a civil commitment to a nearby state hospital rather than in a commitment to the maximum-security hospital at Atascadero.   Even Atascadero, located midway between San Francisco and Los Angeles, seemed to us in late 1964 to enjoy a much better reputation than its counterparts in New York, Michigan and Illinois.   This is expressed in the willingness of San Francisco lawyers to advise defendants to plead insanity.   They know that psychiatric care will be afforded their clients who plead insanity and are committed to Atascadero and that the release prospects of these persons are not very much worse than in the other state hospitals in California.   They know this because former clients have come back from Atascadero and reported that such is the case.   The California experience suggests that mentally ill defendants generally would plead insanity if the plea were more than a disguised pathway to indeterminate commitment in a maximum-security hospital and were, in fact, a procedure holding the promise of psychiatric treatment.

b. INFORMAL METHODS OF BY–PASSING FORMAL ASSERTION OF THE INSANITY DEFENSE

LEWIN, INCOMPETENCY TO STAND TRIAL: LEGAL AND ETHICAL ASPECTS OF AN ABUSED DOCTRINE, 1969 LAW AND THE SOCIAL ORDER

233, 237–38, 257–61.

On its face, the doctrine of mental incompetency as a disability to take part in criminal proceedings is relatively simple. It has its roots deeply buried in the common law and means that the defendant because of the existence of mental disease, defect, or other reason, does not understand the nature and object of the proceedings pending against him, or cannot appreciate or comprehend his own condition in relation to the proceedings, or is unable to assist his attorney or participate in his own defense in a rational manner. If the defendant is found to be incompetent, all criminal proceedings are suspended, and the state is denied the power to proceed against him. Prosecuting an incompetent is a denial of his right to due process of law. Even if the underlying mental defect is not discovered until the defendant has been convicted and time for appeal has expired, the issue of incompetency may be raised collaterally, and if it is proved, the entire proceeding will be voided and set aside. So fundamental is this principle that incompetency may not be waived, even with the consent of the court. As a consequence, incompetency proceedings are sometimes inaugurated by the prosecution or by the trial judge on his own motion.

*   *   *

One of the most interesting practices discovered in the Michigan study was the custom of many prosecutors, particularly those in the more populous counties, to use the incompetency commitment as the final disposition of a criminal case. While there were many variations, the theme followed generally the illustration below, which was typical of many cases reported from the Detroit Recorder's Court, the busiest single criminal court in Michigan. Because this court has an attached court clinic, the court ordered a defendant examined by the clinic on motion of the prosecutor whenever the prosecutor or the court suspected that he was mentally ill. The staff psychiatrists submitted their findings in the form of a report to the trial judge, and if they found the presence of a psychosis or severe mental retardation, and in addition recommended hospitalization, the court would then appoint a commission of three physicians pursuant to the procedure in existence at the time of the study. The purpose of this commission would be to determine whether the defendant's mental condition would prevent his standing trial or otherwise proceeding with the case. The clinical report would usually contain a finding of the defendant's mental condition both at the time of the crime and at the time of the examination; if serious mental disorder was noted, the doctors would often state whether the alleged crime was a "product" of the psychosis. If the defendant were thereafter found to be incompetent and committed before trial to the state hospital, the prosecution would then have a basis for entering a nolle prosequi when the defendant recovered his sanity and was returned to stand trial. Some judges, though not all, would permit testimony of the defendant's mental condition at the time of the crime at the incompetency hearing. If there was no testimony at the original incompetency hearing, the doctors would often make and testify to this finding at the hearing following the defendant's subsequent recovery and return to court.

* * *

* * * [In one case] the defendant was an alleged murderer, but he was released to the streets a free man within three and one-half years from the date of the crime because the prosecution and the court agreed that since the act was a product of the mental disease and since that disease had been "cured," there was no reason to hold him. Two other alleged murderers and numerous persons accused of lesser crimes had their cases handled in a similar manner during the same period of time in the same court.

* * *

Sometimes, the prosecutors would allege in their petitions for nolle prosequi that the victim no longer wished to prosecute, that eyewitnesses were unavailable, or simply that the period of pretrial confinement plus restoration to sound mental health satisfied the ends of justice. But even where the prosecutors did not specifically rely upon the existence of mental illness at the time of the crime, they nonetheless would admit that the existence of mental illness was a primary, if unspoken, consideration in their determination to dismiss. * * *

A. MATTHEWS, MENTAL DISABILITY AND THE CRIMINAL LAW 162 (1970)

Many persons accused of crime who show signs of mental disturbance can be provided custody and treatment, adequate for the protection of society and more appropriate for their own welfare, by means of civil commitment. This is particularly true of persons whose criminal violations are relatively nonserious, a category which includes most mentally ill persons involved in the criminal process. We found extensive use of the civil commitment procedure in most of the jurisdictions studied, particularly Illinois, but very limited use of it * * * in the District of Columbia. These variations appear to reflect not differences in law or explicit administrative policy, but differences in the connections between the civil commitment procedure and the apparatus of criminal justice.

c.　RESULTS OF SUCCESSFUL ASSERTION OF THE INSANITY DEFENSE: POST–ACQUITTAL COMMITMENT AND RELEASE

BOLTON v. HARRIS

United States Court of Appeals for the District of Columbia, 1968.
130 U.S.App.D.C. 1, 395 F.2d 642.

BAZELON, Chief Judge.　In this appeal from denial of habeas corpus, appellant attacks the mandatory commitment provisions of D. C.Code § 24–301(d) [hereinafter Subsection (d)] [1] and the release provisions of D.C.Code § 24–301(e) [2] These provisions apply after a successful voluntary plea of not guilty by reason of insanity.　The primary contention is that these provisions violate equal protection because they do not afford safeguards available for those civilly committed under the Hospitalization of the Mentally Ill Act of 1964.

Gerald C. Bolton was charged with unauthorized use of a motor vehicle and transportation of a stolen motor vehicle in June 1965. At trial in August 1966 defense counsel stipulated to the facts concerning the alleged offense and relied solely on a plea of insanity.　The only witness at the trial was Dr. George Weichardt, a psychiatrist on the staff of Saint Elizabeths Hospital.　＊　＊　＊　Dr. Weichardt stated that appellant was suffering from mental illness at the time of the stipulated offenses in 1965 and that these offenses were a product of this illness.

He also testified that after the offenses in 1965 and before trial in 1966, Bolton was treated for five months at the Rockland State Hospital in Orangeburg, New York.　But he was not asked and did not say that the hospital reported that appellant "responded to chemo and psychotherapy, and general milieu treatment," and was discharged *"Condition: Recovered* [emphasis added]."　And it further appears that eight months after his release from the New York Hospital the Superintendent of Saint Elizabeths reported that Bolton was "suffering from mental illness　＊　＊　＊　but is competent for trial."　At the

---

1.　If any person tried ＊ ＊ ＊ for an offense ＊ ＊ ＊ is acquitted solely on the ground that he was insane at the time of its commission, the court shall order such person to be confined in a hospital for the mentally ill. [D.C. Code § 24–301(d) (1967)].

2.　Unconditional release, under Subsection (e), requires the superintendent of the mental hospital to certify "(1) that such person has recovered his sanity, (2) *that, in the opinion of the superintendent, such person will not in the reasonable future be dangerous to himself, or others,* and (3) in the

opinion of the superintendent, the person is entitled to his unconditional release from the hospital ＊ ＊ ＊." D.C.Code § 24–301(e) (1967) (emphasis added).　To establish eligibility for release on habeas corpus, the patient must prove "freedom from such abnormal mental condition as would make the individual dangerous to himself or the community in the reasonably foreseeable future."　Overholser v. Leach, 103 U.S.App.D.C. 289, 292, 257 F.2d 667, 670 (1958), cert. denied 359 U.S. 1013, 79 S.Ct. 1152, 3 L.Ed.2d 1038 (1959).

conclusion of trial and with the apparent consent of the Government, Bolton was found not guilty by reason of insanity and committed to Saint Elizabeths Hospital pursuant to Subsection (d).

Three months later he brought this habeas corpus action alleging *inter alia* that shortly after the stipulated offenses he was committed in July 1965 to the Rockland State Hospital where he was treated "for six months and released as cured" of the mental illness which led him to commit the criminal acts. At a habeas corpus hearing held December 12, 1966, Dr. Weichardt, who was respondent's only witness, testified that appellant was still mentally ill and that if released "he'd get in trouble taking automobiles again." Bolton now appeals from the district court's denial of relief.

I

* * *

In Cameron v. Mullen,[10] we held that upon an acquittal by reason of insanity over a defendant's objection, a third inquiry is required for commitment, one that embodies the procedural safeguards of civil commitment. This inquiry, like the one on competence to stand trial, concerns *present* mental condition, but its purpose is to determine whether the defendant is mentally ill, dangerous and in need of treatment.[11] A defendant who was insane for the purpose of responsibility at the time of the offense may not be insane for the purpose of civil commitment at the time of the verdict, or (although competent to stand trial) he may be insane, dangerous and in need of treatment for the purpose of civil commitment.

* * *

In a habeas corpus petition, Mrs. Mullen challenged the validity of her confinement under Subsection (a). After the district court found that subsection unavailable, we held that she was entitled to have the more protective provisions of the 1964 Hospitalization of the Mentally Ill Act. We relied upon our decision in Cameron v. Fisher [15] in which we had held Subsection (a) unavailable by its own terms. We also relied on the principle derived from the Supreme Court's decision in Baxstrom v. Herold,[16] that the commission of criminal acts does not give rise to a presumption of dangerousness which, standing alone, justifies substantial difference in commitment procedures and confinement conditions for the mentally ill. We concluded that "while prior criminal conduct is relevant to the determination whether a per-

---

10. 128 U.S.App.D.C. 235, 387 F.2d 193 (March 2, 1967).

11. The standard for civil commitment is whether "the person is mentally ill and, because of that illness, is likely to injure himself or other persons if allowed to remain at liberty * * *." D.C.Code § 21–545(b) (1967).

15. 116 U.S.App.D.C. 9, 320 F.2d 730, 731 (1963).

16. 383 U.S. 107, 86 S.Ct. 760, 15 L.Ed. 2d 620 (1966).

son is mentally ill and dangerous, it cannot justify denial of procedural safeguards for that determination." And we also concluded that "while prior criminal conduct is a relevant consideration for determining the conditions of custodial care, it does not provide an automatic basis for allowing significant and arbitrary differences in such conditions." We think the principles of *Baxstrom* also apply where, as here, the defendant is acquitted upon his own plea of insanity.

II

Subsection (d) provides for automatic commitment without any hearing, even though acquittal by reason of insanity reflects only a reasonable doubt that the defendant was sane at the time of the offense. Like commitment under Subsection (a), the period of confinement under Subsection (d) is indeterminate and is unrelated to the period for which sentence could have been imposed upon conviction. A patient confined under Subsection (d) may be released only upon order of the court. The order must be based upon either the certificate of the Superintendent of Saint Elizabeths Hospital or the patient's petition for habeas corpus. The Superintendent may certify either that the patient has recovered his sanity, that he will not be dangerous to himself or others in the foreseeable future, and that he is entitled to unconditional release; or that, while not fully recovered, he is eligible for conditional release. In either case, the court may release the patient on the certificate or it may hold an evidentiary hearing concerning his recovery. It has been held that for release on habeas, the patient must prove beyond a reasonable doubt that he is free "from such abnormal mental condition as would make the individual dangerous to himself or others in the foreseeable future." and, according to some cases, that the Superintendent's refusal to issue a certificate is arbitrary and capricious.

So construed, this statutory scheme would conceivably allow a patient committed under Subsection (d) to remain in the hospital for the rest of his life without a judicial determination that he is mentally ill or that he is still likely to commit dangerous acts. In sharp contrast the 1964 Hospitalization of the Mentally Ill Act, enacted subsequent to the decisions referred to above, requires a judicial determination and places the burden of proving insanity on the Government. It also requires the hospital to examine a civilly committed patient at least every six months and to release him without a court order if the chief of the patient's service then deems him recovered.

The present version of § 24–301 prescribing the summary commitment procedures of Subsections (a) and (d) and the release standards of Subsection (e) was enacted after our decision in Durham v. United States. Its purpose was to "achieve a balance of interest between the public and the person charged with the crime" [28] by insuring

---

28.   S.Rep.No.1170, H.R.Rep.No.892, 84th Cong., 1st Sess. 2, 3, 16.

that "in every case where a person had committed a crime as a result of mental disease or defect, such person *shall* be given a period of hospitalization to guard against imminent recurrence of some criminal act by that person." The congressional committees which proposed the legislation thought "a mandatory commitment statute would add much to the public's peace of mind and to the public safety, without impairing the rights of the accused."

Before the advent of *Baxstrom* and the new civil commitment safeguards of the 1964 Hospitalization of the Mentally Ill Act, we said it was reasonable to treat those found not guilty by reason of insanity differently from other mentally ill persons because of the greater likelihood that the former will be dangerous to society, and that habeas corpus provided a sufficient safeguard for their rights. But in view of *Baxstrom* and the 1964 Act prior criminal conduct cannot be deemed a sufficient justification for substantial differences in the procedures and requirements for commitment, and habeas corpus may no longer be deemed to afford adequate protection against unwarranted detention. These principles apply whether a plea of insanity is raised by defendant, prosecutor or court. In each case the defense may be based merely upon "some" evidence, said to be "more than a scintilla" but not necessarily enough to raise a reasonable doubt of sanity. The plea is neither an express nor implied admission of present illness, and acquittal rests only on a reasonable doubt of *past* sanity, *i. e.,* at the time of the offense. It follows that there is no reasonable basis for distinction for commitment purposes between those who plead insanity and those who have the defense thrust upon them. Neither may be automatically deprived of the type of protection which the 1964 Hospitalization of the Mentally Ill Act provides.

* * *

The * * * recent case of Specht v. Patterson [42] renders Subsection (d) constitutionally suspect simply because the subsection fails to provide a hearing on present mental condition. In *Specht,* the Supreme Court held that a defendant convicted under Colorado law for "indecent liberties" could not be given an indeterminate sentence under the Colorado Sex Offenders Act without a full hearing. It rejected the Tenth Circuit's contention that defendant was "afforded all the rights of due process at the time of trial," by pointing out that the imposition of an indeterminate sentence requires "a new finding of fact [that the person convicted constitutes a threat of bodily harm to the public] that was not an ingredient of the offense charged [at trial]."

After acquittal by reason of insanity there is also need for a new finding of fact: The trial determined only that there was a reasonable doubt as to defendant's sanity in the past, present commitment is

42. [386 U.S. 605, 87 S.Ct. 1209, 18 L.Ed.2d 326 (1967.]

predicated on a finding of present insanity. Thus *Specht* would appear to require that this finding be made in a hearing.

The question is whether Subsection (d) can survive this constitutional attack. Rigid application of the equal protection doctrine might suggest that Subsection (d) be wholly supplanted by the Hospitalization of the Mentally Ill Act. But a reasonable application permits Subsection (d) to treat persons acquitted by reason of insanity differently from civilly committed persons to the extent that there are relevant differences between these two groups.

We agree * * * for example, that commitment without a hearing is permissible for the period required to determine present mental condition. The jury's finding of a reasonable doubt as to defendant's sanity at the time of the offense provides sufficient warrant for further examination.

The length of time required for such examination will vary, of course, with the individual case. It will be the responsibility of the court to establish this period, just as it now orders the hospital to make a determination and report its findings when the question of an accused's competency to stand trial is raised. The courts in this jurisdiction have sufficient experience with the problems involved to make individual judgments.

Once the examination period is over, however, there is no rational basis for denying a hearing. It is true that persons acquitted by reason of insanity have committed criminal acts and that this fact may tend to show they meet the requirements for commitment, namely, illness *and* dangerousness. But it does not remove these requirements. Nor does it justify total abandonment of the procedures used in civil commitment proceedings to determine whether these same requirements have been satisfied. Hence persons found not guilty by reason of insanity must be given a judicial hearing with procedures substantially similar to those in civil commitment proceedings. Since nothing in Subsection (d) precludes a hearing and since *Baxstrom* and *Specht* require one, we deem it necessarily implicit in our statute. * * *

III

The question then arises how a person thus committed can obtain release. We uphold the release provisions of § 24–301(e) even though they differ from civil commitment procedures by authorizing court review of the hospital's decision to release a patient. We do not think equal protection is offended by allowing the Government or the court the opportunity to insure that the standards for the release of civilly committed patients are faithfully applied to Subsection (d) patients.

We note, however, that under civil commitment procedures, a patient is entitled to periodic examinations by the hospital staff and has the right to be examined by an outside psychiatrist. If just one of the examining physicians believes he should no longer be hospitalized, he is entitled to a court hearing. Subsection (e) provides none of these safeguards. Because we find no rational justification for withholding these safeguards from a Subsection (d) patient, we construe Subsection (e) to require them.

Subsection (d) patients may also establish their eligibility for release by a writ of habeas corpus. This court has often debated what the burden of proof should be in such habeas proceedings. But it follows from our view of the requirements of equal protection that the burden for Subsection (d) patients must be the same as that for civilly committed patients. While the criminal acts committed by a Subsection (d) patient may be evidence indicating whether or not the burden has been met, they do not justify a different burden.

Unfortunately, the cases in this jurisdiction do not make clear what the burden of proof is in habeas proceedings challenging civil commitment. It could be argued that the Government should have the burden of proving that the patient is still committable, since this is where the burden lies in the initial commitment proceeding. But the traditional rule in habeas corpus proceedings is that the petitioner must prove, by the preponderance of the evidence, that his detention is illegal. We conclude that the traditional rule should apply, particularly since we have previously held that the hospital must assist the court in acquiring all the relevant information on the patient's condition, treatment, etc. Thus, the court must find, by the preponderance of the evidence, that the patient's commitment is no longer valid— i. e., that he is no longer "likely to injure himself or other persons" due to "mental illness." * * *

NOTES

1. How valuable are the procedural rights established in the instant case? If the hospital personnel in the facility housing the patient oppose his release, is a court likely to overrule them? In any case, how does a person demonstrate that he will not pose a danger once released:

> [O]nce a man has shown himself to be dangerous, it is all but impossible for him to prove the negative that he is no longer a menace. The spectors of the murder appellant committed 35 years ago * * * and the murder he may have committed more than 10 years ago obviously haunt the hospital at the very thought of granting him the least measure of freedom within [the hospital]. * * * [This] concern is understandable and may well be fully justified. But for all that appears, the murders and the unpredictable consequences will still be there after twenty years or after fifty.

Covington v. Harris, 136 U.S.App.D.C. 35, 419 F.2d 617 (1969).

2.   Might the problems be reduced by according defendants acquitted on insanity grounds certain limited "rights"?   Consider the following questions:

a.   Should post-acquittal hospitalization be available no matter what offense was charged?   Are there some offenses of so minimal dangerousness that a prosecution for them should not be permitted to result in hospitalization?   Should some limits be placed upon the length of time which an acquitted defendant can be hospitalized?   If so, what—if any—relationship should such limits have to the penalties provided for the offense charged?   See generally Overholser v. O'Beirne, 112 U.S.App. D.C. 267, 302 F.2d 852 (1961).

b.   Does—or should—a defendant acquitted on insanity grounds and committed to a psychiatric institution have a "right to treatment"?   Consider Wyatt v. Stickney, page 297, supra. Does—or should—he have a right to be treated in the manner involving the least restriction upon his liberty?   Cf. Ashe v. Robinson, 146 U.S.App.D.C. 220, 450 F.2d 681 (1971).   See generally, Chambers, Alternatives to Civil Commitment of the Mentally Ill: Practical Guides and Constitutional Imperatives, 70 Mich.L.Rev. 1107 (1972).

c.   Under what, if any, circumstances should a person hospitalized following a verdict of not guilty by reason of insanity have a right to be examined by an "independent" psychiatrist, i. e., one not affiliated with the institution in which he is hospitalized?   See State ex rel. Hoover v. Bloom, 461 S.W.2d 841 (Mo. 1971), holding that a patient hospitalized seventeen years following acquittal on a charge of child molesting had no such right.

d.   In a judicial proceeding brought in an attempt to obtain release following acquittal by reason of insanity, where should the burden of proof lie and what should it be?   See State v. Shackford, 262 A.2d 359 (Me.1970), holding that the patient must establish beyond a reasonable doubt that his release could be effected without danger to the public within the foreseeable future.

3.   Consider the following findings of the President's Commission on Crime in the District of Columbia relating to defendants acquitted on grounds of insanity and subsequently committed to Saint Elizabeth's, a large public psychiatric hospital.   Are they relevant to an evaluation of the propriety of an insanity defense as well as to the issues raised by post-acquittal hospitalization?

Duration of Confinement

As of December 31, 1965, 203 of the 361 persons who were charged with felonies and found not guilty by reason of insanity in the United States District Court had been released from Saint Elizabeths Hospital; 144 of these obtained their first release conditionally and 59 were released the first time unconditionally. * * * 23 persons originally charged with felonies were released from the hospital in less than six months and 25 more were released in less than a year; 19 of the 48 were conditionally released and 29 were unconditionally released. Thus, among the 361 persons found not guilty by reason of insanity in the District Court, 13 percent (48 of 361) were released in less than a year. * * * 153 (42 percent) of the 361 persons committed to Saint Elizabeths have not been released, conditionally or unconditionally.

Limitations of available data prevent a precise comparison of confinement in Saint Elizabeths Hospital with length of time spent by convicted felons in prison. * * *

However, an approximate comparison can be made * * *. [T]he median confinement at Saint Elizabeths Hospital appears to be greater than the median confinement of District felons in prison in every crime category with the very important exception of homicide and the less important exceptions of forgery, "other felonies," and possibly narcotics.

Medians may also be calculated for the length of time spent in the hospital by persons charged with misdemeanors in the Court of General Sessions. Whereas the maximum prison sentence for a misdemeanor is 12 months or less, the median length of confinement for *released* misdemeanor patients is 15.8 months.

Escapes

The Commission has concluded that the number of escapes from Saint Elizabeths Hospital is a serious problem which requires immediate attention and remedial action. During the calendar years 1955 through 1965, 202 (34 percent) of the 591 persons committed after a finding of not guilty by reason of insanity left the hospital without permission. 139 (39 percent) of the persons who had been charged with felonies eloped, and 63 (27 percent) of those who had been charged with misdemeanors eloped. As of December 31, 1965, Saint Elizabeths had 384 insanity acquittal patients on its rolls and 39 (10 percent) were on unauthorized leave.

Although 80 percent of these escapes lasted for a day or less, 7 percent lasted longer than a year. Many had serious consequences. * * * [A]pproximately one-third of the escaped persons were arrested on criminal charges.

Most of the escapes from Saint Elizabeths Hospital are made from the West Side Service or from other facilities housing prisoner-patients; they are not made from John Howard Pavilion. These escapes are usually "walk-offs," which occur when the patients are enjoying ground privileges incident to progress in the treatment program, and are generally attributable to the lack of staff and proper facilities.

Criminal Conduct After Release

One of the few available measures of the effectiveness of treatment at Saint Elizabeths of patients found not guilty by reason of insanity is the extent to which persons released subsequently engage in criminal conduct. Of the 360 patients who were released conditionally or unconditionally prior to December 31, 1965, 134 (37 percent) were rearrested a total of 406 times after their release. Ninety-five of these arrests were for felonies.

Although these figures are alarmingly high, they are roughly comparable to the incidence of rearrest of felons after a prison term. A leading authority on recidivism statistics has reported that about 50 percent of male felons released from prison acquire a record of subsequent arrests within 2 to 5 years after release. Any comparison with the 37 percent subsequent arrest rate for persons charged with felonies in the United States District Court and released from Saint Elizabeths Hospital must be qualified, since only 52 percent of the District Court releasees had been out more than 3 years and only 69 percent had been released for more than 2 years as of April 1966.

The same authority on recidivism also concludes that about one-third of the felons released from prison are convicted of subsequent felonies. Forty-one of 203 District Court insanity releases (20 percent) acquired a record of felony arrests and their convictions can only be a smaller proportion.

President's Commission on Crime in the District of Columbia, Report 545–549, 555–557, 558–559 (1966).

C. PSYCHOLOGICAL ABNORMALITY AND THE REQUIREMENT OF A "WILLED ACT"

STATE v. MERCER

Supreme Court of North Carolina, 1969.
275 N.C. 108, 165 S.E.2d 328.

[This case is reprinted at page 320, supra.]

NOTES

1. To what extent must the defendant's consciousness be affected to bring the rule applied in the instant case into play? Consider the following comment from People v. Newton, 8 Cal.App.3d 359, 87 Cal.Rptr. 394, 405 (1970):

"Unconsciousness," as the term is used in the rule * * *, need not reach the physical dimensions commonly associated with the term (coma, inertia, incapability of locomotion or manual action, and so on); it can exist * * * where the subject physically acts in fact but is not, at the time, conscious of acting.

Is this helpful?

2. Was the assertion by the defendant in *Mercer* properly considered as raising the issue of whether a sufficient "act" upon which to base lia-

bility had been performed? If the trier of fact should believe the defendant's testimony would the result under the instant case (acquittal) be proper, especially when compared to that which would be reached if the defendant's testimony was considered as raising a defense of "insanity"? See infra.

3. How is it to be determined whether evidence of modified consciousness should be held as raising the issue of the existence of a voluntary act or as raising the "insanity" defense. The instruction which was held erroneously refused in People v. Wilson, 66 Cal.2d 749, 59 Cal.Rptr. 156, 427 P.2d 820 (1967) included the following:

> [The rule holding that an act committed while unconscious is not criminal] does not apply to a case in which the mental state of the person in question is due to insanity [or] mental defect * * * but applies only to persons of sound mind as, for example, somnambulists or persons suffering from the delirium of fever, epilepsy, a blow on the head or the involuntary taking of drugs or intoxicating liquors, and other cases in which there is no functioning of the conscious mind and the person's acts are controlled solely by the subconscious mind.

Is this an appropriate criterion? If so, did the evidence here tend to show that the defendant was a person of "sound mind"? Does a person of "sound mind" black out under the circumstances in which the defendant testified he had blacked out? See Sprague v. State, 52 Wis.2d 89, 187 N.W.2d 784 (1971), apparently holding that psychomotor epilepsy "or other pathological conditions of impaired consciousness" should be considered only as raising the insanity issue and not as raising "a defense under the principle requiring that an act be voluntary in order to be criminal." Consider also the following, from Commonwealth v. Crosby, 444 Pa. 17, 279 A.2d 73, 75, 76 (1971):

> Appellant, an auxiliary policeman, later that day went to his wife's apartment. He testified as follows with respect to what thereafter transpired: Upon entering the apartment, he discovered his wife having sexual relations in front of his children with Robert Cliett. He left the bedroom and walked into another room, where his wife soon joined him. When he told her that he would report her conduct to the Court, she shouted to Cliett, "Get him!" Cliett picked up a large wooden slat and charged toward appellant, who then fired the gun in Cliett's direction. Appellant was unable to remember anything after firing the first shot. His first recollection afterwards was that he had a gun in his hand in an alley about one-half a block from his wife's apartment.

> * * *

> Appellant's next contention involves the lower Court's refusal to admit the testimony of Dr. Robert L. Sadoff, a psychiatrist. This psychiatric testimony was *not offered to show insanity* under the M'Naghten Rule * * * nor for the purpose of showing a mental state *incapable of forming the specific intent* necessary for a finding and verdict of first-degree murder * * *[.]

> Appellant's purpose in offering this testimony was to corroborate his narration and theory of the crime—i. e., that he *blacked out*

after firing the first shot at Cliett, so that he was thereafter *unconscious of what he was doing* and, therefore, lacked the requisite criminal intent for the commission of any crime.[2]

A careful examination of the cases in those jurisdictions which allow and apply this defense of unconsciousness reveals that in no instance has it been applied to a factual situation such as related by this appellant. Unconsciousness as a defense has been permitted only where the defendant's state of unconsciousness resulted from a physical ailment such as epilepsy, Smith v. Commonwealth, 268 S.W.2d 937 (Ky.), or a physical disability such as that resulting from a blow on the head, People v. Cox, 67 Cal.App.2d 166, 153 P.2d 362, or the mental condition of somnambulism, Fain v. Commonwealth, 78 Ky. 183.

More specifically, the defense of unconsciousness resulting from a blackout—a complete defense—has never been recognized in Pennsylvania where, as here, the defendant's state of unconsciousness is the result of the excitement or emotion naturally engendered by the commission of an unlawful, cold-blooded killing. We believe that the defense of unconsciousness has no application whatever in a situation such as this.[3]

The Court below did not err in excluding the psychiatric testimony of Dr. Sadoff.

4. If an offense is committed during an epileptic seizure, would this raise an issue of "insanity" or "automatism"? For a study suggesting that acts of violence are unusual—but possible—during an epileptic seizure, see Knox, Epileptic Automatism and Violence, 8 Med., Sci. & L. 96 (1968).

5. The American cases are discussed in Fox, Physical Disorder, Consciousness, and Criminal Liability, 63 Colum.L.Rev. 645 (1963), who concluded that as of that date the opportunity to exploit the ambiguity in early cases as to the existence of a defense of "unconsciousness" had been largely neglected. Id. at 655. Foreign discussions are numerous. See, e. g., N. Morris and C. Howard, Studies in Criminal Law, 61–78 (1964); Williams, Automatism, in Essays in Criminal Science (G. Mueller ed. 1961); Blackwell, Automatism and Amnesia, 79 S.A.L.J. 16 (1962); Cross, Reflections on Bratty's Case, 78 L.Q.Rev. 236 (1962); Edwards, Automatism and Criminal Responsibility, 21 Mod.L.Rev. 375 (1958), supplemented by Edwards, Automatism and Social Defense, 8 Crim.L.Q. 258 (1965); Elliott, Responsibility for Involuntary Acts: Ryan v. The Queen, 41 Aust.L.J. 497 (1968); Jennings, The Growth and Development of Automatism as a Defense in Criminal Law, 2 Os.H.L.J. 370 (1962); Kahn, Automatism, Sane and Insane, 1965 N.Z.L.J. 113, 128; Keene, The Problem of Automatism, 1968

2. Since appellant claims that the blackout occurred after he fired the first shot at Cliett, this testimony could only be relevant, if at all, to the conviction in the subsequent killing of his wife.

3. If we were to accept appellant's theory of this defense, it would follow that a murderer who lines up seven innocent persons, intending to kill them, shoots and wounds five of them, and then becomes so emotionally excited or upset that he "blacks out," but thereafter shoots and kills the remaining two persons, he would not be guilty of any crime against these two victims.

Auckland U.L.Rev. 15; Leigh, Automatism and Insanity, 5 Crim.L.Q. 160 (1962); Scoble, Amnesia, Automatism and Insanity, 79 S.A.L.J. 338 (1962). The application of the defense to strict liability offenses is discussed in Clark, Automatism and Strict Liability, 5 V.U.W.L.Rev. 12 (1968).

D. PSYCHOLOGICAL ABNORMALITY AND THE DEGREE OF CRIMINAL LIABILITY

DIAMOND, CRIMINAL RESPONSIBILITY OF THE MENTALLY ILL

14 Stan.L.Rev. 59, 62 (1961).

Central to the difficulties with any definition of legal insanity is the all-or-none conceptualization of the law. A defendant is either sane and totally responsible, or insane and not at all responsible. Such all-or-none concepts are peculiarly foreign to modern psychiatric thinking. Neither normal persons nor mentally disturbed persons are ever "all-or-none" in their psychological functioning. When such an arbitrary division is required of the psychiatric expert he is liable to testify capriciously and not in accord with all of the psychological facts of the case.

1. "DIMINISHED CAPACITY"

PEOPLE v. WELLS

Supreme Court of California, 1949.
33 Cal.2d 330, 202 P.2d 53, certiorari denied 338 U.S. 836,
70 S.Ct. 43, 94 L.Ed. 510.

SCHAUER, Justice. Wesley Robert Wells appeals from a judgment entered upon a jury verdict that he is guilty of violation of section 4500 of the Penal Code, and from an order denying his motion for new trial. Section 4500 provides that certain kinds of assault committed by life-term prisoners "with malice aforethought" are capital offenses. Defendant contends: * * * (4) The trial court erred to his prejudice by excluding evidence of medical experts offered to show that he did not act with "malice aforethought." * * * [W]e conclude that the proffered evidence should have been received but that the error in rejecting it is not prejudicial.

* * *

In every crime there must exist a union or joint operation of act and intent. In the present case there is little dispute as to the act done by defendant; the crucial factual question is whether such act was done with the intent or motive which is an essential element of the crime denounced by section 4500 of the Penal Code; i. e., "with malice aforethought".

This issue, then, necessarily involves proof of a mental state (the specific intent or motive amounting to malice aforethought) and, as pertinent and material to resolving such issue, the prosecution (as has been shown hereinabove) was properly allowed to introduce evidence of various objective manifestations by defendant from which it could be inferred that he bore such "malice aforethought" toward prison guards as a class and toward Brown in particular.[4] Defendant was likewise properly allowed to give testimony as to his state of mind which tended to show lack of "malice aforethought."[5] But defendant was not allowed to introduce proffered evidence of physicians who had observed objective manifestations by defendant from which it could be inferred that, because he was suffering from an abnormal physical and mental condition (not insanity) at the time he injured Brown, defendant acted, not with "malice aforethought," but, as he himself testified, under fear for his personal safety and in the honest belief that he was defending himself from attack by Officers Robinson and Hogan. Defendant made and the trial court refused the following offer of proof: Two days before the assault upon Guard Brown the chief medical officer of the prison, making his customary rounds, saw defendant and was impressed by defendant's apparently abnormal state; he required defendant to report to the prison hospital where he examined defendant and caused defendant to be examined by the consulting psychiatrist of the prison; both physicians concluded that defendant was suffering from a "state of tension"; i. e., a condition in which "the whole body and mind are in a state of high sensitivity to external stimuli, and the result of this state is to cause the victim

4. In addition to the above summarized evidence of other instances of misconduct, the prosecution introduced the following evidence tending to show "malice aforethought": Testimony of a prisoner (contradicted by defendant) that on the night before the assault defendant said, "I will demand that son-of-a-bitch [Brown] be in the Warden's office [at the time of the disciplinary hearing] and I will hit him with the first thing I can get my hands on"; testimony of prison officials as to defendant's conduct, as evidencing his state of mind, immediately before the disciplinary hearing (defendant said, when he was told that he should enter the hearing room, "You'll be sorry you took me first"), at the hearing (defendant "became very noisy and upset"), and immediately after he left the hearing room and before he injured Brown (defendant was weeping and "trembling all over").

5. Defendant testified as to his feelings toward prison officers in general and Brown in particular; as to his state of mind at the time he picked up and threw the cuspidor; and as to the attitude engendered when he learned (in 1946) that, after his 1944 conviction, the deputy district attorney who prosecuted that case (and the present case) recommended to the Adult Authority that it "not fix a definite term in this case. As long as you fail to do so, his maximum sentence will remain at life, and he will be subject to prosecution under the statute which makes it a capital offense for a life term prisoner to commit an assault."

or patient to react abnormally to situations and external stimuli. *One of the characteristics of this state is that the patient possesses an abnormal fear for his personal safety and that an external stimulus apparently threatening that personal safety will cause the patient to react to it more violently and more unpredictably than the same stimulus applied to a normal person. In other words, that the threshold of the fear of the patient is lower to the extent where stimuli which would normally not cause fear in the patient will cause fear in the patient suffering from this state.*" (Italics added.) The psychiatrist, pursuant to the results of his examination, "made to the prison authorities certain recommendations for the alleviation of this condition; [before these recommendations were acted upon defendant injured Brown]; * * * also he examined the defendant after the occurrence out of which this charge arose and is prepared to testify to his then mental and physical condition."

The proffered evidence above summarized would be incompetent to establish the defense known as "self-defense" because one's rights in self-defense are limited to such acts as are either *actually* reasonably necessary or which would appear to a *reasonable* person, under the same circumstances, to be reasonably necessary. But here the evidence was not offered to prove self-defense; it was offered solely in relation to the specific mental state which was necessarily put in issue by the charge and the not guilty plea and concerning which the prosecution had already produced substantial evidence. Under the circumstances the materiality of this evidence in defendant's case is patent. If he acted only under the influence of fear of bodily harm, in the belief, honest though unreasonable, that he was defending himself from such harm by the use of a necessary amount of force, then defendant, although he would not be guiltless of crime, would not have committed that particular aggravated offense with which he is charged, for the essential element of "malice aforethought" would be lacking. In resolving this question in a close case the jury could well be materially aided by the knowledge that, in the opinion of qualified experts, the defendant's condition was such that he might readily have acted from genuine fear rather than from a desire for vengeance or from any other malicious purpose.

* * *

The issue upon which the improperly excluded evidence was offered does not, however, appear to have been a close one. In accord with the mandate of section 4½ of article VI of the state Constitution we have examined the entire cause, including the evidence, and have concluded that the rejection of the physicians' proffered testimonies did not result in a miscarriage of justice. Able and conscientious counsel have not on behalf of defendant pointed out, nor have we discovered, any reason for the jury's having been in doubt or difficulty in resolving against defendant the question of his state of mind. It is apparent from defendant's own frank testimony[6] that he set up for himself and for the prison officials standards of conduct different from those recognized by the law of this state and the rules of the prison, and that, fully aware of the probable consequences, he conducted himself in accord with such standards rather than according to law. The jury determined—and it is almost impossible to imagine that either with or without the proffered, excluded testimonies they could have determined otherwise—that defendant at the time of the charged offense was acting pursuant to such just mentioned personal standards, and malice for those who breached them, rather than under the influence of honest, mistaken fear.

For the reasons above stated the judgment and order appealed from are affirmed.

NOTES

1. In Fisher v. United States in the District of Columbia, 328 U.S. 463, 66 S.Ct. 1318, 90 L.Ed. 1382 (1946) the defendant had been charged with first degree ("premeditated") murder. At trial, he contended that his "mental and emotional qualities" were "of such a level at the time of the crime that he was incapable of deliberation and premeditation although he was then sane in the usual legal sense." Testimony of psychiatrists tending to support this was introduced. Fisher requested that the jury be instructed to consider his "personality" in determining whether he had the state of mind required for first degree murder. This was refused, the defendant was convicted, and an appeal was taken. The Supreme Court affirmed:

> We express no opinion whether the theory for which petitioner contends should or should not be made the law of the District of Columbia. Such a radical departure from common law concepts is more properly a subject for the exercise of legislative power or at least for the discretion of the courts of the District.

2. Assuming that evidence of psychological abnormality is admissible on the issue of state of mind, should it be permitted to disprove any state of

---

6. "Q. [Referring to the night before Brown was injured, when defendant violated a prison rule by creating a disturbance.] You made sufficient noise to awaken every one in that immediate vicinity? * * * A. I would say yes. Q. In other words, you at that time were not concerned with awaking people, although you had been making all this fuss when you had been awakened when the officer was doing his duty in counting the cells? A. I am interested in looking out for Wells' welfare. I was due to appear before the court the next morning for disciplinary action, and I wanted to be able to present some kind of a case. * * * I rattled my cup on the door, which is proper to do if wou want to speak to the guard. The guard came up and I made my request and he said he would make his report, and I told him that I must see Lieutenant Stevenson * * * I said, 'I will give him about twenty minutes. I don't want to create any disturbance to cause anybody any trouble, but I want to see him this morning, because I am going to court.' Q. In other words, you were laying down an ultimatum? A. If you want to put it that way * * * I was going to continue to make a noise until I saw Lieutenant Stevenson * * * Any time I feel I am being misused by an officer or by anyone I resent it, and I will let them know I resent it, and if they haven't given occasion to show any different use toward me, I conduct myself as a gentleman."

mind? Would there be a likelihood of complete acquittals? If so, is this desirable in a jurisdiction which has a distinct "insanity" defense? How might such a situation be avoided? Might psychological abnormality be admitted only to disprove a "specific" intent? Could this be justified? Reconsider the limitations upon the use of intoxication raised at pages 546–60, supra. See also People v. Noah, 5 Cal.3d 469, 487 P.2d 1009 (1971).

Suppose the evidence is offered in support of a defendant's contention that a killing is voluntary manslaughter rather than murder because of the "provocation" rule. The Pennsylvania Supreme Court had evidenced its hostility to psychiatric evidence in a series of cases holding that such testimony was not admissible to disprove a "specific intent to kill" and thereby reduce a killing from first degree murder to second degree murder. See Commonwealth v. Rightnor, 435 Pa. 104, 253 A.2d 644 (1969); Commonwealth v. Phelan, 427 Pa. 265, 234 A.2d 540 (1967); Commonwealth v. Ahearn, 421 Pa. 311, 218 A.2d 561 (1966). But in Commonwealth v. McCusker, 448 Pa. 382, 292 A.2d 286 (1972) the same court reversed a conviction for second degree murder because the trial court had excluded psychiatric testimony offered in support of the defendant's contention that he had acted in the "heat of passion" and was therefore guilty of only voluntary manslaughter:

> Our law is quite explicit that the determination of whether a certain quantum of provocation is sufficient to support the defense of voluntary manslaughter is purely an objective standard. * * *
>
> Having found in a given situation that an accused was confronted with adequate provocation, the focus then shifts to defendant's response to that provocation. * * * Applying the established principles of relevancy to a murder prosecution where a defendant asserts that he acted in the heat of passion, it seems clear that any evidence—lay or psychiatric—pertinent to that defense should be admissible.

292 A.2d at 290–91.

3. What effect should "diminished capacity" have in a homicide case prosecuted on the felony-murder theory? Consider the following comments concerning California law:

> [T]he court should require that the defense apply with as much force in felony-murder cases as it now does in murder cases. This change in the law could best be implemented through a new jury instruction that will apply the diminished capacity defense correctly and effectively, yet will not undermine the rationale of the felony-murder rule. The jurors are presently instructed that if they believe that the defendant, prior to the commission or attempted commission of the felony, was suffering from such a diminished capacity due to intoxication or mental defect or disease so that he could not form the intent to commit the underlying felony, they may not convict him of felony-murder. Such a finding normally results in a conviction of involuntary manslaughter, the same result reached in murder cases in which evidence of diminished capacity—approaching unconsciousness or insanity—successfully rebuts the proof of specific intent of the defendant to take human life.

The jurors should be further instructed that if they find the specific intent to commit the underlying felony, yet believe that the defendant, due to his diminished capacity, was unable to form this intent as a result of premeditation and deliberation, or was unable to recognize and reflect upon the degree of risk involved, they should find him guilty of no more than second degree murder. This instruction would not alter the mechanics of the felony-murder rule; if specific intent to commit the felony were shown, the offender would still be presumed guilty of murder in the first degree. The presumption could be rebutted, however, by a showing that the defendant's mental state precluded him from engaging in the requisite premeditation and deliberation. The felony-murder rule should not be allowed to produce results materially different from regular murder, when the defendant could not be guilty of first degree murder due to his inability to premeditate and deliberate. Indeed, to hold a defendant responsible for first degree murder under these circumstances is contrary to the underlying rationale of the felony-murder rule.

While the defense of diminished capacity would thus be given its appropriate effect in an area where it was formerly of only nominal value, the essence of the felony-murder rule would remain intact. In addition, the deterrent purpose of the rule would be unaltered since felons who claim only that they did not intend to kill are still subject to the traditional operation of the rule. The injustice of convicting people of crimes for which they lacked the requisite mental capacity would be eliminated. Only when the defendant could not, due to diminished mental capacity, have arrived at the intent to commit the felony by means of premeditation and deliberation would the rule no longer operate to convict him of murder in the first degree. Any other result is clearly at odds with the rationale of the *Wells-Gorshen* doctrine as well as that of the felony-murder rule.

Note, The Diminished Capacity Defense to Felony-Murder, 23 Stan.L.Rev. 799, 809–10 (1971).[n]

4. Consider the wisdom of legislative enactment of the following statute:

Diminished Responsibility of Offender

1. Definition of Diminished Responsibility. An offender shall be regarded as being of diminished responsibility if the trier of fact finds that at the time of the offense his psychological condition was such that he should not be regarded as fully responsible for his offense.

2. Effect of Diminished Responsibility. In any case in which the trier of fact makes a finding of diminished responsibility, the sentencing judge should consider this as a mitigating factor and should impose a less severe penalty than would be imposed had there not been such a finding. In no case in which there

has been a finding of diminished responsibility may the sentence imposed exceed, in minimum or maximum term, two-thirds of the minimum and maximum that would otherwise be authorized for offense.

3. Admissibility of Evidence of Diminished Responsibility. Any evidence tending to establish that the defendant was mentally ill or otherwise psychologically abnormal at the time of an alleged offense for which he is being tried shall be admissible.

4. Burden of Proof on Responsibility. A defendant shall be presumed to be fully responsible. Where a defendant introduces evidence which raises the issue of his responsibility, however, the prosecution must prove full responsibility beyond a reasonable doubt. If the prosecution fails to carry that burden, the defendant is entitled to a finding of diminished responsibility.

5. Instruction to Jury. In any jury trial in which the evidence raises an issue of diminished responsibility, the trial jury should be instructed on the definition of diminished responsibility, on the burden of proof on that issue, and that in evaluating responsibility they should consider any evidence of the defendant's reduced capacity to conform his conduct to the requirements of law at the time of the offense as well as any evidence of his reduced capacity to understand the nature, quality, or criminality of his action. The jury should also be told that if they find that the defendant committed the crime and was not insane at the time of the crime, but that the prosecution has not proved full responsibility at the time of the crime, they should indicate on their verdict that the defendant should be regarded as being of diminished responsibility. The jury should further be instructed that if they find that the defendant was of diminished responsibility the trial judge will be required by law to impose a less severe penalty than would otherwise be the case.

6. Nonjury Trials. Where trial of a criminal case is to the court rather than the jury, the court should consider evidence of mental illness or psychological abnormality and, where appropriate, make a specific finding of diminished responsibility.

Reconsider the matter after examination of the materials that follow.

5. For general treatment of "diminished capacity," see Diamond, Criminal Responsibility of the Mentally Ill, 14 Stan.L.Rev. 59 (1962); Dix, Psychological Abnormality as a Factor in Grading Criminal Liability: Diminished Capacity, Diminished Responsibility, and the Like, 62 J.Crim.L., C. & P.S. 313 (1971); Hasse, Keeping Wolff From the Door: California's Diminished Capacity Concept, 60 Cal.L.Rev. 1641 (1972); Keedy, A Problem of First Degree Murder: Fisher v. United States, 99 U.Pa.L.Rev. 26 (1950); Taylor, Partial Insanity as Affecting the Degree of Crime—A Commentary on Fisher v. United States, 34 Cal.L.Rev. 625 (1946); Weihofen, Partial Insanity and Criminal Intent, 24 Ill.L.Rev. 505 (1930); Comment, A Punishment Rationale for Diminished Capacity, 18 U.C.L.A.L.Rev. 561 (1971). The California cases are discussed in Cooper, Diminished Capacity, 4 Loyola U.L.A.L.Rev. 308 (1971); Comment, Diminished Ca-

pacity: Its Potential Effect in California, 3 Loyola U.L.A.L.Rev. 153 (1970). The American cases are collected in Annot., Mental or Emotional Condition as Diminishing Responsibility for Crime, 22 A.L.R.3rd 1228 (1968).

MODEL PENAL CODE

(P.O.D.1962).

Section 4.02.   Evidence of Mental Disease or Defect Admissible When Relevant to Element of the Offense; [Mental Disease or Defect Impairing Capacity as Ground for Mitigation of Punishment in Capital Cases]

(1) Evidence that the defendant suffered from a mental disease or defect is admissible whenever it is relevant to prove that the defendant did or did not have a state of mind which is an element of the offense.

[(2) Whenever the jury or the Court is authorized to determine or to recommend whether or not the defendant shall be sentenced to death or imprisonment upon conviction, evidence that the capacity of the defendant to appreciate the criminality [wrongfulness] of his conduct or to conform his conduct to the requirements of law was impaired as a result of mental disease or defect is admissible in favor of sentence of imprisonment.]

STATE v. SIKORA

Supreme Court of New Jersey, 1965.
44 N.J. 453, 210 A.2d 193.

FRANCIS, J.   [Defendant shot and killed Douglas Hooey in a tavern on January 15, 1962. Following a fight between the two, defendant returned to his apartment, got a gun, and returned to the tavern where he shot Hooey. At his apartment, police found a note saying, "The first bullet is for Doug and the second is for Stella Miller." Stella Miller was defendant's former girlfriend. He was tried and convicted of first degree premeditated murder.]

The error asserted in this Court as requiring reversal of the conviction had its origin in one hypothetical question put by defense counsel to Dr. Noel C. Galen, a psychiatrist produced on behalf of the defendant.

* * *

Dr. Galen specializes in psychiatry and psychoanalysis. He received his M.D. degree in 1949. In addition to postgraduate work in neurology and psychiatry, he had three years of training as a psychoanalyst. This last training, he said, dealt with psychodynamics on a very detailed and sophisticated level. It taught him that people are a product of their own life history, their own genetic patterns, and that they all react differently under the stresses of their daily lives. As a result of his study and experience, he believes that mental disturbance and disorder, as distinguished from objective disease, are merely gradients, that people range from being essentially normal, perceiving the world substantially in its normal appearance, all the way to marked distortion of the thinking mechanism, and between the two extremes is a rather jagged line which is prone to and open to many variations.   *   *   *   Mental illness or disorder in this context is a relative term as he sees it; it is a disorganization of the personality which causes a person to react in a specific way to a specific kind of stress in a way characteristic for him.

*   *   *

The idea seems to be that every deed, no matter how quickly executed, is never fully the result of the apparent immediate cause, and must be judged according to the probable unconscious motivations of an individual with the actor's lifelong history.   Therefore, if in the opinion of the psychodynamically oriented psychiatrist, the deed, when evaluated against a background of the individual's life history, was probably produced by unconscious rather than conscious motivations, there was no *mens rea,* no criminal intent, and therefore no criminal guilt.   In his view the conduct must be considered as having been conditioned by internal and external forces quite beyond the actor's control.

[At trial, defense counsel asked Dr. Galen whether, given the facts of the case, in Dr. Galen's opinion the defendant was capable of premeditating a murder.   The prosecution's objection was sustained; the following represents what Dr. Galen would have testified if he had been permitted to answer.]

According to Dr. Galen, tensions had been building up in Sikora, particularly since his female friend rejected him.   When he was humiliated in the tavern by the remarks about her availability for other men because she had broken with him, and then physically beaten by Hooey and his companions, the tensions mounted to the point where they represented a situation in life with which he felt unable to cope.   So he began to act in an automatic way;   the manner in which a person with his personality inadequacy would characteristically act.   He responded to the stress in the way which inevitably would be his way of dealing with that kind of stress.   He reacted automatically in the fashion of Dr. Galen's physician friend when he was cut off by another motorist.   His successive actions, walking home from the tavern, reporting the assault upon him to the police, deciding against a criminal complaint, obtaining his gun from its place of concealment in the apartment, putting the extra bullets in his pocket, writing the note that the first bullet was for Doug and the second for Stella Miller, contemplating suicide, test-firing the gun, rejecting the idea of suicide, reloading the gun on the stairway of his apartment while thinking about Hooey and the beating in the tavern, walking to the tavern to "talk" to Hooey, deciding to use the alley entrance in an effort to draw Hooey out that way, and putting four bullets into Hooey after backing some distance from the tavern while warning him not to come closer and advising him he was "liable" to find out the gun would fire if he came closer, and then walking to the Miller woman's apartment still carrying the gun and searching for her, all showed strong elements of automatism. The beating administered by Hooey in the tavern precipitated the disorganization of his personality to the extent that from then on he probably "acted in at least a semi-automatic way, and probably an automatic way."

The doctor went on to say that from the defendant's course of conduct it could be seen that he was acting in an automatic way "rather than being totally aware of his environment, and the situation * * *." Although the state was not completely an automatic one there were "strong elements of automatism" present. He was not "fully conscious of his activities" and not "completely aware" of what he was doing. The stress to which he had been subjected had distorted his personality mechanism. His personality disorder, the kind of man life had made him, when subjected to that stress prevented him from "seeing reality, or premeditating or forming a rational opinion of what is going on in his life." He had been confronted with a situation and reacted with conduct which was his characteristic way of dealing with the particular kind of stress. * * *

In short the doctor opined that the circumstances to which Sikora had been subjected imposed on his personality disorder a stress that impaired or removed his ability consciously to premeditate or weigh a design to kill. The tension was so great that he could handle it only by an automatic reaction motivated by the predetermined influence of his unconscious. Plainly the doctor meant that Sikora's response was not a voluntary exercise of his free will. The stress was such as to distort his mechanisms. During the various actions Sikora took leading up to the killing, which so clearly indicate conception, deliberation and execution of a plan to kill, he was thinking but the thinking was automatic; it was simply subconscious thinking or reaction; it was not conscious thinking. The doctor said Sikora's anxieties at the time were of such a nature that conceivably, his reaction in that automatic way and the commission of the homicide, actually prevented a further disorganization of his personality. The killing, said the doctor, was "a rational murder" but "everything this man did was irrational," and engaged in when he could not conceive the design to kill. * * *

The question now presented is whether psychiatric evidence of the nature described is admissible in first degree murder cases on the issue of premeditation. Defendant argues that it should have been received at the trial on that issue.

In [State v.] Di Paolo [, 34 N.J. 279, 168 A.2d 401, cert. denied, 368 U.S. 880, 82 S.Ct. 130 (1961)] the Chief Justice said that evidence of "any defect, deficiency, trait, condition, or illness which rationally bears upon the question" whether the defendant did in fact premeditate is admissible at a first degree murder trial. But he indicated also that if such evidence was unreliable or too speculative or incompetent when tested by concepts established in law for the determination of criminal responsibility, it should not be received on the issue of guilt or innocence. That is the situation here. * * *

Criminal responsibility must be judged at the level of the conscious. If a person thinks, plans and executes the plan at that level, the criminality of his act cannot be denied, wholly or partially, because, although he did not realize it, his conscious was influenced to think, to plan and to execute the plan by unconscious influences which were the product of his genes and his lifelong environment. So in the present case, criminal guilt cannot be denied or confined to second degree murder (when the killing was a "rational murder" and the product of thought and action), because Sikora was unaware that his decisions and conduct were mechanistically directed by unconscious influences bound to result from the tensions to which he was subjected at the time. If the law were to accept such a medical doctrine as a basis for a finding of second rather than first degree murder, the legal doctrine of *mens rea* would all but disappear from the law. Applying Dr. Galen's theory to crimes requiring specific intent to commit, such as robbery, larceny, rape, etc., it is difficult to imagine an individual who perpetrated the deed as having the mental capacity in the criminal law sense to conceive the intent to commit it. Criminal responsibility, as society now knows it, would vanish from the scene, and some other basis for dealing with the offender would have to be found. At bottom, this would appear to be the ultimate aim of the psychodynamic psychiatrists.

WEINTRAUB, C. J. (concurring). * * *

It seems clear to me that the psychiatric view expounded by Dr. Galen is simply irreconcilable with the basic thesis of our criminal law, for while the law requires proof of an evil-meaning mind, this psychiatric thesis denies there is any such thing. To grant a role in our existing structure to the theme that the conscious is just the innocent puppet of a nonculpable unconscious is to make a mishmash of the criminal law, permitting—indeed requiring—each trier of the facts to choose between the automaton thesis and the law's existing concept of criminal accountability. It would be absurd to decide criminal blameworthiness upon a psychiatric thesis which can find no basis for personal blame. So long as we adhere to criminal blameworthiness, *mens rea* must be sought and decided at the level of conscious behavior.

NOTES

1. Diamond, With Malice Aforethought, 2 Archives of Criminal Psychodynamics 1, 29 (1957):

* * * I believe that the psychiatrist's job in cases in which psychiatric evidence is offered to prove the absence of malice aforethought is to make as thorough-going investigation as possible of the defendant, searching for the hidden psychodynamics which will explain the unique act of criminal behavior. The clinical information which is obtained can then be formulated in terms of the vast body of psychoanalytic knowledge * * * This must then be translated into terms which are meaningful to the judge and jury.

Actually, the law is not interested in the psychiatrists' speculations about free will. Nor is it interested in medical categorizing of who does or does not have malice aforethought. What it wants to know is whether, in the case of the particular individual on trial, did the criminal action result from a voluntary, deliberate choice such as normal, reasonable persons appear to make in their daily lives, or was it the result of pathological forces arising far below the conscious level over which the defendant had little power of control.

How accurate is Doctor Diamond's description of the legal issue in a homicide case raising "diminished capacity"?

2. Consider the following from Dix, Mental Illness, Criminal Intent, and the Bifurcated Trial, 1970 Law and the Social Order 559, 567:

To most mental health personnel, the conscious awareness and desires of an individual at any one specific time are of minimal importance in understanding his behavior. His learned or developed reactions to stress are of primary importance, and although they may affect his conscious awareness and desire as well as his behavior, this impact upon conscious awareness and desire is of minimal significance. Therefore, when called upon in court to explain the dynamics of an offender's behavior, they will tend to explain it in terms they feel are significant. Legally speaking however, the insight is relevant only insofar as it explains how the offender's conscious awareness was affected. Theoretically, an alert trial court judge could limit testimony to that logically relevant to the state of mind defined by the substantive criminal law. But as a matter of practice it is unlikely that any such restriction will be placed on the evidence.

* * *

3. In Stewart v. United States, 107 U.S.App.D.C. 159, 275 F.2d 617 (1960), the Court of Appeals for the District of Columbia reconsidered its earlier rejection of "diminished capacity." In reaffirming its prior holdings, the court explained:

The problem of classifying, assessing and analyzing the results of the application of modern psychiatry to administration of criminal law as it relates to gradations of punishment according to the relative intelligence of the defendant is beyond the competence of the judiciary. Courts are neither trained nor equipped for this delicate and important task. The basic framework for sentences of punishment must be established by the legislative branch. Indeed, one can hardly conceive of a process less suited to formulating general rules in this sensitive area, than an adversary proceeding. That must be done by long range studies by competent public and quasi-public entities and by legislative committees with trained staffs aided by objective technical and scientific witnesses who can deal with all aspects of the problem, not confined as we are to the facts of an individual case. In this process legislative committees can call upon the best scientific resources of the country without limit as has been done in studies conducted by Royal Commissions in England and Canada.

In United States v. Brawner, 471 F.2d 969 (D.C.Cir. 1972) the court, in dicta, indicated that it would accept evidence of mental illness as disproving state of mind. Why might the reasons given by the court in 1960 for the rejection of the "diminished capacity" rule not apply in 1972?

---

2. "DIMINISHED RESPONSIBILITY": THE ENGLISH EXPERIMENT

HOMICIDE ACT, 1957

5 & 6 Eliz. II, c. 11, § 2.

(1) Where a person kills or is a party to the killing of another, he shall not be convicted of murder if he was suffering from such abnormality of mind (whether arising from a condition of arrested or retarded development of mind or any inherent causes or induced by disease or injury) as substantially impaired his mental responsibility for acts and omissions in doing or being a party to the killing.

(2) On a charge of murder, it shall be for the defence to prove that the person charged is by virtue of this section not liable to be convicted of murder.

(3) A person who but for this section would be liable, whether as principal or as accessory, to be convicted of murder shall be liable instead to be convicted of manslaughter.

(4) The fact that one party to a killing is by virtue of this section not liable to be convicted of murder shall not affect the question whether the killing amounted to murder in the case of any other party to it.

REGINA v. BYRNE

Queens Bench, 1960.
[1960] 2 Q.B. 396.

LORD PARKER, C. J. The appellant was convicted of murder before Stable J. at Birmingham Assizes and sentenced to imprisonment for life.   The victim was a young woman whom he strangled in the Y.W.C.A. hostel, and after her death he committed horrifying mutilations upon her dead body.   The facts as to the killing were not disputed, and were admitted in a long statement made by the accused. The only defence was that in killing his victim the accused was suffering from diminished responsibility as defined by section 2 of the Homicide Act, 1957, and was, accordingly, guilty not of murder but of manslaughter.

Three medical witnesses were called by the defence, the senior medical officer at Birmingham Prison and two specialists in psychological medicine.   Their uncontradicted evidence was that the accused was a sexual psychopath, that he suffered from abnormality of mind, as indeed was abundantly clear from the other evidence in the case, and that such abnormality of mind arose from a condition of arrested or retarded development of mind or inherent causes.   The nature of the abnormality of mind of a sexual psychopath, according to the medical evidence, is that he suffers from violent perverted sexual desires which he finds it difficult or impossible to control. Save when under the influence of his perverted sexual desires he may be normal.   All three doctors were of opinion that the killing was done under the influence of his perverted sexual desires, and although all three were of opinion that he was not insane in the technical sense of insanity laid down in the M'Naughten Rules it was their view that his sexual psychopathy could properly be described as partial insanity.

Before the passing of the Homicide Act, 1957, a person who killed or was party to a killing could escape liability for murder— as for any other crime requiring mens rea—if he showed that at the time of the killing he was insane within the meaning of the M'Naughten Rules.   *   *   *   The test is a rigid one: it relates solely to a person's intellectual ability to appreciate: (a) the physical act that he is doing, and (b) whether it is wrong.   If he has such intellectual ability, his power to control his physical acts by exercise of his will is irrelevant.

*   *   *

To satisfy the requirements of [subsection 2 of the Homicide Act, and thereby reduce a killing from murder to manslaughter] the accused must show: (a) that he was suffering from an abnormality of mind, and (b) that such abnormality of mind (i) arose from a condition of arrested or retarded development of mind or any inherent causes, or was induced by disease or injury and (ii) was such as substantially impaired his mental responsibility for his acts in doing or being a party to the killing.

"Abnormality of mind," which has to be contrasted with the time-honoured expression in the M'Naughten Rules "defect of reason," means a state of mind so different from that of ordinary human beings that the reasonable man would term it abnormal. It appears to us to be wide enough to cover the mind's activities in all its aspects, not only the perception of physical acts and matters, and the ability to form a rational judgment as to whether an act is right or wrong, but also the ability to exercise will power to control physical acts in accordance with that rational judgment. The expression "mental responsibility for his acts" points to a consideration of the extent to which the accused's mind is answerable for his physical acts which must include a consideration of the extent of his ability to exercise will power to control his physical acts.

* * *

As already indicated, the medical evidence as to the appellant's ability to control his physical acts at the time of the killing was all one way. The evidence of the revolting circumstances of the killing and the subsequent mutilations as of the previous sexual history of the appellant pointed, we think plainly, to the conclusion that the accused was what would be described in ordinary language as on the border-line of insanity or partially insane. Properly directed, we do not think that the jury could have come to any other conclusion than that the defence under section 2 of the Homicide Act was made out.

The appeal will be allowed and a verdict of manslaughter substituted for the verdict of murder. The only possible sentence having regard to the tendencies of the accused is imprisonment for life. The sentence will, accordingly, not be disturbed.

Appeal allowed.

NOTES

1. If ability to control is not relevant to "insanity," on what basis can the court's decision to so define diminished responsibility as to make it relevant to that issue be defended?

2. Wootton, Diminished Responsibility: A Layman's View, 76 L.Q. Rev. 224 (1960) reports an attempt to ascertain how the diminished responsibility section of the Homicide Act was being administered in practice. She examined the first seventy-three homicide prosecutions following enactment of the Homicide Act in which the diminished responsibility issue was raised. Fifty-three had resulted in acquittal, although in fifteen of these diminished responsibility was not the only argument made upon which a conviction of manslaughter rather than murder might have been based. After comparing the successful assertions of diminished responsibility with those that were unsuccessful, Wootton concluded that "a previous history of mental disorder is the type of evidence most likely to prove convincing." The evidence in a majority of the successful assertions of the matter included a history of "mental instability," but "comparatively few" of the unsuccessful ones did so.

More surprisingly, however, Wootton was unable to find any other distinction. The nature of the crime had little effect. "The crimes in which pleas of diminished responsibility succeeded were not in general either more, or less, rationally motivated than those for which the defendant was held to be fully responsible." Killings which followed long periods of domestic disharmony were included in the successful group, as well as those which appeared to be the result of no more than minor annoyances." [C]rimes of apparently straightforward sexual jealousy are represented just as much as those in which sexual aberrations appear to have played a part." Diminished responsibility always failed only in cases of "straightforward killing for gain."

Turning to the medical evidence in the cases, Wootton concluded that "the experts" agreed well "in principle" as to what sort of mental abnormality amounted to diminished responsibility. Most of the opinions concluding that the subject was of diminished responsibility contained diagnoses of "emotional immaturity," "mental instability," or "psychopathic personality." But there were widely varying views concerning what evidence was necessary to justify applying these diagnostic labels to a particular defendant. Basically, Wootten concluded, the experts' conclusion that a specific defendant was of diminished responsibility is based upon a conclusion that he is within a category consisting of persons more likely than others to commit crimes of violence.

If this is accurate, what is its significance for evaluating the diminished responsibility doctrine? Wootten is critical of the doctrine. Experts, she concludes, can only help establish that an individual does not control his conduct. "Any judgments as to whether he could do so must necessarily be governed by the philosophical position of those who make them on the eternally unresolved question of the reality of free will." Thus diminished responsibility requires juries composed of laymen to answer questions "which are not only beyond the competence of experts, but are by their very nature unanswerable by anybody." Is this supported by her study? Is it accurate? If it is accurate, would it require a conclusion that the substantive criminal law should not have a diminished responsibility doctrine?

See also, B. Wootton, Crime and the Criminal Law 85–90 (1963), containing the results of a study of second series of cases under the diminished responsibility portions of the Homicide Act. Power, Diminished Responsibility, 7 Medicine, Science and The Law 185 (1967) contains a number of illustrative case descriptions.

3. A further investigation of the actual operation of the Homicide Act is reported in N. Walker, Crime and Insanity in England 158–59 (1968):°

[Statisticians, analyzing the impact of the Homicide Act, demonstrated that the effect of the statute was neither as simple nor as spectacular as some had first suggested.] Gibson and Klein[28] compared the percentages of murderers committed for trial who benefited from the loopholes of 'insanity on

o. Reprinted with permission from Crime and Insanity in England (2 vols.), 1969–72, N. P. Walker, Professor of Criminology, University of Cambridge. Edinburgh University Press (U.S.A.: Aldine-Atherton, Inc., Chicago).

28. E. Gibson, and S. Klein, Murder: A Home Office Research Unit Report (HMSO, 1961).

arraignment', 'guilty but insane', or 'diminished responsibility' in the years immediately before and after the Act, and drew attention to the startling fact that in both periods the combined percentages totalled very much the same. A comparison which extends over a longer period confirms their observation, as figure 2 shows. This diagram is based on the Criminal Sta-

FIGURE 2. 'Murderers' found 'guilty but insane', 'insane on arraignment', or of diminished responsibility, 1947–63

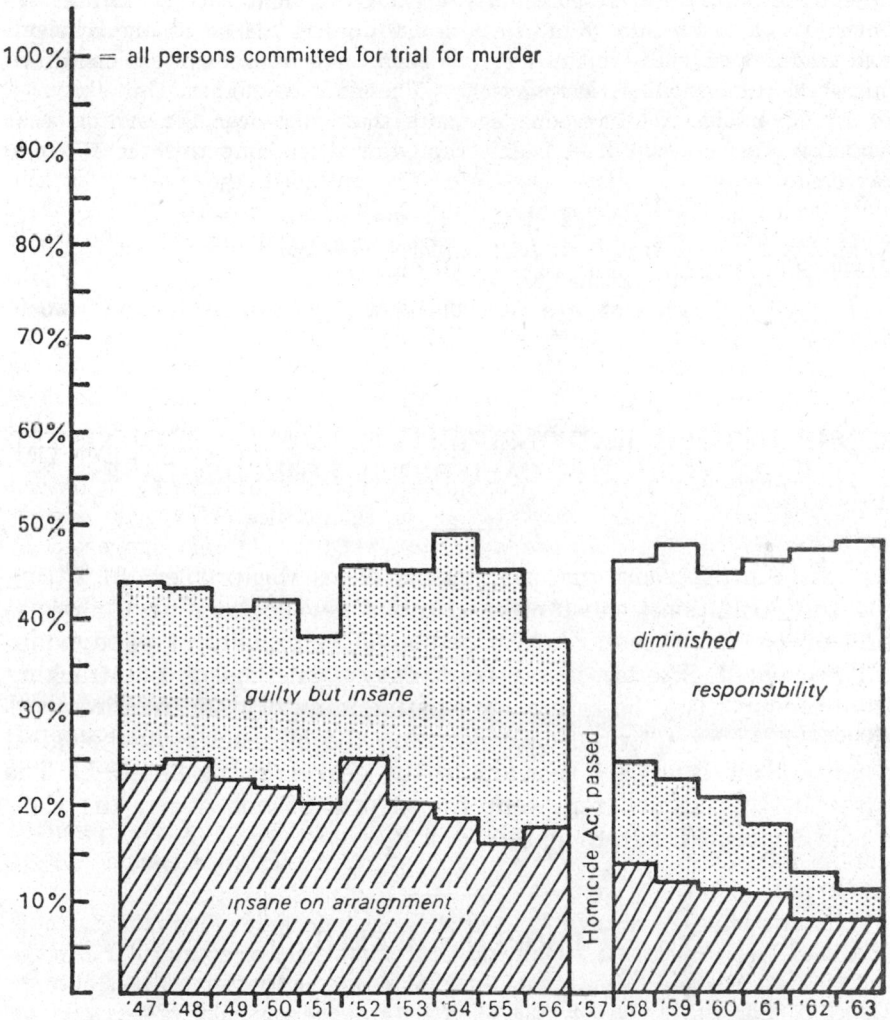

Percentages are shown as sliding three-year averages for 1946–8. They are also shown cumulatively: thus in 1946–8 the percentages found 'insane on arraignment' or 'guilty but insane' *together* averaged 44 per cent.

[A9018]

tistics from 1946 to 1963. It shows sliding three-year averages (i. e. the percentage shown for 1947 is the average percentage for 1946, 1947, and 1948); and is based on persons committed for trial for murder in those calendar years. Gibson and Klein's figures are for a shorter period, are not averaged, and group murderers according to the year of the homicide. But the same picture emerges.

Two separate trends are discernible. First, there has been the recent reduction * * * in 'murderers' [29] who escaped trial altogether by reason of insanity. This was compensated by the gradual increase in the percentage of 'murderers' who were found 'guilty but insane'. But as soon as the defence of diminished responsibility became available, this percentage too began to fall. The steady fall in both findings of 'insane on arraignment' and findings of 'guilty but insane' has been compensated by verdicts of 'diminished responsibility', *but no more*. These trends suggest that section 2 of the Homicide Act has done no more than take over the sort of case which previously would have been accepted by courts as within the M'Naghten Rules.

4. Would an approach similar to that provided for in the English Homicide Act be desirable in American law? If so, how might substantive criminal law doctrine be changed so as to provide for it? Could this be done judicially? If such a change were made, what changes in practice would be likely?

---

3. "DIMINISHED RESPONSIBILITY" THROUGH "DIMINISHED CAPACITY": THE CALIFORNIA HOMICIDE CASES

As the preceding material makes clear, the problem of fitting together traditional substantive criminal law doctrine and information provided by mental health personnel (especially psychodynamically-oriented experts) is far from easy. One means of attacking the problem might be to modify existing state of mind requirements so as to render information concerning the offender's psychological condition more directly relevant to the degree of his liability. The cases in this section represent the efforts of one court, the California Supreme Court, to do this.

PEOPLE v. WELLS

Supreme Court of California, 1949.
33 Cal.2d 330, 202 P.2d 53, certiorari denied 338 U.S. 836,
70 S.Ct. 43, 94 L.Ed. 510.

[The report of this case appears at page 1313, supra.]

29. The term 'murderers' is used, in inverted commas, as a less cumbersome way of referring to persons committed for trial on charges of murder.

PEOPLE v. GORSHEN

Supreme Court of California, 1959.
51 Cal.2d 716, 336 P.2d 492.

SCHAUER, Justice. Defendant pleaded not guilty to a charge of murder. Trial by jury was waived (as authorized by Cal.Const., art. I, § 7) and the court (see Pen.Code, § 1167) found defendant guilty of second degree murder. Defendant appeals from the ensuing judgment. He urges that uncontradicted psychiatric testimony, accepted by the trial court, establishes that defendant did not intend to take human life or, at least, that he did not act with malice aforethought, and that therefore he should be acquitted or, as a minimum of relief, that the offense should be reduced to manslaughter.
* * *

Defendant, a longshoreman, shot and killed his foreman, Joseph O'Leary, at about 2:30 a. m. on March 9, 1957. The record discloses the following events leading up to the homicide: At 5 p. m. on March 8 defendant reported to the dispatching hall. Between 6 and 7 o'clock he and a fellow worker ate and consumed a fifth of a gallon of sloe gin. Defendant worked until 11 p. m. Between 11 and 12 o'clock defendant and the fellow worker ate and consumed a pint of sloe gin. Shortly after 12 midnight O'Leary saw defendant standing on the deck of the ship drinking a glass of coffee. O'Leary told defendant to go to work. Defendant threw the glass to the deck, exchanged "a few words" with O'Leary, and went to work. Thereafter O'Leary told defendant that he was drunk and was not doing his work properly and directed defendant to go home. They argued, defendant spat in O'Leary's face, and O'Leary knocked defendant down and kicked him. At the request of other workers O'Leary walked away from defendant. Defendant threw a piece of dunnage and brandished a carton at O'Leary.

Paul Baker, a "walking boss," took defendant to a hospital. Defendant was bleeding and bruised; his left eye was swollen shut and a deep cut under it required five or six stitches. Defendant was discharged at 1:45 a. m. The hospital records bear the notation, "Alcoholic Breath." As Baker drove defendant back to the pier where they worked, defendant said "that he was going to go home and get a gun and kill this fellow."

When he reached the pier defendant said that he wished to return to work but his superiors insisted that he go home. Defendant said, "I'll go home and get my gun. I'll come back and take care of him." Defendant drove to his home, got a .25 caliber automatic pistol which contained two bullets, fired one shot in his living room, put the gun in his apron, and drove back to the pier. He arrived there about 30 minutes after he had been sent home and went onto the ship looking for O'Leary.

O'Leary and Nelson, a union business agent, had followed defendant to his house and, when they saw defendant leave his house, had driven to a police station. Police officers went to the pier. They searched defendant but did not find his gun. Defendant told the officers that he "had a fight with Mr. O'Leary, and * * * that he couldn't forget about the eye that he had obtained during the fight." One of the officers described defendant as "angry," "almost tearsome," "emotional," but not incoherent or boisterous.

O'Leary and Nelson then appeared. Defendant said, "My buddy. Hah, my buddy," and produced the gun. O'Leary shouted, "Look out, he's got the gun." Defendant shot. The single bullet entered O'Leary's abdomen, killing him; it also wounded Nelson's arm. The officers subdued defendant after a brief struggle. Defendant told the authorities, shortly after the homicide, that O'Leary was "looking at me, smiling, so I just let him have it. * * * Nelson was standing by; I had to take chance to hit him, because I had only one bullet."

Defendant had a very good reputation for peace and quiet and did not usually drink to excess. He testified as follows: During the 15 years he had known O'Leary prior to the night of the homicide they had been friends and had had no trouble. Defendant's recollection of the events of that night was "kind of hazy." He considered it unfair of O'Leary to order him to go home but to retain the fellow worker with whom defendant had been drinking. "The argument starts about he wants me to go home and I * * * tell him that I intend to wait until business agent comes in, so apparently he, he hit me and knocked me off, off the floor and when I jumped up, he got on and hit me again, and that's—then I tried to defend myself. I, I didn't hit him * * * ; he was apparently too fast for me or stronger, bigger." Defendant did not recall throwing a piece of dunnage or brandishing a carton or threatening to go home and get a gun. When he discharged the gun in his home, "I didn't know it was on the safety or not, I was shaky, I didn't know what I was doing." Defendant recalled little of his return to the pier, but did recall that the police searched him. Then he saw O'Leary "grinning, looking at me. I don't know what, what become of me. I just grabbed the gun and shot."

Dr. Bernard L. Diamond, a psychiatrist who examined defendant, testified as follows: [2]

After described examinations and tests of defendant, the doctor concluded that defendant suffers from chronic paranoiac schizophrenia, a disintegration of mind and personality. For 20 years defendant has had trances during which he hears voices and experiences visions, particularly of devils in disguise committing abnormal sexual acts, sometimes upon defendant. Defendant recognizes that these

2. It should be noted that no question
of legal insanity is here involved.

experiences are "not real" but believes that they are forced upon him by the devil. Apparently defendant, prior to his examination by Dr. Diamond, had not disclosed these experiences to anyone.

A year before the shooting defendant (who was 56 years of age at the time of trial) became concerned about loss of sexual power. With this concern his sexual hallucinations occurred with increased frequency and his ability in his work became increasingly important to him as a proof of manhood.

On the night of the shooting, O'Leary's statement that defendant was drunk and should leave his work was to defendant the psychological equivalent of the statement that "You're not a man, you're impotent, * * * you're a sexual pervert." Then, according to defendant's statements to Dr. Diamond, O'Leary applied to defendant an epithet which indicated sexual perversion. At this point, according to Dr. Diamond's opinion, defendant was confronted with "the imminent possibility of complete loss of his sanity. * * * [A]s an alternate to total disintegration * * *, it's possible for * * * an individual of this kind, to develop an obsessive murderous rage, an unappeasable anger * * *. The strength of this obsession is proportioned not to the reality danger but to the danger of the insanity * * *. [F]or this man to go insane, means to be permanently in the world of these visions and under the influence of the devil. * * * [A]n individual in this state of crisis will do anything to avoid the threatened insanity, and its this element which lends strength to his compulsive behavior so that he could think of nothing else but to get O'Leary, so he went home and got the gun and shot him; and [as] is usually the case in this type of event, the shooting itself released the danger of [defendant's complete mental disintegration]."

Defendant told Dr. Diamond that from the time he was taken to the emergency hospital until the time of the shooting "That is all I was thinking about all of this time is to shoot O'Leary. I forgot about my family, I forgot about God's laws and human's laws and everything else. The only thing was to get that guy, get that guy, get that guy, like a hammer in the head."

In the opinion of the doctor, defendant acted almost as an automaton; "even the fact that policemen were right at his elbow and there was no possibility of getting away with this, still it couldn't stop the train of obsessive thoughts which resulted in the killing * * *. [H]e did not have the mental state which is required for malice aforethought or premeditation or anything which implies intention, deliberation or premeditation."

Dr. Diamond quoted section 188 of the Penal Code, which provides that the "malice aforethought" which is an essential element of murder "may be express or implied. It is express when there is manifested a deliberate intention unlawfully to take away the life of a fellow-creature. It is implied, when no considerable provocation appears, or when the circumstances attending the killing show an abandoned and malignant heart." He then gave his opinion of the "medical essence" of "malice aforethought"; i. e., "whether an individual performs an act as a result of his own free will or intentionality, or * * * whether the action is directly attributable to some abnormal compulsion or force, or symptom or diseased process from within the individual." [3]

The doctor further explained that in his opinion "actions, like the threat to kill, the going home to get the gun and so forth"—actions which "in an ordinary individual" would be evidence "that he intended to do what he did do, and that this was an act of free will and deliberation"—in defendant's case were, rather, "just as much symptoms of his mental illness as the visions and these trances that he goes into."

* * *

The trial court stated at some length the matters which it considered in reaching its decision. It said, "up till the time that Dr. Diamond testified in this case, there was no explanation of why this crime was committed. * * * [The doctor is] the first person that has any reasonable explanation. Whether it's correct or not, I don't know * * *. [I]f I would follow Diamond's testimony in toto, I should acquit this man. * * *

"I'm willing to go on the record, that in all probability his theories are correct * * * that he had no particular intent to commit this crime.

"I like to be advanced. But it seems to me that my hands are tied with the legal jurisprudence as it stands today, and that's why I'm saying this for the purposes of the record. The Appellate Court might say that my hands are not tied, but I think they are. * * * [E]ven accepting in part the testimony of Dr. Diamond, I still feel that this man is guilty of second degree murder."

In reply to defense counsel's assertion that "There is not one scintilla of malice," the court said, "it all depends on how you view it * * *. Some other person or another Judge, might say, 'Malice, why, it's full of it. He planned it. He said he was going to do it, he went home, he had an hour.' "

Again defense counsel asked, "Does your Honor feel that there is malice here?" The court replied, "there was some intent. Now, whether you have free will or not free will, that's so advanced, we're

3. The trial court correctly overruled the People's objection that by this testimony the doctor gave "a medical interpretation of a legal principle." The court did not permit the doctor to usurp the judicial function of interpreting legislative language; rather, it properly permitted him to explain what he meant by his opinion that defendant lacked malice aforethought. * * *

not prepared for that * * * There's plenty, plenty of malice as far as statements are concerned, and plenty of malice as far as actions are concerned. Now, whether he was compelled to do this because of some mental condition, that is so advanced and so far from us that we don't understand it. * * * [I]t would be a perfect first degree if it wasn't for the fact that he's never been in trouble and because of the statement of the Psychiatrist."

Dr. Diamond's testimony was properly received in accord with the holding of People v. Wells (1949), 33 Cal.2d 330, 346–357, 202 P.2d 53. * * *

A * * * problem arises as to whether evidence of defendant's abnormal mental or physical condition (whether caused by intoxication, by trauma, or by disease, but not amounting to legal insanity or unconsciousness) can be considered to rebut malice aforethought and intent to kill in a case such as the one at bar, where the prosecution evidence shows infliction of a mortal wound for the purpose of killing and the evidence does not show provocation which would meet the law's definition of voluntary manslaughter, an unlawful killing upon a sudden quarrel or in a heat of passion such as would naturally be aroused in the mind of an *ordinarily reasonable person* under the circumstances. In such a case the question whether the intent to kill was formed as the result of deliberation and premeditation can be answered by evidence that the particular defendant, because of impairment of his mental ability by intoxication, injury, or disease, could not and therefore did not deliberate, as well as by evidence of objective circumstances, but the question whether defendant was guilty of murder or manslaughter is traditionally answered on the basis of the objective (reasonable man) standard of the provocation which, by rule of law, removes malice aforethought (even though it may in fact exist) from manslaughter. So it has been held that voluntary intoxication, although it can be considered on the question of the degree of murder, cannot be considered on the question whether defendant is guilty of murder or manslaughter. * * *

It would seem elementary that a plea of not guilty to a charge of murder puts in issue the existence of the particular mental states which are essential elements of the two degrees of murder and of manslaughter (a crime traditionally regarded as necessarily included in murder although in some cases the mental element of manslaughter may be more accurately described as differing from, rather than included in, the mental element of murder). Accordingly, it appears only fair and reasonable that defendant should be allowed to show that in fact, subjectively, he did not possess the mental state or states in issue.

* * *

Defendant and amici curiae urge that in the present case statements of the trial court affirmatively show that it believed the expert testimony that defendant, because of the concurrence of mental disease and the objective circumstances with which he was confronted, in fact lacked intent to kill and malice aforethought, yet erroneously concluded that the law required it to find that those elements were present. * * *

The trial court's informally expressed opinion was that defendant's threats and actions evidenced intent to kill and malice aforethought, but that "whether he was compelled to do this because of some mental condition, that is so advanced and so far from us that we don't understand it." A fair interpretation of the quoted statement is, not that the expert testimony was as a matter of law incomprehensible or unacceptable to the court as a finder of fact or as a judge of the law, but rather that the court as a trier of fact did not have a reasonable doubt that this particular defendant, when he killed, lacked intent to kill and malice aforethought. * * *

Thus it is apparent that whatever the trial judge may have had in mind when he stated in the course of his pro and con deliberations that "I like to be advanced. But it seems to me that my hands are tied with the legal jurisprudence as it stands today," he did in truth finally decide that his fact-finding hands were not tied; he must have so concluded because he received, considered and gave effect to the expert's testimony on the issues to which it was pertinent. Some of those issues he resolved in favor of the prosecution (he found the defendant guilty of murder), but others he determined in favor of the defendant (he found that the murder was *not* of the first degree). In other words, within the area of culpability for the crime charged the testimony of the expert apparently created a reasonable doubt that the homicide was murder of the first degree but not that it was murder. * * *

For the reasons above stated, the judgment is affirmed.

NOTES

1. If the trial judge had accepted Dr. Diamond's testimony, would the appropriate finding have been guilty of voluntary manslaughter? How can the traditional definition of that offense—a killing that would be murder except for adequate provocation—be avoided? Did the California Supreme Court attempt to explain what impact the mental illness must have had— what effect it must have had upon the defendant's conscious awareness— before a finding of manslaughter would have been proper? Or does the distinction turn upon the impact of the mental illness upon something other than conscious awareness. Do the existing definitions of manslaughter and murder provide the basis for answering these questions?

2. Was it proper for Dr. Diamond to be permitted to give his opinion as to the "medical essence" of "malice aforethought?" Was his opinion consistent with the law? Did the court adopt his opinion as the proper definition? If the court did not accept Dr. Diamond's definition, why was not his testimony inadmissible as being based upon an erroneous understanding of the issues in the case?

3.   Was the California Supreme Court correct in its conclusion that the trial judge found facts which, under a correct interpretation of the diminished capacity rule, would support a finding that the defendant was guilty of murder? Did the trial judge have in his mind a clear and accurate picture of what impact the mental illness must have had before he should find the defendant guilty of manslaughter rather than murder?

PEOPLE v. WOLFF

Supreme Court of California, 1964.
61 Cal.2d 795, 394 P.2d 959, 40 Cal.Rptr. 271.

SCHAUER, Justice.   Defendant appeals from a judgment imposing a sentence of life imprisonment (with recommendation that he be placed in a hospital for the criminally insane) after he pleaded not guilty by reason of insanity to a charge of murder, the jury found that he was legally sane at the time of the commission of the offense, and the court determined the killing to be murder in the first degree. [Defendant was fifteen years of age at the time of the alleged offense.]

* * *

[T]here was evidence that in the year preceding the commission of the crime defendant "spent a lot of time thinking about sex." He made a list of the names and addresses of seven girls in his community whom he did not know personally but whom he planned to anesthetize by ether and then either rape or photograph nude. One night about three weeks before the murder he took a container of ether and attempted to enter the home of one of these girls through the chimney, but he became wedged in and had to be rescued. In the ensuing weeks defendant apparently deliberated on ways and means of accomplishing his objective and decided that he would have to bring the girls to his house to achieve his sexual purposes, and that it would therefore be necessary to get his mother (and possibly his brother) out of the way first.[6]

The attack on defendant's mother took place on Monday, May 15, 1961. On the preceding Friday or Saturday defendant obtained an axe handle from the family garage and hid it under the mattress of his bed. At about 10 p. m. on Sunday he took the axe handle from its hiding place and approached his mother from behind, raising the weapon to strike her. She sensed his presence and asked him what he was doing; he answered that it was "nothing," and returned to his room and hid the handle under his mattress again. The following morning defendant arose and put the customary signal (a magazine) in the

6.   Defendant lived with his mother and older brother since his parents were divorced some 13 years previously. However, his father remained on good terms with the family; he drove by their house each morning to ascertain that they had not overslept, and he often ate with them in the evening.

front window to inform his father that he had not overslept. Defendant ate the breakfast that his mother prepared, then went to his room and obtained the axe handle from under the mattress. He returned to the kitchen, approached his mother from behind and struck her on the back of the head. She turned around screaming and he struck her several more blows. They fell to the floor, fighting. She called out her neighbor's name and defendant began choking her. She bit him on the hand and crawled away. He got up to turn off the water running in the sink, and she fled through the dining room. He gave chase, caught her in the front room, and choked her to death with his hands. Defendant then took off his shirt and hung it by the fire, washed the blood off his face and hands, read a few lines from a Bible or prayer book lying upon the dining room table, and walked down to the police station to turn himself in. Defendant told the desk officer, "I have something I wish to report. * * * I just killed my mother with an axe handle." The officer testified that defendant spoke in a quiet voice and that "His conversation was quite coherent in what he was saying and he answered everything I asked him right to a T."

Defendant's counsel repeatedly characterizes as "bizarre" defendant's plan to rape or photograph nude the seven girls on his list. Certainly in common parlance it may be termed "bizarre;" likewise to a mature person of good morals, it would appear highly unreasonable. But many a youth has committed—or planned—acts which were bizarre and unreasonable. This defendant was immature and lacked experience and judgment in sexual matters. But it does not follow therefrom that the jury were precluded as a matter of law from finding defendant *legally* sane at the time of the murder. From the evidence set forth hereinabove the jury could infer that defendant had a motive for his actions (gratification of his sexual desires),[7] that he planned the attack on his mother for some time (obtaining the axe handle from the garage several days in advance; abortive attempt to strike his mother with it on the evening before the crime), that he knew that what he was doing was wrong (initial concealment of the handle underneath his mattress; excuse offered when his mother saw him with the weapon on the evening before the crime; renewed concealment of the handle under the mattress), that he persisted in the fatal attack (pursuit of his fleeing mother into the front room; actual infliction of death by strangling rather than bludgeoning), that he was conscious of having committed a crime (prompt surrender to the po-

7. This does not mean, of course, that it was his *only* motive. At different times defendant offered as reasons for the murder the fact that his mother nagged him, that they constantly bickered, and that he was ashamed to bring friends home because his mother did not keep house well. However, the issue is not whether in the opinion of an appellate court such other reasons may somehow be deemed evidence of insanity, but whether the record supports an inference that defendant had an actual—not just imagined or hallucinatory—motivating reason to commit these acts. As observed above, our inquiry must be to determine whether there is substantial evidence to support—not to undermine —the verdict of the jury.

lice), and that he was calm and coherent (testimony of desk officer and others). * * *

[Four psychiatrists testified—and no one disputed on appeal—that at the time of the crime the defendant suffered from an illness characterized by a "disintegration of the personality" and a "complete disassociation between intellect and emotion," that the defendant was "not capable of conceptual thinking" but only of "concrete" thinking, and that his judgment was affected "to a considerable degree."]

The Degree of the Murder

From what has been said it follows that there was no substantial error in the trial on the issue raised by the plea of not guilty by reason of insanity and that the evidence adequately supports the jury's verdict. But another and more substantial problem remains to be considered: the contention that the evidence is insufficient to support the trial court's finding that the murder was of the first, rather than the second, degree. * * * To confidently resolve the issue it is essential that we identify the elements which (insofar as relevant to the facts of this case) should as a matter of law be given weight as characterizing, distinguishing, or differentiating, the two degrees of murder. In People v. Holt (1944) supra, 25 Cal.2d 59, 83, 153 P.2d 21 [9], we said "Murder, and this, of course, includes murder of the *second* degree as well as murder of the first degree, is defined as 'the unlawful killing of a human being, with malice aforethought.' (Pen.Code, § 187.) * * *

* * * The malice which is one of the two essential elements of the offense—whether of the first or of the second degree—is defined by section 188 of the Penal Code. 'Such malice may be express or implied. It is express when there is manifested a deliberate intention unlawfully to take away the life of a fellow creature. It is implied, when no considerable provocation appears, or when the circumstances attending the killing show an abandoned and malignant heart.' "

As noted in Holt there has sometimes appeared to be a tendency to emasculate the distinction between the two degrees of murder. In Holt we declared firmly against any such emasculation: * * * Dividing intentional homicides into murder and voluntary manslaughter was a recognition of the infirmity of human nature. Again *dividing the offense of murder into two degrees is a further recognition* of that infirmity and *of difference in the quantum of personal turpitude of the offenders.* * * * The victim of manslaughter or second degree murder is just as dead as is the victim of first degree murder. The law has fixed standards by which such *personal depravity of the offender;* i. e., the character of the particular homicide, *is to be measured.* When the homicide is perpetrated by means of poison, or lying in wait, or torture, or in the perpetration of or attempt to perpetrate the enumerated felonies the standard is definite and no difficulty in fixing the degree ensues. But when it is claimed that the homicide is by 'any other kind of willful, deliberate, and premeditated killing' there is necessity for an appraisal which involves something more than the ascertainment of objective facts. This appraisal is primarily a jury [or trial court] function and within a wide field of discretion its determination is final. But as is true as to all factual issues resolved by a jury [or trial court], the evidence upon which the determination is made is subject to review on the question of its legal sufficiency to support the verdict. To the extent that the character of a particular homicide is established by the facts in evidence the jury is bound, as are we, to apply the standards fixed by law." (Italics added.)

* * * In the case at bench there is no question that the defendant had the intent to kill; but the mental infirmity of this defendant presents a very serious factual problem as to the quantum of his personal turpitude and depravity as inherently related to the degree of the murder.

* * *

" * * * Neither the statute nor the court undertakes to measure in units of time the length of the period during which the thought must be pondered before it can ripen into an intent which is truly deliberate and premeditated. The time would vary with different individuals and under differing circumstances. The true test is not the duration of time as much as it is the *extent of the reflection*." (Italics added.) In the case now at bench, in the light of defendant's youth and undisputed mental illness, all as shown under the California M'Naghton rule on the trial of the plea of not guilty by reason of insanity, and properly considered by the trial judge in the proceeding to determine the degree of the offense, the true test must include consideration of the somewhat limited extent to which this defendant could *maturely and meaningfully reflect* upon the gravity of his contemplated act. * * *

Certainly in the case now at bench the defendant had ample *time* for any normal person to maturely and appreciatively reflect upon his contemplated act and to arrive at a cold, deliberated and premeditated conclusion. He did this in a sense—and apparently to the full extent of which he was capable. But, indisputably on the record, this defendant was not and is not a fully normal or mature, mentally well person. He knew the difference between right and wrong; he knew that the intended act was wrong and nevertheless carried it out. But the extent of his understanding, reflection upon it and its consequences, with realization of the enormity of the evil, appears to have been materially—as relevant to appraising the quantum of his moral turpitude and depravity—vague and detached. We think that our analysis in Holt of the minimum essential elements of first degree murder, especially in respect to the quantum of reflection, comprehension, *and turpitude of the offender*, fits precisely this case: that the use by the Legislature of "wilful, deliberate, and premeditated" in conjunction indicates its intent to require as an essential element of first degree murder (of that category) substantially more reflection; i. e., more understanding and comprehension of the character of the act than the mere amount of thought necessary to form the intention to kill. It bears repeating (People v. Holt (1944) supra, 25 Cal.2d 59, 89 [12], 153 P.2d 21) that "Dividing intentional homicides into murder and voluntary manslaughter was a recognition of the infirmity of human nature. Again dividing the offense of murder into two degrees is a further recognition of that infirmity and of difference in the quantum of personal turpitude of the offenders. The difference is basically in the offenders. * * *"

* * *

Upon the facts, upon the law, and for all of the reasons hereinabove stated we are satisfied that the evidence fails to support the finding that the murder by this defendant, in the circumstances of his undisputed mental illness, was of the first degree, but that it amply sustains conviction of second degree murder.

NOTES

1. Did *Wolff* represent a significant alteration of, or addition to, the definition of first degree murder under California law?

2. Does the opinion in *Wolff* explain helpfully what impact mental illness must have to reduce a killing from first degree murder to second degree murder? The defendant must have "maturely and meaningfully" reflect upon the gravity of his contemplated crime. Does this mean that mental illness is relevant only if it impairs the defendant's reasoning ability? Would it be relevant that there were strong unconscious factors in the causation of the crime?

3. Might there be other crimes which require "mature and meaningful" reflection, or does *Wolff* apply only to first degree murder? The offense of which *Wells* was convicted consisted of assault by a life-term prisoner with malice aforethought. Does *Wolff* affect the definition of this offense?

PEOPLE v. CONLEY

Supreme Court of California, 1966.
64 Cal.2d 310, 411 P.2d 911, 49 Cal.Rptr. 815.

TRAYNOR, Chief Justice. Defendant appeals from a judgment of conviction entered on jury verdicts finding him guilty on two counts of first degree murder, finding him sane at the time of the commission of the crimes, and fixing the penalty on each count at life imprisonment. He contends that the court erred in instructing the jury on the elements of murder [and] in refusing to give requested instructions on manslaughter * * * [.]

Defendant shot and killed Clifton and Elaine McCool on Sunday July 19, 1964, in Ukiah. The victims, who were married and the parents of three children, had recently reconciled after a period of separation and were preparing to move to the State of Washington. They occupied cabin No. 7 of a bungalow court near the home of defendant's sister, Goldie Haley, with whom defendant was living at the time of the killings. While the McCools were separated, Elaine became romantically involved with defendant and told him that she would get a divorce and marry him.

Defendant injured his back in an industrial accident several months before the killings and had no regular employment since that accident. On July 15, the Wednesday before the shooting, he received two compensation checks and, as was his habit when he had funds, began a prolonged period of steady drinking. He and several other witnesses testified that he drank whiskey, vodka, and finally wine continually for over three days before the homicides. Defendant also testified that he had been taking medication to relieve the pain of his back injury and an ulcer. A medical expert testified that some of the medication prescribed for defendant could have increased the effect of alcohol.

On Thursday, July 16, the defendant took Elaine and the McCool children on an outing and apparently engaged in intimate relations with Elaine. When he brought her and the children back to their cabin, she told him that she had decided to return to her husband.

On Sunday, July 19, defendant purchased a .30-.30 rifle and early that evening tried it out with two friends at a nearby dump. His friends testified that on their way back defendant said that he ought to kill the McCools, but they dismissed the remark as "just the booze talking" and changed the subject. Thereafter, defendant went to his sister's home and drank wine until about 9:00 p. m. He then went to cabin No. 3 of the bungalow court and told other friends who lived there that he was going to kill the McCools because, "I have been hurt by three different woman before. I can't take any more. She promised to marry me." They attempted to dissuade him, but he said he had made up his mind. Once again, however, he was not taken seriously and his friends allowed him to leave with his rifle.

A few minutes later four shots rang out. Upon hearing the first shots, the occupants of cabin No. 1 went to their front porch and saw defendant shoot Elaine as she was running from him. Defendant walked back to cabin No. 3, told his friends that he had killed the McCools, and then went to his sister's house and told her what he had done. He left and was found two hours later in a nearby field.

Defendant testified that he did not intend to kill the McCools and remembered nothing from the time he was drinking at his sister's house until his arrest. The results of a blood alcohol test given about three hours after the shooting showed that his blood then contained .21 per cent alcohol. A medical expert testified that this alcohol level would be sufficient to impair fine muscular coordination and judgment in the average individual and that if defendant had consumed no food or alcohol between 9:00 p. m. and midnight, the blood alcohol level at 9:00 p. m. could have been .27 per cent, but that it might have been even less than .21 per cent.

A defense psychologist testified that in his opinion defendant was in a dissociative state at the time of the killings and because of personality fragmentation did not function with his normal personality.

Both sides requested manslaughter instructions. The court ruled that even if initially there had been adequate provocation to reduce the killing from murder to manslaughter, a sufficient cooling period had elapsed as a matter of law to preclude consideration of the crime as having been committed in the heat of passion. The court suggested that if either party could present an evidentiary theory upon which a manslaughter instruction could be based it would be given but ultimately refused any such instruction, although diminished capacity and intoxication were both suggested as theories upon which instructions on manslaughter were required. This refusal was prejudicial error.

* * *

Hoping to gain complete exculpation, defendant based his defense in part on a theory of unconsciousness. In support of that defense he introduced evidence of intoxication and mental illness and testified that he had no recollection of the shootings and did not intend to kill the McCools. Implicit in such a defense is also the defense of diminished capacity. The jury could well reject the claim of complete unconsciousness and yet believe that the evidence introduced to establish unconsciousness was sufficient to indicate that defendant's mental capacity was substantially reduced. Counsel for both sides made known to the court defendant's reliance on the defense of diminished capacity. Since the jury was not advised that diminished capacity could negate the existence of malice and that if malice were absent the offense could not be murder, a material issue was withheld from its consideration. * * *

The Attorney General contends, however, that the jury necessarily determined this issue under the instructions given by finding defendant guilty of first rather than second degree murder. There is no merit in this contention, for the issue of malice aforethought was not presented to the jury. * * * In returning a verdict of first degree murder, the jury found that defendant's act was intentional, voluntary, deliberate, and premeditated. They did not necessarily find, however, that defendant acted with malice aforethought.

We have previously noted the difficulty of formulating a comprehensive definition of malice aforethought that will serve to distinguish murder and manslaughter. Penal Code, section 188 provides that malice "may be express or implied. It is express when there is manifested a deliberate intention unlawfully to take away the life of a fellow creature. It is implied, when no considerable provocation appears, or when the circumstances attending the killing show an abandoned and malignant heart." These provisions create a presumption of malice when the commission of a homicide by the defendant has been proved and place the burden on him to raise a reasonable doubt in the minds of the jurors that malice was present. The "conclusive presumption" of a malicious and guilty intent set forth in section 1962 of the Code of Civil Procedure offers no help to the jury. To bring it into operation the jury must find "the deliberate commission of an unlawful act for the purpose of injuring another," which involves subjective factors on which evidence of diminished capacity is also relevant. * * *

The mental state constituting malice aforethought does not presuppose or require any ill will or hatred of the particular victim. * * * When a defendant "with wanton disregard for human life, does an act that involves a high degree of probability that it will result in death," he acts with malice aforethought. * * * This mental state must be distinguished from that state of mind described as "wilful, deliberate, and premeditated," however. The latter phrase encompasses the mental state of one who carefully weighs the course of action he is about to take and chooses to kill his victim after considering the reasons for and against it. * * * A person capable of achieving such a mental state is normally capable also of comprehending the duty society places on all persons to act within the law. If, despite such awareness, he does an act that is likely to cause serious injury or death to another, he exhibits that wanton disregard for human life or antisocial motivation that constitutes malice aforethought. An intentional act that is highly dangerous to human life, done in disregard of the actor's awareness that society requires him to conform his conduct to the law is done with malice regardless of the fact that the actor acts without ill will toward his victim or believes that his conduct is justified. In this respect it is immaterial that he does not know that his specific conduct is unlawful, for all persons are presumed to know the law including that which prohibits causing injury or death to another . An awareness of the obligation to act within the general body of laws regulating society, however, is included in the statutory definition of implied malice in terms of an abandoned and malignant heart and in the definition of express malice as the deliberate intention unlawfully to take life.

Thus, one who commits euthanasia bears no ill will toward his victim and believes his act is morally justified, but he nonetheless acts with malice if he is able to comprehend that society prohibits his act regardless of his personal belief. If because of mental defect, disease, or intoxication, however, the defendant is unable to comprehend his duty to govern his actions in accord with the duty imposed by law, he does not act with malice aforethought and cannot be guilty of murder in the first degree. The situation of an individual who kills with intent, deliberation, and premeditation, but without malice aforethought is illustrated by the evidence in the *Gorshen* case. Had the trial court in that case believed the defendant's testimony, it might have concluded that he acted without malice when, after an altercation with his foreman and after consuming a large quantity of alcohol, he went to his home, got his pistol, fired a shot in his living room, drove back to his place of employment, and then after being searched by two police officers (who did not find his gun) and while still in their company shot the foreman. The psychiatric expert urged that because of personality disintegration and paranoiac schizophrenia the defendant believed the act necessary to prevent his own insanity and that the defendant was incapable of having the "mental state which is required for malice aforethought, or premeditation or anything which implies intention, deliberation, or premeditation." (People v. Gorshen, supra, 51 Cal.2d 716, 723, 336 P.2d 492, 496.) The defendant had testified that he had forgotten about "God's laws and human's laws and everything else." (Id.) Confronted with this evidence, the court or a jury could conclude that the defendant killed intentionally, with premeditation and deliberation, but did not do so with malice aforethought. Although legally sane according to the M'Naughton test, such a defendant could not be convicted of murder if mental illness prevented his acting with malice aforethought. * * *

Similarly in the present case, the jury could have found that although defendant deliberated and premeditated the killings, his intoxication and mental disorder precluded malice aforethought. In finding him guilty of first degree murder under the instructions given it therefore did not necessarily determine that he acted with malice aforethought.[4]

* * *

The judgment is reversed.

---

4. In adapting its instructions to a case such as this in which diminished capacity and unconsciousness because of voluntary intoxication are relied on by the defense, the felony murder doctrine is not involved, and there is no evidence of poisoning, torture, or lying in wait, the court might advise the jury:

* * *

Malice aforethought, either express or implied, is manifested by the doing of such an act by a person who is able to comprehend this prohibition and his obligation to conform his conduct to it. There is a presumption that the defendant was able to understand this prohibition but he may rebut the presumption by evidence of diminished capacity on which I shall instruct you shortly.

* * *

The defendant has offered evidence that because of mental illness and intoxication he was unconscious. If you find that he was conscious of the shootings, but had substantially reduced mental capacity because of mental illness or intoxication, you must consider what effect, if any, this diminished capacity had on the defendant's ability to form any of the specific mental states that are essential elements of murder, which I have

NOTES

1. Did *Conley* represent a significant alteration of, or addition to, the definition of murder under California law?

2. Does the opinion in *Conley* explain helpfully what impact mental illness must have had to reduce a killing from murder to manslaughter? A person does not act with "malice aforethought" if he is "unable to comprehend his duty to govern his actions in accord with the duty imposed by law." Does this mean that mental illness is relevant only if it impairs the defendant's reasoning ability? Suppose the trier of fact believed that the defendant had an intellectual understanding of "the duty imposed by law," but that because of a dissociative state he lacked the "normal" emotional aversion to noncompliance with that duty. What result? Suppose the trier of fact believed that the defendant had an intellectual understanding of the legal duty not to kill except in limited situations. But in addition it believed that the defendant lacked an emotional aversion to disobeying that requirement because of his early life situation, i. e., he had been raised in a ghetto community in which many violent confrontations were considered appropriate even if not sanctioned by law. What result?

3. If Wolff's case were retried after *Conley*, would he have been entitled to an instruction on manslaughter? If convicted of murder, would he have been entitled to have the verdict set aside as against the weight of the evidence?

PEOPLE v. MORSE

Supreme Court of California, 1969.
70 Cal.2d 711, 452 P.2d 607, 76 Cal.Rptr. 391, certiorari denied
397 U.S. 944, 90 S.Ct. 959, 25 L.Ed.2d 124.

SULLIVAN, Justice. A jury found defendant guilty of first degree murder (Pen.Code, §§ 187, 189) and fixed the penalty at death (§ 190). The trial judge denied defendant's motions for a new trial and for reduction of penalty. This appeal is automatic. (§ 1239, subd. (b).)

On August 6, 1964, a jury determined that defendant, who in 1962 had been found guilty of murdering his mother and sister, should

---

defined for you, or of manslaughter, which I will define shortly.

* * *

Manslaughter is the unlawful killing of a human being without malice. Two kinds of manslaughter, the definitions of which are pertinent here, are:

1. Voluntary manslaughter, an intentional killing in which the law, recognizing human frailty, permits the defendant to establish the lack of malice * * * by

* * *

b. Showing that due to diminished capacity caused by mental illness, mental defect, or intoxication, the defendant did not attain the mental state constituting malice.

* * *

Thus, if you find that the defendant killed while unconscious as a result of voluntary intoxication and was therefor unable to formulate a specific intent to kill or to harbor malice, his killing is involuntary manslaughter.

* * *

suffer life imprisonment. On August 14, 1964, while defendant was confined in the San Diego County jail awaiting formal sentencing for these crimes, he garrotted Thomas Larry Taddei, another prisoner, with part of a mattress cover braided into a cord.

Both defendant and Taddei occupied separate cells in a cellblock on the fifth floor of the jail. Deputy Sheriff Murkerson, who was assigned to jail duty on the floor below, was delivering medicine to another inmate in the same cellblock as defendant when he found the victim lying outside defendant's cell with his head and neck suspended by a sort of woven rope attached to the bars. Defendant was in his cell. Murkerson called to defendant "Cut him loose, Joe." Defendant, standing in the center of the cell and looking at the jailer, shrugged his shoulders, lay down on the bunk behind him, and folded his hands behind his head. Murkerson went for help and returned shortly with two other officers and a trusty. One of the officers cut the cord which had been knotted at the back of the victim's neck and looped around and knotted behind a bar of defendant's cell. Murkerson noticed that the victim was pale and cold and that there was paper sticking out of his mouth. An attempt was made to revive Taddei. Finally it was determined that he was dead.

At the trial Murkerson testified on *voir dire* outside the jury's presence that approximately two or three minutes after he had returned with help and while he and another officer were attempting to use artificial respiration on Taddei, he had a conversation with defendant. At this time the two officers were outside defendant's cell and Murkerson was kneeling beside the victim and facing defendant's cell. The jailer looked up toward defendant, who was lying on his bunk, and asked "Joe, did you do this?" Defendant nodded his head in the affirmative and said, "Yeah." The jailer then immediately asked, "Why?" and defendant replied, "The sonofabitch wouldn't pay his debts." The jailer then asked, "What did he owe you?" and defendant immediately answered, "Cigarettes." * * *

Defendant * * * contends that the court erroneously failed to give instructions on manslaughter. He urges that there was here presented evidence which, if believed, would negate the malice required for murder, and he contends * * * that refusal to instruct on manslaughter in the face of such evidence constitutes reversible error.

* * * [T]he defense in the instant case was based entirely upon the testimony of the defense psychiatrist, Dr. David Wilson, relative to defendant's capacity to entertain the mental states necessary to first degree murder. At defendant's request the court gave the standard instructions on how intent is manifested * * * and on defendant's diminished capacity to form the requisite specific intent or have the requisite mental state to constitute the crime charged * * *, commonly referred to as the *Wells-Gorshen* rule. But the

court did not give instructions on manslaughter and in fact refused three instructions requested by defendant, presumably on the theory that the evidence presented, while tending to negate premeditation and deliberation, did not tend to negate malice aforethought.

*　*　*

The success of defendant's efforts to find some evidence negating malice aforethought and compelling instructions on manslaughter depends on the testimony of defendant's witness Dr. Wilson, upon which the entire defense rested. We may fairly summarize his testimony as to the mental condition of defendant at the time of the homicide thusly: Defendant suffers from a medically recognized character disorder known as sociopathic personality, anti-social type. One of the qualities of this type of disorder is that it renders the subject to some extent incapable of relating to the world outside him in terms of customary social morality, so that he becomes in some sense a law unto himself, answerable in moral terms only to himself. Superimposed upon this character disorder in the case of defendant is the fact that a great portion of his life has been spent in a custodial environment, wherein the value of practical comforts tends to be exaggerated —especially for a person suffering from a sociopathic character disorder. Further, within such a culture retaliation is both the expected and the acceptable method of dealing with personal affronts. Therefore, within this context of personality disorder and custodial environment, defendant's reaction to Taddei's conduct was both consistent and psychologically predictable. In sum, because of such disorder and the cultural pressures of defendant's environment, Taddei's behavior provoked defendant into committing the homicide. Once this situation arose, defendant had no control over the following events and his actions were instinctual.[15]

15. Illustrative of Dr. Wilson's opinion are the following excerpts of his testimony: "I felt that he is described clinically as being [sic] a sociopathic personality disorder, the anti-social type. * * * It was my opinion that the cultural pressures which were just mentioned, which was namely, the culture that a person exists in when he lives in a prison environment for the majority of his life, and also the cultural environment of living on death row for an extended period of time, changed his value systems. In other words, the things that might provoke one into an act are considered in light of all the circumstances. One can be provoked at one time and not another. One person can be provoked by different things.

"Because of the personality disorder and because of the environment in which he lived, it was my opinion that the

acts of the victim which led to the homicide in question did in truth provoke his particular actions, namely that of the homicide."

Dr. Wilson further explained: "Q [Mr. Rickles, attorney for defendant] Did you form an opinion, Doctor, as to whether or not once this situation arose that Mr. Morse had any control over the events that followed, sir?

"A Yes, I formed such an opinion.

"Q What was your opinion as to that, sir?

"A Once the act began, his actions were those of an instinctual nature. * * * Instinct. In other words, there was an automatic response. Given the circumstances and the precipitating factors, he then acted without any particular thought. It was merely the appropriate thing to do, and no thought was given to the act. The

We may therefore distill from the foregoing testimony the following theories of defense: First, defendant did not act deliberately or with premeditation but automatically and "instinctually"; secondly, the victim's conduct was adequate provocation for the killing. Defendant's position is that either theory eliminates malice aforethought.

We consider the latter theory first. * * * It is clear that the provocation here involved was not such that it would have the indicated result upon "ordinary men of average disposition," and that the evidence of defendant's extraordinary character and environmental deficiencies was manifestly irrelevant to the inquiry.

We now turn to consider whether there is any evidence under the first theory which will negate malice aforethought. As we indicated in People v. Conley (1966) 64 Cal.2d 310, 318, 49 Cal.Rptr. 815, 411 P.2d 911, the enumeration of nonmalicious homicides contained in section 192 is not complete. * * *

act merely took place as a matter of course. * * *

"MR. RICKLES: Q Doctor, could you advise us as to what the defendant's action would be attributable to? * *

"A The circumstances of the homicide were, as according to the defendant's statements, were that there was a game in which the victim lost and, therefore, was expected to pay a carton of cigarettes as the gambling debt and announced that he was not able to do this because he had no funds.

"This angered the defendant, but they agreed upon a substitute payment, namely, that of one dessert for each of the ten packs of cigarettes over ten to sixteen days.

"At a later time the victim welched on his gambling debt, which again angered the defendant, at which time he decided that he would retaliate by beating him up or punishing him in some way.

"Subsequent to this, in the final last straw, was an act that was provocative in the eyes of the defendant, namely, the victim came to the wall or the bars of the cell and had the temerity to ask him or try to bum a cigarette from him. That was the precipitating factor that resulted in the homicide.

"Now, where this in itself might be considered annoying to the normal mind, to the mind of the defendant here, this was the justifiable basis for the act, for two reasons:

"One, because of his personality disorder, he doesn't have the capacity to think in terms of usual values of morality.

He is without the ability, in other words, to think in moral terms. In other words, taking of a life can be justified on many means. We think of it as being the supreme sort of act. To a person of this sort, it is just another act, and it can follow as a result of many things, even something minor such as this.

"Furthermore, we have, in addition to the mental condition of this person without a moral sense, in other words, we have the cultural environment wherein it is understood in this particular setting, since life is itself no longer of great consequence on death row, everything else becomes extremely important. They have nothing else but cigarettes. This is the only value they have, because life has been already forfeited. Consequently, things assume an exaggerated proportion, including something like this. Furthermore, we have the cultural factor that when a person provokes another person in this culture, retaliation is expected. In other words, a person asks for it. By doing a certain act, he can expect a retaliation. Retaliations can vary. Under the circumstances here, this would be an appropriate sort of thing in this particular culture, so we have a series of circumstances that, taken in the abstract, appear to be of no great value. Under the circumstances of this particular mental condition and the environment, it explains quite satisfactorily from a psychological sense the act that occurred."

We * * * delineated in *Conley* a standard to be applied in the determination of whether, in cases involving diminished capacity, the state of mind amounting to malice aforethought is present * * *.

The evidence heretofore summarized by us provides no basis whatsoever for a finding that defendant's act was accomplished in the absence of malice aforethought. Nowhere is it intimated that defendant lacked an awareness that his act was contrary to the laws of society. Rather, the testimony of Dr. Wilson posits such awareness and proceeds upon the theory that defendant's personality disorder and the effects of his environment rendered him disinclined to or incapable of conforming his conduct accordingly. Such a state of mind cannot amount to an absence of malice aforethought as we have defined that term in *Conley*. Though defendant's conduct may in fact have been in some sense "psychologically predictable," under the present law of the State of California this fact does not of itself affect his criminal liability.

It therefore appears that, since defendant presented no evidence in support of a finding that his diminished capacity rendered him incapable of entertaining malice aforethought, and further, since he presented no evidence indicating provocation of the sort required by section 192, the trial court properly refused to instruct on the law of manslaughter. * * *

PETERS, Justice (concurring and dissenting). * * *

Whether there is any evidence of lack of malice depends entirely upon the testimony of Dr. Wilson. * * * Not only does Dr. Wilson's testimony show that defendant was incapable of premeditation and deliberation, but it also shows that he was unable to harbor the state of mind called malice aforethought. * * *

[U]ntil I read the majority opinion, I believed the matter had been settled by *Gorshen,* which involved a conviction of second degree murder, thus an acquittal of first, and which squarely held that the defense of irresistible impulse was applicable not as a complete defense but as rebutting malice aforethought. * * *

A conclusion that there is no evidence negating malice aforethought in the present case can only be reached by ignoring *Gorshen,* and the discussion of *Gorshen* in *Conley,* and thereby impliedly overruling those cases or by ignoring the testimony of Dr. Wilson in the instant case. The evidence in this case is as strong as that in *Gorshen.*

NOTES

1. Does the majority hold that if the impact of psychological abnormality has been to render a person incapable of conforming his conduct to the laws of society, the defendant nevertheless may act with malice aforethought as defined in *Conley*? In People v. Noah, 5 Cal.3d 469, 487 P.2d 1009, 96

Cal.Rptr. 441 (1971) the court quoted with approval from *Gorshen* to the effect that evidence of irresistable impulse is received not as a "complete defense" but rather as "a 'partial defense' negating specific mental states essential to a particular crime." Is this helpful in interpreting the *Morse* opinion?

2. Is the result in *Morse* based more upon the nature of the psychological abnormality than upon its impact upon the defendant? In other words, does *Morse* stand for the proposition that loss of control does not establish lack of malice aforethought where that loss of control was caused only by a "personality disorder" and "the effects of [the defendant's] environment?" If so, is this defensible? Explain.

3. To what extent does *Morse* represent a decision on the part of the California Supreme Court to abandon the efforts which *Wells*, *Gorshen*, *Wolff*, and *Conley* represented? Insofar as it does represent such a decision, what might explain it? Consider the following possibilities:

a. The legal criteria that the court developed in an effort to make the expert testimony and the law compatible were so vague that they were of little help in resolving particular cases. No more specific criteria could be formulated. The diminished capacity rule thus became inherently unmanagable.

b. If diminished capacity were limited to consideration of the impact of psychological abnormality upon defendants' intellectual processes, it did not accommodate a large number of cases in which it would be desirable to assign a lower grade of liability. But there was no way in which to define the various homicide offenses other than in terms of conscious awareness, i. e., "state of mind." The diminished capacity rule thus proved ineffective in accomplishing its basic objective of providing a vehicle for consideration of psychological abnormality in assigning the degree of criminal liability.

c. As the concept of diminished capacity broadened, it became clear that it would be difficult or impossible to restrict it to cases involving traditional serious "mental illnesses." Yet once it was applied beyond such cases, there was no reasonable method of halting its application short of unacceptable expansion. Thus the diminished capacity rule floundered on an inability to distinguish those who should be permitted to invoke it.

4. Is the California Supreme Court's treatment of the diminished capacity issue analagous to the United States Court of Appeals for the District of Columbia's treatment of the insanity issue? To the extent that they are analagous, what lessons do they teach for efforts to integrate the substantive criminal law and what are arguably greater insights into the nature of human behavior?

*

INDEX

References are to Pages